THE
HOWARD UNIVERSITY
BIBLIOGRAPHY OF AFRICAN
AND
AFRO-AMERICAN
RELIGIOUS STUDIES

•

WITH LOCATIONS
IN
AMERICAN LIBRARIES

Compiled by

Ethel L. Williams
and
Clifton F. Brown

SR *Scholarly Resources Inc.*
1508 Pennsylvania Avenue · Wilmington, Delaware 19806

© 1977 by Ethel L. Williams and Clifton F. Brown
All rights reserved
First published 1977
Printed in the United States of America

Scholarly Resources, Inc.
1508 Pennsylvania Avenue
Wilmington, Delaware 19806

Library of Congress Cataloging in Publication Data

Williams, Ethel L.
　　The Howard University bibliography of African and
Afro-American religious studies.

　　Includes indexes.
　　1. Afro-Americans—Religion—Bibliography—Union lists.
2. Africa—Religion—Bibliography—Union lists.　3. Slavery
in America—Bibliography—Union lists.　4. Afro-Americans—
Civil rights—Bibliography—Union lists.　5. Catalogs, Union—
United States.　I. Brown, Clifton F., 1943—joint author.
II. Howard University, Washington, D.C.　III. Title.
IV. Title: Bibliography of African and Afro-American religious
studies.
Z1361.N39W555　[BR563.N4]　016.299'6　76-5604
ISBN 0-8420-2080-2

CONTENTS

II. CHRISTIANITY AND SLAVERY IN THE NEW WORLD

III. THE BLACK MAN AND HIS RELIGIOUS LIFE IN THE AMERICAS
(for contemporary status, see Section V)

A. Religious Development of the American Negro

    1. The Negro Church

       a. Denominations

       b. Storefront Churches and Sects

PREFACE

The Howard University Bibliography of African and Afro-American Religious Studies is a comprehensive bibliographical guide to more than thirteen thousand primary and secondary sources in the areas of African, Afro-Caribbean, and Afro-American religious studies. Drawing on more than 230 repositories throughout the United States, we have provided at least one location for each entry. A brief annotation is provided when the title of an entry does not suggest the subject of the item. The books, periodical articles, and analyticals of books in this volume are listed under five major headings: (1) African Heritage, (2) Christianity and Slavery in the New World, (3) The Black Man and His Religious Life in the Americas, (4) Civil Rights Movement, (5) The Contemporary Religious Scene. In addition to a general index, *The Howard University Bibliography* includes a comprehensive appendix of some six thousand autobiographical and biographical works and a guide to unpublished manuscripts.

Although the present work is comprehensive, it can in no way be considered definitive. Additional work remains to be done, particularly in the areas of mimeographed studies on indigenous religion in African repositories, Islam in Africa, studies on cults and sects in the Caribbean and Brazil, and denominational records and publications of Black churches.

The compilers are grateful to all who have assisted in making this volume possible. We wish to especially express our gratitude to Dr. Lorraine A. Williams, Vice President for Academic Affairs, Howard University, who acted as consultant for various stages of this project. We also would like to express our deep appreciation to those who assisted in the research for this volume: Blanche Allen, Esme Bhan, Reginald Biddle, Anthony Clark, Carole Walls Cody, Leroy Davis, Yemane Haile, Lee Ingham, Karen Jefferson, James Johnson, Patricia Jones, Hermela Kebede, Dolores Leffall, Clifford Muse, Charmaine Roberts, and Florestine Sampson. This volume was made possible by partial support from the Faculty Research Program in Social Sciences, Humanities and Education of Howard University through the Office of the Vice President for Academic Affairs and the Lilly Endowment, Inc.

Ethel L. Williams
Clifton F. Brown

INTRODUCTION

All entries are numbered consecutively and listed topically under five general headings. These general headings are divided and subdivided into particular topics relating to the general area. Individual entries are alphabetically arranged by authors under these particular topics. Therefore, in order for the bibliography to be of maximum benefit, it is suggested that the user first consult the topics as outlined in the Table of Contents. An index of authors is provided.

A service that is provided by this bibliography for the user is that all entries note at least one location from which an item can be obtained (see Key to Location Symbols). Also, in those instances where a title does not suggest the subject of entry, a brief annotation is included.

At the conclusion of the volume are two appendices. Appendix I lists major manuscript collections on Black American ministers, religious figures, and institutions. Appendix II lists citations providing autobiographical or biographical data on Black American religious figures.

KEY TO LOCATION SYMBOLS

AA/IES	Institute of Ethiopian Studies Addis Ababa, Ethiopia	CMIG	Golden Gate Baptist Theological Seminary Mill Valley, California
AAP	Auburn University Auburn, Alabama	CoDI	Iliff School of Theology Denver, Colorado
A&M	Florida Agriculture and Mechanical University Tallahassee, Florida	CoDU	University of Denver Denver, Colorado
AMAU	Air University, Maxwell Air Force Base Montgomery, Alabama	CoU	University of Colorado Boulder, Colorado
ArU	University of Arkansas Fayetteville, Arkansas	CSmH	Henry E. Huntington Library San Marino, California
ATC	Talledega College Talledega, Alabama	CSt	Stanford University Stanford, California
ATT	Tuskegee Institute Tuskegee, Alabama	CSt-H	Stanford University, Hoover Institution on War, Revolution and Peace Stanford, California
CBPac	Pacific School of Religion Berkeley, California	CU	University of California Berkeley, California
CL	Los Angeles Public Library Los Angeles, California	CU-S	University of California San Diego, California
CLolC	Loma Linda University Loma Linda, California	CtHC	Hartford Seminary Foundation Hartford, Connecticut
CLSU	University of Southern California Los Angeles, California	CtW	Wesleyan University Middletown, Connecticut
CLU	University of California Los Angeles, California	CtY	Yale University New Haven, Connecticut
CLUM	White Memorial Medical Center Library Los Angeles, California	CtY-D	Yale University, Divinity School New Haven, Connecticut

CtY/DML — Yale University, Day Missionary Library New Haven, Connecticut

DAU/W — American University, Wesley Theological Seminary Washington, D. C.

De-Ar — Delaware Public Archives Commission Library Dover, Delaware

DGU — Georgetown University Washington, D. C.

DGU-M — Georgetown University, Medical Dental and Nursing Library Washington, D. C.

DGU/TH — Georgetown Theological Library, Georgetown University Washington, D. C.

DHC — Holy Cross College Washington, D. C.

DHEW — U. S. Department of Health, Education, and Welfare Washington, D. C.

DHU — Howard University, University Library Washington, D. C.

DHU/AA — Howard University, African Studies Library Washington, D. C.

DHU/L — Howard University, Law School Library Washington, D. C.

DHU/MO — Howard University, Moorland-Spingarn Research Center Washington, D. C.

DHU/R — Howard University, School of Religion Library Washington, D. C.

DHU/SW — Howard University, Social Work School Library Washington, D. C.

DLC — U. S. Library of Congress Washington, D. C.

DNAL — U. S. National Agricultural Library Washington, D. C.

DOUM/EUB — United Methodist Commission on Archives (Formerly EUBC) Dayton, Ohio

DPL — District of Columbia Public Library Washington, D. C.

DPU — Pan American Union Washington, D. C.

DSI/M — Smithsonian Institution Museum Library Washington, D. C.

DT — Trinity College Library Washington, D. C.

DWTC — Washington Theological Coalition Library Washington, D. C.

FSU — Florida State University Tallahassee, Florida

FU — University of Florida Gainesville, Florida

GAU — Atlanta University Atlanta, Georgia

GAU/ITC	Atlanta University, Inter-denominational Theological Center Library Atlanta, Georgia		ICT	Chicago Theological Seminary Chicago, Illinois
GAuP	Paine College Augusta, Georgia		ICU	University of Chicago Chicago, Illinois
GEU	Emory University Atlanta, Georgia		ICU-D	University of Chicago, Divinity School Chicago, Illinois
GEU-T	Candler School of Theology Atlanta, Georgia		IEG	Garrett Theological Seminary Evanston, Illinois
GMM	Mercer University Macon, Georgia		IEN	Northwestern University Evanston, Illinois
IaAS	Iowa State University of Science and Technology Ames, Iowa		In	Indiana State Library Indianapolis, Indiana
ICA	Art Institute Chicago, Illinois		INE	Evangelical Theological Seminary Library Naperville, Illinois
ICF	Chicago Natural History Museum Chicago, Illinois		InElkB	Mennonite Biblical Seminary Elkhart, Indiana
IC/H	Chicago Public Library, Hurst Collection Chicago, Illinois		InNd	University of Notre Dame Notre Dame, Indiana
ICHi	Chicago Historical Society Chicago, Illinois		InRE	Earlham College Richmond, Indiana
ICJ	John Crerar Library Chicago, Illinois		InU	Indiana University Bloomington, Indiana
ICLT	Lutheran School of Theology Chicago, Illinois		IObB	Bethany Theological Seminary Oak Brook, Illinois
ICMcC	McCormick Theological Seminary Chicago, Illinois		IObNB	Northern Baptist Theological Seminary Oak Brook, Illinois
ICRL	Center for Research Libraries Chicago, Illinois		IU	University of Illinois Urbana, Illinois

IW-CBFMS	Conservative Baptist Foreign Mission Society Wheaton, Illinois	MB	Boston Public Library Boston, Massachusetts
IWW	Wheaton College Wheaton, Illinois	MBAt	Boston Athenaeum Boston, Massachusetts
KH-MBMS	Kansas State Historical Society Topeka, Kansas	MBGIL	General Theological Library Boston, Massachusetts
KKcB	Central Baptist Theological Seminary Kansas City, Kansas	MBU	Boston University Boston, Massachusetts
KyBB	Berea College Berea, Kentucky	MdBE	Enoch Pratt Free Library Baltimore, Maryland
KyLoS	Southern Baptist Theological Seminary Louisville, Kentucky	MdBFr	Friends Meeting, Stony Run Baltimore, Maryland
KyLoU	University of Louisville Louisville, Kentucky	MdBJ	The Johns Hopkins University Baltimore, Maryland
KyLx	Lexington Public Library Lexington, Kentucky	MdBP	Peabody Institute Baltimore, Maryland
KyLxCB	Lexington Theological Seminary Lexington, Kentucky	MdHi	Maryland Historical Society Baltimore, Maryland
L	Louisiana State Library Baton Rouge, Louisiana	MH	Harvard University Cambridge, Massachusetts
LN	New Orleans Public Library New Orleans, Louisiana	MH-AH	Andover-Harvard Theological Library Boston, Massachusetts
LNAA	Amistad Archives New Orleans, Louisiana	MH-H	Harvard University, Houghton Library Cambridge, Massachusetts
LNB	New Orleans Baptist Theological Seminary New Orleans, Louisiana	MH-P	Harvard University, Peabody Museum Cambridge, Massachusetts
LND	Dillard University New Orleans, Louisiana	MH-W	Harvard University, Widener Library Cambridge, Massachusetts

MiBsA	Andrews University Berrien Springs, Michigan	MWA	American Antiquarian Society Worcester, Massachusetts
MiEM	Michigan State University East Lansing, Michigan	MWelC	Wellesley College Wellesley, Massachusetts
MiU	University of Michigan Ann Arbor, Michigan	NB	Brooklyn Public Library Brooklyn, New York
MiU-C	University of Michigan William L. Clements Library Ann Arbor, Michigan	NcD	Duke University Durham, North Carolina
MiU-H	Michigan Historical Collection University of Michigan Ann Arbor, Michigan	NcHiC	North Carolina Historical Commission Raleigh, North Carolina
MnHi	Minnesota Historical Society St. Paul, Minnesota	NcMHi	Historical Foundation of the Presbyterian and Reformed Churches Montreat, North Carolina
MnMohT	Moorhead State College Moorhead, Minnesota	NcMjHi	United Methodist Church Commission on Archives and History Library Lake Junaluska, North Carolina
MNtcA	Andover Newton Theological School Newton Center, Massachusetts	NcSalL	Livingstone College Salisbury, North Carolina
MnU	University of Minnesota Minneapolis, Minnesota	NcU	University of North Carolina Chapel Hill, North Carolina
MoS	St. Louis Public Library St. Louis, Missouri	NcWfSB	Southeastern Baptist Theological Seminary Wake Forest, North Carolina
MoSIP	Missouri Institute of Psychiatry St. Louis, Missouri		
MoSU	St. Louis University St. Louis, Missouri	NhD	Dartmouth College Hanover, New Hampshire
MsBsS	Divine Word Seminary of Saint Augustine Bay St. Louis, Mississippi	NHi	New-York Historical Society New York, New York
MtU	University of Montana Missoula, Montana	NjMD	Drew University Madison, New Jersey

NjMD-T	Theological School, Drew University Madison, New Jersey
NjP	Princeton University Library Princeton, New Jersey
NjP-T	Theological Seminary Princeton, New Jersey
NjPlaSDB	Seventh Day Baptist Historical Society Plainfield, New Jersey
NN	New York Public Library New York, New York
NNA	American Geographical Society New York, New York
NNAG	American Gas Association New York, New York
NNC	Columbia University New York, New York
NN-CMA	Christian Missionary Alliance New York, New York
NNCor or NIC	Cornell University Ithaca, New York
NNC-T	Teachers College, Columbia University New York, New York
NNG	General Theological Seminary of the Protestant Episcopal Church New York, New York
NNJ	Jewish Theological Seminary of America New York, New York

NNM	American Museum of Natural History New York, New York
NNMB	Methodist Board of Missions New York, New York
NN-MPUML	Methodist-Presbyterian United Missions Library New York, New York
NNMR	Missionary Research Library New York, New York
NNNAM	New York Academy of Medicine New York, New York
NNRIS	Research Institute for the Study of Man New York, New York
NN/Sch	New York Public Library Schomburg Collection New York, New York
NNUN	United Nations New York, New York
NNUT	Union Theological Seminary New York, New York
NRAB	Samuel Colgate Baptist Historical Library of the American Baptist Historical Society Rochester, New York
NRCR	Colgate-Rochester Divinity School Rochester, New York
NRU	University of Rochester Rochester, New York
NSy	Syracuse Public Library Syracuse, New York

NsyU	Syracuse University Syracuse, New York	OWibfU	Wilberforce University Carnegie Library Wilberforce, Ohio
O	Ohio State Library Columbus, Ohio	OWoC	College of Wooster Wooster, Ohio
OC	Public Library of Cincinnati and Hamilton County Cincinnati, Ohio	PBL	Lehigh University Bethlehem, Pennsylvania
OCH	Hebrew Union College, Jewish Institute of Religion Cincinnati, Ohio	PCarlD	Dickinson College Carlisle, Pennsylvania
OCl	Cleveland Public Library Cleveland, Ohio	PCC	Crozer Theological Seminary Chester, Pennsylvania
OCIWHi	Western Reserve Historical Society Cleveland, Ohio	PFL	Friends Library Philadelphia, Pennsylvania
OGK	Kenyon College Gambier, Ohio	PGC	Gettysburg College Gettysburg, Pennsylvania
OHi	Ohio State Historical Society Columbus, Ohio	PGraM	Messiah College Grantham, Pennsylvania
OO	Oberlin College Library Oberlin, Ohio	PHarH	Pennsylvania Historical and Museum Commission Harrisburg, Pennsylvania
OOxM	Miami University Oxford, Ohio	PHC	Haverford College Haverford, Pennsylvania
OrU	Oregon University Eugene, Oregon	PHi	Historical Society of Pennsylvania Philadelphia, Pennsylvania
OU	Ohio State University Columbus, Ohio	PLU	Lincoln University Oxford, Pennsylvania
OUM/EUB	United Methodist Evangelical Library Dayton, Ohio	PP	Free Library of Philadelphia Philadelphia, Pennsylvania
OWibfP	Payne Theological Seminary Wilberforce, Ohio	PPAmP	American Philosophical Society Philadelphia, Pennsylvania

PPEB	Eastern Baptist Theological Seminary Philadelphia, Pennsylvania
PPiD	Duquesne University Pittsburgh, Pennsylvania
PPL	Library Company of Philadelphia Philadelphia, Pennsylvania
PPMHi	Methodist Historical Association Philadelphia, Pennsylvania
PPPD	Philadelphia Divinity School (Formerly Divinity School of the Protestant Episcopal Church) Philadelphia, Pennsylvania
PPPrHi	Presbyterian Historical Society Philadelphia, Pennsylvania
PPT	Temple University Philadelphia, Pennsylvania
PPULC	Union Library Catalogue of Pennsylvania Philadelphia, Pennsylvania
PSC-Hi	Friends Historical Library Swarthmore College Swarthmore, Pennsylvania
PSW or PSC	Swarthmore College Swarthmore, Pennsylvania
PU	University of Pennsylvania Philadelphia, Pennsylvania
PU-Mu	University Museum, University of Pennsylvania Philadelphia, Pennsylvania
PV-ABFMS	American Baptist Foreign Mission Society, Villanova University Villanova, Pennsylvania
RPB	Brown University Providence, Rhode Island
RPCJB	John Carter Brown Library Providence, Rhode Island
SCBHC	Samuel Colgate Baptist Historical Collection, Colgate-Rochester Divinity School Rochester, New York
ScHi	South Carolina Historical Society Charleston, South Carolina
ScU	University of South Carolina Charleston, South Carolina
T	Tennessee State Library Nashville, Tennessee
TJaL	Lane College Jackson, Tennessee
TN/DCHS or TNDC	Disciples of Christ Historical Society Nashville, Tennessee
TNF	Fisk University Nashville, Tennessee
TNJ	Joint University Libraries Nashville, Tennessee
TNMph	Methodist Publishing House Nashville, Tennessee
TNSB	Southern Baptist Convention Historical Commission Nashville, Tennessee
TNU	Upper Room Devotional Library and Museum Nashville, Tennessee

TSewU-T	School of Theology, University of the South Sewanee, Tennessee	ViHa	Charles H. Taylor Memorial Library Hampton, Virginia
TxD	Perkins School of Theology, Southern Methodist University Dallas, Texas	ViHi	Virginia Historical Society Richmond, Virginia
TxDaTS	Dallas Theological Seminary and Graduate School of Theology Dallas, Texas	ViU	University of Virginia Charlottesville, Virginia
TxFS	Southwestern Baptist Theological Seminary Forth Worth, Texas	WaS	Seattle Public Library Seattle, Washington
TxU	University of Texas Austin, Texas	WaU	University of Washington Seattle, Washington
TxWB	Baylor University Waco, Texas	WHi	State Historical Society of Wisconsin Madison, Wisconsin
USID	Church of Jesus Christ of Latter-Day Saints, Historian's Office Salt Lake City, Utah	WMCHi	Milwaukee County Historical Society Milwaukee, Wisconsin
Vi	Virginia State Library Richmond, Virginia	WNa	Nashotah House Nashotah, Wisconsin
ViAlTH	Virginia Theological Seminary Alexandria, Virginia	WU	University of Wisconsin Madison, Wisconsin
		WvU	West Virginia University Morgantown, West Virginia

I. AFRICAN HERITAGE

A. ANCIENT EGYPT AND KUSH

1. Adams, William Y. "Post Pharaonic Nubia in the Light of Archaeology I, II, III." Journal of Egyptian Archaeology (50; 51; 52, 1964; 1965; 1966), pp. 102-120; 147-62; 160-178. DCU/SE

2. ----- "An Introductory Classification of Christian Nubia Pottery." Kush (10; 1962), pp. 245-88 DLC

3. Arkell, Anthony John. A History of the Sudan: From the Earliest Times to 1821. London: University of London, Athlone Press, 1961. (2nd Ed.). DHU/MO
   Sections on the early Christian States in Nubia.

4. ----- "The Influence of Christian Nubia in the Chad Area between A.D. 800-1200." Kush (11; 1963), pp. 315-19. DLC

5. Bates, William N. (ed.). Archaeological News. Notes on Recent Excavations and Discoveries; Other News. Egypt. - Luxor. - "The Prayer for the Dead in Christian Nubia." American Journal of Archaeology (13:3, Jl.-Sept., 1909), p. 376. DLC

6. Bayer, Wilheim. "De Religion der Altesten Agyptischen Inschriften." Anthropos (22:3, 4, Sept.-Dec.; 22:5, 6, My.-Ag., 1927 & 23:3, 4, My.-Ag., 1928), pp. 511-37. DLC
   Dr. Wilheim Bayer, Aachen.

7. Beardsley, Grace M. H. The Negro in Greek and Roman Civilization; A Study of the Ethiopian Type. New York: Russell & Russell, 1967. DHU/MO

8. Ben-Jochannan, Yosef. Black Man of the Nile and His Family. New York: Alkebu-Ian Books Associates, 1972. DHU/MO
   Chapter 10, Mother of the Gods of Man.

9. Blackman, Winifred S. The Fellahin of Upper Egypt: Their Religious, Social and Industrial Life With Special Reference to Survivals From Ancient Times. London: F. Cass, 1968. DHU/MO

10. Breasted, James H. Development of Religion and Thought in Ancient Egypt. Gloucester, Mass.: Peter Smith, 1970. DLC
    Originally published in 1959.

11. Brooks, Lester. Great Civilizations of Ancient Africa. New York: Four Winds Press, 1966. DHU/R
    Black Egypt discussed including religion.

12. Budge, Ernest Alfred T. W. The Dwellers of the Nile:Chapters on the Life, History, Religion, and Literature of the Ancient Egyptians. New York: R. Blom, 1972. DLC
    Reprint of 1962 edition.

13. ----- The Egyption Heaven and Hell; Being the Book of Am-Tuat, the Shorter Form of the Book of Am-Tuat, the Book of the Gates and the Contents of the Book of the Other World, Described and Compared. London: Martin Hopkinson, 1925. DLC

14. ----- From Fetish to God in Ancient Egypt. New York: Benjamin Blom, Inc., 1972.
    "With 240 black and white illustrations."

15. Carter, Howard. The Tomb of Tutankhamen. New York: E. P. Dutton & Co., 1972. DHU/R
    Burial practices in Ancient Egypt.

16. Clayson, Rodman R. Egypt's Ancient Heritage. San Jose, Calif.: Supreme Grand Lodge of Amove, Inc., 1971. DHU/R

17. Davis, Simon. Race-relations in Ancient Egypt. London: Metheuen, 1951. MSohG

18. Desroches-Noblecourt, Christiane. Tutankhamen; Life and Death of a Pharaoh. New York: New York Graphic Society, 1963. DHU/R

19. "The Deities of Ancient Egypt." (Historical Criticism, Ancient Religions). Andover Review (3; Apr., 1885), pp. 374-90. DHU/R

20. Dixon, O. M. "The Origin of the Kingdom of Kush (Napata-Meroe)." Journal of Egyptian Archaeology (50; 1964), pp. 121-32. DCU/SE

21. Doresse, Jean. The Secret Books of the Egyptian Gnostics. n.p.: Hollis & Carter, 1960. DLC; MH; NNC; ANiU

22. Dunham, Dows. The Royal Cemetries of Kush. Cambridge, Mass.: Published for the Museum of Fine Arts, Harvard University, 1950-58, Vols. I-IV. DLC

23. Erman, Adolf. The Ancient Egyptians. Harper and Row Publications, 1966. NUC; DLC; ICU; MB; NjP

24. ----- A Handbook of Egyptian Religion. London: Archibald Constable & Co., 1907. DHU/R; DLC: OrCs; ICN; MB

25. Evans, Luther. The Book of Thoth. New York: Comet Press, 1960. DHU/MO
    Egyptian God of time.

26. "The Forgotten Kingdom." BBC-TV, London. Released in the U. S. by Time-Life Films, 1971. 30 min. sd. color. 16 mm. DLC
    Film. "Shows the ruined temples and pyramids of the kingdom of Kush in the Sudanese desert."

27. Frankfort, Henri. Ancient Egyptian Religion, An Interpretation. New York: Columbia University Press, 1948. DHU/R
    Chapter I, The Egyptian Gods.

28. Getty, Marie Madeleine of Jesus (Sister). The Life of the North Africans as Revealed in the Sermons of Saint Augustine. Doctoral dissertation. Catholic University of America, 1931. DCU

29. Hansberry, William Leo. "Ancient Kush, Old Aethiopia, and the Balad es Sudan." Journal of Human Relations (8; Spr.-Sum., 1960), pp. 357-87. DAU; DCU/SW

30. Hasan, Yusuf F. The Arabs and the Sudan From the Seventh to the Early Sixteenth Century. Edinburgh: The University Press, 1967.   DLC

31. Hawks, Francis Lister. The Monuments of Egypt; or Egypt, a Witness for the Bible. New York: G. P. Putnam, 1854.
DHU/MO

32. Hordern, Peter J. C. Geographical Influences on Religious Conceptualization With Special Reference to Ancient Egypt. Doctoral dissertation. McMaster University, 1972.

33. Mercer, Samuel A. B. Horus, Royal God of Egypt. Grafton, Mass.: Society of Oriental Research, 1942.
DLC: PBm; PCC:OO

34. ----- The Religion of Ancient Egypt. London: Luzac & Co., 1949.   DHU/MO

35. Mileham, Geoffrey S. Churches in Lower Nubia. Philadelphia: The University Museum, 1910.   DHU/MO

36. Moore, Charlean DeBerry. The Educational System of Ancient Egypt. Master's thesis. New Orleans Baptist Theological Seminary, 1950.

37. Moret, Alexandre. Kings and Gods of Egypt. New York: G. P. Putnam's Sons, 1911.   DHU/MO

38. Oates, J. F. A. "A Christian Inscription in Greek from Nubia." Journal of Egyptian Archaeology (49; 1963), pp. 161-71.   DCU/SE

39. Petrie, William Matthew Flinders. History of Egypt. London: Methuen & Co., 1898-1905.   DHU/MO; DHU/R

40. ----- Personal Religion in Egypt before Christianity. New York: Harper & Brothers, 1909.   NN/Sch

41. ----- Religion and Conscience in Ancient Egypt; Lecture Delivered at University College, London. London: Methuen, 1898.   DHU/R

42. ----- Religious Life in Ancient Egypt. New York: Cooper Square Publishers, 1972.   DHU/R

43. Pirenne, Jacques. La Religion et la Morale Dans l'Egypte Antique. Neuchâtel: La Baconnière, 1965.   NN/Sch

44. Price, Ira Maurice. The Monuments and the Old Testament; Evidence from Ancient Records.... Chicago: The Christian Culture Press, 1907.   DHU/MO
Chapter 9, "Israel Under the Glow of Egypt."

45. Pritchard, James B., (ed.). Ancient New Eastern Texts Relating to the Old Testament. Princeton, New Jersey: Princeton University Press, 1954.   DHU/R
Includes practice of religion in Egypt.

46. Prorok, Byron Khun De. "The Ancient Basilicas of Carthage and the Early Christian Ruins of North Africa." Art and Archaeology (19:3, Mr., 1925), pp. 147-51.   DHU/R

47. Read, Frederick William. Egyptian Religion and Ethics. London: Watts, 1925.   DLC; CtY; PHC; PU

48. St. Laurent, Phillip. "The Dawning of Monotheism." (8:4, Dec., 1972), pp. 27-8. Pam. File,   DHU/R
The beginnings of Monotheism in Egypt in the 18th dynasty.

49. Schar, Hans. "Ancient Egyptian Idea of Gods." Istvan Rácz. The Unknown God. (New York: Sheed and Ward, 1970), pp. 41-66.   DHU/R

50. Scott-Moncrieff, Philip David. Paganism and Christianity in Egypt. Cambridge: Cambridge University Press, 1913.
DLC; PU; MiU; NN

51. Seligman, C. G. "Ancient Egyptian Beliefs in Modern Egypt." E. C. Quiggin, (ed.). Essays and Studies Presented to William Ridgeway ... on His Sixtieth Birthday, 6 August, 1913. Cambridge: University Press, 1914.   DLC

52. Shinnie, Peter L. "New Light on Medieval Nubia." Journal of African History (6:3, 1965), pp. 263-73.   DHU/MO

53. Spence, Lewis. The Mysteries of Egypt or the Secret Rites and Traditions of the Nile. Blauvett. New York: Rudolph Steiner Pub., 1972.   DHU/R

54. Velde, H. T. Seth, God of Confusion: A Study of His Role in Egyptian Mythology and Religion. Leiden: E. J. Brill, 1967.
DHU/R

55. Wainwright, Gerald A. The Sky-Religion in Egypt: Its Antiquity and Effects. Westport, Conn.: Greenwood Press, 1971. Reprint of 1938 edition.   DLC

56. Wake, C. Staniland. "Traits of an Ancient Egyptian Folk-tale, Compared with Those of Aboriginal American Tales." Journal of American Folk-Lore (17:67, Oct.-Dec., 1904), pp. 255-64.
Microcard.   DHU/R

57. Whitley, E. H. "Ancient and Modern Pantheism." The East and the West (14; Ja., 1916), pp. 1-16.   DHU/R
Includes Ancient Egypt.

58. Wiedemann, Alfred. "Die Religiöse Bedeutung der Ägyptischen Pyramiden." Anthropos (16-17: 4-6, Jl.-Dec., 1921-1922), pp. 657-80.   DLC

59. Wilkinson, J. G. "Manners and Customs of the Ancient Egyptians, Including Their Private Life, Government, Laws, Arts, Manufacture, Religion and Early History." Christian Examiner (31:1, 1841), pp. 38-60.   DHU/R

60. Yashuda, Abraham S. The Language of the Pentateuch in its Relation to Egypt... London: Oxford University Press, 1933.
DHU/MO

B. CHRISTIANITY AND JUDAISM IN EGYPT AND ETHIOPIA (See also I-Eld)

61. Abir, Mordechai. Ethiopia: The Era of the Princes: The Challenge of Islam and the Re-Unification of the Christian Empire 1769-1855. New York: Praeger, 1969.   DHU/MO

62. Abraham Demoz. "Moslems and Islam in Ethiopic Literature." Journal of Ethiopian Studies (10:1, Ja., 1972), pp. 1-11.
DHU/R

63. "The Abyssinian Church." Quarterly Review (Ja., 1936), pp. 10-13.   AA/IES; DLC

64. Allotte de la Fuye, Maurice, (ed. and tr.). Actes de Filmona. Louvain: Secrétariat du CorpusSCO, 1958. 2 Vols. Corpus Scriptorum Christianorum Orientalium, Vols. 181-182; Scriptores Aethiopici, t. 35-36.   AA/IES

65. Amero, Constant. Le Negus Menelik et L'Abyssinie Nouvelle ... Paris: J. Lefort, 1897.   NN/Sch

66. "The Ancient, Serene Ethiopian Church." Time (Jan. 6, 1967), pp. 60-61.   DHU

67. Andersen, Knud Tage. Ethiopiens Orthodokse Kirke. Udg. of Dansk Ethiopei Mission. Kobenhaven: Savanne, D. B. K., 1971.   DLC

68. Apostolical Constitutions. Ethiopic Version. The Ethiopic Didascalia; or, the Ethiopic Version of the Apostolical Constitutions, Received in the Church of Abyssinia. With an English translation. Edited and Translated by Thomas Pell

Platt. London: Published for the Oriental Translation Fund of Great Britain and Ireland by R. Bently, 1834.   NN/Sch

69. Arce, Laurent d'. ...L'Abyssinie, Étude D'Actualite (1922-24). Avignon: Librairie Aubanel Frères, 1925.   NN/Sch

70. Alvares, Francisco. Narrative of the Portuguese Embassy to Abyssinia, 1520-1527. New York: Burt Franklin Publishing, 1964.   DHU/R; INU

71. Arnhard, Carl von. "Die Wasserweike nach dem Ritus der Athiopischen Kirche." Zeitschrift der Deutschen Morgen-landischen Gesellschaft (41; 1887), pp. 403-14.   AA/IES

72. Arras, Victor, (ed.). Miraculorum S. Georgii Megalomar-tyris Collectio Altera. Louvain: L. Durbecq, 1953. 2 Vols. Corpus Scriptorum Christianorum Orientalium, Vols. 138-139; Scriptores Aethiopici, t. 31-32.   DLC
       Ethiopic and Latin.

73. Assad, Maurice Mikhail. "The Coptic Church and Social Change in Egypt." International Review of Mission (61:242, Apr., 1972), pp. 117-29.   DHU/R

74. ..... Education in the Coptic Orthodox Church Strategies for the Future. Doctoral dissertation. Columbia University,1970.

75. Aymro Wondmagegnehu. Monasteries and Churches of Ethi-opia. Papers prepared for the Conference of Patriarchs, Addis Ababa, Jan., 1965.   AA/IES

76. Aymro Wondmagegnehu and Joachim Motovu, (eds.). The Ethiopian Orthodox Church. Addis Ababa, Ethiopia: The Ethiopian Orthodox Mission, (1970).   DHU/R

77. Baars, W. and R. Zuurmond. "A New Edition of the Ethiopi-an Book of Jubilees." Journal of Semitic Studies (9:1, Spring, 1964), pp. 67-74.   AA/IES

78. Bahru Damese. "External Policy of Zagwe Kings." History Journal (2:2, 1968), pp. 32-36.   AA/IES

79. Bairu Tafla. "The Establishment of the Ethiopian Church." Tarikh (2:1, 1967), pp. 28-42.   AA/IES; DLC

80. Baker, Samuel White. Nile Tributaries of Abyssinia, and Sword Hunters of the Hamran Arabs. London: Macmillan, 1868.   PPA; NUC; DLC; RPB; PHC; PP; CU; OCIW; PV; PU.

81. Beckingham, Charles Fraser. The Achievements of Prester John: an Inaugural Lecture Delivered on 17 May 1966. London: University of London, School of Oriental and African Studies; Distributed by Luzac, 1966.
       MiU; IEN; NIC; CST; IEdS; MiEM

82. ..... "A Note on the Topography of Ahmad Gran's Campaigns in 1542." Journal of Semitic Studies (4:4, Oct., 1959), pp. 362-73.   DHU/R
       A discussion of the nature and impact of the Islamic jihad on Christian Ethiopia.

83. Bent, James T. The Sacred City of the Ethiopians: Being a Record of Travel and Research in Abyssinia in 1893, With a Chapter by H. D. Muller on the Inscriptions from Yeha and Ak-sum, and an Appendix on the Morphological Character of the Abyssinians by J. G. Garson. London: Longmans, Green and Co., 1896. NUC; DLC; CoDU; PPULC; WaS; OrU; CoD; NcD; NIC; IEN; WU; NN; MiU; PBa; PPM; PU; PPL;MH; MdBP; OCI; NjP; ViHai; CU; MBr-Z.

84. Bezold, Carl. Kebra Nagast. München: K. Akademie der Wissenschaften, 1905.   AA/IES

85. Bible. John Coptic. ...The Gospel of St. John According to the Earliest Coptic Manuscript. Edited with Translation, by Sir Herbert Thompson. London: British School of Archaeolo-gy in Egypt, 1924.   DHU/MO

86. Bible. The New Testament of Our Lord and Saviour Jesus Christ. Translated into Galla language by Oresimus Nesib. London: St. Chrischona, 1899. Galla text.   AA/IES

87. Bidder, Irmgard. Lalibela: the Monolithic Churches of Lali-bela. New York: Praeger, 1960.   DLC

88. "Black Jews in Israel." Our World (10:11, Nov., 1955), pp. 27-31.   DHU/MO
       Ethiopian Falashas in Israel.

89. Blyth, E. M. E. "The Church of Ethiopia." Hibbert Journal (34:1, Oct., 1935), pp. 80-91.   AA/IES; DHU/R

90. Borchardt, Paul. "Die Falaschajuden in Abessinien im Mitte-lalter." Anthropos (16-17: 1, 2, 3, Ja.-Je., 1923-24), pp. 258-66.   DLC

91. Bosworth, C. E. "Christian and Jewish Religious Dignitaries in Mamluk Egypt and Syria: Qalqashandi's Information on their Hierarchy, Titulature, and Appointment (II)." International Journal of Middle East Studies (3:2, Apr., 1972), pp. 40-46.   DLC

92. Brightman, F. E. (ed.) Liturgies: Eastern and Western. V.1. Oxford: Clarendon Press, 1965.   DHU/R
       Includes discussion of the Anaphora of the Ethiopic Church Ordinances, pp. 189-93.

93. Brooke, Marcus. "Back to Biblical Beauty." Washington Post (Sunday; January 7, 1973).   DHU

94. Brown, Clifton F. "The Conversion Experience in Axum Dur-ing the Fourth and Fifth Centuries." Lorraine A. Williams (ed.) Africa and the Afro-American Experience (Washington, D. C.: Howard University, The Department of History, 1973), pp. 5-30.   DHU/R

95. ----- "The Ethiopian Orthodox Church." Negro History Bulle-tin (35:1, Ja., 1972), pp. 10-11. Pam. File; DHU/R; DHU/MO

96. Browne, P. W. "Ethiopia in its Ecclesiastical Aspects." Ec-clesiastical Review (94:2, Feb., 1936), pp. 113-24.   AA/IES; DLC

97. Bruce, James. Interesting Narrative of the Travels of James Bruce into Abyssinia to Discover the Source of the Nile. n. p.: Symondo, 1800.   DLC; MHi; InU; TU; ANIiU

98. Budge, Ernest Alfred T. W. The Alexander Book in Ethiopia. London: Oxford University Press, 1933.   AA/IES

99. -----, (tr.). The Book of the Saints of the Ethiopian Church. Cambridge: The University Press, 1928.   DLC

100. ----- The Contendings of the Apostles. A translation of the Gadla Hawâryât (Acts of the Apostles). 2 vols. London: Henry Frowde, 1901.   AA/IES

101. ----- A History of Ethiopia, Nubia and Abyssinia. Vols. I & II. Oosterhout N. B., The Netherlands: Anthropological Pub-lications, 1966.   DHU/M; DLC
       Rich discussion on the development of Christianity in Ethi-opia. (Originally publ. 1928, Methuen & Co. Md.)

102. ----- Legends of Our Lady Mary, the Perpetual Virgin & Her Mother Hanna. Translated from the Ethiopic Manuscripts... London: Medici Society, Ltd., 1922.   AA/IES

103. ----- The Life of Takla Haymanot... and the Miracles of Takla Haymânôt, the version of Dabra Libanos, and the Book of the Riches of Kings. The Ethiopic texts... with English translation. London: Priv. Pr. for Lady Meux, 1906. 2 vols.   AA/IES

104. ----- The Lives of Maba Seyon and Gabra Kristos. London: Griggs, 1898.   AA/IES

105.   -----, (tr.). The Miracles of the Blessed Virgin Mary and the
Life of Hanna (Saint Anne) and the Magical Prayers of Abeta
Mikael. The Ethiopic texts with English. London: Griggs, 1900.
                                                        AA/IES

106.   ----- One Hundred and Ten Miracles of Our Lady Mary,
Translated from Ethiopic Manuscripts for the Most Part in the
British Museum with Extracts from Some Ancient European
Versions and Illustration from the Paintings in Manuscripts by
Ethiopian Artists. London: Oxford University Press, 1933.
                                                        T Sew U-T

107.   -----, (ed. & tr.). The Queen of Sheba and Her Only Son
Menyelek. Translated from Bezold's edition of the Ethiopic
text. London: Oxford University Press, 1932.   DLC
        Translation of the Kebra Negast which includes a recount-
ing of the Solomonic and Queen of Sheba legend.

108.   -----, (ed.). Texts Relating to Saint Mena of Egypt and
Canons of Nicaea. London: British Museum, (etc.), 1909.
                                                        AA/IES

109.   Butler, Alfred J. Ancient Coptic Churches of Egypt. Oxford:
Clarendon Press, 1970.   DHU/R
        Reprint of 1884 edition.

110.   Buxton, David R. The Abyssinians. New York: Praeger
Publishers, 1970.   DHU/R
        Contains information on the Ethiopians, their religion and
way of life.

111.   ----- "The Christian Antiquites of Northern Ethiopia." Archaeologia (42; 1948), pp 1-42.   DHU

112.   ----- "Ethiopian Medieval Architecture - The Present State
of Studies." Journal of Semitic Studies (9; 1964), pp. 239-44.
                                                        DHU
        Discusses Christian architecture in the Ethiopian highlands.

113.   ----- "Ethiopian Rock-hewn Churches." Antiquity (20;1946),
pp. 60-69.   DHU

114.   ----- Travels in Ethiopia. New York: Praeger, 1948.
                                                        DHU/MO
        Includes discussion on local churches and monasteries.

115.   Caquot, André. "Aperçu preliminaire sur le Mashafa Tefut
de Gechen Amba." Annales d'Ethiopie (1: 1955), pp. 89-108.
                                                        AA/IES

116.   ----- "L'homelie en l'honneur da l'archange Ouriel (Dersana
Urael)." Annales d'Éthiopie (1; 1955), pp. 61-88.   AA/IES

117.   ----- "Note Sur Berber Maryam." Annales d'Ethiopie (1;
1955), pp. 109-16.   AA/IES

118.   ----- "Une version Geez du traité d'Hippolyte de Rome sur
l'Antichrist." Annales d'Éthiopie (6;1965), pp. 165-214.
                                                        AA/IES

119.   Caulk, R. A. "Religion and the State in Nineteenth Century
Ethiopia." Journal of Ethiopian Studies (10:1, Ja., 1972), pp.
23-41.   DHU/R

120.   Cerulli, Enrico, (ed. and tr.). Atti di Giulio di Aqfahs.
Louvain: Secrétariat du CorpusSCO, 1959. 2 vols. Corpus
Scriptorum Christianorum Orientalium, vols. 190-191;
Scriptores Aethiopici, t. 37-38. DLC Ethiopic and Italian.

121.   -----, (ed.). Atti di Krestos Samra. Louvain: L. Durbecq,
1956. 2 vols. Corpus Scriptorum Christianorum Orientalium,
vols. 163-164; Scriptores Aethiopici, t. 33-34. DLC
Ethiopic and Italian.

122.   ----- "The 'Kalilah wa-Dimnah' and the Ethiopic 'Book of
Barlaam and Josaphat' (British Museum MS Or. 534)." Journal
of Semitic Studies (9:1, Spring, 1964), pp. 75-99. AA/IES

123.   ----- "Two Ethiopian Tales on the Christians of Cyprus."
Abba Salama (1; 1970), pp. 178-85.   AA/IES

124.   ----- "Two Ethiopian Tales on the Christians of Cyprus."
Journal of Ethiopian Studies (5:1, Ja., 1967), pp. 1-8.
                                                DHU/MO; DHU/R

125.   Chaine, Marius, (ed. and tr.). Apocrypha de B. Maria Vir-
gine. Romae: K. de Luigi, 1909. 2 vols. Corpus Scriptorum
Christianorum Orientalium, vols. 39-40; Scriptores Aethiopici,
ser. 1, t. 7.   DLC

126.   ----- "Le Rituel du Baptême." Bessarione (17:123, 1913),
pp. 38-71.   AA/IES

127.   Charles, Robert Henry. The Ascension of Isaiah. London:
S. P. C. K., 1919.   AA/IES

128.   ----- The Book of Enoch. London: Richard Clay, 1917.
                                                        AA/IES

129.   ----- The Book of Jubilees or the Little Genesis. London:
Macmillan Co., 1917.

130.   ----- The Ethiopic Version of the Book of Enoch. Edited
from twenty-three MSS. Together with the fragmentary Greek
and Latin Versions. Oxford: Clarendon Press, 1906. AA/IES

131.   Cheeseman, Major R. E. Lake Tana & the Blue Nile: An
Abyssinian Quest. London: Frank Coss & Co., 1968.
        Includes discussion of local churches and monasteries.

132.   Chojnacki, Stanislaw. "Notes on a Lesser-known Type of St.
Mary in Ethiopian Painting." Abba Salama (1; 1970), pp. 162-
72.   NcD

133.   ----- "Notes on Art in Ethiopia in the 15th and Early 16th
Century." Journal of Ethiopian Studies (8:2, Jl., 1970), pp.
21-65.   DHU/R
        Religious Art of Ethiopia.

134.   ----- "Notes on Art in Ethiopia in the 16th Century: An Inquiry into the Unknown." Journal of Ethiopian Studies (9:2,
Jl., 1971), pp. 21-97.   DHU/R
        Ethiopian religious art.

135.   ----- and Mergia Diro, (comps.). Ethiopian Publications:
Books, Pamphlets, Annuals and Periodical Articles Published
in 1962 Ethiopian and 1970 Gregorian Calendar. Addis Ababa:
Institute of Ethiopian Studies, Haile Sellassie I University,
1971.   AA/IES
        Includes titles in Ethiopian languages.

136.   ----- and Sahle-Mariam Kifle, (comps.). List of Current
Periodical Publications in Ethiopia. Addis Ababa: Institute of
Ethiopian Studies, Haile Sellassie I University, 1972. AA/IES

137.   The Church of Ethiopia: A Panorama of History and Spiritual
Life. Addis Ababa: Ethiopian Orthodox Church, 1970. DHU/R

138.   The Church of Ethiopia: An Introduction to the Contemporary
Church of Ethiopia. Addis Ababa: Ethiopian Orthodox Church,
1973.   DHU/R

139.   Clapham, Christopher. Haile-Selassie's Government. New
York: Praeger, 1969.   DHU/MO; DHU/R
        Sub-section on the Church and religion.

140.   Cleve, Hugh Craswall. The Ethiopic Version of the Song of
Songs. London: Taylor's Foreign Press, 1951. AA/IES

141.   Conacher, John Roy Hamilton. General Survey Concerning
Christian Literature in Ethiopia. Addis Ababa: Christian Literature Development Project, 1970.   AA/IES

142.   Constantine II Augustus. "Letter of Constantius to the Ethiopians against Frumentius." Nicene and Post-Nicene Fathers of
the Christian Church. Vol. 4, Second Series (Grand Rapids,
Michigan: W. B. Eerdmans Publishing Co., 1953), pp. 250-51.
                                                        DHU/R

143. Conti Rossini, Carlo, (ed. and tr.). Documenta ad Illustr-
      andam Historiam. I. Liber Axumae. Parisiis: E typogra-
      pheo Reipublicae, 1909-1910. 2 vols. Corpus Scriptorum
      Christianorum Orientalium, vols. 54, 58; Scriptores Aethio-
      pici, ser. 2, t. 8.   DLC Ethiopic and French.

144. -----, (ed.) "Due Capitoli del libro del Mistero di Giyorgis
      da Sagla." Rassegna di Studi Etiopici (7:1, 1948), pp. 13-53.
                                                              AA/IES

145. -----, (ed. and tr.). Historia regis Sarsa Dengel (Malak
      Sagad). Edidit et interpretatus est K. Conti Rossini. Accedit
      Historia gentis Galla, curante et interprete I. Guidi. Parisiis:
      E typographeo Reipublicae, 1907. 2 vols. Corpus Scriptorum
      Christianorum Orientalium, vols 20-21; Scriptores Aethiopici,
      ser. 2, t. 3. DLC   Ethiopic and Latin.

146. ----- "Lo 'Awda Nagast scritto divinatorio etiopico." Ras-
      segna di Studi Etiopici (1; 1941), pp. 127-45.   AA/IES

147. ----- "Note per la storia letteraria abissina." In: Reale
      accademia dei Lincei. Rendiconti: Classe di scienze morali,
      storiche e filologiche (ser. 5, 8; 1900), pp. 197-220; 263-285.
                                                              AA/IES

148. -----, (ed. and tr.). Vitae Sanctorum Antiquiorum (Gadla
      Yared, seu Acta Sancti Yared; Gadla Pantalewon, seu Acta S.
      Pantaleonis). Romae: K. de Luigi, 1904. 2 vols. Corpus
      Scriptorum Christianorum Orientalium, vols. 26-27; Scriptores
      Aethiopici, ser. 2, t. 17. DLC   Ethiopic and Latin.

149. -----, (ed. and tr.). Vitae Sanctorum Indigenarum (Gadla
      Abuna Abakerazun, seu Acta Sancti Abakerazun; Gadla Takla
      Hawaryat, sive Acta Sancti Takla Hawaryat). Romae: K. de
      Luigi, 1910. 2 vols. Corpus Scriptorum Christianorum
      Orientalium, vols. 56-57; Scriptores Aethiopici, ser. 2, t.24.
      DLC   Ethiopic and Latin.

150. -----, (ed. and tr.). Vitae Sanctorum Indigenarum (Gadla
      Basalota Mika'el, seu Acta Sancti Basalota Mika'el; Gadla
      Anorewos, seu Acta Sancti Honorii). Romae: K. de Luigi,
      1905. 2 vols. Corpus Scriptorum Christianorum Orientalium,
      vols. 28-29; Scriptores Aethiopici, ser. 2, t. 20. DLC
      Ethiopic and Latin.

151. -----, (ed. and tr.). Vitae Sanctorum Indigenarum (Gadla
      'Emna Walatta Petros, seu Acta Sanctae Walatta Petros, Edi-
      dit Karolus Conti Rossini; Ta'amera Zar'a-Buruk, seu Mira-
      cula Sancti Zara-Buruk, edidit C. Jaeger). Romae: K. de
      Luigi, 1912. Corpus Scriptorum Christianorum Orientalium,
      vol. 68; Scriptores Aethiopici, ser. 2, t. 25. DLC Ethiopic.

152. -----, (ed. and tr.). Vitae Sanctorum Indigenarum (Gadla
      Marqorewos, seu Acta Sancti Mercurii). Parisiis: E typo-
      grapheo Reipublicae, 1904. 2 vols. Corpus Scriptorum Chris-
      tianorum Orientalium, vols. 33-34; Scriptores Aethiopici, ser.
      2, t. 22.   DLC   Ethiopic and Latin.

153. Conzelman, William E., (ed.). Chronique de Galawdewos
      (Claudius). Roi d'Ethiopie. Paris: Emile Bouillon, 1895.
                                                              DLC

154. Coppet, Maurice de. "Sanctuaires et Pélegrinages Chrétiens
      d'Ethiopie." L'Illustration (#4239; 1924), pp. 531-32. AA/IES

155. ----- "Le Tabot." Gebra Sellase (ed.). Chronique du Re-
      gne de Menelik II, Roi des Rois d'Ethiopie (Paris: Maisonne-
      uve Freres, 1930), pp. 549-51.   AA/IES

156. "The Coptic Church in Egypt." Christian Union (5:12, Dec.,
      1854), pp. 555-59.   DHU/R

157. Cosmas. The Christian Topography of Cosmas, An Egyp-
      tian Monk. J. W. McCrindle, ed. London: Hakluyt Society,
      1897.   AA/IES; DLC

158. Coulbeaux, Jean Baptiste. Histoire Politique et Religieuse
      d'Abyssinie. 3 vols. Paris: Paul Geunthner, 1929. AA/IES

159. Cowley, Roger. "The Beginnings of the andem Commentary
      Tradition." Journal of Ethiopian Studies (10:2, 1972), pp. 1-16.
                                                              DHU/R

160. ----- "The Ethiopian Church and the Council of Chalcedon."
      Sobornost (6:1, Sum., 1970), pp. 33-38. Pam. File, DHU/R;
                                                              DCU

161. ----- "The Study of Geez Manuscripts in Tegre Province."
      Journal of Ethiopian Studies (9:1, Ja., 1970), pp. 21-25. DHU/R
      Religious manuscripts.

162. -----, (ed.). Tsidke Haymanot: Ye-Bete Kristian Haymanot
      Wusanawoch. (Addis Ababa): Berhanena Selam, 1963. (EC)
                                                              AA/IES

163. ----- and Fitawrari Alem Teferu. "The Study of Geez Manu-
      scripts in Tégre Province." Journal of Ethiopian Studies (9:1,
      Jan., 1970), pp. 21-25.   DHU/R

164. Crummey, Donald E. "The Introduction and Expansion of
      Orthodox Christianity in Oelem Auraja, Western Wallaga, from
      about 1886-1941." Journal of Ethiopian Studies (10:1, 1972),
      pp. 103-12.   AA/IES; DHU/R

165. Daoud, Marcos. Church Sacraments. Addis Ababa: Tinsae
      Zegoubae Printing Press, 1952.   AA/IES

166. ----- The Liturgy of the Ethiopian Church. Addis Ababa:
      Berhanena Selam Printing Press, (1954).   AA/IES

167. Daskalakis, Apostolos V. "Evangelisation of Ethiopia and Re-
      lations Between Greeks and Ethiopians in the Byzantine Era."
      Lecture delivered at Haile Selassie I University on February
      25, 1963. Addis Ababa: 1963. Mim.   AA/IES

168. Davies, Donald M. The Old Ethiopic Version of Second Kings;
      A Critical and Comparative Study of its Provenance. Doctoral
      dissertation. Princeton Theological Seminary, 1946.

169. Davis, Asa Johnson. "The Church-State Ideal in Ethiopia: A
      Synopsis. (Part One)." Ibadan (No. 21, 1965), pp. 47-52.
                                                    AA/IES; ANIiu

170. ----- The Mazgaba Haimanot, an Ethiopic Monophysite Text,
      Critically Edited, with Translation, Notes and Introduction.
      Doctoral dissertation. Harvard University, 1960.

171. ----- "The Orthodoxy of the Ethiopian Church." Tarikh (2:1,
      1967), pp. 62-69.   AA/IES; DLC

172. ----- "The Sixteenth Century Jihad in Ethiopia and its Im-
      pact on Culture." Journal of the Historical Society of Nigeria
      (2:4, 1963), pp. 567-92.   DHU/MO

A172. Davis, Raymond J. Fire on the Mountains. Grand Rapids, Mich.:
      Zondervan Pub. Co., 1966. DHU/R; MN+CA
      The Story of a miracle in the church of Ethiopia. Written
      by the general director of the Sudan Interior Mission, who
      has been a missionary in Africa since 1934.

173. Deramey, I. "Introduction et Restauration du Christianisme
      en Abyssinie, 330-480." Revue de l'Histoire des Religions
      (31; 1895), p. 131.   AA/IES

174. Dillmann, August. Das Buch der Jubilaen, oder die Kleine
      Genessis. Leipzig: R. Reisland, 1874.   AA/IES

175. ----- Catalogus Codicum Manuscriptorum Bibliothecae Bod-
      leianae Oxoniensis. Part VII. Codices Aethiopiei. Oxford:
      University, Bodleian Library, 1848.   DLC

176. ----- Liber Henoch, Aethiopice, ad Quinque codicum Fidem
      editus, cum Variis Lectionibus. Lipsiae: Guil Vogelii, 1865.
      Geez text.   AA/IES

177. ----- Liber Jubilaeorum. Londini: Apud Williams et Nor-
      gate, 1859.   AA/IES

178. Dombrowski, Joanne. "Preliminary Report on Excavations in Lalibela and Natchabiet Caves, Begemder." Annales d'Ethiopie (8; 1970), pp. 21-29.   AA/IES

179. Doresse, Jean. Ethiopia. Translated from French by Elsa Coult. London: Elek Books (New York: G. P. Putnam's Sons), 1959.   DHU
     Rich discussion of the Church included.

180. ----- "Ethiopia in the Early Christian and Byzantine Era." Abba Salama (2; 1971), pp. 108-18.   AA/IES

181. ----- "Le Fêtes d'Axoum." Connaissance du Monde (1956), pp. 119-28.   AA/IES

182. ----- "La Saison et ses Fetes: de Noel au Timkat." L'Ethiopie d'aujourd'hui (#8; 1963), pp. 5-8.   AA/IES

183. Dowling, Theodore Edward. The Abyssinian Church.... London: Cope and Fenwick, 1907.   TSewU-T

184. Duensing, Hugo. Der Aethiopische Text der Kirchenordnung des Hippolyt. Gottingen: Vandenhoeck and Ruppracht, 1946.   AA/IES

185. ----- "Die Abessinier in Jerusalem." Zeitschrift des Deutschen Palatina-Vereins (Jahr., 1916), pp. 98-115. AA/IES

186. Duff, Douglass V. "Viceroy of Judah's Lion." The Cornhill Magazine (152:911, Nov., 1935), pp. 513-24.   AA/IES

187. Dye, William McEntyre. Moslem Egypt and Christian Abyssinia. New York: Atkin & Prout Printers, 1880.   DHU/MO; DHU/R

188. Eadie, Douglas G. "Chalcedon Revisited." Journal of Ecumenical Studies (10:1, Wint., 1973), pp. 140-5.   DHU/R
     An interview with Abuna Theophilus, Patriarch of the Ethiopian Orthodox Church.

189. Elliston, Edgar James. An Ethnohistory of Ethiopia: Factors which Affect Planting and Growing of the Church. Masters thesis. School of World Mission, Fuller Theological Seminary, 1971.

190. Endalkachew Makonnen. "Religion of Our Forefathers." Abba Salama (1; 1970), pp. 191-99.   AA/IES

191. Ephraim Isaac. The Ethiopian Church. Boston: Henry N. Sawyer Co., 1968.   DHU/R

192. ----- "The Hebraic Molding of Ethiopian Culture." Mosaic (6:1, 1965), pp. 8-15.   AA/IES

193. ----- A New Text--Critical Introduction to the Mashafa Berhān: With a Translation of Book I. Leiden: E. J. Brill, 1973.   AA/IES

194. ----- "Social Structure of the Ethiopian Church." Ethiopian Observer (14:4, 1971), pp. 240-88.   DHU/MO

195. Esteves Pereira, Francisco Maria, (ed. and tr.). Acta Martyrum. Romae: K. de Luigi, 1907. 2 Vols. Corpus Scriptorum Christianorum Orientalium, Vols. 37-38; Scriptores Aethiopici, ser. 2, t. 28.   DLC
     Ethiopic and Latin. Contents: Gadla Fasiladas seu Martyrium S. Baslidis; Gadla Yostos, seu Martyrium Sanctorum Iusti et Aboli eius filii, et Theocliae eius uxoris; Gadla Tēwoderos, seu Martyrium S. S. Theodori Anatolii; Gadla Abādir, seu Martyrium Sanctorum Apatris et Irenis sororis eius; Gadla Galāwedēwos, seu Martyrium Sancti Claudii; Gadla Fiqtor, seu Martyrium Sancti Victoris; Gadla Susenyos, seu Martyrium Sancti Sisinnii.

196. ----- Martyrio do Abba Isaac de Piphre segundo a versao ethiopica. Coimbra: Imper. da Universidade, 1903. AA/IES

197. ----- Vida do Abba Samuel do Mosteiro do Kalamon versao Ethiopica. Lisboa: Imperensa Nacional, 1894. AA/IES Spanish and Amharic texts.

198. "Ethiopia: Africa's Ancient Kingdom." Color. University of Minnesota.
     Film. Explains different racial and religious backgrounds of the people.

199. "Ethiopia: The Black Jews." Newsweek (67; My. 9, 1966), p. 50+.   DHU

200. "Ethiopia: Cultures in Change." National Geographic Society. Released by Films Incorp., 1971. 20 min. sd. color. 16 mm.   DLC
     Film. "Traces the history of Ethiopia, and points out that it is a natural fortress protected by mountains and deserts. Describes the peoples of Ethiopia, including the Christian, Moslem, and Jewish communities."

201. Ethiopia: Illuminated Manuscripts. Introduction by Jules Leroy and Texts by Stephen Wright and Otto A. Jäger. New York: Published by the New York Graphic Society by Arrangement with UNESCO, 1961.   DHU

202. Ethiopia: Ministry of Information. National Festivals in Ethiopia: Kulubi. Addis Ababa: Published by the Publications and Foreign Languages Press Department, 1967.   AA/IES

203. "Ethiopian Church: Obstacle to Progress." Christianity Today (XIV: 14, Apr. 10, 1970), p. 50.   DHU/R

204. Ethiopian Coptic Church. "Music of the Ethiopian Coptic Church." Record #4 of UNESCO Collection, An Anthology of African Music.   Phonodisc.

205. "Ethiopian Orthodox Church." Ebony (15; Aug., 1960), pp. 125+.   DHU/MO

206. Ethiopian Orthodox Church. The Church of Ethiopia: A Panorama of History and Spiritual Life. Addis Ababa: n.p., 1970.   DHU/R

207. The Ethiopian Orthodox Church Development Commission. The Gospel of Development. (n.p.: n.p., n.d.) DHU/R

208. Ethiopian Orthodox Mission, Addis Ababa. Activities of the Ethiopian Orthodox Mission. Addis Ababa: Berhanena Selam Printing Press, 1970.   AA/IES

209. "Ethiopian Patriarch Visits World Council of Churches." Ecumenical Press Service (40:17, Je., 1973), pp. 9-10. DHU/R

210. Ewald, Heinrich. Abhandlung uber des Athiopischen Buches Henokh, Entstehung Sinn und Zusammensetzung. Gottingen: Dieterich, 1854.   AA/IES

211. Faitlovitch, Jacques. Mota Muse, (La Mort de Moise), Texte Ethiopien. Paris: Paul Geuthner, 1906.   AA/IES
     Geez, French and Hebrew.

212. "Falashas." Encyclopedia Judaica, V.6 (New York: Macmillan & Co., 1971), pp. 1143-55.   Pam. File,   DHU/R

213. "The Falashas." Jewish Quarterly Review (17; 1905), pp. 142-47.   DHU/R

214. Farag, Farag Rofail. Sociological and Moral Studies in the Field of Coptic Monasticism. Leiden: E. J. Brill, 1964.   TSewU-T

215. Fellowship of Reconciliation. "To His Majesty, Haile Selassie: An Open Letter." Christian Century (52; Ag. 14, 1935), pp. 1033-34.   DHU/R

216. The Fetha Nagast (The Law of the Kings). Translated from the Geez by Abba Paulos Tzadua and edited by Peter L. Strauss. Addis Ababa: Faculty of Law, Haile Selassie I University, 1968.   AA/IES

Includes laws on the regulation of the Ethiopian Orthodox Church.

217. Findlay, L. The Monolithic Churches of Lalibela in Ethiopia. Le Caire, 1944.   DLC

218. Forget, I. Synaxarium Alexandrinum. Louvain: Imprimerie Orientaliste L. Dubrecq Secretariat du CorpusSCO, 1953-1963. 2 vols. Corpus Scriptorum Christianorum Orientalium; Scriptores Arabici, vols. 3-5, 13.   DLC

219. Fuhs, Hans Ferdinand. Die äthiopische übersetzung Propheten Hosea. Bonn: Peter Hanstein Verlag, 1971.   AA/IES

220. Funk, F. X. "Die Liturgie der Äthiopischen Kirchenordnung." Theol. Quartalschrift (80:4, 1898), pp. 513-47.

221. Gamst, Federick Charles. The Qemant Agaw of Ethiopia: A Study in Culture Change of a Pagan Hebraic People. Doctoral dissertation. University of California, Berkeley, 1967.

222. Gerster, Georg. Churches in Rock. Early Christian Art in Ethiopia. London: Phaidon Press Ltd., 1970. DHU/R; DLC

223. ----- "Searching Out Medieval Churches in Ethiopia's Wilds." National Geographic (138:6, Dec., 1970), pp. 856-84.
                                                              DHU; DLC

224. Giel, R. and J. N. van Luijk. "Patterns of Marriage in a Roadside Town in South-Western Ethiopia." Journal of Ethiopian Studies (6:2, Jl., 1968), pp. 61-69.   DHU/R

225. Gillard, John Thomas. "Are There any Colored Saints?" The Catholic World (144:859, Oct., 1936), pp. 78-84.
                                                       AA/IES; DCU

226. Gilroy, H. "Falasha Jews from Ethiopia Studying in Israel." New York Times (Mr. 4, 1955).   DHU

227. Giusto da Urbino. Philosophi Abessini (sive Vita et philosophi magistri Zar'a-Ya'qob eiusque discipuli Walda-Heywat philosophia). Edidit et interpretatus e Enno Littmann. Parisiis: E typographeo Reipublicae, 1904. 2 vols. Corpus Scriptorum Christianorum Orientalium, vols. 18-19; Scriptores Aethiopici, ser. 1, t. 31.   DLC Ethiopic and Latin.

228. Gizachew Adamu. "The City of Castles and 44 Churches." The Ethiopian Herald (Sunday, Aug. 13, 1972 - Nehase 7, 1964).
                                                              DCU

229. Glenday, D. K. "Mary in the Liturgy; an Ethiopian Anaphora." Worship (47; Apr., 1973), pp. 222-26.   DCU/TH; DGU

230. Goldschmidt, Lazarus. Vida do Abba Daniel do Mosteiro de scete, versao Ethiopica. Lisboa: Imprensa Nacional, 1897.
AA/IES   Geez and Spanish texts.

231. Goldstein, Israel. "Falashas: Ethiopia's Jews." The National Jewish Monthly (Dec., 1969), pp. 14-15+.   AA/IES

232. Gondal, I. L. Il Cristianesimo nel Paese di Menelik. Dalla Secondo Edizione Francese. Roma: Desclee, 1908. AA/IES

233. The Gospel of Development: The Orthodox Church Development Commission. n.p.: n.p., n.d.   DHU/R

234. Gotthard, Herbert. Der Text des Buches Nehemia. Kiel: n.p., 1952.   AA/IES

235. Graham, Douglas. "Reports on the Manners, Customs and Superstitions of the People of Shoa, and on the History of the Abyssinian Church." Journal of the Asiatic Society (12; 1843), pp. 625-728.   AA/IES

236. Grebaut, Sylvain. "Deux Notes Theologiques fums. Ethiopien." Aethiops (#64, 1930), pp. 46.   AA/IES

237. Gregorius (Bishop). "The Sacraments of Baptism and Chrism in the Rite of the Coptic Orthodox Church." Abba Salama (2; 1971), pp. 219-30.   AA/IES

238. Griaulle, Marcel. Abyssinian Journey. Translated by E. G. Rich. London: J. Miles, 1935. DLC; OrU; MBU; IEN; NcD; MiU; IU; PBm; NN; Cty

239. Guidi, Ignazio, (ed. and tr.). Annales Iohannis I, Iyasu I, Bakaffa. Parisiis: E typographeo Reipublicae, 1903-1905. 4 vols. Corpus Scriptorum Christianorum Orientalium, vols. 22-25; Scriptores Aethiopici, ser. 2, t. 5. DLC Ethiopic and French.

240. ----- Annales Regum Lyasu II et Iyo'as. Parisiis: E typographeo Reipublicae, 1910-1912. 2 vols. Corpus Scriptorum Christianorum Orientalium, vols. 61, 66: Scriptores Aethiopici, ser. 2, t. 6.   DLC   Ethiopic and French.

241. ----- Vita Za-Mikael Aragawi. Romae: R. Accademia dei Lincei, 1896.   AA/IES   Geez text.

242. Guidi, Michelangelo. "Contributo all'agiografia etiopica, La Vita di Aron di Sarug." Rendiconti della R. Accademia dei Lincei (25; 1916), pp. 659-701.   AA/IES

243. Haberland, E. "Christian Ethiopia." Roland Oliver (ed.). The Middle Age of African History (New York: Oxford University Press, 1967), pp. 7-12.   DHU/MO

244. Halevy, J. Teezaza Sanbat (Commandements du Sabbat): Texte Ethiopien. Publie et traduit par J. Halevy. Paris: Emile Bouillon, 1902.   AA/IES

245. Hamer, John H. "Folktales, Socialization, and the Content of Social Relationships: An Ethiopian Example." Anthropos (67:3-4, 1972), pp. 388-404.   DLC; DHU/MO

246. Hammerschmidt, Ernst. "Jewish Element in the Cult of the Ethiopian Church." Journal of Ethiopian Studies (3:2, Jl., 1965), pp. 1-12.   AA/IES; DHU/R

247. ----- "The Liturgical Vestments of the Ethiopian Church: A Tentative Survey." Proceedings of the Third International Conference of Ethiopian Studies. V. I (Addis Ababa: Institute of Ethiopian Studies, Haile Selassie I University, 1969), pp. 151-56.
                                                              DLC

248. ----- "Das pseudo-apostolische Schrifttum in äthiopischer Überlieferung." Journal of Semitic Studies (9:1, Spring, 1964), pp. 114-21.   AA/IES

249. ----- "Some Remarks on the History of, and Present State of Investigation into the Coptic Liturgy." Bulletin de la Societe d'Archeologie Copte (19; 1970), pp. 89-113.   AA/IES

250. ----- ...Stellung und Bedeutung des Sabbats in Aethiopien. Stuttgart: W. Kohlhammer Verlag, 1963.   AA/IES

251. ----- Studies in the Ethiopic Anaphoras. Berlin: Akademie-Verlag, 1961. Berliner Byzantinistische Arbeiten, Bd. 25.
                                                              AA/IES

252. ----- "Zur Christologie der Äthiopischen Kirche." Ostkirchliche Studien (13; 1964), pp. 203-07. AA/IES

253. Hansberry, William Leo. "Sources for the Study of Ethiopian History." Howard University Studies in History. (No. 11, Nov., 1930).   DHU/MO

254. Hapte Mariam Workneh,(Like Siltanat). Tintawi Ye-Itiopiya Timhirt. (Addis Ababa); Berhanena Selam, n.d. AA/IES

255. Harden, John. The Anaphoras of the Ethiopic Liturgy. London: Society for Promoting Christian Knowledge (New York: the Macmillan Co.), 1928.   AA/IES

256. ----- The Ethiopic Didascalia. New York: The Macmillan Co., 1920.   AA/IES

257. ----- An Introduction to Ethiopic Christian Literature. London: Society for Promoting Christian Knowledge, 1926. AA/IES

258. Harris, Joseph E. (ed.). The William Leo Hansberry African Notebook. Pillars in Ethiopian History. Wash., D.C.: Howard University Press, 1974.   DHU/R; DLC
       Includes explanations of "the Queen of Sheba legend," and explores the legend of Prester John and provides data to substantiate the claim that he was, in fact, an Ethiopian King.

259. Harris, William Cornwallis. The Highlands of Aethiopia. n.p.: Longman, Brown and Green, 1844.
       DLC; IEN; WU; CtY; CU; MH; NcD; OCIW; TxU

260. Haupt, Paul. "Hebrew AZ=Ethiopic ENZA." Journal of the Society of Oriental Research (7:1, Ja., 1923), pp. 41-44. DHU/R

261. Hempel, Christa and Ernst Hammerschmidt. "Position and Significance of Sabbath in Ethiopia." Mundus (1:4, 1965), pp. 305-06.

262. Herbert, Mary Elisabeth (A'Court), (Baroness.). Abyssinia and Its Apostle. London: Burns, Oates and Co., 1867. AA/IES

263. Hess, Robert L. Ethiopia: The Modernization of Autocracy. New York: Cornell University Press, 1970. DHU; DLC
       Discussion of the relationship of the Church with the state included.

264. ----- "An Outline of Falasha History." Proceedings of the Third International Conference of Ethiopian Studies. V. I (Addis Ababa: Institute of Ethiopian Studies, Haile Selassie I University, 1969), pp. 99-112.   DLC

265. Heyer, Friedrich. Die Kirche Athiopiens. Berlin: W. de Gruyter, 1971.   DLC

266. Hinsley, Arthur. "Abyssinia." Dublin Review (197:395, Oct., 1935), pp. 187-209.   AA/IES, DLC

267. Hippolytus. "Heads of the Canons of Abulides or Hippolytus, Which are Used by the Aethiopian Christians." Ante-Nicene Fathers Down to A.D. 325. V.5 (Grand Rapids, Michigan: W. B. Eerdmans Publishing Co., 1952), pp. 256-57, DHU/R

268. Hofmann, Josef, (ed.). Die Äthiopische Übersetzung der Johannes--Apokalypse. Louvain: Secrétariat du CorpusSCO, 1967. 2 vols. Corpus Scriptorum Christianorum Orientalium, vols. 281-282; Scriptores Aethiopici, t. 55-56. AA/IES
       Ethiopic and Latin.

269. Hogans, J. H. "Ethiopian Hebrews Mark End of Holiday Season." New York Age Defender (Oct. 22, 1955). DHU/MO
       N.Y. Age Defender (sic). Journal of Ecumenical Studies (8:1, Wint. 1971), p. 114.

270. ----- "Ethiopian Jews to Mark Advent of the New Year." New York Age (Sept. 29, 1951).   DHU/MO

271. Hoskins, George Alexander. Travels in Ethiopia Above the Second Cataract of the Nile, Exhibiting the State of That Country, and Its Various Inhabitants Under the Dominion of Mohammed Ali, and Illustrating the Antiquities, Arts, and History of the Ancient Kingdom of Meroe. London: Longmans, 1835.
                                                                                NBB; DLC

272. Huntingford, George W. B., (tr. and ed.). The Glorious Victories of Amda Seyon: King of Ethiopia. Oxford: Clarendon Press, 1965.   DLC
       Record of the reign of Amda Seyon (1312-42), and the conflict between Christians and Muslims.

273. ----- "The Lives of Saint Takla Haymanot." Journal of Ethiopian Studies (4:2, 1966), pp. 35-40. AA/IES; DHU/R

274. Hyatt, Harry Middleton. The Church of Abyssinia. London: Luzac and Co., 1928.   AA/IES; DLC

275. Imbakom Kalewold. Traditional Ethiopian Church Education. New York: Teachers College Press, 1970.   TSewU-T

276. "Israel Acknowledges Jewishness of Tribe in Northern Ethiopia." The Washington Post (Ja. 5, 1973). Pam. File, DHU/R

277. Jäger, Otto A. Antiquities of North Ethiopia: A Guide. Stuttgart: F. A. Brockhaus, 1965.   AA/IES
       Discusses archeological remains of early Christianity in Ethiopia.

278. Jesman, Czealaw. "Theodore II of Ethiopia." History Today (22:4, Apr., 1972), pp. 255-64.   DHU; DGU
       Some discussion of Theodore's relations with the Orthodox Church.

279. Jones, Arnold Hugh Martin and Elizabeth Monroe. A History of Abyssinia. New York: Negro Universities Press, 1969.
                                                                         IC/H; DHU/R
       Reprint of 1935 edition.

280. ----- A History of Ethiopia. Oxford: Clarendon Press, 1970.
                                                                         DHU/R; IC/H
       The Abyssinian Church, pp. 35+. The Jesuit Mission — Quiedo, Paez, Mendez, pp. 88-101.

281. Jungmann, Josaf. The Early Liturgy. Notre Dame: University of Notre Dame, 1959.   DHU/R
       Ethiopian liturgy discussed, pp. 225-26.

282. Kallimachos, D. "The Patriarchate of Alexandria in Abyssinia." Abridged and translated into English by Metropolitan Methodios of Aksum. Abba Salama (2; 1971), pp. 151-60.

283. Karmiris, Lannis. "Relations Between the Orthodox and the non-Chalcedonian Churches and the Beginning of the Preparatory Dialog Between Them." Abba Salama (1; 1970), pp. 138-53.
                                                                                AA/IES

284. Karpozilos, Apostolos D. "Anglican and Orthodox Relations to 1930." Abba Salama (1; 1970), pp. 206-17. AA/IES

285. Kolmodin, Johannes, (ed.). Tradition de Tsazzega et Hazzega. Textes Tigrigna. Archives d'études orientale, vol.5:1. Roma: Carlo de Luigi, 1912.   AA/IES

286. Korabiewicz, D. W. The Ethiopian Cross. Addis Ababa: Holy Trinity Cathedral, 1973.   AA/IES

287. Korten, David C. with Frances F. Korten. Planned Change in a Traditional Society: Psychological Problems of Modernization in Ethiopia. New York: Praeger Publ., 1972.
                                                                         DLC; DHU/R

288. Kur, Stanislas, (ed. and tr.). Actes de Marha Krestos. Louvain: Secrétariat du CorpusSCO, Waversebaan, 49, 1972. 2 vols. Corpus Scriptorum Christianorum Orientalium, vols. 330-331; Scriptores Aethiopici, t. 62-63.   DLC
       Ethiopic and French.

289. ----- Actes de Samuel de Dabra Wagag. Louvain: Secrétariat du CorpusSCO, 1968. 2 vols. Corpus Scriptorum Christianorum Orientalium, vols. 287-288; Scriptores Aethiopici, t. 57-58.   DLC   Ethiopic and French.

290. ----- Gadla Iyasus Mo'a (Actes de Iyasus Mo'a, Abbé du Couvent de St.-Étienne de Hayq). Louvain: Secrétariat du CorpusSCO, 1965. Corpus Scriptorum Christianorum Orientalium, vols. 259-260; Scriptores Aethiopici, t. 49-50. DLC

291. Lantschoot, A. "Abba Salama, métropolite d'Ethiopie (1348-1388) et son role de traducteur." Atti del convegno internazionale di studi etiopici (Roma, 1959), pp. 397-401. AA/IES

292. Laurence, Ricardo. The Book of Enoch the Prophet: An Apocryphal Production... Translated from an Ethiopic MS. in the Bodleian Library. Oxford: John Henry Parker, 1838. 3rd ed., rev. and enl.   AA/IES

293. ----- Libri Enoch, prophetae versio Aethiopica. Londini:
Typis Academicis, Impensis Editoris, 1838.   AA/IES
Geez text.

294. Lefèvre, Renato. "L'Abissinia Nella Politica Orientale di
Gregorio XIII." Gli Annali Dell'Africa Italiana (#1; 1938),
pp. 1171-1209.   AA/IES

295. Leiris, Michel. La Possession et ses Aspects Théatraux
chez les Ethiopiens de Gondar. Paris: Librairie Plon, 1958.
                                                    DLC
     Book review by Wolf Leslau in Journal of American Folk-
     Lore (73:288, Apr.-Je., 1960), pp. 175-76.
     Microcard, DHU/R

296. Leslau, Wolf. "Arabic Loan-Words in Geez." Journal of
Semitic Studies (3:2, Apr., 1958), pp. 146-68.   DHU/R

297. ----- An Annotated Bibliography of the Semitic Languages of
Ethiopia. The Hague: Mouton, 1965.   DLC; CLU

298. ----- Falasha Anthology: The Black Jews of Ethiopia. New
York: Schocken Books, 1951.   DHU/R

299. ----- The Land of Prester John, Problems and Challenges.
                                                    CLU
     "Faculty Research Lecture, University of California,
     Los Angeles, 1968."

500. Lipsky, George A. Ethiopia: Its People, Its Society, Its Culture. New Haven: HRAF Press, 1962. DHU/MO; DHU/R
     Chapter on religion.

301. The Liturgy of the Ethiopian Church. Translated by Marcos
Daoud. Revised by M. E. Blatta Marsie Harzen. N.p.: Egyptian Book Press, (1959).   DHU/R; DHU/MO
     English translation in one column and Arabic in other
     column.

302. Lobo, Jeronymo. A Voyage to Abyssinia. Translated by
Joachin LeGrand from the French. n.p.: A. Bettesworth and
C. Hitch, 1735.   NNMR

303. Lods, Adolphe. Le livre d'Henoch. Fragments grecs décou-
verts à Akhmim (Haute Egypte) publiés avec les variantes du
texte éthiopien. Paris: Leroux, 1892.   AA/IES

304. Löfgren, Oscar. Die Äthiopische Übersetzung, des propheten
Daniel... Paris: Paul Geuthner, 1927.   AA/IES   Amharic and
German text.

305. ----- Jona, Nahum, Hababuk, Zephanja, Haggai Sacharja und
Maleachi Athiopisch. Paris: H. Champion, 1930.   AA/IES
Amharic text.

306. ----- "The Necessity of a Critical Edition of the Ethiopian
Bible." Proceedings of the Third International Conference of
Ethiopian Studies. V.2 (Addis Ababa: Institute of Ethiopian
Studies, Haile Selassie I University, 1970), pp. 157-61. DLC

307. Lowenstern, Edward S. Exotic Jewish Communities of
Eurasia and Africa. Northbrook, Illinois: Whitehall Co., 1971.
                                                    DHU/R
     Includes a chapter on the Falashas of Ethiopia.

308. Luka, Ibrahim. "The Coptic Orthodox Church." Christian
East (17:3-4, Jl.-Dec., 1937), pp. 99-120.   DHU/R

309. Lundgreen, F. "Die Einführung des Christentums in Athio-
pien. Eine Quellenkritische Studie als Beitray zur Geschichte
der Kirche." Neue Kirchliche Zeitschrift (10; 1899), pp. 736-
69.   AA/IES

310. Luther, Ernest W. Ethiopia Today. Stanford, California:
Stanford University Press, 1958. DLC; NcD; NN; CtY

311. Malan, S. C. The Book of Adam and Eve, also called the
Conflicts of Adam and Eve with Satan. London: Williams and
Norgate, 1882.   AA/IES

312. Manley, G. T. "The Policy of the Christian Church in Egypt."
The Church Missionary Review (73:838, Je., 1922), pp. 143-54.
                                                    DHU/R

313. Mara, Yolande. The Church of Ethiopia: The National
Church in the Making. Asmara, Ethiopia: Il Poligrafico, 1972.
                                                    DLC

314. Marsie-Hazen, (Blatta). "The Ethiopian Church." Ecumenical Review (1:2, Wint., 1949), pp. 179-87.   DHU/R

315. Matthew, Austin Frederic. "The Abyssinian Church." The
Christian East (14:3, 1933), pp. 112-16.   AA/IES

316. ----- The Church of Ethiopia During the Italian Occupation.
(Addis Ababa, 1943.)   AA/IES

317. ----- The Church of Ethiopia, 1941-1944. (Addis Ababa,
1944).   AA/IES

318. ----- The Teaching of the Abyssinian Church, as set up by
the Doctors of the Same. London: The Faith Press, 1936.
                                                    AA/IES

319. Matthews, Derek H. "The Restoration of the Monastery
Church of Debra Damo, Ethiopia." Antiquity (23; 1949),
pp. 188-204.   DHU

320. ----- and Mordini, Antonio. "The Monastery of Debra Damo,
Ethiopia." Archaeologia (97:1959), pp. 1-58.   DLC

321. McClure, Bryan. "Religion and Nationalism in Southern
Ethiopia." Current Bibliography on African Affairs (5; Nov.,
1972), pp. 497-508.   DHU/MO; DLC

322. McNeile, R. F. "Sidelights on the Coptic Church." The
Church Missionary Review (62; Jl., 1911), pp. 407-10. DHU/R

323. Meinardus, Otto F. Christian Egypt, Ancient and Modern.
Cairo: Cahiers d'Historie Egyptienne, 1965.   DHU

324. ----- "Notizen Über das Eustathische Kloster Debra Bizen."
Annales d'Éthiopie (6; 1965), pp. 285-91.   AA/IES

325. ----- "The Zequala, the Holy Mountain of Ethiopia." Orien-
talia Suecanie (13; 1964), pp. 34-47.   AA/IES

326. Mendelssohn, Sidney. The Jews of Africa: Especially in the
Sixteenth and Seventeenth Centuries. London: Kegan Paul,
Trench, Trubner and Co., 1920. DLC; MB; NJD; NN
     Two chapters on the Falashas of Ethiopia.

327. Mercer, Samuel A. B. "The Anaphora of Our Lord in the
Ethiopic Liturgy." Journal of the Society of Oriental Research
(1:1, 1917), pp. 24-40.   DHU/R

328. -----, (tr.). "The Anaphora of Our Lady Mary (Keddase
Maryam)." Journal of the Society of Oriental Research (3:1,
Oct., 1919), pp. 51-64.   DHU/R

329. -----, (tr.). "The Anaphora of St. Gregory." Journal of the
Society of Oriental Research (7:1, Ja., 1923), pp. 27-34.

330. ----- "Christian Abyssinian." The American Church
Monthly (28:5, Nov., 1930), pp. 391-95. AA/IES; DLC

331. ----- The Ethiopic Liturgy. Its Sources, Development and
Present Form. New York: AMS Press, 1970.   DHU/R
     Reprinted from the edition of 1915.

332. Mesehafa Kidasse: Geezena Amarigna Kenemilikitu. Addis
Ababa: Berhanena Selam, 1964 (E. C.).   AA/IES

333. Mesehafa Zik: Keamit Iske Amit. (Addis Ababa): Berhanena
Selam Printing Press, 1964 (E.C.).   AA/IES

334. Methodios, Metropolitan of Aksum. "The First Meeting of
the Orthodox-Anglican Theological Sub-Commissions of Joint

(Methodios, cont.)

Doctrinal Discussions in Chambesy September 12-14, 1972, by Metropolitan Methodios of Aksum." Ekkleseastikos Paros (55:1, 1973), pp. 5-38.   AA/IES

335. ----- "The Introduction of Christianity into Aksum." Abba Salama (1; 1970), pp. 186-90.   AA/IES

336. ----- "Letters of the Greek Patriarchs of Alexandria to Ethiopia, Translated into English and Edited by Metropolitan Methodios of Axum." Abba Salama (1; 1970), pp. 131-37.
                                                        AA/IES

337. ----- "Patriarch Bailios of Ethiopia in Memoriam." Abba Salama (2; 1971), pp. 338-39.   AA/IES

338. Mezmure Dawit. (Addis Ababa): Berhanena Selam, 1959 (E.C.).   AA/IES

339. Michael Geddes. The Church History of Ethiopia. London: Printed for R. Chiswell, 1696.   DHU/MO

340. Molnar, Enrico C. Selley. The Ethiopian Orthodox Church: a Contribution to the Ecumenical Study of Less Known Eastern Churches. Pasadena: Bloy House Theological School, 1969.
                                                        TSewU-T

341. Montet, Pierre. Egypt and the Bible. Philadelphia: Fortress Press, 1968.   DLC

342. ----- Eternal Egypt. London: Weidenfeld and Nicolson, 1964.   DLC; NNC; CtY; TU

343. Montule, Edward de. Travels in Egypt During 1818 and 1819. n.p.: Richard Phillips, 1821.   DLC; CtY; NNC

344. Moore, Dale H. "Christianity in Ethiopia." Church History (5:3, Sept., 1936), pp. 271-84.   DHU/R

345. Moore, Eine. Ethiopian Processional Crosses. Addis Ababa: Institute of Ethiopian Studies, Haile Selassie I University, 1971.
                                                        DLC

346. Moretz, Rufus L. The Textual Affinity of the Earliest Coptic Manuscripts of the Gospel of John. Doctoral dissertation. Duke University, 1969.

347. Morrison, S. A. "The Church in Egypt." The Church Missionary Review (78:858, Je., 1927), pp. 134-46.   DHU/R

348. Mosley, Leonard Oswald. Haile Selassie, the Conquering Lion. London: Weidenfeld & Nicolson, 1964.
                                      DLC; NjP; RP; AAP; NcRR

349. Munro, Eleanor C. "While the King Slept His Soul Went to Heaven; When He Awoke He Built Lalibela." New York Times (Sept. 26, 1971).   DHU
          Description of the rock-hewn Churches at Lalibela.

350. Negaso Gidada with Donald Crummey. "The Introduction and Expansion of Orthodox Christianity in Qelem Awraja, Western Wallaga from about 1896 to 1941." Journal of Ethiopian Studies (10:1, Ja., 1972), pp. 103-12.   DHU/R

351. Nelson, J. Robert. "No Myopia in Ethiopia." Christian Century (88:6, Feb. 10, 1971), pp. 180-82.   DHU/R

352. Nemoy, Leon. "A Modern Egyptian Manual of the Karaite Faith." Jewish Quarterly Review (62:1, Jl., 1971), pp. 1-11.
                                                        DHU/R

353. Newman, Edward W. New Abyssinia. London: Rich & Cowan, Ltd., 1938.   DLC; ICU; OU; ANiiU

354. Norden, Hermann. Africa's Last Empire; Through Abyssinia to Lake Tana and the Country of the Falasha. London: H. F. & G. Witherby, 1930.   DHU/MO

355. ----- "The Black Jews of Abyssinia." Travel (59; Ja., 1930), pp. 25-29.   AA/IES

356. Noshy, Ibrahim. The Coptic Church. Washington: Ruth Sloan Associates, 1955.   DHU/MO

357. O'Hanlan, Douglas. Features of the Abyssinian Church. London: Society for Promoting Christian Knowledge, 1946.
                                                        AA/IES

358. O'Leary, de Lacy Evans. The Ethiopian Church, Historical Notes on The Church of Abyssinia. London: Society for Promoting Christian Knowledge, 1936.   AA/IES; DLC

359. Oudenrijn, Marcus van den. Helenae aethiopum reginae quae feruntur preces et carmina. 2 vols. Louvain: Secretariat du CorpusSCO, 1960. Corpus Scriptorum Christianorum Orientalium, vols. 208 and 211; Scriptores Aethiopici, t. 39-40.
                                                        AA/IES

360. Pankhurst, Richard K. "The Saint Simonians and Ethiopia." Proceedings of the Third International Conference of Ethiopian Studies. V. I (Addis Ababa: Institute of Ethiopian Studies, Haile Selassie I University, 1969), pp. 169-223.   DLC

361. ----- State and Land in Ethiopian History. Addis Ababa: Institute of Ethiopian Studies and the Faculty of Law, Haile Selassie I University, 1966. MH/L; FU/L; NIC; NjR; CU; WaU/L; NhD; CLU/L; ICU
          Includes discussion of Church's role in development of land tenure.

362. Pankhurst, Sylvia. "The Monolithic Churches of Lalibela: One of the Wonders of the World." Ethiopia Observer (4:7, Ag., 1960), pp. 214-24.   AA/IES

363. Pawlikowski, John T. "The Judaic Spirit of the Ethiopian Orthodox Church: A Case Study in Religious Acculturation." Journal of Religion in Africa (4:3, 1972), pp. 178-99. DHU/R

364. Pearce, Ivy. "An Andrews Adventure and Pearce's Pilgrimage to the Cave and Rock Churches of Lasta." Ethiopia Observer (12:3, 1969), pp. 142-63.   AA/IES

365. Perham, Margery. The Government of Ethiopia. Evanston: Northwestern University Press, 1969.   DHU/MO; DHU/R
          A chapter and several sub-sections on the Church.

366. Perruchon, Jules. Le Livre des Mysteres du ciel et de la terre. Paris: P. Fages, 1903.   AA/IES Geez and Italian text.

367. Pétridès, Stephanos Pierre. "Essai sur l'Evangélisation de l'Ethiopie, la Date et son Protagoniste." Abba Salama (2; 1971), pp. 77-104.   AA/IES

368. (Abuna) Philippos (Ethiopian Archbishop). Know Jerusalem. Addis Ababa: Berhanena Selam Haile I Printing Press, 1972.
                                      DHU/R; AA/IES

369. Plant, Ruth. "Rock-hewn Churches of the Tigre Province with Additional Churches by David R. Buxton." Ethiopia Observer (8:3, 1970), entire issue.   AA/IES

370. Polandian, Terenig, (bp.). The Doctrinal Position of the Monophysite Churches. Addis Ababa: Central Printing Press, 1963.
                                                        AA/IES
          Also in: Ethiopia Observer (7;1964), pp. 257-64 and Bulletin de la Société d'Archeologie Copte (17;1963), pp. 157-75.

371. Quinton, G. G. H. Ethiopia and the Evangel. London: Marshall, Morgan, and Scott, 1949.   DHU/MO

372. Ranger, Terence O. "African Religion in the History of Ethiopia." African Religious Research (3:1, Apr. 1973), pp. 30-33.
                                                        DHU/R
          A review article of Journal of Ethiopian Studies (10:1, Ja., 1972).

373. Rathjens, Carl. Die Juden in Abessinien. Hamburg:
W. Gente, 1921.   DHU/MO

374. Rayner, Decourcy H. "Persecution in Ethiopia." Christianity
Today (17:3, Nov. 10, 1972), pp. 54-55.   DHU/R
     Report on the jailing of Pentecostal Christians and the
     closing of their churches.

375. Rees, A. Herbert. "Ethiopia and Her Church." The East and
West Review (2; 1936), pp. 22-29.   DHU/R

376. Reminick, Ronald A. "The Evil Eye Belief Among the Amhara
of Ethiopia." Ethnology (13:3, Jl., 1974), pp. 279-91. DHU/R

377. Revised Constitution of Ethiopia. Negarit Gazeta (15th year:
2, Nov. 4, 1955), entire issue.
     Several sections of Constitution deal with the nature of
     the relationship of the Church with the State.

378. Rey, Charles F. The Real Abyssinia. New York: Negro
Universities Press, 1969.   DHU/R
     Reprint of 1935 edition.
     Includes chapters on slavery, religion and the National
     Church.

379. Ricci, L., (tr.). Gadla 'Emna Walatta Pētros (Vita di Walatta Piētros). Louvain: Secrétariat du CorpusSCO, Waversebaan, 1970. Corpus Scriptorum Christianorum Orientalium,
vol. 316; Scriptores Aethiopici, t. 61.   DLC

380. Riley, Willard D. Wisdom in Ethiopia. New York: Vantage
Press, 1959.   DLC; NN/Sch

381. Ross, Sheila. "Linking Aksum and Medieval Nubia." Addis
Reporter (1:5, 1969), pp. 18-19.   AA/IES

382. Rubenson, Sven. King of Kings: Tewodros of Ethiopia. Addis
Ababa: Haile Selassie I University, 1966. InU; MH; CaOTP;
CSt; CaQML
     Discussion of Tewodros' relations with the Church is covered.

383. Russell, Michael. ... Nubia and Abyssinia Comprehending
their Civil History... Illustrated by a Map, and Several Engrav-
ings. New York: J. & J. Harper, 1833.   DHU/MO

384. Samuel, V. C. "The Fourth Unofficial Consultation of Theologians Belonging to the Eastern and the Oriental Churches."
Abba Salama (3; 1972), pp. 176-80.   AA/IES

385. ----- "Proceedings of the Council of Chalcedon and its Historical Problems, a Paper written From a Critical Point of View."
Abba Salama (1; 1970), pp. 73-93.   AA/IES

386. Sanford, Christine. Lion of Judah Hath Prevailed: Being the
Biography of His Imperial Majesty Haile Selassie I.
n. p.: Dent, 1955.   NNMR

387. Schäfers, Joseph. Die Äthiopische Ubersetzung des propheten
Jeremias. Freiburg: Herderschen Verlagshandlung, 1912.
                                               AA/IES

388. Schneider, Madeleine, (ed. and tr.). Actes de Za-Yohannes
de Kebran. Louvain: Secrétariat du CorpusSCO, Waversebaan,
49, 1972. 2 Vols. Corpus Scriptorum Christianorum Orientalium, Vols. 332-333; Scriptores Aethiopici, t. 64-65. DLC
     Ethiopic and French.

389. Schodde, George Henry. "The Rules of Pachomius Translated
from the Ethiopic." Presbyterian Review (6; 1885), pp. 678-89.
                                               AA/IES; DHU/R

390. Schultz, Harold J. "Reform and Reaction in Ethiopia's Orthodox Church." Christian Century (85; Ja. 31, 1968), pp. 142-43.
                                               DHU/R

391. Sergew Hable Sellassie, (comp.). Bibliography of Ancient and
Medieval Ethiopian History. Addis Ababa: History Department,
Haile Sellassie I University, 1969.   DHU/R

392. ----- "Church and State in the Aksumite Period." Proceed-
ings of the Third International Conference of Ethiopian Studies.
V. I (Addis Ababa: Institute of Ethiopian Studies, Haile
Selassie I University, 1969), pp. 5-8.   DLC

393. ----- "New Historical Elements in the 'Gedle Aftse.'" Journal of Semitic Studies (9:1, Spring, 1964), pp. 187-99. DLC

394. ----- "The Problem of Gudit." Journal of Ethiopian Studies
(10:1, Ja., 1972), pp. 113-24. Pam. File, DHU/R
     Discussion of the Jewish or pagan queen who destroyed
     Christian Axum.

395. ----- "State and Church in the Aksumite Period." Proceed-
ings of the Third International Conference of Ethiopian Studies.
V. I (Addis Ababa: Institute of Ethiopian Studies, Haile
Selassie I University, 1969), pp. 5-8.   DLC

396. ----- "Yared." Ye Memhiran Dimts (1:1, 1965), pp. 15-17.
                                               AA/IES

397. Shack, William A. "The Mascal-Pole: Religious Conflict and
Social Change in Gurageland." Africa (38:4, Oct., 1968),
pp. 457-68.   DHU/MO

398. Shenk, Calvin E. The Development of the Ethiopia Orthodox
Church and Its Relationship With the Ethiopian Government From
1930 to 1970. Doctoral dissertation. New York University, 1972.

399. ----- "The Italian Attempt to Reconcile the Ethiopian Orthodox Church (the use of religious celebrations and assistance to
Churches and monasteries)." Journal of Ethiopian Studies
(10:1, Ja., 1972), pp. 125-35.   DHU/R

400. Simoons, Frederick J. Northwest Ethiopia: Peoples and
Economy. Madison: University of Wisconsin Press, 1960.
                                               DLC; AU; GU; LU

401. Skinner, Elizabeth. Haile Selassie: Lion of Judah.
New York: Nelson, 1967.   DLC

402. Smith, Joseph F. Egyptian Alphabet and Grammar. Salt
Lake City, Utah: Modern Microfilm Co., 1966.   CSt

403. Snowden, Frank M. Blacks in Antiquity. Ethiopians in the
Greco-Roman Experience. Cambridge, Mass.: The Belknap
Press of Harvard University Press, 1970. DHU/R; DHU/MO
     Chapter IX, "Early Christian attitude toward Ethiopians:
     Creed and Conversion."

404. Socrates. "In What Manner the Nations in the Interior of
India (Ethiopia) were Christianized in the Times of Constantine." Hist. Eccl. 1.19. Nicene and Post-Nicene Fathers of
the Christian Church. V. 2, Second Series (Grand Rapids,
Michigan: W. B. Eerdmans Publishing Co., 1952), p. 23. DHU/R

405. Sozomen. "Some Indian (Ethiopian) Nations Received Chris-
tianity at that Time Through the Instrumentality of Two Cap-
tives, Frumentius and Edesius." Hist. Eccl. 24. Nicene and
Post-Nicene Fathers of the Christian Church. V. 2, Second
Series (Grand Rapids, Michigan: W. B. Eerdmans Publishing
Co., 1952), pp. 274-75.   DHU/R

406. Spencer, Diana. "In Search of St. Luke Ikons in Ethiopia."
Journal of Ethiopian Studies (10:2, Jl., 1972), pp. 67-95. DHU/R

407. Stan, Liviu. "L'Église d'Ethiopie, Nouveau Patriarcal."
Abba Salama (2; 1971), pp. 119-50.   AA/IES

408. Stern, Henry Aron. Wanderings Among the Falashas in Abyssinia. London: Frank Cass and Co., 1968.
                         NUC; DLC; WU; OrU; FMU
     Reprint of 1862 edition.

409. Stigand, Chauncey Hugh. To Abyssinia, Through an Unknown
Land. New York: Negro Universities Press, 1969. NNMR
     Also: London: Seeley & Co., 1918.

410. Stitz, Volker. Distribution and Foundation of Churches in Ethiopia. Addis Ababa: n. p., 1973. (A paper prepared for the Conference of the Historical Society of Ethiopia, Addis Ababa, 1973).   AA/IES

411. Stone, Michael E. "Judaism at the Time of Christ." Scientific American (228:1, Ja., 1973), pp. 80-87.
     Mention of Ethiopic texts.

412. Strelcyn, S. "La Chretiente dans la Region de la Mer Rouge." Journal of Religion in Africa (5:3, 1973), pp. 161-70. DHU/R

413. Sumner, Claude. "The Ethiopic Liturgy: an Analysis." Journal of Ethiopian Studies (1:1, 1963), pp. 40-46. AA/IES

414. ----- The Ethiopic Liturgy; Liturgy of the Apostles. Addis Ababa: n. p., 1958.   AA/IES

415. Taddesse Tamrat. "The Abbots of Dabra-Hayq, 1248-1535." Journal of Ethiopian Studies (8:1, Ja., 1970), pp. 87-117.
                                                           DHU/R; DLC

416. ----- Church and State in Ethiopia: 1270-1527. Oxford: Clarendon Press, 1972. DHU/MO; DHU/R

417. ----- "Hagiographies and the Reconstruction of Medieval Ethiopian History." Rural Africana (10; Spr., 1970), pp. 12-20.
                                                                   DLC

418. ----- "A Short Note on the Tradition of Pagan Resistance to the Ethiopian Church (14th and 15th Centuries)." Journal of Ethiopian Studies (10:1, Ja., 1972), pp. 137-50. DHU/R

419. ----- "Some Notes on the Fifteenth Century Stephanite Heresy in the Ethiopian Church." Rassengne di Studi Etiopici (22; 1968), pp. 103-15.

420. ----- "Traditions of Pagan Resistance to the Expansion of the Ethiopian Church (14th and 15th Centuries)." Historical Society of Ethiopia, Papers of the Annual Conference, Addis Ababa, 1971.   AA/IES

421. Talalak Yemister Haymanot Megirachoch. Trans. Teshager Wube. Addis Ababa: Berhanena Selam Printing Press, n. d.
                                                              AA/IES

422. Tasoma Adara. "Maskal: Mystique and Mystery." Addis Reporter (1:39, 1969), pp. 6-10.   AA/IES

423. The Teachings of the Abyssinian Church, As Set Forth by the Doctors of the Same. London: The Faith Press Ltd., 1936.
                                                              TSewU-T

424. Theodoret. "Conversion of the Indians (Ethiopians)." Hist. Eccl. 1.21. Nicene and Post-Nicene Fathers of the Christian Church. V. 3, Second Series (Grand Rapids, Michigan: W. B. Eerdmans, 1953), p. 58.   DHU/R

425. Thornton, Douglas M. "The Educational Problem in Egypt." Church Missionary Intelligencer (57; Sept., 1906), pp. 651-58.
                                                                   DHU/R
     An appeal for the founding of a Christian college in Egypt.

426. Thurston, Herbert. "Abyssinian Devotion to Our Lady." Dublin Review (198:396, Ja., 1936), pp. 29-42. AA/IES

427. Tito Lepisa, (Abba). "The Three Modes and the Signs in the Ethiopian Liturgy." Proceedings of the Third International Conference of Ethiopian Studies. V. II (Addis Ababa: Institute of Ethiopian Studies, Haile Selassie I University, 1970), pp. 162-87.   DLC

428. Turaev, Boris A. Acta Sancti Fere-Mika'el. Louvain: Imprimerie Orientaliste, 1955.   AA/IES

429. ----- Vita et miracula Eustathii. Petropoli: Sumptibus Universitatis Caesareae Petropolitanae, 1905. AA/IES

430. ----- Vita Philippi Dabralibanensis. Lipsia: F. A. Brockhaus, 1902. Geez text.   AA/IES

431. ----- Vita Samuelis Valdebani. Petropoli: S. C. U. P., 1902. Geez text.   AA/IES

432. -----, (ed. and tr.). Vitae Sanctorum Indigenarum (Gadla Aron, seu Acta Sancti Aaronis; Gadla Filpos, seu Acta Sancti Philippi). Romae: K. de Luigi, 1908. 2 vols. Corpus Scriptorum Christianorum Orientalium, vols. 30-31; Scriptores Aethiopici, ser. 2, t. 20. Ethiopic and Latin.   DLC

433. -----, (tr.). Vitae Sanctorum Indigenarum (Gadla Ewostatewos, sive Acta Sancti Eustathii). Romae: K. de Luigi, 1906. Corpus Scriptorum Christianorum Orientalium, V. 32; Scriptores Aethiopici, ser. 2, t. 21. Latin translation. DLC

434. -----, (ed. and tr.). Vitae Sanctorum Indigenarum (Gadla Fere-Mika'el, seu Acta Sancti Fere-Mika'el; Gadla Zar'a-Abreham, seu Acta Sancti Zar'a-Abreham). Romae: K. de Luigi, 1905. 2 vols. Corpus Scriptorum Christianorum Orientalium, vols. 35-36; Scriptores Aethiopici, ser. 2, t. 23. Ethiopic and Latin.   DLC

435. Ullendorff, Edward. "Candace (Acts viii. 27) and the Queen of Sheba." New Testament Studies (2; 1955-56), pp. 53-56.
                                                                   DHU/R

436. ----- Ethiopia and the Bible. New York: Oxford University Press, 1968.   DHU/MO; DHU/R

437. ----- The Ethiopians. London: Oxford University Press, 1973.   DHU/R
     Includes chapter on religion and the church, Muslim conquests and Portuguese interlude.

438. ----- "Hebraic-Jewish Elements in Abyssinian (Monophysite) Christianity." Journal of Semitic Studies (1:3, Jl., 1956), pp. 216-56.   AA/IES; DHU/R

439. Vadasy, Tibor. "Ethiopian Folk-Dance." Journal of Ethiopian Studies (8:2, Jl., 1970), pp. 119-46.   DHU/R

440. ----- "Ethiopian Folk-Dance II: Tegre and Gurage." Journal of Ethiopian Studies (9:2, Jl., 1971), pp. 191-217. DHU/R

441. Van Deusen, Robert E. A Study of a Church-Related International Broadcasting Project in Addis Ababa, Ethiopia. Doctoral dissertation. American University, 1968.

442. Velat, Bernard. "Chantres, Poetes, Professeurs: Les Dabtara Ethiopiens." Les Cahiers Coptes (#5, 1954), pp. 21-29.   AA/IES

443. ----- Etudes sur le Meeraf Commun de l'Office Divin Ethiopien. Paris: Firmin-Didot, 1966.   AA/IES

444. ----- Meeraf Commun de l'office divin Ethiopien Pour Toute l'Annee. Paris: Firmin-Didot, 1966.   AA/IES

445. Vivian, Herbert. Abyssinia: Through the Lion-Land to the Court of the Lion of Judah. New York: Negro Universities Press, 1969.   DHU/R
     "Originally published in 1901."
     Chapter 10, Abyssinian Christianity.

446. Walker, C. H. The Abyssinian at Home. London: The Sheldon Press, 1933.   AA/IES

447. Walkin, Edward. A Lonely Minority, the Modern Story of Egypt's Copts. New York: Morrow, 1963.   TSewU-T

448. Walsh, Martin de Porres. The Ancient Black Christians. San Francisco: Julian Richardson Associates, 1969. DHU/MO
     Includes discussion on Ethiopia.

449. Ward, Algernon. "The Egyptian (Coptic) Church." The East and the West (6; Oct., 1908), pp. 429-36.   DHU/R

450. Watkin, Edward. "Ethiopia's Coptic Christians." The Lamp/
A Christian Unity Magazine (70:2, Feb., 1972), pp. 14-17+.
DHU/R

451. Weischer, Bernd Manuel. "Historical and Philological Problems of the Axumitic Literature (especially in the Qérellos)."
Journal of Ethiopian Studies (9:1, Jan., 1971), pp. 83-93. DHU/R

452. Wendt, Kurt. "Des Kamf un den Kanon Heiliger Schriften in
der Athiopischen Kirche der Reformen des XV Jahrhunderts."
Ethiopian Studies (1964), pp. 107-13.   AA/IES

453. -----, (ed.). Das Mashafa Milad (Liber Nativitatis) und
Mashafa Sellase (Liber Trinitatis) des Kaisers Zar'a Yaqob.
Louvain: Secrétariat du CorpusSCO, 1962-63. 4 vols. in two.
Corpus Scriptorum Christianorum Orientalium, vols. 221-
222, 235-236. Scriptores Aethiopici, vols, 41-44. DLC

454. Wilkinson, A. H. "The Scriptures in Ethiopia." The East
and West Review (2; 1936), pp. 30-34.   DHU/R

455. Windsor, Rudolph R. From Babylon to Timbuktu. A History
of the Ancient Black Races Including the Black Hebrews.
New York: Exposition Press, 1969.   DHU/R

456. Ye-Kristian Imnet Tiru Minch. (Addis Ababa): Showa Printing Press, 1959 (E.C.).   AA/IES

457. Ye-Qwanqwe Kirsina Ye-Washa Abyate Kristian. Addis
Ababa: Nigd Printing Press, 1962 (E.C.)   AA/IES

458. Zar'a Ya'qob. Il Libro della Luce, Mashafa Berhan. Edito
e tradotto a cura di C. Conti Rossini, col concorso di .
L. Ricci. Louvain: Secrétariat du CorpusSCO, 1964-65. 4
vols. Corpus Scriptores Christianorum Orientalium, vols
250-251, 261-262; Scriptores Aethiopici, t. 47 etc. DLC
Ethiopic and Italian.

459. Zotenberg, Herman. "Un Document sur les Falashas."
Journal Asiatique (Sixieme Série, 9; 1867), pp. 265-68. AA/IES

C. AFRICA: INDIGENOUS RELIGIONS—ISLAM AND CHRISTIANITY

460. Abd, Al-Magid A. "Some General Aspects of the Arabization
of the Sudan." Sudan Notes and Records (40; 1959), pp. 48-74.
DCU/AN; DLC; ICF; MH; NN; NjP

461. Abdul, M. O. A. "Syncretism in Islam Among the Yoruba."
West African Religion (No. 15, Mr., 1974), pp. 44-56. DHU/R

462. ----- "Yoruba Divination and Islam." Orita, The African
Journal of Religious Studies (4:1, Je., 1970), pp. 17-25. DHU/R

463. Abraham Demoz. "Moslems and Islam in Ethiopic Literature."
Journal of Ethiopian Studies (10:1, Jan., 1972), pp. 1-11. DHU/R

464. Abrahams, R. G. "Spirit, Twins, and Ashes in Labwor,
Northern Uganda." Jean Sibyl LaFontaine (ed.). The Interpretation of Ritual (London: Tavistock Publications, 1972),
pp. 115-34.   DHU/R

465. Abrahams, Willie. The Mind of Africa. Chicago: University
of Chicago Press, 1963.   DHU/R

466. Abrahamsson, Hans. The Origin of Death: Studies in African Mythology. Uppsala: Almguist and Wikesell, 1951. DLC;
ICU; MiU; CU; NIC; PPULC; UU; KU; OCU; MH

467. Abu-Lughod, Ibrahim. "Africa and the Islamic World."
John N. Paden and Edward W. Soja, (eds.). The African
Experience V. 1 (Evanston: Northwestern University, 1970),
pp. 545-67.   DHU/MO

468. ----- "The Islamic Factor in African Politics." Orbis
(8:2, Sum., 1964), pp. 425-44.   DCU/HU; DGU; DHU

469. Adams, Charles Clarence. Islam and Modernism in Egypt:
A Study of the Modern Reform Movement Inaugurated. London:
Oxford University Press, 1933. DLC; CoDU; IdU; NcD

470. Addison, James Thayer. "Ancestor Worship in Africa."
Harvard Theological Review (17:2, 1924), pp. 155-71. DHU/R

471. ----- The Christian Approach to the Moslem: A Historical
Study. New York: Columbia University Press, 1942. DLC;
MiU; OrU; OC; OT

472. Addo, Peter E. A. Ghana Folk Tales. Jericho, N. Y.:
Exposition Press, Inc., 1968.   DHU/MO

473. Adeney, Miriam A. "What is "Natural" About Witchcraft and
Sorcery?" Missiology, an International Review (2:3, Jl., 1974),
pp. 377-95.   DHU/R

474. Africa (8:4, Oct., 1935), Special Issue on Witchcraft in Africa.
DHU/MO

475. "African Names in Christian Initiation." African Ecclesiastical Review (14:4, 1972), pp. 350-52.   DHU/R

476. "African Religions." Frank Gardonyi and Clifford Janoff.
Released by BFA Educational Media, 1970. 44 fr. color.
35 mm. & phonodisc: 2 s.   DLC
Filmstrip. "Depicts the major African religions of
Christianity, Islam, and ancient tribal beliefs, showing
the customs and observances unique to each and the develop-
ment of new sects that are a blend of tribal and Christian
Beliefs."

477. "African Religions and Ritual Dances." WCAU-TV. Released by Carousel Films, 1971. 19 min. sd. color. 16 mm.
DLC
Film. "Shows the rarely-seen African religious cult
dances the Invocation to Igunnu and the Ritual fire dance
to Shango, and portrays how dance itself is an expression
of religous devotion."

478. Ahamdou Hampate Bâ. "The Fulbe or Fulani of Mali and
Their Culture." Abbia (Jl.-Dec., 1966), pp. 55-87. DHU/MO

479. Ahmed, Jamal M. "The Islamic Factor in the Awakening of
Algeria." C. Allen and R. W. Johnson (eds.). African Perspectives (New York: Cambridge University Press, 1970),
pp. 113-14.   DHU/MO
Islamic-Arabic roots of Algerian revolution.

480. Ajami, S. M. "La Societé Musulmane et ses Regles Face
á l'Evolution." Etudes Conglaises (11; Oct.-Dec., 1968),
pp. 40-49.   DLC

481. Akalu Walda-Mikael. "Buhe." Ethnological Society Bulletin
(7; 1957), pp. 57-63.   AA/IES

482. Alagoa, Ebiegberi J. The Small Brave City State. Madison,
Wisconsin: University of Wisconsin Press, 1964. DHU/MO

483. Alberti, Ludwig. Account of the Tribal Life and Customs
of the Xhosa in 1807. Translated by Dr. William Fehr. From
the original manuscript in German of the Kaffirs of the South
Coast of Africa. Cape Town: A. A. Balkema, 1968. DHU/MO

484. Alexander, David and Bill Rau. Spirit Possession at Chalumbe
Primary School. Lusaka, Zambia: Conference on the History
of Central African Religions Systems, Ag. 31-Sept. 8, 1972.
Pam. File, mim.   DHU/R

485. Alexandre, Pierre. "L'animisme." Monde Non-Chrétien
(61-62, Ja.-Je., 1962), pp. 70-76.   DLC
Religion in Africa.

486. ----- "A West African Islamic Movement: Hamalism in
      French West Africa." Robert I. Rotberg and Ali A. Mazrui
      (eds.). Protest and Power in Black Africa (New York: Oxford
      University Press, 1970), pp. 497-512.   DHU/R

487. Allen, Christopher and R. W. Johnson, (eds.). African Per-
      spectives. Cambridge: University Press, 1970.   DHU/R
           "Includes information on Islam in the history of West
      Africa" and "colonial misfortune and religious response."

488. Allen, Roland. "Islam and Christianity in the Sudan," Inter-
      national Review of Missions. (9; Oct., 1920), pp. 31-48. DHU/R

489. Al-Rayyah Hashim, M. A. "Free Will and Pre-destination in
      Islamic and Christian Thought." Kano Studies (3; Je., 1967),
      pp. 27-34.   DLC

490. Amorium, Deolindo. Africanismo e Espiritismo. Traduccion
      de Cristoforo Postiglione. Buenos Aires: Editorial Constancia,
      1958.   NNCor
           First published in the Periodical Estudos Psiguicos, Lisbon,
      in March, August and October, 1946.

491. Ancestors, Negroes and God; the Principles of Akan-Ashanti
      Ancestor Worship. Gold Coast: George Boakye Pub. Co., 1938.
                                                      DHU/MO

492. Anderson, J. N. D. Islamic Law in Africa. London: H. M. S.
      O., 1954.   DHU/MO

493. Anderson, Vernon Andry. Witchcraft in Africa: A Mission-
      ary Problem. Doctoral dissertation. Southern Baptist Theo-
      logical Seminary, 1942.

494. Andre, Pierre J. L'Islam Noir: Contribution a L'Etude des
      Confreries Religieuses Islamiques en Afrique Occidentale,
      Suivie d'Une Etude sur l'Islamen Dahomey. Paris: Geuthner,
      1924.   MH

495. Arberry, A. J. Revelation and Reason in Islam. New York:
      Macmillan, 1957.   DHU/R

496. Archdeacon, Ward. "The Druzes and Their Religion." The
      East and the West (8; Ja., 1910), pp. 32-41.   DHU/R
           Islam-Egypt.

497. Ardener, Edwin. "Belief and the Problem of Women." Jean
      Sibyl La Fontaine (ed.) The Interpretation of Ritual (London:
      Tavistock Publications, 1972), pp. 135-58.   DHU/R
           The Bakweri of Cameroon--traditional religion.

498. Arinze, Francis A. Sacrifice in Ibo Religion. Ibadan: Ibadan
      University Press, 1970. WvU; MH-P; InNd

499. Arnoux, P. Alex. "Le Culte de la Societe Secrete des Iman-
      dwa au Ruanda." Anthropos (7:3, My.-Je., 1912), pp. 273-95.
                                                      DLC
           des Peres Blancs, Kabgayi, Ruanda (Afrique Orientale
      Allemande).

500. ----- "Le Culte de la Societe Secrete des Imandwa au
      Ruanda." Anthropos (7:4, 5, Jl.-Oct., 1912), pp. 529-58. DLC
           des Peres Blancs, Kabgayi, Ruanda (Afrique Orientale
      Allemande).

501. ----- "Le Culte de la Societe Secrete des Imandwa au Ruanda."
      Anthropos (7:4, 5, Jl.-Oct., 1912), pp. 840-75.   DLC
           des Peres Blancs, Kabgayi, Ruanda (Afrique Orientale
      Allemande).

502. ----- "Le Culte de la Societe Secrete des Imandwa au Ruanda."
      Anthropos (8:1, Jan.-Feb., 1913), pp. 110-34.   DLC
           des Peres Blancs, Kabgayi, Ruanda (Afrique Orientale
      Allemande).

503. ----- "Le Culte de la Societe Secrete des Imandwa au Ruanda."
      Anthropos (8:4, 5, Jl.-Oct., 1913), pp. 754-74.   DLC
           des Peres Blancs, Kabgayi, Ruanda (Afrique Orientale
      Allemande).

504. "Ashanti Fetishes and Oracles." (Readings.). American
      Journal of Folk-Lore (13:48, Ja.-Mr., 1900), pp. 61-65. DHU/R
      Microcard.

505. Ashton, E. H. Medicine, Magic and Sorcery Among the South-
      ern Sotho. Cape Town: University of Cape Town, 1949. NN/Sch.
           "Communications from the School of African Studies,
      University of Cape Town."

506. The Association for the Study of Negro Life & History, Inc.
      "Negro-Mohammedan Kingdoms." Africa Then and Now, 1801-
      1899 (Washington, D.C.: The Associated Publishers, Inc.,
      1971), pp. 8-9.   DHU/R

507. Atterbury, Anson Phelphs. Islam in Africa. New York:
      G. P. Putnam's Sons, 1899.   DHU/R

508. Avon, R. P. "Vie Sociale des Wabende au Tanganika."
      Anthropos (10-11:1, 2, Ja.-Apr., 1915-16), pp. 98-113. DLC
           des Peres Blancs, au Tanganika, Afrique.

509. Awolaln, J. Omosade. "Cultic Functionaries in the Yoruba
      Traditional Religion." Journal of Religious Thought (28:2,
      Aut.-Wint., 1971), pp. 85-94.   DHU/R

510. Ayliff, John and Joseph Whiteside. History of the Abambo
      Generally Known as the Fingo. Cape Town: C. Struik, 1962.
      (orig. Butterworth, Transkei: "The Gazette," 1912.)

511. Aycdele, Stephen A. The Social Factors That Contributed to
      the Spread of Islam Among the Hausa and the Yoruba Tribes of
      Nigeria. Masters thesis. Howard University, School of
      Religion, 1973.

512. Azikiwe, Ben N. "Fragments of Onitsha History." Journal
      of Negro History (15:4, Oct., 1930), pp. 474-97.   DHU

513. Azikiwe, Nnamdi. Renascent Africa. London: Frank Cass &
      Co. Ltd., 1968.   DHU/R
           pp. 120-23, Toward Spiritual Balance.
           pp. 107-13, A Heaven on Earth.

514. Ba Amadou, Hampate. "Animisme En Savane Africaine
      (Animism in the African Savanah)." Rencontres Internationales
      De Bouacke, Les Religions Africaines Tradionnelles. Paris:
      Editions du Seuill, 1965. NjPt; InU; NcD; PPULC; NhD; CSt-H;
      IEN; NjP; MMC; ICU; MiU

515. Balandier, Georges. "Femmes 'Possedees' et Leurs Chants.
      Presence Africaine (5:3, 1948), pp. 749-55. Cty; IEN; MH;
      NN; NhD; TNF; ICB; DHU/MO
           The Lebu tribe of Sengal consecration of the possessed
      person, dances and the sacrifice of an animal which is
      eaten.

516. ----- and P. Mercier. Les Pecheurs Lebou du Senegal:
      Particularisme et Evolution. Et. Senegalaises, 1952. DLC
           "A study of the influence of Islam and modern commerce
      on our fishing people."

517. Balogun, Ismail Ayinla Babatundo. "The Introduction of
      Islam into the Etsako Division of the Mid-Western State of
      Nigeria." Orita (6:1, Je., 1972), pp. 27-38.   DHU/R

518. ----- The Penetration of Islam into Nigeria. Khartoum:
      Sudan Research Unit, Faculty of Arts, University of Khartoum,
      (African Studies Seminar Paper no. 7), 1969. DLC; ANIiU. Mim

519. Banton, Michael. West African City; a Study of Tribal Life in
      Freetown. London: Oxford University Press, 1957. DHU/R
           Chapter on Tribal groups and religious alignments.

520. Barlow, Jerome H. "Hausa Women and Islam." Canadian
      Journal of African Studies (6:2, 1972), pp. 317-28. DHU/MO

521. Barton, George A. "Sacrifice Among the Wakamba in British
      East Africa." Journal of American Folk-Lore (12:45, Apr.-
      Je., 1899), pp. 144-45.   DHU/R
      Microcard.

522.   Bascom, William R. "African Culture and the Missionary."
Civilizations (3:4, 1963), pp. 491-502. DAU; DGW; DLC

523.   ----- and Melville J. Herskovits. Continuity and Change in
African Cultures. Chicago: University of Chicago Press, 1959.
                                                    DHU/R
       "Religious acculturation among the Anang Ibibio of
       Southeastern Nigeria." pp. 279-99.

524.   Bascom, William R. "Drums of the Yoruba." Folkways
Records and Service Corporation, 1953.
       Phonodisc.

525.   ----- "Ifa Divination. Comments on the Paper by J. D.
Clarke." Journal of the Royal Anthropological Institute
(69; 1939), pp. 235-56.   CLU

526.   ----- "Ifa Divination." Man (42:14-28, Mar.-Apr., 1942),
pp. 41-43.   DHU/MO

527.   ----- Ifa Divination: Communication Between Gods and Men
in West Africa. Bloomington, Ind.: Indiana University Press,
1969. NcGU; KyLxCB; GU, KU; LU, NRU; InU; MoSW; NSyU;
NBuC; MH; KyU; NjP; DAU; CLU

528.   ----- "Odu Ifa: the Names of the Signs." Africa (36:4,
Oct., 1966), pp. 408-21.   DHU/MO

529.   ----- "Odu Ifa: the Order of the Figures of Ifa." Bulletin
de l'Institut Francis d'Afrique Noire (23:3/4, Jl.-Oct., 1961),
pp. 676-82.   DHU/MO

530.   ----- "The Principle of Seniority in the Social Structure of
Yoruba." American Anthropologist (n.s. 44; 1942), pp. 37-64.
                                                    CLU

531.   ----- "The Relationship of Yoruba Folklore to Divining."
Journal of American Folk-Lore (56:220, Apr.-Je., 1943),
pp. 127-31.   DHU/R
       Microcard.

532.   ----- "The Sanctions of Ifa Divination." Royal Anthropological Institute of Great Britain and Ireland Journal (71; 1941),
pp. 43-54.   CLU

533.   ----- "Secret Societies," Religious Cult-Groups and Kinship
Units Among the West African Yoruba. Doctoral dissertation.
Northwestern University, 1939.

534.   ----- "Social Status, Wealth and Individual Differences
Among the Yoruba." American Anthropologist (53; 1951),
pp. 490-505.   CLU

535.   ----- "The Sociological Role of the Yoruba Cult-Group."
American Anthropologist (n.s. 46:1 pt. 2, Memoir no. 63,
Ja., 1944), pp. 1-75. Pam. File, DHU/R; Cty; DCU; DLC;
ICU; NN; OrU; Txd; CLU

536.   ----- The Yoruba of Southwestern Nigeria. New York: Holt,
Rinehart, and Winston, 1969.   DHU/SW
       Contains chapters on the Yoruba Spiritual Cycle, and
       the Deities.

537.   Basden, George Thomas. "After Paganism-What?" East
and Review (5:1, Ja., 1939), pp. 22-34.   DHU/R

538.   ----- Among the Ibos of Nigeria: An Account of the Curious
and Interesting Habits, Customs and Beliefs of a Little Known
African People by One Who Has for Many Years Lived Amongst
Them on Close and Intimate Terms. n.p. Frank Cass, 1966.
                                                    IEN

539.   ----- Niger Ibos: A Description of the Primitive Life, Cus-
toms and Animistic Beliefs, of the Ibo People of Nigeria by One
Who, for Thirty-Five Years, Enjoyed the Privilege of Their
Intimate Confidence and Friendship. n.p.: Cass, 1966. NNMR

540.   Bastide, Roger. Elements de Sociologie Religieuse. Paris:
A. Colin, 1935. DLC; CaBVa; PPULC; PBM; TU; NcD

541.   ----- "Reflexions sans Titre Autour d'une des Formes de
la Spiritualité Africaine (Polytheismes des Nigeriens ou Daho-
meens)." Présence Africaine (17-18, Feb.-My., 1958),
pp. 9-16.   DHU/MO
       Religion in Africa.

542.   ----- "Religions Africaines et Structure de Civilisation."
Présence Africaine (66:2d quarter, 1968), pp. 98-111.
DHU/MO; DGW; NIC; NjP

543.   Baudin, Noel. Fetichism and Fetich Worshippers. New York:
Benziger Brothers, 1885. DHU/MO; NB; DCU/H
       Religious beliefs in Africa.

544.   ----- "Le Fetichisme, ou La Religion des Negres de la
Guinee." Les Missions Catholiques (16; 1884), pp. 190-260+.
CaO; CtHC; CtY-D; DCU

545.   Beattie, John H. M. "The Ghost Cult in Bunyoro." Ethnology (3:2, Apr., 1964), pp. 127-51.   DHU/R
       The Bunyoro of western Uganda.

546.   ----- "Group Aspects of the Nyoro Spirit Mediumship Cult."
Rhodes-Livingstone Journal (30; 1961), pp. 25-28. DAU

547.   ----- "Initiation into the Chwezi Spirit Possession Cult in
Bunyoro." African Studies (16:3, 1957), pp. 150-61. DHU/MO

548.   ----- "Ritual and Social Change." Man (1:1, Mr., 1966),
pp. 60-74.   DLC

549.   ----- and John Middleton. Spirit Mediumship and Society in
Africa. New York: Africana Pub. Co., 1969.   DHU/R
       Anthropologists investigate comparatively the relationship
       between forms of mediumship and the social order in Africa.

550.   Beavon, Harold W. E. An Analysis of Religious Elements in
African Animism. Masters thesis. Seventh-day Adventist
Theological Seminary, 1955.

551.   Becker, C. H. Christianity and Islam. London: Harper and
Brothers, 1909.   DLC

552.   Beckett, Lemuel Morgan. Rational Thoughts Concerning the
Supreme Being of the Universe and the True Primitive Religion.
Washington, D.C.: n.p., 1919.   OWibfU

553.   Beecham, John. Ashantee and the Gold Coast: Being a Sketch
of the History, Social State, and Superstitions of the Inhabitants
of Those Countries: With a Notice of the State and Prospects of
Christianity Among Them. London: Mason, 1841. CtY; OrU;
PPULC; InU

554.   Behrman, Lucy Creevey. Muslim Brotherhoods and Politics
in Senegal. Cambridge, Mass.: Harvard University Press, 1970.
                                                    DHU/MO; DHU/R

555.   ----- The Political Influence of Muslim Brotherhoods in
Senegal. Doctoral dissertation. Boston University, 1967.

556.   Beidelman, Thomas O. "Eight Kaguru Texts: A Contribution
Toward a Survey of Kaguru Folklore and Cosmology."
Anthropos (62:3-4, 1967), pp. 369-93. DLC; DHU/MO

557.   ----- The Kaguru, a Matrilineal People of East Africa.
New York: Holt, Rinehart, 1971.   DLC

558.   ----- "Myth, Legend and Oral History: A Kaguru Traditional
Text." Anthropos (65:1 & 2, 1970), pp. 74-97.   DLC

559.   Beier, Ulli (ed.). Origin of Life and Death: African Creation Myths. London: Heinemann, 1966.   CLU

560.   Bell, Henry Hesketh Joudou (Sir.). "The Fetish-Mountain of
Krobo." Macmillan's Magazine (July, 1893), pp. 210-19.
                                CtY; DLC; MH; NN; NNC

561.   Bell, Richard. The Origin of Islam in Its Christian Environment ... Edinburgh: Macmillan and Co., 1926. DLC; NN; MB

562. Bender, C. ... Religious and Ethical Beliefs of African Negroes, Duala and Wakweliland. Girard, Kan.: Haldeman-Juluis Co., 1925.   NN/Sch

563. Benedict, Burton. People of the Seychelles. London: H. M. Stationery Off., n. d.   DLC
     Includes some discussion of religion.

564. Bengtson, Dale Raymond. The Issue of 'Meaning' and 'Function' in the Study of African Traditional Religions: Illustrated by a Religio-Historical Inquiry into the Phenomenon of the 'Founder'. Doctoral dissertation. Hartford Seminary Foundation, 1971.   DHU/R

565. "Benin Kingship Rituals." Ibadan, Nigeria: Medical Illustration Unit, University of Ibadan.   Film.

566. Ben-Jochannan, Yosef. African Origins of the Major "Western Religions." New York: Alkebu-Lan Books, 1970.   DHU/R
     African roots of contemporary black religion in America.

567. Bennett, Robert A. "Africa and the Biblical Period." Harvard Theological Review (64:4, Oct., 1971), pp. 483-500.   DHU/R

568. Berger, Morroe. Islam in Egypt Today. Social and Political Aspects of Popular Religion. Cambridge: Cambridge University Press, 1970.   DHU/R
     Current religious organization in Egypt.

569. Berglund, Axel-Ivar. "Communion With the Shades in Traditional Zulu Society." Missionalia (1:2, Ag., 1973), pp. 39-41.
                                                                  DHU/R
     Cult of the shades (the forefathers) in Zulu society.

570. Bergsma, Harold M. "Tiv Proverbs as a Means of Social Control." Africa (40:2, Apr., 1970), pp. 151-61.   DHU/MO

571. Beyerhaus, P. "The Christian Approach to Ancestor Worship." Ministry (6:4, Jl., 1966), pp. 137-46.   DLC
     Religion in Africa.

572. Bhebe, N. M. B. The Ndebele and Mwari Before 1893: A Religious Conquest of the Conquerors by the Vanquished. Lusaka, Zambia: Conference on the History of Central African Religious Systems, Ag. 31-Sept. 8, 1972. Pam. File, DHU/R Mim.

573. Bible, N. T. Matthew. Matthew's Gospel Translated into the Grebo Language. West Africa: Cape Palmas, 1836. DHU/MO

574. Biebuyck, Daniel. Lega Culture; Art, Initiation, and Moral Philosophy Among a Central African People. Berkeley: University of California Press, 1973.   DHU/R
     See pp. 52-54, for the essential features of Lega religion.

575. Biranda. (Prince). La Bible Secrete Des Noirs Selon Le Bouity, Doctrine Initiatique de l'Afrique Equatoriale. Illustrations par la Comtesse S. de Villermont et R. Kempf d'après l'auteur. Commentaires de Jean-Rene Legrand. Paris: Omnium Litteraire, 1952.   DLC

576. Bleeker, Sonia. The Ibo of Biafra. New York: William Morrow & Co., 1969.   DHU
     Chapter 5, "Religion and the Arts."

577. Bloch, Maurice. "Tombs and Conservation Among the Merina of Madagascar." Man (3:1, Mr., 1968), pp. 94-104.
                                                                  DHU/MO

578. Bloomhill, Greta. The Sacred Drum: A Collection of Stories Based on Folklore of Central Africa. Cape Town, South Africa: Howard Timmins, 1960.   DLC; CtY; CLU

579. ----- Witchcraft in Africa. Cape Town: Timmins, 1962. CLU

580. Blyden, Edward Wilmot. African Life and Customs. London: C. M. Phillips, 1908.   NNCor
     Also Microfilm, Library of Congress Photoduplication Service, 1961.

581. ----- The Arabic Bible on the Soudan; an idea for Transliteration. London: C. M. Phillips, 1910.   DHU/MO
     Negro author.

582. ----- Christianity, Islam and the Negro Race. Edinburgh: University Press, 1967. DHU/R; FSU
     Reprint of 1888 ed.

583. ----- "Islam in Western Sudan." Journal of the African Society (2; Oct., 1902), pp. 11-37. CtY; DLC; NN

584. ----- "The Koran in Africa." Journal of the African Society (4; Ja., 1905), pp. 157-77. CtY; DLC; NN

585. ----- "Mohammedanism and the Negro." Fraser's Magazine (96; 1875), pp. 598+.   DLC; OO

586. ----- "Mohammedanism and the Negro Race." Methodist Quarterly Review (59:1, Ja., 1877), pp. 100-27.   DHU/R

587. ----- "Mohammedans in Africa." The Church at Home and Abroad (6; 1889), pp. 408-09.   DHU/R

588. Boerakker, Hans. "Traditional Marriage Versus Customary Marriage." African Ecclesiastical Review (15:2, 1974), pp. 142-51.   DHU/R

589. Bolink, Peter. "God in Traditional African Religion; A Deus Otiosus." Journal of Theology For Southern Africa (5; Dec., 1973), pp. 19-28.   DHU/R

590. Bond, John. "The Barrier of African Mysticism." Optima (Mr., 1958), pp. 1-7.   DLC

591. Boone, C. C. "Some African Customs and Superstitions on the Congo." Southern Workman (39:11, Nov., 1910), pp. 625-27.   DHU/MO; DLC

592. Bosch, Pere Fridolin. "Le Culte des Ancetres chez les Banyangwezi." Anthropos (20:1, 2, Ja.-Apr., 1925), pp. 200-09.   DLC

593. Bouisson, Maurice. Magic, its Rites and History. London: Rider & Co., 1960.   DHU/R
     Part 2: Magic and Religion, Rite and Prayer.

594. Bourdillon, M. F. C. The Cults of Dzivaguru and Karuva Amongst the North-Eastern Shona Peoples. Lusaka, Zambia: Conference on the History of Central African Religious Systems, Ag. 31-Sept. 8, 1972.   Pam. File; DHU/R

595. ----- "The Manipulation of Myth in a Tavara Chiefdom." Africa (42:2, Apr., 1972), pp. 112-21.   DHU/MO

596. Bourguignon, Erika. "Divination. Transe et Possession en Afrique Transsaharieene." A. Caquot and M. Liebovici (eds.). La Divination. Paris: Presses Universitaires de France, 1968.   CLU

597. Bowdich, Thomas Edward. An Essay on the Superstitions, Customs, and Arts, Common to the Ancient Egyptions, Abyssinians, and Ashantees. Paris: Smith, 1821.
                                   DLC; CtY; NN; PPULC

598. Bowers, Aidan. "Towards an Understanding of Islam." African Ecclesiastical Review (13:4, 1971), pp. 305-14. DHU/R

599. Bradbury, R. E. "Ezomo's Ikengobo and the Benin Cult of the Hand." Man (61; Ag., 1961), pp. 129-38. NNU; DLC; OkU

600. Braimah, B. A. R. "The Concept of Sin in Islam." Ghana Bulletin of Theology (4:1, Dec., 1971), pp. 31-40. DHU/R

601. ----- "Islamic Education in Ghana." Ghana Bulletin of Theology (4:5, Dec., 1973), pp. 1-16.   DHU/R

602. Brain, James L. "Kingalu, A Myth of Origin from Eastern Tanzania." Anthropos (66:5-6, 1971), pp. 817-38.
                                   DLC; DHU/MO

603. ----- "More Modern Witch-Finding." Tanganyika Notes and Records (No. 64, Mr., 1964), pp. 44-48.   DCU/AN

604. Brelvi, Mahmud. Islam in Africa. Lahore, Pakistan: Institute of Islamic Culture, 1964. NN; MH; IEN; InU; DLC

605. ----- Muslims in Arabia and Africa. Karachi: Ferozsons, 1951. CU; ICU; MiU; NN; NcD; MH; C

606. Brinton, Daniel Garrison. Religions of Primitive Peoples. New York: G. P. Putnam's Sons, 1897. InU; DHU/R; NN; PPULC; MH; PU; DCU

607. Brown, Sheila. "De L'Adhésion à un Nouveau Système Religieux à la Transformation d'un Système de Valeurs: Étude d'une Communauté Rurale Africaine. Social Compass (Louvain: 19:1, 1972), pp. 83-91.   DHU/R

608. Bruwer, J. P. "Remnants of a Rain-Cult Among the Achewa." African Studies (11:4, Dec., 1952), pp. 179-82.   DHU/MO

609. Bryant, Alfred T. Zulu Medicine and Medicine Men. 2nd ed. Mystic, Conn.: Lawrence Verry, Inc., 1970.   DHU

610. Burns, R. I. "Christian-Islamic Confrontation in the West; the Thirteenth-Century Dream of Conversion." The American Historical Review (76:2, Dec. 1971), pp. 1386-1412+.
                                        DCU; DHU; DAU; DGW;DGU

611. Burton, Richard Francis. A Mission to Gelele, King of Dahome. With Notices of the So Called "Amazons", the Grand Customs, the Yearly Customs, the Human Sacrifices, the Present State of the Slave Trade, and the Negro's Place in Nature. London: Tinsley, 1864.   DHU/MO

612. Burton, William F. Luba Religion and Magic in Custom and Belief. Tervuren: n.p., 1961.   CLU

613. Buthelegi, Manas. "Polygyny in the Light of the New Testament." African Journal of Theology (2; Feb., 1969), pp. 59-70.
                                                            DHU/R
      "One in a series of articles on Polygyny and the Church in Africa."

614. Butin, Romain Francois. "New Archaeological Discoveries in Southern Abyssinia." Art and Archaeology (24:1-2, Aug., 1927), pp. 21-26.   AA/IES

615. Butt-Thompson, Frederick W. West African Secret Societies, Their Organizations, Officials and Teaching. Westport, Conn.: Negro Universities Press, 1970.   DHU/R
      Reprint of 1929 edition.

616. Buxton, Jean. Religion and Healing in Mandari. New York: Oxford University Press, 1973.   DHU/R

617. Byaruhanga-Akiiki, A. B. T. Religion in Bunyoro. Kampala: Makerere University, 1971.   ANAU

618. Cabrera, Lydia. "Ritual y Simbolos de la Iniciación en la Sociedad Secreta Abakua." Journal de la Société des Américanistes de Paris (58; 1969), pp. 139-71.   DLC

619. Cagnolo, C. Akikuyu; Their Customs, Traditions and Folklore. English Translation. Nyeri, Kenya: Printed by Akikuyu in the Mission Printing School, 1933. NUC; NN; DCU; CU; OCI; NcD; MH-P; LU; DLC; ICU; C; NNC; WaU; TxU; CaQML; KU; IEN; CtY-D

620. Callaway, Godfrey. "Witchcraft." International Review of Missions (25; 1936), pp. 216-26.   DHU/R
      Africa.

621. Calloway, Henry. The Religious System of the Amazulu. London: Trubner and Co., 1868-70. NN/Sch; DHU/MO

622. Cambridge History of Islam. Edited by P. M. Holt, Ann K. S. Lambton and Bernard Lewis. Cambridge University Press, 1970.   DHU/R

623. Campbell, Dugald. In the Heart of Bantuland, a Record of Twenty-Nine Years Pioneering in Central Africa Among the Bantu Peoples, With a Description of Their Habits, Customs, Secret Societies, and Languages. Philadelphia: Lippin Cott, 1922.   DHU/MO

624. Camphor, Alexander P. Missionary Story Sketches, Folklore From Afrika. New York: BFL Communications, Inc., 1909.   DHU/MO

625. Cantori, Louis Joseph. Political Implications of Islam in the Middle Belt of Northern Nigeria. Doctoral dissertation. University of Chicago, 1963.

626. Cardi, C. N. de (Comte). "Ju-Ju Laws and Customs in the Niger Delta." Journal of Anthropological Institute (29; 1899), pp. 51-61.   DCU/A

627. ----- "A Short Description of the Natives of the Niger Coast Protectorate, With Some Account of Their Customs, Religion, Trade, Etc." Mary H. Kingsley, West African Studies. London: Macmillan, 1899.   CLA

628. Cardinall, Allan Walsey. The Natives of the Northern Territories of the Gold Coast; Their Customs, Religion and Folklore. London: Negro University Press, 1920.
                            DLC; NcD; NN; NNC; ICJ; INu

629. Carles, Fernand. La France et l'Islam en Afrique Occidentale. Contribution A l'etude de la Politique Coloniale dans l'Afrique Francaise. Toulouse: Riviere, 1915.
                            NUC; DLC; CU; CtY; OU; MiU

630. Carrington, John F. "African Music in Christian Worship." International Review of Missions (37; 1948), pp. 198-205. DHU/R
      Yakusu district of the Upper Congo.

631. Carroll, Kevin. Yoruba Religious Carving: Pagan and Christian Sculpture in Nigeria and Dahomey. New York: Praeger, 1967.   DHU/MO

632. Carter, Fay. "The Education of African Muslims in Uganda." Uganda Journal (29:2, 1965), pp. 193-99. NcD; CU; WU; NIC; NNIG

633. Carter, Mary. Origins and Diffusion of Central African Cults of Affliction. Lusaka, Zambia: Conference on the History of Central African Religions Systems. Ag. 31-Sept. 8, 1972.
                    Pam. File, DHU/R   mim.

634. Cash, W. Wilson. "Religious Life in Egypt." The East and the West (21; Oct., 1923), pp. 319-24.   DHU/R
      Christianity versus Islam in Egypt.

635. Cerulli, Enrico. "The Folk-Literature of the Galla of Southern Abyssinia." Harvard African Studies (3; 1922), pp. 9-215.
                                                CtY; DLC; NN; NjP

636. ----- "Islam u Ethiopi (Islam in Ethiopia)." Przeglad Orientalistyczny (Warsaw) (no. 1/65, 1968), pp. 3-13. DAU

637. Ceston, P. Jean Marie. "Le 'Gree-Gree Bush' (Initiation de la Jeunesse) chez les Negres-Golah, Liberia." Anthropos (6:5., Sept.-Oct., 1911), pp. 729-54.   DLC
      des Miss. Africaines de Lyon, Kekou, Liberia. Religious institution.

638. Challis, W. A. "Swaziland from Within." The East and the West (6; Jl., 1908), pp. 307-21.   DHU/R
      Swaziland religion, witchcraft and Christian evangelism, pp. 312-21.

639. Chambard, Roger. "Notes sur Quelques Croyances Religieuses des Galla." Revue d'Ethnographie et des Traditions Populaires (25; 1926), pp. 121-24.   AA/IES

640. Champagne, P. Emery. "La Religion des Noirs du Nord de la Gold Coast." Anthropos (23; 5, 6, Sept.-Dec., 1928), pp. 851-60.   DLC

641. Chapelle, Jean. Nomades Noirs du Sahara. Paris: Plon, 1957.   CtY; CU; NhD; TxU

642. ----- "La Religion Des Toubous (Tubu Religion)." Nomades Noirs du Sahara. Paris: Librarie Plon, 1957. CtY; TxU; WU; IU

643. Charles-Picard, Gilbert. Les Religions de l'Afrique Antique. Avec 11 gravures hors texte, 21 gravures et une carte dans le texte.... Paris: Plon, 1954.   NN/Sch

644. Chatelain, Heli. "African Fetishism." Journal of American Folklore (7:3, Jl.-Sept., 1894), pp. 303-04. Pam. File, DHU/R Manifestations and Paraphernalia in African religion.

645. ----- "African Folk-Life." Journal of American Folklore (10: 36, Ja.-Mr., 1897), pp. 21-34.   DHU/R Microcard.

646. ----- "African Races." Journal of American Folklore (7:3, Jl.-Sept., 1894), pp. 289-302. Pam. File, DHU/R American Ethnology.

647. ----- "Folk-Lore in an African's Life." Southern Workman (25:8, Ag., 1896), pp. 164-66.   DLC; DHU/MO A general idea of the province of Angola's personal folk-lore.

648. Chavaillon, Jean. Prehistoric Finding in Melka Kunture and Omo Valley. Addis Ababa: (Ethiopian Archaeological Institute), 1970.   AA/IES

649. Chikopela, E. K. "Marriage Commitment." African Ecclesiastical Review (14:4, 1972), pp. 327-31. DHU/R Author feels that many years of study and survey is needed before a solution can be reached for the present marital situation in Africa.

650. Childs, Gladwyn Murray. Umbundu Kinship and Character; Being a Description of the Social Structure and Individual Development of the Ovimbundu of Angola, With Observations Concerning the Bearing of the Enterprise of Christian Missions of Certain Phases of the Life and Culture Described. Doctoral dissertation. Columbia University, 1950.

651. Christensen, James Boyd. "The Adaptive Functions of Fanti Priesthood." William R. Bascom and Melville J. Herskovits, (eds.). Continuity and Change in African Cultures (Chicago: University of Chicago Press, 1959), pp. 257-78.   DHU/R

652. Christensen, Thomas G. Gbya Value Orientation as Opportunities for Dialogue with the Christian Mission. Masters thesis. Lutheran School of Theology at Chicago, 1971.

653. Clarke, J. D. "Ifa Divination." Journal of the Royal Anthropological Institute (69:2, 1939), pp. 235-56. DLC

654. Clarke, Virginia Maltby. A Study of Primitive Religion in the Congo. Masters thesis. College of Missions, 1926. TN/DCHS

655. Cleene, Nide. Introduction a L'Ethnographie du Congo Belge et du Rwanda-Burundi. Anvers: Editions de Sikkel, 1957.   DHU/MO

656. Cobern, Camden McCormick. The New Archeological Discoveries and their Bearing upon the New Testament and upon the Life and Times of the Primitive Church... Introduction by Edward Naville... New York and London: Funk & Wagnalls Co., 1917.   DHU/MO

657. Collins, Robert Oakley. The Mahdist Invasions of the Southern Sudan, 1883-1898. Doctoral dissertation. Yale University, 1959.

658. Colson, Elizabeth. "Ancestral Spirits Among the Plateau Tongas." Simon and Phoebe Ottenberg. Cultures and Societies of Africa. (New York: Random House, 1960), p. 372. DHU/MO

659. ----- "Rain-Shrines of the Plateau Tongo of Northern Rhodesia." Africa (18:4, Oct., 1948), pp. 272-83.   DHU/MO

660. Comhaire, Jean L. "Crimes et Superstitions Indigénes." Revue Juridique du Congo Belge (2:4, 1926). MH-L; CtY Congo.

661. ----- "La Vie Religieuse a Lagos." Zaïre (3:5, My., 1949), pp. 549-56. DCU/AN; DLC; ICU; NN; DHU/MO Women in Lagos turning to Mohammedanism causing the decline of the Christian religions in Lagos.

662. Conant, Francis P. Dodo of Dass: A Study of a Pagan Religion of Northern Nigeria. Doctoral dissertation. Columbia University, 1960.

663. Cooksey, Joseph J. The Land of the Vanished Church: A Survey of North Africa. London: World Dominion Press, 1926. NC; DLC; CtY-D; OCI; MH; CtY

664. Cooley, William D. The Negroland of the Arabs Examined and Explained; or, An Enquiry into the Early History and Geography of Central Africa. With a Bibliographical Introduction by John Ralph Willis. n.p.: Frank Cass, 1966. NNMR

665. Cooper, Joseph. Un Continent Perdu, ou l'esclavage et la Traite en Afrique (1875) Avec Quelques Observations Sur la Manière dont ils se Pratiquent en Asie et Dans d'autres Contrées Sous le nom de Système Contractuel de la Main-d' oeuvre. Ouvrage Traduit del 'anglais et Contenant une Pref. de M. Ed. Laboulaye. Paris: Hachette, 1876. CtY-D

666. Correia, R. P. J. Alves. "L'animisme Ibo et les Divinities de la Nigeria." Anthropos (16-17: 1-3, Ja.-Je., 1921-22), pp. 360-66. DLC; DAU; DCU/AN

667. ----- "Le sens Moral chez les Ibos de la Nigeria." Anthropos (16-17: 4-6, Jl.-Dec., 1923-24), pp. 880-89.   DLC; DAU; DCU/AN

668. Courlander, Harold. Tales of Yoruba Gods and Heroes. New York: Crown Publishers, Inc., 1973.   DHU/R

669. Cousin, Charles. Etude sur le Droit Martrimonial dans la Coutume de Soudan. Paris (Doct. d'Etatdroit) 1908-9. DLC

670. Cousins, William Edward. Malagasy Customs: Native Accounts of the Circumcision, the Tangena, Marriage, and Burial Ceremonies. Antanarivo: L.M.S. Press, 1876. MH:NC

671. Crawford, J. R. Witchcraft and Sorcery in Rhodesia. London: Oxford University Press, 1967.   DHU/MO

672. Cross, Sholto. The Watch Tower, Witch-Cleansing, and Secret Societies in Central Africa. Lusaka, Zambia: Conference on the History of Central African Religions Systems. Ag. 31-Sept. 8, 1972 (mim.). Pam. File; DHU/R

673. Crossley, John. "The Islam in Africa Project." International Review of Mission (61:242, Apr., 1972), pp. 150-60. Pam. File, DHU/R

674. ----- "Ten Years of Islam in Africa Project." The Bulletin of Christian Institutes of Islamic Studies (3:3-4, Ja./Apr., 1970), pp. 60-63. Pam. File, DHU/R

675. Crowder, Calvin Ray. An Inquiry Into the Influences of Islam in Nigeria and its Challenge to Christian Missions. Masters thesis. New Orleans Baptist Theological Seminary, 1961.

676. Crowder, M. "Islam in Northern Nigeria." Geographical Magazine (31; 1958), pp. 304-16.   DHU

677. ----- "Islam on the Upper Niger." Geographical Magazine (31; 1958), pp. 222-35. Mi; WM; OO; PP

678. Crowther, Samuel Adjai, (bp.). Experiences with Heathens and Mohammedans in West Africa. London: Society for Promoting Christian Knowledge, 1892. NC; MH

679. Crummey, Donald E. "Shaikh Zakaryas: An Ethiopian Prophet." Journal of Ethiopian Studies. (10:1, Jan., 1972),
pp. 55-66.   Pam. File,   DHU/R

680. "Cults of Affliction and of Mass Possession." African
Religious Research (2:2, Nov., 1972), pp. 17-26. Pam. File,
DHU/R
A summary of some of the papers given at the Conference
of Central African Religious Systems, University of
Zambia, August 31st to September 8th, 1972.

681. Cunnison, I. "Perpetual Kinship: A Political Institution of
the Luapala Peoples." Rhodes-Livingstone Journal (20; 1956),
pp. 31-36.   DAU

682. Dale, Godfrey. The Contrast Between Christianity and
Muhammadanism. London: Society for Promoting Christian
Knowledge, 1913.   DLC; ODW

683. ----- Islam and Africa. London: Society for Promoting
Christian Knowledge; N. Y. & Toronto, The Macmillan Co.,
1925.   DLC; WaU; NN; CU

684. ----- The Peoples of Zanzibar; Their Customs and Religious
Beliefs. New York: Negro University Press, 1969.
DHU/R; InU; NN/Sch
Reprint of 1920 publication.

685. Dammann, Ernst. Die Religionen Afrikas. Stuttgart:
W. Kholhammer, 1963.   NNCor; DHU/MO
Die Religionen der Menschheit, bd. 6.

686. Daneel, Marthinus L. "The Christian Gospel and the Ancestor
Cult." Missionalia (1; 2, Ag., 1973), pp. 46-73.   DHU/R

687. Danquah, Joseph Boakye. The Akan Doctrine of God.
London: Lutterworth Press, 1944.   DHU/MO

688. ----- Ancestors, Negroes and God; the Principles of Akan-
Ashanti Ancestor-Worship. Gold Coast: George Boakye Pub. Co.
1938.   DHU/MO

689. Dapper, Olfert. Description de l'Afrique, Contenant les Noms,
la Situation et les Confins de Toutes ses Parties, Leurs Rivieres,
Leurs Villes et Leurs Habitations, Leurs Plantes et Leurs Ani-
maux, les Moeurs, les Coutumes, la Langue, les Richesses, la
Religion et le Gouvernement de ses Peuples. Amsterdam: Wolfgang, Waesbergers, Boom & Van Someren, 1686.   DLC; RPJ-
CB; IEN; CtY; CU; PP; PU-MU; IN; InU; NN

690. Debrunner, Hans W. Witchcraft in Ghana. New York:
Panther House, 1971.   DHU/MO

691. Decle, Lionel. "Funeral Rites and Ceremonies Amongst the
'Tshinyai' (or 'Tschinyungwe')." Journal of Anthropological
Institute (23; 1893-1894), pp. 420-21. CtY; CU; IU; CaTU; ICN

692. Dekmejian, Richard H. and Margaret J. Wyozomirski.
"Charismatic Leadership in Islam: The Mahdi of the Sudan."
Comparative Studies in Society and History (14: 2, Mr., 1972),
pp. 193-214.   DHU/R

693. Delafosse, Maurice. "Islam in Africa: First Paper." International Review of Missions (15:3, July, 1926), pp. 533-46.
DHU/R

694. "Demonical Possession in Angola, Africa." Journal of
American Folk-Lore (6:23, Oct.-Dec., 1893), p. 258. DHU/R
Microcard.

695. Dennett, Richard Edward. At the Back of the Black Man's
Mind. London: Macmillan & Co., 1906. DLC; NcD; PPAN;
OU; DHU/R
Traditional African religions and customs.

696. ----- Notes on the Folklore of Fjort (French Congo). Published for the Folk-lore Society, by David Nutt, 1898.
DLC; OCU; MiU; PP

697. ----- The Religious and Political System of the Yoruba.
Nigerian Studies. London: Macmillan & Co., 1910. DLC

698. Dery, P. P. "Traditional Healing and Spiritual Healing in
Ghana Christian Attitudes." The Ghana Bulletin of Theology
(4:4, Je., 1973), pp. 53-64.   DHU/R

699. Deschamps, Hubert Jules. ... Les Religions de L'Afrique
Noire. Paris: Presses Universitaires de France, 1954. NN/Sch

700. Dewar, Emmeline H. "Katete." Southern Workman (42:1,
Ja., 1913), pp. 43-44.   DLC; DHU/MO
Author is of King Williams Town, South Africa.
"An African folk-lore story explaining why the children
never let pots fall off their heads."

701. Dickson, Kwesi A. "Christian and African Traditional Ceremonies." Practical Anthropology (18:2, Mr.-Apr., 1971),
pp. 64-71.   DHU/R; DAU/W; DCU/AN

702. ----- and Paul Ellingworth (eds.). Biblical Revelation and
African Beliefs. London: Lutterworth Press, 1969.   MiEM;
ICU; DHU/R; NjP

703. Dieterlen, Germaine. "Les Ceremonies Soix Antenaires du
Sigui Chel les Dogon." Africa (41:1, Ja., 1971), pp. 1-11.
DHU/MO
Complex religious ceremony.

704. ----- Essai sur la Religion Bambara. Paris: Presses
Universitaries de France, 1951.   DHU/MO
The Bambara are a West African people living in Guinea,
Senegal, Mauritania, Upper Volta, Mali, Ivory Coast.

705. ----- and Béatrice Appia, et al. Textes Sacrés d'Afrique
Noire, Choisis et Présentés. Préface de Amadou Hampaté Ba.
Paris: Gallimard, 1965.   NjP

706. "Divination in South Africa." (Folk-Lore Scrap-Book.)
Journal of American Folk-Lore (11:42, Jl.-Sept., 1898),
pp. 231-34.   DHU/R
Microcard.

707. Doane, Thomas W. Bible Myths and Their Parallels in Other
Religions; Being a Comparison of the Old and New Testament and
Miracles, With Those of Heathen Nations of Antiquity; Considering also Their Origin and Meaning. N. Y.: The Truth Seeker Co.,
1882-1910. ND; OU; DLC; NN/Sch

708. Dobbins, Frank Stockton. Error's Chains: How Forged and
Broken. A Complete Graphic and Comparative History of the
Many Strange Beliefs, Superstitious Practices, Domestic
Peculiarities, Sacred Writings, Systems of Philosophy, Legends
and Traditions, Customs and Habits of Mankind Throughout the
World, Ancient and Modern. New York: Standard Publishing
House, 1883.   DHU/MO

709. Doi, A. R. I. "An Aspect of Islamic Syncretism in Yorubaland." Orita Ibadan Journal of Religious Studies (5:1, Je.,
1971), pp. 36-46.   DHU/R

710. ----- "The Yoruba Mahdi." Journal of Religion in Africa
(4:2, 1971), pp. 119-38.   DHU/R

711. Donaldson, Stuart A. Church Life and Thought in North
Africa, A.D. 200. Cambridge: The University Press, 1909.
DLC; MdBP; CtY; OO; NNC; PPP; PU; PPStC; MB-Z

712. Dorsey, George A. "The Ocimbanda, or Witch-Doctor of the
Ovimbundu of Portuguese Southwest Africa." Journal of
American Folk-Lore (12:46, Jl.-Sept., 1899), pp. 183-88.
DHU/R
Microcard.

713. Douglas, Mary. "Social and Religious Symbolism of the Lele
of the Kasai." Zaire (9:4, 1955), pp. 385-402.   DHU/MO

714. Downes, Rupert M. Tiv Religion. Ibadan: Ibadan University
Press, 1971.   DLC

715. Driberg, Jack Herbert. "The Secular Aspect of Ancestor-Worship in Africa." Journal of the Royal African Society (35; Ja., 1936), p. 21.   DHU/MO

716. Dubois, H. M. "L'idée de Dieux chez les Anciens Malgaches." Anthropos (24:1, 2, Ja.-Apr., 1929), pp. 281-311.   DLC

717. DuBois, William E. B. The Negro... London: Oxford University Press, 1970.   DHU/R
      Repr. of 1915 ed. Chapt. IV, "The Niger and Islam." Negro author.

718. Dunger, George A. The Dynamics of Religious Behavior of the Northwestern Bantu. Doctoral dissertation. Hartford Seminary Foundation, 1950.

719. Earthy, E. Dora. Valenge Women: the Social Economic Life of the Valenge Women of Portuguese East Africa. An Ethnographic Study. London: Oxford University Press, 1933.
      NN; DAU; OCI; PU; DLC
      Deals with social organization, economic life, life cycle, religion and magic.

720. Eberhardt, Jacqueline. "Messianisme en Afrique du Sud." Archives de Sociologie des Religions (2:4, Jl.-Dec., 1957), pp. 31-56.   DCU

721. Eby, Omar. The Sons of Adam. Scottsdale, Pa.: Herald Press, 1970.   DHU/R
      Brief accounts of Americans in Africa and their experiences of Muslim-Christian encounters.

722. Echeruo, Michael J. C. "The Religious Culture of 19th Century Lagos." West African Religion (12; Jl., 1972), pp. 16-25.   DHU/R

723. Edel, May. The Chigo of Western Gyanda. New York: Oxford University Press, 1957. DLC; DHU/MO; CtY; IU; ICU; KU; MoU

724. Edinburgh University Centre of African Studies. Religion in Africa; Proceedings of a Seminar Held in the Centre of African Studies, University of Edinburgh, 10th-12th April, 1964. Edinburgh: n.p., 1964.   NNCor

725. Edwards, A. "Study of Religion in West Africa, 1959-69 (Bibliography)." Religion; a Journal of Religion and Religions (2:1, Spr., 1972), pp. 42-56.   DCU; DLC

726. Egboh, E. O. "Conflicts Between Traditional Religion and Christianity in Iboland, South-Eastern Nigeria." West African Religion (10; Jl., 1971), pp. 7-17.   DHU/R

727. Egidi, P. V. M. "La Religione e le Conoscenze Naturali dei Kuni (Nuova Guinea Inglese)." Anthropos (8:1, Ja.-Feb.,1913), pp. 202-18.   DLC

728. Elder, J. D. "The Yoruba Ancestor Cult in Gasparillo." Caribbean Quarterly (16:3, Sept., 1970), pp. 5-20. Pam. File, DHU/R

729. Ellenberger, Victor. Afrique avec cette Peur Venue du Fond des Ages Sorcellerie, Initiation, Exorcisme. Paris: Livre Contemporain, 1958.   DLC

730. Ellingworth, Paul. Biblical Revelation and African Beliefs. London: Lutterworth Press, 1969.   CLU; TSewU-T

731. Ellis, Alfred B. The Ewe-Speaking Peoples of the Slave Coast of West Africa. Their Religion, Manners, Customs, Laws, Language, ... London: Chapman and Hall, 1890.   DHU/MO

732. ----- The Tshi-Speaking People of the Gold Coast of West Africa. Their Religion, Manners, Customs, Laws, Language, etc. London: Chapman & Hall, 1894.   DHU/MO

733. ----- "Vodu and Voodoo." Journal of American Folklore (4:2, Apr.-Je., 1891), pp. 181-82. Pam File, DHU/R
      Definition of Pagan and African practice.

734. ----- The Yoruba-Speaking Peoples of the Slave Coast of West Africa. Their Religion, Manners, and Customs, Laws, Languages, etc. London: Chapman & Hall, 1894. DHU/MO

735. Ellis, George Washington. Negro Culture in West Africa. New York: Neale, 1914.   OWibfU

736. The Encyclopaedia of Islam. New Edition. Prepared by a Number of Leading Orientalists, Under the Patronage of the International Union of Academies. Leiden: E. J. Brill, 1960.   DHU/R

737. Entwistle, Mary. The Call Drum. New York: Friendship Press, 1928.   DHU/MO

738. Epega, David Onadele. The Mystery of Yoruba Gods. Lagos: The Hope Rising Press, 1931.   MH

739. Erivwo, S. U. "The Holy Ghost Devotees and Demonday's Ministry—An Evaluation." West African Religion (No. 15, Mr., 1974), pp. 19-31.   DHU/R

740. Esa, Raqib. "Islam in the African World." Transition (1:2, 1973), pp. 73-79.   DHU/MO

741. Euba, Akin. "The Music of Nigeria. A Short General Study." Vada E. Butcher. Development of Materials for a One Year Course in African Music for Undergraduate Students. (Wash., D.C.: U. S. Dept. of Health, Education and Welfare, 1970), pp. 93-98.   DHU/R
      "Religion and music are most inseparable."
      "Entertainment music was very likely originally used for celebrating religious festivals."

742. Evans, Melvin O. Spirit Possession Among Certain Southern Bantu Tribes in Relation to the Bible and Church Growth. Masters thesis. School of World Mission, Fuller Theological Seminary, 1971.

743. Evans, St. John. "Marriage Problems in West Africa." The Church Overseas (7; 1934), pp. 29-35.   DHU/R
      Christianity versus African tradition.

744. Evans-Pritchard, E. E. The Divine Kingship of the Shilluk of the Nilotic Sudan. Cambridge: University Press, 1948.
      OCI; NN; ICU; CtY; DLC

745. ----- Kinship and Marriage Among the Nuer. Oxford: Clarendon Press, 1951.   DHU/AA; DHU/MO

746. ----- Nuer Religion. Oxford: Oxford University Press, 1956.   DHU/R

747. ----- Theories of Primitive Religion. Oxford: Clarendon Press, 1965.   DHU/MO

748. ----- Witchcraft, Oracles and Magic Among the Azande. Oxford: Clarendon Press, 1937. DHU/R; DHU/AA

749. Even, A. "Les Propriétés Maléfiques et Bénéfiques du Sexe de la Femme Selon les Croyances des Babamba et Mindassa (Moyen Congo, A. E. F.)." Bulletin et Memoires de la Société d'Anthropologie de Paris (10:8th series, 1-3, 1939), pp. 51-72.   MBAt; NN
      Women and their sex life and ceremonies of a ritual nature including dances and songs with exorcising powers.

750. Ewing, Ethel E. The Culture of Africa South of the Sahara. Chicago, Ill.: Rand McNally, 1967.   DHU/AA
      Includes religion.

751. Ezeanya, S. N. "Christianity and African Traditional Religions." West African Religion (Nos. 13-14, Sept.-Dec., 1972), pp. 29-38.   DHU/R

752. ----- "Igbo Religious Proverbs as a Means of Interpreting the Traditional Religion of the Igbo People." West African Religion (No. 15, Mr., 1974), pp. 3-18.   DHU/R

753. Fabunmi, M. A. Ife Shrines. Ife: University of Ife Press, 1969.   NNCor
     Yoruba religion.

754. Faduma, Orishetukeh. "Religious Beliefs of the Yoruba People, West Africa." J. W. E. Bowen, (ed.). Africa and the American Negro: Addresses and Proceedings of the Congress on Africa (Miami, Fla.: Mnemesyne Publishing Co., 1969), pp. 31-36.   DHU/R

755. Falkner, D. "Witch or What?" Nigeria (23; 1946), pp. 105-11.   CtY; CtHC
     Story of a young girl in Lagos thought to be a witch.

756. Farrow, S. S. Faith Fancies and Fetish, or Yoruba Paganism. New York: Macmillan Company, 1926.   DHU/R

757. Faublee, Jacques. Les Esprits de la Vie a Madagascar. Paris: Presses Universitaires de France, 1953. WaU; MH-P; CtY; NNC

758. Faust, Arthur J. The Religious Conceptions of the Pero People, Historical, Economic and Social Background, With a Comparison of Religious Beliefs With Those of Other African Tribes. Doctoral dissertation. Harford Seminary Foundation, 1945.

759. Ferguson, John. "Aspects of Early Christianity in North Africa." L. A. Thompson and J. Ferguson. Africa in Classical Antiquity... Nigeria: Ibadan University Press, 1969.
                                                              DHU/R

760. ----- Christian Byways: Deviations from the Christian Path. Ibadan: Daystar Press, 1968.   DLC
     Indigenous religions, Islam, the sects, Jehovah's Witnesses, Christian Science, The Rosicrucians, Astrology, Secret Societies, Moral Rearmament, Humanes in the failure of the churches.

761. Feldmann, Susan, (ed.). African Myths and Tales. New York: Dell Publishing Co., 1963.   TSewU-T

762. Fernandez, James W. "The Affirmation of Things Past: Alar Ayong and the Bwiti as Movements of Protest in Central and Northern Giaban." Robert I. Rotberg and Ali A. Mazrui (eds.). Protest and Power in Black Africa (New York: Oxford University Press, 1970), pp. 427-57.   DHU/R

763. ----- "African Religious Movements, Types and Dynamics." Journal of Modern African Studies (2; 1964), pp. 531+. DHU/MO

764. ----- "Christian Acculturation and Fang Witchcraft." Cahiers d'Etudes Africaines (Paris)(2; 1961), pp. 244-55.
                                                        DAU; DGU

765. ----- "The Idea and Symbol of the Saviour in a Gabon Syncretistic Cult: Basic Factors in the Mythology of Messianism." International Review of Missions (53; 1964), pp. 281-89. DHU/R

766. ----- Microcosmogency and Modernization in African Religious Movements. Quebec: Center for Developing Asia Studies, McGill University, 1969.   DLC

767. ----- "Revitalized Words from the Parrot's Egg and the Bull that Crashes in the Kraal; African Cult Sermons." Proceedings of the 1966 Annual Spring Meeting (Wash., D.C.: American Ethnological Society, 1967), pp. 45-63.   DLC

768. ----- "Unbelievably Subtle Words— Representation and Integration in the Sermons of an African Reformative Cult." Journal of the History of Religions (6:1, 1966), pp. 43-69. DHU/R

769. Ferrere, F. La Situation Religieuse de l'Afrique Romaine Depuis la Fin du IV Siecle Jusqu'a l'Invasion des Vandales (429). Paris: Alcan, 1897.   NjP
     Religious situation in Africa during the 4th Century, A.D.

770. Fiawoo, D. K. "Ancestral Worship Among the Ewe-Speaking People of Southern Ghana: A Study in Religious Change." Ghana Journal of Sociology (5; Oct., 1969), pp. 18-22.   DHU/MO

771. Field, M. J. Religion and Medicine of the Ga People. London: Oxford University Press, 1937. DLC; MtU; OrU; Ct-Y

772. Finnegan, Ruth. "How to Do Things with Words: Performative Utterances Among the Limba of Sierra Leone." Man (4:4, 1969), pp. 537-52.   DCU/AN
     Folklore of a group of agricultural people living in the hills and swamps of Northern Sierra Leone.

773. ----- Oral Literature in Africa. Oxford: Clarendon Press, 1970.   DHU/R
     Chapter 7, Religious Poetry.

774. Fischer, Oskar. Divinations— Formen der Primitiven Afrikas. Munchen: Parcas Buchdruckerei, 1929.
                                        MiU; CtY; IU; DCU

775. Fisher, Allan G. B. and J. Humphrey. Slavery and Muslim Society in Africa. New York: Doubleday & Co., 1971.
                                            DHU/R; DLC; TSewU-T
     Chapter II discusses slave status and religion.

776. Fisher, H. J. Ahmadiyyah: A Study in Contemporary Islam on the West African Coast. London: Oxford University Press, 1963.   DHU/MO

777. Fitzgerald, M. L. "Crusade and Jihad." Dini Na Mila (5:1, Mr., 1971), pp. 5-8.   DHU/R
     Religious character of Jihad and Crusade.

778. ----- "Factors Influencing the Spread of Islam in East Africa." Orita: Ibadan Journal of Religious Studies (5:2, Dec., 1971), pp. 93-104.   DHU/R

779. Flatt, Donald C. "The Cross-Cultural Interpretation of Religion in Africa." Missiology (1:3, Jl., 1973), pp. 325-38.
                                                              DHU/R

780. ----- "Methodology in the Cross-Cultural Interpretations of Religion in Africa." Missionary Research Library. Occasional Bulletin (13:12, Oct., 1973), pp. 1-9.   DHU/R

781. "Folk-Tales of Angola." Journal of American Folklore (7:1, Ja.-Mr., 1894: 7:3, Jl.-Sept., 1894), pp. 61-65; 311-16.
                                        Pam. File,   DHU/R

782. Forde, Cyril Daryll, (ed.). African Worlds: Studies in the Cosmological Ideas and Social Values of the African Peoples. London: Oxford University Press for the International African Institute, 1954.   DLC
     Studies of aspects of the religious life of the Lele, Aboluheya, Lovedu, Dogon, Meude, Shilluk, Ruanda & Ashanti.

783. ----- The Context of Belief: A Consideration of Fetishism Among the Yako. Liverpool: Liverpool University Press, 1958. CU; OrU; NNC; ICU; MH; CLU; NN; WaU; NjP; MH-P; IEN; TxU; IU
     Nigeria.   Book review by William A. Lessa in Journal of American Folk-Lore (72:287, Ja.-Mr., 1960, pp. 83-84.
     DHU/R   Microcard.

784. ----- "Spirits, Witches and Sorcerers in the Supernatural Economy of the Yako." Journal of the Royal Anthropological Institute of Great Britain and Ireland (88:2, Jl.-Dec., 1958), pp. 165-78.   DCU/AN; DGW

785. ----- and P. M. Kaberry, (eds.). West African Kingdoms in the Nineteenth Century. New York: Oxford Press, 1971. DHU/R

786. Fortes, Meyer. The Dynamics of Clanship Among the Tallensi. London: Published for the International African Institute by the Oxford University Press, 1945.   DHU/MO

787. ----- Oedipus and Job in West African Religion. Cambridge: Cambridge University Press, 1959. NIC; CU; ICU; MH; MiU;

(Oedipus and Job, cont.)
   WU; OO; TU; NjPT; CLU; WaU; KU; DCU; CtY-D; LU; OCU;
   MiEM; NbU; DHU/R
      Book review by J. David Saper in Journal of American
      Folk-Lore (73:288, Apr.-Je., 1960), pp. 182-83. DHU/R
      Microcard.

788. France, H. "Worship of the Thunder God Among the Awuna."
   Journal of African Society (8; Oct., 1908), pp. 78-81.
                                                    CtY; DLC; NN

789. Franklin, John Hope. From Slavery to Freedom. New York:
   Alfred A. Knopf, 1967.   DHU/R
      African ideas of religion, pp. 31-34.
      Negro author.

790. Frazer, James George. The Golden Bough: A Study in Magic
   and Religion. London: Macmillan & Co., 1913-15. 12 vols.
                                                    DHU/R; DHU

791. ----- The Fear of the Dead in Primitive Religion; Lectures
   Delivered on the William Wyse Foundation at Trinity College,
   Cambridge. London: Macmillan & Co., 1933-36. DHU/MO

792. Frease, E. F. "Islam in North Africa." Missionary Review
   (38; Je., 1915), pp. 408-15.   DHU/R

793. Friedrich, Adolf. Afrikanische Priestertumer; Vorstudien zu
   Einer Untersuchung. Stuttgart: Strecker and Schroder, 1939.
                                  MiBsA; NNCor; PPT
      Religion in Africa.
      Also N.Y.: Johnson Reprint Corp., 1968.

794. Froelich, Jean Claude. Les Musulmans D'Afrique Noire.
   Paris: Editions de l'Orante, 1962. DeU; NNC; NcU; MH; NjP;
   NN; IEN; MBU; CSt; NNG; WU; WrU; NcD; CLU; CtY; MiU;
   KStMC; TNJ; MnU

795. ----- Les Nouveaux Dieux d'Afrique ... Paris: Orante, 1969.
                        MBU; NjP; MiBsA; PPT
      Religion in Africa.

796. Gaba, Christian R. "Contemporary Research in African Traditional Religion." Ghana Bulletin of Theology (3:4, Je., 1968),
   pp. 1-13.   DLC

797. ----- "The Idea of A Supreme Being Among the Anlo People of
   Ghana." Journal of Religion in Africa (2:1, 1969), pp. 64-79.
                                                    DHU/R

798. ----- "Prayer in Anlo Religion." Orita (2:2, Dec., 1968),
   pp. 71-78.   DHU/R

799. ----- "Sin in African Traditional Religion." Ghana Bulletin of
   Theology (4:1, Dec., 1971), pp. 21-30.   DHU/R; DLC

800. Gairdner, G. D. A. "Mohammedanism in South Africa." South
   African Quarterly (1; Dec., 1914; Feb., 1915), pp. 53+.
                                                    IU; NN; NNC

801. Gairdner, W. H. "Islam in Africa: The Sequel to a Challenge."
   International Review of Missions (13; Ja., 1924), pp. 3-25. DAU/W

802. Gallagher, Joseph Thomas. Islam and the Emergence of the
   Ndondeuli. Doctoral dissertation. Boston University, 1971.

803. Garcia, Samuel Ruiz. "The Incarnation of the Church in Indigenous Cultures." Missiology; an International Review (1:2, Apr.,
   1973), pp. 21-30.   DHU/R

804. Garner, R. O. "Superstitions of the West African Tribes."
   Australian Association for the Advancement of Science (6; 1895),
   pp. 589-95.   DLC; CtY; INU; MH; WU

805. Garnier, Christine and Jean Fralon. Le Fetichisme en Afrique
   Noire (Togo-Cameroun). Paris: Payot, 1951. ICU; NcD;CtY;DLC

806. Gartlan, Jean. "The Christening of Pagan Customs in Ghana."
   Catholic World (190:1136, Nov., 1959), pp. 101-06. DHU/R

807. Gbadamosi, G. O. The Growth of Islam Among the Yoruba,
   1841-1908. Doctoral dissertation. University of Ibadan, 1968.

808. Gebauer, Paul. Spider Divination in the Cameroons. Milwaukee: Published by Order of the Board of Trustees, Milwaukee Public Museum, 1964.   NNMR
      Public Museum Publications in Anthropology, 10.

809. Gelfand, Michael. An African's Religion; The Spirit of Nya-
   jena. Case History of a Karanga People. Capetown: Juta and
   Co., 1966.   DLC; CLU

810. ----- The African Witch. London: E. & S. Livingstone, 1967.
                                                    DHU/MO

811. ----- Medicine and Magic of the Mashona. Capetown, S.A.:
   Juta, 1956.   DLC

812. ----- Shona Religion With Special Reference to the Makore-
   kore. Capetown: Juta, 1962.   DHU/MO; DLC; CLU

813. ----- Shona Ritual. With Special Reference to the Chami-
   nuka Cult. Capetown: Juta, 1959.   CLU

814. ----- Witch Doctor: Traditional Medicine Man of Rhodesia.
   London: Harvill Press, 1964.   DHU/MO

815. Georgetown University. Washington, D. C. Institute of Ethnic
   Studies. The Arab Middle East and Muslim Africa. Thames
   and Hudson, 1961. (History and Its Making)   DGU
      "Seven Studies originally presented at the Third Annual
      Roundtable Conference of the Georgetown University's
      Institute of Ethnic Studies."

816. Gilliland, Dale Stewart. African Traditional Religion in Tran-
   sition: The Influence of Islam on African Traditional Religion in
   North Nigeria. Doctoral dissertation. Hartford Seminary
   Foundation, 1971.   DHU/R

817. Gilliland, Dean S. "The Indigenous Concept in Africa."
   Missiology (1:3, Jl., 1973), pp. 325-38.   DHU/R

818. Glave, E. J. "Le Fétishisme au Congo." Société Nouvelle:
   Revue Internationale (Brussels) (14; 1891), p. 518.
                                                    DLC; NN; NNC

819. Gleason, Judith. Orisha; the Gods of Yorubaland. New York:
   Atheneum, 1971.   DLC

820. Gluckman, Max. Custom and Conflict in Africa. Oxford:
   Blackwell, 1955.   DHU/MO
      Chapter 4, "The Logic in Witchcraft," pp. 81-108.

821. ----- Essays on the Ritual of Social Relations. Manchester:
   University Press, 1962.   DHU

822. ----- Rituals of Rebellion in South-East Africa. Manchester:
   Manchester University Press, 1954. PP; CtY; ICU; DLC; CU
      Bantus and religion.

823. ----- "Zulu Women in Hoe Cultural Ritual." Bantu Studies
   (9:3, Sept., 1935), pp. 255-71. DAU; DLC; CLU; DHU/MO
      Sexual division of labour in the hoe culture. Men are
      excluded from performing in the ritual.

824. Goblet d' Alviella (Comte). "Croyances Religieuses des
   Peuples du Congo." Bulletin de la Societe Royal Belge de
   Geographie (8; 1884).   CtY; DLC; NNC

825. Goody, Esther N. Contexts of Kinship. An Essay in the
   Family Sociology of the Gonja of Northern Ghana. Cambridge:
   Cambridge University Press, 1973.   DHU/R

826. Goody, Jack. Death, Property and Ancestors. A Study of the
   Mortuary Customs of the LoDagaas of West Africa. Stanford,
   California: Stanford University Press, 1962. DHU/MO; CSt;
                                                    DLC

327. ----- "Religion and Ritual: The Definitional Problem."
British Journal of Sociology (12:2, Je., 1961), pp. 142-64.
                          DHU; DCU/SW
     LoDagaas of Northern Ghana.

328. Gouilly, Alphonse. L'Islam dans L'Afrique Occidentale Francaise. Paris: Larose, 1952.   DHU/MO

329. Graham, Lorenz B. How God 'Fix' Jonah ... New York:
Reynal and Hitchcock, 1946.   DHU/MO
     "Stories on Verses from the Bible... in the
     idiom of the West African native."

330. Gray, Ernest. "Some Present-day Problems for African
Christian Marriage." International Review of Missions (45;
1956), pp. 267-77.   DHU/R

331. Greenberg, Joseph H. The Influence of Islam on a Sudanese
Religion. Seattle and London: University of Washington Press,
1966.   DHU/R

332. ----- The Religion of a Sudanese Culture as Influenced by
Islam: A Study in Non-European Acculturation. Doctoral dissertation. Northwestern University, 1941.

333. ----- "Some Aspects of Negro-Mohammedan Culture ——
Contact Among the Hausa." American Anthropologist (43:1,
Ja.-Mr., 1941), pp. 51-61.   DLC

334. Grenville-Grey, Wilfrid. All in an African Lifetime. New
York: Friendship Press, 1971.   DHU/R
     Includes African beliefs about God, soul and spirit.

335. Greschat, Hans-Jurgen. "Understanding African Religion."
Orita (2:2, Dec., 1968), pp. 59-69.   DHU/R

336. Griffith, Francis Llewellyn. Christian Documents from Nubia.
London: H. Milford, 1928.   NN/Sch

337. Grunebaum, Gustave E. Medieval Islam: A Study in Cultural
Orientation. Chicago: University of Chicago Press, 1946.
          DHU/MO
     Discussion includes Islam in Medieval North Africa.

338. Gulliver, P. H. Social Control in an African Society. A Study
of the Arusha Agricultural Masai on Northern Tanganika.
London: Kegan Paul, 1963.   DHU/R
     How the Masai worship their God and why only a small
     percentage of the Arusha have become Christians.

339. Hadfield, Percival. Traits of Divine Kingship in Africa.
London: Watts, 1949.   DHU/MO

340. Haines, C. R. Islam As A Missionary Religion.
London: S.P.C.K., 1889.   DHU/R

341. Hair, Paul Edward Hedley. "Christianity in Medieval Nubia
and the Sudan: a Bibliographical Note." Bulletin of the Society
for African Church History (1: 3-4, 1964), pp. 67-73. DLC

342. Haitz, Linn. Juju Gods of West Africa. Saint Louis:
Concordia Publishing House, 1961.   DHU/R

343. Hallpike, Christopher R. The Konso of Ethiopia: A Study of
the Values of a Cushitic People. Oxford: Clarendon Press, 1972.
          DHU/R
     A discussion of religious practices is included.

344. Hambly, Wilfrid D. Serpent Worship in Africa. Chicago:
Field Museum of Natural History, 1931. Publication 289;
Anthropological ser., V. 21, No. 1. PU; PPAmP; OCI; ViU;
OU; OCU; DLC; OrU; CaBVaU; NBuU

345. ----- Source Book for African Anthropology. Chicago:
Field Natural History Museum, Anthropological Series, Vol.26,
1937, pp. 541-85.   DHU/MO

846. Hamilton, R. A. "Oral Tradition: Central Africa."
R. A. Hamilton (ed.). History and Archaeology in Africa
(London: University of London, 1955), pp. 11-99. DHU/MO

847. Hamson, Ruth H. Islam in South Africa: A Bibliography.
Cape Town: University School of Librarianship, 1964.
     NhD; CLU; CSt-U; CU; NcD

848. Hansberry, William Leo. "Indigenous African Religions."
Africa Seen by American Negroes. Paris: Presence Africaine,
1958.   DHU/MO
     Negro author.

849. Hardyman, Marjorie. "The Church and Sorcery in Madagascar."
David B. Barrett (ed.). African Initiatives in Religion (Nairobi:
East Africa Publishing House, 1971), pp. 208-21.   DHU/R

850. Harlock, G. "Amaxosa and Fingo Traditions." The East and
The West (15; Apr., 1917), pp. 190-95.   DHU/R
     South Africa, indigenous religion.

851. Harries, Lyndon P. Islam in East Africa. London: Universities' Mission to Central Africa, 1954. DHU/MO; DHU/R

852. Harris, Grace. "Possession Hysteria in a Kenya Tribe."
American Anthropologist (59; 6, 1957), pp. 1046-66.
DAU; DCU/AN; DGU; DHU

853. Harris, Joseph E. African Presence in Asia. Evanston, Ill.:
Northwestern University Press, 1971.   DLC

854. Harris, P. G. "Notes on Yauri (Sokoto Province), Nigeria."
Journal of the Royal Anthropological Institute (60; 1930),
pp. 283-334.   DCU/AN; DGW

855. Harris, Rendel. "Egypt and Abyssinia: A Prehistoric Study."
The Hibbert Journal (35:1, Oct., 1936), pp. 250-53. DHU/R

856. Harris, William T. The Springs of Mende Belief and Conduct.
Freetown, Sierra Leone: Sierra Leone University Press, 1968.
      DHU/MO; DHU/R

857. Hartland, F. S. "Problems of Early Religion in the Light of
African Folklore." Man (1:2, 1901). CtY; DLC; OO

858. Hartmann, M. "Islam and Culture in Africa." Moslem World
(1; 1911), pp. 373-80.   DHU/R

859. Harwood, Alan. Witchcraft, Sorcery, and Social Categories
Among the Safwa. London: Oxford University Press, 1970.
      DHU/R
     A tribe located in the Livingstone Mountains which
     was in 1962 a part of the Tanganyika.

860. Hassan, Y. F. "Penetration of Islam in the Eastern Sudan."
Sudan Notes and Records (44; 1963), pp. 1-8. DLC

861. Hasselblatt, G. "Islam i Etiopien; övers B. Hällgren."
Svensk Missionstidskrift (59:4, 1971), pp. 289-93.
      CtY; ICU; CtHC

862. Hatch, J. E. "Some African Customs and Superstitions in
Rhodesia." Southern Workman (39:11, Nov., 1910), pp. 624-25.
      DLC; DHU/MO

863. Haule, Cosmos. Bantu "Witchcraft" and Christian Morality:
the Encounter of Bantu Uchawi with Christian Morality: An
Anthropological and Theological Study. Schöneck-Beckenried:
Neue Zeitschrift für Missionswissenschaft, 1969. TxDaM-P

864. Havens, Mary Sue McDonald. A Study of Bantu Childhood.
Masters thesis. College of Missions, 1925. TN/DCHS

865. Hayley, Thomas Theodore Steiger. The Anatomy of Lango
Religion and Groups. New York: Negro Universities Press,
1970.   DHU/R; DLC; TxU; FTaSU; CtY
     Originally published in 1947 by Cambridge University Press.

866. Heintzen, H. "The Role of Islam in the Era of Nationalism."
      W. H. Lewis, (ed.). New Forces in Africa (Washington: Pub-
      lic Affairs Press, 1962), pp. 42-50.   DHU/MO

867. Heinwick, J. O. "Religion and State in the Songhay Empire,
      1464-1591." Ioan M. Lewis, (ed.). Islam in Tropical Africa
      (London: Oxford University Press, 1966), pp. 296-318. CLU

868. Herskovits, Melville J. The Human Factor in Changing Africa.
      New York: Alfred A. Knopf, 1962.   DHU/R
          Chapter 13, "Religion and the Arts."

869. ----- and Frances S. "Tales in Pidgin English from Ashanti."
      Journal of American Folk-Lore (50:195, Ja.-Mr., 1937),
      pp. 52-101.   DHU/R
          Microcard.

870. ----- An Outline of Dahomean Religious Beliefs. Menasha,
      Wisc.: George Banta Co., 1933.   DHU/MO

871. Hetherwick, Alexander. "Islam and Christianity in Nyasaland."
      Moslem World (17; Apr., 1927), pp. 184-86.   DHU

872. ----- "Some Animistic Beliefs Among the Yaos of British
      Central Africa." Journal of Anthropological Institute (32; 1902),
      pp. 89-95.   DCU/A

873. Hitchens, William. "Music: A Triumph of African Art." Art
      and Archaeology (33:1, Ja.-Feb., 1932), pp. 37-41. DHU/R

874. Hill, Richard. On the Frontiers of Islam: Two Manuscripts
      Concerning the Sudan Under Turco-Egyptian Rule 1822-1845.
      London: Oxford University Press, 1970.   DHU/R

875. Hinnant, John. "Spirit Possession, Ritual, and Social Change:
      Current Research in Southern Ethiopia." Harold G. Marcus
      and Donald E. Crummey (eds.). Ethiopia: Land and History.
      Rural Africana, #11, Spring, 1970 (East Lansing, Michigan:
      The African Studies Center, Michigan State University, 1970),
      pp. 107-11.   Pam. File, DHU/R

876. Hiskett, Mervyn. The Sword of Truth: The Life and Times of
      the Shehu Usuman Dan Fodio. New York: Oxford University
      Press, 1973.   DHU/R
          The history of the Holy War led by a hausa Shehu
          Usuman Dan Fodio to reform Islam in Hausaland
          (now, Northern Nigeria).

877. Hobley, Charles William. Bantu Beliefs and Magic with
      Particular Reference to the Kikuya and Kamba Tribes of
      Kenya Colony. London: H. F. and G. Witherby, 1922.
                                                      DHU/MO
          East Africa after the war, pp. 286-302.

878. Hoernle, Agnes W. "Certain Rites of Transition and the
      Conception of Inau Among the Hottentots." Harvard African
      Studies (2; 1918), pp. 65-82. CtY; DLC; NN; NjP

879. Hogben, Sidney John. An Introduction to the History of the
      Islamic States of Northern Nigeria Ibadan. Nigeria: Oxford
      University Press, 1967.   MSohG

880. Holas, Bohumil. L'Afrique Noire. Religions du Monde.
      Paris: Bloud, 1964.   NjP

881. ----- Arts de la Cote d'Ivoire. (2nd ed.). Paris: Presses
      Universitaires de France, 1966. CU; NNC; MH; NcU

882. ----- Le Culte de Zie: Elements de la Religion Kono
      (Haute Guinee Francaise). Dakar: IFAN, 1954. DHU/MO
          Study of a river cult among the Kono tribe of Guinea.

883. Hollis, Alfred Claud. The Nandi, Their Language and Folk-
      Lore. London: Oxford University Press, 1909.   DHU/R
          Tribe of East Africa.

884. Holway, James D. "Christianity and Islam in Africa--Look-
      ing Ahead." Missionalia (2:1, Apr., 1974), pp. 3-17. DHU/R

885. ----- "Contact with Islam in East Africa Before 1914."
      Journal of Religion in Africa (4:3, 1972), pp. 200-12. DHU/R

886. ----- "Islam and Christianity in East Africa." David B.
      Barrett, (ed.). African Initiatives in Religion (Nairobi: East
      Africa Publishing House, 1971), pp. 262-77.   DHU/R

887. ----- "The Quran in Swahili," Muslim World (61:2, Apr.,
      1971), pp. 102-10.   DHU/R

888. Hopewell, James Franklin. Muslim Penetration into French
      Guinea, Sierra Leone and Liberia before 1850. Doctoral dis-
      sertation. Columbia University, 1958.

889. Hopkins, Elizabeth. "The Nyabingi Cult of Southwestern
      Uganda." Robert I. Rotherg and A. Mazuri, (eds.). Protest
      and Power in Black Africa (New York: Oxford University
      Press, 1970), pp. 258-336.   DHU/R

890. Horton, Robin. "African Conversion." Africa (41:1, Apr.,
      1971), pp. 85-108.   DHU/MO
          Summary of the Aladura or 'prayer' churches.

891. ----- "God, Man and the Land in a Northern Ibo Village
      Group." Africa (26:1, Ja., 1956), pp. 17-28.
                      DAU; DCU/AN; DGW; DHU; DLC; CLU; DHU/MO

892. ----- "The Kalabari World-View, an Outline and Interpreta-
      tion." Africa (32:3, Jl., 1962), pp. 197-220.
                      DAU; DCU/AN; DGW; DHU; DLC; CLU; DHU/MO

893. Hostetter, R. "Missions Today and African Traditional
      Religion." Christian Standard (Nov. 21, 1971), pp. 7+
                          CtY-D; DLC; OrU; NjMD
          World missions.

894. Howell, E. Milford. Tribal Laws and Social Customs Which
      Effect Mission Work in Southern Nigeria. Masters thesis.
      Southwestern Baptist Theological Seminary, 1952.

895. Howells, William. The Heathens: Primitive Man and His
      Religions. Garden City: Doubleday and Company, Inc. 1946.
                                                      NN
          Study of Mana, tabu, white magic, black magic witch-
          craft, ancestor worship, demons, gods, ghosts, and
          shamans.

896. Huber, Hugo. "Ideas of God Among African Peoples."
      Istvan Racz. The Unknown God (New York: Sheed and Ward,
      n.d.), pp. 155-84.   DHU/R

897. Hugo, H. C. "The Mashona Spirits." Nada (13; 1935-40),
      pp. 52-58.   DLC

898. Huntingford, George W. B. The Galla of Ethiopia and The
      Kingdoms of Kafa and Janjero. London: International African
      1st., 1955. (Ethnographic Survey of Africa. North Eastern
      Africa. Pt. 2). PBm; OAU; OrPR; GU; IU; TU; CaBVaU;
      OrU; DLC; LU; NN; NIC; NcD; OCI; NNC; ICU; MH-P; CtY

899. ----- "Notes on the Charms Worn by Nandi Women." Man
      (27: 140, Nov., 1927), pp. 209-10.   DCU/AN
          Charms consisting of vegetables to drive away
          illness and the evil spirits.

900. ----- "The Social Institutions of the Dorobo." Anthropos
      (46:1-2, 1951), pp. 1-48.   DLC

901. Hurt, Lewis Albert. The Role of Magic in Social Control
      Among Central African Peoples. Masters thesis. College of
      Missions, 1925.   TN/DCHS

902. Hylander, Fride. "Onesinus Nesib: Some Remarks on Cer-
      ulli's 'The Folk-Literature of the Galla'." Journal of Ethiopi-
      an Studies (7:2, Jl., 1969), pp. 79-87.   DHU/R

903. Idowu, E. Bolaji. African Traditional Religion: a Definition.
      New York: Orbis Books, 1973.   DHU/R; MNtcA

904. ----- "The Challenge of Witchcraft." Orita, The African Journal of Religious Studies (4:1, Je., 1970), pp. 3-16. DHU/R

905. ----- God in Yoruba Belief. London: Longmans, 1962.
DHU/MO

906. ----- Olodumare, God in Yoruba Belief. London: Longmans, 1962.   DHU/MO; MiBsA
Religion and ritual of the Yoruba.

907. ----- "Religions on Peace." Orita: Ibadan Journal of Religious Studies (5:2, Dec., 1971), pp. 83-92.   DHU/R
Author is Professor and Head of the Dept. of Religious Studies at the University of Ibadan.

908. Ikenga-Metuh, Emefie E. "Igbo World View: A Premise for Christian-Traditional Religion Dialogue." West African Religion (13 & 14, Sept. and Dec., 1972), pp. 51-58.   DHU/R

909. Ilogu, Edmund. "Christianity and Ibo Traditional Religion." International Review of Missions (54; 215, Jl., 1965), pp. 335-42.
DHU/R

910. ----- "Worship in Ibo Traditional Religion." West African Religion (10; Jl., 1971), pp. 18-25.   DHU/R

911. Imran, Muhammad. "Muslim Liberation Movement in Africa." Islamic Literature (5; 1971).   DLC

912. International African Seminar, 3d, Salisbury Southern Rhodesia, 1960. African Systems of Thought; Studies Presented and Discussed at the Third International African Seminar in Salisbury, December, 1960. New York: Oxford University Press, 1965.   NNCor

913. International African Seminar, 5th, Zaria, Nigeria, 1964. Islam in Tropical Africa; Studies Presented and Discussed at the Fifth International African Seminar, Ahmadu Bello University Zaria, January 1964. Edited by I. M. Lewis... London: Oxford University Press, 1966.   A&M; DHU/MO

914. International African Seminar, 7th, University of Ghana, 1965. Christianity in Tropical Africa: Studies Presented and Discussed at the Seventh International African Seminar, University of Ghana, April, 1965. London: Oxford University Press, 1968. NNM; MH; NN; NjP

915. Inyamah, Nathaniel G. N. "Polygamy and the Christian Church." Concordia Theological Monthly (43:3, Mr., 1972), pp. 138-43.   DHU/R
The Ibo of Nigeria.

916. Irstam, Tor. The King of Ganda, Studies in the Institutions of Sacral Kingship in Africa. Sweden: Hakan Ohlssons Boktryskeri, 1944.   DHU/MO

917. Isichei, Elizabeth. "Seven Varieties of Ambiguity, Some Patterns of Igbo Response to Christian Missions." Journal of Religion in Africa (3:3, 1970), pp. 209-27.   DHU/R

918. "Islam in the History of West Africa." C. Allen and R. W. Johnson, (eds.). African Perspectives (New York: Cambridge University Press, 1970), pp. 3-108. DHU/MO

919. "Islam is Spreading Quickly Among the Black Africans and Growing as a Force for Political Change." New York Times (Mr. 25, 1973). Pam. File,   DHU/R

920. Ismail, Osman Sid Ahmed. "The Historiographical Tradition of African Islam." T. O. Ranger, (ed.). Emerging Themes of African History (Nairobi, Kenya: East African Publishing House, 1968), pp. 7-13.   DHU/R

921. Iwarsson, J. "Moslem Mass Movement Toward Christianity in Abyssinia." Moslem World (14; Jl., 1924), pp. 286-89.
DHU

922. Jackman, Edward J. R. The History of Islam in Hausaland. Masters thesis. Aquinas Institute of Theology, 1971.

923. Jackson, John G. Introduction to African Civilizations. New York: University Books, 1970.   DHU/R; DHU/MO
Contains information on religion in Ghana, Mali, Songhay and other African nations.

924. Jacobs, Donald R. "African Culture and African Church." World Student Christian Federation (A WSCF Book) (2:2, 1972), pp. 3-8.   DHU/R

925. ----- The Culture Themes and Puberty Rites of the Akamba: a Bantu Tribe of East Africa. Doctoral dissertation. New York University, 1961.

926. Jadin, Louis. "Les Sectes Religieuses Secretes des Antoniens (1703-1709)." Cahiers des Religions Africaines (2; 1968), pp. 109-20.   DLC

927. Jahoda, Gustav. "Social Aspirations, Magic and Witchcraft in Ghana: A Social, Psychological Interpretation." P. C. Lloyd, (ed.). The New Elites of Tropical Africa (London: Oxford University Press for International African Institute, 1966), pp. 199-212.   DHU/MO

928. Janssens, P. A. "Het Ontstaan der Dingen in de Folklore der Bantu's." Anthropos (21: 3, 4, My.-Ag., 1926), pp. 546-65.   DLC

929. Jarrett-Kerr, Martin. "Christian Faith and the African Imagination." Religion in Life (41:4, Wint., 1972), pp. 554-68.   DHU/R

930. Jedrej, M. C. "An Analytical Note on the Land and Spirits of the Sewa Mende." Africa (44; Ja., 1974), pp. 38-44.

931. Jeffreys, M. D. W. "Ikenga: the Ibo Ram-Headed God." African Studies (13:1, Apr., 1954), pp. 25-40. DHU/MO

932. ----- "A Triad of Gods in Africa." Anthropos (67:5-6, 1972), pp. 723-35.   DLC: DHU/MO
"A study of some elements in the Ibo or Igbo religion among the Umundri group that lives near Awka, some 25 miles east of Onitsha on the Niger."

933. Jennings, George J. "Islamic Culture and Christian Missions." Practical Anthropology (18:3, My.-Je., 1971), pp. 128-44.   DHU/R

934. Jensen, Adolf E. Myth and Cult Among Primitive People. Chicago: University of Chicago Press, 1963.   DHU/R

935. Johanssen, Ernst. "The Idea of God in the Myths and Proverbs of Some East African Bantu Tribes." International Review of Missions (20; 1931), pp. 345-55+.   DHU/R

936. Johnson, Samuel. The History of the Yorubas from the Earliest Times to the Beginning of the British Protectorate. London: G. Routledge & Sons, 1921.   DHU/MO
Chapter III, Religion, pp. 26-39.

937. Johnson, S. Jangaba M. "The Traditions, History and Folklore of the Belle Tribe." Liberian Studies Journal (1:2, Spr., 1969), pp. 45-73.   DHU/MO

938. The Journal of Conflict Resolution (5:1, Mr., 1961), pp. 16-26.
DAU; DCU/SW; DGW/LW; DHU
Articles on the traditional religious system in Africa.

939. Jumbale, Anderson. "Traditional Religion of the Chonyi." Dini Na Mila (5:2, Je., 1971), pp. 29-44.   DHU/R
Traditional Religion of the Chonyi of Kenya.

940. Junod, Henri A. "Bantu Heathern Prayers." International Review of Missions (11; 1922), pp. 561-71.   DHU/R

941. ----- The Life of a South African Tribe. London: Macmillan, 1927. ICF; CU; MB; NcD; NcU
Includes information on rituals and religion.

942. ----- "Moral Sense Among the Bantu." International Review of Missions (16; Ja., 1927), pp. 85-90.   DHU/R

943. ----- "The Psychology of Conversion Among Primitive People." International Review of Missions (15:1, Ja., 1926), pp. 119-25.   DHU/R

944. Junod, Henri Philippe. "Les Cas de Possession et l'Exorcisme Chez Les Va Ndau." Africa (7:3, Jl., 1934), pp. 273-75.   DHU/MO

945. Kabore, D. Y. "Les Mangeuses d'Ames Chez les Mossi." Notes Africaines (24; 1944), pp. 17-18.
          NRU; PU/Mu; DLC; DSI/M; ICF; NN
          How the Mossi discover and punish women that they
          believe "eat" souls of new-born children and adults.

946. Kaemer, John. A Study of the Factors Involved in the Use of Indigenous Music in the Christian Church in Africa South of the Sahara. Masters thesis. Scarritt College for Christian Workers, 1957.

947. Kagame, Alexis. La Philosophie Bantu-Rwandaise de l'Etre. Bruxelles: Académie Royale des Sciences d'Outre-Mer, 1955.   DHU/MO
          A study of Bantu religion.

948. ----- "La Place de Dieu et de l'Homme dans la Religion des Bantu." Cahiers des Religions Africaines (2; Jl., 1968), pp. 213-22.   DLC

949. Kale, S. I. "Polygamy and the Church in Africa." International Review of Missions (31; 1942), pp. 220-23.   DHU/R

950. Kamil, 'Abd-al-'Aziz 'Abd-al-Qādir. Islam and the Race Question. Paris: UNESCO, 1970. VtU; NIC; CaOTP; DAU
          The race question and modern thought.

951. Kanyua, Jesse Ndwiga. "The Traditional Religion of the Embu People." Dini Na Mila (5:1, Mr., 1971), pp. 1-58.
                                                              DHU/R
          Describes the religious aspects of this tribe
          of Kenya before the British came.

952. Kasozi, A. B. K. "The Impact of Koran Schools on the Education of African Muslims in Uganda, 1900-1968." Dini Na Mila (4:2, My., 1970), pp. 1-22.   DHU/R

953. ----- "The Maulid An-Nabbi in Uganda." Dini Na Mila (5:3, Dec., 1971), pp. 1-10.   DHU/R

954. Kaula, Edna Mason. "African Village Folktales." Vols. 1, 2, 3. Caedmon TC 1309, 1310, 1312.
          Audiotape.

955. Kay, Stephen. Travels and Researches in Caffraria: Describing the Character, Customs, and Moral Condition of the Tribes Inhabiting that Portion of Southern Africa. New York: Harper, 1834.   DLC; PMA; TU; MdBP

956. Kennedy, John G. and Hussein Fahim. "Nubian Dhikr Rituals and Cultural Change." Muslim World (64:3, Jl., 1974), pp. 205-19.   DHU/R

957. Kenyatta, Jomo. "Kikuyu Religion Ancestor-worship and Sacrificial Practices." Africa (10:3, 1937), pp. 308-28. DLC

958. Khun de Prorok, Byron. Digging for Lost African Gods. The Record of Five Years Archaeological Excavation in North Africa. New York: Putnam, 1926. CLU

959. Kibicho, Samuel Gakuhi. "African Traditional Religion and Christianity." World Student Christian Federation (A WSCF Book) (2:2, 1972), pp. 14-21.   DHU/R

960. ----- The Kikuyo Conception of God, Its Continuity Into the Christian Era, and the Question It Raises for the Christian Idea of Revelation. Doctoral dissertation. Vanderbilt University, 1972.   DHU/R

961. Kidder, B. F. "Some Superstitions of North Africa and Egypt." John Henry Barrows, (ed.). The World's Parliament of Religions. V. 2 (Chicago: Parliament Publishing Co., 1893), p. 1362.   DHU/R

962. Kietzman, Dale W. "Folklore: A Tool For the Missionary." Practical Anthropology (2:1, Ja.-Feb., 1955), pp. 5-12. DHU/R

963. Kilhefer, Donald W. "The Christian Kingdoms of the Sudan, 500-1500." Africanist (1:1, Je., 1967), pp. 1-13. DHU/MO

964. Kilson, Marion. "Ambivalence and Power: Mediums in Ga Traditional Religion." Journal of Religion in Africa (4:3, 1972), pp. 171-77.   DHU/R

965. ----- Kpele Lala. Ga Religious Songs and Symbols. Cambridge, Mass.: Harvard University Press, 1971. MH; DLC

966. ----- "Taxonomy and Form in Ga Ritual." Journal of Religion in Africa (3:1, 1970). pp. 45-66.   DHU/R

967. ----- "Twin Beliefs and Ceremony in Ga Culture." Journal of Religion in Africa (5:3, 1973), pp. 171-97.   DHU/R

968. King, Anthony Vincent. Yoruba Sacred Music From Ekiti. Nigeria: Ibadan University Press, 1961.
          DLC; MiEM; NNC; DHU/MO

969. King, Noel Quinton. Christian and Muslim in Africa. New York: Harper and Row, 1971.   DHU/R; DLC

970. ----- The Religions of Africa. New York: Harper and Row, 1970.   DHU/R

971. Kinney, Sylvia. "Drummers in Dagbon: The Role of the Drummer in the Damba Festival." Ethnomusicology (14:2, May, 1970), pp. 205-27. DAU; DCU/MU; DGW; DHU

972. Kirby, P. R. The Musical Instruments of the Native Races of South Africa. New York: Humanities Press, Inc., 1965.
                                                              DHU

973. Kirkland, James E. Some Foreign Elements in the Sudanese Religions. Doctoral dissertation. Dropsie College, 1957.

974. Kitagawa, Joseph M. and Charles H. Long, (eds.). Myths and Symbols: Studies in Honor of Mircea Eliade. Chicago: University of Chicago Press, 1969.   DHU/R
          Includes an article by E. G. Parrinder entitled: "God in
          African Mythology."

975. Kitt, Eartha. "Folk Tales of the Tribes of Africa."
          Phonodisc.
          African folk tales.

976. Kiwovele, Judah B. M. "Polygyny as a Problem to the Church in Africa." Africa Theological Journal (2; Feb., 1969), pp. 7-26.   DHU/R

977. Klein, Martin A. Islam and Imperialism in Senegal: Sine-Saloum, 1847-1914. Stanford, Calif.: Published for the Hoover Institution by Stanford University Press, 1968. DHU/R
DHU/MO; WaU; NNC; KyU

978. Klipple, May A. African Folk Tales With Foreign Analogies. Doctoral dissertation. Indiana University, 1938.

979. Knappert, Jan. "Swahili Religious Terms." Journal of Religion in Africa (3:1, 1970), pp. 67-80.   DHU/R

980. Koelle, Sigismund Wilhelm. African Native Literature, or Proverbs, Tales, Fables, and Historical Fragments in the Kanuri or Bornu Language. London: Church Missionary Society, 1854.   DHU/MO; NN/Sch

981. Kourouma, K. "Sur une Formule de Purification des Femmes en Pays Somba." Notes Africaines (43; 1954), pp. 82-83.   AMAU; CLU; CSt/H; CU; DLC

A ritualistic purification formula done by future brides to initiate them into adult life.

982. Krige, E. J. and J. D. The Realm of a Rain-Queen. London: Oxford University Press, 1943.   DHU/MO
Chapters 1, 8, 13 and 15 — on cults of the drum and of the rain, ancestral cults, and fertility rites.

983. Kirtzeck, James, (ed.). Islam in Africa.... New York: Van Nostrand-Reinhold Co., 1969.   DHU/R

984. Kudadjie, J. N. "Does Religion Determine Morality in African Societies? — a Viewpoint." Ghana Bulletin of Theology (4:5, Dec., 1973), pp. 30-49.   DHU/R

985. Kuitse, R. "Islam in Africa Project — Ghana Survey." The Bulletin of Christian Institutes of Islamic Studies (3:3-4, Ja./ Apr., 1970), pp. 34-50.   Pam. File,   DHU/R

986. Kumm, Herman K. W. Khont-Hon-Nofer. Westport, Conn.: Negro Universities Press, 1970.   DHU/R
Originally published in 1910 by Marshall Brothers, Ltd., London.

987. ----- Mohammed in Africa. Indianapolis: CWBM, n. d.
TN/DCHS

988. La Fontaine, Jean Sibyl (ed.). The Interpretation of Ritual. London: Tavistock Publications, 1972.   DHU/R
Includes an article by the editor on traditional religion among the Gisu of East Africa — "Ritualization of Women's Life — Crises in Bogisu," pp. 159-86.

989. Laing, George E. F. A King for Africa. London: United Society for Christian Literature, 1945.   DHU/MO
Includes discussion of African Religion. Negro author.

990. Lane, Michael. "The Aku-Akwa and Aku-Maga Post-Burial Rites of the Jukun Peoples of Northern Nigeria." African Music (2:2, 1959), pp. 29-31.   DLC
Songs used in the funeral rites by the people of northern Nigeria.

991. Langlands, Brian W. Studies on the Geography of Religion in Uganda. Kampala, Uganda: Dept. of Geography, Makerere University College, 1967.   DLC
(Occasional paper, no. 4).

992. Langworthy, Harry W. A History of Undi's Kingdom to 1890. Aspects of Chewa History in East Central Africa. Doctoral dissertation. Boston University, 1961.

993. Laoye, John Anjola. The Confrontation of Christianity with the Yoruba Traditional Faiths. Masters thesis. Southern Baptist Theological Seminary, 1969.

994. La Roche, Robert. La Divination. Avec un Supplement Sur la Superstition en Afrique Centrale. Doctoral dissertation. Catholic University of America, 1957.

995. Larson, Thomas J. "The Spirits of the Ancestors and the Mandengure Ceremony of the Hambukushu of Ngamiland." Anthropos (66:1-2, 1971), pp. 52-69. DLC; DHU/MO
"This paper is a preliminary study of some of the beliefs of the Hambukushu of Ngamiland, Botswana, concerning the hathimo (the spirits of the ancestors), and the Mandengure Ceremony in which hathimo are propitiated."

996. The Last Great Muslim Empires. Pt. 3 of The Muslim Empires World: A Historical Survey. Leiden: E. J. Brill, 1969.
DHU/R
Discussion of Islam and its penetration of North and East Africa.

997. Le Chatelier, Alfred. L'Islam dans l'Afrique Occidentale. Paris: Steinheil, 1899.   NNMR

998. Leeder, S. H. Veiled Mysteries of Egypt and the Religion of Islam. New York: C. Scribner's Sons, 1913.   DLC
Book review in International Review of Missions (2; 1913), pp. 595-98.   DHU/R

999. Leeuwen, Arend Theodoor Van. Christianity in World History. The Meeting of the Faiths of East and West. New York: Charles Scribner's Sons, 1964.   DHU/R
Part V, "The Challenge of Islam."

1000. Legum, Colin. Africa, a Handbook. London: Anthony Blond, 1965.   DLC
Religion, pp. 458-75.

1001. Leonard, Arthur Glyn. The Lower Niger and Its Tribes. London: Frank Cass & Co., Ltd., 1968.   DHU/R
Religion in Africa.

1002. Leslau, Charlotte and Wolf. "African Proverbs: Daughters of Experience." Freeing the Spirit (1:4; 11:1, Fall-Wint., 1972, Spr., 1973), pp. 66-67.   DHU/R; CLU

1003. Le Tourneau. Almohad Movement in North Africa in the 12th and 13th Centuries. Princeton, New Jersey: Princeton University Press, 1969.   DHU/MO
Islamic reform movement.

1004. Levine, Ellen Deborah. The Second Eden: Myth and Religion in Afrikaaner Political Community. Doctoral dissertation. University of Chicago, 1946-1947.

1005. Levonian, Luftfi. Studies in the Relationship Between Islam and Christianity. London: George Allen & Unwin, 1940.
DHU/R

1006. Levtzion, Nehemia. "Commerce et Islam Chez la Dagomba du Nord-Ghana." Annales, Economies, Societes, Civilisations (23, Jl.-Ag., 1968), pp. 723-43.   DAU; DGU

1007. ----- Muslims and Chiefs in West Africa: A Study of Islam in the Middle Volta Basin in the Pre-Colonial Period. Oxford: Clarendon Press, 1968.   DLC

1008. ----- The Spread and Development of Islam in the Middle Volta Basin in the Pre-Colonial Period. Doctoral dissertation. University of London, 1965.

1009. Lewis, Archibald R. (ed.). The Islamic World and the West, A.D. 622-1492. New York: John Wiley & Sons, Inc., 1970.   DHU/R
Chapter I, Selections from the Koran concerning Jesus and Christianity.

1010. Lewis, Ioan M. Estatic Religion: An Anthropological Study of Spirit Possession and Shamanism. Baltimore: Penguin Books, 1971.   DHU/R
Includes information on African traditional religions and voodoo in Haiti.

1011. -----, (ed.). Islam in Tropical Africa. Oxford: Oxford University Press, 1966.   DHU/R; CLU

1012. ----- "The Names of God in Northern Somali." Bulletin of the School of Oriental and African Studies (22; 1959), pp. 134-40.   DHU/MO

1013. ----- Peoples of the Horn of Africa: Somali, Afar, and Saho. London: International African Institute, 1955. CLA
Includes some discussion of Islam.

1014. ----- "Sufism in Somaliland — A Study in Tribal Islam." Bulletin of the School of Oriental and African Studies (17:3, 1955; 18:1, 1956), pp. 581-602; 146-60.   DHU/MO

1015. Lewy, Guenter. Religion and Revolution. New York: Oxford University Press, 1974.   DHU/R
Chapter 9: Messianism and Rebellion in Twentieth century Africa.

1016. Lienhardt, G. Divinity and Experience; the Religion of the Dinka. Oxford: Clarendon Press, 1961.   DHU/MO

1017. ----- "Some Notions of Witchcraft Among the Dinka." Africa (21:4, Oct., 1951), pp. 303-18.   DHU/MO

1018. Lighton, George. "The Numerical Strength of Islam in the Sudan." Moslem World (26; 1936), pp. 253-73.   DHU/R

1019. Linden, Ian. The Shrine of the Karongas at Mankhamba: Some Problems in the Religious History of Central Malawi. Lusaka, Zambia: Conference on the History of Central African Religious Systems, Ag. 31-Sept. 8, 1972. Pam. File, DHU/R mim.

1020. Lloyd, Peter C. "Yoruba Myths — A Sociologist's Interpretation." Odu (2; 1956), pp. 20-28.   DAU

1021. Loeb, Edwin M. "Kuanyama Ambo Magic." Journal of American Folk-Lore (68:267, Ja.-Mr., 1955), pp. 35-50; (68:268, Apr.-Je., 1955), pp. 153-68; (68:269, Jl.-Sept., 1955), pp. 291-311.
        Microcard.

1022. ----- and Carl Koch, et al. "Kuanyama Magic." Journal of American Folk-Lore (69:272, Apr.-Je., 1956), pp. 147-74.
        DHU/R
        South West Africa.
        Microcard.

1023. Loewen, Jacob A. "The Function of Myth in Society." Practical Anthropology (16:4, Jl.-Ag., 1969), pp. 159-70.
        DHU/R

1024. ----- "Myth Analysis." Practical Anthropology (16:4, Jl.-Ag., 1969), pp. 178-85.   DHU/R

1025. ----- "The Structure and Content of Myths." Practical Anthropology (16:4, Jl.-Ag., 1969), pp. 150-59.   DHU/R

1026. Long, Charles H. "Primitive Religion." Charles J. Adams, (ed.). A Reader's Guide to the Great Religions (New York: The Free Press, 1965), pp. 1-30.   DHU/R
        Negro author.

1027. Lucas, Jonathan Olumide. The Religion of the Yoruba. Lagos, Nigeria: C.M.S. Bookshop, 1948. DHU/MO
        Also: Robert O. Collins, (ed.). Problems in African History (Englewood Cliffs, N.J.: Prentice-Hall, 1968), pp. 29-35.   DHU/MO

1028. Lugira, A. M. "African Traditional Religion Vis-a-Vis Christianity." Dini Na Mila (4:2, My., 1970), pp. 23-34.
        DHU/R

1029. Luttig, Hendrik Gerhard. The Religious System and Social Organization of the Herero. Utrecht: Kemink en Zoo, N.V.-over den dom, 1933.   NCU; NcD

1030. Luzbetak, Louis J. "Worship of the Dead in the Middle Wahgi (New Guinea)." Anthropos (51:1-2, 1956), pp. 81-96.
        DLC; DHU/MO

1031. Lystad, Robert A. The Ashanti; a Proud People. New Brunswick, N.J.: Rutgers University Press, 1958.   NjR

1032. "Macabro." Trans-American Films, 1966. 88 min. sd. color. 35 mm.   DLC
        Film. "A documentary account of the many strange rituals and activities performed around the world."

1033. MacDonald, James. "Manners, Customs, Superstitions, and Religions of South African Tribes." Journal of the Anthropological Institute (19), pp. 264-96.   DLC; CtY; CU

1034. ----- Religion and Myth. London: D. Nutt, 1893. DHU/R; NjP; IC/H; MiBsA; MNtcA; PPT

Reprinted by Negro Universities Press, 1969.
Religious observance and social customs of African tribes.

1035. MacKenzie, Agnes E. "African Folk Stories." Southern Workman (54:7, Jl., 1925), pp. 319-25. DLC; DHU/MO

1036. ----- "African Folk Tales." Southern Workman (50:9, Sept., 1921), pp. 423-26.   DLC; DHU/MO
        Collected from the Gonde tribe of Livingstonia Mission, Nyasaland.

1037. ----- "Central African Folk Stories." Southern Workman (43:6, Je., 1914; 43:9, Sept., 1914), pp. 362-64; 509-13.
        DLC; DHU/MO

1038. MacKenzie, D. R. The Spirit-Ridden Konde. London: Seeley, Service, 1925.
        Southern Africa traditional religion.

1039. Mackrell, J. E. C. "The Dinka Oath on Ashes." Sudan Notes and Records (25:1, 1942), pp. 131-34.   DHU/MO

1040. Madziyire, Salathiel. An Obstacle, Race Towards Understanding Bernard Mizeki, the Mashonaland Martyr. Lusaka, Zambia: Conference on the History of Central African Religious Systems. Ag. 31-Sept. 8, 1972. Pam. File, DHU/R mim.

1041. Mafeje, Archie. "The Ideology of Tribalism." Journal of Modern African Studies (9:2, Ag., 1971), pp. 253-61.
        DHU/MO

1042. Magrath, Oswin. "Taking African Tradition Seriously." African Ecclesiastical Review (14:4, 1972), pp. 348-49. DHU/R

1043. Mahmud, Khalil. "The Concept of Al-Mahdi According to the Ahmadiyya Movement in Islam." Orita (2:2, Dec., 1968), pp. 103-08.   DHU/R

1044. Mair, Lucy. "Witchcraft as a Problem in the Study of Religion." Cahiers d'Etudes Africaines (4:15, 1964), pp. 335-48.
        DAU; DGU; DHU/MO

1045. Malcolm, L. W. G. "Islam in the Cameroons." Journal of the African Society (21; 1921), pp. 35-46. CtY; DLC; NN

1046. ----- "Short Notes on Soul-Trapping in Southern Nigeria." Journal of American Folk-lore (35:137, Jl.-Sept., 1922), pp. 219-22.   DHU/R
        Microcard.

1047. ----- "The Social-Political Organisation of the E-yap Tribe, Central Cameroon." Anthropos (21:1,2, Ja.-Apr., 1926), pp. 233-43.   DLC

1048. Mandrin, J. "Les Sorcières Mangeues d'Ames." Grand Lacs (54:4-6, 1937-38), pp. 189-90.   DLC
        Mostly beliefs and superstitions concerning eaters of souls.

1049. Manley, G. T. "A Survey of Islam in Africa." The Church Missionary Review (67; Ja., 1916), pp. 8-15.   DHU/R

1050. Manolesco, John. Vaudou et Magie Noire. Montréal: Editions du Jour, 1972. NNCor; NjP; PPT
        Voodooism.

1051. Marais, Ben. "Islam: Political Factor in Africa." Bulletin of the Africa Institute of South Africa (9:2, Mr., 1971), pp. 51-64.   DHU/MO

1052. Markovitz, Irving L. "Traditional Social Structure: the Islamic Brotherhoods, and Political Development in Senegal." Journal of Modern African Studies (3:2, Apr., 1970), pp. 73-96.
        DHU/MO

1053. Marsh, Zoë and George William Kingsnorth. An Introduction to the History of East Africa. (3rd. ed.). New York: Cambridge University Press, 1965.   DHU/MO

1054. Martin, Earl R. The Ahmadiyy. A Movement in Tanzania. Master's thesis. Baptist Theological Seminary, 1966.

1055. Marty, Paul. Etudes sur l'Islam au Senegal. Paris: E. Leroux, 1917.   MH; DLC

1056. ----- Etudes sur l'Islam en Cote d'Ivoire. Paris: E. Leroux, 1922. DLC; WU; MH; MBU; NjPT

1057. ----- Etudes sur l'Islam et les Tribus de Soudan. Paris: E. Leroux, 1920-21. 4V. DLC; WU; MH

1058. ----- Etudes sur l'Islam Maure: Cheikh Sidia - les Fadelia, les Ida Ou Ali. Paris: E. Leroux, 1916.   DLC

1059. ----- L'Islam en Guinée: Fouta-Diallon. Paris: E. Leroux, 1921.   DLC; OGK; OGC

1060. ----- L'Islam en Mauritanie et du Sénégal. Paris: Collection de la Revue du Monde Musulman, 1917.   MH

1061. ----- L'Islam et les Tribus dans la Colonie du Niger. Paris: Paul Geuthner, 1931. IEN; MBU; NIC; NNC; INU; CtY-D; OU

1062. Marwick, Marvin G. "African Witchcraft and Anxiety Load." Theoria (No. 2, 1948), pp. 115-29.   DLC

1063. ----- "Another Modern Anti-Witchcraft Movement in East Central Africa." Africa (20:1, Ja., 1950); (20:2, Apr., 1950), pp. 100-12; 110-12. DCU/AN; DGW; DHU; DLC; CLU; DHU/MO

1064. ----- "The Continuance of Witchcraft Beliefs." Prudence Smith (ed.) Africa in Transition; Some BBC Talks on Changing Conditions in the Union and the Rhodesias. (London: Reinhardt, 1958), pp. 106-14.   DLC

1065. ----- "The Sociology of Sorcery in a Central African Tribe (Cewa)." African Studies (22:1, 1963), pp. 1-21. DAU; DCU/AN; DHU; DHU/MO

1066. ----- "The Social Context of Cewa Witch Beliefs." Africa (22:2, Apr., 1952), pp. 120-35.   DHU/MO

1067. Masamba, Jean. "Une Approche Pastorale du Probleme de la Sorcellerie." Revue du Clerge Africain (26;1, Ja., 1971), pp. 3-26.   DHU/R

1068. Matee, H. S. "Witchcraft From the Native Point of View." East and West Review (2; 1936), pp. 199-209. DHU/R South Africa.

1069. Mathews, Basil Joseph. "Islam and Western Civilization. The Influence of Western Nations and Western Science, Commerce and Thought on the Mohammedan World." Missionary Review of the World. (49; Dec., 1926), pp. 937-44. DHU/R

1070. Matringe, G. "Chrétienté et Islam au Maroc (du XVIᵉ a XXᵉ Siècle)." Revue Historique de Droit Francais et Etranger (4:43), pp. 588-643.   DCU/TH

1071. Mawinza, Joseph. Reverence for Ancestors Among Bantu Tribes in Tanzania with Special Reference to Uluguru. Paper presented at workshop in Religious Research, University College, Nairobi, Dec. 28, 1967 to Ja. 12, 1968. Nairobi: University College, 1968.

1072. Mazrui, Ali A. On Heroes and Uhuru-Worship: Essays on Independent Africa. London: Longman Group Limited, 1967. DHU/R
        Chapter 11, "Islam, Political Leadership and Economic Radicalism in Africa."

1073. Mba, Cyriac S. "Marriage Law in Need of Further Elaboration." African Ecclesiastical Review (15:4, 1973), pp. 340-44. DHU/R
        Discuss the practice in Eastern Nigeria.

1074. Mbiti, John S. "African Concept of Time." Africa Theological Journal (No. 1, Feb., 1968), pp. 8-20.   DHU/R

1075. ----- "African Names of God." Orita (6:1, Je., 1972), pp. 3-14.   DHU/R

1076. ----- African Religions & Philosophy. New York: Frederick A. Praeger, 1969.   DHU/R

1076. ----- African Religions & Philosophy. New York: Frederick A. Praeger, 1969.   DHU/R
        Native Kenyan theologician surveys the religion of Africa.

1077. ----- Akamba Stories. Oxford: Clarendon Press, 1966.
                                                        DHU/R
        Oral stories of the Akamba tribe of Ukambani located in the eastern region of Kenya.

1078. ----- "Christianity and Traditional Religions in Africa." International Review of Missions (59:236, Oct., 1970), pp. 430-40.   DHU/R

1079. ----- Concepts of God in Africa. New York: Praeger Publishers, 1970.   DHU/R

1080. ----- "Growing Respectability of African Traditional Religion." Lutheran World (19:1, 1972), pp. 54-58. DAU/W; DGW; DCU/TH; DGU/TH

1081. ----- New Testament Eschatology in Relation to Evangelisation in Africa. Paper presented at workshop in Religious Research, University College, Nairobi, Dec. 28, 1967 to Jan. 12, 1968. Nairobi: University College, 1968. DHU/MO

1082. Mbunga, Stephen B. G. Church Law and Bantu Music; Ecclesiastical Documents and Law on Sacred Music as Applied to Bantu Music... Schoneck-Beckenried, Switzerland: Nouvelle Revue de Science Missionaire, 1963.   DLC

1083. McCall, Daniel F., (ed.). Western African Religion. New York: Frederick A. Praeger, 1969.   DHU
        Boston University Papers on Africa, V. 4.
        Chapters on Islam, Christianity and tribal religions.

1084. Mc Lean, David A. and Ted J. Solomon. "Divination Among the Bena Lulua." Journal of Religion in Africa (4:1, 1971), pp. 25-44.   DHU/R
        Divination among the Bena Lulua of Zaire.

1085. McClelland, E. M. "The Significance of the Number in the Odu of Ifa." Africa (36:4, 1966), pp. 421-30.   DLC

1086. McVeigh, Malcolm J. The Interaction of the Conceptions of God of African Traditional Religion and Christianity in the Thought of Edwin W. Smith. Doctoral dissertation. Boston University, 1971.

1087. Mead, Margaret. "Pastoral Psychology: The Next 20 Years ... As Seen by a Social Scientist." Pastoral Psychology (21: 201, Feb., 1970), pp. 8-15.   DHU/R
        Article contains bibliographic references to African Religion.

1088. Means, John E. A Study of the Influence of Islam in Northern Nigeria. Doctoral dissertation. Georgetown University, 1965.

1089. Meek, C. K. The Northern Tribes of Nigeria: An Ethnographical Account of the Northern Provinces of Nigeria, Together with a Report on the 1921 Decennial Census. Oxford: Clarendon Press, 1925.   DHU/MO

1090. ----- "The Religions of Nigeria." Africa (London) (14; 1943), pp. 106-18.   DLC

1091. Meinhof, Carl. Die Religionen der Afrikaner in Ihrem Zusammenhang Mit Dem Wirtschaftsleben, Dargestellt. Oslo: H. Aschehoug & Co., (W. Nygaard); Cambridge, Mass.: Harvard University Press, 1926.   NjP

1092. ----- "The Moslem Advance in Africa." E. M. Wherry and S. M. Zwemer, et al. (ed.). Islam and Missions (New York: Fleming H. Revell Company, 1911), pp. 76-86. DHU/R

1093. Melland, Frank H. In Witch-Bound Africa: An Account of the Primitive Kaonde Tribe and Their Beliefs. New York: Barnes & Noble, 1923. DHU/MO; ICU; OCL; MLU

1094. Memoirs of Naimbanna, a Young African Prince. Philadelphia: Printed for Thomas Dobson, at the Stone-House, No. 41, South Second Street, 1799.   NN/Sch

1095. Mendelsohn, Jack. God, Allah and JuJu; Religion in Africa Today. New York: Thomas Nelson & Sons, 1962. DHU/R

1096. Mends, E. H. "Some Aspects of Periodic Ritual Ceremonies of the Anomabo Fante." Ghana Journal of Sociology (5:1, Feb., 1969), pp. 39-48.   DHU/MO

1097. ----- "The Concept of Mbusu in the Ritual Ceremonies of the Fante." Ghana Bulletin of Theology (4:2, Je., 1972), p. 24.   DHU/R

1098. Mensah, Thomas K. "Some Cultural Values and Marriage Expectations Among the Ashantis of Ghana." City of God (4:2, Feb., 1972), pp. 9-11. Pam. File, DHU/R

1099. Merker, M. "Religion und Tradition der Masai." Zeitschrift fur Ethnologie (XXXV; 1903), pp. 733-44. CLU; CtY; DCU; DLC; ICU; NN; NNC; OrU

1100. Merriam, D. P. "Death and the Religious Philosophy of Basongye." Antioch Review (21:3, 1961), pp. 292-304.
                                        DAU; DGU; DHU

1101. Merwe, Willem Jacob van der. The Shona Idea of God. Ft. Victoria, South Rhodesia: Morgenster Mission Press, 1957.   WaU; DLC

1102. Messenger, John C. "Religious Acculturation Among the Anang Ibibio." William R. Bascom and Melville J. Herskovits (eds.). Continuity and Change in African Cultures (Chicago: University of Chicago Press, 1959), pp. 279-99. DHU/R

1103. Metraux, Alfred. "La Comedie Rituelle Dans La Possession." Diogeno (Jl., 1955), pp. 1-24.   DPU

1104. Metuh, Emefir E. "The Supreme God in Igbo Life and Worship." Journal of Religion in Africa (5:1, 1973), pp. 1-11.
                                                        DHU/R

1105. Meyerowitz, Eva L. Akan of Ghana; Their Ancient Beliefs. London: Faber and Faber Ltd., 1958. DLC; NeD; MH; CtY; NN; CtY-D

1106. ----- Akan Traditions of Origin. London: Faber and Faber, 1952.   NcD; NcU

1107. ----- Divine Kingship in Ghana and Ancient Egypt. London: Faber and Faber, 1960.   DLC; NNC; CtY; PU; CtY-D

1108. ----- The Sacred State of the Akan. London: Faber and Faber, 1951.   IEN; CtY; NcU; NcD

1109. Middleton, John. Lugbara Religion: Ritual and Authority Among an East African People. New York: Oxford University Press, 1960. DHU/R; DLC; MtU; MiU; NcD; NbU; WaU; NN/Sch

1110. ----- The Lugbara of Uganda. New York: Rinehart & Winston, 1965. DLC; MH-P; CtY; NcD
        Chapter 6.

1111. ----- "Secrecy in Lugbara Religion." History of Religions (12:4, My., 1973), pp. 299-316.   DHU/R
        Result of field work carried on in Uganda 1949-53.

1112. ----- "The Yakan Cult Among the Lugbara." Man (58; Jl., 1958), p. 156.   DHU/MO

1113. ----- and E. H. Winter, (eds.). Witchcraft and Sorcery in East Africa. New York: Praeger, 1963.   DHU/MO

1114. Migeod, Frederick William Hugh. "The Basis of African Religion." Journal of the African Society (19; Oct., 1919), pp. 20-34.   CtY; NN; DLC

1115. Milimo, John. "African Traditional Religion." World Student Christian Federation (A WSCF Book) (2:2, 1972), pp. 9-13.   DHU/R

1116. Miller, Walter R. "Islam in Africa." International Review of Missions (15; 1926), pp. 556-68.   DHU/R

1117. ----- "Islam in West Africa." S. M. Zwemer and E. M. Wherry, et al. (eds.). The Mohammedan World of To-day (New York: Fleming H. Revell Company, 1906), pp. 41-50.
                                                        DHU/R

1118. Milligan, Robert H. The Fetish Folk of West Africa. New York: AMS Press, 1970.   DHU/R
        Reprint of 1912 edition.
        Religion and folklore.

1119. "Missionaries and Moslems in Africa." Missionary Review of the World (26; Je., 1903), p. 461.   DHU/R

1120. Mitchell, J. Clyde. "Chidzere's Tree: A Note on a Shona Land-Shrine and its Significance." Nada (38; 1961), pp. 28-35.
                                                        DLC

1121. Mitchell, Richard P. The Society of the Muslim Brothers. London: Oxford University, 1969.   DHU/R
        Chapter 9 discusses the spiritual solution of problems in Egypt.

1122. Moggridge, L. T. "The Nyassaland Tribes, Their Customs and Their Poison Ordeal." Journal of Anthropological Institute (32; 1902), pp. 467-72.   DCU/A

1123. Molema, S. M. The Bantu Past and Present. An Ethnological and Historical Study of the Native Races of South Africa. Cape Town: C. Struik, 1963.   DHU/MO
        Original edition, Edinburgh: W. Green, 1920.

1124. Molla, Claude F. "The Rapid Growth of Islam South of the Sahara." The Christian Minister (5:3, Mr., 1969), pp. 24-30+.
                                                        DHU/R

1125. ----- "Some Aspects of Islam in Africa South of the Sahara." International Review of Missions (56:224, Oct., 1967), pp. 459-68.
                                                        DHU/R

1126. Monfouga-Nicolas, Jacqueline. Ambivalence et Culte de Possession. Contribution a l'Etude du Bori Hausa. Paris: Anthropos, 1972.   DLC

1127. Monteil, Vincent. L'Islam Noire. Paris: Editions du Seuil, 1964.   DLC; CtY; CLU; InU; OrU; NjP

1128. Montgomery, W. W. "The Political Relevance of Islam in East Africa." International Affairs (London, 42; 1966), pp. 35-44.   DLC

1129. Moore, G. "The Ila Oso Festival at Ozuakoli." Nigeria Magazine (No. 52; 1956), pp. 61-69. CtY; CtHC; NN; OU; DHU/MO

Ibo ceremony which occurs twice yearly marking the
end of the agricultural cycle.

1130. Moore, R. J. B. "The Development of the Conception of
God in Central Africa." International Review of Missions
(31; 1942), pp. 412-20.   DHU/R
African traditional religion.

1131. Moorehead, Alan. The White Nile. New York: Harper &
Row, 1971.   DHU/R
Part 3, The Moslem Revolt; Part 4, The Christian
Victory.

1132. Moorish Literature: Comprising Romantic Ballads, Tales
of the Berbers, Stories of the Kabylie, Folk-lore and National
Traditions. Translated into English by René Basset.
New York: The Colonial Press, 1902.   DLC

1133. Morel, Edmund D. Nigeria, its Peoples and its Problems.
London: Smith, Elder & Co., 1912. DLC; CtY; PBm; ICJ; NN
Christianity and Islam in Nigeria. Book Review in
International Review of Missions (1:2, 1912), pp. 323-27.
DHU/R

1134. Morton-Williams, Peter. "An Outline of the Cosmology and
and Cult Organization of the Oyo Yoruba." Africa (34:3, Jl.,
1964), pp. 243-61.   DHU/MO

1135. Mosmans, Guy. L'Eglise a L'Meure de L'Afrique.
Tournai: Casterman, 1961.   NjP

1136. Mpongo, Laurent. "La Liturgie du Mariage dans la Per-
spective Africaine." Revue du Clergé Africain (26: 3-4, My.-
Jl., 1971), pp. 177-97.   DHU/R
Christian marriage in Africa.

1137. Mufassir, Sulayman S. "Solutions to the Problem of Slavery
(Then and Now): Islam vs. Christianity." Black World
(19:9, Jl., 1970), pp. 12-18.   DHU/MO

1138. Muhammed, Said Abdulla. Mzimu Wa Watu Wa Kale.
(Swahili. The Home of the Spirits of the Ancestors.) Dar es
Salaam (Tanganyika): The Eagle Press; East African Litera-
ture Bureau, 1960. CLU; WU; INU; DHU/MO

1139. Mukendi, Placide. "La Jamaa et son Avenir." Revue du
Clerge Africain (36:2, Mr., 1971), pp. 142-68.   DHU/R

1140. Mukenge, Godefroid. "Une Approche d'Une Spiritualite du
Mariage Chretien en Afrique." Revue du Clergé Africain
(26; 3-4, My.-Jl., 1971), pp. 162-76.   DHU/R
Christian Marriage in Africa.

1141. Mulago gwa Cikala Musharhamina. "Symbolisme dans les
Religions Traditionnelles Africaines et Sacramentalisme."
Revue du Clergé Africain (27: 4-5, Jl., 1972), pp. 467-502.
DHU/R

1142. Mulago, Vincent. "Le Mariage Traditionnel Bantu." Revue de Clergé Africain (26: 3-4, My.-Je., 1971), pp. 5-61.
DHU/R

1143. ----- Un Visage Africain du Christianisme: L'Union Vitale
Bantu Face a L'Unite Vitale Ecclesiale. Paris: Presence
Affricaine, 1965.   DLC

1144. Mumba, Levi. "The Religion of My Fathers." The Inter-
national Review of Missions (19; 1930), pp. 362-76. DHU/R
Written by a member of a tribal group in Nyasaland
(Malawi) who first came under the influence of
Christianity in 1884.

1145. Munday, J. T. "The Witchcraft Ordinance of Northern
Rhodesia." International Review of Missions (37; 1948),
pp. 181-87.   DHU/R

1146. Murphree, Marshall W. Christianity and the Shona. New
York: Humanities Press, 1969. DLC; NjR; DAU; MH-P;DHU/R
Adaptation of Budjga to Christianity.

1147. Mutwa, Credo Vusa'mazula. My People, My Africa. New
York: The John Day Co., 1969.   DHU/R
Written by a Bantu of South Africa whose thesis is that
Christianity will never be completely understood and
accepted by the Bantu.

1148. Mveng, Englebert. L'Art d'Afrique Noire; Liturgic Cos-
mique et Langage Religieux. Tours: Mame, 1964. NcD

1149. Mwanza, R. Mwari: The God of the Karanga. Lusaka,
Zambia: Conference on the History of Central African Reli-
gious Systems. Ag. 31-Sept. 8, 1972. Mim. Pam. File,
DHU/R

1150. Nadel, Siegfried Frederick. A Black Byzantium. London:
Oxford University Press, 1942.   DHU/MO
Effect of Mohammedanism on Nupe culture in Nigeria.

1151. ----- Nupe Religion. London: Routledge & Paul, 1954.
DHU/MO

1152. ----- "Witchcraft in Four African Societies." American
Anthropologist (54:1, Feb., 1952), pp. 18-29. DHU

1153. "The Names of God in Northern Somali." Bulletin of the
School of Oriental and African Studies (22: 1959), pp. 134-40.
DAU; DGU; DGW

1154. Nassau, Robert Hamill. Fetichism in West Africa. New
York: Charles Scribner's Sons, 1904.   DHU/MO

1155. ----- Where Animals Talk: West African Folk Lore Tales.
Boston: Badger, 1912.   DHU/MO; NN/Sch

1156. Nenquin, Jacques. Contributions to the Study of the Prehistoric Cultures of Rwanda and Burundi. Tervuren: Musée
Royal de l'Afrique Centrale, 1967.   DLC

1157. Nesbitt, Lewis Mariano. Desert and Forest: the Exploration of Abyssinian Danakil. London: J. Cape, 1934. DLC

1158. Nipperdey, H. "Der Fetisch und Fetisch-Glaube in West-
Afrika." Ausland (59; 1886), p. 712. CtY; DLC; ICU; MH; NN;
00

1159. Nketia, Joseph H. K. African Gods and Music. Legon:
Institute of African Studies; University of Ghana, 19__? DLC

1160. ----- African Music in Ghana: A Survey of Traditional
Forms. Evanston: Northwestern Univ. Press, 1963. DHU/R

1161. ----- Folk Songs of Ghana. Lagon: University of Ghana,
1963.   DLC

1162. ----- Funeral Dirges of the Akan People. Achimota:
James Townsend & Sons, 1955.   DHU/MO

1163. ----- "The Role of the Drummer in Akan Society."
African Music (1:1, 1954), pp. 34-43.   DLC

1164. Noble, Lowell Lappen. Ashanti Acculturation: With Special
Emphasis on Its Effect Upon Ancestor Worship. Master's
thesis. Hartford Seminary Foundation, 1966.

1165. Norbeck, Edward. "African Rituals of Conflict." American Anthropologist (65:6, Dec., 1963), pp. 1254-79. DLC
African traditional religion.

1166. Norris, H. T. "Papers on Islam and West Africa. Third
Conference on African History and Archaeology, 3-7 July
1961." Journal of African History (3:2, 1962), pp. 317-36.
DAU; DGU; DGW

1167. Noss, Philip A. "An Interpretation of Gbaya Religious
Practice." International Review of Mission (61:244, Oct.,
1972), pp. 357-74.   DHU/R

1168. Nottingham, John. "Sorcery Among the Kamba in Kenya." Journal of African Administration (11:1, Ja., 1959), pp. 2-14.
DAU; DGW; DHU

1169. Nukunya, K. G. "The Yewe Cult Among Southern Ewe-Speaking People of Ghana." Ghana Journal of Sociology (5:1, Feb., 1969), pp. 1-7.   DHU/MO
Salient features of religious cults in Anlo areas.

1170. Nwabara, Samuel N. "Christian Encounter with Indigenous Religion at Onitsha (1857-1885)." Cahiers d'Etudes Africaines (11:4, 1971), pp. 589-601.   DAU; DGU

1171. "Nyangweso.' "The Cult of Mumbo in Central and South Kavirondo." The Journal of the East Africa and Uganda Natural History Society (38-39, 1930), pp. 13-17. DHU/MO

1172. O'Brien, Donald C. "The Saint and the Squire. Personalities and Social Forces in the Development of a Religious Brotherhood." Christopher Allen and R. W. Johnson, (eds.). African Perspectives (New York: Cambridge University Press, 1972), pp. 157-69.   DHU/MO
About the merging of two Muslim groups, one led by Amadu Bamba (Saint) and the other by Shaikl Iba Fall (Squire) groups in Africa.

1173. ----- "Towards an Islamic Policy in French West Africa, 1854-1914." Journal of African History (8:2, 1967), pp. 303-16.   DHU/MO

1174. O'Connell, James. "Government and Politics in the Yoruba African Churches: The Claims of Tradition and Modernity." Odu (2; 1965), pp. 92-108.   DHU/MO

1175. ----- "The Problems of Baptising the High God." African Ecclesiastical Review (15:3, 1973), pp. 218-26.   DHU/R

1176. ----- "The Withdrawal of High God in West African Religion: An Essay in Interpretation." Man (62; My., 1962), pp. 67-69.   DHU/MO

1177. Odiong, Udo. "Abasi Ibom: The Supreme God in Ibibo Land." West African Religion (Nos. 13 & 14, Sept. & Dec., 1972), pp. 59-61.   DHU/R

1178. Odita, E. Okechukwu. "Universal Cults and Intra-Diffusion: Igbo Ikenga in Cultural Retrospection." African Studies Review (16:1, Apr., 1973), pp. 73-82.   DHU/MO

1179. O'Donohue, J. "The Dead are Thirsty." African Ecclesiastical Review (15:4, 1973), pp. 345-46.   DHU/R
Dogon of West Africa and the practice of slaking the thirst of their dead.

1180. Oduyoye, Modupe. The Vocabulary of Yoruba Religious Discourse. Ibadan, Nigeria: Daystar Press, 1971.   DLC

1181. Oger, Louis. Spirit Possession Among the Bemba; A Linguistic Approach. Lusaka, Zambia: Conference on the History of Central African Religions, Ag. 31-Sept. 8, 1972.
Pam. File, DHU/R   mim.

1182. Ogot, B. A. and J. A. Kiéran. Zamani: A Survey of East African History. New York: Humanities Press, Inc., 1971.
DHU/R
Published for the Historical Association of Kenya.

1183. Ogunba, Oyinade. Ritual Drama of the Ijebu Peoples: a Study of Indigenous Festivals. Doctoral dissertation. Ibadan University, 1967.

1184. Ogutu, G. E. M. "Islam in My Home Area (Nyanza Province)." Dini Na Mila (5:2, Je., 1971), pp. 1-6.   DHU/R
Nyanza Province, Kenya.

1185. Ojo, William. "Folk History of Imesi Ile." Nigeria: A Quarterly Magazine of General Interest (42; 1953), pp. 98-117.
Pam. File, DHU/R

Imesi Ile is a remote town in North Yorubaland. This article taken from unpublished work of William Ojo, a native of the town.

1186. Okonji, D. Ogbolu. "Ogbanje: an African Conception of Predestination." African Scholar (1:4, 1970), pp. 1-2.
DHU/MO
Ogbanje ritual at Ibusa on Western bank of River Niger.

1187. Olatunji, Kwame. "Flaming Drums." African Spirituals. Arranged and Concluded by Fred Karlen. Phonodisc.

1188. Olisa, Michael S. O. "Taboos in Ibo Religion and Society (Social and Religious Values of Abominations Among the Ibo)." West African Religion (11; Ja., 1972), pp. 1-18.   DHU/R

1189. Omari, C. K. "Ancestral Cult Among the Vasu (Pare) of Tanzania." Dini Na Mila (5:3, Dec., 1971), pp. 12-32. DHU/R
This paper contains extracts from the author's Ph.D. thesis entitled "God and Worship in ASU Traditional Society" submitted to the University of East Africa in 1970.

1190. ----- "The Role of Witchcraft and Sorcery in Society." Psychopathologie Africaine (Dakar) (8:1, 1972), pp. 115-25. DLC

1191. Omijeh, Matthew. "EHI— The Concept of the Guardian." The Nigerian Christian (5:5, My., 1971), pp. 14-15+.
Pam. File, DHU/R
Bini religion.

1192. ----- "Ehi— Some Notes on the Paradox of Self Predestination in Bini Religion." West African Religion (10; Jl., 1971), pp. 1-6.   DHU/R
The Bini of Nigeria.

1193. Omoyajowo, Joseph A. "Christian Expression in African Indigenous Churches." Presence (5:3, 1972), pp. 9-12. DHU/R

1194. ----- "Human Destiny, Personal Rites and Sacrifices in Africa Traditional Religion." Journal of Religious Thought (30:1, Spr.-Sum., 1973), pp. 5-15.   DHU/R

1195. Opoku, Kofi Asare. "Aspects of Akan Worship." The Ghana Bulletin of Theology (4:2, Je., 1972), pp. 1-13.   DHU/R

1196. Orr, Charles William J. The Making of Northern Nigeria. London: Macmillan & Co., 1911. PW-Mu; NN; DLC; MB
Christianity and Islam in Nigeria.
Book review International Review of Missions (1:2, 1912), pp. 323-27.   DHU/R

1197. Osei, Gabriel K. The African Philosophy of Life. London: The African Publication Society, 1971.   DHU/R
Chapter 2, The Spread of Islam in Africa and Chapter 5, Religion in Africa.

1198. "Oshogbo Celebrates Festival of Shango." Nigeria: A Quarterly Magazine of General Interest (40; 1953), pp. 298-312.
Pam. File, DHU/R
"Oshogbo is a Nigerian town where tradition and progress are marching side by side."

1199. Osir, Clerah. "An Analysis of the Religious and Philosophical Contents of the Names of God from the Luo of Kenya." Dini Na Mila (5:1, Mr., 1971), pp. 1-7.   DHU/R

1200. Ottenberg, Simon. Leadership and Authority in an African Society: The Afikpo Village-Group. Seattle: University of Washington Press, 1971.   DHU/R
Includes information on religious agents as leaders, ritual, oath shrines, Yam Priest, etc.

1201. Owolalu, J. Omosade. "Yoruba Sacrificial Practice." Journal of Religion in Africa (5:2, 1973), pp. 81-93. DHU/R

1202. Owomoyela, Oyakan. Folklore and the Rise of Theater Among the Yoruba. Doctoral dissertation. University of California, 1970.

1203. Paden, John Naber and Edward W. Soja. The African Experience. Evanston: Northwestern University, 1970.
DHU; DHU/MO
V. 2, pp. 48-55, Conceptual Systems and Religion; pp. 81-84, Islam in Africa; pp. 201+ , Impact of Christianity. Islamic Reformation Movements.
V. 3, pp. 89+ , The Impact of Islam in Africa.

1204. Palmer, H. Richmond. "Trident — Gods in Sahara and Western Sudan." Man (41; Mr.-Apr., 1941), p. 15+. DCU/AN

1205. Park, George K. "Divination and Its Social Contexts." Journal of the Royal Anthropological Institute (93: 2, 1963), pp. 195-209.   DLC

1206. Parkin, David. "Politics of Ritual Syncretism: Islam Among the Non-Muslim Giriama of Kenya." Africa (40:3, Jl., 1970), pp. 219-33.   DHU/MO

1207. Parrinder, Geoffrey   see   Parrinder, Edward Geoffrey.

1208. Parrinder, Edward Geoffrey. A Dictionary of Non-Christian Religions. Philadelphia: The Westminster Press, 1971.
DHU/R

1209. ----- African Mythology. London: Paul Hamlyn, 1967.
DHU/AA

1210. ----- "African Religions." The Expository Times (83:11, Ag., 1972), pp. 324-28.   DHU/R
Six in a series, Learning From Other Faiths.

1211. ----- African Traditional Religion. London: Hutchinson's University Library, 1954.   DHU/MO; CoDI

1212. ----- La Religion en Afrique Occidentale... Paris: Payot, 1950.   DLC

1213. ----- "Monotheism and Pantheism in Africa." Journal of Religion in Africa (3:2, 1970), pp. 86-88.   DHU/R

1214. ----- Religion in Africa. Balto., Md.: Penguin Books, Inc., 1969. DHU/R; DLC; CoDI; NjP, T Sew U-T; MiBsA; NNCor; MNtcA

1215. ----- Religions of the World. New York: Grosset and Dunlap, 1971.   DHU/R
Includes sections on Traditional Africa, Ancient Egypt, Christianity and Islam.

1216. ----- West African Psychology: A Comparative Study of Psychological and Religious Thought. London: Lutterworth Press, 1951.   DHU/MO

1217. ----- West African Religion, Illustrated from the Beliefs and Practices of the Yoruba, Ewe, Akan, and Kindred Peoples. With a Foreword by Edwin Smith. London: Epworth Press, 1949. DHU/R; DHU/MO; OWibfU; CoDI

1218. ----- West African Religion: A Study of the Beliefs and Practices of Akan, Ewe, Yoruba, Ibo, and Kindred Peoples. New York: Humanities Press, 1970. DHU/MO; CoDI
Reprint of 1961 2nd rev. and enl. ed.

1219. ----- Witchcraft: A Critical Study of the Belief in Witchcraft From the Records of Witch Hunting in Europe Yesterday and Africa Today. Baltimore: Harmonds, 1958.

1220. ----- Witchcraft: European and African. New York: Barnes & Noble, Inc., 1963.   DHU/R; DHU/MO

1221. Parsons, Q. N. Notes of Oral Presentation. Lusaka, Zambia: Conference on the History of Central African Religious Systems. Ag. 31-Sept. 8, 1972. Pam. File, DHU/R Mim.

1222. Parsons, Robert T. Religion in an African Society. A Study of the Religion of the Kono People of Sierra Leone In Its Social Environment, With Special Reference to the Function of Religion In That Society. Leiden: E. J. Brill, 1964. NN/Sch

1223. Patton, Cornelius Howard. The Lure of Africa. New York: Missionary Education Movement of the United States and Canada, 1917.   NN/Sch
Mohammedanism in Africa.

1224. Pauw, Berthold A. Religion in a Tswana Chiefdom. London: Oxford University Press, 1960. NIC; MH; OCI; OrU; ICU; MnU; NcU; DHU/R

1225. Pauwels, Marcel. "Le Culte de Nyabingi (Ruanda)." Anthropos (46:3-4, My.-Ag., 1951), pp. 337-57. DAU; DCU/AN; DLC

1226. Payne, Roland J. "The Influence of the Concept of the Traditional African Leadership on the Concept of Church Leadership (some personal impressions I)." Africa Theological Journal (No. 1, Feb., 1968), pp. 69-74.   DHU/R

1227. p'Bitek, Okot. African Religions in Western Scholarship. Kampala: East African Literature Bureau, 1970.
MiBsA; DLC; DHU/R; NNCor; MBU

1228. Pearson, J. D. (comp.). Index Islamicus 1906-1955; A Catalogue of Articles on Islamic Subjects in Periodicals and Other Collective Publications. Cambridge, Eng.: W. Heffer, 1958. DLC; FtaSu; CtY-D; CLSU; CBPac

1229. Pearson, Roger. "Ancestor Worship in Sub-Saharan Africa." The Southern Quarterly (10:3, Apr., 1972), pp. 223-44.
Pam. File,   DHU/R

1230. Peel, John D. Y. "Religious Change in Yorubaland." Africa (37:3, Jl., 1967), pp. 292-306.   DHU/MO

1231. Peirot, Claude-Hélène. "Un Culte Messianique Chez les Sotho au Milieu de 19 siecle." Archives de Sociologie des Religions (9:18, Jl.-Dec., 1964), pp. 147-52.   DCU

1232. Penick, C. C. "The Devil Bush of West Africa." Journal of American Folklore (9:34, Jl.-Sept., 1896), pp. 220-22.
Pam. File,   DHU/R

1233. Perregaux, E. "Ashanti Fetishes and Oracles." Journal of American Folklore (13:14, Ja.-Mr., 1900), pp. 61-64.
Pam. File,   DHU/R
Gold Coast Religion.

1234. Person, Yves. "Pour une Histoire des Religions Africaines." Archives de Sciences Sociales des Religions (18:36, Jl.-Dec., 1973), pp. 91-101.   DHU/R

1235. Pettersson, Olof. Afrikas Religioner. Stockholm: Svenska Bokforlaget (Bonnier), 1966.   NNCor

1236. ----- Chiefs and Gods: Religious and Social Elements in the South Eastern Bantu Kingship. Lund: Gleerup, 1953.
DHU/MO; DLC

1237. Phillips, J. E. Tracy. "Observation on Some Aspects of Religion Among the Azande 'Niam-Niam' of Equatorial Africa." Journal of the Anthropological Institute (56; 1926), pp. 178-88.
CtY; DLC

1238. Philipps, Tracy. "An African Culture of Today in the Country Between the Bantu Negro and the Semitic Arab." Anthropos (41-44: 1-3, n.m. 1946-49), pp. 193-211.
"Some aspects of spiritual religion of the aZande, nick-named "Niam-naim," peoples of African Equatoria."

1239. Pich, V. Merlo. "Les Aspects Religieux du Mouvement Mau-Mau." Devant les Sectes non-Chrétiennes (XXXIe Semaine de Missiologie, Louvain, 1961). Louvain: Desclée de Brouwer, n.d. (imprimatur, 1961), pp. 125-39. DLC

1240. "Pilgrimage to the Sacred Ruins of the Basilicas of Africa." The Catholic Historical Review (14:1, Apr., 1924), pp. 90-91.
DHU/R
Christianity in Africa.

1241. Plaatje, Solomon Tshekisho. Native Life in South Africa: Before and Since the European War and the Boer Rebellions. New York: Negro Universities Press, 1969.   DHU/R
Originally published in 1916 by P.S. King and Son, Ltd., London.

1242. Platt, Marjorie Elizabeth. The Effects of Mohammedanism in Central Africa. Master's thesis. New Orleans Baptist Theological Seminary, 1949.

1243. Plotnicor, Leonard. "'Nativism' in Contemporary Nigeria." Anthropological Quarterly (37:3, Jl., 1964), pp. 121-37.
DCU/AN

1244. Pommerol, Jean. L'Islam Africain, Ches Ceux Gui Guettent. Paris: Fontemoing, 1905.   NNMR

1245. Prempeh, Samuel. Attitudes and Policies of the Protestant Churches to Traditional Birth, Puberty, Marriage, and Funeral Rites in Ghana. Master's thesis. New College, Faculty of Divinity, University of Edinburgh, 1970.

1246. Pretorious, Pauline. "An Attempt at Christian Initiation in Nyasaland." International Review of Missions (39; Jl., 1950), pp. 284-91.   DHU/R

1247. Prince, Raymond Hubert. Ifa; Yoruba Divination and Sacrifice. Ibadan: Medical Illustration Unit, University of Ibadan, 1964.

1248. "Progress Report on Churches' Research on Marriage in Africa." African Ecclesiastical Review (14:4, 1972), p. 371.
DHU/R

1249. Proyart, Lievain Bonaventure. Histoire de Loango, Kakongo, et Outres Royaumes d'Afrique. ..par M. L'Abbe Proyart. Paris: C. P. Berton, 1776. (Farnborough: Gregg, 1968.)   NjP

1250. Prussin, Lebelle. "The Architecture of Islam in West Africa." African Arts/Arts d'Afrique (1:2, Wint., 1968), pp. 32-35+.   DHU/MO

1251. "Psalms of Cameroons." Collected and Edited by John Phillipson. Folkway Records. Lyrics included in English and Cameroon language.
Phonodisc.

1252. Quatrefoges de Breau, Armond. The Pygmies. New York: Macmillan Co., 1895.   DHU
"Religious beliefs of the Hottentots and the Bushmen."

1253. Quechon, Martine. "Réflexions Sur Certains Aspects du Syncrétisme Dans l'Islam Ouest-Africain." Cahiers d'Etudes Africaines (11:42, 1971), pp. 206-30. DAU; DGU

1254. Quinn, Charlotte Alison. Traditionalism, Islam and European Expansion: the Gambia, 1850-1890. Doctor dissertation. University of California at Los Angeles, 1967.

1255. Racz, Istvan. The Unknown God. New York: Sheed and Ward, n.d.   DHU/R
Includes "Ideas of God among African Peoples," and "Ancient Egyptian Ideas of God."

1256. Radcliffe-Brown, Alfred Reginald, et al. (eds). African Systems of Kinship and Marriage. London: Oxford University Press, 1950.   DHU/R

1257. Radin, Paul and Elenor Marvel, (eds.). African Folktales and Sculpture. New York: Pantheon Books, 1966. DHU/R
(Bollingen series, V. 32.)
"Special nature of African folk literature."

1258. ----- ...Primitive Religion: its Nature and Origin. New York: The Viking Press, 1937.   DHU/MO
African tribal religions.

1259. Ramponi, Egidio. "Religion and Divination of the Logbara Tribe of North Uganda." Anthropos (32; 1937), pp. 571-94.
DLC

1260. Rangeley, W. H. J. "M'bona the Rain Maker." The Nyasaland Journal (5:1, 1953), pp. 8-27.   DLC

1261. ----- "Two Nyasaland Rain Shrines." The Nyasaland Journal (5:2, Jl., 1952), pp. 31-50.   DLC

1262. Ranger, Terence O. Mchape and the Study of Witchcraft Eradication. Lusaka, Zambia: Conference on the History of Central African Religious Systems. Ag. 31-Sept. 8, 1972.
Pam. File,   DHU/R   mim.

1263. ----- and Isaria N. Kimambo, (eds.). The Historical Study of African Religion. Berkeley: University of California Press, 1972.   DHU/R; MiBsA; CoDU; TSewU-T
Papers presented at a conference sponsored by the University of Dar es Salaam and the African Studies Center of the University of California at Dar es Salaam in June, 1970.

1264. Rattray, Robert Sutherland. Akan-Ashanti Folk Tales. Oxford: The Clarendon Press, 1930. DLC; CU; PU; CtY; NcD

1265. ----- Ashanti. Oxford: Clarendon Press, 1923.   DHU/R
Traditional religion in Ghana.

1266. ----- Hausa Folklore Customs, Proverbs, ... Oxford: Clarendon Press, 1913.   DLC

1267. ----- Religion and Art in Ashanti. Oxford: The Clarendon Press, 1927.   DHU/MO

1268. Raum, Johannes. "Die Religion der Landschaft Moschi am Kilimandjaro." Archiv fur Religionswissen-Schaft (XIV; 1911), pp. 159-211. CtY; DLC; ICU; NN; NNC; OO; NcD

1269. Raum, J. "Christianity and African Rites." International Review of Missions (16; 1927), pp. 581-91.   DHU/R

1270. Raum, Otto F. "Magic and a Christian Policy." International Review of Missions (24; 1935), pp. 358-65. DHU/R

1271. Ray, Benjamin C. African High Gods. Doctoral dissertation. University of Chicago, 1971.

1272. ----- "'Performative Utterances' in African Rituals." History of Religions (13:1, Ag., 1973), pp. 16-35. DHU/R

1273. ----- "Recent Studies of African Religion." History of Religions (12:1, Aug., 1972), pp. 75-89.   DHU/R

1274. Reeck, Darrell L. "Islam in a West African Chiefdom: An Interpretation." The Muslim World (62:3, Jl., 1972), pp. 183-94.   DHU/R

1275. Rehse, H. "Die Priestersprache und Die Frauensprache der Basinza." Zeitschrift für Kolonialsprachen (6; 1947), pp. 244-50.   DLC; ICU; NN; OU; NNC

1276. Les Religions Africaines Comme Source de Valeurs de Civilisation. Colloque Organiso par la Societe Africaine de Culture. Paris: Presence Africaine, 1972. NNCor; NjP

1277. "The Religions of Black Africans." Family Films. Released by Society for Visual Education, 1970. 58 fr. color. 35 mm. & phonodisc: 1s., 12 in., 33-1/3 rpm., 10 min.   DLC
Filmstrip. "Shows African art and sculpture which express religious ideas and feelings and reveal the African's interrelationship with nature. Focuses on the three living religions in Africa: traditional, Christian, and Islamic.

1278. "The Religion of My Fathers: The Religion of an African."
International Review of Missions (19; 1930), pp. 362-76.
DHU/R
Nyasaland.

1279. Rencontres Internationales de Bouaké, Oct., 1962. Les
Religions Africaines Traditionnelles. Paris: Editions du
Seuil, 1965. DLC; NjP; InU; NcD; PPULC; NNCor

1280. Rennie, J. K. Some Revitalization Movements Among the
Ndau and Inhambane Thonga, 1915-1935. Lusaka, Zambia:
Conference on the History of Central African Religious
Systems, Ag. 30-Sept. 8, 1972. Pam. File, DHU/R
Mim.

1281. Reyburn, William D. Out of the African Night. New York:
Harper & Row, 1968.   DHU/R
Chapter 2, A Grain Falls into the Earth. An episode
which illustrates the position of respect that ancestors
have in traditional African religions.

1282. Reynolds, Barries. Magic, Divination and Witchcraft
Among the Barotse of Northern Rhodesia. Berkeley: University of California Press, 1963.   DHU/R

1283. Richard, Audrey I. "A Modern Movement of Witchfinders."
Africa (8:4, Oct., 1935), pp. 448-61.   DAU; DCU/AN;
DGW; DHU; DLC; CLU; DHU/MO
Also in Marwick, Max. Witchcraft and Sorcery. London:
Penguin Modern Sociology Readings, 1970, pp. 164-77.

1284. ----- (ed.). East African Chiefs: A Study of Political
Development in Some Uganda and Tanganyika Tribes. New
York: Praeger, 1960.   DHU/MO

1285. Rita-Ferreira, A. "The Nyau Brotherhood Among the
Mozambique Cewa." South African Journal of Science
(64:1, Ja., 1968), pp. 20-24.   DLC

1286. Roberts, Bill. Life and Death Among the Ibos. London:
Scripture Union, 1970.   DLC; DHU/R
Includes information on their worship.

1287. Robinson, David. "Abdul Qadir and Shaykh Umar: a Continuing Tradition of Islamic Leadership in Futa Toto." International Journal of African Historical Studies (6:2, 1973),
pp. 286-303.

1288. Robson, James. Christ in Islam. London: J. Murray,
1929.   DLC; NN; NcD;   MH-AH

1289. Roome, William John Waterman. "The Dead Weight of
Islam in Equatorial and Southern Africa." Moslem World
(4; 1914), pp. 273-91.   DHU

1290. Roscoe, John. The Baganda; an Account of Their Native
Customs and Beliefs. London: Macmillan and Co., 1911.
DHU/MO

1291. Rose, Brian W. "African and European Magic: A First
Comparative Study of Beliefs and Practices." African Studies
(23:1, 1969), pp. 1-9.   DAU; DCU/AN; DHU

1292. Ross, Brownlee John. "The Religion of the Bantu, and that
of Early Israel." South African Outlook. (56; Jl. 1, 1926),
pp. 156-58.   OO; CtY

1293. Ross, Emory W. Fetishism: What It Is. Indianapolis:
Christian Woman's Board of Missions, 19?   TN/DCHS

1294. Rotberg, Robert I. A Political History of Tropical Africa.
New York: Harcourt, Brace, 1965.   DHU/MO
Conflict between Christian and Islamic traditions in Africa.

1295. Rouch, Jean. La Religion et la Magie Songhay (Religion
and Magic of Songhay). Paris: Presses Universitaires de
France, 1960. CU; CaQMU; InU; CLU; NN; MH

1296. Ruel, M. J. "Religion and Society Among the Kuria of East
Africa." Africa (35:3, Jl., 1965), pp. 295-306. DHU/MO

1297. ----- "Witchcraft, Morality and Doubt." ODU (2:1, Jl.,
1965), pp. 3-27.   DHU/MO

1298. Ruffin-Pierre, M. P. "Femmes 'Zebola' ou Femmes
Hantées Par Un Esprit." Voix du Congolais (14; 1947),
pp. 613-14.   DLC; NN; PU/Mu
Operations done through sorcery which Mongo women
have to undergo who are thought to be haunted by spirits.

1299. "The Rules of the African Society." Thomas R. Frazier,
(ed.). Afro-American History: Primary Resources (New
York: Harcourt, Brace & World, Inc., 1970), pp. 43-45.
DHU/R; DHU/MO

1300. Rusillon, Henry. "Islam in Madagascar," Moslem World
(12; 1922), pp. 286-89.   DHU

1301. Ruud, Jorgen. Taboo: A Study of Malagasy Customs and
Beliefs. New York: Humanities Press, 1960.
NcD; TNJ; CLU; DLC
Book Review by J. L. Fischer in Journal of American
Folklore (74:293, Jl.-Sept., 1961), pp. 264-65. DHU/R
Microcard.

1302. Ruxton, F. H. "Pagan Conceptions of God." The East and
the West (10; Oct., 1912), pp. 368-76.   DHU/R
Africa.

1303. Samarin, William J. "Gbeya Prescientific Attitudes and
Christianity." Practical Anthropology (6:4, Jl.-Ag., 1959),
pp. 179-82.   DHU/R

1304. Sangree, Walter H. "The Dodo Cult, Witchcraft, and Secondary Marriage in Irigwe, Nigeria." Ethnology (13:3, Jl.,
1974), pp. 261-78.   DHU/R

1305. Sankey, Lugano W. T. "African Concept of Time."
Reader's Comments. Africa Theological Journal (2; Feb.,
1969), pp. 94-101.   DHU/R
In opposition to John S. Mbiti's February, 1968 essay.

1306. Santos, Eduardo dos. Sabre a Religias dos Quiocos.
Lisboa: Jienta de Investigacoes do Ultramar, 1962. DCU
Kioko tribe and religion.

1307. Sarpong, Peter K., (bp.). "Aspects of Akan Ethics." The
Ghana Bulletin of Theology (4:3, Dec., 1972), pp. 40-44.
DHU/R

1308. ----- "The Sacred Stools of Ashanti." Anthropos (62:1-2,
1967), pp. 1-60.   DLC; DHU/MO
The Ashanti Stool and the ancestral blackened stool.

1309. Sawyerr, Harry A. E. "The African Concept of Death."
World Student Christian Federation (2:2, 1972), pp. 22-34.
DHU/R

1310. ----- God: Ancestor or Creator? Aspects of Traditional
Belief in Ghana, Nigeria and Sierra Leone. London: Longman, 1970.   DLC; DHU/R; TSewU-T; PPT

1311. Scarborough, William S. "Proverbs and Sayings from Africa and the West Indies." Southern Workman (25:10, Oct.,
1896), pp. 205-06.   DLC; DHU/MO

1312. Schapera, Issac. A Handbook of Tswana Law and Custom.
London: Oxford University Press, 1938. DHU/MO

1313. ----- "Marriage of Near Kin Among the Tswana." Africa
(27:2, Apr., 1957), pp. 140-42.   DHU/MO

1314. ----- "Sorcery and Witchcraft in Bechunaland." African
Affairs (51; 1952), pp. 41-50.   DAU; DGU; DHU

1315. Schebesta, P. P. "Die Zimbabwe - Kultur in Afrika."
Anthropos (21:3, 4, My.-Ag., 1926), pp. 484-545.   DLC

1316. Schneider, Wilhelm. Die Religion der Afrikanischen
Naturvolker. n.p.: Aschendorff, 1891.   NNMR; PPT

1317. Schoffeleers, J. M. The Chisumphi and M'Bona Cults in
Malawi: A Comparative History. Lusaka, Zambia: Confer-
ence on the History of Central African Religious Systems.
Ag. 30-Sept. 8, 1972.   Pam. File, DHU/R   Mim.

1318. ----- "The History and Political Role of the M'Bona Cult
Among the Mang'anja." Terrence O. Ranger and I. Kimambo,
(eds.). Historical Study of African Religion (Berkeley: University of California Press, 1972), pp. 73-94.   DHU/R

1319. ----- M'Bone the Guardian Spirit of the Mang'anja.
Master's thesis. Oxford University, 1966.

1320. ----- Social and Symbolic Aspects of Spirit Worship Among
the Mang'anja. Doctoral dissertation. Oxford University, 1968.

1321. Schurtz, Heinrich. "The Costumes of Africa." Journal of
American Folklore (4:13, Apr.-Je., 1891), pp. 176-77.
                    Pam. File,   DHU/R
           Dress as reflection of ethos and religion.

1322. Seats, V. Lavell. Conceptions of Deity in West African
Animism. Doctoral dissertation. Southwestern Baptist
Theological Seminary, 1946.

1323. Seidel, H. "Islam und Moscheen im Westlichen Sudan."
Globus (61; 1892), pp. 328-31.   CtY; DLC; ICU; NjP

1324. Seligman, Charles Gabriel and Brenda Z. Pagan Tribes of
the Nilotic Sudan. Boston: Routledge & Kegan Paul, 1932.
                                        DHU/MO

1325. Sell, Canon E. "The Dervish Orders in Africa." E. M.
Wherry and S. M. Zwemer, et al. (eds.). Islam and Missions
(New York: Fleming H. Revell Company, 1911), pp. 63-75.
                                        DHU/R

1326. Sempa, Katende. "Emperical Foundations of the Concept of
a Soul." Dini Na Mila (5:2, Je., 1971), pp. 7-28. DHU/R
           Article shows the empirical foundations of the concept
           of a soul by using data of the author's African environ-
           ment. Buganda, Uganda.

1327. Setiloane, Gabriel M. "Modimo: God, Among the Sotho-
Tswana." Journal of Theology for Southern Africa
(4; Sept., 1973), pp. 6-17.   DHU/R

1328. Shannon, Alexander Harvey. "Christian Slavery in North
Africa." Methodist Review (Quarterly) (72:2, Apr., 1923),
pp. 288-96.   DHU/R

1329. Shejavali, Abisai. "The Influence of the Concept of the
Traditional African Leadership on the Concept of the Church
Leadership (some personal impressions II)." Africa Theo-
logical Journal (No. 1, Feb., 1968), pp. 75-82.   DHU/R

1330. Shelton, A. G. "On Recent Interpretations on Dews Otiosus:
The Withdrawn God in West African Psychology." Man (64;
1964), pp. 53-54.   DCU/AN

1331. ----- "The Presence of the Withdrawn High God in North
Ibo Religious Belief and Worship." Man (65; 1965), p. 18.
                                         DCU/AN

1332. Shelton, Austin J. The Igbo-Igala Borderland; Religion and
Social Control in Indigenous African Colonialism. Albany,
N.Y.: State University of New York Press, 1971. DHU/R
           Chapter 2, Nsukka Religion.

1333. Shepperson, George. "The Jumble of Kota Kola and Some
Aspects of the History of Islam in British Central Africa."
Ioan M. Lewis (ed.). Islam in Tropical Africa (London:
Oxford University Press, 1966), pp. 193-208.   CLU

1334. Shinnie, Peter L. and H. N. Chittick. Ghazali – a Monastery in the Northern Sudan (Sudan Antiquities Service Occasional Papers, No. 5), Khartum: 1961.   MH

1335. Shorter, Aylward. "African Traditional Religion and Religious Education." African Ecclesiastical Review (14:4,
1972), pp. 304-17.   DHU/R

1336. ----- "The Migawo: Peripheral Spirit Possession and
Christian Prejudice." Anthropos (65:1-2, 1970), pp. 111-26.
                    DLC; DAU; DCU/AN
           The Migawo is a pre-dominantly women's spirit pos-
           session cult among the Kimbu of Tanzania.

1337. ----- "Religious Values in Kimbu Historical Charters."
Africa (39: 3, Jl., 1969), pp. 227-37.   DHU/MO

1338. ----- "Three More African Eucharistic Prayers."
African Ecclesiastical Review (15:2, 1973), pp. 152-60. DHU/R

1339. Shropshire, Denys W. "Bantu Ancestor Worship: Its Moral
Value." The Church Overseas (5; 1932), pp. 135-51. DHU/R

1340. ----- "Can the Religion of the Bantu Be Preserved?" The
Church Overseas (2:8, Oct., 1929), pp. 315-23.   DHU/R

1341. ----- Church and Primitive Peoples: the Religious Institutions and Beliefs of the Southern Bantu... London: Society for
Promoting Christian Knowledge, 1938. DLC; PPT;MNtcA;ICU

1342. Sibree, James Jr. "Curious Words and Customs Connected
With Chieftainship and Royalty Among the Malagasy." Journal
of the Anthropological Institute (21; 1891-1892), pp. 230-44.
                                             DCU/A

1343. ----- "Relationships and the Names Used for Them Among
the Peoples of Madagascar, Chiefly the Hovas; Together With
Observations Upon Marriage Customs and Morals Among the
Malagasy." Journal of Anthropological Institute (9; 1880),
pp. 35-49.   DCU/A

1344. Simmons, William S. Eyes of the Night: Witchcraft Among
a Senegalese People. Bostom: Little, Brown, 1971.   DLC

1345. Simpson, George E. "Selected Yoruba Rituals: 1964." The
Nigerian Journal of Economic and Social Studies (7; 1965),
pp. 311-24.   DHU/MO

1346. ----- "The Shango Cult in Nigeria and in Trinidad."
American Anthropologist (64:6, Dec., 1962), pp. 1204-19.
                                             NNRIS

1347. Skinner, Elliot P. "Christianity and Islam Among the Mossi."
American Anthropologist (60:6, Dec., 1958), pp. 1102-19.
                                             DCU/AN

1348. ----- "The Spread of Islam in an African Society." Annals
of the New York Academy of Sciences (96:2, Ja., 1962),
pp. 659-69.   DAU; DGW/M; DHU/MO

1349. Smart, Ninian. The Religious Experiences of Mankind.
New York: Charles Scribner's Sons, 1968. DHU/R; DLC
           Religion in Africa.

1350. Smith, Alfred W. "The Advance of Islam in Africa." The
Church Missionary Review (64; Nov., 1913), pp. 656-60. DHU/R

1351. Smith, Cynthia. Notes on Giriama Religious Persistence in
the Face of Islam and Christianity. Unpublished Research
Seminar paper. University of California, Los Angeles, 1972.
                                             CLU

1352. Smith, Edwin W. African Beliefs and Christian Faith. An
Introdution to Theology for African Students, Evangelists and
Pastors. London: The United Society for Christian Literature,
1937.   DHU/R

1353. -----, (ed.). African Ideas of God, a Symposium. London:
Edinburgh House, 1950. DHU/MO; DLC; CoDI

1354. ----- Golden Stool. n. p. : Holborn Publishing House, 1927.
       IC/H; MiBsA
       The use of the stool in African indigenous religions.

1355. ----- The Secret of the African. London: Student Christian
       Movement, 1929. MiBsA; CtY; PPT
       Religion in Africa.

1356. Smith, Robert. Kingdoms of the Yoruba. London: Methuen,
       1969.   MiBsA; DHU/R

1357. Some, Bernard B. "La Religion Traditionnelle Mossi
       Comme Source de Valeurs de Civilisation Politique." Cahiers
       des Religions Africaines (4; Jl., 1970), pp. 205-27. DAU; DGU
       Traditional religion as source of Mossi political culture.

1358. Sourey, J. Ch. Sorciers Noirs et Sorcier Blanc: la Magie,
       la Sorcellerie et Ses Drames en Afrique. Bruxelles, Lib. :
       Encyclopédique, 1952.   DHU/MO

1359. Southall, Aidan. "Twinship and Symbolic Structure." Jean
       Sibyl La Fontaine (ed.). The Interpretation of Ritual (London:
       Tavistock Publications, 1972), pp. 73-114. DHU/R
       African traditional religion.

1360. Sowande, Fela. African Religion and Philosophy. A Per-
       spective in Outline. 1971. Pam. File, DHU/R
       Typescript.

1361. Speel, C. J. "The Disappearance of Christianity from
       North Africa in the Wake of the Rise of Islam." Church
       History (29:4, Dec., 1960), pp. 379-97.   DHU/R

1362. Spieth, J. Die Religion der Eweer in Sud-Togo.
       Leipzig: Dieterich, 1911. DLC; MiU; OCH; NN

1363. Ssekamwa, J. C. "Witchcraft in Buganda Today."
       Transition (6:5, Apr.-My., 1967), pp. 31-39. DAU

1364. Stam, N. "The Religious Conceptions of the Kavifondo."
       Anthropos (5:2-3, Mr.-Je., 1910), pp. 359-62. DLC

1365. ----- "The Religious Conception of Some Tribes of Buganda
       (British Equatorial Africa)." Anthropos (3:2, 1908), pp. 213-18
                                                        DLC

1366. Stebbing, M. "Mamhepo" — Spirit Possession Among the
       Shona. Lusaka, Zambia: Conference on the History of Cen-
       tral African Religious Systems, Ag. 31-Sept. 8, 1972.
                        Pam. File, DHU/R   Mim.

1367. Stefaniszyn, Bronislaw. Social and Ritual Life of the Ambo
       of Northern Rhodesia. London: Oxford University Press,
       1964.   NN/Sch

1368. Stevenson, R. C. "Some Aspects of the Spread of Islam in
       the Nuba Mountains." Sudan Notes and Records (44; 1963),
       pp. 9-20.   DLC

1369. Stewart, Charles Cameron. Islam and Social Order in
       Mauritania: A Case Study From the Nineteenth Century.
       Oxford: Clarendon Press, 1973.   DHU/R

1370. Stow, N. "The Religious Conceptions of the Kanironda."
       Anthropos (5; 1910), pp. 359-62. DCU/AN; DLC; CtY

1371. ----- "The Religious Conceptions of Some Tribes of
       Buganda in British Equatorial Africa." Anthropos (3; 1909),
       pp. 213-18. DCU/AN; CtY; DLC

1372. Strelcyn, S. "Magie, Medecine et Possession a Gondar."
       Journal of Religion in Africa (4:3, 1972), pp. 161-70. DHU/R

1373. Stuart, Richard G. Mchape and The U.M.C.A., 1933.
       Lusaka, Zambia: Conference on the History of Central Afri-
       can Religious Systems, Ag. 30-Sept. 8, 1972. Pam. File,
                                                DHU/R

1374. Stuart-Watt, Eva. The Quest of Souls in Qua Iboe.
       Edinburgh: Marshall, Morgan & Scott, 1951. NNMR

1375. Sulayman, Shahid Mufassir. "Islam Has Soul, It is the
       Natural Religion." Encore (2:6, Je., 1973), pp. 39-40.
                        Pam. File, DHU/R

1376. Swantz, Marja-Liisa. Ritual and Symbol in Transitional
       Zaramo Society with Special Reference to Women.
       Lund: Gleerup, 1970.   DLC
       Rites, ceremonies, social life and customs of Tanzania.

1377. Swithenbank, Michael. Ashanti Fetish Houses. New York:
       Panther House, 1971.   DLC
       Ashanti temples.

1378. Talbot, Percy A. Life in Southern Nigeria: The Magic,
       Beliefs and Customs of the Ibibio Tribe. New York: Barnes
       & Noble, Inc., 1967. DHU/R; DLC; FMU; CSt; NNMR

1379. ----- Some Nigerian Fertility Cults. New York: Barnes
       & Noble, 1967.   DHU/MO; DLC
       Phallicism, cultus, and religion in Nigeria.

1380. ----- Tribes of the Niger Delta: Their Religion and Cus-
       toms. London: Sheldon Press, 1932. PLI; NcD; NN; ViU; OCl

1381. Tamuno, Tekena and Robin Horton. "The Changing Position
       of Secret Societies and Cults in Modern Nigeria." African
       Notes (5:1, Ja., 1969), pp. 36-62.   DHU/MO

1382. Tanner, Ralph E. S. "Conversion to Christianity and Islam
       From African Religions: Some Social and Ritual Factors."
       The Heythrop Journal (15:2, Apr., 1974), pp. 144-65. DHU/R

1383. ----- Transition in African Beliefs: Traditional Religion
       and Christian Change. A Study in Sukumaland. Maryknoll,
       N. Y.: Maryknoll Publications, 1967. DHU/MO; CLU

1384. Tasie, Godwin Onyemeachi Mgbechi. "Priesthood and Social
       Change in the Traditional Religion of the Kalabari People."
       Journal of Religion in Africa (3:2, 1970), pp. 96-105. DHU/R
       Kalabari forms part of the Rivers people who occupy
       the southern portion of the Niger Delta.

1385. Tauxier, Louis. La Religion Bambara. Paris:
       P. Geuthner, 1927.   DCU/A
       West Africa.

1386. ----- Religion, Moeurs et Coutumes des Agnis de la
       Cote-d'Ivoire. Paris: Paul Geuthner, 1932.
                        CtY; PU; DLC;   CU

1387. Taylor, John Vernon. "The Development of African Drama
       for Education and Evangelism." International Review of
       Missions (39; Jl., 1950), pp. 292-301.   DHU/R

1388. ----- The Primal Vision. Christian Presence Amid Afri-
       can Religion. Philadelphia: Fortress Press, 1963. DHU/R

1389. ----- Processes of Growth in an African Church.
       London: SCM Press, 1958. OWibfU; DLC

1390. Tegnaeus, Harry. Le Héros Civilisateur; Contribution à
       L'Etude Ethnologique de la Religion et de la Sociologie
       Africaines. Stockholm, 1950.   DHU/MO

1391. Tempels, Placide. Bantu Philosophy. Paris: Presence
       Africaine, 1969.   DHU/MO; DHU/R
       "Bantu ethics, ontology, wisdom and mission to
       civilize."

1392. "Territorial Cults in Central Africa." African Religious
       Research (2:2, Nov., 1972), pp. 6-16.   DHU/R
       A Summary of some of the papers given at the Con-
       ference on the History of Central African Religious
       Systems, University of Zambia, August 31st to
       September 8th, 1972.

1393. Tesfai, Yacob. Hebrew and African Understanding of Death: A Comparison. Master's thesis. Lutheran School of Theology at Chicago, 1971.

1394. ----- Theories of Primitive Religion. Oxford: Clarendon Press, 1965.   DHU/MO

1395. Thiemes, Darius. "Music History in Africa." Vada E. Butcher. Development of Materials for a One Year Course in African Music for the General Undergraduate Student (Wash., D.C.: U.S. Dept. of Health, Education, and Welfare, 1970), pp. 101-04.   DHU/R
     Howard University, Washington, D.C.
     Project of the Fine Arts Dept.
     "Spirit possession ceremonies."

1396. ----- "Music in Yoruba Society." Vada E. Butcher. Development of Materials for a One Year Course in African Music for the General Undergraduate Student (Wash., D.C.: U.S. Dept. of Health, Education, and Welfare, 1970), pp. 107-11.   DHU/R
     "Howard University, Wash., D.C., Project of the Fine Arts Dept."

1397. Thom, Gideon. "A Reform Perspective on African Belief in Ancestors." Missionalia (1:2, Ag., 1973), pp. 73-85. DHU/R

1398. Thomas, Louis V. "Courte Analyse des Religions Négro-Africaines Traditionnelles (l'Exemple de l'Afrique 'Anglophone' Orientale et Australe)." Notes Africaines (113; Ja., 1968), pp. 1-10.   DLC

1399. ----- Les Religions d'Afrique Noire, Textes et Traditions Sacrés. Paris: Fayard Denoël, 1969. MiBsA; NjP; DHU/MO; PPT
     Religion in Africa.

1400. ----- "The Study of Death in Negro Africa." Lalage Brown and Michael Crowder, (eds.). Proceedings of the First International Congress of Africanists (London: Longmans, 1964), pp. 146-68.   DAU

1401. Thompson, Virginia and Richard Adloff. Djibouti and the Horn of Africa. Stanford, Calif.: Stanford University Press, 1968.   CSt; ViU; KyU
     Part 2 includes a discussion of religion.

1402. Thompson, W. "Moslem and Pagan in Cameroon." Asia (24; Oct., 1924), pp. 764-67. DLC; MH; CtY; DCU

1403. Thomson, Joseph. "Mohammedanism in Central Africa." Contemporary Review (50; 1887), pp. 876-83. CLU; CtY; DCU; DHU; DLC; ICU; InU; KyU; NN; NNC; OO; OrU

1404. Tippett, Alan R. Peoples of Southwest Ethiopia. South Pasadena, Calif.: William Carey Library, 1970.   DLC
     Chapters on indigenous religions and the impact of Christianity.

1405. Tomlinson, G. J. F. History of Islamic Political Propaganda in Nigeria. London: Waterlow & Sons, 1927. IEN

1406. Torrend, F. J. "Likenesses of Moses' Story in the Central Africa Folk-Lore." Anthropos (5:1, Ja.-Feb., 1910), pp. 54-70.   DLC

1407. Torrend, Jules. Specimens of Bantu Folk-Lore from Northern Rhodesia. New York: E. P. Dutton & Co., 1921.
                                    DHU/MO; NN/Sch

1408. Torrey, E. Fuller. "What Western Psychotherapists Can Learn from Witchdoctors." American Journal of Orthopsychiatry (42:1, 1972), pp. 67-76.   DLC; TxU

1409. ----- "The Zar Cult in Ethiopia." Proceedings of the Third International Conference of Ethiopian Studies. V. III (Addis Ababa: Institute of Ethiopian Studies, Haile Selassie I University, 1970), pp. 51-59.   AA/IES

1410. Tremearne, Arthur J. N. The Ban of the Bori: Demons and Demon-Dancing in West and North Africa. London: Frank Cass & Co., Ltd., 1968.   DHU/R

1411. ----- Hausa Superstitions and Customs. London: Frank Cass & Co. Ltd., 1970.   DLC

1412. Trimingham, John Spencer. "Africa's Own Brand of Islam." New Society (66; Ja. 2, 1964), pp. 14-15.   DAU

1413. ----- The Christian Church and Islam in West-Africa. London: SCMP, 1956.   DHU/MO; DHU/R

1414. ----- A History of Islam in West Africa. Oxford: Clarendon Press, 1962.   DHU/R

1415. ----- The Influence of Islam Upon Africa. New York: Frederick A. Praeger, 1968. DHU/MO; DHU/R

1416. ----- Islam in East Africa. New York: Barnes and Noble, 1965.   DHU/R

1417. ----- Islam in Ethiopia. London: Frank Cass & Co., 1965. (New York: Barnes and Noble, 1965).   DHU/R

1418. ----- Islam in the Sudan. London: Oxford University Press, 1949.   DLC; ICU; CSt-H; NNUN; MH

1419. ----- Islam in West Africa. Oxford Clarendon Press, 1959.
                                    DHU/R

1420. ----- "Notes on the Tribes, Regions and Emirates of Northern Nigeria." African Studies Bulletin (8; 1965).
                                    DLC

1421. Tshibangu, Tharcisse. "Problématique d'une Pensée Religieuse Africaine." Cahiers des Religions Africaines (2:1, Ja., 1968), pp. 11-21.   DLC

1422. Turnbull, Colin M. "Tribalism and Social Evolution in Africa." The Annals of the American Academy of Political and Social Science (354; Jl., 1964), pp. 22-31. DAU; DGU; DCU/SW; DGU; DHU

1423. Turner, Harold W. Living Tribal Religions. London: Ward Lock Educational Ltd., 1971.   DLC

1424. ----- "Resource Materials on the African Spiritual Heritage." Current Bibliography on African Affairs (4:5, Sept., 1971), pp. 339-41.   DHU/MO
     Lists scholarly journals on African religions.

1425. Turner, Henry McNeal, (bp.). "The American Negro and His Fatherland." J. W. E. Bowen (ed.). Africa and the American Negro: Address and Proceedings of the Congress on Africa (Miami, Fla.: Mnemosyne Publishing Co., Inc., 1969), pp. 195-98.   DHU/R
     Negro author.

1426. Turner, Philip. "The Wisdom of the Fathers and the Gospel of Christ: Some Notes on Christian Adaptation in Africa." Journal of Religion in Africa (4:1, 1971), pp. 45-68.   DHU/R

1427. Turner, Victor W. The Drums of Affliction: A Study of Religious Processes Among the Ndembu of Zambia. Oxford: Clarendon Press for the International African Institute, 1968.
                                    DHU/R

1428. ----- The Forest of Symbols; Aspects of Ndembu Ritual. New York: Cornell University Press, 1967. DHU/MO; NNCor

1429. ----- "An Ndembu Doctor in Practice in Magic, Faith and Healing." Ari Kiev, (ed.). Magic, Faith, and Healing: Studies in Primitive Psychiatry Today (New York: Free Press of Glencoe, 1964), pp. 230-63.   DLC

1430. ----- The Ritual Process: Structure and Anti-Structure. Chicago: Aldine, 1969. DHU/R; DLC; MU

Analyzes the ritual of "Isoma" by which Ndembu
cure persons and the Wubwangu which strengthens
a woman who bears twins.

1431. Tutu, Desmond. "Some African Insights and the Old Testament." Journal of Theology for Southern Africa (1; Dec.,
1972), pp. 16-22.   DHU/R

1432. ----- "The Ancestor Cult and Its Influence on Ethical
Issues." Ministry (9:3, 1969), pp. 99-104.   DLC

1433. Tyler, J. "Native Worship in South Africa — Zulu Hades-
Doctors of Divination and Spiritualism." Andover Review
(5:30, Je., 1886), pp. 656-59.   DHU/R

1434. Tylor, Edward B. Primitive Culture; Researches into the
Development of Mythology, Philosophy, Religion, Language,
Art, and Custom. London: John Murray, 1903.   DHU/R

1435. Tyms, James Daniel. "African Contributions to World Religion." J. S. Roucek and Kiernan (eds.). The Negro Impact
on Western Civilization (New York: Philosophical Library,
1970), pp. 109-37.   DHU/R
       Negro author.

1436. Umunna, V. N. "Nigerian Paganism as a Preparation for
the Gospel." East and West Review (5:2, Apr., 1939),
pp. 139-45.   DHU/R

1437. Usher, Roland G. "Primitive Law and the Negro." Journal
of Negro History (4:1, Ja., 1919), pp. 1-6.   DHU

1438. Uzoho, V. N. "The Sacred and the Profane in the Traditional
Religion of Africa." West African Religion (No. 15, Mr., 1974),
pp. 36-43.   DHU/R

1439. Van Binsbergen, Wim J. J. Bituma: Preliminary Notes on
a Healing Movement Among the Nkoya of Kaoma District and
of Lusaka, Zambia. Lusaka, Zambia: Conference on the History of Central African Religious Systems, Aug. 31-Sept. 8,
1972. Pam. File,   DHU/R   Mim.

1440. Van der Merwe, Willem J. "Religions of Africa." Bulletin
of the Africa Institute of South Africa (9:6, Jl., 1971),
pp. 231-45.   Pam. File,   DHU/R

1441. ----- "The Shona Idea of God." Nada (34-37; 1959-60),
pp. 39-63.   DLC

1442. Van der Westhuizen, P. J. W. S. "Life After Death
Amongst the Bushmen." Missionalia (1;2, Ag., 1973), pp. 42-6.
                                                DHU/R

1443. Vanneste, A. "Le Mariage en tant que Sacrement." Revue
du Clerge Africain (26; 3-4, My.-Jl., 1971), pp. 128-45.
                                                DHU/R
       Christian marriage in Africa.

1444. Vermel, Pierre. "L'Influence du Madhisme au Nigeria."
L'Afrique et L'Asie (1971), pp. 93-94, 47-60. DLC;CtY;OU

1445. Vernier, Charles. Islamisme et Christianisme et Afrique.
Montauban: Imprimeri Cooperative (Ancien Maison Granie,
1908).   NN/Sch

1446. Vernon-Jackson, Hugh. West African Folk Tales. London:
University of London Press, 1958.   IEN; NNC

1447. Vincent, Jeanne-Francoise. "Divination et Posession chez
les Mofu, Montagnards du Nord-Cameroun." Journal de la
Societe des Africanistes (41:1, 1971), pp. 71-132. DCU/A

1448. Voil, John. "Two Biographies of Ahmad Ibn Idris Al-Fast
(1780-1837)." International Journal of African Historical
Studies (6:4), pp. 633-45.

1449. Voll, John. "The British, the Ulama, and Popular Islam in
the Early Anglo-Egyptian Sudan." International Journal of

Middle East Studies (2; 1971), pp. 212-18.
                        DLC; CLU; DGW; CtY-L

1450. ----- "Islam: Its Future in the Sudan." Muslim World
(63:4, Oct., 1973), pp. 280-96.   DHU/R

1451. von Grunebaum, Gustave E. Modern Islam, the Search for
Identity. Berkeley: University of California Press, 1962. DLC

1452. Walk, Leopold. "Initiationszeremonien und Pubertatsriten
der Sudafrikanischen Stamme." Anthropos (23:5-6, Sept.-Dec.,
1928), pp. 861-966.   DLC

1453. Walker, Andre R. Rites et Croyances des Peuples du Gabon;
Essai sur les Pratiques Religieuses d'Autrefois et d'Aujourd'
hui... Paris: Presence Africaine, 1962.   NN/Sch

1454. Walker, Shelia S. Ceremonial Spirit Possession in Africa
and Afro-America, Forms, Meanings, and Functional Significance for Individuals and Social Groups. Leiden: Brill, 1972.
                                                DLC; DHU/R

1455. Wallace, Anthony F. C. "Revitalization Movements."
American Anthropologist (58; 1956), pp. 121-33. CtY; DCU;
DHU; DLC; IcU; NN; OrU; TxD
       Includes information on "cargo cult", "religious revival",
       "Messianic movements" and "Charismatic movements."

1456. Wanger, W. "The Zulu Notion of God." Anthropos (18-19;
1923-24; 21; 1926), pp. 656-87; 351-85. DLC; DCU/AN

1457. Ward, Edward. The Yoruba Husband-Wife Code. Washington, D. C.: The Catholic University of America, Anthropological Series No. 6, 1938.   DCU/AM

1458. Warmelo, N. J. Contributions Toward Venda History, Religion and Tribal Ritual. Pretoria: The Government Printer,
1932.   DHU/MO

1459. Watson, A. "Islam in Egypt and Sudan." Missionary Review of the World. (30; My., 1907), pp. 351-58. DHU/R

1460. Watson, Charles R. "Islam Under Pagan Rule." E. M.
Wherry and S. M. Zwemer, et alii, (eds.). Islam and Missions (New York: Fleming H. Revell Company, 1911), pp. 76-
86.   DHU/R
       The major portion of this chapter is about Islam in Africa.

1461. ----- "Statistical and Comparative Survey of Islam in Afri-
ca." S. M. Zwemer and E. M. Wherry, et alii, (eds.). The
Mohammedan World of To-day (New York: Fleming H. Revell
Company, 1906), pp. 279-85.   DHU/R

1462. Watt, E. S. The Quest of Souls in Qua-Iboe. London:
n. p., 1951.

1463. Webster, Hutton. Primitive Secret Societies. A Study in
Early Politics and Religion. New York: Macmillan Co., 1908.
                                                DHU/R
       "Development of tribal societies."

1464. Weeks, John H. Among the Primitive Bakongo. A Record
of Thirty Years' Close Intercourse With the Bakongo and Other
Tribes of Equatorial Africa, with a Description of Their Habits, Customs, and Religious Beliefs. London: Seeley, Service
and Co., 1914.   DHU/MO

1465. Welbourn, Frederick Burkewood. "Mary Douglas and the
Study of Religion. A Review Article." Journal of Religion in
Africa (3:2, 1970), pp. 89-95.   DHU/R

1466. Welch, Galbraith. Africa Before They Came. The Continent North, South, East, and West, Preceding the Colonial
Powers. New York: William Morrow & Co., 1965. DHU

1467. Welch, James W. "Witchcraft in Nigeria II. The Christian
Answer." The Church Overseas (5; 1932), pp. 31-45. DHU/R

1468. ----- "Witchcraft and Christianity in the Niger Delta." The Church Overseas (4; 1931), pp. 318-33.   DHU/R

1469. ----- Religious Studies in an African University. Ibadan: University Press, 1950.   DHU/MO
An inaugural lecture delivered on the Foundation Day ceremonies at the Ibadan University College, Nigeria. Lecture covers Islam, West African indigenous religion, Christian theology, and Graeco-Christian theology.

1470. Welsh, Isabel M. Islam in Senegal: A Study of the Islamic Brotherhoods. Masters thesis. University of California at Berkeley, 1965.

1471. Welton, Michael R. "Themes in African Traditional Belief and Ritual." Practical Anthropology (18:1, Ja.-Feb., 1971), pp. 1-18.   DHU/R

1472. Were, Gideon S. and Derek A. Wilson. East Africa Through a Thousand Years... New York: Africana Publishing Corp.,1970.   DHU/MO
Chapter I, "Dhous and Mosques: the Coast, 1000 to 1500."

1473. Werner, Alice. Myths and Legends of the Bantu. London: George G. Harra & Co., Ltd., 1932.   DHU/MO

1474. Werner, Douglas. Aspects of History in the MIAO Spirit System of the Southern Lake Tanganyika Region: The Case of Kapembwa. Lusaka, Zambia: Conference on the History of Central African Religious Systems, Aug. 31-Sept. 8, 1972.
Pam. File,   DHU/R   Mim.

1475. ----- "Some Developments in Bemba Religious History." Journal of Religion in Africa (4:1, 1971), pp. 1-24. DHU/R
Bemba is a part of the African nation of Zambia.

1476. Westermann, Diedrich. Africa and Christianity. London: Oxford University Press, 1937. DHU/R; NN/Sch; OU; NcD; NjPT

1477. ----- "Islam in the Eastern Sudan." International Review of Missions (2; Mr., 1913), pp. 454-85; (1; Apr., 1912), pp. 618-58.   DAU/W

1478. ----- "Islam in the West and Central Sudan." International Review of Missions (1:4, 1912), pp. 618-53.   DHU/R

1479. Westermarck, E. A. "The Magic Origin of Moorish Designs." Journal of the Anthropological Institute of Great Britain and Ireland (34; 1904), pp. 211-22. DCU/AN; DGW

1480. White, Charles M. N. Elements in Luvale Beliefs and Rituals. Manchester: Published on Behalf of the Rhodes Livingstone Institute by the Manchester University Press, 1961.   DHU/MO

1481. ----- "Stratification and Modern Changes in an Ancestral Cult." Africa (19:4, Oct., 1949), pp. 324-31.   DHU/MO

1482. Wilberforce, Daniel F. Sherbro and the Sherbros: or a Native African's Account of His Country and People. Dayton, Ohio: United Bretheren Publishing House, 1886. DOUM/EUB

1483. Wilder, George Albert. The White African; the Story of Mafavuke "Who Dies and Lives Again." Told by Himself, at the Request of His Relatives and Friends... Bloomfield, N.J.: Morse Press, 1933.   NN/Sch

1484. Wilks, Ivor. "Islam in Ghana History: An Outline." Ghana Bulletin of Theology (2:3, 1962), pp. 20-28. CLU; DLC; NNMR

1485. ----- "The Transmission of Islamic Learning in the Western Sudan." John R. Goody, (ed.). Literacy in Traditional Societies (New York: Cambridge University Press, 1969), pp. 162-97.   CLU

1486. Willett, Frank. On the Funeral Effigies of Owo and Benin and the Interpretation of the Life-size Bronze Heads From Ife, Nigeria. Evanston Ill.: 1966.

1487. Williams, F. R. J. "The Pagan Religion of the Madi." Uganda Journal (13:2, 1949).   CtY; DLC

1488. Williams, Joseph J. Africa's God... Chestnut Hill, Mass.: Boston College Press, 1936-38.   DHU/MO

1489. ----- Hebrewisms of West Africa: From Nile to Niger with the Jews. New York: Biblo and Tanner, 1967.
DHU/R; DHU/MO
Chapter 7 "The Lion of the Tribe of Juda." pp. 159-185. Originally published in 1930.

1490. Williamson, Sydney George. Akan Religion and the Christian Faith: A Comparative Study of the Impact of Two Religions. Accra: Ghana Universities Press, 1965. DHU/MO; MNtcA; PT

1491. Willis, John Ralph. "The Historiography of Islam in Africa: the Last Decade (1960-1970)." African Studies Review (14:3, Dec., 1971), pp. 403-24.   DHU/MO

1492. ----- "The Spread of Islam (C.A.D. 500-1500)." The Horizon History of Africa (New York: American Heritage Publishers Co., 1971), pp. 136-68.   DHU/MO

1493. Willis, Roy G. "Changes in Mystical Concepts and Practices Among the Fipa." Ethnology (7:2, Apr., 1968), pp. 139-57.   DHU/R
Fipa of Southwest Tanzania.

1494. ----- "Kamchape: An Anti-Sorcery Movement in South West Tanzania." Africa (38:1, Ja., 1968), pp. 1-14.
DAU; DCU/AN; DGW; DHU; DLC; CLU; DHU/MO

1495. ----- "Kaswa: Oral Tradition of a Fipa Prophet." Africa (40:3, Jl., 1970), pp. 248-56.   DHU/MO

1496. Willoughby, William Charles. Nature-Worship and Taboo. Hartford, Conn.: Hartford Seminary Press, 1932. DHU/R

1497. ----- The Soul of the Bantu. Garden City, N.Y.: Doubleday, Doran & Co., Inc., 1928.   DHU/R

1498. Wilson, Bryan R. Magic and the Millennium: A Sociological Study of Religious Movements of Protest Among Tribal and Third-World Peoples. New York: Harper and Row, 1973. DLC

1499. Wilson, Monica. Communal Rituals of the Nyakyusa. New York: Oxford University Press, 1959.
DHU/R; DHU/MO; NNM; CU; NjR; CtY
Southern Tanganyika (Tanzania).
Book review by Melville J. Herskovits in Journal of American Folk-Lore (73:293, Oct.-Dec., 1960), pp. 341-43.
DHU/R
Microcard.

1500. ----- Rituals of Kinship Among the Nyakyusa. New York: Oxford University Press, 1957. DLC; ICU; NIC; CtY; DHU/MO

1501. ----- "The Wedding Cakes: a Study of Ritual Change." Jean Sibyl La Fontaine, (ed.). The Interpretation of Ritual (London: Tavistock Publications, 1972), pp. 187-201. DHU/R
Influence of Christian missions upon traditional religious customs in South Africa.

1502. ----- "Witchcraft Beliefs and Social Structure." American Journal of Sociology (56; 1951), pp. 307-13.
DAU; DCU/SW; DGW; DHU
Study of the Nyakyusa and Ponod.

1503. ----- and Archie Mafeje. Langa, A Study of Social Groups in an African Township. Cape Town: Oxford University Press, 1963.   DLC; DHU/MO
"South Africa."

1504. Wilson, Samuel G. Modern Movements Among Moslems. New York: Fleming H. Revell Company, 1916. DHU/R
The penetration of Africa by Islam, pp. 94-105.
The Mahdi of the Sudan, pp. 139-46.

1505. Wilson-Haffenden, J. R. The Red Men of Nigeria. An
Account of a Lengthy Residence Among the Fulani, or "Red
Men" and Other Pagan Tribes of Central Nigeria, With A De-
scription of Their Headhunting, Pastoral and other Customs,
Habits and Religion. New York: Barnes & Noble, 1930.
                                                    DHU/MO

1506. Wipper, Audrey. "The Gush Rebels." Robert I. Rotberg
and Ali A. Mazrui, (eds.). Protest and Power in Black Africa
(New York: Oxford University Press, 1970), pp. 377-426.
                                                    DHU/R

1507. "Witchcraft Eradication Movements." African Religious
Research (2:2, Nov., 1972), pp. 27-34.   DHU/R
      A summary of some of the papers given at the Con-
      ference of Central African Religious Systems, Univer-
      sity of Zambia, August 31st to September 8th, 1972.

1508. Witchcraft, Oracles, and Magic Among the Azanale.
Oxford: Oxford University Press, 1937.   DHU/R

1509. Wordsworth, J. "Islam and Christianity in Africa."
Missionary Review of the World (32; Sept., 1909), pp. 691-95.
                                                    DHU/R

1510. Wurz, Friedrich. "Pan-Islamism in Africa." E. M.
Wherry, S. M. Zwemer, et alii, (eds.). Islam and Missions
(New York: Fleming H. Revell Company, 1911), pp. 53-62.
                                                    DHU/R

1511. Wyndham, John. The Curse of Obo: A Tradegy of Benin.
London: Duckworth, 1926.   NNMR
      See Harris, John Blynon.

1512. ----- "The Divination of Ifa (A Fragment)." Man
(19:80, 1919), pp. 151-53.   DLC
      Reprinted in Wyndham, 1921: 65-70.

1513. Young, Crawford. "Materials for the Study of Islam in the
Congo." Cahiers Economiques et Sociaux (4:4, Dec., 1966),
pp. 461-64.   DAU

1514. Young, Thomas C. "Ancestor-Worship or Ancestor-
Partnership?" The Church Overseas (6; 1933), pp. 241-49.
                                                    DHU/R
      African traditional religion.

1515. ----- "The Communal Bond in Bantu Africa." International
Review of Missions (22; 1933), pp. 105-14.   DHU/R
      African traditional religion.

1516. Zahan, Domonique. Religion, Spiritualité, et Pensée
Africaines. Paris: Payot, 1970.   NjP

1517. Zankovsky, S. "Zar and Tambura as Practised by the Wom-
en of Omdurman." Sudan Notes and Records (31:1, 1950),
pp. 65-81.   DCU/AN; DLC; ICF; MH; NN; NjP
      Names of ceremonies held in order to calm the spirits.
      The dance of possession is performed by women.

1518. Zaretsky, Irving I. Bibliography of Spirit Possession and
Spirit Mediumship. Evanston: Northwestern University Press,
1966.   DLC; CSt

1519. Zempleni, A. "La Dimension Therapeutique du Cult des Rab.
Ndop, Tuuru et Samp, Rite de Possession chez les Lebou et les
Wolof." Psychopathologie Africaine (2; 1966), pp. 295-343.
                        DLC; CtY; ICU; WaU; MH

1520. Zuesse, Evan M. "On the Nature of the Demonic: African
Witchery." Numen (18:3, 1971), pp. 210-39. DAU; DCU/TH;DGU

1521. Zuure, Bernard. "Immana le Dieu des Barundi." Anthropos
(21:5, 6, Sept.-Dec., 1926), pp. 733-76.   DLC

1522. Zwemer, Samuel M. The Influence of Animism on Islam.
London: Central Board of Missions and S.P.C.K., 1920. DLC

1523. ----- "Islam in Africa." Moslem World (15; Jl, 1925),
pp. 217-22.   DHU

1524. ----- "Islam at Cape Town." Moslem World (15; Oct.,
1925), pp. 327-33.   DHU

D. EARLY MISSIONARY ACTIVITIES (to 1800)

1525. ----- "Islam in Africa: Second Paper." International
Review of Missions (15:3, Jl., 1926), pp. 547-55. DHU/R

1526. Conference of Missionary Societies in Great Britain and
Ireland. Bibliography of African Christian Literature. Compiled by Rev. Canon F. Rowling... and Rev. C. E. Wilson...
London: Conference on Missionary Societies of Great Britain
and Ireland, 1933.   CtY-D; DLC

1527. Cuvelier, Jean, (ed.). Documents sur une Mission Francaise au Kakongo, 1766-1776. Bruxelles: n.p., 1953. NN/Sch

1528. Duignan, Peter and Clarence C. Clendenen. The United
States and the African Slave Trade 1619-1862. (Stanford,
Calif.) Hoover Institution on War, Revolution and Peace,
Stanford University, 1963.   DHU/MO

1529. Equiano, Olaudah. The Interesting Life of Olaudah Equiano,
Gustavas Vassa, the African. London: n.p., 1789. DHU/MO
      "The slave who helped to end the slave trade."

1530. Fage, J. D. and R. A. Oliver, (eds.). Papers in African
Prehistory. London: Cambridge University Press, 1970.
                                                    DHU/R

1531. Gray, John M. Early Portuguese Missionaries in East
Africa. London: Macmillan, 1958. MH-AH; NIC; ICU; CtY-D;
NjPT; CST; TxDaM; WaU; CLU; NNCor

1532. Hair, Paul Edward Hedley. "Guides to the Records of Early
West African Missions." Journal of Religion in Africa.
(1:2, 1967), pp. 129-37.   DHU/R

1533. ----- "Protestants as Pirates, Slavers, and Proto-Mission-
aries: Sierra Leone 1568 and 1582." Journal of Ecclesiastical History (21:3, Jl., 1970), pp. 203-24.   DHU/R

1534. Klingberg, Frank J. "Sir William Johnson and the Society
for the Propagation of the Gospel, 1749-1774." The Historical
Magazine of the Protestant Episcopal Church (8; 1939), pp. 4-37.
                                                    DHU/R

1535. Kup, Alexander Peter. "Jesuit and Capuchin Missions of the
Seventeenth Century." Sierra Leone Bulletin of Religion
(5:1, 1963), pp. 27-34.   DLC

1536. Laurent de Lucques, (Father). Relations sur le Congo du
Pere Laurent de Lucques (1700-1717) Traduits et Annotees
par Mgr. J. Cuvelier. Bruxelles: n.p., 1953.   NN/Sch

1537. Legassick, Martin Chatfield. The Griqua, the Sotho-Tswana,
and the Missionaries, 1780-1840: The Politics of a Frontier
Zone. Doctoral dissertation. The University of California at
Los Angeles, 1969.

1538. Richie, C. I. A. "Impressions of Senegal in the Seventeenth
Century: Excerpts From Louis Chamboneau's 'A Treatise on
the Origin of the Negroes of Senegal, on the African Coast,
About the Country, Religion and Habits'." African Studies
(26; 1967), pp. 59-94.   DLC
      "African Studies published in Johannesburg."

1539. Silva, Antonio da. "A Familia Mocambicana Vista Relos
Missionanos Jesuitas Anteriores a 1759." Arquioo Historico
de Portugal (2a:1, 1964), pp. 394-428.   PU

1540. Welch, Sidney R. Portuguese Rule and Spanish Crown in
       South Africa, 1581-1640. Cape Town: Juta, 1950. NjP; PPT

1541. ----- South Africa Under King Sebastian and the Cardinal,
       1557-1580.

                    E. CHRISTIAN CHURCH AND AFRICA

                    1. Later Missionary Activities (since 1800)

a. Cameroon

1542. Beanland, Lillian L. African Logs. Illustrated by
       Lois McNeil. n.p., 1945.   NN/Sch
           "Copyright... by the Board of Foreign Missions of
           the Presbyterian Church in the U.S.A."

1543. Brutsch, Jean René. "A Glance at Missions in Cameroon."
       International Review of Missions (37; Jl., 1950), pp. 302-10.
                                                        DHU/R

1544/45. Christol, Frank. ...Quatre ans au Cameroun. Paris:
       Sociéte des Missions Evangéliques de Paris, 1922. NN/Sch

1546. Dussercle, Roger. ... Du Kilimandjaro au Cameroun.
       Monseigneur F. X. Vogt (1870-1943). Paris: La Colombe,
       1954.   NN/Sch

1547. Gelzer, David Georg. "Missions and Colonization: Educa-
       tion in Cameroun in the Days of the Germans." The Bulletin
       of the Society for African Church History (3:1-2; 1969-70),
       pp. 1-14.   DHU/R

1548. Hallden, Erik. The Culture Policy of the Basel Mission in
       the Cameroons 1886-1905. Uppsala: Institutet for allman och
       jamforande etnografi, 1968. NhD; InU; NcD; CtHC; MH-P; CU;
       NjPT; PPULC; IaU; IU; NcGU; GU; LU; MU; CtY-D; OrU; NRU

1549. Halsey, Abram W. "Romance of Cameroun Mission."
       Missionary Review (40; My., 1917), pp. 330-38. DHU/R

1550. Hawker, George. An Englishwoman's Twenty-five Years in
       Tropical Africa. Being the Biography of Gwen Elen Lewis,
       Missionary to the Cameroons and the Congo. London and New
       York: Hodder and Stoughton, 1911. DLC; OrP; ICRL; CLU
           Book review in International Review of Missions
           (1:2, 1912), pp. 342-44.   DHU/R

1551. Hitcher, B. 'Basel Mission in the Southern Cameroons."
       Missionary Review (35; My., 1912), pp. 375-76. DHU/R

1552. Horner, Norman Aste. "Polygyny Among the Bantu of
       French Cameroun." International Review of Missions (43;
       1954), pp. 173-73.   DHU/R
           Christian missions and African traditions.

1553. ----- Protestant and Roman Catholic Missions Among the
       Bantu of Cameroun: A Comparative Study. Doctoral disserta-
       tion. Hartford Seminary, 1956.

1554. Johnson, Thomas Lewis. Africa for Christ. Twenty-eight
       Years a Slave. London: Alexander and Shepheard, 1892.
                                                        NN/Sch

1555. Kwast, Lloyd E. The Disciplining of West Cameroon: a
       Study of Baptist Growth. Grand Rapids, Mich.: Eerdmans,
       1971.   DLC

1556. Mackenzie, Jean Kenyon. African Adventures. West Med-
       ford, Mass.: Central Committee on the United Study of For-
       eign Missions, 1917.   NN/Sch

1557. ----- Black Sheep; Adventures in West Africa. New York:
       Houghton Mifflin Co., 1916.   NN/Sch

1558. Reyburn, William D. "Polygamy, Economy and Christianity
       in the Eastern Cameroun." Practical Anthropology (6:1, Ja.-
       Feb., 1959), pp. 1-19.   DHU/R

Capetown and Johannesburg: Juta and Co.,Ltd., 1949.
Also deals with the status and function of the Catholic
Church in South Africa.

1559. Scheve, E. Die Mission der Deutschen Baptisten in Kame-
       run Von 1884 bis 1901. Berlin: F. G. Oncken, 1908. CtY

1560. Skolaster, Hermann. Die Pallottiner in Kamerun; 25 Jahre
       Missions-Arbeit. Limburg-Lahn: Kongregation der Pallottiner,
       1924.   NN/Sch

1561. Steiner, P. Kamerun als Kolonie und Missionsfeld. Basel:
       Basler Missions-buchhandlung, 1909.   NjP

1562. Trobisch, Ingrid Hult. On Our Way Rejoicing! New York:
       Harper & Row, 1964.   NN/Sch
           Annals of a missionary family: the African field of
           reference is mainly Cameroun, though some parts
           relate to Tanzania and elsewhere.

1563. Zoa, Jean. "The African Church Now." International
       Documentation on the Contemporary Church. North American
       Edition. (No. 10; Sept. 26, 1970), pp. 45-49.   DHU/R
           Archbishop of Yaounde, Cameroon, opinions on the
           future of the Catholic Church in Africa.

b. Chad, Niger, Mali, Mauretania

1564. Addison, James Thayer. Francois Coillard. Hartford,
       Conn.: Published for the National Council of the Protestant
       Episcopal Church by Church Missions Publishing Co., 1929.
                                                        NN/Sch

1565. Anderson, August Magnus. Ukanya; Life Story of an Afri-
       can Girl. Anderson, Ind.: The Warner Press, 1931. NN/Sch

1566. DuBois, Felix. Timbuctoo. New York: Negro Universities
       Press, 1969.   DHU/R
           Reprint of 1896 edition.
           West Africa.

1567. Ligers, Ziedonis. Les Sorko (Bozo): Maitres du Niger:
       Ethnographique. 3 vols. Paris: Libraire des Cinq Continents,
       1964-67.
           In V.II is a discussion of religion in Mopti region of Mali.

1568. Marty, Paul. Etudes sur l'Islam et les Tribus Maures:
       les Brakna. Paris: E. Leroux, 1921.   DHU/MO

1569. Venberg, Rodney W. The Southern Brethren Church in
       Chad and Camerouns. Masters thesis. Fuller Theological
       Seminary, 1970.

c. Dahomey (Benin)

1570. Akindélé, Adolphe and Cyrille Aguessy. Contribution a
       L'Etude de L'Histoire de L'Ancien Royaume de Porto-Nuvo.
       Dakar: IFAN, 1953.   DHU/MO
           Includes some discussion of religion in the former
           Kingdom of Porto-Nuvo (Dahomey).

1571. Argyle, William Johnson. The Fon of Dahomey: A History
       and Ethnography of the Old Kingdom. Oxford: Clarendon Press,
       1966.   DHU/MO
           Some discussion of religion included.

1572. Endicott, Mary Austin. Spotlight on Africa. Illustrations
       by courtesy of Methodist Prints-- New York, D. G. Ridout--
       Toronto. Toronto: Committee on Missionary Education, Lit-
       erature Dept., Woman's Missionary Society, United Church of
       Canada, 1945.   NN/Sch

1573. Forbes, Frederick Edyn. Dahomey and the Dahomans: Being the Journals of Two Missions to the King of Dahomey and Residence at His Capital in the Years 1849 and 1850. London: Longmans, Brown, Green and Longmans, 1851. DLC;NN;PPL;NcU

1574. Freeman, Thomas Birch. "Wesleyan Mission in Guinea (Dahomey)." Missionary Herald (40:2, Feb., 1844), pp. 63-67. DHU/R

1575. Guilcher, Rene François. ...Au Dahomey Avec le Pere Dorgère. L'Activité Pacificatrice d'un Missionaire. Lyon: Procure des Missions Africaines, 1939. NN/Sch

1576. Laffitte, J. Le Pays des Negres, et la Cote des Esclaves, par M. L'Abbe Laffitte. Tours: A. Mame, 1878. NN/Sch

1577. Lawyer, Zelma Wood. I Married a Missionary. Abilene, Tex.: Abilene Christian College Press, 1943. NN/Sch

1578. Marty, Paul. Etudes sur l'Islam au Dahomey: Le Bas Dahomey, Le Haut Dahomey. Paris: E. Leroux, 1926. DHU/MO

c. Ethiopia (see also I-B)

1579. Alamé Esaté. Activities Politiques de la Mission Catholique (Lazariste) en Ethiopie (Sous la Règne de l'Empereur Johannés), 1868-1889. Paris: Études Documentaires, 1970. AA/IES

1580. Alays (Père). Capucins Missionaires en Afrique Orientale. Pays Galla en Ethiopie, Côte Francaise des Somalis. Toulouse: Les Voux Franciscaines, 1931. AA/IES

1581. Alvares, Francisco. The Prester John of the Indies; a True Relation of the Lands of the Prester John Being the Narrative of the Portuguese Embassy to Ethiopia in 1520. The Translation of Lord Stanley of Alderley (1881) Revised and Edited with Additional Material by G. F. Beckingham and G. W. B. Huntingford. Cambridge, Eng.: Published for the Hakluyt Society at the University Press, 1961. MNtcA

1582. Baeteman, Joseph. Etiopia: Tradusione di Giulio Barsotti. Parma: Istituto Missioni Estere, 1935. NN; NB

1583. Barsotti, Giulio. Etiopia Christiana; Prefazione di Piero Bargelini. Milano: Editrice Ancora, 1939. NN/Sch

1584. Bartnicki, Andrzej and Joanna Mantel-Niećko. "The Role and Significance of the Religious Conflicts and People's Movements in the Political Life of Ethiopia in the Seventeenth and Eighteenth Centuries." Rassegna di Studi Etiopici (24; 1971), pp. 5-39. AA/IES

1585. Bergama, Stuart. Rainbow Empire; Ethiopia Stretches Out Her Hands. Grand Rapids, Mich.: W. B. Eerdmans Publishing Co., 1932. NN/Sch

1586. Bernoville, Gaetan. Monseigneur Jarosseau et la Mission des Gallas. Mission d'Éthiopie. Paris: Librairie St. Francois, 1950. DLC; CoDU; IEN; WU

1587. Betta, Luigi. "Fondazione Della Missione Lazzarista in Abissinia (1838)." Annali della Missione (62:45, 1955), pp. 274-316. AA/IES

1588. Beylot, Robert. "Un Episode de l'Histoire Ecclesiastique de l'Éthiopie. La Mouvement Stéphanite. Essai sur sa Chronologie et sa Doctrine. Annales d'Éthiopie (8; 1970), pp. 103-16. AA/IES

1589. Bockelman, Wilfred and Eleanor. Ethiopia: Where Lutheran is Spelled "Mekane Yesus." Minneapolis: Augsburg Publishing House, 1972. AA/IES; DLC

1590. Catholic Cathedral, Addis Ababa. The Consecration of a Bishop According to the Ethiopic Rite. Addis Ababa, 1958. AA/IES

1591. "The Catholic Church in Ethiopia." African Ecclesiastical Review (13:1, 1971), pp. 89-91. DHU/R

1592. Cerulli, Enrico. "La Dea Mater ed il suo Culto Presso le Genti dell'Etiopia Meridionale (Galla Caffa). Rivista di Antropologia (43; 1956), pp. 3-12. AA/IES

1593. "The Church Blesses Murder." Editorial. Pittsburgh Courier (Nov. 9, 1939). DHU/MO
Roman Catholic Church accused for sanctioning murder in Ethiopia during Italian-Ethiopian crisis.

1594. Cleland, C. S. "Seen in Abyssinia." The Missionary Review of the World (47:12, Dec., 1924), pp. 964-70. AA/IES; DHU/R

1595. Congregazione Delle Figlie di S. Anna. Asmara. Le Figlie di S. Anna in Etiopia in 1866-1966, 8 Dicembre, 1° Centenario. Roma: 1966. AA/IES

1596. Cooksey, Joseph J. A Serious Aspect of the Abyssinian Situation... London: New Midway Press, 1935. NN/Sch

1597. Cotterell, F. P. "An Indigenous Church in Southern Ethiopia." The Bulletin of the Society for African Church History (3:1-2, 1969-70), pp. 68-104. DHU/R

1598. Coulbeaux, Jean Bapiste. Mission d'Abyssinie. Paris: Librairie Armand Colin, 1901. AA/IES

1599/1600. Crawford, O. G. S., (ed.). Ethiopian Itineraries: circa 1400-1524. Cambridge: Published for the Hakluyt Society University Press, 1958. DHU/MO
Includes activities of Missionaries.

1601. Crummey, Donald E. European Religious Missions in Ethiopia, 1830-1868. Doctoral dissertation. London University, 1967.

1602. ----- "Foreign Missions in Ethiopia, 1829-68." The Bulletin of the Society for African Church History (2:1, Dec., 1965), pp. 15-36. DHU/R

1603. ----- Priests and Politicians: Protestant and Catholic Missions in Orthodox Ethiopia, 1830-1868. London: Oxford University Press, 1973. DHU/R

1604. De Carouge, Alfred, O. M. Cap. Une Mission en Ethiopie d'Apres les Memoires du Cardinal Massaia et d'autres Documents. Paris: Poussielgue, 1902.

1605. Galbiati, Giovanni. "L'apostolo dell' Abissinia." Nuova Antologia (Ottava Serie), 1936. AA/IES

1606. Gianazza, Elvira. Guglielmo Massaia, Missionario ed Esploratore nell' Olta Etiopia. Torino: G. B. Paravia, 1939. AA/IES

1607. (Keis) Gidada Solon. The Other Side of Darkness. New York: Friendship Press, 1972. AA/IES

1608. Gobat, Samuel. Journal of Three Years' Residence in Abyssinia. Proceeded by an Introduction, Geographical and Historical, on Abyssinia. Translated from the French by Rev. Sereno D. Clark. Accompanied with a Biographical Sketch of Bishop Gobat, by Robert Baird... New York: M. W. Dodd, 1850. NN/Sch

1609. Hahn, Heinrich. "Von der Katholischen Missionsthätigkeit in der Berberi, Aegypten und Abyssinien." Geschichte der Katholischen Missionen seit Jesus Christus bis auf die Neueste Zeit (1; 1858), pp. 223-53. AA/IES

1610. Hanson, Herbert M. and Della. For God and Emperor. Mountain View, Calif.: Pacific Press Publishing Association, 1958. AA/IES

1611. Häylä-Dengel (Abba). "Lettre d'un Prêtre Indigène de la Mission Galla.' L'écho de St. Francois et de St.-Antoine de Padoue (15:183, 1926), pp. 367-68.   AA/IES

1612. Hodson, Arnold W. Seven Years in Southern Abyssinia. London: T. F. Unwin, 1927. DLC; WU; DAU; NcD; MH; PPAmP; OCl; CSt-H; NN

1613. Holy Savior Church, Addis Ababa. Ordo Missae. Addis Ababa, 1970.   AA/IES

1614. Iwarson, Jonas. Notizie Storiche e Varie Sulla Missione Evangelica Svedese dell 'Eritrea, 1866-1916. Asmara: Missione Evangelica Svedese, 1918.   AA/IES

1615. Jones, Rex R. A Strategy of Ethiopian-Christian Missionary Fellowship. Masters thesis. School of World Mission, Fuller Theological Seminary, 1971.

1616. Kjaerland, Gunnar. Planting the Church Among the Nomadic Borana. Masters thesis. School of World Mission, Fuller Theological Seminary, 1971.

1617. Lambie, Thomas Alexander. Boot and Saddle in Africa. Philadelphia: The Blakiston Co., Distributed by Fleming H. Revell Co., New York and London, 1943.   NN/Sch

1618. ----- "Pioneer Missions in Abyssinia." Bibliotheca Sacra (85; Ja., 1928), pp. 31-36.   AA/IES

1619. Lasserre, (Louis de Gonzaque, Padre). "En Pays Gallas. Lettre de Mgr. Lasserre, Capucin, Vicaire Apostolique d'Aden." (De Zeila à Farré). Les Missions Catholiques (20; 1888), pp. 382-84, 392-95, 405-09.   AA/IES

1620. Lass-Westphal, Ingeborg. "Protestant Missions During and After the Italo-Ethiopian War, 1935-1937." Journal of Ethiopian Studies (10:1, Ja., 1972), pp. 89-101.   DHU/R

1621. Lauro, Raffaele. "Etiopia Vecchio Regime: Il Massacro della Missione Canadese nel 1936." Gli Annali dell' Africa Italiana (1; 1938), pp. 673-79.   AA/IES

1622. Liesel, Nikolaus. The Eastern Catholic Liturgies: A Study in Words and Pictures. Westminster, Maryland: Newman Press, 1960.   DHU/R
      Chapter II. "The Ethiopic Liturgy," pp. 17-29.
      Catholic rite.

1623. Lombard, Pascal (Padre). "Nouvelles de nos Missions d'Abyssinie." L 'écho de St.-Francois (26:297, 1936), pp. 155-58.   AA/IES

1624. Lucatello, Enrico. Ventidue anni in Etiopia. La Missione del Beato Giustino de Jacobis. Prefazione di Piero Bargellini. Roma: Annali della Missione, 1939. AA/IES; NN/Sch

1625. Maly, Zbynek. "The Visit of Martin Lang, Czech Francis-can, in Gondar in 1752." Journal of Ethiopian Studies (10:2, Jl., 1972), pp. 17-25.   DHU/R

1626. Massaja, Guglielmo (Cardinal). I Miei Trentacinque anni di Missione nell 'alta Etiopia; Memorie Storiche di Fra Guglielmo Massaja... Illustrate da Incisioni e Carte Geografiche. Roma: Tipografia Poliglota di Propaganda Fide, 1885-1886. AA/IES

1627. ----- I Miei Trentacinque anni di Missione nell 'alta Etiopia; Memorie Storiche di fra Guglielmo Massaja. Roma: Coop. Tipografia Manuzio, 1921-30.   AA/IES

1628. Matthew, A. F. "Slavery in Abyssinia." The Church Over-seas (6; 1933), pp. 325-33.   DHU/R
      Christianity and Slavery in Ethiopia (Abyssinia).

1629. McClure, William Donald. Red-headed, Rash and Religious; The Story of a Pioneer Missionary. Edited and compiled by Marion Fairman. Pittsburgh, Penn.: Board of Christian Ed-ucation of the United Presbyterian Church of North America, 1954.   AA/IES

1630. Meinardus, Otto F. "Peter Heyling in the Light of Catholic Historiography." Ostkirchliche Studien (18:1, 1969), pp. 16-22.   AA/IES

1631. Metodio da Nembro, (Padre). La Missione dei Minori Cap-puccini in Eritrea (1894-1952). Rome: Institutum Historicum ord. fr. min. cap., 1953.   AA/IES

1632. ----- Vita Missionaria in Eritrea. Roma: Edizioni "Il Massaia, " 1953.   AA/IES

1633. Missione Catholica. Asmara. I Settant 'Anni Della Mis-sione Catholica dei Padri Cappucini in Eritrea (1894-1964). Asmara: Scuala Tipografica Francescana, 1964.   AA/IES

1634. O'Mahoney, Kevin. A Chapter of Church History: the Po-lemic Between Missionaries to Maintain the Ethiopian Rite: 1840-1970. Historical Society of Ethiopia. Papers of the Annual Conference, Addis Ababa; n.p., 1971.

1635. Pankhurst, Richard K., (ed.). Travellers in Ethiopia. London: Oxford University Press, 1965.   DLC; NjP; CSt-H; CtY; NNC; CaQmL
      Accounts of missionaries are included.

1636. Pankhurst, Rita. "Michael Aragawii, Ethiopia's First Protestant Missionary." Ethiopia Observer (10:3, 1966), pp. 215-19.   AA/IES

1637. Paton, William and Margaret Sinclair. "Survey of Mis-sions in Ethiopia." The International Review of Missions (32: 125, Ja., 1943), pp. 34-35.   AA/IES; DHU/R

1638. Rice, Esme Ritchie, (ed.). Eclipse in Ethiopia and its Corona Glory. Toronto: Evangelical Publishers, 1938.   NN/Sch

1639. Richard, J. "Leo Premiers Missionaires Latins en Ethiopie (XIIe-XIVe siècles)." Atti del Convegno Internazion-ale di Studi Etiopici (1959), pp. 323-29.   AA/IES

1640. Salvatore, Arata. Abuna Yakob: L'apostolo dell' Abissinia, (Mons. Giustino de Iacobis C. M.), 1800-1860. Roma: Dire-zione Annali della Missione, 1934.   AA/IES

1641. Salviac, Martial de. ... Un Peuple Antique: ou, Une Colonie Gauloise au Pays de Menelik Les Galla, Grande Nation Afri-caine. Cahors F. Plantade, Imprimeur de L'eveche, 1900.   NN/Sch

1642. Sottochiesa, Gino. ... La Religione in Etiopia... Torino: Tip. G. Damonte, 1936.   NN/Sch

1643. Täklä-Haymanot (Abba). Abuno Yacob, ou le Vénérable de Jacobis. Scènes de sa vie d' apostolat Racontées par un Temoin Abba Tekla-Haimanot. Paris: Procure des Laza-ristes, (1914).   AA/IES

1644. ----- Vita di Abuna Jacob Ossia il Venerabile Padre Giustino de Jacobis. Traduzione dal Francese per P. Celes-tine da Desio. Asmara: Tipografia Francescana, 1922.   AA/IES

1645. Trimingham, John Spencer. The Christian Church and Missions in Ethiopia (Including Eritrea and the Somaliland.) London: World Dominion Press, 1950.   NN/Sch

1646. United Presbyterian Church in the United States of America. Ethiopia, The Church Moves Forward in Mission. (New York, 1965.)   AA/IES

1647. Waldmeier, Theophilus. The Autobiography of Theophilus Waldmeier, Missionary; Being an Account of Ten Years' Life in Abyssinia; and Sixteen Years in Syria. London: S. W. Partridge & Co., 1886.   NN/Sch

1648. Willmott, Helen Mary. The Doors Were Opened; The Re-markable Advance of the Gospel in Ethiopia. London: Sudan Interior Mission (1961 ?).   AA/IES

e. Ghana (Gold Coast)

1649. Adams, Frater Williams. "Gold Coast Calling: Mississippi Crusaders go to Africa." Shield (21; Mr., 1942). DCU/ST Negro author.

1650. Alleyne, Cameron Chesterfield, (bp.). Gold Coast at a Glance. New York: The Hunt Printing Co., 1931. DHU/MO; NN/Sch; DLC

1551. Antubam, Kofi. Ghana's Heritage of Culture. Leipzig: Koehler and Amelang, 1963.   DHU/MO

1552. Ayandele, E. A. "A Legitimate Branch of the Church Universal— A Review Article." Orita, the African Journal of Religious Studies (4:1, Je., 1970), pp. 44-61. DHU/R

1553. Barnes, Roswell P. "The Ghana Assembly in the Evolution of Missions." Religion in Life (27:1, Spr., 1958), p. 362. DHU/R

1554. Bartels, Francis Lodowic. The Roots of Ghana Methodism. Cambridge: University Press in Association with Methodist Book Depot, Ghana, 1965.   NN/Sch

1655. Belshaw, Harry. "Church and State in Ashanti." International Review of Missions (35; Oct., 1946), pp. 408-15. DAU/W; DCU/TH

1656. ----- "Religious Education in the Gold Coast." International Review of Missions (34; 1945), pp. 267-72.   DHU/R

1657. Bourret, F. M. The Gold Coast, A Survey of the Gold Coast and British Togoland, 1919-1946. Stanford: Stanford University Press, 1949.   CS; DLC

1658. Christaller, J. G. "Recent Explorations in the Basin of the Volta (Gold Coast) by Missionaries of the Basel Missionary Society." Proceedings of the Royal Geographical Society (8, 1886), pp. 246-56. CtY-D; DLC; NN; NNC; NcD; CLU; RPB

1659. Claridge, W. Walton. A History of the Gold Coast and Ashanti from the Earliest Times to the Commencement of the Twentieth Century. London: J. Murray, 1915. DLC; CaBViP; NIC; CU

1660. Dauphine, John W. "Catholic Mission in Accra." St. Augustine's Messenger (18; Oct., 1940), pp. 182-84. DCU/ST Negro author.

1661. Debrunner, Hans W. History of Christianity in Ghana. Accra: Waterville Press, 1967. MH-AH; DLC; NjPt; InU; IEN; NcD; NN; CtY-D

1662. ----- Owura Nico, the Rev. Nicholas Timothy Clerk, 1862-1961, Pioneer and Church Leader. Accra: Waterville Publishing House, 1965.   DHU/MO

1663. ----- "Pioneers of Church and Education in Ghana: Danish Chaplains to Guinea, 1661-1850." Kirkehistoriske Samlinger Syvende Raekke (4:3, 1963), pp. 374-425. CtY; DLC

1664. Grau, Eugene E. The Evangelical Presbyterian Church (Ghana and Togo) 1914-1946. Doctoral dissertation. Hartford Seminary Foundation, 1964.

1665. Haliburton, Gordon Mackay. "The Anglican Church in Ghana and the Harris Movement in 1914." Bulletin of the Society of African Church History (1; 1964), pp. 101-06. DLC

1666. ----- "The Calling of a Prophet: Sampson Oppong." The Bulletin of the Society for African Church History (2:1, Dec., 1965), pp. 84-96.   DHU/R
        "Between 1920 and 1926 travelled among the Ashanti as a Christian evangelist under Methodist auspices."

1667. "The I. M. C. Assembly in Ghana." International Review of Missions (46; 1957), pp. 197-200.   DHU/R
        The International Missionary Council Assembly Broadcast of B. B. C. General Overseas and Far Eastern Services on February 27, 1957.

1668. Jack, Homer A. "Conversation in Ghana." Christian Century (79: 15, Apr. 10, 1957), pp. 446-48.   DHU/R

1669. Kemp, Dennis. Nine Years at the Gold Coast. London: Macmillan, 1898.   NN/Sch

1670. Klingberg, Frank J. "Phillip Quaque: Pioneer Native Missionary on the Gold Coast, 1765-1816." The Journal of Negro Education (8; 1939), pp. 666-72.   DHU/R

1671. Kyeremater, E. A., (tr.). "A History of the Presbyterian Church at Bompata in Asante Akyem by M. P. Frempong." Ghana Notes and Queries (11; Je., 1972), pp. 38-43. DLC

1672. "Missionary Adventure in the Gold Coast." Society for Visual Education, 1955. 58 fr., color, 35 mm.   DLC
        Filmstrip. "Glimpses of geographical, social, and religious aspects of the Gold Coast."

1673. Mobley, Harris. The Ghanian's Image of the Missionary. Leiden: E. J. Brill, 1970.   DHU/R

1674. Odonkor, S. S. "A Missionary Tour of Adangme Land: Evangelism in the Gold Coast." International Review of Missions (34; 1945), pp. 144-49.   DHU/R

1675. O'Rorke, M. "Religion in the Gold Coast." Hibbert Journal (22; Oct., 1924), pp. 773-81.   DHU/R

1676. Parsons, Robert T. The Churches and Ghana Society 1918-1955: A Survey of the Work of Three Protestant Mission Societies and the African Churches Which They Established in Their Assistance to Societary Development. Leiden: E. J. Brill, 1963. DHU/MO; MNtcA
        The Presbyterian, Evangelical Presbyterian and Methodist Churches.

1677. Pawelzik, Fritz. I Lie On My Mat and Pray. New York: Friendship Press, 1964.   DHU/R
        Collection of prayers written by Ghanaians.

1678. Pobee, J. S. "Funerals in Ghana." Ghana Bulletin of Theology (4:5, Dec., 1973), pp. 17-29.   DHU/R

1679. Ramseyer, Friedrich August. Dark and Stormy Days at Kumasai, 1900; or Missionary Experiences in Ashanti According to the Diary of Rev. F. Ramseyer. London: S. W. Partridge and Co., 1901.   NNMR

1680. ----- Four Years in Ashantee by the Missionaries Ramseyer and Kuhne. Edited by Mrs. Weitbrecht; with Introduction by Rev. Dr. Gundert and Preface by Prof. Christleib. New York: R. Carter, Brothers, 1875. DHU/MO; NN/Sch

1681. Sackey, Isaac. "A Brief History of the A. M. E. Zion Church, West Gold Coast District 1903-1953." Pam. File, DHU/R

1682. Smith, Noel. The Presbyterian Church of Ghana, 1835-1960; A Younger Church in a Changing Society. London: University of Oxford Press, 1967.   DLC

1683. Wilkie, A. W. "An Attempt to Conserve the Work of the Basel Mission to the Gold Coast." International Review of Missions (9; 1920), pp. 86-94.   DHU/R

1684. Williamson, S. G. "Missions and Education in the Gold Coast." International Review of Missions (41; 1952), pp.364-73.   DHU/R

1685. Williamson, Sydney G. and J. Bardsley. The Gold Coast, What of the Church? London: Edinburgh House Press, 1953.   NcD; NjPT

1686. Wiltgen, Ralph M. Gold Coast Mission History, 1471-1880. Techny, Ill.: Divine Word Publications, 1956. DHU/MO; NN/Sch

f. Gabon

1687. Deschamps, Hubert Jules. Quinze Ans de Gabon: Les
Debuts de l'Etablissement Francais, 1839-1853. Paris: Société
Française d'Histoire d'Outre-Mer et Librairie G. P.
Maisonneuve et Larose, 1965.   IEN; NUC
     Part 3 discusses Catholic and Protestant Missions.

1688. ----- Traditions Orales et Archives au Gabon: Contribution a L'Ethno-Histoire. Paris: Berger-Levrault, 1962.
                                                 DHU/MO

1689. Grebert, F. ... Au Gabon (Afrique Equatoriale Française).
Paris: Société des Missions Evangeliques de Paris, 1948. NN/Sch

1690. Nassau, Robert Hamill. Corisco Days; the First Thirty
Years of the West Africa Mission. Philadelphia: Allen Lane
& Scott, 1910.   NN/Sch

1691. Reading, Joseph H. "En Route to Gabon." The Church at
Home and Abroad (4; 1888), pp. 38-39.   DHU/R
     Presbyterian mission.

g. Guinea, Ivory Coast, Senegal

1692. Billy, Ed. de. En Côte d'Ivoire; Mission Protestante
d'A.O.F. Paris: La Société des Missions Evangeliques, 1931.
                                                 NN/Sch

1693. Gorja, Joseph. La Côte d'Ivoire Chretienne. Lyon:
E. Vitte, 1915.   NN/Sch

1694. Holas, Bohumil. Les Toura: Esquisse d'Une Civilization
Montagnarde de Côte D'Ivoire. Paris: Presses Universitaires de France, 1962.   DHU/MO

1695. Joseph, Gaston. Côte d'Ivoire. Paris: A. Fayard, 1944.
                                                 NN/Sch

1696. Marty, Paul. Etudes Sénégalaises, 1785-1826. Paris:
Société de l'Histoire des Colonies Françaises et Editions
Leroux, (192__.)   DLC

1697. Platt, William James. African Prophet: the Ivory Coast
Movement and What Came of It. London: Student Christian
Movement Press, 1934.   DLC; CU; CtY

1698. Smith, John. Trade and Travels in the Gulph of Guinea,
Western Africa, With an Account of the Manners, Habits,
Customs, and Religion of the Inhabitants. London: Simkin
and Marshall, 1851.   NN/Sch

1699. Thompson, E. W. "The Ivory Coast: A Study in Modern
Missionary Method." International Review of Missions (4;
1928), pp. 630-44.   DAU/W; DCU/TH

1700. Walker, Frank Deaville. The Story of the Ivory Coast.
London: Cargate Press, (1928).   CtY
     About the Prophet Harris and his movement in West Africa.

h. Kenya

1701. Barrett, David B. Urban Pressure on Religion and Church.
A Study of the Luo of Kenya. Master of Sacred Theology Thesis.
Union Theological Seminary, 1963.

1702. Beecher, Leonard J. "The Revival Movement in Kenya."
World Dominion (29; Ja.-Feb., 1951), pp. 29-34. CtY-D;DLC;NN

1703. Bennett, Norman Robert. "The Church Missionary Society
at Mombasa 1873-94." Jeffrey Butler, (ed.). Boston University Papers in African History, I (Boston: Boston University
Press, 1964), pp. 159-94.   DHU/MO

1704. Bewes, Thomas Francis Cecil. Kikuyu Conflict. Mau Mau
and the Christian Witness. London: Highway Press, 1954.
                                                 NN/Sch

1705. Blakeslee, Helen Virginia. Beyond the Kikuyu Curtain.
Chicago: Moody Press, 1958.   NN/Sch

1706. Britton, J. "The Missionary Task in Kenya." International
Review of Missions (12; 1923), pp. 412-20.   DHU/R

1707. Carey, Walter. Crisis in Kenya. London: A. R. Mowbray
& Co., 1953.   DHU/MO

1708. Cayzac, P. P. "La Religion des Kikuyu (Afrique Orientale)."
Anthropos (5:2, 3, Mr.-Je., 1910), pp. 309-19.   DLC
     C. Sp. S. : Congregation of the Holy Spirit and of the
     Immaculate Heart of Mary.

1709. Chadwick, W. "The Kikuyu Conference: How it Arose and
What it Did." Church Missionary Review (65; Ja., 1914),
pp. 25-28.   DHU/R

1710. ----- and J. J. Willis. "Kikuyu Missionary Conference."
Missionary Review of the World (37;Mr., 1914), pp. 208-13.
                                                 DHU/R

1711. Church Conference on African Affairs. New York. African
Committee of the Foreign Missions and Conference of North
America, 1942.   DHU/MO

1712. Dougall, James W. C. Missionary Education in Kenya and
Uganda: A Study of Co-Operation. London: International Missionary Council, 1936.   ND; NcD; IEN; NN; NcU

1713. Gogarty, Henry Aloysius, (bp.). Kilima-njaro; an East-
African Vicariate. New York: Society for the Propagation of
the Faith, 1927.   NN/Sch

1714. Hannington, James. The Last Journals of Bishop Hannington; being Narratives of a Journey Through Palestine in 1884
and a Journey through Masai-land and U-Soga in 1885. London: Seeley, 1888.   MH; CtY

1715. Harries, Lyndon. "Bishop Lucas and the Masasi Experiment." International Review of Missions (34; Oct., 1945),
pp. 389-96.   DAU/W; DCU/TH

1716. Hooper, H. D. "Kikuyu Churches in United Action."
Church Missionary Review (70: 825, Mr., 1919), pp. 15-23.
                                                 DHU/R

1717. Kushner, G. "An African Revitalization Movement: Mau
Mau." Anthropos (60; 1965), pp. 763-802. DAU; DCU/AN

1718. Ludwig, Charles. Witch Doctor's Holiday. Anderson,
Ind. : The Warner Press, 1945.   NN/Sch

1719. Macpherson, R. The Presbyterian Church in Kenya; An
Account of the Origins and Growth of the Presbyterian Church
of East Africa. Nairobi: Presbyterian Church of East Africa,
1970.

1720. McGregor, A. W. "Kikuyu and Its People." The Church
Missionary Review (60; Ja., 1909), pp. 30-36.   DHU/R

1721. McIntosh, Brian G. The Scottish Mission in Kenya, 1891-
1923. Doctoral dissertation. University of Edinburgh, 1969.

1722. Nystrom, Gertrude Evelyn. Seeking Kenya's Treasures.
The Life of Charles F. Johnston, Pioneer Missionary of the
Africa Inland Mission. Grand Rapids, Mich. : Zondervan
Publishing House, 1949.   NN/Sch

1723. "Our Believing World." Unitarian Universalist Service
Committee.
     Film.   An account of Kenya at independence and
     the UUSC's African Student Program.

1724. Perlo, Filippo. ... Karoli, il Constantine Magno del Kenya.
Torino: Instituto Missioni Consolata.   NN/Sch

1725. Ranger, Terence O. "Missionary Adaptation of African
Religious Institutions: the Masasi Case." Terence O. Ranger
and I. Kimambo, (eds.). Historical Study of African Religion
(Berkeley: University of California Press, 1972), pp. 221-51.
                                                 DHU/R

1726. Robinson, Arthur W. "The Kikiyu Decision." The East and the West (12; Jl., 1915), pp. 249-58. DHU/R

1727. Sangree, Walter H. Age, Prayer and Politics in Tiriki, Kenya. Oxford: Oxford University Press, 1966. DHU/R

1728. Schneider, Fred D. "Kikuyu and Ecclesia Anglicana." Historical Magazine of the Protestant Episcopal Church (41:1, Mr., 1927), pp. 37-65. DHU/R
    Arising from the specific problems of missionary enter-prise in East Africa; this conference held in 1913, raised issues which were of world-wide importance and which were to affect subsequent schemes for union between Episcopal and non-Episcopal churches.

1729. Scott, Henry E. (Mrs.). Saint in Kenya: a Life of Marion Scott Stevenson. London: Hodder and Stoughton, 1932. IEN

1730. Simonson, Jonathan D. A Cultural Study of the Masai to Determine an Effective Program of Evangelism. Masters thesis. Luther Theological Seminary. St. Paul, Minn., 1955.

1731. Spencer, Leon P. "Defence and Protection of Converts: Kenya Missions and the Inheritance of Christian Widows, 1912-1931." Journal of Religion in Africa (5:2, 1973), pp. 107-27. DHU/R

1732. Stowe, David M. "A Marriage in Nairobi." The New Missionary Herald, United Church Board for World Minis-tries (12:2, Fall, 1970), pp. 10-11. Pam File, DHU/R

1733. Willis, John Jamieson (bp.). The Kikuyu Conference: A Study in Christian Unity, Together With the Proposed Scheme of Federation Embodied in the Resolutions of Conference. London: Longmans, 1914. NcD

1734. ----- (bp.). "The Kikuyu Conference: The Proposed Scheme of Federation." Church Missionary Review (65; Ja., 1914), pp. 28-37. DHU/R

i. Liberia
1735. Anderson, Robert Earle. Liberia, America's African Friend. Chapel Hill: University of North Carolina Press, 1952. NN/Sch

1736. Ashmum, Jehudi. "History of the American Colony in Liberia, 1821-1823." Washington City: Printed by Way & Gideon, 1826.
    Microfilm.

1737. Bane, Martin J. The Catholic Story of Liberia. New York: McMullen, 1950. DHU/MO; NN/Sch

1738. Bellamy, V. Nelle. "The Library and Archives of the Church Historical Society: Domestic and Foreign Missionary Society Papers, Liberia Papers, 1822-ca. 1911." Historical Magazine (37:1, Mr., 1968), pp. 77-82. DHU/R

1739. Blyden, Edward Wilmot. A Chapter in the History of Liberia. A Lecture Delivered in the Baptist Church at Edina, Grand Bassa County, Liberia, October 26, 1891. Printed at T. J. Sawyer's Excelsior Printing Works, Freetown, 1892. CtY

1740. ----- Elements of Permanent Influence. Discourse De-livered in the Fifteenth Street Presbyterian Church, Washing-ton, D.C., Sunday, February 16, 1890. Published by Request. Washington: R. L. Pendleton, Printer, 1890. NUC; DLC; PPULC; PPPrHi

1741. ----- "Liberia." The Church at Home and Abroad (4; 1888), p. 149. DHU/R

1742. ----- Liberia as She Is; and The Present Duty of Her Cit-izens: Annual Address Before the Common Council and the

Citizens of Monrovia, Liberia-July 27, 1857, Being the Cele-bration of the National Independence. Monrovia: Gaston Killian, 1857. NUC; PHi; PPPrHi; PPULC

1743. ----- Liberia: Past, Present and Future. An Adress Delivered July 26, 1866, on Mount Lebanon, Syria, at the Celebration of the Nineteenth Anniversary of the Independence of Liberia, Held by American Missionaries and other Citizens of the U. S. Residing in Syria. Washington: M'Gill and Witheraw, 1869. DLC

1744. ----- Liberia's Offering; Being Addresses and Sermons, etc. New York: John A. Gray, 1862. OWibfu; NN/Sch

1745. ----- "On Mixed Races in Liberia." Smithsonian Report (25; 1870), pp. 386-89. DLC

1746. ----- Our Origin, Dangers, and Duties. The Annual Address Before the Mayor and Common Council of the City of Monrovia, July 26, 1865. New York: Gray and Green, 1865. DHU/MO; NN/Sch

1747. ----- The Problems Before Liberia. A Lecture Delivered in the Senate Chamber in Monrovia, July 18, 1909. London: Phillips, 1909. DHU/MO; NN/Sch

1748. ----- "The Republic of Liberia." The Church at Home and Abroad (2; 1887), pp. 525-28. DHU/R

1749. ----- The Three Needs of Liberia. A Lecture Delivered at Lower Buchanan, Grand County, Liberia, January 26, 1908. London: Phillips, 1908. DHU/MO; NN/Sch

1750. Boone, Clinton C. Liberia as I Know It. Richmond, Va.: n. p., 1929. NN/Sch

1751. Browne, George D. "History of the Protestant Episcopal Mission in Liberia up to 1838." Historical Magazine of the Protestant Episcopal Church (39:1, Mr., 1970), pp. 17-27. DHU/R

1752. Campbell, Robert E. "Church Has Served Liberia One Hundred Years." Spirit of Missions (101; Mr., 1936), pp. 103-07. DLC

1753. Cason, John Walter. The Growth of Christianity in the Liberia Environment. Doctoral dissertation. Columbia University, 1962.

1754. Cox, Melville Beveridge. Remains of Melville B. Cox, Late Missionary to Liberia. With a Memoir. Boston: Light & Horton, 1835. NN/Sch
    Edited by Gershom F. Cox.

1755. Crummell, Alexander. The Duty of a Rising Christian State to Contribute to the World's Well-Being and Civilization, and the Means by Which it May Perform the Same. The Annual Oration Before the Common Council and the Citizens of Monrovia, Liberia-July 26, 1855. London: Wertheim & Macintosh, 1856. DHU/MO
    Negro author.

1756. ----- The Future of Africa: Being Addresses, Sermons, etc., Delivered in the Republic of Liberia. New York: Scribner, 1862. NN/Sch
    Negro author.

1757. ----- Sermons Preached in Trinity Church, Monrovia, West Africa. Boston: Press of J. R. Marion & Sons, 1865. DHU/MO
    Negro author.

1758. Donohugh, T. S. "The Christian Mission in Liberia." International Review of Missions (34; Apr., 1945), pp. 136-43. DAU/W; DCU/TH; DHU/R

1759. Durrant, R. E. Liberia: A Report. London: African
International Corporation, 1925.   DHU/MO
Includes section on missions.

1760. Dyer, Alfred Stace. Christian Liberia, the Hope of the
Dark Continent. With Special Reference to the Work and
Mission of E.S. Morris of Philadelphia. London: n.p.,
1879.   MH; DN; PPL; PH

1761. Edward, (Brother). "Plenty how-do" from Africa;
Letters and Stories from the Liberian Bush. West Park,
N.Y.: Holy Cross Press, 1941.   NN/Sch

1762. Emery, M.T. Bishop Auer of Cape Palmas. Hartford,
Conn.: Junior Auxiliary Pub. Co., n.d.   NN/Sch

1763. Farguhar, Charles W. "The Liberian Republic and the
West Indian Mission to West Africa." The East and The
West (16; Ja., 1918), pp. 27-37.   DHU/R

1764. Flora, George R. New Turns on the Liberia Road; a
Mission Study Book. Philadelphia: Board of Foreign Missions
and Women's Missionary Society of the United Lutheran
Church in America, 1945.   NN/Sch

1765. Forbes, Edgar Allen. "The American Church on the
West Coast of Africa." Spirit of Missions (74:8, Ag., 1909),
pp. 673-81.   DHU/R
Illus. account of missionary activity in Liberia.

1766. Fox, George Townshand. A Memoir of the Rev. C.
Colden Holfman, Missionary to Cape Palmas, West Africa.
With a Preface by Samuel Waldegrave. London: Seeley,
Jackson and Holliday. New York: A.D.F. Randolph, 1868.
DLC; ViU; IEN; PPRETS; CtY; PPL; NjP; MWA; ViHal

1767. Green, Ashbel. Presbyterian Missions, by Ashbel Green;
With Supplemental Notes by John C. Lowrie. New York:
A.D.F. Randolph, 1895.   NN/Sch

1768. Gurley, Ralph R. Life Jehudi Ashmun Late Colonial
Agent in Liberia... with a Brief Sketch of the Life of the Rev.
Lott Carey... Washington, D.C.: Printed by J.C. Dunn,
1835.   DHU/R

1769. Harris, John Hobbis. Africa: Slave or Free? With
Preface by Sir Sydney Olivier. London: Student Christian
Movement, 1919.   DHU/R; CtY-D

1770. Haywood, Dolores C. (ed.). "Domestic and Foreign
Missionary Society Liberia Papers; 1822-Ca. 1911."
Engage/Social Action (2:4, Apr., 1974), pp. 77-82. DHU/R

1771. Haywood, Dolores C. and Patricia L. Davis. "The
Domestic and Foreign Missionary Society Papers. The
Liberia Papers: 1822-1939." Historical Magazine of the
Protestant Episcopal Church. (39:1, Mr., 1970), pp. 91-94.
                                          DHU/R
Article describes papers.

1772. Holt, Dean Arthur. Change Strategies Initiated in the
Protestant Episcopal Church in Liberia from 1836 to 1950
and Their Differential Effects. Doctoral dissertation.
Boston University, School of Education, 1970.

1773. Hoyt, William B. Land of Hope. Reminiscences of
Liberia and Cape Palmas, With Incidents of the Voyage.
Hartford: H.J. Fox & W.B. Hoyt, 1852. NNCor
Missions in Liberia.

1774. Jordan, Lewis Garnett. Pebbles from an African Beach.
Philadelphia: Lisle-Carey Press, 1917.   NN/Sch
Negro author.

1775. King, Willis J., (bp.). History of the Methodist Church
Mission in Liberia. n.p., 1945.   IEG
Negro author.

1776. "Liberia as a Missionary Field." Southern Workman
(5:12, Dec., 1876), p. 91.   DLC; DHU/MO

1777. Methodist Church (United States) Conference. Liberia.
Journal of Sessions... Monrovia: 19--.   NN/Sch

1778. Officer, Morris. A Plea for a Lutheran Mission in
Liberia. Springfield, Ohio: Nonpareil Office, 1855. DLC

1779. "One Face of Africa." Association Films, Inc.
Film
Gives an over-all view of the country and focuses on
Liberia's YMCA movement.

1780. Parson, A.B. "The Beginnings of the Church in Liberia."
Historical Magazine of the Protestant Episcopal Church
(12; 1938), p. 154 +.   DLC

1781. Peabody, George Barh-Fofoe. Barh-Fofoe: a Bassa Boy.
Story of His Childhood and Youth at His Home in the Doh
Country, and at the Mission School in Quibie Country, near
Marshall, Liberia, West Coast, Africa. Told by Himself.
Lancaster, Pa.: New Era Printing House, 1891. NN/Sch
Negro author.

1782. "Portrait of Promise." National Council for the Protestant
Episcopal Church.
Film
Work of the Episcopal Church in the interior of Liberia.
Includes views of Cuttington College.

1783. Protestant Episcopal Church in the U.S.A. Liberia
(Missionary District). Annual Report to the Board of Mission.
                                          NN/Sch

1784. Protestant Episcopal Church in the U.S.A. Souvenir
of the Twenty-Fifth Anniversary Celebration of the Consecration of the Rt. Rev. Samuel David Ferguson (June 24th,
1885 to June 26th, 1910), as Observed in Trinity Parish,
Monrovia, Sunday, June 26th, 1910. Cape Palms, Liberia:
P.E. Mission Printing Office, 1910.   NN/Sch

1785. Ramsaur, William Hoke. The Letters of William Hoke
Ramsaur; Compiled by his Friends Elwood Henry Haines,
Jeannie Ogden Miller Cornell and his Sister, Mary Alex-
ander Ramsaur. Jacksonville, Fla.: 1928. NN/Sch

1786. "Report of the Commission to Liberia." Spirit of Missions
(83; Je., 1918), pp. 393-402.   DLC; DHU/R

1787. Rice, Edwin Botts. Historical Sketch of the African Mission.
New York: Church Missions House, 1903.   NN/Sch

1788. Schofield, Thomas A. "Impressions of Liberia." Spirit
of Missions (83; 1918), pp. 459-75.   DLC; DHU/R

1789. Schofield, William. "A Hampton Missionary in Africa."
Southern Workman (33:10, Oct., 1904), pp. 569-70.
                                          DLC; DHU/MO
Report of missionary, Rev. Wm. Schofield and his work
in Liberia.

1790. Scott, Anna M. Day Dawn in Africa; or, Progress of the
Protestant Episcopal Mission at Cape Palmas, West Africa.
New York: Prot. Episc. Soc. for the Promotion of Evan-
gelical Knowledge, 1858.   DHU/MO; NN/Sch

1791. Seebach, Margaret Rebecca. Man in the Bush. Philadelphia: The Board of Foreign Missions and the Women of
the United Lutheran Church in America, 1945. NN/Sch

1792. Sibley, James L. Liberia...Old and New: A Study of its
Social and Economic Background with Possibilities of
Development. Garden City, N.Y.: Doubleday, 1928. NN/Sch

1793. Smith, Charles Spencer, (bp.). Liberia in the Light of
Living Testimony. A Pamphlet Compiled by C.H. Smith.
Nashville, Tenn.: Pub. House of A.M.E. Church Sunday
School Union, 1895.   NN/Sch

1794. Smith, Lucius Edwin. Heroes and Martyrs of Modern Missionary Enterprise, a Record of Their Lives and Labors. Including a Historical Review of Earlier Missions. Providence, R.I.: O.W. Potters, 1857. NN/Sch

1795. Spirit of Missions (88; Sept., 1923).   DLC; DHU/R
Whole issue on Protestant Episcopal Church and missions in Liberia.

1796. Stewart, Thomas McCants. "Climate." Charles Spencer Smith, (comp.). Liberia in the Light of Living Testimony (Nashville: Publishing House of the A.M.E. Sunday School Union, 1895), pp. 6-15.   NN/Sch
Written by a lawyer, author and A.M.E. minister.

1797. Swingle, Albert Edwin. The Growth of the Ministry in the Lutheran Church in Liberia. Masters thesis. The Lutheran School of Theology (Chicago, Illinois).

1798. Williams, Walter B. Adventures with the Krus in West Africa. New York: Vantage Press, 1955.   NN/Sch

j. Malawi (Nyasaland)

1799. Alexander, Frank. Missions in Malawi. Masters thesis. Fuller Theological Seminary School of World Mission, 1969.

1800. Ambali, Augustine. Thirty Years in Nyasaland. Westminster, London: Universities' Mission to Central Africa, 1923.
Negro author.

1801. Barnes, Bertram H. Johnson of Nyasaland. A Study of Life and Work of William Percival Johnson... Archdeacon of Nyasa, Missionary, Pioneer, 1867-1928. London: Universities' Mission to Central Africa, 1933.

1802. Booth, Joseph. Africa for the African. Dedicated First to Victoria, Queen of Great Britain, Second, to the British and American Christian People, Third, and Specially to the Afro-American People of the United States of America. Nyasaland, East Central Africa: n.p., 1897. NN/Sch

1803. Douglas, Arthur Jeffreys. Arthur Douglas, Missionary on Lake Nyasa. The Story of his Life. London: Universities' Mission to Central Africa, 1912.   NN/Sch

1804. Fraser, Donald. The Autobiography of an African. Retold in Biographical Form and in the Wild African Setting of the Life of Daniel Mtusu. Connecticut: Negro Universities Press, 1970.   DHU/R
Originally published in 1925 about an African who became a Presbyterian minister in Malawi, for Nyasaland.

1805. ----- Winning a Primitive People: Sixteen Years Work Among the Warlike Tribe of the Ngoni and the Senga and Tumbuka Peoples of Central Africa. New York: E.P. Dutton & Co., 1914.   NN/Sch; DHU/R

1806. Livingstone, William Pringle. Laws of Livingstonia. A Narrative of Missionary Adventure and Achievement. London: Hodder and Stoughton, 1921.   NN/Sch

1807. Macdonald, Duff. Africans; or, The Heart of Heathen Africa. London: Simpkin, Marshall & Co., 1882. N & P
              NN/Sch

1808. Mackintosh, Catharine Winkworth. ...Some Pioneer Missions of Northern Rhodesia and Nyasaland. Livingstone, Northern Rhodesia: Rhodes-Livingstone Museiu, 1950.
              NN/Sch

1809. Maclean, Norman. Africa in Transformation. London: J. Nisbet & Co., Ltd., 1914.   NN/Sch

1810. Pineau, Henry. Evèque, Roi des Brigands. Monseigneur Dupont, Premier Vicaire Apostolique du Nyassa (1850-1930). Paris: La Province de France de Pères, 1937. NN/Sch

1811. Pretorious, J.L. "The Story of the Dutch Reformed Church Mission in Nyasaland." The Nyasaland Journal (10:1, 1957), pp. 11-22.   DLC

1812. Room, William John Waterman. A Great Emancipation: A Missionary Survey of Nyasaland, Central Africa. London: World Dominion Press, 1926.

1813. Schoffeleers, J.M. and I. Linden. "The Resistance of the Nyau Societies to the Roman Catholic Missions in Colonial Malawi." Terrence O. Ranger and I. Kimambo, (eds.). Historical Study of African Religion (Berkeley: Univ. of Calif. Press, 1972), pp. 252-73.   DHU/R

1814. Shepperson, George. Independent African; John Chilembwe and the Origins, Settings and Significance of the Nyasaland Native Rising of 1915. Edinburgh: University Press, 1958.
              NN/Sch

1815. Van Velsen, Jaap. "The Missionary Factor Among the Lakeside Tonga of Nyasaland." The Rhodes-Livingstone Journal (26; Dec., 1959), pp. 1-22.   DAU

1816. Waldman, Marilyn R. "The Church of Scotland Mission at Blantyre, Nyasaland: Its Political Implications." Bulletin of the Society for African Church History (2:4, 1968), pp. 299-310.   DHU/R

1817. Wellens, Stephen C. "The Influence of Village Environment on the Stability of Roman Catholic Marriages in a Rural Parish of Malawi." Africa Theological Journal (2; Feb., 1969), pp. 84-93.   DHU/R

1818. Wishlade, R.L. Sectarianism in Southern Nyasaland. London: Oxford University Press, 1965.   DHU/MO

1819. Young, Thomas C. Notes on the History of the Tumbuka-Kamanga Peoples in the Northern Province of Nyasaland. Second edition with a new introduction by Ian Nance. London: F. Cass, 1970.   FMU

k. Nigeria

1820. Afigbo, A.E. "The Calabar Mission and the Aro Expedition of 1901-1902." Journal of Religion in Africa (5:2, 1973), pp. 94-106.   DHU/R

1821. Agbebi, Mojola. Inaugural Sermon, Delivered at the Celebration of the First Anniversary of the "African Church," Lagos, West Africa, December 21, 1902. Yonkers, N.Y.: Efgar F. Howorth, 1903.   TNF
Biographical sketch of this African clergyman, pp. 21-23.

1822. Ajayi, J. Christian Missions in Nigeria, 1841-1891; the Making of a New Elite. Evanston, Ill.: Northwestern Univ. Press, 1965.   DHU/MO; NN/Sch

1823. Ajayi, W.O. A History of the Yoruba Mission, 1843-1880. Masters Thesis, University of Bristol, 1959.

1824. ----- "The Beginnings of the African Bishopric on the Niger." Bulletin of the Society for African Church History (1:3-4, 1964), pp. 92-99.   DLC

1825. ----- "The Niger Delta Pastorate Church, 1892-1902." The Bulletin of the Society for African Church History (2:1, Dec., 1965), pp. 37-54.   DHU/R

1826. ----- "Christian Involvement in the Ijaye War." Bulletin of the Society for African Church History (2:3, 1967), pp. 224-238.   DHU/R

1827. Anderson, Susan. "So This is Africa" (to the Missionary Minded). Nashville, Tenn.: Broadman Press, 1943.
              DHU/MO; NN/Sch

1828. Ayandele, E.A. Holy Johnson: Pioneer of African Nationalism, 1836-1917. London: Cass, 1970. DHU/MO

(Ayandele, E.A., cont.)
   A full-scale study of Bishop James Johnson in Sierra
   Leone and Nigeria.

1829. ----- "The Missionary Factor in Brass, 1875-1900:
   A Study in Advance and Recession." The Bulletin of the
   Society for African Church History (2:3, 1967) pp. 249-258.
                                                    DHU/R

1830. ----- "Missionary Enterprise Versus Indirect Rule
   Among the Angass of the Bauchi Plateau, 1906-14." The
   Bulletin of the Society for African Church History (2:1,
   Dec., 1965), pp. 73-83.   DHU/R
      "Case study of the conflict that obtained between
      Christian missionary endeavour and 'Indirect Rule'
      among a pagan tribe of Northern Nigeria, the Angass."

1831. ----- The Missionary Impact on Modern Nigeria,
   1842-1914. New York: Humanities, 1967.
                                   DHU/MO; DLC; RL

1832. Barber, Mary Ann Serrett. Oshielle: or Village
   Life in the Yoruba Country; from the Journals and
   Letters of a Catechist There, Describing the Rise of
   a Christian Church in an African Village. London:
   J. Nisbet and Co., 1857.   NN/Sch

1833. Basden, George Thomas. Edith Warner of the Niger;
   the Story of Thirty-three Years of Zealous and Coura-
   geous Work Amongst Ibo Girls and Women. London:
   Seeley, 1927.   NN/Sch

1834. ----- "The Niger Mission, 1910." The Church Missionary Review (62; Sept., 1911), pp. 563-70.   DHU/R

1835. Bible, N.T. Romans. Yoruba. The Epistle of Paul,
   the Apostle to the Romans. Translated into Yoruba, for the
   use of the Native Christians of That Nation. By the Rev.
   Samuel Crowther, Native Missionary. n.p., Church Missionary Society, 1850.   DLC

1836. Broadbent, T. David S. The World Before Them; Stories
   of Northern Nigeria. London: Edinburgh House, 1949.
                                                  NN/Sch

1837. Broom, Wendell Wright. Growth of Churches Among
   Ibidios of Nigeria. Masters thesis. Fuller Theological
   Seminary. Sch. of World Mission, 1970.

1838. Bulifant, Josephine Christiana. Forty Years in the African
   Bush. Grand Rapids, Mich.: Zondervan, 1950. NN/Sch

1839. Calabar. Report of Missionary Conference Nov. 1911.
   Calabar: Hope Waddell Training Institution, 1913.
                                                  NC; CtY-D

1840. Campbell, Robert. A Pilgrimmage to My Motherland and
   Account of a Journey Among the Egbas and Yorubas of Central
   Africa in 1859-1860. New York: T. Hamilton, 1861. OWibfU

1841. Catchings, Anna Delois. History of the Ogbomosho Baptist
   Hospital. Masters thesis. New Orleans Baptist Theological
   Seminary, 1948.

1842. Christian Council of Nigeria. Building for Tomorrow;
   a Pictorial History of the Protestant Church in Nigeria.
   Lagos: Christian Council of Nigeria, 1960. DHU/MO

1843. Church Missionary Society. Nigeria the Unknown: a
   Missionary Study Text-Book on Nigeria...London: n.p.
   1921.   NN/Sch

1844. Cooksey, Joseph J. Religion and Civilization in West
   Africa. London: World Dominion Press, 1931.
                                   DHU/MO; NN/Sch

1845. Crowther, Samuel Adjai, (bp.). Bible, N.T. Romans.
   Yoruba. The Epistle of Paul, the Apostle to the Romans.

Translated into Yoruba for the Use of the Native Christians
of That Nation. London: Church Missionary Society,
1850.   DLC

1846. ----- (bp). Bible. O.T. Genesis. Yoruba. First
   Book of Moses, Commonly Called Genesis. Translated
   into Yoruba, for the use of the Native Christians of that
   Nation by the Rev. Samuel Crowther. London: British
   and Foreign Bible Soc., 1853.

1847. ----- (bp.). Grammar and Vocabulary of the Nupe
   Language. London: Church Missionary House, 1864.
                              DLC; CtY; OCI; NN; MH

1848. ----- (bp.,). Niger Mission, Bishop Crowther Report
   of the Overland Journey from Lokoja to Bida, on the River
   Niger, and thence to Lagos or the sea coast, from November
   10th, 1871 to February 8th, 1872. London: Church Missionary House, 1872.   MH

1849. ----- (bp.). A Vocabulary of the Yoruba Language.
   Together With Introductory Remarks by the Rev. O.E.
   Vidal. London: Seeleys, 1852.   DLC; PU; NcD

1850. ----- and J.C. Taylor. The Gospel in the Banks of the
   Niger: Journals and Notices of the Native Missionaries
   Accompanying the Niger Expedition of 1857-1859. New York:
   Humanities, 1968.   DHU/SP

1851. Daly, John. "Iboland: the Background to the Vocation
   Explosion." African Ecclesiastical Review (15:3, 1973),
   pp. 259-66.   DHU/R
      History of Catholic missionary activity in Iboland and
      the present situation with African priests and nuns.

1852. Delano, Isaac O. The Singing Minister of Nigeria;
   the Life of the Rev. Canon J.J. Ransome-Kuti. London:
   United Society for Christian Literature, 1942. NN/Sch
      Negro author.

1853. ----- The Soul of Nigeria. London: T. Werner Laurie
   Ltd., 1937. DLC; CU; CtY; NN

1854. Dike, Kenneth Onwuka. Origins of the Niger Mission,
   1841-1891. A Paper Read at the Centenary of the Mission
   at Christ Church, Onitsha on 13 November 1957. Ibadan
   University: Press for the C.M.S. Niger Mission, 1957.
                                                  NNMR
      Church Missionary Society.

1855. Dodds, Fred W. (ed.). Nigerian Studies, by Nigerian
   Missionaries. London: Holborn Press, 1920? NN/Sch

1856. Duval, Louis M. Baptist Missions in Nigeria. Richmond,
   Va.: Southern Baptist Convention, 1928. DLC; CCovB; CtY

1857. Ekechi, Felix Kamalu. "Colonialism and Christianity
   in West Africa: the Igbo Cass, 1900-1915." Journal
   of African History (12:1, 1970), pp. 103-15. DHU/MO

1858. ----- Missionary Enterprise and Rivalry in Igboland,
   1857-1914. London: Cass, 1972.   DLC
      Revision of author's dissertation, University of Wis-
      consin, 1969.

1859. Fitzpatrick, F.J. "Christian Missions in Nigeria."
   Twentieth Century (52; Oct., 1925), pp. 550-59.
                        DAU; DGU; DCU/SL; DCU/SW; DGW; DHU
      Title was formerly Nineteenth Century.

1860. Flint, John E. Nigeria and Ghana. Englewood Cliffs,
   N.J.: Prentice Hall, 1966.   DHU/MO
      Includes discussion of the impact of Christianity
      and Islam on Modern Nigeria and Ghana.

1861. Florin, Hans W. The Southern Baptist Foreign Mission
   Enterprise in Western Nigeria: An Analysis. Doctoral
   dissertation. Boston University, 1960.

1862. Goldie, Hugh. Calabar and Its Mission. Edinburgh:
Oliphant Anderson and Co., 1890. NG; NcD; PPWe;
NjPT; OCl

1863. Green, Charles Sylvester. New Nigeria: Southern
Baptists at Work in Africa. Richmond, Va.: Foreign
Mission Board, Southern Baptist Convention, 1936. NN/Sch

1864. Helser, Albert David. Education of Primitive People:
A Presentation of the Folklore of the Bura Animists with
a Meaningful Experience Curriculum. New York: Negro
Universities Press, 1969.   DHU/R
Originally published in 1934 by Fleming H. Revell Co.,
New York.

1865. ----- In Sunny Nigeria, Experiences Among a Primitive People in the Interior of North Central Africa;
Introduction by Otho Winger... New York: F.H. Revell,
1926.   NN/Sch

1866. High, Thomas O'Connor. A History of the Educational
Work Related to the Nigerian Baptist Convention 1850-1959.
Doctoral dissertation. Southern Baptist Theological
Seminary, 1960.

1867. Hinderer, Anna (Martin). Seventeen Years in the Yoruba
Country. Memorials of Anna Hinderer, Gathered From
Her Journals and Letters; With an Introduction by Richard
B. Hone ... London: Seeley, Jackson and Halliday, 1872.
                                             NN/Sch

1868. Howell, E. Milford. Nigerian Baptist Leaders and Their
Contributions. Doctoral dissertation. Baptist Seminary,
(Texas), 1956.

1869. Ifeka-Moller, Caroline. "White Power: Social-Struc-
tural Factors in Conversion to Christianity, Eastern
Nigeria, 1921-1966." Canadian Journal of African
Studies (8; 1974), pp. 55-72.

1870. Ikenga Metuh, E. E. Beliefs About God in Igbo
Traditional Religion. Masters thesis. London Univ-
sity, 1971.

1871. "In Memoriam: The Beloved Bishop -- I Remember
Crowther." The Nigerian Christian (2:6, Je., 1968),
p. 5. Pam. File, DHU/R

1872. Irving, Dr. "The Yoruba Mission." The Church
Missionary Review (4; 1853), pp. 123-37+. DLC

1873. Johnson, Dorothy. A Missionary Survey of Nigeria.
Masters thesis. Columbia Bible College (S. C.), 1956.

1874. Johnston, G. D. "Ohafia 1911-1940: A Study in
Church Developments in Eastern Nigeria." The Bulletin of the Society for African Church History (2:2,
1966), pp. 139-54.   DHU/R

1875. Jones, F. Melville. "The Mass Movement in the
Yoruba Country." Church Missionary Review (70:825,
Mr., 1919), pp. 47-56.   DHU/R
Christianity versus Islam in Yorubaland, Nigeria.

1876. ----- "The Mass Movement to Christianity in
Southern Nigeria." Church Missionary Review (65;
Feb., 1914), pp. 90-95.   DHU/R

1877. Jordan, John P. Bishop Shanahan of Southern
Nigeria; With an Introduction by His Grace, Most
Rev. David Mathew, and a Note by His Excellency Rt.
Rev. Charles Heerey. Dublin: Clonmore & Reynolds,
1949.   NN/Sch; NNMR

1878. Kiessling, Nicolas. "Statesmanship in the Nigerian
Mission." Concordia Historical Institute Quarterly
(34:2, Jl., 1961), pp. 54-61.   MSL/CHI

1879. Knight, Charles William. A History of the Expansion
of Evangelical Christianity in Nigeria. Doctoral dissertation. Southern Baptist Theological Seminary, 1951.

1880. Lasbrey, Bertram. "The Church in Nigeria: Its
Position and Its Opportunity." The East and the West
(23; Apr., 1925), pp. 113-18.   DHU/R

1881. Livingstone, William Pringle. Dr. Hitchcock of Uburu:
an Episode in Pioneer Medical Missionary Service in Nigeria.
Edinburgh: Foreign Mission Committee of the United Free
Church of Scotland, 1920.   NN/Sch

1882. ----- Mary Slessor of Calabar; Pioneer Missionary.
New York: Doran, 1916?   NN/Sch; DHU/R

1883. Lucas, Jonathan Olumide. An Oration on the History
of the Anglican Church in Lagos, 1852 to 1952. Lagos:
Tika-Tore Press, 1952.   DLC

1884. Mac Keown, Robert L. Twenty-Five Years in Qua
Iboe: the Story of the Qua Iboe Mission. London: Marshall
Brothers, 1909.   MH; CtY/DM

1885. Maddry, Charles E. Day Dawn in Yoruba Land.
Nashville: Broadman Press, 1939.   NN/Sch

1886. Martin, Samuel Wadiei. The Autobiography of Rev.
S. W. Martin (Founder and President of the Pilgrim Baptist
Mission Nigeria). Issele-Uku: The Author, 1966.

1887. Maxwell, J. Lowry. Half a Century of Grace, A
Jubilee History of the Sudan United Mission, Nigeria.
London: Sudan United Mission, n. d. DOUM/EUB

1888. McFarlan, Donald Maitland. Calabar, The Church of
Scotland Mission founded in 1846. London: Nelson, 1957.
MH-AH; IEN; TxU; WU; NN/Sch

1889. Mercier, Paul. Civilizations du Benin. Paris: Société
Continentale d'Editions Modernes Illustrées, 1962. DHU/MO

1890. Miller, Lillian Ewing. Medical Missions: Nursing in
Nigeria. Master's thesis. New Orleans Baptist Theological
Seminary, 1949.

1891. "The Mission." Our Lady of Apostles Missionary Society,
Ardfoyle, Ireland. Made and Released in the U.S. by Desi
Bognar, 1962. 33 min., sd., color, 16 mm.
Film.
"Surveys mission work in Nigeria, West Africa."

1892. M'Keown, Robert L. Twenty-five Years in Qua Iboe;
the Story of a Missionary Effort. London: Morgan & Scott,
1912.   NN/Sch

1893. Montroy, Edythe. Womanhood and Christianity in Nigeria.
Master's thesis. New Orleans Baptist Theological Seminary,
1946.

1894. Morgan, Lily Mae Wingate. The Work of Southern
Baptists in Nigeria. Master's thesis. New Orleans Baptist
Theological Seminary, 1945.

1895. Murray, A. Victor. "A Missionary Educational Policy for
Southern Nigeria." International Review of Missions (21; 1932),
pp. 516-31.   DHU/R

1896. Nadel, Siegfried Frederick. The Kingdom of Nupe in
Nigeria: A Black Byzantium. New York: Routledge &
Paul, 1942.   DHU/MO; DLC

1897. Nau, Henry. We Move Into Africa; the Story of the
Planting of the Lutheran Church in Southeastern Nigeria.
St. Louis, Mo.: Concordia Pub. House, 1945. NN/Sch;
MSL/CHI

1898. Nsasak, I.V. "Collecting Church Historical Materials in South-East Nigeria." Bulletin of the Society for African Church History (2:2, 1966), pp. 196-99.   DHU/R

1899. Ochiagha, Gregory O. A History of Education in Eastern Nigeria to 1960. Doctoral dissertation. Catholic University of America, 1965.

1900. Oduyoye, Modupe. The Planting of Christianity in Yorubaland, 1842-88. Ibadan, Nigeria: Daystar Press, 1969. CtY-D; ICU; NcD

1901. Official Nigeria Catholic Directory, 1967. Lagos: African Universities Press, 1967.   DLC

1902. Okon, Gabriel. The Role of the Catholic Mission in the Developing of Education in Eastern Nigeria, 1902-1960. Masters thesis. Howard University, 1968.

1903. Olatunji, Olatunde. "Religion in Literature: the Christianity of J. S. Sowande (Sobo Arobiodu)." Orita (8:1, Je., 1974), pp. 3-21.   DHU/R
     Christianity in the Yoruba poetry of J. S. Sowande.

1904. Oluwole, Isaac. "After Fifty Years in an African Colony: Extracts from an Address to the Synod of Western Equatorial Africa, Held at Lagos, May 16-19, 1911." The Church Missionary Review (62; Nov., 1911), pp. 660-68. DHU/R

1905. Paden, John Naber. The Influence of Religious Elites on Political Culture and Community Integration in Kano, Nigeria. Doctoral dissertation. Harvard University, 1968.

1906. Page, Jesse. The Black Bishop, Samuel Adjai Crowther. London: Simpkin, Marshall, Hamilton, Kent & Co., 1910. DHU/MO; NN/Sch

1907. ----- Samuel Crowther, the Slave Boy Who Became Bishop of the Niger. London: S. W. Partridge & Co., 1889. NN/Sch

1908. Pakenham, E. T. "Polygamy: A Problem in Nigeria." The Church Missionary Review (74:841, Mr., 1923), pp. 15-21.   DHU/R
     A problem for the Christian Church in Nigeria.

1909. Parrinder, Edward Geoffrey. Religion in an African City. London: Oxford University Press, 1953. DHU/MO; DHU/R; CoDI
     Missions-Nigeria, pp. 86-106.

1910. Peak, Lynda S. "Nigerian Church Aid Continues." Christian Advocate (14:3, Feb. 5, 1970), p. 24. Pam File, DHU/R

1911. Phillips, Earl H. The Church Missionary Society, the Imperial Factor, and Yoruba Politics, 1842-1873. Doctoral dissertation. University of Southern California, 1966.

1912. Pilkington, Frederick. "Bookshop Evangelism in Nigeria." Congregational Quarterly (23; 1945), pp. 251-55. DHU/R
     Missionary Societies' Bookshops.

1913. Pinnock, Samuel George. The Romance of Missions in Nigeria. Richmond, Va.: Educational Department, Foreign Mission Board, Southern Baptist Convention, 1917. NRAB; NcWsW; ODW

1914. Ray, Stanley. The History and Evaluation of Baptist Mission Policy in Nigeria, 1950-1960. Master's thesis. Southwestern Baptist Theological Seminary, 1970.

1915. Roberson, Cecil. "Life Sketch of the Late Rev. I. A. Adejumobi." Nigerian Baptist (47:4, Apr., 1969), pp. 16-18. Pam File, DHU/R

1916. Ryder, Alan Frederick Charles. "The Benin Missions." Journal of the Historical Society of Nigeria (2:2, 1961), pp. 231-59.   DHU/MO

1917. Sadler, George W. A Century in Nigeria. Nashville: Broadman Press, 1950.   NN/Sch

1918. Saunders, Davis Lee. The Life and Labors of William Henry Carson. Master's thesis. Southern Baptist Theological Seminary, 1955.

1919. Schauffler, A. F. "White 'Ma' of Calabar; a Review of the Life of Mary Slessor, of Calabar." Missionary Review (39; Oct., 1916), pp. 767-72.   DHU/R

1920. Schön, James Frederick. Journals of the Rev. James Frederick Schön and Mr. Samuel Crowther, who, with the Sanction of Her Majesty's Government, Accompanied the Expedition up the Niger, in 1841, in Behalf of the Church Missionary Society. London: Hatchard & Son, 1842. NN/Sch

1921. Schwab, W. B. The Growth and Conflicts of Religion in a Modern Yoruba Community." Zaire (6:8, Oct., 1952) pp. 826-35.   DCU/AN

1922. "Sharing the Word in West Africa." Foreign Mission Board, Southern Baptist Convention, 1957. Made by Church-Craft Pictures. 64 fr., Color, 35 mm.
     Filmstrip.
     "The story of a century of Southern Baptist missionary progress in Nigeria and the extension of the program into Ghana."

1923. Tasie, Godwin Onyemeachi Mgbechi. "Denominational Cooperation and Rivalry in South-East Nigeria, 1880-1918." The Bulletin of the Society for African Church History (3:1-2, 1969-70), pp. 44-52.   DHU/R

1924. Tucker, Sarah. Abbeokuta; or, Sunrise Within the Tropics: an Outline of the Origin and Progress of the Yoruba Mission. New York: R. Carter & Brothers, 1854. NN/Sch; CtY-D

1925. Uchendu, Victor C. "Missionary Problems in Nigerian Society." Practical Anthropology (11:3, My.-Je., 1964), pp. 105-17.   DHU/R

1926. Udo, Edet Akpan. The Methodist Contribution to Education in Eastern Nigeria, 1893-1960. Doctoral dissertation. Boston University Graduate School, 1965.   DHU/R

1927. Veenstra, Johanna. Black Diamonds. Grand Rapids, Mich.: Meyer-Book Co., 1929.   NN/Sch

1928. Volz, Paul M. The Evangelical Lutheran Church of Nigeria, 1936-1941. Calabar, Nigeria: Hope Waddell Press, 1961. MSL/CHI; DHU/MO

1929. Walker, Frank Deaville. A Hundred Years in Nigeria, the Story of the Methodist Mission in the Western Nigeria District, 1842-1942. London: The Cargate Press, 1942. NN/Sch; DLC

1930. ----- The Romance of the Black River; the Story of the C. M. S. Nigeria Mission. London: Church Missionary Society, 1938.   NN/Sch

1931. Ward, William J. ...In and Around the Oron Country or, The Story of Primitive Methodism in S. Nigeria. London: W. A. Hammond, 190-?   NN/Sch

1932. Webster, James Bertin. The African Churches Among the Yoruba, 1888-1922. Oxford: Clarendon Press, 1964. DHU/R; DHU/MO.

1933. Weeks, Annie Florence. Builders of a New Africa, a Compilation. Nashville, Tenn.: Broadman Press, 1944. NN/Sch

1934. West, Ralph Lee. A Study of Indigeneity Among Nigerian Baptists. Doctoral dissertation. New Orleans Baptist Theological Seminary, 1954.

1935. Young-O'Brien, Albert Hayward. ...She had a Magic; the Story of Mary Slessor. London: J. Cape, 1958. NN/Sch
     Author's pseud., Brian O'Brien, at head of title.

l. (Portuguese Africa) — Angola, Mozambique and Guinea-Bissau

1936. Allison, Madeline G. "The Churches." The Crisis
(22:2, Je., 1921), p. 84.   DHU/MO; DLC
      Methodist in Africa bought 8,000 acres of land in Portuguese
West Africa.

1937. Alves Correia, Manuel. ...Missões Franciscanas
Portuguesas de Moçambique e da Guiné. Braga, Tip. das
Missoes franciscanas.   NN/Sch

1938. Barmento, Alexandre. ...Temas Angolanos. Lisboa:
Tipografia Ideal, 1957.   NN/Sch
      Missions in Angola, pp. 51-64.

1939. Berthoud, Paul. Les Negrès Gouamba; ou, Les Vingt
Premières Années de la Mission Romande. Lausanne:
Le Conseil de la Mission Romande, 1896.   NN/Sch

1940. Brásio, António D. Angola (Spiritana Monumenta Historica
Series Africana), I-V. Pittsburgh: Duquesne Univeristy Press,
1967-71.   DLC
      Aspects of the history of the mission of the Holy Ghost
Fathers in Angola between 1882 and 1967, mostly in Portu-
guese and French. All are documents.
      Book review: P. E. H. Hair. Journal of Religion in
Africa (4:2, 1973; 5:2, 1973), pp. 146-9; 153-4. DHU/R

1941. ----- Monumenta Missionaria Africa. Ocidental...
Coligida e Antada Pelo Padre António Brasio...
Lisboa: Agencia Geral do Utramar, Divisao de Publicacões
e Biblioteca, 1952.   NN/Sch

1942. Cancela, Luis Lourenco. Surpresas do Sertão; Cartas
de um Missionário a Seus Sobrinhos. Lisboa: Editorial
L.I.A.M., 1946.   NN/Sch

1943. Chatelain, Heli. "Angolan Customs." Journal of American
Folk-Lore (9:32, Ja.-Mr., 1896), pp. 13-18.   DHU/R
      Microcard.
      Traditional beliefs of the Tombo near Loanda, Angola.

1944. ----- "Demoniacal Possession in Angola, Africa."
Journal of American Folklore (6:3, Jl.-Sept., 1893), p. 258.
                              Pam File, DHU/R

1945. -----Folk Tales of Angola. Fifty Tales, With Ki-
Mbundu Text, Literal English Translation, Introduction
and Notes. Boston: Houghton, Mifflin, 1894.   DHU/MO

1946. Cushman, Mary Floyd. Missionary Doctor, the Story of
Twenty Years in Africa, by Mary Floyd Cushman, M.D.
New York: Harper & Bros., 1944.   NN/Sch

1947. Okuma, Thomas Masaji. The Social Response of
Christianity in Angola: Selected Issues. Doctoral
dissertation. Boston University, 1964.

1948. Grenfell, W.D. The Dawn Breaks; The Dawn Breaks; the
Story of Missionary Work at Sao Salvador, Portuguese Congo.
London: Carey Press, 1948.   NN/Sch

1949. Kaan, Fred. "Summary of Events Concerning the Arrest
and Suicide of Mozambique Presbyterian Church Leaders."
Reformed World (32:5, 1973), pp. 225-39.   DLC

1950. Maio, Augusto. No Coraco da Africa Negra. Lisbon:
Editorial L.I.A.M., 1947.   NN/Sch
      Missions, Angola.

1951. Parsons, M.E. "Revival in Angola, West Africa."
Missionary Review. (62; Ja., 1939), p. 40.   DHU/R

1952. Soremekun, Fola. A History of the American Board
of Missions in Angola, 1880-1940. Doctoral dissertations.
Northern University, 1965.

1953. ----- "Religion and Politics in Angola: the American
Board of Missions and the Portuguese Government 1880-
1922." Cahiers d'Etudes Africaines (11:43, 1971), pp.
341-77.   DAU; DGU

1954. Tucker, John T. Angola, the Land of the Blacksmith
Prince. London: World Dominion Press, 1933. NN/Sch

1955. Tucker, Theodore. "Protestant Missionaries in Angola."
Africa Today (15:3, Je.-Jl., 1968), p. 4.   DHU/MO

1956. Weld, Alfred. The Suppression of the Society of Jesus
in the Portuguese Dominions. London: Burns and Oates,
1877.   DCU; ICN; DLC

m. Rhodesia—Northern and Southern, Zambia, Zimbabwe

1957. Butt, G.E. My Travels in North West Rhodesia: or,
A Missionary Journey of Sixteen Thousand Miles. London:
E. Dalton, 19--.   NN/Sch

1958. Christiansen, Ruth. ...For the Heart of Africa. Minneapolis: Augsburg Pub. House, 1956.   NN/Sch

1959. Coillard, F. "Expedition Missionaire du Zambeze."
Journal des Missions Évangéliques (54; 1879), pp. 9-13.
                              CtY; MH

1960. Dominion Sister. In God's White Robed Army. The
Chronicle of the Dominican Sisters in Rhodesia, 1895-1934.
Cape Town: M. Miller, 1951.   DLC

1961. Evans, John T. The Church in Southern Rhodesia.
London: S. P. C. K. and S. P. G., 1945.   IEN; NE

1962. Gann, Lewis Henry. The Birth of a Plural Society:
The Development of Northern Rhodesia Under the British
South Africa Company, 1894-1914. Manchester, Eng.:
Manchester University Press, 1961. NcD; IU; OCU; LU;
                              NjP; CaBVaU; FTaSu
      Missionary impact is discussed.

1963. Hassing, Per. Christian Missions and the British
Expansion in Southern Rhodesia, 1888-1923. Doctoral
dissertation. American Univeristy, 1960.

1964. Hobby, Alvin. African Missions of the Church of Christ
in Northern Rhodesia. n.p., n.p., 19?   TN/DCHS

1965. Hostetter, John Norman. Mission Education in a
Changing Society: Brethren in Christ Mission Education in
Southern Rhodesia, Africa, 1889-1959. Doctoral disser-
tation. State University of New York at Buffalo, 1967.

1966. Mackintosh, Catharine Winkworth. The New Zambesi
Trail; A Record of Two Journeys to North-Western Rhodesia
(1903 and 1920). London: Marshall, 1922. NN/Sch

1967. Marimazhira, Xavier. "Acculturation in Rhodesia."
African Ecclesiastical Review (15:2, 1973), pp. 130-33.
                              DHU/R

1968. Martin, Marie-Louise. "The Mai Chaza Church in
Rhodesia." David B. Barrett, (ed.). African Initiatives
in Religion (Nairobi: East African Pub. House, 1971), pp.
109-21.   DHU/R

1969. Masters, Henry. In Wild Rhodesia. A Story of
Missionary Enterprise and Adventures Where Livingstone
Lived, Laboured and Died. London: F. Griffiths, 1920.
                              NN/Sch

1970. Miller, Charles M. The Financial Support of the
Ordained Ministry: An Historical Study of the Ministry
in the Rhodesia Annual Conference of the Methodist Church.
Master's thesis. Wesley Theological Seminary, 1965.

1971. Moffat, Malcolm. "Chitambo Mission Station Northern
Rhodesia." Southern Workman (58:5, My., 1929), pp.
211-15.   DLC; DHU/MO

1972. Moore, R. J. B. Man's Act and God's in Africa.
London: Livingstone Press, 1940.   NNtcA
Missions in Northern Rhodesia.

1973. North West Rhodesia. General Missionary Conference.
Report of the Proceedings. 1st-9th, 1914; 1919; 1927;
1931; 1935; 1939; 1944.   NNMR

1974. Quick, Griffith. "Some Aspects of the African Watchtower Movement in Northern Rhodesia." International
Review of Missions (29; Apr., 1940), pp. 216-26.
                                           DHU/R

1975. Rea, Fred B. "The Need for a Unified Church in Southern
Rhodesia." International Review of Missions (47; 1958),
pp. 84-9.   DHU/R

1976. Rea, W. F. "Livingstone's Rhodesian Legacy."
History Today (23:9, Sept., 1973), pp. 633-39.
Discusses missionary successes of Livingstone and
some of his colleagues on the Zambia River.

1977. Rotberg, Robert I. Christian Missionaries and the
Creation of Northern Rhodesia, 1880-1924. Princeton,
N.J.: Princeton University Press, 1965. MNtcA; NjP;
DHU/MO; DHU/R; NN/Sch; A&M

1978. ----- "The Lenshina Movement of Northern Rhodesia."
Rhodes-Livingstone Journal (29; Je., 1961), pp. 63-78.
                                           DAU

1979. ----- "Missionaries as Chiefs and Entrepreneurs:
Northern Rhodesia, 1882-1924." Jeffrey Butler (ed.).
Boston University Papers in African History I (Boston:
Boston University Press, 1964), pp. 197-215. DHU/MO;
                                           MBU

1980. ----- "The Missionary Factor in the Occupation of
Trans-Zambezia." Northern Rhodesia Journal (5:4, 1964),
pp. 330-38.   DLC

1981. Savage, Murray J. Achievement: Forty Years of
Missionary Witness in Southern Rhodesia. Wellington,
N.Z.: A.H. & A.W. Reed for the Foreign Mission Exec-
utive Committee, Associated Churches of Christ, New
Zealand, 1949.   TN/DCHS

1982. Shaw, Mabel. God's Candlelights; an Educational
Venture in Northern Rhodesia. London: The Livingstone
Press, 1936.   DHU/MO; NN/Sch

1983. Shewmaker, Stanford. A Study of the Growth of the Church
of Christ Among the Tonga Tribe of Zambia. Masters thesis.
Fuller Theological Seminary, 1969.

1984. ----- Tonga Christianity. South Pasadena, Calif.:
William Carey Library, 1970.   DLC
Christianity among the Tonga of Zambia.

1985. Smith, Edwin William. The Way of the White Fields in
Rhodesia. A Survey of Christian Enterprise in Northern and
Southern Rhodesia. London: World Dominion Press, 1928.
                                           NN/Sch
"List of African tribes in Southern Rhodesia."

1986. Steere, Douglas V. God's Irregular Arthur Shearly
Cripps: A Rhodesian Epic. London: S.P.C.K., 1973.
                                           DHU/R
Rhodesian history and church history.

1987. Taylor, John Vernon, and Dorothea A. Lehmann.
Christians of the Copperbelt: The Growth of the Church in
Northern Rhodesia. London: SCM Press, 1961. DHU/MO

1988. Thomas, Norman E. Christianity, Politics, and the
Manyika: A Study of the Influence of Religious Attitudes and
Loyalties on Political Values and Activities of Africans in
Rhodesia. Doctoral dissertation. Boston University, 1968.

1989. Von Hoffman, Carl. Jungle Gods. New York: Holt,
1929.   NN/Sch

1990. Wallis, John Peter Richard, (ed.). The Matabele
Mission, a Selection from the Correspondence of John and
Emily Moffat, David Livingstone and Others, 1858-1878.
London: Chatto & Windus, 1945.   NN/Sch
(Government Archives of Sothern Rhodesia. Oppenheimer
Series. No. 2).

n. Sierra Leone
1991. Alldridge, Thomas Joshua. A Transformed Colony,
Sierra as it Was and as it Is, Its Progress, Peoples, Native
Customs and Undeveloped Wealth. London: n.p., 1910.
INU; DHU/MO; DLC; MiU; OCL; NcD; CtY

1992. Bacon, Ephriam. Abstract of a Journal of Ephriam Bacon,
Assistant Agent of the United States, to Africa; with an
Appendix, containing extracts from Proceedings of the Church
Missionary Society in England, for the Years 1819-20. To
Which is prefixed an Abstract of the Journal of the Rev.
J.B. Cates...on an Overland Journey, performed in Company
with Several Natives, in the Months of February, March, and
April, 1819. The Whole Showing the Successful Exertions of
the British and American Governments in the Repressing the
Slave Trade. Philadelphia: S. Potter & Co., 1821. NN/Sch

1993. Baker, Earl D. Development of Secondary Education in
Sierra Leone Until Independence. Doctoral dissertation,
University of Michigan, 1963.
Author is a missionary to Sierra Leone for United
Brethren Church in Christ.

1994. Bell, T. M. Outrage by Missionaries; A Report of the
Whole Proceedings on the Trial in Sierra Leone of William
Fortunatus John, Phoebe John, John Williams, and Kezia
Williams, for the Murder of Aurelia John, at Onitsha, River
Niger. Liverpool, n.p., 1883.   NN/Sch

1995. Blyden, Edward Wilmot. From West Africa to Palestine.
Freetown, Sierra Leone: T. J. Sawyer, 1873. DLC; NB; MH

1996. ----- Report on the Falaba Expedition, 1872. Addressed to His Excellency, Governor Pope Hennessy...
Sierra Leone: Printed at the Government Office, 1827.
                                           NUC; DLC

1997. ----- The West African University: Correspondence
Between Edward W. Blyden and His Excellency J. Pope
Hennessy, Administratior-in-Chief of the West African
Settlements. Freetown: "Negro" Printing Office, 1872.
                                           DLC

1998. Bowen, John, (bp.). Memorials of John Bowen,
L.L.D., Late Bishop of Sierra Leone Compiled From His
Letters and Journals by His Sister. London: J. Nisbet, 1862.
                                           DHU/R
     Microfilm.

1999. Boxer, C.R. "A Christian Experiment: the Early Sierra
Leone Colony." G. J. Cuming (ed.). The Mission of the
Church and the Propagation of the Faith (Cambridge: Univ-
versity Press, 1970), pp. 107-129. DHU/R; DLC

2000. Charlesworth, Maria Louisa. Africa's Mountain Valley; or
the Church in Regent's Town, West Africa... London: Seeley,
Jackson and Halliday, 1874.   NN/Sch

2001. Corby, Richard Andrew. The Mende Uprising of 1898
in Sierra Leone as it Related to the United Brethren in
Christ Missions. Masters Thesis, Western Illinois University, 1971.

2002. Ellis, Malcolm. The Christian Mission in Sierra Leone,
West Africa. Masters thesis. Butler University, 1954.

2003. Flickinger, Daniel Kumler. Fifty-five Years of Active
Ministerial Life...; With a Preface by Bishop E. W. Mathews.

Dayton, Ohio: U. B. Publishing House, 1907.
Missionary to Sierra Leone.   DOUM/EUB

2004. Hair, Paul Edward Hedley. "Material on Religion in
Sierra Leone Before 1780." Sierra Leone Studies (no. 21;
J1., 1967), pp. 80-86.   DHU/MO

2005. ----- "Niger Languages and Sierra Leonean Missionary
Linguists, 1840-1930." The Bulletin of the Society for
African Church History (Vol. II, 2, 1966), pp. 127-138.
                                               DHU/R

2006. Harris, J.H. "Dawn in Darkest Africa." Missionary
Review (37; Sept., 1914), pp. 685-92.   DHU/R

2007. Hughson, Shirley Carter. The Green Wall of Mystery;
Venture and Adventure in the Hinterland of West Africa.
Holy Cross Press, 1928.   NN/Sch

2008. Johnson, William A. B. A Memoir of the Rev. W. A. B.
Johnson, Missionary of the Church Missionary Society in
Regent's Town, Sierra Leone, A. D. 1816-1823. Compiled
from his Journals, etc. by R. B. Seeley With Some Prefatory
Remarks by the Rev. William Jowett. n.p.: Seeleys,
1853.   ViU; MWA; CtY; OO

2009. Leone, John Sierra. "First Impressions of Sierra Leone."
The Church Missionary Review (63; My., 1912), pp. 272-78.
                                               DHU/R

2010. Medbery, Rebecca B. Memoir of William G. Crocker,
Late Missionary in West Africa Among the Bassas, Including
a History of the Bassa Mission. Boston: Gould, Kendall, &
Lincoln, 1847.   NN/Sch

2011. "Mendi Mission, Good Hope Station, Near Freetown,
Sierra Leone, West Africa." (Letter to the editor). Southern
Workman (7:2, Feb., 1878), p. 12.   DLC; DHU/MO
   Hampton Institute Graduate Missionary Ackral E. White
   writes of his interesting experiences.

2012. Mills, Job Smith, (bp.). Mission Work in Sierra Leone,
West Africa. Memorial ed. Dayton, Ohio: n.p., 1898.
                           DOUM/EUB; NN/Sch; DHU/MO

2013. Olson, Gilbert W. Church Growth in Sierra Leone: A
Study of Church Growth in Africa's Oldest Protestant Mission
Field. Eerdmans: Grand Rapids, 1969.   DLC; DHU/R

2014. Peacock, Amjogollo E. Missionary Work in Sierra Leone.
Masters thesis. Howard University, 1940.

2015. Pierson, Arthur Tappan. Seven Years in Sierra Leone.
The Story of the Work of William A.B. Johnson, Missionary
of the Church Missionary Society from 1816-1823 in Regent's
Town, Sierra Leone, Africa. New York: Fleming H.
Revell, 1897.   NN/Sch

2016. Reeck, Darrell L. "Innovators in Religion and Politics in
Sierra Leone, 1875-1896." International Journal of African
Historical Studies (5:4, 1972), pp. 587-909. DLC

2017. "Sierra Leone." Christian Spectator (8:1, Ja., 1826),
pp. 48-9.   DHU/R
   Effect of missionary education on "liberated Africans."

2018. Statton, Arthur B. Diary Kept ... When he Represented
and was Sent by the United Brethren Church to Sierra
Leone, Africa: 1928-1929.   DOUB/EUB
   Mim.

2019. Thompson, George. Thompson in Africa: or, An
Account of the Missionary Labors, Sufferings, Travels,
and Observations of George Thompson in Western Africa,
at the Mendi Mission. New York: Printed for the author,
1852.   DHU/MO; NN/Sch

2020. Tyng, Stephen Higginson. A Memoir of the Rev. W. A. B.
Johnson, Missionary of the Church Missionary Society, in
Regent's Town, Sierra Leone, Africa. New York: R. Carter
& Bros., 1853.   NN/Sch

2021. United Brethren Mission. Twelve Mendi Songs; Lord's
Prayer, Child's Prayer; Apostles Creed and Ten Commandments. Freetown, Sierra Leone: Albert Academy Press,
1907.   DOUM/EUB

2022. Vivian, William. A Captive Missionary in Mendiland:
the Story of the Rev. C. H. Goodman's Wonderful Deliverance From Death, and His Strange Experiences During
the Sierra Leone Rebellion. London: Crombie, 1899.
                                           DOUM/EUB

2023. Walmsley, John. John Walmsley, Ninth Bishop of
Sierra Leone. London: Society for Promoting Christian
Knowledge, 1923.   PPStc

o. South Africa including Swaziland, Botswana

2024. Adventures of a Missionary; or, Rivers of Water in a
Dry Place; Being an Account of the Introduction of the Gospel
of Jesus into South Africa and of Mr. Moffat's Missionary
Travels and Labors. Miami, Fla.: Mnemosyne Pub., 1969.
                                               IC/H

2025. Abdy, Dora C. David Livingstone, the Story of His Life.
Westminster, Eng.: Universities Mission to Central Africa,
1947.   MiBsA

2026. Anderson, W. H. On the Trail of Livingstone. Mountain
View, Calif.: Pacific Press, 1919.   MiBsA

2027. Andrews, Charles Freer. John White of Masonaland.
Westport, Conn.: Negro Universities Press, 1969.
                                  IC/H; InU; DHU/MO
   The story of a missionary of South Africa.

2028. Arbousset, Jean Thomas. Narrative of an Exploratory Tour
to the North-East of the Colony of the Good Hope. Cape
Town: Struik, 1968.   NjP; PPT

2029. "Archbishop Approves Apartheid." Christian Century (81;
Mr. 11, 1964), p. 325.   DHU/R

2030. Astrop, Nils. "Progress of Mission Work in Natal
and Zululand." The East and the West (5; Oct., 1907),
pp. 383-92.   DHU/R

2031. Badertscher, Jean. La Ségrégation Raciale en Afrique du
Sud. Lausanne: Editions du Soc, 1962.   DLC

2032. Battey, D. S. "Separation of Black and White in Church."
The East and the West (12; J1., 1914), pp. 330-38. DHU/R

2033. Baynes, Hamilton. "The 'Raw' Kaffir and the Christian."
The East and the West (3; Oct., 1905), pp. 438-47. DHU/R

2034. Bedwell, H. Kenneth. Black Gold; the Story of the International Holiness Mission in South Africa which United with
the Church of the Nazarene, Nov. 29, 1952. Acornhoek,
Transvaai, Union of South Africa. Kansas City, Mo.:
Beacon Hill Press, 1953.   NN/Sch

2035. Benham, Marian S. Henry Callaway, M.D., D.D.
First Bishop for Kaffraria, His Life History and Work.
London: Macmillan, 1896.   NN/Sch

2036. Berthoud, Alexander. "The Birth of a Church: The
Church of Basutoland." International Review of Missions
(38; Ja.-Oct., 1949), pp. 156-64.   DHU/R

2037. Birtwistle, Norman A. William Threfall: a Study in
Missionary Vocation. London: Oliphants, 1966.
                                           DHU/MO

   Early Methodist missionary in South Africa.

2038. Blaxall, A. W. "The Cape Coloured People and the Church." The Church Overseas (5; 1932), pp. 243-252.
DHU/R

2039. "Boers and Christianity in South Africa." Missionary Review of the World (23; Je., 1900), pp. 462-7.
DHU/R

2040. Bokwe, John Knox. Ntsikana. Lovedale, So. Africa: Printed at the Mission Press, 1914.   DHU/MO

2041. Booth, Newell S. "The Ministry in Bantu Religion." International Review of Missions (26; 1937), pp. 334-44.
DHU/R

2042. Botha, Johannes M. A. History of the Afrikaans Baptist Church From Its Inception to the Present. Masters thesis. Wheaton College, 1965.

2043. Broadbent, Samuel. A Narrative of the First Introduction of Christianity Amongst the Barolong Tribe of Bechuanas, South Africa; With a Brief Summary of the Subsequent History of the Wesleyan Mission to the Same People. London: Wesleyan Mission House, 1865.   NN/Sch

2044. Brookes, Edgar Harry. Bishop Gray and the Nature and Mission of Anglicanism. Cape Town: Church of the Province of South Africa, 1962.   DLC

2045. ----- A Century of Missions in Natal and Zululand. Durban: Natal Missionary Conference, n. d. (ca. 1935).
DLC

2046. ----- A Retrospect and a Forecast: Fifty Years of Missionary Work in South Africa, 1875-1925. Lausanne: Mission Suisse Romande, 1925.   NNMR

2047. Brown, John Tom. Among the Bantu Nomads. London: Seeley, Service & Co., 1925.   DHU/MO
"Gives customs, religious beliefs, and history of the Bechuana."

2048. ----- The Apostle of the Marshes: The Story of Shomolekae. London: The Religious Tract Society, 1925. NN/Sch

2049. Brown, William E. The Catholic Church in South Africa: From its Origins to the Present Day. Edited by Michael Derrick. New York: J.P. Kennedy, 1960. DHU/MO; DLC

2050. Brownlee, Charles. Reminiscences of Kaffir Life and History, and Other Papers by the Late Hon. Charles Brownlee; with a Brief Memoir by Mrs. Brownlee. Lovedale, So. Africa: Lovedale Mission Press, 1896.   NN/Sch

2051. Brownlee, Margaret. The Lives and Work of South African Missionaries. Cape Town: University of Cape Town, School of Librarianship, 1952.   DHU/MO

2052. Bryant, Alfred T. Olden Times in Zululand and Natal Containing Earlier Political History of the Eastern-Nguni Clans. London: Longmans Green, 1929.   DLC

2053. Burkhardt, Gustav E. Die Evangelische Mission unter Volkerstammen in Sud-Afrika. Bielefeld: Velhagen und Klasing, 1860.   MiBsA

2054. Butterfield, Kenyon Leech. ...Report of Dr. Kenyon L. Butterfield on Rural Conditions and Sociological Problems in South Africa. New York: n.p., 1929. NN/Sch

2055. Cains, Earle Edwin. Political and Humanitarian Activities of the London Missionary Society in South Africa, 1799-1857. Doctoral dissertation. University of Nebraska, 1942.

2056. Calderwood, Henry. Caffres and Caffre Missions, With Preliminary Chapters on the Cape Colony as a Field for Emigration and the Basis of Missionary Operation. London: James Nisbet, 1858.   DLC

2057. Callaway, Godfrey. Mxamli, the Feaster; a Pondomisi Tale of the Diocese of St. John's, So. Africa. New York: Macmillan Co., 1919.   NN/Sch

2058. ----- "The Native Problem in South Africa and Its Challenge to Christianity." Cowley Evangelist (Oct.; 1926), pp. 647-61.   NNG

2059. ----- The Pilgrim Path; a Story of an African Childhood; with an Introduction by the Rt. Rev., the Lord Bishop of St. John's. London: Society for the Propagation of the Gospel in Foreign Parts, 1933.   NN/Sch

2060. ----- A Shepherd of the Weld: Bransby Lewis Key, Bishop of St. John's, Kaffraria. London: Wells Gardner, 1912.   MNtcA

2061. ----- The Soul of An African Padre. ...With a preface by the Most Rev. W.M. Carter... Milwaukee: Morehouse Pub. Co., 1932.   NN/Sch

2062. ----- "A Transkei Experiment: Training in Self Government." The East and West Review (3; 1937), pp. 52-61.
DHU/R

2063. ----- "Colour Antipathies: A Study of Conditions of Church Life in South Africa." The East and the West (8; Ja., 1910), pp. 57-62.   DHU/R

2064. Campbell, John. Africaner; or, Missionary Trials. Philadelphia: Presbyterian Board of Publication 1840.
NN/Sch

2065. ----- The Life of Africaner: a Namacqua Chief of South Africa. Prepared for publication by the editors. New York: G. Lane & P.P. Sandford for the Sunday School Union of the Methodist Episcopal Church, 1841.
NN/Sch

2066. ----- Travels in South Africa, Undertaken at the Request of the London Missionary Society; being a Narrative of a Second Journey in the Interior of that Country. London: F. Westley, 1822.   NN/Sch

2067. Carlyle, J. E. South Africa and Its Mission Fields. London: n.p., 1878.   DLC

2068. Carstens, Kenneth. "The Churches on Trial." George M. Daniels. Southern Africa: A Time for Change (New York: Friendship Press, 1969), pp. 71-5.
DHU

2069. Casalis, Eugene. My Life in Basuto Land: A Story of Missionary Enterprise in South Africa. Capetown: C. Struik, 1971.   DHU/R

2070. "Catalogue of South African Missions." Missionary Review of the World (23; Apr., 1900), p. 318. DHU/R

2071. Chalmers, John A. Tiyo Soga; A Page of South African Mission Work. Edinburgh: Andrew Elliott, 1877. NN/Sch

2072. Chamberlin, David. Moffat of Kuruman. London: Sheldon Press, 1931.   NN/Sch

2073. Champion, George. The Journal of an American Missionary in the Cape Colony, 1835. Cape Town: South African Library, 1968.   PPT

2074. ----- Journal of the Rev. George Champion, American Missionary in Zululand, 1835-1839. Cape Twon: C. Struik, 1967.   NjP; NNCor; MNtcA

2075. Chapman, Louise Robinson. Africa, O Africa. Kansas City: Beacon Hill Press, 1945.   DHU/Mo

The author tells of her twenty years as a missionary under the Church of the Nazarene in Swaziland, southern Africa.

2076. Cheeseman, Thomas. The Story of William Threlfall. Missionary Martyr of Namaqualand, with Some Account of Jacob Links and Johannes Jager Who Fell with Him. Cape Town: Methodist Publishing Office, 1910. DLC

2077. Chirgwin, A. M. "The Wilberforce of Africa." Congregational Quarterly (7; 1929), pp. 297-306.
DHU/R
The work of Dr. John Philip of the London Missionary Society for the colored people of South Africa.

2078. Christian Literature for the Bantu of Southern Africa. Johannesburg: Committee of South African Churches, 1957.
CLU

2079. Christianity and the Natives of South Africa. A Year-book of South African Missions. V. 1, 1929.
Published under the auspices of the General Missionary Conference of South Africa. Lovedale, C.P. South Africa. Printed by the Lovedale Institution Press. Rev. J. Dexter Taylor.

2080. Christofersen, Arthur Fridjof. Adventuring With God: The Story of the American Board Mission in South Africa. Durban: Inanda Seminary, 1967.
DLC

2081. Clark, Samuel. Missionary Memories. Cape Town: Methodist Book Depot & Publishing House, 1927.
NN/Sch

2082. Clinton, Desmond K. The South African Melting Pot. A Vindication of Missionary Policy, 1799-1836. London: Longmans Green, 1937.
DLC

2083. Clinton, Iris A. "A Congregational Assembly in South Africa." Congregational Quarterly (18; 1940), pp. 316-19.
DHU/R

2084. Conference on Christian Citizenship in a Multi-Racial Society, Rosettenville, South Africa, 1949. The Christian Citizen in a Multi-Racial Society: A Report of the Rosettenville Conference, July, 1949. With Aids to Study and Discussion. Strand, C. P.: Christian Council of South Africa, 1949.
NN/Sch

2085. Coppin, Levi Jenkins, (bp.). Letters from South Africa. Philadelphia: A.M.E. Book Concern, 1902. NN/Sch
Negro author.

2086. -----, (bp.). Observations of Persons and Things in South Africa, 1900-1904. n.p., 1905. NN/Sch; NcD
Part second (210p.) has special t.-p.: Letters from So. Africa, by Bishop L.J. Coppin. Philadelphia.

2087. Cousins, Henry Thomas. From Kafir Kraal to Pulpit; the Story of Tiyo Soga, First Ordained Preacher of the Kafir Race. London: S. W. Partridge, 1899. NN/Sch

2088. Crawshaw, C.J. A First Kafir Course. Capetown: J.C. Juta, 1901.
OWibfU.

2089. Dachs, Anthony J. "Missionary Imperialism--the Case of Bechuanaland." Journal of African History (13:4, 1972), pp. 647-58. DAU; DGU; DGW; DHU/MO

2090. Dalziel, Jack. The History of the Presbyterian Church in South Africa. Johannesburgh: St. Columbia's Presbyterian Church, n.d. DLC
Mim.

2091. Daniell-Bainbridge, H. G. "The Mission of Help to the Church in South Africa." The East and the West (3; Jl., 1905), pp. 284-93. DHU/R

2092. Davidson, Hannah Frances. South and South Central Africa; a Record of Fifteen Years' Missionary Labors among Primitive Peoples. Elgin, Ill.: Printed for the author by Brethren Pub. House, 1915. NN/Sch

2093. Davies, Horton, (ed.). South African Missions, 1800-1950. An anthology compiled by Horton Davies and R.H.W. Shepherd. London: Nelson, 1954.
DHU/MO; NN/Sch

2094. Dubé, J.L. "Native View of Christianity in South Africa." Missionary Review of the World (24; Je., 1901), pp. 421-26. DHU/R

2095. DuPlessis, Johannes. The Evangel in South Africa. Cape Town: Cape Times, Ltd., Printers, 1912. NN/Sch

2096. ----- "The Missionary Situation in South Africa." International Review of Missions (1:4, 1912), pp. 573-86.
DHU/R

2097. The Dutch Reformed Churches in South Africa and the Problems of Race Relations. Transvaal: Dutch Reformed Churches of Transvaal, n.d. DHU/MO
Report of the Ad Hoc Comission for race relations appointed by the Federal Council of Dutch Reformed Churches in South Africa; as approved by the Synodical Commission of the Dutch Reformed Church in the Transvaal.

2098. Du Toit, Henrik A. Die Kerstening van die Bantoe. Pretoria: N. G. Kerk-boekhandel, 1967. DLC
Outline of a method of working with the Bantu in Southern Africa.

2099. Du Toit, Stefanus. Die Heilige Skrif en Rasseverhoudinge, met Besondere Toepassing op Suid-Afrikaanse Toestande. Potchefstroom: Pro Reg-Pers, 1959. DLC

2100. Ellenberger, V. A Century of Mission Work in Basutoland. Morija: Sesuto Book Depot, 1938. Njp; DLC MH; ICU; CtY

2101. Etherington, Norman Alan. The Rise of the Kholwa in Southeast Africa: African Christian Communities in Natal, Pondoland, and Zululand. Doctoral dissertation. Yale University, 1971.

2102. The Evangelisation of South Africa: Being the Report of the Sixth General Missionary Conference of South Africa, Held at Johannesburg, June 30 to July 3, 1925. Cape Town: Nasionale Pers., 1925. NNMR

2103. Favre, Edouard. ...Les Vingt-Cinq Ans de Coillard au Lessouto. Paris: Société des Missions Evangéliques, 1931. NN/Sch

2104. Ferguson, George P. Cusa: The Story of the Churches of the Congregational Union of South Africa. Paarl: A. H. Fisher & Sons, 1940. DLC; CtY-D

2105. Florin, Hans. Lutherans in South Africa. Durban: Lutheran Publishing House, 1967. WU; CSt; CLU

2106. Frame, George. Blood Brother of the Swazis; the Life Story of David Hind. Kansas City, Mo.: Beacon Hill Press, 1952. NN/Sch

2107. France, Dorothy. "South Africa a Strange Society." World Call (54:9, Oct. 1972), pp. 5-6. DHU/R
"Mrs. Carl G. France is a minister of the Christian Church (Disciples of Christ) from Pulaski, Virginia X."

2108. Fraser, Donald. "The Building of the Church in Africa." The Church Missionary Review (77:854, Je., 1926), pp. 117-23. DHU/R

2109. Fuller, J. Latimer. "The Separation of Black and White in Church." The East and The West (10; Oct., 1912), pp. 382-94. DHU/R

2110. ----- South African Native Missions; Some Considerations. Leed: R. Jackson, 1907.   NN/Sch

2111. Gelfand, Michael, (ed.). Mother Patrick and Her Nursing Sisters. Based on Letters and Journals of the Dominican Sisterhood, 1890-1900. Capetown: Juta, 1904.   CLU

2112. Gerdener, Gustav Bernhard August. The Story of Christian Missions in South Africa. Linden, Johannesburg: Linden Christian Church, 1950.   TN/DCHS

2113. ----- Studies in the Evangelisation of South Africa. London: Longmans, Green & Co., 1911. DLC; McBE CtY-D; MH
     Missions in South Africa. Book review in International Review of Missions (1:2, 1912), pp. 328-31. DHU/R

2114. Germond, Robert C., (ed.). Chronicles of Basutoland; A Running Commentary on the Events of the Years 1830-1902 by the French Protestant Missionaries in Southern Africa. Morija: Morija Sesuto Book Depot, 1967.   MH

2115. Gibson, Alan G. S. "Christianity Among the Bantu in South Africa." The East and The West (11; Oct., 1913), pp. 383-96.   DHU/R

2116. ----- Eight Years in Kaffraria, 1882-1890. London: W. Gardner, Darton, 1891.   PPT

2117. ----- "Polygamy and Christianity in South Africa." The East and The West (5; Apr., 1907), pp. 135-50.   DHU/R

2118. ----- "The South African Church and the Church at Home." The East and The West (12; Oct., 1914), pp. 374-82.   DHU/R

2119. Good, James I. "Francis Coillard, the Great Missionary to the Zambesi." The Christian Intelligencer (75:38, Sept., 1904), p. 600.   DHU/R
     Includes notes on a Christian mission among the Basutos in Southern Africa.

2120. Green, Betrand W. The Impact of Christianity on the Position of the Bantu Chief in the Union of South Africa, 1887-1958. Masters thesis. Howard University, 1960.

2121. Hance, Gertrude Rachel. The Zulu Yesterday and Today; Twenty-Nine Years in South Africa. New York: Fleming H. Revell Co., 1916.   NN/Sch

2122. Helander, Gunnar. Must We Introduce Monogamy? A Study of Polygamy as a Mission Problem in South Africa. Pietermaritzburg: Shuter & Shooter, 1958. NN/Sch

2123. Hewitt, James. Sketches of English Church History in South Africa, 1795-1848. Cape Town: Juta, 1887.   NH; NcD

2124. Hewson, Leslie A. An Introduction to South African Methodists. Cape Town: Printed by the Standard Press, 1951?   NN/Sch

2125. Hinchcliff, Peter (Bingham). The Anglican Church in South Africa: an Account of the History and Development of the Church of the Province of South Africa. London: Darton, Longman and Todd, 1963. DHU/MO; DLC; ICU; MiU; WvU

2126. Holden, W.C. A Brief History of Methodism, and of Methodist Missions in South Africa. London: Wesleyan Conference Office, 1887.

2127. Holt, Basil. Joseph Williams and the Pioneer Mission to the South-Eastern Bantu. Lovedale: Lovedale Press, 1954.   DLC; IU; NBuU; NcD

2128. Howe, Sonia E. "Seventy-Five Years in Basutoland." The Church Missionary Review (64; Apr., 1913), pp. 225-31.   DHU/R

2129. Hubbard, Ethel Daniels. The Moffats. New York: Missionary Education Movement of the United States and Canada, 1917.   NN/Sch

2130. Humphreys, Nicholas. Missionary in South Africa. With a Foreword by the Rt. Rev. Bishop Count David O'Leary. London: Blackfriars Publications, 1953.   NN/Sch

2131. Hunter, D. A. "The Lovedale Institute in South Africa." Southern Workman (54:7, Jl., 1925), pp. 305-11.   DLC; DHU/MO
     The Lovedale Mission started by the Glasgow Missionary Society "is situated in the division of South Africa known as Victoria East."

2132. Ireland, William B. Historical Sketch of the Zulu Mission in South Africa. Boston: American Foreign Missions, 1864.   NN/Sch; DHU/MO

2133. Jacottet, E. "The French Mission in Basutoland." International Review of Missions (2; 1913), pp. 486-500.   DHU/R

2134. Jalla, Adolphe. Pionniers Parmi les Ma-Rotse, par le Missionaire Adolphe Jalla. Avec de Nombreuses Gravures. Florence: Imprimerie Claudienne, 1903.   NN/Sch

2135. Johannesburg, Arthur. "Africa and South Africa." The Church Overseas (1:4, Oct., 1928), pp. 320-29.   DHU/R

2136. Johnson, William Percival. My African Reminiscences, 1875-1895. Westport, Conn.: Negro Universities Press, 1970.   IC/H; NN/Sch
     "Originally published in 1925."

2137. Jones, J. D. Rheinallt. "Missionary Work Among the Bantu in South Africa." International Review of Missions (17; 1928), pp. 175-85.   DHU/R

2138. Junod, Henri Philippe. "Anthropology and Missionary Education." International Review of Missions (24; Apr., 1935), pp. 213-28.   DHU/R
     About the Bantu of South Africa.

2139. Kelly, Herbert. "Methods of Missionary Work in South Africa: A Criticism." The East and The West (1:2, Apr., 1903), pp. 156-70.   DHU/R

2140. Kicherer, Johannes Jacobus. "The Rev. Mr. Kicherer's Narrative of his Mission to the Hottentots." London Missionary Society, Transactions of the Missionary Society... (2:1, 1804), pp. 1-48.   NN/Sch
     Illustrations and portraits.

2141. ----- An Extract from the Rev. Mr. Kicherer's Narrative of his Mission in South Africa; Together With a Sketch of the Public Conference with the Hottentots in London, Nov. 21, 1803. Wiscasset: Printed by Babson & Rust, 1805.   NN/Sch

2142. Knight-Bruce, Geo. Wyndham Hamilton. Gold and Gospel in Mashonaland, 1888, Being the Journals of the Mashonaland Mission of Bishop Knight-Bruce and Concession Journey of Charles Dunell Rudd. London: Chatto and Windies, 1949.   DHU/MO

2143. Kotze, D. J. Letters of the American Missionaries, 1835-1838. Cape Town: Van Riebeeck Society, 1950.   DLC; CU-S; MH-AH; FU

2144. Krüger, Bernard. The Pear Tree Blossoms: The Story of Moravian Church in South Africa, 1737-1869. Genadendal: Moravian Book Depot, 1966. NjP; MiBsa; MNtcA

2145. Kuper, Hilda. The Uniform of Color, A Study of White-Black Relationships in Swaziland. Johannesburg: University of Witwatersrand Press, 1947.   DLC

2146. Latrobe, Christian Ignatius. Journal of a Visit to South Africa in 1815 and 1816, with Some Account of the Missionary Settlements of the United Brethren, Near the Cape of Good Hope. New York: Negro Universities Press, 1969. IC/H; NjP

        Reprint of 1818 edition.

2147. Lea, Allen. Across South Africa. East London, South Africa: Central Missions Office, 1925.   NNMR
        Concerns the Wesleyan Methodist Church in South Africa.

2148. Lee, Albert William. Charles Johnson of Zululand. Westminister: Society for the Propagation of the Gospel in Foreign Parts, 1930.   NNMR

2149. ----- Once Dark Country. Recollections and Reflections of a South African Bishop. London: SPCK, 1949. NN/Sch

2150. Ledward, Sally Ann. The Constitutional Development of the Church of the Province of South Africa, 1848-1936. Cape Town: 1957. (Univ. of Cape Town. School of Librarianship. Bibliographical series)   CLU
        mim.

2151. Lewis, Cecil, and G.E. Edwards. Historical Records of the Church of the Province of South Africa. London: Society for Promoting Christian Knowledge, 1934.   DLC

2152. The Life of Robert Moffat of South Africa, Founded on the Biography of His Son, John S. Moffat and Other Reliable Sources. Concinnati: Revivalist Press, 1915. MiBsA

2153. A Life's Labours in South Africa; The Story of the Life-Work of Robert Moffat, Apostle to the Bechuana Tribes... London: J. Snow, 1871.   NN/Sch

2154. Livingstone, David. Missionary Travels and Researches in South Africa... New York: Johnson Reprint Corporation, 1971.   DHU/R
        Reprint of 1858 edition.

2155. Loram, Charles T. "The Phelps-Stokes Education Commission in South Africa." International Review of Missions (10; 1921), pp. 496-508.   DHU/R

2156. Mackenzie, John. Day-Dawn in Dark Places. A Story of Wandering and Work in Bechuanaland. London: Cassell, 1883.   NN/Sch

2157. MacKenzie, William Douglas. John MacKenzie, South African Missionary and Statesman. London: Hodder & Stoughton, 1902.   NN/Sch

2158. Mabuda, Fanny. "Mission Work in Natal, South Africa." Southern Workman (39:3, Mr., 1910), pp. 181-83.
                                             DLC; DHU/MO

2159. Maimane, H. Mashite. "The Christian Church in Relation to the Social and Religious Life of Bantu." The Church Overseas (1:3, Jl., 1928), pp. 212-219. DHU/R

2160. Main, John K. Africa Looks Ahead. New Advance in Africa. London: Livingstone Press, 1947. NN/Sch

2161. Majeke, Nosipho. The Role of the Missionaries in Conquest. Johannesburg, South Africa: Society of Young Africa, 1952.
                                             DHU/MO

2162. Malan, Major C. H. Rides in the Mission Field of South Africa, Between the Kel and the Bashee Rivers, Kaffraria. Also a Visit to the Missionary Colleges of Lovedale and Healdtown, in British Kaffraria. London: Morgan & Scott: n. d., 1872.
                                             NjNST

2163. Maples, Ellen, (ed.). Journals and Papers of Chauncy Maples, Late Bishop of Likoma, Lake Nyasa, Africa. New York: Longmans, 1899.   DHU/MO

2164. Marais, Barend J. Colour, Unsolved Problem of the West. Cape Town: H.S. Timmins, 1962.   NN/Sch

2165. Marks, Shula. "Christian African Participation in the 1906 Zulu Rebellion." The Bulletin of the Society for African Church History (2:1, Dec., 1965), pp. 55-72.   DHU/R

2166. Mayr, F. R. "Zulu Proverbs." Anthropos (7:6, Nov.-Dec., 1912), pp. 957-63.   DLC
        Pietermaritzburg, Natal.

2167. McCarter, John M. The Dutch Reformed Churches in South Africa with Notices of Other Denominations. Edinburgh: Inglis, 1869.
                                             MB; NcD

2168. Mears, W.J. Gordon. Barnabas Shaw, Founder of South African Methodism. Rondebosch, South Africa: Methodist Missionary Dept., 1957.   IEN

2169. ----- The Rev. James Allison, Missionary: A Biographical Outline. Durban, South Africa: Mission and Extension Dept., Methodist Church of South Africa, 1967.   MH-AH; NjMD

2170. Mears, William. The Church and the Bantu. Cape Town: Methodist Book Depot and Pub. House, 1933. NN/Sch

2171. Moffat, John Smith. John Smith Moffat, C. M. G. Missionary; a Memoir. New York: Universities Press, 1969. IC/H

2172. ----- The Lives of Robert & Mary Moffat. London: T. Fisher Unwin, 1885.   MiBsA

2173. Moffat, Robert. Missionary Labours and Scenes in South Africa... New York and Pittsburgh: Robert Carter, 1845.
                            DHU/MO; NN/Sch; DHU/R; NjP

2174. Montgomery, Henry H. Francis Balfour of Basutoland: Evangelist and Bishop... London: Society for the Propagation of the Gospel in Foreign Parts, 1925.   DLC

2175. Morshead, Anne Elisabeth. Mary Anderson. A Pioneer and Founder; Reminiscences of Some Who Knew Robert Gray, First Bishop of Cape Town and Metropolitan South Africa. n. p. : Skeffington & Son, 1905.   NNMR

2176. Nash, J. O. "Education Problems in South Africa." East and West (14; Ja., 1916), pp. 25-32.   DHU/R
        The Church and Christian involvement in education in South Africa.

2177. Northcott, William Cecil. Robert Moffat: Pioneer in Africa, 1817-1870. New York: Harper, 1961. MiBsA; NjP; MNtcA
        Missions in South Africa.

2178. Nunns, Theodora. The Land of Storms and Hope. A Short History of the English Church in South Africa. Wynberg: Rustica Press, 1921.   NN/Sch

2179. Oglethorpe, James. "Crisis in Dutch Reformed Churches." Africa South in Exile (5:3, Apr. -Je., 1961), pp. 44-48.
                                     DAU; DHU; DHU/MO

2180. Olinton, Desmond Kenilworth. The South African Melting Pot: A Vindication of Missionary Policy 1799-1836. London: Longman-Green, 1937.
                                             NN/Sch

2181. Orchard, Ronald Kenneth. Tomorrow's Men in Africa. London: Livingstone Press, 1948.   NN/Sch

2182. Oosthuizen, Gerhadus C. Shepherd of Lovedale.
Johannesburg: Keartland, 1970.   MiBsA

2183. "The Outer Pocket. A Missionary Wrties from the Union
of South Africa." The Crisis (21: 1, Nov., 1920), p. 20.
DHU/MO; DLC
Letter to the editor written by H. A. Payne and how
how he received "a most unwelcome and humiliating landing
at Cape Town."

2184. Paterson, Edward. "The Church's Work at Cyrene, South
Africa." East and West Review (2; 1936), pp. 133-41. DHU/R

2185. Paton, Alan C. Apartheid and the Archbishop: The Life and
Times of Geoffrey Clayton. New York: Scribner's, 1973. DHU/R

2186. Paton, David MacDonald, (ed.). Church and Race in South
Africa. Papers from South Africa, 1952-57, illustrating the
Churches' Search for the Will of God. London: SCM Press, 1958.
DHU/MO; NN/Sch

2187. Paton, William. The White Man's Burden...
London: The Epworth Press, 1939.   DLC

2188. Patterson, Sheila. Colour and Culture in South Africa:
A Study of the Status of the Cape Coloured People Within the
Social Structure of the Union of South Africa. n.p.: Routledge
& Paul, 1953.   DHU/MO

2189. Pederson, Pernie C. Mission in South Africa; Studies in
the Beginning and Development of the Indigenous Lutheran
Church in the Union of South Africa. Minneapolis, Minn.:
Augsburg Pub. House, 1957.   NN/Sch

2190. Philip, John. Researches in South Africa; Illustrating the
Civil, Moral, and Religious Condition of the Native Tribes,
Including Journals of the Author's Travels in the Interior,
Together With Detailed Accounts of the Progress of the British
Christian Missions, Exhibiting the Influence of Christianity in
Promoting Civilization. n.p.: James Duncan, 1828.
Ic/H; MiBsA
"Reprint 1968."

2191. Phillips, Ray E. The Bantu are Coming; Phases of South
Africa's Problem London: S.C.M. Press, 1930. NN/Sch
The Christian Mission in relation to industrial problems in
Asia and Africa--the official statement of the International
Missionary Council, pp. 219-36.

2192. Plaatje, Solomon Tshekisho. Mhudi; An Epic of South African
Native Life a Hundred Years Ago.
Lovedale, South Africa: Lovedale Press, 1930. DLC; NN/Sch
DHU/MO

2193. Presbyterian Church in the U.S.A. Board of Foreign Missions.
Historical Sketches of the Missions under the Care of the...
Philadelphia: Woman's Foreign Missionary Society of the
Presbyterian Church, 1886.   DHU/R
Includes chapter on South Africa.

2194. Price, Elizabeth Lees (Moffat). Journals Written in Bech-
uland, Southern Africa, 1854-1883; With an Epilogue: 1889
and 1900. Edited with Introd., Annotations, etc. by Una Long
for Rhodes University, Grahamstown, South Africa. London:
E. Arnold 1956.

2195. Puaux, Frank. Les Bassoutos; une mission Francais
au Sud l'Afrique. Paris: Librarie G. Fishbacher, 1881.
NN/Sch

2196. Pudule, Elias Stowell. The Role of an Africanist Ideology
in the Religious Struggle: a Study of the Congregation of Christ
of South Africa. Masters thesis. Howard University, 1973.

2197. Read, A.C. "Have we Spoilt the Natives in South Africa?"
The East and the West (5; Jl., 1907), pp. 304-14.   DHU/R

2198. Reuling, Eleanor S. First Saint to the Zulus. Boston:
American Board of Commissioners for Foreign Missions,
1960. DLC; MBU-T; H-I-AH; CBPac; NjR

2199. Ricardo, James D. The Catholic Church and the Kaffir.
London: Burns, 1880.   NjP

2200. Robertson, Henrietta. Mission Life Among the Zulu Kirfirs.
A Memoir of Henrietta, Wife of the Rev. R. Robertson, S. P. G.
Missionary, Compiled from Letters and the Journals Written to
the Late Bishop MacKenzie and His Sisters. Edited by Anne
MacKenzie. London: Bemrose, 1875.   DHU/R
Microfilm.

2201. Ross, Brownlee John. Brownlee J. Ross, His Ancestry and
Some Writings. Lovedale: C.P., So. Africa, Lovedale Press,
1948.   NN/Sch

2202. Sadler, Celia, (ed.). Never a Young Man. Extracts From
the Letters and Journals of the Rev. William Shaw. Capetown:
Haum, 1967.   DHU/MO

2203. Sales, Jane Magorian. The Mission Station as an Agency of
"Civilization"; the Development of a Coloured Christian
Community in the Eastern Cape Colony, 1800-1859. Doctoral
dissertation. University of Chicago, 1972.

2204. ----- The Planting of the Churches in South Africa. Grand
Rapids, Mich.: Eerdmans, 1971. MiBsA; NjP; MNtcA

2205. Sales, Richard, (ed.). Christofersen, Arthur Fridjof,
Adventuring With God: The Story of the American Board
Mission in South Africa. Durban: Inanda Seminary, 1967.
DLC

2206. Scenes and Services in South Africa. The Story of Robert
Moffat's half-century of Missionary Labours... London:
J. Snow, 1876.   NN/Sch

2207. Schebesta, P. P. Portuoals Konguistamission in Südost-
Afrika: Missions geschichte Sambesiens und des Monomota-
pareiches 1560-1920. St. Augustin: Steyler, 1966-7. NjP

2208. Schimlek, Francis. Against the Stream, Life of Father
Bernard Huss, C. M. M., The Social Apostle of the Bantu.
Mariannhill: Mariannhill Press, 1949.   DLC

2209. Schlyter, Herman. The History of the Cooperating Missions
in Natal, 1912-1951. Durban: Lutheran Pub. House, 1953.
CtY-D

2210. Shaw, Barnabas. Memorials of South Africa. New York:
Negro Universities Press, 1970. MiBsA; NjP
Missions in South Africa, Methodist Church.

2211. Shaw, William. Memoir of the Rev. William Shaw...
London: Wesleyan Conference Office, 1874.   PPT

2212. ----- The Story of My Mission Among Native Tribes of
South Africa. London: Wesleyan Mission House, 1872.
NN/Sch

2213. Shepherd, Robert Henry Wishart. Bantu Literature and Life.
South Africa: Lovedale Press, 1955.   NN/Sch

2214. ----- Children of the Veld: Bantu Vignettes. London:
J. Clarke & Co., Ltd., 1937.   MNtcA

2215. ----- Lovedale, South Africa. n.p.: Lovedale Press, n.d.
IC/H

2216. ----- Where Aloes Flames; South African Missionary
Vignettes. London: Lutterworth Press, 1948.   NN/Sch

2217. Smit, M.T.R. African Greatheart; the Story of Cornelius
Sejosing. London: Lutterworth Press, 1945.   NN/Sch

2218. Smith, Charles Spencer, (bp.). The Relations of the British
Government to the Natives of South Africa. Address of Bishop
C. S. Smith, Resident Bishop of the African Methodist Episcopal
Church in South Africa, 1904-1906, Delivered at the Negro Young

People's Christian and Education Congress, in Convention Hall, Washington, D. C., Wednesday, August 1, 1906. (Wash., D. C.: n.p., 1906)   NN/Sch
Negro author.

2219. Smith Edwin W. The Blessed Missionaries, Being the Phelps-Stokes Lectures Delivered in Cape Town in 1949. Cape Town: Oxford University Press, 1950.   NN/Sch

2220. ----- The Life and Times of Daniel Lindley (1808-80). Missionary to the Zulus. New York: Literary Publishers, 1952.   NN/Sch; DHU/MO

2221. ----- The Religion of Lower Races, as Illustrated by the African Bantu. New York: Macmillan Co., 1923.   NN/Sch

2222. ----- Robert Moffat, One of God's Gardeners. London: Student Christian Movement, 1925.   DHU/R
Biography which seeks to place Moffat in the historical and ethnological setting of South Africa.

2223. ----- The Shrine of a People's Soul. New York: Friendship Press, 1947.   DHU/R; MNtcA
"Missionary in South Africa and Northern Rhodesia writes of the literary work of the missionary."

2224. Smith, J. Allister. A Zulu Apostle, Joel Mbambo Matunfwa. London: Salvationist Pub. and Supplies, 1953.   NN/Sch

2225. Snell, C. D. "Missions and Problems in South Africa." Church Missionary Review (63; Jl., 1912), pp. 420-26. DHU/R

2226. Snipes, Esther Wacknitz. The Advance of Culture in Bantu Africa. Master's thesis. College of Missions, 1925. TN/DCHS
Disciples of Christ (Christian Churches) and missions in Africa.

2227. Snipes, Percy Doyle. Social Ethics of the Bantu. Master's thesis. College of Missions, 1924.   TN/DCHS
Disciples of Christ (Christian Churches) and missions in Africa.

2228. "South Africa." The American Quarterly Register (6:2, Nov., 1833), pp. 94-96.   DHU/R

2229. "South African Bishops." Commonweal (79; Mar. 13, 1964) pp. 704-05.   DHU

2230. "South African Churches Asked to Consultation." Interchurch News (1; Jl., 1960), p. 1.   DLC

2231. South African Deputation Papers: Presenting Some Aspects and Problems of the Work of the two South African Missions of the American Board, Prepared for the Information of the Deputation of 1903. Natal: American Zulu Mission, 1904.
MNtcA

2232. Starbuck, Charles C. "South Africa." Andover Review (8:46, Oct., 1887), pp. 427-38.   DHU/R

2233. ----- "Southern Africa." Andover Review (12; 69, Sept., 1889), pp. 314-24.   DHU/R

2234. Strassberger, Elfriede. The Rhenish Mission Society in South Africa, 1830-1950. Cape Town: C. Struik, 1969.
MiBsA; NjP

2235. Student Christian Association. Christian Students and Modern South Africa. A Report of the Bantu-European Student Christian Conference. Fort Hare, June 27-July 3, 1930. Fort Hare: Alice C.P., 1930.   DHU/MO

2236. Taylor, James D. "Native Progress in Natal." Southern Workman (38:1, Ja., 1909), pp. 27-36.   DLC; DHU/MO

2237. Taylor, William, (bp.). Christian Adventures in South Africa... New York: Nelson & Phillips, 1877. NN/Sch

2238. Thomas M. "Mariannhill: The Work of the Catholic Trappist in South Africa." The Crisis (25:2, Dec., 1922), pp. 63-5.
DHU/MO; DLC

2239. Tindall, Joseph. The Journal of Joseph Tindall, Missionary in South West Africa, 1839-1855. Cape Town: Van Riebeeck Society, 1959.   DHU/MO

2240. Tlou, Thomas. The Batawana of Northwestern Botswana and Christian Missionaries- 1877-1906. Lusaka, Zambia: Conference on the History of Central African Religions 30 Ag. - 8 Sept., 1972. Pam. File, DHU/R
mim.

2241. Trollope, Anthony. South Africa. 2 Vols. London: Dawson, 1968.   DHU/MO
Reprint of 1878 edition.

2242. "Two Views on Race: Archbishop W. P. Whelan and South African Bishops' Conference." America (110; Mr. 14, 1964), p. 328.   DHU

2243. Tyler, Josiah. "Missionary Experiences Among the Zulus." J. W. E. Bowen, (ed.). African and the American Negro: Addresses and Proceedings of the Congress on Africa (Miami, Fla.: Mnemosyne Publishing Co., Inc., 1969), pp. 117-18.
DHU/R

2244. "Umtwalumi, An Industrial School in South Africa." Southern Workman (5:8, Ag., 1876), p. 61.   DLC; DHU/MO
The building of the Umtwalumi Mission Station.

2245. "A Unique Foreign Mission, A Work Kindred to Hampton's In South Africa." The Lovedale Industrial Mission. Southern Workman (23:1, Ja., 1894), pp. 13-15. DLC; DHU/MO
"The Rev. Dr. James Stewart and Mrs. Stewart, from the Lovedale Mission, under the Free Church of Scotland, in Cape Colony South Africa give an interesting account of their work."

2246. Van der Merwe, Willem J. The Development of Missionary Attitudes in the Dutch Reformed Church in South Africa. Doctoral dissertation. Hartford Seminary Foundation, 1934.

2247. Victor, Osmund. The Salient of South Africa. London: Society for the Propagation of the Gospel in Foreign Parts, 1931.   N & P; NN/Sch

2248. Vilakazi, A. Isonto Lamanazeretha: The Zulu Church of the Nazarites in South Africa. Masters thesis. Kennedy School of Mission, (Hartford, Conn.) 1954.

2249. Visser't Hooft, Willem Adolph. Christianity, Race and South African People: Report on an Ecumenical Visit. New York: World Council of Churches, 1952.
TxDAM; CtY; IEN; NcD

2250. Walters, William. Life and Labours of Robert Moffat, Missionary in South Africa. London: W. Scott, 1885.
MiBsA; MNtcA

2251. Watts, C. C. "Up-Country Work in South Africa." The East and The West (17; Apr., 1919), pp. 145-51. DHU/R

2252. Welsh, David. The Roots of Segregation. Native Policy in Colonial Natal, 1845-1910. London: Oxford Press, 1971.
DHU/R
Deals with system created by Sir Theophilus Shepstone in Natal for the administration of the Zulu people. His policy was the precursor of aparthied. Chapters on Missionaries and the Shepstonian System.

2253. White, Amos Jerome. Dawn in Bantuland; an African Experiment; or, An Account of Missionary Experiences and Observations in South Africa. Boston: Christopher Pub. House, 1953.
Negro author.

2254. Whiteside, J. History of the Wesleyan Methodist Church of
South Africa. London: Eliot Stock, 1906.   NNMR

2255. Widdicombe, John. Fourteen Years in Basutoland. A
Sketch of African Mission Life. London: The Church Printing
Co., 1891.   DHU/MO

2256. Williams, Donovan. When Races Meet: the Life and Times
of William Ritchie Thomson, Glasgow Society Missionary, Government Agent and Dutch Reformed Church Minister, 1794-1891.
Johannesburg: A. P. B. Publishers, 1967.   NjP

2257. Willoughby, William Charles. "Khama: A Bantu Reformer."
International Review of Missions (13; 1924), pp. 74-83. DHU/R

2258. Wirgman, A. Theodore. English Church and People in South
Africa. New York: Negro Universities Press, 1969. DHU/R

2259. World Council of Churches. Report on the World Council of
Churches' Mission in South Africa, April-December 1960.
Geneva: n. p., 1961.   NcD; DLC

2260. Woronoff, Jon. "Black Policies for South Africa." Worldview (15:8, Ag., 1972), pp. 18-21.   DHU/R

2261. Wright, Charlotte. Beneath the Southern Cross; the Story
of an American Bishop's Wife in South Africa. New York:
Exposition Press, 1955.   OWibfU; DHU/MO; NN/Sch; DLC;
TNF; CtY-D

2262. Wright, Richard Robert, Jr., (bp.). "South Africa Has
Its Own Color Line." Opportunity (27:5, My., 1939), pp. 138-
41.   DHU/MO
       Negro author.

2263. ----- (bp.). "Wilberforce in South Africa." Opportunity
(13; Oct., 1934), pp. 306-10.   DHU/MO
       Negro author.

2264. Wright William. Slavery at the Cape of Good Hope. New
York: Negro Universities Press, 1969.   DHU/R
       Originally published in 1831 by John Rodwell, London.
       Includes section on religious instruction of the slaves.

2265. "The Y. M. C. A. in South Africa." Southern Workman
(53:8, Ag., 1924), pp. 339-40.   DLC; DHU/MO
       An editorial.

2266. Zululand, Wilmot. "A Native Episcopate for South Africa."
East and West (19; Ja., 1921), pp. 50-53. DHU/R

2267. ----- "Zululand Today." The East and the West (6; Apr.,
1908), pp. 153-9.   DHU/R
       Christian missionaries a cause of unrest in Zululand.

p. Sudan
2268. Beacham, C. New Frontiers in the Central Sudan. Toronto Evangelical Publishers, 1928.   NN/Sch

2269. Beshir, Mohamed Omer. The Southern Sudan: Background
to Conflict. New York: Praeger, 1968.   DHU/MO
       A study of pagan and Catholic peoples.

2270. Bingham, Rowland V. Seven Sevens of Years and a Jubilee!
The Story of the Sudan Interior Mission. New York: Evangelical Publishers, 1943.   NN/Sch

2271. Chapman, William. A Pathfinder in South Central Africa.
A Story of Pioneer Missionary Work and Adventure. London:
W. A. Hammond, 1910.   NN/Sch

2272-73. Collins, Robert Oakley. The Southern Sudan, 1883-
1898: A Struggle for Control. New Haven: Yale University
Press, 1962.   DLC
       Discussion of the Mahdist state.

2274-75. Fuller, W. Harold. Run While the Sun is Hot. New
York: Sudan Interior Mission, 1967.   DLC
       Work of the Sudan Interior Mission and related bodies.

2276. Geyer, Franz Xaver, (bp.). Durch Sand, Sumpf und Wald;
Missionsreisen in Zentral-Afrika; mit 395 Bildern und 9 Karten.
Neue Ausgabe. Freiburg im Breisgau: Herdersch Verlagshand-
lung, 1914.   NN/Sch

2277. Giffen, John Kelly. The Egyptian Sudan. New York: F. H.
Revell, 1905.   NN/Sch

2278. Gowan, Richard. "The Religious Imperative: Gordon in
the Sudan." Perspective (11; Wint., 1970), pp. 319-32.
                                          DHU/R

2279. Gwynne, L. H. "Missionary Work in the Sudan," Church
Missionary Review of the World (72; Sept., 1926), pp. 245-50.
                                          DHU/R

2280. Hofmayr, F. S. C., P. W. "Religion der Schilluk."
Anthropos (6:1, Ja.-Feb., 1911), pp. 120-31.

2281. Kumm, Herman K. W. The Sudan; a Short Compendium of
Facts and Figures About the Land of Darkness. London:
Marshall Bros., 1907.   NN/Sch

2282. ----- "Sudan an Unevangelized Land." Missionary Review
of the World (27; Mr., 1904), pp. 212-6. DHU/R

2283. Milligan, Robert H. The Jungle Folk of Africa... New York:
F. H. Revell Co., 1908.   NN/Sch

2284-85. Mills, W. L. "Work in Eastern Kordofan." East
and West Review (4; 1938), pp. 65-71.   DHU/R
       Missionary work in the Sudan.

2286. "Outposts of the Nile." Presbyterian Church in U. S. A.
Film.
       Foundation work of Christian leaders in building a national
       church in the southern Sudan.

2287. Percy, Douglas Cecil. Doctor to Africa; the Story of
Stirrett of the Sudan. New York: Sudan Interior Mission,
1948.   NN/Sch

2288. Sudan United Mission. Executive Committee. Annual Report
and Review. 190- NN/Sch

2289. Trimingham, John Spencer. The Christian Approach to
Islam in the Sudan. London: New Oxford Univ. Press, 1948.
                                          NN/Sch

2290. Trimingham, John Spencer. The Christian Church in Post-
War Sudan. London: World Dominion Press, 1949. DLC; MH;
NcD

2291. Watson, Charles R. The Sorrow and Hope of the Egyptian
Sudan: A Survey of Missionary Conditions and Methods of
Work in the Egyptian Sudan. Philadelphia: Board of Foreign
Missions of the United Presbyterian Church of North America,
1913.   DLC

q. Tanzania (Tanganyika and Zanzibar) and Madagascar
2292. American Sunday School Union. History of Madagascar;
Embracing the Progress of the Christian Mission and an
Account of the Persecution of the Native Christians. Philadelphia: American Sunday School Union, 1839. NN/Sch

2293. Auf Der Maur, Ivo. "Beitrag der Benediktiner-Missionäre
von St. Ottilien in Tansania zur Liturgchen Erneuerung
"(1887-1970)." Neue Zeitschrift für Missionswissenschaft
(Schöneck, Suisse) (27:2, 1971), pp. 126-35. DCU/TH

2294. Bernander, Gustav A. Lutheran Wartime Assistance to
Tanzanian Churches, 1940-1945. Lund: Gleerup, 1968.
                                          CtHC

2295. Birkeli, Fridtjor. "The Church in Madagasar." International Review of Missions (46; 1957), pp. 155-63. DHU/R

2296. Boudou, Adrien. Les Jesuites a Madagascar au XIX. Siecle.
Paris: Beauchesne, 1942. 2 Vols.   NB; NN

2297. ----- Le Père Jacques Berthieu de la Compagnie de Jesus,
Missionnaire à Madagascar. Tananarive: Imprimerie Catholique, 1933.   NB; CtY-D

2298. Briggs, J. In the East African War Zone. London: Church
Missionary Society, 1918.   NN/Sch

2299. Camboue, S. J., P. Paul. "Education et Instruction en
Madagascar." Anthropos (10-11: 5, 6, Sept.-Dec., 1915-16),
pp. 844-60.   DLC
     S. J.: Society of Jesus. Missionnarie du district de N. D.
     de Lourdes d'Ambohiberloma, Madagascar Central.

2300. Chambers, George Alexander. Tanganyika's New Day.
London: Church Missionary Society, 1931. IEN; CtY; NjPT;
CtY-D; CSt-H

2301. Chirgwin, A. M. "The Growth of the Church in Madagascar."
International Review of Missions (22; 1933), pp. 94-104. DHU/R

2302. ----- "Madagascar as a Mission Field." Congregational
Quarterly (10; 1932), pp. 294-300.   DHU/R

2303. Clinch, B. J. "Roman Catholic Missions in Madagascar."
American Catholic Quarterly Review (18; 1893), p. 392+.
CtY; MH; DCU; DLC; DGU; ICU; RPB

2304. Cole, Henry. Children of the Dark Continent. Foreword by
the Rev. Canon Copner. London: F. Griffieths, 1933. NN/Sch

2305. Copland, Samuel. A History of the Island of Madagascar,
Comprising a Political Account of the Island, the Religion,
Manners, and Customs of the Inhabitants, and Its Natural Production; With an Appendix Containing a History of Several Attempts to Introduce Christianity into the Island. London: 1822.
                                       NN/Sch

2306. Cornish, Robert Kestell. Journal of a Tour of Exploration
in the North of Madagascar by the Right Reverend Bishop Kestell
Cornish, June 15-October 22, 1876. London: Society of the
Propagation of the Gospel in Foreign Parts, 1877. NK; IEN;
OU; DHU/MO; NN/Sch

2307. Couve, Daniel. "Co-operation in Madagascar." International
Review of Missions (3; 1914), pp. 313-22.   DHU/R

2308. Crouzet. ...Dix ans d'Apostolat Dans le Vicariat Apostolique
de Madagascar Meriodional, 1896-1905. Lille: Desclee, de
Brouwer et cie, 1912.

2309. Decary, Raymond. Moeurs et Coutumes des Malgaches.
Paris: Payot, 1951. DLC; CU; OCI; NN; PU; PU-Mu; WU;
KU; CSt; CtY
     A general study which includes information on social organ-
     ization and religion.

2310. Deschamps, Hubert Jules. Les Antaisaka. Tanarive:
Pilot de la Beaujardiere, 1936. ND; DLC; CtY; NNC

2311. Dubois, Henri Marie. La Mission de Madagascar Betsiléo.
PP. Jésuites Francais (Province de Champagne) Son Histoire,
son Organisation, ses Oeuvres. Lille, France: Procure des
Missions, 1925.   NN/Sch

2312. Eggert, Johanna. Missionsschule und Sozialer Wandel in
Ostafrika; der Beitrag der Deutschen Evangelischen Missions-
gesellschaften Zur Entwicklung des Schulwesens in Tanganyika
1891-1939. Bielefeld: Bertelsmann Universitätsverlag, 1970.
NjP

2313. Ellis, William. History of Madagascar. Comprising also
the Progress of the Christian Mission Established in 1818;

and an Authentic Account of the Persecution and Recent Martyrdom of the Native Christians. Comp. chiefly from original documents, by the Rev. Wm. Ellis, London: Fisher, Son & Co.,
1838.   NN/Sch

2314. ----- Madagascar Revisited. Describing the Events of a
New Reign and the Revolution Which Followed; Setting Forth
also the Persecutions Endured by the Christians, and Their
Heroic Sufferings, With Notices of the Present State and
Prospects of the People... London: J. Murray, 1867.
                                       NN/Sch

2315. ----- The Martyr Church. A Narrative of the Introduction,
Progress, and Triumph of Christianity in Madagascar. With
Notices of Personal Intercourse and Travel in that Island.
London: J. Snow, 1870.   NN/Sch

2316. ----- and James Cameron. "Christianity in Madagascar."
Missionary Herald (50:2, Feb., 1854), pp. 54-56. DHU/R

2317. Frank, Cedric N. The Life of Bishop Steere; a Christian
Interpreter in East Africa. Dar es Salaam, Africa: Eagle Pr.,
1953. ANAU; CSt-H; IU; NcD; IEN; ITU; MH; DHU/MO

2318. Freeman, Joseph and John D. A Narrative of the Persecution
of the Christians in Madagascar; With Details of the Escape of
Six Christian Refugees, Now in England. London: Snow, 1840.
DLC; CtY; OCI; MiD; MH

2319. Gale, William Kendell. Church Planting in Madagascar.
With a foreward by Dr. T. Cochrane... London: The World
Dominion Press, 1937.   NN/Sch

2320. Gamperle, Lukas. "Examples of Christian Political Commitment in Tanzania." Concilium (4:9, 1973), pp. 146-51.
                                       DAU/W

2321. Groselaude, Étienne. ...Un Parisien à Madagascar;
Aventures et Impressions de Voyage. Ouvrage Illustré de
138 Gravures. Paris: Hachette, 1898.   NN/Sch

2322. Hardyman, J. "Church, Politics and Nationalism in Madagasar." International Review of Missions (37; 1948), pp.
194-97.   DHU/R

2323. ----- "A History of the Church in Madagascar." Bulletin
of the Society for African Church History (3:1-2, 1969-70),
pp. 105-08.   DHU/R

2324. ----- Madagascar on the Move. London: Livingstone Press,
1950.   DHU/MO

2325. Hawkins, F. H. "The Centenary of Missions in Madagascar."
International Review of Missions (9; 1920), pp. 570-80. DHU/R

2326. ----- "Christian Missions in Madagascar." The East and
The West (12; Apr., 1914), pp. 121-36.   DHU/R

2327. Hore, Edward Goode. Missionary to Tanganyika, 1877-1888:
The Writings of Edward Coode Hore, Masted Mariner. Edited
by James B. Wolf. London: F. Cass, 1971. DHU/MO;
DHU/R

2328. ----- Tanganyika; Eleven Years in Central Africa. London:
Stanford, 1892.   NN/Sch

2329. Jacques, Oliver. Africa Called Us. Washington, D.C.:
Review and Herald Pub. Assoc., 1952.   NN/Sch

2330. Johnson, Donald E. The Doctrine of the Church as Related
to Church and Society in Northern Tanganyika. Masters thesis.
The Biblical Seminary in New York, 1958.

2331. Jouen, Louis. "Le Christianisme à Madagascar." Revue
de l'Orient (12; 1852), p. 41.   CtY; NN

2332. Keck, Daniel. Histoire des Origines du Christianisme à
Madagascar. Paris: Impr. de Caix, 1898. NK; TxDAM; MH

2333. Kibira, Josiah. "The Church in Buhaya: Crossing Frontiers." The Church Crossing Frontiers (Uppsala, Sweden:
Gleerup, 1969), pp. 190-205.   DHU/R
    North-Western Diocese of the Evangelical Lutheran Church
    in Tanzania.

2334. King, G. L. "The Preparation of a Native Ministry." The
East and The West (7; Apr., 1909), pp. 162-74.   DHU/R
    Madagascar.

2335. Kootz-Kretschmer, Elise. Sichyajunga; ein Leben Unruhe.
Herrnhut: Missions-Buchhandlung, 1938.   CtY-D

2336. La Vaissiere, Camille de. Histoire de Madagascar, ses
Habitants et ses Missionnaires, par le p. de La Vaissiere...
Paris: V. Lecoffre, 1884.   NN/Sch

2337. Lhande, Pierre. Madagascar, 1832-1932. Paris: Plon,
1932.   NN/Sch

2338. Mac Mahon, Edward Oliver. Christian Missions in Madagascar. Westminister Society for the Promotion of the Gospel,
1914.   CtY; NjPT; NcD

2339. Madagascar for Christ; Impressions of Nine Missionary
Visitors to Madagascar, July to October, 1913. Paris:
P. M. S., 1914.   NN/Sch

2340. Munthe, Ludvig. La Bible à Madagascar. Les Deux Premières Traductions du Nouveau Testament Malgache. Oslo:
Egede Instituttet, 1969.   DLC
    Book review by T. T. Hardyman in Journal of Religion
in Africa (5:2, 1973), pp. 156-58.   DHU/R

2341. Newman, Henry Stanley. Banani; the Transition from
Slavery to Freedom in Zanzibar and Pemba. New York:
Negro Universities Press, 1969. IC/H; NjP

2342. Nyblade, Orville W. "An Idea of Theological Education in
Tanzania." Africa Theological Journal (3; Mr., 1970), pp.
69-79.   DHU/R

2343. Raum, Johannes. "Educational Problems in Tanganyika
Territory." International Review of Missions (19; 1930),
pp. 563-75.   DHU/R
    German Christian missions in Tanganyika.

2344. Richardson, James. Lights and Shadows; or Chequered
Experiences Among Some of the Heathen Tribes of Madagascar. The London Missionary Society, 1877. NN/Sch

2345. Rugambwa, Laurian. "Bishop of Tanganyika: Made a
Cardinal by Pope John XXIII." Negro History Bulletin
(24; Ja., 1961), pp. 94-95.   DHU/MO

2346. Rusillon, Henry. "The Effect of the Gospel on the Natives
of Madagascar." International Review of Missions (23; 1934),
pp. 530-8.   DHU/R

2347. Shaw, George A. Madagascar of To-day: An Account of
the Island its People, Resources and Development. London:
Religious Tract Society, 1886.   CtY

2348. Sibree, James. "Christian Missions in Madagascar."
The East and the West (7; Ja., 1909), pp. 26-39. DHU/R

2349. ----- Fifty Years in Madagascar: Personal Experiences
of Mission Life and Work... Boston: Houghton Mifflin,
1924.   NN/Sch

2350. ----- Madagascar and its People. London: The Religious
Tract Society, 1870. DLC; IEN; PPCC; PPWa; PPL; PU;
CtY

2351. Sicard, Siguard von. "The First Ecumenical Conference in
Tanzania, 1911." The Bulletin of the Society for African Church
History (2:4, 1968), pp. 323-33.   DHU/R

2352. ----- The Lutheran Church on the Coast of Tanzania 1887-
1914. With Special Reference to the Evangelical Lutheran
Church in Tanzania. Synod of Uzaramo-Uluguru. Gleerup:
n. p., 1970.   DHU/R

2353. Smith, Herbert Maynard. Frank Bishop of Zanzibar; the
Life of Frank Weston, D. D., 1871-1924. London: Society
for Promoting Christian Knowledge. New York: Macmillan,
1926.   NN/Sch; DHU/R

2354. Stirling, Leader. Bush Doctor; Being Letters from Dr.
Leader Stirling, Tanganyika Territory. Westminster, London:
Published by Parrett & Neves for the Universities' Mission to
Central Africa, 1947.   NN/Sch

2355. Strawbridge, Jean A. A Missionary Survey of Tanganyika;
an Analysis of the Work of Eighteen Missions Active in
Tanganyika. Masters thesis. Columbia Bible College, (S. C.),
1954.

2356. Stuart-Watt, Eva. Africa's Dome of Mystery. Comprising
the First Descriptive History of the Wachagga People of
Kilimanjaro, Their Evangelization, and a Girl Pioneer Climb
to the Crater of Their 19,000 ft. Snow Shrine. London:
Marshall, Morgan & Scott, 1930.   NN/Sch

2357. Swanson, S. Hjalmar. Touring Tanganyika. Rock Island,
Ill.: Augustana Book Concern, 1948. MSL/CH
    Lutheran missions in Africa.

2358. Vaagenes, Morris G. C., Jr. A Definitive Biography of
Dr. John O. Dyrnes, Missionary to South Madagascar from
1900-1943. Masters thesis. Luther Theological Seminary,
(St. Paul), Minnesota, 1970.

2359. Webster, Allan Neill. ...Madagascar. London: Society
for the Propagation of the Gospel in Foreign Parts, 1932.
                                                NN/Sch

2360. White, Paul Hamilton Hume. ...Doctor of Tanganyika.
Illustrated by Thirty-four Original Photographs Taken by
the Author. London: Paternoster Press, 1952. NN/Sch

2361. ----- ...Jungle Doctor's Enemies. With thirty-two
illustrations by Harry Swain and Boothroyd. London:
Paternoster Press, 1951.   NN/Sch

2362. Wright, Marcia. German Evangelical Missions in
Tanganyika, 1891-1939, With Special Reference to the Southern
Highlands. Doctoral dissertation. University of London,
1966.
    Also: Oxford: Clarendon Press, 1971.   DLC

r. Zaire (Belgian Congo), Uganda and Rwanda

2363. Alexis, M. G. La Barbarie Africaine et l'Action Civilisatrice des Missions Catholiques au Congo et dans l'Afrique
Equatoriale. Liege: H. Dessain, 1889.   CU; NBuU

2364. Almquist, Lars Arden. Covenant Missions in Congo;
Issued under the Auspices of the Board of Missions of the
Evangelical Covenant Church of America. Chicago Covenant
Press, 1958.   MNtcA

2365. Andre, Marie. Les Martyrs Noirs de L'Ouganda. Paris:
Bloudeet Gay, 1936.   NN/Sch

2366. Anet, Henri. Message of the Congo Jubilee and West Africa
Conference, Leopoldville, Congo Belge, Africa, Sept. 15,
to 23, 1928. Leopoldville, Congo Belge: Conseil Protestant
du Congo, 1929.   NN/Sch

2367. ----- "Protestant Missions in Belgian Congo." International Review of Missions (28; 1939), pp. 415-25. DHU/R

2368. Arnot, Frederick Stanley. Bihé and Garenganze; or, Four
Years' Further Work and Travel in Central Africa... London:
J. E. Hawkins, 1893.   NN/Sch

2369. ----- Missionary Travels in Central Africa. London: A Holness, 1914. NN/Sch

2370. Ashe, Robert P. Chronicles of Uganda. New York: Randolph, 1895. MNtcA; DHU/R

2371. Axelson, Sigbert. Culture Confrontation in the Lower Congo. Falkoping, Sweden: Gummessons, 1970. DHU/R
A Doctoral Dissertation written under the Theological Faculty of the Univ. of Uppsala which focuses on the clash of cultures with special reference to the Swedish Missionaries in the 1880's and 1890's.

2372. Baesten, V. "La Nouvelle Mission Belge de la Compagnie de Jésus dan l'Etat Independant du Congo." Precis Historiques (XLI; 1892), pp. 193-202. CtY; NN

2373. Balandier, George. Daily Life in the Kingdom of the Kongo From the Sixteenth to the Eighteenth Century. New York: Pantheon Books, 1968. DHU/MO

2374. Banks, Emily (Tiptaft). White Woman on the Congo. New York: Revell, 1943. TN/DCHS

2375. Baptist Missionary Society. Rise and Progress of the Work on the Congo River. By the Treasurer. 2d ed. London: Alexander & Sheppard, 1885. GAU

2376. Bedinger, Robert Dabney. Triumphs of the Gospel in the Belgian Congo. Richmond: Presbyterian Committee of Publication, 1920. DHU/MO

2377. "The Beginning and Formative Years of The Church in Buganda (1927-1942)." Dini Na Mila (6:1, 1972), pp. 25-36. DHU/R

2378. Bell, John. A Miracle of African Missions; the Story of Matula, a Congo Convert. New York: London: F. H. Revell Co., 1903. NN/Sch

2379. Bentley, H. Margo. W. Holman Bentley...the Life and Labours of a Congo Pioneer, by his widow, H. M. Bentley. London: Religious Tract Society, 1907. NN/Sch

2380. Beslier, Genevieve G. ...L'apotre du Congo, Mgr. Augouard; Avant-Propos de S. G. Mgr. Le Roy... Paris: Editions de la Vraie France, 1926. NN/Sch

2381. Bittremieux, P. Leo. "Overblijfselen van den Katholieken Godsdienst in Lager Kongoland." Anthropos (21:5, 6, Sept.-Dec., 1926), pp. 797-805. DLC
Scheut, Belgïe.

2382. Boone, Clinton C. Congo as I Saw It. New York: Ives, 1927. NN/Sch
Negro author.

2383. Braekman, E. M. Historie du Protestantisme du Congo. Bruxelles: Editions de la Librarie des Eclaireurs Unionistes, 1961. KyLxCB; NNUT; CoDl; CLU; NjPT

2384. Brown, H. D. "The Church and its Missionary Task in Congo." International Review of Missions (41; 1952), pp. 301-09. DHU/R

2385. Browne, Stanley G. "The Indigenous Medical Evangelists in Congo." International Review of Missions (35; Ja., 1946), pp. 59-67. DAU/W; DCU/TH

2386. Buchner. "Congo Expedition: Lecture Extract on 1878 Exploration of Lunda." Journal of American Folklore (6:4, Oct.-Dec., 1893), pp. 316-17. Pam File; DHU/R
The Black man of the Congo's non-Western approach to Religion.

2387. Burton, William F. Congo Sketches. Illustrated by the author. London: Victory Press, 1950. NN/Sch

2388. ----- Missionary Pioneering in Congo Forests. A Narrative of the labours of William F. P. Burton and his companions in the native village of LubaLand. Compiled from letters, diaries and articles by Max W. Moorhead--- Preston, Eng.: R Seed & Sons, printers, 1922. DHU/MO

2389. Buxton, T. F. V. "Uganda: A Retrospect and an Inquiry." The East and the West (3; Jl., 1905), pp. 248-61. DHU/R
Discussion of Christianity in Uganda.

2390. Calcraft, G. "Problems of Growth in Elgon." East and West Review (3; 1937), pp. 311-21. DHU/R

2391. Carpenter, George Wayland. Highways for God in Congo; Commemorating Seventy-Five Years of Protestant Missions 1878-1953. Leopoldville: La Librairie Evangelique au Congo, 1952. MNtcA; NC; IEG; CtY-D

2392. Carter, Fay. "Co-operation in Education in Uganda: Mission and Government Relations in the Inter-War Period." The Bulletin of the Society for African Church History (2:3, 1967), pp. 259-75. DHU/R

2393. Christ and the Congo: Findings of Conferences Held Under the Leadership of Dr. John F. Mott at Leopoldville, Mutoto and Elisabethville, Congo Belge, 1934. Leopoldville-Quest: Consiel Protestant du Congo. London and New York: International Missionary Council, 1934. DLC

2394. "Congo Journey." Methodist Publishing House. Film.

2395. Congo Missionary Conference. A Report of the Sixth General Conference of Missionaries of the Protestant Missionary Societies Working in Congoland. Bolobo, Congo Belge: Baptist Mission Pr., 1911. TN/DCHS

2396. Conseil Protestant du Congo. Findings of Conferences Held Under the Leadership of Dr. John R. Mott... at Leopoldville, Mutoto and Elisabethville, Congo Belge, 1934... Leopoldville-Quest, Congo Belge, Conseil Protestant du Congo. New York: International Missionary Council, 1934.

2397. Constance, Marie, (Sister). ...Essai d'Adaption... preface du Revernd Père P. Charles, S. J. Namur, Edition Grands Lacs: Anvers, En Vente Chez les Soeurs Missionaries de Notre Dame d'Afrique, 1947. NN/Sch

2398. Cook, Albert R. "The Church in Uganda To-day." International Review of Missions (20; 1931), pp. 254-64. DHU/R

2399. ----- "Forty Years in Uganda." East and West Review (3; 1937), pp. 209-17. DHU/R

2400. Coxill, H. Wakelin. "The Growth of the Church in the Congo." The East and West Review (5:1, Ja., 1939), pp. 62-9. DHU/R

2401. ----- "Protestants in the Belgian Congo." International Review of Missions (34; 1945), pp. 273-79. DHU/R

2402. Crawford, John R. "Aspects of Culture Clash in the Congo 1878-1920." Missiology (1:3, Jl., 1973), pp. 368-375. DHU/R

2403. ----- Protestant Missions in Congo, 1878-1969. Kinshasa, Democratic Republic of Congo: Librarie Evangelique du Congo, n.d. DHU/R

2404. "Crisis: Congo Fifteen Million People Search for a Nation." Methodist Publishing House. Film.
Methodist mission film.

2405. Croydon, Edward. "The Uganda Church To-Day." The Church Overseas (7; 1934), pp. 229-36. DHU/R

2406. Cultrera, Samuele. ...Eroismo ed Avventure di Missionari al Congo nel Secolo XVII. Torino: Societa Editrice Internationale, 1926.   NN/Sch

2407. Cunningham, James Frances. Uganda and Its Problems: Notes on the Protectorate of Uganda, Especially the Anthropology and Ethnology of Its Indigenous Races. London: Hutchinson and Co., 1905.   NN/Sch

2408. Cuvelier, Jean, (bp.). L'ancien Congo d'après les Archives Romaines (1518-1640) par Mgr. J. Cuvelier et L'Abbe L. Jadin... Bruxelles: n.p., 1954.   NN/Sch

2409. Cuypers, L. "La Coopération de l'Etat Indépendant du Congo avec les missions Catholiques." Revue D'Histoire Ecclésiastique (65:1, 1970), pp. 30-55.   DHU/R

2410. Davis, William Ellsworth. Ten Years in the Congo. New York: Sheed & Ward, 1951.   NN/Sch; TN/DCHS
      Negro author.

2411. Denis, Leopold. ...Les Jésuites Belges au Kwango, 1893-1943. Monographie sur la Mission du Kwango, Devenue Actuellement les Vicariats apostoliques du Kwango et de Kisantu. Bruxelles: L'Edition Universelle, 1943.   NN/Sch

2412. Devresse, L. Le Captaine Joubert. Leverville, Congo Belge: Bibliotheque de l'Etoile, 1951.   NN/Sch

2413. Dieu, Léon. ...Dans la Brousse Congolaise. (Les Origines des Missions de Scheut au Congo), Liège: Marechial, 1946.
                                                              NN/Sch

2414. Doering, Alma E. Leopard Spots or God's Masterpiece, Which? ...Attempting the Answer After 18 Years of Missionary Service among Races of Three Colors, White, Black, and Copper. Chicago: Evangel Pub. House, 1916.   NN/Sch

2415. Dreves, Francis M. The African Chronicles of Brother Giles. London: Sands & Co., 1929.   NN/Sch
      Story of the work accomplished in Uganda by the first missionary to set forth from England. Cf. Author's note.

2416. Duncan, Sylvia. Bonganga; Experiences of a Missionary Doctor. London: Odhama Press, 1958.   NN/Sch

2417. Dye, Eva (Nichols). Bolenge: A Story of Gospel Triumphs on the Congo. Cincinnati: FCMS, 1909.   TN/DCHS; NN/Sch; DHU/MO

2418. ----- Ten Years on the Congo, 1898-1909. Cincinnati: Foreign Christian Missionary Society, 19? DHU/MO; NN/Sch; TN/DCHS

2419. L'Eglise au Congo et au Ruanda-Urundi. Bruxelles: Oeuvres Pontificales Missionaries, 1950.   NN/Sch

2420. Ellis, James J. Dan Crawford of Luanza; or, 37 Years' Missionary Work in Darkest Africa. London: Hulbert, 1927.

2421. Eucher, F. Le Congo. Essai Sur l'Histoire Religieuse de ce Pays Depuis sa Découverte (1484) Jusqu'a nos Jours. Huy (Belgium): Charpentier and Emond, 1894.   DLC; IEN; NN

2422. Evangelical Covenant Church of America. "Congo."
                                                  Pam. File, DHU/R
      Pamphlet on missionary activity of the Board of Missions of the Evangelical Covenant Church of America.

2423. Fahs, Sophia Blanche. ...Uganda's White Man of Work; a Story of Alexander M. Mackay. New York: Young People's Missionary Movement, 1907.   NN/Sch

2424. Faupel, John Francis. African Holocaust; the Story of the Uganda Martyrs. London: Chapman, 1965. IEN; CLU; NjPT; DHU/R; DHU/MO; CU

2425. Ford, W. H. "Conversion and its Recognition in Congo Converts." International Review of Missions (22; 1933), pp. 377-87.   DHU/R

2426. Frank, Louis. ...Le Congo Belge... Bruxelles: La Renaissance du Livre, 1930.   NN/Sch

2427. Fullerton, William Young. The Christ of the Congo River. London: Carey Press, 1929.   NN/Sch

2428. Gale, Hubert P. Uganda and the Mill Hill Fathers. London: Macmillan, 1959.   NN/Sch

2429. Garlick, Phyllis Louisa. Uganda Contrasts. London: Church Missionary Society, 1927.

2430. Gochet, F. Alexis M. La Barbarie Africaine et l'action Civilisatrice des Missions Catholiques au Congo et dans l'Afrique Equatoriale. Liege: Dessain, 1889.   NG; MiU

2431. Golola, Moses L. "The Origins and Development of the Seventh-Day Adventist Church in Buganda (1927-1962)." Dini Na Mila (6:1, 1972), pp. 17-24.   DHU/R

2432. Graham, Robert Haldane Carson. Under Seven Congo Kings, by R. H. Carson Graham, for Thirty-Seven Years a Missionary in Portuguese Congo. London: Carey Press, 1931. NN/Sch

2433. Grubb, Norman Percy. Christ in Congo Forests; the Story of the Heart of Africa Mission. London: Lutterworth Press, 1945.   NN/Sch

2434. Guebels, Léon. ...Les Anciens Rois de Congo... Namur: n.p., 1948.   NN/Sch

2435. Guiness, Fanny Emma. The First Christian Mission on the Congo. London: Hodder & Stoughton, 1882.   CtY; NGj; NN

2436. ----- The New World of Central Africa; With a History of the First Christian Mission on the Congo. Chicago: F. H. Revell, 1890.   NN/Sch; DHU/R

2437. Harford, Charles Forbes. Pilkington of Uganda. Chicago: Fleming H. Revell Co., 1890.   NN/Sch

2438. Harrison, Alexina (Mackay). A. M. Mackay, Pioneer Missionary of the Church Missionary Society to Uganda. New York: A. C. Armstrong and Son, 1890.   DHU/MO

2439. Hattersley, Charles W. The Baganda at Home: With One Hundred Pictures of Life and Work in Uganda. London: The Religious Tract Society, 1908.   NN/Sch

2440. Hawker, George. The Life of George Grenfell, Congo Missionary and Explorer. London: The Religious Tract Society, 1909.   DLC; OOXM

2441. Hemmens, Harry Lathey. Congo Journey. London: Carey Press, 1939.   NN/Sch

2442. Hemptinne, Jean Felix de. La Politique des Missions Protestantes au Congo. Examen du Rapport de la Conference Générale Tenue a Leopoldville, Septembre 1928. Par Monseigneur de Hemptinne. Elisabethville: Editions de l'Essor du Congo, 1929.   NN/Sch

2443. Hendrickson, Francis Harry. A Study of the Reactions of Selected Congo Missionaires Toward Presumed Criticisms of Missionary Education in Africa Presented at the Salisbury Conference on Christian Education. Doctoral dissertation. Columbia University, Teachers College, 1964.

2444. Hensey, Andrew Fitch. My Children of the Forest... With an Introduction by President Charles T. Paul. New York: George H. Doran Co., 1924.   NN/Sch

2445. Hertefelt, Marcel d', and André Coupez, (eds.). La Royaute Sacree de l'Ancien Rwanda: Texte, Traduction et Commentaire de Son Rituel. Tervuren: Musée Royal de l'Afrique Centrale, 1964.   ICU

2446. Hilgers, Walter. "The Roman Catholic Church and Development in Rwanda and Burundi." David B. Barrett (ed.). African Initiatives in Religion (Nairobi: East Africa Pub. House, 1971), pp. 253-61.   DHU/R

2447. Hulme, Kathryn Cavarly. The Nun's Story... Boston: Little Brown, 1956.   NN/Sch

2448. Industrial, Self-Supporting Missionaries. A Practical Scheme Inaugurated by the Congo Training Institute, Colwyn Bay, North Wales. Colwyn Bay: Printed by E. R. Jones, 1892?   NN/Sch

2449. Johnson, T. Broadwood. Tramps Round the Mountains of the Moon, and the Back Gate of the Congo State. Boston: D. Estes, 1909.   NN/Sch

2450. Jones, Herbert Gresford. Uganda in Transformation, 1876-1926. London: Church Missionary Society, 1926.   NN/Sch

2451. Jump, Chester Jackson and Margaret. Congo Diary. New York: American Baptist Foreign Mission Society, 1951. NN/Sch

2452. "The Kabaka of Uganda and the Church Missionary Society." The Church Missionary Review (64; Oct., 1913), pp. 626-27.   DHU/R

2453. Kavulu, David. The Uganda Martyrs. Kampala: Longmans of Uganda, 1969.   DLC

2454. Kellersberger, Julia Lake (Skinner). Congo Crosses; a Study of Congo Womanhood. Boston: The Central Committee on the United Study of Foreign Missions, 1936.   NN/Sch

2455. ----- God's Ravens. New York: Fleming H. Revell Co., 1941.   NN/Sch

2456. ----- A Life for the Congo; the Story of Althea Brown Edmiston. New York: Fleming H. Revell Co., 1947.   NN/Sch

2457. Kitching, Arthur. On the Backwaters of the Nile; Studies of Some Child Races of Central Africa. New York: C. Scribner's Sons, 1912.   NN/Sch

2458. ----- "The Present Position in Uganda." The Church Missionary Review (72: 836, Dec., 1921), pp. 303-11.   DHU/R

2459. Kittler, Glenn D. The White Fathers. Introduction by Bishop Laurian Rugambwa. New York: Harper, 1957.   NN/Sch

2460. Kiwanuka, M. S. M. Semakula. A History of Buganda: From the Foundation of the Kingdom to 1900. New York: Africana Pub. Corp., 1972.   DHU/R
      Includes references to religion.

2461. Lagergren, David. Mission and State in the Congo. Sweden: Gleerup, 1970.   DHU/R
      A study of the relations between Protestant Missions and the Congo Independent State Authorities with special reference to the Equator District, 1885-1903.

2462. Lerrigo, Peter Hugh James. Omwa? Are You Awake? New York: Fleming H. Revell Co., 1936.   NN/Sch

2463. ----- "Protestant Missions in Relation to the Future of Congo." International Review of Missions (25; Apr., 1936), pp. 227-34.   DHU/R; DAU/W; DCU/TH

2464. ----- Rockbreakers; Kingdom Building in Kongo Land... Edited by the Department of Missionary Education, Board of Education of the Northern Baptist Convention... Philadelphia: The Judson Press, 1922. DLC; MNtcA; WN/Sch

2465. Lillingston, Kathleen M. E. Glimpses of Uganda. London: Church Missionary Society, 1939.   NN/Sch

2466. Lloyd, Albert Bushnell. Apolo the Pathfinder; Who Follows? London: Church Missionary Society, 1934.   NN/Sch

2467. ----- Uganda to Khartoum; Life and Adventure on the Upper Nile. London: T. F. Unwin, 1906.   NN/Sch

2468. Loewen, Melvin J. Three Score. Elkhart, Ind.: Congo, Inland Mission and African Inter-Mennonite Mission, 1972.   NNMR
      History of a Mennonite Church in Zaire.

2469. Lory, Maris Joseph. ...Face a l'Avenir; L'Eglise au Congo Belge et au Ruanda-Urundi. Tournai: Casterman, 1958.   NN/Sch

2470. Low, D. A. Religion and Society in Buganda 1875-1900. Kampala: East African Institute of Social Research, 195?   NcD

2471. Mabie, Catharine Louise Roe. Congo Cameos. Philadelphia: Judson Press, 1952.   NN/Sch

2472. ----- Our Work on the Congo. Philadelphia: American Baptist Publication Society, 1917.   DLC

2473. MacDonnell, John de Courey. King Leopold II, His Rule in Belgium and the Congo. New York: Cassell & Co., 1905.   NN/Sch

2474. Mackay, Alexander Murdoch. A. M. Mackay, Pioneer Missionary of the Church Missionary Society of Uganda. By his Sister. New York: A. C. Armstrong, 1890. NN/Sch

2475. MacKenenzie, George S. "The Troubles in Uganda." Magazine of Christian Literature (6:5, Ag., 1892), pp. 363-72.   DLC

2476. Marvel, Tom. The New Congo. New York: Duell, Sloan, and Pearce, 1948.   DHU/MO

2477. A. M. McKay, Pioneer Missionary of the Church Missionary Society to Uganda. By his Sister... London: Cass, 1970.   DHU/R

2478. Moore, Loren Ellsworth. The Origin and Development of Education in the Congo, Belge. Master's thesis. Southern Baptist Theological Seminary, 1956.

2479. Myers, John Brown. The Congo for Christ; the Story of the Congo Mission. London: S. W. Partridge, 1911. NN/Sch

2480. ----- Thomas J. Comber, Missionary Pioneer to the Congo. Negro Univ. Press, 1888.   INU

2481. "The Native Anglican Church of Uganda." The Church Missionary Review (64; Jl., 1913), pp. 431-38. DHU/R

2482. Nelson, Robert Gilbert. Congo Crisis and Christian Mission. St. Louis: Bethany Press, 1861.   NN/Sch; TN/DCHS

2483. "News from Uganda." The Church at Home and Abroad (23; 1898), pp. 298-300.   DHU/R
      Presbyterian missions in Africa.

2484. Oldham, Joseph Houldsworth. Florence Allshorn and the Story of St. Julian's. New York: Harper, 1950. NN/Sch

2485. Padmore, George. "The Missionary Racket in Africa." The Crisis (42:7, Jl., 1935), pp. 198+. DLC; DHU/MO
      Uganda. "Missionaries in the service of imperialism."

2486. Paul, Austin. Trumpet Notes in Congo. Foreword by Howard W. Ferrin. Brooklyn: Africa Inland Mission, 1949.   NN/Sch

2487. Pearce, Gordon James Martin. Congo Background. London: Carey Kingsgate Press, 1954.   NN/Sch

2488. Peeters, Paul. Henry Beck de la Compagnie de Jesus, Missionaire au Congo Belges. Lille: Desolee de Brouwer, 1898.   NN/Sch

2489. Pierpont, Ivan de. Au Congo et aux Indes: Les Jesuites Belges aux Missions. Kwango, par Ivan de Pierpont; Ceylan, par Victor Le Cocq; Bengale Occidental. Bruxelles: C. Bulens, 1906.   NN/Sch

2490. Pirouet, M. Louise. The Expansion of the Church of Uganda from Buganda into Northern and Western Uganda between 1891 and 1914, with Special Reference to the Work of African Teachers and Evangelists. Doctoral dissertation. Makerere University College, 1968.
      University is located in Kampala, Uganda Africa.

2491. "Powder Keg in the Congo." United Church of Christ. Film.

2492. Probert, Herbert. Life and Scenes on the Congo. Phila.: n.p., 1889.   MNtcA

2493. Purvis, John Bremner. Through Uganda to Mount Elgon. New York: American Tract Society, 1909.   NN/Sch

2494. Robins, Catharine. "Rwanda: Case Study in Religious Assimilation."   CLU
      "Paper read for University of California Los Angeles, Dar es Salaam Conference, 1970."

2495. Rombauts, Hugo. ...Les Soirées de Saint-Broussebourg... Namur; Grands Lacs; Scheut-Bruxelles: Editions de Scheut, 1948.   NN/Sch

2496. Roome. William John Waterman. Apolo, the Apostle to the Pygmies. London: Marshall, Morgan & Scott, 1935.
                                                      NN/Sch

2497. ----- Through the Lands of Nyanza, Central Africa. London: Marshall, Morgan & Scott, 1920.   NN/Sch

2498. Roscoe, John. "Native Pastorate in Uganda." The East and the West (12; Oct., 1914), pp. 432-39.   DHU/R

2499. Rowling, F. "The Building of the Uganda Cathedral." The International Review of Missions (8; 1919), pp. 227-37.   DHU/R

2500. Russell, John Keith, (Bp.). Men Without God? A Study of the Impact of the Christian Message in the North of Uganda. London: Highway Pub., 1966.   MNtcA

2501. Salotti, Carlo, (Cardinal). ...La Rancon de l'Uganda... Namur: Grands Lacs, 1939.   NN/Sch

2502. Schaloff, Stanley. The American Presbyterian Congo Mission: A Study in Conflict, 1890-1921. Doctoral dissertation. Northwestern University, 1967.

2503. Scholler, Clement. Contrasts... Evolutions... Bruxelles: C. Bulens, 1941.   NN/Sch

2504. Shaloff, Stanley. "Presbyterians and Belgian Congo Exploitation." Journal of Presbyterian History (47:2, Je., 1969), pp. 173-94.   DHU/R

2505. Sheppard, William Henry. Presbyterian Pioneers in Congo. Presbyterian Committee of Publication, 1917.   NN/Sch; IC/H
      Negro author.

2506. Slade, Ruth N. English-Speaking Missions in the Congo Independent State (1878-1908). Bruxelles: Academie Royale des Sciences Coloniales, 1959. CtY; ICU; DCU; MH-P; CLU MiU; DS; DHU/MO

2507. Sly, Virgil Adolph. The Congo Mission of Disciples of Christ. Indianapolis: UCMS, 1966.   TN/DCHS

2508. ----- Report on the Congo Mission. Indianapolis: UCMS, 1946.   TN/DCHS

2509. Smith, A. C. Stanley. "The Story of the Ruanda Mission." The East and West Review (4:1, Apr., 1938), pp. 150-59.
                                                      DHU/R

2510. Smith H. Sutton. Fifty Years in Congo. Disciples of Christ at the Equator. Indianapolis: n.p., 1949.   DLC

2511. ----- "Yakusu" the Very Heart of Africa, Being Some Account of the Protestant Mission at Stanley Falls, Upper Congo. London: Marshall, n.d.   DHU/MO

2512. Snipes, Paul David. Congo Christians. (n.p.: n.p., 19?)
                                                      TN/DCHS

2513. Springer, John McKendree. Christian Conquests in the Congo. New York: Methodist Book Concern, 1927. NN/Sch

2514. ----- Pioneering in the Congo. New York: The Katanga Press, 1916.   NN/Sch

2515. Springes, Helen Emily (Chapman). Camp Fires in the Congo. Boston, Mass.: Central Committee on the United Study of Foreign Missions, 1936.   NN/Sch

2516. Stock, Sarah Geraldina. The Story of Uganda and the Victoria Nyanza Mission. New York: Fleming H. Revell, n.d.
                                              NN/Sch; DHU/R

2517. Stonelake, Alfred R. Congo, Past and Present. London: New York City, World Dominion Press, 1937.   MNtcA

2518. -----"The Missionary Situation in Congo." The International Review of Missions (8; 1919), pp. 314-30.   DHU/R

2519. Streicher, Henri. Les Bienheureux Martyrs de l'Ouganda. Alger: Maison-Carrée, 1920.   NN/Sch

2520. Sulzer, Peter. Christ Ersheint am Kongo. Heilbronn: Salzer, 1958. WU; CtY; DHU/MO; MH; NN/Sch

2521. Sweeting, Rachael. "The Growth of the Church in Buwalasi-II." The Bulletin of the Society for African Church History (3:1-2, 1969-70), pp. 15-27; (2:4, 1968), pp. 334-49. DHU/R

2522. Taylor, John Vernon. The Growth of the Church in Buganda: An Attempt at Understanding. London: SCM Press, 1958. DHU/R; OWibfu; MNtcA; DHU/MO

2523. Thoonen, J. P. Black Martyrs. London: Sheed & Ward, 1941.   DHU/MO; NN/Sch

2524. Tilsley, George Edwin. Dan Crawford, Missionary and Pioneer in Central Africa. New York: Revell, 1929.
                                                      NN/Sch

2525. Tucker, Alfred R., (bp.). "Bishop Tucker on the State of Uganda." Church Missionary Intelligencer (Oct., 1898), pp. 748-52.   CtY-D; ICU; NN

2526. -----(bp.). Eighteen Years in Uganda and East Africa. Westport, Conn.: Negro Universities Press, 1970.
                                              MiBsA; IC/H; NjP
      Reprint of the 1911 edition.

2527. Uganda, J. J., (bp.). "Buganda Teachers and Mass Movements." Church Missionary Review (69:823, Sept., 1918), pp. 304-13.   DHU/R

2528. ----- (bp.). "Marriage: Pagan and Christian." The Church Overseas (4; 1931), pp. 238-47.   DHU/R
      Uganda.

2529. ----- (bp.). "Mboga." The Church Overseas (5; 1932), pp. 52-58.   DHU/R
      Christian missions in Mboga of Zaire (Belgian Congo).

2530. United Christian Missionary Society. The Congo Mission Handbook. Indianapolis: n.p., 1955.   TN/DCHS

Disciples of Christ (Christian Churches) and Missions in Africa.

2531. United Missionary Conference on the Congo, 1902-1924. A Report of the First-Ninth Conference Generale des Missionnaires Protestants du Congo, Held et Leopoldville-Est Congo Belge, Sept. 25-Oct. 2, 1924. Leopoldville-Est., Congo Belge: Congo Protestant Council, 1902-1925. NNMR

2532. Van Ronsle, Camillus. "Le Development des Missions Catholiques dans la Colonie. Belge (Vicariat de Leopoldville)." Revue Illustrée de l'Exposition Missionaire Vaticane (11; 1925), pp. 625-30. DLC

2533. Vassal, Gabrielle M. Life in French Congo. London: Fisher Unwin, 1925. DHU/MO
Includes information on Roman Catholic missions.

2534. Warburton, Mabel C. "Uganda, 1877-1927, 'Go Forward' The Jubilee of the Mission." Church Missionary Review (73: 859, Sept., 1927), pp. 220-29. DHU/R

2535. Weatherhead, H. T. C. "Educational Experiment in Uganda." The East and The West (15; Apr. 1917), pp. 211-21. DHU/R

2536. Weeks, John H. Among Congo Cannibals. Experiences, Impressions and Adventures During a Thirty Years Sojourn Amongst the Boloki and Other Congo Tribes, With a Description of Their Curious Habits, Customs, Religions and Laws. London: Seeley, Service; Philadelphia: Lippincott, 1913. NN/Sch

2537. ----- A Congo Pathfinder: W. Holman Bentley Among African Savages. London: Religious Tract Society, 1910. NN/Sch

2538. Welbourn, Frederick Burkewood. Religion and Politics in Uganda, 1952-1962. Nairobi: East African Publishing House, 1965 NN/Sch

2539. Wells, Goldie Ruth. Sila, Son of Congo. St. Louis, Mo.: Bethany Press, 1945. NN/Sch

2540. Willis, John Jamieson, (bp.). An African Church in Building. London: Church Missionary Society, 1925. NN/Sch

2541. ----- (bp.). "Christian Missions in Uganda: A United Church." The East and the West (12; Apr., 1914), pp. 199-208. DHU/R

2542. ----- (bp.). "Christianity and the Native Government of Uganda." The Church Missionary Review (72:836, Dec., 1921), pp. 294-301. DHU/R

2543. ----- (bp.). "Church and State in Uganda." The Church Missionary Review (78:857, Mr., 1927), pp. 6-13. DHU/R

2544. ----- (bp.). "The Mission of the Uganda Church." Church Missionary Intelligencer (57; Feb., 1906), pp. 81-86. DHU/R

2545. ----- (bp.). "The Organization of the Anglican Church in Uganda." International Review of Missions (7; 1918), pp. 481-91. DHU/R

2546. ----- (bp.). "What Uganda Owes to Missions." The Church Missionary Review (76:850, Je., 1925), pp. 102-09. DHU/R

2547. Wilson, Christopher James. Uganda in the Days of Bishop Tucker. London: Macmillan, 1955. NN/Sch

2548. "Witch Doctor's Decision." Conservative Baptist Foreign Mission Society, 1956. Made by Films Afield. 25 min., sd., color, 16 mm. DLC
Film.
"A story about a witch doctor living in a 'heathen village' in the Congo who becomes a Christian when the missionaries and African Christians witness for Christ."

2549. Yates, Barbara Ann. The Missions and Educational Development in Belgian Africa, 1876-1908. Doctoral dissertation. Columbia University, 1967.

2550. Zuure, Bernard. Croyances et Pratiques Religieuses Barundi. Bruxelles: Editions de l'Essorial, 1929. DLC

s. General

2551. Aberly, John. An Outline of Missions. Philadelphia: Muhlenberg Press, 1945. MSL/CHI

2552. "Address by Dr. Blyden." President of Liberia College. To the students of Hampton Institute. Southern Workman (12:1, Ja., 1883), p. 9. DHU/MO; DLC

2553. "Africa." Quarterly Register of the American Education Society. (3:1, Ag., 1830), pp. 30-37. DHU/R

2554. Africa Committee of the Foreign Missions Conference of North America. Abundant Life in Changing Africa: Report of the West Central Africa Regional Conference Held at Leopoldville, Congo Belge July 13-24, 1946. N. Y.: Foreign Missions Conference of North America, 1947. MNtcA

2555. "Africa: Livingstone Mission Expedition." Southern Workman (5:5, My., 1876), p. 37. DLC; DHU/MO

2556. "Africa: The London Missionary Society." The Southern Workman (5:4, Apr., 1876), p. 29. DHU/MO; DLC

2557. African Education Commission. Education in Africa; a Study of West, South, and Equatorial Africa by the Africa Education Commission, Under the Auspices of the Phelps-Stokes Fund and Foreign Mission Societies of North America and Europe; Report Prepared by Thomas Jesse Jones, chairman of the Commission. New York: Phelps-Stokes Fund, 1922. MNtcA

2558. African Education Commission. Education in East Africa. A Study of East, Central and South Africa by the First and Second African Education Commission. New York: Phelps-Stokes Fund, 1925. DHU/R
"Report prepared by Thomas Jesse Jones." Includes information on the role of Christian missions in Africa.

2559-60. African Education Commission, 1923-1924. Education in East Africa; a Study of East, Central and South Africa by the Second African Education Commission Under the Auspices of the Phelps-Stokes Fund, in Cooperation With the International Education Board. Report prepared by Thomas Jesse Jones. New York: Negro Universities Press, 1970. IC/H; MiBsA

2561. "African Missionary in Africa." Missionary Review (28; Oct. -Nov., 1905), pp. 739-43+ DHU/R

2562. "African Missionary Work. Letter from an African Graduate of Hampton Institute." (letter to the editor). Southern Workman (16:10, Oct., 1887), p. 99. DHU/MO; DLC
"The Rev. J. P. Farler, of the Universities' Mission to Central Africa, has made a spirited reply to a Professor Lenz's attack on British missions in that region."

2563. The African Squadron. Petition of the Committee of the Church Mission Society Deprecating the Diminishing or Removal of the Squadron. n.p., 1850. DHU/MO

2564. "Africa's Challenge to the Church." National Council Outlook. (5; Feb., 1955), pp. 18+. DHU/R

2565. Afrika in Wort und Bild; Mit Besonderer Berücksichtigung der Evangelischen Missionsarbeit. Hrsg. Vom Calwer Verlagsverein. Calw: Verlag der Vereinsbuchhandlung, 1904. NjP

2566. "After Lincoln." By a Missionary. Christian Century. (59:17, Apr. 29, 1942), pp. 564-65. DHU/R
A letter by a missionary concerning the mistreatment of Negroes in the United States.

2567. Aggrey, James. A Selection of Sayings of a Great African Christian. London: Sheldon Press, n.d. MiEM

2568. Ajayi, J. F. Ade and E. A. Ayandele. "Writing African Church History." The Church Crossing Frontiers (Uppsala, Sweden: Gleerup, 1969), pp. 90-108.   DHU/R

2569. Akeley, Delia J. (Denning). Jungle Portraits: with Original Photographs. New York: Macmillan Co., 1930. DHU/MO

2570. A l'Assaut des Pays Nègres; Journal des Missionnaires D'Alger dans L'Afrique Equatoriale. Paris: Oeuvre des Ecoles D'Orient, 1884.   NjP

2571. Allen, Belle Jane. A Crusade of Compassion for the Healing of the Nations. A Study of Medical Missions for Women and Children; Compiled by Belle J. Allen, edited by Caroline Atwater Mason. West Medford, Mass.: The Central Committee on the United Study of Foreign Missions, 1919.   NN/Sch

2572. Allen, Roland. Le Zoute: A Critical Review of "The Christian Mission in Africa." London: World Dominion Press, 1927.   DLC; CtY

2573. Allier, Raoul. "The Social Outreach of Protestant Missions." International Review of Missions (21; 1932), pp. 547-65.   DHU/R

2574. Allison, Madeline G. "The Churches." The Crisis (22:1, My., 1921), p. 30-31.   DHU/MO; DLC
          Progress of the Presbyterian Church in Africa over the past 20 years.

2575. Alston, Leonard. The White Man's Work in Asia and Africa. A Discussion of the Main Difficulties of the Colour Question. London: Longmans, Green and Co., 1907.   DHU/R
          See Chapter II, "Christian Ethics & Philosophy in Relation to the Lower Races."

2576. American Board of Commissioners for Foreign Missions. Historical Sketch of the Missions of the American Board in Africa. Boston: n.p., 1898.   MiBsa

2577. Amor, Frank. "The African and the Religious Life." The Church Overseas (3:12, Oct., 1930), pp. 379-87.   DHU/R

2578. Amu, E. "The Position of Christianity in Modern Africa." International Review of Missions (29; Oct., 1940), pp. 477-85.   DAU/W; DCU/TH; DHU/R

2579. Anderson, Benjamin J. K. Appendix to Ben Anderson's Journey to Musadu. New York: Lithographing, Engraving and Printing Co., 1870.   DHU/MO; NN/Sch
          Translated by Edward Wilmot Blyden.

2580. Anderson, Llewellyn Kennedy. Bridge to Africa. New York: Board of Foreign Missions of the Presbyterian Church in the United States of America, Foreign Missions and Overseas Interchurch Services, 1952.   NN/Sch

2581. Anderson, William T. "The Church in African Universities." Clergy Review. (53:3, Mr., 1968), pp. 191-98.   DCU/Th

2582. Anderson-Morshead, A. E. M. The History of the Universities' Mission to Central Africa, 1859-1896. London: Office of the Universities' Mission to Central Africa, 1909. ANAU; NjPT
          History covers parts of Tanzania, Zanzibar, Mozambique, Zambia, Malawi and Rhodesia.

2583. "Anti-Christian Movements in Africa." Missionary Review of the World (33; 1910), pp. 723-40.   DHU/R

2584. Arnot, Frederick Stanley. Garenganze, or Seven Years' Pioneer Mission Work in Central Africa. Chicago: n.p., 1889.   NjP; NN/Sch

2585. Asiegbu, Johnson U. J. Slavery and the Politics of Liberation, 1787-1861. London: Longmans, 1970. DHU/MO
          A study of Liberated African Emigration and British Anti-Slavery Policy.

2586. Atwater, Anna (Robison). Forms of Work Conducted by the Christian Woman's Board of Missions. Indianapolis: CWBM, n.d.   TN/DCHS

2587. Auf der Maur, P. I. "Werden, Stand und Zukunft des Africanischen Monchtums." Neue Zeitschrift fur Missionswissenschaft (23:4, 1967), pp. 284-95; (24:1, 1968), pp. 21-35.   DLC

2588. Baeta, C. G. Christianity in Tropical Africa. London: International Africa Institute, 1968.   DLC; DHU/R

2589. Baines, Thomas. Journal of a Residence in Africa, 1842-1853. Cape Town: Van Riebeeck Society, 1961-64. NIC; CaOTP; ViU; MiEM; NN; NcD; CSt

2590. Baird, James B. Children of Africa. Chicago: F. H. Revell Co., 1910.   NN/Sch

2591. Bakke, N. J., comp. Unsere Negermission in Wort Und Bild. St. Louis: Concordia Publishing House, 1914. MSL/CHI

2592. Bane, Martin J. Catholic Pioneers in West Africa. Dublin and London: Clonmore and Reynolds 1956.   DHU/MO

2593. ----- The Popes and Western Africa: An Outline of Mission History, 1460's-1960's. Staten Island, N. Y.: Alba House, 1968.   DLC; MiBsA

2594. Barclay, Wade Crawford. The Methodist Episcopal Church, 1845-1939: Widening Horizons, 1845-95. (Vol. III of the History of Methodist Missions). New York: Board of Missions of the Methodist Church, 1957.   DHU/R
          Chapter IX, Expanding Foreign Missions--Africa.

2595. Barr, Mary. The Gowa Story: A Series of Missionary Lessons for Sunday Schools. Birmingham, Engl.: Berean Press, n.d.   TN/DCHS; DLC

2596. Barron, Jack Terrill. Pages from an African Notebook. Indianapolis: Missionary Education Dept., UCMA, 1959.   TN/DCHS

2597. Barrow, A. H. Fifty Years in Western Africa: Being a Record of the Work of the West Indian Church on the Banks of the Rio Pongo. London: Society for Promoting Christian Knowledge, 1900.   NN/Sch; DHU/R

2598. Bartlett, S. C. Historical Sketch of the Missions of the American Board in Africa. Boston: Pub. by the Board, 1880.   DHU/MO

2599. Battle, Vincent M. and Charles H. Lyons, (eds.). Essays in the History of African Education. New York: Center for Education in Africa Series, Teachers College, 1970. DHU/R
          Includes three chapters on the The Church and Missionaries, Methodists in Liberia and Presbyterians in the Sudan.

2600. Baudert, S. Die Evangelische Mission. Leipzig: B. G. Teubert, 1913.   MSL/CHI

2601. Baumann, Julius. Missions und Ökumene in Südwestafrika, Dargestellt am Lebenswerk von Hermann Heinrich Vedder. Leiden: E. J. Brill, 1965.   MiBsa; MNtcA
          Missions in Southwest Africa.

2602. Beach Harlan. A Geography and Atlas of Protestant Missions; their Environment, Forces, Distribution, Methods, Probelms, Results and Prospects at the Opening of the Twentieth Century. New York: Student Volunteer Movement for Foreign Missions, 1901-1903.   NN/Sch; DHU/R

2603. ----- and Burton St. John. World Statistics of Christian Missions. New York: The Committee of Reference and Counsel of the Foreign Missions Conference of North America, 1916.   DHU/R

2604. Beecham, John. The Claims of the Missionary Work in Western Africa, and the Importance of Training a Native Ministry. London: Mason, 1842. NB; IEG; IEN; MBU

2605. Bell, William Clark. African Bridge Builders. New York: Friendship Press, 1936.   NN/Sch; DHU/MO

2606. ----- "Christian Civilization in Africa." Southern Workman (54:11, Nov., 1925), pp. 504-11.   DLC; DHU/MO

2607. Bennett, Norman Robert. "The Holy Ghost Mission in East Africa, 1858-1890." Studies in East African History (Boston: Boston University Research Studies, No. 4, 1963), pp. 54-75.   MB

2608. Bernardi, Bernardo. The Migwe: A Failing Prophet. Oxford: Oxford University Press, 1959.   DHU/R

2609. Béthune, León (Baron). Les Missions Catholiques d'Afrique. Lille: Société Saint-Augustin, 1889.   NB; IEN

2610. Bickersteth, E. Memoirs of Simeon Wilhelm, a Native of the Susoo Country, West Africa; Who Dies at the House of the Church Missionary Society, London, Aug. 29, 1817; Aged 17 Yrs. Together with Some Accounts of the Superstitions of the inhabitants of West Africa. New Haven: S. Converse, 1819.   DHU/MO

2611. Bird, Mary E. Adaora: Romance of West African Missions. New York: Revell, 1903.   NNMR

2612. Birtwistle, Norman A. Thomas Birch Freeman: West African Pioneer. London: Cargate Press, 1950.   DHU/MO

2613. Bliss, Edwin M. The Encyclopedia of Missions. Discriptive, Historical, Biographical Statistical. New York: Funk & Wagnalls, 1891.   DHU/R
Includes Africa and West Indies.

2614. Blyden, Edward Wilmot. The African Problem and Other Discourses, Delivered in America in 1890. London: W. B. Whittingham, 1890.   NB; WU

2615. ----- The African Problem, and the Method of Its Solution. Washington: Gibson, 1890.   DHU/MO; NN/Sch

2616. ----- The Aims and Methods of a Liberal Education for Africans, Inaugural Address, Delivered January 5, 1881. Cambridge: Wilson, 1882.   DHU/MO; NN/Sch

2617. ----- Phillip and the Eunuch; or the Instruments and Methods of Africa's Evangelization. A Discourse Delivered in the Park Street Church, Boston, U. S. A., Sunday, Oct. 22, 1882. Cambridge: John Wilson and Son, 1883. DHU/MO
Negro author.

2618. ----- "The Political Outlook for Africa." Alice Ruth Nelson. Masterpieces of Negro Eloquence: The Best Speeches Delivered by the Negro From the Days of Slavery to the Present Time. New York: Bookery Publishing Company, 1914, pp. 663-64.   DHU/MO

2619. ----- Return of the Exiles and the West African Church. A Lecture Delivered at the Breadfruit School House, Lagos, West Africa, January 2, 1891. London: Whittingham, 1891.   NNCOR
Microfilm.

2620. ----- Vindication of the African Race; Being a Brief Examination of the Arguments in Favor of African Inferiority... With an Introduction by Alexander Crummell. Monrovia: Gaston Killian, 1857.   NUC; NcD; DLC; PPULC

2621. ----- A Voice from Bleeding Africa, on Behalf of Her Exiled Children. Monrovia: Killian, 1856.   DHU/MO

2622. ----- West Africa Before Europe, and Other Addresses, Delivered in England in 1901 and 1903. London: C. M. Phillips, 1905.   DLC; OO

2623. Blyth, George. Reminescences of Missionary Life, with Suggestions to Churches and Missionaries. Edinburgh: Oliphant, 1851.   NNUT

2624. Bois, G. "L'Afrique, l'Inde et le Christianisme d'Apres Raymond Panikkar." Le Monde Non Chretien (74, Avril-Juin, 1965), pp. 102-106.   Pam. File DHU/R

2625. Booth, Newell Snow. The Cross Over Africa. New York: Friendship Press, 1945.   NN/Sch

2626. ----- This is Africa South of the Sahara. New York: Friendship Press, 1959. MiBsa; NN/Sch
Missions in sub-saharan Africa.

2627. Bouchoud, Joseph. L'Eglise en Afrique Noire. Paris: La Palatine, 1958.   NjP

2628. Bouniol. Joseph. The White Fathers and Their Missions. London: Sands, 1929. DLC; CBBD; DCU; MoSU; NcD; CtY; FU; WaU; NN

2629. Bourne, Henry Richard Fox. Slavery and Its Substitutes in Africa. A Paper Submitted to the Anti-Slavery Conference, Held in Paris in August, 1900. London: Aborigines Protection Society, 1900?   CtY-D

2630. Bovet, Pierre. "Education as Viewed by the Phelps-Stokes Commissions." International Review of Missions (15:3, July, 1926), pp. 483-92.   DHU/R
Christian education in Africa.

2631. Bowen, John Wesley Edward, (ed.). Africa and the American Negro. Atlanta: Franklin Press, 1896.   DHU/MO

2632. -----(ed.). Congress of Africa. Atlanta, 1895. Africa, and the American Negro. Addresses and Proceedings of the Congress on Africa, Held Under the Auspices of the Stewart Missionary Foundation for Africa of Gammon Theological Seminary, in Connection with the Cotton States and International Exposition, December 13-15, 1895. Atlanta: Gammon Theological Seminary, 1896.   DHU/MO; NN/Sch

2633. Bowen, Thomas J. Central Africa. Adventures and Missionary Labors in Several Countries in the Interior of Africa from 1849 to 1856... Charleston, Southern Baptist Publication Society, 1857.   DHU/MO; NN/Sch; DHU/R

2634. ----- Meroke; or, Missionary Life in Africa. Philadelphia: n. p., 1858.   NB; CtY; PPAMS; PPULC

2635. Boyce, William B. Memoir of the Rev. William Shaw, Late General Superintendent of the Wesleyan Missions in South Eastern Africa, Edited by His Oldest Surviving Friend. London: Wesleyan Conference Office, 1874?   NB; MH; CtY

2636. Brain, B. "Africaner, a Twice-Born Black Man." Missionary Review (35; Jl., 1912), pp. 487-94. DHU/R

2637. Branson, William H. Missionary Adventures in Africa. Washington, D. C.: Review and Herald, 1925. MiBsa; NjP
Seventh-day Adventist.

2638. Brásio, António D. A Accão Missionária No Perído Henriquino. Lisboa: Comissao Executiva das Comemoracoes du Quinto Centenario da Morte do Infante D Henrique, 1958.   NNCor; NjP
Missions in Africa.

2639. Bratton, Michael. American Doctoral Dissertations on Africa, 1886-1972. Waltham, Mass.: African Studies Association, Research, 1973.   DLC

2640. Brodhead, Chloe A. S. Our Free Methodist Missions in Africa to April, 1907. Pittsburg: Aldine Printing Co., 1908.   DLC

2641. Brown, Ina Corinne. Training for World Friendship; a Manual in Missionary Education for Leaders of Young People. Nashville, Tenn.: Cokesbury Press, 1929. NN/Sch; DHU/R

2642. Browning, Louise. They Went to Africa: Biographies of Missionaries of the Disciples of Christ. Indianapolis: Missionary Education Dept., UCMS, 1952.   TN/DCHS

2643. Brownlie, Ian, (ed.) Basic Documents on African Affairs. Oxford: Clarendon Press, 1971.   DLC

2644. Bruls, R. P. and A. Roux. "L'Ouevre Culturelle des Missions Chrétiennes en Afrique Noire." Revue de Psychologie des Peuples (20:4, 4th Quarter, 1965), pp. 436-40.   DLC

2645. Bühlmann, Walbert. Afrika. Mainz: M. Grünewald, 1963.
                                                    MiBsA
      Missions in Africa.

2646. ----- Die Predigtweise in Afrika. Schoneck Beckenried, Schweiz, Administration der Neuen Zeitschrift fur Missionswissenschaft, 1956.   NNCOR
      Missions in Africa.

2647. Buntrock, Orville A. "The History of American Lutheran Missions in Asia, Africa, and Oceana Since World War I." Concordia Historical Institute Quarterly (21:2, Jl., 1948), pp. 88-96; (21:3, Oct., 1948), pp. 114-28; (21:4, Ja., 1949), pp. 187-92; (22:2, Jl., 1949), pp. 84-89; (22:3, Oct., 1949), pp. 127-33.   MSL/CHi

2648. Burkhardt, Gustav E. Die Evangelische Mission unter den Negern in West-Afrika. Bielefeld: Velhagen und Klasing, 1856.   MiBsA
      Missions in West Africa.

2649. Burridge, William. Destiny Africa: Cardinal Lavigerie and the Making of the White Fathers. London and Dublin: Geoffrey Chapman, 1966.   DHU/MO

2650. ----- "Mission and Reality, The Role of History in the Development of the Church in Sub-Saharan Africa." World-Mission (23:4, 1972-73), pp. 6-12+   IEG; IMC

2651. Burton, E. D. and A. K. Parker. "Expansion of Christianity in the Twentieth Century." Biblical World (41; Je., 1913), pp. 402-07.   DHU/R

2652. Burton, William F. When God Changes a Man. A True Story of this Great Change in the Life of a Slave-raider. London: Victory Press, 1929.   NN/Sch

2653. Butler, Annie Robins. By the Rivers of Africa, from Cape Town to Uganda; with a Map and Sixty Illustrations. London: Religious Tract Society, 188?   NN/Sch

2654. Butler, Rosa Kate (Smith). "Mrs. Thomas Butler." Missions As I Saw Them: An Account of a Visit to the Important Centres of the United Missionary Society in China and Africa, With an Interesting Description of Many of the Places Passed Through and Incidents of the Journey Both Grave and Gay. London: Seeley, Service & Co., 1924.   NNCor

2655. Capper, Joseph. The Negro's Friend. Consisting of Anecdotes, Designed to Exemplify the Moral, Intellectual, and Religious Attainments of the African Race, and the Cruelties and Oppressions to Which They have been Subjected by the Europeans. London: S. Bagster, n.d.   DHU/MO

2656. Carpenter, George Wayland. Church, State and Society in Central Africa: Some Sociological Concomitants of Government and Missionary Policy in Central Africa, With Special Reference to Education. Doctoral dissertation. Yale University, 1937.

2657. ----- ...The Way in Africa. New York: Friendship Press, 1959.   NN/Sch
      "A selected reading list," pp. 161-65.

2658. Cash, W. Wilson. "Church Building in East Africa." East and West Review (4:1, Ja., 1938), pp. 21-28. DHU/R

2659. "The Catholics in Africa." Southern Workman (6:12, Dec., 1877), p. 93.   DLC; DHU/MO

2660. Césard, Père Edmond. "Le Muhaya (L'Afrique Orientale)." Anthropos (32: n.i., n.m. 1937), pp. 15-60.
                                                    DLC
      Des Blancs. Cath. Miss. of Kashozi, P.O. Bukoba. xll. La religion.

2661. Chaney, Charles. God's Glorious Work: A Study in the Theological Foundations of the Early Missionary Societies in America, 1762-1817. Doctoral dissertation. Univerisity of Chicago, 1968.

2662. "Chart, Showing Societies at Work in the Dark Continent." Missionary Review (37; Je., 1914), p. 422.   DHU/R

2663. Chirgwin, A. M. The Forward Tread. London: The Livingston Press, 1932.   DHU/MO

2664. Christian Action in Africa; Report of the Church Conference on African Affairs Held at Otterbein College, Westerville, Ohio, June 25, 1942. New York: Africa Committee of the Foreign Missions Conference of North America, 1942.
                                          MiBsA; DHU/MO

2665. Christian Council of the Gold Coast. Christianity and African Culture: the Proceedings of a Conference Held at Accra, Gold Coast, May 2nd-6th, 1955. Under the Auspices of the Christian Council. The Council, 1955.   NNMR

2666. "Christian Education in Africa." Harmon Foundation, 1930. 15 min., si., b & w, 16 mm.
      Film.
      "Describes courses of study in mission schools in Africa, and shows activities of boy scouts and girl guides."

2667. "The Christian Mission in Africa." International Review of Missions (15:3, Jl., 1926), pp. 323-26.   DHU/R

2668. The Christian Occupation of Africa. Proceeding of a Conference of Mission Boards Engaged in Work in... Africa, New York City, Nov. 20-22, 1917. New York: Committee of Reference and Council of Foreign Missions Conference of North America, 1917.   NNMR
      Offical record concerning the evangelization of Africa.

2669. "Christian Union Is Coming to a Section of Africa." The Christian Century (39:31, Ag. 3, 1922), p. 980. DHU/R

2670. Christianity and Native Rites. London: Central Africa Home Press, 1956.   NN/Sch

2671. Christy, David. Ethiopia: Her Gloom and Glory as Illustrated in the History of the Slave Trade and Slavery, the Rise of the Republic of Liberia, and the Progress of African Missions. New York: Negro Universities Press, 1969. PPT; NN/Sch; Cty-D
      Reprint of the 1857 ed.

2672. "The Church." The Crisis (10:3, Jl., 1915), p. 115.
                                                    DLC; DHU/MO
      The bishops of Mombassa and Uganda have been adjudged not guilty in the Kikuyu case by the Archbishop of Canterbury.

2673. Church Conference on African Affairs. Otterbein College, 1942. Christian Action in Africa. Report of the Church Conference on African Affairs held at Otterbein College, Westerville, Ohio, June 19-25, 1942. New York: Africa Committee of the Foreign Missions Conference of North America, 1942.
                                                    DHU/MO

2674. Church Missionary Society. Centenary Volume of the Church Missionary Society for Africa and the East: 1799-1899. n.p.: Church Missionary Society, 1902.   NNMR

2675. Church Missionary Society for Africa and the East. Proceedings... Twentieth Year... London: Watts, 1820. NjP

2676. Clarke, Virginia Maltby. Disciples of Christ in Africa. Indianapolis: Missionary Education Dept., UCMS, 1945.
TN/DCHS

2677. Clendenen, Clarence C. and Peter Duignan. Americans in Black Africa Up to 1865. Stanford University: The Hoover Institution on War, 1964. DHU/R
Part II, Missionaries and colonization, societies, revolution and peace.

2678. Cloete, Stuart. The African Giant; The Story of a Journey. Boston: Houghton Mifflin, 1955. DHU/MO

2679. Coan, Josephus R. "The Missionary Presence in Africa." A. M. E. Church Review (104:246, Apr.-Je., 1971), pp. 65-72. DHU/R
Negro author

2680. Coillard, Francois. On the Threshold of Central Africa; a Record of Twenty Years' Pioneering Among the Barotsi of the Upper Zambesi. London: Hodder, 1897. NjP; PPT

2681. Coldham, Geraldine E. A Bibliography of Scriptures in African Languages. London: British and Foreign Bible Society, 1966. DLC

2682. Collier, Casa. Meet Ngombi... New York: Board of Foreign Missions of the Presbyterian Church, U.S.A., 1934.
NN/Sch

2683. Collins, Robert Oakley. The Mahdist Invasions of the Southern Sudan, 1883-1898. Doctoral dissertation. Yale University, 1959

2684. Comhaire, Jean L. "Religious Trends in African and Afro-American Urban Societies." Anthropology Quarterly (1; Ja., 1928), pp. 95-108. DHU

2685. Commission on the Enlistment of Educated Negroes for Work in Africa. "The Task of the Christian Church in Africa." Arcadius S. Trawick, (ed.). The New Voice in Race Adjustment. (New York: Student Volunteer Movement, 1914), pp. 201-09. DHU/R

2636. Conference of Mission Boards Engaged in Work in the Continent of Africa, New York, 1917. The Christian Occupation of Africa: the Proceedings of a Conference of Mission Boards Engaged in Work in the Continent of Africa, Held in New York City, November 20, 21 and 22, 1917, together with the Findings of the Conference. New York: Committee of Reference and Counsel of the Foreign Missions Conference of North America, 1917.
NN/Sch

2687. Congress on Africa, Atlanta, 1895. Africa and the American Negro; Addresses and Proceedings. Miami, Fla.: Mnemosyne Pub. Inc., 1969. NjP
Reprint of 1896 ed.

2688. Conover, Helen F. Africa South of the Sahara. Washington: Library of Congress, 1957. DHU/MO

2689. Cook, Albert R. and Bishop Tucker. "A Cry from Central Africa." The Church Missionary Review (60; Je., 1909), pp. 363-66. DHU/R

2690. Cooke, Raymond McIntyre. British Evangelicals, Native Peoples and the Concept of Empire, 1837-1852. Doctoral dissertation. University of Oregon, 1963.

2691. Cooley, John K. Baal, Christ, and Mohammed; Religion and Revolution in North Africa. London: John Murray, 1967.
DHU/R
Part III, "Christian Missionaries and Moslem Rulers."

2692. Coppinger, William. Winning an Empire. Hampton, Va.: Normal School Steam Press, 1884. NN/Sch

2693. Corey, Stephen Jared. Among Central African Tribes: Journal of a Visit to the Congo Mission. Cincinnati: Foreign Christian Missionary Society, 1912. NN/Sch; TN/DCHS

2694. Correia, Joaquim Alves. A Dilatacao da fe no Imperio Portugues. Lisboa: Agencia Geral das Colonias, Divisao de Publicacoes e Biblioteca, 1936. NNCor

2695. Corry, Joseph. Observations Upon the Windward Coast of Africa, the Religion, Character, Customs of the Natives Made in the Years 1805 and 1806. London: Nicol, 1807.
DHU/MO

2696. Coston, Herbert R. An Evaluation of the First Group of Methodist Short-Term Missionaries to Africa. Masters thesis. Garrett Biblical Institute, 1956.

2697. Crawford, Daniel. Thinking Black: 22 Years Without a Break in the Long Grass of Central Africa. New York: Doran, 1912. NN/Sch

2698. Crawford, E. May. By the Equator's Snowy Peak; a Record of Medical Missionary Work and Travel in British East Africa. London: Church Missionary Society, 1913. ANAW; DHU/R; CU; WU; IU; DLC; NNC; Cty

2699. Cripps, Arthur S. "Saint Francis of Assisi: His Mission to Africa and Elsewhere: 700 Years Ago and Now." The East the West (24; Oct., 1926), pp. 289-96. DHU/R

2700. Cronk, Katharine S. and Elsie Singmaster. Under Many Flags. New York: Presbyterian Church in the U.S.A., 1921. DHU/R
Includes chapters on Mary Slessor, Missionary of Nigeria and David Day, missionary to Liberia.

2701. Crowther, Samuel Adjai, (bp.). Journal of an Expedition up the Niger and Tshadda Rivers, Undertaken by Macgregor Lavid, Esq., in Connection With the British Government, in 1854. London: Church Missionary Society, 1855.
DHU/MO

2702. ----- and James Frederick Schon. Journals of the Rev. J. F. Schon and Mr. S. Crowther, Who, With the Sanction of Her Majesty's Govt. Accompanied the Expedition up the Niger in 1841 ... Church Missionary Society. London: Hatchard and Son, 1942. DLC

2703. ----- and Townsend. "Mission Parmi les Yorubas." Journal des Missions Evangeliques (30; 1850), pp. 241-60.
CtY; MH

2704. Crummell, Alexander. "The Absolute Need of an Indigenous Missionary Agency in Africa." J. W. E. Bowen, (ed.). Africa and the American Negro: Addresses and Proceedings of the Congress on Africa (Miami, Fla.: Mnemosyne Pub. Co., Inc., 1969), pp. 137-42. DHU/R
Negro author.

2705. ----- Africa and America: Addresses and Discourses. Springfield, Mass.: Willey, 1891. NN/Sch; A&M
Missions - Africa, West, pp. 405-53.

2706. ----- "Civilization a Collateral Agency in Planting the Church in Africa." J. W. E. Bowen, (ed.). Africa and the American Negro: Addresses and Proceedings of the Congress on Africa (Miami, Fla.: Mnemosyne Pub. Co., Inc., 1969), pp. 119-24. DHU/R

2707. ----- Hope for Africa. A Sermon on Behalf of the Ladies Negro Education Society. London: Seeleys, 1853. NN

2708. ----- The Relations and Duties of Free Colored Men in America to Africa. Hartford: Press of Case, Lockwood and Company, 1861. DHU/MO
A letter to B. Dunbar.

2709. Culwick, Arthur Theodore. Good Out of Africa. Livingstone, Northern Rhodesia: The Rhodes-Livingstone Institute, 1942. DHU/MO

2710. Dagadu, P. K. "Africa Asks Questions of the Western World." The African Methodist Episcopal Church Review (70:182, Oct. - Dec., 1954), pp. 59-64+.   DHU/R
     Written by General Secretary of the Christian Council of the Gold Coast A. M. E. Church.

2711. "Dan Crawford of Africa." Literary Digest (47; Sept. 20, 1913), pp. 474-75.   DHU

2712. Davies, Edward. An Illustrated Handbook on Africa, Giving an Account of its People, its Climate, its Resources, its Discoveries, and Some of Its Missions. Reading, Mass.: Holiness Book Concern, 1886-1887.   NjP

2713. Davis, John Merle. The Cinema and Missions in Africa.   NN/Sch
     "Reprinted from the International Review of Missions for July, 1936."

2714. Davy, Yvonne. African Adventure Unlimited; a Collection of Stories. New York: Greenwich Book Publishers, 1958.   MiBsA
     Missions in Central Africa.

2715. ----- Going With God; on Missions of Mercy in Central Africa. Washington, D.C.: Review and Herald Pub. Association, 1959.   MiBsa
     Seventh-day Adventist missions in Central Africa.

2716. Dawson, Edwin Collas. James Hannington...First Bishop of Eastern Equatorial Africa; A History of His Life and Work, 1847-1885. London: Seeley, 1889. ANAU; DHU/R; ViU; NjP; PP

2717. Day Missions Library. Catalogue of the Foreign Missions Library of the Divinity School of Yale University. New Haven: Tuttle, Morehouse & Taylor, 1892.   CtY

2718. De la Cote des Esclaves aux rives de Nil, par une Religieuse Missionnaire. Lyon: Librarie E. Vitte Venissieux, Soeurs Missionnaires de N. D. des Aportres, 1931. NN/Sch

2719. Dealtry, William. Duty and Policy of Propagating Christianity. A Discourse Delivered Before the Church Missionary Society for Africa and the East, May 4, 1813. Pub. at the request of the General Meeting. London: Sold by L. B. Seeley, 1813.   NN/Sch

2720. Dean, Christopher. The African Traveler; or, Prospective Missions in Central Africa. Boston, Mass.: Sabbath School Society, 1838.   DHU/MO

2721. Deedy, J. "Missions as Problem." Commonweal (97; Feb. 9, 1973), p. 410.   DHU/R

2722. Delany, Martin Robinson and Robert Campbell. Search for a Place: Black Separatism and Africa, 1860. Introduction by Howard H. Bell. Ann Arbor: University of Michigan Press, 1969.   DHU/R
     Chapter 10, "Missionary Influence," pp. 102-06.

2723. De Montmorency, James Edward Geoffrey. Francis William Fox. A Biography. London: n.p., 1923. DLC; MtU; CtY; NN
     Life of a Quaker, including an account of his anti-slavery activities in the Sudan and Eastern Africa, 1876-97.

2724. Dempsey, James. Mission on the Nile. New York: Philosophical Library, 1956.   NN/Sch

2725. Dennett, Richard E. "Mission Work in West Africa." The East and the West (14; Jl., 1916), pp. 278-89. DHU/R

2726. Dickinson, Charles Henry. "Samuel Armstrong's Contribution to Christian Missions." International Review of Missions (10; 1921), pp. 509-24.   DHU/R

2727. Dieterlen, H. Eugène Casalis (1812-1891). Paris: Société des Missions Evangeliques, 1930.   NjP

2728. Directory of North American Protestant Foreign Missionary Agencies. New York: Missionary Research Library Agencies, 1960.   RL; DLC

2729. Dodge, Ralph E. Missions and Anthropology: A Program of Anthropological Research for Missionaries Working Among the Bantu-Speaking Peoples of Central and Southern Africa. Doctoral dissertation. Hartford Seminary Foundation, 1944.

2730. Döring, Paul. Morgendämmerung in Deutch-Ostafrika. Ein Rundgang durch die Ostafrikanische Mission. Berlin: Warneck, 1900.   NjP

2731. Doty, James E. Reverence for Life in the Career of Albert Schweitzer. Doctoral dissertation. Boston University School of Theology, 1959.

2732. Dougall, James W. C. "Christian Education and the Life of the African Church." East and West Review (2; 1936), pp. 341-9.   DHU/R

2733. ----- (ed.). Christianity and the Sex-Education of the African. London: Society for the Promotion of Christian Knowledge, 1937.   DLC; NN; PU; LU; CtY

2734. ----- "The Relationship of Church and School in Africa." International Review of Missions (26; 1937), pp. 204-14.   DHU/R

2735. ----- "Religious Education." International Review of Missions (15; 1926), pp. 493-505.   DHU/R

2736. ----- Religious Education in Africa: A Provisional Statement Submitted for Criticism and Experiment. New York and London: International Missionary Council, 1929. NjPT; WU; IEN; MB

2737. ----- "Thomas Jessee Jones: Crusader for Africa." International Review of Missions (39; 1950), pp. 311-17.   DHU/R

2738. Drach, George, (ed.). Forces in Foreign Missions. Philadelphia: United Lutheran Publication House, 1925. MSL/CHI

2739. ----- (ed.). Our Church Abroad. Columbus, Ohio: Lutheran Book Concern, 1926.   MSL/CHI

2740. "Dramatizing Missions: Work of Converting Africans Filmed by Harmon Foundation." Newsweek (12; Oct. 17, 1938), p. 27.   DHU

2741. Draper, Charlotte. For the Presbyterian Female of Color's Enterprising Society in Baltimore. A Free-Will Offering. For the Benefit of Africa. The Island of Corsica, in Western Africa, January 25, 1860. Baltimore: Frederick A. Hanzche, 1860.   DHU/MO

2742. Dubois, Henri Marie. ...Chez les Betsiléos; Impressions et Croquis. Paris: Casterman, 1907.   NN/Sch

2743. ----- ...Le Répertoire Africain. Rome: Sodalite de S. Pierre Claver, 1932.   NN/Sch

2744. Dubose, Hampden C. Memoirs of Rev. John Leighton Wilson, ...Missionary to Africa and Secretary of Foreign Missions. Richmond, Va.: Presbyterian Committee of Publications, 1895.   DHU/R; NNCOR

2745. DuPlessis, Johannes. The Evangelisation of Pagan Africa; a History of Christian Missions to the Pagan Tribe of Central Africa. Published under the auspices of the University of Stellenbosch. Cape Town: Juta, 1930.   NN/Sch

2746. Dwight, Henry Otis, (ed.). The Blue Book of Missions For 1907. New York: Funk & Wagnalls Co., 1907. DHU/R

2747. Dwight, Theodore. "Condition and Character of Negroes in Africa." The Mercersburg Review (16; Ja., 1864), pp. 77- .   DLC

2748. East, David J. Western Africa; Its Condition, and Christianity, the Means of Its Recovery. n. p.: Houlston and Stoneman, 1844.   NNMR

2749. East, J. E. "Colored Baptist Missions." The Crisis (36:11, Nov., 1929), pp. 372; 391-92. DHU/MO; DLC
Dr. East, Secretary of the Foreign Missionary Board of the National Baptist Convention (Inc.), in this article tells what Negro Baptists were trying to do in Africa.

2750. Edwards, Josephine C. Tales from Africa. Nashville: Southern Publishing Association, 1956.   MiBsa
Seventh Day Adventist African mission series.

2751. Ellingworth, Paul. "As They Saw Themselves, More About the Beginnings of Methodism in Ouidah." The Bulletin of the Society for African Church History (1:2, Dec., 1963), pp. 35-41.
DHU/R

2752. ----- "Methodism on the Slave Coast 1842-1870." Bulletin of the Society for African Church History (2:3, 1967), pp. 239-58.   DHU/R

2753. Eriksson, Linne. Det Afrika vi sag Af. Orebro: Bokforlaget Libris, 1963.   NNCOR

2754. Eubank, Richard. "Roman Catholic Missions." The East and the West (3; Ja., 1905), pp. 46-67.   DHU/R
Africa, pp. 62-7.

2755. "Evangelism in Africa." World Parish (13:5, Feb., 1974), pp. 1-2.   DHU/R
Delegates from seventeen African countries meet in Nairobi under the auspices of the Evangelism Committee of the World Methodist Council. The theme of the meetings was, "Evangelism -- Our Continuing mission."

2756. Faduma, Orishetukeh. "Success and Drawbacks to Missionary Work in Africa." J. W. E. Bowen, (ed.). Africa and the American Negro: Addresses and Proceedings of the Congress on Africa. (Miami, Fla.: Mnemosyne Publishing, Inc., 1969), pp. 125-36.   DHU/R

2757. Fahs, Charles Harvey. The Open Door; a Challenge to Missionary Advance. Cincinnati: Jennings & Pye, 1903.
NN/Sch

2758. Faulkner, Rose E. Joseph Sidney Hill: First Bishop in Western Equatorial Africa. London: H. R. Allenson, 1895.
TSewU-T

2759. Favre, Edouard. Francois Coillard; D'Apres Son Autobiographie, Son Journal intime et sa Correspondance. Paris: Société des Missions Evangéliques, 1908-13.   NjP

2760. Findlay, G. G. and W. W. Holdsworth. The History of the Wesleyan Methodist Missionary Society. Vol. 2, London: Epworth Press, 1921.   NNUT

2761. Finney, Rodney E. Judy Goes to Africa. Nashville: Southern Pub. Association, 1962.   MiBsa
Seventh-day Adventist and Missions in Africa.

2762. Fisher, A. B. "Mission Among the African Pygmies." Missionary Review of the World (27; Apr., 1904), pp. 297-98.
DHU/R

2763. Fisher, Lena Leonard. Under the Crescent and Among the Kraals; a Study of Methodism in Africa. Boston, Mass.: The Women's Foreign Missionary Soc. Methodist Episcopal Church, 1917.   NN/Sch

2764. Fisher, Miles Mark. "Lott Carey, the Colonizing Missionary." Journal of Negro History (7:4, Oct., 1922), pp. 380-418.
DHU
Negro author.

2765. Flickinger, Daniel Kumler. Ethiopia: or Thirty Years of Missionary Life in Western Africa... Dayton: United Brethren Publishing House, 1885.   DHU/MO

2766. ----- History of the Origin, Development and Condition of Missions Among the Sherbro and Mende Tribes in Western Africa. Dayton: n. p., 1885.   MiBSa

2767. Floyd, Olive Beatrice. Partners in Africa. New York: The National Council, Protestant Episcopal Church, 1946?
DHU/MO

2768. Forcinelli, Joseph. The Interrelation of Religions and the Theology of the Christian Mission. Doctoral dissertation. Claremont Graduate School, 1967.

2769. Ford, Jefferson W. "Industrial Work in African Missions." Southern Workman (51:3, Mr., 1922), pp. 121-4.
DHU/MO; DLC
Of the Friends' Mission, British East Africa.

2770. Forde, H. A. Black and White Mission Stories. New York: E. & J. B. Young & Co., 1881.   NN/Sch

2771. Fountain, O. C. "Religion and Economy in Mission Station-Village Relationships." Practical Anthropology (13:2, Mr.-Apr., 1966), pp. 45-58.
The role of missionary activity in regional economy development.

2772. Fox, William. A Brief History of the Wesleyan Mission on the Western Coast of Africa. Including Biographical Scetches of All the Missionaries Who Have Died in That Important Field of Labour. With Some Account of the European Settlements, and of the Slave-Trade. London: Aylott & Jones, 1851. CtY-D

2773. Fraser, Agnes R. "The Place of Missions In Spreading a Knowledge of Health and Hygiene in Village Life." International Review of Missions (19; 1930), pp. 377-87.   DHU/R

2774. Fraser, Donald. Africa Idylls; Portraits & Impressions of Life on a Central African Mission Station... London: Seeley, Service, 1923.   NN/Sch

2775. ----- "The Evangelistic Approach to the African." International Review of Missions (15:3, Jl., 1926), pp. 438-449.
DHU/R

2776. ----- The Future of Africa. London: Church Missionary Society, 1911.   NN/Sch

2777. ----- The New Africa. New York: Missionary Education Movement of the United States and Canada, 1928. DHU/MO

2778. "Freedmen for Africa." The Church at Home and Abroad (2; Ag., 1887), pp. 166-67.   DHU/R
Discusses possibility of Negroes as Missionaries in Africa.

2779. Freeman, Thomas Birch. Journals of Various Visits to the Kingdoms of Ashanti, Aku and Dahomi in Western Africa. London: Cass, 1968. DLC; PPT; IEG; MB; CtY-D; CtY
"Cass Library of African Studies. Missionary Researches and Travels, no. 1."

2780. Frere, H. Bartle. Eastern Africa as a Field for Missionary Labour. London: Murray, 1874.   DHU/MO

2781. Friends of the Missions. ...For the Missions. The Apostolate in Africa... Quebec: The Model Print Shop, 1911. NN/Sch

2782. "From Our Missionary in Africa." (letter to the editor). Southern Workman (12:12, Dec., 1883), p. 124. DHU/MO; DLC
Letter from Mr. Samuel Miller, graduate of the Hampton Institute class of '76, and for two years a missionary teacher in Benguela, Africa, under the American Board.

2783. Fulani Bin Fulani. "Christianity and Labour Conditions in Africa." International Review of Missions (9; 1920), pp. 544-51.
DHU/R
Influence of the Church missions in Africa.

2784. ----- "Religion and Common Life: A Problem in East African Missions." The International Review of Missions (8; 1919), pp. 155-72.   DHU/R

2785. Furlong, C. W. "White Fathers of North Africa." Scribners Magazine (41; Feb., 1907), pp. 140-51.   DHU

2786. Fyfe, Christopher (Hamilton). "The West African Methodists in the Nineteenth Century." Sierra Leone Bulletin of Religion (5: 2, 1963), pp. 55-60.   DLC

2787. "Gaboon and Corisco Mission." The Church at Home and Abroad (1; 1887), pp. 552-54.   DHU/R
      Protestant missions in West Africa.

2788. "The Gaboon Mission." (letter to the editor). Southern Workman (8:4, Apr., 1879), p. 38. DLC; DHU/MO
      A letter to the editor written by Albert H. Tolman on the Gaboon Mission in Western Africa.

2789. Gammon Theological Seminary. Stewart Missionary Foundation on Africa. Africa and the American Negro. Addresses and Proceedings of the Congress on Africa... Dec. 13-15, 1896.   DHU/MO

2790. Garritt, J. B. Historical Sketch of the Missions Among the North American Indians Under the Care of the Board of Foreign Missions of the Presbyterian Church. Philadelphia: Published by Woman's Foreign Missionary Society of the Presbyterian Church, 1881.   DHU/R
      pp. 1-24, Missions in Africa.

2791. Gavan Duffy, Thomas. Mission Tours - Africa, ... or For Short Let's Go. Boston: Propagation of the Faith Office, 1928.   NN/Sch

2792. "General Statistics of Missions in Africa." Missionary Review of the World (35; Je., 1912), p. 460.   DHU/R

2793. George, C. T. T. "Early Baptist Christians in the Niger Delta." Orita: Ibadan Journal of Religious Studies (5:1, Je., 1971), pp. 77-79.   DHU/R
      Summary of C. T. T. George, Baptist Work in the Niger Delta-from the Beginning to 1950, B. A. Extended Essay University of Ibadan, 1968.

2794. George, Poikail John. "Racist Assumptions of the 19th Century Missionary Movement." International Review of Mission (59:235, Jl., 1970), pp. 271-84.   DHU/R

2795. "German Missions in Africa." The Church at Home and Abroad (1; 1887), pp. 557-60.   DHU/R

2796. Gilbert, John W. "The Southern Negro's Debt and Responsibility to Africa." Arcadius M. Trawick, (ed.). The New Voice in Race Adjustment (New York: Student Volunteer Movement, 1914), pp. 129-33.   DHU/R
      Written by President of C. M. E. Miles College.

2797. Glover, Robert H. The Progress of World-Wide Missions. New York: George H. Doran Co., 1924.   DHU/R

2798. Gochet, Jean Baptiste. La Traite des Nègres et la Croisade Africaine, Comprenant la Lettre Encyclique de Léon XIII sur l'Esclavage, le Discours du Cardinal Lavigeri à Paris, les Temoignages des Grands Explorateurs: Livingstone, Cameron, Stanley, des Missionnaires. Francais, etc. Ainsi que l'Organisation des Sociétés Anties Clavagistes en France et en Europe. Paris: Ch. Poussielgue, 1891. NN/Sch; NcD

2799. Goerner, H. C. "Race Factor in World Missions." Review and Expositor (59; Jl., 1959), pp. 288-94. DLC; CtY-D

2800. Gollmer, Charles. Charles Andrew Gollmer, His Life and Missionary Labours in West Africa, Compiled from His Journals and the Church Missionary Society's Publications. London: Holder and Stoughton, 1889. NG; NN; NjPT; CtY

2801. Gollock, Georgina Anne. Sons of Africa. New York: Friendship Press, 1928.   IC/H; NNCor; PPT
      Missions in Africa.

2802. ----- "Uganda, Masasi and the Upper Nile: Three African Dioceses." International Review of Missions (16; 1927), pp. 235-49.   DHU/R

2803. Good, A. C. "Africa." (Letters from the Field). The Church at Home and Abroad (1; 1887), pp. 93-4.   DHU/R

2804. Goodall, Norman. A History of the London Missionary Society, 1895-1945. London: Oxford University Press, 1954.   NjPT

2805. Grahame, Nigel B. M. Arnot of Africa, a Fearless Pioneer, a Zealous Missionary and a True Knight of the Cross. New York: George H. Doran Co., 1926.   DHU/MO

2806. Grayston, E. Allison. ...Africa; Comp. by E. Allison Grayston and Clifton Ackroyd. London: Edinburgh House, 1950.   NN/Sch

2807. Gregory, John Walter. The Foundation of British East Africa. New York: Negro Universities Press, 1969. DLC; NN; FU; WU; MiU; PPL; ICN; PP
      Reprint of the 1901 edition.

2808. Griggs, John Paul. Opportunities and Strategies for Christian Missions in the Light of Rival Forces Seeking to Capture Africa. Masters thesis. Southern Baptist Theological Seminary, 1961.

2809. Groves, Charles Pelham. Jesus Christ and Primitive Need: A Missionary Study in the Christian Message... London: The Epworth Press, 1934.   CtY; NcD

2810. ----- "Missionary and Humanitarian Aspects of Imperialism from 1870-1914." L. H. Gann and P. Duignan (eds.). Vol. 1 of Colonialism in Africa: 1870-1960. (New York: Cambridge University Press, 1969), pp. 462-96.   DLC

2811. ----- The Planting of Christianity in Africa. London: Lutterworth Press, 1948-1955.   DHU/MO

2812. Grundemann, R. "Contributions to the Statistics of Protestant Missions." Condensed Translation by Rev. C. C. Starbuck. Andover Review (4:22, Oct., 1885), pp. 370-76; (5:26, Feb., 1886), pp. 202-18.   DHU/R

2813. ----- "Die Mission in den Deutschen Schutzoebieten in West Afrika." Deutche Kolonialzeitung (5; 1888), pp. 129-34.   DLC

2814. Hallett, Robin. Africa to 1875. A Modern History. Ann Arbor: The University of Michigan Press, 1970.   DHU/R

2815. Halsey, Abram W. "Can Africa be Christianized?" Missionary Review (33; Je., 1910), pp. 433-9.   DHU/R

2816. ----- A Visit to the West Africa Mission of the Presbyterian Church, in the U. S. A. New York: Board of Foreign Missions of the Presbyterian Church in the U. S. A., 1905.   NN/Sch

2817. Hamilton, Benjamin A. The Environment, Establishment, and Expansion of Protestant Missions in French Equatorial Africa. Doctoral dissertation. Grace Theological Seminary, 1959.

2818. Hammond, E. W. S. "Africa in its Relation to Christian Civilization." J. W. E. Bowen, (ed.). Africa and the American Negro: Addresses and Proceedings of the Congress on Africa. (Miami, Fla.: Mnemosyne Publishing, Inc., 1969), pp. 205-10.   DHU/R

2819. Hansberry, William Leo. "Africa and the Western World." Midwest Journal (7:2, Sum., 1955), pp. 129-55. DHU/MO

"The African and the Christian West, " pp. 147-48.
Negro author.

2820. Harnack, H. "Principles of Protestant Missions." Missionary Review of the World (24; Apr., 1901), pp. 286-7.
DHU/R

2821. Harr, Wilber Christian, (ed.). Frontiers of the Christian World Mission Since 1938. New York: Harper 1962. DHU/R; NN/Sch
Christian Mission since 1938: Africa South of the Sahara, pp. 83-114.

2822. ----- The Negro as an American Protestant Missionary in Africa. Doctoral dissertation. University of Chicago, 1945.

2823. Harris, J. H. "Day of Opportunity in West Central Africa." Missionary Review (35; Sept., 1912), pp. 673-81.   DHU/R

2824. Hartford, Charles F. "Missions and the African Liquor Traffic." The Church Missionary Review (73:839, Sept., 1922), pp. 227-31.   DHU/R

2825. Hartwig, Gerald. "Bukerebe, The Church Missionary Society, and East African Politics, 1877-1878." African Historical Studies (1:2, 1968), pp. 211-32.   DHU/MO

2826. Hartzell, Joseph Crane, (bp.). "American Methodism in Africa." Missionary Review (32; Ag., 1909), pp. 565-76.
DHU/R

Negro author.

2827. ----- (bp.). "The Continent of Africa." Arcadius S. Trawick, (ed.). The New Voice in Race Adjustments (New York: Student Volunteer Movement, 1914), pp. 115-20.   DHU/R

2828. ----- (bp.). Forward Movements in Africa: the Quadrennial Report to the General Conference of 1908. New York: Africa Diamond Jubilee Commission... Methodist Episcopal, 1908-1909.   NH
Methodist Episcopal Church and Missions in Africa.

2829. Hastings, Adrian. Missions and Ministry. London: Sheed and Ward, 1971.   MiBsA

2830. Heard, William Henry. The Bright Side of African Life. New York: Negro Universities Press, 1969. DHU/R
Originally published in 1898.
Protestant Episcopal bishop of Cape Palmas, Liberia.
Negro author.

2831. ----- The Missionary Fields of West Africa. Philadelphia: A.M.E. Book Concern, n. d.   DHU/MO

2832. Heggoy, W. N. Fifty Years of Evangelical Missionary Movement in North Africa. Doctoral dissertation. Hartford Seminary, 1960.

2833. Hellberg, Carl J. Missions on a Colonial Frontier West of Lake Victoria. Lund: Gleerups, 1965. NcD; ICU; CtHC

2834. Helser, Albert David. Africa's Bible; the Power of God Unto Salvation. New York: Sudan Interior Mission, 1951.
DHU/MO

2835. ----- Education of a Primitive People. New York: Negro Universities Press, 1969.   DHU/R
"Originally published in 1934."
Study made with the Bura people of Northeastern Negewa.

2836. ----- The Glory of the Impossible. New York: Evangelical Publishers, 1940.   DHU/MO

2837. Hening, E. F. History of the African Mission of the Protestant Episcopal Church in the United States With Memoirs of Deceased Missionaries and Notices of Native Customs. New York: Stanford and Swords, 1853. DLC; NH; NN; DHU/R; NN/Sch

2838. Hertlein, Siegfried. Christentum und Mission im Urteil der Neoafrikanischen Prosaliteratur. Munster Schwarzach: Vier-Turme-Verlag, 1962.   NNCor
Missions in Africa.

2839. Hess, Robert L. and Dalvan M. Coger. Semper ex Africa... A Bibliography of the Primary Sources for Nineteenth Century Tropical African History, as Recorded by Explorers, Missionaries, Travelers... California: Board of Trustees of the Leland Stanford Junior University, 1972. (Hoover Bibliographical Series #47).   DHU/R; CSt-H

2840. Hewitt, Gordon. The Problem of Success: A History of the Church Missionary Society, 1910-1942. London: S.C.M. Press, 1971.   DLC

2841. Hilford, M. R. "Solving the African Problem." Missionary Review (39; Je., 1916), pp. 408-18.   DHU/R

2842. Hine, J. E. "The Use of Ritual in Missionary Churches." The East and The West (2; Jl., 1904), pp. 241-8. DHU/R

2843. Historia Missionum Ordinis Fratrum Minorum. Praefatio: Alphonsus Schnusenberg. Romae: Secretariatus Missionum O. F. M., 1967.   NNCor
Missions in Africa.

2844. Hodge, Alison. "The Training of Missionaries for Africa: The Church Missionary Society's Training College at Islington, 1900-1915." Journal of Religion in Africa (4:2, 1971), pp. 81-96.   DHU/R

2845. Holdsworth, W. W. "The Missionary Motive." The East and The West (8; Apr., 1910), pp. 132-40.   DHU/R

2846. Holland, Frederick E. Kulikuwa Juton: a Way, a Walk, and a Warfare of Forty-three Years in Africa as Nimrod, Named and Missionary. New York: Exposition Press, 1963. DHU/MO
Autobiography of a missionary of the Africa Inland Mission.

2847. Holmes, John Beck, (bp.). Historical Sketches of the Mission of the United Brethren for Propagating the Gospel Among the Heathen from Their Commencement to the Year 1817. London: Printed for the author and sold by J. Nisbet, 1827. NN/Sch

2848. Hopkins, A. J. Trail Blazers and Road Makers; A Brief History of the East Africa Mission of the United Methodist Church. London: n. p., n. d.   NNMR

2849. Horstead, J. L. C. "Co-Operation with Africans." International Review of Missions (24; 1935), pp. 203-12. DHU/R
Christian missions in Africa.

2850. ----- "The Future of the Church in West Africa." The Church Overseas (2:8, Oct., 1929), pp. 324-31. DHU/R

2851. Hotchkiss, Willis Ray "A Glimpse into Central Africa." Southern Workman (34:9, Sept., 1905), pp. 488-93. DLC; DHU/MO
Author, a Nandi Industrial Mission.
Missionary discusses work among the Bantu race and the Christian Missionary Society.

2852. ----- Sketches from the Dark Continent. Cleveland, O.: The Friends Bible Institute and Training School, 1901. NN/Sch

2853. Hubbard, John Waddington. "The Cause and the Cure of African 'Immorality': African Marriage Problems." International Review of Missions (20; 1931), pp. 241-53. DHU/R

2854. "Hubbard-Missionary." The Crisis (29:1, Nov., 1924), pp. 10-11.   DLC; DHU/MO
" ... the Hubbard Industrial Mission established by the Foreign Mission Board of the National Baptist Convention ... in West Africa. "

2855. Huckel, W. "Des Religions de l'Afrique." Journal des Missions Evangeliques Paris (Apr., 1922), pp. 315-33.
OO;CtY

2856. Hughes, W. Dark Africa and Way Out, or A Scheme for
Civilizing and Evangelizing the Dark Continent. New York:
Negro Universities Press, 1969.   DHU/R

2857. Humphreys, Guy E. The Report of the African Christian
Mission for 1951. n.p.: n.p., 195?   TN/DCHS

2858. Hunter, C. Earl. "American Baptist Foreign Missions,
1814-1845."   PPEB
Typescript.
A Study made at The Eastern Baptist Theological Seminary
1945.

2859. Hutchinson, Bertram. "Some Social Consequences of
Missionary Activity Among South African Bantu." Practical
Anthropology (6:2, Mr.-Apr., 1959), pp. 67-76. DHU/R

2860. Ifemesia, Christopher C. "The Social and Cultural Impact
of Christian Missionaries on West Africa in the 19th and 20th
Centuries." West African Religion (12; Jl., 1972), pp. 1-15
DHU/R

2861. Ingham, E. Graham, (bp.). "Church and Empire Building
in Central Africa." The Church Missionary Review (60;
Feb., 1909), pp. 65-73.   DHU/R

2862. Inter-Missionary Council. Department of Social and Industrial Research. Modern Industry and the African. An Inquiry
into the Effect of the Copper Mines of Central Africa Upon
Native Society and the Work of Christian Missions Made Under
the Auspices of the Department of Social and Industrial Research
of the Inter-Missionary Council ... London: Macmillan &
Co., 1933.   DHU/MO

2863. International Missionary Council. Assembly, Accra, 1957-
1958. The Ghana Assembly of the International Missionary
Council, 28th December, 1957 to 8th January, 1958; Selected
Papers with an Essay on the Role of the I. M. C. Edited by
Ronald K. Orchard. London: Published for the International
Missionary Council by Edinburgh House Press, 1958. DHU/R

2864. International Missionary Council. Dept. of Social and Eco-
nomic Research and Counsel. Modern Industry and the African;
an Inquiry into the Effect of Copper Mines of Central Africa
Upon Native Society and the Work of Christian Missions Made
Under the Auspices of the Department of Social and Industrial
Research of the International Missionary Council; J. Merle
Davis, Chairman of the Commission of Enquiry and Editor
of the Report ... London: Macmillan and Co., 1933. DHU/R

2865. International Missionary Council. Ibadan, Nigeria, 1958.
The Church in Changing Africa: Report of the All-Africa
Church Conference, Held at Ibadan, Nigeria, January 10-19,
1958. N. Y.: International Missionary Council, 1958.

2866. Irle, Frau Hedwig. Unsere Schwarzen Landsleute in Deutch-
Sudwestafrika... Gütersloh: n.p., 1911. NjP

2867. Jack, James William. Daybreak in Livingstonia; the Story of
the Livingstonia Mission, British Central Africa. New York:
Negro Univerisities Press, 1969. NjP; DHU/MO

2868. Jackson, Samuel Macauley. Bilbiography of Foreign Missions. New York: Funk & Wagnalls, 1891.   NN/Sch

2869. James, J. A. The Path to the Bush. Boston, Mass.:
Sabbath School Society, 1843.   DHU/MO

2870. James, S. P. "The Bible is Not Enough." The Crisis
(42:2, Feb., 1935), pp. 54-58.   DLC; DHU/MO
"Dr. James, a native of British Guiana, returned recently
from several years in Africa and brings the advice that
Christian missionaries will have greater success with their
religion if they will carry along with it more practical medical work."

2871. Jesse, C. "De l'Heresie a l'Emeute: Les Mefaits du
Kitawala." Grands Lacs (61; 1946), pp. 82-84. MH/P

2872. Jesuits. Letters from Missions. Missions de l'Amérique.
Paris: La Society Catholique des Bons Livres, 1827. NN/Sch

2873. Johnson, Thomas Sylvester. The Story of a Mission.
London: S. P. C. K., 1953.   DHU/MO

2874. Johnson, V. E. Pioneering for Christ in East Africa.
Rock Island, Ill.: Augustana Book Concern, 1948. MSL/CHI

2875. Johnson, William Percival. Nyasa: The Great Water.
New York: Negro Universities Press, 1969. DHU/R
"Originally published in 1922."
Written by the Archdeacon of Nyasa under the sponsorship
of the Universities Mission to Central Africa.

2876. Johnston, Harry Hamilton. "The Missionary Attitude
Towards Negro Labour in Africa." The East and the West
(1:3, Jl, 1903), pp. 264-74.   DHU/R

2877. Johnston, James. Missionary Landscapes in the Dark
Continent... New York: A.D.F. Randolph & Co., 1892.
DHU/MO

2878. Johnston, W. C. "A Missionary Lady in the Bush."
The Church at Home and Abroad (23; 1898), p. 34. DHU/R

2879. Jones, Charles H. Africa, the History of Exploration and
Adventure. New York: Henry Holt and Co., 1875. DHU/R
IC/H
Chapt. 20, Christian Missions in Africa.

2880. Jones, David Benjamin, (Mrs.). David Jones, Ambassador
to the Africans. Kansas City, Mo.: Beacon Hill Press, 1955.
NN/Sch

2881. Jones, F. Melville. "An African Church." The East and
the West (16; Apr., 1918), pp. 122-30.   DHU/R

2882. ------ "A Growing Mission in West Africa." The Church
Missionary Review (61; Sept., 1910), pp. 547-51. DHU/R

2883. ------ "The Work of the Church Missionary Society in West
Africa." International Review of Missions (1:2, 1912), pp. 240-
57.   DHU/R

2884. Jones, Thomas Jesse. "The Educational Needs of the
People of Equatorial Africa." Address at 29th Annual Ses-
sion, Foreign Mission Conference of North America, New
York, 1922.   DHU/R

2885. Jordaan, Bee. Splintered Crucifix: Early Pioneers for
Christendom on Madagascar and the Cape of Good Hope.
Cape Town: C. Struik, 1969.   DLC

2886. Joy, Charles R. Africa of Albert Schweitzer. New York:
Harper, 1948.   IC/H

2887. Kennedy, John Herron. Sympathy, Its Foundation and
Legitimate Exercise Considered, in Special Relation to
Africa. A Discourse Delivered on the 4th of July, 1828. In
the Sixth Presbyterian Church. Philadelphia: W. F. Geddes,
1828.   DLC

2888. Keppel, Frederick P. "A Comment on Christian Missions
to Africa." International Review of Missions (18; 1929), pp.
503-08.   DHU/R

2889. Kiazi, Nzita E. "Mariage Chretien vu par un Laic."
Revue du Clerge Africain (26; 3-4, My.-Jl., 1971), pp.
146-52.   DHU/R

2890. Kibicho, Samuel G. God in the African Experience and
the Problem of Revelation in Christianity. Doctoral dissertation. Vanderbilt Univeristy, 1972.

2891. Kieran, John A. "Some Roman Catholic Missionary Attitudes to Africans in Nineteenth Century East Africa." Race
(10:3, Ja., 1969), pp. 341-59. DAU; DGW; CtY; NN; MH

2892. "The Kikuyu Conference: The Controversy Arising from the Kikuyu Conference." Church Missionary Review (65; Feb., 1914), pp. 96-104.   DHU/R

2893. "The Kikuyu Conference: Expressions of Public Opinion and Article in 'The Times' Newspaper." Church Missionary Review (65; Ja., 1914), pp. 38-41.   DHU/R

2894. "The Kikuyu Conference: Resolution of the Committee, 8 November, 1910." Church Missionary Review (65; Ja., 1914), pp. 37-38.   DHU/R

2895. "The Kikuyu Conference: The Primate's Statement." Church Missionary Review (65; Mr., 1914), pp. 170-76. DHU/R

2896. King, Kenneth James. Pan-Africanism and Education: A Study of Race Philanthropy and Education in the Southern States of America and East Africa. London: Oxford University Press, 1971.   DHU/R; DLC; CLU
      Chapter 2, Tuskegee, Philanthropy and the Missionary Societies.

2897. Kingston, Vera. Any Army With Banners; the Romance of Missionary Adventure. London: S. Low, Marston & Co., Ltd., 1931.   NN/Sch

2898. Kirkpatrick, Lois. Methodist at Work in Africa, A Source for those Studying about Africa. Boston: The Methodist Publishing House, 1945.   NN/Sch

2899. Kitching, Arthur L. "A New African Diocese." The Church Missionary Review (77:856, Dec., 1926), pp. 319-28. DHU/R
      Catholic missions in Africa.

2900. Knak, Siegfried. Zwischen Nil und Tafelbai; eine Studie Li er Evangelium, Volkstum und Zivilisation, am Beispiel der Missionsprobleme unter den Bantu, von d. Siegfried Knak...
      1.-3. Tausend. Berlin: Heimatdienst-verlag, 1931. NN/Sch

2901. Krapf, J. Lewis. Travels, Researches, and Missionary Labours During an Eighteen Years Residence in Eastern Africa... London: Frank Cass & Co., 1968. DHU/R; DHU/MO; NN/Sch
      Reprint.

2902. Krueger, Hilmar C. "Reactions to the First Missionaries in Northwest Africa." The Catholic Historical Review (32:3, Oct., 1946), pp. 275-300.   DHU/R

2903. Kumm, Hermann, K. W. African Missionary Heroes and Heroines. New York: The Macmillan Company, 1917. PPT; DHU/R

2904. Lagos, Frank Melville. "The Future of the Church in Africa." The East and the West (22; Apr., 1924), pp. 125-36. DHU/R

2905. Lankenau, F. J. The World is Our Field. St. Louis: Concordia Publishing House, 1928.   MSL/CHI

2906. Latourette, Kenneth S. The Great Century in the Americas, Australasia, and Africa, A.D. 1800-1914. New York: Harper & Bros., 1943.   DHU/R
      In History and Expansion of Christianity, V. 5.

2907. ----- "The Spread of Christianity: British and German Missions in Africa." Prosser Gifford and W. R. Louis, (eds.). Britain and Germany in Africa (New Haven: Yale Univ. Press, 1967), pp. 393-416.   DHU/MO

2908. Laury, Preston A. A History of Lutheran Missions. Reading, Penn.: Pilger Publishing House, 1899.   MSL/CHI

2909. Leclercq, Henri. L'Afrique Chretienne. 2nd ed. Paris: V. Lecoffre, 1904.   NjP

2910. Lecompte, Ernest. "La Mission de Sainte-Marie de Bailoundo." Missions Catholiques (Lyons) (28; 1896), pp. 486-91. CtY; DCU; ICU
      See also Missioni Catholiche (Milan) (26; 1897), pp. 209-11.

2911. Leopard, Donald D. "Africa-Related Materials in European Missionary Archives." African Studies Bulletin (10:2, Sept., 1967), pp. 1-5.   DHU/MO

2912. Le Roy, Alexandre, (bp.). The Evangelization of Africa, 1822-1912. New York: Soc. for Propagation of the Faith, 1911.   DCU

2913. ----- (bp.). The Religion of the Primitives. New York: Negro Universities' Press, 1969. NN; NcD; PCC
      Reprint of the 1922 ed.

2914. "Les Idées Principales du Cardinal Lavigerie Sur l'Evangélisation de l'Afrique. Une Père Blanc." Revue d'Historie des Missions (?49; Sept., 1925), pp. 351-96.   DCU/ST

2915. Leuking, Frederick Dean. Shaping of the Lutheran Missionary Idea. Doctoral dissertation. University of Chicago, 1960.

2916. Levo, John Ernest. The West Adventure. London: Westminster Society for the Propagation of the Gospel in Foreign Parts, 1929.   CtY/DML

2917. Leys, N. "A Problem in East African Missions." International Review of Missions (8; 1919), pp. 155-72. DHU/R
      Criticism of Western missionaries in Africa.

2918. Light and Darkness in East Africa; a Missionary Survey of Uganda, Anglo-Egyptian Sudan, Abyssinia, Eritrea and the Three Somalilands. London: World Dominion Press, 1927.
                         MiBsA; NN/Sch

2919. Lindeman, Esther M. A Survey of Missions in French Equatorial Africa. Masters thesis. Columbia Bible College, (S. C.) 1959.

2920. "The Liquor Traffic in Africa." The Church at Home and Abroad (1; 1887), pp. 560-63.   DHU/R
      Includes account of missionary and missionary societies' protests.

2921. Livingstone, David. Dr. Livingstone's Cambridge Lectures, Together with Prefatory Letter by the Rev. Prof. Sedgwick... Cambridge: Dieghton, Bell & Co., 1858.   NN/Sch

2922. ----- ...Family Letters, 1841-1856... Edited with an introduction by I. Schapera. London: Chatto & Windus, 1959.
                         NN/Sch

2923. ----- Missionary Correspondence, 1841-1856. Berkeley: University of California Press, 1961.   DHU/MO

2924. Livingstone, William Pringle. Christina Forsyth of Fingoland; the Story of the Loneliest Woman in Africa. New York: Hodder and Stoughton, 1918.   NN/Sch

2925. Lloyd, Thomas Ernest. African Harvest. London: Lutterworth Press, 1953.   NN/Sch

2926. Lord, F. Townley. Achievement: A Short History of the Baptist Missionary Society, 1792-1942. London: The Carey Press, 1942.   DLC

2927. Loth, Heinrich. Die Christliche Mission in Südwestafrika; Zur Destruktiven Rolle der Rheinischen Missionsgesellschaft beim Prozess der Staatsbildung in Südwestafrika (1842-1893). Berlin: Akademie-Verlag, 1963.   NjP

2928. Lowrie, John C. A Manual of the Foreign Missions of the Presbyterian Church in the United States of America. New York: William Rankin, Jr., 1868.   DHU/R
      Includes discussion of missions in Western Africa and in the West Indies.

2929. Luck, Anne. African Saint; the Story of Apolo Kivebulaya.
London: SCM Press, 1963.   MNtcA; DHU/MO

2930. Luke, James. Pioneering in Mary Slessor's Country. London
Epworth Press, 1929.   NN/Sch

2931. Macdonald, Allan John. Trade, Politics and Christianity in
Africa and the East. London: Longmans, Green, 1916. NN/Sch

2932. Macgregor, J. K. "Christian Missions and Marriage Usage
in Africa." International Review of Missions (24; 1935), pp.
379-91.   DHU/R

2933. MacGregor-Hastie, Roy. Africa, Background for Today.
New York: Criterion, 1967.   DHU/R
     Chapter 5 and 8, information on "Ethiopia, the first Christian
Empire & Missionary Influence in West Africa."

2934. Mackenzie, Jean Kenyon. An African Trail. West Medford,
Mass.: The Central Committee on the United Study of Foreign
Missions, etc., 1917.   DHU/MO

2935. ----- Spiritual Clinic in Africa." Missionary Review (41;
My., 1918), pp. 339-42.   DHU/R

2936. Mackintosh, Catharine Winkworth. Coillard of Zambesi;
the Lives of Francois and Christina Coillard, of the Paris
Missionary Society, in South and Central Africa (1858-1904).
New York: American Tract Society, 1907.   NN/Sch

2937. Maples, Ellen. Chauncy Maples, Pioneer Missionary in
East Central Africa for Nineteen Years and Bishop of Likoma,
A.D. 1895. London: Longmans, Green & Co., 1899. DLC

2938. Marett, R. R. Faith, Hope and Charity in Primitive Religion.
New York: n.p., 1932.   DHU/R
     Anthropological evaluation of primitive religion to determine
the extent to which it furthers morality by stimulating the
appropriate emotions. Ashanti, Bantu, Dinka and religious
rites in Dahomey and ancient Egypt.

2939. Marriott, H. P. Fitzgerald. "The Secret Societies of West
Africa." Journal of Anthropological Institute (29; 1899), pp. 21-
24.   DCU/A

2940. Mason, Madison Charles B. Solving the Problem: a Series
of Lectures. Chicago: n.p., 1917.   NN/Sch
     Negro author.

2941. Matheson, Elizabeth M. African Apostles. Staten Island,
New York: Alba House, 1963.   DCU
     "White Fathers Missionary work in Africa.

2942. Mathews, Basil Joseph. Black Treasure; the Youth of Africa
in a Changing World. New York: Friendship Press, 1928.
                NN/Sch

2943. ----- Consider Africa. New York: Friendship Press, 1936.
                NN/Sch

2944. Maze, Jules. La Collaboration Scolaire des Gouvernements
Coloniaux et des Missions. Afrique Britannique, Afrique
Belge, Afrique Francaise. Alger: Maison-Carree, 1933.
                NjP

2945. McGavran, Donlad Anderson. The Disciplining of Africa
in This Generation. New York: n.p., 1955. MiBsA

2946. McKee, William. History of the Sherbro Mission, West
Africa, Under the Direction of the Missionary Society of
The U. B. in Christ. Dayton, Ohio: n.p., 1874. DOUM/EUB

2947. McKenzie, P. R. "Samuel Crowther's Attitude to Other
Faiths - The Early Period." The Bulletin of the Society for
African Church History (3:1-2; 1969-70), pp. 28-43. DHU/R
     Discusses his attitude toward the traditional religions of
Africa.
     Also: Orita: Ibadan Journal of Religious Studies (5:1, Je.,
1971), pp. 3-17.   DHU/R

2948. McLanaham, Samuel. Isabella A. Nassau of Africa. New
York: Women's Board of Foreign Missions of the Presbyterian
Church, 190-.   NN/Sch

2949. Meinhof, Carl. "Changes in African Conceptions of Law Due
to the Influence of Christian Missions." International Review
of Missions (18; 1929), pp. 430-35.   DHU/R

2950. Methodist Overseas Missions; Gazetteer and Statistics.
New York: n. p., 1946.   NN/Sch

2951. Miller, Basil William. Twenty Missionary Stories from
Africa. Grand Rapids: Zondervan Pub. House, 1951. NN/Sch

2952. Milum, John P. Thomas Birch Freeman: Missionary Pioneer to Ashanti, Dahomey, and Egbe. n.p.: Partridge, 1893.
                NNMR

2953. Misiones Capuchinas en Africa. Madrid: Consejo Superior
de Investigaciones Cientificas, Instituto Santo Toribio de
Mogrovejo, 1950.   NNCor
     Missions in Africa of the Capuchins order.

2954. Missionary Atlas, A Manual of the Foreign Work of the
Christian and Missionary Alliance. Harrisburg, Pa.:
Christian Publications, Inc., 1964.   DHU/R
     Includes sections on West Africa, Congo and Gabon.

2955. Moffat, John Smith. "The Second Stage of Missionary Work."
The East and The West (5; Oct., 1907), pp. 436-43.   DHU/R
     Africa- General.

2956. Moffat, R. Adventures of a Missionary; or Rivers of Water in
a Dry Place. Miami: Mnemosyne, 1969.   INU

2957. Moister, William. Memorials of Missionary Labours in
Western Africa and the West Indies; With Historical and Descrip-
tive Observations. New York: Lane and Scott, 1851. CtY;
NN/Sch

2958. Mondini, A. G. Africa or Death; A Biography of Bishop
Daniel Comboni, Founder of Missionary Societies of the Verona
Fathers (Sons S. H.) and the Verona Sisters. Boston: St. Paul
Editions, 1964.   IC/H
     Missions in East Africa.

2959. Montgomery, H. H. "Education in Tropical Africa."
East and West (23; Ja., 1925), pp. 1-7.   DHU/R
     An evaluation of Missionary education in Africa.

2960. Moore, George F. "Protestant Missions in East Africa."
Andover Review (1:4, Apr., 1884), pp. 387-407+. DHU/R

2961. Moorhouse, Geoffrey. The Missionaries. London: Eyre
Methven, 1973.   DLC; TxDaTS; MiBsA
     Protestant missions in Africa.

2962. Morcelli, Stafano Antonia. Africa Christiana. Bresoia:
Ex Officina Bettoniana, 1816.   DLC; MH; NjPT

2963. Morrill, Madge (Haines). Dans la Brousse Africaine; le
Dr. E. G. Marcus en Face de la Maladie et de la Superstition
dans l'EstAfricain. Dammarie - les- Lys Editions "Les Signes
des Temps", 1951.   MiBsA

2964. Morrison, James Horne. The Missionary Heroes of Africa.
New York: George H. Doran Co., 1922.   NN/Sch

2965. ----- Streams in the Desert; a Picture of Life in Livingstonia.
New York: Doran, 1919?   MiBsA; NjP
     Missions in Central Africa.

2966. Morshead, Anne Elisabeth M. The History of the Universities
Mission to Central Africa, 1859-1909. London: Office of the
Universities Mission to Central Africa, 1909.   NjP

2967. Mott, John Raleigh. The Decisive Hour of Christian
Missions... New York: Student Volunteer Movement for Foreign
Missions, Association Press, 1911.   DHU/MO

2968. Mouezy, Henri. ...Assinie et le Royaume de Krinjabo, Histoire et Coutumes. Paris: Larose, 1953. NN/Sch

2969. Mueller, John Theodore. Brightest Light for Darkest Africa. St. Louis: Concordia Publishing House, 1936. MSL/CHI

2970. ----- Great Missionaries to Africa. Grand Rapids, Mich.: Zondervan Pub. House, 1941.   NN/Sch

2971. ----- How We Got to Africa. St. Louis: Evangelical Lutheran Synod of Missouri, Ohio, and Other States, n.d.   MSL/CHI

2972. Murray, Albert Victor. "Christianity and Rural Civilization." International Review of Missions (19; 1930), pp. 388-97. DHU/R Includes Africa.

2973. ----- "Education in East Africa." The East and West Review (4:1, Ja., 1938), pp. 76-82.   DHU/R
Christian missions urging that education continue to Christianize.

2974. ----- The School in the Bush; A Critical Study of the Theory and Practice of Native Education in Africa. New York: Longmans Green & Co., 1929.   NN/Sch

2975. Nassau, Robert Hamill. Crowned in Palm Land. A Story of African Mission Life... Philadelphia: J. B. Lippincott & Co., 1874.   NN/Sch

2976. ----- "Ibiya--a West African Pastor." Missionary Review of the World (37; Je., 1914), pp. 442-44.   DHU/R

2977. Naylor, Wilson Samuel. Daybreak in the Dark Continent. New York: Missionary Education Movement of the United States and Canada, 1915.   DHU/R; NN/Sch

2978. Neckebrouck, V. L'Afrique Noire et la Crise Religieuse de L'Occident. Tabora, Tanzania: T.M.P. Book Dept., 1971.   PPT

2979. Neill, Stephen Charles. Colonialism and Christian Missions. New York: McGraw-Hill, 1966.   DHU/R

2980. Nevinson, Henry W. A Modern Slavery. New York: Schocken Books, 1968.   DHU/R
Chapter VII, Savages and Missions.

2981. New York, Missionary Research Library. Directory of North American Protestant Foreign Missionary Agencies. New York: Missionary Research Library, 1960.   DLC

2982. "Nineteenth-Century Crisis and Religious Systems in East and Central Africa." T. O. Ranger and I. Kimambo, (eds.). Historical Study of African Religion (Berkeley: Univ. of Calif. Press, 1972), pp. 151-217.   DHU/R

2983. Noble, Frederic Perry. Outlook for African Missions in the Twentieth Century." J. W. E. Bowen, (ed.). Africa and the American Negro: Addresses and Proceedings of the Congress on Africa. (Miami, Fla.: Mnemosyne Publishing Inc., 1969), pp. 61-67.   DHU/R

2984. ----- The Redemption of Africa; A Story of Civilization. With Maps, Statistical Tables and Select Bibliography of the Literature of African Missions ... Chicago: F. H. Revell, 1899.   NN/Sch

2985. North, Eric McCoy. The Kingdom and the Nations. West Medford, Mass.: The Central Committee on the United Study of Foreign Missions, 1921.   NN/Sch

2986. Northcott, William Cecil. David Livingstone: His Triumph, Decline and Fall. Philadelphia: The Westminister Press, 1973.   DHU/R
A re-appraisal of Livingstone written by a secretary for fifteen years of the London Missionary Society.

2987. ----- and Joyce Reason. Six Missionaries in Africa: Robert Moffat, David Livingstone, James Stewart, Alexander Mackay, Mary Slessor and Albert Cook. London: Oxford University Press, 1960.   PPT

2988. Notice sur la Société des Missions Evangéliques, Chez les Peuples non Chretiens. Paris: Chez J. J. Risler, Librarie, 1839.   DHU/MO

2989. Nyblade, Orville W. Factors Related to Persistence in the Protestant Missionary Vocation in Sub-Saharan Africa: 1961-1967. Doctoral dissertation. University of Pittsburgh, 1970.

2990. Oldham, Joseph Houldsworth. "Christian Education in Africa." The Church Missionary Review (75:848, Dec., 1924), pp. 305-14.   DHU/R

2991. ----- "Christian Missions and African Labor." International Review of Missions (10; Apr., 1921), pp. 183-95.   DHU/R

2992. ----- "The Christian Opportunity in Africa: Some Reflections on the Report of the Phelps-Stokes Commission." International Review of Missions (14; 1925), pp. 173-87. DHU/R

2993. ----- "Dr. Siegfried Knak on the Christian Task in Africa." International Review of Missions (20; 1931), pp. 547-55.   DHU/R

2994. ----- The Remaking of Man in Africa. London: Oxford University Press, H. Milford, 1931.   NN/Sch

2995. Orchard, Ronald Kenneth. Africa Steps Out. London: Edinburgh House, 1952.   NN/Sch

2996. Osmunson, Robert L. Crash Landing. Mountain View, Calif.: Pacific Press, 1963.   MiBsA
Seventh-day Adventist missions in Africa.

2997. Overs, Walter Henry. Stories of African Life. New York: E. S. Gorham, 1924.   NN/Sch

2998. Pan-African Catechetical Study Week, 1st, Katigondo, 1964. Katigondo: Presenting the Christian Message to Africa. Edited by Robert J. Lodogar and Geoffrey Chapman. Deacon Books, 1965.   NNC; DLC; ICU

2999. Pan-African Catholic Education Conference, Leopoldville, Aug. 16-23, 1965. Catholic Education in the Service of Africa: Report.... Brussels: Regional Secretariat for Africa and Madagascar, Catholic International Education Office, 1966.   DLC; MBU

3000. Parker, Joseph I., (ed.). Directory of World Missions. New York: International Missionary Council, 1938. DHU/R Includes directory material on Protestant missions in Africa and the West Indies.

3001. Parsons, Ellen C. Christus Liberator; an Outline Study of Africa. New York: Macmillan, 1905. DHU/MO; NN/Sch

3002. Parsons, Robert T. "Missionary - African Relations." Civilizations (3:4, 1953), pp. 505-16.   DAU; DGU

3003. -----(ed.). Windows on Africa: A Symposium. Leiden: E. J. Brill, 1971.   DHU/R; DLC
Written by African and Western writers representing seven African countries and nine different Protestant denominations.

3004. Patton, C. "Continental Program for Africa." Missionary Review (41; Ja., 1918), pp. 29-36.   DHU/R

3005. Payne, John. A Full Description of the African Field of the Protestant Episcopal Church with Statistics from All the Mission Stations. (Corrected to 1st January, 1866)...New York: Foreign Committee of the Board of Missions, 1866?   NN/Sch

3006. p'Bitek, Okot. "DeHellenising the Church." East Africa Journal (6:8, Ag., 1969), pp. 8-10.   DHU/MO

3007. Peltola, Matti. Afrikan Valtiollisen Murroksen Vaikutus Lahetystyohon Der Politische Umbruch in Afrika und die Christliche Mission, Zusammenfassung. Helsinki: Suomen Lähetystieteelinen Seura, 1962.   NNCor

3008. "Peril to Missionary Africa." Literary Digest. (56; Feb. 9, 1918), p. 33.   DHU/R

3009. Personnalite Africaine et Catholicisme. Paris: Presence Africaine, 1963.   DLC; MBU; NNC

3010. Peters, Erna Alma. The Contribution to Education by the Pentecostal Assemblies of Canada. Homewook, Manitoba: By the Author, 1971.   DHU/R
    Chapters 6-8, Educational work in Africa.

3011. Peters, G. "Pauline Patterns of Church-Mission Relationships." Evangelical Missions Quarterly (9; Wint., 1973), pp. 111-18.   DAU/W
    Indigenous churches.

3012. Petersen, William J. Another Hand on Mine: The Story of Dr. Carl K. Becker of the Africa Inland Mission. Michigan: Zondervan Publishing House, 1967.   DHU/R

3013. Philip, Robert. The Life, Times and Missionary Enterprises of the Rev. John Campbell. London: John Snow, 1841. CtY-DM

3014. Phillips, Gene D. The Attitudes and Practices of Southern Baptist Missions in Africa to the Problems of Polygamy. Masters thesis. Southeastern Baptist Theological Seminary, 1965.

3015. Pierson, Arthur Tappan. "Khama, the Good--Christian Chief of Africa." Missionary Review of the World (24; Feb., 1901), pp. 93-99.   DHU/R

3016. ----- The Miracle of Missions; or, The Modern Marvels in the History of Missionary Enterprise. New York: Funk & Wagnalls Co., 1895.   NN/Sch

3017. ----- "One of the Miracles of Missions." Missionary Review of the World (32; Je., 1908), pp. 418-22.   DHU/R

3018. Polack, W. G. Into All the World. St. Louis: Concordia Publishing House, 1930.   MSL/CHI
    Lutheran Church and missions in Africa.

3019-20. Porter, Dorothy B., (comp.). A Catalogue of the African Collection in the Moorland Foundation Howard University Library. Washington, D.C.: Published for the Moorland Foundation and the Program of African Studies by Howard Univ. Press, 1958. Negro author.

3021. Price, Thomas. "The Task of Mission Schools in Africa." International Review of Missions (27; 1938), pp. 233-38.   DHU/R

3022. Price, William Salter. My Third Campaign in East Africa: A Story of Missionary Life in Troublous Times. London: W. Hunt & Co., 1891.   DHU/MO

3023. Pringle, M. A. A Journey in East Africa Towards the Mountains of the Moon. Freeport, New York: Books for Libraries Press, 1972.   DHU/R
    Reprint of 1886 edition.
    Universities mission project in East Africa.

3024. "Racialism and Missions: The Papal Injunction." East and West Review (5:2, Apr. 1939), pp. 161-65.   DHU/R

3025. Ragi, Otto. "Uber Die Aufgaben der Missionsschule in Afrika." Evangelisches Missions-Magazin (8; 1925), pp. 242-49.   DLC

3026. Ransom, C. N. "South Africa, a Burden, a Vision, and a Duty." Missionary Review of the World (26; Je., 1903), pp. 427-30.   DHU/R

3027. Rauscher, Fridolin. Die Mitarbeit der Eihmeimischen Laien am Apostolat in den Missionen der Weissen Vater. Munster: Westfalen, Aschendorffsche Verlagsbuchandlung, 1953.   NNCor
    Missions in Africa. White Fathers.

3028. Reeck, Darrell L. A Socio-Historical Analysis of Modernization and Related Mission Influences in Two Chiefdoms in West Africa, 1875-1940. Doctoral dissertation. Boston University, 1970.

3029. Reed, James Eldin. "American Foreign Policy, the Politics of Missions and Josiah Strong, 1890-1900." Church History (41:2, Je., 1972), pp. 230-45.   DHU/R

3030. Rego, Antonio da Silva. Alguns Probemas Sociologico-Missionârios da Africa Negra. Lisboa: Junta de Investigacoes do Ultramar, Centro de Estudos Politicos e Sociais, 1960.   NNCor

3031. Renault, Francois. Lavigerie, L'Escalvage Africain, et L'Europe, 1868-1892. Paris: E. de Boccard, 1971. NjP; PPT

3032. Retief, Malcolm Wilheim. A Program of Religious Education in Africa. Doctoral dissertation. Southern Baptist Theological Seminary, 1930.

3033. Richards, Charles Granston. Krapf, Missionary and Explorer. London: Nelson, 1950.   NN/Sch

3034. Richardson, Kenneth. Garden of Miracles: A History of the African Inland Mission. London: Africa Inland Mission & Victory Press, 1968.   MiBsA; MNtcA
    Missions in Central Africa.

3035. Ridgel, Alfred L. Africa and African Methodism. Atlanta: Franklin Printing and Publishing Co., 1896. TNMph

3036. Roberts, Thomas H. "Preaching in the Vernacular." The Church at Home and Abroad (2; 1887), pp. 406-07. DHU/R
    Glimah, Vei Country, West Africa.
    Presbyterian mission.

3037. Robinson, Charles Henry. History of Christian Missions. Edinburgh: T. & T. Clark, 1915.   MNtcA
    Missions in Africa.

3038. Robinson, James Herman. "Africa and Asia's Challenge to Missions." The African Methodist Episcopal Church Review (68:176, Apr.-Je., 1933), pp. 90-4.   DHU/R
    Negro author.

3039. ----- Tomorrow is Today. Philadelphia: Christian Education Press, 1954.   DHU/R
    Negro author.

3040. Robinson, Virgil Eugene. Ye Shall Reap. Nashville: Southern Pub. Association, 1964.   MiBsA
    Missions in Africa, Seventh Day Adventists.

3041. Rodeheaver, Homer Alvan. Singing Black; Twenty Thousand Miles With a Music Missionary. Chicago: The Rodeheaver Company, 1936.   MiBsA
    Missions in Africa.

3042. Roesler, Calvin L. The American Negro as a Foreign Missionary. Master's thesis. Columbia Bible College (S.C.), 1953.

3043. Roome, William John Waterman. Can Africa be Won? London: A. & C. Black, 1927.   NN/Sch

3044. ----- "A Chain of Mission Stations Across Africa." The
Church Missionary Review (73:837, Mr., 1922), pp. 35-46.
                                                    DHU/R

3045. ----- Through Central Africa for the Bible. London:
Edinburgh, Marshall, Morgan and Scott, ltd., 1929. MiBsA

3046. Roosevelt, T. "African Missions." Missionary Review
(34; Ja., 1911), pp. 55-56.   DHU/R

3047. Roseberry, Robert Sherman. The Niger Vision. A Modern
Miracle of Missions. The Record of the Opening of the Western
Soudan to the Lighthouse along the Niger with its Tributaries,
Program for Immediate Evangelization of Vast Pagan Areas.
Harrisburg, Pa.: Christian Publications, 1934. NN/Sch

3048. ----- The Soul of French West Africa. Harrisburg, Pa.:
Christian Publication, 1947.   PPT
        Missions in French West Africa.

3049. Ross, Emory. Africa in Crisis: Address. New York: Africa
Committee of the Foreign Missions Conference of North America,
1947.

3050. ----- African Heritage. New York: Friendship Press, 1952.
                                                    DHU/MO

3051. Roux, Andre. L'Evangile dans la Foret: Naissance d'une
Eglise en Afrique Noire. Paris: Editions du Cerf, 1971.
                                                    DLC

3052. Rowe, John Allen. "The Purge of Christians at Mwanga's
Court." Journal of African History (5:1, 1964), pp. 55-72.
DAU; DGW; DGU; DHU/MO

3053. Russel, B. T. What are the Policies, Practices and Attitudes
of the Foreign Mission Boards in North America. With Reference to the Sending of American Negroes as Foreign Missionaries. Master's thesis. College of Missions, 1924.
Education, 1945.

3054. Russell, Harvey Gray. Influence of the White Man Upon
Central Africa. Masters thesis. College of Missions, 1924.

3055. Rutherford, J. "North Africa from a Missionary Point of
View." Missionary Review of the World (34; Je., 1911), pp.
415-24.   DHU/R

3056. Sailer, Thomas Henry Powers. Christian Adult Education
in Rural Asia and Africa. New York: Friendship Press, 1943.
                                                    NN/Sch

3057. St. John, B. "Missionary Occupation of Africa." Missionary Review (40; Nov., 1917), pp. 811-14.   DHU/R

3058. Sanders, W. H. and F. A. Walter. "The West Central
African Mission." Missionary Herald (81:5-7, 10-12, My.-Jl.,
Oct.-Dec., 1885), pp. 194-5, 240-2, 278-9, 397-9, 465-7,
523.   DHU/R

3059. Santadrea, Stefano. Bibliografia Di Studi Africani Della
Missione Dell'Africa Centrale. Verona: Instituto Missioni
Africane, 1948.   DLC

3060. Sartre, Robert. "Christianisme et Cultures Africaines."
Tam-Tam Review Des Etudiants Catholiques Africains (6; 1957),
pp. 12-23.   DLC

3061. Scheel, M. "Missionary Work and Healing." International
Review of Missions (53; 1964), pp. 265-71.   DHU/R

3062. Schieffelin, Henry Maunsell. People of Africa. New York:
Anson D. F. Randolph & Co., 1871.   PPAmP; PH; NjP

3063. Schön, Jakob Friedrick and Samuel H. Crowther. Journals
of the Rev. J. F. Schon and Mr. Samuel Crowther, who...
Accompanied the Expedition up the Niger in 1841, in Behalf of
the Church Missionary Society. London: Hatchard, 1842.
                                                    NN/Sch

3064. Setiloane, Gabriel M. "I Am an African." International
Review of Mission (58:230, Apr., 1969), pp. 204-07. DHU/R
"The testimony of an African Christian" delivered in a
United Worship Service of the Selly Oak College.

3065. Shaffer, Grace Duffield. Africa's "Floating Logs". Washington: Review and Herald, 1972.   MiBsA
        Missions in Africa. Seventh-day Adventist missions in Africa.

3066. Sharp, W. "Cardinal Lavigerie's Work in North Africa."
Atlantic (74; Ag., 1894), pp. 214-27.   DHU

3067. Shaw, Trever. Through Ebony Eyes; Evangelism Through
Journalism in West Africa. London: United Society for
Christian Literature, Lutterworth Press, 1956.   NN/Sch

3068. Sheppard, William Henry. "Light in Darkest Africa."
Extracts from two addresses given at Hampton in Feb., 1905,
by Rev. William H. Sheppard, F. R. G. S., an African Missionary
of the Southern Presbyterian Church, and a Hampton ex-student.
Southern Workman (34:4, Apr., 1905), pp. 218-27. DLC;
                                                    DHU/MO
        Negro author.

3069. ----- "Response of Africa to the Gospel." Arcadius S.
Trawick, (ed.). The New Voice in Race Adjustments (New
York: Student Volunteer Movement, 1914), pp. 120-28.
                                                    DHU/R
        Negro author.

3070. Shillito, Edward. Craftsmen All; Fellow Workers in the
Younger Churches... New York: Friendship Press 1933.
                                                    DLC; NN/Sch

3071. Simon, Jean Marie, (bp.). Bishop for the Hottentots; African
Memories, 1882-1909. Translated by Angeline Bouchard.
New York: Benriger, 1959.   DLC; NN/Sch

3072. "Simple Walk with Christ: Bishop Festo Kivengere." World
Vision (17; My., 1973), p. 20.   DGW
        Missions and converts in Africa.

3073. Singleton, George A. "God, the Bible, and the African."
The African Methodist Episcopal Church Review (78:213, Jl.-
Sept., 1962), pp. 81-91.   DHU/R
        Negro author.

3074. Smith, Charles Spencer, (bp.). Glimpses of Africa, West
and Southwest Coast, Containing the Author's Impressions and
Observations During a Voyage of Six Thousand Miles from Sierra
Leone to St. Paul de Loanda and Return, Including the Rio del
Ray and Cameroons Rivers, and the Congo River from its mouth
to Matadi, Introduction by Bishop H. M. Turner... Nashville,
Tenn.: Publishing House A. M. E. Church Sunday School Union,
1895.   NN/Sch
        Negro author.

3075. Smith, Edwin W. Aggrey of Africa: A Study in Black and
White. London: Student Christian Movement, 1929. DLC;
PPFA; PCC; NNC; MNtcA

3076. ----- The Christian Mission in Africa, a Study Based on the
Work of the International Conference at Le Zoute, Belgium
September 14th to 21st, 1926. New York: The International
Missionary Council, 1926. MiBsA; DHU/MO; NNCor; MNtcA

3077. ----- Knowing the African. London: United Society for
Christian Literature, 1946.   NN/Sch

3078. Smith, Eli. An Address on the Missionary Character. Boston:
Printed by Perkins & Marvin, 1840.   DHU/R
        Microfilm.

3079. Smith, Robert. "A Scene in African Missionary Life."
Baptist Magazine (London) (60; 1863), pp. 122-23. GMM; OC

3080. ----- "Trials of the Converts in Africa." Baptist Magazine
(London) (60; 1863), p. 804.   GMM; OC

3081. Smith, S. R. "The Development of the Church in West
       Africa." The Church Missionary Review (78:857, Mr., 1927),
       pp. 31-41.   DHU/R

3082. Society for Promoting Christian Knowledge... Publication
       for East and Central Africa. London: n.p., 1928. NNAB

3083. Society of African Missions. One Hundred Years of Mission-
       ary Achievement, 1856-1956. Cork, Ireland: African Missions,
       1957?   DLC

3084. Speer, Robert Elliott. Missiona and Modern History; a
       Study of the Missionary Aspects of Some Great Movements of
       the Nineteenth Century. New York: Fleming H. Revell Co.,
       1904.   NN/Sch

3085. Springer, Eva Alice. As I Saw Africa: Land of Tragedy and
       Triumph. Cincinnati: Powell & White, 1936. TN/DCHS.
       Disciples of Christ (Christian Churches) and missions in
       Africa.

3086. Stanley, M. W. "Friends Industrial Mission in Africa."
       Missionary Review (40; Nov., 1917), pp. 815-22. DHU/R

3087. Stanton, H. U. Weitbrecht. "A Study of African Missions."
       The Church Missionary Review (74:844, Dec., 1923), pp. 227-34.
                                           DHU/R

3088. Starbuck, Charles C. "Central and Eastern Africa."
       Andover Review (9:49, Ja., 1888), pp. 90-102; (11:45, My.,
       1889), pp. 533-59; (12:67, Jl., 1889), pp. 103-12. DHU/R

3089. ----- (A General View of Missions). "Western Africa."
       Andover Review (12: 71, Nov., 1889), pp. 537-45. DHU/R

3090. Statton, Arthur B. and Samuel G. Ziegler. The Deputation
       to Africa 1928-1929... Foreign Missionary Society, United
       Brethren Church in Christ, 1929.   DOUM/EUB
       Mim.

3091. Stauffer, Milton Theobald, ed. ...Thinking with Africa.
       Chapters assembled and edited. New York: Published for the
       Student Volunteer Movement for Foreign Missions by the Mission-
       ary Education Movement of the United States and Canada, 1927.
                                           DHU/MO

3092. Stevens, D. A. "African Christianity and the Sacraments."
       East and West (22; Oct., 1924), pp. 330-45.   DHU/R

3093. Stewart, James. Dawn in the Dark Continent. New York:
       Fleming H. Revell Co., 1903.   DHU/MO

3094. Stinetorf, Louise A. Beyond the Hungry Country. Philadel-
       phia: Lippincott, 1954.   NN/Sch

3095. ----- White Witch Doctor. Philadelphia: Westminster
       Press, 1950.   NN/Sch

3096. Stock, Eugene. "C. M. S. Native Church Organization."
       International Review of Missions (3; 1914), pp. 266-83.
                                           DHU/R

3097. ----- The History of the Church Missionary Society, its
       Environment, its Men and its Work. London: Church Mission-
       ary Society, 1899-1916.

3098. ----- "Livingstone." The Church Missionary Review (64;
       Mr., 1913), pp. 135-43.   DHU/R
       David Livingstone and the Christian Missionary Society.

3099. ----- "A Notable African Bishop." Church Missionary
       Review (68; Ag., 1917), pp. 323-32.   DHU/R

3100. Stock, Sarah Geraldina. Missionary Heroes of Africa.
       London: Missionary Society, 1897.   CtY; PPT

3101. Stone, W. Vernon. "The Livingstonia Mission and the Bemba."
       Bulletin of the Society for African Church History (2:4, 1968),
       pp. 311-22.   DHU/R
       Central Africa.

3102. Streit, Robert, and Johannes Dindinger. Bibliotheca Missionum.
       Munster I. W.: Aachen, 1916-63.   DLC
       Tremendous bibliographical enterprise covering the literature
       of Catholic missions Throughout the world from earliest times
       to the present day.

3103. Sundermeier, T. "Gesetz und Geseslzlichkeit in den
       Afrikanischen Kirchen." Evangelische Theologie (31; Feb.,
       1971), pp. 99-114.   DAU/W; DCU/TH

3104. Talbot, Percy A. "Aspects of West African Religions."
       Edinburgh Review (220; Jl., 1914), pp. 96-114.   DHU

3105. The Task of the Christian Church; a World Survey. London:
       World Dominion Press, 1926.   NN/Sch

3106. Taylor, Stephen Earl. The Price of Africa. New York:
       Young People's Missionary Movement, 1902.   NN/Sch
       The forward mission study courses; ed. by A. R. Wells
       and S. E. Taylor.

3107. Taylor, William, (bp.). The Flaming Torch in Darkest
       Africa. New York: Eaton & Maine, 1898.   NN/Sch

3108. Teilhard de Chardin, Joseph Michel. La Guinée Supérieure
       et ses Missions Etudes Geographique, Sociale et Religieuse des
       Contrées Evangelisées Par les Missionaires de la Société des
       Missions Africaines de Lyon. Tours: A. Cattier, 1889.
                                           NN/Sch

3109. Thiessen, John Caldwell. A Survey of World Missions.
       Chicago: Inter-Varsity Press, 1955.   DHU/R

3110. Thompson, George. The Palm Land; or West Africa, Illus-
       trated. Being a History of Missionary Labors and Travels, With
       Descriptions of Men and Things in Western Africa. Cincinnati:
       Moore, Wilstach, Keys, 1859.   MiBsA; NjP
       Also published in London: Dawson, 1969.

3111. Thornton, Douglas Montagu. Africa Waiting; or, The Prob-
       lem of Africa's Evangelization. London: Student Volunteer
       Missionary Union, 1898.   NN/Sch

3112. Timothy, Bankole. Missionary Shepherds and African Sheep;
       How Does Christianity as Preached and Practiced by Europe
       and America Appear to Africans. Ibadan: Daystar Press,
       1971.   PPT

3113. Todd, John M. African Missions; A Historical Study of the
       Society of African Missions Whose Priests Have Worked on the
       Coast of West Africa and Inland, in Liberia, the Ivory Coast,
       Ghana, Togoland, Dahomey and Nigeria, and in Egypt, Since
       1856. London: Burns and Oates, 1962.   MNtcA; DLC

3114. Toenjes, Hermann. Ovambaland, Land, Lente, Missions,
       Mit Besonderer Berücksichtigung Seines Grossten Stammes
       Onkuanjama. Berlin: M. Warneck, 1911.   CtY; IEN

3115. Toppenberg, Valdemar E. Africa Has My Heart. Mountain
       View, Calif.: Pacific Press Pub. Association, 1958. MiBsA
       Seventh-Day Adventist missions in Africa.

3116. "The Training of Village Teachers in Africa." International
       Review of Missions (18; 1929), pp. 231-49.   DHU/R
       British missions in Africa.

3117. Tucker, Alfred R., (bp.). Toro. Visits to Ruwenzari,
       "Mountains of the Moon." London: Church Missionary Society,
       1899.   CtY

3118. Tutuola, Amos. My Life in the Bush of Ghosts. London:
       Faber and Faber, 1954. New York: Grove Press, 1954.
                                           DHU/MO; CtY; NN/Sch; CLU; CU

3119. Uganda, J. J., (bp.). "The Proposed East African Province."
       The Church Overseas (2:6, Apr., 1929), pp. 133-39. DHU/R

3120. Underhill, Edward Bean. _Alfred Saker, Missionary to Africa._
London: n. p. , 1884.   CtY

3121. Universities' Mission to Central Africa. _The History of the_
Universities' Mission to Central Africa. London: n. p. , 1955-
62.   MiBsA

3122. Vandegrift, Eileen Gordon. _The Christian Missionary Society._
Masters thesis. Butler Univ. , 1945.   TN/DCHS
Disciples of Christ (Christian Churches) and Missions.

3123. Vandervort, Eleanor. _A Leopard Tamed: The Story of an_
African Pastor, His People and His Problems. New York:
Harper & Row, 1968.   DHU/R

3124. Van Dyke, D. "Letter From Africa." _The Christian Intel-_
ligencer (82:32, Ag. 9, 1911), pp. 511-12.   DHU/R
Dutch Reformed Church mission in East Africa.

3125. Van Rensselaer, Cortland. "God Glorified by Africa."
Presbyterian Magazine (27; Feb. , 1857), p. 30. DHU; DLC
Written by white Presbyterian minister.

3126. Vaughan, Edward Thomas. _A Sermon Preached at St._
Andrew by the Wardrobe and St. Anne Black Friars, on Tues-
day, May 2, 1815, before the Church Missionary Society for
Africa and the East, being their Fifteenth Anniversary; also the
Report of the Committee to the Annual Meeting, held on the
Same Day and a List of Subscribers and benefactors. London:
Whittingham & Rowland, 1815.   NN/Sch

3127. Wagner, C. Peter. "Missions From the Third World."
Christianity Today (17; Je. 22, 1973), pp. 11-14. DHU/R

3128. Wakefield, E. S. _Thomas Wakefield, Missionary and Geo-_
graphical Pioneer In East Equatorial Africa. London: Religious
Tract Society, 1904.   PPT

3129. Walker, Frank Deaville. _The Call of the Dark Continent;_
A Study in Missionary Progress, Opportunity and Urgency.
London: Wesleyan Methodist Missionary Society, 1911.
NN/Sch

3130. ----- _The Day of Harvest in the White Fields of West Africa._
London: Cargate, 1925.   NjP

3131. Walker, Samuel Abraham. _Missions in Western Africa,_
Among the Soosoos, Bulloms, &c. Being the First Undertaken
by the Church Missionary Society for Africa and the East.
With an introduction containing: I. A Sketch of Western
Africa; with a description of the principal tribes inhabiting
that coast. II. A Brief History of the Slave Trade to the
Present Day. III. Some Account of the Early African
Churches. IV. A Condensed Survey of all the Missionary
Exertions of Modern Times, in Favor of Africa. Dublin:
W. Curry, 1845.   CtY-D; NN/Sch

3132. Wall, Martha. _Splinters From An African Log._ Chicago:
Moody Press, 1962.   MiBsA
Missions in West Africa.
Seventh-day Adventist Church and African missions.

3133. Wallace, Archer. _Blazing New Trails._ With an introduction
by Rev. George A. Little. New York: Doubleday, Doran, 1928.
NN/Sch

3134. Wallis, Patrick. "Daniel Faragi - Catechist. A Missionary
Tale of African Slave Days." _Missionary Annals, Rathmines_
(8; 1926), pp. 132-44.

3135. Walsh, William P. _Modern Heroes of the Missionary Field._
New York: Thomas Whittaker, 1895.   DHU/R
Biographies of missionaries to Africa in the eighteenth and
nineteenth centuries.

3136. Ward, A. "Missionaries in Egypt." _Nineteenth Century_
(48; Ag. , 1900), pp. 207-18.   DHU

3137. Warnke, Mabel. _Partners the World Around._ St. Louis:
Concordia Publishing House, 1966.   MSL/CHI
Lutherans and missions in Africa.

3138. Webb, Allan B. "From Bloemfontein to the Zambesi; a Great
Missionary Journey by the Bishop of Bloemfontein." _Mission_
Field (34; 1899).   CtY-D

3139. Webb, James Morris. _The Black Man, the Father of Civil-_
ization. Proven by Biblical History... Chicago, Ill.: Wm.
H. Poole, Printer, 1914.   DHU/MO

3140. Weeks, John H. "Mission Work in West Africa: A Reply
to Mr. Dennett." _The East and the West_ (14; Oct. , 1916), pp.
460-65.   DHU/R

3141. Weitfrecht, H. U. "A Study of African Missions." _Church_
Missionary Review (74; Dec. , 1923), pp. 227-34.   DHU/R

3142. Welbourn, Frederick Burkewood. _East African Christian._
London: Oxford University Press, 1965.   MiBsA

3143. Welch, James W. "Can Christian Marriage in Africa be
African?" _International Review of Missions_ (22; 1933), pp. 17-32.
DHU/R

3144. Welldon, J. E. C. "The Problem of Christian Missions."
The East and the West (19; Oct. , 1921), pp. 302-18. DHU/R
Includes Christian Missions in Africa.

3145. Weller, John C. "Msoro Mission Under Leonard Kamungu
and his Successors." David B. Barrett (ed.). _African Initia-_
tives in Religion (Nairobi: East Africa Pub. House, 1971), pp.
35-49.   DHU/R

3146. West Africa Conference. _Annual Conference Minutes, 1947-_
1950.   DOUM/EUB
Evangelical United Brethren Church and missions.

3147. ----- _Minutes of the Annual Session of the West Africa_
Conference of the United Brethren Church in Christ, 1881-
1946.   DOUM/EUB
Typescript.

3148. West Central African Regional Conference. _Abundant Life_
in Changing Africa: Report, Leopoldville, Congo Belge (July,
13-24, 1946). New York: Africa Committee of the Foreign
Missions Conference of North America, 1946. DLC; CtY-D;
NN; MH; NcD

3149. West, E. Courtenay. "The Call From Africa." _East and_
the West (24; Apr. , 1926), pp. 156-65.   DHU/R
Discusses evangelization potential in Africa.

3150. Westermann, Diedrich. _The African Today._ Published for
the International Institute of African Languages and Cultures.
n. p. : Oxford University Press, 1934.   MNtcA

3151. ----- _The Missionary and Anthropological Research._
London: Oxford University Press, International African
Institute, 1948.   DHU/MO

3152. Westervelt, Josephine H. _On Safari for God: An Account_
of the Life and Labors of John Stauffacher a Pioneer Mission-
ary of the African Inland Mission. New York: n. p. , n. d.
NNMR

3153. Wetherell, Phyllis J. "The Foundation and Early Work
of the Church Missionary Society." _Historical Magazine of_
the Protestant Episcopal Church (18; 1949), p. 350+. DLC

3154. "What Makes A Missionary." Conserving Foreign Mission
Society, 1954. Made by Colburn Laboratory. 140 fr. color.
35 mm. & disc: 2 s. , 12 in. , 33 1/3 r p m, 30 min.
Filmstrip.
"Describes the factors which influence a missionary's
decision to go to the foreign field, showing step-by-step
the training and procedures in becoming a missionary."

3155. White, Ackrel E. "Mission Work in Africa." Southern
Workman (11:3, Mr., 1882), p. 31. DHU/MO; DLC
Article has map of these Protestant Mission stations in
Africa.

3156. White, Diana. Timbuctoo the Mysterious. New York:
Negro Universities Press, 1969.   DHU/R
Originally published in 1896 by Longmans, Green, and Co.,
New York.

3157. White, George. A Brief Account of the Life, Experience,
Travels, and Gospel Labours of George White, an African:
Written by Himself and Revised by a Friend. New York:
John C. Totten, 1810.   DHU/MO

3158. Whiton, Samuel J. Glimpses of West Africa, With Sketches
of Missionary Labor. Boston: American Tract Society, 1866.
NjP

3159. Wilcox, W. D. "Need of Industrial Missions in Africa."
Biblical World (41; Feb., 1913), pp. 103-08.   DHU/R

3160. "William Sheppard: Christian Fighter for African Rights."
Southern Workman (89: 1, Ja., 1910), pp. 8-12. DLC;
DHU/MO
"Dr. Wm. H. Sheppard, tried and acquitted before a Belgium
court in Africa for exposing the Kassai Company's cruel
methods of extortion of Africans."

3161. Williams, Chancellor. The Destruction of Black Civiliza-
tion. Great Issues of a Race From 4500 B. C. to 2000 A. D.
Dubuque, Iowa: Kendall Hunt Pub. Co., 1971. DHU/R; DLC
Part IV includes a chapter on Christian Africa.
Negro author.

3162. Williams, Lorraine A., (ed.). Africa and the Afro-American
Experience. Washington, D.C.: Howard University, The
Department of History, 1973.   DHU/R

3163. Williams, W. B. "Fighting the Devil in Africa." Missionary
Review (39; Ag., 1916), pp. 597-601.   DHU/R

3164. Willis, John Jamieson, (bp.). "The Appeal to the African."
Church Missionary Review (63; Ja., 1912), pp. 27-34. DHU/R

3165. ----- (bp.). "The Gain of Christianity." The Church
Missionary Review (71:830, Je., 1920), pp. 104-14.
DHU/R

3166. Willoughby, William Charles. "Building the African Church:
First Paper." International Review of Missions (15:3, Jl., 1926),
pp. 450-66.   DHU/R

3167. ----- Race Problems in the New Africa. A Study of the
Relation of Bantu and Britons in Those Parts of Bantu Africa
Which are Under British Control. Oxford: Clarendon Press,
1923.   DHU/MO
Contrast between Muslims and Christians, pp. 256-9.

3168. Wilson, C. E. "The Provision of a Christian Literature
for Africa." International Review of Missions (15:3, Jl., 1926),
pp. 506-14.   DHU/R

3169. Wilson, Charles Thomas. "A Journey from Kagei to Tabora
and Back." Proceedings of the Royal Geographical Society.
New Series (11; 1880), pp. 616-20.   NcD; NIC; OO

3170. Wilson, Elizabeth A. G. History of the Assemblies of God
in Africa, Including Egypt. Masters thesis. Texas Christian
University, 1955.

3171. Wilson, George Herbert. The History of the Universities'
Mission to Central Africa. Freeport, New York: Books for
Libraries Press, 1971. MiBsA; MNtcA; NjP
Reprint of 1936 edition.

3172. Wilson, Jesse R. "They Want Us Everywhere." Missions:
An International Baptist Magazine (147:1, Ja., 1949), pp. 21-24.
Pam. File, DHU/R

3173. Wilson, William E. "A Note on Christian Captives in North
Africa." The Catholic Historical Review (28:4, Ja., 1943), pp.
491-98.   DHU/R

3174. Woman's Congress of Missions, Chicago, 1893. Women in
Missions; Papers and Addresses Presented at the Woman's
Congress of Missions, October 2-4, 1893, in the Hall of Colum-
bus, Chicago. Compiled by Rev. E. M. Wherry. New York:
American Tract Society, 1894.   NN/Sch

3175. Woodworth, C. Historic Correspondences in Africa and
America. A Discourse Delivered Before the Faculty and
Students of Atlanta University, May 27, 1888, by C. L.
Woodworth. Boston: Beacon Press, 1889. NN/Sch

3176. World Missionary Conference. Edinburgh, June 1-23, 1910.
Statistical Atlas of Christian Missions... Edinburgh: The
Conference, 1910.   DLC; CtY-D

3177. World Missionary Conference, Edinburgh, 1910. ...Report
of Commission I-VIII... N.Y.: F. H. Revell Co., 1910.
DLC; DHU/R

3178. Wright, Richard Robert, (bp.). "African Bishop in Africa:
The Story of Missionary's Journey." Missionary Review of
the World (60:12, Dec., 1937), pp. 589-91.   DHU/R
Negro author.

3179. Wrong, Margaret. Africa and the Making of Books; Being a
Survey of Africa's Need of Literature. New York: International
Committee on Christian Literature for Africa, 1934. NN/Sch

3180. ----- "The Church's Task in Africa South of the Sahara."
International Review of Missions (36; 1947), pp. 206-31. DHU/R

3181. The Young African Prince; or, Memoirs of Naimbana.
Boston: Printed and sold by Lincoln & Edmands, Cornhill,
1822.   NN/Sch
Religious conversion of an African Prince.

3182. Young, Rosa. Light in the Dark Belt. St. Louis: Concordia
Publishing House, 1929, 1930. Rev. ed. 1950, 1952. MSL/CHI
Lutherans and missions in Africa.

3183. Zwemer, Samuel Marinus. The Unoccupied Mission Fields
of Africa and Asia. New York: Student Volunteer Movement
for Foreign Missions, 1911.   NN/Sch

t. Other areas
3184. "African Islands." The American Quarterly Register
(6:2, Nov., 1833), pp. 96-98.   DHU/R

3185. Allier, Raoul. Une Énigne Troublante La Race Nègre et
la Malédiction de Cham. Paris: Société des Missions Evangeliques, 1930.   mim, Pam. File, DHU/R
"Les Cahiers Missionnaires #16."
Biblical study on curse of Ham theory.

3186. Amiji, Hatim M. "Some Notes on Religious Dissent in
Nineteenth-Century East Africa." African Historical Studies
(4:3, 1971), pp. 603-16.   DHU/MO

3187. Andersen, Esther. Sobetab gotab Kristianindet. Kijabe:
A. I. M. Publications, 1963.   ANAU
English title: Christian Family Life, in Kalenjin.

3188. Anderson, James-Forrester. Esquisse de l'Histoire du
Protestantisme à l'Ile Maurice et aux Iles Mascaregnes (1502-
1902). Paris (Thèses de baccalauréat-Theol.). 1902-03.
A history of Protestants in Mauritius.

3189. Anderson, Llewellyn Kennedy. "Twenty-Six Thousand Africans
were Converted; an Experience of the Church in West Africa."
Missionary Review. (62; My., 1939), pp. 233-35. DHU/R

3190. Barrow, Alfred H. Fifty Years in Western Africa. New
York: Negro Universities Press, 1969.   DHU/R

A record of the Work of the West Indian Church in Guinea and Sierra Leone.

3191. Becken, Hans-Jürgen. "The Constitution of the Lutheran Bapedi Church of 1892." The Bulletin of the Society for African Church History (2:2, 1966), pp. 180-89.   DHU/R

3192. Beiderbecke, Heinrich. Life Among the Hereros in Africa; the Experiences of H. Beiderbecke, Lutheran Pastor. Rendered into English by J. A. Weyl... New York: E. Kaufmann, 1923.   NN/Sch

3193. Bordeaux, Henry. L'Épopée Noir: La France en Afrique Occidentale. Paris: Denoel et Steele, 1936. NN/Sch

3194. Burkhardt, Gustav E. Die Evangelische Mission auf dem Festland und den Inseln von Ost-Afrika. Bielefeld: Velhagen und Klasing, 1860.   MiBsA
            Missions in East Africa.

3195. Chailley, Marcel. Histoire de L'Afrique Occidentale Francaise, 1638-1959. Paris: Editions Berger-Levrault, 1968. WU
            First section includes some discussion of religion in Africa.

3196. Cummings, George D. Life of Mrs. Virginia Hale Hoffman Late of the Protestant Episcopal Mission to Western Africa. 2nd ed. ... Philadelphia: Lindsay and Blakiston, 1859.   DHU/MO

3197. Daigre, Father. ...Oubangui-Chari; Témoignage sur son Evolution (1900-1940). Issoudun, Indre: Dillen & Cie, 1947.   NN/Sch

3198. Dean, John M. Cross of Christ in Bolo-Land. Edinburgh: Oliphant, Anderson and Ferrier, 1902. New York: Revell, 1902. DLC; NIC; NcC; OCI; PBm

3199. DeBrunner, Hans W. A Church Between Colonial Powers, a Study of the Church in Togo. London: Lutterworth Press, 1965.   DHU/R; ICU; MH; MBU-T

3200. Doutte, Edmond. Magie et Religion dans l'Afrique du Nord. Alger: Adolphe Jourdan, 1909.   DCU

3201. Earthy, E. Dora. "The Customs of Gazaland Women in Relation to the African Church." International Review of Missions (15:4, Oct., 1926), pp. 662-74.   DHU/R
            Describes ritual practices of women and how they can be adapted to the Christian religions.

3202. "Eastern Africa." The American Quarterly Register (6:2, Nov., 1833), p. 96.   DHU/R

3203. Faure, Jean. ...Togo Champ de Mission. Paris: Société des Missions Evangéliques, 1943.   NN/Sch

3204. Fenton, Thomas. Black Harvester... London: Cargate Press, n.d.   NN/Sch

3205. Fintan, Father. Light and Laughter in Darkest Africa. Dublin: M. H. Gill & Son, 1943.   NN/Sch

3206. Fisher, Ruth B. On the Borders of Pigmy Land. Chicago: F. H. Revell Co., 1905.   NN/Sch

3207. Fisher, William Singleton. Africa Looks Ahead. The Life Stories of Walter and Anna Fisher of Central Africa. London: Pickering & Inglis, 1948.   NN/Sch

3208. Flickinger, Daniel Kumler and William McGee. Missions of the United Brethren in Christ. History of the Origin, Development, and Condition of Missions Among the Sherboro and Mendi Tribes, in Western Africa. Dayton, O.: United Brethren Publishing House, 1885.   DHU/MO

3209. Fouroadier, Etienne. ...La Vie Héroique de Victoire Rasoamanrivo. Paris: Dillen, 1937.   NN/Sch

3210. Gelfand, Michael, (ed.). Gubulawayo and Beyond. Letters and Journals of the Early Jesuit Missionaries to Zambesia (1879-1887). London: Chapman, 1968.   DLC

3211. Giffen, John Kelly. "Fifteen Years of Progress in Egypt." Missionary Review of the World (27; Nov., 1904), pp. 835-41.   DHU/R

3212. Goyau, Georges. ...Un Grand "Homme," Mere Javouhey, Apôtre des Moirs; Avec Quatre Gravures Hors Texte. Paris: Plon, 1929.   NN/Sch

3213. Groffier, Valérien. ...Héros Trop Qubliés de Notre Epopée Coloniale. Afrique Occidentale, Centrale et Orientale. Lyon: E. Vitte, 1928.   NN/Sch

3214. Guilcher, Rene Francois. ...La Société des Missions Africaines; ses Origines, sa Nature, sa Vie, ses Oeuvres. Lyon: Procure des Missions Africaines, 1956.   NN/Sch

3215. Hayford, Mark Christian. West Africa and Christianity. A Lecture Delivered at the Rochester Theological Seminary, N. Y., U.S.A., September 28th, 1900, by Rev. Mark C. Hayford... London: Pub. for the author by the Baptist Tract and Book Society, 1903.   NN/Sch

3216. Hepburn, James Davidson. Twenty Years in Khama's Country and Pioneering Among the Batauana of Lake Ngami; told in the letters of the Rev. J. D. Hepburn. London: Hodder, 1895.   NN/Sch

3217. Hopkins, A. J. Trail Blazers and Road Makers. A Brief History of the East Africa Mission of the United Methodist Church. London: H. Hooks, U. M. Pub. House, 1928.   NH; NcD; NN

3218. "How Missionaries Work in Africa; Extracts from Letters of Pastors, Teachers, Doctors, and Industrial Missionaries of the American Presbyterian Mission in West Africa." Missionary Review (62; Ja., 1939), pp. 2 +, 20-28.   DHU/R

3219. Howard, Cecil, (ed.). West African Explorers. London: Oxford University Press, 1952.   DHU/MO

3220. Hurst, Leonard. There Blossoms Red. London: Livingstone Press, 1949.   NN/Sch

3221. Jackson, Joseph Harrison. A Voyage to West Africa and Some Reflections on Modern Missions. Philadelphia: n. p., 1936.   DLC

3222. Jenkins, Thomas (An African Prince). "Chamber's Miscellany." William Armistead. A Triubute for The Negro: Being a Vindication of the Moral, Intellectual, and Religious Capabilities of the Colored Portion of Mankind... (Conn.: Negro Univ. Press, 1848), pp. 317-23.   DHU/R
            Missionary to Mauritius and teacher.

3223. Kiéran, J. The Holy Ghost Fathers in East Africa, 1863-1914. Doctoral dissertation. University of London, 1966.   DLC

3224. Kilham, Hannah. The Claims of West Africa to Christian Instruction. London: Harvey and Darton, 1830. DHU/MO

3225. Kinch, Emily Christmas. West Africa, An Open Door. Philadelphia: Pr. by the A. M. E. Book Concern, 1917.   NN/Sch; CtY-D

3226. Knight-Bruce, George Wyndham Hamilton, (bp.). Memories of Mashonaland. London: E. Arnold, 1895.   NN/Sch

3227. "Krapf of East Africa." The East and West Review (3; 1937), pp. 259-69.   DHU/R
            A letter written by Dr. J. L. Krapf from Mombas, 1845.

3228. Lloyd, Albert Bushnell. Apolo of the Pygmy Forest. London: Church Missionary Society, 1936. TNF; CtY; NcD

3229. ----- In Dwarf Land and Cannibal Country; a Record of
Travel and Discovery in Central Africa. New York: C.
Scribner's Sons, 1899.   NN/Sch

3230. Mears, Walter. Wesleyan Missionaries in Great Namaqualand,
1820-1967. Capetown: Struik, 1970.   NjP

3231. Morgan, W. T. W., (ed.). East Africa: Its Peoples and
Resources. Nairobi, Kenya: Oxford University Press, 1969.
                                                DLC

3232. Nassau, Robert Hamill. My Ogowe: Being a Narrative of
Daily Incidents During Sixteen Years in Equatorial West Africa.
New York: The Neal Pub. Co., 1914.   NN/Sch

3233. New, Charles. Life Wanderings, and Labours in Eastern
Africa, with an Account of the First Successful Ascent of the
Equatorial Snow Mountain, Kilimanjaro, and Remarks Upon
East African Slavery. London: F. Cass, 1971. MiBsA;
NjP; DHU/R

3234. Oliver, Roland. The Missionary Factor in East Africa.
New York: Humanities, 1967.   DHU/MO

3235. Padwick, C. E. Temple Gairdner of Cairo. London: Society
for Promoting Christian Knowledge, 1930.   MH; CtY
    Story of an Anglican missionary in Egypt during the first
    quarter of the twentieth century. Missions in Egypt.

3236. Parsons, Ellen C. A Life for Africa; Rev. Adolphus Clemens
Good, Ph. D. American Missionary in Equatorial West Africa.
2nd ed. New York: Fleming H. Revell, 1900. DHU/MO; NN/Sch

3237. Radford, Lewis B. "The Gambia Bishopric." East and West
Review (1:2, Apr., 1935), pp. 146-54.   DHU/R

3238. Reading, Joseph Hankinson. The Ogowe Band. A Narrative
of Africa Travel. Philadelphia: Reading & Co., 1890. NN/Sch

3239. Rowley, Henry. The Story of the Universities' Mission to
Central Africa; from its Commencement, under Bishop
Mackenzie, to its Withdrawal from the Zambesi. London:
Saunders, Otley, 1866. CtY; PPl; MB; NN; IC/H; CtY

3240. Shoemaker, Gertrude Mae. A History of Protestant Missions
in West Central Africa. Master's thesis. College of Missions,
1924.   TN/DCHS

3241. Smith, Edwin W. Great Lion of Bechuanaland. The Life
and Times of Roger Price, Missionary and Statesman. London:
Published for the London Missionary Society by Independent
Press, 1957.   DHU/MO; DHU/R; MNtcA

3242. Snyder, DeWitt C. "Among the Bakuba." Southern Workman
(32:4, Apr., 1903), p. 203.   DLC; DHU/MO
    A mission located at Luebo in Central Africa.

3243. Springer, John McKendree. The Heart of Central Africa;
Mineral Wealth and Missionary Opportunity. New York: The
Methodist Book Concern, 1909.   NN/Sch

3244. Stewart, James. The Zambesi Journal of James Stewart,
1862-1863, With Selection of His Correspondence. London:
Chatto and Windus, 1952.   NNMR

3245. Tildsley, Alfred. The Remarkable Work Achieved by Dr.
Mark C. Hayford, in Promotion of the Spiritual and Material
Welfare of the Natives of West Africa, and Proposed Develop-
ments. London: Morgan & Scott, 1926.   DHU/MO; NN/Sch

3246. Ward, Gertrude. Letters from East Africa. London: Universities' Mission to Central Africa, 1901.   NN/Sch

3247. ----- The Life of Charles Alan Smythies, Bishop of the
Universities' Mission to Central Africa. London: Office of the
Universities' Mission to Central Africa, 1899. NN/Sch

3248. Watt, Rachel S. In the Heart of Savagedom. Reminiscences
of Life and Adventure During a Quarter of a Century of Pioneering
Missionary Labours in the Wilds of East Equatorial Africa.
London: Marshall, 192?   NN/Sch

3249. "Western Africa." The American Quarterly Register (6:2,
Nov., 1833), pp. 93-94.   DHU/R

3250. Wrong, Margaret. West African Journey, in the Interests
of Literacy and Christian Literature, 1944-45. London:
Livingstone Press, 1946.   DHU/MO; NN/Sch

3251. Zwemer, Samuel Marinus and H. E. Phillips. A Survey of
the Missionary Occupation of Egypt: With a Special Section on
Cario: Nile Mission Press, 1924.   NNMR

2. Independent Churches and Separatist Movements

3252. "The African Brotherhood Church." Ecumenical Review
(24:2, Apr., 1972), pp. 145-59.   DHU/R
    Origin of this independent African Church begun in Nairobi,
    Kenya in 1945.

3253. "African Religious Movements, Types and Dynamics."
Journal of Modern African Studies (2; 1964), pp. 531+. DHU/MO

3254. Aina, J. Ade. The Present-day Prophets and the Principles
upon which They Work. Nsukka: Crowther College of Religion,
1964.   DHU/MO; CtHe, ANIiu
    mim.
    Materials for the Study of Nigerian Church History, No. 1.
    Reproduction of an apologia published in Ibadan ca. 1930,
    with a historical and theological introduction.

3255. Aldén, Karl. "The Prophet Movement in Congo." International
Review of Missions (25; 1936), pp. 347-53. DHU/R
    Kimbangu and the Ngunza movement. Indepenent church
    vs. Protestant missions.

3256. Andersson, Efraim. Messianic Popular Movements in the
Lower Congo. London: William Heinemann, Ltd., 1958.
                              CtY-D; DHU/MO
    Also in: Studia Ethnographia Upsaliensia (Stockholm)
    (14; 1958) CtY; DCU; CLU; ViU; WaU

3257. Avery, Allen, Jr. African Independency: A Study of the
Phenomenon of Independency and the Lessons to be Learned
from It for Greater Church Growth in Africa. Masters thesis.
Fuller Theological Seminary, 1971.

3258. Ayandele, E. A. "The Aladura Among the Yoruba: A Challenge
to the 'Orthodox' Churches." The Nigerian Christian (3:7, Jl.,
1969), pp. 15-16.   Pam. File, DHU/R

3259. ----- A Visionary of the African Church: Mojola Agbebi
(1860-1917). Nairobi: East African Pub. House, 1971. DLC

3260. Baëta, C. G. Prophetism in Ghana. London: SCM Press,
1962.   DHU/MO

3261. Balandier, George. "Messianism and Nationalism in Black
Africa." Pierre L. Van den Berghe, Africa, Social Problems
of Change and Conflict (San Francisco: Chandler Pub. Co., 1965),
pp. 443-48; 457-58.   DLC

3262. Banton, Micheal. "African Prophets." Race (5; Oct., 1963),
pp. 42-55.   DHU/MO; DAU

3263. Barrett, David B. "The African Independent Churches."
World Christian Handbook (New York: Abingdon Press, 1967),
pp. 24-28.   DHU/R

3264. ----- Reaction to Mission: an Analysis of Independent Church Movements Across Two Hundred African Tribes. Doctoral dissertation. Columbia University, 1965.

3265. ----- Schism and Renewal in Africa: An Analysis of Six Thousand Contemporary Religious Movements. New York: Oxford University Press, 1968.   DLC

3266. ----- "Separatisme et Renouveau en Afrique." Monde Non-Chrétien (88; Oct.-Dec., 1968), pp. 3-22.   DLC

3267. ----- Two Hundred Independent Church Movements in East Africa. Kampala: n.p., 1967.   DLC

3268. Becken, Hans-Jürgen. "A Healing Church in Zululand: The New Church Step to Jesus Christ Zion in South Africa." Journal of Religion in Africa (4:3, 1972), pp. 213-22.   DHU/R

3269. ----- "On the Holy Mountain: A Visit to the New Year's Festival of the Nazaretha Church on Mount Nhlangakazi, 14 January, 1967." Journal of Religion in Africa (1:2, 1967-68), pp. 138-49.   DHU/R

3270. Beecher, Leonard J. "African Separatist Churches in Kenya." World Dominion (31; Ja.-Feb., 1953), pp. 5-12.   CtY-D; DLC; NN

3271. Benz, Ernst, (ed.). Messianische Kirchen, Sekten und Bewegungen im Heutigen Afrika. Leiden: E. J. Brill, 1965.   CtHc; MH-AH; NN; NNC; NNCor

3272. Bergliend, A. Rituals of an African Zionist Church. Johannesburg: Univ. of the Witwatersrand, 1967. MH; CtY African Studies Programme, Occasional paper, 3. Zion Jerusalem Church of the Twelve Apostles, a South African Christian denomination.

3273. Bernard, G. and P. Caprasse. "Religious Movements in the Congo: A Research Hypothesis. Cahiers Economiques et Sociaux (3; 1965), pp. 49-60.   DAU

3274. Berndt, Manfred. Adaptation of the Religious Dance and Similar Physical Movements in the Indigenous Church. Master's thesis. Concordia Seminary, 1971.

3275. Bertsche, James E. "Kimbanguism: A Challenge to Missionary Statesmanship." Practical Anthropology (13:1, Ja.-Feb., 1966), pp. 13-33.   DHU/R

3276. Beyerhaus, Peter. "An Approach to the African Independent Church Movement." Ministry (9:2, Apr., 1969), pp. 62-65.   DLC

3277. ----- (ed.). Begegnung mit Messianischen Bewegungen in Afrika. Stuttgart: Missionsverlag, 1967.   DLC; NUC "A synthetic study of African and Oceanian independent churches, combining theological, sociological and other points of view in respect ot Messianic movements as one type."

3278. Bridgman, Frederick B. "The Ethopian Movements in South Africa." Missionary Review of the World (27; Oct., 1904), pp. 434-45.   DHU/R

3279. Brown, Kenneth I. "An African Experiment in Christian Union." The Christian (103:4, 1965; Ibid., 103:5, 1965), pp. 4-5; 8-9.   DLC Union of an "older" with an "independent" church.

3280. ----- "Forms of Baptism in the African Independent Churches of Tropical Africa." Practical Anthropology (19; Jl., 1972), pp. 169-82.   DHU/R

3281. ----- "A Weekend with an African Independent Church in Natal." Ministry (11:1, 1971), pp. 8-16.   DLC

3282. ----- "Worshiping with the African Church of the Lord (Aladura)," Practical Anthropology (13: 2, Mr.-Apr., 1966), pp. 59-84.   DHU/R

3283. Buerkle, H. "The Message of the 'False Prophets' of the Independent Churches of Africa." Makerere Journal (11; Dec., 1965), pp. 51-55.   DHU/MO; DLC

3284. Burnet, Amos. "Ethiopianism." The Church Missionary Review (73:837, Mr., 1922), pp. 29-34.   DHU/R South Africa.

3285. Calmettes, Jean Loup. The Lumpa Church and Witchcraft Eradication. Lusaka, Zambia: Conference on the History of Central African Religions, Ag. 30-Sept. 8, 1972.   Pam File, DHU/R mim.

3286. Cameron, W. M. "The Ethiopian Movement and the Order of Ethiopia." The East and the West (2; Jl., 1904), pp. 375-97.   DHU/R A discussion of "Ethiopianism" in South Africa.

3287. Chinguku, Alkuin and J. Kunirum Osia, et al. "Africans Talk About Church/Liturgy in Africa." Freeing the Spirit (1:1, Ag., 1971), pp. 18-25.   DHU/R

3288. Chome, Jules. La Passion de Simon Kimbangu, 1921-1951. Brussels: n.p., 1959.   DHU/MO

3289. "The Church of the Lord (Aladura)." Ecumenical Review (24:2, Apr., 1972), pp. 121-29.   DHU/R

3290. Comhaire, Jean L. "Societes Secretes et Mouvements Prophetiques au Congo Belge." Africa (25:1, Ja., 1955), pp. 54-59.   DHU/MO

3291. Crane, William H. "The Kimbanguist Church and the Search for Authentic Catholicity." Christian Century (87:22, Je. 3, 1970), pp. 691-95.   DHU/R Deals with first independent African Church admitted to the World Council of Churches.

3292. Cross, Sholto. "A Prophet Not Without Honour: Jeremiah Gondwe." Christopher Allen and R. W. Johnson, (eds.). African Perspectives (New York: Cambridge University Press, 1972?) pp.   DHU/Mo "Colonial misfortune and Religious Response.

3293. Dallimore, H. "The Aladura Movement in Ekiti." Western Equatorial Africa Magazine (36; 1931), pp. 93-97.   NNMR

3294. Dammann, Ernst and Katesa Schlosser, et al. Messianische Kirchen, Sekten und Bewegungen im Heutigen Afrika. Leiden: E. J. Brill, 1965, 1966.   NjP

3295. Daneel, Marthinus L. The God of the Matopo Hills: an Essay on the Mwari Cult in Rhodesia. Leiden: Africa Study Centre Communications, 1970.   DLC; CLU; NSyU; NjR; MH-P

3296. ----- Independent Churches in Rhodesia: Old and New in Southern Shona Independent Churches. The Hague: Mouton 1970.   CLU

3297. ----- Old and New in Southern Shona Independent Churches: Background and Rise of the Major Movements. New York: Humanities, 1972.   MiGrC

3298. ----- "Shona Independent Churches and Ancestor Worship." Barrett, David B., (ed.). African Initiatives in Religion (Nairobi: East African Publishing House, 1971), pp. 160-70.   DHU/R

3299. ----- Shona Independent Churches and the Eradication of Wizardry. Lusaka, Zambia: Conference on the History of Central African Religious Systems. Ag. 31-Sept. 8, 1972.   Pam. File, DHU/R Mim.

3300. ----- Zionism and Faith-Healing in Rhodesia: Aspects of African Independent Churches. New York: Humanities, 1970.   CoFS; NSyU

3301. de Queiroz, Maria Isaura Pereira. "Maurice Leenhardt et les 'Eglises Ethiopiennes.'" Le Monde Non-Chretien (74; Apr.-Je., 1965), pp. 84-101.   Pam. File, DHU/R

3302. Dougall, James W. C. "African Separatist Churches." International Review of Missions (45; 1956), pp. 257-66.
                                                                        DHU/R

3303. Epelle, E. M. T. "Development of the Sects in Eastern Nigeria." West African Religion (Nos. 13 & 14, 1972), pp. 41-50.   DHU/R

3304. Fabian, Johannes. Jamaa: A Charismatic Movement in Katanga. Evanston, Ill.: Northwestern University Press, 1971.
                                                                        DLC; DHU

3305. Farmer, E. 'Separate Churches in South Africa." The East and The West (15; Apr., 1917), pp. 135-42.   DHU/R

3306. Fehderau, Harold W. "Enthusiastic Christianity in an African Church." Practical Anthropology (8:6, Nov.-Dec., 1961), pp. 279-80+.   DHU/R

3307. ----- "Kimbanguism: Prophetic Christianity in Congo." Practical Anthropology (9:4, Jl.-Ag., 1962), pp. 157-78.
                                                                        DHU/R

3308. Fernandez, James W. "Politics and Prophecy: African Religious Movements." Practical Anthropology (12:2, Mr.-Apr., 1965), pp. 71-75.   DHU/R

3309. ----- "The Precincts of the Prophet: a Day With Johannes Galilee Shembe.' Journal of Religion in Africa (5:1, 1973), pp. 32-53.   DHU/R
        A South Africa Zulu.

3310. ----- "Rededication and Prophetism in Ghana." Cahiers d'Etudes Africaines (Paris) (10:2, 1970), pp. 228-305.
                                                                        DAU; DGU

3311. Fisher, Humphrey J. "Muslim and Christian Separatism in Africa." Religion in Africa (1964), pp. 9-23. DLC

3312. Foster, Raymond S. The Sierra Leone Church. An Independent Anglican Church. London: S.P.C.K. Press, 1961.
                                                                        DHU/MO; DLC
        Former Anglican Church, now The Sierra Leone Church. The Church Missionary Society withdrew its missionaries in 1907.

3313-14. Fraser, Elizabeth. "Christianity in Tribal Idiom: Causes and Characteristics of African Separatists." African World (Nov. 1965), pp. 4-5.

3315. Gibson, Alan G. S. "Native Church Organisation in South Africa." The East and The West (6; Oct., 1908), pp. 398-411.
                                                                        DHU/R

3316. Haliburton, Gordon Mackay. The Prophet Harris; a Study of an African Prophet and His Mass Movement in the Ivory Coast and the Gold Coast, 1913-1915. New York: Oxford Univ. Press, 1973.   ICT

3317. ----- The Prophet Harris and His Work in Ivory Coast and Western Ghana. Doctoral dissertation. University of London, 1966.

3318. Hayward, Victor E. W., (ed.). African Independent Church Movements. London: Edinburgh House, 1963.   DHU/MO;
CoDI

3319. ----- "African Independent Church Movements." International Review of Missions (52:206, Apr., 1963), pp. 163-72. DHU/R

3320. Heimer, Haldor Eugene. The Kimbanguists and the Bapostole: A Study of Two African Independent Churches in Luluabourg, Congo, in Relation to Similar Churches and in the Context of

Lulua Traditional Culture and Religion. Doctoral dissertation. Hartford Seminary Foundation, 1971.   DHU/R

3321. Herzog, H. "The Pentecostal Groups in Camroon. A Challenge to the Churches." Ministry (9:4, 1969), pp. 147-51.   DLC

3322. Hinchliff, Peter Bingham. "African Separatists: Heresy, Schism or Protest Movements?" Derek Baker, (ed.). Schism, Heresy and Religious Protest (Cambridge: Cambridge University Press, 1972), Vol. 9, pp. 391-404.   DHU/R

3323. Hodgson, E. Out of the Darkness; the Story of an Idigenous Church in the Belgian Congo. London: Victory Press, 1946.
                                                                        NN/Sch

3324. Holas, Bohumil Le Separatisme Religieux en Afrique Noire. Paris: Presses Universitaires de France, 1965. NUC; NjP; NNUC; PPULC; MH-AH; NjPT; NIC; CtY; CU; ICU; IEN; INU; MH; MBU; NNCor

3325. Hostetter, R. "African Independent Churches." Christian Standard (Apr. 16, 1972), pp. 7+. Cty-D; DLC; OrU; NjMD

3326. Hutchison, W. F. "African Prophets." Pt. I; Pt. II. Southern Workman (58:2, Feb., 1929; 58:3, Mr., 1929), pp. 77-84; pp. 123-30.   DLC; DHU/MO
        A preacher, William Wade Harris, was a Kruman, a member of the Grebo tribe, born in the little village of Graway, near Cape Palmas, in the Republic of Liberia became a Christian prophet.
        "Samson Oppon, an Ashanti who became a Christian prophet."

3327. Idowu, E. Bolaji, Towards an Idigenous Church. London: Oxford University Press, 1965. NcD; CBPac; CtY-D; NjP; NRU; InU; IEN; NjPt; MH-AH; CLU; ICU; MiBsa

3328. Jabavu, Davidson D. T. An African Idigenous Church. Lovedale, South Africa: Lovedale Press, 1942. NJ; IEN; DLC

3329. Janosik, Robert J. "African Sects and Political Involvement." Journal for the Scientific Study of Religion (13:2, Je., 1974), pp. 161-75.   DHU/R
        Comparative study of the involvement of religious sects in Africa in political activities.

3330. "The Kimbanguist Church in the Congo." Ecumenical Review (19:1, Ja., 1967), pp. 29-36.   DHU/R

3331. Lane, Eric. Prophecy and Power in Rwanda and Malawi. Lusaka, Zambia: Conference on the History of Central African Religious Systems, Ag. 31-Sept. 8, 1972.   Pam. File, DHU/R Mim.

3332. Lanternari, Vittorio. The Religions of the Oppressed: A Study of Modern Messianic Cults. New York: Alfred A Knopf, Inc., 1963.   DHU/R
        Chapter I. Nativistic Religions in Africa.
        Chapter IV. Religious Movements in Central and South America.

3333. ----- "Syncrétismes, Messianismes, Néo-Traditionalismes. Postface à une Étude des Mouvements Religieux de L'Afrique Noire." Archives de Sociologie des Religions (21; 1966), pp. 101-10.   DHU/R
        II. La Situation Post-Coloniale.

3334. Lea, Allen. Native Separatist Church Movement in South Africa. Capetown: Juta, 1926.   CLU

3335. Lehmann, J. P. and H. Memel Fote. "Le Cercle du Prophete et du Sorcier." Psychopatologie Africanine (Dakar) (1; 1967), pp. 81-119.   DLC; CtY; ICU; WaU; MH

3336. Lohrentz, Kenneth P. "Joseph Booth, Charles Domingo, and the Seventh Day Baptists in Northern Nyasaland, 1910-1912." Journal of African History (12:3, 1971), pp. 461-80. DHU/MO
        Establishment of Seventh Day Baptist separatist churches and independent schools by Africans.

3337. Loram, Charles T. "The Separatist Church Movement."
International Review of Missions (15; 1926), pp. 476-82. DHU/R

3338. MacDonald, Roderick J. "Religious Independency as a Means
of Social Advance in Northern Nyasaland in the 1930's." Journal
of Religion in Africa (3:2, 1970), pp. 106-29.   DHU/R

3339. McIntosh, Brian G. "Archival Resources of the University
College, Nairobi, Relating to Missionary Work and Independent
Churches in Kenya." The Bulletin of the Society for African
Church History
(2:4, 1968), pp. 350-51.   DHU/R

3340. Messenger, John C. "Reinterpretations of Christian and
Indigenous Belief in a Nigerian Nativist Church." American
Anthropologist (62; 1960), pp. 268-78. CtY; DCU; DHU; DLC;
ICU; NN; OrU; TxD; IMC; ICNB; INE

3341. Messianische Kirchen, Sekten und Bewegungen in Heutigen
Afrika. Unter Mitarbeit von Ernst Dammann, Katesa Schlosser,
O. F. Raumua. Hrsg. von Ernst Benz. Leiden: E. J. Brill,
1965.   DLC; CtHC; NjPT; NcD; MiBsA; CBPaC; PPT
Nativistic movements in Africa.

3342. Microcosmogency and Modernization in African Religious
Movements. Quebec: Center for Developing-Asia Studies,
McGill University, 1969.   DLC

3343. Mitchell, Robert Cameron. A Comprehensive Bibliography
of Modern African Religious Movements. Evanston, Ill.:
Northwestern University Press, 1966.   DHU/MO; DHU; NjP;
MiBsA; NNCor

3344-45. ----- "Religious Protest and Social Change: The Origins
of the Aladura Movement in Western Nigeria." Robert I. Rotberg
and Ali A. Mazrui, (eds.). Protest and Power in Black Africa
(New York: Oxford University Press, 1970), pp. 458-96.
DHU/R

3346. ----- "Towards the Sociology of Religious Independency."
Journal of Religion in Africa (3:1, 1970), pp. 2-21. DHU/R

3347. Moede, Gerald F. "The African Brotherhood Church."
Ecumenical Review (24:2, 1972), pp. 145-59.   DHU/R

3348. Mqotsi, L. & M. Mkele. "A Separatist Church Ibandla
Laka Kristu." African Studies (5; 1946), pp. 119-123.
DAU; DCU/AN; DGW; DHU; CLU; DLC; DHU/MO

3349. Murray, Jocelyn. "The Kikuyu Spirit Churches." Journal
of Religion in Africa (5:3, 1973), pp. 198-234.   DHU/R

3350. "Simon Kimbangu et le Kimbanguisme sous l'Eclairage de
l'Histoire." Revue du Clerge Africain (27:6, 1972), pp. 631-45.
CtHC
Religious prophet of Zaire.

3351. Okite, O. "Africa: Independent Churches Thrive, but Face
Hurdles." Christianity Today (15; Mr. 12, 1971), pp. 54-55.
DHU/R

3352. Oosthuizer, Gerhardus C. Post-Christianity in Africa: A
Theological and Anthropological Study. Grand Rapids, Mich.:
Eerdmans, 1968.   DHU/MO
"A study of Christian and nativistic movements."

3353. ----- The Theology of a South African Messiah: An Analysis
of the Hymnal of "The Church of the Nazarites." Leiden:
E. J. Brill, 1967.   DHU/R

3354. Oruoch, Ogada. "How Newcomers are Welcomed to One of
Africa's Fastest Growing Churches." Voice of Missions
(8 : 1-2, Sept.-Oct., 1972), pp. 21-22.   DHU/R
About the Nomiya Luo Church in Kenya, an independent
African church.

3355. Peaden, W. R. "Zionist Churches in Southern Mashonaland
1924-1933." The Bulletin of the Society for African Church
History (3: 1-2; 1969-70), pp. 53-67.   DHU/R

3356. Peel, John D. Y. "The Aladura Movement in Western
Nigeria." Tarikh (3:1, 1969), pp. 48-55.   DHU/MO

3357. ----- Aladura: A Religious Movement Among the Yoruba.
London: Oxford University Press, 1968.   DHU/R

3358. ----- "Syncretism and Religious Change." Comparative
Studies in Society and History (10:2, Ja., 1968), pp. 121-41.
DHU/R
A study of the independent churches in Western Nigeria.

3359. Pentecost, E. C. "Mission Outreach of the Third World."
World Vision (17; Mr., 1973), pp. 10-11.   DGW
Indigenous churches.

3360. Phillips, Ray E. "Why Africa Turns from the Gospel."
The Christian Century (47:1, Ja. 15, 1930), pp. 80-82.
DHU/R

3361. Pritchard, John. "The Prophet Harris and Ivory Coast."
Journal of Religion in Africa (5:1, 1973), pp. 23-31. DHU/R

3362. "Prophet Movement in Africa Subsides." Editorial. The
Christian Century (39:27, Jl. 6, 1922), p. 860. DHU/R

3363. Puller, F. W. "The Ethiopian Order." East and West
(1:1, Ja., 1903), pp. 75-91.   DHU/R
Article explores the connection between the "Ethiopian
Movement" in South Africa and the A. M. E. Church.

3364. Ranger, Terence O. The African Churches of Tanzania.
Nairobi: East African Pub. House, 1969. NN; InU; WaU; CSt

3365. ----- "The 'Ethiopian' Episode in Barotseland, 1900-1905."
Rhodes-Livingstone Journal (37; 1965), pp. 26-41. DAU

3366. Raymaekers, Paul. "Historie de Simon Kimbangu Prophete,
d'apres les Ecrivains Nfinangani et Nzungu." Archives de
Sociologie des Religions (16:31, Ja.-Je., 1971), pp. 7-49.
DHU/R

3367. Reeh, Günther. "The Half-Opened Door: The Herero Church
in South West Africa." International Review of Missions (50;
1961), pp. 293-6.   DHU/R

3368. Richardson, Lincoln. "Congo's Kimbanguist Church." Presbyterian Life (23:14, Ag. 1, 1970), pp. 18-21+.   DHU/R

3369. Roberts, Andrew D. "The Lumpa Church of Alice Lenshina." Robert I. Rotberg and Ali A. Mazrui, (eds.). Protest
and Power in Black Africa (New York: Oxford Univ. Press,
1970), pp. 513-68.   DHU/R

3370. Roke, Alfred G. An Indigenous Church in Action. Acukland,
N. Z.: Sudan Interior Missions, 1938.   MNtcA

3371. Rotberg, Robert I., (ed.). Rebellion in Black Africa.
London: Oxford Univeristy Press, 1971.   DHU/R
Six essays which discuss revolts which were organized
by or around religious leaders.

3372. Sales, Jane M. "Worship in African Separatist Churches."
Missionary Research Library: Occasional Bulletin (22:4,
Apr., 1971), pp. 1-11.   DHU/R

3373. Schlosser, Katesa. Propheten in Afrika. Braunschweig:
A. Limbach, 1949. MiBsA; DLC; NNCor; PPT; NjP
Sects in Africa.

3374. Setiloane, Gabriel M. The Separatist Movement in South
Africa: Its Origin, Danger to the Church, and Comparison
With American Negro Cults. Masters thesis. Union Theolog-
ical Seminary, New York, 1955.

3375. Shepherd, Robert H. W. "The Separatist Churches of South Africa." International Review of Missions (26; 1937), pp. 453-63.   DHU/R

3376. Shepperson, George. "The Politics of African Church Separatist Movements in British Central Africa, 1892-1916." Africa (24:3, Jl., 1954), pp. 233-46.   DHU/MO

3377. Singleton, Michael. "On Gas Bottles and Gospels." African Ecclesiastical Review (15:2, 1973), pp. 119-29.   DHU/R
Roman liturgists and Africanizing the Mass.

3378. Sithole, Ndabaningi. Obed Mutezo: the Muzimu Christian Nationalist. Nairobi: Oxford University Press, 1970. DHU/R; DLC

3379. Spanton, E. F. "Building the African Church: Second Paper." International Review of Missions (15:3, July, 1926), pp. 467-75.   DHU/R

3380. Steele, F. "Roots of Two Missions Tensions." Evangelical Missions Quarterly (9; Wint., 1973), pp. 90-93.   DAU/W

3381. Stone, W. Vernon. "The Alice Movement in 1958," in "The Alice Movement in Northern Rhodesia." International Missionary Council Occasional Papers (1, 1958), pp. 5-10.   NNUT Mim.

3382. Sundkler, Bengt G. M. "Bantu Messiah and White Christ." Practical Anthropology (7:4; Jl.-Ag., 1960), pp. 170-6. DHU/R

3383. ----- Bantu Prophets in South Africa. London: Oxford University Press, 1961.   DHU/MO

3384. ----- The Concept of Christianity in the African Independent Churches. Durban University of Natal: Institute for Social Research, 1958.   DLC

3385. Thomas, George B. "Kimbanguism, African Christianity." International Documentation on the Contemporary Church (Mar. 13, 1971), pp. 2-29.   DHU/R

3386. Turner, Harold W. "African-Prophet Movement." Hibbert Journal (61:242, Apr., 1963), pp. 112-16. DAU; DAU/W; DCU/TH; DGU; DGW; DHU

3387. ----- (ed.). "Bibliography of Modern African Religious Movements: Supplement 1." Journal of Religion in Africa (1:3, 1968), pp. 173-210.   DHU/R

3388. ----- "The Church and the Lord: the Expansion of a Nigerian Independent Church in Sierra Leone and Ghana." Journal of African History (3:1, 1962), pp. 91-110. DAU; DGW; DGU; DHU/MO

3389. ----- History of an African Independent Church. Oxford: Clarendon Press, 1967.   DHU/MO; OWibfU; DHU/R

3390. ----- "The Litany of an Independent West African Church." Practical Anthropology (7:6, Nov.-Dec., 1960), pp. 256-62.   DHU/R

3391. ----- "A Methodology for Modern African Religious Movements." Comparative Studies in Society and History (8:3, Apr. 1966), pp. 281-94.   DHU/R

3392. ----- "Pagan Features in West African Independent Churches." Practical Anthropology (12:4, Jl.-Ag., 1965), pp. 145-51.   DHU/R

3393. ----- "The Place of Independent Religious Movements in the Modernization of Africa." Journal of Religion in Africa (2:1, 1969), pp. 43-63.

3394. ----- Profile Through Preaching; a Study of the Sermon Texts Used in a West African Independent Church. London: Edinburgh House Press, 1965.   TSewU-T; INU; MH/AH; MBU/T
Review: International Review of Missions (55:217, Ja., 1966), pp. 114-15.   DHU/R

3395. ----- "Prophets and Politics: A Nigerian Test-Case." The Bulletin of the Society for African Church History (2:1, Dec., 1965), pp. 97-118.   DHU/R

3396. ----- "A Typology for African Religious Movements." Journal of Religion in Africa (1:1, 1967), pp. 1-34. DHU/R

3397. Turner, Henry McNeil, (bp.). "The Church of the Lord." Journal of African History (3:1, 1962), pp. 91-100. DHU/MO
Negro author.

3398. Van der Post, Laurens. The Dark Eye in Africa. New York: William Morrow & Co., 1955.   DHU/MO
David Stirling and the Capricorn Society, formulated in British Africa, dedicated to forming a new society free of hate, color and religious discrimination.

3399. Wagner, Jean-Michel. Histoire et Sociologie Politiques de la Republique du Congo (Brazzaville). Paris: Librarie Générale de Droit et de Jurisprudence, 1963. DHU/MO
A discussion of Separatist Churches is included.

3400. Wainwright, Geoffrey. "Theological Reflections on the Catechism Concerning the Prophet Simon Kimbangu of 1970." Orita: Ibadan Journal of Religious Studies (5:1, Je., 1971), pp. 18-35.   DHU/R

3401. Walls, A. F., (ed.). "Bibliography of the Society, for African Church History." Journal of Religion in Africa (1:1, 1967), pp. 46-94.   DHU/R

3402. Weaver, Edwin I. and Irene. The Uyo Story. Elkhart, Indiana: Mennonite Board of Missions, 1970.   DLC
"An account of an experiment in fellowship with independent churches in South Eastern Nigeria."

3403. Webster, James Bertin. "Independent Churches in Africa." Tarikh (3:1, 1969), pp. 56-81.   DHU/MO

3404. Welbourn, Frederick Burkewood. East African Rebels: A Study of Some Independent Churches. London: SCM Press, 1961. DLC; MH; CtY-D; NNCor; MBU-T; NjPT; ICU; KyLxCB; DHU

3405. ----- A Place to Feel at Home; a Study of Two Independent Churches in Western Kenya. London: Oxford Univ. Press, 1966.   NN/Sch

3406. Welch, F. G. Towards an African Church. Nairobi: Christian Council of Kenya, 1962. ViAlTh; DLC; KyLxCB; NjPT; CtY-D

3407. Welton, Michael R. "The Holy Aruosa: Religious Conservatism in a Changing Society." Practical Anthropology (16:1, Ja.-Feb., 1969), pp. 18-27.   DHU/R

3408. Yengwa, M. B. "World Church Support for Liberation Movements." Sechaba (5:4, Apr., 1971), pp. 8-9. DHU/MO
African liberation movements.

3409. Young, Parker C. The Development of an Indigenous United Brethren in Christ Christ Church in Sierra Leone, West Africa. Masters thesis. Bonebrake Theological Seminary, 1941.
                                        DOUM/EUB

a. Central Africa

3410. Adelman, Kenneth Lee. "Christ and Culture in Zaire." Worldview (17:8, Ag., 1974), pp. 37-40.   DHU/R

3411. ----- "President Mobutu and Religion." St. Croix Review (72:2, Apr., 1974), pp. 15-22.   DHU/R

3412. Andersson, Efraim. Churches at the Grass-Roots; a Study in Congo-Brazzaville; Translated [from the French] by Dorothea M. Barton. London: Lutterworth Press, 1968.   MNtcA

3413. Balandier, George. The Sociology of Black Africa; Social Dynamics in Central Africa. New York: Praeger, 1970.   DHU/MO; DLC

3414. Bokeleale, Itofo B. "From Missions to Mission: The Church in Zaire and New Relationships." International Review of Mission (62:248, Oct., 1973), pp. 433-36.   DHU/R

3415. Bokeleale, Jean. "Letter Addressed to All Missionaries in-Congo-Tunshasa (Zaire) by the General Secretary of the Newly Consititued Church of Christ in Zire." Ecumenical Review (24:2, Apr., 1972), pp. 214-16.   DHU/R

3416. Bolink, Peter. Towards Church Union in Zambia: A Study of Missionary Co-operation and Church - Union Efforts in Central Africa. Franeker, Netherlands: T. Wever, 1967.   DLC

3417. Bright, John Douglas, Sr. "Central Africa and African Methodism." The African Methodist Episcopal Church Review (94:236, J1-Sept., 1968), pp. 63-68.   DHU/R
    Negro author.

3418. Broomfield, Gerald Webb. Towards Freedom. With a foreword by the Archbishop of New York. London: The Universities' Mission to Central Africa, 1957.   NN/Sch

3419. Brown, Wesley Haddon. Marriage Payment: a Problem in Christian Social Ethics among Kongo Protestants. Doctoral dissertation. University of Southern California, 1971.   DHU/R

3420. "Burundi Statement Adopted by the Central Committee of the World Council of Churches." The Ecumenical Review (25:4, Oct., 1973), p. 512.   DHU/R
    "Urge staff and others to continue their efforts to effect reconciliation in the area."

3421. Chona, M. Mainza. Speech at the Opening Ceremony of the Conference on Central African Religion. Lusaka, Zambia: Ag. 31- Sept. 8, 1972.   Pam. File, DHU/R
    mim.

3422. "Church Crisis in Zaire." Voice of Missions (79:4, Dec., 1972), pp. 10-11.   DHU/R

3423. Cline, Catherine Ann. The Church and the Movement for Congo Reform." Church History (32:1, Mr., 1963), pp. 45-56.

3424. Crawford, John R. "Money in the Congo Churches." Occasional Bulletin (20:10, Dec. 1969), pp. 1-13.   DHU/R

3425. Delano, R. F. and Williard A. Scofield. "School for Bush Preachers." American Baptist Magazine (172:2, Feb., 1974), pp. 20-22.   DHU/R
    Abouth the Kikongo Pastoral Training School established by American Baptists in Zaire.

3426. Elmslie, Walter A. Among the Wild Ngoni. Being Some Chapters in the History of the Livingstonia Mission in British Central Africa. London: F. Cass, 1970.   WU; DAU; MH; NN; DHU/R

3427. Fehderau, Harold W. "Planting the Church in the Congo, and the Merging Situation Today." Practical Anthropology (8:1, Ja. -Feb., 1961), pp. 25-30.   DHU/R

3428. Greschat, Hans-Jurgen. Kitawala; Ursprung, Ausbreitung und Religion der Watch-Tower-Bewegung in Zentralafrika. Marburg: N. G. Elwert Verlag Marburg, 1967. DHU/MO
    V. 4 of the Marburger Theologische Studien.
    Jehovah's Witnesses in Central Africa.

3429. Harris, Alton Louis. A United Ministry for a United Church in Congo. Masters thesis. Lexington Theological Seminary, 1966.   TN/DCHS

3430. Hetherwick, Alexander. The Gospel and the African; The Croall Lectures for 1930-1931 on the Impact of the Gospel on a Central African People. Edinburgh: T. & T. Clark, 1932.   NN/Sch

3431. Jadot, Jean. "The Church in the Congo." Catholic World (201:1, 204, J1., 1965). pp. 247-53.   DHU/R

3432. Jones, Arthur Gordon. Bridge of Friendship. London: Cargate Press, 1955.   NN/Sch

3433. Keable, Robert. Darkness or Light; Studies in the History of the Universities' Mission to Central Africa. Illustrations to the theory and practice of missions; with a preface by the Rt. Rev. Frank Weston. London: Universities' Mission to Central Africa, 1914.   NN/Sch

3434. Keller, Jean. "The Churches of Equatorial Africa." Practical Anthropology (10:1, Ja.-Feb., 1963), pp. 27-31.   DHU/R

3435. Kingsnorth, John S. Come Back Africa; the Review of the Work of 1962. London: Universities' Mission to Central Africa, 196-.   NN/Sch

3436. Laverdiere, Lucien. "Evolution et Revolution Pastorales en Afrique Centrale." Revue du Clerge Africain (27:2, Mr., 1972), pp. 117-200.   DHU/R

3437. Martin, Marie-Louise. "Prophetic Christianity in the Congo." Pro Veritate (7:4, Ag., 1968), pp. 14-17.   DLC

3438. "Mission in Congo." American Baptist Films, 1963. 84 fr., color. 35 mm.
    Filmstrip.
    "Shows the present-day missions in a changing Congo as they are carried on by national leaders and American Baptist missionaries."

3439. Morris, Colin M. Anything but This; the Challenge of Race in Central Africa. London: United Society for Christian Literature, 1958.   NN/Sch

3440. Niklaus, Robert L. "Politics Goes to Church in Zaire." Christianity Today (17; Nov. 24, 1972), pp. 9-13. DHU/R
    "Church and State in Zaire."

3441. ----- "Zaire Zaps its Religious Press." Christianity Today (17:13, Mr. 30, 1973), p. 689.   DHU/R

3442. ----- "Zaire's Super-Church." Christianity Today (16:14, Apr., 14, 1972), pp. 4-10.   DHU/R

3443. Norton, H. Wilbert. "Zaire: The Church in Crisis." Moody Monthly (73:1, Sept., 1972), pp. 64 +.   DHU/R

3444. Parr, Martin W. "Church and State in Equatoria." East and West Review (5:3, J1., 1939), pp. 214-19.   DHU/R

3445. Perraudin, Jean. Naissance d'une Eglise: Histoire du Burundi Chretien. Usumbura: Presses Lavigerie, 1963.
    Cst-H

3446. Phipps, William E. "The Influence of Christian Missions on the Rise of Nationalism in Central Africa." International Review of Missions (57; 1968), pp. 229-32.   DHU/R

3447. "Sending Words to be Witnesses." Board of World Missions, Presbyterian Church in the U. S., 1961. 45 fr., color, 35 mm. and disc: 1 s., 33 1/3 rpm, 13 min.
   Filmstrip.
   "Surveys recent revents in the Congo mission, pointing out the opportunity for Christian literature to be of service in that area."

3448. Shepperson, George. "Church and Sect in Central Africa." The Rhodes-Livingstone Journal (23; 1963), pp. 82-94. DLC

3449. Truby, David W. Regime of Gentlemen: Personal Experiences of Congolese Christians During the 1964 Rebellion. London: Marshall, Morgan and Scott, 1971.   DLC

3450. Widman, Ragnar. "Skolmission Och Kolonial Politik i Kongo." Svensk Missionstidskrift (60:4, 1972), pp. 212-32. CtY; ICU; CtHC; DLC
   Mission schools and politics in Zaire.

3451. Wing, Joseph van. Etudes Bakongo: Sociologie, Religion et Magie. Bruges: Desclee, De Brower, 1959. MH; NNC; RPB; MiU; CU; TxU

3452. Zaire. Church of Christ in the Congo. "Letter to All Missionaries in the Congo-Kinshasa (Zaire) From Dr. Jean Bokeleake, General Secretary." Ecumenical Press Service (No. 2/39th yr., Ja. 20, 1972), pp. 1-3.   DHU/R
   "Requests all missionaries to hold a Congress to discuss the future of Protestantism in Zaire."

3453. "Zaire." World Parish (11:7, Apr., 1972), p. 4+. DHU/R
   World Methodist Council.

3454. "Zaire Today: People, Government, Church." IDOC International (12; Oct., 1973), pp. 7-12.   DHU/R
   "Report issued by a group of European Catholic missionaries in Zaire, August, 1973."

b. Eastern Africa

3455. Andersen, Esther. Mutũũrĩrie wa mũcĩi wa Mũkristiano. Kiahbe A. I. Publications, 1964.   ANAU; DLC
   English title: Christian Family Life, in Kikuyu.

3456. Anderson, William B. Ambassadors by the Nile: The Church in North-east Africa. London: Lutterworth, 1963. CtY; CtY-D; IEG; KyWAT; DLC

3457. ----- "The Role of Religion in the Sudan's Search for Unity." David B. Barrett, (ed.). African Initiatives in Religion (Nairobi: East African Pub. House, 1971), pp. 73-87. DHU/R

3458. Benson, Stanley. "Christian Communication Among the Masai." Africa Theological Journal (4; 1971), pp. 68-75.   DHU/R

3459. Bernander, Gustav A. The Rising Tide- Christianity Challenged in East Africa. Rock Island: Augustana Press, 1957. DLC; CtY-D; CLU; ICU; NN; MNtcA

3460. Bhushan, Kul. "Hare Krana Safari." Back to Godhead (No. 51, 1973), pp. 21-23.   Pam. File, DHU/R

3461. Chittick, H. N. "The Last Christian Stronghold in the Sudan." Kush (11; 1963), pp. 264-72.   DLC

3462. Clark, Leon E. Nation-Building: Tanzania and the World (Through African Eyes: Cultures in Change, Unit VI). New York: Frederick A. Praeger, 1970.   DHU/MO

3463. Dain, Ronald. "Religious Education in Kenya Today." Bulletin of the Association for Religious Education (4:1, Spr., 1972), pp. 8-14.   Pam. File, DHU/R

3464. Diamond, Stanley, and Fred G. Burke, (eds.). The Transformation of East Africa: Studies in Political Anthropology. New York: Basic Books, 1966.   DHU/MO

3465. Elwes, Columba Cary. "Some Reflections on the Church in East Africa." African Ecclesiastical Review (13:1, 1971), pp. 69-75.   DHU/R

3466. "Episode in Rwanda." White Sisters of Africa. Color. Film.
   Social work being done by the White Sisters of Africa in Rwanda.

3467. Fordham, Paul and H. C. Wiltshire. Some Tests of Prejudice in an East African Adult College. London: Journal of the Institute of Race Relations, 1963.   DLC; ANAU
   Tests conducted at the College of Social Studies, Kikuyu, Kenya.

3468. Francis, Michael D. The Views of Students in Teachers' Colleges in Tanzania on The Teaching of Religion in Schools. Masters thesis, University of East Africa (Nairobi) 1968.

3469. Fuller, W. Harold. "Social Action in Sudan: Evangelicals Lend a Hand." Christianity Today (17:12, Mr. 16, 1973), pp. 638-40.   DHU/R

3470. Gingyera-Pinycwa, A. G. G. "The Missionary Press and the Development of Political Awareness in Uganda in the Decade 1952-62: a Case Study from Northern Uganda." Dini Na Mila (4:2, My., 1970), pp. 35-61.   DHU/R

3471. Goovaerts, Leo. "Les Catechistes au Rwanda et au Burundi." Lumen Vitae (27:2, 1972), pp. 217-18.   DLC; DCU; MB

3472. Gray, Betty and Bill. "East Africa is Turning to Christ." Episcopalian (138:9, Sept., 1973), pp. 8-11+   DHU/R

3473. Greschat, Hans J. and H. Jungraithmayr, (eds.). Wort und Religion-Kalima na Dini. Stuttgart: Evang. Missionsverlag, 1969.   DLC
   Studies in linguistics, Christian missions and religion in East Africa.

3474. Gunda, Zephania. The Significance of the Arusha Declaration as Seen in the Teaching and Practices of the Christian Church in Tanzania Today. Master's thesis. The Lutheran School of Theology at Chicago, 1971.

3475. Hake, A. "The De-Colonization of the Church in East Africa." East Africa Journal (3:11, Feb., 1967), pp. 7-12. DCU/AN

3476. Harjula, Raimo. "On the Role of the Laity and Their Equipping." Africa Theological Journal (No. 1, Feb., 1968), pp. 30-48.   DHU/R

3477. Harries, Lyndon P. "Religion and the Secular State in Tanzania." The Christian Century (89:36, Oct. 11, 1972), pp. 1014-16.   DHU/R

3478. Hastings, Adrian. Church and Mission in Modern Africa. Bronx, N. Y.: Fordham University Press, 1968. DHU/R; NjP; CLU

3479. Heywood, R. S. "Movements Towards Union in East Africa." The East and West Review (3; 1937), pp. 28-34.   DHU/R

3480. Holman, Ernest. "The Lutheran Church in Tanzania." Lutheran Brotherhood Bond (Apr., 1965), pp. 8-9. DLC; IU; MnHi; PGC

3481. Holway, James D. "The Religious Composition of the Population of the Coast Province of Kenya." Journal of Religion in Africa (3:3, 1970), pp. 228-39.   DHU/R

3482. Ijlst, Wim. A Present for Cold Mornings. Dublin, Ireland: Gill and Macmillan, 1968.   DLC MH
   Missions in East Africa.

3483. Jack, Homer A. "Uganda, Human Rights and the UN Agenda." America (127:11, Oct. 14, 1972), pp. 282-85. DHU/R

"Secretary General of the World Conference of Religion for Peace."

3484. Jasper, Gerhard. "The East African Church Union Discussions." Africa Theological Journal (No. 1, Feb., 1968), pp. 49-58.
DHU/R

3485. Kamfer, Pieter P. Die Volksorganiese Sendingmetode. By Bruno Gutmann. Amsterdam: Swets & Zeitlinger, 1955. NN/Sch Summary in English.

3486. Kibira, Josiah M. "Revival in Tanzania." Lutheran World (21:3, 1974), pp. 282-84.   Pam. File, DHU/R
Excerpts from author's Church, Clan and World. Uppsala, 1974. Author is bishop of the Northwest Diocese of the Evangelical Lutheran Church in Tanzania.

3487. Lacy, Creighton. "'Christian' Activism in Kenya." The Christian Century (89:13, Mr.29, 1972), pp. 364-69. DHU/R

3488. ----- "'Christian Socialism in Tanzania, An Interview with President Julius Nyerere." The Christian Century (89:9, Mr. 1, 1972), pp. 245-49.   DHU/R

3489. Langford-Smith, N. "Revival in East Africa." International Review of Missions (43; 1954), pp. 77-81.   DHU/R

3490. Low, D. A. "Converts and Martyrs in Buganda." International African Seminar. Christianity in Tropical Africa (London: International Africa Institute, 1968), pp. 28-68.
CLU

3491. Lutheran Church. Ministry to East Africa. "Washington, D. C. Church Provides Special Ministry to East Africans Living in Washington Area." The Lutheran (10:7, Apr. 5, 1972), p. 57.   Pam. File, DHU/R

3492. "A Lutheran Comment on the Progress of the East African Church Union Consultation." Africa Theological Journal (3; 1970), pp. 115-16.   DHU/R

3493. Mazrui, Ali A. "The Sacred and the Secular in East African Politics." Dini Na Mila (6:1, 1972), pp. 1-17.   DHU/R

3494. McAllister, Dorothy. "Notes on an East African Journey." The Crisis (79:9, Nov., 1972), pp. 304-07. DHU/R
Discusses her impressions of religion in the life of African people, several churches she visited and some of the educational activities sponsored by church groups.
Negro author.

3495. Middleton, John and Greet Kershaw. The Kikuyu and Kamba of Kenya. London: International African Institute, 1972. DHU/R
Religion - pp. 60-63; 83-85.
Sorcery - pp. 64-67; 86-87.

3496. Miller, Paul M. Equipping for Ministry in East Africa. Dodoma, Tanzania Cential: Tanganyika Press, 1969. DHU/R

3497. ----- "Vocation to the Ministry as Seen by 445 East African Secondary School Pupils." Presence (5:3, 1972), pp. 25-29.
DHU/R

3498. Muga, Erasto. The Impact of Western Christian Religion on the Development of Leadership Groups in East Africa (Kenya, Uganda, Tanzania). Doctoral dissertation. New School for Social Research, 1967.

3499. Mutembei, Richard. "Den Kristnes Ansvar; Tanzania Idag" Svensk Missionstidskrift (60:4, 1972), pp. 232-37. CtY; ICU; CtHC
The role of the church in Tanzania.

3500. Nass, Eef A. H. "Christian Communication Among the Masai." Africa Theological Journal (4; 1971), pp. 56-67.   DHU/R

3501. Newing, Edward G. "The Baptism of Polygamous Families: Theory and Practice in an East African Church." Journal of Religion in Africa (3:2, 1970), pp. 130-41.   DHU/R

3502. Ney, Joseph S. Unity and Diversity in East Africa: A Bibliographical Essay. Durham, N. C.: Committee on African Studies. Commonwealth Studies Center, Duke University, 1966.
"Reprinted from South Atlantic Quarterly (65:1, Wint., 1966), pp. 104-23." DLC

3503. Ochsner, Knud. "Church, School and the Clash of Cultures: Examples From North-West Tanzania." Journal of Religion in Africa (4:2, 1971), pp. 97-118.   DHU/R

3504. "Of People and a Vision." Maryknoll Fathers. Made and released by World Horizon Films, 1970. 19 min. sd. color. 16mm.   DLC
Film.
"Portrays the emerging nation of Tanzania a vibrant young nation working toward development. Shows the role of the church in this developmental progress and the efforts of the people to achieve social and economic stature."

3505-06. Painter, Levinus K. The Hill of Vision; the Story of the Quaker Movement in East Africa, 1902-1965... [Nairobi] East Africa Yearly Meeting of Friends, [1966.] DLC

3507-08. Pirouet, M. Louise. "Recovering the Sources for Church History in East Africa." Bulletin of the Society for African Church History (2:2, 1966), pp. 193-96.   DHU/R

3505. O'Grady, Desmond. "Conscience Crunch in Mozambique." U. S. Catholic (38:6, Je., 1973), pp. 30-33.   Pam. File DHU/R

3506. Painter, Levinus K. The Hill of Vision; the Story of the Quaker Movement in East Africa, 1902-1965... [Nairobi] East Africa Yearly Meeting of Friends, [1966.] DLC

3507. Perret, Edmond. "The Faithful Witness of the Presbyterian Church of Mozambique." Church and Society (64:6, Jl.-Ag., 1974), pp. 8-17.   DHU/R

3508. Pirouet, M. Louise. "Recovering the Sources for Church History in East Africa." Bulletin of the Society for African Church History (2:2, 1966), pp. 193-96.   DHU/R

3509. "Planning for the Church in Eastern Africa in the 1980's." African Ecclesiastical Review (16: 1 & 2, 1974.)   DHU/R
Issue devoted entirely to the December 1973 association meeting of the "members of the Episcopal Conference of Eastern Africa". (AMECEA)
Includes guidelines, message and position papers.

3510. Price, Thomas. "The Church as a Land Holder in Eastern Africa." Bulletin of Society for African Church History (1:1, 1963), pp. 8-13.   DLC

3511. Ranger, Terence O. "Christian Independency in Tanzania." David B. Barrett, (ed.). African Initiatives in Religion (Nairobi: East Africa Pub. House, 1971), pp. 122-45.   DHU/R

3512. Robinson, Isaiah. Religion As a Potent Factor in Social Stability and Traditional Continuity Among the Nilotic Nuer. Master's thesis. Howard University, 1969.

3513. Rogers, Cornish. "The Search for Black Identity in East Africa." Christian Century (88:39, Sept. 29, 1971), pp. 1124-25.
DHU/R

3514. ----- "The Ugandan Caper: Rights or Racism?" The Christian Century (89:36, Oct. 11, 1972), pp. 1001-02. DHU/R
Sees the Ugandan expulsion of Asians as part of the legacy of British Colonial rule and an "unmistakable sign that the colonial era is coming to an end."

3515. Saunders, Davis L. "Baptists in East Africa: the Birth of Two Conventions." Baptist History and Heritage (6:4, Oct., 1971), pp. 226-32.   DHU/R
Southern Baptist missions in East Africa.

3516. Schofield, J. V. "Where is the Prophet?" East Africa
Journal (6:5, My., 1969), pp. 23-4   DHU/MO
    Role of Christian church in Kenyan politics and social affairs.

3517-18. Shenk, David W. A Study of Mennonite Presence and
Church Development in Somalia From 1950 Through 1970.
Doctoral dissertation. New York University, 1972.
    Abstract: The Mennonite Quarterly Review (47; Ja., 1973),
    pp. 62-3.

3519. Shorter Aylward and Eugene Kataza. Missionaries to Your-
selves. African Catechists Today. New York: Orbis Books,
1972.   DHU/R

3520. "A Sick Church." Target (74; June, 1970), p. 1.   DHU/R
    An examination of the American Church of Uganda,
    Rwanda and Burundi.

3521. Simpson, Donald H. "The Dictionary of East African Biography Project and Its Missionary Material." Bulletin of the
Society for African Church History (2:2, 1966), pp. 190-93.
                                             DHU/R

3522. Swantz, Lloyd W. Church, Mission, and State Relations in
Pre and Post Independent Tanzania, 1955-1964. New York:
Syracuse University, Maxwell Graduate School of Citizenship
and Public Affairs, 1965.   Pam. File, DHU/R
    Mim. "Occasional Paper #19."

3523. Tanner, Ralph E. S. "Economic Factors in East African
Ecumenism." Journal of Ecumenical Studies (10:1, Wint., 1973),
pp. 51-69.   DHU/R

3524. "Tanzania: New Marriage Act." African Eccliastical Review
(13:4, 1971), p. 378.   DHU/R

3525. "Tanzania Quickly Rescinds Ban on Jehovah's Witnesses."
New York Times (Feb. 15, 1965).   DHU

3526. Tate, Francis V. Patterns of Church Growth in Nairobi.
Masters thesis. Fuller Theological Seminary, 1970.

3527-28. "Uganda Government Formulates Policy on Religion."
African Ecclesiastical Review (13:4, 1971), pp. 378-79.
                                             DHU/R

3529. Vidal, Henri. La Separation des Eglises et de l'Etat a
Madagascar. Paris: Pichon et Durand-Auzias, 1970.   DLC
    Book review by J. T. Hardyman in Journal of Religion in
    Africa (5:2, 1973), pp. 158-60.   DHU/R

3530. Vincent, Joan. African Elite. The Big Men of a Small Town.
New York: Columbia University Press, 1971. DHU/R; DLC
    Results of a field study in Leso, Uganda, 1966-67.
    Includes statistics on religious affiliation of adult males in
    Gondo parish.

3531. Walker, Alice. "The Diary of an African Nun." Toni Cade,
(ed.). The Black Woman (New York: New American Library,
1970), pp. 38-41.   DHU/MO
    A short story set in Uganda.

3532. Walker, R. H. "Christian Unity in East Africa." The Church
Missionary Review (50; Oct., 1909), pp. 621-23. DHU/R

3533. Welch, F. G. Training for the Ministry in East Africa.
Limuru, Kenya: Association of East African Theological
Colleges, 1963.   NNMR

3534. Westink, D. E. "The Orthodox Church in East Africa."
Ecumenical Review (20:1, Ja., 1968), pp. 33-43.   DHU/R
    A discussion of the African Greek Orthodox Church.

3535. Whittle, Stephen. "How Your Church Helps in the Sudan."
A. D. Presbyterian Life Edition (2:3, Mr., 1973), pp. 14-20.
DHU/R
    "The World Council of Churches helped negotiate the peace
    in the Sudan. Now through one great hour of sharing, we
    are playing a key role in reconstruction."

3536. Willie, Wilhelm. "Popular Bible Interpretation in Uganda."
African Ecclesiastical Review (15:3, 1973), pp. 227-36. DHU/R

3537. Wilson, Bryan R. "Jehovah's Witnesses in Kenya." Journal
of Religion in Africa (5:2, 1973), pp. 128-49.   DHU/R

3538. Wilson, Monica. Good Company: A Study of Nyakyusa Age-
Villages. Boston: Beacon Press, 1971.   DHU/R
    Chapter 5, Mystical Interdependence.

3539. Wolfe, Raymond W. Scott Theological College and the Africa
Inland Church, Kenya. Masters thesis. Trinity Evangelical
Divinity School of World Mission, 1971.

3540-41. Wrigley, C. C. "The Christian Revolution in Buganda."
Comparative Studies in Society and History (2; 1959), pp. 33-48.
                                             DHU/R

c. Southern Africa

3542. Adam, Heribert. Modernizing Racial Domination. The
Dyanamics of South African Politics. Berkeley, Calif.: University of South African Politics. Berkeley, Calif.: University
of California Press, 1971.   DHU/R
    Churches, pp. 56-67.

3543. Adendorff, R. Desmond. Churches' Urban Planning Commission. Capetown: Churches' Urban Planning Commission, 1973.
                                             DHU/R

3544. Alant (C. J.). "The Relevance of Socio-Economic Groups in the
Analysis of the Nederduitse Gereformeerde Kerk in South Africa."
Social Compass (Louvain: 19, 1, 1972), pp. 21-28.   DHU/R

3545. All Africa Conference of Churches. Lusaka, Zambia, May
11-24, 1974. "Living no Longer for Ourselves but for Christ."
Ecumenical Press Service (171:41, Je. 20, 1974), pp. 1-13.
    Extracts from three speeches delivered at the conference.

3546. "Andrew Walter Molise Makhene." Voice of Missions (80:7,
Mr., 1974), pp. 11-12.   DHU/R
    Native minister of South Africa.

3547. Ankrah, Kodwo E. "Why Stop White Migration." Ecumenical
Press Service (5:41st year, Feb. 21, 1974), pp. 5-9.   DHU/R
    Describes actions taken by British Council of Churches and
    World Council of Churches to prohibit South Africa, Rhodesia
    and Portugal from continuing the policies of attracting white
    immigrants to their countries.

3548. Anstrey, Roger T. "Christianity and Bantu Philosophy:
Observations on the Thought and Work of Placide Tempels."
International Review of Missions (52; 1963), pp. 316-22.
                                             DHU/R

3549. "Apartheid and the Church in South Africa." Worldview
(16:8, Aug., 1973), pp. 21-28.   DHU/R

3550. "Archbishop Hurley on Apartheid." African Ecclesiastical
Review (15:3, 1973), pp. 276-79.   DHU/R

3551. Baartman, Ernest N. "The Significance of the Development
of Black Consciousness for the Church." Journal of Theology
For Southern Africa (Mr. 2, 1973), pp. 18-22.   DHU/R
    Author is General Secretary of the Christian Education
    and Youth Department of the Methodist Church of South
    Africa.

3552. Bailey, J. Martin. "World Spotlight Hits Africa." United
Church Herald (13:11, Dec., 1970), pp. 44-7.   DHU/R
    Churches collide with white regimes in South Africa,
    Rhodesia and Angola."

3553. Barker, Anthony. "Thoughts from NQUTU (Religion and
Migrant Labour). "South African Outlook (104; Feb., 1974),
pp. 24-26+.

3554. Becken, Hans-Jürgen. "A Challenge to the Theological Education in Southern Africa." The Ghana Bulletin of Theology (4:4, Je., 1973), pp. 42-50. DHU/R

3555. Beckers, Gerhard. Religiöse Faktoren in der Entwicklong der Sudafrikanischen Rassenfrage. Ein Beitrag Zur Rolle des Kalvinismus in Kolonialen Situationen. München: W. Fink, 1969. NNCor
Church on race problems in South Africa.

3556. Berglund, Axel-Ivar. "The South African Missiological Society." Journal of Theology for Southern Africa (2; Mr., 1973), pp. 53-56. DHU/R
A report of The South African Missiological Society, Sixth Annual Congress.

3557. Berthoud, Alexander. "The Missionary Situation in South Africa." International Review of Missions (49; 1960), pp. 83-90. DHU/R

3558. "Black African Rights Sought by Churches." The Churchman (186:8, Oct. 1972), p. 19. DHU/R

3559. Bloom, Leonard. "An Interdisciplinary Study of Social, Moral and Political Attitudes of White and Non-white South African University Students." Journal of Social Psychology (54; 1961), pp. 3-12. DHU

3560. Bobo, John. "Congregation Explores on-the-job Christianity." National Council Outlook (8; Sept., 1958), pp. 11-12. DHU/R

3561. Bockelman, Wilfred. An Exercise in Compassion: the Lutheran Church in South Africa. Minneapolis: Augsburg Pub. House, 1972. MiBsA; DHU/R; MSL/CHI

3562. ----- and Eleanor Bockelman. An Exercise in Compassion. The Lutheran Church in South Africa. Minneapolis, Minn.: Augsburg Publishing House, 1972. DHU/R

3563. Bosch, David J., (ed.). Church and Change in Africa. Pretoria: N. G. Kerkboekhandel, 1971. DLC; ICT
"Papers read at the third annual meeting of the South African Society for Missionary Studies, 1971."

3564. ----- "The Question of Mission Today." Journal of Theology for Southern Africa (1; Dec., 1972), pp. 5-15. DHU/R

3565. Boud, S. "Apartheid and the Church." Commonweal (72; Je. 3, 1960), pp. 250-3. DHU

3566. Brady, J. E. Trekking for Souls. Cedara, Natal: Missionary Association of Mary Immaculate, 1952. NB; CSt-H; MiEM; CtY-D

3567. Brandel-Syrier, Mia. Reeftown Elite: A Study of Social Mobility in a Modern African Community on the Reef. London: Routledge & Kegan Paul, 1971. DHU/MO
The influence of missionaries on South Africa.

3568. Brayshaw, E. Russell. "The Racial Problems of South Africa." Friends Intelligencer (109:33, Ag. 16, 1952), pp. 467-69. DHU/R

3569. Brennecke, Gerhard. Bruder im Schatten. Das Bild Missionsreise durch Sudafrika Gesehen, Bedacht und Aufgezeichnet. Berlin: Evangelische Verlagsanstalt, 1954. MiBsA

3570. British Council of Churches. International Dept. The Future of South Africa. A Study by British Christians. Published for the British Council of Churches. London: SCM Press, 1965. DLC

3571. Brown, Sheila. A Sociological Study of the Influence of the Christian Religion on the Bantu Community at Rwarwa. Masters thesis. University of South Africa at Pretoria, 1970.

3572. Bucher, Hubert. "Black Theology in South Africa." African Ecclesiastical Review (15:4, 1973), pp. 329-39. DHU/R

3573. Calder, Ralph F. G. "Congregationalism in South Africa." Congregational Quarterly (31:2, Apr., 1953), pp. 149-56. DHU/R

3574. Calkins, Thomas M. Umfundisi, Missioner to the Zulus. Milwaukee: Bruce Pub. Co. 1959. MiBsA; DLC PPT

3575. Carlson, Joel. "The Americans Decision on South Africa." World Call (53:11, Dec., 1971), pp. 12-14. DHU/R

3576. Carstens, Kenneth N. "Apartheid: How Much Longer?" Metanoia An Independent Journal of Radical Lutheranism (5:3, Sept., 1973), pp. 4-5. DHU/R

3577. ----- "South Africa, the Churches and the Future." Concern (8:22, Dec. 15, 1966), pp. 4-7. DHU/R

3578. Carter, John Stanley. Methods of Mission in Southern Africa. London: S.P.C.K., 1963. MNtcA

3579. Cassidy, M. "A South African Christian Confronts Apartheid." Christianity Today (16:4, Nov., 1971), pp. 3-6. DHU/R; DAW/W; DCU/Th

3580. ----- "White South African Views His Country From America." World Vision (17; My., 1973), p. 14. DGW

3581. Cawood, Lesley. The Churches and Race Relations in South Africa. Johannesburg: South African Institute of Race Relations, 1964. NcD; DLC

3582. Chavunduka, G. L. Social Change in a Shona Ward. Salisbury: University of Rhodesia, 1970. DLC
University of Rhodesia. Department of Sociology. Occasional paper, no. 4.

3583. "The Christian and Southern Africa--a Conversation on Dialogue." Presence (5:2, 1971), pp. 32-3. DHU/R

3584. "A Christian Approach, Social Antipathies and the Christian Remedy." Interracial Review (34; My. 1961), pp. 281-82. DHU/MO

3585. The Christian Handbook of South Africa. Die Suid-Afrikaanse Kristen-Handboek... Lovedale, So. Africa. Published by the Lovedale Press on behalf of the Christian Council of South Africa, 1938. NN/Sch

3586. Christian Principles in Multi-Racial South Africa. Pretoria: Dutch Reformed Church, 1953. DLC

3587. Christian Responsibility Toward Areas of Rapid Social Change. Johannesburg: Report of the Multi-Racial Conference, 1959. CStH

3588. "The Church and Apartheid." Lutheran Standard (129; Oct. 5, 1971), p. 25. ICLT; IMC

3589. "Church and Race in South Africa." Race Today (5:2, Feb., 1973), p. 50. DHU/MO

3590. "Churches in Rhodesia Speak." IDOC International (46; Apr. 29, 1972), pp. 59-66. DHU/R

3591. Churchmen Report on U. S. Businesses in Southern Africa. Charles C. Diggs. Washington, D. C., Congressional Record, 92nd Congress, Second Session, March 22, 1972. DHU/R

3592. "Circular from Individual Christians in Rhodesia." IDOC International (46; Apr. 29, 1972), pp. 44-48. DHU/R

3593. Coates, Austin. Basutoland. London: Her Majesty's Stationery Office, 1966. NN/Sch
See "The Coming of Christianity"- pp. 24-30 and "The Rival Doctrine"- pp. 101-11.

3594. Collins, Colin B. Catholic Bantu Education. Pretorio: n.p., 1957. DHU/R

3595. "Cool-mannered Bishop Leads Black African's World
Pleas." Christian Advocate (16:6, Mr. 16, 1972), pp. 19-20.
                                        Pam File, DHU/R
Bishop Abel T. Muzorowa, bishop of United Methodism's
Southern Rhodesia area. He spoke as chairman of the
African National Council in December, 1971, to oppose
implementation of a proposed settlement between Rhodesians
and the British government.

3596. Creighton, William F. & William Booth. "Repression in
South Africa." International Documentation on the Contemporary
Church. (n.a. Ed.) (Ag. 28, 1971), pp. 6-22.   DHU/R

3597. Crowther, E. "Church's Task in South Africa." Christian
Century (83:30, Jl. 27, 1966), pp. 933-35.   DHU/R

3598. Cunningham, Robert J. A Brief Survey of Southern Africa:
a Contemporary Review of the Peoples and the Church.
Maryknoll, N.Y.: Maryknoll Publications, 1956. MNtcA

3599. Cushman, Mary Floyd. Missionary Doctor, the Story of
Twenty Years in Africa. New York: Harper & Bros., 1944.
                                        NN/Sch

3600. Daniels, George M. "Rhodesia: Crisis for America's
Conscience." Christian Herald (95:10, Oct., 1972), pp. 36-39;
(95:11, Nov., 1972), pp. 20-22+.   DHU/R
Captioned under heading of "what black Christians are
thinking." "Mr. Daniels is director of Interpretive Services
of the United Methodist Board of Missions."
Negro author.

3601. ----- "South African Methodists Pushing for Desegregation."
The African Methodist Episcopal Church Review (81:221,
Jl.-Sept., 1964), pp. 27-28.   DHU/R

3602. ----- (ed.). Southern Africa: A Time for Change. New
York: Friendship Press, 1969.   DHU/R
pp. 18-21, "What God Hath Joined Together;" pp. 71-75,
"The Churches on Trial."

3603. Davies, Horton. Great South African Christians. New York:
Oxford Univ. Press, 1951. MiBsA; INU; DLC; DHU/R

3604. ----- "South Africa and Ourselveles." Congregational
Quarterly (32:3, Jl., 1954), pp. 241-46.   DHU/R
The Congregational Union of South Africa.

3605. DeBeer, Z.J. Multi-Racial South African: The Reconciliation of Forces. Issued under the auspices of the Institute
of Race Relations. London: Oxford Univ. Press, 1961.
                                        A & M; DHU/MO

3606. De Gruchy, John W. "Church Union in South Africa."
South African Outlook (104; Feb., 1974), pp. 20-23+.

3607. ----- The Local Church and the Race Problem in South
Africa. Masters thesis. Chicago: The Chicago Theological
Seminary, 19??

3608. "Divided Church in Rhodesia." America (124; My. 29,
1971), p. 556.   DHU/R
"Catholic church in Rhodesia."

3609. "Do You Enjoy Saying Mass?" African Ecclesiastical
Review (13:4, 1971), pp. 348-51.   DHU/R
Article signed by a pastor of Zambia.

3610. Dodge, Ralph E. "The Church's Dilemma in Southern
Africa." Africa Today (15:3, Je.-Jl., 1968), pp. 12-14.
                                        DHU/MO

3611. Du Preez, Andries Bernardus. Eiesoortige Ontwikkeling
Tot Volksdiens, die Hoop van Suid-Afrika. Kaapstad:
H. A. U. M., 1959.

3612. ----- Inside the South African Crucible. Kaapstad, So.
Africa: H. A. U. M., 1959.   DLC; NN/Sch

3613. Dutch Reformed Conference of Church Leaders, Pretoria,
1953. Christian Principles in Multi-Racial South Africa;
A Report. Pretoria: n.p., 1954.
Conference held Nov. 17-19, 1953.

3614. Du Toit, Stefanus. Holy Scripture and Race Relations, with
Special Application to South African Conditions. Potchefstroom:
Pro Rege-Pers, 1960.   DLC; NcD

3615. Ecumenical Consultation on Christian Practice and Desirable
Action in Social Change and Race Relations in Southern Africa.
Report: Christians and Race Relations in Southern Africa.
Kitwe, Northern Rhodesia, 1964.   MiBsA

3616. Freilem, Helene. "Kirke, Utvikling og Politik: Zambia
(Church, Development and Politics in Zambia)." Norsk
Tidsskrift for Misjon (26:3, 1972), pp. 174-84. CtHC; CtY-D
MH/AH

3617. "Gandhi and South Africa Today." IDOC-International
(Ja. 29, 1972), pp. 51-54.   DLC; DHU/R
Address delivered by Denis E. Hurley, archbishop of
Durbin, during a prayer service held at Phoexin, Natal
on October 2, 1971. Text first appeared in the November
15, 1971 issue of Pro Veritate.

3618. Garrett, A. E. F. South African Methodism. Her Missionary Witness. Cape Town: Methodist Pub. House, 1966. MH

3619. Gerdener, Gustav Bernhard August. Recent Developments
in the South African Mission Field. London: Marshall, Morgan,
& Scott, 1958.   DHU/MO; MiBsA

3620. Go Ye Therefore. The Missionary Work of the Dutch Reformed
Church (Nederduitse Gereformeerde Kerk) of South Africa. Cape
Town: Church Information Offices, 1962.   NNMR

3621. "God-Talk in Southern Africa." Editorial. Journal of
Theology for Southern Africa (5; Dec., 1973), pp. 3-6.
                                        DHU/R

3622. Gqubule, T. Simon N. "The White Missionary and the S. A.
Churches Today." South African Outlook (103; Nov., 1973), pp.
190-91.

3623. Groth, Siegfried. "The Condemnation of Apartheid by the
Churches in South West Africa." International Review of
Missions (61:242, Apr., 1972), pp. 183-95.
                                        Pam. File, DHU/R

3624. Hadfield, F. L. Christ and the Colour Bar in Southern
Africa. South Africa: Central News Agency, 1953. TN/DCHS

3625. Harvey, Pharis J. "UCM's Demise." The Christian Century
(89:31, Sept. 6, 1972), pp. 875-76.   DHU/R
Response to item in Aug. 2nd issue of folding of University
Christian Movement in South Africa.

3626. Haselbarth, Hans. Rassenkonflikt und Mission; zum Beitrag
der Christlichen Kirchen in Sudafrika. Berlin: Lettner-Verlag,
1970.   NNCor
Church and race problems in South Africa.

3627. "Heart of Darkness." Newsweek (28:15, Oct., 1973), p. 119.
                                        Pam. File, DHU/R
The Catholic Church and the struggle for Mozambique.

3628. Heaton, Jane. "Zambia, Women Find Role in a New Africa."
The Disciple, A Bi-Weekly Journal of the Christian Church
(Disciples of Christ) (1:2, Ja., 1974), pp. 21-22. DHU/R
Disciples of Christ contribute personnel and finance to the
Women's Training Centre in Kitwe, Zambia.

3629. Higgins, Edward. "Les Roles Religieux Dans le Contexte
Multiracial Sud-Africain: Le Profil du Ministere Dans le
Calvinisme et le Catholicisme." Social Compass (19:1, Je.,
1972), pp. 29-47.   DHU/R

3630. ----- "The Sociology of Religion in South Africa." Archives De Sociologie Des Religions (32, Jl.-Dec., 1971), pp. 143-64.
DHU/R

3631. Hinchliff, P. The Anglican Church in South Africa. London: Longman & Todd, 1963.   DHU/MO

3632. Hoagland, Jim. South Africa: Civilizations in Conflict. Boston: Houghton Mifflin Co., 1972.   DHU/R
Church and State, p. 67.

3633. Hofmeyr, Jan Hendrick. Christian Principles and Race Problems. Johannesburg: S.A. Institute of Race Relations, 1945.   DHU/MO

3634. ----- Hoernlé Memorial Lectures for 1945--1946--1947. Johannesburg: S.A. Institute of Race Relations, 1948. NN/Sch
Church and race relations.

3635. Homdrom, Theodore. The Problem of Lutheran Unity in South Africa. Masters thesis. Luther Theological Seminary (St. Paul), 1959.

3636. Hooker, J. R. "Witnesses and Watchtower in the Rhodesias and Nyasaland." Journal of African History (6:1, 1965), pp. 91-106.   DHU/MO

3637. Horrell, Muriel. A Survey of Race Relations in South Africa. Johannesburg: South African Institute of Race Relations, 1971.   DHU/R
Churches and Missions, p. 258.

3638. Houtart, Francois and André Rousseau. The Church and Revolution. Maryknoll, N.Y.: Orbis Books, 1971. DLC; DHU/R
Southern Africa is included.

3639. Hurley, Denis E. Apartheid: A Crisis of the Christian Conscience. Delivered under the auspices of the South African Institute of Race Relations. Pietermaritzburg: Printed by the National Witness, 1964.   NN/Sch

3640. ----- "The Churches and Race Relations." N. J. Rhoodie. South African Dialogue, Contrast in South African Thinking on Basic Race Issue (Philadelphia: Westminster Press, 1972), pp. 459-79.   DHU/R

3641. "Implementation of "Motu Proprio" on Mixed Marriages, in South Africa." African Ecclesiastical Review (13:1, 1971), pp. 85-86.   DHU/R
"Bishops of Southern Africa Resolution."

3642. Inter-Racial Conference of Church Leaders, Johannesburg, 1954. God's Kingdom in Multi-Racial South Africa; A Report on the Inter-Racial Conference of Church Leaders, Johannesburg, 7-10 December, 1954. Johannesburg: Printed by Voortrekkerpers Beperk, 1955? NN/Sch; NcD; CtY; IaU

3643. "Is Prayer Enough? Apartheid in South Africa." Newsweek (55; Apr. 25, 1960), p. 100.   DHU

3644. Jackman, Stuart Brooke. The Numbered Days. London: SCM Press, 1954.   DHU/R; NN/Sch; DLC

3645. Jennings, James R. "A Visit to the Fourth Reich." Catholic World (214:1, 280, Nov., 1971), pp. 56-59. DHU/R
Written by the Associate Director of the Division of World Justice and Peace on apartheid in South Africa.

3646. Johanson, Brian. "The South African Congress on Mission and Evangelism." Journal of Theology For Southern Africa (3; Je., 1973), pp. 57-63.   DHU/R
A report of meeting held at Durban, March 12-22, 1973.

3647. Juhnke, James C. "South African Church Council Moves to Oppose Racism." Christian Century (89:39, Nov. 1, 1972), pp. 1109-12.   DHU/R

3648. Kalilombe, Patrick Augustine. "Rector of Kachebere Major Seminary in Mchinji, Malawi will be Consecrated First Malawian Bishop of Lilongwe Diocese on August 27, /1972/." Target (101; Sept., 1972), p. 7.   DHU/R

3649. Keet, B. Wither--South Africa? Translated by N. J. Marquard. Stellenbosch: University Publishers and Booksellers, 1958.   NN/Sch

3650. Kellerman, A. P. R. "Religious Affiliation in South Africa." Social Compass (19:1, 1972), pp. 7-20.   DHU/R

3651. Kemp-Blair, Henry J. The Problem of Racial Tensions in South Africa and the Challenge They Present to Protestants in the United States. Masters thesis. Southern California School of Theology, 1957.

3652. Kendall, R. Elliott. "Rhodesia: A Crucial Issue for the Christian Conscience." Christian Century (88:37, Sept. 15, 1971), pp. 1086-88.

3653. Klepzig, Fritz. Kinderspiele der Bantu. Mesenheim am Glam: Verlag Anton Hain, 1972.   DLC

3654. Kotzé, Jacobus Cornelius Gideon. Principle and Practice in Race Relations, According to Scripture. Stellenbosch: S. C. A. Publishers, 1962.   DLC; NcD

3655. Kuper, Leo and Hilstan Watts, et alii. Durban, A Study in Racial Ecology. London, New York: Columbia University Press, 1958.   DHU/R
page 83, Statistical table of Religious affiliation of the population of Durban, South Africa by race: 1951 census.

3656. Lacy, Creighton. "Christian Humanism in Zambia, An Interview with President Kenneth Kaunda." Christian Century (89:7, Feb. 16, 1972), pp. 191-95.   DHU/R

3657. ----- "Christian Optimism in South Africa." Christian Century (89; Apr. 19, 1972), pp. 445-51.   DHU/R

3658. Lamprecht, J. A. Theology Here and Now or a Theology of Acceptance. An Inaugural Lecture Given in the University of Fort Hare on the 14th September, 1973. n.p.: Printed by the Lovedale Press, 1973.   Pam. File, DHU/R
Author is professor of Systematic Theology, South Africa. Discusses movements toward indigenisation of Christianity in South Africa.

3659. Landman, W. A. A Plea for Understanding; A Reply to the Reformed Church in America. Cape Town: N. G. Kerkuitgewers for the Information Bureau of the Dutch Reformed Church in South Africa, 1968.   DLC

3660. Lawson, Jennifer. "Education for Equality." A. D. United Herald Edition (2:1, Ja., 1972), pp. 56-58. DHU/R
United Church of Christ, founder of Inanda Seminary, the only private school in South Africa which has an interracial staff.

3661-62. "Liberal Wins South Africa Church Election." Christian Century (79; Nov. 7, 1962), p. 1346.   DHU/R

3663. Lockwood, Ted. "Trial by Terror in South Africa." Christianity and Crisis (31:22, Dec., 1971), pp. 278-84.
Pam. File, DHU/R

3664. Løken, Andreas. "Forsätt Medansvar for det sørlige Afrika (Continued co-responsibility for Southern Africa.)." Norsk Tidsskrift for Misjon (27:1, 1973), pp. 47-56. CtHC; CtY-D; MH/AH

3665. Long, Norman. Social Change and the Individual. A Study of the Social and Religious Responses to Innovation in a Zambian Rural Community. Manchester: Manchester Univ. Press for Institute of Social Research, Univ. of Zambia, 1968. NN; MH-P; MiEM; CU-SC; GW; IEdS; WaU; NjR; MH; MdU

(Long, Norman, cont.)
Analysis of how the Jehovah's Witnesses integrated into the wider Zambian society.

3666. Lorraine, Guy. "Clergy Protest Apartheid Laws." Christian Science Monitor (Dec. 22, 1972).   Pam. File, DHU/R
Clergy march across South Africa protesting apartheid labor laws.

3667. Lutheran Church. South Africa. "Committee Stresses Need for Contact Between Lutheran World Federation and the Federation of Evangelical Lutheran Churches in Southern Africa." Target (101; Sept., 1972), pp. 1+.   DHU/R

3668. Lutheran Church. South Africa. "Nambia Lutherans Confer with United Nation Heads." The Lutheran (10:7, Apr. 5, 1972), pp. 28-29.   Pam File, DHU/R

3669. Lutheran Church. South West Africa. "African Church Leader Asks Continued U. S. Support." The Lutheran (10:15, Ag. 16, 1972), pp. 28-29.   Pam. File, DHU/R

3670. MacDonald, Roderick J. "Reverend Hanock Msokera Phiri and the Establishment in Nyasaland of the African Methodist Episcopal Church." African Historical Studies (3:1, 1970), pp. 75-87.   DHU/MO

3671. "Malawi: Difficult Choice." Africa (17; Ja., 1973), p. 32.

3672. Martin, Marie-Louise. The Biblical Concept of Messianism, and Messianism in Southern Africa. Morija, Basutoland, Africa: Morija Sesuto Book Depot, 1964. CLU; DLC; MH-AH; CtHC; NcD; InU; NNMR

3673. Mary Aquina, (Sister). "Christianity in a Tribal Trust Land." African Social Research (1; Je., 1966), pp. 1-40.   DLC

3674. ----- "The People of the Spirit: An Independent Church in Rhodesia (The Apostles)." Africa (37:2, Apr., 1967), pp. 203-19.   DHU/MO; DAU; CLU

3675. Matthews, A. H. "Graham in South Africa: Showing How it Can Work." Christianity Today (17;14, Apr. 13, 1973), p. 748.   DHU/R
Evangelistic work.

3676. ----- "South African Congress: Breaking New Ground." Christianity Today (17:14, Apr. 13, 1973), pp. 747-48. DHU/R
Evangelistic work in South Africa & religious institutions.

3677. Mayer, Philip. Townsmen or Tribesmen. Conservatism and the Process of Urbanization in a South African City. Cape Town: Oxford Univ. Press, 1963.   DHU/MO

3678. Mbali, E. Z. "Asati Staff Institute." Journal of Theology for Southern Africa (5; Dec., 1973), pp. 60-2.   DHU/R

3679. Mdlalose, W. J. "The Bantu Presbyterian Church of S. A." South African Outlook (103; Nov., 1973), p. 182.

3680. Mechem, D. "Zambia -- a Call for Workers." Christian Standard (Dec. 26, 1971), pp. 4+. CtY/D; DLC; OrU; MD

3681. "The Methodist Church Acts." Africa Today (15:3, Je.-Jl., 1968), p. 27.   DHU/MO
"Recognizing their involvement in Southern Africa began as early as 1885, the Methodist Church declared it could no longer maintain its old relationships."

3682. Milingo. Emmanuel. "Patronado and Apartheid. Text of a radio speech delivered as a Easter Sermon. March 29, 1970." International Documentation on the Contemporary Church, North American Edition (10; Sept. 26, 1970), pp. 51-57. DHU/R
Archbishop of Lusaka, Zambia, discusses the moral duty of the Catholic Church to censure the government.

3683. Mitchell, Constance. History and Development of the Seventh-Day Adventist Church in the Union of South Africa. Master's thesis. Howard University, 1959.

3684. Mitchell, James Clyde. Kalela Dance: Aspects of Social Relationships Among Urban Africans in Northern Rhodesia. Manchester: Univ. Press for the Rhodes-Livingstone Institute, 1956.   NNMR

3685. Moodie, T. D. "Power, Apartheid, and the Afrikaner Civil Religion." Harvard Theological Review (65:41, Oct., 1972), pp. 600-1.   DHU/R
Abstract of Ph.D. dissertation, Harvard University.

3686. Moore, Basil. The Challenge of Black Theology in South Africa. Atlanta: John Knox Press, 1974.   DHU/R

3687. ----- "South Africa: UCM, Church and Bible. Communio Viatorum (16:1-2, Spr., 1973), pp. 77-84. DHU/R
UCM --University Christian Movement has a majority of Black Students.

3688. Morris, Colin M. The Hour After Midnight: a Missionary's Experiences of the Racial and Political Struggle in Northern Rhodesia. New York: Longmans, 1961. WU; NNC; CLU; MH; NN; T Sew U-T

3689. Morrison, Lionel. "The Church and Apartheid." Race Today (4; 1, Ja., 1972), pp. 14-15.   DHU/MO

3690. Morton, Don. Partners in Apartheid. Should United States Companies Withdraw from South Africa. n.p.: n.p., n.d.
                                          Pam. File, DHU/R
A Christian assessment, written by Rev. Morton for the Council for Christian Social Action, United Church of Christ.

3691. Multi-Racial Conference on Christian Responsibility Toward Areas of Rapid Social Change. Johannesburg, 1959. Christian Responsibility Toward Areas of Rapid Social Change; Report to the Multi-Racial Conference Held at the University of Witwatersrand...from 7 to 10 Dec. 1959. Johannesburg: Voortrekkerpers Beperk, 1960.   NN/Sch

3692. Muzorewa, Abel. "Black vs. White in Rhodesia." Crisis (79:5, My., 1972), pp. 151+.   DHU/R
Bishop Muzorewa of the Methodist Church is chairman of the Nationalist Council of Rhodesia.

3693. Nash, J. O. "The Church of the Province of South Africa. The Church Overseas (3:11, Jl., 1930), pp. 268-78. DHU/R

3694. Nelson, Robert G. "Justice in Rhodesia is a Christian Concern." World Call (54:5, My., 1972), pp. 24-25.   DHU/R
The author is executive secretary of the Department of Africa in the Overseas Ministries of the Christian Church (Disciples of Christ).

3695. Nesbitt, Rozell William Prexy. Prophets or Profits? The "Concern" of the American Protestant Church With Southern Africa. Evanston: Northwestern University, English Department, 1973.   IEN; DHU/R
Typescript.

3696. "New National Seminary of Zambia." African Ecclesiastical Review (15:4, 1973), p. 378.   DHU/R

3697. Niederberger, Oskar. Kirche - Mission - Rasse; die Missionsauffassung der Niederlandisch-reformierten Kirchen von Sud-Afrika. Schoneck-Beckenriea, Schweiz (Suisse): Administration der Neven Zeitschrift fur Missionwissenschaft, 1959.
                                          MiBsA

3698. Noble, Walter James. The Black Trek; From Village to Mine in Africa. London: Livingstone Press, 1931.   NN/Sch

3699. Ntlabati, Gladstone. "Ethics and Violence in South Africa." Africa Today (15:3, Je.-Jl., 1968), pp. 8-11.   DHU/MO

3700. ----- "The Two Apartheids: White Man's Heaven--Black Man's Hell." Social Action (34:8, Apr., 1968), pp. 26-34.
                                          DHU/R

3701. Nurnberger, Klaus. "A Relevant Theology for Africa: Reflections on the Missiological Institute at Mapumulo 1972." Journal of Theology for Southern Africa (1; Dec., 1972), pp. 59-64.   DHU/R
    Southern Africa and comments on Black Theology.

3702. ----- "Relevant Theology in Action." Journal of Theology For Southern Africa (1; Dec., 1972), pp. 59-63.   DHU/R
    Author, a teacher at the Lutheran Theological College, Mapumulo, Natal, gives his impressions of the Missiological Institute's consultation held at the College on "A Relevant Theology for Africa: An Examination of Black Theology - African Theology."

3703. Onokpasa, B. E. Hero of Sharpeville. Ibadan (Nigeria): Augustinian Publishers of Nigeria, 1961.   CLU
    Brutal shooting by police of South African blacks when they met peacefully to protest against apartheid. Bishop of Johannesburg and Anglican church took active role in protest.

3704. "Open Letter to South Africa." IDOC-International (32; Sept. 25, 1971), pp. 64-96.   DHU/R
    "Addressed to all South Africans signed by over forty church men and women regarding apartheid."

3705. Orpen, Christopher and Quentin Rookledge. "Dogmatism and Prejudice in White South Africa." The Journal of Social Psychology (66:1, 1972), pp. 151-53.   CEY; PU

3706. "Our Church Has Let Us Down." Presence (5:2, 1971), pp. 38-40.   DHU/R
    "Excerpts from a Manifesto issued by five black Roman Catholic priests, South Africa, January 23, 1970."

3707. Parker, Daniel Otis. The Problem of Apartheid and the Blacks of the Church in the Union of South Africa. 1957.
    Typescript.
    Paper submitted in A.N.T.S. for Mission Seminar, May 8, 1957.

3708. Paton, Alan C. "A Christian Perspective on South Africa." Princeton Seminary Bulletin (64:3, Dec., 1971), pp. 30-7.
          Pam. File, DHU/R

3709. ----- Christian Unity: A South African View. Grahamstoun, S.A.: Rhodes Univ.; Indianapolis: Association for the Promotion of Christian Unity, 1951.   TN/DCHS

3710. ----- "Church and State in South Africa." Christianity and Crisis (34:16, Sept. 30, 1974), pp. 205-10.   DHU/R

3711. ----- The Long View. Edward Callan, (ed.). New York: Frederick A. Praeger, 1968.   DHU/R
    Chap. II is entitled "Christian Conscience in a Racial Society."

3712. ----- "The Price of Segregation: The Effects of Apartheid on Culture." Social Action (34:8, Apr. 1968), pp. 19-25.
          DHU/R

3713. Paton, David M., (ed.). Church and Race in South Africa. London: SCM Press, 1958. DLC; NjP; DHU/MO; NN/Sch

3714. Pauw, Berthold A. "Patterns of Christianisation Among the Tswana and the Xhosa-Speaking Peoples." African Systems of Thought. Studies Presented and Discussed at the Third International African Seminar in Salisbury, December, 1960. London: Oxford University Press, 1965.   DHU/MO

3715. Pedersen, Odd Kvaal. Afrika i Dag-Og i Morgen? Oslo: Egede Instituhet, 1969.   DLC
    Church and race problems in South Africa.

3716. Perret, Edmond. "Prospects for South Africa." The Presbyterian Outlook (156:7, Feb. 18, 1974), p. 5. Pam. File, DHU/R

3717. Pistorius, Philippus Villiers. No Further Trek. Johannesburg: Central News Agency, 1957.   DLC

3718. Pitts, S. G. "Churches Protest South Africa Law." Christian Century (74; Je. 5, 1957), pp. 714-16.   DHU

3719. "Political Strangulation for South African Churches?" Christian Century (71:45, Nov. 10, 1954), pp. 1355+.   DHU

3720. Pretorius, H. L. "The Future of Missions in the Transkei." Missionalia (2:1, Apr. 1, 1974), pp. 17-29. DHU/R

3721. Proudfoot, M. "Christian Liberalism in South Africa: Defeat at Hand?" Christian Century (90; Sept. 12, 1973), pp. 869-98.   DHU/R

3722. "Racial Good Will Wins a Round in South Africa." Christian Century (83; Nov. 16, 1966), p. 1401.   DHU

3723. Ramaila, Henry S. Christian Education Endeavor in a Culturally Changing South Africa. Master's thesis. Columbia University and Union Theological Seminary, 1955.

3724. Randall, Max Ward. New Proposals for Zambia Missions. Masters thesis. Fuller Theological Seminary, 1969.

3725. ----- Profile for Victory; New Proposals for Missions in Zambia. South Pasadena, Calif.: Wm. Carey Library, 1970.
    Author proposes a new type of missions which would accept indigenous type of worship.

3726. Randall, Peter, (ed.). Apartheid and the Church. Report of the Church Commission of the Study Project on Christianity in Apartheid Society. Johannesburg: Spro-Cas, 1972.   DLC

3727. Rea, Fred B. "The Future of Mission Education in Southern Rhodesia." International Review of Missions (49; 1960), pp. 195-200.   DHU/R

3728. Reaves, A. "South Africa: the Sin of Racism." Christian Century (78; Dec. 13, 1961), pp. 1490-3.   DHU

3729. Reeves, Richard Ambrose, (bp.). Shooting at Sharpville; the Agony of South Africa. Boston: Houghton Mifflin Company, 1961.   DHU/R
    Author is Bishop of Johannesburg.
    With a foreword by Chief Albert Luthuli.

3730. ----- (bp.). South Africa, Yesterday and Tomorrow: A Challenge to Christians. London: Gollancz, 1962. DHU/R; NcD

3731. ----- (bp.). "South African Church vs. Racism." Christian Century (74; Ag. 7, 1957), pp. 936-99.   DHU

3732. "The Relation of Mission Boards to the Angolan People." International Review of Missions (62:46, Apr., 1973), pp. 202-05.
          DHU/R
    Summary of the Report of the American Task Force.

3733. "Response of Rhodesian Bishops." IDOC International (46; Apr. 29, 1972), pp. 67-74.   DHU/R

3734. "The Responsibility of United States Catholics and Racism in Southern Africa." IDOC International North American Edition (My. 29, 1971), pp. 6-15.   DHU/R

3735. "Rhodesian Bishops Still Object to Land Tenure Act." African Ecclesiastical Review (15:3, 1973), pp. 283-84.
          DHU/R

3736. "Rhodesia: By and For Europenas?" IDOC International (43; Mr. 11, 1972), pp. 25-6.   DHU/R
    This article is a statement by the English and Welsh Catholic Commission for International Justice and Peace on the settlement reached between the British and Rhodesian Governments concerning majority rule in Rhodesia.

3737. "Rhodesia." World Parish (11:7, Apr., 1972), pp. 4-5.
          DHU/R
    World Methodist Council.

3738. "Rhodesian Settlement Proposals: Zimbabweans Say 'No.'" IDOC International (46; Apr. 29, 1972), pp. 2-9. DHU/R

3739. Rogers, Cornish. "Portuguese Ploy in Angola and WCC Response." The Christian Century (89:12, Mr. 22, 1972), pp. 329-30.   DHU/R

3740. Rogers, Cyril A. and C. Frantz. Racial Themes in Southern Rhodesia: The Attitudes and Behavior of the White Population. New Haven: Yale University, 1962.   DHU/R
        Includes information on religion.

3741. Ross, Emory. ... Colour and Christian Community. Delivered Under the Auspices and in the 25th Anniversary Year of the South African Institute of Race Relations, by Emory Ross, at Johannesburg on 4 August 1854, and at Cape Town on 6 August 1954. Johannesburg, S. A.: Institute of Race Relations, 1954.   NN/Sch; TN/DCHS

3742. Sachs, Bernard. The Road from Sharpeville. London: D. Dobson, 1961.   DHU/R; NN/Sch; DLC

3743. Schmale, Karl-Heniz. "Lutheran Churches in Southern Africa. A Report." Lutheran World (21:3, 1974), pp. 285-95.
                                                 Pam. File, DHU/R

3744. Schneider, T. "The Divine Names in the Tsonga Bible." The Bible Translator (21:2, Apr., 1970), pp. 89-99. DHU/R

3745. Schulte, G. "Die Politische Funktion Religiöser Bewegungen Im Sudlichen Afrika." Zeitschrift für Evangelische Ethik (17; Ja., 1973), pp. 17-25.   DAU/W; DGW

3746. Setiloane, Gabriel M. "The Adventures of a Black Minister in a Multiracial Church." South African Outlook (103; Nov., 1973), pp. 186-89.

3747. ----- "Youth Work in African Churches in South Africa." Ecumenical Review (15:2, Ja., 1962), pp. 144-48.
                                                          DHU/R

3748. Sheerin, John B. "South African Bishops Defy the Government Catholic World (185; Sept., 1957), pp. 401-02.   DHU/R

3749. Shepherd, Robert Henry Wishat. "Apartheid in South Africa's Churches." Christian Century (76:4 Ja. 28, 1959), pp. 103-05.
                                                          DHU

3750. Sithole, Ndabaningi. "The Five Principles: Rhetorics vs. Reality." IDOC International (46; Apr. 29, 1972), pp. 49-58.
                                                          DHU/R
        Memo sent to Sir Alec Douglas-Hume by Rev. Sithole on the Rhodesian settlement.

3751. Snyder, Ross. "A 'Confessing Church' for South Africa." Christian Century (90:16, Apr. 18, 1973), pp. 446-7. DHU/R
        Schlebusch Commission, an organized body of Christians is investigating the activities of four antiapartheid organizations. The Christian Institute was organized to confront the organization.

3752. "South Africa: Geography and Natural Divisions." The American Quarterly Register (5:1, Ag., 1832), pp. 46-55.   DHU/R

3753. "South Africa." News and Views. Africa Theolgocial Journal (2; Feb., 1969), pp. 102-03.   DHU/R
        Lutherans in South Africa.

3754. South Africa. "Two Views on Black Theology." IDOC-International (Ja. 29, 1972), pp. 45-50.   DHU/R
        "Two letters written by members of the Christian Institute, a group of concerned white church leaders and affiliated black groups in South Africa."

3755. "South African Churches Race Against Time." Christian Century (74:27, Jl. 31, 1957), pp. 910-11. DHU

3756. "South African Lutherans Urged to Fight Apartheid." Ecumenical Press Service (23; Aug. 16, 1973), pp. 6-7. DHU/R

3757. "South African Racists Fear the Light." Christian Century (79; My. 30, 1962), p. 682.   DHU

3758. "Southern Africa: Four Churches to Merge by '75." Lutheran World (21:3, 1974), pp. 280-81.   Pam. File, DHU/R
        Four black churches in South Africa agreed to unite their Churches by December, 1975.

3759. "Spreading the Gospel." South African Panorama (18; Mr., 1973), pp. 44-47.

3760. Squire, J. "South Africa Wracked by Conflict Between State, Liberal Clergy." Christian Century (88; Mr. 31, 1971), pp. 406-07.   DHU/R

3761. Sundkler, Bengt G. M. "Black Man's Church." Libertas (Johannesburg) (5:10, 2, Sept., 1945), pp. 28-9. DLC; CtY

3762. Taylor, John Vernon and Dorothea A. Lehmann. Christians of the Copperbelt. The Growth of the Church in Northern Rhodesia. London: SCM Press, 1961.   MNtcA; DHU/MO

3763. Thebehall, David. "Has Christianity Any Relevance and Any Future?" World Student Christian Federation (2:2, 1972), pp. 40-45.   DHU/R

3764. Thomas, David. "Self-Help for Zululand." Ecumenical Press Service: This Month (9; Apr., 1974), pp. 3-4.   DHU/R
        Self help programs set up by World Council of Churches through the Zululand Churches' Health and Welfare Association, known as "Helwel."

3765. Tiryakian, Edward A. "Apartheid and Education in the Union of South Africa." Harvard Educational Review (25; 1955), pp. 242-59.   DHU; DLC

3766. ----- "Apartheid and Religion." Theology Today (14:3, 1957), pp. 385-400.   DHU/R

3767. Ungar, Andre. "Jews and Apartheid; Can Neutrality Be Justified?" Jewish Digest (9; Ja., 1964), pp. 37-40. DLC

3768. "U. S. Church Leaders." IDOC International (46; Apr. 28, 1972), pp. 75-79.   DHU/R
        Statement by major Protestant denominations in U. S. on the settlement conflict in Rhodesia.

3769. United Church of Christ. Board for World Ministries. "Resolution on Southern Africa." Social Action (38:7, Mr., 1972), p. 25.   DHU/R

3770. United Church of Christ. Eighth General Synod. "Goals on Racial Justice, Church Action Against Racism and Resolutions on Southern Africa." Social Action (38:1, Sept., 1971), pp. 15-21.   DHU/R
        "Actions of the Eighth General Synod United Church of Christ, June 25-29, 1971."

3771. "United States Churches Challenge 22 Firms Doing Business in Southern Africa." Ecumenical Press Service (no. 2; Ja. 17, 1974), p. 6.   DHU/R

3772. Verkuyl, Johannes. "The Dutch Reformed Church in South Africa and the Ideology and Practice of Apartheid." Reformed World (31:7, Sept., 1971), pp. 291-301.   DHU/R

3773. ----- L'Eglise Reformee Hollandaise en Afrique du Sud et l'Ideologie et la Pratique de l'Apartheid." Parole et Societe (Strasbourg) (80:4, 1972), pp. 353-65.   DLC

3774. Verryn, Trevor D. "Anglican and Roman Catholic Priests in South Africa: Some Questionnaire Responses." Social Compass (19:1, 1972), pp. 93-99.   DHU/R

3775. ----- The Vanishing Clergyman. A Sociological Study of the Priestly Role in South Africa. Braamfonteyn: The South African Council of Churches, 1971.   DLC

3776. Vika, G. T. "The Bantu Presbyterian Church in 1973." _South African Outlook_ (103; Nov., 1973), pp. 181+.

3777. _Violence in Southern Africa: A Christian Assessment._ London: S.C.M. Press, 1970.   MBU-T

3778. "Voice of the Shepherds; Protesting of Apartheid Measures in South Africa." _America_ (101; My., 30, 1959), p. 384. DHU

3779. Wadlow, René. "An African Church and Social Change." _Practical Anthropology_ (16:6, Nov.-Dec., 1969), pp. 257+.
                                                          DHU/R

3780. "Warning for South Africa; Study Project on Christianity in Apartheid Society's Report." _America_ (128; Je. 23, 1973), p. 568.   DHU/R

3781. Watts, Hilstan L. "Some Structural Problems of Urban Religion. A Case Study From the City of Durban." _Social Compass_ (19:1, 1972), pp. 63-81.   DHU/R
        "The city of Durban is the major port for the Republic of South Africa."

3782. "WCC Decisions: Southern African Churches Respond." _Presence_ (5:2, 1971), pp. 34-5.   DHU/R

3783. "WCC on Rhodesia." _IDOC International_ (46; Apr. 29, 1972), pp. 78-9.   DHU/R

3784. "WCC Race Commission Says Break Investment Links With S. Africa." _Ecumenical Press Service_ (39:13, My. 11, 1972), pp. 2-3.   DHU/R

3785. "WCC Tugs at the Vines of Investments in Southern Africa." _The Christian Century_ (89:35, Oct. 4, 1972), p. 987. DHU/R

3786. Weber, Hans-Ruedi. "South African Travel Diary." _Ecumenical Review_ (25:3, Jl., 1973), pp. 337-41.   DHU/R
        "South African Council of Churches black majority attempt to bring about changes in black and white relationships."

3787. Weil, Ulrich. "Christian Care in Rhodesia." _Race_ (12:4, Apr., 1971), pp. 127-29.   DHU/MO

3788. West, Martin. "Therapie et Changement Social dans les Eglises Urbaines D'Afrique du Sud." _Social Compass_ (19:1, 1972), pp. 49-62.   DHU/R

3789. "The White Fathers Leave Mozambique." _African Ecclesiastical Review_ (13:4, 1971), pp. 356-68.   DHU/R

3790. "White Man's God: Apartheid and the Churches." _Time_ (70; Jl. 29, 1957), p. 21.   DHU

3791. _White Power: The Cunene River Scheme._ Committee for Freedom in Mozambique, Angola and Guine. London: Committee for Freedom, n.d.

3792. Whyte, Quintin. _Behind the Racial Tensions in South Africa._ Johannesburg: South African Institute of Race Relations, 1953.
                                                          NN/Sch

3793. Williamson, Lamar. "Reflections on a Year in Zaire." _Presbyterian Outlook_ (157:3, Ja., 1974), p. 5. DHU/R
        Written by a theological professor spending a year as teacher, National University of Zaire under the Board of World Missions of the Presbyterian Church, U.S.

3794. "Witness Against Odds in South Africa." _Christian Century_ (79:27, Jl. 4, 1962), p. 832.   DHU/R

3795. Wood, C. T. "The Parochial System in South Africa." _The East and West Review_ (3;1937), pp. 163-70. DHU/R

3796. "World Board Continues to Train Black Leadership for South Africa." _A. D. United Church Herald Edition._ (2:10, Oct., 1973), pp. 34-35.   DHU/R

3797. World Council of Churches. _Christianity, Race and South African People. Report to the Central Committee on a Visit to the South African Churches, April and May, 1952 by W. A._ Visser't Hooft. New York: 1952.   MNtcA
        Interracial publication no. 78.

3798. World Council of Churches. Committee to Combat Racism. _A Profile of Frelimo (Frente de Libertacao de Mozambique)._
                                         Pam. File, DHU/R
        Mim.
        Profile of a liberation movement which was given $15,000 by the WCC to combat racism in Mozambique. Other liberation movements given financial assistance are listed.

3799. World Council of Churches. Committee to Combat Racism. International Advisory Committee. _Recommendations for Money Allocations to Liberation Movement in South Africa._ Geneva: World Council of Churches, 1970-72. Pam. File, DHU/R
        Mim.

3800. World Council of Churches. Executive Committee. "Resolution on Rhodesia." _Ecumenical Review_ (24:2, Apr. 1972), p. 214.   DHU/R
        Passed February 8-12 in Auckland, New Zealand, by Committee.

3801. World Council of Churches. _Mission in South Africa, April-December, 1960._ Geneva: n.p., 1961.   MiBsA
        Report prepared by the World Council of Churches delegation to the consultation.

3802. World Council of Churches. Programme to Combat Racism. _Time to Withdraw Investments in Southern Africa._ Pam. File, DHU/R
        Mim.
        Resolutions adopted by the 120 member Center Committee of the World Council of Churches.

3803. World Council of Churches. _Report on the World Council of Churches Mission in South Africa, April-December, 1960._ Prepared by the WCC Delegation to the Consultation in December, 1960: Franklin Clark Fry, Chairman. Geneva: 1961. MNtcA
        "Half title: Mission in South Africa."

3804. Woronoff, Jon. "The Activist Church." _Africa Report_ (17:2, Feb., 1972), pp. 20-22.   DHU/MO
        Resistance of Christian Churches to apartheid.

3805. Young, Ernle W. D. "A Theological Reflection on Church/State Relations in South Africa Today." _Journal of Theology for Southern Africa_ (1; Dec., 1972), pp. 37-44.   DHU/R

3806. Zulu, A. H. "Message from Africa." _Christian Century_ (79:3 Ja. 10, 1962), pp. 60-61.   DHU/R

d. Western Africa

3807. "Accra, Ghana--A. M. E. Zion Church." _The A. M. E. Zion Quarterly Review_ (83:3, Fall, 1971), pp. 152-78.   DHU/R

3808. Adesina, Segun, "Christian Missions Versus State Governments in Nigeria: The Battle for the Nations Schools." _Religious Education_ (68:4, Jl.-Aug., 1973), pp. 483-496.   DHU/R

3809. "Africa." _World Parish_ (12:7, Apr., 1973), pp. 4, 6.
                                                          DHU/R
        "United Methodist in Sierra Leone and Liberia, Africa."

3810. "Africa in Change: West Africa (Nigeria)." Boston University, 1962.
        Film.
        Pictures the cultural, religious and economic differences of the various regions.

3811. "Africa: Mali." Avid Corp., 1972. 48 fr. color. 35 mm. & phonodisc: 2s., 12 in., 33 1/3 rpm., 15 min.   DLC
        Filmstrip.
        "Describes the agriculture, trade, religion, transportation, and government of Mali."

3812. Agbebi, Mojola. The Christian Handbook, New Calabar,
West Africa. n. p., n. d.   NN/Sch

3813. Akande, S. T. Ola. "The People Called Baptists." Nigerian
Baptist (47:5, My., 1969), pp. 19-20.   Pam. File, DHU/R

3814. Akiwowo, Akinsola. "Christian Denominations in Nigeria
Today." The Nigerian Christian (3:5, My., 1969), pp. 2-3.
                                         Pam. File, DHU/R

3815. Anozie, Ifeanyichukwu. "Theology and the Contemporary
Nigerian Society." West African Religion (11:Ja., 1972), pp.
19-27.   DHU/R

3816. Awa, E. O. "The Religious Situation in Nigeria Today."
West African Religion (Nos. 13 & 14, Sept. & Dec., 1972), pp.
4-8.   DHU/R

3817. Ayivi, Emmanuel. "Joint Apostolic Action in Dahomey."
International Review of Mission (61:242, Apr., 1972), pp.
144-149.   Pam. File, DHU/R

3818. Belshaw, Harry. Facing the Future in West Africa. London:
Cargate Press, 1951.   NN/Sch

3819. Boetzkes, William. "West Cameroon: a Success Story."
World Mission (15:3, 1964), pp. 83-87.   DCU

3820. Booth, Alan. "The Churches in the Nigerian War." Round
Table (Apr., 1970), pp. 121-27.   DLC

3821. "Building A House of Prayer." Conservative Baptist Foreign
Mission Society, 1953. Made by Colburn Laboratory. 68 fr.,
color, 35 min. and disc: 25, 10 in., 33 1/3 rpm. 17 min.
    Filmstrip.
    "A story about the new converts of West Africa who, released
    from the curse of fetish worship, band together to build a mud
    and thatch hut where they can gather to worship God."

3822. "Children of the World: Dahomey." Bloomington, Ind.:
Indiana Univ., National Education Television, 1971. 29 min.
Color.
    Film.
    Religion of Dahomey.

3823. Christian Council of Nigeria. Christian Responsibility in an
Independent Nigeria. Ibadan: Abiodun Printing Works, 1960.
MoSCS; MBU-T

3824. Cox, Emmett Dean. The Church of the United Brethren
in Christ in Sierra Leone; Its Program and Development.
Masters thesis. Fuller Theological Seminary School of World
Mission, 1969.

3825. Currens, Gerald E. "A Policy of Baptizing Polygynists
Evaluated." Africa Theological Journal (2; Feb., 1970), pp.
71-83.   DHU/R
    "The Lutheran church in Liberia took a step unprecedented
    among Lutherans in Africa."

3826. Dean, Curtis L. Missions in French West Africa. Masters
thesis. Columbia Bible College, 1957.

3827. Dekar, Paul. "Alfred Saker and the Baptists in Cameroon."
Foundations: a Baptist Journal of History and Theology (14:4
Oct.-Dec. 1971), pp. 325-43.   DHU/R

3828. Derrick, Jonathan. "Church and People in Cameroon."
America (127:12, Oct., 1972), pp. 314-16.   DHU/R

3829. Diara, Agadem L. Islam and Pan-Africanism. Detroit:
Agascha Productions, 1973.   DHU/R
    "In memory of Amilcar Cabral, 1925-1973, revolutionary
    leader of the African Party for the Independence of Guinea-
    Bissau and the Cape Verde Islands. (PAIGC)."

3830. Donegan, Charles Edward. "Marriage and Divorce Law in
Sierra Leone: a Microcosm of African Legal Problems."

Cornell International Law Journal (5:1, 1972), pp. 43-74.
                                          Pam. File, DHU/R
    Negro author.

3831. "Duminea." Ibadan, Nigeria: Medical Illustration Unit, University of Ibadan.
    Film.
    Community festivals to the water spirits in Eastern Niger
    Delta.

3832. Ekechi, Felix Kamalu. "The Holy Ghost Fathers in Eastern
Nigeria, 1885-1920: Observations on Missionary Strategy."
African Studies Review (15:2, Sept., 1972), pp. 17+. DHU/MO

3833. Elango, Lovett Z. "Dilemmas of the Church in Cameroun."
The Black Church (1:2, 1972), pp. 73-82.   DHU/R

3834. Epelle, Emmanuel M. Tobiah. The Church in the Niger Delta.
n. p.: Niger Delta Diocese, 1955.   NE; ICU; CtY-D; MH

3835. ----- "The Collection of Church Historical Materials in South-
Eastern Nigeria." Bulletin of the Society for African Church
History (2:3, 1967), pp. 276-80.   DHU/R

3836. ----- Writing a Local Church History; a Short Guide. Nsukka,
Eastern Nigeria: n. p., 1965.   MH; NUC

3837. Erivwo, S. U. "Christian Churches in Urhoboland." Orita:
Ibadan Journal of Religious Studies (7:1, Je., 1973), pp. 32-45.
                                                 DHU/R

3838. ----- "The Concept of God Among the Urhobo of the Niger
Delta." The Ghana Bulletin of Theology (4:6, Je., 1974), pp.
48-58.   DHU/R

3839. "The Evangelization of West Africa To-day." International
Review of Missions (54; 1965), pp. 484-94.   DHU/R
    A statement issued by the Consultation on the Evangelization
    of West Africa To-day held at Yaounde, Cameroun, June
    23-30, 1965.

3840. Fyfe, Christopher (Hamilton). "The Baptist Churches in
Sierra Leone." Sierra Leone Bulletin of Religion (5:2, 1963),
pp. 55-60.

3841. Goody, Jack. "Reform and Resistance: a Mahdi in Northern
Ghana." Christopher Allen and R. W. Johnson, (eds.). African Perspectives (Cambridge: Cambridge University Press,
1970), pp. 143-56.   DHU/MO
    "Colonial misfortune and religious response."

3842. Grimley, John B. and Gordon E. Robinson. Church Growth
in Central and Southern Nigeria. Grand Rapids, Michigan:
Wm. B. Eerdmans Pub. Co., 1966. DHU/R; MNtcA

3843. Gusimana, Bartholome. "L'Homme et l'Unite de la Race
Humaine." Revue du Clerge Africain (26:2, Mr., 1971), pp.
169-80.   DHU/R

3844. Hair, Paul Edward Hedley. "Freetown Christianity and
Africa." Sierra Leone Bulletin of Religion (6:2, 1964), pp.
13-21.   OLC

3845-46. Houston, W. J. "Readings in Colossians, Related to the
Religious Situation in Nigeria." West African Religion (Nos.
13 & 14, Sept. & Dec., 1972), pp. 9-28.   DHU/R

3847. Ilogu, Edmund. "Nationalism and the Church in Nigeria."
International Review of Missions (51; 1962), pp. 439-50.
                                                 DHU/R

3848. ----- The Problems for Christian Ethics in Nigeria - An
Organic Society Undergoing A Change Under the Influence of
Technical Civilization. Masters thesis. Union Theological
Seminary, (New York), 1958.

3849. ----- "The Religious Situation in Nigeria Today." West
African Religion (12; Jl., 1972), pp. 26-39.   DHU/R

3850. ----- "Theological Education for the Ministry in the Age of Technology." West African Religion.(11; Ja., 1972), pp. 28-38.   DHU/R

3851. Jahoda, Gustav. "Social-Psychological Reflections on Religious Changes in Ghana." Religion; a Journal of Religion and Religions (1:1, Spr., 1971), pp. 24-31.   DCU; DLC

3852. Kretzmann, Justus P. "The Synodical Conference Begins work in Nigeria." Concordia Historical Institute Quarterly (45:3, Ag., 1972), pp. 181-91.   MSL/CHI

3853. Lair, Lena Valinda. Implications of Governmental, Educational, and Social Changes in Developing a Baptist College in Nigeria. Doctoral dissertation. Southern Baptist Theological Seminary, 1960.

3854. Lasbrey, Bertram. "Problems of a Church in Tropical Africa: The Niger Diocese." East and West Review (4:4, Oct., 1938), pp. 312-19.   DHU/R

3855. Little, Kenneth Lindsay. West African Urbanization: A Study of Voluntary Associations in Social Change. London: Cambridge University Press, 1965.   DLC
    Included is a discussion of Christian voluntary associations.

3856. Lynch, Hollis R. "The Native Pastorate Controversy and Cultural Ethnocentrism in Sierra Leone." Journal of African History (5:3, 1964), pp. 395-413.   DAU; DGW; DGU

3857. Marioghae, Michael Ajobona and John Ferguson. Nigeria Under the Cross. London: Highway Press, 1965. MNtcA

3858. Marwieh, Augustus B. Bible Study and Training Program in a New Field Such as Liberia. Master's thesis. Golden Gate Baptist Theological Seminary, 1960.

3859. McGarey, Margaret. "The Resolve Not to be Useless." The Message Magazine (38:5, Ag., 1972), pp. 7-10. DHU/R; MiBsA
    About Dr. Samuel DeShay and his missionary service in Sierra Leone and Nigeria. Seventh-day Adventist.

3860. Meinerts, Oryn G. West African Culture Change and the Christian Approach. Masters degree. North American Baptist Seminary, 1970.

3861. Nicolas, Jacqueline. "Culpabilité, Somatisation et Catharsis au Sein d'un Culte de Possessionik Bori Hausa." Psychopathologie Africaine (6:2, 1970), pp. 147-80.   DLC

3862. North American Baptist General Conference. Cameroon Baptist Mission. Annual Report. Pam. File, DHU/R
    Reports for 1968-1971.

3863. North American Baptist General Conference. Mambilla Baptist Mission. Annual Report. Pam. File, DHU/R
    Report for 1971.

3864. Ong, Walter J. "Mass in Ewondo." America (131:8, Sept. 28, 1974), pp. 148-51.   DHU/R
    Mass in Cameroun is "authentic employing quite naturally the profoundest music, dance and ceremonial customs of God's people."

3365. Parratt, J. K. "Religious Change in Yoruba Society-A Test Case." Journal of Religion in Africa (2:2, 1969), pp. 113-28.   DHU/R

3366. Pilkington, Frederick. "The Church in Nigeria." African Affairs (56), pp. 158-60.   DHU

3867. Porter, A. T. "Religious Affiliation in Freetown, Sierra Leone." Africa (23:1, Ja., 1953), pp. 3-14.   DHU/MO

3368. Rasilly, Gilles de. "Les Catéchistes de Haute-Volta." Lumen Vitae (26:3, 1971), pp. 411-26.   DCU/TH

3869. Reeck, Darrell L. "Transformations of Missionary Christianity in Rural Sierra Leone." Genève-Afrique Acta Africana (11:2, 1972), pp. 45-61.   DGW

3870. ----- and John H. Ness, Jr. "Research Notes: Sierra Leone Holdings in United Methodist Archives." Methodist History (10:3, Apr., 1972), pp. 48-53.   DHU/R

3871. "Report from West African Church Conference on Science, Technology and the Future of Man and Society, Accra, March 24-30, 1972." The Ecumenical Review (24:3, Jl., 1972), pp. 341-47.   DHU/R

3872. "Report of the Presiding Elder of the Accra District of the East Ghana Conference of the A. M. E. Zion Church." A. M. E. Zion Quarterly Review (83:3, Fall 1971), pp. 157-65. DHU/R
    Report issued by Rev. Dr. Samuel K. Asante, Presiding Elder, Accra District.

3873. Robinson, Oren Charles, Jr. The Indigenous Development of the Baptist Churches of Nigeria. Master's thesis. Southern Baptist Theological Seminary, 1951.

3874. Ross, Philip J. It is Marvellous in our Eyes: an Account of the Celebrations in Connection With the Centenary of the Niger Mission of the Church Missionary Society, 1957. Freetown: Church Missionary Society, 1959.   NNMR

3875. Salamone, Frank A. "Structural Factors in Dukawa Conversions." Practical Anthropology (19:5, Sept.-Oct., 1972), pp. 219-25.   DHU/R
    Catholic missions in Nigeria.

3876. Sawyeer, Harry A. E. "Christian Evangelistic Strategy in West Africa: Reflections on the Centenary of the Consecration of Bishop Samuel Adjayi Crowther on St. Peter's Day, 1864." International Review of Missions (54:215, Jl., 1965), pp. 343-52.   DHU/R

3877. Schuyler, Joseph B. "Church, State and Society in Nigeria." Insight and Opinion (5 :3, 1972), pp. 57-74.   DHU/MO

3878. "Scripture Selections in West Africa." World Parish (11:7, Apr., 1972), p. 5.   DHU/R
    World Methodist Council.

3879. "Sierra Leone." World Parish (11:7, Apr., 1972), p. 4.   DHU/R
    World Methodist Council.

3880. Simpson, George E. "Religious Changes in Southwestern Nigeria." Anthropological Quarterly (43; 1970), pp. 79-92. CLU; CtY; DGU; ICU; NN; NNC; NjP; OrU

3881. Soras, Alfred de. Relations de l'Eglise et de l'Etat dans les Pays d'Afrique Francophone; vues Prospectives. /Paris/: Mame /1963/.   DLC
    Study of the relations between Catholic Church and State in French-speaking Africa.

3882. Stern, Irven. Land Tenure and Christianity in Northern Nigeria. Masters thesis. Northwestern University and Garrett Biblical Institute, 1959.

3883. Stevens, R. S. O. The Church in Urban Nigeria. Birmingham, Eng.: The Press of Frank Juckes, 1963? TxFTC

3884. Tasie, Godwin Onyemeachi Mgbechi. "Research Note: Instrumenta Studiorum at the Scottish Institute of Missionary Studies Relating to Ibo Studies." West African Religion (No. 15, Mr., 1974), pp. 32-35.   DHU/R

3885. Thomas, J. C. "Society and Liturgical Reform." The Ghana Bulletin of Theology (4:6, Ja., 1974), pp. 1-18.   DHU/R
    Examines the idea of liturgical reform in relation to the Christian churches in Ghana.

3886. "To Mankind with Love." Catholic Relief Services. Film.

("To Mankind With Love", cont.)

    Distribution of food and technical assistance activities in Senegal and Morocco.

3887. Toupet, Charles. "Orientation Bibliographique sur la Mouritanie." Bulletin de l'Institut Francais d'Afrique Noire (21:1-2, Ja.-Apr., 1959), pp. 201-39. DAU; DLC; DHU/MO

3888. "Tragedy in Timbuktu. Africa's Creeping Calamity." Christianity Today (17:24, Sept. 14, 1973), pp. 42-46. DHU/R
    Assistance American Church Mission societies are giving to victims of the famine in Africa.

3889. Truly, Mary Elizabeth. Baptist Educational Program for Girls in Nigeria. Doctoral dissertation. Southwestern Baptist Theological Seminary, 1960.

3890. Turner, Harold W. "Pentecostal Movements in Nigeria." Orita (6:1, Je., 1972), pp. 39-47. DHU/R

3891. Tyms, James Daniel. "Role of the Church in the Emergence of Modern Ghana." Journal of Human Relations (8:3-4, Spr.-Sum., 1960), pp. 793-809. DAU; DCU/SW
    Negro author.

3892. Varney, Peter D. "Religion in a West African University." Journal of Religion in Africa, (2:1, 1969), pp. 1-42. DHU/R

3893. Verner, Gene. "Ghana: Emerging Baptist Leadership." The Commission (35; Feb., 1972), p. 19+. DLC

3894. Willis, Jeannie. "Liberia: From Outpost to Church." The Episcopalian (137:8, Ag., 1972), pp. 16-23. DHU/R
    An Episcopal Church mission becomes independent after 150 years of struggle.

3895. Wold, Joseph C. God's Impatience in Liberia. Grand Rapids Mich.: Eerdmans, 1968. DHU/MO; MNtcA; DHU/R
    Religious institutions in Liberia.

3896. World Council of Churches. Committee to Combat Racism. Profile of Paige Partido Africano de Independencia da Guinee e Cabo Verde. Pam. File, DHU/R
    Mim.
    Liberation movement in Africa given $20,000 from WCC for developing economic, educational, social welfare and health programs.

3897. Yates, Walter L. The History of the African Methodist Episcopal Zion Church in West Africa, Liberia, Gold Coast and Nigeria, 1900-1939. Doctoral dissertation. Hartford Seminary Foundation, 1955.

3898. Yerokun, J. O. "A Pentecostalist Speaks on Pentecost." The Nigerian Christian (2:6, Je., 1968), p. 11. Pam. File, DHU/R

3899. Ziegler, Samuel G. Proclaiming the Gospel in Africa; Sierra Leone, Nigeria. Dayton, Ohio: Dept. of World Missions, E.U.B. Church, 1952. DOUM/EUB
    Evangelical United Brethren Church and missions in Africa.

e. General

3900. Abouadaou, Said. I Was an Algerian Preacher. New York: Vantage Press, 1971. DLC
    Convert from Islam.

3901. "Acts of Holy See." African Ecclesiastical Review (15:3, 1973), p. 282. DHU/R

3902. Addo, Peter E. A. "How a Black African Views His American Black Brothers." The Christian Century (89:31, Sept. 6, 1972), pp. 871-72. DHU/R

3903. Adegbola, A. "A Christian Interpretation of the African Revolution." All African Conference of Churches Bulletin (2:3, Je., 1965), pp. 11-122. DLC; CLU; CtY-D; IEN; NjPT; MBU

3904. "Africa." International Review of Missions (57:225, Ja., 1968), pp. 33-54. DHU/R

3905. Africa Today: A Selection of Articles which First Appeared in Sudan Witness. London: Sudan Interior Mission, 1968. NNCor

3906. "Africa: Unprecedented Response." Christianity Today (16; Feb. 18, 1972), p. 60. DHU/R
    "Missions - Africa"

3907. "L'Afrique Chretienne." Tam-Tam (17:4-5, 1969), pp. 31-48. DLC

3908. Agbeti, J. K. "African Theology: What it is." Presence (5:3, 1972), pp. 5-8. DHU/R

3909. ----- "New Perspectives in Theological Education With Special Reference to Ghana." The Ghana Bulletin of Theology (4:6, Je., 1974), pp. 19-36. DHU/R

3910. All Africa Church Conference. Africa in Transition; the Challenge and the Christian Response. Geneva: Published by All African Church Conference in Collaboration with the Dept. on Church and Society, Division of Studies, World Council of Churches, 1962. MiBsA

3911. All-Africa Church Conference, Ibadan, Nigeria, 1958. "The Church in Changing Africa; Report of the All-Africa Church Conference, Held at Ibadan, Nigeria, January 10-19, 1958." New York: International Missionary Council, 1958. NN/Sch

3912. All African Church Conference, Kampala, Uganda, 1963. Drumbeats from Kampala; Report of the First Assembly of the ... held at Kampala, Apr. 20-30, 1963. London: United Society for Christian Literature, Lutterworth Press, 1963. DLC; ICU; CtY; MBU

3913. "All-Africa Conference Designs Far-Reaching Program for '72-'73." The Presbyterian Outlook (154:35, Oct. 2, 1972), p. 10. DHU/R
    News note on the All-Africa Conference of Churches (AACC) program for 1972-73.

3914. "All Africa Conference of Churches and the Lusaka Assembly." African Ecclesiastical Review (16:3, 1974), pp. 329-38. DHU/R
    Report of the conference held May 12th to 21st, 1974.

3915. All Africa Conference of Churches. Drumbeats from Kampala; Report of the First Assembly of the All Africa Conference of Churches, held at Kampala, April 20 to April 30, 1963. London: Lutterworth Press, 1963.

3916. All African Conference of Churches. "Kinshasa Declaration." International Review of Mission (61:242, Apr., 1972), pp. 115-116. Pam. File, DHU/R

3917. "The All-Africa Conference of Churches and the WWC." Presence (5:2, 1971), p. 35. DHU/R

3918. Anderson, Gerald H. "A Moratorium on Missionaries?" Christian Century (91:2, Ja., 1974), pp. 435. DHU/R
    An African church leader request the World and U.S. Nat. Councils of Churches that there be a moratorium on sending missionaries to Asia, Africa and Latin America.

3919. Andriamanjato, R. R. "Women in the Church and in Society." International Review of Mission (61:242, Apr., 1972), pp. 166-76. Pam. File, DHU/R
    Discussion of women in the Church with special references to Africa.

3920. Armstrong, Roger D. Peace Corps and Christian Mission. New York: Friendship Press, 1965. DLC

3921. Asamoa, E. A. "The Christian Church and African Heritage." International Review of Missions (44; 1955), pp. 292-301. DHU/R

3922. Ayaga, Odeyo. "The Implications of Pope Paul VI's African Pilgrimage in 1969." Pan-African Journal (4:1, Wint., 1971), pp. 55-74.   DHU/MO
Critical essay on historical relations between Christian Church and African race.

3923. Baal, J. van. Symbols for Communication: an Introduction to the Anthropological Study of Religion Studies of Developing Countries. New York: Humanities Press, 1971.   DHU/R

3924. Baëta, C. G. Christianity in Tropical Africa: Studies Presented and Discussed at the Seventh International African Seminar, University of Ghana, April 1965. London: Published for the International African Institute by the Oxford University Press, 1968.   NjMD; MBU; NN; ICU; MH

3925. ----- "Le Rôle de l'Eglise Chrétienne et des Chrétiens dans l'Afrique d'Aujourd 'hui." Revue du Clerge Africain (27; 4-5, Jl., 1972), pp. 503-17.   DHU/R

3926. ----- "The Younger Churches: An African Viewpoint." Religion in Life (34:1, Wint., 1964-65), pp. 15-24. DHU/R

3927. Banks, Arthur Leslie, (ed.). The Development of Tropical and Subtropical Countries with Particular Reference to Africa. London: Arnold, 1954.   DHU/MO

3928. Barrett, David B. "AD 2000: 350 Million Christians in Africa." International Review of Mission (59:233, Ja., 1970), pp. 39-54.   DHU/R

3929. -----(ed.). African Initiatives in Religion. Nairobi: East Africa Pub. House, 1971.   DHU/R

3930. ----- "Analytical Methods of Studying Religious Expansion in Africa." Journal of Religion in Africa (3:1, 1970), pp. 22-44.   DHU/R

3931. ----- "Interdisciplinary Theories of Religion and African Dependency." David B. Barrett. (ed.). African Initiatives in Religion (Nairobi: East Africa Pub. House, 1971), pp. 146-59.   DHU/R

3932. Bascom, William R. Continuity and Change in African Cultures... Chicago: Univ. of Chicago Press, 1962.   CLU

3933. Bates, Gerald E. "Mission Church Tensions in Africa as a Function of Goal Discrepancy." Practical Anthropology (18:6, Nov.-Dec., 1971), pp. 269-78.   DHU/R

3934. Beaver, Robert Pierce, (ed.). Christianity and African Education: The Papers of a Conference at the Univeristy of Chicago. Grand Rapids, Mich.: Wm. Eerdmans Pub. Co., 1966.   NN/Sch

3935. Beckmann, Klaus-Marten. "German Churches and Missions Face the Race Question." International Review of Mission (59:235, Jl., 1970), pp. 311-15.   DHU/R

3936. Beethan, Thomas A. Christianity and the New Africa. New York: Frederick A. Praeger, 1967.   DHU/R
Attempts to answer the question "Can the Christian religion continue in the face of Nationalism, Islam, and Secularism in Africa?"

3937. Bennett, George. "Christianity and African Nationalism." Mawazo (1:3, Je., 1968), pp. 63-68.   DAU; DLC

3938. Berglund, Axel-Ivar. "Crisis in Missions; a Pastoral/Liturgical Challenge (Healing on the Africa Scene)." The Lutheran Quarterly (25:1, Feb., 1973), pp. 22-23.   DHU/R

3939. Bernard Michael (Sister). "This is the School That We Built." Navy Chaplains Bulletin (1; Fiscal Year, 1974), pp. 8+ DHU/R

3940. Bernardi, Bernardo. Le Religioni in Africa. Roma: Istituto Italiano per L'Africa, 1964.   NNCor

3941. Beyerhaus, Peter and Carl F. Hallenereutz, (eds.). The Church Crossing Frontiers. Days in the Native Mission. Lund: Gleerup, 1969.   DLC;CU
Includes writings on the African church.

3942-43. Blomjous, Joseph. "The Church in a Developing World." Cross Currents (20:3, Sum., 1970), pp. 287-314.   DHU/R
Church in Africa today.

3944. Brett, E. A. African Attitudes: A Study of the Social, Racial and Political Attitudes of Some Middle-Class Africans. Johannesburg: South African Institute of Race Relations, n.d.   DHU/MO

3945. Brice, E. W. "Development of Social Welfare Institutions and Services in Africa." Journal of Human Relations (8; Spr.-Sum., 1960), pp. 668-81.   DAU; DCU/SW

3946. "British Churches Respond." IDOC International (46; Apr. 29, 1972), pp. 34-43.   DHU/R
British Churches response to "Proposals for Settlement" in Rhodesia.

3947. Brookes, Edgar Harry and Army Vanderbosch. The City of God and the City of Man in Africa. Lexington: University of Kentucky Press, 1964. MiBsA; MSohG; DHU/R; NjP; PPT

3948. Buetu, A. "Les Dimensions Oecumeniques de l'Action du Christianisme en Afrique." Revue du Clerge Africain (27; 4-5, Jl., 1972), pp. 443-552.   DHU/R

3949. Burgess, Andrew S., (ed.). Lutheran Churches in the Third World. Minneapolis: Augsburg Pub. House, 1970.   MNtca

3950. ----- Winning the Nations. Minneapolis: Augsburg Publishing House, 1955.   MSL/CHI

3951. Burkle, Horst. "Patterns of Sermons from Various Parts of Africa." David B. Barrett, (ed.). African Initiatives in Religion (Nairobi: East African Pub. House, 1971), pp. 222-31.   DHU/R

3952. Carney, Joseph P. "Liberating Portuguese Africa." Commonweal (100:4, Mr. 29, 2974), pp. 79-83. DHU/R
Catholic Church and Portuguese Africa.

3953. Carpenter, George Wayland. "The Role of Christianity and Islam in Contemporary Africa.: C. G. Haines, (ed.). Africa Today (Baltimore: Johns Hopkins Press, 1955), pp. 90-113.   DHU/MO

3954. Carpenter, Kathleen. Fire in the Jungle. London: Highway Press, 1961.   NNCor
Missions in Africa.

3955. Carstens, Kenneth N. "Christianity and Violent Revolution." Africa Today (15:3, Je.-Jl., 1968), pp. 6-7.   DHU/MO

3956. Cascudo, Luis de Camara. Made in Africa; Pesquisas e Notas. Rio de Janeiro: Editôra Civilização Brasileira, 1965.   NjP

3957. Cason, J. Walter. "An Evaluation of Theological Education in Africa Today." Reformed World (31:6, Je., 1971), pp. 252-57.   Pam. File, DHU/R
Author is responsible for the Africa Desk, Theological Fund, London.

3958. Catholic Church. Secretariatus pro Non-Christianis. Meeting the African Religions. Roma: Ancora, 1969.
MiBsA; DLC
Religion in Africa.

3959. Chandler, R. "Enterprising Africans; Black Evangelists in African Enterprise." Christianity Today (18; Nov. 9, 1973), p. 54.   DHU/R

3960. Chrisia, Dunduza Kalui. Africa: What Lies Ahead? New York: African-American Institute, 1962.   MiBsa
Religion in Africa.

3961. Christ in the Art of Africa. Commission on Ecumenical Mission and Relations, United Presbyterian Church in the U.S.A. Released by United Presbyterian Church in the U.S.A., 1964. 105 fr. color. 35mm. & phonodisc: 25., 33 1/3 rpm. Filmstrip.
"Portrays the life of Christ through reproductions of sculptures, wood carvings, and paintings by Christian artists in Africa. "

3962. "Christianity Is on the Move in Africa. " The Mennonite (87; Feb. 22, 1972), pp. 140+   IOBB

3963. "Christianity's Future. " America (124; Mr. 6, 1971), pp. 220-21.   DHU/R
"Christianity in Africa. "

3964. Clark, Leon, (ed.). Through African Eyes. New York: Frederick Praeger Pub., 1970.   DHU/MO
Interspersed with material about missionary workers.

3965. Classen, A. J. A Christian Educational Manual for African Churches. Masters thesis. Dallas Theological Seminary, 1964.

3966. Coan, Josephus R. "Redemption of Africa: The Vital Impulse of Black American Overseas Missionaries. " Journal of the Interdenominational Theological Center (1:2, Spr., 1974), pp. 27-37.   DHU/R

3967. Collins, Robert Oakley and Peter Duignan. Americans in Africa: a Preliminary Guide to American Missionary Archives and Library Manuscript Collections on Africa. Stanford, California: Hoover Institute on War, Revolution and Peace, 1963.
DHU/MO; MiBsa; NNCor; NjP

3968. "The Congregation for the Evangelization of Peoples. " African Ecclesiastical Review (15:3, 1973), pp. 282-83.   DHU/R

3969. Considine, John J. "Africa--Birth of a Great Black Church. " Catholic World (190:1, 136, Nov., 1959), pp. 93-100. DHU/R

3970. Coutinho, J. DaVeiga. "The Church and the Third World. " Cross Currents (18:4, Fall, 1968), pp. 435-49.   DHU/R

3971. Crane, William H. "Indigenization in the African Church. " International Review of Missions (53; 1964), pp. 408-22. DHU/R

3972. Dalbey, E. Gordon, Jr. "Anti-biotic Christ. " The Christian Century (87:22, Je., 1970), pp. 34-7.   DHU/R
Critic of the Western influence of Christianity upon non-Western Africa.

3973. Damboriena, Prudencio. Tongues As of Fire: Pentecostalism in Contemporary Christianity. Washington: Corpus Books, 1969.   DHU/R
Chapter 9, Mission and Ecumenism.

3974. Daniels, George M. "The Church in New Nations. " Christian Herald (95:11, Nov., 1972), p. 20.   DLC; DHU/R

3975. Daniels, George M. This is the Church in New Nations. New York: Friendship Press, 1964. IC/H; MiBsa
Missions in Africa.

3976. Dargitz, Robert Earl. A Selected Bibliography of Books and Articles in the Disciples of Christ Research Library in Mbandaka. Indianapolis: Dept. of Africa and Jamaica, Div. of World Mission, UCMS, 1967.   TN/DCHS

3977. Davis, Jeanne. "Negro Missionary Reaction to Africa. " Practical Anthropology (11:2, Mr., 1964), pp. 61-70.
DAU; DHU

3978. Davy, Yvonne. Sunrise Over Africa. Nashville: Southern Pub. Association, 1961.   MiBsa
Seventh-day Adventist, missions in Africa.

3979. Day, Philip. "Secularisation and Africa. " African Ecclesiastical Review (14:4, 1972), pp. 332-36.   DHU/R

3980. De Cock, J. "Le Concile de Trente et Mariage. " Revue du Clerge Africaine (26;3-4, My.-Jl., 1971), pp. 107-127. DHU/R
Christian marriage in Africa.

3981. Deeken, A. "New World Language? A Chance to Mediate the Christian Message. " America (126; Jan. 8 1972), pp. 11-14.
DHU/R
"Catholic church in Africa. "

3982. Dehoney, Wayne. African Diary. Nashville: Broadman Press, 1966.   MiBsA; MNtcA
Missions in Sub-Saharan Africa.

3983. De Mestral, Claude. Christian Literature in Africa. London: Distributed by the Christian Literature Council, 1959. DLC

3984. De Reeper, J. "Responsible Parenthood. " African Ecclesiastical Review (14:4, 1972), pp. 318-26.   DHU/R
Theological developments as regards 'Humanae Vitae'.

3985. Desai, Ram, (ed.). Christianity in Africa as Seen by Africans. Denver: Swallow, 1962.   NN/Sch; DHU/MO

3986. Desroche, Henri C., (ed.). Socialisme et Sociologie Religieuse. Paris: Cujas, 1965.   DLC

3987. Dickson, Kwesi A. "The Old Testament and African Theology. " The Ghana Bulletin of Theology (4:4, Je., 1973), pp. 31-41.
DHU/R

3988. Dodge, Ralph E. The Unpopular Missionary. Westwood, N. J.: F. H. Revell, 1964.   MiBsa

3989. Dougall, James W. C. "Christian Education and the African Church. " East and West Review (2; 1936), pp. 341-49. DHU/R

3990. ----- Christians in the African Revolution. Edinburgh: The Saint Andrew Press, 1963.   DHU/R

3991. Dovlo, C. K. Africa Awakes. Accra: Scottish Mission Book Depot, 1952.   DHU/MO
Some of the problems facing Africa today as seen from the Christian point of view.

3992. Dubb, A. A. The Role of the Church in an Urban African Society. Masters thesis. Rhodes University, 1962.

3993. Early, Tracy. "All Africa Church Conference Steps Up Campaign on Racism. " World Call (53:6, Je., 1971), pp. 22-23.   DHU/R

3994. Ebben, B. "Africanization ... Why?" African Ecclesiastical Review (15:2, 1973), pp. 179-81.   DHU/R

3995. "Editors and Managers Reflect on Their Task. " African Ecclesiastical Review (15:4, 1973), pp. 347-52. DHU/R
Editors and managers of Christian literature in east and central Africa hold workshop.

3996. Edwards, Herbert O. "The Third World and the Problem of God-Talk. " Harvard Theological Review (64:4, Oct., 1971), pp. 525-39.   DHU/R

3997. Edwards, Josephine C. "From Africa to America. " The Message Magazine (24:3, My.-Je., 1963), pp. 12+. DHU/R

3998. ----- Kamwendo. Nashville: Southern Publishing Association, 1966.   MiBsA

3999. ----- Sibande and Other Stories. Mountain View, Calif.: Pacific Press Publishing Association, 1967.   MiBsA

4000. Ellis, Joan. "Reprints of Books and Journals on Africa. " African Studies Bulletin (11:3, Dec., 1968), pp. 329-62.
DHU/R

4001. Ellwanger, Joseph W. Racism and the Christian World Mission. Masters thesis. Concordia Theological Seminary, 1958.

4002. Engström, Olle. "Experiences in Africa." Reformed World (32:1, Mr., 1972), pp. 23-29.   DHU/R
The author, principal of the Theological Seminary of the Mission Covenant of Sweden, visited ten countries to study the training of ministers.

4003. Engstrom, Ted W. "Challenge of Africa." World Vision (17; My., 1973), pp. 4-6.   DGW
Missions in Africa.

4004. Eppstein, John. Does God say Kill? An Investigation of the Justice of Current Fighting in Africa. London: Tom Stacey, Ltd., 1972.   DLC

4005. Evans, Stanley George. Christians and Africa... London: Society of Socialist Clergy and Ministers, 1950.   NN/Sch

4006. "Facts of a Field: Africa." World Vision (17; My., 1973), pp. 13-14.   DGW
Missions in Africa.

4007. Fanon, Frantz. The Wretched of the Earth. New York: Grove Press, 1963.   DHU/R
Author discusses the part that religious rivalries play in developing nations.

4008. Fedry, J. "Langage et Ethnographie; Une Étude de J. S. Mbiti Sur l Eschatologie en Afrique." Recherches de Science Religieuse (61; Ja.-Mr., 1973), pp. 139-51.   DCU/TH

4009. Fernandez, James W. "Contemporary African Religion -- Confluents of Inquiry." Gwendolen M. Carter and Ann Paden, eds. Expanding Horizons in African Studies (Evanston: Northwestern Univ. Press, 1969), pp. 27-46. ICU; LU; NbU; ViU; IENN; NBUU; MiU; CtY; NjP; TNJ; IaU; NcD; MH; KU

4010. Forman, Charles W. "A Study in the Self-Propagating Church: Madagascar." W. C. Harr, (ed.). Frontiers of the Christian World Mission Since 1938 (New York: Harper, 1962). NN/Sch; DHU/R

4011. Forsberg, Malcolm. Land Beyond the Nile. New York: Harper, 1958.   NN/Sch

4012. Francis, Everett W. "Africa: Same Mission, New Strategy." Church and Society. (62:4, Mar.-Apr., 1972), pp. 22-24.   DHU/R

4013. "Freedom in Their Souls." American Bible Society in Cooperation with Canadian Bible Society. Released by American Bible Society, 1964. 26 min., sd., color, 16 mm. DLC Film.
"Presents glimpses of the emerging African nations, explaining the part played by churches and missionaries in their search for freedom.

4014. Fueter, Paul D. "The African Contribution to Christian Education." Practical Anthropology (11:1, Ja.-Feb., 1964), pp. 1-13.   DHU/R

4015. Fuller, W. Harold. "Association of Evangelicals of Africa and Madagascar Battle for Africa's Mind." Christianity Today (17:12, Mr. 16, 1973), p. 44.   DHU/R

4016. Garlick, Peter C. "Theses on Africa by Howard University, Washington, D. C." African Studies Bulletin (11:3, Dec., 1968), pp. 259-68.   DHU/R

4017. Gatewood, R. D. Some American Protestant Contributions to the Welfare of African Countries in 1963. New York: National Council of the Churches of Christ in the U. S. A., 1964. NNC; ICU; KyLxCB; MNtcA; DHU/MO

4018. Genischen, H. W. "Theological Education in Africa. The Special Africa Programme of the Theological Education Fund."
International Review of Missions (52:206, Apr., 1963), pp. 155-62.   DHU/R

4019. Gluckman, Max. "The Logic of Witchcraft." Peter J. McEwan and Robert B. Sutcliffe, (eds.). Modern Africa (New York: Thomas Crowell, 1965), pp. 79-92. DLC

4020. Goddard, Burton L., (ed.). The Encyclopedia of Modern Christian Mission: The Agencies. Camden, N. J.: Thomas Nelson & Sons, 1967. DLC; KyLxCB; MH-AH

4021. Gogan, C. "Engaged to the Whole World." African Ecclesiastical Review (13:4, 1971), pp. 333-36.   DHU/R
An aspect of the missionary vocation.

4022. Grenville-Grey, Wilfrid. "Mindolo: a Catalyst for Christian Participation in Nation Building in Africa." International Review of Missions (58:229, Ja., 1969), pp. 110-17. DHU/R

4023. Haines, A. Grove. Africa Today. Baltimore: Johns Hopkins Press, 1955.   DHU/MO

4024. Hallencreutz, Carl Fredrik. "Svart Eller Afrikansk? Notiser Fran ett Missionsseminarium (Black or African Theology)." Svensk Missionstidskrift (60:4, 1972), pp. 197-201. CtY; ICU; CtHC

4025. Harold, Turner. "Dynamic Religion in Africa." Learning for Living (12:5, My., 1973), pp. 3-7.   DHU/R

4026. Häselbarth, H. "Afrika: Neues Zentrum der Christen." Evangelische Theologie (33; My.-Je., 1973), pp. 311-22.   DAU/W; DCU/TH

4027. Hassing, P. "Christian Theology In Africa." Religion in Life (40:4, Wint., 1971), pp. 510-18.   DHU/R

4028. Hawley, Edward A. "Dawn in 'Portuguese' Africa." A. D. (United Presbyterian Edition) (3:11, Nov., 1974), pp. 18-23.   DHU/R

4029. Haynes, George Edmund. Africa, Continent of the Future. New York: Association Press; Geneva, Switzerland: World's Committee of Young Men's Christian Associations, 1950.   NN/Sch
Negro author.

4030. Hellberg, J. H. "Church and State in Relation to Health Care." International Review of Mission (61:242, Apr., 1972), pp. 161-65.   Pam. File, DHU/R
Discussion of church-related medical work in Africa.

4031. Henriet, M. "The Malagasy Churches Under the Sign of 'All Things New'." International Review of Missions (58:229, Ja., 1969), pp. 107-09.   DHU/R

4032. Herrick, Mary D. "Report on Africana in American Collections." African Studies Bulletin (3:2, My., 1960), pp. 5-12.   DHU/MO

4033. Hess, Mahlon M. "African Political Systems and African Church Polity." Practical Anthropology (4:5, Sept.-Oct., 1957), pp. 170-84.   DHU/R

4034. Hillman, Eugene. "Towards a New Approach to the Polygamy Problem." African Ecclesiastical Review (16:3, 1974), pp. 301-10.   DHU/R

4035. Hinchliff, Peter. "'Indigenizing' Church History." The Bulletin of the Society for African Church History (1:2, Dec., 1963), pp. 29-34.   DHU/R

4036. Huddleston, Trevor. "The Christian Churches in Independent Africa." African Affairs (68:270, Ja., 1969), pp. 42-48.   DHU/MO

4037. Innes, G. Mac. "Preaching and Teaching in the African Parish." African Ecclesiastical Review (13:1, 1971), pp. 53-61.   DHU/R

4038. International Missionary Council. Assembly, Accra, 1957-
1958. Minutes of the Assembly of the International Missionary
Council, Ghana, December 28th, 1957 to January 8th, 1958.
London: International Missionary Council, 1958?   NN/Sch

4039. Inter-Varsity Missionary Convention, 8th, University of
Illinois, 1967. God's Men, From All Nations. Chicago:
Inter-Varsity Press, 1968.   DLC
    Religion in Africa.

4040. "An Interview With Rev. A. Adegbola." Presence (5:3, 1972),
pp. 13-16.   DHU/R
    African minister.

4041. Ismael, T. Y. "Religion and U.A.R. African Policy."
Journal of Modern African Studies (6; 1968), pp. 49-58. DLC

4042. "Israel Faces Growing Arab Political Campaign in Black
Africa." Washington Post (Je. 5, 1973). Pam. File, DHU/R
    Israel embassies closed in Chad, Congo-Brazzaville and
    Niger.

4043. Jahn, Janheinz. Muntu: An Outline of the New African Culture. Translated by Marjorie Grene. New York: Grove Press,
Inc., 1961   DHU/MO

4044. Johnson, H. B. "The Location of Christian Missions in
Africa." Geographical Review (57; 1967), pp. 168-202. DHU;
DGW; DAU; DCU

4045. Jones, LeRoi (Imamu Amiri Baraka), (ed.). African Congress.
A Documentary of the First Modern Pan-African Congress.
New York: Wm. Morrow & Co., 1972.   DHU/R
    Religion, pp. 249-62.

4046. Kalilombe, Patrick A. "The Theology of Communications
From an African Point of View." African Ecclesiastical Review
(15:4, 1973), pp. 291-303.   DHU/R

4047. Karefa-Smart, John. The Halting Kingdom: Christianity and
the African Revolution. New York: Friendship Press, 1959.
                                      CoDI; NN/Sch

4048. Karefa-Smart, Rena. "Christian Effort in Tropical Africa."
Congregational Quarterly (33; 1955), pp. 47-54. DHU/R

4049. Kearney, Vincent S. "Africa: Church on a Tightrope."
America (129:9, Sept. 29, 1973), pp. 207-09.   DHU/R

4050. Keats, Ezra Jack. God is in the Mountains. New York:
Holt, Rinehart & Winston, Inc., 1966.   DLC
    Contrasting thoughts of Christians, Jews, Africans, etc.

4051. Kehler, L. "African Churches Grew But Against Heavy
Odds." The Mennonite (87; Mr. 7, 1972), pp. 166+. IOBB;
IOB

4052. Kennedy, William B. "African Education and the Churches."
Ecumenical Press Service (This Month) (#6; Mar., 1973), pp.
5-6.   DHU/R

4053. King, Léon. "Christian Imperialism and Negro Charity."
Cross Currents (9; Wint., 1959), pp. 86-8.   DHU/R

4054. "Kinshasa Declaration." International Review of Missions
(61:242, Apr., 1972), pp. 115-16.   DHU/R
    All Africa Conference of Churches.

4055. Kiplagat, B. A. "Christianity and African Novelists." International Review of Missions (61:242, Apr., 1972), pp. 130-43.
                                      DHU/R

4056. Kitagawa, Daisuke. "Church and Race in Today's Africa."
The African Methodist Episcopal Church Review (78:210, Oct.-
Dec., 1961), pp. 58-63.   DHU/R

4057. Kiwanicka, Joseph. "Silver Jubilee of Colored Bishop." St.
Augustine's Messenger (31:9, Nov., 1954), pp. 313-17. DHU/R
    "Biographies of African Bishops."

4058. Kolarz, Walter. Religion and Communism in Africa. London:
Sword of the Spirit, 1963?   DLC; IEN; NBuU; WU

4059. Kotto, Jean. "L'Evangelisation en Afrique." Flambeau
(1; Feb., 1964), pp. 7-15.   Pam. File, DHU/R

4060. Kozak, Igor G. Religions in Africa. Washington, D.C.:
Associated Publishers, Inc., 1971.   DHU/R

4061. Kretzmann, Martin Luther. "Theological Education: A
Critique." Africa Theological Journal (3; Mr., 1970), pp. 17-
29.   DHU/R

4062. Kunambi, B. N. "Women in Africa: Awake!" African Ecclesiastical Review (13:4, 1971), pp. 301-04.   DHU/R
    African womens' contribution to development.

4063. Lamson, Byron S. To Catch the Tide. Winona Lake, Indiana:
General Missionary Board, 1963.   MiBsA
    Missions in Africa, Free Methodist Church.

4064. Larson, Peter A. "Third World Missionary Agencies: Research in Progress," Missiology: an International Review
(1:2, Apr., 1973), pp. 95-111.   DHU/R

4065. Lavanoux, Maurice. "African Religious Art Looks Forward."
Catholic World (190:1, 136, Nov., 1959), pp. 107-11. DHU/R

4066. Lee, Annabelle. "African Nuns: an Anthropologist's Impression." New Blackfriars (My., 1968), pp. 401-09. DAU/W;
DCU/TH; DGU

4067. Lehmann, Paul. "A Theological Defense of Revolutions."
Africa Today (15:3, Je.-Jl., 1968), pp. 18-21.   DHU/MO

4068. Lobinger, F. "A Plea for Team Ministry." African Ecclesiastical Review (13:4, 1971), pp. 344-47.   DHU/R

4069. Lobo, G. "Towards a Theology of Development." African
Eccleseastical Review (13:1, 1971), pp. 18-24.   DHU/R

4070. Loth, Heinrich. Kolonialismus Unter der Kutte. Berlin:
Dietz, 1960.   NN/Sch

4071. Luntadila, Jean-Cl. L. "Has Christianity a Future in Africa?" Ministry (9:4, 1969), pp. 147-51.   DLC

4072. Luykx, B. "Les Nouveaux Documents Liturgiques Romains
et Leur Reception." Revue du Clerge Africain (26;1, Ja.,
1971), pp. 27-42.   DHU/R

4073. Magesa, Lawrence. "Catholic Yet African: Authentic Self-
Assertion of the Church and African Culture." African Ecclesiastical Review (15:2, 1973), pp. 110-17.   DHU/R

4074. ----- "Return to the World; Towards a Theocentric Existen-
tialism in Africa." African Ecclesiastical Review (16:3, 1974),
pp. 277-84.   DHU/R

4075. Makunike, Ezekiel C. "Evangelism in the Cultural Context
of Africa." International Review of Missions (63:249, Ja.,
1974), pp. 57-63.   DHU/R

4076. ----- "Voices for the New Africa." Ecumenical Press Service (Je., 1971), pp. 3-4.   DHU/R

4077. Malik, Charles. "Asia and Africa Ask Searching Questions."
Congregational Quarterly (33; 1955), pp. 37-46.   DHU/R
    Problems relating to Christianity in Asia and Africa.
    A paper read at the Second Assembly of the World Council
    of Churches at Evanston, August, 1954.

4078. Malula, Joseph A. "Place du Chretien dans la Societe et
Role de la Hierarchie." Revue du Clerge Africain (26; Ja.,
1971), pp. 77-86.   DHU/R

4079. Maquet, Jacques. Africanity: The Cultural Unity of Black Africa. New York: Oxford University Press, 1972. DHU/R pp. 141-74, One Hundred Traditional Societies of Black Africa which includes for each, art, religion and basic culture.

4080. Margull, Hans Jochen. Aufbruch zur Zukunft: Chiliastich-Messianische Bewegungen in Afrika und Sudostasien. Guters-loher: Gerd Mohn, 1962.   NNMR

4081. Maro, Nick. "Self-reliance and the Church." Presence (4:2, 1970), pp. 43-47.   DHU/R

4082. Martin, Denis. "Christianity and Development in Africa." Cross Currents (15; Wint., 1975), pp. 19-31.   DHU/R

4083. Martin, V. Notes d'Introduction à une Etude Socio-religieuse des Populations de Dakar et du Senegal. Dakar: Fraternité Saint Dominique, 1964.   MH
      Also contains material on Gambia, Portuguese Guinea and the Cape Verde Islands.

4084. Matthews, Z. K. "Christian Education in a Changing Africa." International Review of Missions (52; 1963), pp. 38-46. DHU/R

4085. Maurier, Henri. Religion et Développement; Traditions Africaines et Catécheses. Paris: Mame, 1965.   NNCor Missions in Africa.

4086. Mbaeyi, P. M. "The 'Mist of Life', Religion and Politics." Orita: Ibadan Journal of Religious Studies (5:1, Je., 1971), pp. 46-66.   DHU/R

4087. Mbiti, John S. "African Concept of Human Relations." Ministry (9:4, 1969), pp. 158-68.   DLC

4088. ----- "African Theology." Worldview (16:8, Aug., 1973), pp. 33-39.   DHU/R

4089. ----- "Church and State: A Neglected Element of Christianity in Contemporary Africa." Africa Theological Journal (5; Dec., 1972), pp. 31-46.   DHU/R

4090. ----- The Crisis of Mission in Africa. Mukono, Uganda: P.O. Box 4, 1971.   DHU/R

4091. ----- "Future of Christianity in Africa, 1970-2000." Communio Viatorum (13:1-2, Spr., 1970), pp. 19-38. DHU/R

4092. ----- "Harmony, Happiness and Morality in African Religion." The Drew Gateway (43; Wint., 1973), pp. 108-15. DAU/W

4093. McFall, Ernest A. Approaching the Nuer of Africa Through the Old Testament. South Pasadena, Calif.: William Carey Library, 1970.   DLC

4094. McGrath, Oswin. "Training for the Ministry in the Africa of Tomorrow." Ministry (11:4, 1971), pp. 103-8.   CLWM; CLoIC

4095. McVeigh, Maldolm J. "Sources for an African Christian Theology." Presence (5:3, 1972), pp. 2-4. DHU/R

4096. Melady, Margaret Badum. "The Church in Independent Africa. How is its Future Based on the Present." Worldmission (23:2, 1972), pp. 17-20.   DCU

4097. Melady, T. P. "The Impact of Africa on Recent Developments in the Roman Catholic Church." Race (7:2, 1965), pp. 147-56.   DAU

4098. Merle, Marcel. Les Eglises Chretiennes et la Decolonisation. Paris: A. Colin, 1967.   DLC

4099. M'Gabe, Davis. "Is the Church a Stumbling Block to Revolution?" Africa Today (15:3, Je.-Jl., 1968), pp. 15-17.   DHU/MO

4100. Missiology in Africa Today; Thought-Provoking Essays by Modern Missionaries. Dublin: M. H. Gill, 1961. NNCor

4101. "The Missionary Aspect of Priestly Formation." African Ecclesiastical Review (12:2, 1973), pp. 169-70.   DHU/R

4102. "The Missionary Role of the Laity." African Ecclesiastical Review (13:1, 1971), pp. 80-85.   DHU/R

4103. Moehlum, Helge. "Migonsansvar og Språkutdanneng (Missionary Responsibility and Language Training) Norsk Tidssrift for Misjon (27:2, 1973), pp. 93-108.   CtY-D; MH-AH

4104. Moore, Clark D. and Ann Dunbar. Africa Yesterday and Today. New York: Frederick A. Praeger, 1969. DHU/R pp. 350-57, Missionaries and the Peace Corps.

4105. Moore, James R. "Literature of Countercultural Religion." Christianity Today (16:15, Apr. 28, 1972), pp. 14-16. DHU/R Includes Africa.

4106. Morris, Colin M. Church and Challenge in a New Africa: Political Sermons. London: Epsworth Press, 1964. MH; ICU; NIC; NjPY; InU; MNtcA

4107. ----- "The Cross Over Africa." Christian Century (87:22, Je. 3, 1970), pp. 688-91.   DHU/R

4108. ----- Nothing to Defend. London: Cargate Press, 1963.   NNCor
      Missions in Africa.

4109. ----- Out of Africa Crucible; Sermons from Central Africa. London: Lutterworth Press, 1960.   NN/Sch

4110. Mosothome, Ephraim K. "Communio Sanctorum in Africa." Missionalia (1;2, Ag., 1973), pp. 86-95.   DHU/R

4111. Mshana, Eliewaha E. "Church and State in the Independent States in Africa." Africa Theological Journal (5; Dec., 1972), pp. 46-58.   DHU/R

4112. ----- "Nationalism: a Problem of the Church." Pro Veritate (11:9, 1973), pp. 20-22.   DLC

4113. ----- "Nationalism in Africa as a Challenge and Problem to the Christian Church. Africa Theological Journal (No. 1, Feb., 1968), pp. 21-29.   DHU/R

4114. "Mukaba and His Bible." American Bible Society, 1965. 45 fr. color. 35 mm. and phonodisc: 1 s., 10 in., 33 1/3 rpm., 7 min.   DLC
      Filmstrip.
      "The story of an African boy's desire to own a Bible and his willingness to forego a boy's normal pleasure in order to achieve his goal."

4115. Mullin, Joseph. The Catholic Church in Modern Africa; A Pastoral Theology. London: G. Chapman, 1965. DHU/MO; MiBsA; NNCor

4116. Murray, M. M. "The Witness of a Servant Church." African Ecclesiastical Review (13:1, 1971), pp. 3-11.   DHU/R
      "There is a new Africa, and there must be a new church, one distinguished by her service to the poorest."

4117. Musa, Thomas. "Training for Ministry in Contemporary Africa." Credo (18:1, Mr., 1971), pp. 26-35.   DLC

4118. Mushanga, Musa T. "Church Leadership in a Developing Society." African Ecclesiastical Review (13:1, 1971), pp. 33-40.   DHU/R

4119. Mwasaru, Dominic. "The Challenge of Africanising the Church." African Ecclesiastical Review (16:3, 1974), pp. 285-94.   DHU/R

4120. Nabeeta, Tom. "The Aims of Religious Education." African Ecclesiastical Review (14:4, 1972), pp. 296-303.   DHU/R
      Makes plea that the study of religious education in the schools of Africa be ecumenical.

4121. Ncube, Pius A. "A Christian Feast of Tabernacles for Africa?" African Ecclesiastical Review (16:3, 1974), pp. 269-76.
DHU/R

4122. Neill, Stephen Charles. "Crisis in Tropical Africa." The Ecumenical Review (3:1, Oct., 1950), pp. 14-25. DHU/R

4123. Nelson, Robert G. "God's Church in Africa." World Call (53:7, Jl.-Ag., 1971), pp. 22-23. DHU/R

4124. "New Faces of Africa." Methodist Publishing House. 1959. Film.
Emphasis is on Protestant activity in Africa.

4125. "A New Look at Christianity in Africa." World Student Christian Federation (A WSCF Book, no. 5) (2:2, 1972), pp. 3-80.
DHU/R; MNtcA

4126. Newing, Edward G. "A Study of Old Testament Curricula in Eastern and Central Africa." Africa Theological Journal (3; Mr., 1970), pp. 80-98. DHU/R

4127. Ngindu A. "L'effervescence des 'Eglises Africaines'." Revue du Clergé Africain (26; 1971), pp. 437-45. CtHC
An examination of the role of the church in the typical African community.

4128. Ngoumou, P. C. "Musique, Eglise et Vie Africaine." Flambeau (2; My., 1964), pp. 44-55. Pam. File, DHU/R

4129. Ngoyi, Louis. "Le Mariage Chretien vu par un Conglais Critique." Revue du Clergé Africain (26; 3-4, My.,-Jl., 1971), pp. 153-61. DHU/R
Christian marriage in Africa.

4130. Ngugi, James. "The Role of the Church in Africa Today." Presence (4:3, 1971), pp. 4-6. DHU/R

4131. Nketia, J. H. "The Contribution of African Culture to Christian Worship." International Journal of Missions (47:4, 1958), pp. 265-78. DHU/R

4132. Nomenyo, Seth. "Vie Chretienne en Afrique Hier et Aujourd' hui." Flambeau (27; Ag., 1970), pp. 147-58. Pam. File, DHU/R

4133. Nordby, Juel A. The Role of the Methodist Class Meeting in the Growth of an African City Church: A Historical Study. Doctoral dissertation. Boston University, 1967.

4134. North American Assembly of African Affairs, Wittenberg College, 1952. Africa is Here; Report of the North African Assembly of African Affairs, Held at Wittenberg College, Springfield, Ohio, June 16-25, 1952. New York: Africa Committee of the Division of Foreign Missions of the Churches of Christ in the U. S. A., 1952. PPT

4135. Northcott, William Cecil. Christianity in Africa. London: Westminster Press, 1963. NN/Sch; DLC; A&M

4136. ----- "Ecumenical Reaches Africa." Christian Century (75; Dec. 17, 1958), pp. 1454-55. DHU/R

4137. Obiechina, Emmanuel. An African Popular Literature. A Study of Onitsha Market Pamphlets. Cambridge: At the University Press, 1973. DLC
Chapter 9, Religion and Morals.

4138. Odhiambo, Abel Ouma. "Religious Titles Under Fire." African Ecclesiastical Review (15:4, 1973), p. 377. DHU/R

4139. Oduyoye, Mercy Amba. "Unity and Freedom in Africa." The Ecumenical Review (26:3, Jl., 1974), pp. 453-58. DHU/R
Includes information on the agenda of Christians in Africa.

4140. Ojiako, J. "The Challenge of the Religious Situation to Parish Life - Analytical Survey of Some of the Challenges." West African Religion (13 & 14; Sept. & Dec., 1972), pp. 39-40. DHU/R

4141. Okafor-Omali, Dilim. "The First Christian in the Village." The Bulletin of the Society for African Church History (1:2, Dec., 1963), pp. 49-61. DHU/R; DLC

4142. Okite, Odhiambo. "African Challenge: Christian Literature." Christianity Today (14:17, My. 22, 1970), p. 36. DHU/R

4143. Okullu, J. Henry. "Comment on Tribal Hatred." African Ecclesiastical Review (14:4, 1972), pp. 341-42. DHU/R

4144. ----- "Consultation in Kampala." The Christian Century (89:7, Feb. 16, 1972), pp. 185-86. DHU/R
Author is from Nairobi, Kenya, discusses conference of African theologians at Makerere University "early this year." The theme of the conference was "African Theology and Church Life." Author's summation of the conference was that "Africa will no longer accept Christianity on Western terms."

4145. ----- "Nonchurch Marriages in Africa: the Church Takes a Second Look; A Hastings Survey." Christian Century (89; My. 10, 1972), pp. 536-37. DHU/R

4146. Olumide, Y. "Christian Broadcasting in Africa." International Review of Mission (60:4, Oct. 1971), pp. 505-11.
DHU/R; DCU; DAU/W

4147. Onwuachi, P. Chike. African Identity, Black Liberation. New York: Black Academy Press, Inc., 1973. DHU/R

4148. Oosthuizen, Gerhardus C. "Causes of Religious Independentism in Africa." Ministry (11:4, 1971), pp. 121-33. CLWM; CLoIC

4149. ----- "The Church Among African Forces." Practical Anthropology (11:4, Jl.-Ag., 1964), pp. 161-80. DHU/R

4150. ----- Theological Battleground in Asia and Africa: the Issues Facing the Churches and the Efforts to Overcome Western Divisions. London: C. Hurst & Co., 1972. DHU/R; DLC

4151. ----- Theological Discussions and Confessional Developments in the Churches of Asia and Africa. Franeker: T. Wever, 1958. MNtcA

4152. Opaleye, 'Biodun. "About 4,000 Delegates Attend the 56th Session of the Nigerian Baptist Convention." Nigerian Baptist (47:6, Je., 1969), pp. 1+. Pam. File, DHU/R

4153. ----- "Nigerian Baptist Convention Holds 58th Annual Session in Jos." Nigerian Baptist (49:6, Je., 1971), pp. 1+.
Pam. File, DHU/R

4154. Ouma, Joseph P. B. M. "The Christian and the Integral Development in Africa." African Ecclesiastical Review (13:1, 1971), pp. 12-17. DHU/R

4155. "The Outlook for Christianity in Africa." Interview with Ambassador Thomas P. Melady. The Lamp/A Christian Unity Magazine (70; 2, Feb., 1972), pp. 2-5. DHU/R
Ambassador to Central African Republic of Burundi is interviewed on Catholic ecumenism and racial understanding.

4156. Parker, Everett C. "All African Christianity." The African Methodist Episcopal Church Review (78:217, Jl.- Sept., 1968), pp. 66-70. DHU/R
Report on All-Africa Conference of Churches held at Kampala, Uganda, Apr. 20-30, 1963.

4157. Pawelzik, Fritz. I Sing Your Praise All the Day Long. New York: Firendship Press, 1967. DHU/R
Collection of prayers written by Ghananians.

4158. Payne, Denis. African Independence and Christian Freedom: Address Delivered at Makerere University College, Uganda, in 1962. London: Oxford Univ. Press, 1965. DLC; DHU/R

4159. Perrin-Jassy, Marie France. Basic Community in the African Churches. New York: Orbis Books, 1973.   DHU/R

4160. Philpot, David. "Evaluation of Theological Education in East Africa Today." Reformed and Presbyterian World (Mr.. 1970), pp. 25-29.   DAU/W

4161. Pius XII, Pope. The Future of Africa: The Encyclical Fidei Donum, of Pope Pius XII. London: Sword of the Spirit, 1957.   DCU

4162. Pluralism in Africa. Edited by Leo Kuper and M. G. Smith. Berkeley: University of California Press, 1969.   DCU/A

4163. "La Politique Gouvernementale et l'Eglise dans les Territoires Portugais d'Afrique." Pro Mundi Vita (Bruxelles) (No. 43; 1972), pp. 18-40.   DCU/TH

4164. "Pope Paul on 'Evangelization and Development'." African Ecclesiastical Review (13:1, 1971), pp. 76-79.   DHU/R
        From Pope Paul's Message for Mission Sunday, 1970.

4165. Pratt, S. A. J. "Spiritual Conflicts in a Changing African Society." Ecumenical Review (8:2, Ja., 1956), pp. 154-62.
        DHU/MO; DHU/R

4166. "Problem -- and Promise- In African Journalism." Occasional Bulletin (19:11, Nov., 1968), pp. 1-15.   DHU/R
        Twenty editors of Christian newspapers and magazines in Africa came together to discuss the challenges of their work.

4167. Pulliam, R. "Importing the Gospel; Africa Inland Mission." Christianity Today (18; Oct. 12, 1973), p. 58.   DHU/R

4168. Ranger, Terence O. "The Church in the Age of African Revolution." East Africa Journal (Nairobi) (5:8, Ag., 1968), pp. 11-16.   DHU/MO
        Catholic Church in Africa.

4169. ----- and I. N. Kimambo, (eds.). The Historical Study of African Religion. London: Heinemann Educational Books, 1972.   DHU/R
        Missionary adaptation of African religious institutions. The Masai case, pp. 221-51. Also efforts to use African rituals in Southern Tanzania by Bishop Vincent Lucas.

4170. Rawson, David P. "Africa's Social and Political Demands on the Church." Practical Anthropology (16:1, Mr.-Apr., 1969), pp. 75-83.   DHU/R

4171. "Religion Courses Begin New Phase." African Ecclesiastical Review (14:4, 1972), pp. 369-70.   DHU/R

4172. Reuschle, Helmut. "Blackboards for Freedom." This Month (5; Je., 1974), pp. 3-5.   DHU/R
        Author questions if money given to Africa by the World Council of Churches for humanitarian and social programs is being used for liberation.

4173. Reyburn, William D. "Africanization and African Studies." Practical Anthropology (9:3, My.-Je., 1962), pp. 97-110.   DHU/R
        Discusses the subtle reorientation of Christianity as it is exposed to African influences.

4174. ----- "Christian Responsibility Toward Social Change." Practical Anthropology (7; My., 1960), pp. 124-31.   DHU/R

4175. ----- "Conflicts and Contradictions in African Christianity." Practical Anthropology (4:5, Sept.-Oct., 1957), pp. 161-69.   DHU/R

4176. ----- "The Message of the Old Testament and the African Church--I." Practical Anthropology (7:4, Jl.-Ag., 1960), pp. 152-56.   DHU/R

4177. ----- "Sickness, Sin and the Curse: The Old Testament and the African Church--II." Practical Anthropology (7:5, Sept.-Oct., 1960), pp. 217-22.   DHU/R

4178. Roberts, James Deotis, Sr. "African Religion and Social Consciousness." The Journal of Religious Thought (29:1, Spr.-Sum., 1972), pp. 43-56.   DHU/R

4179. ----- Africanisms and Spiritual Strivings." Journal of Religious Thought (30:1, Spr.-Sum., 1973), pp. 16-27.   DHU/R

4180. Robinson, James Herman. Africa at the Crossroads. Philadelphia: Westminster Press, 1962.   NN/Sch

4181. ----- Christianity and Revolution in Africa. Chicago: Christian Century Foundation, 1956.   NNMR
        Negro Presbyterian minister.

4182. Rogers, Cornish. "A Visit With African Leaders." Christian Century (88:38, Sept. 22, 1971), pp. 1099-1100.   DHU/R
        Negro author.

4183. Rotberg, Robert I. and Ali A. Mazrui, (eds.). Protest and Power in Black Africa. New York: Oxford Univeristy Press, 1970.   DHU/R
        "Thirty-four essays describe and analize various forms of sub-Saharan African protests against alien rule, with Dr. Rotberg, Editor, stressing these three themes: dissent, diversity, reintegration."

4184. Rubingh, Eugene. "The African Shape of the Gospel." His (33:1, Oct., 1972), pp. 10-13.   IOBNB

4185. ----- "Theology From Africa." Banner (Sept. 24, 1971), pp. 4+.   CtY-D; NN

4186. Ruch, Ernst A. "African Christianity, African Theology." Ministry (11:4, 1971), pp. 166-200.   CLWM; CLoIC

4187. Said, Dibinga Wa. "An African Theology of Decolonization." Harvard Theological Review (64:4, Oct., 1971), pp. 501-24.   DHU/R

4188. Sarpong, Peter K., (bp.). "The Search for Meaning: the Religious Impact of Technology in Africa." The Ecumenical Review (24:3, Jl., 1972), pp. 300-09.   DHU/R

4189. ----- (bp.). "What Does Africa's Laity Ask." African Ecclesiastical Review (14:4, 1972), pp. 285-95+.   DHU/R

4190. Saunders, David L. "Changing Concepts of Vocation in Southern Baptist Foreign Missions, 1845-1973." Baptist History and Heritage (8:4, Oct., 1973), pp. 213-24.   DHU/R
        Author is secretary for Eastern and Southern Africa Foreign Mission Board.

4191. Sawyerr, Harry, A. E. "The Basis of a Theology for Africa." International Review of Missions (52:207, Jl., 1963), pp. 266-78.   DHU/R

4192. ----- Christian Theology in Independent Africa. Freetown, Sierra Leone: n.p., 1961.   DLC

4193. ----- Creative Evangelism Towards a New Christian Encounter With Africa. London: Lutterworth, 1968.   DLC; WU

4194. ----- "Salvation Viewed From the African Situation." Presence (5:3, 1972), pp. 16-22.   DHU/R

4195. ----- "Theological Faculty Conference for Africa. An Appreciation." Africa Theological Journal (3; Mr., 1970), pp. 7-10.   DHU/R

4196. ----- "What is African Theology." Africa Theological Journal (4; Ag., 1971), pp. 7-24.   DHU/R

4197. Scanlon, David G. Church, State, and Education in Africa. New York: Teachers College Press, Teachers College Columbia University, 1966.   DLC

4198. Schuyler, Philippa. *Jungle Saints. Africa's Heroic Catholic Missionaries.* Rome, Italy: Casa Editrice Herder, 1963.
DHU/MO
Author's work with Catholic missionaries in Africa.

4199. Scott, Michael. *Experiment in Time.* London: The Africa Bureau, 1954.   DHU/MO
A Sermon on Africa preached by Rev. Michael Scott at New York Cathedral, New York City.

4200. Sekwa, Castor. "Liturgy and Building Up of the Christian Community." *African Ecclesiastical Review* (15:3, 1973), pp. 243-49.   DHU/R

4201. Serapiao, Luis B. "The Preaching of Portuguese Colonialism and the Protest of the White Fathers." *Issue* (2:1, Spr., 1972), pp. 34-41.   DLC; DHU/MO

4202. Shockley, Grant S. *Understanding the New Generation in Africa.* New York: Friendship Press, 1971.   DHU/R
Negro author.

4203. Shorter, Aylward. *African Culture and the Christian Church.* Maryknoll, N.Y.: Orbis Books, 1974.   DHU/R

4204. Sicard, Harold von. "Language and Theological Training in Africa." *The International Review of Missions* (44; 1955), pp. 147-52.   DHU/R

4205. Sievers, E. K. "Christian Prayer in an African Setting." *The Ghana Bulletin of Theology* (4:6, Je., 1974), pp. 37-47.
DHU/R

4206. Simensson, Tord. "On Theological Education in Non-Western Countries." *Africa Theological Journal* (3; Mr., 1970), pp. 30-6.   DHU/R

4207. Singleton, M. "The Eucharistic Meal and the African's Eating Habits." *African Ecclesiastical Review* (15:4, 1973), p. 375.   DHU/R

4208. Smith, Brian H. "Pastoral Strategy in the Third World." *America* (130:19, My. 18, 1974), pp. 389-92.   DHU/R

4209. Smith, Donald Eugene, (ed.). *Religion, Politics and Social Change in the Third World: a Sourcebook.* New York: Free Press, 1971.   DLC

4210. "The Society for African Church History." *The Bulletin of the Society for African Church History* (2:2, 1966), pp. 200-06.
DHU/R

4211. "The Southern African Catholic Bishops' Conference." *African Ecclesiastical Review* (16:3, 1974), pp. 345-54. DHU/R
Theme of conference was Pastoral Directive on Family Planning held in February, 1973.

4212. Stuyvesant, Carolyn. *Storytime in Africa, Book One and Two.* Washington: Review and Herald, 1968, 1969.   MiBsA
Seventh-day Adventist missions in Africa.

4213. Sundermeier, Theo. "The Concept of Law and the Problem of Legalism in the Churches of Africa." *Credo* (17:1-2, Je., 1970), pp. 5-17.   DLC

4214. Sundkler, Bengt G. M. *The Christian Ministry in Africa.* Uppsala: Swedish Institute of Missionary Research, 1960.
OWibfU; DLC

4215. ----- "Historical Factors in the Development of the Various Forms of Ministry in Africa." *Credo* (18:1, Mr., 1971), pp. 17-25.   DLC

4216. Tanner, Ralph E. S. "Married Clergy in East and Central Africa: The Clash of Roles." *Heythrop Journal* (11:3, Jl., 1970), pp. 278-93.   DHU/R

4217. Taylor, John Vernon. "Thoughts on an African Passion Play." *Practical Anthropology* (3:6, Nov.-Dec., 1956), pp. 114-18.   DHU/R

4218. ----- *Christianity and Politics in Africa.* London: 1957. CSt-H; KyLxCB; NcD; CtY-D; DHU/MO; OWibfU; NN/Sch

4219. Teasdale, Charles W. *An Evaluation of the Ecclesiology of the Africa Inland Church.* Masters thesis. Wheaton College, 1956.

4220. Thomas, J. C. "What is African Theology." *The Ghana Bulletin of Theology* (4:4, Je., 1973), pp. 14-30. DHU/R

4221. Thompson, Vincent B. *African and Unity; The Evolution of Pan-Africanism.* New York: Humanities Press, 1969.
DHU/MO
Information on religious overtones and undertones in the African Resistance.

4222. "Three Views of Catholicism in Africa." *Africa Report* (8:3, Mr., 1963), pp. 13-20.   DHU/MO

4223. Thunberg, Anne Marie. *Kontinente im Aufbruch; Kirche und Mission Angesichts der Afro-Asiatischen Revolution.* Göttingen: Vandenhoech, 1960.   NjP

4224. Trobisch, Walter A. "Church Discipline in Africa." *Practical Anthropology* (8:5, Sept.-Oct., 1961), pp. 200-06.
DHU/R

4225. "'True' African Leadership is Urged." *Presbyterian Outlook* (156:2, Ja. 14, 1974), p. 4.   DHU/R
All Africa Conference of Churches & the World Council of Churches draw up communique that urges more African leadership and the participation of women and youth.

4226. Turner, Harold W. "Bibliography of Modern African Religious Movements." *Journal of Religion in Africa* (1:3, 1968; 3:3, 1970), pp. 173-210; 161-208.   DHU/R

4227. Uba, Sam. "An African Pope?" *Encore* (2:7, Ag., 1973), pp. 44-46.   Pam. File, DHU/R

4228. ----- "The Papacy: Africa's Turn?" *Africa* (43:2, Apr., 1973), pp. 17-21.   DHU/MO
Speculates on possibility of a Black African ever becoming Pope.

4229. "Under the Banner of Unity: African National Council." *IDOC International* (46; Apr. 29, 1972), pp. 80-85. DHU/R

4230. Van Horne, Marion. "African Women Stand Tall and Shout Loud." *World Call* (54:4, Apr., 1972), pp. 22-25. DHU/R

4231. Vaughan, Benjamin N. Y. *The Expectation of the Poor: The Church and the Third World.* London: S. C. M. Press, 1972.
DLC

4232. Vonck, Pol J. "Theological Faculty Conference for Africa. Personal Comment." *Africa Theological Journal* (3; Mr., 1970), pp. 11-16.   DHU/R

4233. Wa Said, Dibinga. "An African Theology of Decolonization." *Harvard Theological Review* (64:4, Oct., 1971), pp. 501-24.
DHU/R

4234. Wadlow, René. "Planning for Change and Social Action: The Role of an African Church." *International Review of Missions* (56; 1967), pp. 489-98.   DHU/R

4235. Wagner, C. Peter. "Evangelical Missions and Revolution Today." *Missiology* (1:1, Ja., 1973), pp. 91-8. DHU/R

4236. Wainwright, Geoffrey. "Localization of Worship." *Studia Liturgica* (8:1, 1971-72), pp. 26-41.   DHU/R
Indigenization of the church's worship in the African churches.

4237. Walls, A. F. "African Church History; Some Recent Studies (review article)." *The Journal of Ecclesiastical History* (23:2, Apr., 1972), pp. 161-9.   DHU/R

4238. Wambutda, Daniel N. "An African Looks at Christian Missions in Africa." Practical Anthropology (17:4, Jl-Ag., 1970), pp. 169-76.   DHU/R

4239. Warren, Max. Problems and Promises in Africa Today; the Lichfield Lectures in Divinity for 1963. London: Hodder and Stoughton, 1965.   MNtcA

4240. Webster, James Bertin. "Source Material for the Study of the African Churches." The Bulletin of the Society for African Church History (1:2, Dec., 1963), pp. 41-49.   DHU/R

4241. Wellmer, G. "All Africa Conference of Churches." Ministry (10:1, 1970), pp. 30-44.   DLC

4242. Wenzel, Kristen. Clergymen's Attitude Toward Black Africa; Role of Religious Beliefs in Shaping Them. Washington: Center for Applied Research in the Apostolate, 1971. MiBsA; PPT; MNtcA
        Missions in Sub-Saharan Africa.

4243. ----- The Relationships Between Religious Beliefs and Missionary Attitudes Held Towards Black Africa: A Study of Protestant and Catholic Clergymen Serving Churches Within the Five Boroughs of New York City. Doctoral dissertation. The Catholic University of America, 1970.

4244. Werman, Henry. "The New Praise in Ancient Tunes." The Church Crossing Frontiers (Uppsala, Sweden: Gleerup, 1969), pp. 177-88.   DHU/R
        New songs of praise in the young African churches.

4245. West, Martin. "Conflict and Cooperation in African Churches." This Month; Ecumenical Press Service (Oct., 1971), pp. 5-7.   DHU/R
        Lecturer in Anthropology. University of Capetown, South Africa.

4246. Wilson, Frank T. "Future of Missionary Enterprise in Africa South of the Sahara." Journal of Negro Education (30; Sum., 1961), pp. 324-33.   DHU
        Negro author.

4247. Wilson, Monica. Religion and the Transformation of Society: A Study of Social Change in Africa. Cambridge: The University Press, 1971. DHU/R; DCU; NNCor; TSewU-T; MNtcA; NjP; PPT

4248. Wilson, William J., (ed.). The Church in Africa: Christian Mission in a Context of Change. A Seminar. Maryknoll, N. Y.: Maryknoll Publications, 1967.   DHU/MO; DLC

4249. World Council of Churches. Commission on World Mission and Evangelism. The Mission of the Church in Urban Africa; Report on the Consultation Held in Nairobi March, 1961. All-Africa Church Conference, Kitwe, Northern Rhodesia. N. Y.: World Council of Churches, 1962.   MNtcA

4250. World Council of Churches. Committee to Combat Racism. First and Second List of Corporations Directly Involved in Investment in or Trade With South Africa, Namibia, Zimbabwe, Angola, Mozambique, and Guine-Bissao. Pam. File, DHU/R Mim.
        Two lists issued December, 1972 and August, 1973.

4251. World Council of Churches. Committee to Combat Racism. A Profile of the African National Congress. Pam. File,   DHU/MO
        Mim.
        Liberation movement in Africa which received $10,000 from the WCC.

4252. "World Council of Churches: More Funds to Combat Racism." IDOC - International. (no. 36; Nov. 27, 1971), pp. 32-54.   DHU/R

4253. Wright, Marcia. "African History in the 1960's: Religion." African Studies Review (14:3, Dec., 1971), pp. 439-45.   DHU/MO

4254. Young, Robert. Modern Missions, Their Trials and Triumphs. New York: Cassell & Co., 1882.   DHU/R
        Includes Protestant missions in Africa, Western, South Central, Gold Coast and Madagascar.

4255. Zanzibar, Frank. "Mr. Keable's Indictment of African Priest." East and West (17; Ja., 1919), pp. 165-75. DHU/R

4256. Zulu, Lawrence B. "A Black Assessment of Nineteeth Century Missionaries." World Student Christian Federation (2:2, 1972), pp. 35-9.   DHU/R

II. CHRISTIANITY AND SLAVERY IN THE NEW WORLD

A. SLAVERY IN THE WEST INDIES AND SOUTH AMERICA

4257. Bennett, J. Harry. Bondsmen and Bishops; Slavery and Apprenticeship on the Codrington Plantations of Barbados, 1710-1838. Berkeley: University of California Press, 1958.
CtY-D

4258. Bird, Mark Baker. The Black Man; or, Haytian (sic) Independence. Deduced from historical notes, and Dedicated to the government and people of Hayti. New York: Published by the author, 1869.
NN/Sch

4259. Bleby, Henry. Romance Without Fiction: or, Sketches from the Portfolio of an Old Missionary. London: Published for the author at the Wesleyan Conference Office, 1872.
NN/Sch

4260. Bowser, Frederick P. The African Slave in Colonial Peru, 1524-1650. Stanford, Calif.: Stanford University Press, 1974.
DHU/R

4261. ----- Negro Slavery in Colonial Peru, 1529-1650. Doctoral dissertation. University of California, 1967.

4262. Brathwaite, Edward. Folk Culture of the Slaves in Jamaica. London: New Beacon, 1970.
NjP

4263. Breathett, George A. "Religious Protectionism and the Slave in Haiti." Catholic Historical Review (55:1, Apr., 1969), pp. 26-39.
DHU/R

4264. Buchner, J. H. The Moravians in Jamaica. History of the Mission of the United Brethren's Church to the Negroes in the Island of Jamaica, from the Year 1754-1854...London: Longman, Brown & Co., 1854.
DHU/MO

4265. Bury, Herbert. A Bishop Amongst Bananas. Milwaukee: Young Churchman Co., 1911.
NN/Sch

4266. Candler, John. Narrative of a Recent Visit to Brazil, by John Candler and Wilson Burgess; to Present an Address on the Slave-Trade and Slavery, issued by the Religious Society of Friends. London: E. Marsh, 1853.
INRE

4267. Carneiro, Edison de Souza. O Quilombo dos Palmares, 1630-1695. Sao Paulo: Editora Brasiliense, 1947. DHU/MO

4268. Caswell, Henry. The Martyr of the Pongas being a Memoir of the Rev. Hamble James Leacock, Leader of the West Indian Mission to Western Africa. London: Rivingtons, 1857. NN/Sch

4269. Coke, Thomas, (bp.). A History of the West Indies; Containing the natural, civil, and ecclesiastical history of each island; with an account of the missions instituted in those islands, from the commencement of their civilization; but more especially of the Missions which have been established in that Archipelago by the Society late in connexion with the Rev. John Wesley...Liverpool: Printed by Nuttal, Fisher & Dixon, 1808.
DHU/MO; NN/Sch

4270. Comitas, Lambros, (comp.). Slaves, Free Men, Citizens: West Indian Perspectives. Garden City, N. Y.: Anchor Books, 1973. T Sew U-T
Social conditions in West Indies.

4271. The Conference: or, Sketches of Wesleyan Methodism. In two parts. By the author of "Amusements of a Mission,"...Bridgeton, West N.J.: J. Clarke, 1824. DHU/MO
Part II contains short sections on bringing God to the blacks of South and West Africa and the slaves of the West Indies.

4272. Conrad, Robert Edgar. The Struggle for the Abolition of the Brazilian Slave Trade, 1808-1853. Doctoral dissertation. Columbia Univ., 1967.

4273. Degler, Carl N. Neither Black Nor White; Slavery and Race Relations in Brazil and the United States. New York: Macmillan, 1971. T Sew U-T

4274. Drew, Samuel. The Life of the Rev. Thomas Coke. Including in detail his various travels and extraordinary missionary exertions, in England, Ireland, America, and the West Indies. New York: Published by T. Manson and G. Lane, for the Methodist Episcopal Church, at the Conference Office, 200 Mulberry Street; J. Collord, printer, 1837. NN/Sch

4275. Edwards, Bryan. History of the British Colonies in the West Indies. London: Stockdale, 1793-1801. DHU/MO; NN/Sch
Book 4, Chapters 3, 4 and 5 deals with religion of the First Slaves.

4276. Eliot, Edward. Christianity and Slavery; in a Course of Lectures Preached at the Cathedral and Parish Church of St. Michael, Barbados. London: J. Hatchard, 1833. NNCor

4277. Freyre, Gilberto. The Masters and the Slaves, A Study in the Development of Brazilian Civilization. New York: Knopf, 1964.
DHU/R
Catholicism and the slave in Brazil, pp. 358-99.

4278. Handler, Jerome S. The Unappropriated People: Freedmen in the Slave Society of Barbados. Baltimore: John Hopkins University Press, 1974.
DHU/R

4279. Hibbert, Robert, Jr., (ed.). Facts Verified Upon Oath in Contradiction of the Report of the Rev. Thomas Cooper Concerning the General Condition of Slaves in Jamaica and ...Relative to the...Treatment of Slaves Upon Georgia Estate. London: Murray, 1824. LU; CtY; NIC; NNC; TNF; TxU; NN

4280. Hovey, Sylvester. Letters from the West Indies Relating Especially to the Danish Island St. Croix, and the British Islands Antigua, Barbadoes and Jamaica. New York: Gould and Newman, 1838.
NN/Sch

4281. Jesse, C. "Religion Among the Early Slaves in the French Antilles." Journal of the Barbados Museum and Historical Society (28:1, Nov., 1960), pp. 4-10.
NN

4282. Klingberg, Frank J. (ed.). Codrington Chronicle: An Experiment in Anglican Alturism on a Barbados Plantation, 1710-1834. Berkeley and Los Angeles: University of California Press, 1949.   NN/Sch; DHU/MO

4283. Knibb, William. Facts and Documents Connected in the Late Insurrection in Jamaica, and the Violations of Civil and Religious Liberty Originating Out of It. London: Holdsworth & Ball, 1832.   DLC

4284. ----- and Peter Borthwick. Colonial Slavery. Defence of the Baptist Missionaries from the Charge of Inciting the Late Rebellion in Jamaica. A Discussion Dec. 15, 1832, at Bath. London: Published at the Tourist Office, 1832.   DLC

4285. Laing, Samuel. Slaveholding Missionaries. Correspondence of Mr. S. Laing, With the Secretary of the Edinburgh Association in Aid of the United Brethren's (Moravian) Missions, on Their Holding Slaves in the Danish West Indies Islands. Edinburgh: Printed by W. Forrester, 1844.   NN/Sch

4286. Latimer, James. "The Foundations of Religious Education in the French West Indies." Journal of Negro Education (40:1, Wint., 1970), pp. 91-98.   DHU/R; DHU/MO

4287. ----- "The Foundations of Religious Education in the Spanish West Indies." Journal of Negro Education (39:1, Wint., 1970), pp. 70-75.   DHU/R; DHU/MO

4288. Linde, J. M. van der. "De Emancipatie der Negerslaven in Suriname en de Zendingsarbeid der Moravische Broeders." West-Indische Gids (34; 1953), pp. 23-37.   NNC

4289. May, Samuel Joseph. Address of Rev. Mr. May, on Emancipation in the British West Indies; Delivered in the First Presbyterian Church in Syracuse, August 1, 1845. Syracuse: J. Barber, 1845.   DHU/MO

4290. Murray, William. "Christianity in the West Indies." Philip Schaff and S. L. Prime. Evangelical Alliance Sixth General Conference. Held in New York Oct. 2-12, 1873 (New York: Harper & Bros., 1874), pp. 133-36. DHU/R

4291. Nisbet, Richard. The Capacity of Negroes for Religious and Moral Improvement, considered; With Cursory Hints, to Proprietors and to Government, for the Immediate Melioration of the Condition of Slaves in the Sugar Colonies. London: James Philips, 1789.   DLC

4292. Oldendorp, Christian Georg Andreas. C. G. A. Oldendorps Geschichte der Mission der Evangelischen Bruder auf den Cariabischen Inseln S. Thomas. S. Croix und S. Jan Herausgegben durch Johann Jakob Bossart... Barby: Bey C. F. Laux, und in Leipzig in Commission bey Weidmanns Erben und Reich, 1777.   NN/Sch

4293. Pitman, Frank Wesley. "Slavery on British West India Plantations in the Eighteenth Century." Journal of Negro History (11:4, Oct., 1926), pp. 584-660.   DHU
      Religious instruction of the slaves.

4294. Porter, Dorothy B. "The Negro in the Brazilian Abolition Movement." Journal of Negro History (37; Ja., 1952), pp. 54-80.   DHU/MO

4295. Ramos, Arthur. ...Las Culturas Negras en el Nuevo Mundo; Version Espoñola de Ernestina de Champourcín, Glosario de Voces. Mexico: Fondo de Cultura Economica, 1943.   NcD

4296. Ramsay, James. An Essay on the Treatment and Conversion of African Slaves on the British Sugar Colonies. London: J. Phillips, 1784.   DLC; FSU

4297. Riot in Barbadoes, and Destruction of the Wesleyan Chapel and Mission House. London: J. & T. Clarke, Printers, St. John-Square, 1823.   NN/Sch

4298. Robb, Alexander. Gospel to the Africans: A Narrative of the Life and Labours of the Rev. William Jameson in Jamaica and Old Calabar. By his son-in-law, the Rev. Alex. Robb. Edinburgh: Elliot, 1861.   NN; PPM; CtY

4299. Rose, George Henry. ...A Letter on the Means and Importance of Converting the Slaves in the West Indies to Christianity. By the Rt. Hon. Sir G. H. Rose. London: J. Murray, 1823.   NN/Sch

4300. Shirmer, Charles Frederic. Account for the Mission Established by the Protestant Church of the United Brethren Among the Negroes in Tobago. Extracted from the Reports and Diaries of the Missionary, Received by the Secretary of the Brethren's Society for the Furtherance of the Gospel Among the Heathen in the Year 1799. London: Printed by J. Marshall, 1799.   NN/Sch

4301. Smith, Robert W. "Slavery and Christianity in the British West Indies." Church History (19:3, Sept., 1950), pp. 171-86.   DHU/R

4302. Society for the Conversion and Religious Instruction and Education of Negro Slaves in the British West Indian Islands. n.p., n.d.   DHU/MO

4303. Truman, George. Narrative of a Visit to the West Indies, in 1840 and 1841. By George Truman, John Jackson and Thos. B. Longstreth. Philadelphia: Merrihew and Thompson, Printers, 1844.   NN/Sch
      A missionary journey by members of the Society of Friends to various islands of the Lesser Antilles. Slavery in the West Indies.

4304. Vernon, B. J. History of Jamaica. London: J. Hodges, 1790.   DLC
      pp. 306-38. Religion of the first Africans brought to this country.

4305. Watson, Richard. A Defense of the Wesleyan Methodist Missions in the West Indies: Including a Refutation of the Charges in Mr. Marryat's "Thoughts on the Abolition of the Slave Trade" and in Other Publications; With Facts and Anecdotes Illustrative of the Moral State of the Slaves, and of the Operation of Missions. London: T. Cordeux, 1817. NNCor
      Slavery and the Methodist Church.

4306. ----- The Religious Instruction of the Slaves in the West-India Colonies Advocated and Defended. A Sermon ... London: Printed for J. Butterworth and J. Kershaw, 1825. NNCor

4307. ----- Sermons and Sketches of Sermons... New York: Pub. by T. Mason and G. Lane, for Methodist Episcopal Church, 1838.   NN/Sch

4308. Weiss, H. "One Suriname;" Handbook Voor Zendingsstudie. Den Hang: Boekhandel van den Zendings-Studie-Raad, 1911.   NN/Sch

4309. West Indian Mission. Prepared for the American Sunday School Union and Revised by the Committee of Publication. Philadelphia: American Sunday-School Union, 1834. NN/Sch

4310. West Indian Societies for the Instruction and Christian Education of the Negro Slaves. Bristol: Wright and Bagnall, n.d.   DHU/MO

4311. Wilberforce, William. An Appeal to the Religion, Justice, and Humanity of the Inhabitants of the British Empire, in Behalf of the Negro Slaves in the West Indies. London: Printed for J. Hatchard & Son, 1823.   DHU/MO

B. RELIGIOUS INSTRUCTION OF THE SLAVES

4312. Adger, John Bailey. The Religious Instruction of the Colored Population. A Sermon, Preached by the Rev. John Adger, in the Second Presbyterian Church, Charleston, S. C., May 9th, 1847. Published by request. Charleston: T. W. Haynes, 1847.   CtY-D; NcD

4313. An Address to the Presbyterians of Kentucky, Proposing a Plan for the Instruction and Emancipation of Their Slaves, By a Committee of the Synod of Kentucky. Newburyport: Whipple, 1836.   NcD

4314. Association for the Religious Instruction of the Negroes in Liberty County, Ga. Ninth Annual Report of the Association... Together with the Address to the Association by the President the Rev. Robert Quarterman. Savannah: T. Purse, 1844.
                              NNCor

4315. Bacon, Thomas. Four Sermons Preached at the Parish Church of St. Peter in Talbot County, in the Province of Maryland, Two Sermons on Black Slaves, and two for the Benefit of a Charity Working-School, in the Above Parish, For the Maintenance and Education of Orphans and Poor Children, and Negroes. London: Printed by J. Oliver, 1753. Reprinted at Bath, by R. Cruttwell, 1783.   DLC

4316. ----- Four Sermons. Upon the Great and Indispensible Duty of all Christian Masters and Mistresses to Bring up their Negro Slaves in the Knowledge and Fear of God. London: J. Oliver, 1750.   DLC

4317. Barker, S. C. "A Sermon to Servants." Lettie J. Austin. The Black Man and the Promise of America (Glenview, Ill.: Scott, Foreman & Co., 1970), pp. 32-37. DHU; DCU/HU
    Printed from Harper's Magazine (20:175, Dec. 1864), pp. 664-66.   DHU

4318. Bearcroft, Phillip. Sermon. London: Willis, 1738. IC/H
    A sermon dealing with the conversion of Negro slaves to the Christian faith.

4319. Bible. Parts of the Holy Bible, Selected for the Use of Negro Slaves in the British-West India Islands. London: Printed by Law and Gilbert, 1808.   TNF

4320. Bolton, S. C. "South Carolina and the Reverend Doctor Francis Le Jau: Southern Society and the Conscience of an Anglican Missionary." Historical Magazine of the Protestant Episcopal Church (40:1, Mr., 1971), pp. 63-79.   DHU/R
    "Religious instruction to Negro Slaves and Indians."

4321. Bruce, J. G. A Sermon on the Duty of Instructing Slaves. Delivered Sabbath Evening, August 23, 1846. Georgetown: Wise, 1846.   NcD; DLC

4322. Bruner, Clarence Vernon. The Religious Instruction of the Slaves in the Antebellum South. Doctoral dissertation. George Peabody College, 1933.   NcD; DLC

4323. Burger, Nash Kerr. "A Side-light on an Ante-Bellum Plantation Chapel." Historical Magazine of the Protestant Episcopal Church (12; 1943), p. 69.   DLC

4324. Campbell, Alexander. "Queries on Master's Duties." The Millenial Harbinger (21; Sept., 1851), p. 529. TN/DCHS; CtY

4325. A Catcehism for the Religious Instruction of Persons of Color. Charleston: Printed for the author, 1844. NN/Sch; NcD
    "The subjects have been treated in accordance with the views of the Protestant Episcopal Church."

4326. Charleston, S. C. Committee of Fifty on Calvary Church. Public Proceedings. Relating to Calvary Church and the Religious Instruction of Slaves. Published by Order of Council. Charleston, S. C.: Printed by Miller & Browne, 1850. CLU

4327. Charleston, S. C. Meeting on Religious Instruction of Negroes. Proceedings of the Meeting in Charleston, S. C., May

13-15, 1845, on the Religious Instruction of the Negroes, Together with the Report of the Committee, and the Address to the Public. Pub. by Order of the Meeting. Charleston, S. C.: Pr. by B. Jenkins, 1845.   DLC; NN/Sch
    Daniel E. Huger, chairman of the meeting and of the standing committee.

4328. Child, Lydia Maria (Francis). Anti-Slavery Catechism. Newburyport: C. Whipple, 1839.   CtY-D

4329. Clark, Elmer Talmage. ...The Negro and His Religion... Nashville: Cokesbury Press, 1924.   DLC; NN/Sch
    Reprinted from "Healing Ourselves; the First Task of the Church in America."

4330. Clerical Teachings on Slavery. n.p.: n.p., 1850? NNCor

4331. Cohen, Sheldon S. "Elias Neau, 1662-1722, Instructor to New York's Slaves." New York Historical Society Quarterly (55:1, Jan., 1972), pp. 7-27. DGU; CU; CtY; DLC; IU; MH; NN; TxU

4332. Davies, Samuel. The Duty of Christians to Propagate their Religion among Heathens, Earnestly Recommended to the Masters of Negroe Slaves in Virginia. A Sermon Preached in Hanover, January 8, 1757. London: Pr. by J. Oliver, 1758.
                              DLC

4333. Dickson, Andrew Flinn. Plantation Sermons, or, Plain and Familiar Discourses for the Unlearned. Philadelphia: Presbyterian Board of Publication, 1856. DHU/MO; DLC; NcD

4334. "The Established Virginia Church and the Conversion of Negroes and Indians, 1620-1760." Journal of Negro History (46:1, Jan., 1961), pp. 12-23.   DHU/MO

4335. Fickling, Susan Maria Markey. Slave-Conversion in South Carolina, 1830-1860. Columbia, S. C.: University of South Carolina, 1924.   DHU/MO; DLC

4336. Fisk University. Social Science Institute. God Struck Me Dead: Religious Conversion Experiences and Autobiographies of Negro Ex-Slaves. Nashville: Social Science Institute, 1945. DCU; DLC; CtY-D; NN/Sch

4337. Fleetwood, William, (bp.). A Sermon Preached Before the Society for the Propagation of the Gospel in Foreign Parts, at the Parish Church of St. Mary-le-Bow, on Friday, the 16th of February... London: Joseph Downing, 1711. DLC; MH; IU; NcD
    Criticises owners who would not permit their slaves to receive Christian instruction.

4338. Gibson, Edmund. A Letter of the Lord Bishop of London to the Masters and Mistresses of Families in the English Plantations Abroad. Exhorting Them to Encourage and Promote the Instruction of Their Negroes in the Christian Faith. London: n. p., 1727.   DLC; NN/Sch

4339. Glennie, Alexander. Sermons Preached on Plantations to Congregations of Negroes. Charleston: A. B. Hiller, 1844.
                              NN/Sch; NcD; DHU/R

4340. [Godwin, Morgan] Trade Preferr'd Before Religion and Christ Made to Give Place to Mammon: Represented in a Sermon Relating to the Plantations. London: B. Took, 1685.
                              CtY; DLC

4341. ----- Some Proposals Toward Propagating of the Gospel in Our American Plantations ... To which is Prefixed Mr. Morgan Godwin's Brief Account of Religion in the Plantations. With the Causes of Neglect and Decay thereof in Those Parts. London: G. Sawbridge, 1708.   DLC
    "On the Duty of Giving Religious Instruction to Slaves."

4342. ----- The Happy Negro; Being a True Account of a Very Extraordinary Negro in North America, and of an Interesting

(...The Happy Negro, cont.)

Conversation He Had With a Very Respectable Gentleman
From England. To Which is Added, The Grateful Negro.
London: Printed by W. Clowes for the Religious Tract Society,
1830.   NN/Sch; DHU/MO; TNF

4343. Greene, Lorenzo J. "Slaveholding New England and Its
Awakening Conversion of the Slaves." Journal of Negro History
(13:4, Oct., 1923), pp. 492-533.   DHU

4344. Grout, L. "Religious Instruction of Negroes." New England
Magazine (42; 1883), p. 723.   DLC

4345. Harrison, William Pope. The Gospel Among the Slaves.
A Short Account of Missionary Operations Among the African
Slaves of the Southern States. Compiled from original sources
and edited by W. P. Harrison... Nashville, Tenn.: Publishing
House of the M. E. Church, South, 1893. NcD; DHU/MO; DLC

4346. Hayden, J. Carleton. "Conversion and Control: Dilemma
of Episcopalians in Providing for the Religious Instructions of
Slaves, Charleston, South Carolina, 1845-1860." Historical
Magazine of the Protestant Episcopal Church (40:2, Je., 1971),
pp. 143-71.   DHU/R
   Negro author.

4347. Hoff, John F. Manual of Religious Instruction; Specially
Intended for the Oral Teaching of Colored Persons but Adapted
to the General Use in Families and Schools. Richmond, Va.:
P. B. Price, 1857.   DHU/MO; NcD

4348. "Instruction of Slaves." Christian Spectator (8:2, Feb.,
1826), p. 102.   DHU/R
   Effects of Missionary efforts on "liberated Africans."

4349. Jackson, James Conroy. "The Religious Education of the
Negro in South Carolina Prior to 1850." Historical Magazine
(36:1, Mr., 1967), pp. 35-61.   DHU/R

4350. Jackson, Luther P. "Religious Development of the Negro
in Virginia from 1760-1860." Journal of Negro History (16:2,
Apr., 1931), pp. 168-239.   DHU

4351. ----- "Religious Instruction of Negroes, 1830-1860 with
Special Reference to South Carolina." Journal of Negro History
(15:1, Ja., 1930), pp. 72-114.   DHU

4352. Jernegan, Marcus W. "Slavery and Conversion in the American Colonies." American Historical Review (21:3, Apr.,
1916), pp. 504-27.   DHU

4353. Jones, Charles Colcock. A Catechism for Colored Persons.
Charleston: Observer Office Press, 1834.   NcD

4354. ----- A Catechism of Scripture and Practice for Families
and Sabbath Schools Designed also for the Oral Instruction
of Coloured Persons. Philadelphia: Presbyterian Board of
Publication, 1852.   NcD

4355. ----- The Religious Instruction of the Negroes. A Sermon,
Delivered Before Associations of Planters in Liberty and
M'Intosh Counties, Georgia, by the Rev. Charles Colcock
Jones,... Princeton, N. J.: D'Hart & Connolly, 1832.   NcD

4356. ----- The Religious Instruction of the Negroes in the United
States. Savannah: T. Purse, 1842. DHU/R; NN/Sch; NcD
   Reprinted 1969, Kraus Reprint Co.

4357. ----- Suggestions on the Religious Instruction of the Negroes
in the Southern States: Together With an Appendix Containing
Forms of Church Registers, Form of a Constitution, and Plans
of Different Denomination of Christians. Philadelphia: Presbyterian Board Publication, 1847.   NcD; NN/Sch

4358. Jones, Jerome W. "The Established Virginia Church and the
Conversion of Negroes and Indians 1620-1760." Journal of
Negro History (46:1, Ja., 1961), pp. 12-23.   DHU

4359. Knight, Edgar Wallace. A Documentary History of Education
in the South Before 1860... Chapel Hill: University of North
Carolina Press, 1949-53.   NN/Sch

4360. Knox, William. Three Tracts Respecting the Conversion
and Instruction of the Free Indians and Negro Slaves in the
Colonies. London: n.p., 1768.   DHU/MO

4361. Letters Respecting a Book, "Dropped From the Catalogue"
of the American Sunday School Union... New York: American
and Foreign Anti-Slavery Society. William Harned, Pub.
Agent... 1848.

4362. Mallard, Robert. Plantation Life Before Emancipation.
Richmond, Va.: Whittet & Shepperson, 1892.   NN/Sch

4363. Mather, Cotton. The Negro Christianized. An Essay to
Excite and Assist that Good Work, the Instruction of Negro
Servants in Christianity... Boston: Printed by B. Green,
1706.   MHU/H

4364. McTyeire, H. N. Duties of Masters to Servants. A History
of Methodism. Nashville, Tenn.: n.p., 1884.   NN/Sch

4365. Meade, William. Pastoral Letter... on the Duty of Affording
Religious Instruction to those in Bondage. Delivered in the
year 1834-. Reprinted by the Convocation of Central Virginia
in 1853. Richmond: Ellyson, 1853. In his sermons, V. 2,
no. 4.   NcD

4366. ----- Sermons, Dialogues and Narratives for Servants, to
be Read to them in Families; Abridged Altered, and Adapted
to their Condition, Chiefly by the Right Rev. William Meade,
D. D. Richmond: Southern Churchman, 1836.   NcD

4367. Noel, Baptist W. Freedom and Slavery in the United States
of America. Westport, Conn.: Negro Universities Press,
1970.   DHU/R
   Reprint of 1863 edition. Chapter 2, Section 5: "Opposition
   to Religious Instruction" (for slaves).

4368. Palmer, Benjamin M. A Plain and Easy Catechism Designed
Chiefly for the Benefit of Coloured Persons, to Which Are Annexed Suitable Prayers and Hymns. Charleston, S. C.: Observer Office Press, 1828.   GU

4369. Pascoe, C. F. Two Hundred Years of the Society for the
Propagation of the Gospel. 2 Vols. London: n.p., 1901.

4370. Pennington, Edgar Legare. The Reverend Francis Le Jau's
Work Among Indians and Negro Slaves. Baton Rouge: Franklin
Press, 1935?   NN/Sch; DHU
   "Reprinted from the Journal of Southern History (1:4, Nov.,
   1935)."

4371. ----- ...Thomas Bray's Associates, and Their Work among
the Negroes... Worcester, Mass.: The Society, 1939. DHU/MO
NN/Sch

4372. Perkins, Haven P. "Religion for Slaves: Difficulties and
Methods." Church History (10:3, Sept., 1941), pp. 228-45.
                                         DHU/R

4373. Pierre, C. E. "The Work of the Society for the Propagation
of the Gospel in Foreign Parts Among the Negroes in the Colonies." Journal of Negro History (1:4, Oct., 1916), pp. 349-60.
                                         DHU/MO

4374. Plumer, William Swan. Thoughts on the Religious Instruction
of the Negroes of this Country. First Published in the Princeton
Review. Princeton, N. J.: Printed by J. T. Robinson, 1848.
                              DLC; NcD; NN/Sch; CLU

4375. Protestant Episcopal Church in the U. S. A. Diocese of
Virginia. Journal of Sixty-Fifth Annual Convention, 1860.
Richmond: n.p., 1860.   DLC
   Report of a committee appointed to ascertain the provisions
   to be made to instruct Negroes in religion and determine
   the best way to keep them in the church.

4376. Raymond, Charles A. "The Religious Life of the Negro Slave." Harper's Monthly (27; 1863), pp. 479-88+; 676-82; 816-25. DAU

4377. "Religion Among Slaves." Christian Spectator (12:3, Dec., 1821), pp. 656-57. DGU
"From the London Methodist Magazine, being extracts from Mr. Hyde's Journal, dated Parham, Antigua, May 7, 1821."

4378. The Religious Instruction of the Black Population. n.p.:n.p., 1847. NNUT; NcD
"Extracted from The Southern Presbyterian Review."

4379. Religious Instruction of the Slaves. London: Ellerton and Henderson, n.d. DHU/MO

4380. Reynolds, Grant. Religious Education of the Negro During the Colonial Period. New York: n. p., n. d. NN/Sch
Negro Author

4381. Richmond, Legh. The African Servant; an Authentic Narrative. New York: American Tract Society. (Publication no. 53.) NN/Sch

4382. Ryland, Robert. The Scriptural Catechism for Colored People, the Church Members Guide. Richmond: Harrold & Murry, 1948. DLC

4383. Sims, Charles F. The Religious Education of the Southern Negroes. Doctoral dissertation. Southern Baptist Theological Seminary, 1926.

4384. Singleton, George Arnett. Religious Instruction of the Negro in the United States Before the Rebellion. Masters thesis. University of Chicago, 1929.
Negro author.

4385. "A Slave Catechism." Leslie H. Fishel, Jr. and Benjamin Quarles, (eds.). The Black American, A Documentary History (New York: Morrow, 1970), p. 114. DHU/R; DHU/MO

4386. Smedes, Susan Dabney, (ed.). Memorials of a Southern Planter. New York: James Pott and Co., 1900. DHU/MO
Pro-Slavery argument, pictures of a good master giving moral and religious training to his slaves.

4387. Stowe, Charles E. "The Religion of Slavery." The Crisis (5:1, Nov., 1912), pp. 36-8. DLC; DHU/MO

4388. Thornwell, James Henley. A Review of Rev. J. B. Adger's Sermon on the Religious Instruction of the Coloured Population. Charleston, S. C.: Burges, James and Paxton, Printers, 1847. NcD

4389. ----- The Rights and the Duties of Masters. A Sermon Preached at the Dedication of a Church Erected in Charleston, S. C., for the Benefit and Instruction of the Coloured Population. Charleston, S. C.: Press of Walker & James, 1850. NcD; NN/Sch

4390. Trew, J. M. An Appeal to Christian Philanthropy of the People of Great Britian and Ireland, in Behalf of the Religious Instructions and Conversion of Three Hundred Thousand Negro Slaves. London: M. Richardson, Cornhill, 1826. DHU/MO

4391. Vibert, Faith. "The Society for the Propagation of the Gospel in Foreign Parts: Its Work for the Negroes in North America Before 1783." Journal of Negro History (18:2, Apr., 1933), pp. 171-212. DHU/MO

4392. Wilson, J. Leighton. "Religious Instruction of the Colored People." The Southern Presbyterian Review (16; Oct., 1863), pp. 190+. DLC; NjP

C. SLAVERY AND BIBLICAL INTERPRETATION

4393. "Alexander Campbell and James Hartzell Interpret the Bible on Slavery." The Iliff Review (30:1, Wint., 1972), pp. 59-71. Pam. File, DHU/R

4394. Allen Isaac. Is Slavery Sanctioned by the Bible? A Premium Tract of the American Tract Society. Boston: American Tract Society, 1860. DLC; CtY-D; NcD

4395. American Reform Tract and Book Society. The Bible Gives No Sanction to Slavery, by a Tennessean. Cincinnati, O.: American Reform Tract and Book Society, n. d. DHU/MO

4396. American Reform Tract and Book Society. Hebrew Servitude and American Slavery. Cincinnati, O.: American Reform Tract and Book Society, n. d. DHU/MO
Tract no. 2. Pamphlets on Slavery and Christianity, V. 2.

4397. American Reform Tract and Book Society. Slavery and the Bible. Cincinnati, O.: American Reform Tract and Book Society, n. d. DHU/MO

4398. American Reform Tract and Book Society. A Tract for Sabbath Schools. Cincinnati, O.: American Reform Tract and Book Society, n. d. DHU/MO
Tract No. 7. On Evils of Slavery and Christianity, Pamphlets on Slavery and Christianity, vol. 11.

4399. An Ancient Landmark, or The Essential Element of Civil and Religious Liberty: Dedicated to the Young Men of New England. By a Pastor. Middletown: C. H. Pelton, 1838. DHU/MO
Pamphlets on Slavery and the Church.

4400. Armstrong, George Dodd. The Christian Doctrine of Slavery. New York: Negro Universities Press, 1969. DLC; DHU/R; DHU/MO; CtY-D
Reprint of the 1857 ed.

4401. Atkins, Thomas. African Slavery. A Reply to the Letter of Bishop Hopkins, of Vermont on This Important Subject. New York: W. C. Green, n. d. DHU/MO

4402. ----- American Slavery Just Published: A Reply to the Letter of Bishop Hopkins of Vermont, on this Important Subject. New York: Scobell, n. d. DHU/MO

4403. Bacon, Leonard. The Higher Law. A Sermon Preached on Thanksgiving Day, Nov. 27, 1851. New Haven: B. L. Hamlen, 1851.

4404. ----- "Noah's Prophecy: Cursed be Cannan." The New Englander (21; Apr., 1862), pp. 341-61. DCU/ST; DHU

4405. Barnes, Albert. An Inquiry into the Scriptural Views of Slavery. Philadelphia: Perkins and Purves, 1846. DHU/MO

4406. Barnes, William. American Slavery. A Sermon, Preached at Hampton, Conn., Apr. 14, 1843, the Day of the Annual Public Fast. Hartford: Elihu Geer, 1843. DLC

4407. Barrow, David. Involuntary, Unmerited, Perpetual, Absolute, Hereditary Slavery Examined, on Principles of Nature, Reason, Justice, Policy and Scripture. Lexington: D. & C. Bradford, 1808. NcD; NIC

4408. Bartlett, T. R. The Black Apostle; Ancient Biblical History of the Black of Negro Race, Proven by the Holy Bible...by J. Justice (Pseud.) Shreveport: Shreveport Journal, 1946. DHU/MO

4409. Baxter, Richard. Baxter's Directions to Slave-Holders, Revived; First Printed in London in the Year 1673. To which is subjoined, a letter From the Worthy Anthony Benezet ... to the Celebrated Abbe Raynal ... Philadelphia: F. Baily, 1785. NNCor

4410. ----- A Christian Directory: Or, a Summary of Practical
Theologie, and Cases of Conscience. London: n.p., 1673.
                                                        DLC

4411. Beecher, Charles. The God of the Bible Against Slavery.
New York: American Anti-Slavery Society, 1855. CtY-D

4412. Berdiaev, Nikolai Aleksandrovich. Slavery and Freedom.
London: G. Bles, the Centenary Press, 1943.   DLC
Philosophical account of effect of slavery on human nature.

4413. Bible. English. Selections. Scripture Evidence of the
Sinfulness of Injustice and Oppression. Respectfully submitted
to Professing Christians, in Order to Call Forth their Sympathy
and Exertions, on Behalf of the Much-Injured Africans. London: Harvey and Darton, 1828.   NN/Sch

4414. The Bible on the Present Crisis. The Republic of the United
States, and its Counterfeit Presentment; the Slave Power and the
Southern Confederacy; the Copperhead Organization and the
Knight of the Golden Circle; the Civil War in Which They are
Involved, its Duration and Final Results, Described in Daniel
and the Revelations, and Other Prophecies of the Old and New
Testaments. New York: S. Tousey, 1863.   CtY-D; DHU/MO

4415. The Bible View of Slavery Reconsidered. Letter to the Right
Rev. Bishop Hopkins. Philadelphia: Henry B. Ashmead, 1863.
                                                        NcD

4416. Birney, James Gillespie. Letter to Ministers and Elders,
on the Sin of Holding Slaves and the Duty of Immediate Emancipation. Mercer County, Ky.; Sept. 2, 1834. New York:
S. W. Benedict & Co., 1834.   DHU/MO

4417. ----- The Sinfulness of Slaveholding in all Circumstances;
Tested by Reason and Scripture. Detroit: C. Wilcox, 1846.
                                                        DHU/MO

4418. Bolles, John R. A Reply to Bishop Hopkins' View of Slavery,
and a Review of the Times. Philadelphia: J. W. Daughaday,
1865.   NN/Sch

4419. Booth, Abraham. Commerce in the Human Species, and the
Enslaving of Innocent Persons, Inimical to the Laws of Moses,
and the Gospel of Christ. A Sermon Preached in the Little
Prescot Street, Goodman's Fields, London, Ja. 29, 1792.
Philadelphia: Reprinted and sold by Daniel Lawrence, 1792.
                            NmU; PPu; PPULC

4420. Bourne, George. The Book and Slavery Irreconcilable.
With Animodversions Upon Dr. Smith's Philosophy. Philadelphia: J. M. Sanderson & Co., 1816. DHU/MO; NN/Sch

4421. ----- A Condensed Anti-Slavery Bible Argument, by a Citizen of Virginia. New York: S. W. Benedict, 1845. DHU/MO;
NN/Sch; CtY-D

4422. Bradley, L. Richard. "The Curse of Canaan and the American Negro." Concordia Theological Monthly (42:2, Feb.,
1971), pp. 100-10.   DHU/R

4423. Brisbane, William Henry. Slaveholding Examined in the
Light of the Holy Bible. New York: The American and Foreign
Anti-Slavery Society, 1849.   NN/Sch; DHU/MO

4424. ----- Speech of the Rev. Wm. H. Brisbane, Lately a Slaveholder in South Carolina; Containing an Account of the Change in
his Views on the Subject of Slavery. Delivered before the Ladies
Anti-Slavery Society of Cincinnati, February 12, 1840. Hartford:
S. S. Cowles, 1840.   DHU/MO; NN/Sch

4425. Brooke, Samuel. Slavery and the Slave-Holder's Religion;
as Opposed to Christianity. Cincinnati: the Author, 1845.
                                    DHU/MO; DLC

4426. Broomfield, Gerald Webb. The Chosen People or the Bible,
Christianity and Race. London: Longmans, Green & Co., 1954.
                                                        DHU/MO

A study to re-examine what the Bible and Christianity says
about racial distinction.

4427. Buckingham, G. The Bible Vindicated from the Charge of
Sustaining Slavery. Columbus: Temperance Advocated Office,
1837.   CtY

4428. Buswell, James Oliver. Slavery, Segregation, and Scriptures. Grand Rapids: Eerdmans, 1964.   DHU/R; NN/Sch;
CtY-D

4429. Cannon, Noah Calwell. The Rock of Wisdom; an Explanation
of the Sacred Scripture. To Which are Added Several Interesting Hymns. n.p., 1833. NN/Sch; TNF; ICN; DHU/MO; NN/Sch

4430. Capitein, Jacobus Eliza Johannes. Is Slavery Contrary to
Christian Freedom or Not? Leyden, Amsterdam: [sic]
Phillippos Bonk by Gerritt de Groot, 1742. Rare Book, DHU/MO
Written by an African, educated and ordained a minister in
Amsterdam, 1742. Theological professor and minister,
Elimina Castle, Ghana, West Africa.

4431. Chautard, Leon. Escape from Cayenne... Salem, Mass.:
Printed the Observer Office, 1857.   DHU/MO
Contains a brief discussion of slavery as a destruction of
God's work.

4432. Cheever, George Barrell. The Comission from God, of
the Missionary Enterprise, Against the Sin of Slavery; and the
Responsibility on the Church and Ministry for its Fulfilment.
An Address, Delivered in Tremont Temple, Boston, Thursday,
May 27th, 1858. Before the American Missionary Association.
Boston, J. P. Jewett, 1858.   CtY-D; DLC
Tracts for thinking men and women, no. 3.

4433. ----- The Curse of God Against Atheism. Boston: Walker,
1859.   IC/H
A discourse on the duties of Christians in regard to slavery
and some lessons on God's law against the sin of slaveholding.

4434. The Child's Book on Slavery or Slavery Made Plain. Cincinnati: American Reform Tract and Book Society, 1857.
                                                        DHU/MO
"Slavery goes against the Bible and many Biblical passages
are given as examples."

4435. "Christianity and War." The Christian Review (26; Oct.
1861), pp. 603.   ICT; IEG
Old and New Testament as well as religion support the Union
in this war against slavery.

4436. Christy, David. Cotton Is King: or, The Culture of Cotton,
and Its Relation to Agriculture, Manufactures and Commerce;
to the Free Colored People; and to Those Who Hold that Slavery
Is in Itself Sinful; by an American. Cincinnati: Moore, Wil-
stach, Keys & Co. 1855.   DHU/MO

4437. Clebsch, William A. Christian Interpretations of the Civil
War. Philadelphia: Fortress Press, 1969. MNtcA

4438. Cobb, Howell. A Scriptural Examination of the Institution
of Slavery in the United States. Georgia: Printed for the
Author, 1856.   DLC

4439. Coleman, Elihu. A Testimony Against that Anti-Christian
Practice of Making Slaves of Men ... New Bedford: n.p., 1733.
                                                NN/Sch; INRE
    Reprinted by A. Shearman, 1825.

4440. Colver, Nathaniel. The Fugitive Slave Bill; or God's Laws
Paramount to the Laws of Men. A Sermon, Preached on Sun-
day, October 20, 1850... Pub. by Request of the Church.
Boston: J. W. Howes & Co., 1850.   NN/Sch; DHU/MO

4441. Conrad, F. W. "The Hand of God in the War." The Evangelical Quarterly Review (16, Apr., 1865), pp. 225.   DLC

4442. Cox, Francis Augustus. The Scriptural Duty of Churches in Relation to Slaveholders Professing Christianity. London: T. Ward, 1841.   NNCor

4443. Cronan, Edward P. The Dignity of the Human Person. New York: Philosophical Library, 1955.   DLC

4444. Dalcho, Frederick. Practical Considerations Founded on the Scriptures Relative to the Slave Population of South Carolina. Charleston, S.C.: A. E. Miller, 1823.
Minister of St. Michael's Episcopal Church in Charleston, S. C.

4445. Day, Norris. A Lecture Upon Bible Politics. ... Montpelier, Poland and Briggs, 1846.   DHU/MO

4446. De Bow, James Dunwoody Brownson. ...The Interest in Slavery of the Southern Non-Slaveholder. The Right of Peaceful Secession. Slavery in the Bible. Charleston: Evans & Cogswell, 1860. (1860 Association. Tracts no. 5).   NN/Sch

4447. Deeming, D. D. Anti-Spoonerism; or, The Reactionary Forces of the Negro. With a Scriptural View of the "Equality of Man." Also, Considerations on the Dogma of "Man Has No Property in Man." New York: Ross & Tousey, 1860.   CtY-D

4448. Dickey, James H. A Review of a Summary of Biblical Antiquities Compiled for the Use of Sunday School Teachers, and for the Benefit of Families, by John W. Nevin... Ripley: Pub. by the Abolition Society of Paint Valley. Printed by Campbell and Palmer, 1934.   DHU/MO

4449. Does The Bible Sanction Slavery? Pamphlets on Slavery and Christianity, V. 1.   DHU/MO; NN/Sch

4450. "Does the Bible Sustain Slavery?" The Christian Review (27; Oct., 1862), pp. 584+.   DLC

4451. "Domestic Slavery Considered as a Scriptural Institution." Southern Literary Messenger (11; Sept., 1845), p. 513.   IC/H

4452. Doulophilus. Slaveholding Proved to be Just and Right to a Demonstration From the Word of God. South Carolina: n.p., 1846.   DHU/MO
Pamphlets on Slavery and Christianity, V. 1.

4453. Drisler, H. A Reply on the "Bible View of Slavery, by J. H. Hopkins, D. D., Bishop of the Diocese of Vermont." Broadway: Loyal Publications Society, 1863.   NN/Sch; CtY-D; DHU/MO

4454. [Dudley, Miss Mary.]. Scripture Evidence of the Sinfulness of Injustice and Oppression; Respectfully Submitted to Professing Christians, in Order to Call Forth Their Sympathy and Exertions on Behalf of the Much Injured Africans. London: Harvey and Darton, 1828.   DHU/MO

4455. Duncan, James. A Treatise on Slavery. In which is Shown Forth the Evil of Slaveholding Both from the Light of Nature and Divine Revelation. Vevay: Indiana Register Office, 1824.   DHU/MO

4456. Eastman, Mary H. Aunt Phillis's Cabin or Southern Life As It Is. New York: Negro Universities Press, 1968.   DHU/R
Reprint of 1852 edition.
Scripture justification for slavery in the southern states.

4457. Easton, Hosea. An Address Delivered Before the Coloured Population, of Providence, Rhode Island on Thanksgiving Day, Nov. 28, 1828. Boston: David Hooton, 1828.   DLC

4458. Elliott, Charles. Sinfulness of American Slavery: Proved from the Wrongs; its Contrariety to Many Scriptural Commands, Prohibitions, and Principles and to the Christian Spirit; and From its Evil Effects; Together with Observations on Emancipation, and the Duties of American Citizens in Regard to Slavery ... ed. by Rev. B. F. Tefft... Cincinnati: Pub. by L. Swarmstedt & J. H. Power, 1851.   DHU/MO; CtY-D; A & M

4459. ----- The Bible and Slavery: In which the Abrahamic and Mosaic Discipline is Considered in Connection with the Most Ancient Forms of Slavery as Related to Roman Slavery and the Discipline of the Apostolic Churches... Cincinnati: L. Swarmstedt & A. Poe, 1857.   DHU/MO; CtY-D; NN/Sch

4460. Epps, Archie C. "The Christian Doctrine of Slavery: A Theological Analysis." Journal of Negro History (46:4, Oct., 1961), pp. 243-49.   DHU

4461. Esquisses de Doctrines Chrétiennes et Notes Introductives a quelques Livre du Nouveau Testment. Port-au-Prince: Imp. 'Etat, 1950.   DHU/MO

4462. An Essay on Slavery: Its Injustifiableness Proved from the Old and New Testament: the State of the Negro Slaves Investigated and an Equitable Plan for their Gradual Emancipation Proposed... By an Eye-witness. London: Pr. for John and Henry L. Hunt, 1824.   NN/Sch; DHU/MO

4463. Ethics of American Slavery, Being a Vindictication of the Word of God and Pure Christianity in all Ages, from Complicity with Involuntary Servitude and Demonstration that American Slavery is a Crime in Substance and Concomitants, by an American Citizen. New York: Ross and Tousey, 1861.   DHU/MO

4464. Evangelicus. Onesimus or the Directions to Christian Masters, in Reference to their Slaves, Considered. Boston: Gould, Kendall & Lincoln, 1942.   NcD; PU

4465. Ewart, David. A Scriptural View of the Moral Relations of African Slavery. Charleston, S. C.: Walker Evans & Co., 1859.   DLC

4466. Fee, John Gregg. Anti-Slavery Manual: or, The Wrongs of American Slavery Exposed by the Light of the Bible and of Facts; With a Remedy for the Evil... New York: William Harned, 1851.   DHU/MO

4467. ----- Non-Fellowship With Slaveholders the Duty of Christians. New York: John A. Gray, 1851.   DHU/MO

4468. ----- The Sinfulness of Slave-Holding Shown by Appeals to Reason and Scripture. New York: John A. Gray, 1851.   DHU/MO

4469. Fitzgerald, W. P. N. A Scriptural View of Slavery and Abolition. New Haven: n.p., 1839.   DHU/MO

4470. Fletcher, Thomas. The Question, "How Far is Slavery Prohibited by the Christian Religion and the Holy Scriptures?" Impartially examined. London: Robson, Blades & Co., Printers, 1828.   DLC

4471. Ford, Theodore P. God Wills the Negro; an Anthropological and Geographical Restoration of the Lost History of the American Negro People, Being in Part a Theological Interpretation of Egyptian and Ethiopian Backgrounds; comp. from Ancient and Modern Sources with a Special Chapter of Eight Negro Spirituals. Chicago: Geographical Inst. Press, 1939.   DHU/MO

4472. Friedel, Lawrence M. "Is the Curse of Ham on the Negro Race?" American Ecclesiastical Review (106; 1942), pp. 447-53.   DHU/R

4473. A Friend to Mankind. Argument from Scripture, For and Against the African Slave Trade, as Stated in a Series of Letters Lately Published in the Glasgow Courier. Glasgow: n.p., 1792.   DLC

4474. Frost, Maria Goodell. Gospel Fruits: or, Bible Christianity Illustrated; a Premium Essay... Cinn. American Reform Tract and Book Society, 1856.   DHU/MO

4475. Gallaudet, Thomas H. Jacob and His Sons; or The Second Part of a Conversation Between Mary and Her Mother. Pre-

(Gallaudet, Thomas H. cont.)
pared for the American Sunday School Union. Philadelphia:
American Sunday School Union, 1832.   DHU/MO

4476. Ganse, Hervey Doddridge. Bible Slaveholding Not Sinful.
New York: Brinkerhoff, 1856.   InU; NN/Sch; PPL; DLC;
CtY-D; NcU

4477. Garrison, William Lloyd. Lectures of George Thompson,
With a Full Report of the Discussion Between Mr. Thompson
and Mr. Borthwick, the Pro-Slavery Agent, held at the Royal
Ampitheatre, Liverpool, (Eng.) and which Continued for Six
Evenings with Unabated Interest: Compiled From Various
English Editions also, a Brief History of his Connection with
the Anti-Slavery Cause in England. Boston: Knapp, 1836.
                                                      DHU/R

4478. Giddings, Joshua R. The Conflict Between Religious Truths
and American Fidelity. Speech of Mr. Giddings, of Ohio, Upon
the Issues Pending Before the American People in Regard to
Freedom and Slavery Delivered in Committee of the Whole
House on the State of the Union, Feb. 26, 1858. Washington,
D. D.: Buell & Blanchard, n. d.   DHU/MO

4479. Gillis, James M. "The Crime of Cain." Opportunity
(12:6, Je., 1934), pp. 175-185.   DHU/MO

4480. Godwin, Benjamin. On the Essential Sinfulness of Slavery
and its Direct Opposition to the Precepts and Spirit of Christianity. London: T. Ward, 1840.   NNCor

4481. Goodell, William. American Slavery a Formidable Obstacle
to the Conversion of the World. New York: American and
Foreign Anti-Slavery Society, 1854.   NNCor

4482. The Governing Race: a Book for the Time, and For All
Times ... , by H. O. R. ... Washington: Thomas McGill,
Printer, 1860.   TSewU-T
Defence of Negro slavery on scriptural grounds.

4483. Granger, Arthur. The Apostle Paul's Opionion of Slavery
and Emancipation. A Sermon Preached to the Congregational
Church and Society in Meriden, at the Request of Several Respectable Anti-abolitionists. Middletown: Pr. by C. H. Pelton,
1837.   NN/Sch

4484. Green, Beriah. The Chattel Principle and Principle and
Abhorrence of Jesus Christ and the Apostles: or, No Refuge
for American Slavery in the New Testament. New York:
American Anti-Slavery Society, 1839.   DHU/MO; NN/Sch

4485. Hall, Barnes M. The Fugitive Slave Law. A Sermon.
Schenectady: Riggs, printer, 1850.   NN/Sch

4486. Hague, William. Christianity and Slavery. A Review of
the Correspondence Between Richard Fuller and Francis
Wayland on Domestic Slavery, Considered as a Scriptural
Institution. Boston: Gould, Kendall & Loncoln, 1847. NN/Sch;
DHU/MO

4487. Hamilton, W. T. The Duties of Masters and Slaves Respect-
ively: or, Domestic Servitude as Sanctioned by the Bible: A
Discourse Delivered in the Government Street Church, Mobile,
Ala. ...Dec. 15, 1844. Mobile: Brooks, 1845. NN/Sch; NcD

4488. Harris, Raymund. Scriptural Researches on the Licitness
of the Slave Trade, Shewing its Conformity with the Principles
of Natural and Revealed Religion, Delineated in the Sacred
Writings of the Word of God. Liverpool: Pr. by H. Hodgson,
1788.   NN/Sch; DHU/MO

4489. Hartzell, Jonas. "Bible Vindicated." The North Western
Christian Magazine (Ja., 1857), p. 221+.   OCIWH
Slavery and the Bible.

4490. Hatch, Reuben. Bible Servitude Pre-Examined: With Special
Reference to Pro-Slavery Interpretations and Infidel Objections... Cincinnati: Applegate & Co., 1862. DHU/MO

4491-92. Henson, Herbert Hensley, (bp.). Christianity and
Slavery. London: Rivingtons, 1887.   CtY-D

4493. Higginson, Thomas Wentworth. ...Does Slavery Christianize the Negro? ... New York: American Anti-Slavery Society, 1855.   DHU/MO; CtY-D; DLC

4494. Hodgman, Stephen Alexander. The Great Republic Judged,
but not Destroyed; or, The Beginning and End of Slavery and
the Justice of God Displayed in the Doom of Slaveholders...
New York: R. Craighead, Printer, 1865.   DHU/MO

4495. ----- The Nation's Sin and Punishment; or, The Hand of
God Visible in the Overthrow of Slavery. By a Chaplain of
the U. S. Army, who has been, Thirty Years, a Resident of
the Slave State. New York: American News Co., 1864.
                                             DHU/MO

4496. Holmes, Daniel. Dialogue on Slavery, and Miscellaneous
Subjects, Based on the Word of God. Dayton, O.: Gazette
Book and Job Rooms, 1854.   DLC

4497. Hopkins, Daniel C. True Cause of All Contention, Strife,
and Civil War in Christian Communities... New York: M. W.
Dodd, 1862.   NNCor
Discusses the theological ground of the right of slaveholding.

4498. Hopkins, John Henry. Bible View of Slavery. New York:
n. p., 1863.   NN/Sch

4499. ----- Letter from the Right Rev. John H. Hopkins, on the
Bible View of Slavery. New York: Pr. by W. F. Kost. 1861.
                                            NN/Sch

4500. ----- A Scriptural Ecclesiastical, and Historical View of
Slavery, From the Days of the Patriarch Abraham, to the
Nineteenth Century. Addressed to the Right Rev. Alonzo
Potter... New York: W. S. Pooley & Co., 1864. FSU;
DHU/MO; CtY-D

4501. Hopkins, Josiah. An Inquiry Whether We "Ought to Obey
God Rather Than Men," in a Review of a Sermon Preached
by the Rev. J. C. Lard at Buffalo, N. Y. Entitled "The Higher
Law," its Application to the "Fugitive Slave Bill." Cleveland:
Smead and Cowles, 1851.   DHU/MO

4502. Hosmer, William. The Higher Law, in its Relations to
Civil Government: With Particular Reference to Slavery, and
the Fugitive Slave Law... Auburn, N. Y.: Derby and Miller,
1852.   CtY-D

4503. Houghton, James. Slavery Immoral; Being a Reply to a
Letter in Which an Attempt is Made to Prove That Slavery is
not Immoral. Dublin: James McGlashan, 1847. DHU/MO

4504. Hughes, W. An Answer to the Rev. Mr. Harris's "Scriptural Researches on the Licitness of the Slave Trade." London:
Pr. for T. Cadell, in the Strand, 1788.   DHU/MO

4505. ----- Is Negro Slavery Sanctioned by Scriptures? London:
Ellerton & Henderson, n. d.,   DHU/MO

4506. Jones, John Richter. Slavery Sanctioned by the Bible. The
First Part of a General Treatise on the Slavery Question.
Philadelphia: J. B. Lippincott, 1861.   NN/Sch; MH-AH

4507. Jones, Thomas C. "Simon of Cyrene." St. Augustine's
Messenger (20; Apr., 1942), pp. 80-82.   DCU/ST; DGU
Father Francis supports his grandfather's account that Simon
of Cyrene was made to carry the cross because he was a
Negro.
Negro author.

4508. Jocelyn. Conflict Between Christianity and Slavery. Reprinted from the American Missionary for May 1860. n. p., n. d.
                                             DHU/MO

4509. Junkin, George. The Integrity of our National Union, vs.
Abolitionism: An Argument from the Bible in Proof of the

Position that Believing Masters Ought to be Honored and Obeyed by their Own Servants and Tolerated in, not Excommunicated from, the church of God: Being Part of a Speech Delivered Before the Synod of Cincinnati, on the Subject of Slavery, September 19th and 20th, 1843. Cincinnati, O.: Pr. by R. P. Donogh, 1843.   DLC; NcD; NN/Sch

4510. Keefer, Justus. Slavery: Its Sin, Moral Effects and Certain Death. Also, the Language of Nature, Compared With Divine Revelation, in Prose and Verse... With Extracts from Eminent Authors. Baltimore: J. Keefer, 1864.   DHU/MO

4511. Law, William. An Extract from a Treatise on the Spirit of Prayer, or the Soul Rising out of the Vanity of Time into the Riches of Eternity, with Some Thoughts on War... And Considerations on Slavery. Philadelphia: Jos. Cruikshank, 1780.
DLC

4512. Lawrence, John. The Slavery Question. Dayton, O.: Pub. by Order of the Trustees of the Conference Printing Establishment of the United Brethren in Christ. Vonnieda & Kumler, Agents, 1854.   NN/Sch

4513. Lee, Luther. Slavery; a Sin Against God. Syracuse: Wesleyan Methodist Book Room, 1853.   NN/Sch

4514. ----- Slavery Examined in the Light of the Bible. Syracuse, N.Y.: Wesleyan Methodist Book Room, 1855. DHU/R; CtY-D
Republished by Negro History Press, Detroit, Mich.

4515. Leighton, Nathan. The Bible and Pulpit for Freedom; American Slavery in Conflict with the Bible. Why Should not the Ministry Show it? New York: John A. Gray's Fire-Proof Printing Office, 1858.   DHU/MO; DHU/R
Pamphlets on Slavery and Christianity, V. 11.

4516. Longstreet, Augustus Baldwin. Letters on the Epistle of Paul to Philemon, or the Connection of Apostolical Christianity with Slavery. Charleston: Jenkins, 1845.   NcD

4517. Lounsbury, Thomas. The Touchstone of Truth, Applied to Modern Abolition; or Seven Lectures in Answer to the Question, "What Do the Scriptures Teach on the Subject of Slavery?" Geneva, N.Y.: Scotten & Van Brunt, 1844.   NcD

4518. Lovejoy, Joseph Cammet. The Robbers of Adullam; or, A Glance at "Organic Sin." A Sermon Preached at Cambridgeport, Nov. 27, 1845. Boston: D. H. Ela, Printer, 1845.
DHU/MO

4519. Lovejoy, Owen. The Supremacy of the Divine Law. A Sermon Preached at Princeton, Bureau County, Illinois. n.p.
DHU/MO

4520. Lundy, John Patterson. Review of Bishop Hopkins', Bible View of Slavery, by a Presbyter of the Church in Philadelphia. Philadelphia: n.p., 1863.   NN/Sch; CtY-D

4521. Lyons, Adelaide Avery. Religious Defense of Slavery in the North. (Ser. XIII, p. 5-34 in Historical papers of the Trinity College Historical Society.) Durham, N.C.: 1919. NcD; DLC; CtY

4522. Macbeth, James. The Church and the Slaveholder; or, Light and Darkness: an Attempt to Prove, from the Word of God and from Reason, that to Hold Property in Man is Wholly Destitute of Divine Warrant, is a Flagrant Crime, and Demand Excommunication. Earnestly and Respectfully Addressed to the Members of the Approaching Assembly of the Free Church of Scotland, and to the Churches Generally. Edinburgh: J. Johnston, etc., etc., 1850.   DLC

4523. Marsh, Leonard. Review of a "Letter from the Right Rev. John H. Hopkins, Bishop of Vermont, on the Bible View of Slavery" by a Vermonter. Burlington: Free Press, 1861.
CtY-D

4524. Maston, Thomas Bufford. The Bible and Race. Nashville: Boardman Press, 1959.   DHU/R; CtY-D

4525. ----- "Biblical Teachings and Race Relations." Review and Expositor (56; Jl., 1959), pp. 233-43. DLC; CtY-D

4526. M'Caine, Alexander. Slavery Defended From Scripture, Against the Attacks of the Abolitionists, in a Speech Delivered Before the General Conference of the Methodist Protestant Church, in Baltimore, 1842. Baltimore: Pr. by W. Wooddy, 1842.   NcD; NN/SCH

4527. Mc Kitrick, Eric L. Slavery Defended: the Views of the Old South. New Jersey: Prentice Hall, 1963.   DHU/MO

4528. McWright, A. The Sin of Slaveholding: in Two Sermons, Preached in the Methodist Episcopal Church, Madison, Wisc., April 15th and 22d, 1860. Madison, Wisc: Atwood, Rublee & Reed, Printers, 1860.   NN/Sch

4529. Mell, Patrick Hues. Slavery, a Treatise Showing That Slavery is Neither Moral Political nor Social Evil... Penfield, Ga.: Printed by B. Brantly, 1844.   MHU/W

4530. Meredith, Thomas. "Conservative Pro-Slavery Typical Arguments." The Biblical Recorder (9; Oct. 5, 12, 19, 26, Nov. 2, 1844).   NcD

4531. A Minister of the Gospel. Slavery in its Relation to God; a Review of Rev. Dr. Lord's Thanksgiving Sermon, in Favor of Domestic Slavery, Entitled The Higher Law in its Application to the Fugitive Slave Bill. Buffalo: A. M. Clapp, 1851.
MiBsA

4532. Mielzmer, M. "The Institution of Slavery Among the Ancient Hebrews According to the Bible and the Talmud." The Evangelical Quarterly Review (13; Ja., 1862), pp. 311+. DLC

4533. Morrisey, Richard A. Bible History of the Negro... Nashville, Tenn.: n.p., 1915.   NN/Sch; DHU/MO

4534. ----- Colored People in Bible History. Hammond, Ind.: Pr. for the Author by W. B. Conkey Co., 1925.   DHU/MO

4535. Morse, Samuel Finley Breese. ...An Argument on the Ethical Position Relation to the Politics of the Day. New York: 1863. (Papers from the Society for the Diffusion of Political Knowledge. no. 12).   NN/Sch

4536. Morse, Sidney Edwards. The Bible and Slavery. From the N.Y. Observer of Oct. 4, 1855. New York: n.d. DLC

4537. Nelson, William Stuart. "The Christian Church and Slavery in America." Howard University Review (2:1, 1925), pp. 41-71. DHU/MO; NN/Sch
Negro author.

4538. Nevin, Robert. The Bible Versus Slavery: a Tract for the Times. Londonderry: James and John Hampton, 1863. NcD

4539. Newman, Louis C. "The Bible View of Slavery" Reconsidered; Letter to the Rt. Rev. Bishop Hopkins.   NN/Sch
(In: Loyal Publication Society. Tracts, no. 39, pt. 2. 1864.)

4540. The North and South Misrepresented and Misjudged; or, A Candid View of our Present Difficulties and Danger, and their Causes and Remedy. Philadelphia: Pr. for the Author, 1861.
NN/Sch

4541. The Nutshell. The System of American Slavery "Tested by Scriptures," being "a Short Method:" with Proslavery D. D.'s whether Doctors of Divinity, or of Democracy... 2nd ed. New York: Published for the Author, 1862.   DHU/MO

4542. Owen, Robert Dale. The Wrong of Slavery, the Right of Emancipation, the Future of the African Race in the United States... Philadelphia: J. B. Lippincott, & Co., 1864.
DHU/MO; CtY-D

4543. Parker, Theodore. The Law of God and the Statutes of Men. A Sermon, Preached at the Music Hall, in Boston, June 18, 1854. Boston: B. B. Mussey & Co., 1854. DLC

4544. ----- A Sermon on Slavery, Delivered Ja. 31, 1841, Repeated June 4, 1843, and now Published by Request. Boston: Thurston & Torrey, 1843.   DLC

4545. Patton, William Weston. An Attempt to Prove that Pro-Slavery Interpretations of the Bible Are Productive of Infidelity. Hartford: W. H. Burleigh, 1846.   OO

4546. ----- Slavery--The Bible--Infidelity. Pro-Slavery Interpretations of the Bible, Productive of Infidelity. Hartford: W. H. Burleigh, 1847.   DHU/MO

4547. ----- Slavery and Infidelity: or, Slavery in the Church Ensures Infidelity in the World. Cincinnati: Amer. Reform Book and Tract Society, 1856.   NcD; DHU/MO

4548. Paulding, James K. Slavery in the United States. New York: Negro Universities Press, 1968.   DHU/R
        Originally pub. in 1936. "Opposition of Slavery to the Law of God."

4549. Peabody, Ephriam. "Slavery in the United States. Its Evils, Alleviations and Remedies." North American Review (73; Oct., 1851), pp. 347-85. MH; DCU; OKU; FU; GEU

4550. Perry, Lewis. "Adin Ballou's Hopedale Community and the Theology of Anti-Slavery." Church History (29:3, Sept., 1970), pp. 372-89.   DHU/R

4551. Phelps, Amos Augustus. Letters to Professor Stowe and Dr. Bacon, on God's Real Method with Great Social Wrongs, In Which the Bible is Vindicated from Grossly Erroneous Interpretations. New York: Wm. Harned, 1848.   DHU/MO

4552. Priest, Josiah. Bible Defense of Slavery, or, The Origin, History, and Fortunes of the Negro Race. Louisville, Ky.: W. A. Busk, 1851.   NN/Sch; DHU/MO

4553. ----- Slavery, as it Relates to the Negro or African Race, Examined in the Light of Circumstances, History and the Holy Scriptures; with an Account of the Origin of the Black Man's Color, Causes of His State of Servitude and Traces of His Character as well in Ancient as in Modern Times: With Stricutres on Abolitionism. Albany: Pr. by C. van Benthuysen & Co., 1845.   NN/Sch

4554. Prindle, Cyrus. Slavery Illegal. A Sermon, on the Occasion of the Annual Fast, April 12, 1850. Delivered in the Wesleyan Methodist Church, Shelburne, Vt. Burlington: Tuttle & Stacy, 1850.   NN/Sch

4555. The Pro-Slavery Argument; as Maintained by the Most Distinguished Writers of the Southern States. Charleston: Walker, Richards & Co., 1852.   DHU/R
        pp. 181-285, The Morality of Slavery.

4556. Ramsey, James. Examination of the Rev. Mr. Harris' Scriptural Researches on the Licitness of the Slave-Trade. London: James Phillips, 1788.   DLC

4557. Raphall, Morris J. Bible View of Slavery. A Discourse Delivered at the Jewish Synagogue "Bnai Jeshurum" New York, on the Day of National Fast, January 4, 1861. New York: Rudd & Carleton, 1861.   DHU/MO
        Pamphlets on Slavery and Christianity, V. 11.

4558. Remarks on Bishop Hopkins' Letter on the Bible View of Slavery. n.p., n.d.   NcD

4559. Remarks on the Immediate Aboliton Lecture of Rev. Mr. Phelps Delivered in the 2d Baptist Church in Taunton, Sunday Evening, May 24, 1834. By a Hearer. Taunton, Mass.: E. Anthony, Printer, 1834.   NN/Sch

4560. Review of a "letter from the Right Rev. John Hopkins, Bishop of Vermont, on the Bible View of Slavery," by a Vermonter. Burlington: Free Press Print, 1861.   DHU/MO

4561. Robinson, Robert. Slavery Inconsistent with the Spirit of Christianity. A Sermon, Preached at Cambridge, Feb. 10, 1788. Cambridge: J. Archdeacon, Printer to the Univeristy, 1788.   DLC; OO

4562. Robinson, Virgil Eugene. An Investigation of the Use of the Bible by the Protestant Churches of America in the Slavery Controversy... Master's thesis. S. D. A. Theological Seminary.   MiBsA

4563. Rush, Benjamin. On the Slavery of the Negroes in America, in Answer to a Pamphlet Entitled "Slavery not Forbidden by Scripture; or a Defence; 1773. N.Y.: Arno Press, 1969.   DHU/MO; DLC; INU

4564. ----- A Vindication of the Address, to the Inhabitants of the British Settlements, on the Slavery of the Negroes in America, in Answer to a Pamphlet Entitled, "Slavery Not Forbidden by Scripture; Or, A Defense of the West-India Planters From the Aspersions Thrown Out Against Them by the Author of the Address." By a Pennsylvanian. Philadelphia: Printed by J. Dunlap, 1773.   DHU/MO

4565. Russell, Kenneth C. Slavery as Reality and Metaphor in the Pauline Letters. Romae: Catholic Book Agency, 1968. T Sew U-T
        Slavery and the Bible.

4566. Sawyer, Leicester Ambrose. A Dissertation on Servitude: Embracing an Examination of the Scripture Doctrines on the Subject... New Haven: Durrie & Peck, 1837.   NN/Sch

4567. Schaff, Philip. Slavery and the Bible. A Tract for the Times. Chambersburg, Pa.: M. Kieffer & Co.'s Caloric Printing Press 1861.   NN/Sch
        Also in, Mercersburg Review (10:4, Oct., 1858), pp. 614-20.   DHU/R

4568. Shanks, Caroline L. "The Biblical Anti-Salvery Argument of the Decade 1830-1840." Journal of Negro History (16:2, Apr., 1931), pp. 132-57.   DHU/MO

4569. Sharp, Granville.. The Just Limitation of Slavery on the Laws of God, Compared with the Unbound Claims of the African Traders and British American Slave Holders... London: Pr. for B. White & Co. Dilly, 1776.   NN/Sch

4570. ----- The Law of Passive Obedience, or, Christian Submission to Personal Injuries. Wherein is Shown that the Several Texts of Scripture, which Command the Entire Submission of Servants or Slaves to Their Masters, Cannot Authorize the Latter to Exact an Involuntary Servitude, Nor in the Least Degree, Justify the Claims of Modern Slave Holders... London: Pr. for B. White and C. Dilly, 1776.   DHU/MO

4571. ----- The Law of Retribution: or A Serious Warning to Great Britain and Her Colonies, founded on Unquestionable Examples of God's Temporal Vengeance Against Tyrants, Slave Holders and Oppressors... London: B. White, 1776. NN/Sch

4572. ----- Slavery. Proving from Scriptures Its Inconsistency with Humanity and Religion in Answer to a Late Publication Entitled "The African Slave Trade for Negro Slaves Shown to be Consistent with Principles of Humanity and with the Laws of Revealed Religion." Burlington: Pr. and sold by Isaac Collins, 1773.   NN/Sch

4573. Sihler, Wilhelm. Die Sklaverei im Lichte der Heiligen Schrift Betrachtet. Baltimore, n.p., 1863. NN/Sch

4574. Slavery and the Bible. Cincinnati, O.: American Reform Tract and Book Society, n.d.   NcD; DHU/MO

4575. "Slavery and the Bible." Mercersburg Review (13:2, Apr., 1861), pp. 288-320.   DHU/R
        Signed: E. V. G.

4576. Slavery. By a Marylander. Its Institution and Origin. Its Status Under the Law and Under the Gospel... Balto.: J. P. Des Forges, 1860. MH

4577. Slavery vs. the Bible; A Correspondence between the General Conference of Maine and the Presbytery of Tombechee, Miss. by Cyrus P. Grosvenor. Worcester: Spooner and Howland, 1840. DHU/MO

4578. Smith, E. An Inquiry into Scriptural and Ancient Servitude, in which it is Shown that Neither was Chattel Slavery; with the Remedy for American Slavery... Mansfield, O.: Pub. by the Author at the Western Branch Book Concern of the Wesleyan Methodist Connection of America, 1852. DHU/MO

4579. Smith, Goldwin. Does the Bible Sanction American Slavery? Cambridge: Sever & Francis, 1863. DHU/MO; NN/Sch; CtY-D

4580. Smith, Jeremiah. Is Slavery Sinful? Being Partial Discussions of the Proposition, Slavery is Sinful, between Ovid Butler, Esq., a Bishop of the Christian Church at Indianapolis, Ind... Indianapolis: H. H. Dodd & Co., Printers, and Book Binders, 1863. DHU/MO

4581. Steele, Algernon Odell. The Bible and the Human Quest. New York: Philosophical Library, 1956. NN/Sch
Negro author.

4582. Streeter, S. W. American Slavery, Essentially Sinful. A Sermon. Oberlin, O.: J. M. Fitch, 1845. DHU/MO

4583. Stringfellow, Thornton. A Brief Examination of Scripture Testimony of the Institution of Slavery, in An Essay, First Published in the Religious Herald and Republished by Request... Richmond: Relig. Her., 1841. CtY-D

4584. ----- Slavery; its Origin, Nature and History. Its Relation to Society, to Government, and to True Religion, ...to Human Happiness and Divine Glory. Considered in the Light of Bible Teachings, Moral Justice and Political Wisdom. Alexandria, Va.: Pr. at the Virginia Sentinel Office, 1860. DHU/MO; CtY-D; NN/Sch

4585. Stuart, Charles. A Memoir of Granville Sharp, to which is Added Sharp's "Law of Passive Obedience," and an Extract from his "Law of Retribution." New York: The American Anti-Slavery Society, 1836. NN/Sch

4586. Stuart, M. Conscience and the Constitutions with Remarks on the Recent Speech of the Hon. Daniel Webster in the Senate of the United States on the Subject of Slavery. New York: Negro Universities Press, 1969. DHU/R
Originally published in 1850 by Crocker and Brewster. Scriptural validity of Slavery examined.

4587. Sunderland, LaRoy. The Testimony of God Against Slavery; a Collection of Passages from the Bible, which Show the Sin of Holding and Treating the Human Species as Property... Boston: Pub. by D. K. Hitchcock, 1838. NN/Sch; DHU/MO; CtY-D; MBU-T

4588. Thomas, Thomas E. Review of the Rev. Dr. Junkin's Synodical Speech in Defense of American Slavery: Delivered September 19th and 20th, and Published December, 1843; With an Outline of the Bible Argument Against Slavery. Cincinnati: Daily Atlas Office, 1844. OWoC

4589. Thompson, Ernest T. "The Curse Was Not on Ham." The Presbyterian Outlook (137:7, Mr., 1955). DLC

4590. Thompson, Joseph Parrish. Christianity and Emancipation; or, The Teachings and the Influence of the Bible Against Slavery. New York: A. D. F. Randolph, 1863. NN/Sch; DHU/MO

4591. ----- Teachings of the New Testament on Slavery. New York: J. H. Ladd, 1856. NN/Sch

4592. Thompson, L. The Ethics of American Slavery, being a Vindication of the Word of God and a Pure Christianity in all Ages, from Complicity with Involuntary Servitude; and a Demonstration that American Slavery is a Crime in Substance and Concomitants, by an American Citizen. New York: Ross & Tousey, 1861. NN/Sch

4593. Thompson, Thomas. The African Trade for Negro Slaves Shewn to be Consistent with Principles of Humanity, and with the Laws of Revealed Religion. Canterburg: Pr. and sold by Simmons and Kirby, sold also by Robert Baldwin, Bookseller in Pater-Noster Row, London, 1893. DHU/MO

4594. Thrasher, John B. Slavery a Divine Institution. New York: Arno, 1972. DLC
A speech made before the Breckinridge & Lane Club, Nov. 5, 1861.
Reprint of 1861 edition.

4595. Twenty-six Points of Comparison Between Hebrew Slavery Under the Mosaic, and British Colonial and American Slavery Under the Christian Dispensation... Bristol, England: Wright & Bagnall, 182-? NNCor

4596. Tyler, Edward R. Slaveholding "A Malum in se," or, Invariably Sinful... Hartford: S. S. Cowles, 1839. DHU/MO

4597. Valentine, Foy Dan. "The Curse of Ham." Baptist Standard (66; Ag. 12, 1954), p. 3. LNB; TxFS

4598. Vail, Stephen Montford. The Bible Against Slavery with Replies to the "Bible View of Slavery, by John H. Hopkins, Bishop of Diocese of Vermont; and to "A Northern Presbyter's Second Letter and Ministers of the Gospel," by Nathan Lord, late President of Dartmouth College; and to "X" of the New Hampshire Patriot. Concord: Fogg, Hadley & Co., printer, 1864. NcD; NN/Sch

4599. Veal, Frank Richard. The Attitude of the Ante-Nicean Fathers Toward Slavery Prior to 325 A.D. Bachelor of Divinity paper. School of Religion, Howard University, 1937.

4600. View of the Subject of Slavery Contained in the Biblical Repertory for April, 1836, in which the Scriptural Argument it is Believed, is very Clearly and Justly Exhibited. Pittsburgh: A. Jaynes, Printer, 1836. NN/Sch

4601. Ward, James Wilson. Slavery a Sin That Concerns Non-Slaveholding States. A Sermon Delivered on the Day of the Annual Fast in Mass., Mr. 28, 1839. Boston: I. Knapp, 1839. NHi; MB

4602. Ward, Jonathan. Father Ward's Letter to Professor Stuart. n.p., 1837. DHU/MO
Pamphlets on Slavery and Christianity, V. 1. Priest writes letter for publication refuting Professor Stuart's argument justifying slavery by the Bible.

4603. Warren, Ebenezer W. Nellie Norton: or, Southern-Slavery and the Bible. A Scriptural Refutation of the Principal Arguments Upon Which the Abolitionists Rely. A Vindication of Southern Slavery from the Old and New Testaments. Macon, Ga.: Burke, Boykin, 1864. CtY-D; DHU/MO

4604. Wayland, Francis. The Moral Elements of Moral Science. Boston: Gould & Lincoln, 1864. DHU/R
pp. 206-28, views on slavery and biblical authority by a Baptist minister who was president of Brown University, 1827-55.

4605. Weld, Theodore Dwight. The Bible Against Slavery; or, An Inquiry into the Genius of the Mosaic System, and the Teachings of the Old Testament on the Subject of Human Rights. Pittsburgh: United Presbyterian Board of Publication, 1864. DHU/MO; CtY-D; NN/Sch

4606. Wheaton, N. S. A Discourse on St. Paul's Epistle to Philemon; Exhibiting the Duty of Citizens of the Northern States in Regard to the Institution of Slavery Delivered in Christ Church, Hartford, Dec. 22, 1850. Hartford: Case, Tiffany and Co., 1851. DLC

4607. White, B. Modern Apostasy, Slavery, the Two-Horned Beast, and his Image. Respectfully Dedicated to the American People. Cincinnati: n.p., 1856.   NN/Sch

4608. White, William S. The Gospel Ministry in a Series of Letters From a Father to His Sons. Philadelphia: Presbyterian Board of Publications, 1860.   ICRL

4609. Wiley, Calvin Henderson. Scriptural Views of National Trials; or, The True Road to Independence and Peace of the Confederate States of America. Greensboro, N.C.: Sterling, 1863.   NcD

4610. Williston, Seth. Slavery Not a Scriptural Ground of Division in Efforts for the Salvation of the Heathen. New York: M.W. Dodd, 1844.   DLC; NcD; DHU/MO

4611. Wisner, William C. The Biblical Argument of Slavery. New York; n.p. 1844.   NN/Sch

4612. Wolcott, Samuel T. The Bible Against Oppression. Cincinnati, O.: American Tract Society, n.d.   DHU/MO

4613. Woolman, John. Considerations on Slavery, Addressed to the Professors of Christianity of Every Denomination, and Affectionately Recommended to their Sober Unprejudiced Attention. Baltimore: Pr. by T. Maud, 1821.   NN/Sch
Part 2 has title: "Considerations on the keeping of Negroes."

4614. "Words for Working Men." First Series. Slavery and the Bible. n.p.:, n.d.   DHU/MO

4615. Wright, Henry Clarke. Anthropology; or, The Science of Man: In Its Bearing on War and Slaver, and on Arguments from the Bible, Marriage, God, Death, Retribution, Atonement and Government in Support of These and Other Social Wrongs. In a Series of Letters to a Friend in England. Cincinnati: E. Shepard, 1850.   DLC

D. SLAVERY, NEGROES AND THE CHURCH

1. Baptist

4616. Allen, John. An Oration Upon the Beauties of Liberty or the Essential Rights of the Americans. Delivered at the 2nd Baptist Church in Boston Upon the Last Annual Thanksgiving.... Boston: Printed & sold by D. Kneeland & N. Davis in Queen Street, 1773.   DLC; MB; ICN; MiU-C; INU
Baptist minister from England wrote on the "injustices Negroes were experiencing in the Baptist church in New England in the eighteenth century."

4617. American Baptist Free Mission Society. Anti-Slavery Missions. A Brief View of the Origin, Principles and Operations of the American Baptist Free Mission Society. Bristol: 1851.   MB

4618. American Baptist Free Mission Society. Review of the Operations of the American Baptist Free Mission Society for the Past Year. Bristol: Mathews Bros., 1851. MB

4619. American Baptist Free Mission Society. Thirteenth Annual Meeting of the American Baptist Free Mission Society, Norristown, Pa. May 21-22, 1856. Utica, N.Y.: Curtiss and White, Printers, 1856. Pam. File, DHU/R; DHU/MO
A group instrumental in perpetuating slavery in America.

4620. Biddell, William R. "The Baptism of Slaves in Prince Edward Island." Journal of Negro History (4:4, Oct., 1932), pp. 307-09.   DHU/MO

4621. Boyd, Jesse Lansy. A History of Baptists in America, Prior to 1845. New York: American Press, 1957.   NN/Sch

4622. Brisbane, William Henry. A Speech Delivered April 30, 1844, Before the Baptist Home Mission Society, on the Question of the Propriety of Recognizing Slaveholding Ministers as Proper Missionaries of the Gospel. n.p.: n.p., 1844? NNCor

4623. Cheatham, Thomas Richard. The Rhetorical Structure of the Abolitionist Movement Within the Baptist Church: 1833-1845. Doctoral dissertation. Purdue University, 1969. NNCor

4624. Christian, John. A Christian Experience of Grace, by John Christian, (colored man) a Baptist. Columbus, Ga.: n.p., 1859.   DHU/MO
A broadside.
Negro author.

4625. "The Close of the Slaveholders Rebellion." The Freewill Baptist Quarterly (13; Jl., 1865), pp. 298ff. DLC

4626. Colver, Nathaniel. A Review of the Doings of the Baptist Board of Foreign Mission, and of the Triennial Convention at Baltimore, April, 1841, Originally Published in the Christian Reflector, in Dec., 1841. Boston, 1841. NNCor
Slavery and the Church.

4627. Cutting, Sewall Sylvester. Influence of Christianity on Government and Slavery: a Discourse Delivered in the Baptist Church, in West Boylston, Mass., January 15, 1837. Worcester: Pr. by H.J. Howland, 1837. DHU/MO; DLC

4628. Daniel, W. Harrison. "Virginia Baptists and the Negro in the Antebellum Era." Journal of Negro History (56:1, Ja., 1971), pp. 1-16.   DHU/R

4629. Foss, A.T. Facts for Baptist Churches. Collected, Arranged and Reviewed by A.T. Boss and E. Mathews. Utica: American Baptist Free Mission Society, 1850. NNCor
Slavery and the Baptist Church.

4630. Free-Will Baptist Anti-slavery Society. Annual Report... Read at Sutton, Vt., Oct. 13, 1847. Dover: Wm. Burr, Printer, 1848.   DHU/MO

4631. Free-Will Baptist Anti-slavery Society. Fifth Annual Report of the... Read at Lebanon, Maine, October 9, 1851. Dover: Wm. Bun, Printer, 1851.   DHU/MO

4632. Fuller, Richard. Domestic Slavery Considered as a Scriptural Institution: in a Correspondence Between Richard Fuller and Francis Wayland. New York: L. Colby, 1847. NN/Sch; CtY-D

4633. Furman, Richard. Rev. Dr. Richard Furman's Exposition of the Views of the Baptists, Relative to the Coloured Population of the United States, in a Communication to the Governor of South Carolina. Charleston: A.E. Miller, 1823. DLC

4634. Harvey, H. Memoir of Alfred Bennett, First Pastor of the Baptist Church, Homer, N.Y... New York: Edward H. Fletcher, 1852.   DHU/MO

4635. Hopkins, Samuel. A Dialogue Concerning the Slavery of the Africans! Shewing It to be the Duty and Interest of the American States to Emancipate all their Slaves. With an Address to the Owners of Such Slaves. Norwich (Conn.): Judah P. Spooner, 1776. New York: Repr. for Robert Hodge, 1785. DLC

4636. ----- A Discourse upon the Slave Trade and the Slavery of the Africans. Delivered in the Baptist Meeting House at Providence, before the Providence Society for Abolishing the Slave-Trade. At Their Annual Meeting, on May 17, 1793. Providence: J. Carter, 1793.   DLC

4637. Jeansonne, Glen. "Southern Baptist Attitudes Toward Slavery." The Georgia Historical Quarterly (55:4, Wint., 1971), pp. 510-22.   DCU

4638. Leavell, Zachery T. A Complete History of Mississippi Baptists. Jackson, Mississippi: Mississippi Baptists Pub. Co., 1904.   DLC
    Negro Baptists, pp. 53-84.

4639. Maston, Thomas Bufford. The Ethical and Social Attitudes of Isaac Backus. Doctoral dissertation. Yale University, 1939. Chapter 6, Attitudes of New England Baptist ministers on slavery.

4640. Mathews, Edward. The Shame and Glory of the American Baptists; or, Slaveholders Versus Abolitionists. Bristol: T. Mathews, 1852.   CtY; NNCor

4641. McLoughlin, William G. "The First Antislavery Church in New England?" Foundations (15:21, Apr.-Je., 1972), pp. 103-10.   DHU/R
    Action taken by the First Baptist Church of Ashfield, Mass. in Oct., 1773 against slavery.

4642. ----- New England Dissent 1630-1833. The Baptists and the Separation of Church and State. Cambridge, Mass.: Harvard University Press, 1971.   DGW; DGU
    Chapter 39, The Baptists' Views on Government, Morality, and Slavery, 1780-1810, pp. 751-769. Also: pp. 1269-71.

4643. Murdock, John Nelson. Our Civil War: its Causes and its Issues. A Discourse Delivered in the Baptist Church, Brookline, on the Occasion of the National Thanksgiving, August 6, 1863. Boston: Wright & Potter, Printers 1863.   CtY-D

4644. Posey, Walter Brownlow. "The Baptist and Slavery in the Lower Mississippi Valley." Journal of Negro History (41:2, Apr., 1956), pp. 117-30.   DHU

4645. Purefoy, George W. History of Sandy Creek Baptist Association From its Organization in A.D. 1758 to A.D. 1858. New York: n.p., 1859.   AAP; NcD

Information on the restrictions on free Negro ministers' activities after 1831.

4646. Putnam, Mary B. The Baptists and Slavery, 1840-1845. Doctoral dissertation. University of Chicago, 1910. NcD
    Also published by G. Wahr, 1913.

4647. Satterfield, James Herbert. The Baptists and the Negro Prior to 1863. Doctoral dissertation. Southern Baptist Theological Seminary, 1919.

4648. Sweet, William Warren. Religion on the American Frontier: The Baptists. 1783-1830. A Collection of Source Material. New York: Cooper Square Publishers, Inc., 1964. DHU/R
    Chapter V - "Anti-Slavery Movements Among Baptists."
    Chapter XIV - "Documents Relating to the Friends to the Friends to Humanity or the Anti-Slavery Baptists in Kentucky and Illinois."

4649. Todd, Willie G. The Slavery Issue and the Organization of a Southern Baptist Convention. Doctoral dissertation. University of North Carolina, 1964.
    Microfilm 85, School of Religion.

4650. Watkins, Richard H. "The Baptists of the North and Slavery, 1856-1860." Foundations: A Baptist Journal of History and Theology (13:4, Oct.-Dec., 1970), pp. 317-32.   DHU/R

4651. Wayland, Francis. The Limitations of Human Responsibility. Boston: Gould, Kendall & Lincoln, 1838.   DHU/R
    pp. 161-88 The Slavery Question, written by a Baptist minister who was president of Brown University from 1827-55.

4652. Willis, John. The Plea of John Willis, for Withdrawing Himself From the Eben-Ezer Baptist Church. New York: Printed by Smith and Forman, 1810.   MNtcA
    Slavery and the Baptist Church.

2. Congregational (United Church of Christ)

4653. An Affectionate Expostulation with Christians in the United States of America, Because of the Continuance of Negro Slavery Throughout Many Districts of Their Country, Addressed by the Minister, Deacons, and Members of the Congregational Church, Joined by the Congregation, Assembling in Mill Street Chapel, Perth.
    Glasgow: Geo. Gallie, n.d.   DHU/MO

4654. Allen, Benjamin Russell. The Responsibilities and Duties of American Citizens. A Sermon, Preached in the Congregational Church, South Berwick, Me., Thanksgiving Day, Dec. 19, 1850. Boston: Crocker and Brewster, 1851.   NN/Sch

4655. Allen, George. Mr. Allen's Report of a Declaration of Sentiments on Slavery, Dec. 5, 1837. Worcester: H. J. Howland, 1838.   CtY-D

4656. ----- Mr. Allen's Speech on Ministers Leaving a Moral Kingdom to Bear Testimony Against Sin; Liberty in Danger, from the Publication of its Principles the Constitution a Shield for Slavery; and the Union Better than Freedom and Righteousness." Boston: I. Knapp, 1838.   DHU/MO; CtY-D

4657. Bacon, Leonard. Review of Pamphlets on Slavery and Colonization. First published in Quarterly Christian Spectator, for Mar. 1833. New Haven: A. H. Maltby, 1833.

4658. ----- Slavery Discussed in Occasional Essays, from 1833 to 1846. New York: Baker and Scribner, 1846.   CtY-D

4659. ----- Two Sermons Preached to the First Church in New Haven, on the Day of Fasting. Viz.; Good Friday, the 10th of April, 1857. New Haven: Thos. H. Pease, 1857. DHU/MO

4660. Bassett, George W. Slavery Examined by the Light of Nature. Sermon Preached at the Congregational Church, Washington, D.C., Feb. 28, 1858. Washington, D.C.: n.p., 1858.

4661. Beeson, Lewis, (ed.). Congregationalism, Slavery and the Civil War. Lansing: Michigan Civil War Centennial Observance Commission, 1965.   DLC

4662. Blanchard, Hiram W. An Open Letter to the Second Congregational Church of Dorchester, Mass. Boston: Printed by W. Richardson, 1880.   NNCor
    Slavery and the Congregational Church.

4663. Blodgett, C. How to Win a Brother. A Discourse Delivered in the Congregational Meeting House, Pawtuckett; July 10, 1842. Pawtuckett; Chronicle Press, 1842.   DHU/MO

4664. Boynton, Charles Brandon. Separation From Sin and Sinners. Cincinnati: American Reform Tract Society, n.d.   DHU/MO

4665. ----- Thanksgiving Sermon by Rev. C. B. Boynton D.D. Chaplain of the House of Representatives, and Pastor of the First Congregational Church, Washington, D.C., delivered November 29, 1866. Alexandria, Va.: Pr. at the "Virginia State Journal" Job Office, 1866.   DHU/MO

4666. Bulkley, Charles Henry Augustus. Removal of Ancient Landmarks or the Causes and Consequences of Slavery Extension. A Discourse Preached to Second Congregational Church of West Winsted Conn., Mr. 5, 1854.   DLC; CtY

4667. Bushnell, Horace. The Census and Slavery; a Thanksgiving Discourse, Delivered in the Chapel at Clifton Springs, N.Y., November 29, 1860. Hartford: L. E. Hunt, 1860. CtY-D; DHU/MO

4668. ----- A Discourse on the Slavery Question. Delivered in the North Church, Hartford, Thursday Evening, Jan. 10, 1839. Hartford: Case, Tiffany & Co., 1839.   DHU/MO; CtY-D

4669. ----- The Northern Iron. A Discourse Delivered in the North Church, Hartford, on the Annual State Fast, April 14, 1854... Hartford: E. Hunt & Son, 1854.   CtY-D

4670. Cheever, George Barrell. The Fire and Hammer of God's Word Against the Sin of Slavery. Speech of George B. Cheever, D.D. at the Anniversary of the American Abolition Society, May, 1858. New York: American Abolition Society, 1858.   CtY-D; DHU/R

4671. ----- God Against Slavery: and the Freedom and Duty of the Pulpit to Rebuke It, as a Sin Against God. Cincinnati: American Reform Tract and Book Society, 1859. A&M; DHU/MO; DHU/R; CtY-D

4672. ----- The Guilt of Slavery and the Crime of Slave-Holding Demonstrated from the Hebrew and Greek Scriptures... Boston: J. P. Jewett & Co., 1860.   NN/Sch; CtY-D; DHU/MO

4673. ----- The Salvation of the Country Secured by Immediate Emancipation. A Discourse by Geo. B. Cheever Delivered in the Church of the Puritans, Sabbath Evening, Nov. 10, 1861. New York: J. A. Gray, 1861.   CtY-D

4674. Cheever, Henry Theodore. A Tract for the Times, on the Question, Is It Right to Withhold Fellowship from Churches or from Individuals that Tolerate or Practise Slavery! Read by Appointment, before the Congregational Ministers' Meeting, of New London County, Ct. ...New York: J. A. Gray, Printer, 1859.   NN/Sch

4675. Clark, Calvin Montague. American Slavery and Maine Congregationalists; a Chapter in the History of the Development of Anti-Slavery Sentiment in the Protestant Churches of the North. Bangor, Maine: The Author, 1940. MBGTL; DLC; NcD; NN/Sch; CtY-D

4676. Cleaveland, Elisha Lord. The Patriot's Song of Victory. A Thanksgiving Discourse, for Recent Military Successes, Delivered in the Third Congregational Church, New Haven, September 11, and Repeated by Request, in the Same Place, September 18, 1864. By Elisha Lord Cleaveland... New Haven: T. H. Pease, 1864.   CtY-D

4677. Congregational Churches in Massachusetts. General Association. Report of the Committee of Correspondence with Southern Ecclesiastical Bodies on Slavery; to the General Association of Massachusetts. Pub. by the Vote of the Association. Salem: J. P. Jewett and Co., 1844.   DLC; NN/Sch

4678. Congregational Home Missionary Society. Home Missions and Slavery: A Reprint of Several Articles, Recently Pub. in the Religious Journals; with an Appendix. New York: J. A. Gray, 1857.   DLC

4679. Congregational Union of Scotland. Address of the Congregational Union in Scotland to Their Fellow Christians in the United States, on the Subject of American Slavery. New York: American and Foreign Anti-Slavery Society, 1840.   DHU/MO

4680. Convention of Congregational Ministers of Massachusetts. Report of the Committee on Slavery, to the Convention of Congregational Ministers of Massachusetts. Presented May 30, 1849. Boston: Press of J. R. Marvin, 1849. NN/Sch; CtY-D; NcD; DHU/MO; O; NjP

4681. Dickinson, James Taylor. A Sermon, Delivered in the Second Congregational Church, Norwich, on the Fourth of July, 1834, at the Request of the Anti-Slavery Society of Norwich and Vicinity. Norwich: Anti-Slavery Society, 1834. Rochester: Hoyt & Porter, 1835.   DHU/MO

4682. Dickinson, Noadiah Smith. Slavery: the Nation's Crime and Danger. A Sermon Preached in the Congregational Church, Foxborough, Mass., Sept. 30, 1860. Boston: Press of G. Noyes, 1860.   NN/Sch

4683. Dunlop, John. American Slavery. Organic Sins: or, The Iniquity of Licensed Injustice. Edinburgh: W. Oliphant and Sons, 1846.   NN/Sch

4684. Finney, Charles G. An Autobiography. Westwood, N.J.: Fleming H. Revell Co., 1876.   DHU/R
     Chapter 25, views on slavery and church.

4685. Forman, Jacob Gilbert. The Christian Martyrs; or, The Conditions of Obedience to the Civil Government; A Discourse by... Minister of the Second Congregational Church in Nantucket; ... To Which is Added, a Friendly Letter to Said Church and Congregation on the Pro-Slavery Influences that Occasioned His Removal. Boston: W. Crosby and H. P. Nichols, 1851.   DHU/MO

4686. Forster, Daniel. Our Nation's Sins and the Christian Duty. A Fast Day Discourse, by Daniel Forster, Minister in Charge of the Congregational Church of Concord, Mass., Delivered April 10, 1851. Boston: White & Potter, Printers, 1851.   DLC

4687. Gillett, Francis. A Review of the Rev. Horace Bushnell's Discourse on the Slavery Question, Delivered in the North Church, Hartford, January 10, 1839. Hartford: S. S. Cowles, 1839.   DHU/MO; CtY-D

4688. Green, Beriah. Iniquity and a Meeting. A Discourse Delivered in the Congregational Church, Whitesboro, (N.Y.), Jan. 31, 1841. n.p., n.d.   DHU/MO

4689. Gulliver, J. P. The Lioness and Her Whelps. A Sermon on Slavery Preached in the Broadway Congregational Church, Norwich, Connecticut. December 18, 1859. Norwich: Manning Perry & Co., 1860.   DHU/MO; CtY-D

4690. Hall, Edward Brooks. A Discourse Occasioned by the Death of William Ellery Channing; Delivered in the First Congregational Church, Providence R. I., October 12, 1842. Providence: B. Cranston, 1842.   CtY-D

4691. Hall, Nathaniel. The Iniquity: A Sermon in The First Church, Dorchester, on Sunday Dec. 11, 1859. Boston: Pr. by J. Wilson & Son, 1859.   CtY-D

4692. ----- The Limits of Civil Obedience. A Sermon Preached in the First Church, Dorchester, Ja. 12, 1851. Boston: W. Crosby and H. P. Nichols, 1851.   DLC

4693. ----- The Moral Significance of the Contrasts Between Slavery and Freedom. A Discourse Preached in the First Church, Dorchester, May 10, 1864... Boston: Walker, Wise & Co., etc., 1864.   DHU/MO; CtY-D

4694. ----- Righteousness and the Pulpit: A Discourse Preached in the First Church, Dorchester, on Sunday, Sept. 30, 1855. Boston: Crosby, Nichols, 1855.   NN/Sch CtY-D

4695. ----- Truth Not to Be Overthrown Nor Silenced: A Sermon Preached at Dorchester, Sunday, Jan. 27, 1861.   CtY-D

4696. ----- Two Sermons on Slavery and its Hero-Victims. Boston: Pr. by J. Wilson & Son, 1859.   NN/Sch

4697. Hartford, Conn. Fourth Congregational Church. The Unanimous Remonstrance of the Fourth Congregational Church. Hartford, Conn. Against the Policy of the American Tract Society on the Subject of Slavery. New York: American Anti-Slavery Society, 1855. DHU/MO; NN/Sch; NcD; DLC; GAU; NNCor

4698. Home Missions and Slavery. A Reprint of Several Articles, Recently Published in the Religious Journals; with an Appendix. New York: J. A. Gray, Printer, 1857.   CtY-D

4699. Horner, Joseph Andrew. ...The American Board of Missions and Slavery. A Reprint of the Correspondence in the "Non Conformist Newspaper; to Which is Added an Article on the Fall

of Dr. Pomroy. Leeds: J. B. Barry, 1860.   NNCor
Slavery and the Congregational Church.

4700. Humphrey, Heman. Parallel Between Intemperance and the
Slave Trade. An Address Delivered at Amherst College, July
4, 1828. Amherst: J. S. and C. Adams, 1828.   CtY-D

4701. James, Horace. Our Duties to the Slave. A Sermon Preached
Before the Original Congregational Church and Society, in
Wrentham, Mass. on Nov. 28, 1846. Boston: Richardson &
Filmer, 1847.   DLC; DHU/MO

4702. Lackey, Warren. Correspondence Between Warren Lackey,
Baalis Bullard, and John Orcutt, on the one Part, and Augustine
C. Taft on the Other Part, All of Uxbridge, Mass.. Mutually
dissolving Church. Fellowship. Uxbridge, Mass.: n.p., 1846?
                                        NNCor
Slavery and the Congregational church.

4703. Liberty or Slavery; the Great National Question. Three
Prize Essays on American Slavery... Boston: Congregational
Board of Publication, 1857.   NN/Sch; NcD

4704. Locke, Mary S. Anti-Slavery in America From the Introduction of African Slaves to the Prohibition of the Slave Trade.
Gloucester, Mass.: Peter Smith, 1965. (Radcliffe College
Monographs, no. 11)   DHU/R
'Aims to trace the early development of anti-slavery sentiment under the influence of religious and ethical principles
and of political theories. "

4705. McEwen, Able. A Sermon, Preached in the First Congregational Church, New London, Conn., on the Day of Thanksgiving,
November 28, 1850. New London: Daniels & Bacon, 1851.
                                        CtY-D

4706. McLoughlin, William G. The Meaning of Henry Ward Beecher.
An Essay on the Shifting Values of Mid-Victorian America, 1840-
1870. New York: Alfred A. Knopf, 1970.   DHU/R
Chapters 9 and 10 discuss Beecher and the Civil War and his
ideas on white supremacy and Anglo-Saxon destiny.

4707. Morris, Robert. Slavery; its Nature, Evils, Remedy. A
Sermon Preached to the Congregation of the Presbyterian Church,
Newton, Pa. on the Sabbath Morning, July 27, 1845. Philadel-
phia: Wm S. Martien, 1845.   DHU/MO

4708. The National Entail. A Sermon Preached at the First Congregational Church in Brookline, on the 3rd July, 1864. Boston:
Wright & Potter, 1864.   CtY-D

4709. New York City (New York), Church of the Puritans (Congregational). Reply of the Church of the Puritans to the Protest
of their Late Deacons, also to a "Letter" Addressed to the Church
by Sundry Individuals, July 15, 1857. New York: W. C. Bryant,
Printers, 1857.   CtY-D

4710. Nott, Samuel. The Necessities and Wisdom of 1861. A
Supplement to the 6th ed. of Slavery and the Remedy. Boston:
Crocker & Brewster, 1860.   CtY-D

4711. ----- The Present Crisis: With a Reply and Appeal to
European Advisers, from the 6th ed. of "Slavery and the Remedy."
Boston: Crocker & Brewster, 1860.   CtY-D

4712. ----- Slavery and the Remedy; or, Principles and Suggestions
for a Remedial Code, With a Review of the Decision of the
Supreme Court in the Case of Dred Scott. New York: Appleton,
1857.   CtY-D

4713. Patten, William. On the Inhumanity of the Slave-Trade, and
the Importance of Correcting It. A Sermon, Delivered in the
Second Congregational Church, Newport, Rhode Island, Aug. 12,
1792. Providence: J. Carter, 1793.   DLC

4714. Patton, William Weston. The American Board and Slaveholding. Hartford: W. H. Burleigh, Printer, 1846. CtY-D;
DHU/MO; DLC

4715. ----- Freedom's Martyr. A Discourse on the Death of the
Rev. Charles T. Torrey. Hartford: Wm. H. Burleigh, 1846.
                                        DHU/MO

4716. ----- Thoughts for Christians Suggested by the Case of
Passmore Williamson: A Discourse Preached in the Fourth
Congregational Church, Hartford, Conn., Oct. 7, 1855. Hart-
ford, Conn.: Montague & Co., 1855.   DHU/MO

4717. ----- The Unanimous Remonstrance of the Fourth Congrega-
tional Church Hartford, Conn., Against the Policy of the
American Tract Society on the Subject of Slavery. Hartford:
Silas Andrus & Son, 1855.   DHU/MO

4718. Perth, Scot. Congregational Church. An Affectionate Ex-
postulation with Christians in the United States of America
Because of the Continuance of Negro Slavery Throughout the
Many Districts of Their Country. Glasgow: G. Gallie, 18--.
                                        NNCor
Slavery and the Congregational church.

4719. Putnam, George. God and Our Country. A Discourse Delivered in the First Congregational Church in Roxbury, on Fast
Day, April 8, 1847. Boston: W. Crosby and H. P. Nichols,
1847.   CtY-D

4720. Quint, Alonzo Hall. The Christian Patriot's Present Duty.
A Sermon Addressed to the Mather Church and Society, Jamaica
Plain, Mass., April 28, 1861, by the Pastor. Boston: Hollis
& Gunn, 1861.   CtY-D

4721. Rice, Nathan Lewis. Ten Letters on the Subject of Slavery:
Addressed to the Delegates From the Congregational Associa-
tions to the Last General Assembly of the Presbyterian Church.
St. Louis: Keith, Woods, 1856.   NNCor
Slavery and the Congregational Church.

4722. Root, David. A Fast Sermon on Slavery. Delivered April
2, 1835, to the Congregational Church and Society in Dover,
N. H. Dover: Pr. at the Enquirer Office, 1835. DHU/MO

4723. ----- Liberty of Speech and the Press. A Thanksgiving
Sermon Delivered November 26, 1835, to the Congregational
Church and Society in Dover, N. H. Dover: Pr. at the
Enquirer Office, 1835.   DHU/MO

4724. ----- A Memorial of the Martyred Lovejoy... Delivered in
Dover, N. H. Published by Request. Dover: n.p., 1837.
                                        DHU/MO

4725. Salter, William. Slavery and the Lessons of Recent Events.
A Sermon Preached in the Congregational Church. Burlington;
Dec. 4, 185-?   DHU/MO

4726. Sanders, William Davis. Two Anti-Slavery Sermons Delivered in 1853 and 1854. Edited by David Sanders Clark.
Washington; 1964.   NcD

4727. Senior, Robert C. New England and Congregationalist and
the Anti-Slavery Movement, 1830-1860. Doctoral dissertation.
Yale University, 1954.   NcD

4728. Sexton, Jessie Ethelyn. Congregationalism, Slavery and the
Civil War. Lewis Beeson, editor. Lansing: Michigan Civil
War Centennial Observance Commission, 1966. NcD

4729. Shedd, William Greenough Thayer. The Union and the War.
A Sermon Preached November 27, 1862. New York: Scribner,
1863.   CtY-D

4730. Smectymnuus. [Pseud.] Two Letters Addressed to Rev.
M. L. Rice, D.D.. in Reply to His Letters to the Congrega-
tional Deputation on the Subject of Slavery. Also a Letter to
Rev. Nehemiah Adams, D. D.. in Answer to the "South-Side
view of Slavery." Boston: Crocker and Brewster, 1856.
NNCor; DLC; TxU; PPPrHi; NcU

4731. Spooner, Joshoa. Communication to the First Congregational Church in Brookfield. Brookfield, Mass.: n.p., 1845.
NNCor
    Slavery and the Congregational Church.

4732. Starkey, Marion Lens. The Congregational Way; the Role of
the Pilgrims and their Heirs in Shaping America. Garden City:
Doubleday, 1966.   NN/Sch

4733. Stetson, Caleb. A Discourse on the State of the Country, Delivered in the First Church in Medford, on the Annual Fast April
7th, 1842. Boston: J. Munroe, 1842.   CtY-D

4734. Storrs, Richard Salter. American Slavery, and the Means of
its Removal. A Sermon, Preached in the First Congregational
Church, Braintree, April 4, 1844. Boston: T. R. Marvin, 1844.
CtY-D

4735. The Tables Turned. A Letter to the Congregational Association of New York, Reviewing the Report of Their Committee on
"The Relation of the American Tract Society to the Subject of
Slavery.' By a Congregationalist Director. Boston: Crocker
and Brewster, 1855.   CtY-D; NN/Sch

4736. Thompson, L. The Nation's Danger. A Discourse Delivered
in the Congregational Church, West Amesbury, on the Day of the
Annual State Fast, April 10, 1856. Boston: J. M. Hewes,
Printer, 1856.   CtY-D

4737. Tilton, Theodore. The American Board and American Slav-
ery. Speech of Theodore Tilton, in Plymouth Church, Brooklyn,
January 28, 1860. Reported by Wm. Henry Burr. n.p., 1860.
CtY-D

4738. Weiss, John. Discourse Occasioned by the Death of Convers
Francis, D. D. Delivered Before the First Congregational Soci-

ety, Watertown, April 19, 1863. Cambridge: Priv. Print.,
1863.   CtY-D

4739. ----- Northern Strength and Weakness. An Address on Occasion of the National Fast, April 30, 1863. Delivered in Watertown. Boston: Walker, Wise, 1863.   CtY-D

4740. West Brookfield, Mass. Anti-Slavery Society. An Exposition
of Difficulties in West Brookfield, Connected with Anti-Slavery
Operations, Together with a Reply to Some Statements in a Pamphlet Put Forth by "Moses Chase, Pastor of the Church," Pur-
porting to be a "Statement of Facts in the Case of Deacon Hen-
shaw." By the Board of Managers of the W. B. Anti-Slavery
Society. West Brookfield, Mass.: The Anti-Slavery Society,
1844.   NN/Sch

4741. West Brookfield, Mass. First Church. Church Affairs in
West Brookfield: n.p., 1843.
    Slavery and the Congregational Church.

4742. Whipple, Charles King. Relation of the American Board of
Commissioners for Foreign Missions to Slavery. New York:
Negro University Press, 1969. O; NcD; CtY-D
    Congregational church and slavery.

4743. Whitcomb, William Charles. A Discourse on the Recapture
of Fugitive Slaves, Delivered at Stoneham, Mass., Nov. 3,
1850. Boston: Pr. by C. C. P. Moody, 1850. CtY-D; NN/Sch

4744. Withington, Leonard. A Bundle of Myrrh. Thanksgiving
Sermon Preached Nov. 28, 1850, at Newbury, First Parish.
Newburyport: C. Whipple, 1851.   CtY-D; DHU/MO

4745. Wyatt-Brown, Bertram. Lewis Tappan and the Evangelical
War Against Slavery. Cleveland: Press of Case Western
Reserve University, 1969.   CtY-D

3. Disciples of Christ (Christian Churches)

4746. Campbell, Alexander. "Our Position to American Slavery."
The Millennial Harbinger (15; Feb., 1845), p. 49. DLC; LyL;
CtY; TN/DCHS
    Disciples of Christ and slavery.

4647. Crain, James Andrew. The Development of Social Ideas
Among the Disciples of Christ. St. Louis, Mo.: Bethany Press,
1969.   DHU/R; DLC

4748. Fife, Robert Olkham. Alexander Campbell and the Christian
Church in the Slavery Controversy. Doctoral dissertation.
Indiana University, 1960.
    Founder of the Disciples of Christ Church.
    Microfilm

4749. Harrell, David E., Jr. A Social History of the Disciples of
Christ to 1866. Doctoral dissertation. Vanderbilt University,

1962.
    Slavery and the Church. Disciples of Christ.

4750. Haynes, Nathaniel Smith. The Disciples of Christ in Illinois
and Their Attitude Toward Slavery.
    (In Illinois State Historical Society. Papers in Illinois History
and Transactions for the Year 1913. Springfield, 1914. pp.
52-59)

4751. Shannon, James. An Address Delivered Before the Pro-Slavery Convention of the State of Missouri. St. Louis: Printed at
the Republican Book and Job Office, 1855.   TN/DCHS
    Disciples of Christ Christian Church and race relations.

4752. ----- The Philosophy of Slavery, as Identified With the Philosophy of Human Happiness. Frankfort, Ky.: A. G. Hodge,
1849.
    Disciples of Christ Christian Church and race relations.

4. Friends—Quakers

4753. Alexander, Ann. An Address to the Inhabitants of Charleston,
South Carolina. Philadelphia: Kimber, Conrad, 1805. INRE

4754. Alexander, Stella. Quaker Testimony Against Slavery and
Racial Discrimination. An Anthology Compiled by Stella
Alexander. London: Friends Home Service Committee, 1958.
INRE; DHU/R

4755. Anecdotes and Memoirs of William Boen, a Coloured Man,
Who Lived and Died Near Mount Holly, New Jersey to Which
is Added, the Testimony of Friends of Mount Holly Monthly
Meeting Concerning Him. Philadelphia: John Richards, 1834.
NcD

4756. Anti-Slavery Convention of American Women. 3d, Philadelphia, 1839. An Address from the Convention of American Wom-

en, to the Society of Friends, on the Subject of Slavery. Bristol,
Eng.: Printed by J. Wright, 1840.   NNCor

4757. Applegarth, Albert C. ...Quakers in Pennsylvania. Baltimore: Johns Hopkins Press, 1892. (Johns Hopkins University
Studies in Historical and Political Science, 10th ser., viii-ix).

4758. Aptheker, Herbert. "The Quakers and Negro Slavery."
Journal of Negro History (25:3, Jl., 1940), pp. 331-62.
DHU/MO
    "Corrects the impression that Quakers were always 'Anti-
slavery' it shows the gradual evolution."

4759. Association for the Care of Colored Orphans of Philadelphia.
Annual Report. Ist- , 1836.   INRE (1892)

4760. Association of Friends for Promoting the Abolition of Slavery and Improving the Condition of the Free People of Color. Annual Report. Philadelphia: n.p., 1846. DLC; NcD

4761. Association of Friends for the Aid and Elevation of the Freedmen. Philadelphia. Annual Report. Philadelphia: n.p., 1865. DLC; NcD

4762. Bassett, William. Letters to a Member of the Society of Friends, in Reply to Objections Against Joining Anti-Slavery Societies. Boston: Isaac Knapp, 1836. DHU/MO

4763. ----- Society of Friends in the United States: Their View of the Anti-Slavery Question, and Treatment of the People of Color. Darlington: J. Wilson, 1840. PHC
Compiled from Original Correspondence.

4764. Benezet, Anthony. A Caution to Great Britain and her Colonies, in a Short Representation of the Calamitous State of the Enslaved Negroes in the British Dominions. Philadelphia: Printed; London: Reprinted and Sold by J. Phillips, 1784. CtY-D

Restricted circulation.

4765. ----- Notes on the Slave Trade. n.p.: Cruikshank, n.d. INRE

4766. ----- Observations on the Enslaving, Importing and Purchasing of Negroes; with Some Advice Thereon, Extracted from the Epistle of the Yearly Meeting of the People Called Quakers, Held in London in 1748. Germantown: Christopher Sower, 1760. DHU/MO; FSU

4767. ----- "A Quaker's Observation on Slavery." Gilbert Osofsky. The Burden of Race (New York: Harper & Row, 1966), pp. 44-49. DHU/R

4768. ----- A Serious Address to the Rulers of America, on the Inconsistency of Their Conduct Respecting Slavery: Forming a Contrast Between the Encroachments of England on American Liberty, and American Injustice in Tolerating Slavery. London: J. Phillips, 1783. DHU/MO

4769. ----- A Short Account of the Religious Society of Friends, Commonly Called Quakers. Philadelphia: Kimber and Conrad, 1814. DHU/MO

4770. ----- Some Historical Account of Guinea, its Situation, Produce and the General Disposition of its Inhabitants. With an Inquiry into the Rise and Progress of Slave-Trade, its Nature and Lamentable Effects. Also a Republication of the Sentiments of Several Authors of Note, on this Interesting Subject; Particularly an Extract of a Treatise, by Granville Sharp. By Anthony Benezet... Philadelphia: Pr. by J. Cruikshand, 1771. INRE

4771. ----- Views of American Slavery, Taken a Century Ago. Anthony Benezet, John Wesley... Philadelphia: Pub. by the Association of Friends for the Diffusion of Religious and Useful Knowledge, 1858. INRE

4772. Birkett, Mary. A Poem on the African Slave Trade. 2d ed. Dublin: J. Jones, 1792. INRE

4773. Birney, James Gillespie. Correspondence Between James G. Birney, of Kentucky, and Several Individuals of the Society of Friends. Haverhill: Essex Gazette, 1835. DHU/MO

4774. Bousell, John. The Standard of the Lord of Hosts Exalted; the Banner of the Prince of Peace Displayed. Being a Message unto the King... to take Away the Heavy Burthen of Tithes and to Set at Liberty the African Slaves. n.p.: Pr. for the Author, 1790. INRE

4775. A Brief Sketch of the Schools for Black People, and their Descendants, Established by the Religious Society of Friends in 1770. Philadelphia: Pub. by Direction of the Committee Having Charge of the Schools, Friends Bookstore, 1867. INRE

4776. Child, Lydia Maria (Francis). Isaac T. Hopper: A True Life. Boston: J. P. Jewett, 1853. CtY-D

4777. ----- The Progress of Religious Ideas, Through Successive Ages. New York: C. S. Francis & Co., 1855. NN/Sch

4778. Clarkson, Thomas. Cries of Africa, to the Inhabitants of Europe; or, a Survey of that Bloody Commerce Called the Slave-Trade. London: Harvey and Darton, 1821? CtY-D

4779. ----- The History of the Rise, Progress & Accomplishment of the Abolition of the African Slave-Trade, by the British Parliament... Philadelphia: Pub. by J. P. Parke, 1808. (Brown & Merritt, Printers.) CtY-D

4780. Curtis, Anna L. Stories of the Underground Railroad, by Anna L. Curtis; Foreword by Rufus M. Jones, Illustrated by Wm. Brooks. New York: The Island Workshop Press Co-op., Inc., 1941. INRE

4781. Danforth, Mildred E. A Quaker Pioneer: Laura Haviland, Superintendent of the Underground. New York: Exposition Press, 1961. CtY-D

4782. Dillon, Merton Lynn. Benjamin Lundy and the Struggle for Negro Freedom. Urbana: University of Illinois Press, 1966. CtY-D

4783. Drake, Thomas E. "Joseph Drinker's Pleas for the Admission of Colored People to the Society of Friends, 1795." Journal of Negro History (37:1 Ja., 1947), pp. 110-12. DHU/MO

4784. ----- Quakers and Slavery in America. New Haven: Yale University Press, 1950. DHU/R; CtY-D

4785. Edgerton, Walter. A History of the Separation in Indiana Yearly Meeting of Friends Which Took Place in the Winter of 1842 and 1843 on the Anti-Slavery Question... By Walter Edgerton. Cincinnati: Pugh, Printer, 1856. INRE; NcD

4786. Evans, William. Journal of the Life and Religious Service of William Evans, a Minister of the Gospel in the Society of Friends. Philadelphia: n.p., 1870. DHU/MO

4787. Extracts from Writings of Friends on the Subject of Slavery. Published by Direction of the Association of Friends for Advocating the Cause of the Slave and Improving the Condition of the Free People of Color. Philadelphia: Merrihew and Thompson, 1839. NNCor

4788. Ferris, David. Memoirs of the Life of David Ferris, an Approved Minister of the Society of Friends, Late of Wilmington in the State of Delaware. Philadelphia: Merrihew & Thompson's Steam Power Press, 1855. NNCor
Slavery and the Society of Friends.

4789. Forbush, Bliss. Elias Hicks, a Quaker Liberal. New York: Columbia University Press, 1956. NN/Sch

4790. Forster, John. Slavery Inconsistant with Justice and Good Policy, by Philanthropos. Lebanon, O.: McLean and Hale, 1812. INRE

4791. Forster, William. Memoirs. Edited by Benjamin Seebohm. London: A. W. Bennett, 1865. CtY-D

4792. Free Produce Association of Friends of Philadelphia. An Address to Our Fellow Members of the Religious Society of Friends on the Subject of Slavery and the Slave-Trade in the Western World, by Philadelphia Free Produce Association of Friends. Philadelphia: n.p., 1894. DLC

4793. Friends, Society of. American Friends Service Committee. Proceedings in Relation to the Presentation of the Address of the Yearly Meeting of the Religious Society of Friends, on the Slave-Trade and Slavery, to Sovereigns and those in Authority in the Nations of Europe, and in Other Parts of the World Where

(Friends, Society of. cont.)
the Christian Religion is Professed. New York: J. Egbert, 1856.
NN/Sch

4794. ----- Baltimore Yearly Meeting. A Review of a Pamphlet
Entitled, "A Defence of the Religious Society of Friends Who
Constitute the Yearly Meeting of Baltimore Against Certain
Charges Circulated by Joseph John Gurney." Baltimore: Pr.
by John D. Toy, 1840.   DHU/MO

4795. ----- Friends Board of Control. (Representing the Yearly
Meeting of the West) Committee on Freedmen. Report, Third
Month, 1865. Cincinnati, O.: R. W. Carroll, 1865. INRE

4796. ----- Indiana Yearly Meeting. Secession of a Large Body of
Friends from the Yearly Meeting of Indiana, in Consequence of
Anti-Slavery Action and Opinions, and of Extra Disciplinary
Proceedings on the Part of Said Yearly Meeting Against Them.
Indiana: Dublin, Reprinted by Webb and Chapman, 1843. NNCor

4797. ----- Indiana Yearly Meeting. Missionary Board. Annual
Report of the Missionary Board, for Southland, to Indiana Yearly
Meeting of Friends. V. I, 1864. Richmond, Ind.: n.p., 1864.
INRE

4798. ----- Indiana Yearly Meeting. Missionary Board. The
Discipline of the Society of Friends, of Indiana Yearly Meeting,
Revised by the Meeting Held at White Water in the Year 1854,
and Printed by Direction of the Same. Cincinnati: A. Pugh,
Printer, 1854.   NN/Sch
Pp. 89-91, Slavery and the Church.

4799. ----- Institute for Colored Youth. ...Annual Report of the
Board of Managers of the Institute for Colored Youth. Philadelphia: n.p., 1852.   INRE

4800. ----- London Yearly Meeting. An Address on the Conduct of
Christian and Civilized Nations Towards Those Less Civilized
and Enlightened. London: 1858.   NNCor
Slavery and the Society of Friends.

4801. ----- London Yearly Meeting. An Appeal to the Inhabitants
of Europe, on Slavery and the Slave-Trade. Issued on Behalf of
the Religious Society of Friends in Gt. Brit. London: Harvey
and Darton, 1839.   INRE

4802. ----- London Yearly Meeting. Appel sur l'Iniquité de
l'Esclavage et de la Traite des Noirs, Adopté de la Part de
L'Assemblée Annuelle de la Société Religieuse Dite des Amis,
Réunie en Son Assemblée Annuelle de 1844. Paris: Firmin
Didot Fries, 1845.   NN/Sch

4803. ----- London Yearly Meeting, 1783. The Case of Our Fellow
Creatures, the Oppressed Africans, Respectfully Recommended
to the Serious Consideration of the Legislature of Great Britain
by the People Called Quakers. London: Pr. by James Phillips,
George Yard, Lombard Street, 1783.   DHU/MO

4804. ----- London Yearly Meeting, 1822. An Address to the In-
habitants of Europe on the Iniquity of Slave Trade; Issued by the
Religious Society of Friends, Commonly Called Quakers, in
Great Britain and Ireland. London: W. Phillips, 1822. DHU/MO

4805. ----- London Yearly Meeting, 1844. An Appeal on the Iniquity
of Slavery and the Slave-Trade... London: E. Marsh, 1844.
INRE

4806. ----- London Yearly Meeting, 1854. Proceedings in Relation to the Presentation of the Address of the
Yearly Meeting of the Religious Society of Friends, on the
Slave-Trade and Slavery, to Sovereigns and Those in Authority
in the Nations of Europe, and in Other Parts of the World,
Where the Christian Religion is Professed. Cincinnati: Pr.
by E. Morgan and Sons, 1855.   NN/Sch; NcD

4807. ----- London Yearly Meeting. Beroep op de Goddeloosheid
der Slavernij en van den Slavenhandel, Nitgegeven door de
Jaarlijksche Vergadering van het Godsdiestig Genootschap,

der Vrienden. Gehouden in London, 1844. Amsterdam:
Gedrukt Bij C. A. Spin & Zoon, 1845.   NN/Sch

4808. ----- London Yearly Meeting. Committee on the Negro and
Aborigines Fund. Reports of the Committee... Presented to the
Yearly Meetings of 1854 and 1855... London: Book and Tract
Depository of the Society of Friends, 1855.   INRE

4809. ----- London Yearly Meeting. Observations on the Inslaving,
Importing and Purchasing of Negroes; with Some Advice Thereon, Extracted from the Epistle of the Yearly Meeting of the People Called Quakers. Held at London in the Year 1748... 2d ed.
Germantown: Pr. by Christopher Sower, 1760.   INRE

4810. ----- London Yearly Meeting. Proceedings in Relation to the
Presentation Address of the Yearly Meeting... on the Slave-Trade
and Slavery, to Sovereigns and Those in Authority in the Nations
of Europe... London: Newman, 1854.   I NRE

4811. ----- New England Yearly Meeting, 1842. An Appeal to the
Professors of Christianity, in the Southern States and Elsewhere,
on the Subject of Slavery: by the Representatives of the Yearly
Meeting of Friends for New England. Providence: Pr. by
Knowles and Vose, 1842.   CtY-D

4812. ----- New York Yearly Meeting. An Address of Friends of
the Yearly Meeting of New York, to the Citizens of the United
States, Especially to Those of the Southern States, Upon the
Subject of Slavery. New York: M. Day, 1844. NN/Sch; CtY-D

4813. ----- New York Yearly Meeting. Address of the Yearly
Meeting of the Religious Society of Friends, Held in the City
of New York in the Sixth Month 1852, to the Professors of
Christianity in the United States, on the Subject of Slavery.
New York: J. Egbert, Printer, 1852.   DHU/MO

4814. ----- New York Yearly Meeting, 1837. Address to the
Citizens of the United States of America on the Subject of
Slavery, from the Yearly Meeting of the Religious Society of
Friends (called Quakers) Held in New York. New York: New
York Yearly Meeting of Firends, 1837.   CtY-D

4815. ----- Philadelphia Yearly Meeting. An Address to the Quarterly, Monthly and Preparative Meetings, and the Members ther-
of, Composing the Yearly Meeting to Have Charge of the Subject
of Slavery. Philadelphia: Pr. by J. Richards, 1839. CtY-D

4816. ----- Philadelphia Yearly Meeting. The Appeal of the Religious Society of Friends in Pennsylvania, New Jersey, Delaware,
etc., to their Fellow-Citizens of the United Staes on Behalf of
the Colored Races. Philadelphia: Friends Book Store, 1858.
NcD

4817. ----- Philadelphia Yearly Meeting. A Brief Statement
of the Rise and Progress of the Testimony of the Religious
Society of Friends, Against Slavery and the Slave Trade, Pub.
by Direction of the Yearly Meeting, Held in Philadelphia, in
the Fourth Month, 1843. Philadelphia: Printed by J. and W.
Kite, 1843. PPT; INRE; DHU/R; CtY-D

4818. ----- Philadelphia Yearly Meeting. An Exposition of the
African Slave-Trade, from the Year 1840-1850, Inclusive,
prepared from Offical Documents, and Published by Direction
of the Representatives of the Religious Society of Friends, in
Pennsylvania, New Jersey, and Delaware. Philadelphia: J. A.
Rakestraw, Printer, 1851.   DHU/MO

4819. ----- Philadelphia Yearly Meeting. Memorial ... on the
African Slave Trade. Philadelphia: J. & W. Kite, 1840.
INRE

4820. ----- Philadelphia Yearly Meeting. Slavery and The Domestic Slave Trade, In the United States. By the Committee appointed by the late Yearly Meeting of Friends held in Philadelphia, 1839. Phila.: Pr. by Merrihew and Thompson, 1841.
INRE

4821. ----- Philadelphia Yearly Meeting. A View of the Present
State of the African Slave Trade. Published by Direction of

a Meeting Representing the Religious Society of Friends in Pennsylvania, New Jersey, etc. Philadelphia: W. Brown, Printer, 1824.   CtY-D

4822. Fuller, James Cannings. Letter from James Cannings Fuller to The Editors of the British Friend. Bristol: 1843.
                                                  NNCor
       Slavery and the Society of Friends.

4823. Hicks, Elias. Journal of the Life and Religious Labours of Elias Hicks. Written by Himself. New York: Isaac T. Hopper, 1832.   DHU/MO

4824. ----- Letters Including Observations on the Slavery of the Africans and Their Descendants and On the Use of the Produce of Their Labor. Philadelphia: T. E. Chapman, 1861. NNCor
       Slavery and the Society of Friends.

4825. Hilty, Hiram H. North Carolina Quakers and Slavery. Doctoral dissertation, Duke University, 1969.   INRE

4826. Irish, David. Observations on a Living and Effectual Testimony Against Slavery. Introduced with Some Remarks upon Excess and Superfluity. Recommended to the Consideration of the Members of the Society of Friends. New York: Pr. for the Author, 1836.   DHU/MO

4827. James, Sydney Vincent. A People Among People; Quaker Benevolence in Eighteenth-Century America. Cambridge: Harvard University Press, 1963.   NN/Sch

4828. Janney, Samuel M. The Life of George Fox; with Dissertations, or, his Views Concerning the Doctrines, Testimonies and Discipline of the Christian Church... Phila.: Lippincott, Grambo and Co., 1853.   DHU/MO

4829. Jones, Rufus Matthew. The Quakers in the American Colonies. New York: Russell & Russell, 1962.   NN/Sch

4830. Jordan, Richard. A Journal of the Life and Religious Labors of Richard Jordan a Minister of the Gospel in the Society of Friends, Late of Newton, in Gloucester County, New Jersey. Phila.: For Sale at Friends Book Store, 1877.   NN/Sch

4831. Jorns, Auguste. The Quakers as Pioneers in Social Work (Studien Uber die Sozialpolitik der Quaker). New York: Macmillan, 1931.   DHU/R; NN/Sch
       Bibliographical note: p. 7.

4832. Keene, Calvin. "Friends and Negro Slavery." Friends Intelligencer (109:3, Ja., 19, 1952), pp. 33-4.   DHU/R

4833. Keith, George. An Exhortation & Caution to Friends Concerning Buying or Keeping Negroes. New York: Wm. Bradford, 1893. Philadelphia, 1889.   NN/Sch

4834. ----- The First Printed Protest Against Slavery in America. Philadelphia: n.p., 1889.   CtY-D
       "Reprinted from 'The Pennsylvania Magazine of History and Biography.'"

4835. Lewis, Graceanna. An Appeal To Those Members of the Society of Friends, Who, Knowing the Principles of the Abolitionists, Stand Aloof from the Anti-Slavery Enterprise. n.p.: n.p., 18?   NNCor
       Slavery and the Society of Friends.

4836. Marriott, Charles. An Address to the Religious Society of Friends, on the Duty of Declining the Use of the Products of Slave Labor ... New York: I. T. Hopper, 1835. CtY-D; DHU/MO

4837. McKiever, Charles. Slavery and the Emigration of North Carolina Friends. Murfreesboro, N.C.: Johnson Pub. Co., 1970.   INRE

4838. Mordell, Alber. Quaker Militant, John Greenleaf Whittier... Boston and New York: Houghton Mifflin Co., 1933. DHU/MO

4839. Niles, John Milton. Speech of Mr. Niles, of Connecticut, on the Petition of a Society of Friends in Pennsylvania: Praying for the Abolition of Slavery in the District of Columbia. In Senate, Feb. 15, 1836. Washington: Blair & Rives, 1836.
                                                  DHU/MO

4840. The Non-Slaveholder. v. 1-5, 1846-50; n. s. v. 1-2, 1853-54. Philadelphia: Merrihew and Thompson 1846-54. INRE

4841. Nuermberger, Ruth Anna (Ketring). The Free Produce Movement; a Quaker Protest Against Slavery. Durham, N.C.: Duke University Press, 1942.   CtY-D; NN/Sch
       Also in, Trinity College Historical Society, Historical Papers (ser. 25), 1942.   DLC; NcD; CtY

4842. Observations on the Inslaving Importing and Purchasing of Negroes, with Some Advice Thereon Extracted From the Epistle of the Yearly Meeting of the People Called Quakers. Held at London in the Year 1748. n.p., 1760.   DHU/MO

4843. Osborn, Charles. Journal of the Faithful Servant of Christ, Charles Osborn, Containing an Account of Many of His Travels and Exercises in the Service of the Lord, and in Defense of the Truth, as It is in Jesus. Cincinnati: A. Pugh, 1854. DLC; INRE

4844. ----- A Testimony Concerning the Separation Which Ocurred in Indiana Yearly Meeting of Friends, in the Winter of 1842-43; Together with Sundry Remarks and Observations Particularly on the Subjects of War, Slavery and Colonization. Centreville, (Ind.?): R. Vaile, 1849.   DLC

4845. Philadelphia Free Produce Association of Friends. An Address to Our Fellow Members of the Religious Society of Friends on the Subject of Slavery and the Slave-Trade in the Western World. Philadelphia: n.p., 1849.   INRE

4846. Pickett, Clarence Evan. ...For More Than Bread; an Autobiographical Account of Twenty-two Years' Work with the American Friends Service Committee. Boston: Little, Brown, 1953.
       Slavery and the Church-Friends, Society of pp. 369-72.

4847. Review of "An Address" Respecting Slavery, Issued by the Yearly Meeting of Friends, Held at Lombard Street, Baltimore, 11th Month, 1842. [Baltimore: n.p., 1842?] NNCor

4848. Rhoads, Samuel. Considerations on the Use of the Productions of Slavery... 2d ed. Philadelphia: Merrihew and Thompson, 1845.   DLC; INRE

4849. Richman, Irving B. John Brown Among the Quakers and Other Sketches... Des Moins: n.p., 1894.   NN/Sch

4850. Siebert, Wilbur Henry. A Quaker Section of the Underground Railroad in Northern Ohio. Columbus: Heer, 1930. INRE

4851. Smucker, Orden C. The Influence of the Quakers in the Abolition of Negro Slavery in the United States. Master's thesis. University of Chicago, 1933.

4852. Some Thoughts on Slavery, Addressed to the Professors of Christianity, and More Particularly to Those of the Society of Friends. New York: Barker & Crane, 1844.   NNCor

4853. Stanton, Benjamin. Letter From Benjamin Stanton, Henry H. Way and Daniel Puckett, to James Cannings Fuller, Relative to the Present Position of Anti-Slavery Friends Within the Limits of the Indiana Yearly Meeting. n.p.: n.p., 18_. NNCor

4854. Thomas, Allen Clapp. The Attitude of the Society of Friends Towards Slavery in the Seventeenth and Eighteen Centuries, Particularly in Relation to its Own Members. n.p., n.d. DHU/R; CtY-D
       (In American Society of Church History. Papers. New York & London, 1879. 24.5 cm. vol. viii, p. 263-99.) CtY-D; DHU/R

4855. Turner, Edward R. The First Abolition Society in the United States. Philadelphia: L. B. Lippincott, 1912.   NNCor

4856. Weeks, Stephen Beauregard. Southern Quakers and Slavery: a Study in Institutional History. Baltimore: The Johns Hopkins Press, 1896.   DHU/R; CtY-D; DHU/MO

4857. Wigham, Eliza. The Anti-Slavery Cause in America and its Martyrs. London: Bennett, 1863.   INRE

4858. Woodson, Carter G. "Anthony Benezet." Journal of Negro History (2:1, Ja., 1917), pp. 37-50.
     "Author regards him as the greatest Quaker anti-slavery leader."

4859. Woolman, John. Extracts on the Subject of Slavery, from the Journal and Writings of John Woolman, of Mount Holly, New Jersey, a Minister of the Society of Friends, in the City of New York. New York: M. Day and Co., 1840. DLC

4860. ----- A Journal of the Life, Gospel Labours, and Christian Experiences of that Faithful Minister of Jesus Christ. n.p., Pr. by Thos. Hurst, 1840.   DHU/MO

4861. ----- Selections from the Writings of John Woolman... Dublin: Pr. by C. Benthaus, 1823.   DHU/MO

4862. Zilversmit, Arthur. The First Emancipation; the Abolition of Slavery in the North. Chicago: Univ. of Chicago Press, 1967.   DHU/R
     Chapter 3, Quakers and slavery.

5. Lutheran

4863. Fortenbaugh, Robert. "American Lutheran Synods and Slavery, 1830-1860." Journal of Religion (13:1, Ja., 1933), pp. 72-92.   DHU/R

4864. Heathcote, Charles William. The Lutheran Church and the Civil War. Doctoral dissertation. George Washington University, 1918.

4865. "Our General Synod." The Evangelical Quarterly Review (15; Jl., 1864), pp. 390+.   IEG; ICU
     "The delegates reaffirmed unqualified condemnation of slavery and resisted those who sought to prove its acceptability from scripture." The Lutheran Church.

4866. Payne, Daniel Alexander, (bp.). Document: Protestation of American Slavery.   MNtcA
     Photocopy from Journal of Negro History, v. 52, p. 59-64, Jan., 1967.
     Slavery and the Lutheran Church.

4867. Strange, Douglas C. "Our Duty to Preach the Gospel to Negroes: Southern Lutherans and American Slavery." Concordia Historical Institute Quarterly (42:4, Nov., 1969), pp. 171-82.   MSL/CHI

6. Methodist Episcopal (United Methodist)

4868. Abbey, Richard. Peter, Not an Apostle, But a Chattel With a Strange History. Nashville: Southern Methodist Pub. House, 1885.   NcD

4869. Adams, C. An Address to the Abolitionists of the Methodist Episcopal Church. Boston: Reid & Rand, 1843.   NcD

4870. Alexander, Gross. "The History of the Methodist Church, South." Vol. 2. American Church History Series. New York: Christian Literature Co., 1894.

4871. An Appeal on the Subject of Slavery; Addressed to the members of the New England and New Hampshire Conferences of the Methodist Episcopal Church. Together with a Defence of Said Appeal, in Which Is Shown the Sin of Holding Property in Man. Boston: D. H. Ela, 1835.   NNCor; DHU/MO

4872. Asbury, Francis. The Heart of Asbury's Journal. New York: Eaton & Mains, 1904.   NN/Sch

4873. Baker, George C. An Introduction to the History of Early New England Methodism, 1789-1839. Durham, N.C.: Duke University Press, 1941.   DLC
     "Methodism and Slavery Problem."

4874. Bangs, Nathan. A History of the Methodist Episcopal Church. New York: T. Mason & G. Lane, 1839.   DLC

4875. Bascom, Henry Bidleman. Methodism and Slavery; with other Matters in Controversy between the North and the South; Being a Review of the Manifesto of the Majority in Reply to the Protests of the Minority...in the Case of Bishop Andrew. Frankfort: Hodges, 1845.   NcD; DLC

4876. Bassett, John Spencer. "North Carolina Methodism and Slavery." Historical Papers of the Trinity College Historical Society (Durham, N.C., 1900. Ser. IV), pp. 1-11. NcD; PPULC; MB; PU

4877. Beeson, Lewis. The Methodist Episcopal Church in Michigan During the Civil War. Lansing: Civil War Centennial Observance Commission, 1965.   DLC

4878. Betker, John P. The M. E. Church and Slavery, as Described by Revs. H. Mattison, W. Hosmer, E. Bowen, D.D., D. DeVinne, and J. D. Long, With a Bible View of the Whole Subject. Syracuse: S. Lee, 1859.   DLC

4879. Bond, T. E. "The Methodist Episcopal Church, South." Methodist Quarterly Review (31:2, Apr. 1849; 33:3, Jl., 1851), pp. 282-302; 396-428.   DHU/R
     Discusses the problem of slavery and its effects on Methodism in the South.

4880. Boole, William H. Antidote to Rev. H. J. Van Dyke's Pro-Slavery Discourse. Delivered in the M. E. Church, Mount Vernon, New York, on Sunday, January 13, 1861. New York: E. Jones & Co., Printers, 1861.   NN/Sch

4881. Bowen, Elias. Slavery in the Methodist Episcopal Church. Auburn: W. J. Moses, Printer, 1850.   DHU/MO

4882. Bradburn, Samuel. An Address to the People Called Methodists. Concerning the Criminality of Encouraging Slavery. 5th ed. London: M. Gurney, n.d.   CtY; PHC

4883. "Brief Review." The Quarterly Review of the Methodist Episcopal Church South (15; Ja., 1861), pp. 132+ DLC
     Slavery and religion.

4884. Brownlow, William Gannaway. Ought American Slavery to be Perpetuated? A Debate Between Rev. W. G. Brownlow and Rev. A. Pryne. Held at Phila., Sept., 1858. Philadelphia: J. B. Lippincott & Co., 1858.   DHU/MO; CtY-D

4885. ----- A Sermon on Slavery: A Vindication of the Methodist Church, South: Her Position Stated. Delivered in Temperance Hall, in Knoxville, on Sabbath August 9th 1857, to the Delegates and Others in Attendance at the Southern Commercial Convention. Knoxville: Kinsloe & Rice, 1857.   DHU/MO

4886. Bucke, Emory S. History of American Methodism. New York: Abingdon Press, 1964.   DHU/R
 V.1, "Methodists Churches for Negroes" pp. 601-17. Position on Slavery, pp. 251-56.

4887. Buckley, James M. History of Methodism. New York: Harper & Bros., 1898.   DHU/R
 Vol. 2, Slavery issue and the Methodist Church.

4888. Caldwell, John H., (bp.). Slavery and Southern Methodism: Two Sermons Preached in the Methodist Church in Newman, Georgia. Newman, Ga.: Pr. for the Author, 1865. DHU/MO

4889. Carman, Adam. An Oration Delivered at the Fourth Anniversary of the Abolition of the Slave Trade, in the Methodist Episcopal Church, in Second Street, N.Y., Jan. 1, 1811.
 MBU

4890. Carter, Cullen T. History of the Tennessee Conference. Nashville: The Author, 1948.   IEG
 Information on Negro work 1828-1832 and 1862-1866.

4891. Clark, Elmer Talmage, (ed.). The Journal of Francis Asbury. Nashville: Abingdon Press, 1958.   DHU/R
 Views toward slavery and the church.

4892. Coggeshall, Samuel Wilde. An Anti-Slavery Address, Delivered in the Methodist Episcopal Church, Danielsonville, Conn., Jul. 4, 1849. West Killingly: E. B. Carter, 1849.
 MBU; OO

4893. Coles, George. Heroines of Methodism: or, Pen and Ink Sketches of the Mothers and Daughters of the Church. New York: Carlton & Porter, 1857.   NN/Sch

4894. Collyer, Isaac J. P. Review of Rev. W. W. Eell's Thanksgiving Sermon, Delivered in the Methodist Episcopal Church, Newburyport, Dec. 29, 1850... Newburyport: C. Whipple, 1851.   NN/Sch

4895. Coulter, Ellis Merton. When John Wesley Preached in Georgia. Savannah: Georgia Historical Society, 1925. O

4896. ----- William G. Brownlow, Fighting Parson of the Southern Highlands. Knoxville: University of Tennessee Press, 1971.   DHU/R
 Pro-slavery Methodist Episcopal minister who became head of the government in Tennessee in 1865.

4897. Crane, Jonathan Townley. Christian Duty in Regard to American Slavery. A Sermon Preached in the Trinity Methodist Episcopal Church, Jersey City, on Sabbath Morning, December 11, 1859. Jersey City: R. B. Kashov, 1860.
 NN/Sch

4898. Debate on "Modern Abolitionism," in the General Conference of the Methodist Episcopal Church, Held in Cincinnati, May, 1836. With Notes. Cincinnati, O.: Anti-Slavery Society, 1836.   DHU/MO

4899. DeVinne, Daniel. The Methodist Episcopal Church and Slavery. A Historical Survey of the Relation to the Early Methodists to Slavery. New York: F. Hart, 1857. NN/Sch; DHU/MO

4900. Elliott, Charles. History of the Great Secession from the Methodist Episcopal Church in the Year 1845. Cincinnati: Swormstedt & A. Poe, 1855.   DLC

4901. ----- "Martyrdom of Bewley." The Mercersburg Review (15; Oct., 1863), pp. 656+.   DHU/R
 "Bishop Pierce of the Methodist Episcopal Church, South persecuted Methodists who sympathized with the North."

4902. ----- South-Western Methodism; a History of the M.E. Church in the South-West from 1844 to 1864, Compromising the Martyrdom of Bewley and Others, Persecutions of the M.E. Church, and Its Reorganization. Cincinnati: Poe and Hitchcock, 1868.   NNCor
 Slavery and the Methodist Episcopal Church.

4903. Fuller, Erasmus Q. An Appeal to the Records: a Vindication of the Methodist Episcopal Church, in its Policy and Proceedings Toward the South. Cincinnati: Hitchcock and Walden, 1876.   CtY-D

4904. Garber, Paul Neff. The Methodists are One People. Nashville: Cokesbury, 1939.   DHU/R
 Slavery and racial issues divide Methodists.

4905. Gravely, William B. "Methodist Preachers, Slavery and Caste: Types of Social Concern in Antebellum America." The Duke Divinity School Review (34:3, Aut., 1969), pp. 209-29.   Pam. File, DHU/R

4906. Gross, Alexander. "History of the Methodist Episcopal Church, South." American Church History Series, V. 11 (New York: Christian Literature Co., 1894), pp. 1-142.   DHU/R

4907. Guice, John Asa. American Methodism and Slavery to 1844. Bachelor paper. School or Religion, Duke University, 1930.

4908. Harris, William Logan. The Constitutional Powers of the General Conference, with a Special Application to the Subject of Slaveholding. Cincinnati: Methodist Book Concern, 1860.   NcD

4909. Harrison, William Pope. Methodist Union Threatened in 1844. Was Formally Dissolved in 1848 by the Legislation of Dr. (afterward Bishop) Simpson in the Northern General Conference of 1848: Whereby the Reunion of Episcopal Methodism was Rendered forever Impossible... Nashville: Pub. House, Meth. Episcopal Church, South, 1892. DLC; NcD
 "Appeared in the Quarterly Review under the caption: 'Bishop Simpson as a Politician' "

4910. Haven, Gilbert, (bp.). An Appeal to Our People for Our People. New York: n.p., 1875.   DLC

4911. -----(bp.). National Sermons. Sermons, Speeches and Letters on Slavery and its War, from the Passage of the Fugitive Slave Bill to the Election of President Grant. Boston: Lee & Shepard, 1869.   NN/Sch; InU; DHU/MO
 Reprint: New York: Arno Press, 1969

4912. Henkle, Moses Montgomery. The Life Of Henry Biddleman Bascom... Louisville: Morton & Griswold, 1854. NN/Sch

4913. Horton, Joseph P. Religious and Educational Contributions of the Methodists to the Slaves. Bachelor of Divinity thesis. Southern Methodist University, n.d.

4914. How the Action of the Churches Towards the Anti-Slavery Cause Promotes Infidelity. Issued by the "Union Anti-Slavery Society." Composed of Members of the M.E. Church.
 DHU/MO
 Pamphlets on Slavery and Christianity V.1

4915. Johnston, Robert. Four Letters to Rev. J. Caughey, Methodist Episcopal Minister, on the Participation of the American Methodist Episcopal Church in the Sin of American Slavery. Dublin: Samuel J. Machen, 1841.   TNF; MH; ICN; OCIWHi

4916. Jordan, Marjorie Waggoner. Mississippi Methodists and the Division of the Church Over Slavery. Doctoral dissertation. University of Southern Mississippi, 1972.

4917. Lee, Umphrey and William W. Sweet. A Short History of Methodism. New York: Abingdon Press, 1956. DHU/R
 Attitude of church on slavery, pp. 151-53.

4918. Leeds Anti-Slavery Association. Address of the Leeds Anti-Slavery Association to the Wesleyan Conference, Held at Liver-

(Leeds Anti-Slavery Assoc. cont.)
  pool, in 1857. Leeds, n.p., 1857.   NNCor
    Broadside Methodist Episcopal Church and slavery.

4919. Mac Master, Richard K. "Liberty or Property? The Methodists Petition for Emancipation in Virginia, 1785." Methodist History (10:1, Oct., 1971), pp. 44-55.   DHU/R
    Virginia Methodists petitioned their General Assembly for the
    emancipation of all slaves in the state in 1785, but were
    rejected.

4920. Macmillan, Margaret B. The Methodist Episcopal Church in
  Michigan During the Civil War. Lewis Beeson, editor. Lansing,
  Mich.: Civil War Centennial Observance Commission, 1965.
                                                 NcD

4921. ----- "Michigan Methodism in the Civil War." Methodist
  History (3; Ja., 1965), pp. 26-38.   DHU/R

4922. Mason, C. B. "The Methodist Episcopal Church and the
  Evangelization of Africa." J. W. E. Bowen, (ed.). Addresses
  and Proceedings of the Congress of Africa. (Miami, Fla.:
  Mnemosyne Pub., Inc., 1969), pp. 143-48.   DHU/R

4923. Mathews, Donald G. Antislavery, Piety, and Institutionalism:
  the Slavery Controversies in the Methodist Episcopal Church,
  1780-1844. Doctoral dissertation. Duke University, 1962.

4924. ----- Slavery and Methodism: A Chapter in American
  Morality, 1780-1845. Princeton, N.J.: Princeton University
  Press, 1965.   DHU/MO; DHU/R

4925. Matlack, Lucius C. The Antislavery Struggle and Triumph
  in the Methodist Church. New York: Phillips & Hunt, 1881.
                         DHU/MO; NN/Sch; NcD; MBU

4926. ----- The History of American Slavery and Methodism, from
  1780 to 1849; and History of the Wesleyan Methodist Connection
  of America. New York: n.p., 1849. NcD; DHU/MO; NN/Sch;
  MBU

4927. ----- Narrative of the Anti-Slavery Experience of a Minister
  in the Methodist Episcopal Church, Who Was Twice Rejected
  by the Philadelphia Annual Conference, and Finally Deprived of
  License to Preach for Being an Abolitionist. Philadelphia:
  Merrihew & Thompson. 1845.   OO; DLC

4928. Mattison, Hiram. The Impending Crisis of 1860; or, the
  Present Connection of the Methodist Episcopal Church with
  Slavery and our Duty in Regard to it... New York: Mason Bros.,
  1859.   DHU/MO; CtY-D

4929. McCarter, John M. Border Methodism and Border Slavery.
  Being a Statement and Review of the Action of the Philadelphia
  Annual Conference Concerning Slavery at the late Session at
  Easton, Pa... Phila.: Collins, Printer, 1858. DLC; NcD

4930. Mc Neilly, James H. Religion and Slavery; A Vindication
  of the Southern Churches. Nashville: Publishing House of the
  M. E. Church, South, 1911.   NNCor

4931. Merrill, Stephen E. The Organic Union of American Methodism. Cincinnati: Cranston & Stowe, 1892. ICU: GEO

4932. The Methodist Churches, North and South. An Address to
  the Members of the M. E. Church, South. And to All Other
  Friends of Law, Peace, and Righteousness. By a Member of
  the Kentucky Conference. Cincinnati: Wrightson, Printers,
  1866.   NNCor

4933. Methodist Episcopal Church. General Conference, 1836.
  "Modern Abolitionism" in the General Conference of the...
  Held in Cincinnati, May, 1836. Cincinnati: Anti-Slavery
  Society, 1836.   DLC

4934. Minutes of the Fifth Annual Convention for the Improvement
  of the Free People of Colour in the United States, held by
  adjournments in the Wesley Church, Philadelphia from the

First to the Fifth of June, inclusive, 1835. Philadelphia: Pr.
by Wm. P. Gibbons, Sixth and Cherry Streets, 1934. DHU/MO

4935. Mitchell, Joseph. "Southern Methodist Newspapers During
  the Civil War." Methodist History (11:1, Ja., 1973), pp. 20-
  39.   DHU/R

4936. ----- "Traveling of Preacher and Settled Farmer."
  Methodist History (5; Je., 1967), pp. 3-14.   DHU/R
    "Slaveholding interest in Southern Methodism."

4937. Norwood, John Nelson. The Schism in the Methodist
  Episcopal Church, 1844: a Study of Slavery and Ecclesiastical
  Politics... Alfred, N.Y.: Alfred University, 1923. DHU/R;
  CtY-D; NcD

4938. Parks, William Justice. A Diary-Letter Written from the
  Methodist General Conference of 1844 by the Rev. W. J. Parks
  edited by the Franklin Nutting Parker... Atlanta, Ga.: The
  Library, Emory University, 1944.   NcD; CtY-D

4939. Peck, George. Slavery and the Episcopacy: Being an Examination of Dr. Bascom's Review of the Reply of the Majority
  to the Protest of the Minority of the Late General Conference
  of the M. E. Church, in the Case of Bishop Andrew. ... New
  York: G. Lane & C. B. Tippett, 1845.   NcD

4940. Phelan, Macum. A History of Early Methodism in Tennessee.
  Nashville: Cokesbury Press, 1924.   IEG
    Slavery and Methodism.

4941. Posey, Walter Brownlow. "Influence of Slavery Upon the
  Methodist Church in the Early South and Southwest." Missis-
  ippi Valley Historical Review (17:4, Mr., 1931), pp. 530-42.
                                                DHU

4942. Powell, Milton B. The Abolitionist Controversy in the Methodist Episcopal Church, 1840-1864. Doctoral dissertation.
  University of Iowa, 1963.

4943. Pullen, William H. The Blast of a Trumpet in Zion, Calling
  Upon Every Son and Daughter of Wesley, in Great Britain and
  Ireland, to Aid Their Brethren in America in Purifying Their
  American Zion from Slavery. London: Webb, Millington & Co.,
  1860.   DLC

4944. Purifoy, Lewis M. The Methodist Episcopal Church South
  and Slavery, 1844-1865. Doctoral dissertation. University
  of North Carolina, 1965.   DHU/R

4945. Redford, A. H. History of the Organization of the M.E.
  Church in Kentucky. Nashville: Southern Methodist Publishing
  House, 1868-70.   DLC

4946. Scarritt, Nathan. Position of the M.E. Church, South, on
  the Subject of Slavery. St. Louis: Methodist Book Depository
  1860.   NNCor
    Slavery and the Methodist Episcopal Church.

4947. Schreyer, George Maurice. Methodist Work Among the Plantation Negroes in the South Carolina Conference from 1829 to
  1865. B.D. thesis. Duke University, 1939.   NcD

4948. Scott, Orange. Address to the General Conference of the
  Methodist Episcopal Church. A Member of that Body; Pre-
  sented During its Session in Cincinnati, Ohio, May 19, 1836.
  New York: H. R. Piercy, 1836.   DHU/MO

4949. ----- Appeal to the Methodist Episcopal Church. Boston:
  David H. Ela, 1838.   DHU/MO; NcD

4950. ----- The Grounds of Secession from the M. E. Church:
  or, Book for the Times; Being an Examination of Her Connection with Slavery, and Also of Her Form of Government; Revised and Corrected. To Which is Added Wesley upon Slavery.
  New York: L. C. Mallock, 1851. OO; NcD; TNF; MH; GAU;
  CtY-D; MNtcA; NNCor
    Reprinted, New York: Arno Press, 1969.

4951. ----- The Life of Rev. Orange Scott: Compiled from his Personal Narrative, Correspondence, and Other Authentic Sources of Information. In two Parts. By Lucius C. Matlack. New York: Prindle and D. C. Matlack, 1851.   NN/Sch

4952. ----- The Methodist Episcopal Church and Slavery. Containing Also the Views of the English Wesleyan Methodist Church with Regard to Slavery, and a Treatise on the Duty of Seceding from All Pro-Slavery Churches. Boston: Orange Scott, 1844.   MBU

4953. ----- The Wesleyan Anti-Slavery Review, Containing an Appeal to the Methodist Episcopal Church. No. 1, 1838. Boston: Daivd H. Ela, 1838.   PHi

4954. Shrewsbury, William James. British Methodism and Slavery; an Historic Document: Shewing in What Manner Methodism Prepared the Way for Freedom: - and Promoted the Cause of Emancipation. Heywood: J. Howard, 1862.   NNCor

4955. Simpson, Matthew. Cyclopedia of Methodism... Philadelphia: Louis H. Everts, 1881.   DHU/R
Relation of Methodism to the slave trade. p. 803+.

4956. Slicer, Henry. Speech of Rev. Henry Slicer. Delivered in the General Conference at Indianapolis 28th May, 1856, on the Subject of the Proposed Change in the Methodist Discipline, making Nonslaveholding a Test or Condition of Membership in Said Church. Washington: Polkinhorn, n.d.   NcD

4957. Stein, S. L. "George Whitefield on Slavery." Church History (42:2, June, 1973), pp. 243-56.
Methodist minister's views on slavery.

4958. Stevens, Abel. An Appeal to the Methodist Episcopal Church, Concerning What Its General Conference Should Do on the Question of Slavery. New York: Trow, 1859.   OClWHi

4959. ----- A Compendious History of American Methodism. New York: Eaton & Mains, n.d.   DHU/R
Slavery question in general conferences of the Methodist Church, pp. 524-28.

4960. Stokes, James Carlisle. The Methodist Episcopal Church, South and the American Negro from 1844 to the Setting up of the Colored Methodist Episcopal Church. Doctoral dissertation. Boston University, 1938.

4961. Swaney, Charles Baumer. Episcopal Methodism and Slavery, with Sidelights on Ecclesiastical Politics. Boston: R. G. Badger, 1926.   NcD; CtY-D; MBU

4962. Sweet, William Warren. Methodism in American History. Nashville: Abingdon Press, 1954.   DHU/R
Contains information on Missionary Activities and Slavery in the Methodist Church.

4963. ----- The Methodist Episcopal Church and the Civil War. Cincinnati: Methodist Book Concern, 1933.   ODW

4964. Taylor, Thomas J. Essay on Slavery, as Connected with the Moral and Providential Government of God, as an Element of Church Organization. With Miscellaneous Reflections on the Subject of Slavery. New York: J. Longking, Printer, 1851.   DHU/MO; NN/Sch; NcD

4965. Thompson, George. The Substance of Mr. Thompson's Lecture on Slavery, Delivered in the Wesleyan Chapel, Irwell Street, Salford, Manchester, (Eng.). Manchester: Pr. by S. Wheeler; Boston: Repr by I. Knapp, 1836.   CtY-D

4966. Vail, Stephen Montford. The Church and the Slave Power. A Sermon Preached before the Students of the Methodist Biblical Institute Concord, New Hampshire, February 23, 1860. Pub. by the Students. Concord: Fogg, Hadley & Co., 1860.

4967. Wesley, John. ...Thoughts Upon Slavery, Published in the Year 1774. New York: n.p., 1835.   DHU/R; NN/Sch; MBU
Issue of the Wesleyan Extra, (1:1, Apr., 1835).

4968. Whipple, Charles King. The Methodist Church and Slavery. New York: American Anti-Slavery Society, 1859.   DLC

4969. White, Marie S. "The Methodist Anti-Slavery Struggle in the Land of Lincoln." Methodist History (10:4, Jl., 1972), pp. 33-52.   DHU/R

4970. Williams, Thomas L. The Methodist Mission to the Slaves. Doctoral dissertation. Yale University, 1943.

4971. "Words for Working Men." Fourth Series. Wesley's Thoughts on Slavery. n.p., n.d.   DHU/MO

7. Moravian

NC ENTRIES

8. Presbyterian

4972. " Address of the Presbyterian Church in the Confederate States of America to All the Churches of Jesus Christ Throughout the Earth." The Southern Presbyterian Review (14; Ja., 1 1862), pp. 531+.   DHU/R

4973. Adger, John B. "Northern and Southern Views of the Province of the Church." The Southern Presbyterian Review (16; Mar., 1866), pp. 384+.   DHU/R

4974. Aikman, William. The Future of the Colored Race in America: Being an Article in the Presbyterian Quarterly Review of July, 1862. New York: Anson D. F. Randolph, 1862.   DHU/MO

4975. Armstrong, George Dodd. A Discussion on Slaveholding. Philadelphia: J. M. Wilson, 1858.   NN/Sch; DLC

4976. Barber, Verle L. The Slavery Controversy and the Presbyterian Church. Doctoral dissertation. University of Chicago, 1928.   NcD

4977. Barnes, Albert. Life at Three-Score: A Sermon Delivered in the First Presbyterian Church, Philadelphia. Philadelphia Perry & McMillan, 1859.   DHU/MO

4978. ----- Our Position. A Sermon, Preached before the General Assembly of the Presbyterian Church in the United States, in the Fourth Presbyterian Church in the City of Washington, May 20, 1852. New York: Newman & Ivison, 1852. DHU/MO

4979. Basker, Roosevelt A. Pro-Slavery Arguments of Southern Religious Leaders as Illustrated by the Old School Presbyterians. Master's thesis. University of Chicago, 1935.

4980. Beman, Nathan Sidney Smith. Antagonisms in the Moral and Political World. A Discourse Delivered in the First Presbyterian Church, Troy, New York, on Nov. 18, 1858. New York: A. W. Scribner & Co., 1858.   DHU/MO

4981. Birney, James Gillespie. Mr. Birney's Second Letter. To the Ministers and Elders of the Presbyterian Church in Kentucky. n.p., 1834.   DHU/MO

4982. Bittinger, Joseph Baugher. A Plea for Humanity. A Sermon Preached in the Euclid Street Presbyterian Church, Cleveland, Ohio. Cleveland: Medall Cowles & Co., 1854.   CtY

4983. Blanchard, Jonathan. A Debate on Slavery. Held in the City of Cincinnati, on the First, Second, Third, and Sixth days of Oct., 1845, upon the Question: Is Slavery in itself Sinful, and the Relation between Master and Slave, a Sinful Relation? Affirmative: Rev. J. Blanchard. Negative: N. L. Rice. Cincinnati: W. H. Moore & Co.; New York: M. H. Newman, 1846.
DHU/MO; CtY-D

4984. ----- Is Slave-Holding in Itself Sinful, and the Relation Between Master and Slave, A Sinful Relation? Debate on Slavery: Held in the City of Cincinnati, on the first, second, third, and sixth days of October, 1845. New York: Arno Press, 1969.
DHU/R
"Reprint of 1946 edition."

4985. Bourne, George. An Address to the Presbyterian Church Enforcing the Duty of Excluding all Slaveholders from the "Communion of Saints." New York: n.p., 1833. DLC; CtY; NN/Sch
Signed: Presbyter.

4986. ----- Picture of Slavery in the United States of America. Middletown, Conn.: E. Hunt, 1834. DHU/MO; NN/Sch

4987. Christie, John W. and Dwight L. Dumond. George Bourne and "The Book and Slavery Irreconcilable." Philadelphia: Historical Society of Delaware and Presbyterian Historical Society, 1969.
NjP

4988. Cleveland, Charles Dexter. Slavery and Infidelity. Letter to a Certain Elder of a Certain Presbyterian Church. n.p., n.d.
DHU/MO

4989. Cross, Jasper W. "John Miller's Missionary Journal, 1816-1817: Religious Conditions in the South and Midwest." Journal of Presbyterian History (47:3, Sept., 1969), pp. 226-61.
DHU/R
Mentions efforts to preach to "Blacks."

4990. Davidson, Robert. History of the Presbyterian Church in the State of Kentucky with a Preliminary Sketch of the Churches in the State of Kentucky. New York: Carter, 1847. DHU/R
Chapter 13, Slavery and the Church.

4991. Davis, J. Treadwell. "The Presbyterians and the Sectional Conflict." Southern Quarterly (8:2, Ja., 1970), pp. 117-33.
Pam. File, DHU/R

4992. Drury, Clifford Merrill. ...Presbyterian Panorama. Philadelphia: Board of Christian Education, Presbyterian Church in the United States of America, 1952.
NN/Sch

4993. Foster, Robert V. "A Sketch of the History of the Cumberland Presbyterian Church." American Church History Series. V. II (New York: Christian Literature Co., 1894), pp. 258-309.
DHU/R

4994. Gibbs, Jonathan C. The Great Commission, a Sermon Preached Oct. 22, 1856, Before a Convention of Presbyterian and Congregational Ministers in the Shiloh Presbyterian Church, Corner Prince and Marion Streets, New York. New York: Daly, 1857.
DHU/MO

4995. Gilliam, Will D., Jr. "Robert J. Breckinridge: Kentucky Unionist." Kentucky Historical Society (69:4, Oct., 1971), pp. 362-85.
DLC
Minister of Kentucky and his fight to preserve the union.

4996. Gilliland, James and Samuel Crothers. Two Letters on the Subject of Slavery From the Presbytery of Chillicothe, to the Churches Under Their Care. Hillsborough: Whetstone and Buxton, 1830.
NN
"Title varies."

4997. Green, Beriah. Sermons and Other Discourses. With Brief Biographical Hints. New York: S. W. Green, 1860.
DHU/MO; NN/Sch

4998. ----- Things for Northern Men to do: A Discourse Delivered on the Lord's Day Evening, July 17, 1836, in the Presbyterian Church, Whitesboro, N.Y. New York: Pub. by Request, 1836.
CtY-D

4999. Griffin, Edward Dorr. A Plea for Africa. A Sermon Preached Oct. 26, 1817, in the First Presbyterian Church in the City of New York before the Synod of New York and New Jersey, at the Request of the Board of Directors of the African School Established by the Synod. New York: Gould, Printer, 1817.
CtY-D; NN/Sch

5000. Hefele, Karl J. "Slavery and Christianity." The American Presbyterian and Theological Review Series II (3; Oct., 1965), pp. 601+.
DLC

5001. Holifield, E. Brooks. "Thomas Smyth: The Social Ideas of a Southern Evangelist." Journal of Presbyterian History (51:1, Spr., 1973), pp. 24-39.
DHU/R
"Views on slavery of a Presbyterian evangelist, pastor of the Second Presbyterian Church, Charleston, South Carolina from 1831-1870.

5002. Hovet, Theodore R. "The Church Diseased: Harriet Beecher Stowe's Attack on the Presbyterian Church." Journal of Presbyterian History (52:2, Sum., 1974), pp. 167-87. DHU/R

5003. Howard, Victor B. "The Slavery Controversy and a Seminary for the Northwest." Journal of Presbyterian History (43:4, Dec., 1965), pp. 227-53.
DHU/R

5004. Jack, Thomas C. "History of the Southern Presbyterian Church." American Church History Series, V. II (New York: Christian Literature Co., 1894), pp. 313-479.   DHU/R
Slavery and the Church.

5005. Johnson, Herrick. The Nation's Duty: Thanksgiving Sermon, Preached in the Third Presbyterian Church, Pittsburgh, Thursday, November 27, 1862, by the Pastor, Rev. Herrick Johnson. Pittsburgh: Pr. by W. S. Haven, 1862.   CtY-D

5006. Kay, John. The Slave Trade in the New Hebrides; being Papers Read at the Annual Meeting of the New Hebrides Mission, held at Aniwa, July 1871, and Published by the Authority of the Meeting. Edited by the Rev. John Kay, Coatbridge, Secretary Presbyterian Church of Scotland. Edinburgh: Edmonston & Douglas, 1872.
CtY-D

5007. Kull, Irving Stoddard. "Presbyterian Attitudes Toward Slavery." Church History (7:2, Je., 1938), pp. 101-14. DHU/R

5008. Lord, John Chase. "The Higher Law," in Its Application to the Fugitive Slave Bill. A Sermon on the Duties Men Owe God and to Governments. Delivered at the Central Presbyterian Church, Buffalo, on Thanksgiving Day. New York: Published by Order of the "Union Safety Committee," 1851.   CtY-D

5009. Lord, Nathan. A Letter of Inquiry to the Ministers of the Gospel of All Denominations on Slavery. By a Northern Presbyterian. Boston: Little, Brown and Co., 1854. DHU/MO; CtY-D

5010. Lyon, James A. "A Slave Marriage Law." The Southern Presbyterian Review (16; Oct., 1863), pp. 145. DLC; DHU/R
"A marriage law would be a dangerous step towards giving them legal status in the states."

5011. ----- "Slavery and the Duties Growing Out of the Relation." Southern Presbyterian Review (16; Jl., 1863), pp. 1-37. DLC; DyLxCB
"Slavery is part of the good providence of God."

5012. Marsden, George M. The Evangelical Mind and the New School Presbyterian Experience: A Case Study of Thought and

Theology in Nineteenth-Century America. New Haven, Conn.: Yale University Press, 1970.   DHU/R
  Chapter 4, The Abolition of Black Slavery; Chapter 10, The Civil War, the Flag and the Cross; Appendix 1, Historiography of the Causes of the Division of 1837-38: Doctrine of Slavery.

5013. Marvin, Abijah Perkins. _Fugitive Slaves: A Sermon Preached in North Congregational Church, Winchendon, Apr. 11, 1850_. Boston: J. P. Hewett & Co., 1850. DLC

5014. McGill, Alexander Taggart. _The Hand of God with the Black Face. A Discourse Delivered before the Pennsylvania Colonization Society_. Philadelphia: W. F. Geddes, 1862. CtY-D

5015. McLeod, Alexander. _Negro Slavery Unjustifiable. A Discourse, by Alexander McLeod, A. M., Pastor of the Reformed Presbyterian Congregation in the City of New York_. New York: T. & F. Swords, 1802. DLC; NN/Sch

5016. McLoughlin, William G. "Indian Slaveholders and Presbyterian Missionaries, 1837-1861." _Church History_ (42:4, Dec., 1973), pp. 535-551. DHU/R

5017. Memminger, C. G. _Lecture Before the Young Men's Library Association of Augusta, Georgia Shewing African Slavery to be Consistent With the Moral and Physical Progress of a Nation_. Augusta: W. S. Jones, 1851. NNUT

5018. Miller, Samuel. _The Life of Samuel Miller, D.D., LL.D., Second Professor in the Theological Seminary of the Presbyterian Church, at Princeton, New Jersey_. Philadelphia: Claxton, Remsen and Haffelfinger, 1869. NN/Sch

5019. Moore, Edmund Arthur. _Robert J. Breckinridge and the Slavery Aspect of the Presbyterian Schism of 1837_. Chicago: n.p., 1935. NcD; DLC
  Also, Church History (4:4, Dec., 1935), pp. 282-94. DHU/R

5020. Moorhead, James H. "Henry J. Van Dyke, Sr. Conservative Apostle of a Broad Church." _Presbyterian History_ (50: 1, Spr., 1972), pp. 19-38. DHU/R
  "Minister of Old School Presbyterian Church in Brooklyn a fierce opponent of abolitionism."

5021. Nevin, Edwin Henry. _The Religion of Christ at War with American Slavery, or, Reasons for Separating from the Presbyterian Church_. Mt. Vernon: Wm. H. Cochran, Printer, 1849. DHU/MO

5022. Palmer, Benjamin M. _The Duty of the South to Preserve and Perpetuate the Institution as It Now Exists_. New York: n.p., 1861. ICU

5023. ----- _The Rights of the South Deferred in Pulpits..._ Mobile; J. Y. Thompson, 1860. NcD

5024. Patterson, James. _A Sermon on the Effects of the Hebrew Slavery as Connected with Slavery in This Country. Preached in the 7th Presbyterian Church in the City of Phila....July 4, 1825_. Phila.: S. Probasco, 1825. DHU/MO

5025. Philip, John. _Letter ... to the Society of Inquiry on Missions in the Theological Seminary, Princeton, New Jersey_. Princeton: Gray, 1833. NjP

5026. Pickens, Andrew Lee. _Anti-Slavery and Other Memories of Old Richmond Kirkworth. A Heterogeny of Abstracts and Outlines..._ Paducah, Ky.: Meridan States Research, 1943. CtY-D

5027. Posey, Walter Brownlow. _The Presbyterian Church in the Old Southwest, 1788-1838_. Richmond, Va.: John Knox Press, 1952. NN/Sch

5028. ----- "The Slavery Question in the Presbyterian Church in the Old Southwest." _Journal of Southern History_ (15:3, Ag., 1949), pp. 311-24.

5029. Presbyterian Church in the U. S. _The Distinctive Principles of the Presbyterian Church in the United States, Commonly Called the Southern Presbyterian Church, as Set Forth in the Formal Declarations, and Illustrated by Extracts From Proceedings of the General Assembly, from 1861-67; and of the N. S. Assembly, from 1861-66_. 2nd ed. Richmond: Presbyterian Committee of Publication, n. d. NcD

5030. Presbyterian Church in the U. S. A. General Assembly of 1856. "Constitutional Power Over Slaveholding." _Presbyterian Quarterly_ (5:18, Sept., 1856), pp. 312-27. DHU/R

5031. ----- General Assembly of 1857. "The General Assembly's Answer to the Protest on Slavery." _The Presbyterian Quarterly Review_ (6:23, Dec., 1857), pp. 521-27. DHU/R
  Letters received in reference to a statement of the General Assembly of 1857 on Slavery. For original statement see _Presbyterian Quarterly Review_ (6:22, Sept., 1857), pp. 233-43.

5032. ----- General Assembly of 1857. "Slavery." _The Presbyterian Quarterly_ (6:22, Sept., 1857), pp. 233-46. DHU/R

5033. ----- General Assembly of 1858. "The General Assembly's Answer to the Protest on Slavery." _The Presbyterian Quarterly Review_ (6:24, Mr., 1858), pp. 686-90. DHU/R
  Letters received in reference to the General Assembly of 1857 on Slavery. For original statement see _Presbyterian Review_ (6:22, Sept, 1857), pp. 233-43.

5034. ----- General Assembly of 1860. _Presbyterian Quarterly_ (8; Jl., 1860), pp. 88+. IWW; NjP
  "Adopted a resolution against slavery but do not wish to excommunicate individuals or congregations who support slavery."
  Presbyterians and slavery.

5035. ----- General Assembly of 1861. _Presbyterian Quarterly_ (10; Jl., 1861), pp. 58. ICT; NjP
  "Adopted a resolution condemning secession and calling for support of the government." Presbyterians and the war.

5036. ----- General Assembly of 1862. _The Princeton Review_ (34; Jl., 1862), pp. 464+. DLC; NjP
  "This treason is plainly condemned by the revealed will of God. The alternatives are preservation of union or slavery. This assembly adopted a strong statement written by Dr. Breckinridge of Danville, Kentucky. The church has no authority to council treason, anarchy, or rebellion." Presbyterians and slavery.

5037. ----- General Assembly of 1863. _The American Presbyterian and Theological Review_ Ser. II (I; Jl., 1863), pp. 285+. NjP
  "The Assembly is unanimous in its loyalty and the opinion that slavery is the cause of the war."

5038. ----- General Assembly of 1864. _The Princeton Review_ (36; jl., 1864), pp. 538+. NjP
  "This session declared slavery should be abolished once and forever. Either our national life or slavery must be extinguished."

5039. ----- (Old School) Board of Publication. _American Slavery, as Viewed and Acted on by the Presbyterian Church in the United States of America_. Comp. for the Board of Publication by A. T. McGill. Philadelphia: Presbyterian Board of Publication, 1865. NjP

5040. ----- Presbyteries. Chillicothe. _Two Letters on the Subject of Slavery From the Presbytery of Chillicothe to the Churches Under Their Care_. Hillsborough: Pr. by Whetstone & Buxton, 1830. NcD
  Microfilm copy (negative) of the original in New York Public Library.

5041. Presbyterian Church in the U. S. A. Synod of Cincinnati. _An Address to the Churches, on the Subject of Slavery; Georgetown, Ohio, Aug. 5, 1831_. (Georgetown?) D. Ammen & Co. (1831). DLC

5042. "President Lincoln, " The Princeton Review (37; Jl., 1865),
pp. 435+.   NjP
"Abolition of slavery was no more a legitimate object of
civil war than the abolition of false religion ... President
Lincoln's death is a mysterious event and occasion for
national sorrow. "

5043. "Report on Slavery." The Southern Presbyterian Review
(5:3, Ja., 1852), pp. 380-94.   DHU/R

5044. "The Revival of the Slave Trade." Southern Presbyterian
Review (11:1, Apr. 1, 1858), pp. 100-36.   DHU/R
Review of Reports of the Committee to Whom was referred
the Message of Gov. James H. Adams, Relating to Slavery
and the Slave Trade. Columbia, S. C.: Steam Power Press
Carolina Times, 1857.

5045. Rice David. Slavery Inconsistent with Justice and Good
Policy, by Philanthropos (pseud.) Together with a Twentieth
Century Afterword. Lexington: University of Kentucky Library
Associates, 1956.   CtY-D; KYU
(University of Kentucky Library Associates Keepsake no. 3).

5046. Robinson, John. The Testimony and Practice of the Presby-
terian Church in Reference to American Slavery. With an Appen-
dix: Containing the Position of the General Assembly (New
School), Free Presbyterian, Associate, Associate Reformed,
Baptist, Protestant Episcopal, and Methodist Episcopal
Churches. Cincinnati: J. D. Thorpe, 1852. DLC; DHU/MO;
CtY-D

5047. Rogers, Tommy W. "Dr. Frederick A. Ross and the Presbyterian Defense of Slavery." Journal of Presbyterian History
(45:2, Je., 1967), pp. 112-24.   DHU/R

5048. Ross, Frederick Augustus. Position of the Southern Church
in Relation to Slavery, as Illustrated in a Letter of Dr. F. A.
Ross to Rev. Albert Barnes. With an Introduction by a Constitutional Presbyterian. New York: John A. Gray, 1857. NcD

5049. ----- Slavery Ordained of God... Philadelphia: J. B.
Lippincott & Co., 1857.   CtY-D; DHU/R; NcD

5050. Slave Holding. A Disqualification for Church Fellowships.
A Letter to Dr. Joshus L. Wilson and the First Presbyterian
Church, Cincinnati. By "A Brother." n.p., n.d.   CtY-D

5051. "Slavery." Christian Spectator (5:4, Dec., 1833), pp. 631-
55.   DHU/R
Discussion of the work: Letters on Slavery: Addressed to
the Cumberland Congregation, Virginia. By J. D. Paxton,
their former pastor. Lexington, Kentucky, 1833.

5052. "Slavery." Southern Presbyterian Review (9:3, Ja., 1856),
pp. 345-64.   DHU/R

5053. Sloane, James Renwick Wilson. Life and Work of J. R. W.
Sloane in the Reformed Presbyterian Seminary at Allegheny,
Penn., 1868-1886... New York: A. C. Armstrong & Son,
1888.   OWoC

5054. ----- Review of Rev. Henry J. Van Dyke's Discourse on
"The Character and Influence of Abolitionism, " A Sermon
Preached in the Third Reformed Presbyterian Church, Twenty-
third Street, New York, on Sabbath Evening, December 23,
1860. Also, by Special Request, in the Church of the Puritans
(Rev. Dr. Cheever's) on Sabbath Evening, January 6, 1861.
New York: W. Ewing, 1861.   NN/Sch; CtY-D

5055. Slosser, Gaius Jackson. They Seek a Country; the American
Presbyterians, Some Aspects. Contributors: Frank H. Caldwell... and Others. New York: Macmillan, 1955.   NN/Sch

5056. Smith, Asa Dodge. Obedience to Human Law. A Discourse
Delivered on the Day of Public Thanksgiving, December 12,
1850, in the Brainerd Presbyterian Church, New York. New
York: Leavitt, 1851.   CtY-D

5057. Smith, Edward. The Bible Against Slavery. An Address
Delivered in the Sixth Presbyterian Church, Cincinnati, March
19, 1843.   DHU/MO

5058. Smith, Gerrit. Letter of Gerrit Smith to Rev. James
Smylie, of the State of Mississippi. New York: Published by
R. G. Williams, for the American Anti-Slavery Society, 1837.
                                                       CtY-D
(The Anti-Slavery Examiner, No. 3).

5059. ----- Letters of Rev. Dr. Schmaker and Gerrit Smith.
n. p., 1838.   DHU/MO

5060. Smith, Hilrie S. "The Church and the Social Order in the
Old South As Interpreted by James H. Thornwell, " Church
History (7:2, Je., 1938), pp. 115-24.   DHU/R
Slavery and the church by a Presbyterian minister.

5061. ----- "Moral Crisis in a Troubled South. " Journal of Religious Thought (14; Aut. - Wint., 1956-57), pp. 37-42.   DHU/R

5062. Smylie, James. A Review of a Letter, from the Presbytery
of Chillicothe, to the Presbytery of Mississippi, on the Subject
of Slavery. Woodville, Mi.: Printed by W. A. Norris and Co.,
1836.   NN/Sch

5063. Smyth, Thomas. Autobiographical Notes, Letters and Reflec-
tions. Edited by his granddaughter Louise Cheves Stoney.
Charleston, S.C.: Walker Evans & Cogswell Co., 1914.
                                                       DHU/R
Papers relating to Secession and the War, 1860-1865.
Includes Rev. Smyth's, the pastor of the Second Presbyterian
Church, Charleston, S.C., proslavery views.

5064. ----- Complete Works of Rev. Thomas Smyth. Edited by
Rev. Prof. J. Wm. Flinn. Columbia, S.C.: R. L. Bryan Co.,
1910.   DHU/R
Author was Presbyterian pastor of Second Presbyterian
Church, Charleston, S. C. in early twentieth century. Many
chapters included on his views on justification of slavery as
the "will of God. "

5065. Spear, Samuel Thayer. The Law-Abiding Conscience and the
Higher Law Conscience: with Remarks on the Fugitive Slave
Question: a Sermon, Preached in the South Presbyterian Church,
Brooklyn, Dec. 12, 1850. New York: Lambert & Lane, Station-
ers and Printers, 1850.   NN/Sch

5066. Spencer, Ichabod S. Fugitive Slave Law. The Religious Duty
of Obedience to Law; A Sermon Preached in the Second Presbyterian Church in Brooklyn, Nov.-24, 1850. New York: M. W.
Dodd, 1850.   DHU/MO; CtY-D

5067. Staiger, C. Bruce. "Abolitionism and the Presbyterian
Schism of 1837-1838. " Mississippi Valley Historical Review
(36:3, Dec. 1949), pp. 391-414.

5068. Stiles, Joseph Clay. Speech on the Slavery Resolutions, Delivered in the General Assembly which Met in Detroit in May
Last. New York: M. H. Newman & Co., 1850. NcD; NN/Sch

5069. Tappan, Lewis. Proceedings of the Session of Broadway
Tabernacle (New York City), Against Lewis Tappen, with the
Action of the Presbytery and General Assembly. New York:
n. p., 1839.   DHU/MO

5070. Taylor, Hubert Vance. Slavery and the Deliberating of the
Presbyterian General Assembly, 1833-1838. Doctoral dissertation. Northwestern University, 1964.

5071. Thomas, Alfred A., (ed.). Correspondence of Thomas
Ebenezer Thomas, Mainly Relating to the Anti-Slavery Conflict
in Ohio Especially in the Presbyterian Church. n. p.: n. p.,
1909.   CtY-D; NcD; OWoC; DHU/MO

5072. Thompson, Ernest Trice. Presbyterians in the South ...
Richmond, Va.: John Knox Press, 1963-73. 3 Vols.
                                                  DHU/R; NjP

Blacks in the Presbyterian Church during slavery and the present.

5073. Thompson, George. Discussion on American Slavery, between George Thompson and Robert J. Breckinridge, Holden in the Rev. Dr. Wardlaw's Chapel, Glasgow, Scotland; on the Evenings of the 13th, 14th, 15th, 16th, 17th of June, 1836. Boston: I. Knapp, 1836.   CtY-D; DHU/R

5074. Thompson, Robert E. A History of the Presbyterian Churches in the United States. New York: The Christian Literature Co., 1895.   DHU/R
    "American Church History Series, V. 6," Slavery Issue.

5075. Tinker, Reuben. The Gospel, the Hope of Our Nation. A Discourse on Occasion of the Public Thanksgiving Delivered in the Presbyterian Church, Westfield, New York. Buffalo: T. & M. Butler, Publishers, 1851.   DHU/MO

5076. Two Letters on the Subject of Slavery From the Presbytery of Chillicothe to the Churches under Their Care. Hillsborough: Whetstone and Buston, 1830.   DHU/MO

5077. Union Anti-Slavery Society Auxiliary No. II. To the Congregation of the Western Presbyterian Church. Read and adopted December 24, 1838. Philadelphia: Published by Order of the Society, 1838.   DHU/MO

5078. Van Dyke, Henry Jackson. Giving Thanks for all Things. A Sermon Preached in the First Presbyterian Church of Brooklyn on Thanksgiving-day, Nov. 29, 1860. New York: G. F. Nesbitt and Co., Printers, 1860.   NN/Sch

5079. Vander Velde, Lewis George. The Presbyterian Churches a and the Federal Union, 1861-1869. Cambridge: Harvard University Press, 1932.   CtY-D; DHU/R; NcD

5080. White, William S. 4th of July Remininiscences and Reflections: A Sermon Preached in the Presbyterian Church. Charlottesville: Printed by R. C. Noel, 1840.   ViU

5081. "Who is Responsible for the Present Slavery Agitation?" The Presbyterian Quarterly Review (8:32, Apr., 1860), pp. 529-44.
                                                        DHU/R

9. Protestant Episcopal and Anglican

5082. Addison, James Thayer. The Episcopal Church in the United States, 1789-1931. New York: Scribner, 1951.
    For Slavery and the Civil War, see pp. 189-99.

5083. Birney, William. James G. Birney and his Times; the Genesis of Republican Party. New York: Bergman Publishers, 1969.   CtY-D; DHU/R
    "Anti-slavery books before:" pp. 382-83. Bibliographical footnotes.

5084. Brooks, Phillips. Our Mercies of Re-Occupation. A Thanksgiving Sermon, Preached at the Church of the Holy Trinity, Philadelphia, November 26, 1863. Philadelphia: W. S. and A. Martien, 1863.   CtY-D

5085. Burger, Nash Kerr. "The Diocese of Mississippi and the Confederacy." Historical Magazine of the Protestant Episcopal Church (14; 1940), p. 52+.   DLC

5086. Clifton, Denzil T. "Anglicanism and Negro Slavery in Colonial America." Historical Magazine of the Protestant Episcopal Church (39:1, Mr., 1970), pp. 29-70.   DHU/R

5087. Ellerbee, A. W. "The Episcopal Church Among the Slaves." American Church Review (7; 1855), pp. 429-37.   DLC

5088. "The Episcopal Church." Editorial. The Crisis (7:1, Dec., 1913), pp. 83-4.   DLC; DHU/MO
    Slavery and the church.

5089. Goodwin, Mary F. "Christianizing and Educating the Negro in Colonial Virginia." Historical Magazine of the Protestant Episcopal Church (1:3, Sept., 1932), pp. 148-51. DLC; NN

5090. Holly, James Theodore, (bp.). A Vindication of the Capacity of the Negro Race for Self-Government. New Haven: W. H. Stanley, 1857.   NN/Sch
    Negro author.

5091. Jay, John. Caste and Slavery in the American Church. New York: Wiley and Putman, 1843.   NN/Sch; CtY-D

5092. ----- Correspondence Between John Jay, Esq., and the Vestry of St. Mathew's Church, Bedford, N.Y. Bedford, N.Y.: n.p., 1862.   DLC; NcD; MB; MBU

5093. ----- Slavery and the War: Speeches, Letters ... New York: n.p., 1859-68.   DLC

5094. ----- Thoughts on the Duty of the Episcopal Church, in Relation to Slavery: Being a Speech Delivered in N. Y. A. S.

Convention, Feb. 12, 1839. New York: Piercy & Reed, 1839.
                                                        DLC
    "New York Anti-Slavery Society."

5095. Jay, William. A Letter to the Right Rev. L. Silliman Ives, Bishop of the Protestant Episcopal Church in the State of North Carolina; Occasioned by His Late Address to the Convention of His Diocese... New York: W. Harned, 1848.   DHU/MO

5096. Klingberg, Frank J. "The African Immigrant in Colonial Pennsylvania and Delaware." Historical Magazine of the Protestant Episcopal Church (11:1, Mr., 1942), pp. 126-53.
                                                        DCU/TH

5097. ----- Anglican Humanitarianism in Colonial New York. Phila.: The Church Historical Assoc., 1940. NN/Sch; CyY-D

5098. ----- (ed.). The Carolina Chronicle of Dr. Francis Le Jau, 1706-17. Berkeley & Los Angeles: University of California Press, 1956.   DLC
    "Negro's condition in South Carolina written by a Missionary."

5099. ----- "The S. P. G. Program for Negroes in Colonial New York." Historical Magazine of the Protestant Episcopal Church (8:4, Dec., 1939), pp. 306-71.   DLC

5100. Lines, Stiles Bailey. Slaves and Churchmen: The Work of the Episcopal Church Among Southern Negroes, 1830-1860. Doctoral dissertation. Columbia University, 1960.

5101. Murphy, Dubose. "The Protestant Episcopal Church in Texas During the Civil War." Historical Magazine of the Protestant Episcopal Church (1; 1932), pp. 90+.   DLC

5102. Posey, Walter Brownlow. "The Protestant Episcopal Church: An American Adaptation." Journal of Southern History (25; Feb., 1959), pp. 3-30.   DHU

5103. Protestant Episcopal Church in the U. S. A. Diocese of Louisiana. "View of the Bishops of Ohio and Louisana Upon the Secession of the Southern States, and Its Effects Upon the Ecclesiastical Allegiance of the Dioceses." Historical Magazine of the Protestant Episcopal Church (31; 1962), pp. 288-302.
                                                        DHU/R

5104. Seabury, Samuel. American Slavery Distinguished from the Slavery of English Theorists and Justified by the Law of Nature. New York: Mason Bros., 1861.   CtY-D

5105. Shelling, Richard L. "William Sturgeon, Catechist to the Negroes of Philadelphia and Assistant Rector of Christ Church

(Shelling, Richard L. cont.)

1747-1766." Historical Magazine of the Protestant Episcopal Church (8:4, Dec., 1939), pp. 388-401.   DLC

5106. Sweet, Leonard I. "The Reaction of the Protestant Episcopal Church in Virginia to the Secession Crisis: October, 1859-May, 1861." Historical Magazine of the Protestant Episcopal Church (41:2, Je., 1972), pp. 139-51.   DHU/R

5107. Ward, Henry Dana. Diary: As Rector of St. Jude's P.E. Church, N.Y. City Services for Others Including Wm. A. Muhlenberg and Thos. Galladet, Marriages, Births, Deaths;

Church Government; Elections of Bishops, "Wine Bibbing" Bishops; his Family and his School for Young Ladies; Discipline, Teachers and Servants; Current Events; Slavery; Weather; Letter from Fillmore, 1856, etc. n.p., 1850-57.   NN/Sch
View on slavery by a Protestant Episcopal minister.

5108. Wilberforce, Samuel, (bp.). A Reproof of the American Church on the Subject of Slavery. By the Bishop of Oxford. To Which is Added the Opinions of Eminent Persons in All Ages Regarding Slavery and Oppression. London: W. Tweedie, 1853.
                                                                              NN/Sch

10. Reformed Church

5110. How, Samuel Blanchard. Slaveholding not Sinful. Slavery, the Punishment of Man's Sin, its Remedy, the Gospel of Christ. An Argument before the General Synod of Reformed Protestant Dutch, October 1855... New Brunswick, N.J.: J. Terhune, 1856.   CtY-D; DHU/MO; NN/Sch; CtY-D

5109. Delong, Gerald Francis. "The Dutch Reformed Church and Negro Slavery in Colonial America." Church History (40:4, Dec., 1971), pp. 423-36.   DHU/R

11. Roman Catholic

5111. Allen, Cuthbert Edward. "The Slavery Question in Catholic Newspapers, 1850-1865." United States Catholic Historical Society Records and Studies (26; 1936), pp. 99-179.   DGU

5112. Andrews, Rena M. "Slavery Views of a Northern Prelate." Church History (3:1, Mr., 1934), pp. 60-78.   DHU/R

5113. Blied, Benjamin J. Catholics and the Civil War. Milwaukee, Wisc.: n.p., 1945.   NcD; CtY-D; NN/Sch

5114. Brokhave, Joseph D. Francis Patrick Kenrick's Opinion on Slavery. Washington, D.C.: Catholic University of American Press, 1955.   DCU; DLC

5115. Catholic Church Pope, 1922-1939. God and Liberty Against Slavery. A Simplified Edition of the Encyclical "Divini Redemploris", Atheistic Communism by Pope Pius XI. by Rev. Gerald C. Treacy, S.J. New York: The Paulist Press, 1943.   NC; DLC

5116. "The Catholic Church and the Question of Slavery." Metropolitan (3:5, Je., 1955).
"Whole issue."

5117. Clarke, Richard Frederick. Cardinal Lavigerie and the African Slave Trade. New York: Longmans, Green, 1889.
                                                                              CtY-D

5118. Decker, Vincent de. Sous le Signe de la Croix; des Horreurs de la Traite aux Premieres Caravanes. n.p., n.d.   NN/Sch

5119. Decleene, Arnold. Het Rassenvraagstuk Door een Katholiek Gezien. Antwerpen: Uitgeverij "De Schelde," 1937.   DLC

5120. Ellis, John Tracy. American Catholicism. Chicago: University of Chicago Press, 1956.   NN/Sch
Slavery and the church.

5121. ----- Documents of American Catholic History. Milwaukee: Bruce Pub. Co., 1956.   DCU
Slavery and the church.

5122. England, John. Letters of the Late Bishop England to the Hon. John Forsyth on the Subject of Domestic Slavery. Baltimore: J. Murphy, 1844.

5123. Fave, Armand Joseph. Conférence su l'Esclavage. Panégyri que de Saint Pierre Claver... Grenobe: Baratier, 1888. NN/Sch

5124. Fitton, James. The Influence of Catholic Christian Doctrines on the Emancipation of Slaves. Boston: n.p., 1863.   DLC

5125. Fransioli, Joseph. ...Patriotism, a Christian Virtue. A Sermon Preached...at St. Peter's (Catholic) Church, Brooklyn, July 26, 1863. New York: n.p., n.d., 1863.
                                                                              DHU/MO

5126. Gannon, Michael Valentine. Rebel Bishop: The Life and Era of Augustin Verot. Milwaukee: Bruce Pub. Co., 1964. CtY-D

5127. Gibbons, James. Our Christian Heritage. Baltimore: J. Murphy and Co., 1889.   NN/Sch
Slavery and the church, pp. 416-34.

5128. Holland, Timothy J. Catholic Church and the Negro in the United States Prior to the Civil War. Doctoral dissertation. Fordham University, 1950.

5129. Imbart de la Tour, Joseph Jean Baptiste. L'Esclavage en Africae et la Croisade Notre. Paris: Maison de la Bonne Press, 1891.   NN/Sch

5130. La Farge, John. "The Survival of the Catholic Faith in Southern Maryland." The Catholic Historical Review (21:1, Apr., 1935), pp. 1-20.   DHU/R
Also deals with Catholicism in regard to slavery and the Negro.

5131. La Faye, Jean Baptiste de. A Voyage to Barbary, for the Redemption of Captives; Performed in 1720 by the Mathuren-Trinitarian Fathers... Barbary: n.p., 1735.   CtY-D

5132. Lavigerie, Charles Martial Allemand. Documents sur la Foundation de l'Oeuvre Antiesclavagiste. Saint-Cloud: Imprimerie Vve E. Belin et Fils, 1889.   NN/Sch

5133. ----- L'Esclavage Africain. Conference Faite dans L'Eglise de Saint-Sulpice à Paris. Paris: A la Procure des Missions d'Afrique, 1888.   CtY-D

5134. ----- Slavery in Africa; a Speech by Cardinal Lavigerie made at the Meeting Held in London July 31, 1888. Presided over by Lord Granville, Former Minister of English Foreign Affairs. Boston: Cashman, Keating, 1888.   CtY-D

5135. Letter of an Adopted Catholic, Addressed to the President of the Kentucky Democratic Association of Washington City on Temporal Allegiance to the Pope, and the Relations of the Catholic Church and Catholics, both Native and Adopted, to the System of Domestic Slavery and its Agitation in the U.S. n.p., 1856.   NcD

5136. Manaricua, Andres E. de. El Matrimonio de los Esclavos; Estudio Histórico Juridico Hasta la Fijacion De la Disciplina en

el Derecho Canonico. Romae: A Pud Aedes Universitates
Gregorianae, 1940.   NcD
    Slavery and the Catholic Church.

5137. Miller, Richard Roscoe. Slavery and Catholicism. Durham,
N.C.: Morth State Publishers, 1957. DHU/MO; DLC; NcD;
NN/Sch; PPT

5138. Pilkington, George, (ed.). Folhetos de Pilkington. Rio de
Janeiro: Typographia de Laemmert, 1841. NN/Sch

5139. Rice, Madeleine Hooke. American Catholic Opinion in the
Slavery Controversy. New York: Columbia University Press,
1944.   DHU/MO; NN/Sch; NcD

5140. Rigord. Observations sur Quelques Opinions Relatives
l'Esclavage, Emites & la Chambre des Pairs l'Occasion de
la Discussion de la Loi Sur le Régime. Martinique: Typo-
graphie de E. Ruelle, 1845.   NN/Sch

5141. To Catholic Citizens! The Pope's Bull, and the Words of
Daniel O'Connell. New York: J. H. Ladd, 1856. NN/Sch

5142. Wight, Willard E. "Bishop Verot and the Civil War." The
Catholic Historical Review. (47:2, Jl., 1961), pp. 153-66.
                                               DHU/R

12. Seventh Day Adventist

NO ENTRIES

13. Unitarian Universalist Association

5143. American Slavery. A Protest Against American Slavery, by
One Hundred and Seventy Three Unitarian Ministers. Boston:
B. H. Greene, 1845.   DLC

5144. American Slavery. Report of a Meeting of Members of the
Unitarian Body, Held at the Freemasons' Tavern, June 13th,
1851.   DLC

5145. Austin, James Trecothick. Remarks on Dr. Channing's
Slavery. Boston: Russell, Shattuck, and J. H. Eastburn,
1835.   CtY-D

5146. Boston, Courier. Observations on the Rev. Dr. Gannett's
Sermon, entitled "Relation of the North to Slavery." Repub-
lished from the editorial Columns of the Boston Courier, of
June 28th and 38th, and July 6th, 1854. Boston: Reading, 1854,
                                      CtY-D

5147. Channing, William Ellery. An Address Delivered at Lenox, on
on the first of August, 1842, the Anniversary of Emancipation,
in the British West Indies. Lenox, Mass: J. G. Stanly, 1842.
                                      CtY-D

5148. ----- The Duty of the Free States; or, Remarks Suggested
by the Case of the Creole. Philadelphia: n.p., 1842. CtY-D

5149. ----- Emancipation. Boston: E. P. Peabody, 1840. CtY-D

5150. ----- Letter of William E. Channing to James G. Birney.
Boston: J. Munroe, 1837.   CtY-D
    "Prepared for 'The Philanthropist,' an anti-slavery paper,
    published at Cincinnati, and edited by James G. Birney."

5151. ----- Remarks on the Slavery Question, in a Letter to
Jonathan Phillips, esq. Boston: J. Munroe, 1839. CtY-D

5152. ----- Slavery. Boston: J. Munroe, 1835. DHU/MO; CtY-D

5153. ----- The Works of William E. Channing. Boston: American Unitarian Association, 1875.   DHU/R; CtY-D
    Contains sermons on slavery and the church.

5154. Cheetham, Henry H. Unitarianism and Universalism. An
Illustrated History. Boston: Beacon Press, 1962. DHU/R
    Unitarianism and social justice.

5155. Cheever, George Barrell. God's Way of Crushing the Rebellion. A Sermon at the Church of the Puritans. New York,
Sept. 29, 1861. New York: n.p., 1861. DLC; DHU/MO

5156. Clarke, James Freeman. The Rendition of Anthony Burns.
Its Causes and Consequences. A Discourse on Christian
Politics, Delivered in William Hall, Boston, on Whitsunday,
June 4, 1854. Boston: Crosby Nichols, 1854. DHU/MO;

CtY-D
    "Published by request."

5157. ----- Slavery in the United States. A Sermon Delivered in
Amory Hall, on Thanksgiving Day, November 24, 1842. Boston:
B. H. Greene, 1843.   NN/Sch; CtY-D
    "Printed by friend for gratuitous distribution."

5158. Conway, Moncure Daniel. The One Path; or, the Duties of the
North and South; A Discourse in the Unitarian Church, Washington, Ja. 26, 1856. Washington, D. C.: n.p., 1856. DLC

5159. ----- Virtue vs. Defeat. A Discourse Preached on November 9, 1856... in the Unitarian Church. Cincinnati: Cincinnati
Gazette, 1856.   DHU/MO

5160. Dean, Paul. A Discourse Delivered Before the African Society, at Their Meetinghouse, in Boston, Mass. on the Abolition
of the Slave Trade by the United States of America, July 14,
1819, at First Universal Church in Boston. Boston: Nathaniel
Coverly, 1819.   DLC

5161. Dewy, Orville. A Discourse on Slavery and the Annexation
of Texas. New York: C. S. Francis, 1844.   CtY-D

5162. Frothingham, Octavius Brooks. Colonization. New York:
American Anti-Slavery, 1855.   CtY-D

5163. ----- The Last Signs. A Sermon Preached at the Unitarian
Church in Jersey City, on Sunday Morning, June 1, 1856. New
York: John A. Gray, 1856.   TNF; DLC

5164. ----- The New Commandemnt: A Discourse Delivered in
the North Church, Salem, on June 4, 1854. Salem: Pr. at the
Observer Office, 1854.   DLC

5165. Furness, William Henry. Christian Duty. Three Discourses
Delivered in the First Congregational Unitarian Church of Phil-
adelphia May 28, June 4, and June 11, 1854. Philadelphia:
Merrihew & Thompson, 1854.   DLC

5166. ----- A Discourse Delivered, January 5, 1851 in the First
Congregational Unitarian Church. Philadelphia: n.p., 1851.
                                      DHU/MO

5167. ----- A Discourse Occasioned by the Boston Fugitive Slave
Case, Delivered in the First Congreational Unitarian Church,
Phil., April 13, 1851. Phil.: Merrihew and Thompson, Printers,
                                      DHU/MO

5168. ----- The Right of Property in Man. A Discourse Delivered in the First Congregational Unitarian Church, July 3,
1859. Philadelphia: C. Sherman & Sons, 1859.   DLC

5169. ----- A Thanksgiving Discourse Delivered in the First
Congregational Unitarian Church in Phil., April 13, 1862.
Phil.: T. B. Pugh, 1862.   DHU/MO

5170. Gannett, Ezra Stiles. The State of the Country: A Discourse
Preached in the Federal Street Meetinghouse in Boston, on June
8, 1856. Boston: Crosby, Nichols and Co., 1856.   CtY-D

5171. ----- Thanksgiving for the Union: A Discourse Delivered in
the Federal Street Meetinghouse in Boston, on Thanksgiving Day,
Nov. 28, 1850. Boston: W. Crosby & H. P. Nichols, 1850.
CtY-D

5172. Gannett, William C. Ezra Stiles Gannett, Unitarian Minister
in Boston, 1824-1871. A Memoir by His Son... Boston:
Roberts Bros., 1875.   DHU/MO

5173. Martin, John H. The Unitarian and Slavery. Bachelor of
Divinity thesis. University of Chicago, 1954.

5174. May, Samuel Joseph. Speech of Rev. Samuel J. May, to the
Convention of Citizens, of Onondaga County, in Syracuse, on
the 14th of October, 1851, Called "to Consider the Principles
of the American Government, and the Extent to Which they are
Trampled under Foot by the Fugitive Slave Law," Occasioned
by an Attempt to Enslave an Inhabitant of Syracuse. Syracuse:
Agan & Summers, Printers, 1851.   CtY-D

5175. Palfrey, John Gorham. The Inter-State Slave Trade. New
York: American Anti-Slavery Society, 1855.   CtY-D

5176. Parker, Theodore. Collected Works Containing Theological,
Polemical, and Critical Writings, Sermons, Speeches, and
Addresses, and Literary Miscellanies. Edited by Frances Pow-
er Cobbe. London: Trubner, 1863-71.   DLC

5177. ----- The Effect of Slavery on the American People. A
Sermon Preached at the Music Hall, Boston, on Sunday, July
4, 1858. Boston: W. L. Kent, 1858.   CtY-D

5178. ----- A False and True Revival of Religion. A Sermon Delivered at Music Hall, Boston, on Sunday, April 4, 1858...
Boston: Wm. L. Kent and Co., 1858.   DHU/MO

5179. ----- A Letter to the People of the United States Touching
the Matter of Slavery. Boston: J. Munroe, 1848. CtY-D

5180. ----- The Nebraska Question. Some Thoughts on the New
Assault upon Freedom in America, and the General State of the
Country in Relation thereunto, Set Forth in a Discourse Preached
at the Music Hall, in Boston, on Monday, Feb. 12, 1854. Boston:
B. B. Mussey, 1854.   CtY-D

5181. ----- The New Crime Against Humanity. A Sermon,
Preached at the Music Hall, in Boston, on Sunday, June 4, 1854.
Boston: B. B. Mussey, 1854.   CtY-D

5182. Parker, Theodore. A New Lesson for the Day: a Sermon
Preached at the Music Hall, in Boston, on Sunday, May 25, 1856.
Boston: B. H. Greene, 1856.   CtY-D

5183. ----- The Present Aspect of Slavery in America and the
Immediate Duty of the North: A Speech Delivered in the Hall
of the State House, before the Massachusetts Anti-Slavery Convention, on Friday Night, January 29, 1858. Boston: B.
Marsh, 1858.   CtY-D

5184. ----- The Relation of Slavery to a Republican Form of Government. A Speech Delivered at the New England Anti-Slavery
Convention, Wednesday Morning, May 26, 1858. Rev. by the
author. Boston: W. L. Kent, 1858.   CtY-D

5185. ----- A Sermon on the Dangers which Threaten the Rights
of Man in America; Preached at the Music Hall, on Sunday,
July 2, 1854. Boston: B. B. Mussey, 1854. CtY-D; NN/Sch

5186. ----- Speeches, Addresses, and Occasional Sermons....
Boston: n.p., 1861.   NN/Sch
Abolitionist.

5187. ----- The Three Chief Safeguards of Society, Considered in
a Sermon at the Melodeon, on Sunday, July 6, 1851. Boston:
Wm. Crosby and H. P. Nichols, 1851.   DHU/MO

5188. ----- The Trial of Theodore Parker for the "Misdemeanor"
of a Speech in Faneuil Hall Against Kidnapping, before the
Circuit Court of the United States, at Boston, Apr. 3, 1855.
Boston: Pub. for the author, 1855.   DHU/MO

5189. Peabody, Andrew Preston. Position and Duties of the North
with Regard to Slavery. Newburyport, Mass.: C. Whipple,
1847.   CtY-D
"Reprinted from the Christian Examiner of July, 1843."

5190. "Present State of the Slavery Question." Quarterly Christian
Spectator (8:1, Mr., 1836), pp. 112-27.   DHU/R
A discussion of the book Slavery, by Wm. E. Channing.
Boston, 1835.

5191. Staples, Lawrence C. Washington Unitarianism, a Rich
Heritage. Washington, D.C.: n.p., 1970.   DHU/R
Chapter 4, The Specter of Slavery 1854-1860.

5192. Steinhal, S. Alfred. American Slavery. A Sermon Preached
at Christ Church Chapel, Bridgwater, on Sunday, May the
First, 1853. Bridgwater: Pr. by J. Whitby, 1853. CtY-D

5193. Taggart, Charles Manson. Slavery and Law in Light of
Christianity, A Discourse Delivered Before the Congregation
of Unitarian Christians of Nashville, Tenn. on Sunday Evening,
June 22d, 1851. Nashville: J. T. S. Fall, 1851. NNCor;
MB: NN

5194. Willson, Edmund Burke. The Bad Friday: A Sermon
Preached in the First Church, West Roxbury, June 4, 1854;
it Being the Sunday After the Return of Anthony Burns to Slavery. Boston: Pr. by J. J. Wilson, 1854.   CtY-D

14. Others

5195. Campbell, Douglas. The Puritan in Holland, England, and
America... New York: Harper & Brothers, 1893. 2 vols.
DHU/R
Contains information about Puritanism and slavery.

5196. Flynn, John Stephen. The Influence of Puritanism. New
York: E. P. Dutton & Co., 1920.   DHU/R
pp. 202-12, Slave trade and abolition in America.

5197. Free Church Anti-Slavery Society. An Address to the Office-
Bearers and Members of the Free Church of Scotland, on her
Present Connexion with the Slaveholding Churches of America.
From the Committee of the Free Church Anti-Slavery Society.
Edinburgh: Charles Ziegler, 1847.   DHU/MO

5198. Free Church Anti-Slavery Society. The Sinfulness of Main-
taining Christian Fellowship with Slave-Holders. Strictures on
the Proceedings of the Last General Assembly of the Free
Church of Scotland Regarding Communion with the Slave-Holding
Churches of America, Respectfully Addressed to the Office-
Bearers and Members of that Church. From the Committee of
the Free Church Anti-Slavery Society.
Edinburgh: C. Ziegler, 1846.   DHU/R

5199. Fuller, Edward J. A Fast Sermon, Delivered April 7, 1836,
Before the Calvinistic Church and Society in Harwick, Mass. ...
Brookfield, Mass.: E. & L. Merriam, Printers, 1836. NN/Sch

5200. Gilbert, Arthur. "The Bible Speaks on Segregation." Christian Friends Bulletin (14:2, Apr. 1957), pp. 3-6.   DLC

5201. Korn, Bertram Wallace. Jews and Negro Slavery in the Old South, 1789-1865. Elkins Park, Pa.: Reform Congregation Keneseth Israel, 1961.   TSewU-T

5202. Lupton, D. E. "Does the Bible Support Segregation?" Negro Digest (11; Jl., 1962), pp. 77-81.   DHU/MO

5203. McAll, Samuel. Slavery a Curse and a Sin. A Speech Delivered at Bradford, Yorkshire on Wednesday, October 20, 1852, at the Autumnal Meeting of the Congregational Union of England and Wales... London: Charles A. Bartlett, 1852. DHU/MO

5204. "Meetings." The Crisis (9:1, Nov., 1914), p. 6, 2-3.
          DLC; DHU/MO
"The Old Mennonite Church of Germantown where the first American protest against slavery was made, held a celebration of Emancipation with prominent colored speakers."

5205. Morison, Samuel Eliot. Builders of the Bay Colony. Boston: Houghton Mifflin Co., 1930.   DHU/R
Slaves and slave-trading by Puritans pp. 173-74; 191-92.

5206. Philadelphia. First Free Church. The Confession of Faith, and Rules of Government and Discipline, of the First Free Church, Philadelphia. Philadelphia: Merrihew and Thompson, 1840.
          NNCor

5207. Ruchames, Louis, (ed.). Racial Thought in America From the Puritans to Abraham Lincoln, A Documentary History. Amherst, Mass.: University of Massachusetts Press, 1969. DHU/MO
Puritans, Quakers and slavery in the seventeenth century.

5208. Should the Free Church hold Fellowship with Slave-Holders? and, Should the Money Lately Received from Slaveholding Churches be Sent Back? Respectfully Addressed to the Members of the Free Church of Scotland by a Member of the Free Church. Linlithgow: A. Waldie, 1846.   DHU/MO

5209. Stephenson, George Maldolm. The Puritan Heritage. New York: Macmillan, 1952.   NN/Sch
Slavery and the church, pp. 271-73.

5210. Two Hundred Reward. Liverpool: Millenial Star Office, 1911?   NjP
Slavery, the church and the Latter Day Saints.

5211. Werner, M. R. Brigham Young. New York: Harcourt, Brace and Company, 1925.   DHU/R
Morman attitude on slavery, pp. 97, 99, 100, 163.

15. General

5212. The Abrogation of the Seventh Commandment by the American Churches. New York: D. Ruggles, 1835.   DHU/MO

5213. Adams, John Greenleaf, (ed.). Our Day: A Gift for the Times. Boston: B. B. Mussey, 1848.   NN/Sch
Propose and poetery, "The Alleged Inferiority of the African Race, by Rev. C. Stetson;" pp. 66-7. "The Fugitive Slave, by Rev. Henry Bacon;" pp. 77-8. "Anniversary Week in Boston, by J. G. Adams;" pp. 83-105. "To Frederick Douglass, by J. G. Adams;" pp. 106-7. "A Demon to be Exercised by Rev. G. G. Strickland;" pp. 157-9. "Thomas Clarkson, by J. G. Adams;" pp. 171-7.

5214. Adams, William. Christianity and Civil Government: A Discourse Delivered on Sabbath Evening, November 10, 1850. New York: Charles Scribner, 1851.   DHU/MO

5215. "An Address to Ministers and Christian Masters." n.p., 1829.   DHU/MO

5216. "An Address to the Churches, on the Subject of Slavery." Georgetown, O.: D. Ammen and Co., 1831.   DHU/MO

5217. The African Observer. A Monthly Journal Containing Essays and Documents Illustrative of the General Character, and Moral and Legal Effects of Negro Slavery. Philadelphia: Apr. 1827-Mr. 1828. (Edited by Enoch Lewis, a Consistent Contributor to the Genius of Universal Emancipation.)   DLC; NcD

5218. Albert, Octavia V. Rogers. The House of Bondage; or Charlotte Brooks and Other Slaves. New York: Hunt and Eaton, 1891.   OWibfU; DHU/R
Also appeared in the columns of the South-Western Christian Advocate as a serial."

5219. Allard, Paul. Les Esclaves Chretiens Depuis les Premiers Temps de l'Eglise Jusqu' à la Pin de la Dominatic Romaine en Occident. 5. ed. Paris: J. Gabalda. 1914.   CtY

5220. Allen George. Report of a Declaration of Sentiments on Slavery, Dec. 5, 1837 (to a Committee of the Convention of Ministers of Worcester County). Worcester: Henry J. Howland, 1838.   DHU/MO

5221. ----- Speech on Ministers Leaving a Moral Kingdom to Bear Testimony Against Sin; Liberty in Danger, from the Publication its Principles; the Constitution a Shield for Slavery; and the Union Better than Freedom and Righteousness. Boston: I. Knapp, 1838.   DHU/MO

5222. Allen, Joseph Henry. A Reign of Terror. A Sermon Preached in Union Street Church, Bangor, Je. 1, 1856. Bangor: S. S. Smith, 1856.   DLC

5223. Allen, William G. The American Prejudice Against Color. An Authentic Narrative Showing How Easily the Nation Got into an Uproar. London: W. & F. G. Cash, 1853.   DHU/MO

5224. American Missionary Association. Missionary Boards in Relation to Slavery, Caste, and Polygamy. From the American Missionary, "Extra, May, 1854." New York: American Missionary Association, 1854.   DHU/MO

5225. American Reform Tract and Book Society. Opinion of Mrs. Stowe on Excluding Slaveholders from the Church. American Reform and Tract and Book Society, n. d.   DHU/MO
Pamphlets on Slavery and Christianity V. 2.

5226. American Tract Society. Action of the Church in Franklin, Mass., in Regard to the American Board. New York: J. A. Gray, 1854.   DHU/MO

5227. Anti-Slavery Tracts. New York: 1855-1856. DHU/MO
Nos. 4, 12, 16, 17, and 19. Church and Slavery.

5228. Attempt to Enlist Religion on the Side of Colonial Slavery Exposed. London: Ellerton and Henderson, 1830.   NcD

5229. Bacon, Thomas. Sermons Addressed to Masters and Servants, and Published in the Year 1743 [sic] ... Now Republished with other Tracts and Dialogues on the Same Subject, and Recommended to all Masters and Mistresses to be Used in their Families. By the Rev. William Meade. Winchester, V.: John Heiskell, Printer, 1813.   DHU/MO

5230. Baird, Robert. The Progress and Prospects of Christianity in the United States of America; With Remarks on the Subject of Slavery in America, and on the Intercourse Between British

(Baird, Robert   cont.)
   and American Churches. London: Partridge and Oakey, 1851.
                           DLC; DHU/R; NN/Sch

5231. Banks, Frank D. "Plantation Courtship." Journal of Amer-
       ican Folklore (7:2, Apr.-Je., 1894), pp. 147-49. Pam. File,
                                                           DHU/R

5232. Barnes, Albert. The Church and Slavery. New York: Negro
       Universities Press, 1969.   MiBsA; DHU/MO
          Originally published in 1857.

5233. Bascon, John. "The Laws of Political Economy in Their
       Moral Relations." The New Englander (24; Oct., 1862), pp.
       649.   DCU/ST; DHU
          "Property gained by work must be protested by law or the
          motive for production is removed. How about slavery?
          The capitalists neither withdraws goods from the market
          nor is he [sic] ennervated by luxury."

5234. Beecher, Charles. A Sermon on the Nebraska Bill. New
       York: Oliver and Bros., 1854.   DHU/MO

5235. Beecher, Lyman. The Ballot Box a Remedy for National
       Crimes. A Sermon Entitled, "The Remedy for Dueling by Rev.
       Lyman Beecher, D.D., Applied to the Crime of Slaveholding."
       Boston: I. Knapp, 1841.   DLC

5236. Berwanger, Eugen H. The Frontier Against Slavery.
       Urbana: University of Illinois Press, 1967. MNtcA

5237. Bidlake, John. Slave Trade. A Sermon Preached at Stone-
       house Chapel, on Dec. 28, 1788. Second ed. Plymouth: M.
       Haydon & Son, 1789.   CtY

5238. Birney, James Gillespie. The American Churches, the
       Bulwarks of American Slavery. By an American. Newbury-
       port: Charles Whipple, 1835.   DHU/R; DLC; NN/Sch; CtY-D
       DHU/MO

5239. Blagden, C. W. Discourse on Slavery. Boston: Ticknor,
       n.d.   IC/H
          "Evils and unchristian acts of slavery and the endeavors
          of the churches and societies to end it."

5240. Blame, Joshua Rhodes. American States, Church, and Slav-
       ery. New York: Negro Universities Press, 1969. DLC;
       DHU/R; NcD; CtY-D
          Reprint of the 1862 ed.

5241. Blassingame, John W. The Slave Community, Plantation
       Life in the Antebellum South. New York: Oxford University
       Press, 1972.   DHU/R

5242. Bodo, John R. The Protestant Clergy and Public Issues.
       Princeton University Press, 1954.   NN/Sch
          Slavery and the Church.

5243. Boyd, William K. History of North Carolina. The Federal
       Period, 1783-1860. Chicago: Lewis Publishing Co., 1919.
                                                DLC
          Statistics on numbers of Blacks belonging to organized
          churches in North Carolina in 1860.

5244. ----- (ed.). "Benefit of Clergy as Applied to Slaves."
       Journal of Negro History (8:4, Oct., 1923), pp. 443-47.
                                                DHU

5245. Bowditch, William Ingersoll. God or Our Country. Review
       of the Rev. Dr. Putnam's Discourse Deliverd on Fast Day,
       Entitled "God and Our Country." Boston: I. R. Butts, 1847.
                                                DLC

5246. Breckinridge, Robert J. The Question of Negro Slavery and
       the New Constitution of Kentucky. Philadelphia: Biblical Rep-
       ertory and Princeton Review, 1849.   O

5247. Brecht, Theodor. Kirche und Sklaverei; ein Beitrag zur
       Lösung des Problems der Freiheit. Barmen: H. Klein, 1890.
                                                NNCor

5248. British and Foreign Anti-Slavery Society, London. Amer-
       ican Slavery and British Christians of all Denominations...in
       May, 1845 Showing the Connection of American Religious
       Bodies With Slavery and the Article Entitled "The Silent Men"
       From the "Anti-Slavery Reporter" of July, 1853. London:
       British and Foreign Anti-Slavery Society, 1854. DLC; DHU/MO

5249. Brookes, Iveson L. A Defence of Southern Slavery. Against
       the Attacks of Henry Clay and Alex'r. Campbell...By a South-
       ern Clergyman. Hamburg, S. C.: Pr. by Robinson & Carlisle,
       1851.   CtY-D
          This pamphlet contains a review of Mr. Clay's Letter on
          Emancipation and strictures on Mr. Campbell's 'Tract for
          the people of Kentucky.' -Pref.

5250. ----- Defence of the South Against the Reproaches and In-
       croachments of the North. n.p.: n.p., 1850.   CtY-D
          Reply to an article in the Christian Review for January,
          1849, on the extension of slavery.

5251. Brown, James. American Slavery, in its Moral and Political
       Aspects Comprehensively Examined; to Which is Subjoined an
       Epitome of Ecclesiastical History, Shewing the Mutilated State
       of Modern Christianity. Oswego: Printed by G. Henry, 1840.
                                                DHU/R

5252. Brown, Larry. "Historic Roles of Christianity During Slav-
       ery." Transition (1; 1973), pp. 182-92. DHU/MO

5253. Brown, Letitia Woods. Free Negroes in the Distirct of
       Columbia, 1790-1846. New York: Oxford University Press,
       1972.   MNtcA; DHU/R

5254. Brown, Solyman. Union of Extremes: a Discourse on Lib-
       erty and Slavery, as They Stand Related to the Justice, Pros-
       perity, and Perpetuity of the United Republic of North Amer-
       ica... New York: Pr. by D. Fanshaw, 185?   NN/Sch

5255. Brown, William B. Religious Organizations, and Slavery.
       Oberlin: J. M. Fitch, 1850.   DHU/MO; NcD; DLC

5256. Brunner John H. The Union of the Churches. New York:
       Phillips & Hunt, n.d.   NB; NcD
          Section on Slavery and Church. Church Union versus
          Church Schisms.

5257. Burleigh, Charles. Reception of George Thompson in Great
       Britain. Compiled from Various British Publications. Boston:
       I. Knapp, 1836.   CtY-D

5258. Burt, Jairus. The Law of Christian Rebuke, a Plea for
       Slave-Holders. A Sermon Delivered at Middle-town, Conn.,
       Before the Anti-Slavery Convention of Ministers and Other
       Christians, Oct. 18, 1843. Hartford: N. W. Goodrich & Co.,
       1843.   DLC

5259. Cade, John B. "Out of the Mouths of Ex-Slaves: Religion
       and Recreation of Activities." Journal of Negro History (20:3,
       Jl., 1934), pp. 327-34.   DHU

5260. Cairns, Earle Edwin. Saints and Society; the Social Impact
       of Eighteenth Century English Revivals and its Contemporary
       Relevance. Chicago: Moody Press, 1960. CtY-D

5261. Callaway, T. F. "The Old South and the Negro Slaves."
       The Christian Index (118; Ag. 18, 1938), p. 3. LNB; NcWfSB

5262. Capen, Hanum. Letter to Rev. Nathanial Hall, of Dorchester,
       Mass., by Nahum Capen Concerning Politics and the Pulpit.
       Boston and Cambridge: J. Monroe & Co., 1855.   DLC; NN/Sch
          "A protest directed against the activity of ministers of the
          Gospel in the anti-slavery movement."

5263. Carleton, Stephen. Continuity and Change in Southern Re-
       ligion 1820-1845: The Baptists, The Presbyterians and the

Methodists. Doctoral dissertation. University of Chicago, 1968.

5264. Caste and Slavery in the American Church. By a Churchman. New York and London: Wiley and Putnam, 1843.   DHU/MO

5265. Channing, Edward. History of the United States V. 5 (New York: Macmillan Co., 1932), pp. 204-41.   DHU
Chapter VII contains a brief discussion of feeling of the church relative to the question of slavery.

5266. Cheaney, Henry Ellis. Attitudes of the Indiana Pulpit and Press Toward the Negro 1860-1880. Doctoral dissertation. University of Chicago, 1961.

5267. Cheever, George Barrell. The Sin of Slavery, The Guilt of the Church, and the Duty of the Ministry. An Address Delivered Before the Abolition Society at New York, on Anniversary Week 1858. Boston: J. P. Jewett and Co.; Cleveland: H. P. B. Jewett, 1858.   DLC

5268. The Christian Citizen. Negro Emancipation from the Law of Love and Service Involved in White Supremacy. Gaffney, S. C.: n.p., n. d.   DHU/MO

5269. Christianity Versus Treason and Slavery. Religion Rebuking Sedition.... Philadelphia: H. B. Ashmead, 1864. DHU/MO; DLC

5270. Christy, David. Pulpit Politics; or, Ecclesiastical Legislation on Slavery, in its Disturbing Influences on the American Union. New York: Negro Universities Press, 1969. DLC; DHU/R; DHU/MO; CtY-D; NcD

5271. "The Church and the Country." The Princeton Review (33; Apr., 1861), pp. 322f.   DLC
Slavery and religion.

5272. Clark, Rufus Wheelwright. Conscience and Law. A Discourse Preached in the North Church, Portsmouth, New Hampshire, on Fast Day, Apr. 3, 1851. Boston: Tappan & Whittemore; Portsmouth: S. A. Badger, 1851.   DHU/MO

5273. ----- A Review of the Rev. Moses Stuart's Pamphlet on Slavery, Entitled Conscience and the Constitution. Boston: C. C. P. Moody, 1850.   DHU/MO; CtY

5274. Clay, Cassius M. Cassius M. Clay's Appeal to All Followers of Christ in the American Union. n. p., n. d.   DHU/MO

5275. Cohen, Chapman. Christianity, Slavery and Labour. London: Issued for the Secular Society, Limited, by the Pioneer Press, 1936.   NN/Sch

5276. Cole, Arthur C. The Irrepressible Conflict, 1850-1856. A History of American Life. New York: Macmillan Co., 1934.   DHU/R
Chapter X, "The Challenge to the Church."

5277. Conflict Between Christianity and Slavery. From the American Missionary for May, 1860.   DHU/MO
Pamphlets on Slavery and Christianity, V. 1.

5278. Couch, Paul. ...Just Rulers, a Sermon... Boston: Leavitt and Alden, n. d.   DHU/MO

5279. Crothers, Samuel. The Gospel of the Jubilee. An Explanation of the Typical Privileges Secured to the Congregation and Pious Strangers by the Atonement on the Morning of the Jubilee. Lev., XXV, 9046. Reprint from the Author's Edition of 1893. Wtih an Introduction by Rev. John Rankin. Cincinnati: American Reform Tract and Book Society, 1856.   DLC

5280. ----- The Gospel of the Typical Servitude; the Substance of a Sermon Preached in Greenfield, Ja. 1, 1834. Published by the Abolition Society of Paint Valley (Ohio), Hamilton: Gardener & Gibbon, 1835.   DHU/MO

5281. ----- Strictures on African Slavery. Published by the Abolition Society of Paint Valley (Ohio). Rossville: Butler Co., Ohio, Taylor Webster, 1833.   DHU/MO

5282. Cuffel, Victoria. "The Classical Greek Concept of Slavery." Journal of the History of Ideas (17:3, Jl.-Sept., 1966), pp. 323-42.   DHU/R

5283. Curry, Daniel. The Judgements of God, Confessed and Deprecated. A Sermon Preached on the Occasion of the National Fast, Aug. 3, 1849... n. p., 1849.   DHU/MO

5284. Curtis, George Ticknor. Observations on the Rev. Dr. Gannett's Sermon, Entitled "Relation of the North to Slavery." Republished from the Editorial Columns of the Boston Courier, of June 28th, and 30th, and July 6th, 1854. Boston: Redding and Co., 1854.   DHU/MO

5285. Dana, James. The African Slave Trade. A Discourse Delivered in the City of New-Haven, September 9, 1790, before the Connecticut Society for the Promotion of Freedom. New Haven: Pr. by T. and S. Green, 1791. NN/Sch; CtY-D

5286. Davies, Ebenezer. American Scenes and Christian Slavery; a Recent Tour of Four Thousand Miles in the United States. London: J. Snow, 1849.   CtY; NNC; NcU; MnHi

5287. Davies, Samuel. Letters from the Rev. Samuel Davies, Shewing the State of Religion (particularly among the Negroes) in Virginia. Likewise an Extract of a Letter for a Gentleman in London to his Friend in the Country, being Some Observations on the Foregoing. London: n. p., 1757.   DLC

5288. Davis, David Brion. The Problem of Slavery in Western Culture. Ithaca, N. Y.: Cornell University Press, 1966. CtY-D; DHU/R; NN/Sch

5289. Davis, Owen. Sketches of Sermons, Delivered by Rev. Owen Davis, in the First Free Bethel Church, in West Centre Street, Boston. Boston: Pr. for the Author, 1837. DLC

5290. De Charms, Richard. A Discourse on the True Nature of Freedom and Slavery. Delivered before the Washington Society of the New Jerusalem, in View of the One Hundred Eighteenth Anniversary of Washington's Birth. Philadelphia: J. H. Jones, Printer, 1850.   NN/Sch

5291. DeVingut, Gertrude. "Our Unity as a Nation." The New Englander (21; Ja., 1862), pp. 94+.   DLC
Religion and slavery.

5292. Dexter, Henry Martyn. Our National Condition, and its Remedy. A Sermon, Preached in the Pine Street Church, Boston, on Sunday, June 22, 1856. Boston: J. P. Jewett & Co., 1856.   NN/Sch

5293. Dollar, George W. "Churches and the Civil War." Bibliotheca Sacra (118:472, Oct.-Dec., 1916), pp. 327-33. DHU/R

5294. Dorough, Charles D. Religion in the Old South; a Pattern of Behavior and Thought. Doctoral dissertation. University of Texas, 1947.

5295. Douglass, Frederick. "The Free Church and Slavery." Philip S. Foner, (ed.). The Life and Writing of Frederick Douglass. V. 1. (New York: International Publishers, 1950), pp. 173-79.   DHU/R
Speech given in Glasgow, Scotland, May 29, 1846.
Negro author.

5296. Drummond, Andrew Landale. Story of American Protestanism. Boston: Beacon Press, 1931.   NN/Sch
Slavery and the Church, pp. 286-92.

5297. Duffield, George. A Sermon on American Slavery: its Nature, and the Duties of Christians in Relation to It. Detroit: J. S. and S. A. Bagg, Printers, 1840. DHU/MO; DLC; NcD

5298. Dumond, Dwight Lowell. Anti-Slavery Origins of the Civil War in the United States. Ann Arbor, Mich.: University of Michigan Press, 1939.   DHU/MO
   "Earlier phases of the evangelical attack on slavery."

5299. Easton, Hosea. A Treatise on the Intellectual Character and Civil and Political Condition of the Colored People of the United States and the Predjudice Exercised Toward Them: With a Sermon on the Duty of the Church to Them... Boston: Pr. and pub. by Isaac Knapp, 1837.   DHU/MO
   Also in, Negro Protest Pamphlets: A Compendium. New York: Arno Press, 1969.

5300. Edge, Frederick Miles. Slavery Doomed; or, The Contest Between Free and Slave Labour in the United States. London: Smith, Elder & Co., 1860.   NN/Sch
   Slavery and the church, pp. 166-74.

5301. Edwards, Jonathan. The Injustice and Impolicy of the Slave Trade, and of the Africans: Illustrated in a Sermon Preached before the Conn. Society for the Promotion of Freedom, and for the Relief of Persons Unlawfully Holden in Bondage at their Annual Meeting in New Haven, September 15, 1791...4th ed. Newburyport: Charles Whipple, 1834.   DHU/MO; CtY; NN/Sch

5302. Engelder, Conrad J. The Churches and Slavery: A Study of the Attitudes Toward Slavery of the Major Protestant Denominations. Doctoral dissertation. University of Michigan, 1964.   DHU/R

5303. The Enormity of the Slave Trade and the Duty of Seeking the Moral and Spiritual Elevation of the Colored Race... New York: American Tract Society, 1846.   NN/Sch

5304. Evangelical Alliance and American Slavery. Report of a Meeting Held the 7th October 1846, to Review the Proceedings of the Evangelical Alliance in Reference to American Slavery. Bristol: T. H. & H. B. Sealy, 1846.   NNCor

5305. Evangelical Consociation, Rhode Island. Fellowship with Slavery. Report Republished from the Minutes of the Evangelical Consociation, Rhode Island. Cin.: American Reform and Book Society, 1853.   DHU/MO

5306. Evans, Joshua. A Journal of the Life, Travels, Religious Experiences and Labors in the Work of the Ministry. Phila.: J. & I. Comly, 1837.   NNC

5307. Fast Day Sermons; or, The Pulpit on the State of the Country. New York: Rudd & Carleton, 1861.   NN/Sch

5308. Father Ward's Letter to Professor Stuart. Brentwood, N.H.; August, 1837.   DHU/MO
   Pamphlets on slavery and Christianity, V. 1.

5309. Fawcett, Benjamin. A Compassionate Address to the Christian Negroes in Virginia, and other British Colonies in North America. With an Appendix, Containing Some Account of the Rise and Progress of Christianity among that Poor People. 2d ed. Salop: Pr. by F. Eddowes and F. Cotton, 1756.

5310. The Fellowship of Slaveholders Incompatible with a Christian Profession. New York: American Anti-Slavery Society, 1859.   DLC

5311. "The Final Fight to Rid the World of Slavery." Editorial The Christian Century (47:1, Ja., 1930), p. 5.   DHU/R

5312. Fish, Carol Russell. The Rise of the Common Man. New York: Macmillan Co., 1927.   DLC
   V. 6, split of Baptists and Methodists over slavery.

5313. Fish, Henry Clay. Freedom or Despotism. The Voice of our Brother's Blood: Its Source and Its Summons. A Discourse Occasioned by the Sumner and Kansas Outrages. Preached in Newark, June 8, 1856. Newark, N.J.: Douglass & Starbuck, 1856.   DLC

5314. Fisher, George Elisha. The Church, the Ministry, and Slavery. A Discourse, Delivered at Rutland, Mass., July 14, 1850. Worcester: Pr. by H. J. Howland, 1850.   DLC; NN/Sch

5315. Fitzgerald, John. Christian Slaveholders Disobedient to Christ; or, Ten Thousand English Christians Invited to Protest Actively Against the Sin of the Church in the United States; And to Cease from Purchasing the Produce of Slave Labour. London: W. H. Dalton, 1854.   ICN

5316. Fitzbugh, George. Sociology for the South or the Failure of a Free Society. Richmond: Morris, 1854.   CtY; NN

5317. Fletcher, John. Studies on Slavery, in Easy Lessons. Compiled into Eight Studies, and Subdivided into Short Lessons for the Convenience of Readers. Natchez: J. Warner, 1852.   NN/Sch; CtY-D

5318. Foster, Daniel. An Address on Slavery. Delivered in Danvers, Mass., by Daniel Foster, Pastor of the Free Evangelical Church of North Danvers, in Compliance with the Request of the Voters of Danvers. Boston: B. Marsh, 1849.   CtY-D

5319. Foster, Eden B. The Rights of the Pulpits, and Perils of Freedom. Two Discourses Preached in Lowell, Sunday, June 25, 1854. Lowell: J. J. Judkins, 1854.   DHU/MO; CtY-D; DHU/MO

5320. Foster, Stephen Symonds. The Brotherhood of Thieves: or, A True Picture of the American Church and Clergy: a Letter to Nathaniel Barney, of Nantucket. Boston: Anti-Slavery Office, 1844.   DHU/MO; DLC; NcD; NN/Sch

5321. ----- Letter to Nathaniel Barney and Peter Macy, of Nantucket. Part First. Canterbury, N.H.: n.p., 1843. NNCor
   Slavery and the church.

5322. Fox, George. Gospel Family Order, Being a Short Discourse Concerning the Ordering of Families, Both of Whites, Blacks and Indians. Philadelphia: n.p., 1701.   DLC
   Christian conscience section discusses Negro slaves on the new plantations.

5323. Francklyn, G. An Answer to the Rev. Mr. Clarksm's Essay on the Slavery and Commerce of the Human Species. Miami: Mnemosyne, 1969.   INU; DLC

5324. Franklin, John Hope. The Free Negro in North Carolina, 1790-1860. New York: Norton, 1971.   DHU/R; DHU/MO
   Reprint of 1943 edition. Religion, pp. 174-182.

5325. Furfey, Paul H. The Respectable Murderers; Social Evil and Christian Conscience. New York: Herder and Herder, 1966.   DHU/R
   Slavery and the church, pp. 29-49.

5326. Galpin, William. The Churchmen and His Churchmanship. Things Which the Christian Ought to Know and Believe to His Soul's Health. Muskegon, Mich.: The Parish Printer, n.d.   DHU/MO

5327. Galpin, William. Some Why Nots of the Church. Muskegon, Mich.: The Parish Printery, n.d.   DHU/MO

5328. Gannett, Ezra Stiles. Peace--Not War. A Sermon Preached in the Federal Street Meetinghouse, Dec. 14, 1845... Boston: J. Dowe, 1845.   DHU/MO

5329. ------ Relations of the North to Slavery. A Discourse Preached in the Federal Street Meeting House, in Boston June 11, 1854. Boston: Crosby, Nichols and Co., 1854. DHU/MO; CtY-D

5330. Garlick, Phyllis Louisa. Towards Freedom; Evangelicals and Slave Emancipation... London: Church Missionary Society, 1933.   CtY-D

5331. Gaustad, Edwin Scott. A Religious History of America. New York: Harper & Row, 1966.   NN/Sch
       Slavery and the church, pp. 179-201.

5332. Godwyn, Morgan. The Negro and Indians Advocate: Suing for Their Admission into the Church. London: Pr. for the author by J. D., 1680.   CtY; ViU; NcD

5333. [Godwin, Morgan] The Revival: or Directions for a Sculpture, Describing the Extraordinary Case and Diligence of Cur Nation, in Publishing the Faith Among Infidels in America and Elsewhere. Broadside. Rare Book Room.   RPJCB

5334. Goodell, William. One More Appeal to Professors of Religion, Ministers, and Churches Who Are Not Enlisted in the Struggle Against Slavery. Boston: J. W. Alden, n.d.   DHU/MO

5335. Goodell, William. A Voice From America, Touching the Evangelical Alliance and the Wrongs of the Slave... Newcastle: W. B. Leighton, n.d.   DHU/MO

5336. Goodwin, Daniel Raynes. Southern Slavery in its Present Aspects: Containing a Reply to a Late Work of the Bishop of Vermont on Slavery... Philadelphia: J. B. Lippincott,

5337. Gouge, William. Of Domestical Duties: Eight Treatises. London: Goerge Millery, 1622.   DFO
       Includes duties of masters and slaves.

5338. Gray, Edgar Harkness. Assaults Upon Freedom! or, Kidnapping an Outrage Upon Humanity and Abhorrent to God; a Discourse, Occasioned by the Rendition of Anthony Burns. Shelburne Falls: D. B. Gunn, 1854.   MNtcA
       Slavery and the Church- Sermons.

5339. Green, Beriah. Belief Without Confession. A Sermon, Preached at Whitesboro, New York: Utica: R. W. Roberts, 1844.   CtY; PHi; OClWHi
       "I am opposed to slavery; but am not an abolitionist."

5340. ----- The Church Carried Along; or The Opinions of a Doctor of Divinity on American Slavery. New York: W. R. Dorr, 1836.   CtY; PPrHi; OO

5341. ----- Four Sermons, Preached in the Chapel of the Western Reserve College, on Lord's Days, Nov. 18, and 25, and Dec. 2, and 9, 1832. Cleveland: Office of the Herald, 1833. DHU/MO

5342. Green, Fletcher M. "Northern Missionary Activities in the South 1846-1861." Journal of the Southern History (21:2, My., 1935), pp. 147-72.   DHU

5343. Greenslade, Stanley Lawrence. The Church and the Social Order; A Historical Sketch. London: SCM Press, 1948.   NN/Sch
       pp. 109-14, Slavery and the Church.

5344. Greville, Robert Kaye. Slavery and the Slave Trade in the United States of America; and the Extent to Which the American Churches are Involved in Their Support. Edinburgh: W. Oliphan & Sons, 1845.   DLC

5345. Griggs, Leverett Stearns. Fugitives From Slavery. A Discourse Delivered in Bristol, Conn., on Fast Day, Apr. 10, 1857. Hartford: D. B. Moseley, 1857.   NN/Sch

5346. Grimes, Leonard A. "Imprisoned in Richmond, Va., For Assisting Fugitive Slaves to Escape From Slavery, A Lovely Disciple." Wm. J. Simmons, (ed.). Men of Mark... (Cleveland, O.: Geo. M. Rewell & Co., 1887), p. 662.   DHU/R

5347. Grimke, Angelina Emily. Appeal to the Christian Women of the South. New York: American Anti-Slavery Society. 1936.   DHU/MO; NN/Sch

5348. Grosvenor, Cyrus Pitt. A Review of the "Correspondence" of Messrs. Fuller and Wayland on the Subject of American Slavery. To Which is Added a Discourse by Roger Williams, Printed in London, 1692 on "the Hierling Ministry." Utica: Pub. at the Christian Contributor Office, 1847. NN/Sch

5349. Gulzow, Henneke. Christentum und Skldverei in Den Ersten Drei Jahrhunderten. Bonn: R. Hablet, 1969. NNCor; MiBsa; NjP

5350. Hall, P. W. Thoughts and Inquiry on the Principles and Tenure of the Revealed and Supreme Law, Shewing the Utter Inconsistency and Injustice of Our Penal Statutes, and the Illicit Traffic and Practice of Modern Slavery. With Some Grounds of a Plan for Abolishing the Same. To Which is Added a Letter to a Clergyman on the Same Subject. London: J. Ridgway, 1792.   DHU/MO

5351. Hammon, Jupiter. An Address to the Negroes in the State of New-York. By Jupiter Hammon, Servant of John Lloyd, Jun. Esq. of the Manor of Queen's Village, Long Island... New York: Pr., Philadelphia, reprinted by Daniel Humphreys, in Spruce Street, near the Drawbridge, 1787. Tarrytown, N.Y.: Reprinted W. Abbatt, 1925.   DLC

5352. Harlow, Ralph Volney. Gerrit Smith; Philanthropist and Reformer. New York: H. Holt & Co., 1939.   DHU/MO
       Based on primary sources makes a strong plea for abolition of slavery for religious reasons.

5353. Harrell, Isaac S. Gates County to 1860. Durham, North Carolina: n.p., 1916.   CoU; NH; OCl; NcD
       In Historical Papers of Trinity College Historical Society Series 12, pp. 56-106.

5354. Harris, John. "The Church and Slavery: A Great Opportunity." The Church Overseas (6; 1933), pp. 205-09. DHU/R

5355. Helper, Hinton Rowan. The Impending Crisis of the South: How to Meet it. New York: A. B. Burdick, 1859. CtY-D; DHU/MO

5356. Henning, Thomas. Slavery in the Churches, Religious Societies, etc. Toronto: Printed at the Globe Book and Job office, 1856.   NNCor

5357. Hersey, John. An Appeal to Christians, on the Subject of Slavery... Baltimore: Armstrong & Plaskitt, 1833. DHU/MO

5358. Hickok, Laurens P. A Nation Saved from its Prosperity Only by the Gospel. A Discourse in Behalf of the American Home Missionary Society, Preached in the Cities of New York and Brooklyn... New York: American Home Missionary Society, 1853.   DHU/MO

5359. Higginson, Thomas Wentworth. Man Shall Not Live by Bread Alone. A Thanksgiving Sermon, Preached in Newburyport, Nov. 30, 1848. Newburyport: Charles Whipple, 1848.   DLC

5360. ----- Massachusetts in Mourning. A Sermon Preached in Worchester, on Sunday June 4, 1854... Boston: James Munroe and Co., 1854.   DHU/MO

5361. Hillhouse, William. The Crisis, No. 1-2; or Thoughts on Slavery Occasioned by the Missouri Question. New Haven: A. H. Maltby & Co., 1820.   DLC

5362. Hodges, Charles Edward. Disunion Our Wisdom and Our Duty. New York: American Anti-Slavery Society, 1855.   CtY-D

5363. Holcombe, William Henry. Suggestions as to the Spiritual Philosophy of African Slavery, Addressed to the Members and Friends of the Church of the New Jerusalem. New York: Mason Bros., 1861.   NN/Sch

5364. Hosmer, William. Slavery and the Church... Auburn, N.Y.: W. J. Moses, 1853.   DHU/MO; DLC; NN/Sch; CtY-D

5365. Hough, J. Our Country's Mission; or, the Present Suffering of the Nation Justified by its Future Glory. A Discourse Preached at Williston, Vermont, on the Day of the National Fast, August 4th, 1864. By Rev. J. W. Hough. Burlington: Free Press Print, 1864.   CtY-D

5366. Howard, James H. W. Bond and Free, a True Story of Slave Times. Harrisburg: Meyers, 1886.   OWibfU

5367. Howard, V. B. "Southern Aid Society and the Slavery Controversy." Church History (41:2, Je., 1972), pp. 208-24.
DHU/R

5368. Humphrey, Heman. Dr. Humphrey's Charges Against Slavery. Extracts from a Discourse Delivered at Pittsfield, on the National Fast Day, Jan. 4, 1861. Boston: American Tract Society, 1851.   NN/Sch

5369. Ibn Seid, Omar. "A Devout Moslem Sold to the Infidels." Thomas R. Frazier, (ed.). Afro-American History: Primary Sources (New York: Harcourt, Brace & World, Inc., 1970), pp. 22-26.   DHU/MO
          Originally appeared as "Autobiography of Omar Ibn Sied, Slave in North Carolina, 1831," American Historical Review (30; Jl., 1925), pp. 791-95.

5370. The Independent. Politics and the Pulpit: A Series of Articles which Appeared in the Independent, during the year 1850. To Which Is Added an Article from the Independent of Feb. 21, 1850, Entitled "Shall We Compromise?" New York: W. Harned, 1851.
DHU/MO; DLC

5371. An Inquiry into the Condition and Prospects of the African Race in the United States: and the Means of Bettering its Fortunes. Phila.: Haswell, Barrington & Haswell, 1839. O

5372. Jay, William. An Examination of the Mosiac Laws of Servitude... New York: M. W. Dodd, 1854. NN/Sch; DHU/MO; CtY-D

5373. ----- A Letter to the Committee Chosen by the American Tract Society, to Inquire into the Proceedings of its Executive Committee, in Relation to Slavery. New York: n.p., 1857.
DLC; NN/Sch

5374. Jeffrey, George. The Pro-Slavery Character of the American Churches, and the Sin of Holding Christian Communion with Them. A Lecture Delivered at the Request of the Free Church Anti-Slavery Society. Edinburgh: Charles Ziegler, 1847.
DHU/MO

5375. Jenkins, William S. Pro-Slavery Thought in the Old South. Chapel Hill, N.C.: Univ. of North Carolina Press, 1935.
DHU/MO

5376. Jessup, Lewis. God's Honour; or, The Christian's Statesman. A Sermon Preached in Millsbury, June 15, 1856. Worcester: Chas. Hamilton, 1858.   TNF

5377. Johnson, Evan M. "The Communion of Saints." A Discourse Delivered in St. Michael's Church, Brooklyn, N.Y., on Sunday, the 26th of March, A.D., 1848. Brooklyn: I. Van Anden, 1848.
DHU/MO

5378. Jullan, George Washington. Speeches on Political Questions, 1850-1871. With an Introd. by L. Maria Child. New York: Hurd and Houghton, 1872.   NN/Sch
          Slavery and the church, pp. 67-82.

5379. Kemble, Frances Anne. The View of Judge Woodward and Bishop Hopkins on Negro Slavery at the South. Illustrated from the Journal of a Residence on Georgian Plantation. Philadelphia: n.p., 1863.   CtY-D

5380. Ker, Leander. Slavery, Consistent with Christianity. Jefferson City, Mo.: Pr. by W. Lusk & Son, 1842. DHU/MO

5381. Klein, Herbert S. "Anglicanism, Catholicism, and the Negro Slave." Laura Foner and Eugene D. Genovese, (eds.). Slavery

in the New World, A Reader in Comparative History (Englewood Cliffs, N.J.: Prentice-Hall, 1969), pp. 138-66.   DHU/R
          "Comment on 'Anglicanism, Catholicism, and the Negro Slave, '" pp. 167-69.

5382. ----- Slavery in the Americas. A Comparative Study of Virginia and Cuba. Chicago: Univ. of Chicago Press, 1967.
DHU/R
          Part III, Anglicanism, Catholicism, and the Negro slave.

5383. Krebs, John Michael. The American Citizen. A Discourse on the Nature and Extent of our Religious Subjection to the Government under which we Live... New York: Charles Scribner, 1851.   DHU/MO; CtY-D

5384. Lacy, Charles L. A Sermon Preached in Falling Spring Valley, West Va. October 19, 1876. Lacy on His Return Home, Twelve Years After His Escape from Slavery. Together with an Account of His Flight from Bondage, and a Brief Account of His Miraculous Escape from Death. Also, Good News Received by Letters from Friends. Cleveland: T. C. Schenck, 1880.   CtY-D
          Negro author.

5385. Lafon, Thomas. The Great Obstruction to the Conversion of Souls at Home and Abroad. An Address... New York: Union Missionary Society, 1843.   DHU/MO

5386. Lane Seminary. Fifth Annual Report of the Trustees; Together with the Laws of the Institution, and a Catalogue of the Officers and Students. Cincinnati: Corey & Fairbank, 1834.
DLC
          Contains statement by faculty concerning the late controversy with students over slavery.

5387. ----- Fourth Annual Report of the Trustees of the Cincinnati Lane Seminary; Together with a Catalogue of the Officers and Students. Lane Seminar: Students Typographical Association, n.p., 1834.   DLC
          Seminary was actively involved in the slavery issue.

5388. Lane Seminary Students (Theodore D. Weld). A Statement of the Reasons Which Induced the Students to Dissolve Their Connection with That Institution. Cincinnati: n.p., 1834.
DHU/MO

5389. Larroque, Patrice. De L'Esclavage Chez les Nations Chrétiennes. Paris: Librarie Etrangère de Bohne et Schultz, 1860.   NN/Sch; CtY-D

5390. Lay, Benjamin. All Slave-Keepers That Keep the Innocent in Bondage, Apostates Pretending to Lay Claim to the Pure and Holy Christian Religion; of What Congregation So Ever; but Especially in Their Ministers, by Whose Example the Filthy Leprosy and Apostacy Is Spread Far and Near. Philadelphia: Pr. for the Author, 1737.   DLC; NNCor

5391. Lea, Henry Charles. Studies in Church History; the Rise of the Temporal Power, Benefit of Clergy, Excommunication, the Early Church and Slavery. Phila.: Henry C. Lea, 1883.
MBW; NNCor

5392. Lechler, Gotthard Victor. Sklaverei und Christentum. Leipzig: Druck von A. Edelmann, 1877-78.   CtY-D

5393. Leeds Anti-Slavery Association. "Guilty or Not Guilty?" A Few Facts and Feelings Regarding the Religious Bodies of America in the Matter of Slavery; Being a Report of an Anti-Slavery Meeting Held in Belgrave Chapel, Leeds, December 10th, 1855... Leeds: E. Baines, 1855.   NNCor

5394. Le Jau, Francis. The Carolina Chronicle, 1706-1717. Berkeley: University of California Press, 1956. CtY-D

5395. A Letter to an American Planter, From His Friend in London. Printed by H. Reynell, 1781.   DLC
          The letter is dated Oct. 1, 1770.

5396. Letters, Addressed to Dorothy Ripley, From Several
Africans and Indians, on Subjects of Christian Experience.
Chester: J. Hemingway, 1807.   DHU/MO

5397. Lewis, Evan. An Address to Christians of All Denominations,
on the Inconsistency of Admitting Slave-Holders to Communion
and Church Membership... Philadelphia: S. C. Atkinson,
Printer, 1831.   DHU/MO; DLC
     Published by order of the Pennsylvania Society for Promoting
     the Abolition of Slavery.

5398. ----- Address to the Coloured People of Philadelphia. Delivered at Bethel Church, Mr. 12, 1833. Philadelphia: J.
Richards, 1833.   DHU/MO

5399. Lewis, George. Impressions of America and the American
Churches. Edinburgh: W. P. Kennedy, 1845. INU; NN/Sch

5400. Loguen, Jermain Wesley. Correspondence Between the Rev.
H. Mattison and Rev. J. W. Loguen, on the Duty of Ministers
to Allow Contributions in the Churches in Aid of Fugitives
Slaves and the Obligation of Civil Government and the Higher
Law. Syracuse, N.Y.: J. E. Masters, 1857.   DHU/MO

5401. London Missionary Society. The London Missionary Society's
Report of the Proceedings Against the Late Rev. J. Smith, of
Demerara... Who was Tried Under Martial Law, and Condemned
to Death, on a Charge of Aiding and Assisting in a Rebellion
of the Negro Slaves. London: F. Westley, 1824. CtY-D

5402. Long, John Dixon. Pictures of Slavery in Church and State;
Including Personal Reminiscences, Anecdotes, etc., etc.
With an Appendix, Containing the Views of John Wesley and
Richard Watson on Slavery. New York: Negro Universities
Press, 1969.   DHU/MO; DHU/R; DLC
     Reprint of the 1857. ed.

5403. Loring, Eduard N. Christianity and Slavery, Church and
Society and Missions to the Negro. Doctoral dissertation.
Vanderbilt University, 1971.

5404. Lotz, Adolf. Sklaverei, Staatskirche und Freikirche; die
Englischen Bekenntnisse im Kampf um die Aufhebung von
Sklavenhandel und Sklaverei. Leipzig: B. Tauchnitz, 1929.
                                      NN/Sch

5405. Love, Horace Thomas. Slavery in Its Relation to God. A
Review of Rev. Dr. Lord's Thanksgiving Sermon, in Favor
of Domestic Slavery, Entitled the Higher Law, in Its Application
to the Fugitive Slave Bill. Buffalo: A. M. Clapp & Co., 1851.
                                      DLC

5406. Love, William Deloss. The Reopening of the African Slave
Trade. Milwaukee: n.p., 1860?   CtY-D
     From the advanced sheets of 'The New Englander,' for Feb.,
     1860, V. 18.

5407. Lovewell, Lyman. A Sermon on American Slavery Preached
in New Hudson, Michigan, June 18, 1854. Detroit: Baker and
Conover, 1854.   OO

5408. Lunn, Arnold Henry Moore. A Saint in the Slave Trade Peter
Claver (1581-1654)... New York: Sheed & Ward, 1935.
DHU/MO; DLC; GAU; NcD; NN/Sch

5409. Macdonald, Eugene Montague. A Short History of the In-
quisition, what it was and what it Did; to which is Appended
an Account of Persecutions by Protestants, Persecutions of
Witches, the War Between Religion and Science, and the
Attitude of the American Churches Toward African Slavery...
New York: The Truth Seeker Company, 1907.   NN/Sch

5410. March, Daniel. The Crisis of Freedom. Remarks on the
Duty which all Christian Men and Good Citizens Owe to their
Country in the Present State of Public Affairs. Nashua, N.H.:
Pr. by Dodge and Noyes, 1854.   NN/Sch

5411. Marrant, John. Sermon Preached on the 24th Day of June
1789, Being the Festival of St. John the Baptist, at the

Request... Prince Hall, ... of the African Lodge of the
Honorable Society of Free and Accepted Masons... Boston:
n.p., 1789?   NN/Sch

5412. Massie, James William. Slavery the Crime and Curse of
America: An Expostulation with the Christians of That Land.
London: John Snow, 1852.   CtY; MB; ICN

5413. Mather, Cotton. "A Minister's Advice to Boston Slaveholders." Gilbert Osofsky. The Burden of Race (New York:
Harper & Row, 1966), pp. 35-39.   DHU/R

5414. May, George. A Sermon on the Connection of the Church
with Slavery. Lowell, Mass.: W. H. Stevens, 1845. NN

5415. McCabe, Joseph. ...Christianity and Slavery. Girard,
Kan.: Haldeman-Julius Co., 1927.   NN/Sch

5416. McKeen, Silas. A Scriptural Argument in Favor of Withdrawing Fellowship From Churches and Ecclesiastical Bodies
Tolerating Slaveholding Among Them. New York: American
and Foreign Anti-Slavery Society, 1848.   NNCor

5417. McLoughlin, William G. "Red, White, and Black in the Ante-
bellum South." Baptist History and Heritage (7:2, Apr., 1972),
pp. 69-75.   DHU/R
     "Christianity and racial antagonisms between blacks, Indians,
     and whites."

5418. McNeilly, James Hugh. Religion and Slavery; a Vindication of
the Southern Churches. Nashville, Tenn.: Publishing House of
the M. E. Church, South, 1911.   NN/Sch; NcD; FSU

5419. Meacham, Standish. Henry Thorton of Clapham, 1760-1815.
Cambridge: Harvard University Press, 1964.   CtY-D

5420. Michelini, Francesco. Schiavitu, Religione Antiche e
Cristianesimo Primitivo. Manduria: Lacaita, 1963. NNCor
     Slavery and the Church.

5421. Missionary Boards in Relation to Slavery Caste, and Polygamy.
New York: American Missionary Association, 1854.   NNCor

5422. Moore, H. E. "The Attitude of the Church Toward Slavery
and Serfdom from 325 to 1200 A.D." Quarterly Journal (11:1,
Ja., 1942), pp. 13-45.   DHU/MO

5423. "Morality and Religion in Slavery Days." Southern Workman
(26:10, Oct., 1897), p. 210.   DLC; DHU/MO

5424. Morill, Anson Peaslee. Message of Governor Morrill, to
Legislature of the State of Maine, January 6, 1855. Augusta:
Stevens & Blaine, 1855.   NcD

5425. Morse, Jedidiah. A Discourse Delivered at the African
Meeting-House in Boston. July 14, 1808, in Grateful Celebration
of the Abolition of the African Slave-Trade, by the Governments
of the United States, Great Britain and Denmark. Boston: Pr.
by Lincoln & Edmands, 1808.   NN/Sch

5426. Morse, Sidney Edwards. Premium Questions on Slavery,
Each Admitting of a Yes or No Answer; Addressed to the
Editors of the New York Independent and New York Evangelist,
by Sidney E. Morse, lately editor of the New York Observer.
New York: Harper & Bros., 1860.   NN/Sch

5427. Moulton, Phillips. "John Woolman's Approach to Social
Action--As Exemplified in Relation to Slavery." Church History
(35:4, Dec., 1966), pp. 399-410.   DHU/R

5428. Negro Slavery. A Review of Five Books: Each Dealing with
the Subject of Slavery. Reprinted from The American Quarterly
Review.   NN/Sch
     Phila., n.p., 1832?

5429. Negro Slavery. No. XVIII. Attempt to Enlist Religion on
the Side of Colonial Slavery Exposed. London: Ellerton and
Henderson, Printers, 183-. Pam. File, DHU/R; NcD

5430. Neilson, Peter. Life and Adventures of Zama, an African Negro King; and His Experience of Slavery in South Carolina. Written by Himself, Corrected and Arranged by Peter Neilson. Freeport, N. Y.: Books for Libraries Press, 1970.   DHU/R

5431. Nelson, Isaac. Slavery Supported by the American Church Countenanced by Recent Proceedings in the Free Church of Scotland. A Lecture Delivered at the Request of the Free Church Anti-Slavery Society. Edinburgh: C. Ziegler, 1847.
DHU/MO

5432. Newcomb, Harvey. The "Negro Pew" Being an Inquiry Concerning the Propriety of Distinctions in the House of God on Account of Color. Boston: Isaac Knapp, 1837. DHU/MO; DLC

5433. North Carolina. General Assembly. Journals of the House and the Senate, 1800-1860.   NcHiC
        See Journal for 1830-31, p. 139. Cites a bill introduced which prohibited slaves from meeting at night and later was amended to prohibit free Negroes from preaching in the presence of slaves.

5434. Offley, Greenburg W. God's Immutable Declaration of His Own Moral and Assumed Natural Image and Likeness in Man, Declared. (Genesis 1:26-27...) New Bedford: Mercury Stern Printing House, 1875.   DHU/MO

5435. Osofsky, Gilbert, (ed.). Puttin' On Ole Massa, The Slave Narratives of Henry Bibb, William Wells Brown, and Solomon Northup. New York: Harper and Row, Publishers, 1969.
DHU/R

5436. Parker, Joel and A. Rood. The Discussion Between Rev. Joel Parker, and Rev. A. Rood, on the Question "What are the Evils Inseparable from Slavery," which was Referred to by Mrs. Stowe, in "Uncle Tom's Cabin." New York: S. W. Benedict; Phila.: H. Hooker, 1852.   DHU/MO
        Reprinted from the Phil. Christian Observer of 1846.

5437. Parsons, Theophilus. Slavery. Its Origin, Influence, and Destiny. Boston: W. Carter, 1863.   CtY-D

5438. Patterson, Caleb Perry. ...The Negro in Tennessee, 1790-1865... Austin, Tex. The University, 1922. (University of Texas Bulletin no. 2205: Feb. 1, 1922).   NN/Sch

5439. Patton, William Weston. Conscience and Law; or, A Discussion of Our Comparative Responsibility to Human and Divine Government: With an Application to the Fugitive Slave Law. New York: M. H. Newman, 1850. DHU/MO; NN/Sch

5440. ----- Reminiscences of the Late Rev. Samuel Hopkins, D.D., of the Late Rev. Samuel Hopkins, D.D., of Newport, R.I. Illustrative of His Character and Doctrines, with Incidental Subjects... Providence, R.I.: Isaac H. Cady, 1843. DHU/MO

5441. Paxton, John D. Letters on Slavery; Addressed to the Cumberland Congregation, Virginia... Their Former Pastor. Lexington, Ky.: Abraham T. Skillman, 1833.   DHU/MO

5442. Perkins, Justin. American Slavery; In Connection with American Christianity. Our Country's Sin. A Sermon Preached to the Members and Families of the Nestorian Mission, at Oroomiah, Persia, July 3, 1853. Boston: John P. Jewett and Co., 1854.   DHU/MO; NN/Sch

5443. Pierpont, John. National Humiliation. A Sermon, Preached In Hollis Street Church, Apr. 2, 1840. Boston: Samuel N. Dickinson, 1840.   MB; MH

5444. Pillsbury, Parker. The Church as It Is; or, The Forlorn Hope of Slavery. Concord, N.H.: Pr. by the Republican Press Association, 1883.   DLC; CtY-D; DHU/MO

5445. Porter, Anthony Toomer. Led On! Step by Step: Scenes from Clerical, Military, Educational and Plantation Life in the South, 1828-1898. New York: G. P. Putnam's Sons, 1899.   O

5446. Porter, Noah. Two Sermons on Church Communion and Excommunication, with a Particular View to the Case of Slaveholders, in the Church. Hartford: Case, Tiffany & Co., 1853.   CtY; NNC

5447. Posey, Walter Brownlow. Frontier Mission; a History of Religion West of the Southern Appalachians to 1861. Lexington: University of Kentucky Press, 1966.   NN/Sch

5448. Potter, Alonzo. Christian Philanthropy. A Discourse, P Preached in St. George's Church, Schenectady, Sunday Evening Ja. 13, 1833, Before the African School Society. Schenectady, N.Y.: S. S. Riggs, 1833.   DLC

5449. The Praying Negro. An Authentic Narrative. [Andover, Flagg and Gould, 1818].   NcD

5450. "The Princeton Review on the State of the Country and of the Church." The Princeton Review (37; Oct., 1865), pp. 627+. "Slavery was wrong because it is against the unity of the human race, not because of scripture or constitution."

5451. Purvis, Robert. A Tribute to the Memory of Thomas Shipley, the Philanthropist. Delivered at St. Thomas' Church, Nov. 23, 1836. Published by Request. Philadelphia: Merrihew and Gunn, 1838.   DHU/MO

5452. Putnam, George. Our Political Idolatry. A Discourse Delivered in the First Church in Roxbury, on Fast Day, Apr. 6, 1843. Boston: Wm. Crosby & Co., 1843.   DLC

5453. ----- The Sign of the Times. A Sermon, Preached Mar. 6, 1836. Boston: Charles J. Hindee, 1836.   OO

5454. Quinn, William Paul, (bp.). "The Origin, Horrors, and Results of Slavery..." Dorothy B. Porter, (ed.). Early Negro Writing, 1760-1837 (Boston: Beacon, 1971), pp. 614-36. DHU/MO
        Written by a Negro minister.

5455. Rankin, John. Letters on American Slavery, Addressed to Mr. Thomas Rankin, Merchant at Middlebrook, Augusta Co., Va. Boston: I. Knapp, 1838.   CtY-D; NN/Sch; DHU/R

5456. Rathbone, Richard. Observations and Correspondence Relative to the Proceedings of the Evangelical Alliance, so far as They Had Reference to the Admission of Slave-Holders, at Their Recent Conference in London. Liverpool: Printed for G. and J. Robinson, 1846.   NNCor
        Slavery and the Church.

5457. Rawick, George P. (ed.). The American Slave: A Composite Autobiography. Westport, Conn.: Greenwood Publishing Co., 1972.   DLC
        "Contributions in Afro-American and African Studies, no. 11." Religion of the slaves, pp. 30-52.

5458. Redpath, James. The Roving Editor or Talks with Slaves in the Southern States. New York: A. B. Brudick, 1859.
DHU/MO

5459. Reynolds, Elhanan W. The Relations of Slavery to the War: and the Position of the Clergy at the Present Time. Three Discourses, Preached at Watertown, N.Y. Watertown, N.Y.: Sold at the Bookstores and at Rans's, 1861.   DLC

5460. Richmond, Legh. Annals of the Poor: Consisting of the Dairyman's Daughter, the African Servant, and the Young Cottager. With a Brief Memoir of the Author, and an Introductory Letter, by the Rev. Joel Hawes. Springfield, Mass.: G. & C. Meriman, 1852.   NN/Sch

5461. Richmond, Thomas. God Dealing with Slavery. God's Instrumentalities in Emancipating the African Slave in America. Spirit Message from Franklin, Lincoln, Adams, Jackson, Webster, Penn, and others, to the Author. Chicago: Religiophilosophical Publishing House, 1870.   DHU/MO

5462. Ring, Rodney Everett. The Early Christian Church and the Problem of Slavery. Masters thesis. University of Chicago, 1950.

5463. Root, David. A Tract for the Times and for the Churches; Being the Substance of a Discourse Delivered at South Boston, June, 1845. Boston: A. J. Wright, 1845.   OO

5464. Ross, William Stewart. Christianity and the Slave Trade. By Saladin (pseud.) London: W. Stewart, 1894. CtY-D; NN/Sch

5465. Russo, Pasquale. Negro Slavery; or Crime of the Clergy; a Treatise on Chattel and Wage Slavery, Presenting a Brief Historical Discussion of the Negro Problem in America. Chicago, Ill.: Modern School of Pedagogy, 1923.   DHU/MO; DLC

5466. Schaff, Philip. "The Influence of the Early Church on the Institution of Slavery." Mercersburg Review (10:4, Oct., 1858), pp. 614-20.   DHU/R

5467. Schaub, Friederich. Studien Zur Geschichte der Sklaverei im Frühmittel-Alter. Von dr. Friedrich Schaub. Berlin und Liepzig: W. Rothschild, 1913.   NN/Sch; CtY-D; DLC

5468. Schlatter, Richard B. The Social Ideas of Religious Leaders, 660-1688. New York: Octagon Books, 1971.   DHU/R
      Chapter 3, Master and Servant; see also index under slavery. Reprint of 1940 edition.

5469. Schouler, James. History of the United States. New York: Dodd, Mead & Co., 1894-99.   DHU/R
      Schism in the churches over slavery.

5470. Sears, Edmund Hamilton. Revolution or Reform. A Discourse Occasioned by the Present Crisis. Preached at Wayland, Mass., Sunday, June 15, 1856. Boston: Crosby, Nichols, 1856.   CtY-D

5471. Separation From Sin and Sinners. Should Christians Withdraw Themselves from Sinners? American Reform Tract and Book Society.   DHU/MO
      Pamphlets on Slavery and Christianity, V. 1.

5472. A Sermon on the Relations and Prospects of the United States in Regard to Slavery. Milwaukee, Wis.: June 1851. DHU/MO
      In Liberty Preacher (Je., 1851).

5473. Sewall, Samuel. "The Selling of Joseph." Merle Curti and Willard Thorp, et alii, (eds.). American Issues (Chicago: J. B. Lippincott Co., 1960), pp. 65-66.   DHU
      Slavery and the church and Puritanism and the Negro.

5474. Silver, James W. Confederate Morale and Church Propaganda. Tuscaloosa: Confederate Publishing Co., 1957.
                                                  DHU/MO
      "An attempt to show what part religion played in bringing on secession and in promoting the War Between the States."

5475. Sinclair, Upton. The Profits of Religion. New York: AMS Press, 1970.   DHU/R
      Book Four: The Church of the Slavers.

5476. A Sketch of the African Slave Trade and the Slavery of the Negroes Under Their Christian Masters in the European Colonies. n.p., n.d.   DHU/MO

5477. ...Slaveholding Piety. London: Sold by W. and F. G. Cash, 1853.   DLC

5478. "Slavery and the Church: Letters." Journal of Negro History (10:4, Oct., 1925), pp. 754-58.   DHU

5479. "Slavery and the Slave Trade." The Princeton Review (34; Jl., 1862), pp. 524-48.
      "From a historical perspective the proper attitude of government towards slavery is not one of indifference but of moral opposition to its practice and every attempt to increase it."

5480. Slavery in America; With Notices of the Present State of Slavery and the Slave Trade Throughout the World. Conducted by the Rev. Thomas Price, D.D. No. 1-14. July 1836-Aug. 1837. London: G. Wightman, 1837.   DLC

5481. "Slavery in the Church Courts." The Danville Quarterly Review (4; Dec., 1864), pp. 516+.   DLC

5482. "Slavery in the United States: Its Evils, Alleviations and Remedies." North American Review (73:153, Oct., 1951), pp. 347-85.   MH; DHU

5483. The Slavery of the Pulpit and Uncle Tom's Wigwam of the North; A Historical Tale Based on Facts Without Facts by Uncle Tom's Nephew. Salem: D. S. Brooks & Brothers, 1860.
                                          NcD; MH
      "Authors attributed to be John W. Craft and Thomas Driver.

5484. The Slavery Question: Letter From the Protestants of France on Slavery. New York: n.p., 1857.   MH

5485. Smectymnuus, (pseud.). Slavery and the Church. Two letters Addressed to Rev. N. L. Rice, D.D., in Reply to his Letters to the Congregational Deputation, on the Subject of Slavery. Also a Letter to Rev. Nehemiah Adams, D.D., in Answer to the "South Side View of Slavery." By Smectymnuus. Boston: Crocker & Brewster, 1856.   DLC

5486. Smith, Gerrit. A Letter, Addressed to John Tappan, esq., on Missions ... Cazenovia, N.Y.: Union Herald, 1839.
                                          NNCor
      Slavery and the Church.

5487. Smith, Henry B. Report on the State of Religion in the United States of America Made to the General Conferece of the Evangelical Alliance, at Amesterdam, 1867. New York: U.C. Roger, 1867.   DHU/MO

5488. Smith, Timothy L. Revivalism and Social Reform in Mid-Nineteenth Century America. New York: Abingdon Press, 1957.   DHU/R
      Chapters XII and XIII Churches and Slavery.

5489. ----- "Slavery and Theology: The Emergence of Black Christian Consciousness in Nineteenth-Century America." Church History (41:4, Dec., 1972), pp. 497-512. DHU/R

5490. Smith, William Andrew. Lectures on the Philosophy and Practice of Slavery, as Exhibited in the Institution of Domestic Slavery in the United States: With the Duties of Masters to Slaves. Ed. by Thos. O. Summers. Nashville, Tenn.: Stevenson & Evans, 1856.   CtY-D
      "The substance of lectures...delivered to the classes in moral science in Randolph Macon College."

5491. Smulie, H. "Uncle Tom's Cabin Revisted; the Bible, the Romantic Imagination, and the Sympathies of Christ." Interpretation (27:1, Ja., 1973), pp. 67-85.

5492. South Middlesex Conference of Churches. The Political Duties of Christians. A Report Adopted at the Spring Meeting of the South Middlesex Conference of Churches, April 18, 1848. Boston: Andrews & Prentiss, 1848.   DLC

5493. Stampp, Kenneth M. "The Daily Life of the Southern Slave." Nathan Huggins and Martin Kilson, et alii. Key Issues in the Afro-American Experience (New York: Harcourt Brace Jovanovich, 1971), pp. 116-37.   DHU/R

5494. ----- The Peculiar Institution. Slavery in the Ante-Bellum South. New York: Vintage Books, 1956.   DHU/R
      Religion and slavery, pp. 156-62.

5495. Stang, Alan. A Statistical Inquiry Into the Condition of the People of Colour, of the City and Districts of Philadelphia. Philadelphia: Kite and Walton, 1849.   O

5496. Stanton, Robert Livingston. The Church and the Rebellion a Consideration Against the Government of the United States; and the Agency of the Church, North and South, in Relation Thereto. New York: Derby & Miller, 1864. NN/Sch; DLC; GAU; NcD

5497. Stanton, William Ragan. The Leopard's Spots: Scientific Attitudes Toward Race in America, 1815-1859. Chicago: University of Chicago Press, 1960.   DHU/MO; CtY-D

5498. ----- The Leopard's Spots: Scientific Attitudes Towards Race in America, 1815-1859. Chicago: University of Chicago Press, 1960.   DHU/MO; CtY-D

5499. Statement on Behalf of Dr. Cheever and His Church. Edinburgh: n.p., 1861?   NNCor
Slavery and the Church.

5500. Steele, J. The Substance of an Address Delivered by Rev. J. Steele in the Associate Reformed Synod of the West at Their Meeting in Steubenville, on the Evening of October 16th, 1829, on the Question of Making the Holding of Slaves a Term of Communion in the Church. Washington: Geurnsey Co., 1830.   OO; OOXM

5501. Storm, Herbert Edward. Conscience and Law: the Debate in the Churches over the Fugitive Slave of 1850. New Haven: n.p., 1969.   CtY-D

5502. Stowe, Harriet Elizabeth (Beecher). Mrs. H. B. Stowe on Dr. Monod and the American Tract Society; Considered in Relation to American Slavery... Edinburgh: Repr. for the Edinburgh Ladies' Emancipation Society, 1858.   DLC

5503. Strong, Josiah. Our Country: Its Possible Future & Its Present Crisis. New York: The American Home Missionary Society, 1885.   DLC

5504. Sweet, William Warren. The Story of Religion in America. New York: Harper & Bros., 1930.
Discusses the part of religion in the events leading to the Civil War, including the controversy over slavery.

5505. Tannenbaum, Frank. Slave and Citizen: The Negro in the Americas. New York: Alfred A. Knopf, 1947.   DHU/MO

5506. Tappan, Lewis. American Slavery, (a letter) to the Editor of the British Banner. New York: J. A. Gray, 1852? NNCor CtY
Slavery and the church.

5507. ----- Letters Respecting a Book "Dropped from the Catalogue" of the American Sunday School Union in Compliance with the Dictation of the Slave Power. New York: American and Foreign Anti-Slavery Society, 1848.   DHU/MO; DLC

5508. Taylor, Joe G. Negro Slavery in Louisiana. Doctoral dissertation. Louisiana State University, 1951.

5509. Thayer, William Makepeace. A Sermon on Moses' Fugitive Slave Bill, Preached at Ashland, Mass., November 3, 1850. Boston: Pr. by C. P. Moody, 1850.   NN/Sch

5510. Thompson, Andrew. Slavery Condemned by Christianity. Edinburgh: Wm. Whyte and Co., 1847.   DHU/MO
Pamphlets on Slavery and Christianity, V. 1.

5511. Thompson, Joseph Parrish. The Duties of the Christian Citizen. A Discourse, by Joseph P. Thompson, Pastor of the Broadway Tabernacle Church. New York: S. W. Benedict, 1848.   DLC

5512. Thomson, Andrew Mitchell. Slavery Condemned by Christianity. Edinburgh: W. Whyte and Co., 1847. DHU/MO; DLC

5513. "Thoughts on the Discussion of Slavery." Christian Spectator (7:3, Ag., 1865), pp. 405-08.   DHU/R
Article is initialed S. H.

5514. Three Letters from the Reverend Mr. George Whitfield ... Letter III: To the Inhabitants of Maryland, Virginia, North and South Carolina Concerning Their Negroes. Philadelphia: Pr. & Sold by B. Franklin, 1740.   DLC

5515. Tyler, Alice. Freedom's Ferment. New York: Harper, 1962.   DHU/R
Slavery, controversy and religion, pp. 463-503.

5516. Tyson, Bryan. The Institution of Slavery in the Southern States, Religiously and Morally Considered in Connection with our Sectional Troubles. Washington, D.C.: H. Polkinhorn, Printer, 1863.   CtY-D

5517. Union Anti-Slavery Society. How the Action of the Churches Towards the Anti-Slavery Cause Promotes Infidelity. Issued by the Union Anti-Slavery Society. n.p., n.d.   DHU/MO

5518. United States. 33d Cong., 1st Session, 1853-1854. Senate. Right of Petition New England Clergymen. Remarks of Messrs. Everett... Mason, Pettit, Douglas, Butler, Seward, Houston, Adams and Badger. On the Memorial From Some 3,050 Clergymen of all Denominations and Sects in New England... Washington: Buell & Blanchard, Printers, 1854.   DHU/MO

5519. Van der Linde, Jan M. Heren, Slaven, Broeders; Momenten Uit de Geschchiedenis der Slavernij. Nijkerk: G. F. Callenbach, 1963.   NN/Sch

5520. Vaughan, John. "Negro Slavery." American Quarterly (26; Je., 1833), pp. 436-49. DCU; DGW; MHU/W
"An Address to Christians."

5521. Vincent, James. American Slavery Defeated in its Attempts Through the American Board of Commissioners for Foreign Missions, to Find a Shelter in the British Churches... London: W. Tweedie, 1854.   NNCor
Slavery and the Church.

5522. Walker, David. "Our Wretchedness in Consequence of the Preachers of the Religion of Jesus Christ." Thomas R. Frazier, (ed.). Afro-American History: Primary Resources (New York: Harcourt, Brace & World, Inc., 1970), pp. 102-08. DHU/R; DHU/MO
"From David Walker, 'Article III' of David Walker's Appeal in Four Articles... (Boston, 1829)."
Captioned by Frazier as: "The White Church's Oppression of the Black Man." Negro abolitionist.

5523. Wallace, Cyrus Washington. A Sermon on the Duty of Ministers to Oppose the Extension of American Slavery, Preached in Manchester, N. H., Fast Day, April 3, 1857. Manchester, N.H.: Steam Printing Works of Fisk & Gage, 1857.

5524. "The War." The Biblical Repertory and Princeton Review (35; Ja., 1863), pp. 140-69.   DHU/R
"God binds the nations as well as individuals. Preservation of the Union, not abolition, is the cause of this war and this is God's cause."

5525. Warren, Edwin R. The Free Missionary Principle, or, Bible Missions. A Plea for Separate Missionary Action from Slaveholders... Boston: J. Howe, 1847.   DHU/MO

5526. Washington, L. Barnwell. The Use of Religion for Social Control in American Slavery. Masters thesis. Howard University, 1939.

5527. Webster, Noah. Effects of Slavery, on Morals and Industry. Hartford: Printed by Hudson and Goodwin, 1793.   O

5528. Whipple, Charles King. A Chapter of Theological and Religious Experience. Boston: R. F. Wallcut, 1858. NNCor
Slavery and the Church.

5529. ----- The Family Relation, as Affected by Slavery. Cincinati: American Reform Tract and Book Society, 1858. (American Reform Tract and Book Society. Tracts no. 40.) Cty-D

5530. ----- Relations of Anti-Slavery to Religion. New York: American Anti-Slavery Society, 1855. DHU/MO; NN/Sch; CtY-D Anti-Slavery Tracts, no. 19.

5531. ----- Slavery and the American Board of Commissioners for Foreign Missions. New York: American Anti-Slavery Society, 1859.   DLC

5532. Wight, Willard E. Churches in the Confederacy. Doctoral dissertation. Emory University, 1958.

5533. Wilkinson, James Garth. The African and the True Christian, his Magna Charta. A Study in the Writings of Emanuel Swedenborg. London: J. Speirs, 1892. NN/Sch; DLC

5534. Willey, Austin. The History of the Anti-Slavery Cause in State and Nation. Portland: n.p., 1886.
Section on slavery and the church.

5535. Williams, Thomas Scott. The Tract Society and Slavery. Speeches of Chief Justice Williams, Judge Parsons, and Ex-Governor Ellsworth: Delivered in the Center Church, Hartford Branch of the American Tracts Society. January 9th, 1859. Hartford: Steam Press of E. Geer. 1859. NN/Sch

5536. Wilson, Gold Refined. "The Religion of the American Slave: His Attitude Towards Life and Death." Journal of Negro History (8; Ja., 1923), pp. 41-71.

5537. Wolcott, Samuel T. Separation from Slavery. Being a Consideration of the Inquiry, "How Shall Christians and Christian Churches Best Absolve Themselves from all Responsible Connection with Slavery?" Boston: American Tract Society, n.d.
                                                     DHU/MO; CtY-D
Prize essay by Church Anti-Slavery Society.

5538. Woolman, John. Considerations on Keeping Negroes; Recommended to the Professors of Christianity of Every Denomination. Part Second. Philadelphia: B. Franklin and D. Hall, 1762.   DLC

5539. Woolridge, Nancy Bullock. "The Slave Preacher--Portrait of a Leader." Journal of Negro Education (14; Wint., 1945), pp. 28-37.   DHU/MO

5540. Worcester, Mass., Convention of Ministers of Worcester County, on the Subject of Slavery, 1837-1838. Proceedings of the Convention of Ministers of Worcester County, on the Subject of Slavery; Held at Worcester, 1838. Worcester: Mass. Spy Office, 1838.   DHU/MO

5541. A Word on Behalf of the Slave: or, A Mite Cast into the Treasury of Love. London: C. Gilpin, 1848.   NNCor
Slavery and the church.

5542. A Word to Members of the Free Church, in Reference to the Proceedings of the General Assembly of 1847, on the Question of Communion with Slave-Holding Churches. By a Free Churchman. Edinburgh: Charles Ziegler...1847.   DHU/MO

5543. Wright, Henry Clarke. American Slavery: Two Letters from H. C. Wright to the Liverpool Mercury, Respecting the Rev. Drs. Cox and Olin, and American Man-Stealers. Dublin: Webb and Chapman, 1846.   MH
The first of the two letters appeared in the Manchester Examiner, Sept. 26, 1846 and second in the Liverpool Mercury, Oct. 9, 1846.

5544. ----- Christian Church; Anti-Slavery and Non-Resistance Applied to Church Organizations. Boston: Anti-Slavery Office, 1841.   DLC; NNC; OClWHi

5545. ----- Christian Communion with Slaveholders: Will the Alliance Sanction It? Letters to Rev. John Angell James, D.D. and Rev. Ralph Wardlaw, D.D., Shewing their Position in the Alliance. Rochdale: J. Hall, 1846.   DLC

5546. ----- Rev. Doctors Cox and Leifchild and American Man-Stealers. [Manchester?: J. Hall, Printer, 1846?]. NNCor
Slavery and the Church.
May Anti-Slavery Phamphlets, V. 212.

5547. ----- Two Letters From Henry C. Wright to the Liverpool Mercury, Respecting the Rev. Drs. Cox and Olin, and American Man-Stealers. Dublin: Webb and Chapmann, 1846? NNCor
Slavery and the Church.

E. SLAVE REVOLTS

5548. Aptheker, Herbert. "Styron-Turner and Nat Turner: Myth and Reality." Afro-American History, The Modern Era (New York: Citadel, 1971), pp. 80-95.   DHU/MO

5549. Cromwell, John W. "Aftermath of Nat. Turner's Insurrection." Journal of Negro History (5:2, Apr., 1920), pp. 208-34.   DHU/MO

5550. Gruber, Jacob. Defendant. The Trial of the Rev. Jacob Gruber, Minister of the Methodist Episcopal Church, at the March Term, 1819, in the Fredrick County Court, for a Misdemeanor. (The Charge was Preaching in such manner as to incite slave insurrection.) Fredricktown, Md.: David Martin, 1819.   DLC

5551. James, Cyril L. R. A History of Pan-African Revolt. Washington, D.C.: Drum & Spear Press, 1969. DHU/R
Chapter IV, "Religious Revolts in the New Colonies."

5552. Larison, Cornelius Wilson. Silvia Dubois (Now 116 Yers Old.). A Biografy of the Slav who Whipt her Mistres and Gand Her Freedom. New York: Negro Universities Press, 1969.
                                                     DHU/R
Reprint of 1883 edition.
Written in dialect.

5553. Mullin, Gerald W. Flight and Rebellion: Slave Resistance in Eighteenth-Century Virginia. New York: Oxford University Press, 1972.   DHU/R
Chapter 5, Religion, Acculturation, and American Negro Slave Rebellions: Gabriel's Insurrection, 11. 140-63.

5554. "The Original Confessions of Nat Turner," C. M. S. 539. Audiotape.

5555. Straker, David Augustus. Reflections on the Life and Times of Toussaint L'Overture, the Negro Hytien Commander-in-Chief of the Army, Ruler in the Domination of France, and Author of the Independence of Hayti. Columbia, S.C.: C. A. Calvo, Printer, 1886.
Written by an A.M.E. layman.

5556. Suttles, William C. "African Religious Survivals as Factors in American Slave Revolts." Journal of Negro History (56:2, Apr., 1971), pp. 97-99.   DHU/MO

5557. Wish, Harvey. "American Slave Insurrections Before 1861." Journal of Negro History (22:3, Jl., 1937), pp. 299-320.
                                                     DHU/MO

F. ABOLITION, ABOLITIONISTS, AND COLONIZATION

5558. "The Abolition of Slavery." Quarterly Christian Spectator
(6:2, Je., 1833), pp. 332-44.   DHU/R
A discussion of the book: Lectures on Slavery and Its Remedy, by Amos A. Phelps, pastor of Pine Street Church,
Boston. Published by the New England Anti-Slavery Society,
1834.

5559. "Abstract from the Seventh Report of the American Colonization Society." Christian Spectator (6:4, Apr., 1824), pp.
324-28.   DHU/R

5560. An Address to the Disciples on the Sin of Slavery by the
Churches in Trumbull County, Ohio, and Vicinity. Cincinnati:
W. L. Mendenhall, 1841.   TN/SCHS

5561. Action of the Church in Franklin, Mass., in Regard to the
American Tract Society and the American Board. New York:
J. A. Gray, 1854.   DHU/MO

5562. "Address to the Clergy of All Denominations on Colonization."
n.p., n.d.   DHU/MO

5563. Agutter, William. The Abolition of the Slave Trade Considered in a Religious Point of View. A Sermon Preached Before
the Corporation of the City of Oxford, at St. Martin's Church,
on Sunday, February, 3, 1788. London: F. F. and C. Rivington,
1788.   DHU/MO

5564. Albanese, Catherine L. "In Medias Res: Transcendental
Yankees and the Anti-Slavery Cause." Ohio Journal of Religious
Studies (1:1, Apr., 1973), pp. 18-22.   Pam. File, DHU/R
"The New Englanders who formed the transcendental movement
of the 1830's and 1840's emerged mostly from a background
of Unitarian Boston."

5565. Allen, George. Resistance to Slavery Every Man's Duty. A
Report on American Slavery; Read to the Worcester Central
Association, Mr. 2, 1847. Boston: Wm. Crosby & H. P.
Nichols, 1847.   DHU/MO

5566. American and Foreign Anti-Slavery Society. An Address to
the Anti-Slavery Christians of the United States. New York:
Printed by J. A. Gray, 1852.   DHU/MO; NN/Sch; CtY-D; DLC

5567. American and Foreign Anti-Slavery Society. Shall We Give
Bibles to Three Millions of American Slaves? New York: American and Foreign Anti-Slavery Society, 1847.
                                                 NN/Sch

5568. American and Foreign Anti-Slavery Society. Slavery and
the Board of Commissioners for Foreign Missions. New York:
1859   CtY-D

5569. American Board of Commissioners for Foreign Missions.
On Receiving Donations From Holders of Slaves. Boston:
Printed by Perkins and Marvin, 1840?   NNCor

5570. American Board of Commissioners for Foreign Missions.
...Report of the Committee on Anti-Slavery Memorials, Sept.
1845. With a Historical Statement of Previous Proceedings.
Boston: Press of T. R. Marvin, 1845.   NNCor; NjP; CtY-D

5571. American Colonization Society. ...Annual Report. Washington: n.p., n.d.   DHU/MO; CtY-D; NN/Sch

5572. "American Nationality." The Princeton Review (33; Oct.,
1861), pp. 611+.
Deals with slavery and seccession in South Carolina.

5573. American Reform Tract and Book Society. Agitation--the
Doom of Slavery. Cincinnati, O.: American Reform Tract
and Book Society, n.d.   DHU/MO
Tract no. 4 Pamphlets on Slavery and Christianity, V. 2.

5574. ----- On Slavery. Cincinnati, O.: American Reform
Tract and Book Society, n.d.   DHU/MO
Tract no. 3. Pamphlets on Slavery and Christianity, V. 2.

5575. American Tract Society. The Enormity of the Slave Trade;
and the Duty of Seeking the Moral and Spiritual Elevation of the
Colored Race. Speeches of Wilberforce, and Other Documents
and Records. New York: American Tract Society, 1846.
                                                 DHU/R

5576. ----- New York Branch. Testimony of Five of the Society's
Founders. Historical facts limiting its issues to publications
in which Evangelical Christians agree. n.p., n.d.   DLC

5577. Anti-Slavery Convention of American Women. An Appeal to
the Women of the Nominally Free States, Issued by an Anti-
Slavery Convention of American Women. New York: W. S. Dorr,
1837. Boston: I. Knapp, 1838.   DHU/MO

5578. Appeal of Clerical Abolitionists on Anti-Slavery Measures-
Reply by Editor Pro. Tem. of the Liberator- A Layman's
Reply to a "Clerical Appeal"- Reply to the Appeal by Rev. A. A.
Phelps- Declaration of Abolitionists in the Theological Seminary
at Andover, Mass. Boston: n.p., 1837.   NNCor

5579. Aptheker, Herbert. "Militant Abolitionists." Journal of Negro History (26:4, Oct., 1941), pp. 438-84. Pam. File, DHU/R
Included is information about Negro ministers.

5580. Armistead, Wilson. A Cloud of Witnesses Against Slavery
and Oppression. Containing the Acts, Opinions, and Sentiments
of Individual and Societies in All Ages. Selected from Various
Sources and for the Most Part Chronologically Arranged...
London: W. Tweedie, etc., 1853.   DHU/MO

5581. ----- Five Hundred Thousand Strokes for Freedom. A Series
of Anti-Slavery tracts, of which Half a Million are now First
Issued by the Friends of the Negro. London: W. & F. Cash, 1
1853. Nos. 19; 22; 29; 31; 33; 52; 55; 67; and 82.   DHU/MO

5582. ------ A Tribute for the Negro being a Vindication of the
Moral, Intellectual and Religious Capabilities of the Colored
Portion of Mankind; with Particular Reference to the African
Race. Illustrated by numerous biographical sketches, facts,
anecdotes, etc. n.p. 1848.   DHU/MO; INRE; DHU/R

5583. Aunt Sally; or, The Cross The Way of Freedom. A Narrative
of The Slave-Life and Purchase of the Mother of Rev. Isaac
Williams, of Detroit, Michigan. Cincinnati, Ohio: American
Reform Tract and Book Society, 1862.   DHU/MO; InU; DLC

5584. Babington, Churchill. The Influence of Christianity in Promoting the Abolition of Slavery in Europe... Cambridge, Eng.:
University Press, 1846.   NNCor

5585. Bacon, Leonard. A Discourse Preached in the Center Church
in New Haven, Aug. 27, 1828, at the Funeral of Hehudi Ashmun;
Colonial Agent of the American Colony of Liberia. With the
Address at the Grave by R. R. Gurley. New Haven: Hezekiah
How, 1828.   MH-AH
Bacon was a colonizationist and bitter opponent of immediate
emancipation. He was also opposed to slavery and to the
organized anti-slavery effort.

5586. Baer, Helene (Gilbert). The Heart is Like Heaven; the Life
of Lydia Maria Child. Philadelphia: University of Pennsylvania
Press, 1964.   O

5587. Ball, G. H. "Liberty and Slavery." The Freewill Baptist
Quarterly (9; Apr., 1861), pp. 146 ff.
"Our nation was born under the administration of abolitionists. Slavery is involuntary servitude involving the destruction of the person. If there is any justice in slavery, our
religion is false for it requires primary allegiance to God."
Wenzel (1971) #324

5588. Bannan, Phyllis M. Arthur and Lewis Tappan: A Study of
Religious and Reform Movements in New York City. Doctoral
disseration, Columbia, 1950.

5589. Barnes, Gilbert H. The Anti-Slavery Impulse, 1840-1844. New York: D. Appleton-Century, 1933. DHU/MO; DHU/R
Points out that "the religious conviction was translated in to the anti-slavery cause."

5590. ----- and Dwight L. Dumond. Letters of Theodore Dwight Weld, Angelina Grimke Weld, and Sarah Grimke, 1822-1844. Mass.: P. Smith, 1965. 2 vols. DHU/MO
"Discusses the connection between the anti-slavery movement and religious revivalism."

5591. Barnes, W. Graham. Alexander Campbell on Revolution vis-a-vis the Abolitionists. n.p., n.p., 1967. TN/DCHS

5592. Bassett, John Spencer. Anti-Slavery Leaders of North Carolina. Spartanburg, S. C.: The Reprint Co., 1971. DHU/R
Reprint of 1898 edition.
Abolitionists and the church.

5593. ----- The Southern Plantation Overseer as Revealed in His Letters. Northampton, Mass.: Smith College, 1925. KMK; C CoDU; CoU; KU; WaS; TxLT; OrPR; OrU; OrCS; PPULC; MiU; NcD; NcU; OCIWHi; OCU; OO; OcI; WaU; MWA; PHC; PPT; NN; MB; ViU; TU; Nc; DLC
"All the letters in this book...are taken from the correspondence of James Knox Polk..and all are preserved in a manuscript form in the Library of Congress, Washington, D. C."

5594. Beecher, Charles. The Duty of Disobedience to Wicked Laws. A Sermon on the Fugitive Slave Law... New York: J. A. Gray, Printer, 1851. DHU/MO

5595. Beecher, Henry Ward. Speeches of Rev. Henry Ward Beecher on the American Rebellion, Delivered in Great Britain in 1863. New York: F. F. Lovell & Company, 1887. DHU/MO

5596. Belfast Anti-Slavery Society. To the Christian Churches of the United States. The Address of the Belfast Anti-Slavery Society. Belfast: H. M. Kendrick, 1861. NNCor; MBU

5597. Bell, Howard H. A Survey of the Negro Convention Movement. Doctoral dissertation. Northwestern University, 1953.
The role of Black Preachers in the early convention movement.

5598. Berry, Philip. A Review of the Bishop of Oxford's Counsel to the American Clergy, With Reference to the Institution of Slavery. Also Supplemental Remarks on the Relation of the Wilmot Proviso to the Interests of the Colored Class. Washington, D. C.: Wm. M. Morrison; New York: Stanford & Swords, 1848. NcD; DHU/MO

5599. Bibb, Henry. Narrative of the Life and Adventures of Henry Bibb, An American Slave Written by Himself. New York: The Author, 1849. DHU/MO; NN/Sch
Negro author.

5600. ----- "Speech." American and Foreign Anti-Slavery Society. Annual Report New York, May 8, 1849, With Resolutions and Addresses. New York: A & F. Anti-Slavery Society, 1849. NcD

5601. Birney, Catherine H. The Grimke Sisters. Sarah and Angelina Grimke. New York: Haskell House Publishers, 1970. DHU/MO
(Reprint of 1885 edition) "The First American Women Advocates of Abolition and Woman's Rights."

5602. "The Black Radicals." WCBS-TV and Columbia University. Released by Holt, Rinehart and Winston, 1969. 30 min. sd. b & w. 16 mm. DLC
Film
"Vincent Harding discusses the work of black revolutionsDavid Walker, Frederick Douglass, Henry Garnet, Martin Delaney, Ford Douglass, Fred Scott, and others - prior to the Civil War, and explains their role in the surge of black radicalism which followed the war."

5603. Blyden, Edward Wilmot. Black Spokesman: Selected Published Writings of Edward W. Blyden. Edited by Hollis R. Lynch. New York: Humanities Press, 1971. InU; DLC; DHU/R

5604. Blyden, Edward Wilmot. "Blyden, Gladstone and the War (Civil War)." Journal of Negro History (49; Ja., 1964), pp. 56-61. DHU

5605. ----- "The Call of Providence to the Descendants of Africa in America." Okon Edet Uya (ed.). Black Brotherhood, Afro-Americans and Africa (Lexington, Mass.: D. C. Heath and Co., 1971), pp. 83-95. DHU/MO
A call for the colonization of black Christians in Africa.

5606. Boardman, Henry. "Sermon for the Times: Thanksgiving in War." The Princeton Review (34; Ja., 1862), pp. 188 ff
This rebellion is an example of moral insanity. This conflict clearly involves moral principles so the pulpit must make itself felt.

5607. Bormann, Ernest G., ed. Forerunners of Black Power; The Rhetoric of Abolition. Englewood Cliffs, N.J.: Prentice-Hall, 1971. DHU/MO
Evangelical Religion and Antislavery and Black Abolitionists (includes Henry Highland Garnet's An Address to the Slaves of the United States of America)

5608. Bowen, W. H. "Righteousness, the Foundation of National Strength and Glory." The Freewill Baptist Quarterly (13; Jl., 1865), pp. 285ff. DLC

5609. Bowley, Samuel. General Anti-Slavery Convention. Address of the Convention Held in London From the 15th to the 22nd June Inclusive, to Christian Professors. London: Johnston & Barret, Printers, 1843. DHU/MO
Pamphlets on Slavery and Christianity, Vol. 1.

5610. Bracey, John H. and August Meier, et alii., (eds.). Blacks in the Abolitionist Movement. Belmont, California: Wadsworth, 1971. INU; DLC

5611. Brainerd, M. Life of Rev. Thomas Brainerd for Thirty Years Pastor of the Old Pine Street Church, Phila. Phila.: J. B. Lippincott, 1870. DHU/MO

5612. Brawley, Benjamin Griffin. "Lorenzo Dow." Journal of Negro History (1:3, Jl., 1916), pp. 265-75. DHU/MO
Dow, a white Protestant traveled north and south preaching against slavery.

5613. Brayton, Patience. A Short Account of the Life and Religious Labours of Patience Brayton, Late of Swansey, in the State of Mass., Mostly Selected from Her Own Minutes. New York: Printed; London: Repr. and sold by Wm. Phillips, George-Yard, 1802. DHU/MO

5614. Brightwell, Robert M. Abolitionist Sentiment in Northeast Missouri. Masters thesis. Northeast Missouri State Teachers College, 1966.

5615. British and Foreign Anti-Slavery Society. American Slavery. Address of the Committee of British and Foreign Anti-Slavery Society... London: n.p., 1846. NNCor
Slavery and the Church.

5616. Brooks, George S. Friend Anthony Benezet... Phila., University of Pennsylvania Press; London: H. Milford, Oxford University Press, 1937. DHU/MO

5617. Brown, Isaac Van Arsdale. Biography of the Reverend Finley, 1857. New York: Arno Press, 1969. InU; DLC

5618. ----- Memoirs of the Rev. Robert Finley, D. D., late Pastor of the Presbyterian Congregation at Basking Ridge, New Jersey and President of Franklin College, Located at Athens, in the State of Georgia. With brief Sketches of Some of His Contemporaries, and Numerous Notes. New Brunswick: Terhune & Letson, 1819. DHU/R; CtY-D

5619. Brown, William Wells. The Narrative of William W. Brown, a Fugitive Slave. And a Lecture Delivered Before the Female Anti-Slavery Society of Salem, 1847. Reading, Mass.: Addison-Wesley Pub. Co., 1969.   TSewU-T
      "Addison-Wesley's fugitive slave narratives."

5620. Buchanan, George. An Oration upon the Moral and Political Evil of Slavery. Delivered at a Public Meeting of the Maryland Society, for Promoting the Abolition of Slavery, and the Relief of Free Negroes, and Others Unlawfully Held in Bondage, Baltimore July 4, 1791. Baltimore: Philip Edwards, 1793.
                                                                     DLC

5621. Burgess, Thomas. Considerations on the Abolition of Slavery and the Slave Trade, Upon Grounds of Natural, Religious, and Political Duty. Oxford: D. Prince and J. Cooke, 1789. NNC

5622. Burleigh, Charles C. ...Slavery and the North. New York: American Anti-Slavery Society, 1855.   DHU/MO; NN/Sch
      Anti-slavery tracts, no. 10.

5623. Campbell, Alexander. "Fugitive Slave Law." The Millennial Harbinger (1:1-10, Ja.-Dec., 1851). (6:1-12, Ja.-Dec., 1849).
                                                     TN/DCHS; DLC
      Founder of Disciples of Christ Christain Church in American justified slavery because it was sanctioned in the Bible.

5624. Carrol, Daniel Lynn. Sermons and Addresses on Various Subjects. Philadelphia: Lindsay & Blakiston, 1846. NN; IU
      Including: "A Paramount Remedy for the African Slave Trade."

5625. Carroll, Kenneth L. "Religious Influences on the Manumission of Slaves." Maryland Historical Magazine (56; Je., 1961), pp. 176-97.   DAU

5626. Chandler, Elizabeth Margaret. Essays, Philanthropic and Moral, Principally Relating to the Abolition of Slavery in America. Philadelphia: n.p., 1836.   DLC

5627. Chase, Salmon P. and Charles D. Cleveland. Anti-Slavery Addresses of 1844 and 1845. New York: Negro Universities Press, 1867.   DHU/R
      Anti-slavery addresses.

5628. Chatelain, Heli. "African Slavery and the Liberator's League. Southern Workman (25:9, Sept., 1896), pp. 182-85.
                                                     DLC; DHU/MO

5629. Cheever, George Barrell. Rights of the Coloured Race to Citizenship and Representation: and the Guilt and Consequences of Legislation Against Them. A Discourse Delivered in the Hall of Representatives of the United States, in Washington, D.C., May 29, 1864.   DHU/MO

5630. Child, Lydia Maria (Francis). An Appeal in Favor of that Class of Americans Called Africans. Boston: Allen and Ticknor, 1833.   DHU/MO; FSU
      A Book Review: Quarterly Christian Spectator (6:3, Sept., 1834), pp. 445-56.   DHU/R

5631. Christian Anti-Slavery Convention. The Minutes of the Christian Anti-Slavery Convention Assembled April 17-20th, 1850. Cincinnati: Ben Franklin Book & Job Rooms, 1850.
                                                                     DLC

5632. Christian Anti-Slavery Convention, Cincinnati, 1850. The Minutes of the Christian Anti-Slavery Convention. Assembled April 17th-20th, 1850, Cincinnati, Ohio. Cincinnati: Ben Franklin Book and Job Rooms, 1850.   NNCor

5633. Church Anti-Slavery Society of the United States. Circular-- Declaration of Principles and Consitution. Worcester: n.p., 1859.   DLC

5634. Church Anti-Slavery Society of the United States. Proceedings of the Convention Which Met at Worcester, Mass. March 1, 1859. New York: John F. Trow, 1859.   DLC

5635. Clark, Joseph S. "A Lesson from the Past: How Slavery was Abolished in Massachusetts." Congregational Quarterly (2:5, Ja., 1860), pp. 42-8.   DHU/R

5636. Clarke, James Freeman. Causes and Consequences of the Affair at Harper's Ferry. A Sermon Preached in the Indiana Place Chapel, on Nov. 6, 1859. Boston: Walker, Wise & Co., 1859.   DHU/R
      Clarke was a Congregational Clergyman of Cincinnati; Editor of the "Western Messenger," 1836-1839.

5637. Clarke, Walter. The American Anti-Slavery Society at War with the Church. A Discourse, Delivered Before the First Congregational Church and Society, in Canterbury, Conn., June 30th, 1844. Hartford: Press of E. Gear, 1844. NN/Sch DLC

5638. Clarkson, Thomas. An Essay on the Impolicy of the African Slave Trade. In Two Parts. By the Rev. T. Clarkson. To Which is Added, an Oration, Upon the Necessity of Establishing at Paris, Society to Promote the Abolition of the Trade and Slavery of the Negroes. By J. P. Brissot de Warville. Philadelphia: Francis Bailey, 1788.   NN; DLC; DHU/MO

5639. ----- A Letter to the Clergy of Various Denominations, and to the Slave-Holding Planters in the Southern Parts of the United States of America. London: Johnston and Barrett, 1841.
                                                                     DHU/MO

5640. Clough, Simon. A Candid Appeal to the Citizens of the United States, Proving that the Doctrines Advanced and the Measures Pursued by the Abolitionists, Relative to the Subject of Emancipation... New York: A. K. Bertron, 1834.   DHU/MO; DLC

5641. Cohen, David W. and Jack P. Greene, (eds.). Neither Slave nor Free, The Freedman of African Descent in the Slave Societies of the New World. Baltimore: The Johns Hopkins Univeristy Press, 1972.   DHU/R
      "This volume grew out of a symposium on 'The Role of the Free Mulatto in Slave Societies of the New World', held at The John Hopkins University on April 8 & 9, 1970.

5642. Cole, Charles Chester. The Secular Ideas of Northern Evangelists, 1826-1860. Doctoral dissertation. Columbia University, 1951.
      Microfilm 41, School of Religion.

5643. ----- The Social Ideas of Northern Evangelists, 1826-1860. New York: Columbia Univ. Press, 1954.   DHU/R; NN/Sch

5644. "Colonization and Anti-Colonization." Quarterly Christian Spectator (7:3, 4, Sept. and Dec. 1835), pp. 503-20; 521-40,
                                                                     DHU/R
      Remarks on the following works: An Inquiry into the Character and Tendency of the American Colonization and American Colonization and American Anti-Slavery Societies, by William Jay: Being a Reply to his "Inquiry into the American Colonization and American Anti-Slavery Societies." by David M. Reese.

5645. Colver, Nathaniel. "Slavery or Freedom Must Die." The Harper's Ferry Tragedy: A Sympton of a Disease in the Heart of the Nation; or the Nation, from Which There is no Escape but in the Destruction of Slavery Itself. A Sermon Preached... Dec. 11, 1859. Published by Request of the Congregation. Cincinnati: Office of the Christian Luminary, 1860.

5646. "Constitution of the American Society of Free Persons of Colour, for Imporiving their Condition in the United States; For Purchasing Lands; and for the Establishment of a Settlement in Upper Canada. Also the Proceedings of the Convention, With their Address to the Persons of Colour in the United States." Dorothy B. Porter, (ed.). Early Negro Writing, 1760-1837 (Boston: Beacon Press, 1971), pp. 172+. DHU/R; DHU/MO

5647. Converse, John Kendrick. A Discourse, on the Moral, Legal and Domestic Condition of our Colored Population... Burlington, Vt.: E. Smith, 1832.   DHU/MO; CtY-D

5648. Conway, Moncure Daniel. The Golden Hour. Boston: Ticknor & Fields, 1862.   DHU/MO
Conway was the son of a Virginia slaveholder; a Methodist, then Unitarian minister; and a strong anti-slavery writer.

5649. Copley, Esther. A History of Slavery and its Abolition. London: Houlston & Stoneman, 1839.   NN/Sch

5650. Cornish, Samuel E. The Colonization Scheme Considered in its Rejection by the Colored People in its Tencency to Uphold Caste-in its Unfitness for Christianizing and Civilizing the Aborigines of Africa, and for Putting a Stop to the African Slave-trade: In a Letter to the Hon. Theodore Frelinghuysen and the Hon. Benjamin F. Butler. Newark, N.J.: A Guest, 1840.   DHU/R; DLC

5651. Corr, Joseph M. Address Delivered Before the Humane Mechanics' Society, on the 4th of July, 1934 by the Minister of the First African Methodist Episcopal Church. Philadelphia: n.p., 1834.   DHU/MO
Also: Porter, Dorothy B., (ed.). Early Negro Writing, 1760-1337 (Boston: Beacon Press, 1971), pp. 146+. DHU/R; DHU/MO

5652. Correspondence Between Rev. H. Mattison and Rev. J.S. Loguen, on the Duty of Ministers to Allow Contributions in the Churches in Aid of Fugitive Slaves and the Obligation of Civil Government and the Higher Law. Syracuse: J.E. Masters, 1857.   DHU/MO

5653. Cuzuano, Ottobah. Thoughts and Sentiments on the Evil and Wicked Traffic of the Slavery and Commerce of the Human Species, Humbly Submitted to the Inhabitants of Great-Britain, By Ottobah Cuzuano, a Native of Africa... London: T. Becket, 1787.   DHU/MO
Negro author.

5654. Dillon, Merton L. "The Antislavery Movement in Illinois: 1824-1835." Journal Illinois State Historical Society (57; Sum., 1954), pp. 149-67.   DHU

5655. Douglass, Frederick. Eulogy of the late Hon. William Jay, Delivered on the Invitation of the Colored Citizens of New York City in Shiloh Presbyterian Church, N.Y. May 12, 1859. New York: Strong, 1859.   OWibfU

5656. Duberman, Martin B. (ed.). The Anti-slavery Manguard; New Essays on the Abolitionists. Princeton, N.J.: Princeton University Press, 1965.   TSewU-T

5657. DuBois, William E.B. John Brown. Northbrook, Ill.: Metro Books, Inc., 1972.   DHU/R
Reprint of 1909 edition.
Translation of Brown's philosophical thought is the main focus."

5658. Dumon, Dwight Lowell. Anti-slavery: The Crusade for Freedom in America. Ann Arbor: University of Michigan Press, 1949.   DHU/MO; DHU/R

5659. Dunham, Chester Forrester. The Attitude of the Northern Clergy toward the South, 1860-65. Doctoral dissertation. University of Chicago, 1939.

5660. Essays and Pamphlets on Anti-Slavery. Westport, Conn.: Negro Universities Press, 1970.   CLU; NjP
Includes information on religion of the slaves in the United States.

5661. Evangelical Union Anti-slavery Society of the City of New York. Address to the Churches of Jesus Christ, by the Evangelical Union Anti-slavery Society, of the City of New York, Auxiliary to the Am. A.S. Society With the Constitution, Names of Officers, Board of Managers, and Executive Committee. April, 1839. New York: Pr. by S.W. Benedict, 1839. DHU/MO

5662. "First Printed Protest Against Slavery in America." Pennsylvania Magazine and Biography (13; 1889), p. 265.   IC/H
"Reasons against keeping Negroes enslaved."

5663. Forman, Jacob Gilbert. The Fugitive Slave Law; a Discourse Delivered in the Congregational Church in West Bridgewater Mass., Nov. 17, 1850. Boston: Wm. Crosby and H.P. Nichols, 1850.   DHU/MO

5664. Foster, Eden B. A North-Side View of Slavery...A Sermon on the Crime Against Freedom, in Kansas and Washington. Preached at Henniker, N.H., August 31, 1856. Concord: Jone & Cogswell, Printers, 1856.   CtY-D; NN/Sch

5665. Foster, Stephen Symonds. "An Abolitionist View of the American Church and Slavery." Louis Ruchames (ed.). The Abolitionists (New York: Capricorn Books, 1966,) pp. 179-92.   DHU/R

5666. Fox, Early Lee. The American Colonization Society, 1817-1840... Doctoral dissertation. John Hopkins University, 1917.

5667. Freimarck, Vincent and Bernard Rosenthal, (eds.). Race and the American Romantics. New York: Schocken Books, 1971.   DHU/R
Includes essays, The Church and Clergy Again, Attitude of Abolitionist toward the American Church.

5668. Frothingham, Frederick. Significance of the Struggle Between Liberty and Slavery in America. New York: American Anti-Slavery Society, 1857.   NN/Sch

5669. Frothingham, Octavius Brooks. Gerrit Smith; a Biography. New York: G.P. Putnam & Son, 1909.   DHU/MO

5670. Furness, William Henry. The Blessing of Abolition. A Discourse Delivered in the First Congregation Unitarian Church, Sunday, July 1, 1860. Philadelphia: C. Sherman & Son, Printers, 1860.   NN/Sch

5671. ----- Put Up Thy Sword. A Discourse Delivered Before Theodore Parker's Society, at the Music Hall, Boston, Sunday, March 11, 1860... Boston, R.F. Wallcut, 1860.   DHU/MO

5672. Garnet, Henry Highland. "An Address to the Slaves of the United States of America." Dorothy B. Porter, (ed.). Early Negro Writings, 1760-1837 (Boston: Beacon, 1971), pp. 150-57.   DHU/MO

5673. ----- "Communicated." William Armistead, (ed.). A Tribute to the Negro: Being a Vindication of the Moral, Intellectual, and Religious Capabilities of the Colored Portion of Mankind... (Conn.: Negro Univ. Press, 1848), pp. 510-13.   DHU/R
Orator and Negro Presbyterian minister.

5674. ----- "The Past and Present Condition and the Destiny of the Colored Race." Troy, N.Y.: J.C. Kneeland, 1848   DHU/MO

5675. ----- "The Slave Must Throw Off the Slaveholder." Thomas R. Frazier, (ed.). Afro-American History: Primary Sources (New York: Harcourt, Brace & World, Inc., 1970), pp. 113-19.   DHU/MO; DHU/R
From his "An Address to the Slaves of the United States of America," (1843). "Garnet's address ... was bound together with David Walker's APPEAL in a special edition in 1848." Negro author.

5676. ----- Walker's Appeal With a Brief Sketch of His Life. New York: J.H. Tobitt, 1848.   DHU/MO

5677. Garrettson, Freeborn. A Dialogue between Do-Justice and Professing-Christian. Dedicated to the Respective and Collective Abolition Societies, and to all other Benevolent Humane Philanthropists, in America. Wilmington: P. Brynberg, (1820?).   DLC

5678. Gibbs, Mifflin Wister. Shadow and Light: An Autobiography with Reminiscences of the Last and Present Century. New York: Arno Press and the New York Times, 1968. DHU/MO; OWibfU
Reprint of the 1902 edition.
Negro author.
Son of a Preacher, anti-slavery lecturer.

5679. Gibson, Bertha Askew. The Big Three Then, the Big Job. New York: Vantage Press, 1960.   DHU/MO
Study of the Israelites.
Negro author.

5680. Giltner, John H. "Moses Stuart and the Slavery Controversy: A Study in the Failure of Moderation." Journal of Religious Thought (18:1, Wint.-Spr., 1961), pp. 26-37.   DHU/R

5681. Glasgow Anti-Slavery Meeting. Free Church Alliance with Manstealers. Send Back the Money. Great Anti-Slavery Meeting in the City Hall, Glasgow, Containing Speeches Delivered by Messrs. Wright, Douglass and Buffum from America, and by George Thompson of London; with a Summary Account of a Series of Meetings held in Edinburg, by the above Named Gentlemen. Glasgow: G. Gallie, 1846.   NN/Sch
Speech of Frederick Douglass, pp. 19-24.

5682. Glasgow Emancipation Society. Address by the Committee of the Glasgow Emancipation Society of the Ministers of Religion in Particular and the Friends of Negro Emancipation in General on American Slavery. Glasgow: Aird & Russell, 1836.
DHU/MO

5683. Glasgow Emancipation Society. The American Board of Commissioners for Foreign Missions, and the Rev. Dr. Chalmers, on Christian Fellowship with Slaveholders: An Address by the Glasgow Emancipation Society to Christians of all Denominations, but Especially to Members of the Free Church of Scotland. Glasgow: Pr. by D. Russell, sold by G. Gallie, 1845. DLC

5684. Gloucester, Jeremiah. An Oration Delivered on January 1, 1823 in Bethel Church on the Abolition of the Slave Trade. Philadelphia: J. Young, 1823.   MB
Negro author.

5685. Goodell, William. Come Outerism. The Duty of Secession from a Corrupt Church. New York: American Anti-Slavery Society, 1845.   CtY; MH; OO

5686. Gray, Thomas. A Sermon, in Boston, Before the African Society, 14th of July, 1818; the Anniversary of the Abolition of the Slave Trade. Boston: Parmenter & Norton, 1818.
NNC; CtY; DLC

5687. Green, Beriah. The Martyr. A Discourse, in Commemoration of the Martyrdom of the Rev. Elijah P. Lovejoy, Delivered in Broadway Tabernacle, New York; and in the Bleeker Street Church, Utica. (New York): American Anti-Slavery Society, 1838.   DHU/MO

5688. Green, Sue B. "Lucretia Mott-Hicksite', Abolitionist, Feminist." Friends Journal (20:12, Jl. 1/15, 1974), pp. 358-59.   DHU/R

5689. Grimke, Angelina Emily. Letters to Catherine E. Beecher in Reply to an Essay on Slavery and Abolitionism Addressed to A. E. Grimke, 1838. New York: Arno, 1969. DHU/MO; INU; DLC

5690. ----- Slavery in America. A Reprint of an Appeal to the Christian Women of the Slave States of America. By Angelina E. Grimke, of Charleston, South Carolina. With Introduction, Notes and Appendix, by George Thompson. Recommended to the Special Attention of the Anti-Slavery Females of Great Britain. Edinburgh: Oliphant and Sons, 1837.   DLC

5691. Gross, Bella. Clarion Call: the History and Development of the Negro People's Convention Movement in the United States From 1817 to 1840. New York: Springer Publishing Company, 1963.   O

5692. Guthrie, John. Garrisonian Infidelity Exposed; in Two Letters from the Rev. John Guthrie, Greenock in Reply to George Thompson... Glasgow: Pr. by H. Nisbet, 1851. DHU/MO

5693. Hamilton, William. Address to the Fourth Annual Convention of the Free People of Color of the United States. Delivered at the Opening of Their Session in the City of New York, June 2, 1834. New York: S. W. Benedict & Co., 1834.   CtY; NN/Sch
Negro author.

5694. ----- An Address to the New York African Society, for Mutual Relief, Delivered in the Universalist Church, January 2, 1809. New York: 1809.   NN/Sch
Typescript copy

5695. ----- An Oration Delivered in the African Zion Church, on the 4th Day of July 1827, in Commemoration of the Abolition of Domestic Slavery in this State. New York: Gray & Bunce, 1827.   DLC; DHU/MO

5696. ----- "An Oration, on the Abolition of the Slave Trade, Delivered in the Episcopal Asbury African Church in Elizabeth St., New York, January 2, 1815." Dorothy B. Porter, (ed.). Early Negro Writing, 1760-1837 (Boston: Beacon Press, 1971), pp. 391-400.   DHU/R; DHU/MO

5697. Hammon, Jupiter. An Evening Thought; Salvation By Christ With Penetential (!) Cries; Composed by Jupiter Hammon, a Negro Belonging to Mr. Lloyd, of Queen's Village on Long Island, the 25th of Dec., 1760.   NH; DHU/MO
Also: Dorothy B. Porter, (ed.). Early Negro Writing, 1760-1837 (Boston: Beacon Press, 1971), pp. 529-31.
DHU/R; DHU/MO

5698. Harding, Vincent. "Religion and Resistance Among Antebellum Negroes, 1800-1860." August Meir and Elliott Rudwick, (eds.). The Making of Black America: The Black Community in Modern America. New York: Atheneum, 1969, vol. 1, pp. 179+. DHU/MO
Negro author.

5699. Hart, Albert B. Slavery and Abolition, 1831-1841. London: Harper & Bros., 1906.   DHU/R
Schism in churches over slavery issue.

5700. Hart, Levi. Liberty Described and Recommended; in a Sermon, Preached to the Corporation of Freemen in Farmington, Sept. 20, 1774. Hartford: Watson, 1775. DLC
Micrifilm.

5701. Helm, T. G. "Wendell Phillips and the Abolition Movement." Reformed Church Review (20:2, Apr., 1916), pp. 196-226.
DHU/R

5702. Hinman, H. H. "Colored Colonization Proposed. An Arkansas Missionary in Washington--Secret Organization in the South to Separate the Races." Southern Workman (12:10, Oct., 1883), p. 101.   DHU/MO; DLC

5703. Holley, Myron. Address Delivered Before the Rochester Anti-Slavery Society, on the 19th January and Again, by Request of Several Citizens, at the Court House, in Rochester on the 5th Feb., 1837. Rochester: Hoyt & Porter, 1837.
MH

5704. Hough, John A. A Sermon Delivered before the Vermont Colonization Society, at Montpelier, October 18, 1826. Montpelier: Pr. by Walter, E. P., 1826.   CtY-D

5705. Houston, David. "John Woolman's in Behalf of Freedom." Journal of Negro History (2:2, Apr., 1917), pp. 126-38.
DHU/MO
"Points out that Woolman's influence in 1758 was the first important movement toward abolition among the Quakers."

5706. Howard, Victor B. The Anti-Slavery Movement in the Presbyterian Church, 1835-1861. Master's thesis. Ohio State University, 1961.   NcD

5707. Howitt, William. Colonization and Christianity. A Popular History of the Treatment of the Natives by the Europeans in All Their Colonies. London: Longman, Orme, Brown, Green & Lingmans, 1838.   DHU/MO

5708. Hume, John F. The Abolitionists, Together With Personal Memories of the Struggle for Human Rights 1830-1864. New York: AMS Press, 1973.   DHU/MO
        Reprint of 1905 edition.

5709. Hyde, A. B. "Wilberforce--A Study of Freedom." Methodist Review (Bimonthly) (83; Ja., 1901), pp. 46-52.   DHU/R

5710. Illinois Commission for the Observance of the Half-Century Anniversary of Negro Freedom. History and Report of the Exhibition and Celebration to Commemorate the 50th Anniversary of the Emancipation of the Negro. Chicago: Fraternal Press, 1915.   OWibfU

5711. Ivimey, Joseph. The Utter Extinction of Slavery an Object of Scripture Prophecy: A Lecture the Substance of Which was Delivered at the Annual Meeting of the Chelmsford Ladies' Anti-Slavery Association, in the Friend's Meeting - House, on Tuesday the 17th of April, 1832. With Elucidatory Notes. London: Sold by G. Wightman, 1832.   DHU/MO; NN/Sch; CtY-D

5712. Jakobsson, Stiv. Am I Not a Man and a Brother? British Missions and the Abolition of the Slave Trade and Slavery in West Africa and the West Indies 1786-1838. Lund: Gleerup, 1972.   ICLT; PPT

5713. James, H. F. Abolitionism Unveiled! Hypocrisy Unmasked! and Knavery Scouraged... New York: T. V. Paterson, 1850.
                          O

5714. Jay, William. An Address to the Anti-Slavery Christians of the United States. New York: A. Gray, n. d.   DHU/MO

5715. ----- An Inquiry into the Character and Tendency of the American Colonization and American Anti-Slavery Societies. New York: Leavitt, Lord Co., 1856.   DHU/MO

5716. ----- Miscellaneous Writings on Slavery. Boston: J. P. Jewett, 1853.   CtY-D; NN/Sch

5717. ----- Reply to Remarks of Rev. Moses Stuart, Late Professor in the Theological Seminary at Andover on Hon. John Jay, and an Examination of His Scriptural Exegesis, Contained in His Recent Pamphlet Entitled "Conscience and the Constitution." New York: Pr. by J. A. Gray, 1850.   CtY-D

5718. Jocelyn, Simeon S. College for Colored Youth. An Account of the New Haven City Meeting and Resolutions, with Recommendations of the College, and Strictures upon the Doings of New Haven. New York: Published by the Committee, 1831. RPB

5719. Johnson, Clifton H. "John Gregg Fee: Kentucky Abolitionist." Crisis (79:3, Mr., 1972), pp. 91-94.   DHU/R
        Author, director of the Amistad Research Center writes of a Presbyterian minister who under the auspices of American Missionary Association fought slavery in Kentucky for over a quarter of a century.

5720. [Jones, Absalom]. "Petition of Absalom Jones and Seventy-three Others." Dorothy B. Porter. Early Negro Writing, 1760-1837. (Boston: Beacon, 1971), pp. 330-32. DHU/MO; DHU/R
        An anti-slavery petition to the President and Congress, 30 December, 1799.

5721. ----- and Richard, Allen. A Narrative of the Proceedings of the Black People, During the Late Awful Calamity in Philadelphia, in 1793; and a Refutation of Some Censures, Thrown Up on Them in Some Late Publications. n.p., 1794. DLC; DHU/R
        (In reply to a vicious attack upon Negroes by Matthew Carey, colonizationist.) Also in Negro Protest Pamphlets, a Compendium. New York: Arno Press, 1969.
        Negro authors.

5722. Jones, Benjamin S. Abolitionrieties: or Remarks on Some of the Members of the Pennsylvania State Anti-Slavery Society for the Eastern District, and the American Anti-Slavery Most of Whom Were Present at the Annual Meetings, Held in Philadelphia and New York in May, 1840. n.p., n.d. PHC; DHU; ICU

5723. Kingsford, Edward. The Claims of Abolitionism Upon the Church of Christ, Candidly Examined. A Sermon Delivered at the Baptist Church, Harrisburg, on the Morning of Sabbath, February 18th, 1838. Pub. by Request of Several Members of the Senate and House of Representatives of the Legislature of Pennsylvania. Harrisburg: Pr. by E. Guyer, 1838. DLC

5724. Kettell. George F. A Sermon on the Duty of Citizens, with Respect to the Fugitive Slave Law. White Plains, N.Y.: Eastern States Journal, 1851.   DLC

5725. Klingbert, Frank J. An Appraisal of the Negro in Colonial South Carolina. Washington, D.C.: The Associated Press, 1941.   DHU/MO

5726. Kraditor, Aileen S. Means and Ends in American Abolitionism: Garrison and His Critics on Strategy and Tactics, 1834-1850. New York: Vintage Books, 1970.   DHU/R
        Chapter 4, Religion and the Good Society.

5727. Kuhns, Frederick Irving. The American Home Missionary Society in Relation to the Antislavery Controversy in the Old Northwest. Billings, Mont.: n. p., 1959. TSewU-T; CtY-D

5728. Lashley, Leonard C. Anthony Benezet and His Anti-Slavery Activities. Doctoral dissertation. Fordham University, 1939.
        An account of Benezet's anti-slavery movement in England and its effects in America.

5729. Lawrence, George. "Oration on the Abolition of the Slave Trade, Delivered on the First Day of January, 1813, in the African Methodist Episcopal Church, 1813. With an Address by Peter Malachi Eagans." Dorothy B. Porter, (ed.). Early Negro Writing, 1760-1837 (Boston: Beacon Press, 1971), pp. 374-82.   DHU/MO; DHU/R

5730. Leeds Anti-Slavery Association. The Negro Mother or Christian Steadfastness. New York: Negro Universities Press, 1969.   DLC

5731. Lerner, Gerda. The Grimké Sisters from South Carolina; Rebels Against Slavery. Boston: Houghton Mifflin, 1967. CtY-D

5732. Lewis, Robert Benjamin. Light and Truth. Boston: Comm. of Colored Gentlemen, 1844.   OWibfU

5733. The Life of Olaudah Equiano or Gustavus Vassa the African. New York: Negro Universities Press, 1969.   DHU/R
        Reprint of 1837 edition.
        Account of an African captive from Essaka of the kingdom of Benin who eventually became a Christian and a petitioner to England against slavery.

5734. Lloyd, Arthur Young. The Slavery Controversy, 1831-1860. Chapel Hill: The University of North Carolina Press, 1939.
                          NN/Sch

5735. London Emancipation Committee's Tract. The Rev. John Waddington and American Slavery. London: W. M. Watts, 1860.
                          DHU/MO

5736. Lovejoy, Joseph Cammet. Memoir of Rev. Charles T. Torrey Who Died in the Penitentiary of Maryland, Where he was Confined for Showing Mercy to the Poor. New York: Negro Universities Press, 1969.   DHU/R
        Abolitionist and Congregational minister.

5737. Mac Master, Richard K. "Henry Highland Garnet and the African Civilization Society." Journal of Presbyterian History (48:2, Sum., 1970), pp. 95-112.   DHU/R; NcD; NjP

5738. Marsh, William H. God's Law Supreme. A Sermon, Aiming to Point Out the Duty of a Christian People in Relation to the

(Marsh, William H. cont.)
Fugitive Slave Law; Delivered at Village Corners, Woodstock, Conn., Nov. 28, 1850; and Subsequently Repeated by Request in Southbridge, Mass. Worcester: Henry J. Howland, 1850.
DLC; MH

5739. Mathews, Donald G. Agitation for Freedom: The Abolitionist Movement. New York: John Wiley & Sons, Inc., 1972. DHU/R
Stephen S. Foster the Brotherhood of Thieves, or a true picture of the American Church and Clergy (1843), pp. 79-82.

5740. Mathews, Edward. The Autobiography of the Rev. E. Mathews, the "Father Dickson" of Mrs. Stowe's Dred; Also a Description of the Influence of the Slave-Party Over the American Presidents, and the Rise and Progress of the Anti-Slavery Reform. Miami, Mnemosyne, 1969. INU; DHU/MO

5741. May, Samuel Joseph. A Discourse on the Life and Character of the Rev. Charles Follen, who Perished, Jan. 13, 1840, in the Conflagration of the Lexington. Delivered before the Massachusetts Anti-Slavery Society, in the Marlborough Chapel, Boston, April 17, 1840. Boston: Henry L. Devereux, 1849.
DHU/MO

5742. McGiffert, Arthur Cushman. "Charles Grandison Finney." Christendom (5:4, Aut., 1942), pp. 496-506.   DHU/R
Influence of Finney upon Anti-Slavery sentiment in the Church.

5743. "A Memorial to the White People of that City, (Baltimore), Respecting African Emigration." The Christian Spectator (9:1, Ja., 1828), p. 55.   DHU/R
A Memorial on African Colonization by "The people of colour in Baltimore at a meeting in the African church."

5744. Meridith, Robert. "A Conservative Abolitionist at Alton: Edward Beecher's Narrative." Journal of Presbyterian History (42:1, Mr., 1964; 42:2, Je., 1964), pp. 39-53; 92-103.
DHU/R

5745. Miller, Samuel. A Sermon Preached at Newark, October 22, 1823, before the Synod of New Jersey, for the Benefit of the African School under the Care of the Synod. Trenton: Pr. by G. Sherman, 1823.   NN/Sch

5746. Miller, William. A Sermon on the Abolition of the Slave Trade: Delivered in the African Church, New York, on the First of January, 1810. New York: Printed by J. C. Totten, 1810. NN/Sch; MNtcA; PPT
Reprinted 1969.

5747. Moore, Wilbert E. Slavery, Abolition and the Ethical Valuation of the Individual. Doctoral dissertation. Harvard University, 1940.

5748. Mott, Lucretia (Coffin). A Sermon to the Medical Students, Delivered at Cherry Street Meetinghouse, Philadelphia, Feb. 11, 1849. Philadelphia: W. B. Zeiber, 1849.   DLC

5749. Mudge, Zachariah Atwell. The Christian Statesman; A Portraiture of Sir Thomas Fewell Buxton; with Sketches of British Anti-Slavery Reform. New York: Carlton & Porter, 1865.
NN/Sch

5750. Needles, Edward. A Historical Memoir of the Pennsylvania Society for Promoting the Abolition of Slavery. Philadelphia: Merrihew & Thompson 1848.   OWibfU

5751. Nevin, John W. A Review of a Summary of Biblical Antiquities, Compiled for the Use of Sunday School Teachers, and for the Benefit of Families. Ripley: Pr. by Campbell and Palmer, 1834.   DHU/MO
Pamphlets on Slavery and Christianity, V. 1.

5752. Newhall, Fales Henry. The Conflict in America. A Funeral Discourse Occasioned by the Death of John Brown of Ossawattomie, who Entered into Rest, from the Gallows, at Charlestown, Virginia, Dec. 2, 1859. Preached at the Warren St. M. E. Church, Roxbury, Dec. 4. Boston: J. M. Hewes, 1859.   CtY-D

5753. Ohio State Christian Anti-Slavery Convention, Columbus, 1859. Proceedings of the Ohio State Christian Anti-Slavery Convention, held at Columbus, August 10 and 11, 1859. Columbus: n.p., 1859.   DLC

5754. Parker, Theodore. An Address Delivered before the New York City Anti-Slavery Society, at its First Anniversary, Held at the Broadway Tabernacle, May 12, 1854. New York: American Anti-Slavery Society, 1854.   DLC
Parker was a renowned scholar and one of the most active and daring participants in the latter phases of the abolition movement.

5755. Parrish, John. Remarks on the Slavery of the Black Peoples: Addressed to the Citizens of the United States, Particularly to Those Who are in Legislative or Executive Stations in the General or State Government and Also to Such Individuals as Hold Them in Bondage. Philadelphia: Kimber, Conrad & Co., 1806.
DHU/MO

5756. Parrott, Russell. "An Oration of the Abolition of the Slave Trade Delivered on the First of January, 1814, at the African Church of St. Thomas." Dorothy B. Porter, (ed.). Early Negro Writing, 1760-1837 (Boston: Beacon Press, 1971), pp. 383-90.   DHU/MO; DHU/R

5757. Paul, Nathaniel. "The Abolition of Slavery in New York." Dorothy B. Porter (ed.). Early Negro Writings, 1760-1837 (Boston: Beacon, 1971), pp. 64-76.   DHU/MO
Written by a Negro Baptist minister.

5758. ----- An Address, Delivered on the Celebration of the Abolition of Slavery in the State of New York, July 5, 1827... Albany: Printed by John B. Van Stienbergh, 1827. DHU/MO; DHU/R
Also in Negro Protest Pamphlets; A Compendium. New York: Arno Press, 1969.

5759. ----- Reply to Mr. Joseph Phillips' Enquiry Respecting "The Light" In Which the Operations of the American Colonization Society are Viewed by the Free People of Color on the United States. London: n.p., 1832.   NjMD

5760. Paul, Thomas. "Letter Relative to Conditions in Hayti, July 1, 1824. Written to the Editor of the Columbian Sentinel." Dorothy B. Porter, (ed.). Early Negro Writing, 1760-1837 (Boston: Beacon Press, 1971), pp. 279-80. DHU/MO; DHU/R

5761. Peabody, A. P. "Slavery As It Appeared to a Northern Man in 1844." Andover Review (16; 92; Ag., 1891), pp. 155-66.
DHU/R

5762. Peabody, William Bourne Oliver. An Address, Delivered at Springfield, Before the Hampden Colonization Society, July 4th, 1828. Springfield: Pr. by S. Bowles, 1828. CtY-D

5763. ----- The Duties of Those Who Are Born Free. A Sermon, Preached at the Annual Election of Ja. 2, 1833, before His Excellency Levi Lincoln, Governor, and His Honor Thomas L. Winthrop, Lieutenant-Governor, the Honorable Council and Legislature of Massachusetts. Boston: Dutton and Wentworth, 1833.
DLC

5764. Peck, Nathaniel and Thomas S. Price. Report of Messrs. Peck and Price, Who Were Appointed at the Meeting of the Free Colored People of, Held on the 25th of Nov., 1839. Delegates to Visit British Guiana, and the Island of Trinidad; for the Purpose of Ascertaining the Advantages to be Derived by Colored People Migrating to Those Places. Baltimore: n.p., n.d.
DHU/MO
Negro author.

5765. Peckard, Peter. Justice and Mercy Recommended Particularly with Reference to the Slave Trade. A Sermon Preached before the University of Cambridge... Cambridge: Pr. by J. Arch-deacon, Printer to the University... 1788.   DHU/MO

5766. Pennington, James W. C. An Address Delivered at Newark, N.J. at the First Anniversary of West Indian Emancipation, August, 1839. Newark: Aaron Guest, Printer, 1839. DHU/MO
Negro author.

5767. ----- "Communicated." William Armstead. A Tribute for the Negro: Being a Vindication of the Moral, Intellectual, and Religious Capabilities of the Colored Portion of Mankind... (Conn.: Negro Univ. Press, 1848), pp. 406-09.   DHU/R
Presbyterian Preacher. Slave fugitive.

5768. ----- Covenants Involving Moral Wrong are not Obligatory upon Man: A Sermon, Delivered in the Fifth Congregational Church, Hartford, Nov. 17, 1842. Hartford: J. C. Wells, 1842.   DLC

5769. ----- "The Great Conflict Requires Great Faith." Anglo-African (1:2, Ja., 1859), pp. 343-45.   DHU/MO

5770. ----- A Lecture Delivered before the Glasgow Young Men's Christian Association; and Also Before the St. George's Biblical Literary and Scientific Institute... London... New York: n.p., n.d.   DHU/MO

5771. ----- "A Review of Slavery and the Slave Trade." Anglo-African (1:2, Ja., 1859), p. 93.   DHU/MO

5772. ----- "Speeches." Proceedings of the General Anti-Slavery Convention... Held in London From Tuesday June 15th to Tuesday, June 20th, 1843. (London: John Snow, 1843), pp. 16 f.   NcD

5773. ----- A Two Year's Absence; or, A Farewell Sermon, Preached in the Fifth Congregational Church. Nov. 2d, 1845. Hartford: H. T. Wells, 1845.   DHU/MO
Negro author.

5774. ----- The Uncle Tom's Cabin Almanack; or Abolitionists's Momento. For 1858. London: J. Cassell, 1852. DHU/MO

5775. Perry, Lewis. Radical Abolitionism; Anarchy and the Government of God in Antislavery Thought. Ithaca: Cornell University, 1973.   DHU/R

5776. Phelps, Amos Augustus. Lectures on Slavery, and Its Remedy... Boston: New England Anti-Slavery Society, 1834.
                                                     DHU/MO
"Address to Clergymen", pp. 13-24.

5777. Pillsbury, Parker. Acts of the Anti-Slavery Apostles. Concord, N.H.: Clague, Wegman, Schlict & Co., Printer, 1883.   CtY-D; NN/Sch; DHU/R

5778. ----- Letter from Mr. Pillsbury to the Editor of the Anti-Slavery Standard. Boston: n.p., 1862.   NNCor
Slavery and the church.

5779. Porter, Dorothy B., (ed.). Early Negro Writing, 1760-1837. Boston: Beacon Press, 1971.   DHU/MO; DHU/R
Includes speeches by Negro ministers and other Negro leaders on abolition and colonization.

5780. ----- Negro Protest Pamphlets. New York: Arno Press, 1969.   DHU/MO
Anti-Slavery pamphlets written by Absalom Jones, Daniel Coker, Nathaniel Paul and Hosea Easton.
Negro author.

5781. Porter, Noah. Civil Liberty. A Sermon, Preached in Farmington, Conn., July 13, 1856. New York: Pudney & Russell, 1851.   DLC

5782. Presbyterian and Congregational Convention. 2nd. Philadelphia. Minutes and Sermon of the Second Convention; Held in the Central Presbyterian Church, Lombard Street, Philadelphia,

on the 28th Day of October, 1858. New York: Daly, Printer, 1858.   NN/Sch

5783. Presbyterian & Congregational Convention, 3rd. Hartford, 1958. Minutes of the Third Presbyterian and Congregational Convention Together with the Organization of the Evangelical Association of Presbyterian and Congregational Clergy of Color in the United States. Brooklyn: F. A. Brockway, printer, 1858.
                                                     NNUT

5784. Priestly, Joseph. A Sermon on the Subject of the Slave Trade; Delivered to a Society of Protestant Dissenters, at the New Meeting in Birmingham; and Published at Their Request... Birmingham: Printed for the Author by Pearson and Rollason, 1788.
                                                     DHU/MO

5785. Quarles, Benjamin. Black Abolitionists. New York: Oxford University Press, 1969.   DHU/R
Negro Author.
Chapter IV, Pulpit and Press.

5786. ----- Blacks on John Brown. Urbana: Univ. of Illinois Press, 1972.   DHU/R
Documents written by Black leaders, many of which were ministers, which supports the idea that society rather than Brown, was deranged.

5787. Quincy, Ill. Anti-Slavery Concert for Prayer 1842. Narrative of Facts Respecting Alanson Work, Ja. E. Burr & George Thompson, Prisoners in the Missouri Penitentiary for the Alleged Crime of Negro Stealing, Prepared by a Committee. Quincy, Ill.: Quincy Whig Office, 1842.   DHU/MO

5788. Rankin, John. An Address to the Churches; in Relation to Slavery. Delivered at the First Anniversary of the Ohio State Anti-Slavery Society. By Rev. John Rankin. With a Few Introductory Remarks, by a Gentleman of the Bar... Median: Pr. at the Anti-Slavery Office, 1836.   DLC

5789. ----- The Soldier, the Battle, and the Victory; Being a Brief Account of the Work of Rev. J. Rankin in the Anti-Slavery Cause; by the Author of Life and Writings of Samuel Crothers Etc. Cincinnati: Western Tract & Book Society (1852).
                                                     PPPrHi

5790. Redkey, Edwin S. Black Exodus: Black Nationalist and Back-to-Africa Movements 1890-1910. New Haven: Yale University Press, 1969.   DHU/MO; DHU/R

5791. ----- "Bishop Turner's African Dream." Okon Edet Uya, (ed.). Black Brotherhood, Afro-Americans and Africa (Lexington, Mass.: D. C. Heath and Co., 1971), pp. 96-112. DHU/MO
Also: Journal of American History (54:2, Sept., 1967), pp. 271-90.   DHU

5792-93. Religious Anti-Slavery Convention, Boston, 1846. The Declaration and Pledge Adopted by the Religious Anti-Slavery Convention, Held at the Marboro Chapel, Boston, February 26, 1846. Boston: Devereux and Seamen, 1846.   DHU/MO

5794. "Review of African Colonization: Thirteenth Annual Report of the American Society for Colonizing the free people of color in the United States; Washington, 1830. Third Annual Report of the Colonization Society of the State of Connecticut; New Haven, 1830. An Address delivered to the Colonization Society of Kentucky, at Frankfort, Dec. 12, 1829 by Hon. Henry Clay; Lexington, Kentucky, 1829." Christian Spectator (10:3, Sept., 1830), pp. 459-82.   DHU/R

5795. Review of Pamphlets on Slavery and Colonization. First Published in the Quarterly Christian Spectator, for March, 1833. New Haven: Published and Sold by A. H. Maltby, 1833.
                                                     CtY-D

5796. "A Review of the 'Address to the Public,' by the Managers of the Colonization Society of Connecticut: With an Appendix. New Haven." Christian Spectator (2:9, Sept., 1828), pp. 493-96.   DHU/R

5797. "Reviews: Tenth and Eleventh Annual Report of the American Society for Colonizing the Free People of Color in the United States; Washington, 1827, 1828." *Christian Spectator* (10:7, Jl., 1828), pp. 358-70.   DHU/R

5798. *Right and Wrong in Massachusetts.* New York: Negro Universities Press, 1969.   DHU/R
    Originally published in 1839 by Don and Jackson Anti-Slavery Press, Boston.

5799. *Right of Petition. New England Clergymen. Remarks of Messrs. Everett, Mason, Petitt and others on the Memorial Some 3,050 Clergymen of all Denominations and Sects in the Different States in New England, Remonstrating Against the Passage of the Nebraska Bill. Senate of the U.S., Mar. 14, 1854.* Washington, D.C.: Buell & Blanchard, Printers, 1854.
                                                      CtY-D

5800. Rockwood, George J. *George Barrell Cheever, Protagonist of Abolition.* In Proceedings of the American Antiquarian Society, v. 4, 46, pt. 1, April 15, 1936.   DHU/MO

5801. Root, David. *The Abolition Cause Eventually Triumphant. A Sermon Delivered Before the Anti-Slavery Society of Haverhill, Mass. August, 1836.* Andover: Gould and Newman, 1836.
                                                      DHU/MO

5802. Ruchames, Louis. *The Abolitionist: A Collection of Their Writings.* New York: Capricorn Books, 1963.   DHU/R

5803. Ruggles, David. "The Abrogation of the Seventh Commandment by the American Churches." Dorothy B. Porter. *Early Negro Writing, 1760-1837* (Boston: Beacon, 1971), pp. 478-93.
                                                      DHU/MO
    Also: Pamphlets on Slavery and Christianity. V. 1. DHU/MO
    Negro author.

5804. ----- *An Antidote for a Poisonous Combination Recently Prepared by a "Citizen of New York," Alias Dr. Reese, Entitled" An Appeal to the Reason and Religion of American Christians," Also David Meredith Reese "Humburgs"...* New York: W. Stuart, 1838.   DHU/MO; CtY-D

5805. Saunders, Prince. *Address Delivered at Bethel Church, Philadelphia on the 30th September 1818, Before the Pennsylvania Augustine Society for the Education of People of Colour.* Phila.: Joseph Rakestraw, 1818.   NN/Sch; DHU/MO
    Negro author.

5806. ----- *A Memoir Presented to the American Convention for Promoting the Abolition of Slavery.* Phila.: Dennis Hearth 1818.
                                                      DHU/MO; NN/Sch

    Negro author.

5807. Schor, Joel A. *The Anti-Slavery and Civil Rights Role of Henry Highland Garnett, 1840-1865.* Doctoral dissertation. Howard University, 1974.

5808. Seidensticker, Oswald. "The First Anti-Slavery Protest." *Penn Monthly* (5; 1874), pp. 496-503.   NNCor

5809. Sharp, Granville. *Serious Reflections on the Slave Trade and Slavery.* Wrote in March, 1797. London: Pr. by W. Calvert, 1805.   NN/Sch

5810. Sherwin, Oscar. "The Armory of God." *New England Quarterly* (18:1, Mr., 1945), pp. 70-82.   DGU
    "Summarizes the religious arguments of the Abolitionists and illustrates the use of Biblical sanctions on both sides of the Civil War."

5811. Sherwood, Henry Noble. *Paul Cuffe and His Contributions to the American Colonization Society.* n.p., n.p., n.d.
                                                      TN/DCHS

5812. Sidney, Joseph. *An Oration, Commemorative of the Abolition of the Slave Trade in the United States: Delivered Before the Wilberforce Philanthropic Association, in the City of New York, on the Second of January, 1809.* New York: J. Seymour,

Printer, 1809.   DHU/MO
    Also: Porter, Dorothy B., (ed.). *Early Negro Writing, 1760-1837* (Boston: Beacon Press, 1971), pp. 355+.
                                                      DHU/R; DHU/MO

5813. Simmons, George Frederick. *Two Sermons of the Kind Treatment and on the Emancipation of Slaves. Preached at Mobile on Sunday the 10th, and Sunday the 17th of May, 1840.* Boston: W. Crosby & Company, 1840.   DHU/MO

5814. Sipkins, Henry. *An Oration on the Abolition of Slave Trade. Delivered in the African Church in the City of New York, January 2, 1809, By Henry Sipkins, a Descendent of Africa.* New York: Pr. by J. C. Totten, 1809.   DHU/MO; NN/Sch
    Negro Author

5815. "Slavery and Colonization." *Christian Spectator* (5:1, Mr., 1833), pp. 145-68.   DHU/R
    A rebuttal of William Lloyd Garrison's attack on the American Colonization Society.

5816. Smedley, Robert C. *History of the Underground Railroad in Chester and the Neighbouring Counties of Pennsylvania.* Lancaster, Pa.: Office of the Journal, 1883.   OWibfU; DHU/MO
    Reprinted: N.Y.: Arno Press, 1969.

5817. Smith, Gerrit. *Letter of Gerrit Smith on Preaching Anti-Slavery Politics on Sunday.* n.p.: n.p., 1843.   NNCor

5818. ----- *Sermons and Speeches of Gerrit Smith.* New York: Ross and Tousey, 1861.   DLC

5819. Spring, Gardiner. *Memoirs of the Rev. Samuel J. Mills, Late Missionary to the South Western Section of the United States and Agent of the American Colonization Society.* New York: Evangelical Missionary Society, J. Seymour Printer, 1820.
                                                      NN/Sch

5820. Stanton, Henry B(rewster). *Debate at the Lane Seminary, Cincinnati. Speech of James A. Thome, of Kentucky, Delivered At the Annual Meeting of the American Anti-Slavery Society, May 6, 1834.* Boston: Garrison & Knapp, 1834.   DHU/MO

5821. Staundenraus, Philip J. *The History of the American Colonization Society.* Doctoral dissertation University of Wisconsin, 1958.

5822. Stearns, Oliver. *The Gospel Applied to the Fugitive Slave Law: A Sermon Preached to the Third Congregational Society of Hingham on Sunday, March 2, 1851.* Boston: Wm. Crosby and H. P. Nichols, 1851.   DHU/MO

5823. Stewart, Thomas McCants. *Liberia; the Americo-African Republic.* New York: Jenkins, 1886. OWibfU; NN/Sch; MWA; OO; DHU/MO
    Written by a lawyer, author and A. M. E. minister.

5824. Still, William. *The Underground Railroad.* Chicago: John Publishing Co., 1970.   DHU/R
    A reprint of the 1971 classic, noting the hardships, escapes, letters, etc. of slaves.
    Abolitionist.

5825. Stone, Thomas Treadwell. *An Address Before the Salem Female Anti-Slavery Society, at its Annual Meeting, December 7, 1851.* Salem: W. Ives & Co., Printers, 1852.   CtY-D

5826. Stowe, Harriet Elizabeth (Beecher). *The Christian Slave. A Drama Founded on a Portion of Uncle Tom's Cabin.* Dramatized by Harriet Beecher Stowe, Expressly for the Readings of Mrs. Mary E. Webb. Boston: Phillips, Sampson, 1855.   NN/Sch

5827. Stowe, Lyman Beecher. *Saints, Sinners and Beechers...* Indianapolis: The Bobbs-Merrill Co., 1934.   DHU/MO
    Chapter III, Activities of Lyman Beecher, President of Lane Theological Seminary, Cincinnati, Ohio, in the Abolition Movement.

5828. Stuart, Charles. Oneida and Oberlin, or a Call, Addressed to British Christians and Philanthropists Affectionately Inviting their Prayers and their Assistance in Favor of the Christians... Bristol: Pub. by Wright and Albright, 1841.   DHU/MO

5829. Sumner, Charles. Final Protest for Himself and the Clergy of New England Against Slavery in Kansas and Nebraska. Speech of Hon. Charles Sumner, on the Night of the Passage of the Kansas and Nebraska Bill. In Senate of the United States, May 25, 1854. Washington, D.C.: Buell & Blanchard, Printers, 1854.   CtY-D

5830. Sunderland, La Roy. Antislavery Manual, Containing a Collection of Facts and Arguments on American Slavery. New York: Pr. by S. W. Benedict, 1837.   CtY-D

5831. Tappan, Lewis. Letter to the Convention of Ministers and Representatives of the Evangelical Branches in the Church in Brooklyn, New York. n.p.: John A. Gray and Green, 1866. DHU/MO

5832. Thomas, John L. Slavery Attacked; the Abolitionist Crusade. Englewood Cliffs, N.J.: Prentice-Hall, 1965. TSewU-T

5833. Thompson, George (ed.). Slavery in America. A Reprint of an Appeal to the Christian Women of America by Angelina E. Grimke of Charleston, South Carolina. Edinburgh: William Oliphant and Son, 1837.   DLC

5834. Thompson, George and Henry C. Wright. Church of Scotland and American Slavery: Substance of Speeches Delivered in the Music Hall, Edinburgh, During May and June 1846. With an appendix Containing the Deliverances of the Free Church on the Subject of Slavery, 1844, 1845, and 1846, and Other Valuable Documents. Edinburgh: Published for the Scottish Anti-Slavery Society by T. & W. McDonall, 1846.   NNCor

5835. Thompson, George, and Henry Clarke Wright. The Free Church of Scotland and American Slavery. With an Appendix Containing the Deliverances of the Free Church on the Subject of Slavery, 1844, 1845, and 1846, and Other Valuable Documents. Edinburgh: Scottish Anti-Slavery Society, 1846.   DLC

5836. Thompson, J. E. "Lyman Beecher's Long Road to Conservative Abolitionism." Church History (42:1, Mr., 1973), pp. 89-109.   DHU/R
      Slavery and the church.

5837. Tracy, Joseph. Colonization and Missions. A Historical Examination of the State of Society in Western Africa, as Formed by Paganism and Muhammedanism, Slavery, the Slave Trade and Piracy, and of the Remedial Influence of Colonization and Missions. By Joseph Tracy, Secretary of the Massachusetts Colonization Society. Published by the Board of Managers. 4th ed. Boston: Press of T. R. Marvin, 1845. DHU/MO; CtY-D

5838. Troxler, George. "Eli Caruthers: A Silent Dissenter in the Old South." Journal of Presbyterian History (45:2, Je., 1967), pp. 95-111.   DHU/R

5839. Turner, Henry McNeal, (bp.). Emigration of the Colored People of the United States. n.p.: n.p., 1879.   OWibfU

5840. Underground Railroad. Letter From an Unidentified Quaker of Short Creek, Harrison County, Ohio, Signed "X.Y.Z.," to A.B.C." ("to the Care of Thomas Perkins"); Lynchburg, Virginia, Feb. 21, 1844, Relating to Slavery and the "Underground Railroad," 4 p. Accompanied by a Typewritten Transcript.   NN/Sch

5841. Van Dyke, Henry Jackson. The Character and Influence of Abolitionism. A Sermon Preached in the First Presbyterian Church, Brooklyn, on the Sabbath Evening, Dec. 9, 1860. New York: D. Appleton & Co., 1860.   NN/Sch

5842. Wainwright, J. M. A Discourse on the Occasion of Forming the African Mission School Society. Hartford: Published yhe Directors of the Society, 1828.   DHU/MO

5843. Wander, Philip C. The Image of the Negro in Three Movements; Abolitionists, Colonizationist, and Pro-Slavery. Doctoral dissertation. University of Pittsburgh, 1968.

5844. ----- "Salvation Through Separation: The Image of the Negro in the American Colonization Society." Quarterly Journal of Speech (57:1, Feb., 1971), pp. 57-67. DHU; DCU
      "The ACS strongly backed by many Presbyterians, stressed that blacks were to prosper in Liberia, civilize and convert Africa, and prove to the world that they could govern themselves."

5845. Ward, Samuel. "Speech" American and Foreign Anti-Slavery Society. Annual Report, New York, May 8, 1849. With Resolutions and Addresses. New York: A & F, Anti-Slavery Society, 1849. pp. 13-15.   NcD
      Negro author.

5846. Ward, Samuel R. "Speech on the Fugutive Slave Bill." Dorothy B. Porter, (ed.). Early Negro Writings, 1760-1837 (Boston: Beacon, 1971), pp. 193-96.   DHU/MO
      Negro author.

5847. Weiss, John. Life and Correspondence of Theodore Parker, Minister of the Twenty-eighth Congregational Society. Boston: Books for Libraries Press, 1969.   CoU; NbU; KyLxCB
      Reprint of 1864 edition.
      Unitarian minister and abolitionist.

5848. West, Richard. Back to Africa: A History of Sierra Leone and Liberia. New York: Holt, Rinehart and Winston, 1971.
                                                      DHU/R
      Marcus Garvey and the UNIA, pp. 262-275. See index also for American Colonization Society, Church Missionary Society, etc.

5849. Whipple, Charles King. The Non Resistance Principle: with Particular Application to the Help of Slaves by Abolitionists. Boston: R. F. Wallcut, 1860.   CtY-D

5850. Wickstron, Werner T. The American Colonization Society and Liberia -- A Historical Study in Religious Motivation and Achievement. Doctoral dissertation. Hartford Seminary Foundation, 1958.

5851. Williams, Peter, Jr. Discourse Delivered in St. Phillip's Church, for the Benefit of the Colored Community of Wilberforce in Upper Canada, on the Fourth of July, 1830 ... New York: Printed by G. P. Burke, 1830.   NN/Sch; DHU/MO
      Also: Porter, Dorothy B., (ed.). Early Negro Writing, 1760-1837 (Boston: Beacon Press, 1971), pp. 294-302.
                                              DHU/R; DHU/MO

5852. ----- "Slavery and Colonization." Dorothy B. Porter (ed.). Early Negro Writings, 1760-1837 (Boston: Beacon Press, 1971), pp. 77-85.   DHU/MO

5853. Woodson, Carter G. The Mind of the Negro as Reflected in Letters Written During the Crisis, 1800-1860. New York: Russell & Russell, 1926.   DHU/R
      Includes many letters written by Negro ministers.

5854. Woolman, John. "Exercise of a Quaker Abolitionist's Mind." A. B. Hart (ed.). American History Told by Contemporaries (New York: Macmillan, 1897-1929.   DHU

5855. Wright, Elizur. "The Sin of Slavery and its Remedy; Containing Some Reflections on the Moral Influence of American Colonization." Louis Ruchames, (ed.). The Abolitionists (New York: Capricorn Books, 1966), pp. 58-60. DHU/R

5856. Wright, Henry Clarke. Duty of Abolitionists to Pro-Slavery Ministers and Churches. Concord, N.H.: Pr. by J. R. French, 1841.   NN/Sch; CtY-D; DLC

5857. Wright, Theodore S. Prejudice Against the Colored Man. Carter G. Woodson, (ed.). Negro Orators and Their Orations (Wash., D.C.: Associated Publishers, 1925), pp. 92-95.
                                              DHU/R; DHU/MO
      Written by Negro Presbyterian minister and abolitionist.

G. THE FREEDMAN-RECONSTRUCTION

5858. Abott, Richard H. Cobbler in Congress: Life of Henry Wilson, 1812-1875. Doctoral dissertation. University of Wisconsin, 1965.   DHU/R
    Microfilm.

5859. Alvord, John Watson. Letters from the South Relating to the Condition of Freedmen, Adressed to Major General O. O. Howard Commissioner Bureau R., F., and A. L. Washington, D.C.: Howard University Press, 1870.   DHU/MO

5860. American Missionary Association. What Remains of Slavery and the Slave Trade, the Freedmen and Africa. Papers and Addresses at the Twenty-Ninth Anniversary of the American Missionary Association, with Facts and Statistics. New York: American Missionary Association, 1875.   NN/Sch; DHU/MO

5861. ----- Woman's Work for the Lowly, as Illustrated in the Work of the American Missionary Association Among the Freedmen. Boston: South Boston Inquirer Press, 1873.
                                                                        DHU/MO

5862. Anscombe, Francis Charles. The Contribution of the Quakers to the Reconstruction of the South. Masters thesis, University of North Carolina, 1926.

5863. Arnold, S. G. "Education Among the Freedmen." Methodist Quarterly Review (60:1, Ja., 1878), pp. 43-67.   DHU/R

5864. "The Baptist Among the Freedmen." Editorial Southern Workman (14:10, Oct., 1885), p. 1.   DLC; DHU/MO

5865. Beard, August Field. "The Present Religious Condition of the Negro in the United States." American Missionary Magazine (47:7, Jl., 1893), pp. 211-14.   IC/H
    Condition of the Negro after twenty-seven years of freedom.

5866. Bell, W. B. "Everybody's Parish." Crisis (62:3, Mr., 1955), pp. 133-38.   DHU/MO
    The Church of the Transfiguration at 5th Ave. & 29th St., N.Y.C., where Negroes were once harbored during a post-Civil War riot.

5867. The Board of Freedmen's Missions of the United Presbyterian Church. Our Work Among the Freedmen. n.p.: Published by the Board of Freedmen's Missions of the United Presbyterian Church, 1911.   DHU/MO

5868. Botume, Elizabeth Hyde. "First Days Amongst (The Contrabands." Boston: Lee and Shepard, 1893), pp. 325-326.
                                    Pam. File, DHU/R
    Review: The moods, states of mind, effects of emancipation of Negroes.

5869. Boyle, Sarah Patton. The Desegregated Heart: A Virginian's Stand in Time of Transition. New York: William Morrow & Co., 1962.   DHU/MO

5870. Brewe, H. Peers. "The Protestant Episcopal Freeman's Commission, 1865-1878." Historical Magazine of Protestant Episcopal Church (26:4, Dec., 1967), pp. 361-81. DCU/TH

5871. Bruce, Philip A. ...The Plantation Negro as a Freeman; Observations on His Character, Condition and Prospects in Virginia. New York: Putnam, 1889.   DHU/MO; NN/Sch

5872. Bumstead, Horace. "The Freedman's Children at School." Andover Review (4; 24, Dec., 1885), pp. 550-60. DHU/R

5873. Cain, Richard Harvey (bp.) Civil Rights Bill. Speech of Hon. Richard H. Cain of South Carolina Delivered in the House of Representatives Saturday, Jan. 24, 1874. DHU/MO
    Also in: New National Era & Citizenship (5:5, Feb. 5, 1874).
    Carter G. Woodson (ed.). Negro Orators and their Orations.
    (Wash., D.C.: Association for the Study of Negro Life and History, 1925), pp. 328-38.   DHU/R

5874. ----- (bp.). "The Negro Problem of the South." A. M. E. Church Review (2; 1886), pp. 139-45.   DLC; DHU/MO
    Negro author.

5875. Campus of the Freedmen on the Missippi River. Inquirer Print. Office, 1864.   INRE NN/Sch; DHU/MO

5876. Carroll, J. M. History of Texas Baptists. Dallas: Baptist Standard Pub. Co., 1923.   NN/Sch
    Chapter 43, Religious work among the Negroes during Reconstruction 1867-75.

5877. The Church of the Pilgrims - South. Boston: South Boston Inquirer Press, 1875.   IC/H
    "A paper to show the adaptability of the Congregational policy to the colored people."

5878. Coston, William Hilary. A Freedman and Yet a Slave. Burlington, Iowa: Wohlwend Bros., 1884. DHU/MO; NN/Sch; NcD; OWibfU

5879. Donald, Henderson Hamilton. ...The Negro Freedman; Life Conditions of the American Negro in the Early Years After Emancipation. New York: H. Schuman, 1952. DHU/MO; NN/Sch

5880. Douglass, Harlan Paul. Christian Reconstruction in the South. New York: The Pilgrim Press, 1909. NN/Sch; CtY-D; DHU/MO

5881. Drake, Richard Bryant. "Freedmen's Aid Societies and Sectional Compromise." Journal of Southern History (29; My., 1963), pp. 175-86.

5882. Edwards, Lonzy. "Religious Education by Blacks During Reconstruction." Religious Education (69:4, Jl.-Ag., 1974), pp. 412-21.   DHU/R

5883. Emery, E. B. Letters from the South, on the Social, Intellectual, and Moral Condition of the Colored People... Boston: T. Todd, Printer, 1880.   DHU/MO

5884. "Episcopal Church and the Freedman." The Nation (N.Y.) (1:24, Dec. 14, 1865), p. 743. DLC; CL; CLU; C; IEG; ICU; KyL; NcD

5885. "The First Civil Rights Act: Letter from the Past--228." The Friends Journal (13:8, Apr. 15, 1967), pp. 188-89.
                                                                        DHU/R

5886. Fleming, Walter Lynwood. Documentary History of Reconstruction. Cleveland: A. H. Clark, 1906.   DHU/R

5887. "A Fourfold Work." (Freedmen). The Church at Home and Abroad (23; 1898), p. 110.   DHU/R
    Work of the Freedmen's Board.
    Presbyterian church.

5888. "Freedmen for Africa." The Church at Home and Abroad (2; 1887), pp. 166-67.   DHU/R
    Presbyterian Church.

5889. "Freedmen or Free Men?" The Church at Home and Abroad (3; 1888), p. 373.   DHU/R
    Discussion of the terms.
    Presbyterian Church

5890. Friends' Association of Philadelphia and its Vicinity for the Relief of Colored Freedmen. Report of the Executive Board. First, 1864. Philadelphia: 1864.   DHU/MO; INRE

5891. ----- Statistics of the Operations of the Executive Board of Friends' Association of Philadelphia, and its Vicinity, for the Relief of Colored Freedmen, as Presented to a Public Meeting of Friends, held at Arch St. Meeting House, Philadelphia, 1st Month, 1864. Together with the Report of Samuel R. Shipley,

President of the Board, of his Visit to the Campus of the Freedmen on the Mississippi River. Inquirer Print. Office, 1864.
INRE; NN/Sch; DHU/MO

5892. Friends, Society of. Central Committee of Great Britain
and Ireland for the Relief of the Emancipated Slaves of North
America. ...Case and Claims... London: R. Barrett, 1865.
NNCor

5893. ----- Indiana Yearly Meeting. Missionary Board. Report
of Indiana Yearly Meeting's Executive Committee for the Relief
of Colored Freedmen. Richmond, Ind.: Holloway & Davis,
1854.   INRE

5894. ----- New York Yearly Meeting. Third Report of a Com-
mittee of Representatives of New York Meeting of Friends
Upon the Condition and Wants of the Colored Refugees. New
York: n.p., 1864.   CtY-D

5895. Geppert, Dora Higbee. In "God's Country," a Southern
Romance... With Introduction by Henry Watterson. New York:
American Publishers Corporation, 1897.   DHU/MO

5896. Girardeau, J. L. "Our Ecclesiastical Relation to the Freedman." Southern Presbyterian Review (18; 1867), pp. 2-6.
DLC; KyLxCB

5897. Gravely, William B. "A Black Methodist on Reconstruction
in Mississippi: Three Letters by James Lynch in 1868-1869."
Methodist History (11:4, Jl., 1973), pp. 3-18.   DHU/R

5898. Grimke, Francis James. The Religious Aspect of Reconstruction. A Discourse Delivered at the Second Annual Convocation for Pastors and Christian Workers, Under the Direction of the School of Theology, Howard University, February
19th, 1919. Washington, D.C.: n.p., 1919.   DHU/R
Negro author.

5899. Holland, Frederic May. Frederick Douglass: the Colored
Orator. New York: Funk & Wagnalls Co., 1895. DHU/R
Chapter X, "Is God Dead?."

5900. Holland, Rupert Sargent. Letters and Diary of Laura M.
Towne. New York: Negro Universities Press, 1969. DHU/R
Reprint of 1912 edition. Letters written from the Sea
Islands of South Carolina by a pioneer educator of Negro
Freedmen who built and maintained the Penn School.

5901. Ide, George B. The Freedmen of War; a Discourse Delivered at the Annual Meeting of the American Baptist Home Mission
Society, Phila., May 1863 ... Philadelphia: American Baptist Publishing Society, 1864.   DHU/MO

5902. Inaugural Ceremonies of the Freedman's Memorial to
Abraham Lincoln, Washington City, April 14, 1876. St.
Louis: Levison and Blythe, 1876.   OWibfU

5903. Jervey, Edward D. "Motives and Methods of the Methodist
Episcopal Church in the Period of Reconstruction." Methodist
History (4; Jl., 1965), pp. 17-25.   DHU/R

5904. Johnson, Clifton H. "African Missionaries to U.S. Freedmen." The Crisis (78:9, Nov., 1971), pp. 288-90. DLC;
DHU/MO

5905. Kedro, Milan James. The Civil War's Effect Upon an Urban
Church: the St. Louis Presbytery Under Martial Law." Missouri Historical Society Bulletin (27:3, Apr., 1971), pp. 173-
93. WaU; CtY; DLC; NN; NNC; TxU

5906. Kendrick, J. R. "The Spectre of Negro Rule." Andover
Review (12; 92, Dec., 1889), pp. 596-606.   DHU/R
Makes a plea for the white race in America to recognize
the equal rights of blacks and give them full political justice
and equality.

5907. Laney, Lucy C. "Haines Normal School, Augusta, Georgia."
The Church at Home and Abroad (4; 1888), pp. 148-49. DHU/R
Negro school under Board of Missions for Freedmen.

5908. "A Lesson in Giving." (Freedmen). The Church at Home
and Abroad (25; 1898), p. 418.   DHU/R
Presbyterian church.

5909. "Light Wanted in a Dark Place." (Freedmen). The Church
at Home and Abroad (4; 1888), p. 62.   DHU/R
Appeal to the Board of Missions for Freedmen by a Negro
Missionary on St. Helena Island, S.C.

5910. Litwack, Leon F. North of Slavery: the Negro in the Free
States, 1790-1860. Chicago: Univ. of Chicago Press, 1961.
NN/Sch
Negro church, pp. 187-213.

5911. Lynch, John Ray. The Facts of Reconstruction. New York:
Neale, 1913.   OWibfU

5912. Lyon, Ernest. "Emancipation and Racial Advancement."
Alice Ruth Nelson. Masterpieces of Negro Eloquence: The
Best Speeches Delivered by the Negro From the Days of Slav-
ery to the Present Time (New York: Bookley Pub. Co., 1914),
pp. 461-74.   DHU/MO
Methodist Episcopal Negro Minister.

5913. "Mary Allen Seminary." The Church at Home and Abroad
(1; 1887), pp. 161-3.   DHU/R
Christian education for Freedwomen.

5914. Massachusetts Episcopal Society for the Religious Instruction
of Freedmen. ...Annual Meeting of the Massachusetts Episcopal Society for the Religious Instruction of Freedmen...
Boston: Press of Geo. C. Rand & Avery, 1865.   NNUT

5915. Mays, Benjamin Elijah. "Role of the Negro Liberal Arts
College in Post-war Reconstruction." Journal of Negro
Education (11; Jl., 1942), pp. 400-11.   DHU

5916. McKelvey, Blake. "Penal Slavery and Southern Reconstruction." The Journal of Negro History (30:2, Apr., 1935),
pp. 153-79.   DHU/MO

5917. "Missionary Enterprise." Southern Workman (6:11, Nov.,
1877), p. 83.   DLC; DHU/MO
"Freedmen Educated in Southern Colleges and sent as
Missionaries to Africa-- Farewell services in the Central
Congregational Church."

5918. Morrow, Ralph E. The Methodist Episcopal Church, the
South, and Reconstruction, 1865-1880. Doctoral dissertation.
Indiana University, 1954.

5919. ----- Northern Methodism and Reconstruction. East
Lansing, Mich.: Michigan State University Press, 1956.
DHU/MO; NN/Sch

5920. Mosely, B. W. "The Evangelization of the Colored People."
Southern Presbyterian Review (25; Apr., 1874), pp. 230-33.
DLC; KyLxCB

5921. Nicholson, John. "To Mock My Maker -- A Civil War
Letter on Freedom of Conscience." Historical Magazine of the
Protestant Episcopal Church (41:1, Mr., 1972), pp. 67-76.
DHU/R
Statements on the relationship between Church and State by
Alfred Augustine Watson, rector of St. James Church, Wil-
mington, North Carolina, from 1865-1884. The Letter
protests the Union commander's seizure during the recon-
struction period.

5922. Ogilvie, Charles Finney. Alabama Baptist During the Civil
War and Reconstruction. Master's thesis. Southwestern
Baptist Theological Seminary, 1956.

5923. Osborne, William A. "Slavery Sequel: A Freeman's
Odyssey." Jubilee (3; Sept., 1955), pp. 10-23.   DCU

5924. Other Fools and Their Doings; or Life Among the Freedmen, By One Who Has Seen It. New York: J. S. Ogilvie,
1880.   O

5925. Payne, H. N. "Race Pride." (Freedmen). The Church at Home and Abroad (3; 1888), pp. 268-70.　　DHU/R

5926. Pearne, Thomas H. "The Freedmen." Methodist Quarterly Review (37; Ja., 1877), pp. 462-80.　　DHU/R; DLC

5927. Pierce, Paul Skeels. The Freedmen's Bureau. A Chapter in the History of Reconstruction. New York: Haskell House Publishers, Ltd. 1971.　　DHU/R
　　　"Reprint of 1904 edition." Chapter I, Work of religious and benevolent socieities and Freedmen's Aid Societies.

5928. Porter, Lansing. "Education in Atlanta, Ga." (Freedmen). The Church at Home and Abroad (4; 1888), pp. 565-7.　　DHU/R

5929-30. Potter, F. C. "A Voice From Arkansas." The Church at Home and Abroad (1; 1887), p. 66.　　DHU/R
　　　Freedmen and Presbyterian Church.

5931. Presbyterian Church in the U.S.A. Board of Missions for Freedmen. Annual Report of the Board of Missions for Freedmen of the Presbyterian Church in the United States of America. Pittsburgh: n.p., 186-.　　NN/Sch
　　　1874-75-83-84-88.　　DHU/MO
　　　1871-1885.　　NNUT

5932. ----- A Sketch of the Origin and Work of the Presbyterian Board of Missions for Freedmen. Pittsburgh: Presbyterian Board of Missions for Freedmen, 1888.　　NNUT

5933. Rankin, Arthur E. "Interfering with the Work of Missions for Freedmen" and Why. n.p.,: n.p., after 1914.　　NNUT

5934. Rankin, Charles Hays. The Rise of Negro Baptist Churches in the South Through the Reconstruction Period. Master's thesis. New Orleans Baptist Theological Seminary, 1955.

5935. "Report of the Standing Committee on Missions for Freedmen." The Church at Home and Abroad (4; 1888), pp. 41-43.　　DHU/R
　　　The Presbyterian Board of Missions for Freedmen.

5936. Richardson, Joe M. The Negro in the Reconstruction of Florida, 1865-1877. Tallahassee; The Florida State University, 1965.　　DHU/MO
　　　Chapter 8, Negro religion.

5937. Root, Barnabas. "African Missionaries to U.S. Freedmen." Clifton H. Johnson. Crisis (78:9, Nov., 1971), pp. 288-290.　　DHU/R
　　　African prince of Sierra Leone sent to Montgomery, Alabama by the American Missionary Association in 1873.

5938. "Shall We Enter the Regions Beyond?" The Church at Home and Abroad (2; 1887), pp. 370-1.　　DHU/R
　　　Presbyterian Church.
　　　The Board of Missions for Freedmen.

5939. Stanford, Peter Thomas. The Tragedy of the Negro in America; a Condensed History of the Enslavement, Sufferings, Emancipation, Present Condition and Progress of the Negro Race in the U.S.A. Boston: Wasto, 1897.　　OWibfU; DHU/MO
　　　Negro author.

5940. Stewart, Maria W. Meditations From the Pen of ... Now Matron of the Freedman's Hospital, and Presented in 1832 to the First African Baptist Church and Society of Boston, Mass. First Published by W. Lloyd Garrison & Knapp. Now Most

Respectfully Dedicated to the Church Miltant of Washington, D.C. (Washington, D.C.: n.p., 1878), DHU/MO; DLC

5941. Straker, David Augustus. The New South Investigated. Detroit: Ferguson Printing Co., 1888. OWibfU; NN/Sch; DHU/MO
　　　Negro author.
　　　A.M.E. layman

5942. Sweet, William Warren. "Negro Churches in the South: A Phase of Reconstruction." Methodist Review (Quarterly) (104; My., 1921), pp. 405-18.　　DHU/R

5943. Taylor, Alrutheus A. The Negro in South Carolina During the Reconstruction. Washington, D.C.: The Association for the Study of Negro Life and History, 1924.　　DHU/MO
　　　Also, Journal of Negro History (9:3, Jl., 1924), pp. 241-364. DHU
　　　Negro author.

5944. ----- The Negro in the Reconstruction of Virginia. Washington, D.C.: Assn. for Study of Negro Life and History, 1926. DHU; NN/Sch
　　　Also, Journal of Negro History (11:3, Jl., 1926), pp. 243+.　　DHU

5945. /Turner, Henry McNeal, (bp.)./ Celebration of the First Anniversary of Freedom, Held January 1, 1866, and Containing an Outline of an Oration Delivered by Henry M. Turner. Augusta, Ga.: n.p., /1866/.　　NC; MH

5946. ----- Speech on the Eligibility of Colored Members to Seats in the Georgia Legislature, Delivered before that Body September 3, 1868. Augusta, Ga.: E. H. Pugh, Printer, 1868.　　DHU/MO
　　　Negro author.

5947. ----- "There is No Manhood Future in the United States for the Negro." Thomas Wagstaff, (ed.). Black Power: The Radical Response to White America. Beverly Hills: Gencoe Press, 1969, pp. 50-55.
　　　Urges Negroes to emigrate to Africa.
　　　Negro author.

5948. United States Army Dept. of the Southwest. Chaplains Appeal for the Contrabands at Helena, Ark. to the Friends of Humanity in the Loyal States: The Undersigned, Chaplains in the Army of the South West, beg Leave to Repress the Situation of the Colored People. Helena, Ark.; n.p., 1867.　　MH

5949. Wallace, Jesse Thomas. History of the Negroes of Mississippi from 1865-1890. Doctoral dissertation. Columbia University, 1928.

5950-51. Warfield, B. B. "A Calm View of the Freedmen's Case." The Church at Home and Abroad (1; Ja., 1887), pp. 62-65.　　DHU/R

5952. Waterbury, Maria. Seven Years Among the Freedmen. Chicago: T. B. Arnold, 1890.　　NN/Sch

5953. Williamson, Jolt. After Slavery. The Negro in South Carolina During Reconstruction, 1861-1877. Chapel Hill: University of North Carolina Press, 1965.　　DHU/R
　　　Chapter on Religion, Withdrawal and Reformation.

5954. "Young People's Societies." (Freedmen). The Church at Home and Abroad (23; 1898), pp. 108-9.　　DHU/R
　　　Presbyterian Church.

H. SPIRITUALS, GOSPEL SONGS, MUSIC, POETRY, ORAL TRADITIONS AND FOLKLORE

5955. Abrahams, Roger D. Deep Down in the Jungle; Negro Narrative Folklore From the Streets of Philadelphia. Chicago: Aldine Pub. Co., 1970.　　NjP; O

5956. ----- Positively Black. Englewood Cliffs, N.J.: Prentice-Hall, 1970.　　IC/H
　　　Folklore of the Negro.

5957. Adams, Edward C. L. Congaree Sketches; Scenes From Negro Life in the Swamps of the Congaree and Tales by Tad and Scip of Heaven and Hell With Other Miscellany. Chapel Hill: University of North Carolina Press, 1927. IC/H; NjP
　　　Folklore of the Negro.

5958. "African Masks and Secret Societies." (Various Ethnographic Notes.) Journal of American Folk-Lore (12:46, Jl.-Sept., 1899), pp. 208-11.   DHU/R
        Microcard.

5959. Aimes, Hubert H. S. "African Institutions in America." Journal of American Folk-Lore (18:68, Ja.-Mr., 1905), pp. 15-32.   DHU/R
        Microcard.

5960. "Alabama Folk Lore." Southern Workman (33:1, Ja., 1904), pp. 49-52.   DLC; DHU/MO

5961. Alger, A. L. "Folk-Lore From Northern New York." Journal of American Folklore (5:4, Oct.-Dec., 1892), pp. 336-37.   Pam. File, DHU/R

5962. Allen, Richard. "The Folk Sermon." Ruth Miller (ed.). Black American Literature (California: Glencoe Press, 1971), pp. 115-119.   DHU/R

5963. Allen, William F. and Charles Pickard Ware, et alii. Slave Songs of the United States. New York: A. Simpson & Co., 1867.   DHU/MO

5964 Anderson, John Q. "The New Orleans Voodoo, Ritual Dance and Its Twentieth-Century Survivals." Southern Folklore Quarterly (24:2, Je., 1960), pp. 135-43. DLC; CtY; CL; CLSU; CLU; CU; NNC

5965. Anderson, Marian. "He's Got the Whole World in His Hands." Phonodisc.

5966. Armstrong, Mary F. and Helen W. Ludlow, et alii. Hampton and Its Students ... New York: G. Putnam's Sons, 1874.   DHU/R
        Includes fifty cabin and plantation songs arranged by Thomas P. Fenner.

5967. Arnold, Byron. Folksongs of Alabama. Birmingham: University of Alabama Press, 1950.   DLC
        Includes Negro spirituals.

5968. "At the Big House:" Bibliographical Note on Negro & Indian Stories: Journal of American Folklore (17:3, Jl.-Sept., 1904), pp. 212-213.   Pam. File, DHU/R

5969. Aunt Dicy Tales; Snuff-dipping Tales of the Texas Negro. Austin, Texas: n.p., 1956.   O

5970. Backus, Emma M. "Animal Tales from North Carolina." Journal of American Folk-Lore (11:43, Oct.-Dec., 1898), pp. 284-91.   DHU/R
        Microcard.

5971. ----- "Christmas Carols from Georgia." Journal of American Folk-Lore (12:47, Oct.-Dec., 1899), p. 272.   DHU/R
        Microcard.
        First line: "De leetle cradle rocks to-night in glory."

5972. ----- "Cradle-Songs of Negroes in North Carolina." Journal of American Folklore. (7:3, Jl.-Sept., 1894), p. 310.
                                                Pam. File, DHU/R

5973. ----- "Folk-Tales from Georgia." Journal of American Folk-Lore (13:48, Ja.-Mr., 1900), pp. 19-32.   DHU/R
        Microcard.

5974. ----- "Negro Ghost Stories From North Carolina." Journal of American Folklore (9:3, J.-Sept., 1896), pp. 228-230.
                                                Pam. File, DHU/R

5975. ----- "Negro Hymn from Georgia." Journal of American Folk-Lore (10:39, Oct.-Dec., 1897), p. 264.   DHU/R
        Microcard
        First line: "If yo gets ter Heaben befo' I do."

5976. ----- "Negro Hymns from Georgia." Journal of American Folk-Lore (10:37, Apr.-Je., 1897), p. 116.   DHU/R

Microcard
First line: "Wuz yo dar when dey crucified de Lord?"

5977. ----- "Negro Song From Georgia." Journal of American Folk-Lore (10:38, Jl.-Sept., 1897), p. 216.   DHU/R
        Microcard
        First line: "I 'se gwine on er journey, tell yo',"

5978. ----- "Negro Song from North Carolina" Journal of American Folklore (11:1, Ja.-Mr., 1898), p. 60.   Pam. File, DHU/R

5979. ----- "Tales of the Rabbit from Georgia Negroes." Journal of American Folk-Lore (12:45, Apr.-Je., 1899), pp. 108-15.
                                                DHU/R
        Microcard.

5980. Bacon, Alice Mabel. "Conjuring and Conjure-Doctors in the Southern United States." Journal of American Folklore (9:3, J.-Sept., 1896), pp. 224-26.   Pam. File, DHU/R

5981. ----- "Work and Methods of the Hampton Folk-Lore Society." Journal of American Folk-Lore (11:40, Ja.-Mr., 1898), pp. 17-21.   DHU/R
        Microcard.

5982. Bacon, Herron and A. M. "Conjuring and Conjure Doctors in the Southern United States." Journal of American Folklore (9:33, Apr.-Je., 1896), pp. 143-47.   Pam. File, DHU/R

5983. Baker, Frank. "Superstitions Connected with the Human Hand." Journal of American Folklore (1:1, Apr.-Je., 1888), p. 83.   Pam. File, DHU/R
        Healing and other superstitions connected with hands and paws.

5984. Ballanta-Taylor, Nicholas G. J. Saint Helena Island Spirituals. Recoreded and Transcribed at Penn Norman, Industrial and Agricultural School, St. Helena Island, Beaufort County, South Carolina. New York: G. Schirmer Press, 1925.
                                                DHU/MO
        Phono-disc.
        A native of Sierra Leone points out the characteristics which are common to African and Afro-American music.

5985. Ballowe, Hewitt Leonard. The Lawd Sayin' the Same, Negro Folk Tales of the Creole Country. Baton Rouge: Louisiana State University Press, 1947.   NjP

5986. Banks, Lacy J. "Gospel Music: A Short of Black Joy." Ebony (27:7, My., 1972), pp. 161-68.   DHU/MO

5987. "The Baptist, Methodist, and Presbyterian Preachers," from "Negro tales from Bolivar County, Mississippi." Southern Folklore Quarterly (19; 1955), pp. 104-116. DLC; CtY; CL; CLSU; CLU; CU; NNC

5988. Barrett, Harris. "Negro Folk Songs." Southern Workman (41:4, Apr., 1912), pp. 238-45.   DLC; DHU/MO

5989. Barton, William E. "Hymns of the Negro." New England Magazine (n. s.) (19; Ja., 1899), pp. 609-24.   CtY

5990. ----- Old Plantation Hymns: A Collection of Hitherto Unpublished Melodies of the Slave and the Freedman, with Historical and Descriptive Notes. New York: Samson, Wolffe and Co., 1899.   DHU/MO
        (In New England Magazine, v. 19, p. 443-56.)

5991. Bascom, William R. "Acculturation Among the Gullah Negroes." American Anthropologist (42; 1941), pp. 43-50.
                                                DHU

5992. Beaumont, Geoffrey. "Twentieth Century Folk Mass." Frank Weir and his Concert Orchestra with the Peter Knight Singers.
        Phonodisc.

5993. Beckham, Albert S. "The Psychology of Negro Spirituals."
Southern Workman (60:9, Sept., 1931), pp. 391-4.
DLC; DHU/MO

5994. "Beliefs and Customs Connected With Death and Burial."
(Folk-Lore and Ethnology.). Southern Workman (26:1, Ja.,
1897), pp. 18-19.   DLC; DHU/MO

5995. "Beliefs of Southern Negroes Concerning Hags." Journal
of American Folklore (7:1, Ja.-Mr., 1894), pp. 66-67.
Pam. File, DHU/R
Cure for the "Riding" Hag.

5996. Bellinger, Lucius. Stray Leaves from the Portfolio of a
Local Methodist Preacher. Macon, Ga.: n.p., 1870. IC/H
"For Negro singing at white religious services."

5997. Bennett, John. The Doctor to the Dead, Grotesque Legends
& Folk Tales of Old Charleston. New York: Rinehart, 1946.
NjP; O

5998. Bennett, Robert A. "Biblical Hermeneutics and the Black
Preacher." Journal of the Interdenominational Theological
Center (1:2, Spr., 1974), pp. 38-53.   DHU/R

5999. Bergen, Fanny D. "Louisiana Ghost Story." Journal of
American Folklore (12:45, Apr.-Je., 1899), pp. 1
Microcard.

6000. ----- "On the Eastern Shore." Journal of American Folk-
Lore. (2:3, Jl.-Sept., 1889), pp. 295-300.   Pam. File,
DHU/R
Beliefs and sayings of the "Colored" People of the Chesa-
peake Bay Maryland Region.

6001. Beynon, Erdmann D. "Voodoo Cult Among Negro Migrants in
Detroit." American Journal of Sociology (43; My., 1938), pp.
894-907.   DHU

6002. "Black Delta." 1 Hour.
Film
Documentary survey of religious and secular folklore filmed
in the Mississippi Delta.

6003. "Blind Gary Davis." New York: McGraw-Hill, 197? 12
min.   B & W
Film
Rev. Davis (blind) plays blues and religious songs against
a Harlem background.

6004. Boag, E. T. "De Secon' Flood. Story of a Negro Nurse."
Journal of American Folklore (11:42, Jl.-Sep., 1898), pp.
237-38.   Pam. File, DHU/R
Folk expression in dialect.

6005. Boal, Barbara M. "Casting Out the Seven Devils. The Gap
Between Faith and Understanding in Semi-Literate Societies."
International Review of Mission (61: 244, Oct., 1972), pp. 342-
56.   DHU/R

6006. Bolton, Dorothy (ed.). Old Songs, Hymnal, Words and Mel-
odies from the State of Georgia. Music arranged by Harry T.
Burleigh. New York: The Century Co., 1929.   CoDI
Negro author.

6007. Bolton, H. Carrington. "Decoration of Graves of Negroes
in South Carolina." Journal of American Folklore (4:3; Jl.-
Sept., 1891), p. 214.   Pam. File, DHU/R
Pottery fetish.

6008. Bontemps, Arna W. "Rock Church Rock." Sylvester C.
Watkins. Anthology of American Negro Literature (New York:
Random House, 1944).   DHU/MO
Gospel Singers and their religious orientation.

6009. "Book Review: Agola Proverbs." Journal of American
Folklore (5:2, Apr.-Je., 1892), pp. 168-69.   Pam. File,
DHU/R

The potential for ethnological psychology inherent in folk-
lore.

6010. Botkin, Benjamin Albert. "Negro Religious Songs and Ser-
vices." Library of Congress, Division of Music, Recording
Laboratory Album 10 (AAFS 46-AAFS 50), 1943.   DHU/R;
NN/Sch
Phonodisc.

6011. Bourguignon, Erika. "The Self, The Behavioral Environment, and the Theory of Spirit Possession." Melford E. Spiro
(ed.). Context and Meaning in Cultural Anthropology (New
York: Free Press, 1965), pp. 39-60.   MiU; WaU; CtY; MH;
RPB; NjR

6012. ----- and Louanna Pettay. "Spirit Possession, Trance
and Cross-Cultural Research." (Annual Spring Meeting,
American Ethnological Society Seattle, Wash.: 1964), pp. 36-46.

6013. "The Boy and the Ghost." (Ghosts as Guardians of Hidden
Trasure. The Boy and the Ghost.) Journal of American Folk-
Lore (12:44, Ja.-Mr., 1899), pp. 64-5.   DHU/R
Microcard.

6014. Boyer, Horace C. "Thomas A. Dorsey, 'Father of Gospel
Music'." Black World (23:9, Jl., 1974), pp. 20-32.
DHU/R

6015. Bradford, R. "Swing Low, Sweet Chariot; Religious Rites
of the Southern Negro." Colliers (96; Sept. 21, 1935), pp. 16-
17+.   DHU

6016. Brawley, Benjamin Griffin. "The Singing of Spirituals."
Southern Workman (63:7, Jl., 1934), pp. 209-13.   DLC;
DHU/MO

A6016. Brewer, John Mason. American Negro Folklore...
Chicago: Quadrangel Book, 1968.   DHU/MO
Negro autho.
Oral Negro Sermons.

6017. ----- Dog Ghosts and Other Texas Negro Folk Tales. Austin: University of Texas Press, 1958. DHU/MO

6018. ----- "Songs of the Slave." Lippincott's Magazine (2;
1868), pp. 617.   DHU

6019. ----- The Word on the Brazos; Negro Preacher Tales
from the Brazos Bottoms of Texas. Austin: University of
Texas Press, 1953.   DHU/R; NcD; FSU

6020. ----- Worser Days and Better Times; the Folklore of the
North Carolina Negro. Chicago: Quadrangle Books, 1965.
IC/H; NjP

6021. Brinton, Daniel Garrison. "Races and Peoples." Journal
of American Folklore (4:11, Jan.-Mr., 1891), p. 87-88.
DHU/R

6022. Bryant, M. Winifred. "Negro Services." American
Missionary Magazine (46:9, Sept., 1892), pp. 301-02. IC/H
A. M. A. worker gives impression of her first attendance
at a southern Methodist Love Feast on New Year's Eve
watch meeting.

6023. Burlin, Natalie. Negro Folk-Song-Hampton Series, Books
I, II, III and IV. New York: G. Schirmer, 1918-19. DHU/MO
Vols. I and II are spirituals, v. III and IV are work songs
and play songs.

6024. Byrne, Donald Edward, Jr. Methodist Itinerant Folklore
of the Nineteenth Century. Doctoral dissertation. Duke Univ.,
1971.

6025. Carawan, Guy and Caudie. Ain't You Got a Right to the
Tree of Life? The People of Johns Island, South Carolina,
Their Faces, Their Words, and Their Songs. New York:

Simon and Schuster, 1967.   DHU/MO
Examples of songs sung in the churches and praise halls of
the people of Johns Island, South Carolina.

6026. Carmichael, Waverly Turner. From the Heart of a Folk.
A Book of Songs. Boston: The Cornhill Co., 1918. DHU/MO;
DLC; ViU; NN

6027. Carter, Lawrence E. "Black Preaching: Poetry and a Text."
Freeing the Spirit (3:1, Spr., 1974), pp. 33-36.   DHU/R

6028. Chamberlain, Alexander F. "Negro Creation Legend."
Journal of American Folklore (3:3, Oct.-Dec., 1890), p. 302.
Pam. File, DHU/R
Excellent comparative myth. Implications for Black self-
identity.

6029. ----- "Primitive Woman as Poet." Journal of American
Folklore (16:2, Apr.-Je., 1903; 16:3, Oct.-Dec., 1903), pp.
205-221.   DHU/R

6030. Chamberlain, Mary E. "Superstitions of Negroes in New
Orleans." Journal of American Folk-Lore (5:19, Oct.-Dec.,
1892), pp. 330-34.   DHU/R

6031. Chambers, Herbert A. The Treasury of Negro Spirituals.
New York: Emerson Books, 1959.   DHU/R; A&M
Score and lyrics.

6032. Chapman, Maria Weston. Songs of the Free and Humns of
Christian Freedom. Boston: I. Knapp, 1836.   DLC

6033. Charters, Samuel B., (ed.). "An Introduction to Gospel
Song." Record, Book, & Film Sales, 1962. 2 s. 12 in. 33
rpm.
Phonodisc.

6034. Cheek, William F. Black Resistance Before the Civil War.
Beverly Hills, Calif.: Glencoe Press, 1970.   DHU/MO
Chapter 2, includes information on Spirituals and secular
songs and slave religion.

6035. Chirgwin, A. M. "Vogue of the Negro Spiritual." Edinburgh Review (247; Ja., 1928), pp. 57-74.   DHU

6036. Christensen, A. M. H. Afro-American Folk Lore. New
York: Negro Universities Press, 1892.   DHU/R

6037. Clark, Edgar Rogie, (comp.). Copper Sun: A Collection
of Negro Folk Songs, For Voice and Piano. Bryn Mawr, Pa.:
T. Presser, 1957.   DLC

6038. ----- "Negro Folk Music in America." Journal
of American Folk-Lore (64:253, Jl.-Sept., 1951),
pp. 281-7.   DHU/R
Microcard.
Discussion of music as the Negroes' primary means of survival and "cultural self-determination" in a discriminatory
society.

6039. Clark, Joseph D. "North Carolina Popular Beliefs and Superstitions." North Carolina Folklore (18; Ja., 1970), pp. 1-68.
DLC; CtY

6040. Clarke, Mary Olmsed. "Song Games of Negro Children in
Virginia." Journal of American Folklore (3:3, Oct.-Dec.,
1890), pp. 288-90.   Pam. File, DHU/R
Ring games of Negro children.

6041. Cleveland, James T. "Two Sermons." Word Records.
Phonodisc.
Sermons by a Negro minister.

6042. Cocke, Sarah Johnson. Old Mammy Tales from Dixie Land.
New York: Kraus Reprint Co., 1971.   DHU/R
Reprint of 1926 edition.

6043. Cohen, Lily Young. Lost Spirituals, by Lily Young Cohen,
with Thirty-Six Illustrations by Kenneth K. Pointer, and Forty-

One Plates of Musical Compositions as Composed by Negroes
and Set Down in Music by the Author. New York: W. Neale,
1928.   NcD; DLC; DHU/R

6044. "Collecting and Preserving Traditions and Customs Peculiar
to Negroes." Folk-Lore and Ethnology. Southern Workman
(22:12, Dec., 1893), pp. 180-81.   DLC; DHU/MO
"Notes and observation on the following subjects were re-
quested: Folk-tales; Customs; Traditions of ancestry in
Africa; African words surviving in speech or song, etc.
All subjects are defined and explained.

6045. Cone, James H. "Black Spirituals: A Theological Interpre-
tation." Theology Today (29:1, Apr., 1972), pp. 54-69.
DHU/R
Negro author.

6046. ----- The Spirituals and the Blues: an Interpretation.
New York: Seabury Press, 1972.   TSewU-T; DHU/R
Negro author.

6047. "Conjuring and Conjure-Doctors in the Southern United
States." (Folk-Lore Scrap Book.). Journal of American
Folk-Lore (9:33, Apr.-Je., 1896), pp. 143-47.
DHU/R
Microcard.

6048. Courlander, Harold, (ed.). "Negro Folk Music of Africa
and America." Folkways Records.
Phonodisc.
Includes pamphlet on the influence of African music on
American music.

6049. Crane, T. F. "The Diffusion of Popular Tales." Journal
of American Folklore. (1, Apr.-Je., 1888), pp. 14-15.
Pam. File, DHU/R
Negro Folk Origins.

6050. Crawford, George W. "Jazzin'God." The Crisis (36:2,
Feb., 1929), p. 45.   DLC; DHU/MO

6051. Crite, Allan Rohan. Were You There When They Crucified
My Lord; a Negro Spiritual in Illustrations. Cambridge, Mass.:
Harvard University Press, 1944.   MNtcA; DHU/R

6052. "Crossing the Back". (Folk-Lore Scrap Book). Journal of
American Folklore (5:16, Ja.-Mr., 1892), pp. 63-4. DHU/R
Negro superstitions.
Microcard.

6053. Crowley, Daniel John. "Negro Folklore: An Africanist's
View." Texas Quarterly (Aut., 1962), pp. 65-71.   NNRIS

6054. Culin, Steuart. "Concerning Negro Sorcery in the United
States." Journal of American Folklore (3:3, Oct.-Dec., 1890),
pp. 281-87.   Pam.

6055. "Cures by Conjure Doctors." (Folk-Lore Scrap Book.)
Journal of American Folk-Lore (12:47, Oct.-Dec., 1899), pp.
288-89.   DHU/R
Microcard.

6056. "Customs and Superstitions in Louisiana." Journal of Amer-
ican Folklore (1:2, Jl.-Sept., 1888), pp. 136-39.
Pam. File, DHU/R
Plantation life and slavery before the war.

6057. Dana, Marvin. "Voodoo its Effects on the Negro Race."
Donald P. DeNevi and Doris A Holmes (eds.). Racism at the
Turn of the Century: Documentary Perspectives 1870-1910
(San Rafael, Calif.: Leswing Press, 1973), pp. 344-54. DHU/R;
NN; NjR; PPL
Reprint of an article published in The Metropolitan Magazine,
August 1908.

6058. Davidson, Levette J. A Guide to American Folklore. Westport, Conn.: Greenwood, 1951.   NN/Sch

6059. Davis, Henderson Sheridan. The Religious Experience Underlying the Negro Spiritual. Doctoral dissertation. Boston University, 1950.

6060. Davis, M. E. M. "Notes and Queries; Southern Tales." Journal of American Folklore (18:3, Jl.-Sept., 1905), pp. 250-52.   DHU/R

6061. Dean, Emmett S., (ed.). Victory for Christian Work and Worship... Nashville: National Baptist Publishing Board, 1918.   SCBHC
    165 hymns, & 1 p. of index.

6062. Denham, William Ernest. Gospel Song Movement. Doctoral dissertation. Southern Baptist Theological Seminary, 1916.

6063. "Desecration of "Spirituals"." Editorial. Southern Workman (51:11, Nov., 1922), pp. 501-3.   DLC; DHU/MO
    "A considerable protest in the daily press against the use of Negro "spirituals" in theatres."

6064. Dett, R. Nathaniel. "The Emancipation of Negro Music." Southern Workman (47:4, Apr., 1918), pp. 172-76. DLC; DHU/MO

6065. Dillard, James A. Developing Music Activities in the Negro Church with Emphasis Expecially on the Concord Baptist Church of Christ, Brooklyn, New York. Doctoral dissertation, Columbia University, Teachers College, 1951.

6066. "Diviniation with the Sifter." (Folk-Lore Scrap Book). Journal of American Folk-Lore (5:16, Ja.-Mr., 1892), p. 63.
                                                                        DHU/R
    Microcard.
    Guinean survivals among the American Negro.

6067. Dobie, James F. (ed.). Follow de Drinkin Gou'd. Dallas: Southern Methodist University Press, 1965.   IC/H
    "Texas Folk-lore Society, Proceedings 1927."

6068. ----- (ed.). Tone the Bell Easy. Dallas: Southern Methodist Universities' Press, 1965.   IC/H
    Negro folklore.

6069. Dog Ghost, and Other Texas Negro Folk Tales. Austin: Univ. of Texas Press, 1958.   O

6070. Dorson, Richard Mercer. American Negro Folktales. Greenwich, Conn.: Fawcett Publication, 1967. DHU/R
    Selected primarily from the compiler's Negro folktales from Pine Bluff, Arkansas and Calvin, Michigan, 1958.

6071. ----- (ed.). Folklore and Folklife: An Introduction. Chicago: The University of Chicago Press, 1972. CoU; DHU/R
    Chapter 10, Folk religion by John C. Messenger.

6072. ----- Folklore: Selected Essays. Bloomington: Indiana University Press, 1972.   DHU/R

6073. ----- (ed.). Negro Folktales in Michigan. Cambridge: Harvard Univ. Press, 1956.   O

6074. "Dry Bones." Ruth Miller (ed.). Black American Literature (California: Glencoe Press, 1971), pp. 125-27.   DHU/R
    A sermon.

6075. Dunbar, Paul Laurence. "An Ante-Bellum Sermon." Freeing the Spirit (1:4; 2:1, Fall-Wint.; Spr., 1972; 1973), pp. 35-36.   DHU/R
    Folk Negro sermon.

6076. Dungee, John Riley. Random Rhymes, Formal and Dialect, Sermons and Humorous, Racial, Religious, Patriotic and Sentimental. Norfolk, Va.: Guide Publishing Co., Pointers, 1929.   DHU/MO
    Negro author.

6077. Eddington, Neil Arthur. The Urban Plantation: the Ethnography of an Oral Tradition in a Negro Community. Berkeley, Calif.: n.p., 1967.   NjP

6078. Edet, Edna. "Black Protest Music." Afro-American Studies (2:2, Sept., 1971), pp. 107-16.   DHU/R
    "An examination of the evolution of the social commentary songs of the American Slave from the African beginnings up to the end of the Civil War."

6079. Elligan, Irvin. "The Black Spirituals and the Christmas Carols." Spectrum (49:4, Wint., 1973), pp. 18-21. DHU/R
    Negro author.

6080. Emmons, Martha. Deep Like the Rivers; Stories of My Negro Friends. Austin, Tex.: Encino Press, 1969. NjP; DLC; ICN; MH
    Folklore, Negro.

6081. Engelsen, Nils Johan. Glossolalia and Other Forms of Inspired Speech According to I Corinthians 12-14. Doctoral dissertation. Yale University, 1971.

6082. Evans, David K. "Parallels in West African, West Indian and North Carolina Folklore." North Carolina Folklore (27:2, Nov., 1969), pp. 77-84.   DGW

6083. Faulkner, William J. "The Influence of Folklore Upon the Religious Experience of the Ante-Bellum Negro." Journal of Religious Thought (24:3, Aut.-Wint., 1967-68), pp. 26-28.
                                                                        DHU/R

6084. Ferris, William R., Jr. Mississippi Black Folklore: A Research Bibliography and Discography. Hattiesburg, Miss.: Univ. and College Press of Mississippi, 1971.   DHU/R

6085. ----- "The Negro Conversion Experience." Keystone Folklore Quarterly (15; 1970), pp. 35-51.   DLC

6086. Fields, Arlene L. "Revival of Negro Spirituals." Christian Herald (95:4, Apr., 1972), pp. 6+.   DHU/R

6087. "Fish Stories." (Folk-Lore and Ethnology.) Southern Workman (26:11, Nov., 1897), pp. 229-30.   DLC; DHU/MO

6088. Fisher, Miles Mark. "Deep River!" Okon Edet Uya (ed.). Black Brotherhood, Afro-Americans and Africa. (Lexington, Mass.: D. C. Heath and Co., 1971), pp. 2-23.   DHU/MO
    "Examining the slave songs, now increasingly recognized as oral historical documents. Author shows how Africa was central to the slaves's longing for his freedom."

6089. "Folk-Lore from St. Helena, South Carolina." Journal of American Folk-Lore (38:148, Apr.-Je., 1925), pp. 217-38.
                                                                        DHU/R
    Microcard.
    Includes Negro spirituals.

6090. "The Folk Sermon." Ruth Miller (ed.). Blackamerican Literature, 1760-Present (Beverly Hills, Cal.: Glencoe Press, 1971), pp. 115-135.   DHU/MO
    Commentary and examples: C. C. Lovelace, "The Wounds of Jesus;" Anonymous, "Dry Bones;" John J. Jasper, "De Sun Do Move."

6091. "Folk Songs: the South." Folkways Records FA 2457. 1965. 2s. 12 in. 33 1/3 rpm.   DLC
    Phonodisc.
    Sung by Bernice Reagon. Negro spirituals.

6092. Fortier, Alcee. "Customs and Superstitions in Louisiana." Journal of American Folk-Lore, (1:2, Jl.-Sept., 1888), pp. 136-40.
    Microcard.

6093. Franklin, C. L. "The Golden Calf, Four Sermons." Jewel Records.
    Negro minister.
    Phonodisc.

6094. "Games." Our Hampton (Institute) Folk Lorist. (Folk-Lore and Ethnology.). Southern Workman (22:5, My., 1894), pp. 84-85.
DLC; DHU/MO

6095. Georgia Writers' Project, Work Projects Administration. Drums and Shadows, Survival Studies Among the Georgia Coastal Negroes. Garden City, N.Y.: Anchor Books, 1972. TSewU-T; IC/H; DHU/MO; DLC
Folklore.

6096. Gerber, A. "Uncle Remus Traced to the Old World." Journal of American Folklore (4:15, Oct.-Dec., 1891), pp. 245-57.
Pam. File, DHU/R
Also microcard.

6097. The Ghost in Negro Folklore." (Folk-Lore and Ethnology.) Southern Workman (27:3, Mr., 1898), pp. 57-58. DLC; DHU/MO

6098. Gielow, Martha Sawyer. Mammy's Reminiscences, and Other Sketches. New York: A. S. Barnes and Company, 1898.
NjP

6099. Gifford, Edward S. The Evil Eye: Studies in the Folklore of Vision. New York: The Macmillan Company, 1958. ICU; ViU; MiU; NcD; CtY; MH; NIC; NjR; IU; MoU; KU; NjPT; CLU; PP; OCl; NN; CSt; TsU-M; CU; LU; WU; OU; MnU
Book review by Richard M. Dorson in Journal of American Folklore (73:288, Apr.-Je., 1960), pp. 174-75.
Microcard, DHU/R

6100. Gilbert, Mercedes. Aunt Sara's Wooden God. College Park, Md.: McGrath, 1970.
DHU; INU
Reprint of 1938 edition.

6101. Golden Nuggets. "No Man is Sweeter Than Jesus and Keep Pushing for Jesus." Dun Gee. 45 rmp 100.
Phonodisc.

6102. Gonzales, Ambrose Elliott. With Aesop Along the Black Border. New York: Negro Universities Press, 1969., 1924. Ic/H
Negro folklore.

6103. Gonzales, Marie Infanta. "Going Back to the Spirituals." Freeing the Spirit (1:2, Spr., 1972), pp. 3-5. DHU/R
"Excerpts from Master of Music dissertation", by a Catholic.

6104. "Gospel Music in the United States." Harry A. Ploski, (ed.). Reference Library of Black America (New York: Bellwether Pub. Co., 1971), Book 2, pp. 221-23. DHU

6105. Green, David B. "Folk Singing in Worship." Theology Today (26:3, Oct., 1969), pp. 323+. DHU/R

6106. Greenwood, Theresa. Psalms of a Black Mother. Anderson, Indiana: Warner Press, 1970. DHU/R
"Reflects the Black Mother's relationship to God."

6107. "Hags and Their Ways." (Folk-lore and Ethnology). Southern Workman (22:2, Fe., 1894), pp. 26-7. DLC; DHU/MO
"The hag in Negro folk-lore is the very essence of nightmare, about whose personality gather all the morbid fancies of distempered dreams."

6108. Hall, Julien A. "Negro Conjuring and Tricking." Journal of American Folklore (10:38, Jl.-Sept., 1897), pp. 241-243.
Pam. File; DHU/R

6109. Hammon, Jupiter. "Dialogue: The Kind Master and the Dutiful Servant" Ruth Miller (ed.). Blackamerican Literature (California: Glencoe Press, 1971), pp. 7-9. DHU/R

6110. Haskell, Joseph A. "Sacrificial Offerings Among North Carolina Negroes." Journal of American Folklore (4:14, Jl.-Sept., 1891), pp. 267-69. Pam. File, DHU/R

6111. Haskins, James. Witchcraft, Mysticism and Magic in the Black World. New York: Harper & Row, 1974. DHU/R

6112. Hawkins, Edwin R. "The Gospel." Freeing the Spirit (1:2, Spr., 1972), pp. 7-9. DHU/R
"Gospel: soul participation in praise and worship of God."

6113. Hawkins, John. "An Old Mauma's Folklore." Journal of American Folklore (9:33, Apr.-Je., 1896), pp. 129-31.
DHU/R
Microcard.
Superstitious tales from Maum' Sue of lower South Carolina.

6114. Hayes, Roland. My Songs, Afro-American Religious Folk Songs. Boston: Little, Brown & Co., 1949. CoDU

6115. Haywood, Charles. A Bibliography of North American Folklore and Folksong. New York: Doves Pub., 1961. DHU/MO; CoDU; DHU/R

6116. Henry, Mellinger (ed.). "Negro Songs from Georgia." Journal of American Folk-Lore (44:174, Oct.-Dec., 1931), pp. 437-47.
DHU/R
Microcard.
Hymns and spirituals.

6117. Hensey, Andrew Fitch. Animism: The Religion of Fear. n.p.: n.p., n.d.
TN/DCHS

6118. Herskovits, Melville J. "Some Next Steps in the Study of Negro Folklore." Frances S. Herskovits, (ed.). The New World Negro (Bloomington: Indiana University Press, 1966), pp. 174-82.
DHU/R
Also in Journal of American Folklore (55:219, 1943), pp. 1-7.

6119. Hicks, Richard Ross. "Sweetback, Reverend LeRoy, and the Black Gospel Choir on Campus." Toward Wholeness (1:1, Sum., 1972), pp. 20-22.
DHU/R
Written by Southeastern Regional Secretary, United Ministires in Higher Education, Atlanta, Georgia.

6120. "High Priest of the Devil." Sepia (16; Oct., 1967), pp. 20-23.
DHU/MO

6121. Hilger, Rothe. The Religious Expression of the Negro. Master's thesis. Vanderbilt University, 1931.
Author describes worship, including preaching, singing, handshaking and all responses of the participants.

6122. Hobson, Charles. "Hall Johnson: Preserver of the Negro Spiritual." The Crisis (73:9, Nov., 1966), pp. 480-85. DLC; DHU/MO

6123. Holliday, O. L. "Soul Brother, Soul Sister, Soul Devil." Jewel Records.
Phonodisc.
Sermon by Negro minister.

6124. Holzknecht, K. J. "Some Negro Song Variants From Louisville." Journal of American Folk-Lore (41:162, Oct.-Dec., 1928), pp. 558-78. DHU/R
Microcard.
Includes religious songs.

6125. Hood, Ralph W., Jr. "Normative and Motivational Determinants of Reported Religious Experience in Two Baptist Samples." Review of Religious Research (13:3, Spr., 1972), pp. 192-96.
DHU/R

6126. "How to Catch a Hag." Folk-Lore Meeting. Hampton Institute. (Folk-Lore and Ethnology.). Southern Workman (22:3, Mr., 1894), pp. 46-47. DLC; DHU/MO

6127. Howard University. Washington, D.C. Dept. of Sociology and Anthropology. Religion and Magic Among the Negroes of Washington, D.C.: Howard University, 1946. DHU/MO

6128. Howe, R. Wilson. "The Negro and His Songs." Southern Workman (51:8, Ag., 1922), pp. 381-83. DLC; DHU/MO
Classification of Negro folk-songs.

6129. Hsu, Francis L. K. "A Neglected Aspect of Witchcraft
Studies." Journal of American Folk-Lore (73:287, Ja.-Mr.,
1960), pp. 35-38.   DHU/R
   Microcard.
   Contrasts Western and non-Western outlook

6130. Hughes, Langston. "Simple Prays a Prayer." Nick Aaron
Ford, (ed.). Black Insights: Significant Literature by Black
Americans-1760- to the Present (Waltham, Mass.: Ginn and
Co., 1971), pp. 146-47.   DHU/R
   A short story from The Best of Simple by Langston Hughes.

6131. ----- "Trouble with the Angels." Nick Aaron Ford, (ed.).
Black Insights: Significant Literature by Black Americans-1760
to the Present (Waltham, Mass.: Ginn and Co., 1971), pp.
143-45.   DHU/R
   The trials of the black touring company of the play, Green
   Pastures.

6132. ----- "The Virgin of Guadalupe." The Crisis (23:2, Dec.,
1921), p. 77.   DHU/MO; DLC
   Negro author.

6133. ----- and Arna Bontemps, (eds.). The Book of Negro Folk-
lore. New York: Dodd and Mead, 1958.   IC/H; CoDU

6134. Hunter, Rosa. "The Rich Ghost." (Folk-Lore Scrap-Book.)
Journal of American Folk-Lore (12:44, Ja.-Mr., 1899), p. 64.
DHU/R
   Microcard.

6135. Hurston, Zora Neale. Mules and Men. New York: Negro
Universities Press, 1969.   IC/H; NNCor; NjP; PPT
   Voodooism.
   Negro author.

6136. ----- Seraph on the Suwanee. New York: Charles Scribner's
Sons, 1948.   O

6137. ----- Tell My Horse. Phila.: J. B. Lippincott Co., 1938.
PPT; NjH; DHU/MO
   Folklore.

6138. Hyatt, Harry Middleton. Hoodoo, Conjuration, Witchcraft,
Rootwork. Hannibal, Mo.: Western Pub., 1970. CSt; DAU;
NcRS; NN; CU-SB; LU; InU; TxFTC
   "Beliefs accepted by many Negroes and white persons, these
   being orally recorded among Blacks and whites."

6139. Ingersoll, Ernest. "Decoration of Negro Graves." Journal
of American Folk-Lore (5:16, Ja.-Mr., 1892), pp. 68-69.
DHU/R
   Microcard.
   Negro fetishism in Columbia, S. C.

6140. "An Introduction to Gospel Songs." Compiled by Samuel
B. Charters.
   Phonodisc.

6141. Jackson, Mahalia. "Everytime I Feel the Spirit."
   Phonodisc.

6142. ----- "Mahalia Jackson's Greatest Hits."
   Phonodisc.

6143. Jahn, Janheinz. Neo-African Literature: A History of Black
Writing. New York: Grove Press, 1968.   DHU/MO
   Chapter 8, 'Minstrelsy' and Voodoo;
   Chapter 9, The Negro Spiritual.

6144. Jasper, John J. "De Sun Do Move." Ruth Miller, (ed.).
Black American Literature (California: Glencoe Press, 1971),
pp. 128-35.   DHU/R
   Folk sermon.

6145. "Jazz in Our Religion." Produced, Directed and Edited by
John Jeremy. New York: London Film Festival, 1972.

50 min. B & W.
   Film.

6146. Johnson, Guy B. Folk Culture of St. Helena Island. Chapel
Hill: University of North Carolina Press, 1930.   IC/H;
DHU/R
   Includes a discussion of the origin of the Negro spiritual.

6147. ----- John Henry; Tracking Down a Negro Legend.
Chapel Hill: The University of North Carolina Press, 1929.
IC/H

6148. ----- "The Negro Spiritual a Problem in Anthropology."
American Anthropologist (33; 1931), pp. 157-71.   DHU

6149. Johnson, James Weldon. The Autobiography of an Ex-
Coloured Man. New York: Knopf, 1912.   DHU/MO
   See pages 173-82 for a fictional ... but revealing account
   of a religious revival or big meeting.

6150. ----- "The Creation." Nick Aaron Ford, (ed.). Black In-
sights: Significant Literature by Black Americans, 1760 to the
Present. (Waltham, Mass.: Ginn and Co., 1971). DHU/R
   A Negro folk sermon.

6151. ----- "Go Down Death." Thomas R. Frazier, (ed.). A
Afro-American History: Primary Resources (New York:
Harcourt, Brace & World, Inc., 1970), pp. 272-75. DHU/R;
DHU/MO
   A funeral sermon.

6152. ----- "God's Trombones." Folkways, F19788.
   Audiotape.

6153. ----- "James Weldon Johnson, 1871-1938, from God's
Trombones." Ruth Miller, (ed.). Blackamerican Literature,
1760-Present (Beverly Hills, Cal.: Glencoe Press, 1971),
pp. 198-205.   DHU/MO
   Includes brief biographical information on Johnson and two
   poems, The Crucifixion and The Judgment Day from his
   God's Trombones.
   Negro author.

6154. ----- "Listen Lord." Freeing the Spirit (1:4, 2:1, Fall-
Wint., 1972, Spr., 1973), p. 28.   DHU/R
   Excerpt from Trombone's collection.

6155. ----- "Listen, Lord (A Prayer from God's Trombones)."
Nick Aaron Ford, (ed.). Black Insights: Significant Liter-
ature by Black Americans-1760 to the Present (Waltham, Mass.:
Ginn and Co., 1971), p. 65.   DHU/R
   Negro author.

6156. ----- "O Black and Unknown Bards." Nick Aaron Ford, (ed.).
Black Insights: Significant Literature by Black Americans-
1760 to the Present (Waltham, Mass.: Ginn and Co., 1971), pp.
65-66.   DHU/R
   A poem speculating on how Spirituals were conceived, taken
   from St. Peter Relates an Incident by James Weldon Johnson.
   Negro author.

6157. ----- "The Prodigal Son." Arthur P. Davis and Saunders
Redding, (eds.). Cavalcade: Negro American Writing from
1760 to the Present (Boston: Houghton Mifflin, 1971), pp. 254-
57.   DHU/MO
   Negro author.

6158. ----- St. Peter Relates an Incident of the Resurrection Day.
New York: The Viking Press, 1935.   DHU/R
   Negro author.

6159. Johnston, William Preston. "Two Negro Tales." Journal of
American Folk-Lore (9:34, Jl.- Sept., 1896), pp. 194-98.
DHU/R
   Microcard.
   Tales from Avery's Island in southwestern Louisiana.

6160. Jones, Alice Marie. The Negro Sermon, a Study in the Sociology of Folk Culture. Masters thesis. Fisk University, 1942.

6161. Jones, Bessie Washington. "A Descriptive and Analytical Study of the American Negro Folktale." 1967.   NjP
      Film.

6162. Jones, Charles Colcock. Negro Myths From the Georgia C Coast Told in the Vernacular. Boston: Houghton Mifflin, 1888. DHU/MO; CoDU
      New edition: Detroit; Singing Tree Press Book Tower, 1969.

6163. Jones, LeRoi. "A Black Mass." Class Tape 34.
      Audiotape.

6164. Jones-Williams, Pearl. "Afro-American Gospel Music. A Brief Historical and Analytical Survey (1930-1970)." Vada E. Butcher. Development Materials for a One Year Course in African Music for the General Undergraduate Student. Project of Fine Arts Dept., Howard University. (Wash., D.C.: U.S. Dept. of Health, Education and Welfare, 1970), pp. 201-19. DHU/R

6165. Kennedy, Louise. "Voodoo and Vodun." Journal of American Folk-Lore (3:10, Jl.-Sept., 1890), p. 241.   DHU/R
      Microcard.

6166. Kennedy, William T. "The Genius of Black Preaching." A. M. E. Zion Quarterly Review (83:2, Sum., 1971), pp. 100-08.   DHU/R

6167. Kent, G. E. "Ralph Ellison and Afro-American Folk and Cultural Tradition." College Language Association Journal (13; Mr., 1970), pp. 265-76.   DAU

6168. Kershaw, Alvin L. "From the Heart, A Reflection on the Essence of Jazz." Freeing the Spirit (1:2, Spr., 1972), pp. 18-20.   DHU/R
      "True jazz...is for me far more an act of worship than singing some of the so-called religious songs..."

6169. Kiev, Ari, (ed.). Magic, Faith, and Healing. New York: Free Press of Glencoe, 1964.   NN/Sch

6170. King, Ben. Ben King's Southland Melodies. Freeport, N.Y.: Books for Libraries Press, 1972.   DHU/R

6171. King, Dearing H. "Worship." Home Missions (43:4, Apr., 1972), pp. 7-8.   Pam. File, DHU/R

6172. Krueger, E. T. "Negro Religious Expression." American Journal of Sociology (38; Jl., 1932), pp. 22-31.   DHU

6173. Landeck, Beatrice. Echoes of Africa in Folk Songs of the Americas. New York: David Mc Kay Co., 1961. DHU/MO

6174. Leach, Maria (ed.). Standard Dictionary of Folklore, Mythology and Legend. V. I. New York: Funk and Wagnalls Company, 1949.
      Includes "African and New World Negro".

6175. Lee, Collins. "Some Negro Lore From Baltimore." Journal of American Folk-Lore (5:17, Apr.-Je., 1892), pp. 110-12.   DHU/R

      Microcard
      Superstitions.

6176. Lester, David. "Voodoo Death: Some New Thoughts on an Old Phenomena." American Anthropologist (74' 1972), pp. 386-90.   DHU
      Comment by Francis J. Chine, "A Comment on Voodoo Death." American Anthropologist (75; Feb., 1973), p. 312.   DHU

6177. "Let My People Go: Spirituals." Thomas R. Frazier (ed.). Afro-American History: Primary Sources (New York: Harcourt, Brace & World, Inc., 1970), pp. 91-95.
      DHU/R; DHU/MO

6178. Lett, Anna. "Some West Tennessee Superstitions About Conjurers, Witches, Ghosts and the Devil." Tennessee Folklore Society Bulletin (36:2, Je., 1970), pp. 37-45. CtY GEU; NN; OU; TNV; TXU

6179. Lomax, Alan, (ed.). "Afro-American Spirituals, Work Songs and Ballads." From the Archives of American Folk Song. Wash., D.C.: The Library of Congress Music Division Recording Laboratory.
      Phonodisc.

6180. Lomax, John Avery and Alan Lomax. American Ballads and Folk Songs. New York: The Macmillan Company, 1934.
      TSewU-T; DLC

6181. Louis-Jean, Antonio. La Crise de Possession et la Possession Dramatique. Montreal: Lemeac, 1970. NNCor; PPT
      Voodooism.

6182. Lovelace, C. C. "The Wounds of Jesus." Ruth Miller, (ed.). Black American Literature (California: Glencoe Press, 1971), pp. 119-25.   DHU/R
      Folk sermon.

6183. Lovell, John, Jr. Black Song: The Forge and the Flame. The Story of How the Afro-American Spiritual Was Hammered Out. New York: Macmillan, 1972.   DHU/R; TSewU-T; DLC

6184. Mann, Mary and Page Newton. "Aunt Deborah Goes Visiting: A Sketch From Virginian Life." Journal of American Folklore (4:15, Oct.-Dec., 1891), pp. 354-56. Pam. File, DHU/R
      "Sketch of an old colored mammy."

6185. Martin, D. S. "On Religious Excitement: The Peculair Craze of Kentucky Negroes with the Appearance of General Fremont." Journal of American Folklore (4:12, Ja.-Mr., 1891), pp. 5-6.   Pam. File, DHU/R
      Lecture excerpt.

6186. Martin, Kevin. The Complete Book of Voodoo, by Robert W. Pelton. New York: Putnam, 1972
      Robert W. Pelton, pseud. of Kevin Martin.

6187. Mayle, Bessie H. History and Interpretation of the Pre-Reformation Carol and the Negro Spiritual. Masters thesis. Boston University, 1932.   INU
      Negro author.

6188. McAdams, Nettie F. Folk-Songs of the American Negro; a Collection of Unprinted Texts Preceded by a General Survey of the Traits of Negro. Masters thesis. Univ. of Calif., 1923.

6189. McGee, Daniel Bennett. Religious Beliefs and Ethical Motifs of the Negro Spirituals. Masters thesis. Southeastern Baptist Theological Seminary, 1960.

6190. McGhee, N. B. "The Folk Sermon: A Facet of the Black Literary Heritage." College Language Association Journal (13:5, 1969), pp. 51-61.   DAU

6191. McKay, Claude. "Baptism." Wayne F. Cooper, (ed.). The Passion of Claude McKay... (New York: Schocken Books, 1973), p. 125.   DHU/R

6192. ----- "St. Isaac's Church, Petrograd." Wayne F. Cooper, (ed.). The Passion of Claude McKay...(New York: Schocken Books, 1973), p. 127.   DHU/R
      "A poem."
      Negro author.

6193. McKinney, Samuel B. "Hot Winds of Change." William M. Philpot, (ed.). Best Black Sermons (Valley Forge: Judson Press, 1972), pp. 40-9.   DHU/R
      A sermon. Baptist minister.

6194. Miller, Ruth. Blackamerican Literature, 1760-Present. Beverly Hills, Cal.: Glencoe Press, 1971.   DHU/MO

(Miller, Ruth cont.)
        For a consideration of spirituals see sections, Folk Poetry
        and Anonymous, pp. 108-115. For Sermons, pp. 115-35.

6195. Minor, Mary Willis. "How to Keep off Witches (As Related
        by a Negro)." Journal of American Folk-Lore (11:40, Ja.-Mr.,
        1898), p. 76.   DHU/R
        Microcard.

6196. Mitchell, Henry H. "Black Preaching." Freeing the Spirt
        (1:4, 11:1, Fall-Wint., 1972, Spr., 1973), pp. 5-13.   DHU/R

6197. ----- "Celebration of a Stolen Gospel." Home Missions
        (43:4, Apr., 1972), pp. 15-16.   Pam. File, DHU/R

6198. ----- "Negro Worship and Universal Need." Christian
        Century (83:13, Mr. 30, 1966), pp. 396-98.   DHU/R
        "Discussion." Christian Century (83:24, Je. 15, 1966),
        pp. 780+.   DHU/R

6199. "Modern Conjuring in Washington." (Folk-Lore Scrap Book.)
        Journal of American Folk-Lore (12:47, Oct.-Dec., 1899), pp.
        289-90.   DHU/R
        Microcard.

6200. Molette, Carlton W., II. "The Way to Viable Theater?
        Afro-American Ritual Drama." Black World (22:6, Apr.,
        1973), pp. 5-13.   Pam. File, DHU/R; DHU/MO

6201. Moore, LeRoy, Jr. "The Spiritual: Soul of Black Religion."
        Church History (40:1, Mr., 1971), pp. 79-81.   DAU/W
        Also: American Quarterly (23; Dec., 1971), pp. 658-76.
        DHU; DAU

6202. Moore, Ruby A. "Superstitions of Georgia." Journal of
        American Folklore (7:26, Jl.-Sept., 1894; 9:34, Jl.-Sept.,
        1896).   DHU/R
        Microcard.
        Universality of beliefs, traditions, and superstitions among
        "lower" Southern whites and Negroes.

6203. Morand, Paul. Magie Noire. Paris: B. Grasset, 1928.
                                                      O

6204. Moving Star Hall Singers. "Been in the Storm So Long."
        Spirituals and Shouts. Children's Game Songs. Recorded at
        John's Island, South Carolina by Guy Caravan.
        Phonodisc.

6205 Moving Star Hall Singers and Alan Lomax. "Sea Island Folk
        Festival." Recorded at John's Island, South Carolina.
        Phonodisc.

6206. Moyd, Olin P. Black Preaching: The Style and Design of
        Dr. Sandy F. Ray. Masters thesis. Howard University, School
        of Religion, 1973.

6207. ----- "Elements in Black Preaching." Journal of Relgious
        Thought (30:1, Spr.-Sum., 1973), pp. 52-62.   DHU/R

6208. ----- "The Word in the Black Church." Freeing the Spirit
        (1:4; 2:1, Fall-Wint., 1972, Spr., 1973), pp. 22-27. DHU/R
        "Preaching."
        Negro author.

6209. Mtumishi. "Black Soul Creations." Freeing the Spirit (1:1
        Ag., 1971), pp. 32-47.   DHU/R

6210. Murray, Ellen. "One of the Least." A Bit of Folklore.
        Southern Workman (31:10, Oct., 1902).   DLC; DHU/MO

6211. Myers, James G. God's Trombones. Doctoral dissertation.
        Columbia University, 1965.
        Used the text of James Weldon Johnson's God's Trombones
        as the basis for an original work for an original work for sl
        solo voices, mixed choruses and brass instruments.

6212. The National Baptist Hymnal Arranged for Use in Churches,
        Sunday Schools and Young People's Societies, R. H. Boyd,
        editor; William Rosburgh, Musical editor. 3rd ed. Nashville,
        Tenn.: Natl. Baptist Publishing Board, 1903.   SCBHC
        pp. 440-3 "Articles of faith which should be adopted by
        Baptist churches at the time of organization."

6213. Neal, James H. Ju-ju in My Life. London: Herrap, 1966.
                                                      DLC

6214. "Negro Conjuring and Dancing in Arkansas." Journal of
        American Folklore (1:1, Apr.-Je., 1888), p. 83.
                                          Pam. File, DHU/R
        The Negro as a "typical" conjurer.

6215. "Negro Folk-Songs." Southern Workman (24:2, Feb., 1895),
        pp. 31-2.   DHU/MO; DLC

6216. "Negro Hymn of the Judgement Day." Journal of American
        Folklore (9:34, Jl.-Sept., 1896), p. 210. Pam. File, DHU/R
        Microcard.
        North Carolina.

6217. "Negro Spirituals: Origins and Present Significance."
        Robert Murrell Stevenson. Protestant Church Music in Amer-
        ica: A Short Survey of Men and Movements from 1564 to the
        Present. (New York: W. W. Norton, 1966), DLC

6218. "Negro Superstitions of European Origin." Notes and Queries.
        Journal of American Folk-Lore (12:47, Oct.-Dec., 1899), pp.
        294-5.   DHU/R
        Microcard.

6219. Negro Tales from Pine Bluff, Arkansas, and Calvin, Michi-
        gan. Blomington: Indiana Univ. Press, 1958.   O

6220. "The Negro's Contribution to Religious Music." Moody
        Monthly (72:7, Mr., 1972), pp. 36-38.   DHU/R

6221. Neher, Andrew. "A Physiological Explanation of Unusual Be-
        havior in Ceremonies Involving Drums." Human Biology
        (34:2, 1962), pp. 151-61.   DAU; DCU/BI; DGU/S; DHU/MO

6222. Nelson, Alice Ruth (Moore) Dunbar. Masterpieces of Negro
        Eloquence. The Best Speeches Delivered by the Negro From
        the Days of Slavery to the Present Time. New York: The
        Bookery Pub. Co., 1914.   DHU/MO; OWibfU
        Reprinted Johnson Reprint Corp., 1970.
        Includes speeches of Negro ministers.

6223. Nelson, Patricia D. Interpretation of the Negro Spiritual;
        an Annotated Bibliography with an Introduction. May 10, 1972.
        Vertical File,   Vertical File, DHU/MO
        mim.
        Negro author.

6224. Newell, William W. "Additional Collection Essential to
        Correct Theory in Folklore and Mythology." Journal of
        American Folklore (3:8, Ja.-Mr., 1890), p. 28.
                                          Pam. File, DHU/R
        Borrowing phenomenon in Negro lore.

6225. ----- "African Origins of the Caunda Dance and Song."
        Journal of American Folklore (7:24, Ja.-Mr., 1894), p. 70
                                          Pam. File, DHU/R

6226. ----- "The Importance and Utility of the Collection of
        Negro Folk-Lore." Southern Workman (23:7, Jl., 1894),
        pp. 131-32.   DLC; DHU/MO

6227. ----- "Notes from Seven Years Among the Fjort: Toward
        Clearer Uses of the Concept of Folklore." Journal of Amer-
        ican Folklore (2"7, Oct.-Dec., 1898), pp. 302-04.
                                          Pam. File, DHU/R

6228. ----- "Reports of Voodoo Worship in Hayti and Louisiana."
        Journal of American Folk-Lore (2:4, Ja.-Mr., 1889), pp.
        41-47.   DHU/R
        Microcard.

6229. "Nine Negro Spirituals, 1850-61, From Lower South
Carolina." Notes and Queries. Journal of American Folk-
Lore (41:162, Oct.-Dec., 1928), pp. 579-84.   DHU/R
Microcard.

6230. Norvel, William. "The Meaning of Black Liturgy."
Freeing the Spirit (1:1, Ag., 1971), p. 5.   DHU/R

6231. Oertel, Hanns. "Notes on Six Negro Myths From the
Georgia Coast." American Journal of Folklore (2:3, Jl.-Sept.,
1889), p. 309.   Pam. File, DHU/R
European Aimicarities cited.

6232. Ol' King David an' the Philistine Boys. New York: Harper
& Brothers, 1930.   O

6233. Ol' Man Adam an' His Chillun; Being the Tales They Tell
About the Time When the Lord Walked the Earth Like a
Natural Man. New York: Harper & Brothers, 1928.   O

6234. Owen, Mary Alicia. Old Rabbit, the Voodoo and Other
Sorcerers. London: Unwin, 1893.   NjP

6235. ----- Voodoo Tales: As Told Among Negroes of the
Southwest. Freeport, New York: Author, 1971. DHU/R;
NjP; IC/H; NNCor; PPT

6236. ----- "Voodooism in Missouri." Journal of American
Folklore (3:8, Ja.-Mr., 1890), pp. 9-10.   Pam. File, DHU/R
European and African Contributions.

6237. Owens, James Garfield. All God's Chillun; Meditations
on Negro Spirituals. Nashville: Abingdon Press, 1971.
TSewU-T; DHU/R; DLC

6238. Owens, Richard McLaughlin. A Comparison of the Negro
Spirituals and the Psalms. Bachelor of Divinity paper. Andover Newton Theological School, 1937.

6239. Packwood, L. H. C. "Cure for an Aching Tooth." Journal
of American Folk-Lore (13:48, Ja.-Mr., 1900), pp. 66-7.
DHU/R
Microcard.

6240. "Parchman Penitentiary." 23 min.
Film.
About convict work chants and gospel singing at Parchman,
the State Penitentiary of Mississippi.

6241. Parsons, Elsie C. Folk-Lore from the Cape Verde Islands.
New York: Published by the American Fok-Lore Society,
1923.   DHU/R
Author collected materials in 1916 and 1917 from Portuguese Negro immigrants from the Cape Verde Islands in
Massachusetts, Rhode Island and the seaports of Connecticut.

6242. ----- Folklore of the Sea Islands, South Carolina. Cambridge, Mass.: American Folklore Society, 1923. IC/H;
DHU/R

6243. Pelton, Robert W. Voodoo Charms and Talismans. New
York: Drake Publishers Inc., 1973.   DHU/R

6244. Pendleton, Louis. "Negro Folklore and Witchcraft in the
South." Journal of American Folklore (3:10, Jl.-Sept., 1890),
pp. 201-7.   DHU/R
Microcard.

6245. Perkins, A. E. "Negro Spirituals From the Far South."
Journal of American Folklore (35:137, Jl.-Sept., 1922), pp.
223-49.   DHU/R
Microcard.

6246. Phenix, George P. "Religious Folk-Songs of the Negro."
Southern Workman (56:4, Apr., 1927), pp. 149-52. DLC;
DHU/MO

6247. Phillips, Romeo E. "Black Folk Music: Setting the Record
Straight." Music Educators Journal (60:4, Dec., 1973), pp.
41-45.   DHU

6248. ----- "White Racism in Black Church Music." Negro History Bulletin (36; Ja., 1973), pp. 17-20.   DHU/MO

6249. [Pierce, Elijah]. "Sermons in Wood; Carvings of Elijah
Pierce, an Ohio Barber..." Ebony (29:9, Jl., 1974), pp. 67-
69+.   Pam. File, DHU/R

6250. Pipes, William Harrison. "Old Time Negro Preaching: An
Interpretative Study. Doctoral dissertation. University of
Michigan, 1945.

6251. ----- Say Amen, Brother! Old-Time Negro Preaching: a
Study in American Frustration. New York: William-Frederick
Press, 1951.   DHU/R; DHU/MO; DLC

6252. Pitman, Frank Wesley. "Fetishism, Witchcraft, and Christianity Among the Slaves." Journal of Negro History (2:4, Oct.,
1926), pp. 650-68.   DHU/MO

6253. Powdermaker, Hortense. After Freedom, A Cultural Study
of the Deep South. New York: Viking Press, 1939. DHU/R;
NN/Sch
Chapter IV, Religion and superstition.

6254. Powell, Adam Clayton, Sr. "Rocking the Gospel Trains."
Negro Digest (9; Apr., 1951), pp. 10-13.   Pam. File, DHU/R;
DHU/MO
"Jazz musicians should stay in their own back yards and stop
the prostitution of sacred music."

6255. Preece, Harold. "The Negro Folk Cult." The Crisis (43:
12, Dec., 1936), pp. 364+.   DHU/MO; DLC
"The professional folk lorists are taken to task for their
traditional handling of the Negro."

6256. Price, Leontyne. "Swing Low, Sweet Chariot."
Phonodisc.

6257. Proctor, Henry H. "The Theology of the Songs of the Southern Slave. Pt. I." Southern Workman (36:11, Nov., 1907),
pp. 584-92.   DLC; DHU/MO

6258. ----- "The Theology of the Songs of the Southern Slave.
Pt. II." Southern Workman (36:12, Dec., 1907), pp. 652-56.
DLC; DHU/MO
Their belief as to Satan. Their belief as to the future.

6259. Puckett, Newbell Niles. Folk Beliefs of the Southern Negro.
New York: Negro Universities Press, 1968.   DHU/R; NjP;
MiBsA; Ic/H; T Sew U-T
Contains much material on the spiritual life of the Negro.
Originally collected from field work and questionnaires to
various colleges for his Ph.D. degree at Yale University.
Chapter III, Voodooism and Conjuration.

6260. Pugh, Alfred L. "Fly Me to the Moon." Perspective (13:2,
Spr., 1972), pp. 111-17.   DHU/R
Sermon delivered at a Black Preaching seminar.

6261. Pyles, Joseph C. "A Song of Soul." Home Missions (43:4,
Apr., 1972), pp. 17-19.   Pam. File, DHU/R

6262. Reaver, J. Russell. "Louisiana Folklore Miscellany."
Journal of American Folklore (72:285, Jl.-Sept., 1959), pp.
277-78.   DHU/R
Microcard.
Review of collection in Louisiana Folklore Society Publication
No. 3, May, 1958.

6263. Ricks, George Robinson. Religious Music of the United
States Negro. Doctoral dissertation. Northwestern University,
1959.

6264. Rivers, Clarence Joseph. "An American Mass Program
(Roman Catholic Litury)."

(Rivers, Clarence Joseph cont.)
    Phonodisc.
    Negro priest.

6265. ----- "Babel or Pentecost: A Choice." Freeing the Spirit
    (1:3, Sum., 1972), p. 51.   DHU/R
    "A sermon for Pentecost."

6266. ----- "Black Soul Creation." Freeing the Spirit (1:2, Spr.,
    1972), pp. 29-36.   DHU/R
    "Experiences of three parishes in innovative music and
    worship."
    Negro author.

6267. ----- "The Homily in Integrated Worship." Freeing the
    Spirit (1:4, 2:1, Fall-Wint., 1972, Spr., 1973), pp. 35-36.
                                                DHU/R
    Written by a Black priest.

6268. ----- Soulful Worship. Wash., D.C.: National Office for
    Black Catholics, 1974.   DHU/R

6269. Robbins, Rossell Hope. The Encyclopedia of Witchcraft
    and Demonology. New York: Crown Publishers, Inc., 1959.
    Book Review by Arthur Freeman in Journal of American
    Folklore (73:288, Apr.-Je., 1960), pp. 172-4.   DHU/R
    Microcard.

6270. Roberts, Hilda. "Louisiana Superstitions." Journal of
    American Folklore (40:156, Apr.-Je., 1927), pp. 144-208.
                                                DHU/R
    Microcard.

6271. Rogers, Cornish. "Mahalia Jackson: Saturday Night Rhythms
    and Sunday Morning Lyrics." The Christian Century (89:9, Mr.
    1, 1972), pp. 241-42.   DHU/R
    Negro author.

6272. Rogers, Jefferson P. "Balck Worship: Black Church."
    The Black Church (1:1, 1972), pp. 59-67.   DHU/R

6273. Rowland, Ida. A Study of Rituals and Ceremonies of Negroes
    in Omaha. Master's thesis. Omaha University, 1938.

6274. Rublowsky, John. Black Music in America. New York:
    Basic Books, Inc., 1971.   DHU/R; DLC

6275. Scarborough, Dorothy. On the Trail of Negro Folk-Songs.
    Cambridge, Mass.: Harvard University Press, 1925. DLC;
    PNcT; PP; PSC; PU; DHU/MO
    Reprint: Hatboro, Pa., Folklore Assn., 1963.
    Negro author.

6276. Scarborough, William S. "Creole Folk-Tale: Compair
    Bouki and Compair Lapin." Southern Workman (25:9, Sept.,
    1896), p. 186.   DLC; DHU/MO
    Written by the president of Wilberforce University A.M.E.
    Church school.

6277. ----- "Folklore and Ethnology: Creole Proverbs."
    Southern Workman (25:10, Oct., 1896), p. 206. DLC; DHU/MO

6278. ----- Negro Folklore and Dialect. n.p.: n.p., n.d.
                                                NN/Sch
    "Detached from The Arena."

6279. Seale, Lea and Marianna. "Easter Rock: A Louisiana
    Negro Ceremony." Journal of American Folklore (55:218,
    Oct.-Dec., 1942), pp. 212-18.   DHU/R
    Microcard.

6280. Sellers, John. "Brother John Sellers Sings Baptist Shouts
    and Gospel Songs." Monitor MF 335.
    Phonodisc.

6281. Sherwood, William Henry. Soothing Songs. A Collection of
    Songs, Original and Selected, as Used by Rev. Dr. Sherwood,
    the Negro Evangelist in His Gospel Meeting, Adopted to Sunday

School and Gospel Services.... Kansas City: Kansas City
Press, Printer, 1891.   DHU/MO

6282. Simpson, Robert Bruce. A Black Church: Ecstasy in a
    World of Trouble. Washington University, 1969-70.   CoDI
    Microfilm, University of Michigan.

6283. Smiley, Portia. "Folk-Lore from Virginia, South-Caro-
    lina, Georgia, Alabama and Florida." Journal of American
    Folk-Lore (32:125, Jl.-Sept., 1919), pp. 837-83. DHU/R
    Microcard.
    Includes tales on divining and conjuring.

6284. "Some Conjure Doctors We Have Heard Of." Southern
    Workman (26:2, Feb., 1897), pp. 37-38.   DLC; DHU/MO

6285. Songs and Spirituals of Negro Compositions for Revivals
    and Congregational Singing. Chicago: Overton-Hygienic Co.,
    n.d.   OWibfU

6286. "A South Carolina Folk Song." A Plantation Song. Southern
    Workman (54:12, Dec., 1925), p. 568.   DLC; DHU/MO
    Recorded by Dr. E.C.L. Adams of Columbia, S.C. says,
    "it is a fragment from a funeral sermon by a plantation
    Negro."

6287. Southern, Eileen. "An Origin for the Negro Spiritual." The
    Black Scholar (3:10, Sum., 1972), pp. 8-13.   DHU/R;
    DHU/MO
    Negro author.

6288. "Southern Sanctified Singers, 1926-1942." Roots RL 328.
    196-. 2s. 12 in. 33 1/3 rpm.   DLC
    Phonodisc.

6289. Spalding, Henry D. Encyclopedia of Black Folklore and
    Humor. New York: Jonathan David Publishers, 1972.
                                                DHU/R; IC/H

6290. Spears, James E. "Notes on Negro Folk Speech." North
    Carolina Folklore (18:3, Nov., 1970),   Pam. File, DHU/R

6291. Speck, F.G. "The Negroes and the Creek Nation."
    Southern Workman (38; 1908), pp. 106-10.   DHU/MO
    Includes the Negroes influence in Creek mythology and
    folklore.

6292. Spencer, Terrence J. and Clarence J. Rivers. "Afro-
    American Hope: The Style of Langston Hughes as a Play-
    wright." Freeing the Spirit (1:4, 11:1, Fall-Wint., 1972,
    Spr., 1973), pp. 62-3.   DHU/R

6293. "The Spirituals and Race Relations." Christian Century
    (48:7, Feb. 18, 1931), pp. 230-231.   DHU/R

6294. Steele, Algernon Odell. The Concept of Religion Reflected
    in the Early Negro Spirituals. Masters thesis. Garrett
    Biblical Institute, 1931.

6295. Steiner, Roland. "Braziel Robinson Possessed of Two
    Spirits." Journal of American Folklore (13:50, Jl.-Sept.,
    1900), pp. 226-28.   DHU/R
    Microcard.

6296. ----- "Observations on the Practice of Conjuring in Georgia."
    Journal of American Folklore (14:53, Apr.-Je., 1901), pp. 173-
    80.   Pam. File, DHU/R

6297. ----- "Seeking Jesus, a Religious Rite of Negroes in
    Georgia." Journal of American Folklore (14:53, Apr.-Je.,
    1901), p. 172.   Pam. File, DHU/R

6298. ----- "Sol Lockheart's Call." Journal of American Folk-
    lore (13:48, Ja.-Mr., 1900), pp. 67-70.   DHU/R
    Microcard.
    "A Georgia Negro's call to preach".

6299. ----- "Superstitions and Beliefs From Central Georgia."
    Journal of American Folklore (12:47, Oct.-Dec., 1899), pp.

251-71.   DHU/R
    Microcard.

6300. Stoney, S. G. Black Genesis. N.Y.: Macmillan, 1930.
                                           IC/H
    Folklore of the Negro.

6301. Stuckey, Sterling. "Through the Prism of Folklore: The
    Black Ethos in Slavery." Eric Foner (ed.). America's Black
    Past, A Reader in Afro-American History (New York: Harper
    & Row Publishers, 1970), pp. 97-111.   DHU/R
        Reviews slave culture and notes its contribution to spirituals
        and secular songs.

6302. Szecsi, Ladislas. "Primitive Negro Art." Art and Arch-
    eology (34:3, My.-Je., 1933), pp. 137-45+.   DHU/R

6303. Talbot, Edith A. "True Religion in Negro Hymns." South-
    ern Workman (51:5, 6, 7, My., Je., Jl., 1922), pp. 213-16;
    260-64; 334-39.   DLC; DHU/MO

6304. Tallant, Robert. Voodoo in New Orleans. New York: The
    Macmillan Co., 1946.   NjP; DHU/MO

6305. Talley, Thomas Washington. Negro Folk Rhymes; Wise and
    Otherwise With a Study. Port Washington, N.Y.: Kennikat
    Press, Inc., 1922.   DHU/R

6306. Tallmadge, William H. "Dr. Watts and Mahalia Jackson:
    The Development, Decline and Survival of a Folk Style in
    America." Ethnomusicology (5; My., 1961), pp. 95-99. DAU

6307. ----- "The Responsorial and Antiphonal Practice in Gospel
    Song." Ethnomusicology (12; My., 1968), pp. 219-38.   DAU

6308. Taylor, Hycel B. "The Great Black Religious Drama."
    Christian Ministry (3:1, Ja., 1972), pp. 26-29.   DHU/R
        "A poem attempting to transport the sensitive reader into
        the experience of a typical black mass church."

6309. Terrell, Clemmie S. "Spirituals from Alabama." Journal
    of American Folk-Lore (43:169, Jl.-Oct., 1930), pp. 322-24.
                                           DHU/R
        Microcard.

6310. Terry, Richard R. Voodooism in Music and Other Essays.
    Freeport, N.Y.: Books for Libraries Press, 1968.   NNCor

6311. Thanet, Octave. "Folk-Lore in Arkansas." Journal of
    American Folklore (5:17, Apr.-Je., 1892), pp. 121-25.
                                           Pam. File, DHU/R

6312. Thomas, William Henry. Some Current Folk-Songs of the
    Negro. Austin, Texas: Folk-Lore Society of Texas, 1936. O

6313. Thurman, Howard. "Deep River, an Interpretation of
    Five Negro Spirituals." The Spoken Word, Howard Thurman;
    Music, the Howard University Choir.
        Phonodisc.

6314. Tinney, James S. "Gospel Show to Mark Street Academy
    Move." The Washington Afro-American (ag. 25, 1973), p. 11.
                                           Pam. File, DHU/R

6315. Tischler, Nancy M. Black Masks:Negro Characters in
    Modern Southern Fiction. University Park, Pa.: Pennsylvania
    State University Press, 1969.   DHU/MO
        Chapter 6, The Black Christ.

6316. "Two Negro Tales Concerning the Jay." (Folk-Lore Scrap-
    Book.) Journal of American Folk-Lore (11:40, Ja.-Mr.,
    1898), pp. 74-5.   DHU/R
        Microcard.

6317. "Two Negro Witch-Storeis." Journal of American Folk-
    Lore (12:45, Apr.-Je., 1899), pp. 145-6.   DHU/R
        Microcard.

6318. Vance, L. F. "Hoodoo." Journal of American Folklore
    (1:3, Oct.-Dec., 1888), pp. 236-37.   Pam. File,
                                           DHU/R
        Definitive on "Hoodoo."

6319. Vidor, King. "Hallelujah."
        Film.
        Includes: Religious scenes such as sermons and religious
        seizures among the congregation.

6320. "Voodoo." New Catholic Encyclopadia (New York: McGraw-
    Hill, 1967), pp. 752-53.   DHU/R

6321. "Voodoo and Vodun." Journal of American Folklore (3:10,
    Jl.-Sept., 1890), p. 241.   Pam. File, DHU/R

6322. "A Voodoo Festival Near New Orleans." Journal of Amer-
    ican Folklore (10:36, Ja.-Mr., 1897), pp. 21-34. Pam. File,
                                           DHU/R

6323. Wagner, Jean-Michel. Les Poetes Negrés des Etats Unis.
    Paris: Librairie Istra, 1963.   DHU/MO
        Treats the religious and racial sentiment in verse, 1890-
        1940.

6324. Walker, Thomas H. B. Bebbly: or, the Victorious Preach-
    er... Gainsville, Fla.: 1910.   NN/Sch

6325. Walker, Wyatt T. "The Soulful Journal of the Negro Spiritual
    Freedom's Song." Negro Digest (12:9, Jl., 1963), pp. 84-95.
                                           Pam. File, DHU/R

6326. Walmsley, Robert. A Comparative Analysis of the Symbolism
    of Selected Black Spirituals as Reflected in Some Contemporary
    Gospel Songs and its Impact Upon Black Culture. Masters the-
    sis. Howard University, School of Religion, 1973.

6327. Waring, May A. "Negro Superstitions in South Carolina."
    Journal of American Folklore (7:27, Oct.-Dec., 1894), pp.
    318-19.   DHU/R

6328. Waterman, Richard Alan. "African Influence on the Music
    of the Americas." Sol Tax (ed.) Acculturation in the Amer-
    icas (New York: Cooper Square Publishers, Inc., 1967), pp.
    207-18.   DHU/R

6329. ----- and William R. Basom. "African and New World
    Folklore." Funk and Wagnalls Standard Dictionary of Folk-
    lore, Mythology, and Legend, V. 1 (New York: Funk & Wag-
    nall, 1949), pp. 18-24.   DHU

6330. Watson, Andrew Polk. Primitive Religion Among Negroes in
    Tennessee. Masters thesis. Fisk University, 1932.
        Vivid accounts of the preacher, church organization, ser-
        mons, and conversion experiences of the Primitive Hard-
        shell, or Footwashing Baptists of Central Tennessee.
        Their faith is often called "Cornfield Religion."

6331. Watson, Harmon C. "The Golden Gates Fall Down."
    Nick Aaron Ford, (ed.). Black Insights: Significant Literature
    by Black Americans- 1760 to the Present. (Waltham, Mass.:
    Ginn and Co., 1971), pp. 289-96.   DHU/R
        A one-act play which takes place before St. Peter and the
        gates of Heaven.

6332. "We Shall Overcome: Freedom Songs." Thomas R. Frazier,
    (ed.). Afro-American History: Primary Resources (New York:
    Harcourt, Brace & World, Inc., 1970), pp. 426-31. DHU/R;
    DHU/MO

6333. Whalum, W. "Johnson's Theories and Performance Practices
    of Afro-American Folksong." Phylon (32:4, Wint., 1971), pp.
    383-95.   DHU/MO

6334. Whitchurch, S. The Negro Convert, A Poem; Being the Sub-
    stance of the Experience of Mr. John Marrant, A Negro, as
    Related by Himself, Previous to His Ordination, at the Countess
    of Huntingdon's Chapel... On Sunday, the 15th of May, 1787...
    Bath, England: n.p., 1785.   NN/Sch

6335. White, Eugene Walter. That They Might Know. A Book of Gospel Sermons. Baltimore: Clarke Press, 1952. SCBHC

6336. White, Newman, Iney. "Racial Traits in the Negro Song." Sewanee Review (28; Jl., 1920), pp. 396-404.   DHU

6337. Whitney, Anne Weston. "Why the Devil Never Wears a Hat." Journal of American Folklore (12:47, Oct.-Dec., p. 274.
                                                          DHU/R

6338. Whitten, Norman E., Jr. "Contemporary Patterns of Malijn Occultism Among Negroes in North Carolina." Journal of American Folklore (75:298, Oct.-Dec., 1962), pp. 311-25. DHU/R Microcard.

6339. Williams, Jamye C. and McDonald. The Negro Speaks: The Rhetoric of Contemporary Black Leaders. New York: Barnes & Noble, 1970.   DHU; DHU/MO
      Includes speeches by Benjamin E. Mays, Howard Thruman, Archibald Carey and Adam Clayton Powell, Jr.

6340. Williams, Robert. A Study of Religious Language: Stylistic Appraoch to an Interpretation of Selected Black Spirituals and Related Afro-American Folklore. Doctoral dissertation. Columbia University, 1972.

6341. Williams-Jones, Pearl. "Afro-American Gospel Music." Vada E. Butcher (ed.). Development of Materials for a One Year Course in African Music for the General Undergraduate Student. (Wash., D.C.: U.S. Dept. of Health, Education and Welfare, 1970), pp. 201-19.   DHU/R

6342. Williamson, George. "Superstitions From Louisiana." Journal of American Folklore (18:70, Jl.-Sept., 1905), pp. 229-30.   DHU/R
      Microcard.

6343. Winslow, David J. "Bishop E. E. Everett and Some Aspects of Occultism and Folk Religion in Negro Philadelphia." Keystone Folklore Quarterly (14; 1969), pp. 59-80.   DLC

6344. Woodall, N. F. "Old Signs in Alabama." Journal of American Folk-Lore (43:169, Jl.-Oct., 1930), pp. 325-6. DHU/R
      Microcard.
      Superstitions.

6345. Work, Monroe N. "Some Geechee Folklore." Southern Workman (34:11, 12, Nov.-Dec., 1905), pp. 633-5; 696-7. DLC; DHU/MO
      Dialect, customs, and beliefs of Negroes inhabiting the tide-water section of Georgia and South Carolina.

6346. Wright, Jeremiah. The Treatment of Biblical Passages in Negro Spirituals. Masters thesis. Howard University, 1969.

6347. Zenetti, Lothar and Heisse W. Eisen. Jazz, Spirituals, Beatsongs, Schlager in der Kirche. Munchen: J. Pfeifen, 1966.   DLC; NjP; CBDP; OrU

III. THE BLACK MAN AND HIS RELIGIOUS LIFE IN THE AMERICAS
(for contemporary status, see Section V)

A. RELIGIOUS DEVELOPMENT OF THE AMERICAN NEGRO

1. The Negro Church

a. Denominations

(1) African Methodist Episcopal

6348. Adams, Revels A. Cyclopedia of African Methodism in Mississippi. Natchez, Mississippi: n.p., 1902. DLC; ISAR

6349. "A. M. E. Congress." J. W. Hanson, (ed.). The World's Congress of Religions (Chicago: International Pub. Co., 1894), pp. 1102-21.   DHU/MO
Addresses and papers delivered before the Parliament Aug. 25- Oct. 15, 1893.

6350. African Methodist Episcopal Church. Annual State Conferences. DLC; DHU/MO; DHU/R; GAU; TNF; NcD-D; CtY-D; NcSalL

6351. ----- Articles of Association of the African Methodist Episcopal Church of the City of Philadelphia in the Commonwealth of Pennsylvania. Philadelphia: Historic Publications, 1969. DLC
Reprint of the 1799 ed., with "The founding of Mother Bethel and the African Methodist Episcopal Church 1799; a Bibliographical note, by Maxwell Whiteman" added.

6352. ----- Bishop's Address to the Members and Friends of the African Methodist Episcopal Church in America. n.p., 1872.
GAU

6353. ----- The Budget; Containing the Annual Reports of the General Officers of the A. M. E. Church of U.S.A. for 1881. Xenia, Ohio: Torchlight Printing Co., 1881.   OWibfU

6354. ----- The Budget... for 1886. Xenia, Ohio: Aldine, 1886.
OWibfU

6355. ----- Catechisms... n.p. : n.p., n.d. DLC; GAU; NN/Sch; OWibfU; NcSalL; DHU/MO; NcD; CtY-D

6356. ----- Constitution of the Preacher's Meeting of the African Methodist Episcopal Church of Baltimore and Vicinity. Baltimore, Md. : n.p., n.d.   DHU/MO

6357. ----- Bishop's Council. Committee on Deaconesses. Deaconess Manual of the African Methodist Episcopal Church. r.p., 1902.   NN/Sch
Written by Bishop Abraham Grant, Chairman at the Committee, appointed by the Bishop's Council, July 19, 1901. Negro author.

6358. ----- Doctrine and Discipline... DLC; OWibfu; NcSaiL; DHU/MO

6359. ----- Board of Education. Report. n.p., The Board, 1884.
TNF

6360. ----- Conferences. South Carolina. Some Mountain Peak Characters in the Early Days of African Methodism and the Daniel A. Payne Memorial Chautauquas... Columbia, S.C.: Allen University Press, n.d.   NcD

6361. ----- Dept of Christian Education. Quadrennial Report to the Session of the African Methodist Episcopal Church. 19-. GAU; NN/Sch; DLC; DHU/MO; NcSalL

6362. ----- General Conference. Journal of the ... Quadrennial Session of the General Conference of the African Methodist Episcopal Church. 1820- ... GAU; NcSalL; DHU/MO; DLC; TNF; OWibfU

6363. ----- General Conference, 1936. The Episcopal Address Presented by Bishop William Alfred Fountain to the Thirteenth General Conference of the African Methodist Episcopal Church, New York City, N.Y. May 6, 1936. Pub. by Order of the General Conference of the African Methodist Episcopal Church. Philadelphia: A.M.E. Book Concern, 1936. DHU/MO; NN/Sch; GAU; OWibfU; NcSalL

6364. ----- General Conference. Official Directory... GAU; DHU/MO; DLC; NcSalL; OWibfU; CtY-D; NcD

6365. ----- General Conference. Reports of the Quadrennial Sessions... NN/Sch; DHU/MO; NcSalL; OWibfU; CtY-D; TNF

6366. ----- General Conference. Dept. of Finance. Quadrennial Report... TNF; OWibfu: DLC; GAU; NcSalL; DHU/MO

6367. ----- Hand Book, A.M.E. Church, 1909. Nashville, Tenn.: African Methodist Episcopal Church Sunday School Union Pub. House, 1910.   NN/Sch; GAU; TNF

6368. ----- Home and Foreign Missionary Dept. Annual Reports... 18--. NN/Sch; OWibfU; GAU; DLC; NcSalL; DHU/MO

6369. ----- Hymnal, Adapted to the Doctrines and Usages of the African Methodist Episcopal Church. Philadelphia: A.M.E. Book Concern, 1915. DLC; DHU/MO; OWibfU; NcSalL; GAU

6370. ----- Illinois Conference, 39th Ses. An Appeal to the President and Congress of the United States. Resolution on the Proposed Exposition Commemorative of the Semi-Centennial of the Negroes' Freedom in America. Passed by the Illinois Conference of the A.M.E. Church, at Springfield, Illinois, September, 1910. Springfield: n.p., 1910.

6371. ----- Journal of Negro Education (29; Sum., 1960), pp. 319-22.   DHU

6372. ----- Liturgy and Ritual. A.M.E. Church Liturgy. Philadelphia: A.M.E. Book Concern, 1911. NN/Sch; DLC; OWibfU; GAU; DHU/MO

6373. ----- "Minutes of the Four Last Annual Conferences of the African Methodist Episcopal Church Held at Pittsburgh, (Pa.,) Washington, (D.C.,) Philadelphia, and New York, 1833-4..." Dorothy B. Porter (ed.). Early Negro Writing, 1760-1837 (Boston Beacon, 1971), pp. 182-99.   DHU/MO

6374. ----- Missions and Mission Conferences. Indian Mission...
Proceedings of the 28th Session of the Indian Mission Annual
Conference. Nashville, Tenn.: 1907.   DLC

6375. ----- "Operation...Outreach of Love." A.M.E. Church
Review (106:271, Jl.-Sept., 1972), Whole issue.   DHU/R
Request to the church members to give money to help the
church pay $5,000,000.00 indebtedness.

6376. ----- Philadelphia. Centennial Historical Souvenir of
"Mother" Bethel A.M.E. Church. Philadelphia Historical
Society, 1916.   GAU

6377. ----- Reprint of the Discipline of the African Methodist
Episcopal Church, with Historical Preface and Notes, by
C. M. Tanner... Atlanta, Ga.: Counts Printing Office, 1916.
DLC; GAU; CtY-D; TNF; NN/Sch

6378. ----- The Richard Allen A. M. E. Hymnal, With Respon-
sive-Scripture Readings, Adapted in Conformity with the
Doctrines and Uses of the African Methodist Episcopal Church,
by the Committee on Revision of the Hymnal, Bishop John
A. Gregg, Chairman. Philadelphia: The A. M. E. Book Concern, 1946.   DLC; NN/Sch

6379. ----- Survey of the Colleges and Schools of the Colored
Methodist Episcopal Church. Comp. by J. A. Bray. n.p.:
J. W. Perry, n.d.   NcD

6380. ----- Woman's Home and Foreign Missionary Society.
Constitution and By-Laws of the Woman's Home and Foreign
Missionary Society. Adopted at Chicago, Ill. May, 1928.
n.p., 1929. NN/Sch; OWibfU; FSU; CtY-D; NcSalL

6381. ----- Woman's Home and Foreign Missionary Society.
Report... Charleston, S.C.: n.d. CtY-D; DLC; DHU/MO;
NcSalL; GAU; OWibfU

6382. ----- Yearbook. NN/Sch; NcSalL; OWibfU; GAU; DLC

6383. "The African Methodist Episcopal Church and Segregation."
The African Methodist Episcopal Church Review (70:18,
Jl.-Sept., 1954), pp. 9-10.   DHU/R

6384. "The African M. E. Church in Indiana." The African
Methodist Episcopal Church Review (78:209, Jl.-Sept., 1961),
pp. 6-11.   DHU/R
Negro author.

6385. Allen, Richard, (bp.). "Extract from a Discourse...Dec.
29, 1799...African Methodist Church of Philadelphia."
Franklin B. Hough. Washingtonians. (Vol. 2, Roxbury, 1865),
pp. 216-17.   NA; MB

6386. ----- (bp.). "Spiritual Song." Dorothy B. Porter. Early
Negro Writing, 1760-1837 (Boston: Beacon, 1971), pp. 559-61.
                                                  DHU/MO
Negro minister.
Appeared c. 1800 as a broadside; "In this religious chant
he warned his congregation against loud 'groaning and
shouting'; such religion, he states, is 'only a dream.'"

6387. ----- and Absalom Jones. "A Narrative of the Proceedings
of the Black People During the Late Awful Calamity in Philadelphia." Benjamin Brawley (ed.). Early Negro Writers
Selection with Biographical and Critical Introductions. Freeport, New York: Books for Libraries, 1968.   DHU/R
Negro author.

6388. Allison, Madeline G. "Bethel A. M. E. Church, in Columbia,
S. C." The Crisis (25:2, Dec., 1922), p. 75. DHU/MO; DLC

6389. ----- "The Churches." The Crisis (21:4, Feb., 1921), p.
177.   DHU/MO; DLC
A. M. E. Church convention report.
"Cleaves Industrial Hall" erected at Lane College.

6390. ----- "The Horizon." The Crisis (23:6, Apr., 1922), p.
272.   DHU/MO; DLC

Abyssinia Baptist Church purchases property for a new
edifice. Rev. A. Clayton Powell, Sr., pastor.

6391. ----- "Sunday School Enrollment." The Crisis (24:1, My.,
1922), p. 28.   DHU/MO; DLC
St. John's A. M. E. Church in Cleveland, Ohio.

6392. "American Cradles of Methodism." The African Methodist
Episcopal Church Review (75:200, Apr.-Je., 1959), pp. 5-8.
                                                  DHU/R
Negro author.

6393. "An Easter Service for Use in the Public Service and in
the Sunday School of the A. M. E. Church." Jubilee Gem
(1:1, 1883).   OWibfU

6394. Arnett, Benjamin William, (bp.). Address Delivered Before
the Georgia State Industrial College for Colored Youth at College,
Georgia (Near Savannah), June 7, 1889. n.p.: n.p., 1889.
                                                  DLC
Written by seventeenth bishop of the A. M. E. Church.

6395. ----- (bp.). The Budget, Containing Annual Reports of the
General Officers of the African M. E. Church of the United
States of America. Xenia, O.: Torchlight Printing Co., 1881.
                                                  DHU/MO
Negro author.

6396. ----- (bp.). The Budget of 1904. African Methodist Episcopal Church History. Philadelphia: Lampton & Collett, 1924.
                                                  DHU/MO; OWibfU

6397. ----- (bp.). Centennial Budget Containing an Account
of the Celebration (Nov. 1887) in the Different Parts of the
Church, and the Principal Address Delivered in Bethel Church,
Phil., Pa., Together with the Portrait of Each Bishop and his
Wife, Also the Portrait and Sketch of Many of the Prominent
Men of Church ... Dayton, O.: Christian Pub. Co., ca. 1888.
                                                  DHU/MO; OWibfU; DLC
Negro author.

6398. ----- (bp.). "The Mission of Methodism to the Extremes of
Society." Centennial Methodist Conference, Baltimore, Md.
Proceedings, Sermons, Essays, and Addresses of the Centennial
Held in Mt. Vernon Methodist Episcopal Church, Baltimore,
Md., December 9-17, 1884. With a Historical Statement.
Edited by H. K. Carroll, W. Harrison, and J. H. Bayless.
(New York: T. Phillips and Hunt, 1885), pp. 529-34. GAU/ITC

6399. ----- (bp.). Proceedings of Semi-Centenary Celebration ...
1874. Cincinnati: H. Watkins, 1874.   GAU

6400. "Atlanta's Big Bethel A. M. E. Church, the Rev. Richard
H. Singleton, Pastor." The Crisis (27:5, Mr., 1924), pp.
229-30.   DLC; DHU/MO

6401. Barrows, John Henry (ed.). The World's Parliament of
Religions. Chicago: The Parliament Pub. Co., 1893.
                                                  ISAR; DHU/R
A. M. E. Congress, pp. 1394-6.

6402. Baxter, Daniel Minnort. Back to Methodism. Philadelphia:
A. M. E. Book Concern, 1926.   DHU/MO; NN/Sch

6403. ----- Bishop Richard Allen and His Spirit. Philadelphia:
A. M. E. Book Concern, 1923. OWibfU; DLC; NN/Sch

6404. Bentley, D. S. Brief Religious Reflections. Practical
Studies for Christians. In Three Chapters. Philadelphia:
A. M. E. Publsihing House, n.d.   DHU/MO
Negro author.

6405. Berry, Lewellyn Longfellow. A Century of the African
Methodist Episcopal Church, 1840-1940. New York: Gutenberg
Printing Co., Inc., 1942.   DHU/MO; GAU; OWibfU; CtY-D;
NN/Sch
Negro author.

6406. "Bethel A. M. E. Church of Chicago." Crisis (25:6, Apr., 1923), p. 269.   DHU/MO

6407 "Bishop Daniel A. Payne-- Symposium." A. M. E. Church Review (10; Ja., 1894), pp. 393-414.   DLC
A. M. E. bishop.

6408. Blake, Charles C. Handbook for Members of the A. M. E. Church, n.p., n.d.   O WibfU

6409. Brooks, William Sampson, (bp.). Footprints of a Blackman; the Holy Land. St. Louis: Eden Publishing House Print, 1915.
                                                     DHU/MO
Negro author.

6410. ----- (bp.). Three Addresses by Bishop W. Sampson Brooks, A. M. E. Bishop of Texas. n.p.: n.p., n.d.   GAU

6411. Brown, Dorothy J. "The Organization of St. James A. M. E. Church, Atlantic City of New Jersey." The African Methodist Episcopal Church Review (78:210, Oct.-Dec., 1961), pp. 31-33.   DHU/R
Negro author.

6412. The Budget Containing Annual Reports of the General Officers of the African Methodist Episcopal Church of the United States of America: With Facts and Figures, Historical Data of the Colored Methodist Church in Particular, and Universal Methodism in General... 1881. Xenia, O.: 1881. TNF; NN/Sch; DLC (1881-1904)

6413. Butler, William H. H. A. M. E. Church Ecclesiastical Judicial Practice. Philadelphia: A. M. E. Book Concern, 1914.   DHU/MO; O WibfU; GAU

6414. Butt, Israel LaFayette. History of African Methodism in Virginia; or, Four Decades in the Old Dominion. Introduction by Rev. Benjamin F. Lee... Hampton, Va.: Hampton Institute Press, 1908.   DLC; NN/Sch O WibfU

6415. Cain, Richard Harvey, (bp.). Bishop's Pastoral Letter to Ministers and Members of the A. M. E. Church, August 20, 1880.   O WibfU
Typescript.
Written by a bishop of the A. M. E. Church.

6415. Caldwell, J. C. Constitution of the Allen League of the A. M. E. Church by General Secretary. Nashville, Tenn.: A. M. E. Publication Department, 1914.   O WibfU

6417-18. Cannon, Noah Caldwell. A History of the African Methodist Episcopal Church, the Only One in the United States of America, Styled Bethel Church... to be Held Forth in Remembrance of the Right Reverend Richard Allen, First Bishop of the Connection. Rochester: Stron and Dawson, Printers, 1842.   WHi
Negro author.

6419. Chambliss, Carroll R. "The Church of My Choice." The African Methodist Episcopal Church Review (94:236, Jl.-Sept., 1968), pp. 36-38.   DHU/R
Chaplain calls for a probe of general conference action.
Negro author.

6420. "Churches." The Crisis (4:2, Je., 1912), p. 113. DLC; DHU/MO
General conference of the A. M. E. Church elects four bishops, Rev. John E. Hurst; Rev. J. M. Conner; Rev. Joshua H. Jones; Rev. W. D. Chappelle.

6421. "Churches." The Crisis (8: 2, Je., 1914), p. 62. DHU/MO; DLC
Report of financial board of A. M. E. Church.

6422. Clark, M. M. "The Episcopal Mould." The African Methodist Episcopal Church Review (75:200, Apr.-Je., 1959), pp. 44-45.   DHU/R
Negro author.

6423. Coan, Josephus R. The Expansion of Missions of the African Methodist Episcopal Church in South Africa, 1896-1908. Doctoral dissertation. Hartford Seminary Foundation, 1961.

6424. ----- "The Transition from Missions to Church." The African Methodist Episcopal Church Review (72:190, Oct.-Dec., 1956), pp. 43-48.   DHU/R
Negro author.

6425. Collins, G. N. "African Methodism Adventures in Missions. Four Years in Africa." The African Methodist Episcopal Church Review (92:234, Ja.-Mr., 1968), pp. 51-55; (95:236, Jl.-Sept., 1968), pp. 79-82.   DHU/R
Negro author.

6426. ----- "Four Years in Africa." The African Methodist Episcopal Church Review (94:236, Jl.-Sept., 1968), pp. 58-60.   DHU/R
Negro author.

6427. Coppin, Levi Jenkins, (bp.). Relation of Baptized Children to the Church. Philadelphia: AME Publishing Department, 1890.   O WibfU
Negro author.

6428. ----- (bp.). Unwritten History. New York: Negro Universities Press, 1968.   IC/H; DHU/R
Reprint of 1919 edition.
Written by a bishop of the A. M. E. Church.

6429. Cox, John Morris. A Study of the Religious Education Program of the African Methodist Episcopal Churches in the District of Columbia. Masters thesis. School of Religion, Howard University, 1938.
Negro author.

6430. Cunningham, Dorothy Holmes. An Analysis of the A. M. E. Church Review, 1884-1900. The A. M. E. Church Review (68:174, Oct.-Dec., 1952), pp. 12-18; (68:176, Apr.-Je., 1953), pp. 21-29.   DHU/R
Also Masters thesis, Howard Univ., 1950.   DHU/MO

6431. Cunningham, John C. "Fraternal Address of Reverend J. Cunningham." A. M. E. Church Review (70:181, Jl.-Sept., 1954), pp. 42-45.   DHU/R
Delivered at Bethel A. M. E., Phila., May, 1864.

6432. Davis, Emory G. "History of Allen Chapel A. M. E. Church of Terre Haute of Indiana." The African Methodist Episcopal Church Review (74:197, Jl.-Sept., 1958), pp. 37-41. DHU/R
Negro author.

6433. Davis, James A. The History of Episcopacy, Prelastic and Moderate; with an Introduction by the Rev. B. T. Tanner. Nashville: A. M. E. Church Sunday School Union, 1902.
                                                     NN/Sch
Negro author.

6434. Davis, Monroe H. The Dogmas and Precepts of the Fathers. Nashville: A. M. E. Sunday School Union, 1948. ISAR; O WibfU

6435. Detroit. Bethel African Methodist Episcopal Church. One Hundred Years at Bethel Detroit, 1841-1941. Detroit: The Church, 1941.   Pam. File, DHU/MO

6436. Early, Sarah J. W. "Early Procedures of A. M. E. History in Series: Life and L bors of Rev. Jordan W. Early." A. M. E. Church Review (104:246, Apr.-Je., 1971), pp. 15-18.
Negro author.

6437. ----- The Life and Labors of Rev. Jordan Early. Edited by George A. Singleton. Nashville Publishing House, A. M. E. Church Sunday School Union, 1894. DHU/R; INF; O WibfU; NN/Sch

6438. Embry, James Crawford, (bp.). Digest of Christian Theology... Philadelphia: A. M. E. Book Concern, 1890. DLC;

(Embry, James Crawford cont.)
NN/Sch
Negro author.

6439. Embry, James Crawford, (bp.). "Our Father's House" and Family Past, Present, and Future. Philadelphia: A. M. E. Book Concern, 1893.   CN

6440. "The First African M. E. Churches in the South." The African Methodist Episcopal Church Review (78:218, Oct. -Dec., 1963), pp. 7-8.   DHU/R

6441. "Following the Trail of the Fathers: Rev. John M. Wilkerson.' The African Methodist Episcopal Church Review (75:200, Apr. -Je., 1959), pp. 10-16.   DHU/R

6442. Fountain, William A., (bp.). The Episcopal Address Presented by... to the Thirtieth General Conference of the African Methodist Episcopal Church. New York City, N. Y. May 6, of the General Conference. Philadelphia: A. M. E. Book Concern, May 6, 1936.   DHU/MO

6443. Frizzell, Mary E. "Faith in Action?" The African Methodist Episcopal Church (92:234, Ja. -Mr., 1968), pp. 55-57.
                    DHU/R
        Women's work in the A. M. E. Church."
        Negro author.

6444. Gaines, Wesley John, (bp). African Methodism in the South; or, Twenty-Five Years of Freedom. Atlanta, Ga.: Franklin Publishing Co., 1890.   DHU/MO; GAU; TNF; NN/Sch; NjP
        African Methodist Episcopal Church.
        Negro author.

6445. Gainous, Albert. The Mission of the African Methodist Episcopal Church. Masters thesis. Howard University, School of Religion, 1973.

6446. George, Carol V. R. Segregated Sabbaths; Richard Allen and the Rise of Independent Black Churches, 1760-1840. New York: Oxford University Press, 1973. DHU/MO; DLC; DHU/R; TSewU-T

6447. Gibson, A. B. B. The African Methodist Shield (improved) For the Benefit of the Members Sunday Schools, Allen Christian Endeavor League and Missionary Societies of the African Methodist Episcopal Church. A Companion of the Gibson Handbook, The Gibson Catechism. Macon, Ga.: n. p., 1919. OWibfU

6448. Gist, Grace. Educational Work of the African Methodist Episcopal Church. Masters thesis. Howard University, 1949.

6449. Grant, Abraham, (bp.). Deaconess Manual of the African Methodist Episcopal Church. Philadelphia: A. M. E. Book Concern, 1902.   OWibfU

6450. Greene, Sherman L., Jr. "Rationale Underlying the Support of Colleges Maintained by the African Methodist Episcopal Church." Journal of Negro Education (29; Sum., 1960), pp. 319-22.   DHU
        Negro author.

6451. Gregg, Howard D. Richard Allen and Present Day... Social Problems. Nashville: A. M. E. Sunday School Union, 19--.   GAU
        Negro author.

6452. Griffin, Eunice. The Rise of American Missions. The African Methodist Episcopal Church. New York: Coker Press Books, 1960.   DLC; CtY-D; NN/Sch

6453. Grimes, William W. Thirty-three Years' Experience of an Itinerant Minister of the A. M. E. Church. Lancaster, Pa.: S. Speaker, Printer, 1887.   TNF

6454. Gullins, William Richard. The Heroes of the Virginia Annual Conference of the A. M. E. Church. Norfolk, Va.:

n. p., 1899.   DLC; NN/Sch
        Negro author.

6455. Handy, James Anderson, (bp.). Scraps of African Methodist Episcopal History. Philadelphia: A. M. E. Book Concern, 1901.   NN/Sch; TNF; DHU/MO; OWibfU
        Negro author.

6456. Hanson, V. W., (ed.). The World Congress of Religions of the World Columbian Exposition (Chicago: Monarch Book Co., 1894), pp. 1002+.   IEG

6457. Haskell, Antonio L. "Hymn Singing Vital To The African Methodist Episcopal Church." The African Methodist Episcopal Church Review (84:197, Jl. -Sept., 1964), pp. 3-5.   DHU/R
        Negro author.

6458. ----- "The Musical Heritage of the African Methodist Episcopal Church." The African Methodist Episcopal Church Review (68:172, Apr. -Je., 1952), pp. 40-43.   DHU/R
        Negro author.

6459. Heard, William Henry. From Slavery to the Bishopric in the A. M. E. Church. New York: Arno Press, 1969. DLC; TNF; DHU/MO; CtY-D; OWibfU; NjP

6460. Higginbotham, Maurice J. "Education in the A. M. E. Church." The African Methodist Episcopal Church Review (70:191, Jl. -Sept. 1954), pp. 62-71.   DHU/R
        Negro author.

6461. Hill, Charles Leander. "The Episcopacy-- Its Functions, Its Authority, Its Limitations." The African Methodist Episcopal Church Review (78:208, Apr. -Je., 1961), pp. 3-6. DHU/R
        Negro author.

6462. Historical Records Survey. Inventory of the Church, Michigan Conference. Prepared by the Historical Records Survey Program, Division of Professional and Service Projects, Work Projects Administration, Michigan State Administrative Board, Sponsor. Michigan Historical Collections, Co-Sponsor. Michigan Historical Collections, Co-Sponsor. Detroit, Mich.: The Michigan Historical Records Survey Project, 1940.
                    DLC; CtY-D

6463. Hodges, Ruth H. Materials for a Program of Creative Art Activities in the Christian Education of Children. Doctoral dissertation. New York University, 1965.
        A handbook for teachers' use in the African Methodist Episcopal Church.

6464. Hoover, Dorothy E. A Layman Looks With Love at Her Church. Phila.: Dorrance, 1970.   INU; DLC; DHU/R
        Negro author.
        A. M. E. Church

6465. Hopes, W. K., (ed.). African Methodist Episcopal Liturgy. Philadelphia: A. M. E. Book Concern, 1947.   OWibfU

6466. "How AME's Elect Bishops." Ebony (11; Ag., 1956), pp. 17-20.   DHU/MO

6467. Hurst, John, (bp.). AME Year Book. Philadelphia: AME Book Concern, 1918.   OWibfU
        Written by A. M. E. bishop.

6468. Isaacs, Esther B. The Leader of Young Women's Auxiliary. Young People's Department. Woman's Parent Mite Missionary Society of the African Methodist Episcopal Church. n. p.: Brady-Wolfe Co., 1934.   NN/Sch
        Negro author.

6469. Jackson, Edward Junius. The A. M. E. Layman. Tampa, Fla.: Tampa Bulletin Print, n. d.   NN/Sch
        Negro author.

6470. Jackson, Reid E. "A. M. E. Schools Face the East." The African Methodist Episcopal Church Review (74:197, Jl. -Sept.,

1958), pp. 42-46.   DHU/R
Negro author.

6471. Jenifer, John Thomas. Centennial Retrospect History of
the African Methodist Episcopal Church. Nashville: Sunday
School Union Print, 1915.   DHU/MO; NN/Sch

6472. ----- Who Was Richard Allen and What Did He Do? Baltimore: n.p., 1905.   NN/Sch

6473. Johnson, Henry Theodore. Divine Logos. Boston: A. M. E.
Pub. Co., 1890.   DLC
Negro author.

6474. Johnson, James H. A. The Episcopacy of the AME Church,
or the Necessity for an Ample Force of Bishops. Baltimore:
Hoffman & Co., 1888.   DHU/MO

6475. ----- The Pine Tree Mission. Baltimore: J. Lanahan,
Bookseller, 1893.   NN/Sch
Negro author

6476. Johnson, John Albert. Private Journal. Bermuda: n.p., 1
1889.   NN/Sch

6477. Jordan, Artishia. The African Methodist Episcopal Church
in Africa. New York: Board of Missions, African Methodist
Episcopal Church, 1960.   OWibfU; CtY-D
Negro author.

6478. Jordan, Casper Leroy, (comp.). The Benjamin William
Arnett Papers at Carnegie Library. Wilberforce, O.:
Wilberforce Univ., 1958.   DHU/MO; NcD
Negro author.

6479. Jordan, Frederick D., (bp.). "Marching Orders." The
African Methodist Episcopal Church Review (94:236, Jl.-Sept.,
1968), pp. 8-10.   DHU/R
Episcopal address delivered at the 39th Session of General
Conference of the A. M. E. Church.

6480. Kitrell Normal and Industrial Institute, Kitrell, N. C.
Report to the 19th General Conference (AME Church). Philadelphia: n.p., 1892.   OWibfU

6481. Lane, Isaac. Autobiography. With a Short History of the
A. M. E. Church in America and of Methodism. Nashville:
Publishing House of M. E. Church South, 1916.   DHU/MO

6482. Leach, William H. "Sees Great Race in the Making. Cleve-
land Conference." Christian Century (49:23, Je., 1932), p. 750.
                                      DHU/R
Report on the 29th General Conference of the AME Church at
Cleveland, Ohio.

6483. Lee, Benjamin Franklin. Some Statistics of the African
Methodist Episcopal Church, 1916. Xenia, O.: Aldine Pub.
House, 1916?   NN/Sch
Negro author.

6484. Lewis, Woodrow T. "The Influence of Daniel Alexander
Payne Upon African Methodism." The African Methodist Epis-
copal Church Review (80:220, Apr.-Je., 1964), pp. 82-91.
                                      DHU/R
Negro author.

6485. Long, Charles Sumner. History of the A. M. E. Church
in Florida. Philadelphia: A. M. E. Book Concern, 1939.
                                      DHU/MO; OWibfU

6486. Mason, J. Benedict. "African Methodism! Adventures in
Missions: Diary of Rev. J. Benedict Mason, Product of Af-
rican Methodism's Helping Hand." The African Methodist
Episcopal Church Review (93:235, Apr.-Je., 1968), pp. 90-91.
                                      DHU/R
Negro author.

6487. ----- "Strengthening African-American Relations." The
African Methodist Episcopal Church Review (71; 72:185; 186,

Jl.-Sept., Oct.-Dec., 1955), pp. 32-45; 62-67.   DHU/R
Negro author.

6488. Michigan Historical Records Survey. Inventory of the Church
Archives of Michigan African Methodist Episcopal Church,
Michigan Conference. Detroit: The Michigan Historical Records
Survey Project, 1940.   IEG

6489. Mishol, Luna I. "The Present Role of the A. M. E. Church
in Higher Education." The African Methodist Episcopal Church
Review (78:213, Jl.-Sept., 1962), pp. 33-4.   DHU/R
Negro author.

6490. Missionary Society. "Report." John Henry Barrows (ed.).
The World's Parliament of Religions. V. 2 (Chicago: Parliament Publishing Co., 1893), pp. 1394-96.   DHU/R

6491. ----- Young People's Congress, Atlanta, 1914. Official
Programme; Congress of the African M. E. Church, Atlanta,
Georgia, July 8 to 12, 1914... Nashville, Tenn.: A. M. E.
S. S. Union Print, 1914.   NN/Sch; DLC; DHU/R; OWibfU;
GAU; DHU/MO

6492. Mixon, Winfield Henry. History of the African Methodist
Episcopal Church in Alabama, With Biographical Sketches
With Introduction by Rt. Rev. Henry McNeal Turner. n. p. :
n. d.   NcD; TNF
Negro author.

6493. ----- A Methodist Luminary. Selma, Ala.: Selma Printing
Co., 1891.   OWibfU
Written by an A. M. E. minister and editor of the Dallas
Post.

6494. Morgan, Joseph H. Morgan's History of the New Jersey
Conference of the A. M. E. Church from 1872-1887, with
Biographical Sketches of Members of the Conference. Camden,
N. J.: S. Chew, 1887.   TNF

6495. Morris, Samuel Solomon. An African Methodist Primer.
A Digest of the History, Beliefs Organization and Operation
of the African Methodist Episcopal Church. Gary, Ind. :
Harris Printing Co., n. d.   DHU/R
Negro author.

6496. "The New England A. M. E. Conference Vote to Advise
the Secretary of the Navy." The Crisis (2:3, Jl., 1911), p.
98.   DHU/MO; DLC

6497. Newton, Alexander Herritage. Out of the Briars; an Auto-
biography and Sketch of the Twenty-ninth Regiment, Connecticut
Volunteers. With intro. by J. P. Sampson. Miami, Fla.:
Mnemosyne Pub. Co., 1969, 1910.   TNF; DLC; NN/Sch

6498. Nichols, Decatur Ward, (bp.). The Episcopal Addresses
Presented to the Thirty-Fourth Quadrennial Session of the
General Conference of the African Methodist Episcopal Church
at Chicago, Illinois, May 1952. General Conference, 1952.
                                      NcD

6499. Norris, John William. The A. M. E. Episcopacy: a Paper
Read before the Baltimore A. M. E. Preachers' Meeting.
Baltimore: Afro-American Co., 1916.   NN/Sch

6500. "Oldest A. M. E. Church." Ebony (9; Mr., 1954), pp. 17-
20.   DHU/MO

6501. Palmer, John Moore. Was Richard Allen Great? Sermon
Delivered by Rev. John M. Palmer, Allen Chapel A. M. E.
Church, Lombard Street, above Nineteenth. Philadelphia,
Sunday Evening, February 20, '98. Philadelphia: Weekly
Astonisher Print., 1898.   NN/Sch

6502. Parks, Henry Blanton, (bp.). Africa. The Problem of
the New Century. The Part of the A. M. E. Church Is To Have
in its Solution. New York: Board of Home and Foreign Missionary Department of the A. M. E. Church, 1899. DHU/MO

6503. ----- (bp.). "Bishop Henry McNeal Turner as Missionary and Promoter of Missions." Henry McNeal Turner. Quarto-Centennial (n.p.: n.p., 1905), pp. 149-55.   DHU/MO
Negro author.

6504. ----- (bp.). The Redemption of Africa. [n.p.: n.p., n.d.]
OWibfU
First A. M. E. bishop to establish his episcopal residence on the West Coast (Southern California). Was Editor of Voice of Missions and chairman of Missionary Board.

6505. Payne, Daniel Alexander, (bp.). The African Methodist Episcopal Church in Its Relations to the Freedmen. Address Before the College Aid Society. Marietta, Ohio, November 7, 1868. Xenia: Torchlight Co., 1868.   NcD
Negro author.

6506. ----- (bp.). An Appeal to the Common Sense of the Ministry and Laity of the African Methodist Episcopal Church in the United States of America. n.p.: n.p., n.d.   DHU/MO
A. M. E. bishop.

6507. ----- (bp.). "Bishop Payne's Address at the British Methodist Conference, 1867." Zion's Herald (38; Ag. 29, 1867).
MH-AH; IEG

6508. ----- (bp.). Bishop Payne's First Address to the Philadelphia Annual Conference of the First A. M. E. Church, May 16, 1853. Philadelphia: C. Sherman, 1853.   NN/Sch

6509. ----- (bp.). History of the African Methodist Episcopal Church... Nashville, Tenn.: n.p., 1891. NN/Sch; DHU/R DLC; NjP; OWibfU
Reprint: New York: Arno Press, 1969.

6510. ----- (bp.). The Moral Significance of the XVth Amendment.
OWibfU
Transcript.

6511. ----- (bp.). Recollection of Seventy Years. Nashville: A. M. E. Sunday School Union, 1888. NN/Sch; DHU/R; DHU/MO; DLC; NjP

6512. ----- (bp.). The Semi-Centenary and Retrospection of the African Methodist Episcopal Church, in the United States. Baltimore: Sherwood and Co., 1866. INF; NN/Sch; NjP

6513. ----- (bp.). Sermons Delivered by Bishop Daniel A. Payne Before the General Conference of the A. M. E. Church, Indianapolis, Indiana, May, 1888. Edited by Rev. C. S. Smith. Nashville: A. M. E. Sunday School Union, 1888. ICN; NN/Sch

6514. ----- (bp.). Some of the Many Reasons for Opposing the Organic Union of the A. M. E. Church and the B. M. E. Church.
OWibfU
Typescript.

6515. ----- (bp.). "Thoughts on the Past, Present and Future of the African Methodist Episcopal Church." The African Methodist Episcopal Church Review (1:1, Jl., 1884), pp. 1-8; (1:1, Apr., 1885), pp. 314-20.   DHU/MO

6516. ----- (bp.). A Treatise on Domestic Education... Cincinnati: Pr. by Cranston & Stowe, 1889. DHU/MO; NN/Sch

6517. Pearle, C. Baker. "The Meaning of African Methodism." The African Methodist Episcopal Church Review (68:176, Apr.-Je., 1953), pp. 33-38.   DHU/R
Negro author.

6518. Perry, Grace Naomi. The Educational Work of the African Methodist Episcopal Church Prior to 1900. Masters thesis. Howard University, 1948.

6519. Perry, Naomi. The Education Work of the African Methodist Episcopal Church Prior to 1900. Masters thesis. Howard University, 1900.

6520. Pottinger, John Leo. A Manual for Church Members. Phila.: Reading Press, 1942.   DHU/R; OWibfU; NN/Sch; DLC
Negro author.

6521. Rankin, James W. "The Missionary Propaganda of the A. M. E. Church." The African Methodist Episcopal Review (32:3, Ja. 1916), pp. 174-77.   DHU/MO

6522. Ransom, Reverdy Cassius, (bp.). African Methodist Social Creed. n.d.   OWibfU
Transcript.
Negro author.

6523. ----- (bp.). Christianity, The Church and the Episcopacy: An Address at the Bishops' Council of the A. M. E. Church, Baltimore, Maryland, February 19, 1942.   OWibfU
Transcript.

6524. ----- (bp.). A Handbook of the African Methodist Episcopal Church. Nashville: A. M. E. Sunday School Union, 1916.
OWibfU
Forty-eight bishop of the A. M. E. Church.

6525. ----- (bp.). The Pilgrimage of Harriet Ransom's Son. Nashville: A. M. E. Sunday School Union, 1950.   DHU/MO

6526. ----- (bp.). Preface to History of A. M. E. Church. Nashville, Tenn.: A. M. E. Sunday School Union, 1950.
OWibfU

6527. ----- (bp.). Year Book of Negro Churches. Wilberforce: Authority of Bishops of the A. M. E. Church, 1936. DHU/R
With statistics of records of achievements of Negroes in the United States.

6528. Reid, Gaines S., (bp.). The Church and the Layman. Man's Duty to God; a Place for Positive and Dynamic Support of the Christian Church. Foreword by Bishop George W. Barber. New York: Exposition Press, 1959.   DHU/R; DHU/MO

6529. Reid, Wilfred. "A Century of Progress." The African Methodist Episcopal Church Review (78:217, Jl.-Sept., 1963), pp. 78-9.   DHU/R
History Allen Chapel A. M. E. Church, Galesburg, Illinois.
Negro author.

6530. Robinson, H. N. "What Does My Religion Mean to Me." A. M. E. Church Review (68:176, Apr.-Je., 1953), pp. 71-2+.
DHU/R
A. M. E. pastor, Cleveland, Ohio.

6531. Rogers, Alain. "The African Methodist Episcopal Church-- A Study in Black Nationalism." The Black Church (1:1, 1972), pp. 17-43.   DHU/R

6532. Roman, Charles Victor. Fraternal Message from the African Methodist Episcopal Church to the Methodist Church of Canada. Nashville: Hemphill Press, 1920. DHU/MO; NN/Sch
Negro author.

6533. Royston, John E. "The Role of the A. M. E. Church in Our Society." The African Methodist Episcopal Church Review (95: 237, Oct.-Dec., 1968), pp. 63+.   DHU/R

6534. Rush, Christopher, (bp.). Short Account of the Rise and Progress of the African Methodist Episcopal Church in America. Written by the Aid of George Collins. Also a View of the Church Order of Government from Authors Relative to Episcopacy. New York: The Author, 1843.   TNF; DHU/MO; NjP
Negro author.

6535. Sampson, John Patterson. Address of Rev. J. P. Sampson, D. D., Presiding Elder of the New England Conference of the A. M. E. Church, at the 46th Annual Convention of the Monmouth County Sunday School Association. Ocean Grove, N. J.: n.p., n.d.   NN/Sch
Negro author.

6536. Shackleford, William Henry. Sunday School Problems, Written Especially for Sunday School Workers. Nashville, Tenn.: A. M. E. Sunday School Union, 1925. NN/Sch; DHU/MO

6537. Shockley, Grant S. "The A. M. E. and the A. M. E. Zion Church." Emory S. Burke, (ed.). A History of American Methodism. V. 1 (New York: Abingdon Press, 1964). DHU/R
See Chapter 23.
Negro author.

6538. Shorter, Susie I. The Heroines of African Methodism... at the Octogenial Celebration of Bishop Daniel A. Payne, Feb. 24, 1891. Jacksonville, Fla.: 1891. DHU/MO

6539. Singleton, George Arnett. The Autobiography of George Arnett Singleton. Boston: Forum Publishing Co., 1964. DHU/MO
Negro author.

6540. ----- The Romance of African Methodism: a Study of the African Methodist Episcopal Church. New York: Exposition Press, 1952. DHU/R; INF; NN/Sch; NjP
Speech on the eligibility of colored members to seats in the Georgia Legislature, pp. 203-18.

6541. Smith, Charles Spencer, (bp.). Dedicatory Services at the Publishing House of the A. M. E. Church Sunday School Union, Nashville, Tenn., Sunday and Monday, January 20-21, 1889. Nashville, Tenn.: Publishing House A. M. E. Church Sunday School Union, 1894. NN/Sch; DLC
Negro author.

6542. ----- (bp.). Episcopal Address, Delivered by Bishop Chas. S. Smith, D. D., May, Nineteen Hundred Twelve to the Twenty-Fourth General Conference of the African Methodist Episcopal Church, Kansas City, Missouri. Nashville, Tenn.: Sunday School Union Print, 1912. DHU/MO

6543. ----- (bp.). The First Race Riot Recorded in History for the Commission on After-War Problems of the African Methodist Episcopal Church. Detroit, Mich.: n.p., 1920. PCC; DHU/MO
Written by bishop of A. M. E. Church.

6544. ----- (bp.). A History of the African Methodist Episcopal Church. New York: Johnson Reprint Co., 1968. DHU/MO; TNF; NjP; GAU; OWibfU; DHU/R

6545. Smith, Inez W. "The A. M. E. Church Story." The African Methodist Episcopal Church Review (68:174, Oct.-Dec., 1952), pp. 45-47. DHU/R
Negro author.

6546. Smith, James H. Vital Facts Concerning the African Methodist Episcopal Church. Nashville: A. M. E. Book Concern, 1914. DHU/MO; OWibfU; NN/Sch

6547. Spivey, Charles S., Jr. "The African Methodist Episcopal Church -- Its Problems and Its Future." The African Methodist Episcopal Church Review (92:234, Ja.-Mr., 1968), pp. 27-36. DHU/R

6548. "St. John African Methodist Episcopal Church, Norfolk, Virginia." The African Methodist Episcopal Church Review (72:186, Oct.-Dec., 1955), pp. 16-7. DHU/R
Negro author.

6549. Sterrett, N. B. Annual Sermon Delivered at the Commencement of Allen University, 1906. The Development of the Will Power. Charleston, S. C.: John J. Furlong, Printer, n.d. DHU/MO
Negro author.

6550. Steward, Theophilus Gould. From 1864 to 1914, 50 Years in the Gospel Ministry. Philadelphia: A. M. E. Book Concern, 1914.
Negro author.

6551. Talbert, Horace. The Sons of Allen. Together with a Sketch of the Rise and Progress of Wilberforce University, Wilberforce, Ohio. Xenia, O.: The Aldine Press, 1906. DHU/MO; DLC
Negro author.

6552. Tanner, Benjamin Tucker, (bp.). An Apology for African Methodism (Baltimore: n.p., 1867), pp. 183-88. DHU/MO; GAU; NN/Sch; CtY-D
Written by an A. M. E. bishop.

6553. ----- (bp.). The Dispensations in the History of the Church and the Interregnums. Kansas City: The Author, 1899. DH DHU/MO

6554. ----- (bp.). Hints to Ministers, Especially Those of the African Methodist Episcopal Church. Wilberforce, O.: Industrial Student Printers, 1900. NN/Sch

6555. ----- (bp.). An Outline of Our History and Government for African Methodist Churchmen, Ministerial and Lay in Catechetical Form. Two Parts with appendix. ...Introduction by B. F. Lee. Philadelphia: Grant, Faires & Rodgers, Printers, 1884. DHU/R; DHU/MO; TNF

6556. Tanner, Carl M. "Bethel A. M. E. Tabernacle." The African Methodist Episcopal Church Review (78:217, Jl.-Sept., 1963), pp. 26-33. DHU/R
History of "Big Bethel" Church, Atlanta, Ga.

6557. ----- A Manual of the African Methodist Episcopal Church Being a Course of Twelve Lectures for Probationers and Members. Philadelphia: A. M. E. Publishing House, 1900. NN/Sch; DLC

6558. ----- Reprint of the First Edition of Discipline of the A. M. E. Church with Historical Preface and Notes. Atlanta: C. M. Tanner, 1917. OWibfU

6559. Tolbert, Horace. The Sons of Allen. Xenia, O.: n.p., 1906. IEG; OWibfU

6560. Townsend, Vince M. Fifty-Four Years of African Methodism; Reflections of a Presiding Elder on the Law and Doctrine of the African Methodist Episcopal Church. New York: Exposition Press, 1953. DHU/R; TNF; OWibfU; DLC; NjP; NN/Sch

6561. Turner, Henry McNeal, (bp.). African Letters. Nashville: Publishing House A. M. E. Sunday School Union, 1893. DHU/MO
Negro author.

6562. ----- (bp.). An Appeal for Africa From the A. M. E. Church. n.p.: n.p., 1883. OWibfU

6563. ----- (bp.). The Genius and Theory of Methodist Polity; or, The Machinery of Methodism. Practically Illustrated Through a Series of Questions and Answers. Approved by the General Conference of the A. M. E. Church. Philadelphia: Publication Dept., A. M. E. Church, 1885. NN/Sch; DHU/MO; NjP; DHU/R
Negro author.

6564. [----- (bp.)] The Hymn Book of the African Methodist Episcopal Church, Being a Collection of Hymns, Sacred Songs and Chants... Eight Ed. Phila.: Published at the Publication Department of the A. M. E. Church, 1880. NNUT
"Revised by order of General Conference of 1886, by H. M. Turner."

6565. ----- (bp.). Only for the Bishops' Eye. Atlanta: n.p., 1907. DHU/MO
Negro author.

6566. Turner, Henry McNeil, (bp.). Turner's Catechism; Being a Series of Questions and Answers, Upon Some of the Cardinal Topics of Christianity. Designed for the General Use of Adults, by... Edited by B. T. Tanner. Part 1st. Philadelphia: A. M. E. Church Book Rooms, 1917. TNF; GAU; OWibfU

6567. "Union of the A. M. E. and the A. M. E. Zion Churches."
The African Methodist Episcopal Church Review (80:219,
Ja.-Mr., 1964), pp. 38-39.   DHU/R

6568. Valentine, Rachel. "Synopsis of the History of the Women's
Missionary Society A. M. E. Church." The Missionary Magazine (19:11, Sept., 1971), p. 17.   Pam. File, DHU/R

6569. Walker, John S. "Morris Brown: Crisis Leadership of the
African Methodist Episcopal Church -- 1830-1850." Perspective (13:2, Spr., 1972), pp. 138-55.   DHU/R

6570. Ward, A. Wayward. "Can African Methodism Afford to Tolerate Mediocrity." The African Methodist Episcopal Church
Review (68:174, Oct.-Dec., 1952), pp. 58-62.   DHU/R
      Picture of author.
      Negro author.

6571. Washington, Booker Taliaferro. "The Mission Work of the
A. M. E. Church." The African Methodist Episcopal Church
Review (32:3, Ja. 1916), pp. 186-89.   DHU/MO

6572. Washington, R. Francis. The Philosopher Looks at Life.
Detroit: Missionary Press, 1953.   OWibfU

6573. Wayman, Alexander Walker, (bp.). Cyclopaedia of African
Methodism. Baltimore: Methodist Episcopal Book Depository,
1882.   DHU/MO; TNF; NN/Sch
      Negro author.

6574. ----- (bp.). The Life of Rev. James Alexander Shorter, One
of the Bishops of theAfrican Methodist Episcopal Church. Baltimore: J. Lanahan, 1890.   DHU/MO

6575. ----- (bp.). Manual, or Guide Book for the Administration
of the Discipline of the African M. E. Church. Philadelphia:
African Methodist Episcopal Book Rooms, 1886. GAU; DHU/MO

6576. ----- (bp.). My Recollections of African M. E. Ministers.
Philadelphia: African Methodist Episcopal Book Rooms, 1881.
NN/Sch; DHU/MO; GAU; NjP

6577. Welch, Isaiah H. The Heroism of the Rev. Richard Allen,
Founder and First Bishop of the A. M. E. Church in the U. S.
A. and Rev. Daniel Coker, Co-founder and First Missionary
to Africa from Said Church. With a Brief Sketch of Sister Sarah
Allen's Heroism. Nashville: A. M. E. Sunday School Union,
1910.   NN/Sch

6578. Weston, Abraham. "How African Methodism was Introduced
in the Up Country." The African Methodist Episcopal Church
Review (80:219, Ja.-Mr., 1964), pp. 44-46.   DHU/R
      South Carolina and the A. M. E. Church.
      Negro author.

6579. Whitlock, F. Lemoyne. "For Zion's Sake Will I Hold My
Peace!" The African Methodist Episcopal Church Review (93
(93:235, Apr. Je., 1968), pp. 62-64.   DHU/R
      "Calls for reform in the administration of the A. M. E.
      Church."
      Negro author.

6580. Wright, Richard Robert, Jr., (bp.). AME Mission Study
Course, No. 2, Compiled as a Practical Aid for Those Studying
for Missionary Work. n.p.: Women's Missionary Society
African Methodist Episcopal Church, 1944.   OWibfU

6581. ----- (bp.). The Bishops of the African Methodist Episcopal
Church. Nashville: Pr. by the A. M. E. Sunday School Union,
1963.   DHU/R; TNF; InU; DLC

6582. ----- (ed.). ...Centennial Encylcopedia of the African
Methodist Episcopal Church, Containing Principally the Bio-
graphies of the Men and Women, Both Ministers and Laymen,
Whose Labors During a Hundred Years, Helped Make the A. M.
E. Church What it is; Also Short Historical Sketches of Annual
Conferences, Educational Institutions, General Departments,
Missionary Societies of the A. M. E. Church, and General

Information About African Methodism and the Christian Church
in General; Being a Literary Contribution to the Celebration of
the One Hundredth Anniversary of the Formation of the African
M. E. Church... Philadelphia: n.p., 1916. DHU/R; DHU/MO
      Also: 1947 edition. TNF; DHU/R; DHU/MO

6583. ----- (bp.). 87 Years Behind the Black Curtain. An Autobiography. Philadelphia: Rare Book Co., 1965. TNF; DLC;
OWibfU; NjP

6584. ----- (bp.). The Encyclopedia of the African Methodist
Episcopal Church...2d ed. Containing Principally the Biographies of the Men and Women, Both Minister and Laymen,
Whose Labors during a Hundred and Sixty Years, Helped Make
the AME Church What it is; also Short Historical Sketches of
Annual Conferences, Educational Institutions, General Departments, Missionary Societies of the AME Church. Philadelphia:
n.p., 1947.   DHU/R

6585. ----- (bp.). Social Service, Especially Prepared for the
Allen C. E. League of the A. M. E. Church. Phila.: n.p.,
1922.   DHU/MO

6586. ----- (bp.). What the Negro Gives his Church: Two Cents.
Philadelphia: African Methodist Episcopal Sunday School Union,
1940.   DLC

6587. ----- (bp.). Who's Who in the General Conference, 1924,
Containing Sketches and Pictures of Bishops, General Officers,
College Presidents, Delegates and Alternates, Lay and Ministerial, and their Wives, Who are Members of the General Conference of the A. M. E. Church, Convening at Louisville, Kentucky, May, 1924. Philadelphia: A. M. E. Book Concern,
1924.   NN/Sch

6588. Yancy, J. History of the Connectional Departments of the
African Methodist Episcopal Church. Waco, Tex.: n.p.,
n.d.   DHU/R
      Negro author.

6589. Yearbook of Negro Churches; With Statistics and Records
of Achievements of Negroes in the United States. Wilberforce,
O.: Pr. at Wilberforce University, 1935. OWibfU; DHU/MR;
CtY-D; DHU/MR; CtY-D; DHU/MO; (1939-40); DLC NN/Sch
      "Published by authority of the bishops of the A. M. E.
      Church."

6590. Yearbook and Historical Guide to African Methodist Episcopal Church. E. D. Adams, ed. Columbia, S. C.: Bureau of
Research and History, 1955.   GAU

      (2) African Methodist Episcopal Zion

6591. African Methodist Episcopal Zion Church. Annual State
Conference. DLC; NcSa1L; DHU/MO; DHU/R; NcD-D;
CtY-D; GAU

6592. ----- Catechisms ... DHU/MO; NcSa1L; NN/Sch; DLC;
DHU/R; GAU

6593. ----- Code on the Discipline of the African Methodist Episcopal Zion Church. DLC; DHU/MO; OWibfU; GAU; NcSa1L;
NN/Sch

6594. ----- Christian Education Dept. Report. Chicago: n.p.,
n.d.   DLC; NcSa1L; DHU/MO; NN/Sch

6595. ----- Hand Book, 1856-1960. Edited and Compiled by
Willie G. Alstork. Washington, D.C.: n.p., n.d.   DHU/R

6596. ----- Hymnals...   DLC; DHU/R; NN/Sch; NcSa1L

6597. ----- Message of the Bishops...to the General Conference.
Chicago: n.p., n.d.   DLC; GAU; NcSa1L

6598. ----- ...Year Book, 1906- New Bern, N.C.: n.p., 1906-.
DLC; DHU/MO; NcSa1L; GAU

6599. ----- Department of Foreign Missions. ...Quadrennial Report... Washington, D.C.: n.p., n.d. DLC; DHU/MO; GAU; NcSalL; NN/Sch; CtY-D

6600. ----- The Doctrines and Disciplines of the African Methodist Episcopal Zion Church in America... New York: n.p., 18-. TNF; DLC; NcSapL; GAU; DHU/MO

6601. ----- General Conference. Protest of the A. M. E. Zion Church, New York City, Against the Oridnation of Bishops, by the Extraordinary General Conference, to be Held in Harrisburg, Pa., September 20th, 1866, with the Articles of Consolidation. New York: Zion's Standard, n.d.   NcD

6602. ----- Zion's Sesquicentennial, A. M. E. Zion Church, 1796-1946. Official Souvenir Journal...Sept. 8-22, 1946. New York City, N.Y. New York: n.p., 1946.   NN/Sch; NcSalL

6603. "The African Methodist Episcopal Zion Church, Its Theological Position and Polity." The A. M. E. Zion Quarterly Review (84: 3, Fall, 1972), pp. 154-57.   DHU/R

6604. Anderson, James H. Biographical Souvenir Volume of the Twenty-third Quadrennial Session of the General Conference of the African Methodist Episcopal Zion Church. Big Wesley AMEZ Church, Philadelphia, Pa., May 8-30, 1908. Philadelphia: n.p., 1908.   NN/Sch

6605. Baptiste, Louis J. Basic Beliefs of the African Methodist Episcopal Zion Church. n.p.: n.p., 1964.   CoDl

6606. Bradley, David H. A History of the A. M. E. Zion Church. 2 vols. Nashville: Parthenon Press, 1956-70. DHU/R; NN/Sch; DLC; CtY-D; NjP
          Negro author.

6607. Browne, Jackson A. The Holy Communion Worship Service and Membership Guide in the African Methodist Episcopal Zion Church. Norfolk, Va.: Greater Metropolitan A. M. E. Zion Church, 1972.   Pam. File, DHU/R

6608. Coleman, Clinton R. A Study of A Black Ghetto Church, The Pennsylvania Avenue A. M. E. Zion Church, Baltimore, Maryland. M. Div. Paper. School of Religion, Howard University, 1971.
          Negro author.

6609. Cotter, Joseph. "To Bishop Hood." The Crisis (17:3, Ja., 1919), p. 125.   DHU/MO; DLC
          A. M. E. Zion bishop.

6610. Davenport, William Henry. The Anthology of Zion Methodism. Charlotte, N.C.: A. M. E. Zion Publishing House, 1925.   NN/Sch
          Negro author.

6611. ----- Membership in Zion Methodism; the Meaning of Membership in the A. M. E. Zion Church. Charlotte, N.C.: A. M. E. Zion Publishing House, 1936.   DLC

6612. Davis, Arnor S. A Proposed Program of Christian Education for Juniors in Galbraith African Methodist Episcopal Zion Church, Washington, D.C. Masters thesis. Howard University, 1958.

6613. Eason, Vaughn T. "The Gospel of Liberation." The Church School Herald-Journal (57:1, Dec.-Feb., 1972-73), pp. 5-8.   Pam. File, DHU/R
          "An address to the Quadrennial General Conference of the African Methodist Episcopal Zion Church convening at Big Zion Church, Mobile, Ala., May 3-12, 1972, Wednesday Evening, May 10, 1972."

6614. Eichelberger, James William. "African Methodist Episcopal Zion Church: The Rationale and Policies upon which Maintenance of its Colleges is Based." Journal of Negro Education (29; Sum., 1960), pp. 323-29.   DHU
          Negro author.

6615. ----- The Religious Education of the Negro; an Address Delivered at the International Convention of Religious Education, Toronto, Canada, June 26, 1930. Chicago: The Herald Press, 1931.   DHU/MO; DLC

6616. Fortune, T. Thomas. "Rise of a Great Church." The New York Sun (Sept. 27, 1896); (Sept., 1903).

6617. Harris, Cicero R. Historical Catechism of the A. M. E. Zion Church. For use of Families and Sunday Schools. Charlotte, N.C.: A. M. E. Zion Publication House, 1922.   NN/Sch; DHU/R
          Negro author.

6618. Hood, James Walker., (bp.). "The Mission of Methodism to All Calsses." H. K. Carroll, (ed.). Proceedings, Sermons, Essays and Addresses of the Centennial Methodist Conference Held in Mt. Vernon Methodist Episcopal Church, Baltimore, Md., December 9-17, 1884. Cincinnati: n.p., 1885. GAU/ITC

6619. ----- (bp.). The Negro in the Christian Pulpit or, The Two Characters and Two Destinies, as Delineated in Twenty-One Practical Sermons... Raleigh: Edwards Broughton Co., 1884.   DHU/MO; NN/Sch
          Negro author.

6620. ----- (bp.). One Hundred Years of the African Methodist Episcopal Zion Church; or, The Centennial of African Methodism. New York: A. M. E. Zion Book Concern, 1895. DHU/MO; TNF; NN/Sch; NcD

6621. ----- (bp.). Sermons by J. W. Hood... V. II. York, Pa.: P. Anstadt & Sons, n.d.   NN/Sch; DHU/R

6622. ----- (bp.). Sketch of the Early History of the African Methodist Episcopal Zion Church With Jubilee Souvenir And an Appendix. n.p., 1914.   NN/Sch

6623. Hood, Solomon Porter. Sanctified Dollars; How We Get Them, and Use Them. Philadelphia, Pa.: A. M. E. Book Concern, 1908.
          Negro author.

6624. Jones, Singleton T., (bp.). The Negro, Address Delivered at Commencement Exercises of Zion Wesley Institute, Salisbury, N.C., June 5, 1883. n.p.: n.p., n.d.   OWibfU
          Written by Bishop of A. M. E. Zion Church.

6625. ----- (bp.). Sermons and Addresses of the Late Rev. Bp. Singleton T. Jones, D.D., of the African Methodist Episcopal Zion Church, with a Memoir of his Life and Character. York, Pa.: P. Anstadt & Sons, 1892.   DHU/MO; NN/Sch
          Negro author.

6626. Livingstone College, Salisbury, N.C. Carnegie Library. An Index to Biographical Sketches and Publications of the Bishops of the A. M. E. Zion Church. Compiled by Louise M. Roundtree. Salisbury, N.C.: n.p., 1963. DHU/MO; NcD; DLC

6627. Manley, J. H. A Dream, A Sermon of the Virginia Conference of the A. M. E. Zion Church. n.p.: n.p., 1885. OWibfU

6628. Medford, Hampton Thomas, (bp.). Zion Methodism Abroad. Giving the Rise and Progress of the A. M. E. Zion Church on its Foreign Fields. n.p.: n.p., 1937.   NN/Sch; DHU/R
          Negro author.

6629. Miles, John H. The Right Hand of Fellowship. n.p., 1963.   DHU/R
          "A manual on church membership and responsibility written by a A. M. E. Z. ministers."

6630. Miller, John J. History of the A.M.E. Zion Church in America... York, Pa.: Teacher's Journal Office, 1884.   GAU

6631. Moore, John J., (bp.). History of the A. M. E. Zion Church in America. Founded 1796, in the City of New York, Compiled

(Moore, John J. cont.)
and Publsihed by John Jamison Moore. York, Pa.: Teachers
Journal Office, 1884.   DHU/MO; TNF; NN/Sch
Negro author.

6632. Patterson, Thomas B. "Rural Social Service Work."
Southern Workman (46:4, Apr., 1917), pp. 253-5. DLC;
DHU/MO
"Under the patronage of Dr. J. E. Aggrey, professor of
literature in Livingstone College, an effort was made to
start a local farm conference in the neighborhood of
Miller's Chapel, one of the Churches presided over by
him."

6633. Powell, Jacob Wesley. Bird's Eye View of the General Con-
ference of the African Methodist Episcopal Zion Church With
Observations on the Progress of the Colored People of Louisville,
Kentucky... Boston, Mass.: The Lavalle Press, 1918. NcD
Negro author.

6634. ----- Echoes of Christian Education. Miss M. Leonessa
Powell, Secretary. Malden, Mass.: n.p., 1934. DLC

6635. Satterwhite, John H. "African Methodist Episcopal Zion
Theology for a Uniting Church." The Journal of Religious
Thought (29:2, Aut.-Wint., 1972), pp. 61-67. DHU/R

6636. Speaks, Ruben L. "Zion!!! Africa ia Calling." The A. M.
E. Zion Quarterly Review(8:1, Spr., 1973), pp. 18-21.
DHU/R

6637. Stonehouse, Helena M. One Hundred and Forty Years of
Methodism in the Jamestown, New York Area. n.p.: n.p.,
1954.
Includes the history of the African Methodist Episcopal
Church in this community.

6638. Thomas, G. B. "The A. M. E. Zion Church and Theological
Education." The Star of Zion (94:27 & 28, Jl. 8, Jl. 15, 1971),
pp. 8+.   DHU/R

6639. Van Catledge, John. A Critical Evaluation of the Intermediate
Senior Curriculum of the African Methodist Episcopal Zion
Church. Doctoral dissertation. Hartford, 1943.

6640. Walls, William Jacob, (bp.). The African Methodist Epis-
copal Zion Church; Reality of the Black Church. Charlotte,
N.C.: A. M. E. Zion Pub. House, 1974.   DHU/R
Bishop of the A. M. E. Zion Church.
Includes biographical information on the ministers in this
denomination.

6641. ----- (bp.). Joseph Charles Price: Educator and Race
Leader. Boston: The Christopher Publishing House, 1943.
DHU/MO
Negro author.

6642. ----- Living Essentials of Our Methodism. n.p.: n.p.,
n.d.   DHU/R
Negro author.

6643. ----- (bp.). "Negro Burial Also Cause for Sunderance."
The Star of Zion (96:7, Feb. 15, 1973), pp. 1-2. DHU/R
From the New York Sun, Sept. 23, 1903. "History regarding
religious burial for African people started in New York with
the A. M. E. Zion Church."

6644. ----- (bp.). The Romance of a College. New York: Van-
tage Press, 1963.   DHU/R
Founding and history of Livingstone College, Salisbury,
N.C.

6645. Walters, Alexander, (bp.). My Life and Work. n.p.: n.p.,
1917.   NcSalL
Bishop of A. M. E. Zion Church.

6646. Walton, O. M. "A. M. E. Zion Has Lively Session."
Christian Century (73:24, Je. 13, 1956), pp. 732-33. DHU/R

6647. Wheeler, Benjamin F. Cullings from Zion's Poets. Mobile,
Ala.: n.p., 1907.   DHU/R
Negro author.
"Short biographies and pictures of some A. M. E. Zion
bishops along with their religious poetry."

6648. ----- The Varick Family. Mobile, Ala.: n.p., 1907.
DHU/R; DHU/MO
Descendants of James Varick, founder of the African Meth-
odist Episcopal Zion Church.

(3) Christian Methodist Episcopal

6649. Allison, Madeline G. "The General Conference of the
Colored Methodist Episcopal Church." The Crisis (24:3,
Jl., 1922), pp. 126-27.   DHU/MO; DLC
Legislation passed on education work.

6650. Bailey, Augustus Ceasar. The Passion Week. Jackson,
Tenn.: Publishing House of the A. M. E. Church, 1935.
ISAR
Negro author.

6651. Brown, Lorenzo Quincy. A Study of the Sunday School
Literature Provided for the Intermediate Department of the
Colored Methodist Episcopal Church. Masters thesis. Howard
University, 1940.

6652. Carter, Randall Albert, (bp.). A Century of Progress in
Christian Journalism; The Christian Index. Jackson, Tenn.:
C. M. E. Publishing House, 1967.   ISAR
Negro author.

6653. Christian Methodist Episcopal Church. Annual Conference
Yearbooks... GAU; NN/Sch; NcSalL

6654. ----- The Church College Today, Its Nature, Function,
and Responsibility in the American Educational System.
Jackson, Tenn.: Lane College Press, 1957.   NNCor

6655. ----- The Doctrines and Disciplines... GAU; DLC; NN/Sch;
DHU/MO

6656. ----- Episcopal Addresses to Quadrennial Session... DLC
GAU; DHU/MO; NcSalL

6657. ----- Quadrennial Reports... GAU; NN/Sch; DLC; DHU/MO;
NcSalL

6658. ----- Songs of Love and Mercy. Adapted to the Use of Sun-
day Schools, Epworth Leagues Revivals, Prayer Meetings and
Special Occasions. Scores and words. By Rev. F. M.
Hamilton and Bishop L. H. Holsey. Memphis, Tenn.: Publish-
ing House of the C. M. E. Church, 1968.   Pam. File,
DHU/R
Originally published in 1904.

6659. ----- State and District Programs... GAU; DHU/R; NCSalL;
NN/Sch

6660. ----- State Annual Conference. Souvenir Programs...
DHU/R; GAU; NcSalL; NN/Sch; DLC

6661. ----- Youth Conferences... GAU; NN/Sch; DHU/MO; NcSalL

6662. ----- General Board of Religious Education. Annual Reports.
GAU; DHU/R; DLC; DHU/MO

6663. ----- General Board of Christian Education. Christian Ed-
ucation. Christian Education in the C. M. E. Church...A
Handbook for Workers in Christian Education. Jackson, Tenn.:
Christian Methodist Episcopal Church, 1961.   DHU/R

6664. "Churches." The Crisis (7:6, Apr., 1914), p. 271.
DHU/MO; DLC
Colored Methodists contributed $100,000 to Freedmen's
Aid Society.

6665. Colclough, J. G. The Spirit of John Wesley Gibbert.
Nashville: Cokesbury Press, 1925.   IEG

6666. Coleman, C. D. "Christian Methodist Episcopal Church:
The Rationale and Policies upon Which Support of its College
is Predicated." Journal of Negro Education (29; Sum., 1960),
pp. 315-18.   DHU

6667. Hamilton, Fayette M., (bp.). A Conversation of the Colored
Methodist Episcopal Church in America ... Nashville: n.p.,
1884.   DLC

6668. ----- (bp.). Plain Account of the Colored Methodist Episcopal Church in America... Nashville: n.p., 1887. DHU/MO
Negro author.

6669. Holsey, Lucius Henry, (bp.). The Race Problem. Atlanta,
Ga.: By the author, 1899.   DHU/MO

6670. Johnson, William R., Jr. "From the Division of Higher
Education of the General Board of Christian Education of the
Christian Methodist Episcopal Church." The Christian Index
(106:3, Feb. 8, 1973), p. 5.   DHU/R
"Plans for improving C. M. E. colleges."

6671. ----- "Needed: Preachers in Our C. M. E. Pulpits ---
Now." Christian Index (105:22, Nov. 23, 1972), pp. 5-6.
                                             DHU/R

6672. Lakey, Othal Hawthorne. The Rise of "Colored Methodism";
a Study of the Background and the Beginnings of the Christian
Methodist Episcopal Church. Dallas: Crescendo Book Publications, 1972.   MNtcA
C. M. E. church.

6673. McAfee, Sara Jane. History of the Woman's Missionary
Society in the Colored Methodist Episcopal Church, Comprising
its Founders, Organizations, Pathfinders, Subsequent Developments and Present Status. Phenix City, Ala.: Phenix City
Herald, 1945.   DHU/MO; NN/Sch

6674. McLeod, J. R. An Historical Study of the Origin and Early
Development of Miles Memorial Christian Methodist Episcopal
Church. Masters thesis. Howard University, School of Re-
ligion, 1973.

6675. Newborn, Captola D. Proposals for Developing a Program
of Education at William Institutional C. M. E. Church.
Doctoral dissertation. Columbia University, Teachers College,
1955.

6676. Pettigrew, M. C. From Miles to Johnson. Memphis,
Tenn.: C. M. E. Publishing House, 1970.   DHU/R
"One Hundred Years of Progress 1870-1970 of the
Christian Methodist Episcopal Church."
Negro author.

6677. Phillips, Charles Henry, (bp.). The History of the Colored
Methodist Episcopal Church in America; Comprising its Or-
ganization, Subsequent Development, and Present Status.
Jackson, Tenn.: Publishing House, C. M. E. Church, 1898.
                                             DHU/MO; NN/Sch
"Biography of the author, by J. W. Smith;" p. 7-18.

6678. Sideboard, Henry Yergan. The Historical Background of
the Colored Methodist Episcopal Church. B. D. Paper. School
of Religion, Howard Univ., 1938.   Negro author.

6679. Thrall, Homer S. History of Methodism in Texas. Houston:
Cushing, 1872.   IEG
Formation of the C. M. E. Church.

(4) National Baptist

6680. Johnson, Robert Ross. The Mountain of Olivet. A Historical
Sketch of Negro Baptists in Rochester, N.Y. Rochester, N.
n.p., 1946.   SCBHC
Xerox copy.

6681. McGuire, U. M. "A Baptist Golden Jubilee." Baptist
(21), pp. 1068-9.   SCBHC

6682. Newman, Albert H. (ed.). A Century of Baptist Achievement... Philadelphia: American Baptist Publication Society,
1901.   SCBHC

6683. Palmer, F. B. "Negro Baptist Work in Colorado."
Baptist (10; 1929), pp. 694+.   SCBHC

(5) Progressive National Baptist Convention

6684. Tinney, James S. "Progressive Baptists." Christianity
Today (15:1, Oct. 9, 1970), pp. 42-3.   DHU/R

(6) National Baptist Convention, U.S.A., Inc. – Negro Baptist in General

6685. "The Abyssinian Church of New York." The Crisis (26:5,
Sept., 1923), pp. 203-05.   DLC; DHU/MO
"Abyssinian Church was organized 115 years ago and is
the third oldest Baptist Church in America."

6686. Adams, C. C. and Marshall A. Talley. Negro Baptists
and Foreign Missions. Philadelphia: The Foreign Mission
Board of the National Baptist Convention, U. S. A., Inc.,
1944.   DHU/MO; DLC

6687. Allison, Madeline G. "The Churches." The Crisis (19:2,
Dec., 1919), p. 84.   DHU/MO; DLC
The Sunday School Publishing Board of the National Baptist
Convention, financial report.

6688. ----- "The Lott Carey Baptist Foreign Mission Convention."
The Crisis (25: 1, Nov., 1922), p. 27.   DHU/MO; DLC

6689. Anderson, H. C. Annual Report Delivered to Members and
Friends of New Prospect Baptist Church, Williamston, S. C.
and Mountain Spring Baptist Church, Route No. 2 Anderson,
S. C. by the Pastor Rev. H. C. Anderson.   SCBHC

6690. Asher, Jeremiah. Autobiography with Details of a Visit
to England, and Some Account of the History of the Meeting
Street Baptist Church, Providence, Rhode Island and of Shiloh
Baptist Church, Philadelphia, Pa. ... Philadelphia: Pub.
by Author, 1862.   DHU/MO
Negro author.

6691. Augusta, Ga. Tabernacle Baptist Church. Condensed Historical Sketch. By Thomas P. Lewis, with an Introduction by
Rev. C. T. Walker.   SCBHC

6692. Bacote, Samuel William, ed. Who's Who Among the Colored
Baptists of the United States... Kansas City, Mo.: Franklin
Hudson Publishing Co., 1913-.   DHU/MO; DLC;
GAU

6693. Baptist Advance. The Achievements of the Baptist of North
America for a Century and a Half. Nashville: Broadman Press,
1964.   DHU/R
Negro Baptists, pp. 186-226.

6694. "The Baptist Controversy." The Crisis (11:6, Apr., 1916),
pp. 314-6   DLC; DHU/MO
"Split in the National Baptist Convention."

6695. Baptist General Convention of Virginia. Annual Report of
the Executive Secretary. Richmond, Va.: Virginia Union
University, n.d.   Pam. File, DHU/R

6696. The Baptist Standard Hymnal with Responsive Readings. A
New Book for All Services. Edited by Mrs. A. M. Townsend.
Nashville: S. S. Pub. Bd., National Baptist Convention, 1924.
                                             SCBHC

6697. Baugh, J. Gordon. Historical Account of the First African
Baptist Church. Philadelphia: The Author, 1904. DLC

6698. Benedict, David. _A General History of the Baptist Denomination, in America and in Other Parts of the World._ Boston: n.p., 1813.   DLC; CtY-D

6699. Bennett, Ambrose Allen. _The Preacher's Weapon..._ Nashville, Tenn.: Sunday School Publishing Bd., National Baptist Convention, U.S.A., 1922.   NN/Sch
    Negro author.

6700. "Blunting and Cutting Edge; Resolution Adopted by National Baptist Convention, U.S.A., Inc., Tulsa." _Christian Century_ (82:28, Jl. 14, 1965), pp. 883-84.   DHU/R

6701. Boone, Theodore S. "Beginnings in Negro Baptist History." Shann Custom Recordings, 1964.   TNF
    Phonodisc.
    Narration and music by King Solomon Baptist Church.

6702. ----- _The National Training School for Women and Girls, Its Relation to the Woman's Convention and the National Baptist Convention, U.S.A., Inc._ n.p.: National Baptist Convention, U.S.A., 1939.   DHU/R

6703. ----- _Negro Baptist Chief Executives in National Places._ Detroit: n.p., 1948.   DLC
    Negro author

6704. ----- _Negro Baptist in Pictures and History; A Negro Baptist Historical Handbook._ Detroit: Voice of Destiny, 1964.
    DLC

6705. ----- _A Social History of Negro Baptists._ Detroit: Historical Commission, National Baptist Convention, U.S.A., 1952.   DLC

6706. Booth, L. Venchael. _Who's Who in Baptist America..._ Cincinnati, O.: n.p., 1960.   DHU/R
    Includes leaders and workers in the National Sunday School and Baptist Training Union Congress.
    Negro author.

6707. Boothe, Charles Octavius. _The Cyclopedia of the Colored Baptists of Alabama, Their Leaders and Their Work._ Birmingham: Alabama Pub. Co., 1895.   DLC; NcD

6708. Boston, Mass. Twelfth Baptist Church. _One Hundred and Five Years of Faith; a History of the Twelfth Baptist Church._ Boston: Macmillan, Twelfth Baptist Church, 1946.
    DHU/MO; SCBHC

6709. Bowling, Richard H. "Keeping an Old Church Alive." _Southern Workman_ (61:5, My., 1932), pp. 200-08.
    DLC; DHU/MO
    The First Baptist Church of Norfolk, Va., organized in July, 1800, and at that time composed of both white and colored members, this church has maintained a continuous existence marked until today with more than the usual evidences of spiritual prosperity.

6710. Boyd, Richard Henry., (ed.). _National Baptist Hymnal Arranged for use in Churches, Sunday Schools and Young Peoples Societies._ R. H. Boyd, ed. and William Rosborough, musical editor. 6th ed. revised. Nashville: National Baptist Pub. Board, 1903.   SCBHC

6711. ----- _The Separate or "Jim Crow" Car Laws or Legislative Exactments of Fourteen Southern States._ Reply in Compliance With a Resolution of the National Baptist Convention, September 19, 1908. Lexington, Ky.: Nashville, Tenn. National Baptist Publishing Board, 1909.   DLC; NN/Sch

6712. ----- _A Story of the National Baptist Publishing Board. The Why, How, When, Where, and By Whom it Was Established..._ With an Appendix by Rev. C. H. Clark. Nashville: n.p., n.d.   DHU/MO; TNF

6713. Bradley, Fulton C. _An Evaluation of the Junior Sunday School Curriculum Material of the National Baptist Convention,_

United States of America, Inc._ Masters thesis. Howard University, 1957.

6714. Brawley, Edward McKnight. "Baptists and General Education." E. M. Brawley. _The Negro Baptist Pulpit_ (Phila., Pa.: Baptist Publication Society, 1890), pp. 237-50. DHU/MO

6715. ----- Baptists and Sunday-School Work." _The Negro Baptist Pulpit_ (Phila., Pa.: Baptist Publication Society, 1890), pp. 221-32.   DHU/MO

6716. ----- "The Duty of Colored Baptists in View of the Past, the Present, and the Future." E. M. Brawley. _The Negro Baptist Pulpit_ (Phila., Pa.: Baptist Publication Society, 1890), pp. 287-300.   DHU/MO

6717. ----- (ed.). _The Negro Baptist Pulpit; a Collection of Sermons and Papers on Baptist Doctrine and Missionary and Educational Work, by Colored Baptist Ministers._ Philadelphia: American Baptist Publication Society, 1890. DHU/MO; DLC; TNF
    Negro author.

6718. ----- (ed.). _The Special Duty of Baptists to Circulate the Bible._ Petersburg, Va.: Mitchell Manufacture Co., 1893.
    DHU/MO

6719. Braxton, P. H. A. "Baptists and Foreign Missions." E. M. Brawley. _The Negro Baptist Pulpit_ (Phila., Pa.: Baptist Publication Society, 1890), pp. 256-70.   DHU/MO

6720. Brooks, Charles H. _Official History of the First African Baptist Church._ Philadelphia: The Author, 1922. DLC; ATI

6721. Brooks, Walter H. "The Priority of the Silver Bluff Church and Its Promoters." _Journal of Negro History_ (7:2, Apr., 1922), pp. 172-96.   DHU/MO
    Traces the growth of the Negro Baptist Church at Silver Bluff, S.C. and its influence on the establishment of other Baptist Churches.
    Negro author.

6722. ----- "Unification and Division Among Colored Baptists." _The Crisis_ (30:1, My., 1925), pp. 20-22.   DLC; DHU/MO
    "Dr. Brooks, a prominent Baptist leader and long pastor of the Nineteenth Street Baptist Church, Washington, D.C., warns his church of difficulties in property ownership in its various attempts at united action."

6723. Burdette, Mary G. _Twenty-Nine Years' Work Among Negroes._ Chicago: W.B.H.M.S., 1906.   SCBHC

6724. Carter, Eugene J. _Once a Methodist; Now a Baptist. Why?_ _... and "What Baptists Believe and Practice," by R. H. Boyd; "Boyd's National Baptist Paster's Guide;" "The Negro's Place in Ancient History and in American Life at the Present Day."_ Nashville: National Baptist Publishing Board, 1905. SCBHC

6725. Casey's Fork (Ky.). _Baptist Meeting House Church Book, May 3, 1818 to Ag. 3, 1856._   SCBHC
    Contains a list of members, and a list of "coullered brethren."

6726. Chandler, Russell. "Negro Baptists Praise God and Country." _Christianity Today_ (15:1, Oct. 9, 1970), pp. 42-4.   DHU/R

6727. "Churches." _The Crisis_ (7:3, Ja., 1914), p. 116. DLC; DHU/MO
    Miss Eliza Davis & Rev. James I. Simpson... sailed for Africa as missionaries of the National Baptist Convention.

6728. "Churches." _The Crisis_ (9:6, Apr., 1915), p. 271. DLC DHU/MO
    The Foreign Mission Board of the National Baptist Convention.

6729. "Churches." _The Crisis_ (11:4, Feb., 1916), p. 167.
    DLC; DHU/MO
    Colored New England Baptist convention.

6730. "Churches." The Crisis (5:1, Nov., 1912), p. 10. DHU/MO;
DLC
The total membership of the Negro Baptist Church in America
is now reported to be 2,444,055. There are 18,987 churches
worth $25,000,000.

6731. Clanton, Solomon Trumbull. "Baptist and Bible Work."
E. M. Brawley. The Negro Baptist Pulpit (Phila., Pa.:
Baptist Publication Society, 1890), pp. 188-99. DHU/MO

6732. ----- A Special Meeting in Behalf of the American Baptist
Publication Society Held at Indianapolis, Ind., Sept. 18-19,
1889... SCBHC
Negro author.

6733. Coleman, Charles Leroy. A History of the Negro Baptists
in Boston, 1800-1875. Masters thesis. Andover Newton
Theological School, 1956.

6734. Colored Baptist Home Missionary Society. The State of
Illinois. Proceedings... 1844. Alton, Ill.: Pr. at the Tele-
graph Office, 1844. SCBHC
Lacks pp. 5-6.

6735. Cook, Mary V. "The Work for Baptist Women." E. M.
Brawley. The Negro Baptist Pulpit (Phila., Pa.: Baptist
Publication Society, 1890), pp. 271-86. DHU/MO

6736. Cook, Richard Briscoe. Story of the Baptists... 33rd
Thousand. Baltimore: R. H. Woodward & Co., 1891. SCBHC
The supplementary chapter is entitled "The Colored Baptists."

6737. Davis, Felix L. The Young Men as an Important Force, or
the Young Men as an Important Active Spiritual Power on the
Field; Address Delivered by Elder Felix L. Davis...to the
Twenty-Eighth Annual Session of the Ministerial and Deacon's
Convention of Eastern Association of Indiana Baptist, Held
With the Howard's Chapel Baptist Church, New Albany, Ind.
.. August the 9th, 1911. n.p., 1911. DLC

6738. Dehoney, Wayne. Baptists See Black. Waxo, Texas:
Word Books, 1969. DHU/R
Negro Baptists ministers in the south and their struggle
for racial justice.

6739. Dowling, John. Sketches of New York Baptists. Rev. Thos.
Paul and the Colored Baptist Churches." Baptist Memorial and
Monthly Chronicles (9:9, Sept., 1849), pp. 295-301. SCBHC

6740. DuBois, William E. B. "The National Baptist Publishing
House." The Crisis (18:6, Oct., 1919), p. 285. DHU/MO;
DLC

6741. Durden, Lewis Minyon. ...The Small Negro Baptist Church
in Washington, D.C., Its Existing Program of Religious Education and Methods for Improving It... Master's thesis,
Howard University, 1942.

6742. Elmira, New York. Monumental Baptist Church. Historical Sketch of the Elmira Monumental Church. Chemung
Association Minutes (1934), pp. 11-13. SCBHC

6743. "First Negro Baptist Church." Sepia (6:53, Ja., 1958).
DLC

6744. Fisher, Miles Mark. "The Crozer Family and Negro
Baptists." Chronicle (8; Oct. 4, 1945), pp. 181-7. SCBHC
Negro author.

6745. ----- History of Olivet Baptist Church of Chicago. Master's
thesis. University of Chicago, 1922.
Negro author.

6746. ----- A Short History of the Baptist Denomination.
Nashville: Sunday School Pub. Board, 1933. DHU/R

6747. Fowler, Andrew. A Study of Social Welfare Work of the
Shiloh Baptist Church, 1939. B.D. paper. School of Religion,
Howard University, 1940.

6748. Freeman, Edward A. The Epoch of Negro Baptists and the
Foreign Mission Board, National Baptist Convention, U.S.A.,
Inc. Kansas City, Kan.: Central Seminary Press, 1953.
MNtcA; DHU/MO; CtY-D
Also: Author's dissertation, Central Baptist Theological
Seminary, 1952.

6749. Friedman, Lee M. "A Beacon Hill Synagogue." Old Time
New England (33:1, Jl., 1942), pp. 1-5. DLC
Brief history of Joy Street African Baptist Church in Boston.

6750. Fuller, Thomas Oscar, (ed.). Flashes and Gems of Thought
and Eloquence. Heard From the Platform of the National Baptist Convention, 1900-1920. Memphis: n.p., 1920. DHU/MO

6751. ----- History of the Negro Baptists of Tennessee. Memphis:
Haskins Print, 1936. DHU/MO

6752. General Association of the Colored Baptists in Kentucky.
Diamond Jubilee... The Story of Seventy Five Years of the
Association and Four Years of Convention Activities...
Louisville, KY.: American Baptist, 1943. GAU; TNF

6753. General Assocaition of the Colored Baptists in Kentucky.
Louisville: Mayers Printing Co., 1915. GAU

6754. Gray, Henderson. History of Monumental Baptist Church,
West Philadelphia, Pa., June 30, 1891. n.p., n.d. SCBHC
Rev. W. H. Davenport, Pastor.

6755. Grinstead, S. E. Baptist Student Union Handbook. For Baptist Student Union Directors, Pastors and Faculty Advisors
and Baptist Student Union Executive Council Members. Nashville, Tenn.: Nat. Bapt. Student Union Headquarters, n.d.
Pam. File, DHU/R
Negro Baptist denomination.

6756. Hacker, C. Leroy. The History and Program of the Zion
Baptist Church. Masters thesis. Washington, D.C., Howard
University, 1937.

6757. Harris, Solomon Parker. The External Relations of a Baptist Church. n.p. 1936. TNF

6758. Harvey, W. "National Baptists in Foreign Missions."
Mission (Dec., 1968), p. 32.
"Historical Survey of Negro Natl Baptists, Inc."

6759. Hester, William H. One Hundred and Five Years by Faith.
Twelfth Baptist Church, n.p., 1946. GAU

6760. Hicks, William. History of Louisiana Negro Baptists,
1804-1914. Nashville: National Baptist Pub. Board, 1915.
DHU/MO
Negro author.

6761. ----- Nails to Drive, Drawn from the Word of God and the
History of the Earliest Beginnings of Negro Missionary Baptists in America. Los Angeles: n.p., 1947.

6762. Hill, Andrew William. Some Signs of an Orthodox Baptist
Church. Aiken, S.C.: Ideal Printing Press, 1920? TNF

6763. Hill, Richard Hurst. History of the First Baptist Church
of Charleston, West Va. n.p., n.d. DHU/MO
Negro author.

6764. Historical Records Survey. Directory of Negro Baptist
Churches in the United States. Prepared by Illinois Historical
Records Survey, Division of Community Service Programs,
Work Projects Administration. Sponsored by the Governor of
Illinois. Chicago: Illinois Historical Records Survey, Illinois
Public Records Project, 1942. NcD; DHU/MO; DLC; TNF; DH
DHU/R
Reproduced from typewritten copy.

6765. Hodges, S. S. (comp.). Black Baptists in America and
the Origins of Their Conventions. Wash., D.C.: Progressive
National Baptist Convention, Inc. n.d. Pam. File, DHU/R

6766. Houser, Susie A. "A Community-Serving Community."
Southern Workman (54:2, Feb., 1925), pp. 58-59. DHU/MO;
DLC
The Olivet Baptist Church, Chicago, Dr. L. K. Williams,
Pastor, "has evolved a well-organized system of helpfulness"
by establishing a Bureau of Information; free Employment
Agency and a Health Bureau.

6767. Jackson, Benjamin Franklin. An Adequate Program of
Religious Education for the Small Negro Baptist Church in
Northwest Baltimore Which Has Inadequate Facilities.
Master's thesis. School of Religion, Howard University,
1942.

6768. Jackson, Joseph Harrison. Many but One; the Ecumenics of
Charity. New York: Sheed & Ward, 1964.   NN/Sch; DHU/R
Negro author.

6769. ----- "Participating in the Struggle of America." Herbert
J. Storing, (ed.). What Country Have I?: Political Writings
by Black Americans (New York: St. Martin's Press, 1970),
pp. 134-43.   DHU/MO
"Annual Address of President J. H. Jackson, delivered at
the eighty-fourth Annual Session of the National Baptist
Convention, U. S. A., Inc., September 10, 1964, Cobo
Hall-Arena, Detroit, Michigan."
Negro minister.

6770. Jackson, Joseph Julius. A Compendium of Historical Facts
of the Early African Baptist Churches. Bellefontaine, O.:
n.p., 1922.   DLC
Negro author

6771. Jamaica, New York. Amity Baptist Church. Twenty-Fifth
Anniversary, 1916-1941. n.p., n.d.   SCBHC

6772. Jernagin, William H. Annual Address of Rev. W. H.
Jernagin, President of the National Sunday School and B. T. U.
Congress, U.S.A. Delivered Cleveland, Ohio, June 24, 1948.
Pam. File, DHU/R
Negro Baptist minister.

6773. Jeter, Henry Norval. Historical Sketch of the Shiloh
Baptist Church, at Newport, R.I. and the Pastors who Served.
Newport, R.I.: B. W. Pearce-Newport Enterprise, 1891.
DHU/MO

6774. ----- Forty-Two Years Experience as Pastor...Brief
Fifty Years History of the New England Baptist Missionary
Convention, by Rev. H. N. Jeter, D.D. n.p., n.d. SCBHC

6775. Johnson, R.J. History of Walker Baptist Association of
Georgia... Augusta, Ga.: Chronicle Job Print, 1909. NcD

6776. Johnson, William A. A Study of Leadership Training of
Negro Baptist Ministers Attending the Chicago Baptist
Institute. Master's thesis. University of Chicago, 1944.

6777. Jordan, Lewis Garnett. The Baptist Standard Church
Directory and Busy Pastor's Guide. n.p.: Sunday School
Publication Board of National Baptist Convention, 1929.
DHU/MO
Negro author.

6778. ----- In Our Stead. Foreign Missions Board of the
National Baptist Convention. Philadelphia: n.p., n.d.
OWibfU

6779. ----- Negro Baptist History, U.S.A. 1750, 1930.
Nashville, Tenn.: The Sunday School Publishing Board,
N.B.C., 1930.   DHU/MO; DLC; TNF; NcD

6780. ----- Up the Ladder in Foreign Missions. Nashville, Tenn.:
National Baptist Pub. Board, 1901.   DLC; NN/Sch
Negro author.

6781. Kennard, Richard. A Short History of the Gilfield Baptist
Church of Petersburg, Virginia. Compiled by Wm. H.
Johnson. Petersburg: Owen, 1903.   SCBHC

6782. Kennedy, P. Baptist Directory and Year Book 1892-1893.
Henderson, Ky.: n.d.   SCBHC
Negro author.

6783. Koger, Azzie Briscoe. Negro Baptist of Maryland. Baltimore: Clarke Press, 1946.   DHU/MO; DLC; TNF

6784. Lee, William I. One Hundredth Anniversary of the 19th
Street Baptist Church, Washington, D.C., 1839-1939. 57th
Anniversary of Rev. Walter H. Brooks, 1882-1939.
Washington, D.C.: Printed by Murray Brothers, 1939.
DHU/MO

6785. Lewis, Thomas P. Condensed Historical Sketch of Tab-
ernacle Baptist Church, Augusta, Georgia, from its Organ-
ization in 1885 to February, 1904. Augusta, Ga.: The Georgia
Baptist Book Print, 1904.   DHU/MO
Negro church in Georgia.
Negro author.

6786. Lott Carey Baptist Foreign Mission Society of the United
States. Annual Report of the Corresponding Secretary,
1925-1926.   DHU/MO

6787. ----- Proceedings of the Fifth Annual Session of the Lott
Carey Home and Foreign Missions Convention of the United
States and of the Woman's Auxiliary Convention held with the
Liberty Baptist Church. Washington, D.C., Sept. 10-14,
1902. n.p., n.d.   DHU/MO

6788. Love, Emanuel King. History of the First African Church,
From Its Organization, January 20th, 1788, to July 1st, 1888.
Including the Centennial Celebration, Addresses, Sermons,
etc. Savannah, Ga.: The Morning News Print., 1888.
DHU/MO; TNF; NcD

6789. Lucas, George W. "Negro Baptists, the Stormiest Protestants." Negro Digest (Jan., 1962), pp. 32-40. SCBHC

6790. MacKerrow, P. A Brief History of the Coloured Baptists
of Nova Scotia, and Their First Organization as Churches, A.D.
1832... Halifax, N.S.: Nova Scotia Printing Co., 1895.
SCBHC

6791. Maryland State & District of Columbia Missionary Baptist
Convention. Minutes of the Annual Session. Baltimore:
Press of H.S. Patterson, n.d.   DHU/MO; GAU; DLC

6792. Morris, Charles S. "Fiftieth Anniversary of Negro Baptists."
Baptist (2), pp. 1095.   SCBHC

6793. ----- Pastor Henry N. Jeter's Twenty-five Years Experience with the Shiloh Baptist Church, and her History, Corner School and Mary Streets, Newport, R.I.... Providence:
Remington Print. Co., 1901.   TNF

6794. Moses, William Henry. Baptist Missionary Manual.
Listed in: Edward C. Starr, (ed.). A Baptist Bibliography.
Rochester, N.Y.: American Baptist Historical Society,
1971. V. 16.
(Unable to locate).
Negro Baptist minister.

6795. ----- The Colored Baptist Family Tree... Nashville, Tenn.:
Sunday School Publishing Board of Natl. Baptist Convention of
U.S., 1925.   GAU; DHU/MO
Negro author.

6796. ----- The Origin and Growth of Negro Baptist Churches.
Listed in Edward C. Starr, (ed.). A Baptist Bibliography.
Rochester, N.Y.: American Baptist Historical Society,
1971. V. 16.
(Unable to locate).
Negro Baptist minister.

6797. ----- The Reconstruction Program of Colored American
Baptists.
Listed in: Edward C. Starr, (ed.). A Baptist Bibliography.

Rochester, N.Y.: American Baptist Historical Society, 1971. V. 16 (Unable to locate). Negro Baptist minister.

6798. "Mount Olivet Baptist Church in New York City." Crisis (29:4, Feb., 1925), p. 176.   DHU/MO

6799. National Baptist Convention, U.S.A., Inc. Annual Report of the Auditor of the National Baptist Convention of the United States of America. n.p., 1915.   TNF; DLC; NN/Sch; DHU/MO

6800. ----- "The Deplorable Conditions of the Visible Church of Our Day." Proceedings of the Sixty-Third Annual Session of the National Baptist Convention, U.S.A., Inc. Chicago, Sept., 1943.   DHU/MO

6801. ----- Journal ... Nashville, Tenn.: National Baptist Publishing Board, n.d.   DHU/MO; NN/Sch; GAU; TNF

6802. ----- The Tenth Annual Message of Miss Nannie H. Burroughs, President of the Woman's Convention Auxiliary to the National Baptist Convention, U.S.A., Inc. Chicago: Oct. 14, 1958.   KyLoS

6803. ----- Benefit Association. Report ... Nashville: National Baptist Publishing Board, 1905-.   DHU/MO; GAU

6804. ----- Evangelical Board. Report of the National Baptist Evangelical Board ... Kansas City, Mo.: Sept. 6-12, 1916. Nashville: National Baptist Publishing Board, 1916.   TNF

6805. ----- Foreign Mission Board. The Revised Pictorial Review of Mission Stations of the Foreign Mission Board of the National Baptist Convention, U.S.A., Inc. Phila., Pa.: Foreign Mission Board, National Baptist Convention, U.S.A., Inc., 1952-1953.   KyLoS

6806. ----- Home Mission Board. Report ... Nashville: National Baptist Publishing Board, 189-.   DHU/MO; GAU; NN/Sch

6807. ----- Young People's Union Board. Reports ... Nashville: National Baptist Publishing Board, n.d.   DHU/MO; GAU

6808. National Baptist Educational Convention, U.S.A., Inc. Proceedings of the National Baptist Educational Convention, Held in the First Baptist Church of Phila., 1872. New York: Sheldon and Co., 1872.   KyLoS

6809. ----- Proceedings of the National Baptist Educational Convention, Held in the Perrepont Street Baptist Church, Brooklyn: April 19-21, 1870. Brooklyn Baptist Social Union. New York: W. I. Pooley, 1870.   SCBHC

6810. National Baptist Publishing Board. Annual Report. V.1., 1897- Nashville, Tenn.: n.p., 1897.   TNF 1916, 1920.

6811. National Baptist Sunday School Convention of the U.S. 1st Convention, 1869.   OClWHi; ViU

6812. National Jubilee Melodies. Nashville, Tenn.: Natl. Baptist Publishing Board, n.d.   SCBHC

6813. Negro Baptists - Halifax, Nova Scotia. Cornwallis Street Baptist Church. Halifax, N.S.: Royal Print, n.d. SCBHC

6814. Negro Baptist Year Book. The Negro Baptist Year Book. Fiscal Year Ending August 31, 1906. Compiled by Samuel W. Bacote... Kansas City, Mo., n.p., n.d.   DHU/n.d. DHU/MO

6815. Negro Baptists of Georgia. Statistical Report of Negro Baptists of Georgia for the Year 1915; Rev. D.D. Crawford, Statistician. Macon, Ga.: William Pullins, Printer, 1915. GAU

6816. "Negro Baptists of the National Baptist Convention Throng Chicago." Baptist (2), pp. 1080+.   SCBHC

6817. New Brunswick, New Jersey. Ebenezer Baptist Church. History of the Ebenezer Church. In Central N.J. Association Minutes for 1896, p. 33.   SCBHC

6818. New England Baptist Convention. The 1923 and 1924, State of Country, New England and Baptist Convention... At Mt. Zion Baptist Church, Newark, N.J., June 13-18, 1923. Written by Rev. L.B. Brooks, Pastor, Mr. Ararat Baptist Church, Rutherford, N.J. Forty-ninth Annual Session June 13-18, 1923.   DHU/MO

6819. New England Missionary Baptist Convention. The Diamond Jubilee of New England Missionary Baptist Convention and the Annual Meeting of its Auxiliaries, New York City, June 15 to 17, 1949, Dr. William P. Hayes, President, Dr. John C. Jackson, PresidentEmeritus. n.p.: n.p., 1949. MNtcA Negro baptist organization.

6820. New Rochelle, New York. Bethesda Baptist Church. Yearbook, 1939. n.p., n.d.   SCBHC

6821. New York City, (New York) Abyssinian Baptist Church. The Abyssinian School of Religious Education and Community House Activities. N.Y.: n.p., n.d.

6822. ----- Abyssinian Baptist Church. Annual Reports 31st. TNF; NN/Sch

6823. ----- Abyssinian Baptist Church. The Articles of Faith, Church Discipline and By-Laws...New York: J. Post, 1933. NN/Sch

6824. ----- Abyssinian Baptist Church. The One Hundred Thirtieth Anniversary of the Abyssinian Baptist Church and the First Anniversary as Pastor of A. Clayton Powell, Jr. New York: n.p., 1938.   SCBHC

6825. ----- Abyssinian Baptist Church. The Opening and Dedication Programme of the New Abyssinian Baptist Church and Community House... 1923. N.Y.: New York Age Press, nd. d.   SCBHC

6826. ----- Abyssinian Baptist Church. 32nd Annual Report of the Subscribing Members and Firends... from May 1, 1929, Including April 30, 1930. n.p.: Hayley Press, n.d. SCHBC

6827. New York City, (New York). Baptist Education Center. (Negro Auxiliary). Minutes and Correspondence, 1925-1955. SCBHC

6828. Ohsberg, Harry O. The Race Problem and Religious Education Among Baptists in the U.S.A. Doctoral dissertation. University of Pittsburgh, 1964.

6829. Oliver, Pearleen. A Brief History of the Colored Baptists of Nova Scotia, 1782-1953. In Commemoration of Centennial Celebrations of the African United Baptist Association of Nova Scotia, Inc., 1953.   SCBHC

6830. Olivet Baptist Church. Greetings of Olivet Baptist Church Celebrating the Seventy-Second Anniversary of the Church and Six Years Pastorate of Dr. L. K. Williams, 1922. Compiled by Madeline Hawkins.   DHU/MO

6831. Parrish, Charles H. Golden Jubilee of the General Association of Colored Baptists in Kentucky. The Story of Fifty Years' Work from 1865-1915, Including Many Photos and Sketches... Louisville, Ky.: Mayes Printing Co., 1915.   TNF

6832. Pastor Henry N. Jeter's Twenty-Five Years Experience with the Shiloh Baptist Church and Her History. Corner School and Mary Streets, Newport, R.I. (Pref. by Charles S. Morris). Providence: Remington Print. Co., 1901. NN/Sch

6833. Pegues, Albert Witherspoon. Our Baptist Ministers and Schools. Springfield, Mass.: Wiley and Co., 1892. DHU/MO

6834. Pelt, Owen D. and R. L. Smith. The Story of the National Baptist. New York: Vantage Press, 1960.   DHU/R
        Negro author.

6835. Penn, Robert Earl. Missionary Administration in the National Baptist Convention of the United States of America, Incorporated. Doctoral dissertation. Central Baptist Theological Seminary, 1952.

6836. Person, I. S. An Open Door. Augusta, Ga.: Georgia Baptist Book Print, 1901.   NN/Sch
        Negro author.

6837. Philadelphia, Pa. Shiloh Baptist Church. Articles of Faith and Covenant. Philadelphia: W. G. F. Brinkloe, Printer, 1861.   SCBHC
        Bound with J. Asher's autobiography.

6838. ----- Shiloh Baptist Church. A Century of Faith and Service; Shiloh Baptist Church, Philadelphia, Pennsylvania, 1842-1942; Centennial Jubilee and Anniversary Celebration, September 4, October 29, 1942. Rev. W. H. R. Powell, Pastor. Philadelphia: n.p., 1942.   SCBHC

6839. Piepkorn, Arthur Carl. "The Primitive Baptists of North America." Baptist History and Heritage (7:1, Ja., 1972), pp. 33-51.   DHU/R
        pp. 49- Black members of The National Baptist Convention of the U.S.

6840. ----- "The Primitive Baptists of North America." Concordia Theological Monthly (42:5, May, 1971), pp. 297-314.
                                                            DHU/R
        Some information on "Black Primitive Baptists."

6841. "Pilgrimage to First Negro Church." Crisis (79:5, My., 1972), pp. 162-63.   Pam. File, DHU/R
        First Bryan Baptist Church, near Savannah, Georgia visited by members of the First African Church and outgrowth of this historic church.

6842. Pius, N. H. An Outline of Baptist History. Nashville, Tenn.: National Baptist Publishing Board, 1911. DHU/MO' TNF; GAU
        "The Beginning of Negro Baptist History." Contains information about early Negro Baptist Organizers.

6843. "Politics." The Crisis (9:5, Mr., 1915), p. 217.
                                                       DLC; DHU/MO
        The New England colored Baptist convention is mailing reports on the "State of the Country."

6844. Pollard, R. T. "Baptists and Colportage." E. M. Brawley. The Negro Baptist Pulpit (Phila., Pa.: Baptist Publication Society, 1890), pp. 211-20.   DHU/MO

6845. Quarles, Benjamin. "Ante-Bellum Relationships Between the First African Baptist Church of New Orleans and White Agencies." The Chronicle (18; Ja., 1955), pp. 26-36. NcD
        Negro author.

6846. Ransome, William Lee. Christian Stewardship and Negro Baptists. Richmond, Va.: National Ministers' Institute, Virginia Union University. Richmond, Va.: Brown Print Shop, Inc., 1934.   DHU/MO; DLC
        Negro author.

6847. ----- History of the First Baptist Church and Some of her Pastors, South Richmond, Va. By W. L. Ransome, Assisted by the Following Committee: Ch. H. Munford, Mary V. Binga, Mary V. Nelson and others...Richmond: n.p., 1935.

6848. ----- An Old Story for this New Day, and Other Sermons and Addresses. Richmond: Central Pub. Co., 1954. DHU/R

6849. Reid, Barney Ford. A Brief History of Teachers' Training Work as Connected with the Baptist State Sunday School Convention of Kentucky. Louisville: The Convention, 1928. DLC

6850. Reid, Ira De A. The Negro Baptist Ministry: An Analysis of its Profession, Preparation, and Practices. Philadelphia: H & L Advertising Co., 1951.   DLC
        Negro author.

6851. Reid, Stevenson N. History of Colored Baptists in Alabama; Including Facts About Many Men, Women and Events of the Denomination... Gadsden, Ala.: n.p., 1949.   DLC

6852. Reynolds, Mary C. Baptist Missionary Pioneers Among Negroes. Sketches Written by Mary C. Reynolds and Others. n.p., 1915?   GAU; NN/Sch

6853. Richmond, Va. First Baptist Church. "Reminiscences of the First African Church, Richmond, Va." By Basil Manly, Jr. The Baptist Memorial and Monthly Chronicle (14; 1855), pp. 262-65; 289-92; 321-271 353-56.   SCBHC

6854. Rochester, New York. Mount Olivet Baptist Church. Operation Expansion, Oct., 1954. Rochester, N.Y.: n.p., n.d.   SCBHC

6855. Rowley, Dale L. The Pastoral Ministry of Negro Baptists in the San Francisco Bay Area. Master's thesis. Golden Gate Baptist Theological Seminary, 1959.

6856. Rusling, G. W. "A Note on Early Negro Baptist History." Foundation (XI, Oct.-Dec., 1968), pp. 362-68.   NcD

6857. St. Paul, Minn. Pilgrim Baptist Church. 1863 Centennial 1963. St. Paul, F. D. Fredell, n.d.   SCBHC
        Rev. Floyd Massey, Jr., Pastor.

6858. Sargent, Charles J. Negro Churches and the American Baptist Convention. New York: n.p., 1966.   SCBHC
        Delivered by the pastor of the Union Baptist Church, Stamford, Conn., at the Ministers and Missionaries Benefit Board Annual Luncheon, Kansas City, May 11, 1966.

6859. Savannah, Georgia. First African Baptist Church. Constitution and Rules of Order of the F.M.B. Church, Savannah, Ga. Savannah: Morning News Steam Printing House, 1887.
                                                            SCBHC

6860. Semple, Robert Baylor. A History of the Rise and Progress of the Baptist in Virginia. Richmond, Va.: Pitt & Dickinson, 1894.   NcD

6861. Simms, James M. The First Colored Baptist Church in North America, Constituted at Savannah, Georgia, January 20, A.D. 1788. Philadelphia: Lippincott, 1888. SCBHC; DHU/R

6862. Smith, J. Alfred. A Study of Historical Backgrounds and the First Fifty Years of the Allen Temple Baptist Church. Oakland: Color Art Press, 1973.   DHU/R

6863. Snyder, John. "The Baptists." The Crisis (20:1, My., 1920), pp. 12-14.   DLC; DHU/MO
        "The future of the Negro is bound up with the Negro Baptist Church because of its decentralization."

6864. "Social Uplift." The Crisis (11:1, Nov., 1915), p. 8.
                                                       DLC; DHU/MO
        Negro Baptist Publishing House.

6865. Spencer, David. Early Baptist of Philadelphia. Philadelphia: W. Syckelmoore, 1877.   CtY-D; NN

6866. Stackhouse, Perry J. Chicago and the Baptists. Chicago: University of Chicago Press, 1933.   DLC

6867. Stakely, Charles Averett. History of the First Baptist Church of Montgomery, Alabama, with Sketches of the Other Baptist Churches of the City and County, in Papers Presented

at the Hundredth Anniversary of the First Baptist Church Cele-
brated in Montgomery, November 29- December 1, 1929.
Together with a Reprint of the Church's Declaration of Faith,
Constitution, Covenant, and By-Laws... The History Written
and the Papers Compiled in Chapters. Montgomery, Ala.:
The Paragon Press, 1930.
    p. 67-72: the colored Baptist churches of Montgomery.

6868. Steele, Henry M. Common Life Among Negro Baptists in
Georgia, Between the Years 1874-1904. n.p., 1967. SCBHC
    Paper in Baptist history for Dr. W. S. Hudson, Dec. 1,
1967.

6869. Steward, W. H. "Colored Baptists and Journalism." E. M.
Brawley. The Negro Baptist Pulpit (Phila., Pa.: Baptist Publication Society, 1890), pp. 233-36.   DHU/MO

6870. Stewart, Maria W. Productions of Mrs. Maria W. Stewart
Presented to the First African Baptist Church & Society, of
the City of Boston. Boston: Friends of Freedom and Virtue,
1835.   NN/Sch
    Negro author.

6871. Stokes, Olivia P. An Evaluation of the Leadership Training
Program Offered by the Baptist Educational Center, Harlem,
N.Y., with Recommendations for Its Improvement. Doctoral
dissertation. Teachers College, Columbia University, 1952.

6872. Temple, R. J. "Baptists and Publication Work." E. M.
Brawley. The Negro Baptist Pulpit (Phila, Pa.: Baptist Publication Society, 1890), pp. 200-10.   DHU/MO

6873. Thomas, Edgar G. The First African Baptist Church of
North America... Savannah, Ga.: n.p., 1925. DHU/MO;
NcD; DHU/R; TNF
    Negro author.

6874. Thompson, Patrick H. The History of Negro Baptists in
Mississippi. Jackson, Miss.: Bailey Print. Co., 1898.
    CtY-D

6875. Thornton, Edgar T. Developing a Youth Program Among
Churches of the National Baptist Convention of the United States
of America, Inc. Doctoral dissertation. Central Baptist Theological Seminary, 1957.

6876. Torbet, Robert G. A History of the Baptists. Valley Forge,
Pa.: Judson Press, 1969.   IC/H; DHU/R
    pp. 378-79 & 353-55, Negro baptists.

6877. Tupper, H. A. (ed.). The First Century of the First Baptist
Church of Richmond, 1780-1880. Richmond: C. McCarthy,
1880.   DLC; Vi

6878. Tyms, James Daniel. The Rise of Religious Education
Among Negro Baptists; a Historical Case Study. New York:
Exposition Press, 1966.   TNF; DHU/R; NcD
    Negro author.

6879. Unofficial Inter-Racial Conference on Christian Education
for Negroes under Baptist Auspices. Christian Education for
Negroes under Baptist Auspices; Proceedings of an Unofficial
Interracial Conference of the Hundred Texas Baptist Leaders,
Nov. 4, 1941, Baptist Building, Dallas, Texas. Sponsored
and Published by the Board of Trustees... Bishop College,
Marshall, Texas. Marshall, Tex.: n.p., 1941. NN/Sch

6880. Vann, M. "Baptists and Home Missions." E. M. Brawley.
The Negro Baptist Pulpit (Phila., Pa.: Baptist Publication
Society, 1890), pp. 251-55.   DHU/MO

6881. Vass, Samuel Nathaniel. How to Study and Teach the Bible.
Teacher Training Book, National Baptist Convention, U.S.A.
Nashville, Tenn.: Sunday School Pub. Board, 1922. Negro
author.   NN/Sch

6882. Vincent, A. B. Address Delivered Before the Baptist State
Sunday School Convention, Warrenton, N.C., Sept. 19, 1895.
Raleigh: n.p., 1896.   SCBHC

6883. Washington, D.C. Nineteenth Street Baptist Church. One
Hundred Anniversary of the Nineteenth Street Baptist Church.
Washington, D.C.: 1839-1939. Fifty-Seventh Anniversary,
Rev. Walter H. Brooks, D.D., 1882-1939. Washington: Pr.
by Murray Bros., Inc., 1939.   DHU/R; TNF

6884. Washington, D.C. Shiloh Baptist Church. Fiftieth Anniversary (1863-1913). n.p., n.d.   SCBHC

6885. Whitted, J. A History of the Negro Baptists of North Carolina. Raleigh: Edwards and Broughton, Printing Co., 1908.
    DHU/MO; GAU; SCBHC

6886. Williams, Kenny Jackson. They Also Spoke. Nashville:
Townsend Press, 1970.   DHU/R
    Written by daughter of the President of the National Baptist
Convention, U.S.A. Has many references to Negro church.
Negro author.

6887. Williams, Lacey Kirk. First Annual Address of Dr. L. K.
Williams, President, National Baptist Convention, September
5-10, 1923.   DHU/MO
    Negro author.

6888. ----- "Lord! Lord!" Special Occasion Sermons and
Addresses, of Dr. L. K. Williams, edited by Theodore S.
Boone... Ft. Worth, Tex.: Historical Commission, National
Baptist Convention, U.S.A., Inc., 1942.   DLC

6889. Woman's American Baptist Home Mission Society. From
Ocean to Ocean; the Annual Report of the Missionaries Medical
Educational and Evangelistic... New York: 19-. NN/Sch;
DHU/MO

6890. Woman's American Baptist Home Mission Society. Suggestions for Meetings. Boston: W.A.B.H.M.S., 1902. SCBHC
    A mission study manual designed for the study of the Negro.
Contains music.

6891. Wood River (Illinois) Baptist Association. A Historical
Sketch of the Wood River Baptist Association for the State
of Illinois for the Past Fifty Years, (1838-1888). In Wood River
Baptist Association Minutes for 1888. pp. 44-58.   SCBHC

(7) National Convention of America

6892. American National Baptist Convention. Journal...
Louisville: Courier-Journal Job Printing Co., 18-.
    NN/Sch; DHU/MO; GAU; DLC

6893. Baptists. Kentucky. General Association of Colored
Baptists. Diamond Jubilee of the General Association of Colored
Baptists in Kentucky; the Story of Seventy-Five Years of the
Association and Four Years of Convention Activities. Published
per Order of the General Association, by the Diamond Jubilee
Commission... Louisville, Ky.: American Baptist, 1943.
    SCBHC

6894. National Baptist Convention of America. National Baptist
Publishing Board. Golden Gems; a Song Book for Spiritual
and Religious Worship for the Church, the Choir, the Pew, the
Sunday School and Various Auxiliaries. This Book is Presented
After Careful Compilation and Offered to a Discriminating Pub-
lic. Nashville, Tenn.: National Baptist Pub. Board, 19---.
    NN/Sch; GAU

6895. ----- Women's Auxiliary Convention. Guide for Woman's
Home and Foreign Mission Societies. Nashville: National
Baptist Publishing Board, 1946.   SCBHC

(8) General Negro Churches—Negro Church related Colleges—Religious
Historical Societies

6896. Aery, William Anthony. "Negro Teachers and Ministers
Co-Operate in South Carolina." Bettis Academy's Contribution
to Racial Good Will. Southern Workman (50:11, Nov., 1921),
pp. 503-10.   DLC; DHU/MO

6897. Ahlstrom, Sydney E. _A Religious History of the American People._ New Haven: Yale University Press, 1972. DHU/R
Includes information on the rise of the Black churches, as well as information on slavery, and the church during the Civil War and Reconstruction.

6898. Allison, Madeline G. "The Horizon." _The Crisis_ (23:6, Apr., 1922), p. 274.   DHU/MO; DLC
"A new colored Y.W.C.A. erected by National Headquarters in Little Rock, Ark. Colored people furnished cost of building."

6899. Along the Color Line. (editorial). "The Church." _The Crisis_ (7:1, Dec., 1913), p. 62.   DLC; DHU/MO
Appeal to President Wilson against oppression of Washington, D.C. Negro employees.

6900. Arnett, Benjamin William, (bp.). _Annual Address Delivered Before the Faculty, Students, and Friends of Claflin University and the Claflin College of Agriculture and Mechanical Institute, May 22, 1889, Orangeburg, South Carolina._ Columbia: Sloane, 1909.   MBU-T

6901. ----- and S. T. Mitchell, (comp.). _A Comprehensive Review of the Origin, Development and Present Status of Wilberforce University,_ Xenia: Gazette Office, 1885.   MB; DHEW

6902. Baptists. North Carolina. Neuse River Baptist Association. _Minutes of the...Annual Session of the Neuse River Baptist Association... 1st, 1869-_ Weldon, N.C.: n.p., 1869. NcD
1869-1923 as Neuse River Missionary Baptist Association.

6903. Bare, Paul W. _The Negro Churches in Philadelphia._ Master's thesis. Drew University, 1931.

6904. _Blacks in America: Bibliographical Essays._ James M. McPherson and Laurence B. Holland, et alii. New York: Doubleday & Co., Inc., 1971.   DHU/R
Includes information on: American Churches and Slavery; The Black Church, 1865-1915; The Church and the Civil Rights Movement.

6905. Blanton, Robert J. "The Future of Higher Education Among Negroes." _Journal of Negro Education_ (9:2, Apr., 1940), pp. 177-82.   DHU/MO
p. 179, Establishment of faculty for Theology Department at Howard University.

6906. Bowen, John Wesley Edward. "The Call of the Christian Pulpit--An Appeal of a Negro Minister to Negro Students." Arcadius S. Trawick, (ed.). _The New Voice in Race Adjustments._ (New York: Student Volunteer Movement, 1914), pp. 93-6.   DHU/R

6907. Brooklyn, New York. Mount Lebanon Baptist Church. _Souvenir Journal..._ 1905-1955.   SCBHC

6908. Brown, Frank R. "Educational Philosophy and Program for Higher Education of Hood Theological Seminary, A.M.E. Zion Church, Salisbury, N.C." _The A.M.E. Zion Quarterly Review_ (84:3, Fall, 1972), pp. 148-50.   DHU/R

6909. Brown, Hallie Q. _Pen Pictures of the Pioneers of Wilberforce._ Wilberforce, O.: Aldine Pub. Co., 1937. DHU/MO
Negro author.

6910. Brownlee, Frederick L. "Heritage and Opportunity: The Negro Church Related College: A Critical Summary." _Journal of Negro Education_ (29; Sum., 1960), pp. 401-07. DHU

6911. Burgess, Margaret E. _Negro Leadership in a Southern City._ Chapel Hill: Univ. of North Carolina Press, 1962. DHU/R
Negro religious institutions in a typical urban center in the middle south.

6912. Cady, George L. "Hampton Institute and the American Missionary Association." _Southern Workman_ (63:5, My., 1934), pp. 135-39.   DLC; DHU/MO

6913. Carey, Archibald J., Jr. "The Negro Methodist Churches in America." _The African Methodist Episcopal Church Review_ (78:210, Oct.-Dec., 1961), pp. 20-26.   DHU/R
Negro author.

6914. Chritzberg, A. M. _Early Methodism in the Carolinas._ Nashville: Publishing House of the M. E. Church, South, 1897.
                                                              IEG
pp. 32+, Negro churches.

6915. "Church Documents Which Refer to Howard University." Walter Dyson. _Howard University; the Capstone of Negro Education; A History: 1867-1940._ (Washington, D.C.: The Graduate School, Howard Univ., 1941), pp. 505-06.
                                                              DHU/MO

6916. "Churches." _The Crisis_ (5:3, Mr., 1913), p. 220.
                                                        DLC; DHU/MO
Eight Negro Churches raised money for a memorial hospital in East Orange, N.J.

6917. "Churches, Early Negro, in Kingston, Jamaica and Savannah, Georgia." _Journal of Negro History_ (1:1, Ja., 1916), pp. 69-92.   DHU

6918. Coleman, John W. _Criteria for Evaluating a Program of Education for Professional Workers in Oklahoma Metropolitan Negro Baptist Churches._ Doctoral dissertation. Oklahoma A & M University, 1956.

6919. "Colored Churches Will Shun Birmingham." _Christian Century_ (43:12, Mr. 25, 1926), pp. 393-94. DHU/R; DLC
Officials of the A. M. E. and A. M. E. Zion Churches withdrew from the International Council of Religious Education.

6920. "The Colver Theological Institute, at Richmond, Va." _The Southern Workman_ (1:1, Ja., 1872).   DLC
Microfilm.

6921. "Conferences and Institutes." Hampton Institute. _Southern Workman_ (65:10, Oct., 1936), pp. 299-306. DLC; DHU/MO
"The committee to study the organization, program, and value of conferences and institutes held for Negro ministers attempted to secure data from every source possible."

6922. _Convocation of the Colored Clergy. Proceedings of the First Convocation of the Colored Clergy of the Protestant Church in the United States of America, Held at the Church of the Holy Communion, 6th Avenue and 20th Streets, N. Y. City, September 12th, 13th, and 14th, 1883._ Newark, N.J.: Starbuck and Durham, 1883.   DHU/MO

6923. Corey, Charles H. _History of the Richmond Theological Seminary with Reminiscences of Thirty Years' Work Among the Colored People of the South._ Richmond, Va.: J. W. Randolph Co., 1895.   DHU; DHU/MO; FSU

6924. Cromwell, John Wesley. "First Negro Churches in the District of Columbia." _Journal of Negro History_ (7:1, Ja., 1922), pp. 64-106.   DHU/MO

6925. Daniel, Robert P. "Impact of the War Upon the Church Related College and University." _Journal of Negro Education_ (11:3, Jl., 1942), pp. 359-64.   DHU
Negro author.

6926. ----- "Relationship of the Negro Public College and the Negro Private and Church Related College." _Journal of Negro Education_ (29; Sum., 1960), pp. 388-93.   DHU

6927. Daniel, William Andrew. _Negro Theological Seminary Survey._ Doctoral dissertation. University of Chicago, 1925.

6928. Detroit. Bureau of Governmental Research. _The Negro in Detroit ... Prepared for the Mayor's Inter-Racial Committee by a Special Survey Staff Under the General Direction_

of the Detroit Bureau of Governmental Research, Inc. Detroit:
n.p., 1926.   NN/Sch
   V. 3, "The Negro and the Church."

6929. "Discipline, Health, and Religious Work." Hampton A. &
I. Institute. Thrity-Ninth Annual Report of the Principal.
Southern Workman (36:5, My., 1907), pp. 298-300. DLC;
DHU/MO

6930. Dorey, Frank David. "Negro College Graduates in Schools of
Religion." Christian Education (29; Sept., 1946), pp. 350-58.
                                    DHU/R

6931. Dyson, Walter. Howard University, The Capstone of Negro
Education. A History: 1867-1940. Washington, D.C.:
Graduate School, Howard University, 1941.   DHU/R
   Chapter 16, Religion.

6932. Ebony Pictorial History of Black America. Chicago:
Johnson Publishing Co., 1971.   DHU/R
   Vol. 1, Section 7, pp. 160-78, has information and pictures
   of early black churches and ministers.

6933. Ellison, John M. "Policies and Rationale Underlying the
Support of Colleges Maintained by the Baptist Denomination."
Journal of Negro Education (29; Sum., 1960), pp. 330-38.
                                    DHU
   Negro author.

6934. Fisher, Miles Mark, (ed.). Virginia Union University and
Some of Her Achievements. Twenty-Fifth Anniversary, 1899-
1924. Richmond: Brown Print Shop, Inc., 1924. NN/Sch
   Written by a Negro Baptist minister.

6935. Frissell, H. B. "Report of the Pastor." Hampton N. & A.
Institute. Fourteenth Annual Report of the Principal. Southern
Workman (12:6, Je., 1883), pp. 70-71.   DLC; DHU/R
   For the School and Fiscal Year ending July 1st, 1883.

6936. George, Arthur A. The History of Johnson C. Smith University, 1867 to the Present: to Present and Analyze the Growth
and Development of the Administrative and the Curricular Aims
and Practices of Johnson C. Smith University, 1867 to the
Present. Doctoral dissertation. New York University, 1954.
                                    DHU/R
   Microfilm.

6937. Gibson, DeLois. A Historical Study of Philander Smith
College, 1877-1969. Doctoral dissertation. University of
Arkansas, 1972.   DHU/R

6938. Goodwin, George A. "Is it Time for the Negro Colleges
in the South to be Put Into the Hands of Negro Teachers?"
Daniel W. Culp. Twentieth Century Negro Literature.
(Miami, Fla.: Mnemosyne Publishing Co., Inc., 1969), pp.
132-39.   DHU/MO
   Reprint of 1902 edition.
   Negro Baptist minister and teacher.

6939. Graham, John H. Gammon's Recruiting Progress and the
Replacement Needs of Central Jurisdiction. Atlanta: n.p.,
1956.   GAU

6940. ----- The Role of Gammon Theological Seminary in
Ministerial Training and Services for the Negro Churches,
1940-1954. Atlanta: n.p., 1956.   GAITH
   Seminary founded by the Methodist Church for Negroes.

6941. Graham, William L. Patterns of Intergroup Relations in
the Cooperative Establishment, Control, and Administration
of Paine College Georgia by Southern Negro and White People:
A Study of Intergroup Process. Doctoral dissertation. New
York University, 1955.
   Examines the interaction of the Methodist Episcopal Church,
   South and the Colored Methodist Episcopal Church in their
   joint control over Paine College.

6942. Greenleaf, Jonathan. A History of the Churches of All
Denominations, in the City of New York, From the First

Settlement to the Year 1848. New York: E. French, 1846.
                                    NN/Sch

6943. Haley, James. Afro-American Encyclopedia; or the Thoughts,
Doings and Sayings of the Race... Sermons...History of Denominations. Nashville: Haley & Florida, 1895.   DHU/MO

6944. "Hampton N. & A. Institute. Eighteenth Annual Report of
the Principal, For the School and Fiscal Year ending June 30th
1886." Southern Workman (15:6, Je., 1886), pp. 73-76.
                               DHU/MO; DLC
   Other reports in Southern Workman 1897; 1910; 1911;
   1917-19; 1921; 1926

6945. Hampton Negro Conference. Annual Report, Hampton Negro
Conference. Hampton, Va.: Hampton Institute Press, 1898-.
1908-1912, CtY-D; 1898-1912,   DHU/MO
   "Report of first conference July 1897 is contained in (Sept.
   1897) Southern Workman.

6946. Handy, Robert T. "Negro Christianity and American Church
Historiography." Jerald C. Brauch, (ed.). Reinterpretation
in American Church History (Chicago: The University of Chicago: The University of Chicago, 1968), pp. 91-112. DHU/R

6947. Hargett, Andrew H. "Teaching of Religion in State Colleges
for Negroes." Journal of Negro Education (22; Win., 1953), pp.
88-90.   DHU

6948. Haynes, Roland E. The Place of Religiosity in the Self-
reports of Negro Students in a Church-Related College. Doctoral dissertation. Boston University, 1961.

6949. Hirsch, Leo H. "The Negro and New York, 1783-1865."
Journal of Negro History (16:4, Oct., 1931), pp. 382-473.
                                    DHU
   Includes a discussion of the church.

6950. Historical Records Survey. Virginia. Inventory of the
Church Archives of Virginia. Prepared by the Historical
Records Survey of Virginia, Division of Professional and
Service Projects, Work Projects Administration. Sponsored
by the Virginia Conservation Commission. Negro Baptist
Churches in Richmond. Richmond, Va.: The Historical
Records Survey of Virginia, 1940.   DHU/MO; DLC
   Reproduced from typewritten copy.

6951. A History and Interpretation of Wilberforce University,
Wilberforce, Ohio. Blanchester, Ohio: Printed at the
Brown Publishing Co., 1941.   O

6952. Hodges, George Washington. Early Negro Church Life
in New York. n.p., 1945.   DHU/MO; NN/Sch; NcD
   Negro author.

6953. "Hood Seminary, A Unique Training Center." The Church
School Herald-Journal (56:1, Dec.-Feb., 1971), pp. 1-2.
                                    DHU/R

6954. Jenkins, Clara B. A Historical Study of Shaw University,
1865-1963. Doctoral dissertation. University of Pittsburg,
1965.

6955. Johnson, Alandus C. History of Paine College, Augusta,
1903-1946. Doctoral dissertation. University of Georgia,
1970.

6956. Johnson, William Decker, Sr. (bp.). Lincoln University;
or the Nation's First Pledge of Emancipation. Philadelphia:
For the Author, 1867.   OCIWHi
   Written by forty-second bishop of the A. M. E. Church.

6957. Lee, Benjamin Franklin. Sketch of History of Wilberforce
University. Xenia: n.p., 1884.   OWibfU

6958. Lewis, John Henry. "The Role of the Church Related
College." A. M. E. Church Review (68:176, Apr.-Je.,
1953), pp. 38-43.   DHU/R

6959. "Lincoln University." The Church at Home and Abroad
(1; 1887), p. 164.   DHU/R
        Institution of higher learning for Negroes,
        Presbyterian.

6960. Look Magazine. Religions in America: A Completely
Revised and Up-to-Date Guide to Churches and Religious
Groups in the U.S. New York: Simon and Schuster, 1963.
                                                     DHU/R; INR

6961. Matthews, William E. Address Before the Societies and
Faculty of Wilberforce University. 1880. OWibfu
        Negro author.

6962. Mays, Benjamin Elijah. "A Dream Comes True." The
African Methodist Episcopal Church Review (14:197, Jl.-Sept.,
1958), pp. 55+.   DHU/R
        The beginning of the Interdenominational Theological Center,
        Atalnta, Georgia.

6963. ----- "The Negro Church." Vergilius Ferm, (ed.). An
Encyclopedia of Religion (New York: Philosophical Library,
1945), pp. 520-23.   DHU/R

6964. ----- "The Significance of the Negro Private and Church
Related College." Journal of Negro Education (29:3, Sum.,
1960), pp. 245-51.   DHU/MO
        Negro author.

6965. McKinney, Richard I. "Religion in Negro Colleges."
Journal of Negro Education (13; Fall, 1944), pp. 509-19.
                                                     DHU

6966. Mead, Frank Spencer. Handbook of Denominations in
the United States. New York: Abingdon Press, 19-.
                                              INU; DHU/R
        Brief history and current statistics on Negro churches
        in America. Issued yearly.

6967. Murray, Andrew E. "The Founding of Lincoln University."
Journal of Presbyterian History (51:4, Wint., 1973), pp.
392-410.   DHU/R
        Black Presbyterian University.

6968. Murray, V. W. "NNEA: Important Crossroads." Christianity Today (15; My. 7, 1971), p. 37.   DHU/R
        About the National Negro Evangelical Association.

6969. "Negro Denominations: the Baptists and the Methodists."
Harry A. Ploski (ed.). Reference Library of Black America
(New York: Bellwether Pub. Co., Inc., 1971), Book 2, pp. 192-
203.   DHU

6970. Niebuhr, Helmut Richard. The Social Sources of Denom-
inationalism. New York: Holt, Rinehart and Winston, Inc.,
1929.   DHU/R

6971. Paige, Joseph C. Administrator, Faculty and Student Eval-
uations of Science Programs in the Nine Colleges Associated
with the African Methodist Episcopal Church. Doctoral dissertation. American University, 1965.

6972. Paris, Peter. "A Survey of the Chicago Baptist Institute."
National Council of the Churches of Christ in the U.S.A., (ed.).
Manpower for Mission, New Forms of the Church in Chicago
(New York: Council Press, 1967), pp. 86-102. DHU/R
        Negro author.

6973. Payne, Daniel Alexander, (bp.). Annual Report and Retrospective of the First Decade of Wilberforce University...
June 18, 1873. Cinn.: B. W. Arnett, n.d.   OCIWHi

6974. -----(bp.). Historical Sketch of Wilberforce University.
n.p.: n.p., 1879.   NN; MH; OWibfU

6975. ----- "The History of the Development of Wilberforce
University." David Smith. Biography of David Smith of the
A.M.E. Church... (Xenia: Press at the Xenia Gazette Office,
1881), pp. 99-132.   OWibfU

6976. Payne, Enoch George. An Estimate of Our Negro Schools.
New York: The American Church Institute for Negroes, 1943.
                                              DHU/MO; NN/Sch

6977. Pearson, Colbert Hubert. A Non-Denominational Program
of Christian Education for a Group of Negro Churches Serving
the Negro Community of Englewood, New Jersey. New York,
n.p. 1948.   DHU/MO
        Microfilm.

6978. Peirce, Alfred M. A History of Methodism in Georgia.
n.p.: North Georgia Conference Historical Society, 1956.
                                                     IEG
        Founding of Clark College and Gammon Theological Seminary.

6979. Powell, Ruth Marie. Lights and Shadows. The Story of the
American Baptist Theological Seminary, 1924-1964. n.p., 1964.
                                                     SCBHC

6980. Protestant Church Directory... of Metropolitan New York,
Including Nassau and Westchester Counties. New York:
Protestant Council of the City of New York, 1933. NN/Sch;
DLC

6981. Rand, Earl W. An Analysis of the Boards of Control of
a Group of Selected Negro Protestant Church Related Colleges.
Doctoral dissertation. Indiana University, 1952.

6982. ----- "Negro Private and Church College at Mid-
century." Journal of Negro Education (22; Wint., 1953), pp.
77-9.   DHU

6983. ----- "Selection of Board Members in Negro Church-related Colleges." Journal of Negro Education (25; Wint., 1956),
pp. 79-82.   DHU

6984. Ransom, Reverdy Cassius, (bp.). School Days at Wilberforce.
Springfield, Ohio: New Era, n.d.   OWibfu
        Forty-eight bishop of the A.M.E. Church.

6985. The Reformed Zion Union Apostolic Church. Discipline...
                                                     ISAR
        A group that left the A.M.E. and formed this church
        shortly after the Civil War.

6986. Religious Services in the Second African Church, Philadel-
phia, at the Ordination and Installation of the Rev. Andrew
Harris as Pastor of Said church, on the 13th of April, 1841.
Philadelphia: Isaac Ashmead, 1841.   DHU/MO

6987. "The Rise of Wilberforce University." The African Methodist Episcopal Church (78:208, Apr.-Je., 1961), pp. 3-6.
                                                     DHU/R

6988. Rohrer, John H., (ed.). The Eighth Generation Grows
Up: Cultures and Personalities of the New Orleans Negroes.
New York: Harper & Row, 1960.   DHU/R
        pp. 30-34, Negroes, and the church in New Orleans.

6989. Rosten, Leo, (ed.). A Guide to the Religions of America;
The Famous Look Magazine Series on Religion, Facts, Figures,
Tables, Charts, Articles and Comprehensive Reference
Material on Churches and Religious Groups in the United States.
New York: Simon & Schuster, 1963.   DHU/R

6990. Rowley, Margaret Nelson. "The Joseph Kaplan Human
Relations Program At Morris Brown College." The African
Methodist Episcopal Church Review (78:212, Apr.-Je., 1962),
pp. 65-67.   DHU/R
        Negro author.

6991. "Rural Preachers at Bettis Academy." Editorial. Southern
Workman (52:9, Sept., 1923), pp. 422-4.   DLC; DHU/MO
        "Some two hundred Negro rural preachers of western South
        Carolina come together for an institute on everyday problems
        in Trenton, S.C."

6992. Russell, Daniel Hames. History of the African Union Methodist Protestant Church. Philadelphia: Union Star Book & Job Print. & Pub. House, 1920.   DLC

6993. Saunders, Daivs L. "Negro Baptists in Baptist Historiography." Quarterly Review (31:46, Apr., 1971), pp. 46-55.   DLC; DyLS

6994. Short History of the African Union Meeting and School-House, Erected in Providence (R.I.) in the Years 1819, '20, '21; with Rules for its Future Government. Published by Particular Request. Providence: Brown and Danforth, 1821.   NcD

6995. Sims, David. "Religious Education in Negro Colleges and Universities." Journal of Negro History (5:2, Apr., 1920), pp. 166-208.   DHU/MO

6996. Stearns, Alfred E. "Religion in Education." Southern Workman (63:3, Mr., 1934), pp. 67-76.   DLC; DHU/MO
"Education was to strengthen and enlarge the work of the Christian Church."

6997. Stevenson, J. D. "Tuskegee's Religious Work." Southern Workman (39; Jl., 1910), pp. 401+.   DHU/MO

6998. Stewart, Charles E. "The Denominational Negro "College"." The African Methodist Episcopal Church Review (78:210, Oct. -Dec., 1961), pp. 39-42.   DHU/R
Negro author.

6999. "Summer School for Colored Church Workers." Southern Workman (52:10, Oct., 1923), pp. 473-4.   DLC; DHU/MO
St. Paul's School, Lawrenceville, Va., first to hold training of Colored church workers.

7000. Sweet, William Warren. The American Churches. New York: Abingdon, 1948.   DHU/MO
Religious Affiliations of American Negroes.

7001. Tankerson, Richard Earl. Some Sociological Factors Effecting the Organic Merger of the A. M. E. Zion, and C. M. E. Churches. B.D. paper. School of Religion, Howard University, 1967.
Negro author.

7002. Taylor, Clifford H., Jr. Jarvis Christian College; Its History and Present Standing in Relationship to the Standards of the Texas State Department of Education and the Southern Association of Colleges and Secondary Schools. Research paper. Brite College of the Bible, Texas Christian University, 1948.
mim.

7003. Taylor, Paul L. An Analysis of Religious Counseling Practices of Nine Selected Negro Colleges. Doctoral dissertation. Indiana University, 1958.

7004. Taylor, Prince A., Jr. A History of Gammon Theological Seminary. Doctoral dissertation. New York University, 1948.

7005. Thompson, Charles H. "The Present Status of the Negro and Church Related Colleges." Journal of Negro Education (29: 4, Sum., 1960), pp. 236-44.   DHU/MO

7006. Thrall, Homer S. A Brief History of Methodism in Texas. Nashville: Publishing House of the M. E. Church, South, 1894.   IEG
pp. 278, A. M. E. and C. M. E. Church.

7007. Tieuel, Robert C. The Story of Methodism Among Negroes in the U.S. Copyright... by Robert C. D. Tieuel, Jr. Designed by Portia Elaine Harris Tieuel... Hutchinson, Kan.: 1945.   DLC
Negro author.
Reproduced from typewritten copy. "Catologues of educational and reports of denominational philanthropic institutions."

7008. "Tougaloo University." The Church at Home and Abroad (4; 1888), pp. 567-68.   DHU/R

Sustained by Congregationalists of the American Missionary Association.

7009. Trent, William J. "Relative Adequacy of Source of Income of Negro Church-related Private Colleges." Journal of Negro Education (29; Sum., 1960), pp. 356-67.   DHU

7010. United States Works Progress Administration. The Negro Church in New Jersey. Compiled by James A. Pauley. Hackensack, N.J.: n.p., 1938.   DHU/MO
Mim.

7011. ----- The Negro Church in New Jersey. Emergency Education Program. C. B. Coane, State Director. Benjamin F. Seldon, State Supervisor Negro Adult Education. Compiled by James A. Pawley and Staff, Supervisor, Social Problems Unit, Negro Adult Education. (Hackensack, N.J.), 1938. NjPT
Typescript.

7012. Vass, Samuel Nathaniel. Our Needs as Colored People. Philadelphia: A.B.P.S., n.d.   SCBHC

7013. ----- Principles and Methods of Religious Education. Nashville, Tenn.: Sunday School Publishing Board, 1932.   DHU/MO; NN/Sch

7014. Walker, T. C. "How We May Improve Our Colored Churches in the Country." Arcadius S. Trawick, (ed.). The New Voice in Race Adjustments (New York: Student Volunteer Movement, 1914), pp. 139-45.   DHU/R

7015. Wallace, J. P. Q. "The History of Payne Theological Seminary." The African Methodist Episcopal Church Review (68:174, Oct. -Dec., 1952), pp. 62-3.   DHU/R
Negro author.

7016. Wallace, Robert Clayton. A Study of the Role of Chicago Baptist Institute in theTraining of Ministers... Masters thesis. Howard University, School of Religion, 1972.

7017. Weatherford, Willia Duke. American Churches and the Negro; an Historical Study from Early Slave Days to the Present. Boston: Christopher Pub. House, 1957. DHU/R; InU; GAU

7018. Weaver, Robert C. "Negro Private and Church Related College: A Critical Summary." Journal of Negro Education (29; Sum., 1960), pp. 394-400.   DHU
Negro author.

7019. Webster, Sherman N. A Study of the Patterns of Adult Education in Selected Negro Churches. Doctoral dissertation. Indiana University, 1959.

7020. Wilberforce, Ohio. Wilberforce University. A Comprehensive Review of the Origin, Development and Present Status of Wilberforce University by the Alumni. 1885.   O WibfU

7021. ----- Wilberforce University. Carnegie Library. The Levi Jenkins Coppin Collection at Carnegie Library, Wilberforce University, Wilberforce, Ohio. Compiled by Casper LeRoy Jordan, Chief Librarian. Wilberforce, O.: Wilberforce University, 1957.   NN/Sch; O WibfU

7022. ----- Wilberforce University. Committee on Law and Publication. Laws and Historical Sketch of Wilberforce University Near Xenia, Greene County, Ohio, Belonging to The African M. E. Church of America ... Committee on Law and Publication. Rev. Benjamin W. Arnett. Rev. J. P. Underwood. D. A. Payne ... Cincinnati: R. Clarke & Co., Printers, 1876.   NN/Sch; O WibfU

7023. Wilson, Frank T. To Determine the Procedure for Developing a Program of Religious Education in the Liberal Arts College at Lincoln University, Pennsylvania Teachers College. Doctoral dissertation. Teachers College, Columbia University, 1936.
Negro author.

7024. Wilson, Prince E. "Some Aspects of the Morris Brown
College Academic Program. " The African Methodist Episcopal
Church Review (78:212, Apr.-Je., 1962), pp. 48-53. DHU/R
    Negro author.

7025. Woodcock, Eleanor J. "The Personnel Services of Morris
Brown College. " The African Methodist Episcopal Church
Review (78:212, Apr.-Je., 1962), pp. 54-57.   DHU/R
    Negro author.

7026. Work, Monroe N., (ed.). Negro Year Book. An Annual
Encyclopedia of the Negro. Tuskegee, Ala.: Tuskegee Institute, Negro Year Book Co., 1912-47.   DHU/MO
    Statistics on the Negro church.
    Negro author.

7027. Wright, Richard Robert, Jr., (bp.). and Ernest Smith,
(comps.). The Philadelphia Colored Directory; A Handbook of
the Religious, Social, Political, Professional, Business and
Other Activities of the Negroes of Philadelphia. n. p.: Colored
Directory Co., 1907.   DHU/MO

7028. Wright, Stephen J. "Some Critical Problems Faced by the
Negro Church Related College. " Journal of Negro Education
(29; Sum., 1960), pp. 339-44.   DHU

7029. Yearbook of American Churches. New York Council Press,
National Council of Churches in America, 1916. DHU/R
    Published yearly. Included are short histories of Negro
    churches in addition to statistics.

7030. Yonker, Thomas Walter. The Negro Church in North Carolina, 1700-1900. Masters thesis. Duke University, 1955.

7031. Yonkers, N. Y. Messiah Church and Sunday School. "Historical Sketch. " Agnes Kirkwood. Church and Sunday School
Work in Yonkers, pp. 473-83.   SCBHC

b. Storefront Churches and Sects

    (1) Holiness and Pentecostal Churches

7032. Battle Allen O. Status Personality in a Negro Holiness
Sect. Doctoral dissertation. Catholic University, 1961.

7033. Beckmann, David M. "Trance from Africa to Pentecostalism. "
CTM (45:1, Ja., 1974), pp. 11-26.   DHU/R

7034. Bhengu, Nicholas. "Declaration of Faith of Nicholas Bhengu. "
Walter J. Hollenweger. The Pentecostals, the Charismatic
Movement in the Churches. (Minneapolis, Minn.: Augsburg
Publishing House, 1972), pp. 517-18.   DHU/R

7035. Bloch-Hoell, Nils. The Pentecostal Movement, Its Origin
Development and Distinctive Character. Oslo: Universitet-
forlaget, 1964.   DHU/R
    Several pages relating to the Negro and the Pentecostal
    movement.

7036. Chatham, J. G. "Southern Pentecost; Address, with Editorial Comment. " America (109; Jl. 6, 1963), pp. 11-12.
                                               DHU

7037. "Church Celebrates 50th Anniversary; Church of God in
Christ Lauds Founder. " Ebony (13; Mr., 1958), pp. 54-56.
                                               DHU/MO

7038. Connelly, James T. Neo-Pentecostalism. Doctoral dissertation. University of Chicago, 1971.

7039. Corvin, Raymond Othel. History of the Educational Institutions of the Pentecostal Holiness Church. Doctoral dissertation.
Southwestern Baptist Theological Seminary, 1956.

7040. Davis, Arnor S. "The Pentecostal Movement in Black Christianity. " The Black Church (2:1, 1972), pp. 65-88. DHU/R

7041. Dayton, Donald W. The American Holiness Movement.
Wilmore, Ky.: B. L. Fisher Library, Asbury Theological
Seminary, 1971.   MNtcA

7042. Dayton, W. "Holiness Groups Pare Down Creed. " Christianity Today (16:15, Apr. 28 (sic) 1972), pp. 36-37. DHU/R

7043. Goodman, Felicitas D. "Phonetic Analysis of Glossolalia in
Four Cultural Settings. " Journal for the Scientific Study of
Religion (8:2, Fall, 1969), pp. 227-39.   DHU/R

7044. ----- Speaking in Tongues; a Cross-Cultural Study of
Glossolalia. Chicago: Univ. of Chicago Press, 1972. DHU/R

7045. Hine, Virginia H. "Pentecostal Glossolalia: Toward a Functional Interpretation. " Journal for the Scientific Study of Religion (8:2, Fall, 1969), pp. 211-26.   DHU/R

7046. Hollenweger, Walter J. "A Black Pentecostal Concept. A
Forgotten Chapter of Black History. " Concept (no. 30; Je.,
1970), pp. 1-70.   Pam. File, DHU/R
    Papers from the Department of Studies in Evangelism.
    Geneva: World Council of Churches.

7047. ----- The Pentecostals; The Charismatic Movement in the
Churches. Minneapolis, Minn.: Augsburg Publishing House,
1972.   DHU/R

7048. Holt, John B. "Holiness Religion: Cultural Shock and Social
Reorganization. " American Sociological Review (5; 1940), pp.
740-47. DAU; DAU/W; DCU/SW; DGU; DGW; DHU

7049. Johnson, Benton. "Do Holiness Sects Socialize in Dominant
Values? " Social Forces (39; My., 1961), pp. 309-16. DHU

7050. Lovett, Leonard. "Perspective on the Black Origins of the
Contemporary Pentecostal Movement. " Journal of the Interdenominational Theological Center (1:1, Fall, 1973), pp. 36-49.
                                               DHU/R
    Negro author.

7051. Massey, James Earl. An Introduction to the Negro Churches
in the Church of God Reformation Movement. New York: Shing
Light Survey Press, 1957.   DHU/MO
    Negro author.

7052. Moore, Everett LeRoy. Handbook of Pentecostal Denominations in the United States. Master's thesis. Pasadena College,
1954.

7053. Nichol, John Thomas. Pentecostalism. New York: Harper
& Row, 1966.   DHU/R

7054. "Non-affiliated Churches: the Evangelical Movements. "
Harry A. Ploski, (ed.). Reference Library of Black America
(New York: Bellwether Pub. Co., 1971), Book 2, pp. 207-08.
                                               DHU

7055. Oliver, Bernard J. Some Newer Religious Groups in the
United States: Twelve Case Studies. Doctoral dissertation.
Yale University, 1946.
    Includes information of Father Divine's Peace mission and
    Pentecostal churches.

7056. Parsons, A. "Pentecostal Immigrants: Study of an Ethnic
Central Church. " Practical Anthropology (14; Nov., 1967), pp.
249-66.   DHU/R

7057. Smith, Vern E. "The Perpetual Mission of Mother Waddles. "
Ebony (27:7, My., 1972), pp. 50-58.   DHU/MO
    "Detroit Pentecostal evangelist begins 15th year of her
    mission which has a church program that meets physical
    needs of poor in the U.S. and abroad. "

7058. Synan, Vinson. The Holiness-Pentecostal Movement in the
United States. Michigan: William B. Eerdmans Publishing
Company, 1971.   DHU/R; DLC; KyWAT
    Chapter 8, The Negro Pentecostals.

7059. Tinney, James S. "Black Origins of the Pentecostal Movement." Christianity and Crisis (16:1, Oct. 8, 1971), pp. 4-6.
DHU/R

7060. ----- "Gospel Spreading Church Has 4,000 at Baptizing." The Washington Afro-American (Oct. 6, 1973), p. 11.
Pam. File, DHU/R

7061. ----- "New Mission Thrust For United Holy Church." Washington Afro-American (Sept. 22, 1973), p. 14. DHU/MO;
Pam. File, DHU/R

7062. Tracy, Nat. Speaking in Tongues. Doctoral dissertation. New Orleans Baptist Theological Seminary, 1936.

7063. Wallis, Jim. "'New Evangelicals' and the Demands of Discipleship." Christian Century (91:21, My. 29, 1974), pp. 581-83.   DHU/R
Discussion of the Second Annual Calvin College Conference on Christianity and Politics. Black evangelicals make plea for meaningful action to stop exploitation of the poor blacks and other minorities.

7064. Williams, Colin W. Pentecost and Race. New York: Ministers and Missionaries Benefit Board of the American Convention, 1964.   MNtcA

(2) Cults and Sects, General

7065. Alland, Alexander. "Possession in a Revivalistic Negro Church." Journal for the Scientific Study of Religion (1:2, Spr., 1962), pp. 204-13.   DHU/R
Deals with United House of Prayer (Daddy Grace).

7066. Bach, Marcus. They Have Found a Faith. Indianapolis: Bobbs-Merrill Co., 1946.   DHU/R
Chapter 6, The Kingdoms of Father Divine.

7067. Baskin, Wade and Richard N. Runes. Dictionary of Black Culture. New York: Philosophical Library, 1973.
DHU/MO
Gives biographical sketches on various cult leaders--Daddy Grace, Father Divine, etc.

7068. Belstrom, Chester E. 'Come and See' - Attach Yourself to God in Spirit in Mind in Body - Harmonize With God. Minneapolis, Minn.: The Kingdom Publication, 19?? Pam. File,
DHU/MO
Activities in Father Divine's religious cult.

7069. Bender, Lauretta and Z. Yarrell. "Psychiatric Report on Followers of Father Divine in Bellevue Hospital." New York Bellevue Hospital (193?), p. 4.   Pam. File. DHU/MO

7070. Berlack, Freeman Roosevelt. A Study of Religious Cults Among Negroes in Richmond, Virginia. Bachelor of Divinity thesis. Virginia Union University, 1940.
Includes information on the Father Divine Peace Mission and many holiness churches.

7071. Bernhardt, William H., (ed.). Denver Cults; 1944 Series V. Denver: Iliff School of Theology, 1944.   CoDI
Includes information on Father Divine Peace Mission.

7072. Bird, Richard S. "Expansion of the Father Divine Movement." New York Times (Jl. 2, 1939).   DHU

7073. Blessing, William Lester. Divine Seal. Denver: House of Prayer for All People, 1958.   TN/DCHS

7074. ----- Hallowed Be Thy Name. Denver: House of Prayer for All People, 1955.   TN/DCHS

7075. ----- The Key of Knowledge. Denver: House of Prayer for All People, 1953.   TN/DCHS

7076. ----- The Supreme Architect of the Universe. Denver: House of Prayer for All People, 1953.   TN/DCHS

7077. ----- Survival. Denver: House of Prayer for All People, 1955.   TN/DCHS

7078. ----- The Trial of Jesus. Denver: House of Prayer for All People, 1955.   TN/DCHS

7079. ----- White Supremacy. Denver: House of Prayer for All People, 1952.   TN/DCHS

7080. Boaz, R. "My Thirty Years With Father Divine." Ebony (20; My., 1965), pp. 88+.   DHU/MO

7081. Braden, Charles Samuel. These Also Believe. New York: Macmillan Co., 1950.   DHU/R
See Chapter I, "The Peace Mission Movement of Father Divine."

7082. ----- "What Can We Learn From the Cults?" Religion in Life (14:1, Wint., 1944-45), pp. 52-64.   DHU/R

7083. ----- "Why Are the Cults Growing?" Christian Century (61:2, Ja. 12, 1944), pp. 45-47+.   DHU/R

7084. Brean, H. "Prophet Jones in Church and At Home." Life (17; Nov. 27, 1944), pp. 22.   DLC

7085. Brisbane, Robert H. "New Light on the Garvey Movement." Journal of Negro History (36; Ja., 1951), pp. 56-57.
DHU/MO

7086. Brown, Theodore E. The Negro in Syracuse, New York, as Related to the Social Service Program of Dunbar Center. Masters thesis. Syracuse University, 1943.
Includes information of Negro store-front churches in Syracuse.

7087. Burnham, Kenneth E. Father Divine, A Case Study of Charismatic Leadership. Philadelphia: n.p., 1963. PPT

7088. Cantril, Hadley. The Psychology of Social Movements. New York: Wiley, 1941.   DHU/R; INu
Includes section on Father Divine and his Kingdom.

7089. ----- and Muzafu Sherif. "The Kingdom of Father Divine." Journal of Abnormal and Social Psychology (33; Apr., 1938), pp. 147-67.   DHU

7090. Casey, Phil. "Banks in Area Hold Over $1 Million of Daddy's Grace Money." The Washington Post (Mr. 11, 1960), pp. B-1, B-12.   Pam. File, DHU/MO;
DHU/R

7091. ----- "Daddy Grace Came a Long Way From Early Days in New Bedford." The Washington Post (Mr. 7, 1960), p. B-1.
Pam. File, DHU/MO

7092. ----- "Daddy's Outstanding Miracle: Hold on Flock." The Washington Post (Mr. 22, 1960), p. E-1.   Pam. File,
DHU/MO
About Daddy Grace and the House of Prayer.

7093. "The Enigma of Daddy Grace: Did He Play God?" The Washington Post (Mr. 6, 1960), p. E-1.   Pam. File,
DHU/MO

7094. ----- "Friends Say Daddy Grace Didn't Need Money, He Had Everything." The Washington Post (Mr. 10, 1960), p. A-26.   Pam. File, DHU/MO

7095. ----- "Many Setbacks Failed to Deter Daddy Grace." The Washington Post (Mr. 8, 1960), pp. B-1, B-4. Pam. File,
DHU/MO

7096. ----- "Parable Served Daddy Grace to Evade Direct Replies." The Washington Post (Mr. 9, 1960), pp. B-1, B-12.
Pam. File, DHU/MO

7097. Christian, Paul. "The Mystery of Father Divine." Psychology (21:9, Oct., 1935), pp. 32-33.   DLC

7098. Clark, Elmer Talmage. The Small Sects in America.
Nashville, Tenn.: Abingdon, 1937, 1949.   DHU/R; INU
Chapter 4, Negro sects, distinguishing five types of charismatic sects, most of them offshoots of regular churches,
and all of them characterized by revivalism, emotionalism,
and evangelism.

7099. Clarke, John Henrik. Marcus Garvey and the Vision of
Africa. New York: Vintage Books, 1974.   DHU/R

7100. Cotton, W. R. "What Kind of People Does a Religious
Cult Attract?" American Sociological Review (22; Oct., 1957),
pp. 561+.   DAU; DAU/W; DGU/SW; DGU; DGW; DHU

7102. "Court Ousts Daddy Grace Successor, Names Lawyer as
Church Receiver (Walter McCullough)." The Washington
Evening Star (Ag. 25, 1961), pp. A-1-A-2.   Pam. File;
                                                    DHU/MO

7103. Cronon, E. David. "Black Moses: Marcus Garvey and
Garveyism." Ikon Edet Uya, (ed.) Black Brotherhood, Afro-
Americans and Africa (Lexington, Mass.: D. C. Heath and
Co., 1971), pp. 172-93.   DHU/MO

7104. "D. C. Eyes Taxes, Claims Daddy Grace Lived Here."
The Washington Evening Star, (Apr. 14, 1960), p. C-4.
                                    Pam. File, DHU/MO

7105. "Daddy Grace Cult Joins Estate Fight." The Washington
Post (Je. 10, 1960), p. B-2.   Pam. File, DHU/MO

7106. "Daddy Grace; Millionaire With a Bible." Our World (8; Oct.,
1953), pp. 50-53.   DLC; DHU/MO

7107. "Daddy Grace to Use Fire Hose on 300." Amsterdam News
(Jl. 28, 1956).   DHU/MO

7108. Daniel, Vattel Elbert. Ritual in Chicago's South Side Churches
for Negroes. Masters thesis. University of Chicago, 1940.
                                            DLC; CtY-D

7109. Davis, Grady D. A Psychological Investigation of Motivational Needs and Their Gratification in the Father Divine Movement.
Doctoral dissertation. Boston University, n. d.

7110. "Deity Derepresonifitized: Father Divine's Death." Time
(86; Sept. 17, 1965), p. 41.   DAU; DCU/SW; DGU; DGW; DHU

7111. Denlinger, S. "Heaven is in Harlem." Forum Century
(95; Apr., 1936), pp. 211-18.   DCU/St

7112. "Detroit's Prophet Jones, 63; Colorful Preacher of '50's."
The Washington Evening Star (Ag. 13, 1971), p. B-5.
                                    Pam. File, DHU/MO

7113. "The Dini Ya Israel." Sepia (14; Je., 1965), pp. 42-45.
                                                DHU/MO

7114. Dole, Kenneth. "Elder Lightfoor Solomon Michaux, Negro
Religious Leader, Dies at 84." The Washington Post, (Oct.
21, 1968), pp. A-1+.   Pam. File, DHU/MO

7115. Dynes, R. R. "Church-Sect Typology and Socio-Economic
Status." American Sociological Review (20; 1955), pp. 555-60.
ICU; CLU; DCU; CtY; NN; NNC; INU; OO; PHC; RPB

7116. Edwards, Adelph. Marcus Garvey, 1887-1940. London:
New Beacon Publications, 1967.   DHU/MO
Brief biography of Marcus Garvey.

7117. Eister, Allan W. "An Outline of a Structural Theory of
Cults." Journal for the Scientific Study of Religion (11:4, Dec.,
1972), pp. 319-30.   DHU/R
"Many of the idological and organizational characteristics
typically associated with cult movements can be interpreted
as responses to cultural crisis."

7118. Essien-Udom, E. U. "Garvey and Garveyism." Eric Foner
(ed.). America's Black Past, A Reader in Afro-American
History (New York: Harper and Row, 1970), pp. 352-70.
                                                DHU/R
Negro author.

7119. "Father Divine Dies; Noted Evangelist." The Washington
Evening Star, (Sept. 10, 1965), p. B-3-4. Pam. File, DHU/MO

7120. "Father Divine is Dead. Sepia (14; Nov., 1965), pp. 76-81.
                                                DHU/MO

7121. Fauset, Arthur H. Black Gods of the Metropolis. Philadel-
phia: University of Pennsylvania Press, 1944.   DHU/MO;
NjP; DHU/R
"Negro cults in the city."

7122. Fax, Elton C. Garvey: The Story of a Pioneer Black Nationalist. New York: Dodd, Mead & Co., 1972.   DHU/MO; DHU/R

7123. Fisher, Miles Mark. "Organized Religion and the Cults."
The Crisis (44:1, Ja., 1937), pp. 8-10.   DLC; DHU/MO
"The organized denominations of this country have much to
learn from such cult leaders as Elder Michaux, Father Divine
and Mother Horne, delcares this young minister."

7124. Garber, Paul Russell. The Garvey Movement: an Appraisal.
Masters thesis. Southeastern Baptist Theological Seminary,
1960.

7125. Garvey, Marcus M. "An Appeal to the Conscience of the Black
Race to See Itself." Arthur C. Littleton and Mary W. Burger,
(eds.). Black Viewpoints (New York: New American Library,
1964), pp. 62-74.   DHU/R

7126. ----- "The Back to Africa Movement: 1922." Bradford
Chambers, (ed.). Chronicles of Black Protest (New York:
The New America Library, 1968).   DHU/MO

7127. ----- "The Negro's Greatest Enemy." Thomas R. Frazier,
(ed.). Afro-American History: Primary Resources (New York:
Harcourt, Brace & World, Inc., 1970), pp. 275-84. DHU/R;
DHU/MO
Garvey summarizes his life and accomplishments.

7128. Gelman, Martin. Adat Boyt Moshe--the Colored House of
Moses: A Study of a Contemporary Negro Religious Community
and Its Leaders. Doctoral dissertation. University of Pennsylvania, 1965.

7129. Gillard, John T. A Sociological Document About Father Divine,
Christ, Color and Communism.   IC/H

7130. Gillenwater, Charles A. The Sociological and Psychological
Aspects of the Father Divine Movement. Bachelor of Divinity
paper. Andover Newton Theological School, 1948.

7131. Goodman, George. "Harlem's Yorubas." Look (Ja., 1966),
pp. 441-67.   DLC; DGU

7132. Harkness, G. "Father Divine's Righteous Government".
Christian Century (82:41, Oct. 13, 1965), pp. 1259-61.
                                                DHU/R

7133. Harrell, David E. White Sects and Black Men. Nashville:
Vanderbilt Univ. Press, 1971.   DHU/R
Racial views of a segment of white southern Protestantism.
"Churches discussed are not widely known, and the people
who make them up are among the least articulate of southern-
ers."

7134. Harris, Robert. Black Glory in the Life and Times of Marcus
Garvey. New York: African Nationalist Pioneer Movement,
1961.   NN/Sch

7135. Harris, Sara. The Incredible Father Divine. London: Allen,
1954.   DHU/MO; INU

7136. ----- and Harriet Critendon. Father Divine: Holy Husband. Garden City, N.Y.: Doubleday, 1953.   DHU/MO; INU

7137. Hoshor, John. God is in a Rolls Royce; The Rise of Father Divine, Madman, Menace or Messiah. New York: Hillman-Curl, 1936.   DHU/MO

7138. Howell, C. V. "Father Divine: Another View; Reply to F. S. Mead." Christian Century (53:41, Oct., 7, 1936), p. 1332.   DHU/R

7139. Johnson, Benton. "A Critical Appraisal of the Church-Sect Typology." American Sociological Review (22; 1957), pp. 88-92.   DHU
     "Holiness religion may be a powerful agent in socializing lower-class groups in the values and usages of our predominantly middle-class society."

7140. Jones, Raymond Julius. A Comparative Study of Religious Cult Behavior Among Negroes, With Special Reference to Emotional Group Conditioning Factors. Washington, D.C.: Pub. by the Graduate School for the Division of the Social Sciences, Howard University, 1939.   DHU/R; CtY-D
     Negro author.

7141. Kardiner, Abram and Lionel Ovesey. The Mark of Opression. Explorations in the Personality of the American Negro. New York: World Publishing, 1972.   DHU/R
     pp. 349-59, Cults and Religion of the Negro.

7142. Kelley, H. "Heaven Incorporated." American Magazine (121; Ja., 1936), pp. 40-1.   DHU

7143. King, Truxton. "Father Divine's Peace Mission Movement is Truly Wonderful." Pittsburgh Courier. Magazine Section (Nov. 17, 1951), pp. 8-9.   DHU/MO

7144. LaBarre, Weston. They Shall Take Up Serpents: Psychology of the Southern Snake-Handling Cult. New York: Shocken Books, 1969.   DLC

7145. LaCoste, Richard. "Elder Michaux, 'Happy, Am I' Preacher." Pittsburgh Courier. Magazine Section (Feb. 28, 1953), pp. 4-5.   DHU/MO

7146. Langley, Jabez Ayodele. "Garveyism and African Nationalism." Race (11; Oct., 1969), pp. 157-72.   DHU

7147. Lark, E. F. Presenting a Pictorial Review of Elder Lightfoot Solomon Michaux; International Radio Evangelist, His Famous Cross and Radio Choirs and His Civic Activities For Developing a Good Neighbor Spirit Among All Races and Creeds. August 1941. Washington, D.C.: Murray Brothers, Printers, 1941.   DHU/MO

7148. Larsen, Egon. Strange Sects and Cults: A Study of Their Origins and Influence. New York: Hart Publishing Co., Inc., 1971.   DHU/R
     Includes sections on Father Divine, the Cherubim and Seraphim and "Spritualism and Primitives."

7149. Light, Ivan H. Ethnic Enterprise in America: Business and Welfare Among Chinese, Japanese, and Blacks. Berkley: University of California Press, 1972.   DHU/R
     Chapter. 7, Church, Sect, and Father Divine.

7150. Lips, Julius. "God's Chillun Negerseklen in Washington." Mass und Werte, Zurich: (3:1, 1939), pp. 89-116.   NN/Sch
     "Negro Cults, Solomon Lightfoot Michaux and Father Divine."

7151. Lockley, Edith. The Negro Spiritualist Churches of Nashville. Master's thesis. Fisk University, 1935.

7152. Long, Edward Leroy. A Survey of Christian Ethics. London, Toronto: Oxford University Press, 1970.   DHU/R
     Chapter 18, Sects, Guilds, and Causes.

7153. Martin, Walter Ralson. The Kingdom of the Cults: An Analysis of the Major Cults Systems in the Present Christian Era. Grand Rapids: Zondervan Pub. Co., 1965.   INU

7154. Marty, Martin E. "Sects and Cults." The Annals of the American Academy of Political and Social Science (332; Nov., 1960), pp. 125-34.   DLC; DHU
     "Sects and cults are considered a third Christian force, even though they are spatially and psychologically outside of society."

7155. Mathison, Richard R. Faiths, Cults and Sects of America (From Atheism to Zen). Indianapolis: Bobbs-Merrill, 1960.   DLC

7156. McKay, Claude. Harlem: Negro Metropolis. n.p.: n.p., 1940.   IC/H
     Includes information about George Baker, self-named Father Divine.

7157. ----- "'There Goes God!' The Story of Father Divine and His Angels." The Nation (140; Feb. 6, 1935), pp. 151-53.   DCU/SW; DGU; DGW; DHU

7158. Meigs, Paul A. A Study of the Growth, Development and Principle Doctrines of Some Leading American Cults and Their Impact on American Religious Life. Doctoral dissertation. Golden Gate Baptist Theological Seminary, 1955.

7159. Michaux, Lightfoot Solomon. Spiritual Happiness Making Songs. Washington, D.C.: The Author, n.d.   DHU/MO
     Repetory of songs used by the Elder Michaux Radio Choir.

7160. "The Negro Religious Tradition." Harry A. Ploski and Roscoe C. Brown, Jr. The Negro Almanac (New York: Bellwether Publishing Co., Inc., 1967), pp. 894-921. DHU
     Includes information of Father Divine, text of "Black Manifesto."

7161. Nelson, Geoffrey K. "The Membership of a Cult: the Spiritualists National Union." Review of Religious Research (13:3, Spr., 1972), pp. 170-77.   DHU/R
     "Social and psychological sources of cults. Membership of the Spiritualists Nat. Union in Britain."

7162. "New Mrs. Divine, Cult Leader Marries White Woman Who is Much Younger Than He Is." Life (21; Ag. 19, 1946), p. 38.   DHU

7163. Onwauchi, Patrick C. Religious Concepts and Socio-Cultural Dynamics and Afro-American Religious Cults of St. Louis, Missouri. St. Louis University, 1963.

7164. Ottley, Roe. New World A-Coming. Boston: Houghton Miflin Co., 1943.   DHU/R
     Chapter 7, "I Talked with God," an early account of the Father Divine movement.

7165. Parker, Robert A. The Incredible Messiah: the Deification of Father Divine. Boston: Little, Brown & Co., 1937.   DHU/R; DLC

7166. Pollak-Eltz, Angelina. Afro-Amerikaanse Godskiensten en Culten. Roermond: J. J. Romen and Zonen, 1970.   DLC

7167. Rasky, Frank. "Harlem's Religious Zealots." 9:3, Tomorrow (9; Nov., 1949), pp. 11-17.   DHU/R; DHU/MO
     Elder Lightfoot Solomon Michaux, "Happy Am I Prophet," and Mother Rosa Artinus Horne, "Pray for Me Priestess."

7168. Reid, Ira DeA. "Negro Movements and Messiahs, 1900-1949." Phylon (10:4, Quarter, 1949), pp. 362-69.   DHU/MO

7169. Rogers, Ben F. "William E. B. DuBois, Marcus Garvey a and Pan-Africanism." Journal of Negro History (40:2, Apr., 1955), pp. 154-65.   DHU/MO

7170. "Second Front in Harlem: Elder Michaux and His Choir."
Time (40; Dec. 21, 1942), pp. 74+. DAU; DCU/SW; DGU;
DGW; DHU

7171. Singletor, Deborah. "DuBois and Garvey, Similarities and
Dissimilarities on Pan-Africanism." Transition (1:2, 1973),
pp. 52-61.   DHU/MO

7172. Smith, Marian W. "Toward a Classification of Cult Movements." Man (59:2, Ja., 1959), pp. 8-12. DHU/MO

7173. "Spiritual Churches, Sects Mark 35- Years of Growth."
Ebony (15; Oct., 1960), pp. 60+.   DHU/MO

7174. The "Spoken Word." Los Angeles: Spoken Word Publishing
Co., 1934.   NNUT
"Published in the interest of Father M. J. Divine Kingdom,
peace missions, extensions and connections."

7175. Tinker, E. L. "Mother Catherine's Castor Oil; Visiting the
High Priestess of a Negro Cult in New Orleans." North American Review (230; Ag., 1930), pp. 148-54.   DHU

7176. Tinney, James S. "Expansion Plans for United House of
Prayer." The Washington Afro-American (Sept. 15, 1973),
p. 15.   Pam. File, DHU/R

7177. Tyms, James Daniel. A Study of Four Religious Cults
Operating Among Negroes. Master's thesis. Howard Univer-
sity, 1938.
Negro author.

7178. Washington, Joseph R., Jr. Black Sects & Cults. New York:
Doubleday & Co., 1972. DHU/MO; DHU/R; TSewU-T; MNtcA
Negro author.

7179. Weinberg, Arthur and Lila (eds.). Passport to Utopia: Great
Panaceas in American History. New York: Quadrangle, 1969.
                                                                                        DHU/MO
Discussion of Father Divine's cult.

7180. Whiting, Albert N. The United House of Prayer for All
People. A Case Study of a Charismatic Sect. Doctoral Dissertation. American University, 1952.

7181. Williams, Chancellor. Have You Been to the River? New
York: Exposition Press, 1952.   DHU/R
Negro and cults, fiction.
Negro author.

(3) Storefront Churches

7182. Benedict, Dan and George W. Webber. "Proposal for a
Store-Front Larger System." Union Seminary Quarterly
Review (4:3, Mr., 1948), pp. 17-22.   DHU/R
Union Theological Seminary project in Harlem, New York.

7183. Blackwell, James Edward. A Comparative Study of Five
Negro 'Storefront' Churches in Cleveland. Masters thesis.
Western Reserve Univ., 1949.

7184. Darby, Golden B. The Negro in Syracuse, N.Y. A Study
in Community Relations. Syracuse, N.Y.: Syracuse Public
Library, 1937.   NSy
Typescript.
Author concludes, "the store-front churches provide evidence of the most vicious exploitation of the Negro, both
morally and economically."

7185. Eddy, Norman G. "Store-front Religion." Religion in Life
(28:1, Wint. 1958-59), pp. 68-85.

7186. Hallenbeck, Wilbur C. American Urban Communities. New
York: Harper & Brothers, 1951.   ViU; CoU; NN
Contains brief, clear statements on store front churches.

7187. Harrison, Ira E. Diverse Doubts, Observations, and Conversations Among Store-Front Churches. Syracuse, N.Y.:
Youth Development Center, Syracuse University, March, 1962.
                                                                                        NSyU

Typescript.
"Purpose of this paper is to share with interested persons
some diverse doubts, observations and conversations among
store-front churches."

7188. ----- Participant Observations in Store-Front Churches in
Syracuse, New York. Syracuse, N.Y.: Youth Development
Center, Syracuse University, Oct., 1961.   NSyU
Typescript.
Discusses the ritual and atmosphere in these churches.

7189. ----- A Seclected Annotated Bibliography on Store-Front
Churches and Other Religious Writings. Syracuse, N.Y.:
Youth Development Center, Syracuse University, 1962.
                                                                        NSyU; DHU/R
Typescript.

7190. ----- "The Store-front Church as a Revitalization Movement." Hart M. Nelsen & Raytha L. Yokley, et al. The
Black Church in America (New York: Basic Books, 1971), pp.
240-45.   DHU/R
Also in Review of Religious Research (7; Spr., 1966), pp.
160-63.

7191. Hill, Hilley. The Negro Store-front Churches in Washington,
D.C. Masters thesis. Howard University, 1947.
Negro author.

7192. Lee, Rose Hum. The City. New York: J. B. Lippincott Co.,
1955.   NN; DLC
"In the main, the worshipers identify themselves with 'race
churches', and about 10 per cent of the churches in 'Brozer-
ville' are small, store-front or 'house-churches' with an
average membership of fewer than 25 persons."

7193. Lewis, Elsie Freeman. Storefront Pentecostal Church:
an Exploratory Study of the Influence of a Storefront Church on
its Members. Masters thesis. Washington, D.C.: Howard
University, 1972.

7194. The Negro in Chicago. Report of the Chicago Commission
on Race Relations. Chicago: University of Chicago Press,
1922.   DHU/MO; ICU
Includes information on "store-front" church.

7195. "Old Lafayette Gets Religion; Harlem Theater Made Famous
by Lafayette Players Becomes Live Wire Church." Our World
(8; Apr., 1953), pp. 48-51.   DHU/MO; DLC

7196. Reapsome, J. W. "Storefront Chapel that Grew and Grew."
Moody Monthly (68; Dec., 1967), pp. 28-32.   DHU/R

7197. Reid, Ira De A. "Storefront Churches and Cults." Sherman
Richard B. The Negro and the City (Englewood Cliffs, N.J.:
Prentice-Hall, 1970), pp. 104-09.   DHU/R
Negro author.

7198. Schermerhoun, Richard A. These Our People; Minorities
in American Culture. Boston: D. C. Heath, 1949. DHU/MO
Storefront church.

7199. Sherman, Richard B., (ed.). The Negro and the City.
Englewood, N.J.: Prentice Hall, 1970.   DHU/R
Chapter V, storefront churches and cults.

7200. "Storefront Church." Our World (7; My., 1952), pp. 62-5.
                                                                        DHU/MO; DLC

7201. "Store-Front Preacher." The Lamp (167:1, Ja., 1969), pp.
15-19.   DHU/R
"Rev. Helen Archibald, a White Congregationalist minister
runs a one-woman church in the Brownsville section of
Brooklyn, N.Y."

7202. Union Theological Seminary. Black Economic Development
Steering Committee. The Smaller Churches: "Repairers of
the Breach." New York: Media-Modes, Inc.   DHU/R
Filmstrip.
"Inner view of the ways some storefront churches perceive

the Gospel. How they express love and concern for persons who have been victimized in society."

7203. Williams, Chancellor. The Socio-Economic Significance of the Store-front Church Movement in the United States Since 1920. Doctoral dissertation. American University, 1949.
DHU/R

Negro author.

7204. Willoughby, W. "Storefront Churches: Social Stabilizers." Christianity Today (13:16, My. 9, 1969), pp. 44-5. DHU/R

7205. Wright, William A. The Negro Store-Fronts: Churches of the Disinherited. Bachelor of Divinity thesis. Union Theological Seminary, 1942.

2. Black Jews (including contemporary status)

7206. "Balck Israel: Harlem Jews Keep the Fast of Yom Kippur." News-Week (7; Sept., 29, 1928), p. 25. DLC

7207. "Black Israelite Sect Member Showed Prima Facie C. O. Grounds-- Dismissed," The Ecclesiastical Court Digest (9:10, Oct., 1971), p. 2. DHU/R

7208. "Black Jew Says Israel Should Reject 'Other' Black Jews." Jewish Press (Jl. 10, 1970).

7209. "Black Jews." Harry A. Ploski (ed.). Reference Library of Black America (New York: Bellwether Pub. Co., 1971), Book 2, pp. 204-206. DHU

7210. "Black Jews Helped to Integrate." Jewish Chronicle (Jl. 18, 1969).

7211. "Black Migrants to a Promised Land." Life (68:19; My., 22, 1970), pp. 65-8. DHU
Resettlement of thirty-four members of (Black Hebrew-Israelites in Israel.

7212. "Brothers Under the Skin, Black Jews in New York." New York Sunday News (Ag. 7, 1949). NN

7213. Brotz, Howard M. The Black Jews of Harlem: Negro Nationalism and the Dilemmas of Negro Leadership. New York: Free Press of Glencoe, 1964. DHU/R; INU; DLC

7214. ----- "Negro 'Jews' in the United States." Hart M. Nelsen & Raytha L. Yokley, et al. The Black Church in America (New York: Basic Books, 1971), pp. 194-209. DHU/R
Also in Phylon (13; Dec., 1952), pp. 324-37.

7215. Diaz, J. A. "Balck Jews in U. S. A. - Synagogue Increasing." Social Whirl (Apr. 25, 1955), pp. 18-19.

7216. Egerton, John. "Black Adopting Jewish Religion." Relations Reporter (2:1, Ja., 1971), pp. 8-9. DHU/L

7217. Ehrman, Albert. "Explorations and Responses: Black Judaism in New York." Journal of Ecumenical Studies (8:1, Wint., 1971), pp. 103-14. DHU/R

7218. "Ethiopian Hebrews of New York." The Crisis (52:9, Sept., 1945), pp. 252-54. DLC; DHU/MO

7219. Graham, Alfredo. "White Jews, Black Jews Not Kosher." Pittsburgh Courier (Jl. 16, 1960). Pam. File; DHU/R

7220. "Harlem Leader of Black Jews Syas Race Deserted Its Faith." Afro American (Feb. 8, 1936), DHU/MO

7221. Helm, C. "Negro Sect in Harlem Mixes Jewish and Christian Religions." New York Sun (Ja. 29, 1929). NN

7222. Kaufnian, Ishi. "Head of Black Jewish Cult Dies of Burns." Afro-American (Ag. 1, 1936). DHU/MO
Leader of the Gospel of the Kingdom Tempel, a Black Jewish cult in Harlem.

7223. Koppman, L. "Commandment Keepers." Jewish Digest (9; Mr., 1946), pp. 49-52. DLC
Black Jews.

7224. Landers, Ruth. "Negro Jews in Harlem." Jewish Journal of Sociology (9; Dec., 1967), pp. 175-90. DHU; ICU

7225. Malihi, H. "Problems of a Negro in Israel Told to L. Heiman." Jewish Digest (9; Nov., 1963), pp. 78-80. DLC

7226. "Negro in the Synagogue." United Synagogue Review (16; Sum., 1963), pp. 6+. OCH

7227. "Negro Jews Call for End to Anti-Semitism in City." New York Times (Oct. 26, 1968). DLC

7228. "Negro Sect Mixes Jewish and Christian Religions." The New York Sun (Ja. 29, 1929). NN

7229. "New Horror Bared Among Black Jews." Chicago Defender (Jl. 17, 1926). DHU/MO
From the activities of the "notorious Elder Warren Robinson, who claimed to be the Jewish Messiah, but who in reality headed a love cult." Albert Ehrman: "Black Judaism in New York," Journal of Ecumenical Studies (8:1, Wint., 1971), pp. 101-14. DHU/R

7230. "New York's Negro Jews." Literary Digest (100; Mr. 2, 1929), p. 27. DHU

7231. Obatala, J. K. "Exodus: Black Zionism." Liberator (9; Oct., 1969), pp. 14-17. DHU/MO

7232. "Rabbi David Hill." Frank L. Keegan. Blacktown. U.S.A. (Boston: Little, Brown, 1971), pp. 277-95. DHU/MO
Cleveland based and formerly Bishop of the House of Israel, David Hill is now a self-styled Rabbi.

7233. "A Reader Speaks Out About Black Jews." Jewish Press (Jl. 3, 1970).
Contains remarks by 3 recent black converts to Orthodox Judaism, Abraham Abramson, Chaim Bibbins and Robert Coleman.

7234. Reid, B. G. "New York's Black Jews Estimated at 16,000." New York Courier (Ag. 9, 1969). MN

7235. Simor, George. "Black Jews of Harlem." Sepia (17:4, Apr., 1968), pp. 28-32. DHU/MO

7236. Tarr, H. "Elijah in Mississippi." Jewish Digest (8; Sept., 1963), pp. 71-80. DLC
Black Jews.

7237. Tinney, James S. "Black Jews: A House Divided." Christianity Today (18:5, Dec. 7, 1973), pp. 52-53. DHU/R

7238. ----- "Black Jews Active Here, But Not Well-Known." Washington Afro-American (Nov. 10, 1973). Pam. File, DHU/R

7239. Waitzkin, Howard. "Black Judaism in New York." Harvard Journal of Negro Affairs (1:3, 1967), pp. 12-44. DHU/MO; DLC

7240. "Why There Are No Orthodox Black Rabbis." Jewish Press (Jl., 24, 1970).

3. Black Muslims (including contemporary status and Muslim Sects)

7241. Abel, Steven Dwight. The Dynamics of Social Cohesion as Found in the Teaching of a Black Religious Thinker: Elijah Muhammad. Masters thesis. Howard University, School of Religion, 1973.

7242. "Adopts Islamic Religion--Change of Name Application Denied." The Ecclesiastical Court Digest (5:11, Nov., 1967), p. 1.   DHU/R

7243. Allen, Robert L. "Black Nationalism and the Nation of Islam." Carlene Young (ed.). Black Experience (San Rafael, Calif.: Lewsing Press, 1972), pp. 254-58.   DHU/R

7244. Ashmore, Harry S. The Other Side of Jordan. New York: W. W. Norton & Co.   DHU/MO; INU

7245. Baldwin, James. One Day When I Was Lost; a Scenario Based on the Autobiography of Malcolm X. London: Michael Joseph, 1972.   PPT

7246. Balk, A. and Alex Haley. "Black Merchants of Hate." Saturday Evening Post (236:3, Ja. 26, 1963), pp. 68-75. DHU Black Muslims.

7247. Barbee, Bobbie C. "Will Link With Malcolm X Harm Clay's Career. Champ Offers $20,000 to Anyone Changing His Muslim Beliefs." Jet (25:50, Mr. 26, 1964), pp. 40-44. DHU/MO

7248. Berger, Morroe. "The Black Muslims." Horizon (6; Ja., 1964), pp. 48-65.   DAU; DGU

7249. Bibb, L. C. "They Preach Black to be the Ideal." Negro History Bulletin (28:6, Mr., 1965), pp. 132-33.   DHU/MO Black Muslims.

7250. "Black Capitalism in the Muslim Style." Fortune (81; Ja., 1970), p. 44.   DAU; DCU/SW; DGU; DGW; DHU

7251. "Black Muslim Charges not Established." The Ecclesiastical Court Digest (19:3, Mr., 1972), p. 5.   DHU/R

7252. "The Black Muslim Hope." Sports Illustrated (20; Mr. 16, 1964), p. 8.   DAU

7253. "Black Muslim Inmates of a New York State Prison Bring Suit Charging Religious Persecution. U.S. District Court Dismisses the Complaints." Race Relations Law Reporter (8; Spr., 1963), pp. 44-51.   DHU/L

7254. "Black Muslim Prisoner Denied Access to Certain Literature and Food." The Ecclesiastical Court Digest (6:8, Aug., 1968), p. 6.   DHU/R

7255. "Black Muslim Prisoners Denied 8 Quarts of Milk for Certain Hours." Ecclesiastical Court Digest (11:6, Je, 1973), p. 6.   DHU/R

7256. "Black Muslim Prisoners Entitled to Religious Gatherings - But No Other." The Ecclesiastical Court Digest (8:2, Feb., 1970), p. 6.   DHU/R

7257. "Black Muslim Prisoners Held Not to Have Been Deprived of Religious Rights." The Ecclesiastical Court Digest (4:12, Dec., 1966), p. 5.

7258. "Black Muslim Prisoners Petition Denied." The Ecclesiastical Court Digest (6:10, Oct., 1968), pp. 3-4.   DHU/R

7259. "Black Muslim Prisoners Segregated for Security Reasons." The Ecclesiastical Court Digest (10:6, Je., 1972), p. 5.   DHU/R

7260. "Black Muslim Prisoners Succeed on Papers and Books-- Not on Diet." The Ecclesiastical Court Digest (7:11, Nov., 1969), p. 1.

7261. "Black Muslim Prisoners Suit Dismissed." The Ecclesiastical Court Digest (11:5, My., 1973), pp. 1-2.   DHU/R

7262. "Black Muslim Prisoners to Have Hearing on Religious Discrimination." The Ecclesiastical Court Digest (6:6, Je., 1968), p. 1.   DHU/R

7263. "Black Muslim Refused to Submit for Army Physical Examination." The Ecclesiastical Court Digest (6:6, Je., 1968), p. 4.   DHU/R

7264. "Black Muslim Relgion is a Religion--But Prison Inmates Subject to Rules." The Ecclesiastical Court Digest (7: 1, Ja., 1969), p. 6.   DHU/R

7265. "Black Muslim Religion Recognized--Prison Officials Must Draft Rules." The Ecclesiasitical Court Digest (4:7, Jl., 1966), p. 1.   DHU/R

7266. "'Black Muslim' Suit Premature." The Ecclesiastical Court Digest (4:10, Oct., 1966), p. 3.   DHU/R

7267. "Black Muslims: A Call For Unity, Sound Finances Mark Drive for Economic Growth." Black Enterprise (3:5, Dec. 1972), pp. 21-23,   Pam. File, DHU/R

7268. "Black Muslims' Complaints Upheld for Trial." The Ecclesiastical Court Digest (4:3, Mar., 1966), p. 5. DHU/R

7269. "Black Muslim's Conviction for Criminal Anarchy Reversed by Louisiana Supreme Court." Race Relations Law Reporter (8; Sum., 1963), pp. 411-18.   DHU/L

7270. "Black Muslims Denied Collective Worship in Prison." The Ecclesiastical Court Digest (3:3, Mr., 1965), p. 3.   DHU/R

7271. "Black Muslims Given Religious Rights in Prison-Court Order Not Necessary." The Ecclesiastical Court Digest (6:3, Mr., 1968), p. 3.   DHU/R

7272. "Black Muslims in Prison: Of Muslim Rites and Constitutional Rights (Examination of three recent decisions involving religious rights of Black Muslim Prisoners; effect on the developing law of the substantive constitutional rights of prisoners)." Columbia Law Review (62; Dec., 1962), p. 1488. DAU/LW; DCU/LW; DGU/LW; DGW/LW; DHU/LW

7273. "Black Muslims in the U.S.; Black Nationalism." Journal of Intergroup Relations (3:1, Wint., 1961-62), pp. 5-11.   DHU/MO

7274. "Black Muslims on the Rampage." United States News and World Report (53; Ag. 13, 1962), p. 6.   DLC; DHU

7275. "Black Muslims Practices Restricted in Prisons." The Ecclesiastical Court Digest (1:9, Sept., 1963), p. 6. DHU/R

7276. "Black Muslims-Prisoners To Pursue Religious Observances." The Ecclesiastical Court Digest (12:4, Apr., 1974), p. 5.   DHU/R

7277. "Black Muslims Speak From America." British Broadcasting Corp., London. Released in the U.S. by Peter M. Robeck & Co., 1968. 33 min. sd. b & w. 16 mm.   DLC Film. "Malcolm Muggeridge interviews a group of young Black Muslims about their discontent and their beliefs."

7278. "Black Muslims Succeed in Obtaining Order Directing Worship Rights." The Ecclesiastical Court Digest (3:7, Jl., 1965), p. 2.   DHU/R

7279. "Black Supremacists." Time (74:6, Ag. 10, 1959), pp. 24-5.   DHU Black Muslims.

7280. "Black Supremacy Cult in the United States, How Much of
a Threat." United States News and World Report (47; Nov.
9, 1959), p. 12.   DLC; DHU
Black Muslims.

7281. Bontemps, Arna Wendell and Jack Conroy. "Registered with
Allah." David M. Reumers, (ed.). The Black Man in America
Since Reconstruction (New York: Thomas Y. Crowell, 1970),
pp. 263-90.   InU; DHU/MO
Taken from Arna Bontemps and Jack Conroy, Anyplace But
Here (New York: Hill & Wang, Inc., 1966), pp. 216-41.
Copyright published as They Seek a City
Discusses the origin and growth of the Black Muslims.

7282. Braden, Charles Samuel. "Islam in America." International
Review of Missions (48; Jl., 1959), pp. 309-17.   DHU/R
Blacks Muslims.

7283. Breitman, George. The Last Year of Malcolm X, The Evolution of a Revolutionary. New York: Pathfinder Press,
1970.   NNCor; DLC; InU; DHU/R
Black Muslims.

7284. ----- Malcolm X Speaks. New York: Merit Publishers,
1965.   DHU/R

7285. ----- The Assassination of Malcolm X, Unanswered
Questions and the Trial. New York: Merit Press, 1961.
CoDU

7286. Brown, L. P. "Black Muslims ans the Police." Journal
of Criminal Law, Criminology and Police Science (56; Mr.,
1965), pp. 119-26.   DAU; DLC

7287. Buresh, B. (ed.). "Muhammad Speaks: Interview Elijah
Muhammad." Newsweek (79; Ja. 31, 1972), p. 23. DHU

7288. Burnham, L. E. "Our Own Islam." (The Black Muslims
in U.S.) Freedomways (2; Wint., 1962), pp. 29-30. DHU/MO

7289. Burns, W. Haywood. "The Black Muslims in America: A
Reinterpretation." Edward Greer (ed.). Black Liberation
Politics: A Reader (Boston: Allyn and Bacon, 1971), pp. 72-
85.   DHU/MO

7290. California. Investigation; Paramilitary Organizations in
California. Sacramento: 1965. (In Misc. doc., Vol. 1429).
NcS/L
Investigation of actions of Black Muslims.

7291. "California Supreme Court Denies Negro Inmate of California."
State Prison, the Petition for Habeas Corpus, Inmate Said
Prison Officials Beat him and Denied him Access to the Courts
because of his Race and because he is a Black Muslim. Race
Relations Law Reporter (7; Fall, 1962), pp. 775-79. DHU/L

7292. Calverley, Edwin Elliot. Negro Muslims in Hartford.
Hartford: Hartford Seminary Foundation, 1965.   InU

7293. "Case of Harry X; Court Rules Free." Newsweek (76; Jl.
27, 1970), p. 48.   DHU
Black Muslim member.

7294. Clark, Kenneth Bancroft. The Negro Protest: James Baldwin, Malcolm X, Martin Luther King, talk with Kenneth B.
Clark. Boston: Beacon Press, 1963.   NcD; DHU/R

7295. Clark, Michael. "Rise in Racial Extremism." New York
Times (Jan. 25, 1960).   DHU

7296. Clarke, John Henrik. Malcolm X; the Man and His Times.
New York: Macmillan, 1969.   MiBsA; NNCor;
MNtcA

7297. Cleage, Albert B., Jr. and George Breitman. "Myths about
Malcolm X." International Socialist Review (28; Jl.-Ag., 1967),
pp. 43-51.   DHU
Negro author.

7298. "Complaint by Federal Islam Prisoner Dismissed." The
Ecclesiastical Court Digest (5:1, Ja., 1967), p. 3.   DHU/R

7299. "Conscientious Objector and Ministerial Status Denied Professional Boxer." The Ecclesiastical Court Digest (7:2, Feb.,
1969), p. 5.   DHU/R

7300. "Conscientious Objector Status Denied--Not Opposed to all
Wars-- Muslim." The Ecclesiastical Court Digest (7:12, Dec.,
1969), p. 4.   DHU/R

7301. "Constitution Law - Black Muslimism is a Religion Within the
Meaning of the First Amendment." Georgia Bar Journal
(24; My., 1962), pp. 519+.   DHU/L

7302. Cooper, C. L. "Aftermath: The Angriest Negroes Revisited."
Esquire (55; Je., 1961), p. 164.   DLC
Black Muslims.

7303. Crabites, P. "American Negro Mohammedans." Catholic
World (136; Feb., 1933), pp. 559-66.   DHU

7304. Crawford, Marc. "The Ominous Malcolm X Exits from the
Muslims." Life (56; Mr. 20, 1964), pp. 40-40A.   DHU;
DGW; DGU; DAU

7305. Curtis, Richard. The Life of Malcolm X. Philadelphia:
Macrae Smith Co., 1971.   MCE

7306. Cushmeer, Bernard. This is the One: Messenger Elijah
Muhammad, We Need Not Look for Another. Phoenix: Truth
Publications, 1971.   DHU/MO; DLC
Negro author.

7307. Davis, Charles H. Black Nationalism and the Nation of
Islam. Los Angeles: Operation Education, Operation Boot-
strap, 1968.   CoDU

7308. Davis, John H. "Can a Lutheran Work for the Black Muslims?" Metanoia (2; Mr., 1970), p. 14.   ICLT

7309. "Death and Transfiguration." Time (85; Mr. 5, 1965), p.
23.   DAU; DCU/SW; DGU; DHU; DGW
Black Muslims.

7310. "Death of a Desperado; Assassination of Malcolm X."
Newsweek (65; Mar. 8, 1965), pp. 24-25.   DHU; DGW; DAU;
DLC

7311. "Despair Serves Purposes of Bizarre Cult." Christian
Century (77; Ag. 10, 1960), p. 917. DAU; DAU/W; DCU/TH;
DHU; DGW
Black Muslims.

7312. "Discretion of Director of Corrections not Abused in Re-
fusing to Grant Black Muslims Prisoners Rights Afforded Other
Religious Groups." UCLA Law Review (9; Mr., 1962), pp.
501+.   DLC; CLU

7313. "Divide for Black Muslims." Economist (210:6290, Mr.
14, 1964), p. 996.   DHU

7314. Drimmer, Melvin, (ed.). Black History, a Reappraisal.
New York: Doubleday, 1969.   DHU/R
On the role of Martin Luther King, pp. 440+.
The Black Muslims as a Protest movement, pp. 454+.

7315. Ducas, George and Charles Van Doren. Great Documents
in Black American History. New York: Praeger Publishers,
1970.   MNtcA; MCE
Includes, "Letter from Birmingham Jail" by Martin Luther
King. Speeches by Malcolm X.

7316. Eddy, George Norman. Black Racist Religion. Boston:
n.p., 1962.   Pam. File. NcD

7317. Edwards, Harry. "Black Muslim and Negro Christian
Family Relationship." Robert Staples (ed.). The Black Family

(Edwards, Harry cont.)
Essays and Studies. (Belmont, Calif.: Wadsworth Pub. Co.,
1971.   DHU/MO
Also in Journal of Marriage and the Family, Nov., 1968.
pp. 604-11.

7318. ----- The Black Muslim Family: A Comparative Study.
Masters thesis. Cornell University, 1966.   NNCor

7319. "Egypt Plans to Use Black Muslims in U.S.A. Against Jews.
Top Echelon Debates Requires Successor." Jewish Observer
(12; Sept., 1963), pp. 3-4.   DAU

7320. "8,500 Crowd Armory to Hear Muhammed." Amsterdam
News (Ag. 6, 1960).   DHU/MO

7321. Elkholy, Abdo A. Religion and Assimilation in two Muslim
Communities in America. Doctoral Dissertation. Princeton
University, 1960.

7322. "The End of Malcolm X." Sepia (14; My., 1965), pp. 14-19.
                                         DHU/MO

7323. Epps, Archie (ed.). The Speeches of Malcolm X at Harvard.
New York: Morrow, 1968.   IC/H; CoDU; NNCor; DHU/MO

7324. Esa, Raqib. "The Black Muslims in the Technotronic Age."
The Howard University Review of Science (1:3, Nov., 1972), pp
29-32.   DHU/MO;
DHU/AA

7325. Essien-Udom, Essien Udosen. Black Nationalism: a Search
for an Identity in America. Chicago: University of Chicago
Press, 1963.   DHU/R; INU; CtY-D

7326. Essien-Udom, Ruby M. and Essien Udosen. "Malcolm X:
An International Man." Okon Edet Uya (ed.). Black Brother-
hood, Afro-Americans and Africa (Lexington, Mass.: D.C.
Heath and Co., 1971), pp. 257-78.   DHU/MO

7327. Evans, Ronald. The American Press and the Black Muslims.
Masters thesis. North Carolina Central University, 1971.
Mr. Evans also writes under the name of Raqib Esa.

7328. Farrakhan, Louis. [Speech.] Imamu Amiri Baraka (LeRoi
Jones), (ed.). African Congress. A Documentary of the First
Modern Pan-African Congress (New York: Wm. Morrow &
Co., 1972), pp. 44-56.   DHU/R
National spokesman for Elijah Muhammad of the Nation of
Islam.

7329. Garnett, Bernard E. Invaders from the Black Nation; the
"Black Muslims" in 1970. Nashville: Race Relations Information
Center, 1970.   IC/H; CoDU;
NjR
Special Report, no. 10.

7330. Glanville, B. "Malcolm X." New Statesman (67; Je. 21,
1964), p. 901.   DHU; DGU; DAU; DCU/SW

7331. Gleason, R. J. "Lost-Found Nation." New Statesman (61;
Apr. 14, 1961), p. 580.   DAU; DCU/SW; DGU
Black Muslims.

7332. "Go Ahead, Apostle, Black Muslims." Newsweek (57; Mr.
13, 1961), pp. 58-59.   DLC; DHU

7333. Goldman, Peter. The Death and Life of Malcolm X. New
York: Harper & Row, 1973.   DHU/MO;
DHU/R

7334. Gregor, A. James. "Black Nationalism: A Preliminary
Analysis of Negro Radicalism." Science and Society (27:4,
Fall, 1963), pp. 415-32.   DHU
Black Muslims.

7335. "Growth of the Black Muslim Movement in the United States."
Pacifica Archives AL 976.
Audiotape.

7336. Haley, Alex. "Mr. Muhammed Speaks." Readers Digest
(76; Mr. 1960), pp. 110-14.   DHU

7337. Hatchett, John F. "The Moslem Influence Among American
Negroes." Journal of Human Relations (10; Sum., 1962), pp.
375-82.   DHU

7338. Hentoff, Nat. "Elijah in the Wilderness." Reporter (23;
Ag. 4, 1960), pp. 37-40.   DLC

7339. Hernton, Calvin C. "White Liberals and Black Muslims."
Negro Digest (12; Oct., 1963), pp. 3-9.   DLC

7340. Hodge, W. J. "Agent of Liberation and Reconcilation."
Home Missions (43:4, Apr., 1972), pp. 21-22. Pam. File,
                                         DHU/R
Brief historical statement on the Black Church.

7341. "Holy War?" Newsweek (81:6, Feb. 5, 1973), p. 41.
                            Pam. File, DHU/R
Washington, D.C. massacre, aledged Black Muslim and
Hanafi Muslim conflict.

7342. Howard, John R. Becoming a Black Muslim: A Study of
Commitment Processes in a Deviant Political Organization.
Doctoral dissertation. Stanford University, 1965.

7343. Howell, Hazel W. Black Muslim Affiliation as Reflected in
Attitudes and Behavior of Negro Adolescents With its Effect
on Policies and Administrative Procedures in Schools of two
Eastern Cities, 1961-64. Doctoral dissertation. Columbia
University, 1966.

7344. "I Like the Word Black; Increasingly Militant Mood." Newsweek (61; My. 6, 1963), pp. 27-8.   DLC; DHU
Black Muslims.

7345. Ihde, Carleton. "Chicago Keeps a Racial Watch." Christian
Century (74:44, Oct. 30, 1957), pp. 1299-1300.   DHU/R
Black Muslims.

7346. Illo, John. "The Rhetoric of Malcolm X." The Columbia
University Forum (9:2, Sept., 1966), pp. 5-12. Pam. File,
                                         DHU/R

7347. Imari, Brother. War in America: the Malcolm X Doctrine.
n.p.: The Malcolm X Society, 1968.   DHU/AA

7348. "Integration--- as Negro Champ Views it." United States
News and World Report (56; Mr. 16, 1964), p. 20. DHU; DLC
Black Muslims.

7349. Isaacs, H. R. "Integration and the Negro Mood." Commentary (34:6, Dec., 1962), pp. 487-97.   DHU/R
Black Muslims.

7350. Jamal, Hakim A. From the Dead Level: Malcolm X and Me.
New York: Random House, 1972. MH-AH; CoDU; DHU/AA;
IC/H; NNCor

7351. Jarrett, Alfred I. Muslims' Black Metropolis: An Authentic
Report on the Black Muslim Movement in the United States,
Containing Actual Documents and Photographs. Los Angeles:
Great Western Books Publishing Co., 1962.   DLC; DHU/MO

7352. Jones, Le Roi. (Imamu Amiri Baraka). "The Legacy of
Malcolm X, and the Coming of the Black Nation." Arthur C.
Littleton and Mary W. Burger (eds.). Black Viewpoints (New
York: New American Library, 1964), pp. 413-21.   DHU/R

7353. "Judgment of the World is Now, An Album." Muhammad
Mosque of Islam Number Two, Chicago: n.p., 1972.
Phonodisc.
"Elijah Muhammad."

7354. Kaplan, Howard M. "Black Muslims and the Negro Americans
Quest for Communion." British Journal of Sociology (20; Je.,
1969), pp. 164-76.   DGW; DHU

7355. Karpas, Melvin Ronald. The Black Muslims as the Negro Segregationalists. Chicago: Chicago Teachers College, 1964.
INU

7356. Kirman, J. M. "Challenge of the Black Muslims." Social Education (27; Nov., 1963), pp. 365-68.   DHU; DAU

7357. Klausler, Alfred P. "Muslim Rally in Chicago." Christian Century (78:12, Mr. 22, 1961), p. 372.   DHU/R

7358. Krosney, Herbert. "America's Black Supremacists." Nation (192; My. 6, 1961), pp. 390-92.   DHU

7359. Lacy, Leslie A. "African Responses to Malcolm X." LeRoi Jones and Larry Neal (eds.). Black Fire, An Anthology of Afro-American Writing. (New York: William Morrow and Co., 1968), pp. 19-38.   DHU/MO

7360. Landry, Lawrence. "Black Muslims and Sit-ins." New University Thought (2; Wint., 1962), pp. 3-7.   DLC

7361. Laue, James E. "A Contemporary Revitalization Movement in American Race Relations; The Black Muslims." Social Forces (42; Mr., 1964), pp. 315-23.   DGU; DAU

7362. Lieman, Melvin. "Malcolm X." Liberation (10:2, Apr. 1965), pp. 25-27.   DHU/R

7363. Lewis, Joan Elaine (Wilson). A Comparative Study of the Marcus Garvey and Black Muslim Movements. Masters thesis. Howard University, 1967.   DHU/MO

7364. Lightfoot, Claude. "Negro Nationalism and the Black Muslims." Political Affairs (41; J1., 1962), pp. 3+.   DHU; DLC

7365. Lincoln, Charles Eric. "The Black Muslims." Progressive (26:12, Dec., 1962), p. 43.   DGU
Negro author.

7366. ----- The Black Muslims in America. Boston: Beacon Press, 1961.
"This book originated as a dissertation... in the Graduate School of Boston University."

7367. ----- "Extremist Attitudes in the Black Muslim Movement." New South (18:1, Ja., 1963), pp. 3-10.   DHU/R

7368. ----- "Meaning of Malcolm X." Christian Century (82:14, Apr. 7, 1965), pp. 431-33.   DHU/R
Negro author.

7369. ----- My Face is Black. Boston: Beacon Press, 1961.
DHU/R; INU

7370. ----- Sounds of the Struggle: Persons and Perspectives of the Civil Rights. New York: Morrow, 1967.   DHU/R; InU
Black Muslims, pp. 32-75+.

7371. Linn, E. and A. Barnette. "Black Muslims Are a Fraud." Saturday Evening Post (238; Feb. 27, 1965), pp. 23-29.
DHU; DGW

7372. Little, Malcolm. The Autobiography of Malcolm X. New Yor York: Grobe Press, 1965.   DHU/R; INU
Negro author.

7373. ----- "Ballots or Bullets."
Phonodisc.

7374. ----- "Elijah Muhammad: Cutting Loose from the Devil." Robert H. Binstock and Katherine Ely, (eds.). The Politics of the Powerless (Cambridge, Mass." Winthrop Publishers, 1971), pp. 278-84.   DHU/MO
Excerpt from The Autobiography of Malcolm X.

7375. ----- The End of White World Supremacy: Four Speeches by Malcolm X. Edited and with an introduction by Benjamin Goodman. New York: Merlin House, Inc., 1971. DHU/R; NjP; IC/H; NNCor; PPT

7376. ----- "His Wit and Wisdom." Douglas International SD 797.
Audiotape.

7377. ----- "His Wit and Wisdom." Douglas International SD 797. 12.
Phonodisc.

7378. ----- "The Last Message." Discuss LP 1300.
Audiotape.

7379. ----- "The Last Message." Discus LP 1300. 12 in.
Phonodisc.

7380. ----- "Liberation by any Means Necessary." Thomas R. Frazier, (ed.). Afro-American History: Primary Resources (New York: Harcourt, Brace & World, Inc., 1970), pp. 455-67.
DHU/R; DHU/MO
A speech given by Malcolm X at a meeting sponsored by the Militan Labor Forum in New York City, on 8 April 1964.
Negro author.

7381. ----- "Malcolm X: a Retrospective." Pacifica Archives ALW 611.
Audiotape.
A documentary on the life of Malcolm X from his first impact on black power and the Black Muslims in 1960 until his death in 1965.

7382. ----- "Malcolm X and the Black Muslims, 1964." Bradford Chambers, (ed.). Chronicles of Black Protest (New York: The New American Library, 1968), pp. 200-11.   DHU/MO

7383. ----- Malcolm X and the Negro Revolution: the Speeches of Malcolm X; edited with an Introductory Essay by Archie Epps. London: Owen, 1969.   NjP; NNCor
Negro author

7384. ----- Malcolm X on Afro-American History. New York: Merit Publishers, 1967. MNtcA; DHU/MO; IC/H; NNCor;

7385. ----- "Malcolm X Speaking." Ethnic E 1265.
Audiotape.

7386. ----- "Malcolm X Speaking."
Phonodisc.

7387. ----- Malcolm X Speaks: Slected Speeches and Statements. New York: Grove Press, 1966.   DHU/R; INU

7388. ----- "Malcolm X Speaks to Young People."
Phonodisc.

7389. ----- Malcolm X Talks to Young People. New York: Pathfinder Press, 1971.   DHU/R; IC/H
Excerpt from speech delivered December 31, 1964 at Hotel Theresa, New York City.
Negro author.

7390. ----- "Message to the Grass Roots." Grass Roots 1.
Audiotape.

7391. ----- "Message to the Grass Roots." 2s. 12 in.
Phonodisc.
Excerpts from an address delivered at King Solomon's Baptist Church, Detroit, Michigan, Nov., 1963.

7392. ----- The Speeches of Malcolm X at Harvard. Edited, with an Introductory Essay, by Archie Epps. New York: William Morrow & Co., 1968.   DHU/R; NjP; NcD
Negro author.

7393. ----- "Why the Black Man is Powerless." Robert H. Binstock and Katherine Ely, (eds.). The Politics of the Powerless (Cambridge, Mass.: Winthrop Publishers, 1971), pp. 6-8.
DHU/MO
An excerpt from The Autobiography of Malcolm X.
Negro author.

7394. Lokos, Lionel. The New Racism. Reverse Discrimination in America. New Rochelle, N.Y.: Arlington House, 1971.
DHU/R
Chapter 13, "Black Anti-Seminitism and the New York Mayoralty."
Chapter 14, "Black Muslims."

7395. Lomax, Louis E. The Negro Revolt. New York: Harper, 1962.   DHU/R; INU
pp. 164-177, Black Muslims.
Negro author.

7396. ----- When the Word is Given: A Report on Elijah Muhammad, Malcolm X and the Black Muslim World. Cleveland: World Pub. Co., 1963.   CtY-D; DHU/R

7397. Louisiana Legislature. Joint Committee on Un American Activities Cult of Islam. Hearing Held, November 27, 1962, Baton Rouge. Louisiana, 1963/   DLC; OU
"Report no. 3."
Black Muslims.

7398. Love, James E. "A Contemporary Revitalization Movement in American Race Relations: The 'Black Muslims'." Social Forces (42; Mr., 1964), pp. 315-23.   DHU

7399. Maesen, William A. "Watchtower Influences on Black Muslim Eschatology: An Exploratory Story." Journal for the Scientific Study of Religion (9:4, Wint. 1970), pp. 321-25.
DHU/R

7400. Maglangbayan, Shawna. Garvey, Lumumba, and Malcolm: National-Separatists. Chicago: Third World Press, 1972.
NNCor; DHU/AA

7401. "Malcolm X; Founder, Organization of African Unity." Harry A. Ploski (ed.). Reference Library of Black America (New York: Bellwether Pub. Co., Inc.), Book 2, pp. 29-31.   DHU

7402. "Malcolm X." Mert Koplin and Charles Grinker. Released by Time-Life Films, 1970. 4 min. sd. color. 16 mm. DLC Film.
"Presents public remarks by Malcolm X which express the philosophy of the Black Muslim leader concerning race relations."

7403. "Malcolm X- Struggle for Freedom." New York: Grove Press, 197? 22 min. B & W
Film.

7404. "Malcolm X." The Nation (200; Mr. 8, 1965), p. 239.
DHU; DGW; DAU

7405. Massaquo, H. J. "Elijah Muhammad; Prophet and Architect of the Separate Nation of Islam." Ebony (25; Ag., 1970), pp. 78-80.   DHU

7406. "The Meaning of Malcolm X." The Christian Century (82:14, Apr. 7, 1965), pp. 431-33.   DHU/R

7407. Meier, August. "The Black Muslims: Racism in Reverse?" Liberation (8; Apr., 1963), pp. 9.   DHU/R

7408. "Messenger FromViolet Drive." Bloomington, Ind.: Indiana Univ., National Education Television, 1971. 29 min. B & W

7409. "Minister Malcolm, Orator Profundo." Negro History Bulletin (30; Nov., 1967), pp. 4-5.   DHU/MO

7410. Moon, Henry L. "Enigma of Malcom X." Crisis (72; Apr., 1965), pp. 226-7.   DHU/MO

7411. Morsell, John A. "Black Nationalism." Journal of Intergroup Relations. (3; Wint., 1961-62), pp. 5-11.   DLC

7412. "Muslim Denied Conscientious Status." The Ecclesiastical Court Digest (6:12, Dec., 1968), p. 4.   DHU/R

7413. "Muslim Influence Great." Science Newsletter (88; Sept. 11, 1965), p. 165.   DCU/ED; DGW

7414. "Muslim Inmate of New York State Prison Wins Right of Free Exercise of His Religion in New York Court of Appeals." Race Relations Law Reporter (7; Sum., 1962), pp. 440-43. DHU/L; NN/Sch

7415. "Muslim Not Guilty of Criminal Anarchy." The Ecclesiastical Court Digest (1:8, Ag., 1963), p. 6.   DHU/R

7416. "'Muslim' Prisoner Entitled to Practice His Religion." The Ecclesiastical Court Digest (1:1, Ja., 1963), p. 2.   DHU/R

7417. "Muslim Prisoner - Prejudice Found." The Ecclesiastical Court Digest (1:3, Mar., 1963), p. 6.   DHU/R

7418. "Muslim Prisoners Claim Religious Deprivation--Full Hearing Ordered." The Ecclesiastical Court Digest (10:12, Dec., 1972), p. 6.   DHU/R

7419. "Muslim Prisoners' Complaint Dismissed." The Ecclesiastical Court Digest (1:12, Dec., 1963), p. 5.   DHU/R

7420. "Muslim Prisoner's Complaints Rejected." The Ecclesiastical Court Digest (3:2, Feb., 1965), p. 6.   DHU/R

7421. "Muslim Prisoners Entitled to Religious Benefits." The Ecclesiastical Court Digest (8:11, Nov., 1970), p. 6.   DHU/R

7422. "Muslim Prisoner's Petition Denied." The Ecclesiastical Court Digest (2:1, Ja., 1964), p. 4.   DHU/R

7423. "Muslim Prisoners Refuse to Eat Pork-- Plan to be Submitted." The Ecclesiastical Court Digest (7:10, Oct., 1969), p p. 6.   DHU/R

7424. "Muslim Prisoner's Right to Appeal Upheld." The Ecclesiastical Court Digest (2:11, Nov., 1964), p. 4.   DHU/R

7425. "Muslim Prisoners Seek Special Fast Day Meal Hours." The Ecclesiastical Court Digest (1:12, Dec., 1963), p. 6. DHU/R

7426. "Muslim Prisoners Succeed in Religious Rights Suit." The Ecclesiastical Court Digest (3:1, Ja., 1965), p. 5.   DHU/R

7427. "Muslim Prisoners Sue Prison Officials." The Ecclesiastical Court Digest (2:10, Oct., 1964), p. 6.   DHU/R

7428. "Muslim Prisoner's Suit Dismissed." The Ecclesiastical Court Digest (1:10, Oct., 1963), p. 6; (3:4, Apr., 1965), p. 2.
DHU/R

7429. "Muslim Rivalry." Christianity Today (17:10, Feb. 16. 1973), p. 521-22.   DHU/R

7430. "Muslims Ask Leaders to Rally." Amsterdam News (My. 28, 1960).   DHU/MO

7431. "Muslims in Alabama." Time (95; Feb. 2, 1970), p. 12.
DAU; DCU/SW; DGU; DGW; DHU

7432. "Muslims vs. Muslims." Newsweek (81:6, Feb. 5, 1973), pp. 61-2.   Pam. File, DHU/R
Black Muslims and Orthodox Muslims.

7433. N'Daye, Jean Pierre. Les Noirs aux Etats-Unis Pour les Africains. Paris: n.p., 1964.   INU

7434. "Negro Inmate of a Federal Jail Wins Case in U.S. District Court for Relief From Religious Discrimination." A Muslim, He Had Been Removed From the General Prison Population for 2 Years After Engaging in a Muslim Demonstration; Also 2 Negro Federal Prison... Race Relations Law Reporter (7; Fall, 1962), pp. 779-88.   DHU/L

7435. "Negro Muslim Inmates in a New York State Prison Win Suit in U.S. Court of Appeals for Relief from Religious Persecution; (decision given)." Race Relations Law Reporter (6; Wint., 1961), pp. 1059-62.   DHU/L

7436. "New Jersey Supreme Court Upholds the Commissioner of Education's Ruling that Black Muslim Children Who are Prohibited by Their Religion from Pledging Allegiance to the Flage Should Be Reinstated in the Public Schools of Elizabeth, New Jersey." Race Relations Law Reporter (11; Spr., 1966), pp. 185-88.   DHU/L

7437. "New Move by the Black Muslims." U.S. News and World Report (54; Mr. 11, 1963), p. 14.   DCU; DHU

7438. "New York Court of Appeals, Early in 1962, Handed Down an Opinion Recognizing the Black Muslim Brotherhood as a Religion." Interracial Review (35; My., 1962), p. 114. DHU/MO

7439. New York. U.S. Court of Appeals. March 13, 1973. "Black Muslim Would Participate in a War That Had Beneficial Value to Him." The Ecclesiastical Court Digest (11:10, Oct., 1973), p. 3.   DHU/R

7440. Newman, Edwin S., (ed.). The Hate Reader: a Collection of Materials on the Hate Movements in American Society. Dobbs Ferry, N.Y.: Oceana Publications, 1964.   DHU/MO
        Chapter on "Black Muslims- Case History of Negro Hate."

7441. "Now Its Negroes Versus Negroes in America's Racial Violence." U.S. News and World Report (58; Mr. 8, 1965), p. 6.   DHU; DLC
        Black Muslims.

7442. Obatala, J. K. "Islam and Black Liberation." Liberator (10:6, Je., 1970), pp. 4-10.   DHU/R

7443. Ofari, Earl, (ed.). The Black Book. Detroit: Radical Education Project, 1970.   IC/H
        Some of the speeches of Malcolm X.

7444. O'Gara, J. "After Malcolm X." Commonweal (82; Mr. 26, 1965), p. 8.   DAU; DAU/W; DCU/SW; DGU; DGW

7445. Oliver, Revilo P. "The Black Muslims (History and Tenets: the Movement Viewed as a Crypto-Communist Operation)." American Opinion (6; Ja., 1963), pp. 23+.   DLC

7446. Olsen, Jack. "Learning Elijah's Advanced Lesson in Hate." Sports Illustrated (24; My. 2, 1966), pp. 36-38+.   DAU
        Black Muslims.

7447. Parenti, Michael. "The Black Muslims: From Revolution to Institution." Social Research (31; 1964), pp. 175-94.   DGU

7448. Parks, Gordon. Born Black. Philadelphia: Lippincott, 1971.   DHU/MO
        Chapter 2, The Black Muslims; Chapter 3, The Death of Malcolm X; Chapter 7, On the Death of Martin Luther King, Jr.
        Negro author.

7449. "Peking and Malcolm X." New Republic (152; Mr. 27, 1965), p. 8. Reply- L. M. Edwards (152; Apr. 17, 1965), p. 44.   DGW; DHU

7450. Plimpton, G. "Miami Notebook: Cassius Clay and Malcolm X." Harper's Magazine (228; Je., 1964), pp. 54-61. DAU; DCU/HU; DGU; DGW; DHU

7451. Poole, Elijah (Elijah Muhammed). How to Eat to Live. Chicago: Muhammed Mosque of Islam No. 2, 1967. NcD; DHU/R

7452. ----- Message to the Blackman. Chicago: Muhammad Mosque of Islam No. 2, 1965.   INU; NcD; DHU/R

7453. ----- The Supreme Wisdom: The Solution to the So-Called Negroes' Problem. Chicago: University of Islam, 1957.   NN/Sch

7454. ----- "What the Black Muslims Believe - What the Black Muslims Want." Negro Digest (13:1, Nov., 1963), pp. 3-6.   DHU/MO

7455. ----- "What the Muslims Believe." Harvey Wish, (ed.). The Negro Since Emancipation. (Englewood Cliffs, N.J.: Prentice-Hall, Inc., 1964), pp. 181-2.   DHU/R

7456. ----- White Christian Party Attacks Equality, Purity, Beauty and the Religion of the Negro. Chicago: Muhammad Temple of Islam, n.d.   DHU/MO
        Black Muslims.

7457. ----- and E. Arnold. "Now Hear the Message to the Black Muslims From Their Leader." Esquire (59; Apr., 1963), pp. 97-101.   DHU/EG

7458. Poulard, Grady E. "The Black Muslims: Racism on the Rebound." United Church Herald (5:8, Apr. 19, 1962), pp. 14-15.   DHU/R
        Negro author.

7459. "Prisoner Entitled to Practice Islamic Religion Within the Rules of Prison." The Ecclesiastical Court Digest (5:9, Sept., 1967), p. 3.   DHU/R

7460. "Prisoners Entitled to Recieve 'Muhammad Speaks.'" The Ecclesiastical Court Digest (10:7, Jl., 1972), p. 1. DHU/R

7461. "The Protestant Ethic Among the Black Muslims." Phylon (27; 1st Spr., 1962), pp. 5-14.   DHU/MO

7462. Raab, Earl, ed. American Race Relations Today. Garden City, N.Y.: Doubleday, 1962.   DHU/MO
        pp. 179-90, Black Muslims.

7463. Randall, Dudley and Margaret G. Burroughs, (eds.). For Malcolm; Poems on the Life and Death of Malcolm X. Detroit: Broadside Press, 1969.   IC/H; NNCor

7464. Record, Wilson. "Extremist Movements Among American Negroes." Phylon (17; Spr., 1956), pp. 17-23.   DHU/MO
        Black Muslims.

7465. Record, Wilson. "The Negro Intellectual and Negro Nationalism." Social Forces (32; Oct., 1954), pp. 10-18.   DHU

7466. "Recruits Behind Bars, Black Muslims." Time (77:14, Mr. 31, 1961), p. 14.   DHU

7467. "Refused to Submit for Induction - Black Muslim Religious Claim Too Late." The Ecclesiastical Court Digest (5:11, Nov., 1967), p. 3.   DHU/R

7468. "Religious Practice for Muslims Adopted in Jails." The Ecclesiastical Court Digest (1:5, My., 1963), p. 5. DHU/R

7469. Rich, Andrea L. and Arthur L. Smith. Rhetoric of Revolution: Samuel Adams, Emma Goldman, Malcolm X. Durham, N.C.: Moore Pub. Co., 1970.   PPT

7470. "The Right to Practice Black Muslim Tenents in State Prisons." Harvard Law Review (75; Feb., 1962), pp. 837+. DHU/L

7471. Rose, Arnold M. Assuring Freedom to the Free. Detroit: Wayne State University, 1964.   DHU/MO
        "The Black Muslims as a Protest Movement," by C. Eric Lincoln.

7472. Rowan, Carl T. "New Frontiers in Race Relations: Address, June 24, 1961." Vital Speeches (27:21, Ag. 15, 1961), pp. 665-68.   DHU
        Black Muslims.

7473. Rowley, Peter. New Gods in America. New York: David
McKay Co., 1971.   DHU/R
      Chapter VIII, Black Muslims, pp. 67-77.

7474. Samuels, Gertrude. "Feud Within the Black Muslims." New
York Times Magazine (Mr. 22, 1964).   DLC

7475. ----- "Two Ways: Black Muslim and N.A.A.C.P." August
Meier and Eliott Rudwick (eds.). Black Protest in the Sixties
(Chicago: Quadrangle Books, 1970), pp. 37-45.   DHU/R
      Also: New York Times Magazine (May 12, 1963). DLC

7476. Schaller, Lyle E. "Black Muslims and White Protestants."
Christian Advocate (7; Feb. 14, 1963), pp. 9+.   DHU/R;
DAU/W

7477. Seraile, William. "David Walker and Malcolm X: Brothers
in Radical Thought." Black World (12:12, Oct., 1973), pp. 68-
73.   DHU/R

7478. Shack, William S. "Black Muslims: A Nativistic Religious
Movement Among Negro Americans." Race (3; Nov., 1961), pp.
57-67.

7479. Shalaby, Ibramih M. "The Role of the Muslim School in
America in the Process of Cultural Renewal." Majallat Al-
Azhar (III, 40; Ja., 1969), pp. 8-12; (IV, 40; Feb., 1969), pp.
9-13; (V, 41; Mr., 1969), pp. 13-16.   DLC

7480. ----- "The Role of the Muslim School of the Nation of Islam
in America - 2." Majallat Al-Azhar (40; Oct.-Nov., 1968), pp.
13-16.   DLC
      Role of the school in cultural renewal and identity transfor-
      mation.

7481. ----- The Role of the School in Cultural Renewal and Identity
Development in the Nation of Islam in America. Doctoral
dissertation. University of Arizona, 1967.

7482. ----- "The Role of the School in the Nation of Islam in
America in Changing its Students' Attitudes." Majallat Al-
Azkar (I, 41; Apr., 1969), pp. 10-13; (II, 41; My., 1969), pp.
13-16; (III, 41; Je., 1969), pp. 10-13; (IV, 41; Oct., 1969), pp.
8-11-; (V, 41; Mr., 1969), pp. 13-16.   DLC

7483. Sharrieff, Osman. Islam in North America. Chicago: n.p.,
1961.   DLC

7484. Sherwin, Mark. The Extremists. New York: St. Martin's
Press, 1964.   InU
      pp. 190-212, Black Muslims.

7485. Simon, Walter B. Schwarger Nationalisms in der U.S.A. ...
Kohn: Wesldeutscher Verlag, 1963.   DLC
      Black Muslims.

7486. Southwick, Albert B. "James Baldwin's Jeremiad." Christian Century (82:12, Mr. 24, 1965), pp. 362-64.   DHU/R
      Black Muslims.

7487. ----- "Malcolm X: Charismatic Demagogue." Christian
Century (80:23, Je. 5, 1963), pp. 740-41.   DHU/R

7488. Spellman, A. B. "Interview with Malcolm X." Monthly Review (May, 1964).   DHU

7489. Sulayman, Shaid Mufassir. "Return of the Prodigal: The Rise
of Orthodox Islam in Black America." Black World (22:1, Nov.,
1972), pp. 50-61.   DHU/R

7490. "Superior Court of Delaware Order Authorities at Newcastle,
Delaware Correctional Institution to Allow Muslims to Practice
Their Religion." Race Relations Law Reporter (10; Fall 1965),
pp. 971-81.   DHU/L

7491. Thorne, Richard. "Integration or Black Nationalism; Which
Route Will Negroes Choose?" Negro Digest (12; Ag., 1963),
pp. 36-47.   DHU

7492. Tinney, James S. "Black Muslims: Moving Into Mainstream?"
Christianity Today (17:22, Ag., 1973), pp. 44-45.   DHU/R

7493. ----- "Growing Acceptance Seen in Black Muslim Movement."
The Washington Afro-American (Sept. 1, 1973), p. 15.
                                    Pam. File, DHU/R

7494. ----- "Islam Gains Popularity as a Black Religion." The
Washington Afro-American (Ag. 25, 1973).   Pam. File,
                                                    DHU/R

7495. "Tradgedy of Malcolm X." America (112; Mr. 6, 1965), p.
303.   DAU/W; DCU/SW; DGU; DHU

7496. "Tribute to Malcolm X." Bloomington, Ind.: Indiana Univ.,
National Education Television, 1971. 15 min. B & W.
Film.

7497. Tyler, Lawrence L. "The Protestant Ethic Among the Black
Muslims." Phylon (27; Spr., 1969), pp. 51-4.   DHU/MO

7498. "U. S. Court of Appeals in Washington, D. C. Upholds Mus-
lim Prisoners' Request for One Pork-Free Meal a Day and Coffee
Three Times Daily in Conformity with Muslim Dietary Lasw."
Race Relations Law Survey (1' Nov., 1969), pp. 183. DHU/L

7499. "U. S. Court of Appeals Remands Case of Black Muslim Inmates of Atlanta Federal Penitentiary Who Charged That the
Warden Would not Allow Them to Practice Their Religion; The
Court said They have a Case." Race Relations Law Reporter
(11; Wint., 1966), pp. 1934-39.   DHU/L

7500. "U. S. Court of Appeals Reverses U. S. District Court Decision and Upholds Right of Negro Black Muslim Prisoner
in a Virginia State Penitentiary to Be Released from Maximum
Security Unit and Remain with the Rest of the Prisoners." Race
Relations Law Reporter (11; Wint., 1966), pp. 1942-46. DHU/L

7501. "Unites States Court of Appeals Upholds Complaint of Black
Muslim that California State Prison Does Not Allow Him to Practice His Religious Beliefs. New York Supreme Court Reverses
U. S. Court of Appeals and Upholds Officials of New York State
Prison that Black Muslim Inmates' Religious Rights May Be Restricted to Maintain Discipline." Race Relations Law Reporter
(11; Spr., 1966), pp. 55-58.   DHU/L

7502. "U. S. District Court Denies Suit of Seven Negro Inmates of
the Federal Prison at Lewisburg, Pa., Who Charged That Prison
Officials Were Not Allowing Them to Practice Their Muslim
Faith." Race Relations Law Reporter (11; Wint., 1966), pp.
1939-42.   DHU/L

7503. "U. S. District Court Orders Correction Officials of Attica,
N. Y. State Prison to Produce a Set of Rules and Regulations
Governing the Negro Inmates Practice of Their Religion in
Keeping with Prison Discipline and Security." Race Relations
Law Reporter (11; Wint., 1966), pp. 1438-44.   DHU/L

7504. "U. S. District Court Upholds the Warden of the Leavenworth,
Kansas Federal Prison in Restricting the Religious Activities of
Black Muslim Inmates in Violation of their Federal and Civil
Rights. These Restrictions Are Necessary to Maintain Discipline,
They Say." Race Relations Law Reporter (11; Sum., 1966), pp.
906-09.   DHU/L

7505. "U. S. Supreme Court Remands Case of Black Muslim in Ill-
inois Prison Charging Religious Discrimination. Three of the
Muslim's Requests Were Granted; Three Were Denied." Race
Relations Law Reporter (12; Wint., 1967), pp. 2098-102.
                                                    DHU/L

7506. "Vendetta by Rivals Feared." Senior Scholastic (86:6, Mr. 11,
1965), p. 21.   DHU
      Black Muslims.

7507. "Violence versus Non-Violence." Ebony (20; Apr., 1965),
p. 168.   DHU/MO
      Black Muslims.

7508. "Violent End of the Man Called Malcolm X; With Report by Gordon Parks." Life (58; Mr. 5, 1965), p. 26. DHU; DAU; DGU: DGW
    Black Muslims.

7509. Walton, Hames, Jr. and Isaiah McIver. "The Political Theory of the Black Muslims." The Savannah State College Bulletin (27:2, Dec., 1973), pp. 148-59.   Pam. File, DHU/R
    Negro author.

7510. Warren, Robert Penn. "Malcolm X: Mission and Meaning." Yale Review (56; Wint., 1967), pp. 161-71.   DHU

7511. "Way of Cults." Newsweek (47; My. 7, 1956), p. 102. DLC; DHU
    Black Muslims.

7512. Webb, J. M. "Militant Majorities and Racial Minorities." Sewanee Review (63; Spr., 1955), pp. 322+.   OO; DCU; CtY; DGU
    Black Muslims.

7513. Wechsler, James A. "The Cult of Malcolm X." Progressive (28; Je., 1964), p. 24.   DHU
    Black Muslims.

7514. Whalen, William J. Minority Religions in America. New York: Alba House, 1972.   DHU/R
    Black Muslims, pp. 29-37.

7515. "Whatever Happened to the Black Muslims" Negroes Building Farm Empire." U. S. News and World Report (69; Sept. 21, 1970), pp. 83-84.   DCU; DHU

7516. "Why Black Muslims are Focusing on the Nation's Capitol Now." United States News and World Report (54; My. 27, 1963), p. 24.   DHU; DLC

7517. Whyte, A. "Christian Elements in Negro American Muslims Religious Beliefs." Phylon (25:382, Wint., 1964), pp. 382-88.   DHU/MO

7518. Wiley, C. W. "Who Was Malcolm X?" National Review (17:12, Mr. 23, 1965), pp. 239-40.   DHU; DAU; DCU/SW; DGU
    Black Muslims.

7519. Williams, Daniel Thomas. The Black Muslims in the United States: a Selected Bibliography. Tuskegee, Ala.: Hollis Burke Frissell Library, Tuskegee Institute, 1964. CtY-D; DHU/R

7520. Williams, Daniel Thomas. Eight Negro Bibliographies. New York: Kraus Reprint Co., 1970.   IC/H
    Black Muslims.

7521. Wilson, J. Q. "The Strategy of Protest: Problems of Negro Civic Action." Journal of Conflict Resolution (5; Sept., 1961), p. 291.   DHU; DAU; DCU/SW; DGU; DGW
    Black Muslims.

7522. "Without Malcolm X." Economist (214:6340, Feb. 27, 1965), p. 888.   DHU
    Black Muslims.

7523. Worthy, William. "Angriest Negroes: Muslims." Esquire (55; Feb., 1961), pp. 102-5.   DAU; DHU/MO; Pam. File, DHU/R

7524. ----- "The Nation of Islam: Impact and Prospects; Who the Muslims Are, What They Advocate, What is the Emotional Drive Behind Their Extremist Idology, and How a Liberation Negro Intellectual Reacts to Them." Midstream (81; Spr., 1962), pp. 26+.   DHU

7525. Yaker, Henri M. "The Black Muslims in the Correctional Institutions." Welfare Reporter (N. J.) (13; Oct., 1962), pp. 158+.   DHU

4. Evaluation and Aspects of Negro Religion and Church

7526. Abbott, Ernest H. Religious Life in America: A Record of Personal Observation. New York: Outlook Co., 1902.   DHU/R; NN/Sch
    For Negro Church, see pp. 81-104.

7527. ----- "Religious Tendencies of Negroes." Outlook (69; 1901), p. 1070.   DCU/SW

7528. Ackiss, Thelma D. "Changing Patterns of Religious Thought Among Negroes." Social Forces (23; Dec. 1944), pp. 215-15.   DHU

7529. Aldrich, Gustave B. "Arousing Interest in Negro Missions." Chronicle (3; Feb., 1930), p. 28.   ICU; NNC; NNUT; NjPT
    Negro author.

7530. ----- "Church and the Negro." Commonweal (9; Feb. 13, 1929), pp. 432-33.   DGU; DCU/SW

7531. Allen, Easter W. The Negro's Religion and its Effect Upon the Recreational Activities in Bladen County, North Carolina. Masters thesis. Springfield College (Massachusetts), 1936.   IC/H

7532. American Baptist Home Mission Society. The Christian Education of the Negro. n.p., 1910.   NN/Sch

7533. "American Negro Churches, Membership and Contributions; Table." Missionary Review of the World (59; Je., 1936), p. 36.   DHU/R

7534. "Are Negroes Losing Religion?" Ebony (5; Ag., 1950), pp. 44-45.   DHU/MO

7535. Arnett, Benjamin William, (bp.). "Christianity and the Negro." J. W. Hanson, (ed.). The World's Congress of Religions (Chicago: International Pub. Co., 1894), pp. 747-50.   DHU/MO

7536. -----(bp.). Colored Sunday Schools. Nashville: A. M. E. Sunday School Union, 1896.   OWibfU

7537. Arnold, Benjamin. "A Negro Looks at His Church." Zion's Herald (116; Je. 22, 1939), p. 800.   DLC; CtY-D

7538. Ashanin, C. B. "Afro-American Christianity: Challenge and Significance." Journal of Religious Thought (16:2, Sum. -Aut., 1959), pp. 109-20.   DHU/R

7539. ----- "Negro Protestantism in Crisis." Journal of Religious Thought (20:2, Aut.-Win., 1963-64), pp. 123-30.   DHU/R

7540. "Baha'i a Way of Life for Missions." Ebony (20; Apr., 1965), pp. 48-50.   DHU/MO

7541. Baker, Ray Stannard. Following the Color Line: An Account of Negro Citizenship in the American Democracy. New York: Doubleday, Page & Co., 1908.   DHU/MO

7542. Baldwin, James. "Elizabeth's Prayer." Ruth Miller (ed.). Blackamerican Literature, 1760-Present (Beverly Hills, Cal.: Glencoe Press, 1971), pp. 348-382.   DHU/MO
    Includes brief biographical information about Baldwin and an excerpt from his novel, Go Tell It On the Mountain.

7543. ----- "The Threshing-Floor." Arthur P. Davis and Saunders Redding (eds.). Cavalcade: Negro American Writing from 1760 to the Present (Boston: Houghton Mifflin, 1971), pp. 572-83.   DHU/MO
    Fictional account of a religious conversion in a Black church from his first novel, Go Tell It On the Mountain.

7544. Banks, Melvin E. "The Black Sunday School: Its Strength, Its Needs." Christianity Today (18:20, Jl. 5, 1974), pp. 8-11.
DHU/R
"How racial distinctions figure in church education."

7545. Banks, William L. The Black Church in the U. S. ; Its Origin, Growth, Contributions, and Outlook. Chicago: Moody Press, 1972.   MNtcA; DHU/R

7546. Barber, William Joseph. A Historical Survey of the Origin and Development of a Rural Negro Church Group in Eastern North Carolina. n. p., n. p., 1958.   TN/DCHS

7547. Bardolph, Richard. "Negro Religious and Educational Leaders in 'Who's Who in America,' 1936-1955." Journal of Negro Education (26:2, Spr., 1957), pp. 182-92.   DHU/R

7548. Barrett, Leonard E. Soul Force: African Heritage in Afro-American Religion. New York: Doubleday, 1974.   DHU/R

7549. Beatty-Brown, Florence Rebekah. The Negro as Portrayed by the St. Louis Post-Dispatch From 1920-1950. Doctoral dissertation. University of Illinois, 1951.

7550. Bellamy, Donnie D. "The Education of Blacks in Missouri Prior to 1861." Journal of Negro History (59:2, Apr., 1974), pp. 143-57.   DHU/R
Includes information on the role of the church.

7551. Berrigan, P. F. "Christianity in Harlem." Commonweal (81; Nov. 27, 1964), pp. 323-5.   DHU

7552. Betts, John R. "The Negro and the New England Conscience in the Days of John Boyle O'Reilly." Journal of Negro History (51:4, Oct., 1966), pp. 246-61.   DHU

7553. Billings, R. A. "The Negro and His Church: A Psychogenetic Study." Psychoanalytic Review (21; Oct., 1934), pp. 425-41.
DHU/MED

7554. Bingham, Walter. "Black Men Discover Themselves." World Call (51:6, Je., 1969), pp. 22-23.   DHU/R
Negro author.

7555. "The Black Religious Tradition." Harry A. Ploski, (ed.). Reference Library of Black America (New York: Bellwether Pub. Co., Inc., 1971), Book 2, pp. 190-223.   DHU

7556. Blacknall, O. W. "New Departure in Religion Among Negroes." Atlantic Monthly (52; Nov., 1883), pp. 680-85.
DHU; NN/Sch

7557. Blackwell, George L. "Christian Education in the Black Church- U. S. A." Voice of Missions A. M. E. Church (78:7, Mr., 1972), pp. 8-9.   DHU/R

7558. "Blames Negro Ministry for Lagging Churches." Christian Century (67:33, Ag. 16, 1950), p. 964.   DHU/R

7559. Boatright, Mody Coggin and Donald Day, (eds.). From Hell to Breakfast. Dallas: Southern Methodist University Press, 1967.   DLC; NN/Sch
Publications of the Folklore Society, no. 19.

7560. Bond, J. Max. The Negro in Los Angeles. San Francisco: R & E. Research Associates, 1972.   DHU/R
Originally presented as author's Ph. D. dissertation, University of Southern California, June, 1936. Chapter 5, The Negro Church and Social Agencies.

7561. Bowen, John Wesley Edward. "The Negro and the Church." Howard University Record (14:6, Apr., 1920), pp. 284-87.
DHU/MO

7562. Bowen, Trevor. Divine White Right; A Study of Race Segregation and Inter-Racial Cooperation in Religious Organizations and Institutions in the United States, with a Section on "The Church and Education for Negroes," by Ira De A. Reid. New

York and London: Pub. for the Institute of Social and Religious Research, Harper & Bros., 1934.   NN/Sch; DHU/R; DHU/MO
Ch. 3-5, The Negro's Church, Churches & Slavery and Christian Associations.

7563. Boyer, Laura F. Wanted--Leaders! A Study in Negro Development: Suggestions for Groups Discussion and Individual Study. New York: Presiding Bishop and Council, Dept. of Missions and Church Extension, 1922.   NN/Sch

7564. Boysaw, Harold E. "Does Youth Need Religion?" The Crisis (44:7, Jl., 1937), pp. 216+.   DLC; DHU/MO
"Organized religion as represented by the church of today must change to meet a changing world, writes a student in a middle western college."

7565. Brace, Charles Loring. Gesta Christi: or History of Humane Progress Under Christianity... New York: A. C. Armstrong & Son, 1888.   DHU/MO

7566. Bracey, John H. and August Meier. Black Nationalism in America. New York: The Bobbs-Merril Co., 1970. DHU/R
Pt. 1, Foundation of the Black Community: the Church, pp. 3-17+.

7567. ----- and August Meier, et alii., (eds.). The Black Sociologist: The First Half Century. Belmont, California: Wadsworth, 1971.   INU; DLC
Includes information on the Negro church.

7568. Bradford, Arthur. "Were Christ, Solomon and Job White Men?" The African Methodist Episcopal Church (78: 218, Oct.-Dec., 1963), pp. 16-18.   DHU/R
Negro author.

7569. Bradley, L. Richard. "The Curse of Canaan and the American Negro." Concordia Theological Monthly (42:2, Feb., 1971), pp. 100-10.   DHU/R

7570. Bragg, George Freeman. Afro-American Church and Workers. Baltimore, Md.: Church Advocate Printers, 1904.
DHU/MO; NN/Sch
Negro author.

7571. ----- "Beginning of Negro Church Work in the South." Living Church (65; Ag. 20, 1921), p. 505.   CtY; DLC

7572. ----- The First Negro Organization. The Free African Society, Established on April 12th, 1787. Baltimore: Pub. by the author, 1927.   DHU/MO

7573. ----- The First Negro Priest on Southern Soil. Baltimore: Church Advocate Print., 1909. DHU/MO; A & M; NN/Sch

7574. ----- How the Black Man Found the Church. Baltimore, Md.: n. p., n. d.   DHU/MO

7575. Brawley, Benjamin Griffin. A Prayer. Words by B. G. Brawley, music by A. H. Ryder in (Atlanta, Ga.). Atlanta: Baptist College Press, 1899.   DHU/MO
Negro author.

7576. Brawley, Benjamin Griffin. A Short History of the American Negro. New York: The Macmillan Co., 1917. DHU/R; DHU/MO; CtY-D

7577. Brawley, Edward MacKnight. Sin and Salvation. A Text Book on Evangelism. Revised by Benjamin Brawley. Philadelphia: Judson Press, 1925.   DHU/MO
Negro author.

7578. Brisbane, Robert H. The Black Vanguard. Valley Forge: Judson Press, 1970.   DHU/MO
Contains information on the black church.

7579. Brooks, Walter H. "Religion." Washington Conference on the Race Problem in the United States. National Sociological So-

ciety. <u>How to Solve the Race Problem</u> (Washington, D.C.:
Beresford, Printer, 1904), pp. 212-27.   DHU/R
    Minister of the Nineteenth Street Baptist Church, Wash.,
    D.C.
    Negro author.

7580. Brotz, Howard M. <u>Negro Social and Political Thought,
1850-1920; Representative Texts.</u> New York: Basic Books,
1966.   CtY-D; DHU/R
    Part two, Black Christians.

7581. Brown, Agnes. <u>The Negro Churches of Chapel Hill: A
Community Study.</u> Masters thesis. University of North Carolina, 1939.

7582. Brown, Archer W. <u>Did Jesus Christ Have Negro Blood in
Him?</u> Wonder of the Century. Newark, N.J.: Archer W.
Brown, 1908.   DHU/MO

7583. Brown, Ina Corinne. <u>The Story of the American Negro.</u>
New York: Friendship Press, 1936.   DHU/R; OWibfU

7584. Brown, M. R. "The Negro in His Religious Aspect."
<u>Southern Workman</u> (17; 1875), p. 498.   NIC

7585. Brunner, Edmund De S. <u>Church Life in the Rural South; a
Study of the Opportunity of Protestantism Based Upon Data from
Seventy Counties.</u> New York: George H. Doran Co., 1923.
                                         DHU/R
    Chapter 9, The Negro Rural Church.

7586. Buehrer, Edwin T. "Harlem's God." <u>Christian Century</u>
(52:50, Dec. 11, 1935), pp. 1590-93.   DHU/R

7587. Butcher, Charles Simpson. <u>A Historical Study of Efforts
to Secure Church Union Among Independent Negro Methodists.</u>
B. D. Paper. School of Religion, Howard University, 1939.

7588. Butterfield, R. "In Pulpits Negroes Found Their First
Spokesmen." <u>Life</u> (65; Nov. 22, 1968), pp. 96-97.   DHU

7589. Byers, Theodore F. <u>A Comparative Study of Dropouts and
Nondropouts Among the Congregational Methodist Episcopal
Church and the Montello Ingram Baptist Church.</u> M. Div. Paper.
School of Religion, Howard University, 1971.
    Negro author.

7590. Caldwell, Josiah S., (bp.). "Young People's Societies as a
Religious Force in the Church." I. G. Penn. <u>The United
Negro</u> (Atlanta: Luther, 1902), pp. 524+. NcSaIL; DHU/R

7591. <u>A Call Upon the Church for Progressive Action, to Elevate
the Colored American People.</u> Fall River: n.p., 1848. DLC
    "Beginning with a protest against the use of the term "Af-
    rican" by churches of the colored people, the wirter des-
    cribes the various Negro churches of Philadelphia and New
    York."

7592. Campbell, James F. "What Happened to the Negro's Religion?" <u>The African Methodist Episcopal Church Review</u> (78:218,
Oct.-Dec., 1963), pp. 43-45.   DHU/R
    Also in: <u>Negro Digest</u> (12; Apr., 1963), pp. 74-77.

7593. Canzoneri, Robert. <u>I Do So Politely, a Voice from the South.</u>
Boston: Houghton Mifflin Co., 1965.   DHU/R
    Chapters 7 and 9 on the Negro church.

7594. Carrington, William E. "Negro Youth and the Religious Education Program of the Church." <u>Journal of Negro Education</u>
(9; Jl., 1940), pp. 388-96.   DHU

7595. ----- <u>A Study of Christian Character Building Factors in
Evangelical Religion With Special Emphasis on the Negro Church.</u>
New York: n.p., 1934.   NNUT

7596. Carroll, H. K. "The Negro in His Relations to the Church."
J. W. E. Bowen, (ed.). <u>Africa and the American Negro:
Addresses and Proceedings of the Congress on Africa.</u> (Miami,
Fla.: Mnemosyne Pub. Co., 1969), pp. 215-18.   DHU/R

7597. ----- "The Present Religious Condition of America." J. H.
Barrows, (ed.). <u>The World's Parliament of Religions.</u> Vol. II.
(Chicago: Parliament Publishing Co., 1893), pp. 1162-65.
                                         DHU/R

7598. ----- "Religious Progress of Negroes." <u>Forum</u> (14; 1893),
pp. 75+.   DHU

7599. Carter, Edward Randolph. <u>The Black Side; a Partial History
of the Business, Relgious and Educational Side of the Negro in
Atlanta, Ga.</u> Atlanta, Ga.: n.p., 1894.   DHU/MO

7600. Carter, Luther C., Jr. <u>Negro Churches in a Southern
Community.</u> Doctoral dissertation, Yale University, 1955.

7601. Carter, Randall Albert, (bp.). <u>Canned Laughter</u> Cincinnati:
Caxton Press, 1923.   DHU/MO
    Negro author.

7602. ----- (bp.). "What the Negro Church has Done." <u>Journal
of Negro History</u> (11:1, Ja., 1926), pp. 1-7.   DHU
    Negro author.

7603. Cartwright, Colbert S. "Band Together for Genuine Unity."
<u>New South</u> (16; Ja., 1961), pp. 6-10.   DAU/W
    Little Rock minister's speech at Conference on Community
    Action.

7604. ----- "Christian Churches (Disciples of Christ) as Racial
Ferment (in the South) Accelerates Pastors and Congregations
take Divided Stand on Issue." <u>Christianity and Crisis</u> (18; Mr.
3, 1958), pp. 18-20.   DHU/R

7605. Catchings, L. Maynard. <u>The Social Relevance of the School
of Religion of Howard University: A Study of Howard University:
A Study of the Bachelor of Divinity Curriculum Content and its
Bearing Upon the Social Purpose of the School and the Social
Obligation Felt by its Graduates.</u> B. D. Paper. School of Re-
ligion, Howard University, 1941.

7606. Cayton, Horace. "E. Franklin Frazier: A Tribute and a
Review." <u>Review of Religious Research</u> (5; Spr., 1964), pp.
137-42.   DHU/R
    Review of Frazier's post-humously published the Negro
    Church.

7607. "The Ceremony of '"Foot Wash"' in Virginia." <u>Southern Work-
man</u> (25:4,5, Apr., My., 1896), p. 82; 102-12. DLC; DHU/MO
    An account of the '"Foot Wash"' Ceremony in the country dis-
    tricts of Negro Churches in Virginia.

7608. Chappelle, Ezekiel Emerson. <u>An Evaluation of the Program
of Religious Education in Negro Churches in Greater Kansas
City by the Standards of the National Council of Churches.</u>
Doctoral dissertation. Central Baptist Theological Seminary,
1957.

7609. Cheshire, Joseph B. <u>The Church in the Confederate States.</u>
n.p.: n.p., 1912.   GAU
    pp. 106-34, The Church and the Negro.

7610. Chicago. Work Projects. Administration. <u>Churches and
Voluntary Associations in the Chicago Negro Community.</u> Report of Official Project 465-54-3-386. 1940.   O
    Typescript.

7611. Chivers, W. R. "Religion in Negro Colleges." <u>Journal of
Negro Education</u> (9; Ja., 1940), pp. 5-12.   DHU/MO

7612. "The 'Christian Churches' Become a 'Church'." <u>Christianity
Today</u> (13:1, Oct. 11, 1968), pp. 40-41.   DHU/R
    Disciples of Christ.
    Church's urban crisis program.

7613. "The Church and the Negro." <u>Crisis</u> (6: 6, Oct., 1913), p.
290-1.   DLC; DHU/MO

7614. "Church (Census) Report on Colored Colony of African Descent in New York." <u>The Crisis</u> (2: 2, Je., 1911), p. 51.
                                         DHU/MO; DLC

7615. "Churches." The Southern Workman (1:1, Ja., 1872).
DLC; DHU/MO
Microfilm.
The number of members in the churches of Petersburg, Va.

7616. Clair, Matthew W., (bp.). "The Negro Church." The A. M.
E. Zion Quarterly (53:1, Ja., 1943), pp. 7-10; (53:2, Apr.,
1943), pp. 30-31.   DHU/MO

7617. ----- (bp.). Sociological Origins of the Negro Ministry in
the United States. Doctoral dissertation. Iliff School of Theology, 1927.   CoDI

7618. Clark, William A. "Sanctification in Negro Religion."
Social Forces (15; My., 1937), pp. 544-51.   DHU

7619. Clement, Rufus E. "The Church School as a Factor in Negro
Life." Journal of Negro History (12:1, Ja. 1927), pp. 5-12.
DHU/MO

7620. Clemes, W. W. "Heaven Comes to Harlem." Negro Digest
(8:5, My., 1950), pp. 66-71.   DHU/MO
"East Harlem church brings useful Christianity to people in
urban ghetto."

7621. Clinton, George W., (bp.). "The Church and Modern Industry." Elias B. Sanford. Federal Council of the Churches in
America (New York: Revell Press, 1919), pp. 65.   DHU/R

7622. ----- (bp.). "Evangelism." Arcadius S. Trawick, (ed.).
The New Voice in Race Adjustments (New York: Student Vol-
unteer Movement, 1914), pp. 107-12.   DHU/R
Negro author.

7623. ----- (bp.). "The Negro as a Freeman." W. N. Hartshorn.
An Era of Progress and Promise. (Boston: Priscilla Pub.,
1910), pp. 43+.   NcSa1L; DHU/R

7624. ----- (bp.). The Negro in the Ecumenical Conference of
1901. n. p., n. d.   NcSa1L
Negro author.

7625. Clyde, Natnana Lore. ...The Application of the Teachings
and Example of Christ to the Relationship of the Native Citizen
to the Immigrant, by Nathana L. Clyde. First prize, 1913. A
Practical Application of Christianity to the American Race Problem, by William Burkholder. Second prize, 1913. Lawrence:
University of Kansas, 1913. (Hattie Elizabeth Lewis memorial
essays in applied Christianity).   NN/Sch

7626. Cockin, Frederic Arthur, (bp.). The Problem of Race;
Being Outline Studies Based on "Christianity and the Race Problem," by J. H. Oldham... London: Student Christian Movement, 1924.   NN/Sch

7627. Coles, Robert. "When I Draw the Lord He'll Be a Real Big
Man." The Atlantic (My., 1966), p. 69.   DHU

7628. Colton, Calvin. History and Character of American Revivals
of Religion. London: n. p., 1832.   DLC

7629. "Comparison of Some Ethnic and Religious Attitudes of Negro
and White College Students in the Deep South." Social Forces
(30; My., 1952), pp. 426-28.   DHU

7630. Conference on Education for Negroes in Texas. Proceedings
of the Tenth Educational Conference. The Negro Church in
Texas as an Educational Agency. Ed. and Comp. by John B.
Cade and Walter R. Harrison. Bul. V. 31, no. 1. Hempstead
Tex.: Prairie View State Normal & Industrial College, Prairie
View College Branch, 1939.   NN/Sch

7631. Conference on Science, Philosophy and Religion in their Relation to the Democratic Way of Life. Perspectives on a Troubled Decade: Science, Philosophy and Religion, 1939-1949.
Tenth Symposium, ed. by Lyman Bryson, Louis Finklestein
(and) R. M. MacIver, New York: Conference on Science, Phil-
osphy and Religion in their Relation to the Democratic Way of
Life, Inc. New York: Harper, 1950.   DHU/R

7632. Conference on the Relation of the Church of the Colored People
of the South. Conference on the Relation of the Church to the
Colored People of the South. n. p.: Protestant Episcopal Church,
1883.   DHU/MO

7633. Coppin, Levi Jenkins, (bp.). "The American Negro's Religion for the African Negro's Soul." Independent (54; Mr. 27,
1902), pp. 748-50.   DHU
Negro author.

7634. ----- (bp.). Episcopal Addresses Delivered by Bishop Levi
J. Coppin. Philadelphia: A. M. E. Book Concern, May 1916.
DHU/MO

7635. ----- (bp.). Fifty Years of Religious Progress: an Emancipation Sermon. Delivered on the occasion of the Emancipation Semi-Centennial, Philadelphia, Pa., Sunday, September
14th, 1913. Philadelphia: A. M. E. Book Concern Printers
1913.   NN/Sch

7636. Crawford, Evans Edgar. The Leadership Role of the Urban
Negro Minister. Doctoral dissertation, Boston University,
1957.

7637. Cromwell, John Wesley. The Negro in American History...
Washington, D. C.: The American Negro Academy, 1914.
DHU/R; NN/Sch
Chapters 16, 17, Negro Church, Slavery.

7638. Crook, Roger H. No South or North. St. Louis, Mo.:
Bethany Press, 1959.   CtY-D; NN/Sch

7639. Crummell, Alexander. Charitable Institutions in Colored
Churches. Washington, D. C.: R. L. Pendleton, 189?
NN/Sch
Negro author.

7640. Culp, Daniel W. Twentieth Century Negro Literature.
Atlanta: Nicholson & Co., 1902.   DHU/MO
Chapters 18, 20 & 24 deal directly with the Negro Church;
many other chapters are by black churchmen.

7641. Curran, Francis X. Major Trends in American Church
History... New York: The American Press, 1946. NN/Sch
Negro Church, pp. 107-20.

7642. Current, William Chester. God's Promise to His People, by
Homeless and Blind Billy... Nashville, Tenn.: National
Baptist Publishing Board, 1908.   NN/Sch

7643. Dames, Jonathan A. "Camp Meeting Observations." The
African Methodist Episcopal Church Review (70:182, Oct.-Dec.,
1954), pp. 42-48.   DHU/R
Negro author.

7644. Dancy, John C. "The Future of the Negro Church." Alice
Ruth Nelson. Masterpieces of Negro Eloquence: The Best
Speeches Delivered by Negro From the Days of Slavery to the
Present Time (New York: Bookery Publishing, 1914), pp.
474-82.   DHU/MO

7645. Dangerfiled, Abner Walker. Extracts on Religious and
Industrial Training... Washington, D. C.: Murray Bros.,
Printers, 1909.   NN/Sch
Negro author.

7646. Daniel, Vattel Elbert. "Negro Classes and Life in the Church."
Journal of Negro Education (13; Wint., 1944), pp. 19-29.
DHU

7647. ----- "Ritual and Stratification in Chicago Negro Churches."
American Sociological Review (7; Je., 1942), pp. 353-58.
DHU/R
Described types of behavior in ecstatic cults.

7648. Daniel, William Andrew. The Education of Negro Ministers,
based upon a Survey of Theological Schools for Negroes in the
United States made by Robert L. Kelly and W. A. Daniel. New
York: Goe. H. Doran Co., 1925.   DHU/R

7649. Darrow, Clarence and R. E. Jones. "The Religion of the American Negro." Crisis (38; My., 1931), pp. 190-92.
DHU/MO

7650. Davenport, Frederick Morgan. Primitive Traits in Religious Revivals. New York: Macmillan, 1905.   DHU/R
Chapter 5, The Religion of the American Negro.

7651. ----- "The Religion of the American Negro." Eclectic Magazine of Foreign Literature (145; Dec., 1905), pp. 609-14.
DLC

7652. Davie, Maurice Rea. Negroes in American Society. New York: McGraw-Hill Book Co., 1949.   DHU/R; DHU/MO; CtY-D

7653. Davis, D. Webster. "The Sunday-School and Church as a Solution of the Negro Problems." Alice Ruth Nelson. Masterpieces of Negro Eloquence: The Best Speeches Delivered by the Negro From the Days of Slavery to the Present Time. (New York: Bookery Publishing Company, 1914), pp. 291-304.
DHU/MO

7654. DeBerry, William N. "The Possibilities of the Negro Institutional Church." Durham Fact Finding Conference (2; Apr., 1929), pp. 18-19.   DHU/MO

7655. "The Defects of the Negro Church." Editorial. Southern Workman (32:4, Apr., 1903), p. 200.   DLC; DHU/MO

7656. Diggs, James R. "Negro Church Life." Voice of the Negro (1:2, Feb., 1904), pp. 46-50.   DHU/MO; DLC; NN/Sch

7657. Diggs, John R. L. "Negro Church Life." Voice of the Negro (1:2, Feb., 1904), pp. 46-50.   DHU/MO

7658. Dodson, Dan. The Role of Institutional Religion in Ethnic Groups of Dallas. Master's Thesis. Southern Methodist University, 1936.

7659. Dollard, John. Caste and Class in a Southern Town. New Haven: Pub. for the Institute of Human Relations by Yale University Press, 1937.   CtY-D; DHU/MO
Chapter 11, caste patterns in religion.

7660. Douglass, William. Annals of the First African Church, in the United States of America, Now Styled the African Episcopal Church of St. Thomas, Philadelphia. Established by Absalom Jones, Richard Allen and others, in 1787, and Partly from the Minister of the Aforesaid Church. Philadelphia: King & Baird, 1862.   DHU/MO; NN/Sch
Negro author.

7661. Dowd, Jerome. The Negro Races, a Sociological Study. New York: The Macmillan Co., 1907.   DHU/MO; CtY-D
Chapters 23-29, Negro church.

7662. Downs, Karl E. Meet the Negro. Los Angeles: the Methodist Youth Fellowship, Southern California-Arizona Annual Conference, 1943.   DHU/MO; NN/Sch
Negro author.

7663. Drake, St. Clair. Black Metropolis; a Study of Negro Life in a Northern City. By St. Clair Drake and Horace R. Cayton, with an introduction by Richard Wright. New York: Harcourt, Brace & Co., 1945.   DHU/MO; CtY-D
Chapter 15, Power of the Pulpit.

7664. ----- The Redemption of Africa and Black Religion: the Experience of Black Religion in North America. Chicago: Third World, 1970.   Pam. File, DHU/R; TSewU-T; NjP

7665. DuBois, William E. B. "The Church and Religion." The Crisis (40:1-, Oct., 1933), pp. 236-37.   DHU/MO; DLC

"Critics of religion and of the church must distinguish rather carefully between the two."

7666. ----- Darkwater; Voices from Within the Veil. New York: Harcourt, Brace & Howe, 1920.   DHU/MO; DHU/R; CtY-D
Negro author.

7667. ----- The Gift of Black Folk; the Negroes in the Making of America. Boston: The Stratford Co., 1924.   DHU/MO
Chapter 10, The Gift of the spirit.

7668. ----- "Missionaries." The Crisis (36:5, My., 1929), p. 168.   DHU/MO; DLC
"...The attitude on the part of religion in the United States and Europe toward American Negro missionaries."

7669. ----- "The Negro Church in Philadelphia." Richard B. Sherman, (ed.). The Negro and the City. (Englewood Cliffs, N.J.: Prentice Hall, 1970), pp. 100-04.   DHU/R

7670. ----- "Negro Church." Political Science Quarterly (19; Dec., 1904), pp. 703-04.   DHU

7671. ----- (ed.). The Negro Church; Report of a Social Study Made Under the Direction of Atlanta University, Together with the Proceedings of the Eighth Conference for the Study of the Negro Problems, Held at Atlanta University, May 26th, 1903. Atlanta, Ga.: The Atlanta University Press, 1903.   NjP; DLC; DHU/MO
Negro author.

7672. ----- "The Negro in the Black Belt: Some Social Studies." Washington, D.C.: U. S. Dept of Labor Bulletin, (4:22, My., 1899), pp. 401-17.   DHU/MO

7673. ----- The Philadelphia Negro: A Social Study. Philadelphia: University of Pennsylvania Press, 1899.   DHU/MO

7674. ----- "Religion of Negroes." New World (9; 1900), p. 614.
DCU/RE

7675. ----- The Souls of Black Folk. Chicago: A. C. McClurg and Co., 1903.   DHU/R; DHU/MO; CtY-D
Negro Church, pp. 190-01.

7676. Dykes, Charles B. "Theology Versus Thrift in the Black Belt." Popular Science Monthly (60; Feb., 1902), pp. 360-64.   IC/H; DLC

7677. Earnest, Joseph Brummell, Jr. The Religious Development of the Negro in Virginia. Charlottesville, Va.: Michie Co., 1914.   CtY-D; DLC; NN/Sch; TN/DCHS
Issued earlier as doctoral dissertation, University of Virginia.

7678. Eason, James Henry. Pulpit and Platform Efforts. Sanctifications vs. Fanaticism... Nashville, Tenn.: National Baptist Publishing Board, 1899.   DHU/MO; NN/Sch

7679. Edwards, V. A. "Religion and Rural Life... A Description of a Program for Rural Life Improvement Through the Church in Rural Georgia Communities."
"A paper prepared at Fort Valley College, Fort Valley, Ga., 1943."

7680. Eleazer, Robert Burns. Reason, Religion, and Race. New York: Abingdon-Cokesbury, 1950.   NN/Sch

7681. Ellerson, L. B. "The Negro as a Christian." Daniel W. Culp. Twentieth Century Negro Literature. (Miami, Fla.: Mnemosyne Publishing Co., Inc., 1969), pp. 313-14.
DHU/MO
Reprint of 1902 edition.
Negro Presbyterian minister.

7682. Ellison, John Malcus. "The Negro Church in Rural Virginia." Pt. I; Pt. II; Pt. III. Southern Workman (60:2, Feb., 1931), pp. 67-73; pp. 201-10; pp. 307-14.   DLC; DHU/MO

7683. ------ Negro Organizations and Leadership in Relation to Rural Life in Virginia. Virginia. Virginia Agricultural Station, 1933.   DHU/MO

7684. ------ The Story of the Hamitic Peoples in the Holy Bible. Philadelphia: A. J. Holman Co., 194-.   NN/Sch
Negro author.

7685. ------ Tensions and Destiny. Richmond: Knox Press, 1953.
                                           DHU/MO; NN/Sch
Negro author.

7686. ----- and C. H. Hamilton. The Negro Church in Rural Virginia. Blacksburg, Va.: Virginia Polytechnic Institute, Virginia Agricultural Bulletin 27340.   DHU/MO
Negro authors.

7687. Ely, Effie Smith. "American Negro Poetry." Christian Century (40; Mr. 22, 1923), pp. 366-67.   DHU/R
A discussion of religious protest poetry.

7688. Embree, Edwin Rogers. American Negroes, a Handbook. New York: the John Day Co., 1942.   DHU/MO; CtY-D

7689. ----- Brown America; the Story of a New Race. New York: The Friendship Press, 1936.   DHU/R; DHU/MO; CtY-D

7690. Encyclopedia of the Negro, Preparatory Volume with Reference Lists and Reports, by W. E. DuBois and Guy B. Johnson... Prepared with the Cooperation of E. Irene Diggs, Agnes C. L. Donohugh, Guion Johnson and Others. New York: The Phelps-Stokes Fund, Inc., 1946.   DHU/MO; CtY-D

7691. Eppes, Francis Edward. A Study of Determinative Factors in the Development of the Religion of the American Negro. Masters thesis. Southern Baptist Theological Seminary, 1951.

7692. Eubanks, John B. Modern Trends in the Religion of the American Negro. Doctoral dissertation. University of Chicago, 1947.

7693. "Evangelization of the Negro." Public Opinion (34; Mr. 19, 1903), p. 375.   IC/H
Negro author.
"The Negro's greatest need is to deal with ministers of his own race."

7694. Faduma, Orishatukeh. ...The Defects of the Negro Church. Washington, D.C.: The Academy, 1904. DHU/MO; DLC; NN/Sch

7695. Falls, Arthur Grand Pre. "Colored Churches." Chronicle (5; Feb., 1932), pp. 26-7.   DCU/SW
Negro author.

7696. Felton, Ralph Almon. Go Down Moses; a Study of 21 Successful Negro Rural Pastors. Madison, N.J.: Dept. of the Rural Church, Drew Theological Seminary, 1952. DLC; DHU/R

7697. ----- "Negro Pastors Go to Rural Colleges." Christian Century (61:1, Jan. 5, 1944), pp. 22+.   DHU/R

7698. ----- These My Brethren; a Study of 570 Negro Churches and 1542 Negro Homes in the Rural South. Madison, N.J.: Dept. of the Rural Church, Drew Theological Seminary, 1950. DHU/R; CtY-D; NN/Sch

7699. ----- "Untrained Negro Clergy." Christian Century (72:5, Feb. 2, 1955), pp. 141-42.   DHU/R

7700. Ferm, Vergilius Ture Anselm. The American Church of Protestant Heritage. New York: Philosophical Library, 1953.
                                           DHU/R; INU

7701. Fickland, R. William. The Ideal Christian Ministry. Philadelphia: A. M. E. Book Concern, 1910.   NN/Sch
Negro author.

7702. "Finds Colored Pastors Take Varied Attitudes on Race Churches." The Christian Century (47:32, Ag. 6, 1930), p. 994.   DLC; DHU/R

7703. Fisher, Miles Mark. Keep Negro 'Churches' Central: Recognition Address. Durham, N.C.: White Rock Baptist Church, 1946.   Pam. File, DHU/MO
Negro author.

7704. ----- "Negro Church and the World War." Journal of Religion (5:5, Sept., 1925), pp. 483-99.   DHU/R
Negro author.
Discusses effect of World War I on the Negro Church.

7705. ----- "Negroes as Christian Ministers." Journal of Negro Education (4:1, Ja., 1935), pp. 53-59.   DHU/MO

7706. ------ "Negroes Get Religion." Opportunity (14:5, My., 1936), pp. 147-50.   DHU/MO

7707. Flynn, R. O. "Cooperation Between Pastors of White and Colored Churches." Arcadius S. Trawick, (ed.). The New Voice in Race Adjustments (New York: Student Volunteer Movement), pp. 183-8.   DHU/R

7708. Ford, C. E. and G. Schinert. "The Relation of Ethnocentric Attitudes to Intensity of Religious Practice." Journal of Educational Sociology (32; 1958), pp. 157-62. DAU; DCU/ED; DGU

7709. Ford, John E. "Religious Life in Jacksonville." The Crisis (48:1, Ja., 1942), p. 25.   DLC; DHU/MO

7710. Forrest, Edna Mae. The Religious Development of the Negro in South Carolina Since 1865. Masters thesis. Howard University, 1928.

7711. Fowler, Andrew. Negro Churches as Revealed by the U. S. Census of Religious Bodies for 1936. Masters thesis. Howard University, 1943.

7712. Fox, William K. Experiments in Southern Rural Religious Developments Among Negroes. Bachelor of Divinity thesis. University of Chicago, 1943.

7713. Frazier, Edward Franklin. Black Bourgeoisie. Glencoe, Ill.: The Free Press, 1957.   DHU/R
Negro author.
"Rise of the Negro middle class in the United States with corresponding modifications in religious values and behavior." pp. 209-12.

7714. ----- "The Negro and Non-Resistance." The Crisis (27:5, Mr., 1924), pp. 213-4.   DLC; DHU/MO
"Colored people who arrogate to themselves the possession of such Christian humility that they condemn the activities of the so-called agitators and others who insist that the Negro shall enjoy the same rights as other Americans."

7715. ----- The Negro Church in America. New York: Schocken Books, 1964.   DHU/R; DLC

7716. ----- "The Negro Church in America." Carlene Young (ed.). Black Experience (San Rafael, Cal.: Leswing Press, 1972), pp. 134-37.   DHU/R

7717. ----- ...The Negro in the United States. New York: Macmillan, 1949.   DHU/R; NN/Sch; CtY-D
Negro church, pp. 334-66.

7718. Frazier, Thomas. An Analysis of Social Scientific Writings on American Negro Religion. Doctoral dissertation. Columbia University, 1967.

7719. ----- Social Scientists and Negro Religion. Doctoral dissertation. Columbia University, 1967.

7720. Frucht, Richard, (ed.). Black Society in the New World. New York: Random House, 1971.   DHU/R
Part V, Religion.

7721. Fry, C. Luther. The United States Looks at its Churches. New York: Institute of Social and Religious Research, 1930.
                                           DHU/R

Chart showing the white and Negro adult population in churches by sex, 1926.

7722. Fuller, Thomas Oscar. The Story of Church Life Among Negroes in Memphis, Tennessee, for Students and Workers, 1900-1938. Memphis, Tenn.: n.p., 1938. NN/Sch; ViHa
Negro author.

7723. "The Future of the Negro Churches." Editorial. The Christian Century (47:17, Sept. 17, 1930), pp. 1110-01. DHU/R; DLC
"Discussion." (47; Oct. 15, 1930), pp. 1252-53. DHU/R

7724. Gandy, Samuel L. "Negro Church and the Adult Education Phases of its Program." Journal of Negro Education (14; Sum., 1945), pp. 381-84.   DHU
Negro author.

7725. Gibson, John William. Progress of a Race; or, The Remarkable Advancement of the American Negro from the Bondage of Slavery, Ignorance and Poverty to the Freedom of Citizenship, Intelligence, Affluence, Honor, and Trust. Rev. and enl. by J. L. Nichols and W. H. Crogman. Naperville, Ill.: I. L. Nichols & Co., (c1929).   DHU/MO; NN/Sch
Religion and the Negro, pp. 307-28.

7726. Gillard, John Thomas. "Negro's God." Catholic World (151; Je., 1940), pp. 305-13.   DHU/R

7727. Glass, Victor Thomas. An Analysis of the Sociological and Psychological Factors Related to the Call to Christian Service of the Negro Baptist Minister. Doctoral dissertation. Southern Baptist Theological Seminary, 1952.

7728. Glenn, Norval D. "Negro Relgion and Negro Status in the United States." Louis Schneider, (ed.). Religion Culture and Society (New York: Wiley, 1964), pp. 623-39. DHU/R

7729. Gordon, Asa Hines. The Georgia Negro, a History. Ann Arbor, Mich.: Edwards Bros. Inc., 1937. DHU/MO NN/Sch
Negro author.

7730. Gordon, Jan. On Wandering Wheels. New York: Dodd, 1928.
IC/H
An account of the travels along the coast from Maine to Georgia. Includes many features of American life, folkways, tradition, the Negro and religion.

7731. Gordon, Milton M. "The New Liberalism of the Church." Phylon (8:3, 3rd Quarter, 1947), pp. 239-42.   DHU/MO

7732. Graham, B. J. W. "The Negro Problem of the North." Editorial. The Christian Index (99; Ag. 7, 1919), p. 2. LNB; NcWfSB

7733. Graham, John H. Mississippi Circuit Riders, 1865-1965. Nashville: Parthenon Press, 1967.   NjP
Includes discussion of Negroes active in the Methodist Church during this period.

7734. ----- A Study of Revel's Methodist Church of Greenville, Mississippi. Atlanta: Interdenominational Theological Center, 1960.   GAITH

7735. Green, Constance McLaughlin. The Secret City. A History of Race Relations in the Nation's Capital. Princeton, N.J.: Princeton University Press, 1967.   DHU/MO
Information on Negro churches in Washington, D. C.

7736. Griffin, Clifford S. Their Brothers' Keepers. New Brunswick, N.J.: Rutgers University Press, 1960.   DLC
Chapter 1, Negro Church.

7737. Griffin, Maude K. "The Negro Church and its Social Work-St. Mark's." Charities (14; Mr., 1905), pp. 75-76. CCC; CL; CtY; NNC; NB; MB; MnHi; MiU

7738. Grill, C. Frederick. Methodism in the Upper Fear Valley. Nashville: Parthenon Press, 1966.   IEG

7739. Grimke, Francis James. Anniversary Address on the Occasion of the Seventy-Fifth Anniversary of the Fifteenth Street Presbyterian Church, Washington, D.C. Washington, D.C.: R. L. Pendleton, Printer, 1916.   DHU/MO
Also in Woodson, Carter G. Francis J. Grimke, Washington, D.C.: Association Press, 1942.

7740. ----- A Call for a Revival Within the Church. Washington, D.C.: n.p., n.d.   DHU/MO
Negro author.

7741. ----- The Church Faces the College Generation. n.p.: The Author, 1930.   NjPT; DHU/MO

7742. ----- "Earnest Words from a Colored Missionary." The Church at Home and Abroad (1; Ja., 1887), pp. 65-6. DHU/R
Negro author.

7743. ----- Evangelism and Institutes on Evangleism. Washington, D.C.: n.p., 1918.   DHU/MO; DHU/R

7744. ----- Great Preaching. Washington, D.C.: n.p., n.d.
DHU/MO

7745. ----- Religious Attitudes of Negro Youth. Washington, D.C.: The Author, n.d.

7746. ----- Spiritual Life. Washington, D.C.: The Author, n.d.
NjPT

7747. ----- The Things of Paramount Importance in the Negro Race. Delivered in the Fifteenth Street Presbyterian Church. Washington, D.C., Mar. 29, 1903. Washington, D.C.: n.p., 1903.   DHU/MO; DHU/R
Also in, Woodson, Carter G., Francis James Grimke. Washington, D.C.: Associated Press, 1942.

7748. ----- What Is the Trouble With the Christianity of Today? There is Something Wrong About it... Delivered at the Seventh Annual Convention of the School of Religion of Howard University, Washington, D. C., Nov. 20, 1923. Washington, D. C.: n.p., 1923.   DHU/MO

7749. Grissom, Mary Allen. The Negro Sings A New Heaven... Chapel Hill: The University of North Carolina Press, 1930.
DHU/MO

7750. Gustafson, James M. "The Clergy in the United States." Daedalus (92; Fall, 1963), pp. 724-44.   DHU
Includes material on the unsatisfactory state of the Negro Protestant Ministry and their inadequate education.

7751. Gwaltney, Grace. The Negro Church and the Social Gospel, 1877-1944. Master's thesis. Howard University, 1949.

7752. Gwoehr, Wesley M. The Great Awakening in Virginia, 1740-1790. Durham: Duke University Press, 1930.   IC/H
Study of the social and religious development of Virginia.

7753. Hall, W. H. "The Church and Education." The African Methodist Episcopal Church (70:182, Oct.-Dec., 1954), pp. 54-59.   DHU/R
Negro author.

7754. Hamilton, Charles Horace. The Negro Church in Rural Virginia. The Virginia Agricultural Experiment Station and the Virginia State College for Negroes Cooperating. Blacksburg, Va.: n.p., 1930.   CtY-D

7755. Hammon, Jupiter. An Address to Miss Phillis Wheatly, Ethiopian Poetess, in Boston... Hartford, Conn., 1778.
NH; ABS; MH; NN
Negro author.

7756. "Hampton Ministers' Conference." Southern Workman (54; Ag., 1925), pp. 349+.   DLC

7757. Handy, Robert T. Religion in the American Experience: The Pluralistic Style. Columbia, S.C.: University of South Carolina Press, 1972.   DHU/R
    Chapter 25, "Black Protestantism as Indigenous Religious Expression."
    Chapter 15, "The Church and Slavery."

7758. Hargett, Andrew H. "Religious Attitudes as Expressed by Students of Savannah State College." Journal of Negro Education (20; Spr., 1951), pp. 237-40.   DHU

7759. Harrison, Walter R. The Attitudes of the Negro Towards the Church. Doctoral dissertation. Cornell University, 1945.

7760. Harrison, William Henry, Jr. Colored Girls and Boys' Inspiring United States History and a Heart to Heart Talk About White Folks. n.p.: n.p., 1921.   OWibfU; DHU/MO
    pp. 65-78, "In the Churches."
    Lists Negro ministers from some large cities in the U.S.
    Negro author.

7761. Hartshorn, William N. An Era of Progress and Promise 1863-1910; the Religious, Moral and Educational Development of the American Negro Since his Emancipation. Boston: The Priscilla Publishing Co., 1910.   DHU/MO; NN/Sch

7762. Harvey, M. L. "Negro Youth and the Church." Missionary Review of the World (59; Je., 1936), pp. 306-7.   DHU/R

7763. Haygood, Atticus G. "The Negro in the South." Quarterly Review of the M. E. Church, South (19; Jl., 1891), pp. 300-15.
                                                             DLC; CtY

7764. Haynes, George Edmund. "The Church and Negro Progress." Annals of the American Academy of Political and Social Sciences (130:229, Nov., 1928), pp. 264-71.   DHU/R
    Negro author.

7765. ----- "The Church and the Negro Spirit." Survey Graphic (6:6, Mr. 1, 1925), pp. 695-97; 708-9.   Pam. File, DHU/R
    Negro author.

7766. ----- "The Negro Church and the Modern World." Durham Fact-Finding Conference (Durham, N.C.: Christian Print. Co., 1929), pp. 16-17.   DHU/MO
    Negro secretary of the Federal Council of Churches in America. Dept. of Race Relations.

7767. Haynes, Leonard L. The Negro Community Within American Protestantism, 1619-1844. Boston: Christopher Pub. House, 1953.
                                        DHU/R; DHU/MO; NN/Sch
Negro author.

7768. Hedgley, David R. The Attitude of Negro Pastors in Chicago Toward Christian Education. Master's thesis. University of Chicago, 1935.

7769. Henning, C. Garnett. "The Educational Task of the Negro Church." Journal of Religious Education (30:1, Sept., 1969), p. 13.   DHU/R

7770. "Heroism and Sacrifices of Colored Preachers in the South." Editorial. Southern Workman (1:8, Ag., 1872).   DHU/MO; DLC
    Microfilm.

7771. Herskovits, Melville J. The Myth of the Negro Past. Boston: Beacon, 1958.   DHU/R; InU
    Chapter 7, The Contemporary Scene: Africanisms in religious life.

7772. Heston, David, (ed.). Golden Gleanings. A Select Miscellany ... Philadelphia: J. Smedley, 1886.   NN/Sch
    Negroes and the religious life.

7773. Hewitt, Doris W. The Relationship of Security and Religiosity of the Low-Income Southern Negro Youth. Tallahassee: n.p., 1965.   FSU

7774. Hickok, C. T. The Negro in Ohio, 1802-1870. Cleveland: n.p., 1896.   DHU/MO

7775. Hill, Daniel Grafton. The Negro in Oregon: A Survey. Master's thesis. University of Oregon, 1932.   NN/Sch
    Negro author.

7776. ----- The Sociological and Economic Implications of Negro Church Leadership in Colorado. Doctoral dissertation. Iliff School of Theology, 1946.

7777. Hinkle, J. Herbert. Soul Winning in Black Churches. Grand Rapids: Baker Book House, 1973.   DHU/R

7778. Hobart, George H. The Negro Churches of Manhattan New York City. New York: Greater New York Federation of Churches, 1930.

7779. Hoffman, Mamie G. A Survey of Sunday Schools in the Negro Churches of the Chicago Church Federation. Doctoral dissertation. University of Chicago, 1933.

7780. Hoggarth, F. C. "A Black God." Christian Century (45:46, Nov. 15, 1928), pp. 1397-98.   DHU/R; DLC

7781. Holland, Jerome Heartwell. "Role of Negro Church as an Organ of Protest." Journal of Negro Education (11; Ja., 1942), pp. 165-69.   DHU/MO

7782. Holloway, William H. Whither the Negro Church? New Haven: n.p., 1932.   NNUT
    Seminar held at Yale Divinity School, New Haven, Conn., April 13-15, 1931.

7783. Holly, Alonzo P. God and the Negro... Nashville: National Baptist Publishing Board, 1937.   DHU/R
    Biography and photographs of Negro ministers.
    Negro author.

7784. Hoult, Thomas Ford. Sociology of Religion. New York: The Dryden Press, 1958.   DHU/R
    Chapter 11, The Stratification Order and Religion.

7785. Howard University, Washington, D.C., Graduate School. Division of the Social Sciences. ...The Integration of the Negro into American Society. Papers Contributed to the Fourteenth Annual Conference of the Division of the Social Sciences, May 3, and 4, 1951. Edited by E. Franklin Frazier. Washington, D.C.: Pub. by the Howard University Press for the Graduate School, Howard University, 1951.   DHU/R
    Negro church by Frank D. Dorey.

7786. Howell, John A. "The Church and Black Folk." The Crisis (40:2, Feb., 1933), p. 32.   DHU/MO; DLC

7787. Huggins, Nathan. Key Issues in the Afro-American Experience. New York: Harcourt Brace Co., 1971.   DHU/AA

7788. Hughley, Judge Neal. Rethinking Our Christianity. Philadelphia: Dorrance & Co., 1942.   DHU/R
    Negro author.

7789. Imes, G. Lake. "A Service of the Country Church in Helping the Negro." Arcadius S. Trawick, (ed.). The New Voice in Race Adjustments. (New York: Student Volunteer Movement, 1914), pp. 145-53.   DHU/R
    Negro author.

7790. "Is There Too Much Rock 'n' Roll in Religion?" Color (11; Ja., 1957), pp. 12-13.   TNF

7791. Jackson, Algernon Brachear. The Man Next Door. Philadelphia: Neale Publishing Co., 1919.
    Negro church, pp. 53-76.
    Negro author.

7792. Jackson, Giovanna R. Afro-American Religion and Church and Race Relations. Bloomington: Indiana University Libraries, 1959.   MiBsA; INU; DHU/R
A bibliography of holdings in Indiana University Libraries.

7793. James, Samuel Horace. The Religious Experience of the Negro in America. Masters thesis. Andover Newton Theological School, 1943.

7794. Jernagin, W. H. "President's Address to the Fraternal Council of Negro Churches in America, Washington, D.C. 1938." Negro Journal of Religion (4:6, Jl., 1938), pp. 8+.   DHU/R

7795. Johnson, Charles S. Growing Up in the Black Belt. Washington, D.C.; American Council on Education, 1941. INU; DHU/MO
Negro author.
Rural Negro church.

7796. ----- Shadow of the Plantation. Chicago: University of Chicago Press, 1934.   DHU/MO

7797. ----- "Youth and the Church." Hart M. Nelsen & Raytha L. Yokley et alii. The Black Church in America. (New York: Basic Books, 1971), pp. 91-99.   DHU/R
Increasing number of young blacks in plantation areas early become dissatisfied with their church.

7798. Johnson, Edward A. A School History of the Negro Race in America from 1619 to 1890 ... Philadelphia: Sherman & Co., 1892.   DHU/MO
Chapter 30, "Religious Progress."

7799. Johnson, Ethel E. "Church Institutional Work." Southern Workman (46:3, Mr., 1917), pp. 153-58.   DLC; DHU/MO
The Rev. William N. DeBarry, pastor of St. John's Church, Springfield, Mass. conducted a survey of his parish so that he could carry out definite plans for institutional activities.

7800. Johnson, Henry Theodore. Pulpit, Pew and Pastorate... n.p., 1902.   DHU/MO;
NN/Sch
Negro author.

7801. Johnson, James Weldon. God's Trombones. New York: Viking, 1927.   DHU/R
Descriptions of Negro sermons.

7802. Johnson, Livingston. "Different Views Among Negroes." Biblical Recorder (85; Ja. 28, 1920), p. 7. LNB; NcWfSB

7803. ----- "Two Types of Negroes." Biblical Recorder (95; Jl. 10, 1929), p. 7.   LNB; NcWfSB

7804. Johnson, Mordecai Wyatt. "The Faith of the American Negro." The Crisis (24:4, Ag., 1922), pp. 156-58,   DHU/MO; DLC
Negro author.

7805. Johnston, Harry Hamilton. The Negro in the New World. New York: The Macmillan Company, 1910.   TSewU-T

7806. Johnston, Henry Halcro. "Negro and Religion." Current Literature (49; Ag., 1910), pp. 187-8.   DLC

7807. Johnston, Ruby. The Development of Negro Religion. New York: Philosophical Library, 1954.   DHU/R; INU;
DLC
Negro author.

7808. ----- The Religion of Negro Protestants; Changing Religious Attitudes and Practices. New York: Philosophical Library, 1956.   DHU/R; CtY-D; InU; DLC

7809. Jones, Lawrence N. "They Sought a City: The Black Church and Churchmen in the Nineteenth Century." Union Seminary Quarterly Review (26:3, Spr., 1971), pp. 253-72. DHU/R

7810. Jones, Summerfield Frances. The Church as a Factor in the Economic Progress of the Negro in America. Masters thesis. Howard University, 1928.

7811. Jordan, Winthrop D. "The Resulting Pattern of Separation in Negro Churches." Hart M. Nelsen & Raytha L. Yokley, et alii. The Black Church in America (New York: Basic Books, 1971), pp. 49-53.   DHU/R
Triumph of racial prejudice over Christian ideals.

7812. ----- White Over Black: American Attitudes toward the Negro, 1550-1812. Chapel Hill: Published for the Institute of Early American History and Culture at Williamsburg, Va., by the University of North Carolina Press, 1968. CtY-D; DHU/R
Chapter 5, the Negro church.

7813. Jowers, Joseph Bebee. "Negro Baptists and Methodists in American Protestantism; Aspects and Trends, 1957. Doctoral dissertation. New School of Social Research, 1958.

7814. Kaiser, Clyde Vernon. Sea Island to City: A Study of St. Helena Islanders in Harlem and Other Urban Centers. New York: Columbia University Press, 1932.   NNC
Studies of the function of the church in the lives of the Urban Negro.

7815. Karon, Bertram P. The Negro Personality. New York: Springer Publishing Co., 1958.   DHU/MO
Investigation of the effects of culture.

7816. Kealing, Hightower T. "A Race Rich in Spiritual Content." Southern Workman (33:1, Ja., 1904), pp. 41-44. DLC; DHU/MO
H. T. Kealing, editor of the A. M. E. Church Review.

7817. Keil, Charles. Urban Blues. Chicago: University of Chicago Press, 1966.   DHU/R
Chapter 6, discusses the similarity of roles of bluesmen and ministers in the Negro community.

7818. Kirrane, John Philip. The Establishment of Negro Parishes and the Coming of the Josephities, 1853-1871. Masters thesis. Catholic University, 1932.

7819. Kletzing, Henry F. Progress of a Race; or, The Remarkable Advancement of the Afro-American Negro from the Bondage of Slavery, Ignorance and Poverty, to the Freedom of Citizenship, Intelligence; Affluence, Honor and Trust. With an Introduction by Booker T. Washington... Atlanta, Ga. and Naperville, Ill.: J. L. Nichols & Co., 1898.   DHU/MO;
NN/Sch

7820. Knight, Haywood George. Apocalypticism As Found in the Book of Daniel; and Its Effect Upon the Negro Preacher. Bachelor of Divinity paper. Andover Newton Theological School, 1946.

7821. Kyles, Lynwood W., (bp.). "The Contribution of the Negro to Religious Life of America." Journal of Negro History (11:1, Ja., 1926), pp. 8-16.   DHU/MO
Negro author.

7822. Lamar, J. S. "Religious Future of the Negroes of the South." Christian Quarterly (6; 1874), p. 211.   CtY

7823. Lambert, R. E. "Negroes and the Church." Commonweal Oct. 20, 1961), pp. 90-92.   DHU

7824. Lander, Ernest M. A History of South Carolina. Chapel Hill: University of North Carolina Press, 1960.   NN/Sch
Negro church, pp. 163-8.

7825. Lawrence, Charles Radford. Negro Organizations in Crisis: Depression, New Deal, World War II. Doctoral dissertation. Columbia University, 1952.

7826. Lawton, Samuel Miller. ...The Religious Life of South Carolina Coastal and Sea Island Negroes. Nashville, Tenn.: George Peabody College for Teachers, 1939.   DLC
Also Doctoral dissertation.

7827. Leading Afro-Americans of Vicksburg, Mississippi; Their Enterprises, Churches, Schools. Vicksburg: Biographa, 1908.
DLC

7828. Lee, J. Oscar. "Religion Among Ethnic and Racial Minorities." Arnals of the American Academy of Political and Social Science (332; Nov., 1960), pp. 112-24.   DHU; DLC

7829. ----- 'Religious Life and Needs of Negro Youth." Journal of Negro Education (19; Sum., 1950), pp. 298-309.   DHU

7830. Lee, R. L. Racial Episcopacy--Reasons. Greenville, Miss.: M. Kanaga, 1915.   DLC

7831. Lee, Rcbert and Ralph L. Roy. "The Negro Church." Christian Century (74:44, Oct. 30, 1957), pp. 1285-87. DHU/R

7832. Lehman. H. C. and P. A. Witty. "Church and Sunday School Attendance of Negro Children." Religious Education (22; Ja., 1927), pp. 50-56.   DHU/R

7833. Leiffer, Murray H. The Layman Looks at the Minister. Nashville: Abingdon-Cokesbury Press, 1946.   DHU/R
       Chapter 7, The minister and social ideas.

7834. LeMone Archie. "The Afro-American Churches." Ecumenical Review (20:1, Ja., 1968), pp. 44-52.   DHU/R

7835. Lenski, Gerhard Emmanuel. The Religious Factor: A Sociological Study of Religion's Impact on Politics, Economics, and Family Life. Garden City, N.Y.: Doubleday, 1961. DHU/R; INU; NN/Sch
       Based on a survey made in the Detroit area.

7836. Levine, M. H. "The Negro in the Bible." Negro Digest (14; Ja. 1965), pp. 82-83.   DHU/MO

7837. Lewis, Hylan G. Blackways of Kent. Chapel Hill: University of North Carolina Press, 1955.   DHU/MO
       Chapter 6, Religion and Salvation.
       Negro author.

7838. ----- The Social Life of the Negro in a Southern Piedmont Town. Doctoral dissertation. University of Chicago, 1952.

7839. Lewis, John Henry. Social Services in Negro Churches. Masters thesis. University of Chicago, 1914.

7840. Licorish, David Nathaniel. Tomorrow's Church in Today's World; a Study of the Twentieth-Century Challenge to Religion. New York: Exposition Press, 1956.   DHU/MO
       Negro author.

7841. Little, D. D. "The Religious Side of the Negro Question." Southern Workman (36:7, Jl., 1907), pp. 390-401.   DHU/MO

7842. Littleton, Arthur C. and Mary W. Burger, (eds.). Black Viewpoints. New York: New American Library, 1964. DHU/R
       Includes information on the Church.

7843. Lord, Samuel Ebenezer Churchstone. The Negro and Organized Religion, an Attempt at Interpretation. Kingston, Jamaica: n.p., 1935.   DLC

7844. Love, Edgar. "Role of the Church in Maintaining the Morale of the Negro in World Wars I and II." Journal of Negro Education (12; Sum., 1943), pp. 502-10.   DHU

7845. Mannoni, O. "The Lament of the Negro." Cross Currents (1; Sum., 1951), pp. 1-11.   DHU/R

7846. Margolies, Edward. Native Sons: A Critical Study of Twentieth Century Negro-American Authors. Philadelphia: Lippincott, 1969.   DLC
       A chapter entitled, "The Negro Church: James Baldwin and the Christian Vision."

7847. Markoe, William M. "Negro Morality and a Colored Clergy." America (25; Nov. 12, 1921), pp. 78-81.   DLC

7848. Marty, Martin E. Righteous Empire: The Protestant Experience in America. New York: The Dial Press, 1970. DHU/R
       Chapter 3, The Overlooked Protestant, The Black American.

7849. Mason, Madison Charles Butler. "Did the American Negro Make, in the Nineteenth Century, Achievements Along the Lines of Wealth, Morality, Education, Etc., Commensurate With His Opportunities? If So, What Achievements Did He Make?" Dan Daniel W. Culp. Twentieth Century Negro Literature (Miami, Fla.: Mnemosyne Pub. Co., Inc., 1969), pp. 34-37. DHU/MO
       Reprint of 1902 edition.
       Methodist Episcopal minister and Corresponding Secretary of the Freedmen's Aid and Southern Education Society of the Methodist Episcopal Church.

7850. Massey, James Earl. "When Thou Prayest; an Interpretation of Christian Prayer According to the Teachings of Jesus." Anderson, Ind.: Warner Press, 1960.   NN/Sch
       Negro author.

7851. Mayer, Albert J., and Harry Sharp. "Religious Preference and World Success." American Sociological Review (27:2, Apr. 1962), pp. 218-27.   DHU
       "A 1954-59 probability sample of over 9,000 adult White and Negro Detroiters."

7852. Mays, Benjamin Elijah. "The American Negro and the Christian Religion." Journal of Negro Education (8:3, Jl., 1939), pp. 530-8.   DHU/R
       Negro author.

7853. ----- "Christianity in a Changing World." National Educational Outlook Among Negroes (I; 4, Dec., 1937), pp. 18+.
                                                              DHU/MO

7854. ----- "The Church Surveys World Problems." Crisis (44; Oct., 1937), pp. 299+.   DHU/MO

7855. ------ The Development of the Idea of God in Contemporary Negro Literature. Doctoral dissertation. University of Chicago, 1935.

7856. ----- "Fifty Years of Progress in the Negro Church." Pittsburgh Courier (Apr. 8, 1950),   DHU/MO; NN/Sch
       Negro author.

7857. ----- "The Negro Church in American Life." Christendom (5:3, Sum., 1940), pp. 387-98.   DHU/R

7858. ----- "The Negro in the Christian Ministry." A. M. E. Church Review (75:200, Ap.-Je., 1959), pp. 21-9. DHU/R

7859. ------ "Negroes and the Will to Justice." Christian Century (59:43, Oct., 1942), pp. 1316-7.

7860. ----- The Negro's Church. New York: Institute of Social and Religious Research, 1933.   DHU/R; OWibfU

7861. ----- The Negro's God, as Reflected in His Literature. New York: Negro Universities Press, 1969. DHU/R; DLC; CtY-D
       Reprint of the 1938 ed.

7862. ----- "The Religious Life and Needs of Negro College Stude Students." Journal of Negro Education (9; Jl., 1940), pp. 332-43
                                                              DHU/R

7863. ----- "Religious Roots of Western Culture." Child Study (30; Fall, 1953).   HQ
       Negro author.

7864. ----- "Who Will Preach to Negroes in the Year 2000?" Chicago Defender (Ag., 1955).   DHU/MO
       Negro author.

7865. McCabe, Lda R. "Colored Church Work in New York." The Outlook (54; Ag., 1896), pp. 327-29.   DGW

7866. McClellan, G. E. "One Ministry; Seabury Consultation on the Training of Negro Ministers." National Council Outlook (9; My., 1959), pp. 6-8.   DHU/R

7867. Mead, Frank Spencer. "God in Harlem." Christian Century
(53; Ag. 26, 1936), pp. 1133-35.   DHU/R

7868. Meier, August. Negro Thought in America, 1800-1915. Ann
Arbor, Mich.: University of Michigan Press, 1966. DHU/R
Religion, chapters 3 and 8.

7869. ----- and Elliot M. Rudwick. From Plantation to Ghetto:
An Interpretive History of American Negroes. New York:
Hill and Wang, 1966.   DHU/R
For a discussion of the development and the impact of the
Negro churches on ghetto dwellers in the antebellum cities,
see pp. 74-80.

7870. Mencken, H. L. "The Burden of Credulity." Opportunity
(9:2, Feb., 1931), pp. 40-1.   DHU/MO

7871. Miller, Elizabeth W. The Negro in America: A Bibliography.
Cambridge, Mass.: Harvard University Press, 1970. DHU/R
Section on Religion.

7872. Miller, Kelly. Out of the House of Bondage. New York:
The Neal Publishing Co., 1914.   DHU/MO; CtY-D
Negro author.

7873. ----- "Religion and Education." Voice of the Negro (1:4,
Apr., 1940), pp. 163-5.   DHU/MO

7874. Miller, William R. "The Negro Church in the U. S. A."
Risk (10:1, 1968).   DLC

7875. "Ministers' Conference at Bettis." Editorial. Southern Workman (50:9, Sept., 1921), pp. 392-4.   DLC; DHU/MO
Negro rural ministers of western South Carolina meet and
discuss education, farming, health, and community organization.

7876. Mitchell, Henry H. Black Preaching. Philadelphia: J. P.
Lippincott Co., 1970.   DHU/R; DLC
Negro author.

7877. Montgomery, Leroy Jeremiah. An Analysis of Two Distinct
Religions: Organized Christianity and the Religion of Jesus
Christ. New York: New Voices Pub. Co., 1956.   DHU/MO
Negro author.

7878. ----- Two Distinct Religions, Christianity and the Religion
of Jesus Christ. Houston: Informer Publishing Co., n.d.
                                                    DHU/MO
Negro author.

7879. Morland, Kenneth J., (comp.). The Not so Solid South...
Athens, Georgia: University of Georgia Press, 1971. NN/Sch
pp. 4-15 information on the religion of Negroes.

7880. Muelder, Walter. "Recruitment of Negroes for Theological
Studies." Review of Religious Research (5:3, Spr., 1964), pp.
152-6.   DHU/R

7881. Murray, Andrew E. "The Negro Church Must Lead." The
African Methodist Episcopal Church Review (68:176, Apr.-Je.,
1953), pp. 59-61.   DHU/R
Negro author.

7882. Murray, Florence. The Negro Handbook. New York:
Macmillan, 1949.   DHU/R
Negro author.
pp. 288-99, membership of Negro churches.

7883. Myrdal, Gunnar. An American Dilemma. New York: Harper & Bros., 1944.   INU; DHU/R; CtY-D
Chapter 40, vol. II, The Negro church.

7884. "The National Association for the Advancement of Colored
People. The Sixth Annual Conference. The Church and the
Negro." The Crisis (8:2, Je., 1914), pp. 81-2. DLC;
DHU/MO

7885. The National Encyclopedia of the Colored Race: Editor in
Chief, Clement Richardson... Montgomery, Ala.: National
Publishing Company, Inc., 1919.   NN/Sch
Negro author.
Negro church, pp. 573-8.

7886. National Urban League, Dept. of Research and Community
Projects. A Survey of the Economic and Cultural Conditions of
the Negro Population of Louisville, Kentucky and a Review of the
Program and Activities of the Louisville Urban League in Coop-
eration with the Louisville Health and Welfare Council and the
Louisville Community Chest, by J. Harvey Kerns, Assistant
Director, Dept. of Research and Community Projects, National
Urban League... Jan.-Feb., 1948.   NN/Sch

7887. "The Negro-American Church." The Crisis (4:1, My., 1912),
pp. 29-33.   DLC; DHU/MO
"Four leading churchmen representing leading denominations
among colored people give The Crisis a statement of present
condition of these churches."

7888. Negro Christian Student Conference, Atlanta, 1914. The New
Voice in Race Adjustment; Addresses and Reports Presented
at the Negro Christian Student Conference. Atlanta, Ga., May
14-18, 1914. A. M. Trawick, editor... New York: Student
Volunteer Movement, 1914. A & M; DHU/MO; NN/Sch; DHU/R

7889. "The Negro Church." The Crisis (20:1, My., 1920), pp. 9-
11.   DHU/MO; DLC
Census reports of 1890; 1906; 1916. A study of the development of the Negro Church.

7890. "The Negro Church." Harry A. Polski (ed.). Reference
Library of Black America (New York: Bellwether Pub. Co.,
1971), Book 2, pp. 208-10.

7891. ----- Editorial. The Southern Workman (29:9, Sept., 1900),
p. 501.   DHU/MO; DLC

7892. ----- Political Science Quarterly (19; Dec., 1904), pp. 702-
3.   DHU; DLC

7893. "Negro Emotionalism Passing." Literary Digest (115; Mr.
4, 1933), p. 22.   DHU/R; DHU

7894. "Negro God Has Realms on Earth." Newsweek (2; Dec. 23,
1933), p. 26.   DHU/R

7895. Negro Year Book, An Annual Encyclopedia of the Negro.
Tuskegee Institute, Ala.: Negro Year Book Publis ing Co.,
1912.   DHU/MO;
DHU/R
Short historical facts, denominational statistics.

7896. "Negroes in Missouri." The Church at Home and Abroad
(3; My., 1888), pp. 479-80.
Religious orientation of Negroes in Missouri.

7897. New York City, (New York). Greater New York Federation
of Churches. The Negro Churches of Manhattan (New York
City). A Study Made in 1930. New York: n. p., n. d. SCBHC

7898. Newton, John B. The Colored Commission. Alexandria, Va.:
Hill Print, 1888. 2 vols.   NN/Sch
V. 1, The Negro and the Church, pp. 60-65.

7899. O'Connell, P. "The Negro Ministry." Southern Workman
(57:5, My., 1928), pp. 200-4.   DLC;
DHU/MO
"The following are some of the counts in the indictment
against our minstry: ignorance, sensuality, lack of sense
of honor, conservativism, orthodoxy."

7900. Odom, Edward J., Jr. "Community Concern for the Recruitment and Training of Qualified Professional Religious
Leaders." The African Methodist Episcopal Church Review
(71:185, Jl.-Sept., 1955), pp. 66-68.   DHU/R
Negro author.

7901. Odum, Howard Washington. Social and Mental Traits of the Negro: Research into the Conditions of the Negro Race in Southern Towns, a Study in Race Traits, Tendencies and Prospects. New York: Columbia University, 1910.   NN/Sch

7902. Palmer, Edward Nelson. "The Religious Acculturation of the Negro." Phylon (5:3, 1944), pp. 260-65. DAU; DAU/W; DCU/ST; DHU; DHU/MO

7903. Partee, William E. "The Negro as a Christian." Daniel W. Culp. Twentieth Century Negro Literature. (Miami, Fla.: Mnemosyne Publishing Co., Inc., 1969), pp. 309-13. DHU/MO
          Reprint of 1902 edition.
          Negro Presbyterian minister.

7904. Patrick, James Ruey. A Study of Ideals, Intelligence and Achievements of Negroes and Whites. Athens, Georgia: n.p., 1926.   O

7905. Pawley, James A., (comp.). The Negro Church in New Jersey. Hackensack, N.J.: n.p., 1938. Pam File, DHU/R
          Typescript.
          "Work Progress Administration."

7906. Peck, W. H. "Negro Churches in Detroit; Reply to H. A. White." Christian Century (55; Apr. 13, 1938), p. 468. DHU/R

7907. Penn, Irvine Garland. "Negro Religious and Social Life." Missionary Review (45:6, Je., 1922), pp. 447-53.   DHU/R
          Secretary of the Board of Education for Negroes of the Methodist Episcopal Church.
          Negro author.

7908. ----- (ed.). The United Negro: His Problems and His Problems and His Progress, Containing the Addresses and Proceedings the Negro Young People's Christian and Education Congress, Held August 6-11, 1902; Introduction by Bishop W. J. Gaines... edited by Prof. I. Garland Penn... Prof. J. W. E. Bowen... Atlanta, Ga.: D. E. Luther Publishing Co., 1902.   DHU/R; DHU/MO; DLC
          Negro author.

7909. Perkins, A. E. Sunday School Plans and Outlines. New Orleans: The Author, 1923.   DHU/MO
          "Guide and aid for superintendents, teachers, officers, and Sunday School workers."
          Negro author.

7910. Pettigrew, Thomas F. A Profile of the Negro American. New York: D. Van Nostrand Co., Inc., 1964.   DHU/MO
          Religion, pp. 47-8.

7911. Pickens, William. The Vengeance of the Gods and Three Other of Real American Color Line Life. Philadelphia: AME Book Concern, 1922.   OWibfU
          Negro author.

7912. Pipkin, James Jefferson. The Negro in Revelation, in History, and in Citizenship; What the Race has Done and is Doing. New York: Thompson Publishing Col, 1902. DLC; TNF

7913. ----- The Story of a Rising Race. St. Louis: N. D. Thompson, 1902.   DHU/MO

7914. Ploski, Harry A. The Negro Almanac. New York: Bellwether Publishing Co., 1967.   DHU/R; INU
          Negro church, pp. 793-815.

7915. Poinsett, Alex. Common Folk in an Uncommon Cause. Chicago: Liberty Baptist Church, 1962.
          Negro author.

7916. ----- "The Religion, Negroes and the Christian Church." Ebony Editors. The Negro Handbook (Chicago: Johnson Publishing Co., 1966), pp. 307-08.   DHU/R
          Includes membership statistics.

7917. Pollard, Myrtle E. Harlem as It Is. Masters thesis. City College of New York, 1936-37.   NN/Sch

7918. Pope, Liston. "The Negro and Religion in America." Review of Religious Research (5:3, Spr., 1964), pp. 142-52.
                                                                                                  DHU/R

7919. Poteat, Ervin M. "The Contribution of the Negro Race to the Interpretation of Christianity." Arcadius S. Trawick, (ed.). The New Voice in Race Adjustments (New York: Student Volunteer Movement, 1914), pp. 54-56.   DHU/R

7920. Powell, Adam Clayton, Sr. "Give Me That Old Time Religion." Negro Digest (8; My., 1950), pp. 19-21.
                                                    DHU/MO; Pam. File, DHU/R
          Negro author.

7921. Powell, Adam Clayton, Jr. "Sex in the Church." Ebony (Nov., 1951), pp. 27-30.   DHU

7922. Poynter, W. T. "The Church and the Black Man." Methodist Review (20; Mr.-Apr., 1896), p. 79.   DLC;CtY-D

7923. Preston, J. T. L. "Religious Education of Negroes." New England Magazine (37; 1878), p. 680.   DLC

7924. Proctor, Henry H. "The Negro as a Christian." Daniel W. Culp. Twentieth Century Negro Literature (Miami, Fla.: Mnemosyne Publishing Co., Inc., 1969), pp. 317-19.
                                                                                                  DHU/MO
          Reprint of 1902 edition.
          Negro Congregationalist minister.

7925. "Progress for Negro Sunday Schools." Religious Education (8; Ag., 1913), pp. 283-84.   DHU/R

7926. Puckett, Newbell Niles. "The Negro Church in the United States." Social Forces (4; Mr., 1926), pp. 581-87. DHU

7927. Ransom, Reverdy Cassius, (bp.). The Industrial and Social Condition of the Negro: A Thanksgiving Sermon, Nov. 26, 1896 at Bethel A. M. E. Church, Chicago.   OWibfU
          Negro author.
          Transcript.

7928. ----- The Mission of the Religious Press... an Address Before the General Conference of the A. M. E. Church in Kansas City, Mo., May 16, 1912. New York: American Negro Press, 1912.   NN/Sch; OWibfU
          Negro author.

7929. ----- The Negro: the Hope or the Despair of Christianity. Boston: Ruth Hill Publisher, 1935.   NN/Sch
          Negro author.

7930. Reid, Ira De A. "Let Us Pray!" Opportunity (4:45, Sept., 1926), pp. 274-78.   DHU/MO
          Discusses Negro churches in the city.

7931. "Religion and Resistance." WCBS-TV and Columbia University. Released by Holt, Rinehart and Winston, 1969. 30 min. sd. b & w. 16 mm.   DLC
          Film.
          "Vincent Harding exposes the spiritual undercurrent which aided and abetted the active resistance of blacks to enslavement- including the revolutionary messages shrouded in religion that revolt leaders such as Nat Turner and Denmark Vesey used."

7932. "The Religion of the American Negro." New World (19; Dec., 1900).   DCU/RE

7933. "Religious Life of the Negro." North American Review (181; Jl., 1905), pp. 20-23.   DHU

7934. Renard, Alice. "A Negro Looks at the Church." Commonweal (46:9, Je. 13, 1947), pp. 209-12.   DHU

"Typescript." Section on Negro Church.
Negro author.

7935. Reuter, Edward Byron. The American Race Problem. A Study of the Negro. New York: Thomas Y. Crowell Co., 1927.   DHU/R; DHU/MO
The church and religious life of the Negro, p. 13.

7936. Reynolds, L. H. "Why Negro Churches are Necessary." A. M. E. Church Review (4:4, Oct., 1887), pp. 154-57.
DHU/MO

7937. Richardson, Harry Van Buren. Dark Glory, a Picture of the Church Among Negroes in the Rural South. New York: Pub. for Home Missions Council of North America and Phelps-Stokes Fund by Friendship Press, 1947.
DHU/R; DHU/MO;DLC
Negro author.

7938. ----- "The Negro Church -- Its History and Influence." Christian Home (4:3, Nov., 1971; 4:4, Dec., 1971), pp. 22-24; 24-26.   DLC
Also: Foundations (14:6, Feb., 1973), pp. 18-21.   DLC
Negro author.

7839. ----- "The Negro in American Religious Life." John P. Davis, (ed.). The American Negro Reference Book (Englewood Cliffs, N. J.: Prentice-Hall, 1966), pp. 396-413.   DHU/R

7940. ----- "The New Negro and Religion." Opportunity (11:2, Feb., 1933), pp. 41-44.   DHU/MO
Negro author.

7941. ----- The Rural Negro Church; a Study of the Rural Negro Church in Four Representative Southern Counties to Determine Ministerial Adequacy. Doctoral dissertation. Drew Theological Seminary, 1945.

7942. Richardson, Lee and Goodman. In and About Vicksburg. Vicksburg, Miss.: Gibraltar, 1890.   DLC

7943. Richie, Willia Temple. The Contribution of the Negro Churches of Washington, D. C., to the Problem of the Soldier, Defense Worker and the Parishioner During World War II. Master's thesis. Howard University, 1943.

7944. Richings, G. F. Evidences of Progress Among Colored People. Philadelphia: G. S. Ferguson, 1904.
DHU/R; NN/Sch

7945. Robert, Mattie A. Our Immediate Need of an Educated Colored Ministry. n.p., 1878.   SCBHC

7946. Roberts, Harry W. "The Rural Negro Minister: His Personal and Social Characteristics." Social Forces (27; 1948-49), pp. 291-300.   MB; DLC; NcD
A study of 141 predominantly rural Baptist ministers.

7947. Roberts, James Deotis. "The Negro's Contribution to Religious Thought in America." Swarthmore College Bulletin Alumni Issue (68:2, Oct., 1970), pp. 7-14.
Pam. File, DHU/R

7948. Robertson, Archibald Thomas. That Old-Time Religion. Boston: Houghton Mifflin, 1950.   NN/Sch

7949. Roman, Charles Victor. "The Church in Relation to Growing Race Pride." Arcadius S. Trawick, (ed.). The New Voice in Race Adjustments (New York: Student Volunteer Movement, 1914), pp. 40-50.   DHU/R
Negro author.

7950. Rooks, Charles Shelby. "Image of the Ministry as Reflected in the Protestant Fellowship Program." Journal of Religious Thought (18:2, 1961-62), pp. 317-48.   DHU/R
Negro author.

7951. ----- "The Shortage of Negro Theological Students." Christianity and Crisis (25:2, Feb1, 1965), pp. 20-23.
DHU/R

7952. ----- (ed.). Toward a Better Ministry: A Report of the Consultation on the Negro in the Christian Ministry. Held at the Blue Ridge Assembly, Inc., Black Mountain, N. C., Oct. 5-7, 1965. Sponsored by the Edward W. Hazen Foundation and the Fund for Theological Education, Inc., 1965.
Pam. File, DHU/R

7953. Rosenberg, Bruce A. The Art of the American Folk Preacher. New York: Oxford University Press, 1970.
DHU/R; DLC

7954. Rudwick, Elliot M. W. E. B. DuBois: A Study in Minority Group Leadership. Philadelphia: The University of Pennsylvania Press, 1961.   DHU/MO

7955. Russell, James S. "Church Work Among Negroes." Spirit of Missions (86; Nov., 1921), pp. 737-39.   DHU/R

7956. ----- "Enlisting for the Ministry." Southern Workman (46:9, Sept., 1917), pp. 499-504.   DLC; DHU/MO

7957. ----- "Past and Present Among the Negroes of Southern Virginia." Spirit of Missions (74:4, Apr., 1909), pp. 307-10.
DHU/R

7958. Rutledge, A. "God's Dark Children." Outlook (155; Jl. 23, 1930), pp. 446-8.   DHU

7959. Salisbury, W. Seward. Religion in American Culture. Homewood, Ill.: Dorsey Press, 1964.   DHU/R
pp. 472-75, Negro Church.

7960. Schab, Fred. "Attitudinal Differences of Southern White and Negro Adolescent Males Regarding the Home, School, Religion and Morality." Journal of Negro Education (40:2, Spr. 1971), pp. 108-10.   DHU/R

7961. Scheiner, Seth M. The Negro Church and the Northern City 1890-1930. William G. Shade and Roy C. Herrenkohl (eds.). Seven on Black (Philadelphia: L. B. Lippincott, 1969), pp. 91-117.   DHU/R

7962. ----- The Negro in New York City, 1865-1910. Doctoral dissertation. New York University, 1963.

7963. Schomburg, Arthur Alfonso. "The Negro and Christianity." Opportunity (2; Dec., 1924), pp. 362-64.   DHU/MO

7964. Sernett, Milton Charles. Black Religion and American Evangelicalism: White Protestants, Plantation Missions, and the Independent Negro Church, 1787-1865. Doctoral dissertation. University of Delaware, 1972.

7965. Shaw, George Bernard. The Adventures of the Black Girl in her Search for God. New York: Dodd, Mead & Co., 1932.
DHU/MO

7966. Shockley, Grant S. Improvement of the Status and In-Service Education of Negro Methodist Accepted Supply Pastors. Doctoral dissertation. Teachers College, Columbia University, 1952.

7967. Sinclair, Georges H. The Religious Attitudes of Forty Institutionalized Protestant Girls With Implications for Christian Education. A Comparative Study. Doctoral dissertation. Hartford Seminary Foundation, 1964.
"Racial differences were included in this comparative study."

7968. Singh, Raman K. "Christian Heroes and Anti-Heroes in Richard Wright's Fiction." Negro American Literature Forum (6:4, Wint., 1972), pp. 99-104.   Pam. File, DHU/R

7969. Sisk, Glenn N. "Churches in the Alabama Black Belt, 1875-1917." Church History (23:2, Je., 1954), pp. 153-74.   DHU/R

7970. Smith, Allen H. The Negro Church; a Critical Examination of the Christian Church Among Negroes in the United States. New Haven: Yale University Divinity School, 1961.
CtY-D; DHU/R

(Smith, Allen H. cont.)
   Typescript.
   "Study...presented in conjunction with the Special Honors
   Program of Yale University Divinity School...1960-1961."

7971. Smith, Timothy L. "Slavery and Theology: The Emergence
   of Black Christian Consciousness in Nineteenth Century
   America.' Church History (41:4, Dec., 1972), pp. 497-512.
                                                          DHU/R

7972. Snedecor, James G. "Ministers in Cooperation." Arcadius
   S. Trawick, (ed.). The New Voice in Race Adjustments (New
   York: Student Volunteer Movement, 1914), pp. 178-83. DHU/R

7973. Sowande, Fela. Black Experience of Religion. Mim. Speech
   given at Conference on Continuities and Discontinuities in
   Afro-American Societies and Cultures. April 2-4, 1970. Sponsored by Committee on Afro-American Societies and Cultures.
   Social Science Research Council.   Pam. File, DHU/R

7974. Speaks, R. L. "Will the Negro Remain Protestant?"
   Christian Century (7:22, Je. 2, 1954), pp. 668-69.   DHU/R

7975. Spence, Hartzell. The Story of America's Religions. Pub-
   lished in Cooperation with the Editors of Look Magazine. New
   York: Rinehart & Winston, 1960.   NN/Sch
   History and statistics on Negro churches.

7976. Sperry, Willard Learoyd. Religion in America. New
   York: Macmillan Co., 1946.   NN/Sch; DHU/R
   Negro churches, pp. 181-98.

7977. Spiller, Richard. "The Negro Pulpit and its Responsibilities." Southern Workman (28:9, Sept., 1899), pp. 350-1.
                                                    DHU/MO; DLC

7978. Stelzle, Charles. American Social and Religious Conditions.
   New York: Revell, 1912.   NN/Sch

7979. Stevens, George E. "The Negro Church in the City."
   The Missionary Review of the World (49; Je., 1926), pp. 435-39.
                                                          DHU/R

7980. Strange, Robert (bp.). ...Church Work Among the Negroes
   in the South... Chicago: Western Theological Seminary, 1907.
                                                    NcD; CtY-D

7981. Sutherland, Robert L. An Analysis of Negro Churches in
   Chicago. Doctoral dissertation. University of Chicago, 1930.

7982. Tarter, Charles L. The Development of a Program of
   Cooperation Among Some Negro Churches in the Fourth Ward
   of Paterson, New Jersey. Doctoral dissertation. Teachers
   College, Columbia University, 1952.

7983. Tate, Robert, Jr. A Study of Negro Churches in Durham,
   North Carolina. Bachelor of Divinity thesis. Duke University,
   1939.

7984. Terry-Thompson, Arthur C. The History of the African
   Orthodox Church. New York: n.p., 1956.   DLC

7985. Thirkield, Wilbur Patterson, (bp.). "Constructive Sunday
   School Work Among Colored People." Religious Education
   (7; Oct., 1912), pp. 445-50.   DHU/R

7986. ----- "The Peril of the Negro Church." Opportunity
   (11:7, Jl., 1933), pp. 213-15.   DHU/MO

7987. Thomas, Charles Walker. "Historic Action in the Church."
   Negro History Bulletin (29:3, Dec., 1965), pp. 65-66.
                                                          DHU/MO

7988. Thomas, Isaac Lemuel. Separation or Continuity, Which?
   Or a Colored Man's Reply to Bishop Foster's Book, "Union of
   Episcopal Methodisms." Baltimore: H. H. Smith, 1893.
                                                    NjMD; OWibfU
   Negro author.

7989. Thomas, James S. A Study of the Social Role of the Negro
   Rural Pastor in Four Selected Southern Areas. Doctoral
   dissertation. Cornell University, 1952.

7990. Thorpe, Earl E. Black Historians, A Critique. New York:
   Morrow, 1971.   MNtcA; MH-AH; DHU/MO
   Chapter 8, Church Historians.

7991. Thurman, Howard. "The Task of the Negro Ministry."
   Southern Workman (57:10, Oct., 1928), pp. 387-92.
                                                    DLC;DHU/MO

7992. Tobias, Channing H. "Negro Thinking Today." Religion
   in Life (13:2, Spr., 1944), pp. 204-12.   DHU/R

7993. Trawick, Arcadius McSwain. "The City Church and the
   Problem of Crime." American Journal of Sociology (20;
   1914-15), pp. 220-47.   DHU

7994. -----, (ed.). The Negro Voice in Race Adjustments.
   Addresses and Reports Presented at the Negro Christian
   Student Conference, Atlanta, Georgia, May 14-18, 1914. New
   York: Student Volunteer Movement, 1914.   DHU/R

7995. Trawick, Arch, (Mrs.). "The Social Message of the
   Church." Arcadius S. Trawick (ed.). The New Voice in
   Race Adjustments (New York: Student Volunteer Movement,
   1914), pp. 62-5.   DHU/R
   Negro author.

7996. Trollope, Frances. Domestic Manners of the Americans.
   New York: A. A. Knopf, 1949.   DHU
   Camp meetings and the Negro, pp. 237-41.
   Negro author.

7997. Turner, Ronny E. "The Black Minister: Uncle Tom or
   Abolitionist?" Phylon (34:1, Mr., 1973), pp. 86-95. DHU/MO

7998. Tyms, James Daniel. "Church and This New Generation."
   Journal of Religious Thought (18; Win.-Spr., 1961), pp. 57-65.
                                                          DHU/R
   Negro author.

7999. United States. Census Bureau. Negroes in the United States.
   Washington, D.C.: Govt. Prtg. Office, 1915.   DHU/R
   Negro churches, pp. 45-53.

8000. ----- Religious Bodies, 1906, 1916, 1926, 1936... Washington, D.C.: Govt. Prtg. Office, 1910-1941. DHU/R
   Statistics on Negro churches.

8001. ----- Work Project Administration, New Jersey. The
   Negro Church in New Jersey. Emergency Education Project.
   Hackensack, N.J.: n.p., 1938.   DLC; NN/Sch
   Mim.

8002. "The Universal Negro Improvement Association: Speech at
   Liberty Hall, New York City (1922)." Harry A. Ploski, (ed.).
   Reference Library of Black America (New York: Bellwether
   Pub. Co., Inc., 1971), Book 2, pp. 114-18.   DHU

8003. Walker, C. T. "The Negro Church as a Medium for Race
   Expression." The New Voice in Race Adjustments (New York:
   Student Volunteer Movement, 1914), pp. 50-54.
   Negro author.

8004. Walker, George Gilbert. "Colored People and their Religious
   Organizations." Living Church (65; My. 7, 1921), pp. 15-16.
                                                    CtY; DLC

8005. Walker, Harry J. ...The Negro in American Life. New
   York: Oxford Book Co., 1954.   NN/Sch
   Evaluation of the Negro church in American life.
   Negro author.

8006. Wallace, David M. "Beyond Boycotts." World Call (50:1,
   Ja., 1968), pp. 16-18.   DHU/R
   Author, program director of Operation Breadbasket in
   Chicago, is a Disiple of Christ minister.

8007. Walls, William Jacop, (bp.). Connectionalism and the Negro Church. n.p., n.d.   NcSalL

8008. Walsh, Francis Augustine, (ed.). The Religious Education of the Negro; Papers Read at the National Congress of the Confraternity of Christian Doctrine, New York...October, 1936... Cincinnati: Benziger Bros., 1937. DHU/MO; NcD

8009. Warren, Mervyn Alonzo. "The Black Preacher in Retrospect and Prospect." The Message Magazine. (40:6, Sept., 1974), pp. 34-36.   DHU/R

8010. Washington, Booker Taliaferro. "The Religious Life of the Negro." North American Review (181; Jl., 1905). pp. 20-23.   DHU
     Negro author.

8011. ----- The Story of the Negro. New York: Doubleday, Page & Co., 1909. 2 Vols.   DHU/MO
     "The Negro preacher and the Negro church."

8012. ----- and W. E. B. DuBois. "Religion in the South." The Negro in the South. Philadelphia: Geo. W. Jacobs & Co., 1907.   DHU/R; NN/Sch
     Negro authors.

8013. Washington, Joseph R., Jr. "Are American Negro Churches Christian?" Theology Today (20; Apr., 1963), pp. 76-86.   DHU/R
     Negro author.

8014. Watson, James Jefferson. "Churches and Religious Conditions Among the Negroes." Annals of the American Academy (49; Sept., 1913), pp. 120-28.   DHU

8015. ----- The Religion of the Negro. Doctoral dissertation. University of Pennsylvania, 1912.

8016. Weatherford, Allen Ericson. "Recreation in the Negro Church in North Carolina." Journal of Negro Education (13; Fall, 1944), pp. 499-508.   DHU

8017. Weatherford, Willis Duke. The Negro from Africa to America. New York: Doran, 1924.   NN/Sch
     Negroes and the church, pp. 298-337.

8018. ----- Negro Life in the South, Present Conditions and Needs, With a Special Chapter on the Economic Condition of the Negro, by G. W. Dyer... New York: Young Men's Christian Association Press, 1910.   DHU/R; NN/Sch
     Negro church, pp. 117-46.

8019. Webber, W. "Witness and Service in East Harlem." International Review of Missions (54; Oct., 1965), pp. 441-46.   DHU/R

8020. Weeks, Louis B. "Horace Bushnell on Black America." Religious Education (68; Ja.-Feb., 1973), pp. 28-41. DHU/R

8021. Weisenburger, Francis P. "William Sanders Scarborough: Scholarship, The Negro Religion and Politics." Ohio History (72; Ja., 1963), pp. 25+.   NcD

8022. Wengatz, John Christian. Miracles in Black. New York: Fleming H. Revell Co., 1938.   DHU/MO

8023. Wesley, Charles Harris. "The Black Church in America, Its Origin and Development." Washington Star-News Tuesday Magazine (Ja., 1974), pp. 5+.   Pam. File, DHU/R

8024. ----- "The Religious Attitudes of Negro Youth." Journal of Negro History (21:4, Oct., 1936), pp. 376-93.   DHU/MO
     Negro author.

8025. Wharton, Vernon Lane. The Negro in Mississippi, 1865-1890. Chapel Hill: University of North Carolina Press, 1947. DHU/R
     Negro church, pp. 256-65.

8026. White, Horace A. "Who Owns the Negro Churches?" Christian Century (55; Feb. 9, 1938), pp. 176-77.   DHU/R

8027. Whither the Negro Church? Seminary Held at Yale Divinity School, New Haven, Conn., April 13-15, 1931. n.p., n.d.   DHU/MO

8028. Wiley, Bell Irvin. Southern Negroes, 1861-1865. New Haven, Conn.: Yale University Press, 1965. CtY; DHU/R
     Chapter 6, Religious life.

8029. Williams, Fannie B. "Religious Duty of the Negro." J. W. Hanson (ed.). The World's Congress of Religions (Chicago: International Publishing Co., 1894), pp. 893-97.   DHU/MO

8030. ----- "What Can Religion Further do to Advance the Condition of the American Negro." John Henry Barrows (ed.). The World's Parliament of Religions (Chicago: The Parliament Publishing Co., 1893), pp. 1114-15.   DHU/R

8031. Williams, George Washington. History of the Negro Race in American from 1619 to 1880. New York: Putnam, 1883.   DHU/R
     Negro author.

8032. Willie, Charles V. The Family Life of Black People. Columbus, Ohio: Merrill, 1970.   MCE

8033. Wilson, Elizabeth L. Minority Groups in Bronx Churches: A Study of the Extent of Participation of Negro Minority Groups in Protestant Churches in the Bronx, New York City. Masters thesis. Columbia University, 1945.

8034. Wilson, Robert L. The Association of Urban Social Areas in Four Cities and the Institutional Characteristics of Local Churches in Five Denominations. Doctoral dissertation. Northwestern University, 1958.
     Includes social rank, urbanization and segregation.

8035. Wolfram, Walter A. and Ralph W. Fosold. "A Black English Translation of John 3:1-21 with Grammatical Annotations." The Bible Translator (20:2, Apr., 1969), pp. 48-54. DHU/R

8036. Woodson, Carter Godwin. The African Background Outlined; or, Handbook for the Study of the Negro. Washington, D.C.: Association for the Study of Negro Life and History, 1936.   DHU/R; NN/Sch
     Negro church, pp. 363-92.
     Negro author.

8037. ----- The History of the Negro Church. Washington, D.C.: The Associated Publishers, 1945. DHU/R; DHU/MO; DLC; OWibfU

8038. ----- The Rural Negro. Washington, D.C.: Association for the Study of Negro Life and History, 1930. DHU/MO; NN/Sch
     Rural Negro Church.

8039. Woofter, Thomas J. The Basis of Adjustment. Boston: Ginn & Co., 1925.
     Negro church, pp. 212-34.

8040. ----- "The Negroes of Athens, Georgia." Phelps-Stokes Fellowship Studies. Bulletin of the University of Georgia. (14:4, 1913).   DHU/MO
     Includes information on the moral and social conditions of the people.

8041. Woolridge, Nancy Bullock. The Negro Preacher in American Fiction Before 1900. Doctoral dissertation. University of Chicago, 1942.

8042. Work, Monroe N. "Contirbutions of Black People to the Kingdom of God." Student World (16; Apr., 1923), pp. 43-45.   CtY; DLC

8043. ----- "Negro Church and the Community." Southern Workman (37; Ag., 1908), pp. 428+.   DHU/MO

8044. ----- "The Negro Church in the Negro Community." Southern Workman (37:7, Jl., 1908), pp. 428-32. DHU/MO

8045. ----- "The Negroes of Warsaw, Georgia." Southern Workman (37:1, Ja., 1908), pp. 29-40.   DLC; DHU/MO
A description of religious life among the Negroes (Geeches)
living along the seacoast of Georgia.

8046. ----- and William E. B. DuBois. "The Negro Ministry in
the Middle West." Hart M. Nelson & Raytha L. Yokley, et
alii. The Black Church in America (New York: Basic Books,
1971), pp. 265-68.   DHU/R
Also in DuBois, W. E. B., The Philadelphia Negro.

8047. Wright, James Martin. ...The Free Negro in Maryland,
1634-1860. New York: Columbia University, 1921. NN/Sch
(Studies in History, Economics and Public Law; ed. by the
faculty of Political Science of Columbia University, V. 97,
no. 3, whole no. 222).
Negro church.

8048. Wright, Richard. 12 Million Black Voices; a Folk History of
the Negro in the United States. New York: The Viking Press,
1941.   DHU/MO; CtY-D
Negro author.

8049. Wright, Richard Robert, Jr., (bp.). "Social Work and Influence of the Negro Church." Annals of the American Academy
(30; Nov. 1907), pp. 509-21.   DHU/R
Negro author.

8050. Wyche, Robert P. "To What Extent is the Negro Pulpit Uplifting the Race?" Daniel W. Culp. Twentieth Century Negro

Literature. (Miami, Fla.: Mnemosyne Publishing Co., Inc.,
1969), pp. 122-24.   DHU/MO
Reprint of 1902 edition.
Negro Presbyterian minister and one-time Moderator of the
Synod of Catawba, N. C.

8051. Wynn, Daniel Webster. "Do Negroes Lack a Sense of Mis-
sion?" Religious Education (59:2, Mr.-Apr., 1964), pp. 168-70.
DHU/R
Negro author.

8052. Yates, Walter L. An Analysis of the Influence of War Service upon the Religious Views of Eight Hundred Negro Ex-ser-
vice Men in the District of Columbia, United States of America,
World War II. Master's thesis. Howard University, 1947.

8053. ----- "The God-consciousness of the Black Church in Histor-
ical Perspective." James J. Gardiner and J. Deotis Roberts,
Sr. (eds.). Quest for a Black Theology (Philadelphia: United
Church Press, 1971), pp. 44-61.   DHU/MO; DHU
DHU/R

8054. Yinger, J. Milton. Religion, Society and the Individual. New
York: The Macmillan Co., 1957.   DHU/R

8055. Young, Viola Mae. Little Helps for Pastors and Members.
Rosebud, Ala.: n.p., 1909.   NN/Sch
Negro author.

5. Activities of Negro Clergy and Laity

8056. Alexander, William T. History of the Colored Race in
America. New Orleans: Palmetto, 1888.   DHU/MO

8057. Allen, Helen Bernice. The Minister of the Gospel in Negro
American Fiction. Masters thesis. Fisk University, 1937.

8058. Allen, Richard. "Address to the Public, and People of
Colour." Dorothy B. Porter (ed.). Early Negro Writing,
1760-1837 (Boston: Beacon, 1971), pp. 414-26. DHU/MO
An address which accompanied the confession of a convicted
murderer, John Joyce, alias David, and the account of his
trial in 1808.

8059. [Allen, Richard, (bp.).] Confession of John Joyce, Alias
David, Who Was Executed on Monday, the 14th of March 1808.
For the Murder of Mrs. Sarah Cross; With an Address to the
Public, and People of Colour, Together With the Substance of
the Trial, and the Address of Chief Justice Tilghman, on His
Condemnation (Philadelphia: Printed for the Benefit of Bethel
Church, 1808).   DLC

8060. Alleyne, Cameron Chesterfield, (bp.). Our Pilgrim Vanguard. n.p., 1950.   NcSalL

8061. ----- (bp.). Religion and its Requirements. n.p., n.d.
NcSalL

8062. ----- The Negro Faces Christianity. n.p., 1946. NcSalL
Negro author.

8063. Anderson, E. Hutts. Adjustment. New York: Carlton Press,
1965.   DHU/MO
A religious treatise.
Negro author.

8064. Apsey, Lawrence S. and Elinore Atlee. "Defusers of Violence." Friends Journal (13:13, Jl. 1, 1967), pp. 351-52.
DHU/R

8065. Arnett, Benjamin William, (bp.). Biennial Oration Before
the Second B. M. C. of the Grand United Order of Odd Fellows.
Cincinnati, October 10, 1884. Dayton: n.p., 1884. NN/Sch

8066. ----- (bp.). The Black Laws! Speech of...of Greene
County, in the Ohio House of Representatives. March 10, 1886.
n.p.: n.p., n.d.   OWibfU

8067. ----- (bp.). The Centennial Jubilee of Freedom at Columbus,
Ohio, Saturday, September 22, 1888. Historical Oration published by B. W. Arnett. Xenia, Ohio: n.p., 1888.   NN/Sch

8068. ----- (bp.). Centennial Thanksgiving Sermon, Delivered by
...at St. Paul A. M. E. Church, Urbana, Ohio. Urbana:
n.p., 1876.   DLC; OWibfU

8069. ----- (bp.). Duplicate Copy of the Souvenir from the Afro-
American League of Tennessee to Hon. James M. Ashley of
Ohio. Philadelphia: A. M. E. Publishing House, 1894. NcD

8070. ----- (bp.). "The Northwest Territory." Address at the
Music Hall, Chicago, October 11, 1899. Ohio Archaeological
and Historical Quarterly. (8, 1908), pp. 433-64. NcD; DLC
Negro author.

8071. ----- (bp.). The Poetical Works of James Madison Bell.
Lansing: Press of Wynkoop, Hallenbeck, Crawford Co., 1904?
DLC; NN; OWibfU

8072. ----- (bp.). "Remarks of Rev. B. W. Arnett." Ohio
Archaelogical and Historical Publications (2; 1889), pp. 141-44.
NcD

8073. ----- (bp.), and J. M. Ashley. "Addresses of Bishop B. W.
Arnett and the Hon. J. M. Ashley." J. H. Barrows, (ed.).
The World's Parliament of Religions. V. II (Chicago: Parlia-
ment Publishing Co., 1893), pp. 1101-04.   DHU/R

8074. Avery, William Anthony. "Better Education for Negro Rural
Ministers." Southern Workman (49:10, Oct., 1920), pp. 458-
67.   DLC; DHU/MO

8075. Baldwin, James. "Babriel's Prayer." Nick Aaron Ford
(ed.). Black Insights: Significant Literature by Black Amer-
icans--1760 to the Present. (Waltham, Mass.: Ginn and Co.,
1971.   DHU/R
Fictional excerpt form the novel, GO TELL IT ON THE
MOUNTAIN.

8076. -----. Go Tell It on the Mountain. New York: Knopf, 1953.
DHU/R; DHU/MO
Negro author.
Fiction on Negro preacher.

8077. Ballou, Hosea. An Epistle to the Reverend Lemuel Haynes;
Containing a Brief Reply to His Sermon Delivered at West Rut-
land, June, 1805, Designed to Refute the Doctrine of Universal
Salvation (Schenectady, N. Y.: Ryer Schermerhorn, 1807).
NN/Sch

8078. Banks, William L. Jonah, Verse by Verse. New York: Vantage Press, 1963.   DHU/MO
Negro author.

8079. Bardolph, Richard. The Negro Vanguard. New York: Vintage Books, 1961.   DHU/R
Includes biographies of ministers.

8080. Barham, J. E. C. Life of Dr. J. E. C. Barham and an
Original Exposition of Bible Baptism. Wilmington, Del.:
R. B. Jevay, 1917.   O WibfU

8081. Baxter, Daniel Minort. Richard Allen From a Slave Boy to
the First Bishop of African Methodist Epidcopal Church 1760-
1816. A Drama in Four Acts. Philadelphia: A. M. E Book
Concern, 1934.   DHU/MO

8082. Bayley, Solomon. "Narrative and Letters." William
Armistead (ed.). A Tribute for the Negro: Being a Vindication
of the Moral, Intellectual, and Religious Capabilities of the
Colored Portion of Mankind... (Conn.: Negro Univ. Press,
1848), pp. 513-23.   DHU/R
Slave, writer and minister.

8083. Bayliss, John F., ed. Black Slave Narratives. New York:
Macmillan, 1970.   DHU/R
Includes three slaves who became ministers: Henry Bibb,
James W. C. Pennington and Josiah Henson.

8084. Beasley, Delilah L. The Negro Trail Blazers of California.
Los Angeles, Cal.: Times Mirror Printing and Binding House,
1919.   DHU/MO
Includes biographies of local ministers.

8085. Beckett, Lemuel Morgan. True Worshippers. A Sermon.
Anacostia, D.C.: n.p., 1911.   DHU/MO
Negro author.

8086. Belk, Leotis S. "How are You Dying: A Sermon." Freeing
the Spirit (3:1, Spr., 1974), pp. 37-40. DHU/R
Sermon by associate professor of Philosophical Theology,
Colgate Rochester Divinity School and faculty consultant for
the Martin Luther King Program in Black Church Studies.

8087. Bell, Barbara L. Black Bibliographical Sources: An Annotated Bibliography. New Haven, Conn.: Reference Dpt., Yale
University Library, 1970.   DLC; InU

8088. Bernstein, Leonard. "The Participation of Negro Delegates
in the Constitutional Convention of 1868 in North Carolina."
Journal of Negro History (34; Oct., 1949), pp. 391-409.
DHU/MO
Bishop James W. Hood of the A. M. E. Zion Church was
participant.

8089. Billingsley, Andrew. "Edward Blyden: Apostle of Blackness." The Black Scholar (2:4, Dec. 1970), pp. 3-12. DHU/R
Negro author.

8090. Bishop, Shelton Hale. The Romance of the Negro, by the Rev.
S. H. Bishop. New York: n.p., 1910.   NN/Sch
Detached from the Spirit of Missions (75:3, Mr., 1910).

8091. ----- The Wonder of Prayer. Greenwich, Conn.: Seabury
Press, 1959.   DHU/MO;
NN/Sch

8092. "Black Lilly." The Church at Home and Abroad (3; Ja.,
1888), pp. 62-64.   DHU/R
Tribute to the faith of a daughter of a slave.

8093. Blackson, Lorenzo D. The Rise and Progress of the King-
doms of Light and Darkness, or the Reign of Kings, Alpha and
Abadon. Philadelphia: J. Nichols 1967.   DHU/R
Negro author.

8094. Blackwell, George L., (bp.). Cloaks of Sin. n.p., 1904.
NcSa1L

8095. ----- (bp.). Man Wanted. n.p., 1907.   NcSa1L

8096. ----- (bp.). Model Homestead. Boston: Marshall
Printers, 1893.   NcSa1L

8097. Blassingame, James W. "Negro Chaplains in the Civil
War." Negro History Bulletin (27:1, Oct., 1963), pp. 24+.
DHU/MO

8098. Blyden, Edward Wilmot. "The Call of Providence to the
Descendants of Africa in America." Howard Brotz, (ed.).
Negro Social and Political Thought. (New York: Basic Books,
1950), pp. 112+.   DHU/R
Negro author.

8099. ----- Jewish Question. Liverpool: Hart, 1898. NUC;
PPDrop; PPULC

8100. ----- Philip and the Church. Cambridge: John Wilson and
Son, 1883.   DHU/MO

8101. Boddie, Charles Emerson. God's "Bad Boys." Valley
Forge: Judson Press, 1972.   DHU/R; MiBsA; MNtcA; TSewU-T
Biographical sketches of eight ministers including Martin
Luther King, Jr.

8102. Bontemps, Arna W. Five Black Lives, the Autobiographies
of Venture Smith, James Mars, William Grimes, the Rev. G.
W. Offley, James L. Smith. Middletown: Conn.: Wesleyan
University Press, 1971.   DHU/MO
Includes, A Narrative of the Life and Labors of the Rev.
G. W. Offley.
Negro author.

8103. Borders, William Holmes, Sr. God is Real. Atlanta, Ga.:
Fuller Press, 1951.   DHU/MO

8104. ----- "Handicapped Lives." William M. Philpot,
(ed.). Best Black Sermons (Valley Forge: Judson Press,
1972), pp. 18-24.   DHU/R
A sermon.
Baptist minister.

8105. ----- Men Must Live as Brothers. Twenty Sermons Which
Were First Preached in the Wheat Street Baptist Church,
Atlanta. Atlanta, Ga.: n.p., 1947.   DLC
Negro author.

8106. ------ Sermons. Philadelphia: Dorance and Company,
1939.   DHU/MO; DLC

8107. ----- Seven Minutes at the "Mike" in the Deep South.
Atlanta: B. F. Logan Press, 1943.   DHU/MO; DLC

8108. ----- Thunderbolts. Atlanta, Ga.: B. F. Logan Press,
1943.   SCBHC

8109. ----- Twenty-Fifth Pastoral Anniversary of Rev. & Mrs.
William Holmes Borders, 1937-1962. n.p., n.d. DLC;
DHU/MO; NN/Sch
"Wheat Street Baptist Church, Atlanta, Ga."

8110. ----- What Is That in Thine Hand? and Other Sermons.
n.p., n.d.
Negro author.

8111. Bowen, John Wesley Edward, (ed.). Africa and the American Negro. Addresses and Proceedings of the Congress on Africa Held Under the Auspices of the Stewart Foundation for Africa, December 13-15, 1895. Atlanta, Ga.: 1896. DHU/R
Negro author.

8112. ----- "A Psychological Principle in Revelation." Methodist Review (73; 1891), pp. 227-39.   DHU/R; DLC
Negro author.

8113. ----- What Shall the Harvest Be? A National Sermon, or a Series of Plain Talks to the Colored People of America, on Their Problems, by the Rev. J. W. E. Bowen... in the Asbury Methodist Episcopal Church, Washington, D.C. n.p., n.d.
NN/Sch; DHU/MO

8114. Bragg, George Freeman. A Bond Slave of Christ. Entering the Ministry Under Great Difficulties. n.p., n.d. DHU/MO
Negro author.

8115. ----- The Hero of Jerusalem. In Honor of the One Hundredth Anniversary of the Birth of General William Mahone of Virginia. Baltimore: The Author, n.d.
DHU/MO

8116. ----- Men of Maryland. Baltimore, Md.: Church Advocate Press, 1914.   DHU/MO

8117. ----- Richard Allen and Absalom Jones. Baltimore, Md.: The Church Advocate Press, 1915.   DHU/MO; NN/Sch

8118. ----- Seven Speeches and Sermons and a Tribute to Mrs. Nellie G. Bragg, by the Rev. George F. Bragg, Jr... Baltimore: n.p., 1917-37.   NN/Sch

8119. Brawley, Benjamin Griffin. Early Negro American Writers. Freeport, N.Y.: Books for Libraries Press, 1968. DHU/R
Negro author.

8120. ----- History of the English Hymn. New York: Abingdon Press, 1932.   DHU/R

8121. Bright, John Douglas, Sr. "Speech Delivered by Bishop John D. Bright of the Twelfth Episcopal District." The African Methodist Episcopal District." The African Methodist Episcopal Church Review (80:220, Apr.-Je., 1964), pp. 28-31. DHU/R
Negro author.

8122. Brooks, Walter H. The Pastor's Voice. Washington, D.C.: The Associated Press, 1945.   DHU/R
Negro author.

8123. Brooks, William E. From Saddlebags to Satellites. Nashville: Parthenon Press, 1969.   ISAR

8124. Brown, Annie E. Religious Work and Travels. Chester, Pa.: O. T. Pancoast, 1909.   NN/Sch

8125. Brown, Catharine S. Memoir of Rev. Abel Brown, By His Companion... Worcester: The Author, 1849.   O

8126. Brown, Ethelred E. "The God of an Eternal Penitentiary." The Messenger (6; Je., 1923).   IC/H
Exposition by a Negro minister denying the concept of eternal hell as a part of Christian theology.

8127. ----- Jesus of Nazareth the World's Greatest Religious Teacher was Unitarian... A Sermon Delivered on Sunday Evening, March 14, 1943... at the Harlem Unitarian Church. New York: n.p., n.d.   DHU/MO
Negro author.

8128. Brown, Sterling N. Bible Mastery. Washington, D.C.: Merchant's Printing Co., 1907.   OWibfU

8129. Brown, William Wells. The Black Man, His Antecedents, His Genius and His Achievements. Miami, Fla.: Mnemsoyne Pub. Co., 1969.   DHU/R

8130. Browne, Hosea H. A Study in Pastoral Care of a Selected Number of Adults and Adolescents in a Children's Center Utilizing the Approach of Russell L. Dicks. Doctoral dissertation. Howard University, 1973.
Negro author.

8131. Bruce, John Edward, comp. Short Biographical Sketches of Eminent Negro Men and Women in Europe and the United States. With Extracts from their Writing and Public Utterances. Yonkers, N.Y.: Gazette Press, 1910.   DHU/MO

8132. "The Building of a Church." (letter to the editor). Southern Workman (16:10, Oct., 1887), p. 101.   DHU/MO; DLC
An account of how a Hampton Institute graduate, a minister raised funds to build a high school and a church.

8133. Bullock, Ralph W. In Spite of Handicaps; Brief Biographical Sketches with Discussion Outlines of Outstanding Negroes Now Living Who Are Achieving Distinction in Various Lines of Endeavor... with a Foreword by Channing H. Tobias. New York: Associated Press, 1927.   DHU/MO

8134. Bunton, Henry C., (bp.). The Challenge to Become Involved in the Drama of Restoration. n.p., 1966. Pam. File; DHU/R
Negro author.

8135. Burgess, Lois F. No Boot Straps. n.p., 1965. DHU/MO
Negro author.

8136. Burroughs, Nannie Helen. Making Your Community Christian. Washington, D.C.: Woman's Convention, n.d.   DHU/MO
Negro author.

8137. ----- What Do You Think? Washington, D.C.: n.p., 1950.
NN/Sch

8138. Cade, Toni. The Black Woman. New York: New American Library, 1970.   MCE

8139. Caldwell, Ben. "Prayer Meeting, or the First Militant Minister." LeRoi Jones and Larry Neal (eds.). Black Fire, An Anthology of Afro-American Writing (New York: William Morrow and Co., 1968), pp. 589-94.   DHU/MO
One act play with two black characters, a minister and a burglar.
Negro author.

8140. Caldwell, Josiah S., (bp.). "Greatest Need of the Negro Race." W. N. Hartshorn, An Era of Progress and Promise (Boston: Priscilla Pub. Co., 1910), pp. 399+.

8141. Cannon, Noah Caldwell. A Call to Sinners. (A Sermon) Rochester: n.p., 1842.   MBAt
Written by a Negro A. M. E. minister.

8142. ----- Truth. Instruction to Youth. Seek Ye After Knowledge. Rochester: C. S. McConnell & Co., 1843.
DHU/MO; NN/Sch

8143. Carr, Augustus T. "A Resolution Reference to Simon Miller." The African Methodist Episcopal Church Review (78:216, Apr.-Je., 1963), pp. 24-26+.   DHU/R
Negro author.

8144. Carr, Warren. "Notes From an Irrelevant Clergyman." Christian Century (80:28, Jl. 10, 1963), pp. 879-88. DHU/R
"Discovery that laymen are ready to take moral stands in advance of their churches."

8145. Carrington, William Orlando. Carry a Little Honey, and Other Addresses. New York: Fleming H. Revell Co., 1936.
DHU/R; NN/Sch
Negro author.

8146. ----- "Uplifted Desires." G. Paul Butler, (ed.). Best Sermons (New York: Harper & Brothers, Pubs., 1946). pp. 201-09.   DHU/R
Minister of First A. M. E. Zion Church, Brooklyn, N.Y.
Negro author.

8147. Carroll, J. C. The Conquering Mission of Man. A Sermon.
n p.: Published by Vernon Johns and J. Raymond Henderson,
n d.   DHU/MO
Negro Pulpit Opinion.
Negro author.

8148. Carter, Edward Randolph. Biographical Sketches of Our
Pulpit. Chicago: Afro-American Press, 1969. IC/H; PPT;
GAU; NN/Sch; DHU/MO
Reprint of 1888 edition.
Baptists Negro Ministers in Georgia.

8149. Carter, Randall Albert, (bp.). Feeding Among the Lilies.
Cincinnati: Caxton Press, 1923.   NN/Sch; DHU/MO; DHU/R
Negro author.

8150 ----- (bp.). Gathered Fragments. Nashville: The Parthenon
Press, 1939.   DHU/MO; NN/Sch

8151. ----- (bp.). Morning Meditations and Other Selections. Atlanta: Foote & Davis Co., 1917.   NN/Sch; DHU/MO

8152. ----- (bp.). "Whence and Whither?" Carter G. Woodson.
Negro Orators and Their Orations (New York: Russell &
Russell, 1969), pp. 626-36.   DHU/R
Bishop of the C. M. E. Church.

8153. Chappelle, E. E. The Voice of God. New York: Carlton
Press, Inc., 1963.   DHU/MO
Inspirational sermons.

8154. Chisholm, Frank P. "Documents." Journal of Negro History
(5; Apr., 1920), p. 235.   DHU/MO
"A letter of confirmation on Bishop Hood's active participation
in the framing of the Constitution for North Carolina, 1867-
68 and his position as Assistant Superintendent of Public
Instruction of the state of North Carolina.
A. M. E. Zion bishop.

8155. Church, Roberta. "In the Steps of Her Father." Ebony
(14; My., 1959), pp. 61-2.   DHU/R; DHU/MO
Roberta Church, daughter of Robert R. Church, Jr. a Tenn.
politician, was Minority Group's Consultant for Department
of Labor and a member of Memphis' Emmanuel Episcopal
Church, founded in her great-aunt's parlor.

8156. Clark, Davis Wasgatt, (bp.). Life and Times of Rev. Elijah
Hedding... By Rev. D. W. Clark, D.D. With an introduction by
Rev. Bishop E. S. Janes. New York: Carlton & Phillips, 1856.
                                                    NN/Sch

8157. Clark, Robert Donald. The Life of Matthew Simpson. New
York: Macmillan, 1958.   NN/Sch

8158. Cleaver, Eldridge. Soul on Ice. New York: McGraw-Hill,
1968.   DHU/R
pp. 30-39 his religious convictions.
Negro author.

8159. Clement, Goerge W. (bp.). Boards for Life's Building.
...Introduction by Rev. Thos. W. Wallace... Cincinnati, O.:
Pr. for the Author by The Caxton Press, 1924. NN/Sch; DHU/MO

8160. Clinton, George W. (bp.). Christianity Under the Search-
light. Nashville, Tenn.: National Baptist Pub. Board, 1909.
                                                    NN/Sch
Negro author.

8161. ----- (bp.). The Three Alarm Cries. n.p., 1906. NcSalL

8162. ----- (bp.). Tuskegee Lectures. n.p., 1907. NcSalL

8163. ----- (bp.). A Voice From the South. n.p., n.d. NcSalL

8164. Cobbs, Therion E. "Facing the Future." The African Methodist Episcopal Church Review (92:235, Apr.-Je., 1968), pp.
38-39.   DHU/R
Negro author.

8165. Coke, Thomas, (bp.). Journal & Address, etc. London:
1789-1790.   NN/Sch
Information about Harry Hoosier, known as "Black Harry"
a preacher.

8166. Coker, Daniel. A Dialogue Between a Virginian and an African Minister ... Baltimore: Printed by Benjamin Edes, 1810.
                                        DHU/MO; DHU/R
Also: Dorothy Porter. Negro Protest Pamphlets: a Compendium. N.Y.: Arno Press, 1969.   DHU/MO

8167. Cole, S. W. R. Sermons Outlined. 9th ed. Nashville:
National Baptist Publishing Board, 1940.   SCBHC
Bound with it: J. P. Robinson's Sermons and Sermonettes.

8168. Collins, J. G. Practical Theology. New York: Comet Press
Books, 1960.   DHU/MO
Inspirational essays.
Negro author.

8169. Confessions of a Negro Preacher. Chicago: The Cantebury
Press, 1928.   DHU/MO
Anonymous.

8170. Conner, James Mayer. Elements of Success. Philadelphia:
A. M. E. Book Concern, 1911.   NNSch

8171. ----- Outlines of Christian Theology; or Theological Hints.
Little Rock, Ark.: Brown, 1896.   OWibfU
Negro author.

8172. Cooper, Anna Julia. Life and Writings of the Grimke Family.
n.p.: n.p., 1951.   NN/Sch; DHU/MO
Negro author.

8173. ----- A Voice From the South. By a Black Woman of
the South. Xenia: Aldine, 1892.   DHU/MO; OWibfU
Reprinted by Negro Universities Press, 1969.
Written by a Negro layman of the A. M. E. Church.

8174. Cooper, William A. The Awakening Sermons and Sermonettes on Special Occasions. New York: Exposition Press, 1963.
                                                    DHU/MO

8175. Coppin, Fanny Miriam (Jackson). Reminiscences of School
Life and Hints on Teaching. Philadelphia: A. M. E. Book Con-
cern, 1913.   OWibfU
Written by wife of thirteenth bishop of the A. M. E. Church,
Rev. Levi Jenkins Coppin.

8176. Coppin, Levi Jenkins, (bp.). Fifty-two Suggestive Sermon
Syllabi. Philadelphia: AME Book Concern, 1910. OWibfU;
DHU/MO
Negro author.

8177. ----- (bp.). In Memoriam. Catherine S. Campbell Beckett.
n.p.: n.p., 1888.   NcD; OWibfU
Negro author.

8178. ----- (bp.). The Key to Scriptural Interpretation; or Expository Notes on Obscure Passages. Philadelphia: AME Publishing House, 1895.   OWibfU
Negro author.

8179. ----- (bp.). "The Negro's Part in the Redemption of Africa."
Alice Ruth Nelson. Masterpieces of Negro Eloquence (New York:
The Bookery Publishing Company, 1914), pp. 243-50. DHU/MO
Also: African Methodist Episcopal Church Review (19:2, Oct.,
1902), pp. 10-13.   DHU/MO

8180. Corrothers, James David. In Spite of the Handicap; and
Autobiography... With an Introduction by Ray Stannard Baker.
New York
Negro author.

8181. Coston, William Hilary. The Spanish-American War Volunteer: Ninth United States Volunteer Infantry Roster and Muster,
Biographies, Cuban Sketches. Middleton, Pa.: The Author,
1899.   DLC; DHU/MO; OWibfU; NN/Sch

8182. Councill, William Hooper. Synopsis of Three Addresses Delivered at the Waterloo, Iowa, July 10, 14, 15; Chautauqua Assembly at Spirit Lake, Iowa, July 11-12; and at State Normal
School of Iowa at Cedar Falls, July 15, 1900. n.p., 1900.
                                                    NN/Sch
       Negro author.

8183. Crapsey, Algernon Sidney. ...The Last of the Heretics.
New York: Knopf, 1924.   NN/Sch
       About St. Philips P. E. Church, New York City.

8184. Crite, Allan Rohan. All Glory; Brush Drawing Meditations on
the Prayer of Consecration. Cambridge, Mass.: Society of
St. John the Evangelist, 1947.   DHU/MO; NN/Sch
       Negro illustrator.

8185. Crogman, William H. The Negro: His Needs and Claims.
Atlanta: n.p., 1883.   IEG

8186. ----- Talks for the Times. Freeport, N.Y.: Books
for Libraries Press, 1971.   DHU/R
       Reprint of 1896 edition. Written by Negro professor of Greek
       and Latin at Clark University, Atlanta, Georgia.
       Includes "Christian scholars for Negro Pulpits", pp. 289-312.

8187. Crummell, Alexander. The Black Woman of the South, Her
Neglects and Her Needs. n.p.: n.p., n.d. DHU/MO; NN/Sch
       Negro author.

8188. ----- "The Black Woman of the South: Her Neglects and
Her Needs." Alice Ruth Nelson. Masterpieces of Negro
Eloquence: The Best Speeches Delivered By the Negro
From the Days of Slavery to the Present Time (New York: The
Bookery Publishing Company, 1914), pp. 159-72. DHU/MO;
NN/SCH

8189. ----- Civilization the Primal Need of the Race.
Washington, D.C.: The Academy, 1898.   DHU/MO
       (American Negro Academy Occasional Papers, No. 3.)
       Negro author.

8190. ----- Common Sense in Common Schooling. A Sermon...
n.p., n.d.   DHU/MO
       Negro author.

8191. ----- "Communicated." William Armistead, (ed.). A Tribute for the Negro: Being a Vindication of the Moral, Intellectual,
and Religious Capabilities of the Colored Portion of Mankind.
(Conn.: Negro Univ. Press, 1848), pp. 479-90.   DHU/R
       Black Episcopal Clergyman.

8192. ----- The Greatest of Christ and Other Sermons. New York:
Thomas Whittaker, 1992.   NN/Sch; DHU/R
       Negro author.

8193. ----- The Man, the Hero, the Christian; a Eulogium on
Thomas Clark. 2nd ed. London: Houlston and Stoneman, 1849.
                                       OWibfU
       Negro author.

8194. ----- The Race-Problem in America. Washington, D.C.:
W. R. Morrison, 1889.   DHU/MO
       Negro author.

8195. ----- "The Solution of Problems, the Duty and Destiny of
Man." A. M. E. Church Review (April, 1898).   NN/Sch

8196. Cuffe, Paul. A Brief Account... Contains also: Peter
Williams, a Discourse...; Daniel Coker, Journal of Daniel
Coker; D. H. Peterson, The Looking Glass; Nancy Prince,
A Narrative... New York: S. Wood, 1812. Kraus Reprint,
1970.   INU; DLC
       Negro author.

8197. Dabney, Wendell P. Cincinnati's Colored Citizens: Historical,
Sociological and Biographical. New York: Negro Universities
Press, 1970.   DHU/R
       Originally published in 1926 by the Dabney Publishing Co.
       Short biographies of Negro Ministers included.

8198. Daniel, Everard W. The Church on Trial: A Sermon Preached
Before the Conference of Church Workers Among Colored People.
Philadelphia: n.p., 1916.   NN/Sch
       Negro author.

8199. Daniels, Henry E. Scraps Gathered in My Workshop. Tampa:
Tampa Bulletin, 1921.   OWibfU
       African Methodist Episcopal minister.

8200. Dann, Martin E. The Black Press 1827-1890, the Quest for
National Identity. New York: Putnam, 1971.   DHU/MO
       Excerpts from early Negro newspapers and periodicals.

8201. Davis, Daniel W. "Did the American Negro Make, in the
Nineteenth Century, Achievements Along the Lines of Wealth,
Morality, Education, Etc., Commensurate With His Opportun-
ities? If So, What Achievements Did He Make?" Daniel W.
Culp. Twentieth Century Negro Literature (Miami, Fla.:
Mnemosyne Pub. Co., Inc., 1969), pp. 38-41.   DHU/MO
       Reprint of 1902 edition.
       Negro Baptist minister, teacher and poet.

8202. ----- Idle Moments, Containing Emancipation
and Other Poems. Baltimore: Educator of Morgan College,
1895.   OWibfU
       Negro author.

8203. Davis, H. A. "Fundamental Philosophical Problems of
Christian Belief." The African Methodist Episcopal Church
Review (75:200, Apr.-Je., 1959), pp. 39-43.   DHU/R
       Negro author.

8204. Day, Helen Caldwell. Color, Ebony. New York: Sheed &
Ward, 1951.   NN/Sch
       Negro author.

8205. ----- Not Without Tears. New York: Sheed and Ward,
1954.   NN/Sch

8206. D'Elia, Donald J. "Dr. Benjamin Rush and the Negro."
Journal of the History of Ideas. (30:3, Jl.-Sep., 1969), pp.
413-23.   DHU/R

8207. ----- "The Republican Theology of Benjamin Rush."
Pennsylvania History (37; Apr., 1966), pp. 187-203.
                                       DCU/SW; DGW

8208. Derrick, William Benjamin (bp.). Testimony in the United
States Industrial Commission. Reports of the Industrial
Commission on Immigration, Including Testimony With Review
and Digest and Special Reports. Washington, D.C.: Government Printing Office, 1901.   NN/Sch
       The Commission's Report, V. 15. Includes testimony of;
       Bishops Richard R. Wright, Gaines, Grant, Salter and
       Derrick.

8209. Derricks, Cleavant. Crumbs From the Master's Table.
New York: Pageant Press, 1955.   DHU/R
       Negro author.

8210. Detweiler, Frederick G. The Negro Press in the United
States. Chicago: University of Chicago Press, 1922. DHU/MO
       Negro ministers, writers, and periodicals.

8211. Diamond, John C. Jr. "Aulen's Demythologized Interpretation of the Demonic." Journal of the Interdenominational
Theological Center (1:1, Fall, 1973), pp. 21-35.   DHU
       Negro author.

8212. Dickson, Moses. Manual of the International Order of
Twelve Knights and Daughters of Tabor Containing General Laws,
Regulations, Ceremonies, Drills and Landmarks. St. Louis:
A. R. Fleming & Co., 1891.   DHU/MO; MnHi
       Written by A. M. E. minister.

8213. ----- Three Revised Landmarks and Ceremonies of Courts of
Heroines of Jericho. Kansas City, Mo.: M. Dickson, 19-? N
                                       NN/Sch; DLC
       Negro author.

8214. ----- Why You Should Become a Knight and Daughter of Tabor. n.p. :n.p., n.d.   DHU/MO
Written by an A. M. E. minister.

8215. Dillard, James H. "A Christian Philosopher: Booker T. Washington." Southern Workman (54:5, My., 1925), pp. 209-14.   DLC; DHU/MO

8216. Douglass, Frederick. Ceremonies Attending the Unveiling of the Monument Erected to the Memory of Bishop Daniel Alexander Payne, Monday, May 21, 1894. At Laurel Cemetery, Baltimore, Maryland. ...Appendix Sermon by Bishop A. W. Wayman, at the Funeral of Bishop Payne, Preached in Bethel A. M. E. Church, Baltimore, Dec. 5, 1893. n.p., n.d.   DHU/MO
Address by Frederick Douglass, pp. 19-30.
Negro author.

8217. Douglass, William. Sermons Preached. Freeport, N.Y.: Books for Libraries Press, 1971.   PPT; NcD; NN/Sch
Reprint of the 1854 ed. published under title: Sermons Preached at the African Episcopal Church of St. Thomas', Philadelphia.

8218. Douglin, D. "Musings of a Black Missionary." Christian Reader (Ag.-Sept. 18, 1972), p. 12.   DLC

8219. Eddy, Ansel Doane. "Black Jacob," a Monument of Grace. The Life of Jacob Hodges, an African who Died in Canandaigua, N.Y., Feb. 1842... Philadelphia: American Sunday School Union, 1842.   DHU/MO

8220. Elaw, Zilpa. Memoirs of the Life, Relgious Experience, Ministerial Travels and Labours, of Mrs. Zilpa Elaw, An American Female of Colour in London. Published by the Authoress and Sold by T. Dudley, 1846.   DHU/MO

8221. Ellison, John Malcus. They Who Preach. Nashville: Broadman Press, 1956.   DHU/R; NN/Sch
Negro author.

8222. Ewell, John L. A History of the Theological Department of Howard University. Washington, D.C.: Howard University, 1906.   DHU/MO

8223. Faulk, John Henry. Quickened by de Spirit: Ten Negro Sermons. Masters thesis. University of Texas, 1940.

8224. Ferris, William Henry. The African Abroad; or His Evolution in Western Civilization. New Haven: Tuttle, Morehouse and Taylor, 1913.   OWibfU; DHU/MO
Negro author.

8225. Finley, James B. History of the Wyandot Mission. Cincinnati: Wright & Swormstedt, 1840.   NjMD

8226. Fishel, Leslie H. and Benjamin Quarles. Black America: A Documentary History. New York: Morrow, 1970.   DHU/R

8227. Fisher, Miles Mark. "Jobs for Negro Preachers." Opportunity (10:5, My., 1932), pp. 142-43.   DHU/MO
Negro author.

8228. Floyd, Silas Xavier. "The Apostle of the Second Coming." Voice of the Negro (3:6, Je., 1906), p. 441.   DHU/MO
Negro author.

8229. ----- The Gospel of Service, and Other Sermons. Philadelphia: American Baptist Publication Society, 1902.   GAU

8230. Foster, Gustavus L. Uncle Johnson, the Pilgrim of Six Score Years. Philadelphia: Presbyterian Board of Publication, 1867.   Pam. File, NcD

8231. Frazier, Edward Franklin. God and War. n.p., n.d.   DHU/MO
Negro author.

8232. Frazier Thomas R. (Comp.). Afro-American History: Primary Sources, New York: Harcourt Brace Jovanovich, 1971.   MNtcA

8233. Freeman, Thomas Franklin. The Choice of the Pulpit: A Volume of Sermons. New York: The American Press, 1963.   DHU/R
Negro author.

8234. Fuller, Bertha (Mason). The Life Story of Sarah Lue Bostick: A Woman of the Negro Race. Little Rock, Ark., 1949.   Tn/SCHS
Negro layman of Disciples of Christ Church.

8235. Fuller, Thomas Oscar. An Address Delivered at a Mass Meeting Protesting the Persecution of Jews in Germany, November 20, 1938, Ellis Auditorium, Memphis, Tennessee, 1938. n.p.: n.p., n.d.   DHU/MO
Negro Baptist minister.

8236. ----- Banks and Banking. Memphis: Pilcher Printing Co., 1920.   DHU/MO
Written by a Negro Baptist minister.

8237. ----- Notes on Parliamentary Law, Helpful to Persons Active in Organization. Memphis: n.p., 1940. DLC; NF
Written by Black Baptist minister.

8238. ----- Pictorial History of the American Negro. Memphis: Pictorial History, Inc., 1933.   DHU/MO; NN/Sch; ViHa
Negro minister.

8239. Gandy, Samuel L. Prayers of a Chaplain. Petersburg: Virginia State College, 1955.   Pam. File, DHU/R
mim.
Negro author.

8240. ----- "Releasing the Hold of the Ordinary." Daniel G. Hill, (ed.). Well-Springs of Life (Wash., D.C.: Howard University, 1956), pp. 35-39.   DHU/R
A sermon delivered in Andrew Rankin Cahpel, Howard University.

8241. Gardiner, John Sylvester. A Sermon Preached Before the African Society on 14th of July 1812 ... by J.S. Gardiner, Rector of Trinity Church. Boston: Printed by Munroe & Francis, 1810.   MH

8242. Garland, Phyl. "The Unorthodox Ministry of Leon H. Sullivan." Ebony (26:7, My., 1971), pp. 112-20.   DHU/R

8243. Garnet, Henry Highland. A Memorial Discourse; Delivered in the Hall of the House of Representatives, Washington, D.C., on Sabbath, February 12, 1865. With an Introduction by James McCune Smith. Philadelphia: J.M. Wilson, 1865. NN/Sch
Negro author.

8244. Gholson, Edward. Musings of a Minister. Boston: The Christopher Publishing House, 1943.   DHU/MO; NN/Sch
Negro minister.
Poems teaching Christian truth.

8245. Gibbs, Jonathan. The Great Commission, a Sermon Preached Wednesday Evening, October 22, 1856, Before a Convention of Presbyterian and Congregational Ministers, in the Shiloh Presbyterian Church, Cor. Prince and Marion Sts., New York. New York: Daly Printer, 1857.   DHU/MO
Negro Presbyterian minister.

8246. Gilbert, John W. The Problem of the Races. Augusta, Ga.: Georgia Baptist Print, 1904.   DHU/MO
Written by a Negro C. M. E. minister.

8247. Gilbert, Matthew W. "Did the American Negro Prove In the Nineteenth Century, That He is Intellectually Equal to the White Man?" Daniel W. Culp. Twentieth Century Negro Literature. (Miami, Fal.: Mnemosyne Publishing Co., Inc., 1969), pp. 287-90.   DHU/MO

(Gilbert, Matthew W. cont.)
   Reprint of 1902 edition.
   Negro Baptist minister.

8248. Goens, Anna. How God Became Real in Four Years: A
   Spiritual Experience. New York: Exposition Press, 1957.
                                                    DHU/MO
   Negro author.

8249. Gollock, Georgina A. Daughters of Africa. New York: Negro
   University Press, 1969.   PPT
   Reprint of 1932 edition.
   Chapter 12, Leaders in Religious Life.

8250. Gordon, Buford F., (bp.). The Negro in South Bend. n.p.,
   n.d.   NcSalL
   Negro author.

8251. Gordon, Buford F., (bp.). Pastor and People. n.p., 1930.
                                                   NcSalL

8252. ----- (bp.). The Quest of the Restless Souls. n.p., n.d.
                                                   NcSalL

8253. ----- (bp.). Reflections in Prose and Poetry. n.p., n.d.
                                                   NcSalL

8254. ----- (bp.). Teaching for Abundant Living, Teaching Through
   Sharing and Guiding Experience. Boston: The Christopher Pub.
   House, 1936.   DHU/MO; NN/Sch
   Negro author.

8255. Gordon, Charles Benjamin William. Select Sermons. Peters-
   burg, Va.: C. B. W. Gordon and Co., 1889. DHU/MO; NN/Sch;
   DLC; PCC; MNtcA
   Negro Baptist minister.

8256. Granderson, Elizabeth. Church Chatter. New York: Pageant
   Press, 1950.   DHU/MO
   Negro author.

8257. Grant, John Henry. Am I a Christian or Just a Church Member? Which? Nashville, Tenn.: The Author, n.d.,   NN/Sch

8258. Griffith, T. L. "Negroes in the Baptist Denomination."
   Baptist (8; 1927), pp. 872-73+.   SCBHC

8259. Griggs, Sutton E. Pointing the Way. Nashville: Orion
   Pub. Co., 1908.   DHU/MO; CtY; NN
   Written by a Negro Baptist minister.

8260. Grimke, Francis James. "The Battle Must Go On." Crisis
   (XLI; Ag., 1934), pp. 240-41.   DHU/MO

8261. ----- "Christianity Is Not Dependent Upon the Endorsement
   of Men Great in Worldy Wisdom." Washington, D.C.: The
   Author, 1934.   DHU/MO

8262. ----- "Christianity Needs No New Center of Gravity."
   Washington, D.C.: The Author, 1934.   NjPT

8263. ----- "Christ's Program" for the Saving of the World. n.p.,
   n.d.   DHU/MO

8264. ----- Conditions Necessary to Permanent World Peace. A
   Discourse Delivered by the Rev. Francis J. Grimke in the
   Fifteenth Street Presbyterian Church, Washington, D.C., Nov.
   3, 1935. Washington, D.C.: n.p., 1935.   DHU/MO

8265. ----- Divine Fellowship. Washington, D.C.: The Author,
   n.d.   NjPT

8266. ----- "Doctor Toyohiko Kagawa." Pub. by the author, n.d.
                                          DHU/MO; NjPT

8267. ----- Effective Christianity in the Present World Crisis.
   Wash., D.C.: The Author, 1918.   DHU/MO

8268. ----- Eulogy...of the Late Major James E. Walker.
   Washington, D.C.: Mu-So-Lit. Club, 1916.   DHU/MO

8269. ----- Highest Values. Washington, D.C.: The Author,
   n.d.   NjPT

8270. ----- Human Accountability. Pub. by the Author, n.d.
                                           NjPT

8271. ----- The Inheritance Which All Parents May and Ought to
   Leave to Their Children. Delivered in the Fifteenth Street
   Presbyterian Church, Washington, D.C. Washington, D.C.:
   n.p., n.d.   DHU/MO

8272. ----- Italy and Abyssinia. Washington, D.C., n.p., n.d.
                                          DHU/MO

8273. ----- Jews...A Suffering Persecuted People. Washington,
   D.C.: The Author, 1934.   NjPT; DHU/MO

8274. ----- A Look Backward Over a Pastorate of More Than Forty-
   Two Years Over the Fifteenth Street Presbyterian Church,
   Washington, D.C. ...Delivered Oct. 14, 1923. Washington,
   D.C., n.p., 1923.   DHU/MO

8275. ----- Loyalty to One's Church. n.p.: The Author, n.d.
                                          DHU/MO

8276. ----- Man of Nazareth. Washington, D.C.: The Author,
   n.d.   NjPT

8277. ----- The Negro and Political Parties. Washington, D.C.:
   The Author, n.d.   DHU/MO

8278. ----- The New Year. A Discourse Delivered in the 15th
   Street Presbyterian Church, by the Pastor. Washington, D.C.:
   n.p., n.d.   DHU/MO

8279. ----- Obedience to God. Washingtoj, D.C.: The Author, n.d.
                                           NjPT

8280. ----- One Thing Needful. Washington, D.C.: The Author,
   n.d.   DHU/MO

8281. ----- The Paramount Importance of Right Living...Delivered
   in the Fifteenth Street Presbyterian Church, Washington, D.C.
   ...on Men's Day, May 16, 1926, Under the Auspices of Men's
   Progressive Club of the Church. Washington, D.C.: Pub. by
   the Club, 1926.   DHU/MO

8282. ----- Prize Fighting (Four Tracts). Washington, D.C.:
   The Author, n.d.   DHU/MO

8283. ----- A Resemblance and a Contrast Between the American
   Negro and the Children of Israel; or, The Duty of the Negro to
   Contend Earnestly for his Rights Guaranteed under the Constitution ...Delivered in Fifteenth St. Presbyterian Church, Oct.
   12, 1902 in Connection with the Encampment of the Grand Army
   of Washington. n.p., 1902.   DHU/MO; DHU/R
   Also in Woodson, Carter G., Francis James Grimke, Washington, D.C.: Associated Press, 1942.

8284. ----- Rev. "Billy" Sunday's Campaign in Washington, D.C.
   January 6-March 3, 1918... n.p., 1918.   DHU/MO
   Also in Woodson, Carter G., Francis James Grimke.
   Washington, D.C., Associated Press, 1942.

8285. ----- Scotsboro. Washington, D.C.: The Author, n.d.
                                          DHU/MO

8286. ----- "The Second Marriage of Frederick Douglass."
   Journal of Negro History (19; Jl., 1934), pp. 324-29. DHU/MO

8287. ----- Senator Borah and the Negro. Washington, D.C.:
   The Author, n.d.   NjPT

8288. ----- Some Lessons from the Association of President
   William McKinley. Delivered Sept. 22, 1901. Washington,
   D.C.: n.p., 1901. Washington, D.C.: n.p., 1901. DHU/MO

8289. ----- Some Reflections Growing Out of the Recent Epidemic of Influenza that Affected Our City. Washington, D.C.: The Author, 1918.   DHU/MO

8290. ----- Suicide a Self-Murder. Washington, D.C.: The Author. n.d.   DHU/MO

8291. ----- Three Letters Addressed to the New York Independent, Winston Churchill (and) "Billy" Sunday, by Rev. Francis J. Grimke. Washington, D.C.: Press of R. L. Pendleton, 1915.   NN/Sch; DHU/MO

8292. ----- Two Letters Addressed to Rev. Sol. C. Dickey, General Secretary of the Winona Assembly and Bible Conference, Winona Lake, Indiana, and Rev. Charles Everest Granger, Pastor of Cunton Temple Memorial Presbyterian Church. Washington, D.C.: n.p., 1916.   NN/Sch

8293. ----- "Valiant Men and Free." Opportunity (12; Sept., 1934), pp. 276+.   DHU/MO

8294. ----- "Victory for the Allies and The United States a Ground of Rejoicing, of Thanksgiving." Carter G. Woodson. Negro Orators and Their Orations (New York: Russell & Russell, 1969), pp. 690-708.   DHU/MO; DHU/R
      Sermon delivered at 15th St. Presbyterian Church, Washington, D.C., Dec. 24, 1968.
      Also in Carter G. Woodson, Francis James Grimke. Washington, D.C.: Associated Press, 1942.

8295. ----- A Vision of World Wide Peace. A Talk Given to his Weekly Prayer Meeting. Washington, D.C.: n.p., n.d.   DHU/MO

8296. ----- What Is to Be the Real Future of the Black Man in This Country? Washington, D.C.: The Author, 1934. DHU/MO

8297. ----- A Word of Greeting to Colored Soldiers. Washington, D.C.: The Author, 1918.   DHU/MO

8298. ----- A Word of Warning to the Race. Washington, D.C.: n.p., 1927.   DHU/MO

8299. Hall, A. L. The Ancient Mediaeval and Modern Greatness of the Negro. Memphis, Tenn.: n.p., n.d.   SCBHC
      Containing biographical sketches.

8300. Hall, Ernest N. "A Negro Institutional Church." Southern Workman (50; Mr., 1921), pp. 113+. Illus.   DHU/MO

8301. Hamilton, Fayette M., (bp.). John Parrish. Remarks on the Slavery of the Black People: Addressed to the Citizens of the United States, Particularly to Those Who are in Legislative or Executive Stations in the General or State Governments ... Philadelphia: Kimber, Conrad & Co., 1806.   DLC
      Written by C. M. E. bishop.

8302. Hammon, Jupiter. An Evening's Improvement. Shewing, the Necessity of Beholding the Lamb of God... Hartford, Conn.: Aut., 1790?   NH; CSmH; NHi
      Negro author.

8303. ----- A Winter Piece: Being a Serious Exhortation, With a Call to the Unconverted, and... Hartford, Conn.: 1782?   DHU/MO

8304. Hammond, Lilly Hardy. Southern Women and Racial Adjustment. Lynchburg, Va.: J. P. Bell Co., 1917. DHU/MO; NN/Sch

8305. Harding, Vincent. "The Uses of the Afro-American Past." Donald R. Cutler, (ed.). The Religious Situation, 1969 (Boston: Beacon Press, 1969), pp. 829-40.   DHU/R
      Negro author.

8306. ----- "W. E. B. Du Bois and the Black Messianic Vision." Freedomways (9:1, Wint., 1969), pp. 44-58.   DHU/R
      Negro author.

8307. Harlan, Louis R. and John W. Blassingame (eds.). The Booker T. Washington Papers: Chicago: Univ of Illinois Press, 1972. 2 V.   DHU/R
      Contains speeches Booker T. Washington delivered before the Christian Endeavor Society and other religious organizations.

8308. Harper, Frances Ellen (Watkins). Atlanta Offering. Philadelphia: n.p., n.d.   OWibfU; DHU/MO
      Negro woman of Baltimore, anti-slavery and temperance lecturer. Lectured and wrote on many religious subjects.

8309. ----- Idyllis of the Bible. Philadelphia: n.p., 1901.   OWibfU; DHU/MO
      Negro author

8310. ----- Iola Leroy; or Shadows Uplifted. 2nd ed. Philadelphia: n.p., 1892.   OWibfu; DHU/MO

8311. Harris, Marquis LaFayette, (bp.). Life Can Be Meaningful. Boston: Christopher Pub. House, 1951.   NN/Sch; DHU/MO
      Negro author.

8312. Harrison, Samuel. Pittsfield Twenty-Five Years Ago. A Sermon. Delivered in the Second Congregational Church, Pittsfield, Mass., Jan. 11 and 18th, 1874. Pittsfield, Mass.: Chickering & Axtell, 1874.   NH; CtY-D; MWA; CO
      Negro minister.

8313. ----- "Shall a Nation be Born at Once?" A Centennial Sermon, Delivered in the Chapel of the Methodist Episcopal Church, July 2, 1876. Pittsfield, Mass.: Chickering and Axtell, 1876.   NNC; DLC MHi

8314. Harvey, Claire. "The Black Woman: Keeper of the Faith." The Church Woman (35:9, Nov., 1969), pp. 15-18.   Pam. File, DHU/R

8315. Hatch, Margaret L. D. "Selma Still Has Problems." Friends Journal (12:7, Apr. 1, 1966), pp. 171-72.   DHU/R

8316. Haygood, Atticus G. Our Children... Macon & Atlanta, Ga.: John W. Burke & Co., 1876.   DHU/MO
      Negro author.

8317. Hayne, Joseph E. The Amonian or Hamitic Origin of the Ancient Greeks, Cretans, and all the Celtic Races. A Reply to the New York Sun. Brooklyn: Guide Printing and Publishing Co., 1905.   NN/Sch; PP
      Dean of Theology, Allen University, A. M. E. College.
      Negro author.

8318. ----- Are White People of the South the Negroes' Best Friend? Or, the Only Just, Human Methods of Solving Race Problems. Philadelphia: A. M. E. Book Concern, 1903.   OCIWHi

8319. ----- The Black Man; or, the Natural History of the Hametic Race. Raleigh: Edwards and Broughton, 1894.   NcD; NN/Sch; ICJ; OWibfU; DHU/MO

8320. ----- The Colored Men in American Politics. New York: n.p., 1809.   DLC

8321. ----- A Controversy Between a Brother in White and a Brother in Black Touching the Race Question Generally, or: Two Hours of Very Interesting Reading. New York: Caleb and Theyken, 1901.   DHU/MO

8322. ----- Negro in Sacred History; or Ham and his Immediate Descendents and Their Wonderful Achievements. Charleston: Walker, 1887.   NH; DHU/MO; DLC; NN/Sch; TNF; OWibfU

8323. ----- President Taft Measured by His Most Remarkable Speech on the Hamitic Race Question and the Duty of the American People to This Race. Rock Hill, S. C.: The Record Press, 1910.   DLC; NH

8324. Haynes, George Edmund. The Negro at Work in New York City; a Study in Economic Progress. New York: Longmans, Green & Co., 1912.
NcRS; Pu-L; DLC; MiU; OWibfU; NcD; O; NN/Sch
In: Columbia University. Faculty of Political Science, Studies in History, Economic and Public Law (49:3).

8325. Haynes, Lemuel B. The Character and Work of a Spiritual Watchman Described; A Sermon Delivered at Hinesburgh, Feb. 23, 1791, at the Ordination of the Rev. Reuben Parmerlee. Litchfield, Conn.: n.p., 1791.   NH; MWA; RPJCB; NHi
Written by a Negro Congregationalist minister to Negroes and Whites in the eighteenth and nineteenth centuries.

8326. ----- Divine Decrees, an Encouragement to the Use of Means. A Sermon, Delivered at Granville, (N.Y.) June 25, 1805, Before the Evangelical Society, Instituted for the Purpose of Aiding Pious and Needy Young Men in Acquiring Education for the Work of the Gospel Ministry. Utica: Printed by Seward & Williams, 1810.   DHU/MO

8327. ----- An Entertaining Controversy Between Rev. Lemuel Haynes... and Rev. Hosea Ballou... Consisting... of a Sermon by Mr. Haynes Delivered at West Rutland, in the Year 1805, Entitled "Universal Salvation"... Rutland: Reprinted by W. Fay, 1807.   NN/Sch

8328. ----- The Influence of Civil Government on Religion. A Sermon Delivered at Rutland, West Parish, Sept. 4, 1798... At the Annual Freemen's Meeting... Pastor of a Church in Rutland. Rutland, Vermont: Pr. by John Walker, 1798.
DHU/MO

8329. ----- An Interesting Controversy Between Rev. Lemuel Haynes and Rev. Hosea Ballou. Consisting, First, of a Sermon by Mr. Haynes Delivered at West Rutland... Entitled "Universal Salvation"... Second, an Epistle From Mr. Ballou to Mr. Haynes... Third, a Letter of Mr. Haynes to Mr. Ballou... Middlebury: Ovid Miner, 1828.   NN/Sch

8330. ----- Mystery Developed, or Russell Colvin (Supposed to be Murdered) in Full Life; and Stephen and Jesse Boorn (His Convicted Murderers) Rescued From Ignominious Death by Wonderful Discoveries... Hartford, Conn.: William S. Marsh, 1828.   NN/Sch; DHU/MO

8331. ----- The Nature and Importance of True Republicanism: With a Few Suggestions, Favorable to Independence. A Discourse Delivered at Rutland, (Vermont), the Fourth of July, 1801... Rutland: William Fay, Printer, 1801. NN/Sch

8332. ----- "A Sermon Delivered at Rutland." John Peck. A Short Poem Containing a Descant on the Universal Plan... (Phila.: H. Probasco, 1841).   NN/Sch

8333. ----- "A Sermon Delivered at Rutland, West Parish, October 28th, 1804, Occasioned by the Sudden and Much Lamented Death of the Late Rev. Job Swift." [Job Swift.] Discourses on Religious Subjects... (Middlebury, Vt.: Printed by Huntington and Fitch, 1805), pp. 23-32.
DHU/MO; NN/Sch

8334. ----- Universal Salvation, a Very Ancient Doctrine; With Some Account of the Life and Character of the Author. A Sermon Delivered at Rutland, West Parish in the Year 1805. Boston: Pr. by David Carlisle, 1807.   DHU/MO

8335. ----- "Ye Shall Not Surely Die;" a Short Sermon. n.p.: [The American Tract Society, 1805.]   DHU/MO; NN/Sch

8336. Heacock, Roland T. "Jim Crow Christianity." Southern Workman (63:8, Ag., 1934), pp. 237-42.   DLC; DHU/MO
Negro Congregational minister.

8337. Hearn, Winifred and Betty Stone. "Course in Nonviolence." Friends Journal (10:21, Nov. 1, 1964), pp. 500-01.   DHU/R

8338. Helton, Charles L. "The Tragic in Black Historical Experience." The Duke Divinity School Review (38:2, Spr., 1973),

pp. 78-87.   Pam. File, DHU/R
Written by a Black Seminarian at Duke Divinity School.

8339. Henderson, George W. "Its Colored Ministry: Its Functions and its Opportunities," Southern Workman (33:3, Mr., 1904), pp. 174-77.   DLC; DHU/MO
Written by Rev. George W. Henderson, Dean of the Theological Dept. of Straight Univ., New Orleans.

8340. ----- Studies Upon Important Themes in Religion and Expositions of Difficult Passages of the Scripture. Philadelphia: A. M. E. Book Concern, 1917.   OWibfU

8341. Henry, Caleb Sprague. Politics and the Pulpit: A Series of Articles Which Appeared in the Journal of Commerce and in the Independent During the Year 1850. To Which is Added an Article From the Independent of Feb. 21, 1850, Entitled "Shall We Compromise?" New York: W. Harned, 1851.
NNCor

8342. Henry, Romiche. A Question of Life. New York: Vantage Press, 1963.   DHU/MO
Negro author.

8343. Henson, Josiah. Father Henson's Story of His Own Life. Boston: John P. Jewett & Co., 1858.

8344. Hill, Charles Leander, (tr.). The Communes of Philip Melanchthon... With a Critical Introduction by the Translator... Boston: Meador Publishing Co., 1944.   DHU/MO

8345. ----- The Evangel in Ebony. Boston: Meador Publishing Co., 1960.   DHU/R
A book of sermons.
Negro author.

8346. ----- "The Life of George W. Carver, a Pattern for Christian Living." A. M. E. Church Review (70:182, Oct.-Dec., 1954), pp. 31-36.   DHU/R

8347. ----- "Prophetic Hour." A. M. E. Church Review (68:172, Apr.-Je., 1952), pp. 35-40.   DHU/R
A. M. E. minister

8348. Hill, Daniel Grafton. "Facing the Challenges of Life." The African Methodist Episcopal Church Review (78:216, Apr.-Je., 1963), pp. 54-59.   DHU/R
Former Dean of Howard University School of Religion.
Negro author.

8349. ----- Well-Springs of Life (and other Addresses to College Youth) Delivered at All University Religious Services in Andrew Rankin Memorial Chapel, Howard University. Washington, D.C.: n.p., n.d.   DHU/R; DHU/MO; NN/Sch

8350. Hill, John Louis. When Black Meets White. Cleveland: The Argyle Pub. Co., 1924.   DHU/MO
Religion, pp. 60-80.

8351. Hill, Leslie Pinckney. The Wings of Oppression. Boston: Strafford Co., 1921.   OWibfU
Negro author.

8352. Holly, James Theodore, (bp.). The Word of God Against Ecclesiastical Imperialism. 1880.   OWibfU
In Arnette Papers, V. 76.

8353. Holsey, Lucius Henry, (bp.). Little Gems. Atlanta: Franklin, 1905.   OWibfU
Bishop of the C. M. E. Church.

8354. Hood, James Walker, (bp.). The Plan of the Apocalypse. York, Pa.: Anstadt & Sons, 1900.   NcSalL
Negro author.

8355. ----- (bp.). "Son Remember---Them---Now." Levi Branson, (ed.). North Carolina Sermons. V. 2 (Raleigh: Branson House, 1886), pp. 19-27.   NcD
A sermon.

8356. ----- (bp.). Speech of Rev. James W. Hood of Cumberland County, on the Question of Suffrage, Delivered in the Constitutional Convention of North-Carolina, February 12th, 1868. Raleigh: W. W. Holden & Son, 1868.   OClWHi, NcU

8357. ----- (bp.). "Will it Be Possible for the Negro to Attain in this Country, Unto the American Type of Civilization." Daniel W. Culp. Twentieth Century Negro Literature (Atlanta, Ga.: Nicholson, 1902), pp. 51-56.   DHU/MO
Includes biography and picture of the author.

8358. Hopkins, T. Ewell. The Junior Church. Bachelors thesis. Washington, D.C.: Howard University, 1938.
Negro author.

8359. "How the Stars See God." Ebony (14: Apr., 1959), pp. 101-02.   DHU/MO

8360. Hughes, Langston. The Gospel Glory. A Passion Play. New York: n.p., 1962.   NN/Sch
Negro author.

8361. Hurst, John, (bp.). "Christianity and Women." The Crisis (10:4, Ag., 1915), pp. 179-80.   DLC; DHU/MO

8362. Imes, George Lake. I Knew Carver. Harrisburg, Pa.: J. Horace McFarland Co., 1943.   DHU/MO
Written by a Black Presbyterian minister.

8363. ----- "Negro Ministers and Country Life." Religious Education (7:2, Je., 1912), pp. 169-75.   DHU/R
Negro author.

8364. ----- Remember Booker T. Washington... An Address Delivered Before the Teachers and Students of the Tuskegee Normal and Industrial Institute. n.p.: n.p., 1917. DHU/MO

8365. Imes, William Lloyd. "Faith Versus Success." Daniel A. Poling (ed.). A Treasury of Great Sermons. (New York: Greenberg, 1944), pp. 181-85.   DHU/MO
Written by Black Presbyterian minister.

8366. ----- God's Guiding Hand in Our History: A Sermon for the Dundee Centennial. New York: Dundee Observer, 1947.   DHU/MO
Written by a Negro Presbyterian minister.

8367. ----- Integrity. Meditations on the Book of Job. Nashville: Westminster Press, 1939.   DHU/R
From Today (8:2, My., 1939).

8368. ----- The Negro in Tennessee Before the Civil War, A Sociological Study. Masters thesis. Fisk University, 1912.

8369. ----- The Way of Worship in Everyday Life, a Course of Studies in Devotion. Winona Lake, Indiana: Light and Life Press, 1947.   DHU/MO; DHU/R

8370. ----- and Liston M. Oak. The Plunder of Ethiopia. n.p.: n.p., n.d.   NcD; DHU/MO
Written by Negro Presbyterian minister.

8371. Jackson, Algernon Brashear. Evolution and Life; a Series of Lay Sermons. Philadelphia: Neaula Publishing Co., 1911.   DHU/MO
Negro author.

8372. Jackson, Andrew Webster. A Sure Foundation. Houston, Tex.: n.p., 1940.   NN/Sch
Biographies of Negro ministers.

8373. Jackson, Booker T. God Looks Down... Fort Smith, Ark.: South & West, Inc., 1968.   O
Negro author.

8374. Jackson, Mahalia and Even McLoud Jackson. Movin' on Up. New York: Hawthorne Books, 1966.   DHU/MO; NN/Sch
Negro author.

8375. Jasper, John J. De Sun Do Move: The Celebrated Sermon of a Negro Minister. Richmond: Dietz Press, n.d.   DHU/R

8376. Jenness, Mary. A Course for Intermediates on the Negro in America, Based Primarily on Twelve Negro Americans. New York: Council of Women for Home Missions and Missionary Education Movement, 1936.   DHU/MO; CtY-D; NN/Sch
Biographies of Wm. Lloyd Imes and Howard Thurman.

8377. Johns, Vernon. "A Christmas Sermon." Negro Pulpit Opinion: An Interpretation of Christianity by Colored People (Dec., 1926), pp. 1-8.   DHU/R; DHU/MO
Written by a Baptist minister and editor.

8378. ----- "The Foundation of Immortality." Negro Pulpit Opinion: An Interpretation of Christianity by Colored People (n.d.), pp. 3-7.   Pam. File, DHU/R; DHU/MO

8379. ----- "The Men Who Let Us Drink." Negro Pulpit Opinion: An Interpretation of Christianity by Colored People (n.d.), pp. 3-8.   Pam. File, DHU/R; DHU/MO

8380. ----- "A Negro Agrarian Culture." Opportunity (Nov., 1933), pp. 336-39.   DHU/MO; Pam. File, DHU/R

8381. ----- "Religion and the Open Mind." Negro Pulpit Opinion: An Interpretation of Christianity by Colored People (n.d.), pp. 2-8.   Pam. File, DHU/R; DHU/MO

8382. ----- "Rock Foundations." Negro Pulpit Opinion: An Interpretation of Christianity by Colored People (n.d.), pp. 1-5.   Pam. File, DHU/R; DHU/MO

8383. ----- "What Ails the World?" Negro Pulpit Opinion: An Interpretation of Christianity by Colored People (Ja., 1927), pp. 3-7.   DHU/R; DHU/MO

8384. Johnson, Guion Griffis. Ante-bellum North Carolina. Chapel Hill, N.C.: Univ. of North Carolina Press, 1937.   DHU/MO
Includes information on Negro Methodists.

8385. Johnson, Harvey. The Nations From a New Point of View. Nashville: National Baptist Publishing Board, 1903.   OWibfU
Negro author.

8386. Johnson, Henry Theodore. How to Get On. A Series of Practical Essays for Young and Old. Philadelphia: H. J. Greer, 189?.   NN/Sch
Written by an A.M.E. minister.

8387. ----- Johnson's Gem; Containing of Brief Essays and Dissertations of Literary, Ethical, Religious and Current Topics. n.p.: n.p., 1901.   NN/Sch; OWibfU; CtY
Written by an A.M.E. minister.

8388. ----- Key to the Problem; or Tale of a Sable City. Philadelphia: A.M.E. Book Concern, n.d.   OWibfU
Written by an A.M.E. minister.

8389. ----- Lux Gentis Nigrate. Philadelphia: A.M.E. Book Concern, 1903.   DLC
Written by an A.M.E. minister.

8390. ----- Tuskegee Talks. Ministerial Training and Qualification. Philadelphia: Press of International Printing Co., 1902.   DHU/MO; NN/Sch
Negro author.

8391. ----- Wings of Ebony. Philadelphia: A.M.E. Book Concern, 1904.   OWibfU; NN/Sch
Written by an A.M.E. minister.

8392. Johnson, J. Q. "The Negro as a Writer." Daniel W. Culp. Twentieth Century Negro Literature. (Miami, Fla.: Mnemosyne Publishing Co., Inc., 1969), pp. 270-71.   DHU/MO
African Methodist Episcopal minister, writer and college president -- Allen University, Columbia, S.C.

8393. Johnson, John Howard. Harlem, the War and Other Addresses. New York: W. Malliet & Co., 1942.   DHU/MO; NN/Sch
Negro author.

8394. ----- A Place of Adventure. Essays and Sermons. Greenwich, Conn.: Seabury Press, 1955.   DHU/MO
Negro author.

8395. Johnson, Joseph A., (bp.). The Soul of the Black Preacher. Phila.: Pilgrim, 1970.   DHU/R; NjP
Negro author.
Sermons and meditations by a bishop of the Christian Methodist Episcopal Church.

8396. Johnson, Mordecai Wyatt. "America's Great Hour." G. Paul Butler, (ed.). Best Sermons (New York: McGraw-Hill Book Company, Inc., 1955), pp. 225-30.   DHU/R
A sermon by a baptist minister and president of Howard University.
Negro author.

8397. ----- "The Faith of the American Negro." Carter G. Woodson. Negro Orators and Their Orations (New York: Russell & Russell, 1969), pp. 658-63.   DHU/R
Reprint of 1925 edition.
"Address delivered as one of the three Commencement parts at Howard University Commencement, June 22, 1922."

8398. Johnson, W. Bishop. The Scourging of the Negro. A Sermon delivered at Second Baptist Church, Washington, D.C. By the Pastor...Sunday, April 10, 1904 at 11:00 a.m. Washington, D.C.: Beresford Printer, 1904.   DHU/MO

8399. Johnson, William Decker, Sr., (bp.). Philosophy. A Lecture by...Secretary of Education of the African Methodist Church. Nashville: A.M.E. Sunday School Union Pub. House, 1893.   NcD

8400. ----- (bp.). The Theory of Evolution; To Be Compared With the Book of Genesis. New York: n.p., 1914.   DHU/MO; NN/Sch

8401. Johnson, William Henry. Africans and the Church. To the Afro-American of the United States this Pamphlet is Affectionately Dedicated by the Compiler, Dr. William Henry Johnson, Who is Declining in His Years Has Found in the bosom of the Catholic Church that Peace which Passeth All Understanding, and Hopes that Others of His Race will Study Her Beautiful Doctrines and Her Claim to Their Spiritual Allegiance. Albany, N.Y.: Catholic Chronicle Press, 1916.   NN/Sch
Negro author.

8402. Johnstone, Ronald L. "Negro Preachers Take Sides." Review of Religious Research (2:1, Fall, 1969), pp. 81-89.   DHU/R
Data on sociological change of Negro clergymen.

8403. Jones, Absalom. A Thanksgiving Sermon, Preached January 1, 1808, in St. Thomas's (or the African Episcopal) Church, Philadelphia. Philadelphia: Rhistoric Publications, 1969.   MNtcA: NN/Sch; NcD
Also in: Dorothy B. Porter. Early Negro Writing, 1760-1837. Boston: Beacon, 1971.   DHU/R

8404. Jones, Robert E. "Qualifications of the Minister." Arcadius S. Trawick, (ed.). The New Voice in Race Adjustments. (New York: Student Volunteer Movement, 1914), pp. 96-9.   DHU/R
Negro author.

8405. Jordan, Casper Leroy. "First Freedom Rider." Negro Digest (10; Aug. 1961), pp. 38-42.   DHU/MO
"About Bishop Reverdy C. Ransom of the A.M.E. Church."

8406. Kaplan, Sidney. The Black Presence in the Era of the American Revolution 1770-1800. New York: New York Graphic Society, Ltd., 1973.   DHU/R
Part 3, "The Black Clergy."

8407. Kealing, Hightower T. The Characteristics of the Negro People. A Series of Articles by Representative American Negroes of Today... New York: James Pott & Co., 1903.   DHU/MO
Written by an A.M.E. minister.

8408. ----- "The Colored Ministers of the South." The African Methodist Episcopal Church Review (1:4, Oct., 1884), pp. 139-44.   DHU/MO
Negro author.

8409. ----- How to Live Longer; the Gospel of Good Health. n.p.: n.p., 1905.   OWibfU

8410. Kerr, S. "The Negro as a Christian." Daniel W. Culp. Twentieth Century Negro Literature. (Miami, Fla.: Mnemosyne Publishing Co., Inc., 1969), pp. 320-22.
Reprint of 1902 edition.
West Indian Negro Episcopal priest, missionary and teacher who served in the U.S. and in the West Indies.

8411. King, Dearing E. "The God Who Takes Off Chariot Wheels." William M. Philpot, (ed.). Best Black Sermons (Valley Forge: Judson Press, 1972), pp. 25-30.   DHU/R
A sermon.
Baptist minister.

8412. King, Willis J., (bp.). The Spiritual Pilgrimage of Two Christian Leaders...Saul of Tarsus and John Wesley. Monrovia, Liberia, W. Africa: n.p., n.d.   DHU/MO
Negro author.

8413. Kingsley, Harold M. "The Negro Goes to Church." Opportunity (7:3, Mr., 1929), pp. 90-91.   DHU/MO

8414. LaFarge, John. "Aunt Pigeon's 108 Years." America (56; Mr. 6, 1937), pp. 551+.   DLC

8415. Lawson, R.C. The Anthropology of Jesus Christ Our Kinsman... New York: Church of Christ, n.d.   DHU/MO
Negro author.

8416. Lee, Carleton L. Patterns of Leadership in Race Relations: a Study of Leadership Among Negro Americans. Doctoral dissertation. University of Chicago, 1951.
Negro author.

8417. Lee, Jarena. Religious Experience and Journal...Giving an account of Her Call to Preach the Gospel. Rev. and Cor. From the Original Manuscript, Written by Herself. Phila.: Pub. for the Author, 1849.   DHU/MO; NN/Sch

8418. Lee, John Francis. Building the Sermon. Atlanta, Ga.: A.B. Caldwell Publishing Co., 1921.   NN/Sch
Negro author.

8419. "Letters of Richard Allen and Absalom Jones." Journal of Negro History (1; Oct., 1916), pp. 436-43.   DHU/MO

8420. Levine, Richard M. "The End of the Politics of Pleasure." Harper's Magazine (242:1451, Apr., 1971), pp. 45-60.   DHU/R
"The decline and fall of Adam Clayton Powell, Prince of Harlem."

8421. Lewis, Carlos A. Catholic Negro Bishops; a Brief Survey of the Present and the Past. Bay St. Louis, Miss.: Divine Word Publications, 1958.   CtY-D

8422. Lewis, John W. The Life, Labors and Travels of Elder Charles Bowles, of the Free Will Baptist Denomination.... Together with an Essay on the Character and Condition of the African Race. Watertown: Ingalls and Stowell's Steam Press, 1852.   CtY-D; DHU/MO

8423. Licorish, David Nathaniel. Adventures for Today. New York: Fortuny's, 1939.   DHU/MO
Negro author.

8424. Lincoln, Charles Eric. "Why I Reversed My Stand on
La_ssez-Faire Abortion." Christian Century (90:17, Apr. 25,
1973), pp. 477-79.   DHU/R
Negro author.

8425. Logan, Rayford W. Memoirs of a Monticello Slave. Virginia: University of Virginia Press, 1951.   DHU/R
An intimate photograph of the Thomas Jefferson's household through Isaac.

8426. Long, Charles H. Alpha: Myths of Creation. New York:
G. Braziller, 1963.   DHU/R
Negro author.

8427. ----- "Cargo Cults as Cultural Historical Phenomena."
Journal of the American Academy of Religion (42:3, Sept.,
1974), pp. 403-14.   DHU/R
Negro author.

8428. Massey, James E. The Growth of the Soul: Meditations
on Spiritual Meaning and Behavior. Michigan: James Earl
Massey, 1955.   Pam. File, DHU/R
Negro author.

8429. ----- The Soul Under Siege: A Fresh Look at Christian
Experience. Anderson, Indiana: The Warner Press, 1970
                                                      DHU/R
Negro author.

8430. ----- The Worshipping Church. A Guide to the Experience
of Worship. Anderson, Indiana: The Warner Press, 1961. DHU/R
Negro author.

8431. Masters, Victor I. "As to Unwise Negro Leadership." Ed-
torial. Western Recorder (112; Jl. 7, 1938), p. 8.
                            IObNB; KyLoS; LnB; TND

8432. May, Sherry. Asahel Nettleton: Nineteenth Century American Revivalist. Doctoral dissertation. Drew University, 1969.

8433. Mayard, Aurora. The Inner Guidance. New York: Vantage
Press, 1965.   NN/Sch
Negro author.
On Christian life.

8434. Mays, Benjamin Elijah. Born to Rebel. New York:
Scribner Co., 1971.   DHU/R
Autobiography of Baptist minister and former President
of Morehouse College, Atlanta, Ga.
Negro author.

8435. ----- "College President Responds." Social Action (29;
Sept., 1962), pp. 28-30.   DHU/R

8436. ----- "Color Line Around the World." Journal of Negro
Education (6; Jl., 1937), pp. 134-43.   DHU

8437. ----- "Democratizing and Christianizing America in this
Generation." Journal of Negro Education (14; Fall, 1945), pp.
527-34.   DHU

8438. ----- "Education of Negro Ministers." Journal of Negro
Education (2; Jl., 1933), pp. 342-51.   DHU

8439. ----- "Improving the Morale of Negro Children and Youth."
Journal of Negro Education (19; Sum., 1950), pp. 420-25. DHU

8440. ----- "The Inescapable Christ." G. Paul Butler, (ed.).
Best Sermons (New York: Harper & Brothers, Pubs., 1946),
pp. 26-32.   DHU/R
A sermon by a Baptist minister, theological dean and col-
lege president.
Negro author.

8441. ----- "Role of the Negro Community in Delinquency Pre-
vention Among Negro Youth." Journal of Negro Education
(28; Sum., 1959), pp. 366-70.   DHU

8442. ----- (Contributing Editor). Vergilius Ferm, (ed.). Encyclopedia of Religion (New York: Philosophical Library,
1945)   DHU/R

8443. ----- Weekly Columnist for the Pittsburgh Courier since
1946.   DHU/MO

8444. ----- "What Man Lives By." William M. Philpot, (ed.).
Best Black Sermons (Valley Forge: Judson Press, 1972), pp.
31-9.   DHU/R
A sermon. Baptist minister.

8445. ----- "Why I Believe There is a God." Ebony (17; Dec.
1961), p. 139.   DHU/MO

8446. McDaniel, Charles-Gene. "Funeralizing Mahalia." The
Christian Century (89:9, Mr. 1, 1972), pp. 253-54. DHU/R
Gospel singer.

8447. McDaniels, Geraldine. God is the Answer. New York: Vantage Press, 1965.   DHU/MO
Negro author.

8448. McNeil, Jesse Jai. As Thy Days so Thy Strength. Grand
Rapids, Mich.: Eerdmans Pub. Co., 1960.   DHU/R
Christian living.
Negro author.

8449. ----- Moments in His Presence. Grand Rapids: Eerdmans
Pub. Co., 1962.   DHU/R
Discusses public worship and prayer.
Negro author.

8450. Meachum, John B. An Address to all the Colored Citizens
of the United States. Philadelphia: Pr. for the Author, by
King and Baird, 1846.   NN/Sch
Negro author.

8451. Melanchthon, Philipp. Selected Writings. Translated by
Charles Leander Hill, Elmer Ellsworth Flack & Lowell J.
Satre, (eds.). Minneapolis: Augsburg Pub. House, 1962.
                                                      DHU/R
Doctrines of the Lutheran Church.
Negro translator.

8452. Miller, Ernest J. The Role of Henry Highland Garnet.
Master's of Sacred Theology. Union Theology Seminary, 1969.

8453. Miller, Harriet Parks. Pioneer Colored Christians.
Clarksville, Tenn.: W. P. Titus, 1911. DHU/R; DHU/MO; NjP

8454. Minister's Institute. Proceedings; 1936, held at School of
Religion, Bishop College, Marshall, Texas. Dean H. M. Smith,
director.   DHU/MO

8455. "Ministers (Southern Negro) Meet with Edwin M. Stanton and
General William T. Sherman." Journal of Negro History (16:1,
Ja., 1931), pp. 88-94.   DHU

8456. Moon, Bertha Louise Hardwick. The Bird on the Limb. New
York: Comet Press, 1959.   DHU/MO
Negro author.

8457. Moore, Frank L. The Approach of Nathan A. Scott, Jr., to
the Theology - Literature Dialogue. Doctoral dissertation.
South-Western Baptist Theological Seminary, 1971.

8458. Moorland, Jesse Edward. The Demand and Supply of Increased
Efficiency in the Negro Ministry. Washington, D.C., 1909.
(American Negro Academy, Washington, D.C. Occasional
papers, no. 13).   DHU/MO
Negro author.

8459. Morant, John J. Mississippi Minister. 1st ed. New York:
Vantage Press, 1958.   DLC; DHU/MO; NN/Sch; NcD
Negro author.

8460. Morgan, J. H. "The Negro as a Businessman." Daniel W.
Culp. Twentieth Century Negro Literature. (Miami, Fla.:

(Morgan, J. H. cont.)
Mnemosyne Publishing Co., Inc., 1969), pp. 383-87. DHU/MO
Reprint of 1902 edition.
African Methodist Episcopal minister.

8461. Morris, Elias C. "Is the Young Negro an Improvement,
Morally, on His Father?" Daniel W. Culp. Twentieth Century
Negro Literature (Miami, Fla.: Mnemosyne Pub. Co., Inc.,
1969), pp. 259-64.   DHU/MO
Reprint of 1902 edition.

8462. Morris, Madison C. B. The Gospel Message: Sermons and
Pulpit Talks. Delivered Extemporaneously on Special Occasions.
New York: Eaton & Mains, 1905.   NN/Sch
Negro author.

8463. Morrison, Elizabeth J. There is Something Within. Detroit:
Harlo Press, 1965.   DHU/MO
Series of talks given before religious groups.
Negro author.

8464. Morton, Lena Beatrice. Man Under Stress. New York:
Philosophical Library, 1960.   DHU/MO
Negro author.

8465. Moses, William Henry. Five Commandments of Jesus,
Matthew 5:21-48... n.p., n.d.   DHU/R
Negro author.

8466. ----- The Life of Our Lord: The Four Gospels Interwoven
in One Continuous Narrative... Nashville: National Baptist
Publishing Board, n.d. NRAB; DHU/MO
Negro author.

8467. ----- The White Peril... Philadelphia: Lisle-Carey Press,
1919.   DHU/MO; NN/Sch
Negro author.

8468. Moss, Otis, Jr. "Foundations for Thanksgiving." Freeing
the Spirit (1:4; 11:1, Fall-Wint., 1972, Spr., 1973), pp. 29-32.
                                                       DHU/R
A sermon by the pastor of Mt. Zion Baptist Church in
Lockland, Ohio.

8469. ----- "Going From Disgrace to Dignity." William M.
Philpot, (ed.). Best Black Sermons (Valley Forge: Judson
Press, 1972), pp. 50-7.   DHU/R
A sermon. Baptist minister.

8470. Mossell, Gertrude E. M. (Bustill). The Work of the Afro-
American Woman. Philadelphia: G. S. Ferguson, 1894.
                                                     O WibfU
Negro author.

8471. Mott, Abigail. Narratives of Colored Americans... New
York: Boune & Co., 1882.   DHU/MO; DLC
Includes biographies of ministers.

8472. National Conference of Friends on Race Relations, Black
Mountain, N.C., July 6-9. "Power: Black, White, Shared."
Friends Journal (13:16, Ag. 15, 1967), p. 439.   DHU/R

8473. "Negro Churches Need Educated Ministry." Christian Century (50; Ag. 23, 1933), p. 1052.   DHU/R

8474. "Negro Pastor Nominated for Presbyterian Moderator."
Concern (7; Dec. 1, 1965), p. 23.   DAU/W

8475. "Negro Preachers Serving Whites." The Negro History
Bulletin (3; Oct., 1939), p. 8.   DHU/MO

8476. Nelson, William Stuart, (ed.). The Christian Way in Race
Relations. New York: Harper, 1948. DHU/R; DHU/MO; NN/Sch
Negro author.

8477. Newsome, Effie Lee. "The Negro Minister as an Emancipa-
tor." Negro Journal of Religion (4:10, Nov., 1938), p. 11.
                                                       DHU/R

8478. ----- "Saddlebag Saga." The Negro Journal of Religion (5:
1, Ja., 1940), pp. 7+.   DHU/R
Early Negro Methodist circuit riders.

8479. Newton, Percy John. The Road to Happiness and Other Essays.
Boston: Chapman Grimes, 1955.   DHU/MO
Negro author.

8480. North Carolina. State Board of Public Wel-Fare. The Negro
Population of North Carolina, 1945-1955, by John R. Larkins,
Consultant on Negro Work. Raleight: n.p., 1957.   NN/Sch

8481. O'Neil, Michael J. Some Outstanding Colored People: Interesting Facts in the Lives of Representative Negroes. Baltimore: Franciscan Sisters, 1943.   NN/Sch

8482. "Only Negro Bishop: First Colored Prelate to be Consecrated
by Vatican in Past 1300 Years Visits Catholic Centers in U.S."
Ebony (50; Je., 1950), pp. 40+.   DHU/MO

8483. Parrish, Vestal Willis. Booker T. Washington: The Moral
Leader. Master's thesis. Southeastern Baptist Theological
Seminary, 1959.

8484. Payne, Daniel Alexander, (bp.). "Bishop Daniel A. Payne's
Estimate of Abraham Lincoln." Negro History Bulletin (9; Feb.
1946), p. 111.   DHU/MO
Negro author.

8485. ----- (bp.). "Bishop Payne's Sermon." The African Methodist Episcopal Church Review (68:172, Apr.-Je., 1952), pp.
53-56.   DHU/R
Negro authr.

8486. ----- "Letter From Bishop Payne." Western Christian
Advocate (Mr. 13, Mr. 20, 1867).   NcD

8487. -----(bp.). "The Mournful Lute or the Preceptor's Farewell a Poem Composed for the Soiree of the Vigilant Committee
of Philadelphia, May 7, 1841." Benjamin Brawley, (ed.). Early
Negro American Writers (Westport, New York: Books for Libraries, 1968), pp. 147-59.   DHU/R
Reprint of 1935 edition.
Negro author.

8488. -----(bp.). The Pleasures and Other Miscellanies. Baltimore: n.p., 1850.   RPB

8489. ----- (bp.). "Speech Delivered at the Last Session of the
Franckean Synod in June, 1839 in Favor of the Adoption of the
Report on Slavery." Lutheran Herald (2:15, Ag. 1, 1839), pp.
113+.

8490. -----(bp.). Welcome to the Ransomed; or Duties of the
Colored Inhabitants of the District of Columbia. Baltimore:
Bull & Tuttle, 1862.   PPL; PPPrHi
Also included in: Charles Killian, (ed.). Daniel Alexander
Payne. Sermons and Addresses, 1853-1891. New York
Arno Press, 1972.   DHU/R

8491. Penn, Irvine Garland. The Afro-American Press and its
Editors. Springfield, Mass.:
Biographies of Negro ministers and information about early
religous periodicals
Negro author.

8492. Pettey, Sarah Dudley. "What Role is the Educated Negro
Woman to Play in the Uplifting of Her Race?" Daniel W. Culp.
Twentieth Century Negro Literature. (Miami, Fla.: Mnemosyne
Publishing Co., Inc., 1969), pp. 182-85.   DHU/MO
Reprint of 1902 edition.
Wife of Bishop Charles C. Pettey of the A. M. E. Zion
Church.

8493. Philpot, William M., (ed.). Best Black Sermons. Valley
Forge: Judson Press, 1972.   DHU/R
Includes sermon by Martin Luther King, Jr.

8494. Pierson, Robert H. and Louis B. Reynolds. Bible Answers for for Today's Questions. Nashville: Southern Publishing Association, 1973.   DHU/R

8495. Powell, Adam Clayton, Jr. Keep the Faith, Baby! New York: Trident Press, 1967. DHU/MO; DLC; GAU; NN/Sch; NjP; MiBsA
Negro author.

8496. ----- "My Life With Hazel Scott!" Ebony (4; 1945), pp. 42-50.   DHU

8497. ----- "Rocking the Gospel Train." Negro Digest (9:6, Apr., 1951), pp. 10-13.   DHU/MO
Negro author.

8498. Powell, Adam Clayton, Sr. "H. L. Mencken Finds Flowers in a Dunghill." Opportunity (9; Mr., 1931), pp. 72-4.
                                                        DHU/MO

8499. ----- "The Attitudes of Jesus Toward World Problems." An Address Delivered by... at the Annual Mass Meeting of the N.A.A.C.P., Held in St. Mark's M. E. Church, New York City, Sunday Afternoon, January 3rd, 1932. Pam. File, DHU/R
Baptist minister of Abyssinian Baptist Church, New York City.

8500. ----- "The Church in Social Work." Opportunity (1; Ja., 1923), pp. 15+.   DHU/MO
Negro author.

8501. ----- "Jesus and Wealth." Crisis (40; Oct., 1933), pp. 223-4.   DHU/MO

8502. ----- "The Kind of Christianity Needed to Reconstruct the World." Howard University Record (18:3, Ja., 1924), pp. 172-9.   DHU/MO

8503. ----- Palestine and Saints in Ceasar's Household. New York: R. R. Smith, 1939.   DHU/MO; DLC; NN/Sch

8504. ----- Picketing Hell. New York: Wendell Malliet and Company, 1942.   DHU/MO

8505. ----- "Power of the Spirit: the Need of the Church." American Baptist Historical Society (18; 1915).   SCBHC

8506. ----- Progress, the Law of Life; a Message by A. Clayton Powell Delivered in the Abyssinian Baptist Church ... January 15, 1928. New York: New York Age Press, 1929. DHU/MO; Pam. File, DHU/R

8507. ----- Riots and Ruins. New York: Richard R. Smith, 1945.
                                                        NN/Sch

8508. ----- Upon This Rock. New York: Abyssinian Baptist Church, 1949.   SCBHC

8509. "Powell Says Men Can't Get Jobs." New York Post (Mr. 27, 1935).   NN

8510. "Powell Says Rent Too High." New York Post (Mr. 28, 1935).   DHU

8511. "Powell Wins Council Seat." The New York Age (Nov. 15, 1941).   DHU/MO

8512. Proctor, Henry H. Between Black and White; Autobiographical Sketches. Boston: Chicago: the Pilgrim Press, 1925.
                                                        DHU/MO; CtY-D
Negro author.
Negro ministers, chapters 6 & 7.

8513. Progress of a Race; or the Remarkable Advancement of the American Negro, from the Bondage of Slavery, Ignorance, and Poverty to the Freedom of Citizenship, Intelligence, Affluence, Honor and Trust. Rev. and enl. by J. L. Nichols... and and William H. Crogman... With Special Articles by Well Known Authorities, Mrs. Booker T. Washington, Charles M. Melden...

M. W. Dogan... Albon L. Holsey.. Naperville, Ill.: J. L. Nichols & Co., 1920.   DHU/R
First edition published under the title "The Colored American." Biographies of Negroes including ministers, pp. 329-460.

8514. Randolph, Peter. From Slave Cabin to the Pulpit, the Southern Question Illustrated and Sketches of Slave Life. Boston: J. H. Earle, 1893. MBU; DHU/MO; INU; NN/Sch

8515. Ransom, Reverdy Cassius, (bp.). Address by Rev. Reverdy C. Ransom at Joint Hearing Before Senate Committee on Taxation and Retrenchment and Assembly Excise Committee on the Brackett-Gray Local Opinion Bill, April 14, 1909. Albany, N.Y.: n.p., n.d.   OWibfU

8516. ----- (bp.). Crispus Attucks, a Negro the First to Die for American Independence. An Address at the Metropolitan Opera House, Philadelphia, Pa. March 6, 1930.   OWibfU
Negro author.
Transcript.

8517. ----- (bp.). Deborah and Jael; Sermon to the I. B. W. Woman's Club at Bethel A. M. E. Church, Chicago, Ill. Sunday, June 6, 1897. Chicago: Crystal Print, n.d. OWibfU

8518. ----- (bp.). The Disadvantages and Opportunities of the Colored Youth. Cleveland: Thomas && Mattel, 1894. OWibfU

8519. ----- (bp.). Heredity and Environment. An Address at Literary Congress. Indianapolis, Ind.: n.p., 1898. OWibfU
Transcript.

8520. ----- (bp.). Out of the Midnight Sky: A Thanksgiving Day Address, Nov. 30, 1893 in Mt. Zion Congregational Church, Cleveland, Ohio.   OWibfU
Transcript.

8521. ----- (bp.). Paul Lawrence Dunbar, Poet Laureate of the Negro Race. Phila.: n.p., n.d.   OWibfU
Reprint from A. M. E. Church Review (Apr., 1914).
                                                        DHU/MO; NN/Sch

8522. ----- (bp.). The Spirit of Freedom and Justice. Nashville, Tenn.: A. M. E. Sunday School Union, 1926. DHU/MO; NN/Sch; TNF; CtY

8523. ----- (bp.). Wendell Phillips... Centennial Oration Delivered... in Plymouth Church, Nov. 29, 1911. Brooklyn: n.p., 1910.   NN/Sch

8524. ----- (bp.). "Why Vote for Roosevelt?" Crisis (39; Nov., 1932), p. 343.   DHU/MO
Written by forty-eighth bishop of the A. M. E. Church.

8525. ----- (bp.). William Lloyd Garrison, the Centennial Oration Delivered... in Faneuil Hall, Boston, 1905. Boston: n.p., 1905.   NcD; DHU/MO
Also in: Carter G. Woodson, (ed.). Negro Orators and their Orations (Wash., D.C., The Associated Press, 1925),
                                                        NcD; DHU/MO

8526. Rayl, J. S. "The South." The Church at Home and Abroad (5; 1889), pp. 539-41.   DHU/R
Includes notes on the Negro ministers, Baker Russell and Edward Wilmot Blyden.

8527. Reed, John M. The Devil in Holy Robes. The Bible Against Witchcraft, Fortune Telling, Good, and Bad Luck. Little Rock, Ark.: n.p., n.d.   DHU/R
Negro author.

8528. Reiss, Julian J. "The Future is Yours--Plan and Prepare." Opportunity (25:2, Spr., 1947), pp. 60-2, 115.   DHU/MO
Discusses Negro ministry as a career.

8529. Rev. Calvin Fairbank During Slavery Times. How he "Fought the Good Fight" to Prepare "The Way." Edited from his manu-

(Rev. Calvin Fairbanks.... cont.)
   script. New York: Negro Universities Press, 1969. DHU/R
   Originally published in 1890.
   Abolitionsit preacher who aided many slaves escape from
   bondage.

8530. Revels, Hiram Rhoades. "A Speech on the Georgia Bill."
Carter G. Woodson, (ed.). Negro Orators and Their Orations
(Washington, D.C.: Associated Publishers, 1925), pp. 285-93.
                                                              DHU/MO
   Negro author.

8531. Reynolds, Louis B. The Dawn of a Brighter Day: Light
Through the Darkness Ahead. Nashville, Tenn.: The Southern
Pub. Assn. 1945.   DHU/MO
   Negro author.

8532. Reynolds, Louis B. Great Texts From Romans. Nashville:
Southern Publishing Association, 1972.   DHU/R
   Seventh-day Adventist minister and editor of Southern Pub.
   Assn.
   Negro author.

8533. ----- Look to the Hills... Nashville, Tenn.: Southern Pub.
Assoc., 1960.   DHU/R

8534. Robinson, J. P. Sermons and Sermonettes. Nashville, Tenn.:
National Baptist Publishing Board, 1909.   SCBHC
   Bound up and issued with S.W.R. Cole's Sermons Outlined...
   1940.

8535. Robinson, James Herman. Adventurous Preaching. Great
Neck, N.Y.: Channel Press, 1956.   DHU/R; DHU/MO; DLC
   Negro author.

8536. Rogers, Cornish R. "The Black Minister and his Family."
The Christian Ministry (2:4, Jl. 1971), pp. 19-20. DHU/R
   Negro author.

8537. Rogers, Walter Charles. A Man of God. Boston, The Christopher Publishing House, 1931.   NN/Sch

8538. "Roland T. Heacock Papers Deposited in The Amistad Re-
search Center." The Amistad Research Center News (2:3,
Dec., 1972), p. 1.   Pam. File, DHU/R
   Congregationist Negro minister and chaplain.

8539. Rooks, Charles Shelby. "A Cross to Bear." The Journal
of Religious Thought (20:2, 1963-1964), pp. 131-35. DHU/R
   "A sermon delivered in the Little Chapel School of Religion
   Howard University, October, 1963."

8540. Rush, Christopher, (bp.). Writers Program. New York
City. Negroes at New York. Biographical Sketches. New York:
1938-41. 4 vols.   NN/Sch

8541. Russell, Charles L. Light From the Talmud. New York:
Block Pub. Co., 1942.   DHU/R; DHU/MO
   Hebrew and English on opposite pages.
   Negro author.

8542. Rutledge, D. "Two Dynamic Leaders for Baptists and
Methodists." Sepia (10; My., 1961), pp. 64-67. DHU/MO

8543. Salter, Moses Buckingham (bp.). The Seven Kingdoms; a
Book of Travel, History, Information and Entertainment.
Philadelphia: A. M. E. Publishing House, 1902. OWibfU;
NN/Sch
   Negro author.

8544. Sampson, John Patterson. The Disappointed Bride, or Love
at First Sight. A Drama in Three Acts... Hampton, Va.:
Hampton School Steam Press, 1883.   NN/Sch
   Presiding elder of the New England Conference of the A. M.
   E. Church.

8545. ----- Jolly People. n.p.: Printed by the author, 19?
                                DHU/MO; NN/Sch
   Also in: Plays, Poems and Miscellany.
   Presiding elder of the New England Conference of the A. M.
   E. Church.

8546. Sampson, John Patterson. Mixed Races: Their Environment,
Temperment, Heredity, and Phrenology. Hampton, Va.: Nor-
School Steam Press, 1881.   OWibfU; NN/Sch; DHU/MO

8547. Savory, J. "Descent and Baptism in "Native Son", "Invisible
Man", and "Dutchman." Christian Scholar's Review (3; 173,
1972), pp. 3+.   DAU; DGW

8548. Scarborough, William S. The Birds of Aristophanes. A
Theory of Interpretation. Boston: J. H. Cushing & Co., 1886.
                                DLC; DHU/MO
   Speech read before the American Philological Association,
   July 3, 1886.

8549. ----- ...The Educated Negro and His Mission... Wash.,
D.C., The Academy, 1903.   DHU/MO
   The American Negro Academy. Occasional paper, no. 8.

8550. ----- "Paul Lawrence Dunbar, Poet Laureate of the Negro
Race." A.M.E. Church Review (31; 1914), pp. 135-44.
                                NN/Sch; DHU/MO

8551. Schoener, Allon, (ed.). Harlem on My Mind. Cultural Cap-
ital of Black America, 1900-1968. New York: Random House,
1968.   DHU/R
   Text and pictures of an exhibit in the New York Metropolitan
   Museum. "Political Involvement of Negro ministers in
   Harlem."

8552. Schomburg, Arthur Alfonso. "Two Negro Missionaries to
the American Indians, John Warrant, and John Stewart."
Journal of Negro History (21:4, Oct., 1936), pp. 394-415. DHU

8553. Scott, Nathan Alexander, Jr. "New Heav'ns, New Earth."
--- The Landscape of Contemporary Apocalypse. The Journal
of Religion (53:1, Ja., 1973), pp. 1-35.   DHU/R
   "Anatomy of apocalypticism in literature, art, politics, etc.;
   soulscape of humanity."
   Negro author.

8554. ----- "Reflections on Nathan Scott: After the Death of God."
A. M. Allchin. Theology, A Monthly Review (75:625, Jl., 1972),
pp. 361-69.   DHU/R

8555. ----- "To Stay With the Question of Being: A Consideration
of Theological Elements in the Criticism of Nathan A. Scott, Jr."
Anglican Theological Review (60:1, Ja., 1973), pp. 3-27. DHU/R
   R. Franklin Terry, professor of Morningside College, Siouix
   City, Iowa, examines Scott's theological and critical method.

8556. Scott, Nathan Alexander. Nathanael West. Grand Rapids,
Mich.: Eerdman's Publishing Co., 1971.   DHU/R
   Negro author.

8557. ----- The New Orpheus. Essays Toward a Christian Poetic.
New York: S. Sheed & Ward, 1964.   DHU/R; NN/Sch
   Religion and Literature.

8558. ----- The Tragic Vision and the Christian Faith. New York:
Association Press, 1957.   DHU/R
   Religion and Literature.

8559. Scott, Osborne S. "Chaplain Teacher; Negro Minister In-
structs Chaplains in Army School." Ebony (8; Feb., 1953),
pp. 67-70.   DHU/MO

8560. Scott, Timothy Dwight. Sunday, the Christian Sabbath.
Springfield, Ohio: Whyte Printing Co., n.d. OWibfU; DHU/MO
   Negro author.

8561. Seaton, David P. The Land of Promise; or the Bible Land
and Its Revelation. Philadelphia: Publishing House of the
                                DHU/R

A. M. E. Church, 1895.
Negro author.

8562. Sewell, George A. A Motif for Living and Other Sermons. New York: Vantage Press, 1963. DHU/MO
Negro author.

8563. Shackleford, William Henry. Along the Highway. Nashville: A. M. E. Sunday School Union, 1915. DHU/MO
A. M. E. Minister.

8564. ----- Pearls in Prose and Poetry. Nashville: National Baptist Publication Board, 1907. TNF

8565. Shannon, David T. "A Strange Song in a Strange Land." William M. Philpot (ed.). Best Black Sermons (Valley Forge: Judson Press, 1972), pp. 58-62. DHU/R
A sermon. Baptist minister.

8566. Shaw, Alexander P. "What Must the Negro Do to Be Saved?" Religion in Life (17:4, Aut., 1948), pp. 540-48. DHU/R
A Black churchman discusses the Negro's responsibility for solving the race problem.
Negro author.

8567. Shaw, Talbert O. "A Tentative Profile of the Black Clergy in Chicago." Journal of Religious Thought (30:1, Spr.-Sum., 1973), pp. 39-51. DHU/R
Negro author.

8568. Sherwood, William Henry. Sherwood's Solid Shot, a Few of the Sermons of the Negro Evangelist as Preached by Him in Revival Meetings, North, South, East and West and Reported by George F. Thompson. To Which is Added a Collection of Heavy Hits Which He Deals Upon the Heads of His Congregation at Times Styled Dead Shots. Boston: McDonald, Gill, 1891. NN/Sch; DHU/MO
Negro Evangelist.

8569. Shillito, Edward. "The Poet and the Race Problem." Christian Century (46; Jl. 17, 1929), pp. 915-16. Pam. File, DHU/R
Countee Cullen's religious poetry.

8570. Shockley, Grant S. "Age Groups." Westminster Dictionary of Christian Education (Philadelphia: Westminster Press, 1963), pp. 21-24. DHU/R
Negro author.

8571. ----- "Foundations for a Philosophy of Christian Education." Lawrence C. Little. Religion in Life (31; Aut., 1962), pp. 638-39. DHU/R
Book review.

8572. ----- "Jefferson on Religion in Public Education." Robert M. Healey. Journal of Religious Thought (19; Aut./Wint., 1963), pp. 169-70. DHU/R
Book review.

8573. Simmons, William J. Men of Mark: Eminent, Progressive, and Rising. Cleveland: Geo. M. Rewell & Co., 1887. DHU/R

8574. Simms, Joseph D. Soul-Saving; or, Life and Labors of Henry M. Willis, Evangelist and Missionary. Philadelphia: Robert E. Lynch, 1886. DHU/MO
Negro author.

8575. Small, John Bryan, (bp.). A Cordial and Dispassionate Discussion on Predestination, its Spiritual Support. York, Pa.: Dispatch Pub. Co., 1901. DLC
Negro author.

8576. ----- (bp.). The Human Heart Illustrated by Nine Figures of the Heart, Representing the Different Stages of Life, and Two Death-Bed Scenes; the Wicked and the Righteous. York, Pa.: York Dispatch Print, 1898. DHU/MO; NN/Sch

8577. ----- (bp.). Practical and Exegetical Pulpiteer. York, Pa.: Anstadt & Son, 1895. NcSalL

8578. ----- (bp.). Predestination: Its Scriptural Import. York, Pa.: Dispatch, 1901. NcSalL

8579. Smith, Charles Spencer, (bp.). A Christmas Service. n. p.: n. p., 1882. OWibfU
Written by twenty-eighth bishop of the A. M. E. Church.

8580. ----- (bp.). Some Footprints of the Nineteenth Century, A Sermon by Bishop C. S. Smith...at Bethel A. M. E. Church, Detroit, Mich., Dec. 31st, 1900. n. p.: n. p., 1900. DHU/MO

8581. Smith, Emmitt M. An Analysis of the Professional Activities of One Hundred Negro Ministers with Varied Educational Backgrounds. Masters thesis. Fisk University, 1946.

8582. Smith, George. A Short Treatise Upon the Most Essential and Leading Points of Wesleyan or Primitive Methodism. Poultney, Vt.: L. J. Reynolds, Printer, 1830. NN/Sch
Negro author.

8583. Smith, Hubert W. Three Negro Preachers in Chicago: A Study on Religious Leadership. Masters thesis. University of Chicago, 1935.

8584. Smith, John Wesley, (bp.). "Greatest Need of the Negro Race." W. N. Hartshorn. An Era of Progress and Promise (Boston: Priscilla, 1910), pp. 398. NcSalL; DHU/R
Negro author.

8585. Smith, Kelly Miller. "Time Is Winding Up!" William M. Philpot, (ed.). Best Black Sermons (Valley Forge: Judson Press, 1972), pp. 63-69. DHU/R
A sermon. Baptist minister.

8586. Smith, Paul Dewey. Man's Relationship and Duty to God... New York: Carlton Press, 1964. NN/Sch

8587. Smothers, Felton C. I Am the Beginning and the Ending; A Book of Excerpts from Genesis and the Revelations of St. John, the Divine. Ed. & illustrated by Felton Smothers. New York: Carlton Pr., 1961. DHU/MO; A&M
Negro author.

8588. Spearman, Aurelia L. P. What Christ Means to Us. A Book of Religious Verse. New York: Carlton Press, 1964. DHU/R
Negro author.

8589. Spearman, Henry Kuhns. Soul Magnets; Twelve Sermons from New Testament Texts, compiled as a Memorial by Mrs. Elizabeth F. Spearman. Philadelphia: Pr. by the A. M. E. Book Concern, 1929. NN/Sch
Negro author.

8590. Speers, Wallace Carter. Laymen Speaking. New York: Association Press, 1947. DHU/MO
Negro author.

8591. Spivey, Charles S. A Tribute to the Negro Preacher, and Other Sermons and Addresses. Wilberforce, O.: Xenia, O., Eckerle Printing Co., 1942. NN/Sch; OWibfU
Negro author.

8592. Stanley, A. Knighton. "Only When I Come to My Father Do I Come to Myself." Journal of Religious Thought (29:1, Spr.-Sum., 1972), pp. 82-84. DHU/R

8593. Stephenson, Isaiah H. First Oration on Stephen the First Martyr of the Christian Church. n. p., 1898. DHU/MO
Negro author.

8594. Stevens, Abel. Sketches & Incidents; or, A Budget from the Saddle-Bags of a Superannuated Itinerant... George Peck, ed. Cincinnati: Pub. by Hitchcock & Walden, 1869. NN/Sch; IEG

8595. Stevenson, J. W. How to Get and Keep Churches Out of Debt and Also a Lecture on the Secret of Success in the Art of Mak-

(Stevenson, J. W. cont.)
    ing Money. Albany: Weed, Parsons & Co., 1886. DHU/MO
    Negro author.

8596. Steward, Theophilus Gould. Active Service: or Religious
Work among U.S. Soldiers. A Series of Papers by our Post
and Regiment Chaplains. New York: United States Army Aid
Association, n. d.   DHU/MO
    Negro author.

8597. ----- "The Army as a Trained Force." Alice Ruth Nelson.
Masterpieces of Negro Eloquence: The Best Speeches Delivered
by the Negro From the Days of Slavery to the Present Time.
(New York: Bookery Publishing Company, 1914), pp. 277-90.
    DHU/MO

8598. ----- The Colored Regulars in the United States Army, With
a Sketch of the History of the Colored American, and an Account of his Services in the Wars of the Country, From the
Period of the Revolutionary War to 1899. Philadelphia: A. M. E.
Book Concern, 1904.   OWibfU; NN/Sch

8599. ----- Divine Attributes. Philadelphia: Christian Recorded,
1884. (Tawawa Series in Systematic Divinity, no. 1). OWibfU.
    Written by an A. M. E. minister.

8600. ----- The End of the World; or, Clearing the Way for the
Fullness of the Gentiles. Philadelphia: A. M. E. Church
Book Rooms, 1888.   OWibfU; NN/Sch
    Written by an A. M. E. minister.

8601. ----- Fifty Years in Gospel Ministry. Philadelphia: A. M.
E. Book Concern, 1920.   DHU/MO

8602. ----- Genesis Pre-read or, The Latest Conclusion of
Physical Science Views in their Relation to Mosaic Record,
to which is Added an Important Chapter on the Direct Evidences of Christianity, by Bishop J. P. Campbell. Philadelphia: A. M. E. Book Rooms, 1885.   DHU/MO

8603. ----- Gouldtown, A Very Remarkable Settlement of Ancient
Date; Studies of Some Sturdy Examples of the Simple Life,
Together with Sketches of Early Colonial History of Cumberland
County and Southern New Jersey and Some Early Genealogical
Records. Philadelphia: Lippincott, 1913. NcD; NN/Sch; OWibfU

8604. ----- The Haitian Revolution, 1791 to 1804; or, Side Lights
on the French Revolution. New York: T. Y. Crowell Co.,
1914.   NN/Sch; OWibfU

8605. ----- How the Black Domingo Legion Saved the Patriot
Army in the Siege of Savannah, 1779. Washington: American
Negro Academy Occassional Papers #5, 1899.   NN/Sch

8606. ----- Memoirs of Mrs. Rebecca Steward; Containing a Full
Sketch of Her Life, with Various Selections from her Writings
and Letters. Philadelphia: Publication Department of the
A. M. E. Church, 1877.   PP

8607. ----- "Message of San Domingo to the African Race."
American Negro Academy Papers. Read at 19th Annual Meeting,
December 28-29, 1915. Washington: n. p., 1916.   NN/Sch

8608. ----- My First Years in the Itineracy. Brooklyn: n. p.,
1876.   PHi

8609. Stewart, John. "An Address to the Wyandott Nation and
Accompanying Letter to William Walker Dated May 25, 1817."
Dorothy B. Porter. Early Negro Writing, 1760-1837 (Boston:
Beacon, 1971), pp. 455-59.   DHU/MO
    Negro missionary to the Wyandot Indians. His name appears
    as Steward as well as Stewart.

8610. Stewart, Maria W. Religion and the Pure Principles of Morality the Sure Foundation on which we Must Build. Productions
from the Pen of Mrs. Maria W. Stewart, Widow of the late
James W. Stewart of Boston. n. p., 1831.   DHU/MO
    Negro author.

8611. Stewart, Thomas McCants. "Address Delivered at Bethel
Church, Philadelphia, November 25, 1887." The African
Methodist Episcopal Church Review (78:214, Oct. -Dec., 1962),
pp. 38-47.   DHU/R
    Written by a lawyer, author and A. M. E. minister.

8612. ----- The Impartial Administration of Justice: The Corner-
stone of a Nation, Being an Address Delivered at a Public
Meeting of the Executive Committee of the Liberian National
Bar Association, in the Parlors of the Executive Mansion,
at Monrovia, December 14, 1909. London: Strakers' Printers,
n. d.   NN/Sch

8613. ----- "Popular Discontent." African Methodist Episcopal
Church Review (8; 1891).   DLC
    Microfilm.

8614. ----- The Significance of Newport Day in Liberian National
Life, Being an Address by Prof. T. McCants Stewart, Delivered
in Monrovia, Republic of Liberia, Monday, Dec. 2, 1907. Monrovia, Liberia: College of West Africa Press, 1907. NN/Sch

8615. Stokes, A. Jackson. Select Sermons. n. p., 1914. SCBHC

8616. Straker, David Augustus. "Brief Sketch of the Political Life
of Hon. Robert Browne Elliot of South Carolina." A. M. E.
Church Review (9; April, 1893), pp. 376-87.   DLC; GAU
    Written by a A. M. E. layman.

8617. ----- Citizenship, Its Rights and Duties, - Woman Suffrage;
a Lecture Delivered by D. Augustus Straker at the Israel
A. M. E. Church, and Before the Power League at Hills-
dale, Washington, D. C., April 13, 14, 1874. Washington, D. C.:
New National Era Print, 1874.   DHU/MO; MB

8618. ----- Eulogy on the Life, Character and Public Services
of Robert Browne Elliott, Ex-Member of Congress and Speaker
of the House of Representatives of South Carolina in Bethel
A. M. E. Church, Columbia, S. C., Sept. 24, 1884. Columbia:
W. Sloane, 1884.   TNF

8619. ----- "Introductory Remarks in a Lecture on Commercial
Law Before the Students of the Commercial Business School
of Howard University, Corner of 9th and D Sts., Washington,
D. C." New National Era and Citizen (4:39, Oct. 2, 1874).
    Microfilm.

8620. Swift, Job. Discourse on Religious Subjects... to which
are Prefixed, Skethces of his Life and Character, and a
Sermon Preached at West-Ruthland on the Occasion of his
Death, by the Rev. Lemuel Haynes... Middlesbury, Vt.:
Pr. by Huntington & Fitch, 1805.   DHU/MO

8621. Tanner, Benjamin Tucker, (bp.). Color of Solomon--
What? "My Beloved is White and Ruddy." A Monograph...
with an Introduction by W. S. Scarborough. Philadelphia:
A. M. E. Book Concern, 1895.   DHU/MO

8622. ----- (bp.). Douglass Monthly. (1; Apr. 1859), p. 64. NcD

8623. ----- (bp.). Joel, the Son of Pethuel; His Personage; the
Time in Which He Lived, His Work, the Impression He made.
n. p.: n. p., 1905.   DHU/MO; NN/Sch

8624. ----- (bp.). The Negro in Holy Writ. Philadelphia, Pa.:
n. p., 1902.   DHU/MO

8625. ----- (bp.). The Negro's Origin. Philadelphia: African
Methodist Episcopal Depository, 1869.   DHU/MO

8626. ----- (ed.). Scriptural Means of Producing an Immediate
Revival of Pure Christianity in the Ministry and Laity of Our
Church; Prize Essays. Philadelphia: A. M. E. Pub. Dept.,
1881.   DHU/MO

8627. ----- (bp.)., (ed.). Theological Lectures. Nashville:
A. M. E. Sunday School Union Press, 1894.   DHU/MO

8628. ----- (bp.)., (ed.). To the Memory of Professor O. V. Catto. Respectfully Inscribed to His Fellows of the Institute for Colored Youth and to the Pupils of the Same with Considerations. n. p., 1871.   NN/Sch

8629. Tatum, E. Ray. Conquest of Failure? Biography of J. Frank Norris. Dallas: Baptist Historical Foundation, 1966.   DLC

8630. Taylor, Gardner C. "They Shall Ask the Way." A. M. E. Church Review (68:172, Apr.-Je., 1952), pp. 56-58+. DHU/R

8631. Taylor, James B. Lives of Virginia Baptist Ministers. Richmond: Yale & Wyatt, 1837.   NNUT

8632-33. Taylor, Marshall W. The Life, Travels, Labors, and Helpers of Mrs. Amanda Smith, the Famous Negro Missionary Evangelist. Cincinnati: Pr. by Cranston and Stowe for the Author, 1888.   DHU/MO

8634. Terry, R. Franklin. "To Stay With the Question of Being; a Consideration of Theological Elements in the Criticism of Nathan A. Scott, Jr." Anglican Theological Review (55:1, Ja., 1973), pp. 3-27.   DHU/R
    Nathan A. Scott, Jr. is a Black theologian.

8635. Thirkield, Wilbur Patterson, (bp.). The Training of Physicians and Ministers for the Negro Race. Washington, D.C.: Howard University, 1909.   DHU/R

8636. Thomas, William Hannibal. The American Negro: What He Was, What He Is, and What He May Become. New York: Negro Universities Press, 1969.   DHU/R
    Originally published in 1901. See chapter VI, (Ethnic Beliefs), and chapter VII, (Moral Lapses).

8637. Thompson, Daniel C. The Negro Leadership Class. Englewood Cliffs, N.J.: Prentice-Hall, Inc., 1963.   DHU/R
    Pp. 34-37, Occupational characteristics of the Protestant ministry.

8638. Thurman, Howard. "Christ's Message to the Disinherited." The African Methodist Episcopal Church Review (78:218, Oct.-Dec., 1963), pp. 26-29+.   DHU/R
    Negro author.

8639. ----- The Creative Encounter. New York: Harper & Row, Publishers, 1954.   DHU/R

8640. ----- Deep is the Hunger. New York: Harper & Row, Publishers, 1951.   DHU/R

8641. ----- Footprints of a Dream. New York: Harper & Row, Publishers, 1959.   DHU/R

8642. ----- "Interracial Church in San Francisco." Social Action (11:2, Feb. 15, 1945), pp. 27-28.   DHU/R

8643. ----- Meditations of the Heart. New York: Harper & Row, Publishers, 1953.   DHU/R

8644. ----- The Mood of Christmas. New York: Harper & Row, 1973.   DHU/R

8645. ----- "Mysticism and Ethics." Journal of Religious Thought (27:2, Sum. Suppl., 1970), pp. 23-30.   DHU/R

8646. ----- Mysticism and the Experience of Love. Wallingford, Pendle Hill, Pa.: n.d.   DHU/R

8647. ----- The Search for Common Ground: an Inquiry into the Basis of Man's Experience of Community. New York: Harper & Row, 1971.   DHU/MO; DHU/R

8648. ----- "What Can We Believe In?" Journal of Religion and Health (12:2, Apr., 1973), pp. 111-19.   DHU/R
    "Sixth paper in the series on What Can We Believe In?"

8649. Tilmon, Levin. A Brief Miscellaneous Narrative of the More Early Part of the Life of L. Tilmon, Pastor of a Methodist Congregation in the City of New York. Jersey City: W. W. & L. A. Pratt, 1853.   DHU/MO
    Negro author.
    "Pastor of a Colored Methodist Congregational Church in New York City."

8650. Tindley, Charles A. Book of Sermons. Philadelphia: Edw. T. Duncan, 1932.   DHU/MO; NN/Sch
    Negro author.

8651. Tinney, James S. "Youth Action Center a Miracle of Faith?" The Washington Afro-American (Ag. 25, 1973), p.11.
                    Pam. File, DHU/R
    Negro author.

8652. Toomer, Jean. ... The Flavor of Man... Philadelphia: Young Friends Movement of the Philadelphia Yearly Meetings, 1949.   NN/Sch
    "Delivered at Arch Street Meeting House, Philadelphia."
    Negro author.

8653. Toppin, Edgar A. A Biographical History of Blacks in America Since 1528. New York: David McKay Co., 1971.
                    DHU/MO; DHU/R
    Includes biographical information on Black ministers.

8654. Tross, Joseph Samuel Nathaniel. This Thing Called Religion. Charlotte, N.C.: n.p., 1934.   DHU/MO

8655. Truss, Matthew B. A Sketch of the Life, Death and Funeral of the Rev. Simon Smith, a Man of Colour, and a Member of the Methodist Episcopal Church. Delivered by Matthew B. Truss, One of the Same.   NN/Sch
    Negro author.

8656. Turner, Henry McNeal, (bp.). The Civil and Political Status of the State of Georgia and Her Relations to the General Government, Reviewed and Discussed in a Speech Delivered in the House of Representatives of the Georgia Legislature, Aug. 11, 1870. Atlanta, Ga.: New Era Printing Establishment, 1870.   MH

8657. ----- (bp.). The Conflict for Civil Rights; a Poem. Washington: Judd & Detweiler, Printers and Publishers, 1881.
                    DHU/MO
    Negro author.

8658. ----- (bp.). Memorial Services. Tribute to the Hon. Charles Sumner Held in St. Phillip's A. M. E. Church, Savannah, Georgia, March 18th, 1874. Speeches by Henry McNeal Turner, LL.D., Hon. J. M. Simms, Resolutions, etc. Savannah, Ga.: D. G. Patton, Printer, 1874.   DLC

8659. ----- (bp.). "Races Must Separate, Asserts Bishop Turner." C. E. Dorman, et al. A Solution of the Negro Problem Psychologically Considered. The Negro Not 'A Beast' (Atlanta: Franklin Printing & Publishing Co., n. d.), pp. 30-31.   NcD

8660. ----- (bp.). "Reminiscence of the Proclamation of Emancipation." The African Methodist Episcopal Church Review (80:220, Apr.-Je., 1964), pp. 34-37.   DHU/R

8661. ----- (bp.). Respect Black, The Writings and Speeches of Henry McNeal Turner. Compiled and edited by Edwin S. Redkey. New York: Arno Press, 1971.   DHU/R

8662. ----- (bp.). The World's Expostion; an Address Given at Atlanta, Ga., Sept. 23, 1884. n.p.: n.p., 1844.   DHU/MO

8663. Turner, Maynard P. National Baptist Pulpit, 1969-70. A Treasury of Preaching by Twenty-One National Pulpiteers... Nashville: Townsend Press, 1969-70.   MNtcA
    Negro Baptist sermons.

8664. Tyms, James Daniel. "Excited About Religion." Daniel G. Hill, (ed.). Well-Springs of Life (Wash., D.C.: Howard

(Tyms, James Daniel cont.)
    University, 1956), pp. 108-16.   DHU/R
    A sermon delivered in Andrew Rankin Chapel, Howard
    University.

8665. Tyson, Brady. "Encounter in Ricife." Christian Century
    (87:23, Je. 10, 1970), pp. 720-22.   DHU/R
    "An account of Ralph Abernathy's trip to Brazil."

8666. United States. Senate. The Race Problem Speech. Feb-
    ruary 23-24, 1903. Washington, D.C.: 1903. NcD; DLC
    Includes letter of Henry McNeal Turner to Hon. Benjamin
    R. Tillman, Senator, South Carolina.

8667. Vassall, William F. The Origin of Christianity; a Brief
    Study of the World's Early Beliefs and their Influence on the
    Early Christian Church, Including an Examination of the Lost
    Books of the Bible. New York: Exposition Press, 1952.
                                 DHU/MO; NN/Sch

8668. Vernon, William Tecumseh, (bp.). "A Plea for a Suspen-
    sion of Judgment." Carter G. Woodson. Negro Orators and
    Their Orations (Wash., D.C.: Associated Publ., 1925), pp.
    618-26.   DHU/MO
    Written by Bishop of A.M.E. Church.

8669. ----- (bp.). The Upbuilding of a Race; or, the Rise of a
    Great People, A Compilation of Sermons, Addresses and
    Writings on Education, The Race Question and Public Affairs.
    Introduction by H. T. Johnson. Quindaro, Kansas: Industrial
    Student Printer, 1904.   DLC
    Written by the forty-fifth bishop of the A.M.E. Church.

8670. Wallace, S. B. "Behold we are Servants this Day." The
    Industrial Status of the Colored People of the District of Colum-
    bia. A Sermon Delivered at the Israel C.M.E. Church,
    Washington, D.C., December 30, 1894. Union League Publi-
    cation, no. 5, n.d.   DHU/MO
    Negro author.

8671. ----- What the National Government is Doing for Our
    Colored Boys. The New System of Slavery in the South. Two
    Sermons Delivered at the Israel Colored Methodist Episcopal
    Church, Washington, D.C. by its Pastor... August 16 and
    September 9, 1894. Washington, D.C.: Jones, Printer, 1894.
                        DHU/MO

8672. Walls, William Jacob, (bp.). Baseball: The Parable of
    Life. n.p., n.d.   NcSalL; DHU/R
    Negro author.

8673. ----- (bp.). The Dream of Youth. n.p., n.d.   NcSalL

8674. ----- (bp.). Glimpses of Memory. n.p., n.d.   NcSalL

8675. ----- (bp.). Harriet Tubman. n.p., n.d.   DHU/R

8676. ----- (bp.). Messages of Five Years. n.p., n.d.   NcSalL

8677. ----- (bp.). The Negro in Business and Religion. n.p.,
    n.d.   NcSalL

8678. ----- (bp.). Pastorates and Reminiscences. n.p., n.d.
                        NcSalL

8679. ----- (bp.). Visions for the Times. n.p., n.d.   NcSalL

8680. ----- (bp.). What Youth Wants. n.p., n.d.   NcSalL

8681. Walters, Alexander, (bp.). "Abraham Lincoln and Fifty
    Years of Freedom." Dorothy B. Porter, (ed.). Early Negro
    Writing, 1760-1837 (Boston: Beacon, 1971), pp. 554-61.
                        DHU/MO

8682. ----- (bp.). Frederick Douglass and His Work. Nash-
    ville: National Baptist Publishing Board, 1904.   NcSalL

8683. ----- (bp.). "Greatest Need of the Negro Race." W. N.
    Hartshorn. An Era of Progress and Promise (Boston:
    Priscilla, 1910), pp. 396+.   NcSalL

8684. ----- (bp.). "A Letter to J. W. Thompson." J. W.
    Thompson. Authentic History of The Douglass Monument
    (Rochester: Rochester Herald Press, 1908), p. 196. NcSalL

8685. ----- (bp.) "Possibilities of the Negro in the Realm of
    Politics." W. H. Ferris. The African Abroad (New Haven:
    Tuttle, Morehouse, Taylor, 1913), vol. I, pp. 379-81.
                         DHU/MO; NcSalL

8686. ----- (bp.). "What Should the Next Congress Do?" Irving
    G. Penn. The United Negro (Atlanta: Luther, 1902), pp. 592+.
                         NcSalL

8687. Ward, Thomas Playfair. The Truth that Makes Men Free;
    a Novel. New York: Pageant Press, 1955.
    A novel by a Negro Methodist minister.

8688. Washington, Booker Taliferro. Character Building. New
    York: Doubleday, Pade and Company, 1902.   O

8689. ----- "David Livingstone and the Negro." International
    Review of Missions (2; 1913), pp. 224-35.   DHU/R
    The influence of Christian missionaries on Blacks in
    Africa and America.

8690. ----- Sowing and Reaping. Freeport, N.Y.: Books for
    Libraries Press, 1971.   DHU/R
    Originally published in 1900. "Sunday Evening Talks to
    Students", at Tuskegee Normal and Industrial Institute.

8691. Washington, Joseph R., Jr. "Liberated Women Liberating
    Domestics." The Christian Century (89:36, Oct. 11, 1972),
    pp. 1008-10.   DHU/R
    Written by "Professor of Religious Studies and chairman
    of Afro-American studies at the University of Virginia,
    Charlottesville."
    Negro author.

8692. ----- Marriage in Black and White. Boston: Beacon Press,
    1971.   DHU/R

8693. Watts, Herman H. "What Is Your Name?" William M.
    Philpot, (ed.). Best Black Sermons (Valley Forge: Judson
    Press, 1972), pp. 70-77.   DHU/R
    A sermon.
    Baptist minister.

8694. Wegelin, Oscar. Jupiter Hammon -- American Negro Poet.
    Selections From His Writings and a Bibliography. New York:
    Heartman, 1915.   DHU/MO; NN/Sch

8695. Wheatley, Phillis. An Elegiac Poem, On the Death of That
    Celebrated Divine, and Eminent Servant of Jesus Christ, the
    Reverend and Learned George Whitefield, Chaplain to the Right
    Honourable the Countess of Huntingdon... Newport, Rhode
    Island: Reprinted, 1970. DLC; DHU; CLU; CU; CSt; WU; NNC
    Also: Dorothy B. Porter, (ed.). Early Negro Writing,
    1760-1837 (Boston: Beacon Press, 1971), pp. 532-34.
                        DHU/MO; DHU/R

8696. ----- An Elegy, Sacred to the Memory of That Great Divine,
    the Reverend and Learned Dr. Samuel Cooper, Who Departed
    This Life December 29, 1783. Boston: Printed by Russell,
    1784.   MH; MBAt; MWA
    Negro author.

8697. ----- Memoir and Poems of Phillis Wheatley, a Native
    African and a Slave. Freeport, N.Y.: Books for Libraries,
    1838.   NNCor

8698. ----- Poems on Various Subjects, Religious and Moral.
    Hartford, Conn.: Printed by Oliver Steele, 1804.
            CLU; CU; CSt; WU; DLC; DHU/MO; CtY

8699. ----- Sabbath - June 13, 1779. (A Prayer Written by Miss
    Wheatley, accidently discovered in her Bible.)   NN/Sch

8700. White, William Spottswood. The African Preacher. An Authentic Narative... Philadelphia: Presbyterian Board of Publication, 1849.
Negro author.

8701. ----- William S. White, D.D. and His Times... An Autobiography by his Son. Richmond: Presbyterian Committee of Publication, 1891.   NcD; VC

8702. Whitman, Alberry Allison. An Idyl of the South, an Epic in Two Parts. New York: Metaphysical Publishing Co., 1901.
OWibfU
A. M. E. minister.

8703. ----- Twasinta's Seminoles; or the Rape of Florida. St. Louis: Nixon-Jones, 1884.   OWibfU

8704. Whittier, A. Gerald. Christmas Meditations. New York: Carlton Press, 1961.   DHU/MO
Negro author.

8705. Who's Who of the Colored Race; A General Biographic Dictionary of Men and Women of African Descent. Chicago: n.p., 1915.   DHU/MO
Includes biographical sketches of Negro ministers.

8706. Why I Believe There is a God; Sixteen Essays by Negro Clergymen, with an Introduction by Howard Thurman. Chicago: Johnson Publication Co., 1965.   DHU/R; NN/Sch

8707. Wilkerson, James. Wilkerson's History of His Travels and Labors, in the United States, as a Missionary, in Particular that of the Union Seminary, Located in Franklin Co., Ohio, Since he Purchased His Liberty in New Orleans, La., Etc. Columbus, Ohio: n.p., 1861.

8708. Williams, Ethel L., (ed.). Biographical Directory of Negro Ministers. New York: Scarecrow Press, 1965. 1970- 2d ed., 1976- 3d ed.   DHU/R
Negro author.

8709. Williams, Fannie B. "A Northern Negro's Autobiography." The Independent (57; Jl. 14, 1904), pp. 91-96.   DHU/MO

8710. Williams, Florence D. Guiding Light. Baltimore: National Baptist Training Union Board, 1962.   DHU/MO

8711. Williams, H. M. Preacher's Text and Topic Book with One Hundred Ordination Questions. Nashville, Tenn.: National Baptist Publishing Bd., 1909.   NN/Sch
Negro author.

8712. Williams, Henry Roger. The Blighted Life of Methuselah. Nashville, Tenn.: National Baptist Publishing Board, 1908.
NN/Sch
Negro author.

8713. Williams, Herbert L. Adventures Into Thought. New York: Exposition Press, 1964.   DHU/MO
Man's origin, history and relationship to God.
Negro author.

8714. Williams, Peter, Jr. A Discourse Delivered on the Death of Capt. Paul Cuffe, Before the New York African Institution, in the African Methodist Episcopal Zion Church October 21, 1817. New York: B. Young & Co., Printer, 1817.
Negro author.

8715. ----- "A Discourse on the Death of Captain Paul Cuffee." Benjamin Brawley (ed.). Early Negro American Writers (Freeport, New York: Books for Libraries, 1968), pp. 100-09.
DHU/R; DLC; NN/Sch
Reprint of 1935 edition.

8716. Williams, Preston N. "Black Perspectives on Los Angeles." The Christian Century (89:35, Oct. 4, 1972), pp. 975-76. DHU/R
Editorial on the conference of the International Congress of Learned Societies in the Field of Religion.

8717. Williams, Smallwood E., (bp.). The Worship of God. Address to United States Churchmen Meeting April 2, 1974 in Cincinnati, Ohio.   Pam. File, DHU/R
Typescript.
Black bishop, Bible Way Church, Washington, D. C.

8718. Wilmore, Gayraud S., Jr. "Ethics in Black and Blight." Christian Century (90:32, Sept. 12, 1973), pp. 877-78. DHU/R
Negro author.

8719. ----- "Ethnic Identities and Christian Theology." Nexus Alumni Magazine of Boston University, School of Theology (16: 1, Wint., 1972-73), pp. 8-19.   Pam. File, DHU/R

8720. Wise, Namon. The Namon Wise Story. New York: Carlton Press, 1964.   DHU/MO
Negro author.

8721. Wood, John Wesley, (bp.). Lyrics of Sunshine. n.p., 1922.
NcSalL
Written by Bishop of A. M. E. Zion Church.

8722. Woodson, Carter Godwin. The Mis-Education of the Negro. Washington, D.C.: The Associated Publishers, 1933.
DHU/MO; CtY-D
Chapter 14, Negro ministers.
Negro author.

8723. ----- (ed.). The Works of Francis Grimke. Washington, D.C.: Associated Publishers, 1942.   DHU/R; DHU/MO

8724. Wright, Nathan, Jr. Let's Work Together. New York: Hawthorn Books, 1968.   DHU/MO
Negro author.

8725. ----- One Bread, One Body. Greenwich, Conn.: Seabury Press, 1962.   DHU/MO

8726. ----- The Riddle of Life, & Other Sermons. Boston: Bruce Humphries, 1952.   DHU/MO

8727. Wright, Richard Robert, Jr., (bp.). "The Economic Condition of Negroes in the North. Negro Rural Communities in Indiana." Southern Workman (37:3, Mr., 1908), pp. 158-72.
DLC; DHU/MO

8728. ----- (bp.). "Health the Basis of Racial Prosperity." The New Chivalry - Health (Nashville: Southern Sociological Congress, 1915), pp. 437-46.   DHU/MO

8729. ----- (bp.). "Negro Companions of Spanish Explorers." American Anthropologist (4; Je., 1902), pp. 217-28. DHU/MO
Negro author.

8730. ----- (bp.). The Negro in Pennsylvania: A Study in Economic History... Philadelphia: A. M. E. Book Concern, 1912.
DHU/MO

8731. ----- (bp.) "The Negro in Times of Industrial Unrest Survey Midmonthly." The Negro in the Cities of the North (New York: The Charity Organization Society, 1905), pp. 69-72.
DHU/MO

8732. ----- (bp.). "The Negro in Unskilled Labor." American Academy of Political and Social Science. The Negro's Progress in Fifty Years (Philadelphia: 1913), pp. 19-27.   DHU/MO

8733. ----- (bp.). The Negro Problem... Philadelphia: A. M. E. Book Concern, 1911.   DHU/MO

8734. ----- (bp.). The Negroes of Xenia, Ohio. Washington, D.C.: Gov't. Printing Office, 1903.   NN/Sch
From: U. S. Bureau of Labor Bulletin, No. 48, Sept., 1903.

8735. ----- (bp.). Outline of the Teaching of Jesus, or the Fundamentals of Christian Doctrine. Philadelphia: A. M. E. Book Concern, 1911.   NN/Sch

8736. ----- (bp.). The Philadelphia Colored Directory: A Handbook of the Religious, Social, Political, Professional Businesses and Other Activities of the Negroes of Philadelphia. Philadelphia: Philadelphia Colored Directory Co., 1907.   DHU/MO

8737. ----- (bp.). Self-Help in Negro Education. Cheyne, Pa.: Committee of Twelve for the Advancement of the Interest of the Negro Race, 1909.   DHU/MO

8738. ----- (bp.). A Study of the Industrial Conditions of the Negro Population of Pennsylvania and Especially of the Cities of Philadelphia and Pittsburgh. Pennsylvania Bureau of Statistics. Report. Harrisburgh, 1914. (40; 1912), pp. 21-195.
                                                                NN/Sch

8739. ----- (bp.). "What Does the Negro Want in Our Democracy?" National Conference of Social Work. Proceedings; Selected Papers of the Annual Meetings (1919), pp. 559-65.   DHU/MO

8740. Wynn, Daniel Webster. Moral Behavior and the Christian Ideal. New York: American Press, 1961.   DHU/MO
       Negro author.

8741. ----- Timeless Issues. New York: Philosophical Library, 1967.   DHU/R
       "Sermons delivered by the chaplain at Tuskegee Institute, Alabama."

8742. Yates, William. Rights of Colored Men to Suffrage, Citizenship and Trial by Jury: Being a Book of the Facts, Arguments and Authorities, Historical Notices and Sketches of Debates with Notes. Philadelphia: Merrihew & Gunn, 1838.
                                                                NcD
       p. 61 has repro. of Rev. P. Williams' passport, an early A.M.E. Zion minister.

8743. Young, Andrew J., Jr. "Speech at Thirtieth Anniversary Dinner of Christianity and Crisis." Christianity and Crisis (31:7, My. 3, 1971), pp. 80-2.   DHU/R
       Negro author.

8744. Young, Lucinda (Smith). The Seven Seals. "A Sinner's Dream", "Conversion", "Daniel in the Lion's Den", Meditations", "Distance of Falling", "Vision of After the Judgement"...
       Philadelphia: J. G. Baugh, 1903.   OWibfU; DHU/MO

B. RELIGIOUS DEVELOPMENT OF THE NEGRO IN CENTRAL AND SOUTH AMERICA

1. Brazil

8745. Abrew Felho, Julio. "A Influencia Negra na Religiao Brasileira." Problemas Brasileira (1:5, 1938), pp. 28-35.   DLC

8746. Antoine, Charles. Church and Power in Brazil. Maryknoll: Orbis Books, 1973.   DHU/R

8747. Bachmann, E. Theodore. Lutherans in Brazil: a Story of Ecumenism. Minneapolis, Minn.: Augsburg Publishing House, 1970.   KyLxCB; TxFTC
       "Compressed and helpful, a 'background' book on Brazil, its history, sociology, and religious trends."

8748. "Baptist Missions in Brazil." Discovery (2; Sept., 1972), pp. 12+.

8749. Bastide, Roger. "Le Batuque de Porto Alegre." Sol Tax, (ed.). Acculturation in the Americas, Proceedings and Selected Papers of the 29th International Congress of Americanists V. 2 (Chicago: University of Chicago Press, 1952), pp. 195-206.
                                                                DAU
       Batuque is a contemporary non-Christian Afro-Brazilian religious sect found in every urban center in Brazil.

8750. ----- Brasil Terra de Maria Isaura Pereira de Queiroz. Sao Paulo: Difusao Europeia do Livro, 1959.   DHU/MO

8751. ----- Le Candomblé de Bahia (rite Nagô). Paris: Mouton & Co., 1958.   DHU/MO; MH; ICU; NN; NNCor
       Candomble, the Afro-Brazilian sect of Bahia.

8752. ----- "Contribuicao ao Estudo do Sincretismo Católico-Fetichista e Macumba Paulists." Estudos Afro-Brasileiros 1st Series. Sao Paulo: n. p., 1946.   NNC; TxU

8753. ----- "Contribuicâo ao Estudo de Sincretismo Catolico - Fetichista..." Sociologia (59:1, 1946), pp. 11-50.   DHU/MO
       "Issued by: Universidade de Sao Paulo, Faculdede de Filosofia, Ciencias E Letras."

8754. ----- ...Estudos Afro-Brasileiros. Sao Paulo: Departmento de Cultura, 1944.   DHU/MO
       Also 1946 edition.

8755. ----- Imagens do Nordeste Mistico em Branco e Prêto. Rio de Janeiro: Secâo de Livros da Emprésa Gráfica O Cruzeiro, 1945.   NNCor; DHU1MO
       Voodooism in Brazil.

8756. ----- "A Imprensa Negra do Estado de Sao Paulo." Sociologia (121:2, 2a series), pp. 50-78.   DHU/MO
       "Issued by: Universidade de Filosofia Ciencias E Letras."

8757. ----- "A Macumba Paulista." Sociologia (59:1, 1946), p. 51-112.   DHU/MO
       "Issued by: Universidade de Sao Paulo, Faculdade de Filosofia, Ciencias E Letras."

8758. ----- Les Religions Africaines au Brazil. Paris: Presses Universitaires de France, 1960.   DHU/MO; CLU; PPT

8759. ----- and Florestan Fernandes. Brancos e Negros em São Paulo; Ensaio Sociológico Sôbre Aspectos da Formacão, Manifestacoes Atvais e Efeitos do Preconceito de côr na Sociedade Paulistanta. São Paulo: Companhia Editora Nacional, 1959.
                                                                DHU/MO

8760. Bell, Lester C. Factors Influencing Doctrinal Developments Among the Brazilian Baptists. Doctoral dissertation. Southwestern Baptist Theological Seminary, 1957.

8761. Benton, Peggie. One Man Against the Drylands: Struggle and Achievement in Brazil. London: Collins and Harvill Press, 1972.   DLC
       Priest in N.E. Brazil and community development.

8762. Bezerra, Felte. "Um Xango de Aracaju." Sociologia (10; 1948), pp. 266-71.   DAU
       Xango is an Afro-Brazilian sect.

8763. Blackford, A. L. "Northern Brazil." The Church At Home and Abroad (1; 1887), pp. 89-91.   DHU/R
       Presbyterian missions.

8764. Bottaro, Marcellino. "Rituals and Candombles." Nancy Cunard, (ed.). Negro Anthology (London: Wishart & Co., 1934), pp. 317-20.   DHU/MO

8765. "Brazil is Taking On the Church." Christian Century (90: 36, Oct. 10, 1973), p. 998.   DHU/R
       Political imprisonment of churchmen in Brazil.

8766. Brasil, Padre Etienne Ignace. "Le Fetichisme des Negres du Bresil." Anthropos (3; 1908), pp. 881-904. DAU; DCU/AN

8767. ----- "Os Males." Revista do Instituto Historica e Geographica Brasileiro (62; pt. 2, 1901), pp. 73-126.   DCU/L
       Male is a believer in Islam of African origin.

8768. "Brazil: The Vanishing Negro." Bloomington, Ind.: Indiana Univ., National Education Television, 1971. 30 min. B & W. Film.
       Blacks in Brazil and Afro-Brazilian religious ceremonies.

8769. Carneiro, Edison de Souza. Antologia de Negro Brasileiro.
Rio de Janeiro: Editora Globo, 1950.   DHU/MO
1967 edition.   DHU/MO

8770. ----- "Arthur Ramos: Brazilian Anthropologist (1903-1949)."
Phylon (12; First Quarter, 1951), pp. 73-81.   DHU/MO

8771. ----- Candombles da Bahia. 3rd ed. Rio de Janeiro: Con-
quista. Cascudo, Luis da Camara, 1948.   DHU/MO
Candomble is the Afro-Brazilian sect of Bahia.
1967 edition.   DHU/MO

8772. ----- Folklore in Brazil. Rio de Janeiro: Campanha de
Defesa do Fololore Brasileiro, 1964.   DHU/MO

8773. ----- Ladinos e Crioulos; estudos Sobre O Negro no Brzail.
Rio de Janeiro: Editora Civilizacao Brasileira, 1964. DHU/MO

8774. ----- ... Negros Bantus; Noras de Enthnographia Religiosa
e de Folklore. Rio de Janeiro: Civilizacao Brasileira, s.a.,
1937.   DHU/MO

8775. ----- ... Religioes Negras; Notas de Etnografia Religiosa...
Rio de Janeiro: Civilizacao Brasileira s.a., 1936.   NcD
Biblioteca de divulgacao scientifica, dirigida pelo prof. dr.
Arthur Ramos. V. 7.
Religion of Negroes of Brazil.

8776. ----- "Les Religions du Noir Bresilien." (Brazil. Mini-
tere das Relations Exteriores. La Contribution de l'Afrique a
la Civilisation, Marseille, Sopic, 1966), pp. 21-29. DHU/MO

8777. ----- "The Structure of African Cults in Bahia." Journal
of American Folk-Lore (53: 208-9, Apr.-Sept., 1940), pp.
271-78.   DHU/R
Microcard.
Brazil.

8778. Castro, Jose de. "Paisagem Religiosa do Brazil." Latino-
america, (Mexico) (3:26, Feb. 1, 1951), pp. 72-78.   NN

8779. "Closing the Circle in Brazil." Commonweal (99:21, Mr.,
1974), pp. 525-26.   DHU/R
Unsigned article by a resident of Brazil stating the plight
of Catholic Bishops who oppose policies of the present
regime.

8780. Cossard-Binon, Giselle. "La Fille de Saint." Journal de la
Societe des Americanistes de Paris (58; 1969), pp. 57-78. DLC
Cult of Brazil.

8781. Davis, Horace Victor. The Missionary Relationship of Southern Baptists with Brazilian Baptists with Special Emphasis Upon
the Period Beginning in 1950. Masters thesis. Southeastern
Baptist Theological Seminary, 1972.

8782. Davis, John Merle. How the Church Grows in Brazil. A
Study of the Economic and Social Basis of the Evangelical Church
in Brazil. New York: Dept. of Social and Economic Research
and Counsel. International Missionary Council, 1943.   DHU/R

8783. Dornas, Joao. Capitulos da Sociologia Brasileira. Rio de
Janerio: Edicao da "Organizacao Simoes," 1955.   PPT
Relition in Brazil.

8784. Dos Santos, Juana E. and M. Deoscoredes. "Ancestor
Worship in Bahia: The Equn Cult." Journal de la Societe des
Americanistes de Paris (58; 1969), pp. 79-180.   DLC

8785. "Economic Slavery in Brazil." Idoc (No. 65; Sept., 1974),
pp. 55-68.   DHU/R

8786. Fernandes, Albino G. Xangos do Nordeste; Investigacoes
Sobre os Cultos Negro-Fetichistas do Recife. Rio de Janeiro:
Civilizacao Brasileira, 1937.   PPT
Religion in Brazil.

8787. Figge, Horst H. "Schriftverkehr mit Geistern. Eine Unter-
suchung von Umbanda-Zettelin." Staden-Jahrbuch (Sao Paulo,
Bresil) (20; 1972), pp. 91-102.   DLC
'Umbanda' is a Brazilian cult.
Writings about ghost and other cult investigations.

8788. Figueiredo, Napolean and Anaiza Vergolina e Silva. "Alguns
Elementos Novos Para o Estudo dos Batuques de Belem." Atas
do Simposia Sobre a Biota Amazonica (2; 1966), pp. 101-22. DLC
Batuque is a contemporary non-Christian Afro-Brazilian
religious sect found in urban centers in Brazil.

8789. Fontenelle, Aluzio. A Umbanda Atraves dos Seculos. Rio
de Janeiro: Organizacao Simoes, 1953.   NF; DLC: TxU
Umbanda is an Afro-Brazilian sect originally found in Rio
de Janeiro which has now spread throughout the urban
areas of Brazil.

8790. Freitas, Bryon Torres de and Vladimir Cardoso. Na Gira
da Umbanda. Rio de Janeiro: Editora Eco, 1965. CST; IU
Cult in Brazil.

8791. ----- Os Orixas e a lei de Umbanda. Rio de Janeiro: Editora Eco, 1969.
Codigo sacerdotal umbandista e Afro-brasileiro.

8792. Freitas, Joao de. Orgum Mege Sao Jorge. Rio de Janeiro:
Editora ECO, 1969.   DLC; WU
Umbanda (Cultus).

8793. ----- Oxum Mare. Nossa Senhora da Conceicao. Rio de
Janeiro: Livraria Freitas Bastos, 1965.   DLC; IU; TxU; KU

8794. ----- Umbanda; Reporagens, Entrevistas, Comentarios,
Rituais, etc. Rio de Janeiro: Edicoes Cultura Afro-aborigene,
1957.   NN; CU
Negro religion in Brazil.

8795. ----- Xango Djacuta; Historia, Mitologia, Ritual, Liturgia,
Culinaria, Curandeirismo, Magia, Doutrina, Espiritismo, etc.
Rio de Janeiro: Edicoes Cultura Afro-aborigene, 1957.   NN
Negro Religion in Brazil.

8796. Galvao, Eduardo. Santos e Visagens; um Estudo da Vida
Religiosa da Ita; Amazonas. Sao Paulo: Companhia Editora
Nacional, 1955.   DHU/MO

8797. Gerbert, Martin. Religionen in Brasilien... Berlin: Colloquium Verlag, 1970.   CLU; PPT
Religious sects in Brazil.

8798. Goncalves, Fernandes Albino. O Folclore Magico do Nordeste. Rio de Janeiro: Civilizacao Brasileira S.A., 1938.   NN
Religion in Brazil.

8799. ----- O Sincretismo Religioso no Brasil: Seitas, Cultos,
Cerimonias & Practicas Religiosas e Magico-Curativas entre
as Populacoes Brasileiras. Curitiba: Editora Guaira Limitada,
1941.   DHU/MO
Religious cults and sects in Brazil.

8800. ----- ... Xangos Do Nordeste; Investigacoes Sobre os Cul-
tos Negro-Fetichistas do Recife. Rio de Janeiro: Civilizacao
Brasileira, 1937.   DHU/MO; NcD; DLC
Religion of Negro race in Brazil.

8801. Greenwood, Leonard. "Brazil: Latest Wave of Arrests Aimed
at Union Members and Church Groups Which Help Workers."
Los Angeles Times (Feb. 11, 1974).

8802. Halliday, Fred and Maxine Molyneux. "Brazil: The Under-
side of the Miracle." Ramparts (12:9, Apr., 1974), pp. 14-18,
20.   DHU/R
The Catholic Church's opposition to the policies of the
Brazilian government.

8803. Hayes, Arnold Edmund. Religion in Brazil. Doctoral
dissertation. Southern Baptist Theological Seminary, 1940.

8804. Herskovits, Melville J. "African Gods and Catholic Saints
in the New World Negro Belief." Frances S. Herskovits,

(Herskovits, Melville J. cont.)
(ed.). The New World Negro (Bloomington: Indiana University Press, 1966), pp. 321-29.   DHU/R
Also in American Anthropologist (39:4, 1937), pp. 635-43.

8805. ----- "Drums and Drummers in Afrobrazilian Cult Life."
Frances S. Herskovits, (ed.). The New World Negro (Bloomington: Indiana University Press, 1966), pp. 183-97.   DHU/R
Also in Music Quarterly (30:4, 1944), pp. 477-92. DAU;DHU

8806. ----- "The Panan, an Afrobahian Religious Rite of Transition.
Frances S. Herskovits, (ed.). The New World Negro (Bloomington: Indiana University Press, 1966), pp. 214-26.   DHU/R
Also in Les Afro-Americains (memoirs de l'Insitut Francais d'Afrique Noire, no. 27), pp. 133-40. Dakar: 1953.

8807. ----- "The Social Organization of the Candomblé." Frances S. Herskovits, (ed.). The New World Negro (Bloomington: Indiana University Press, 1966), pp. 226-47.   DHU/R
Afro-Brazilian Cult life.
Also in Anaais do XXXI Congresso Internacional de Americanistas, I, 1954, pp. 505-32. Sao Paulo, 1955.

8808. ----- "The Social Organization of the Candomblé." The Proceeding of the 31st International Congress of Americanists, 1954.   DAU
Candomble in rhe Afro-Brazilian sect of Bahia.

8809. ----- "Some Economic Aspects of the Afrobahian Candomblé."
Frances S. Herskovits, (ed.). The New World Negro (Bloomington: Indiana University Press,1966), pp. 248-266.   DHU/R

8810. ----- "The Southermost Outposts of New World Africanisms."
Frances S. Herskovits, (ed.). The New World Negro (Bloomington: Indiana University Press, 1966), pp. 199-216. DHU/R
Article deals with African religious traditions in Brazil.
Also in American Anthropologist (45:4, pt.1, 1943), pp. 495-510.

8811. Hutchinson, Harry William. "Afro-Bahian Religious Songs."
Washington: Library of Congress, 1947.
Phonodisc.

8812. ----- Village and Plantation Life in Northeastern Brazil.
Seattle: University of Washington Press, 1957. DHU
Chapter 8 discusses religion among Black people.

8813. Ignace, Etienne (Abbe). "La Fetichisme des Negres du Bresil."
Anthropos (3:506, 1908), pp. 881-903.   DLC

8814. Keith, Henry H. and S. F. Edwards. Conflict and Continuity in Brazilian Society. Columbia, S.C.: University of South Carolina Press, 1970.   DLC; WU
"Stimulating and informative essays on key areas of Brazilian history and culture: its economy, its polity, its religious developments."

8815. Kinsolving, L. L. "Brazil and Our Mission." Spirit of Missions (75; Ja., 1910), pp. 13-17.   DHU/R; DLC

8816. Kirchner, Donnell L. "Banned in Brasilia: Bishops Pastoral."
America (129:21, Dec. 22, 1973), pp. 479-81.   DHU/R
Eighteen bishops and superiors of religious congregations issued a letter on conditions in the Northeast of Brazil, which was banned and silenced by the government.

8817. ----- "Old Problems for Brazil's New President." America (130:8, Mr. 2, 1974), pp. 151-52.   DHU/R
"As Brazilian bishops speak out more and more, the Church, traditionally of the state, is on a collision course with the government."

8818. Kloppenburg, Boaventura. A Umbanda no Brasil: Orientacao para as Catolicos. Petropolis: Editora Vezes Limitada, 1961.
NN
Unbandais an Afro-Brazilian sect originally found in Rio de Janeiro which has now spread throughout the urban areas of Brazil.

8819. Kordon, Bernardo. Candomblé; Contribucion al-Estudio de la Raza Negra en el Rio de La Plata. Buenos Aires: Editorial Continente, 1938.   DLC

8820. Lacerda, Pedro Maria de. Carta Pastoral do Bispo de S. Sebastião do Rio de Janeirio Annunciando a Lei n. 2040 de 28 de Setembro de 1871 Sobre Libertacão de Filhos de Escravas e e Sua Criacao, etc. e Recommendando a Todos Sua Execucao.
Rio de Janeiro: Typographia Nacional, 1871.   NNCor
"No. 9, Slavery and the Church."

8821. Landes, Ruth. The City of Women. New York: Macmillan, 1947.   NjP; DHUlMO; PPT; NcD
Discusses the religion of the Negro race, the Negroes in Brazil and Negro folklore.

8822. ----- "Fetish Worship in Brazil." Journal of American Folk-Lore (53: 208-9, Apr.-Sept., 1940), pp. 261-70.   DHU/R
Microcard.

8823. Leacock, Seth and Ruth. Spirits of the Deep: A Study of an Afro-Brazilian Cult. New York: Doubleday Natural History Press, 1972.   DHU/R

8824. Leahy, J. Gordon. "The Presence of the Gods Among the Mortals." Brazil (N. Y.) (29; 4, Fourth Quarter, 1955), pp. 4-13.
The Candomble dances- The Candomble foods.

8825. Lima, Alceu Amoroso. "A Religiosidade do Povo Brasileiro."
A Odrem, Rio de Janeiro (63:3, Marco 1960), pp. 149-54.
DCU/LI

8826. Major, Alfred Roy. The Origin and Development of Spititualism in Brazil. Masters thesis. New Orleans Theological Seminary, 1957.

8827. McIntire, Robert L. Portrait of Half a Century; Fifty Years of Presbyterianism in Brazil. Doctoral dissertation. Princeton Theological Seminary, 1959.

8828. Medeiros, Jose. Candomblé. Rio de Janeiro: Edicoes Ocruzeiro, 1957.   NNCor: NjP
Voodooism in Brazil.

8829. Mein, David. The Contributions of Baptists to the Life of Brazil. Doctoral dissertation. Southern Baptist Theological Seminary, 1945.

8830. Merriam, Alan P. Songs of the Afro-Bahian Cults: An Ethno-musicological Analysis. Doctoral dissertation. Northwestern University, 1951.

8831. Miranda, Osmundo Afonso. Twentieth-Century Brazilian Christianity and Revolution. Tuscaloosa, Ala.: n. p., 1971.
Pam. File. DHU/R
Mim.
"Paper read at the National Annual Meeting of the American Academy of Religion, Atlanta, Georgia, October 29, 1971."
Negro author.

8832. Mombelli, Savino. Umbanda: Origini, Sviluppi e Significati di una Religione Popolare Brasiliana. Milan: n.p., 1971.
Umbanda is an Afro-Brazilian cult.

8833. Monteiro, Duglas Teixeira. "A Macumba de Victoria."
Proceedings of the 31st International Congress of Americanists.
V. 1. (Sao Paulo: Editora Anhembi, 1955), pp. 464-72. DCU/AN
"Macumba" is the popular term for any Afro-Brazilian religion in Brazil.

8834. Moore, Joseph Grassle. Religion of Jamaican Negroes; A Study of Afro-Jamaican Acculturation. Ann Arbor; Mich.: University Microfilms, 1940.   DLC

8835. Morria, James W. "The Church's Message and Mission in Brazil." Spirit of Missions (73; Je., 1908), pp. 431-37.
DHU/R; DLC

8836. Nina Rodrigues, Raymundo. ...O Animismo Fetichista Dos Negros Bahianos; Prefacio e Notas de Arthur Ramos... Rio de Janeiro, Civilazacao Brasiloleira, s.a., 1935. NcD; DHU/M

8837. ----- ...Os Africanos no Brasil; Revisão e Prefacio de Homero Pires. Sao Paulo, Companhia editora Nacional, 1932. NcD; CLW

8838. Pang, Eul-Soo. "The Changing Roles of Priests in the Politics of Northeast Brasil, 1889-1964." The Americas: a Quarterly Review of Inter-American Cultural History (30; Ja., 1974), pp. 341-72.

8839. Panisset, Ulysses. "The Methodist Church in Brazil." World Parish (13:9, Je., 1974), pp. 5+. DHU/R

8840. Pereira, Manoel Nunes. A Casa das Minas: Contribuciao ao Estudo das Sobrevivencias Daomeianas no Brasil. Rio de Janeiro: Publicacoes da Sociedade Brasileira de Antropologia e Etnologia, no. 1, 1947.
Casa da Minas is an exclusive and conservative sect in Sao Luis. It is the most Dahomean of the Afro-Brazilian sects.

8841. Pereira de Queiroz, M. I. Images Messianiques du Bresil. Sondeos no. 87, Cuernavaca, Mexico: DICOC, 1972.

8842. Pierson, Donald. Negroes in Brazil. Carbondale: Southern Illinois University Press, 1967. DHU
Chapter 10, "The Candomble", an Afro-Brazilian cult.

8843 ----- O Candomble da Baia, Gonache de Rebolo Gonzalez. Curitba: Editora Guaíra Limitada, 1942. NjP
Religion of Negroes in Brazil.

8844. Pierson, Paul. A Younger Church in Search of Maturity: Presbyterian in Brazil from 1910 to 1959. San Antonio: Trinity University Press, 1974. NjP

8845. Pinto, Tancredo da Silva. Cabala Umbandista. Rio de Janeiro: Editôra Espiritualista, 1971. DLC

8846. ----- Origens da Umbanda. Rio de Janeiro: Editôra Espiritualista, 1970. DLC
Fundamento doutrinários, fatôres que a influenciaram, ceremônias do culto, ceremônias nascimento, do casamento e do sirrum.

8847. Plett, Donnie W. Evangelical Literature in Brazil. (Factual Survey of Work of all Protestant Missions in Brazil. Masters thesis. Columbia Bible College (S. C.), 1959.

8848. Pollak-Eltz, Angelina. "Notizen uber de Batuquekult de Neger in Porto Alegre (Brasilien)." Mitterlungen der Anthropologischen Gesselschaft in Wien (96-97; 1967), pp. 138-46. DCU

8849. Pressel, Esther J. Umbanda in São Paola: Religious Innovation in a Developing Society. Doctoral dissertation. Ohio State University, 1971.

8850. Ramos, Arthur. O Folclore Negro do Brasil Demosicologia e Psicanalise. Rio de Janeiro: Librariar Editora, da Casa do Estudante do Brasil, 1954. CoDU

8851. ----- O Folk-Lore Negro do Brazil. Rio de Janeiro: Civilizaco Brasileira, s.a., 1935. DHU/MO

8852. Ramos, Jovelino. "Brazil's Economic Miracle: Against Whom?" Church and Society (64:6, Jl.-Ag., 1974), pp. 35-41. DHU/R

8853. Read, William R. New Patterns of Church Growth in Brazil. Grand Rapids: W. B. Eerdmans Pub. Co., 1965. PPT

8854. ----- A Program for Accelerating the Development of an Indigenous Presbyterian Church in Central Brazil. Masters thesis. Louisville Presbyterian Theological Seminary, 1957.

8855. Ribeiro, René. Cultos Afrobrasileiros do Recife: um Estudo de Ajustamento Social. Recife: Instituto Joaquim Nabuco, 1952. DHU/MO; NjP
Also author's Masters thsis at Northwestern University, 1949, written in English - The Afrobrazilian Cult- Groups of Recife - A Study of Social Adjustment.

8856. ----- "Novos Aspectos do Processo de Reinterpretacao nos Cultos Afrobrasileiro do Recife." Proceedings of the 31st International Congress of Americanists (V. 1, Sao Paulo: Editora Anhembi, 1955), pp. 473-91. DCU/AN

8857. ----- "Personality and the Psychosexual Adjustment of Afro-Brazilian Cult Members." Journal de la Société des Américanistes (58; 1969), pp. 109-20. DLC

8858. Rogers, Cornish. "Pride, Repression and Genocide in Brazil." Editorial Correspondence. The Christian Century (91:19, My. 15, 1974), pp. 524-25. DHU/R
The Roman Catholic Church and Brazil.

8859. Sales, Apolonio. "Os Padres Cambonianos no Brasil." Vozes de Petropolis (51:11, Nov., 1957), pp. 801-11. DLC
Religion in Brazil.

8860. Snyder, Howard A. "De Mello the Missionary." Christianity Today (18:15, Apr. 26, 1974), pp. 46-7. DHU/R
De Mello, Brazilian evangelist and his Christ movement.

8861. Souza Carneiro, A. J. de. Os Mitos Africanos no Brazil, Ciencia do Folk-lore. Sao Paulo: Companhia Editora Nacional, 1937. DHU/MO
Folk-lore in Brazil.

8862. Stamato, Jorge. "An Influencia Negra na Religiao do Brazil." Planalto (Sao Paulo) (1; Jl. 1, 1941), pp. 7-8. DLC

8863. Summerlin, Claude. "J.J. Taylor: Seed Sower in Brzil." The Quarterly Review (32; Ja., 1972), p. 54+. DLC
Religion in Brazil.

8864. Swadley, Elizabeth. "Churches in Brazil." Aware (2; Jl., 1972), pp. 42+.

8865. Thomas, William M. M. "History of the Missionary District of Southern Brazil." Historical Magazine of the Protestant Episcopal Church (1; 1942), pp. 362+. DLC

8866. Tôrres, João Camilo de Oliveira. "Observacões Quase Otimistas Sôbre a Situacão Religiosa do Brasil." Vozes de Petropólis (51:1, Ja., 1957), pp. 60-61. DLC

8867. Tucker, Hugh C. The Bible in Brazil: Colporter Experiences. New York: Fleming H. Revell, 1902. DHU/R
"The Churches Missionary Task in Brazil."

8868. Valente, Waldemar. "Influencias Islamicas nos Groupos de Culto Afro-Brasileiros de Pernambuco." Boletin do Instituto Joaquim Nabuco (4; 1957).

8869. ----- Sincretismo Religioso Afro-Brasileiro. Sao Paulo: Companhia Editora Nacional, 1955. PPT; DHU/MO; CLU
Religion in Brazil.

8870. Verger, Pierre. Dieux d'Afrique, Culte des Orishas et Vodouns à l'Ancienne Côte des Esclaves en Afrique et à Bahia, la Baie de Tous les Saints au Brésil. Paris: P. Hartmann, 1954. NNCor; NCD
Voodooism.

8871. ----- Notes sur le Culte des Oritsa et Vodun a Bahia de Tous les Saints au Bresil et a l'Ancienne Côte des Esclaves en Afrique. Dakar: n.p., 1957. CtY; DHU/MO; CU; NNCor
"Study of African religion in South America."

8872. Vernon, Vance Oral. Illiteracy in Brazil. Masters thesis. Southern Baptist Theological Seminary, 1951.

8873. Vieira, Antonio. ...Sermões e Lugares Selectos... Porto: Editora Edicacão Nacional, 1941.   DHU/R
  Written by an Afro-Brazilian priest, 1608-1697.

8874. Villela, Lavinia Costa. "Fiesta de Divino em Sao Luiz do Paraitinga." Sociologia (59:1, 1946), pp. 115-22.   DHU/MO
  "Issued by: Universidade de Filosofia Ciencias E Letras."

8875. Warren, Donald. "The Negro and Religion in Brazil." Race (6:3, 1965), pp. 199-216.   DAU; DGW; DHU; CtY; NN; MH

8876. Wiarda, Ieda S. and Howard J. "The Churches and Rapid Social Change: Observations on the Differences and Similarities Between Protestants and Catholics in Brazil." Journal of Church and State (12:1, Wint., 1970), pp. 13-39.
                    DHU/R; DAU/W; DGU; DGW

2. Caribbean

8877. Adams-Gordon, Veneta H. "The History of the African Methodist Episcopal Church in the Virgin Islands." Voice of Missions (64:2, Feb., 1963), pp. 10-11.   NN

8878. "African Churches Send Greetings to Caribbean Council of Churches." Voice of Missions (80:7, Mr., 1974), pp. 7-8.
                    DHU/R
  The All-Africa Conference of Churches, which includes the Roman Catholic Church for the first time offered congratulations to the Caribbean Conference of Churches. "Together we share a common calling as Black people to renovate history in the future."

8879. African Methodist Episcopal Zion Church. Home Missions of Jamaica, West Indies. Eight Annual Report Missionary Seer (73:4, Apr., 1974), pp. 7-8+.   DHU/R

8880. Allen, Jewett. "The African M. E. Church in Haiti." The African Methodist Episcopal Church. (70:181, July-Sept., 1954), pp. 12-33 con't on 37.   DHU/R
  Negro author.

8881. ----- "Haiti Today." The African Methodist Episcopal Church (70; 71; 72: 182; 185; 186, Oct.-Dec.; July-Sept.; Oct.-Dec., 1954; 1955), pp. 17-25; 34; 71-84; 38-44.   DHU/R

8882. Anderson, Izett and Frank Cundall. Jamaica Negro Proverbs and Sayings. Kingston, Institute of Jamaica, 1910.   DHU/MO

8883. An Appeal to the Churches in Behalf of the West Indian Mission. n. p., n. d.   DHU/MO

8884. Bach, Marcus. Strange Altars. Indianapolis: Bobbs-Merrill, 1952.   NNCor
  Voodooism in Haiti.

8885. Barreal, Isaac. "Tendencias Sincréticas de los Cultos Populares en Cuba." Cuba National Library. Etnologia y Folklore (Núm. 1; 1966), pp. 17-24.   DLC

8886. Barrett, David B. "The Rastafarians - A Study in Messianic Cultism in Jamaica." Caribbean Monograph Series, No. 6 Puerto Rico, 1968.

8887. Barrett, Leonard E. The Rastafarians: A Study in Messianic Cultism in Jamaica. (Caribbean Monograph Series No. 6). Rio Piedras: Institute of Caribbean Studies, University of Puerto Rico, 1968.   DHU/AA; DHU/R
  Revision of Author's Doctoral dissertation. Temple University, 1967.

8888. Bascom, William R. "Fernando Ortiz, 1881-1969." American Anthropologist (72; 1970), pp. 816-17.   DHU
  About anthropologists investigations of African survivals of religion in Cuba.

8889. ----- "The Focus of Cuban Santeria." Southwestern Journal of Anthropology (6:1, Spr., 1950), pp. 64-68.
  DCU/AN; CtY; CLU; ICU; NN; NNC; NjP; OO; OrU
  The worship of African deities as it is practiced in Cuba today is known as "Santeria."

8890. ----- "Two Forms of Afro-Cuban Divination." Sol Tax (ed.). Acculturation in the Americas. Proceedings and Selected Papers of the 29th International Congress of Americanists (Chicago Press, 1952), V. 1, pp. 169-79.   DAU; PU; Pu-Mu
  Reprinted New York: Cooper Square Publishers, 1967.

8891. ----- "Yoruba Acculturation in Cuba." Les Afro-Americains. Memoires de l'Institut Francais d'Afrique Noire. Dakar: (no. 27; 1953), pp. 163-67.   CU; CtY; DSI; NcD

8892. ----- "The Yoruba in Cuba." Nigeria (No. 37, 1951), pp. 14-20.   DHU/MO

8893. Beckwith, Martha W. Black Roadways: A Study of Jamaican Folk Life. Chapel Hill: The University of North Carolina Press, 1929. WaT; CaBViP; WyU; UPB; TxU; MiU; OO; OCI; PP; AzU; ViU; CU; MH; MWA; NN; NcD; OrP; WaS; WaSP; OrU; Or; MChB
  Treatise on Jamaican social life and customs; folk-lore and superstitions.

8894. ----- Christmas Mummings in Jamaica. (Publication of the Folk-lore Foundation). Vassar College, Philadelphia, 1923.
                    DHU/MO

8895. ----- Jamaica Anansi Stories. New York: American Folk-lore Society, 1924.   DHU/MO
  Also Memoires of the American Folklore Society, v. 17, 1961.

8896. ----- Jamaica Folk-lore. New York: The American Folk-lore Society, G. E. Stechert & Co., 1928. MChB; WaS; CaBVaU; UU; CU; ViU; MiU; OU; PP; OCIW; MH; MB
  Memoirs at the American Folk-lore Society, v. 21. Includes Jamaican folk games, Christmas mummings and proverbs.

8897. ----- Jamaica Proverbs. Poughkeepsie, New York: 1922.
                    DHU/MO
  Publication of the Folk-lore Foundation.

8898. ----- "Some Religious Cults in Jamaica." American Journal of Psychology (34:1, Ja., 1923), pp. 32-45.   NNC

8899. Bell, Henry Hesketh Joudou (Sir.). Obeah, Witchcraft in the West Indies. Westport, Conn.: Negro Universities Press, 1970.   CoDl; NN/Sch
  Reprint of 1893 edition.

8900. ----- Witches and Fishes; Illus. by Joanna Dowling. London: E. Arnold, 1948.   NNCor; NjP
  Voodooism.

8901. Bennett, J. Harry. "The Society for the Propagation of the Gospel and Barbadian Politics, 1710-1720." Historical Magazine of the Protestant Episcopal Church (20; 1950), p. 190+.
                    DLC

8902. Bleby, Henry. Scenes in the Caribbean Sea; Being Sketches from a Missionary's Note-Book. London: n. p., 1868. NN/Sch

8903. Booy, Theodoor de. "Certain West-Indian Superstitions Pertaining to Celts." Journal of American Folk-lore (28:107, Ja.-Mr., 1915), pp. 78-82.   NNC

8904. Bourguignon, Erika. "Dreams and Dream Interpretation in Haiti." American Anthropologist (56; 1954), pp. 262-68.
                    DAU; DCU/AN; DGU; DGW; DHU

8905. ----- "The Persistence of Folk Belief: Some Notes on Cannibalism and Zombis in Haiti." American Journal of Folklore (72:283, Ja.-Mr., 1959), pp. 36-46.   DHU/R
  Microcard.

8906. Bowdler, George A. Baptist Missions in the West Indies: A Comparative Study of Methods and Results. Doctoral dissertation. New Orleans Baptist Theological Seminary, 1948.

8907. Bowers, Joseph O. "Our Colored Catholic Neighbors." St. Augustine's Messenger (18; Mr., 1940), pp. 32-34.   DCU
Catholics in the Caribbean.
Negro author.

8908. Bowman, Laura. The Voice of Haiti: Original Ceremonial Songs, Voodoo Chants, Drum Beats. New York: Clarence Williams Music Publishing Co., 1938.   DHU/MO

8909. Bram, Joseph. "Spirits, Mediums, and Believers in Contemporary Puerto Rico." Transactions of the New York Academy of Sciences (20; 1958), pp. 340-47.   NN

8910. Breathett, George A. The Religious Missions in Colonial French Saint Dominque. Doctoral dissertation. State University of Iowa, 1954.

8911. Brown, F. Ross. Mission to Jamaica: A History of Our Congregational Churches. n.p.: n.p., n.d.   NNMR

8912. Brown, Samuel Elisha. "Treatise on the Rastafarian Movement." Caribbean Studies (6:1, Apr., 1966), pp. 39-40.
Pam. File, DHU/R

8913. Bryan, Charles W. "Overview: World Missions -- Middle America and the Caribbean." Accent (3; Oct., 1972), pp. 4+.

8914. Burke, M. E. The History of the Wesleyan-Methodist Contribution to Education in Jamaica in the Nineteenth Century (1833-1900). Masters thesis. University of London, 1966.

8915. Butel, Pierre. De l'impot des successiones a Rome. De l'impot des mutations par deces. Etude comparee de la loi du 22 frimaire an VII et de l'ordonnance du 31 decembre 1828, establissant l'enregistrement a la Martinique, a la Guadeloupe et a la Guyane. Doctoral dissertation. University of Paris, 1893.

8916. Cabon, A. "La Clergé de la Guyane sous la Révolution." Revue de l'Histoire des Colonies Francaises (37: 3-4, 1950), pp. 173-202.   NN

8917. Cabrera, Lydia. El Monte, Igbo, Finda, Ewe Orisha, Vititi y Finda. Miami: Rema Press, 1968.   DHU
Voodooism in Cuba.

8918. ----- La Sociedad Secreta Abakua Narrada por Viejos Adeptos. Habana: Coleccion del Chichereki, 1958.   DHU/MO
Religion from Calabar found nowhere else in Black America except Cuba.

8919. Cadbury, Henry J. "Barbados Quakers- (1683 to 1761: Preliminary list." Journal of the Barbados Museum and Historical Society. (9:1, Nov., 1941), pp. 29-31.   NNM

8920. ----- "Clergymen Licensed to Barbados, 1694-1811." Journal of the Barbados Museum and Historical Society (15:2, Feb., 1948), pp. 62-69.   NNM

8921. ----- "Further Lists of Early Clergy." Journal of the Barbados Museum and Historical Society (16:1-2, Nov.-Feb., 1948-49), pp. 21-24.   NNM

8922. ----- "Glimpses of Barbados Quakerism 1676-9." Journal of the Barbados Museum and Historical Society (20:2, Feb., 1953), pp. 67-70.   NNM

8923. ----- "186 Barbados Quakeresses in 1677." Journal of the Barbados Museum and Historical Society (9:4, Ag., 1942), pp. 195-97.   NNM

8924. ----- "A Quaker Account of Barbados in 1718." Journal of the Barbados Museum and Historical Society (10:3, My., 1943), pp. 118-24.   NNNAM

8925. ----- "Quakers, Jews and Freedom of Teaching in Barbados, 1686." Bulletin of the Friends' Historical Association (29:2, Aut., 1940), pp. 97-106.   ICU; PFL

8926. ----- "Witnesses of a Quaker Marriage in 1689." Journal of the Barbados Museum and Historical Society (14:1-2, Nov.-Feb., 1946-47), pp. 8-10.   NNM

8927. Caires, H. S. de. "The Jesuits in British Guiana." The Month (177:923, Sept.-Oct., 1941), pp. 455-62.   NN

8928. "Caribbean Reflections." A Collection of Lenten Devotions with Folk Music. Based on The Gift of Love edited by Idris Hamid.
Tape.
"Relates love to daily life and enable people in remote areas to hear the Gospel in terms relevant to the Caribbean man."

8929. Carlile, Gavin. Thirty-Eight Year's Mission Life in Jamaica: A Brief Sketch of Rev. Warrand Carlile. London: J. Nisbet & Co., 1884.   DLC; NjPT

8930. Carlin, Francis Maureen. (sister). The Educational Work of the Amityville Dominicans in Puerto Rico (1910-1960). Doctoral dissertation. Fordham University, 1961.

8931. Carr, Andrew T. "A Rada Community in Trinidad." Caribbean Quarterly (3; 1953), pp. 35-54.   DHU; CLU; SCt

8932. Castillo de Aza, Zenón. Trujillo, Benefactor de la Iglesia. (En el Primer Aniversario del Concordato). Ciudad Trujillo: Editora del Caribe, 1955.   NN/Sch
Church and state during life of Trujillo.

8933. Catherall, G. A. The Baptist Missionary Society and Jamaican Emancipation, 1814-1945. Masters thesis. University of London, 1966.

8934. Chaplin, David. "Caribbean Ecumenism." International Review of Mission (60:238, Apr., 1971), pp. 186-91.   DHU/R

8935. Clarke, John. The Memorials of Baptist Missionaries in Jamaica, Including a Sketch of the Labours of Early Religious Instructors in Jamaica. n.p.: n.p., 1869. MWelC; CtY; NRAB

8936. ----- A Voice of Jubilee: A Narrative of the Baptist Mission, Jamaica, from its Commencement. London: J. Snow, 1865.
DLC; CtY; NN; MdBP

8937. Clavel, M. "Items of Folk-Lore from Bahama Negroes." Journal of American Folklore (17:1, Ja.-Mr., 1904), pp. 36-38.   Pam. File, DHU/R

8938. Cleghorn, Robert. A Short History of Baptist Missionary Work in British Honduras 1822-1939. London: Kingsgate Press, 1939.   NNUT

8939. Clouzot, Henri Georges. Le Cheval des Dieux. Paris: Julliard, 1951.   NNCor
Voodooism.

8940. Cohen, Daniel. Voodoo, Devils, and the New Invisible World. New York: Dodd, Mead & Company, 1972.   DHU/R; NjP

8941. Collier, H. C. "Obeah- the Witchcraft of the West Indies- Plain Bugaboo Between Me and You." Canada-West Indies Magazine (30:8, Ag., 1941), pp. 24-25.   NN

8942. Collier, Mary A. Memoir of Thomas Fowell Buxton: Embracing a Historical Sketch of Emancipation in the West Indies, and of the Niger Expedition for the Suppression of the Slave Trade... Boston: American Tract Society, 1861.
DLC; TxU; MB; PHC

8943. Collins, W. E. "The Church in Jamaica, Past and Present." The East and the West (1:1, Ja., 1903), pp. 92-112.   DHU/R

8944. Comhaire-Sylvain, Suzanne. "Survivances Africaines dans le Vocabulaire Religieux d'Haiti." Études Dahoméennes (10; 1955), pp. 8-20.   DLC

8945. "Conference of Denominations in Jamaica." The Christian Century (39:38, Sept. 21, 1973), p. 168.   DHU/R
"Episcopalian leaders..."

8946. Connell, Neville. "Church Plate in Barbados." Connoisseur (London) (134:539, Sept., 1954), pp. 8-13.   DLC
"A little-known collection of Ecclesiastical silver."

8947. ----- "Father Labat's Visit to Barbados in 1700." Journal of the Barbados Museum and Historical Society (24:4, Ag., 1957), pp. 160-74.   NNAMN

8948. ----- "St. George's Parish Church, Barbados." Journal of the Barbados Museum and Historical Society (20: 3, My., 1953), pp. 133-36.   NNM

8949. Cook, Scott. "The Prophets: A Revivalistic Folk-Religious Movement in Puerto Rico." Caribbean Studies (4:4, 1965), pp. 20-35.   DAU; DGU

8950. Cornford, P. H. Missionary Reminiscences: or, Jamaica Retracted. Leeds: Heaton, 1865.

8951. Courlander, Harold. "Cult Music of Cuba." New York: Ethnic Folkways Library, 1949.
Phonodisc.

8952. ----- The Drum and the Hoe. Life and Lore of the Haitian People. Berkely and Los Angeles: University of California Press, 1960.   DHU/MO; DHU/R
Book review by Sidney W. Mintz in Journal of American Folk-Lore (74:293, Jl.-Sept., 1961), pp. 261-62. Micro-card.   DHU/R
Death rites and services for the Loa.

8953. ----- "Gods of the Haitian Mountains." Journal of Negro History (29:3, Jl., 1944), pp. 339-72.   DHU

8954. ----- Haiti Singing. Chapel Hill: The University of North Carolina Press, 1939.   IC/H; NNCor; DHU/R

8955. ----- Religion and Politics in Haiti; Two Essays. Washington: Institute for Cross-Cultural Research, 1966.
DHU/MO; CLU; MiBsA; MNtcA; PPT

8956. ----- and Remy Bastien. Religion and Politics in Haiti. Washington, D.C.: Institute for Cross-Cultural Research, 1966.   DHU/R; NjP

8957. Crabb, J. A. (ed.). Christ for Jamaica. Kingston: The Pioneer Press, 1951.   DHU/MO; DHU; DLC

8958. Craige, John Houston. Cannibal Cousins. New York: Minton, Balch and Company, 1934.   NNCor
Voodooism in Haiti.

8959. "Creole Folk-Lore from Jamaica." Journal of American Folk-Lore (9:33, Apr.-Je., 1869), pp. 121-8.   DHU/R
Microcard.
"Nancy" stories, similar to Anansi stories of Africa, are tales of genius and survival, usually ending in a proverb or moral.

8960. Crooks, Kenneth B. M. "Forty Jamaican Proverbs: Interpretation and Inferences." Journal of Negro History (18:2, Apr., 1933), pp. 132-43.   DHU

8961. Crowley, Daniel John. I Could Talk Old-Story Good: Creativity in Bahamian Folklore. Berkeley, California: University of California Press, 1966.   CoU; DHU/R

8962. ----- "Supernatural Beings in St. Lucia." The Caribbean (8:11-12, Je.-Jl., 1955), pp. 241-44+.   NNRIS

8963. ----- Tradition and Individual Creativity in Bahamian Folktales. Doctoral dissertation. Northwestern University, 1956.

8964. Cundall, Frank. A Brief History of the Parish Church of St. Andrew, Jamaica. Kingston: Institute of Jamaica, 1931.
NN; CaBViP; LNHT; MWelC; MWA; MChB; KyLxCHB Protestant Episcopal Church.

8965. Danneskiold-Samsoe, A. Der Schlangenklut in Oberguinea und auf Hayti. Doctoral dissertation. University of Leipzip, 1907.
Snake cult of Haiti.

8966. Davidson, Lewis. First Things First: A Study of the Presbyterian Church in Jamaica. Edinburgh: William Blackwood, 1945.   NNUT

8967. Davis, John Merle. The Church in the New Jamaica: A Study of the Economic and Social Basis of the Evangelical Church in Jamaica. New York: International Missionary Council, Dept. of Social and Economic Research and Counsel, 1942.   NNUT

8968. ----- The Cuban Church in a Sugar Economy. A Study of the Economic and Social Basis of the Evangelical Church in Cuba. New York: International Missionary Council, Dept. of Social and Economic Research and Counsel, 1942.   DHU/R

8969. Dean, David M. "The Domestic and Foreign Missionary Papers. The Haiti Papers: 1855-1934." Historical Magazine of the Protestant Episcopal Church (39:1, Mr., 1970), pp. 94-95.   DHU/R
Article describes papers.

8970. Delany, Francis X. A History of the Catholic Church in Jamaica B.W.I., 1494 to 1929. New York: Jesuit Mission Press, 1930.   NN/Sch; DHU/R

8971. Delgado, Primitivo. The History of Southern Baptist Missions in Cuba to 1945. Doctoral dissertation. Southern Baptist Theological Seminary, 1948.

8972. Denis, Lorimer and Francois Duvalier. L'Evolution Stadiale du Vodou. Port-au-Prince, Haiti: Imprimerie de l'etat, 1944.   DHU/MO

8973. ----- "L'Evolution Studiale du Vodu." Bulletin de Bureau D'Ethnologie (1955), pp. 1-29.   NNMR

8974. Deren, Maya. Divine Horsemen: The Living Gods of Haiti. London: Longmans, 1953.   DHU/R; DHU/MO; NNCor

8975. Desrosiers, Toussaint. "Haitian Voodoo." Américas (22:2, Feb., 1970), pp. 35-39. DAU; DCU/SW; DGU; DGW; DHU

8976. Detweiler, Charles Samuel. The Waiting Isles; Baptist Missions in the Caribbean. Edited by the Department of Missionary Education, Board of Education of the Northern Baptist Convention... Boston: The Judson Press, 1930.   NN/Sch

8977. Devas, Raymund P. "The Catholic Church in Grenada, B.W.I. (1650-1927)." Irish Ecclesiastical Record (5th ser; Ag. 30, 1927), pp. 188-99; (5th ser; Sept. 30, 1927), pp. 288-307; (5th ser; My. 31, 1928), pp. 474-81; (5th ser; Jl. 22, 1928), pp. 51-56.   NN

8978. ----- Conception Island; or, The Troubled Story of the Catholic Church in Grenada. London: Sands, 1932.   NNRIS

8979. Dewisme, C. H. Les Zombis; on Le Secret des Morts-Vivants. Paris: Grasset, 1957.   NNCor
Voodooism.

8980. Dix, Jabez. "Adolphe-One of the Most Terrible of Obeahmen." Canada-West Indies Magazine (22:2, Ja., 1933), pp. 53-55.   NN

8981. Dorsainvil, Justin C. Vodou et Neurose. Port-au-Prince: Imperimerie "La Presse", 1931.   DHU/MO

8982. Duncan, Peter. Narrative of the Wesleyan Mission to Jamaica, with Occasional Remarks on the State of Society in that Colony. London: Partridge, 1849. DLC; WIC; MU

8983. Dunham, Katherine. Island Possessed. Garden City, N. Y.: Double Day, 1969. NNCor; NjP; PPT
Voodooism in Haiti.

8984. Dunningan, A. "Century of Christian Faith." Sepia (10; Nov., 1961), pp. 56-61. DHU/MO
"Protestant Episcopal Church in Haiti."

8985. Durham, Harriet F. Caribbean Quakers. Hollywood, Florida: Dukane Press, Inc., 1972. DHU/R
Abolition and Emancipation, pp. 79-106.

8986. Easton, Wilfred. West Indies: What of the Church? London: Edinburgh House Press, 1956. NNUT; NAT

8987. Edwards, Charles Lincoln. Bahama Songs and Stories. Boston: Houghton, Mifflin & Co., 1895. O

8988. Elliott, Luke D. History of the Work of the Churches of Christ in Jamaica, B.W.I. n.p.: n.p., 1945. TN/DCHS

8989. Ellis, John B. The Diocese of Jamaica: A Short Account of Its History, Growth, and Organization. London: Society for Promoting Christian Knowledge, 1913. NN; WU; CtY; PPPD

8990. "Epiphany (Theophany) Feast of the Ethiopian Church in Jamaica." One Church (26:3, 1972), pp. 129-31. DHU/R

8991. Facts on Jamaica. "Religion in Jamaica." The Jamaica Information Service, No. 3. Kingston, Jamaica, W. I. DLC

8992. Farrar, P. A. "Christ Church." Journal of the Barbados Museum and Historical Society (2:3, My., 1935), pp. 143-54. NNM

8993. Franco, Raimundo A. and Israel Batiota Guersa. "Christians in Cuba." International Documentation on the Contemporary Church (N. Amer. edition) (45; Apr. 15, 1972), pp. 68-81. DHU/R

8994. Franklin, C. B. A Century and a Quarter of Hanover Methodist Church History, 1809-1934. Port of Spain: Trinidad, 1934. DLC

8995. Franklin, James. The Present State of Hayti (Santo Domingo), With Remarks on its Agriculture, Commerce, Laws, Religion, Finances, and Population... London: J. Murray, 1828. DHU/MC

8996. Friends, Society of. United Meeting. Annual Report of the Wider Ministries Commission in Session April 11-13, 1972. Forty-third Annual Report. Richmond, Indiana: Friends United Meeting, 1972. Pam. File, DHU/R
Reports from East Africa and Jamaica included.

8997. Froude, J. A. "Myths of Voodoo Worship and Child Sacrifice in Haiti." Journal of American Folklore (1:1, Apr.-Je., 1888), pp. 16-30. Pam. File, DHU/R
European origin of Voodoo

8998. Gardiner, Marilyn. "Rastafarian Zealot Has Much to Teach." A. D. Presbyterian Life Edition (3:3, Mr., 1974), p. 58. DHU/R
Rastafarian leader in Jamaica.

8999. George, Thomas P. "Jamaica as a Missionary Centre." The East and The West (6; Apr., 1908), pp. 195-203. DHU/R

9000. Goodwin, Irwin. "A First in the Caribbean. 146 at Remarkable Meeting Discuss Changing Role of Religion in the Area." Washington Post (Dec. 4, 1971). Pam. File; DHU/R

9001. Goveia, Elsa V. Slave Society in the British Leeward Islands at the End of the Eighteenth Century. University of Puerto Rico: Institute of Caribbean Studies, 1965. DHU/R
Christian Missions, pp. 263-310.

9002. Granier de Cassagnac, Bernard Adolphe. Voyage aux Antilles, Francaises, Anglaises Danolaes, Espagnoles: à Saint-Domingus et aux Etats-Unis d' Amérique... Paris: Au Comptoir des Imprimeurs-Unis, 1843-1844. NN/Sch
Slavery and the church in the French West Indies.

9003. Greer, Harold Edward, Jr. History of Southern Baptist Mission Work in Cuba, 1886-1916. Doctoral dissertation. University of Alabama, 1965.

9004. Grose, Howard Benjamin. Advance in the Antilles; the New Era in Cuba and Porto Rico. New York: Literature Dept., Presbyterian Home Missions, 1910.
(Forward mission study courses...)

9005. Guggenheim, Hans and Andrew T. Carr. "Tribalism in Trinidad." Medical Newsmagazine (9:2, Feb., 1965), pp. 138-43. NNRIS

9006. "Haiti." Christian Union (1:5, My., 1850), pp. 230-32.

9007. "Haitians Without Haven." Editorial. Christian Century (91: 8, Feb. 27, 1974), p. 291. DHU/R
Criticism of the fact that the United States offers a haven to refugees in the Middle East and other places and ignores refugees from Haiti.

9008. Hall, Gwendolyn M. Social Control in Slave Plantation Societies. A Comparison of St. Dominique and Cuba. Baltimore: The Johns Hopkins Press, 1971. DHU/R
Includes role of religion in both countries.

9009. Hardie, W. G., (bp.). "A Suffering Church in the West Indies." The East and West Review (4:4, Oct., 1938), pp. 341-47. DHU/R
Church of England mission in Jamaica.

9010. Harris, Wilson. "History, Fable and Myth in the Caribbean and Guianas." Caribbean Quarterly (16:2, Je., 1970), pp. 1-32. Pam. File, DHU/R; DHU/MO

9011. Henderson, George E. Goodness and Mercy: A Tale of a Hundred Years by George E. Henderson, Pastor, 1876-1926, Brown's Town Baptist Church, Jamaica, British West Indies. Kingston: The Gleaner Co., 1931. CtY-D; CtY; PPC

9012. Hendrick, S. Purcell. A Sketch of the History of the Cathedral Church of St. Jago de la Vega, Spanish Town in the Parish of St. Catherine, Jamaica. Kingston: Jamaica Times, 1911. NN

9013. Henney, Jeanette. Spirit Possession Belief and Trance Behavior in a Religious Group in St. Vincent, British West Indies. Doctoral dissertation. Ohio State University, 1968.

9014. Henry, Frances Mischel. "African 'Powers' in Trinidad: The Shango Cult." Anthropological Quarterly (30:2, Apr., 1957), pp. 45-59. DHU

9015. ----- "Social Strification in an Afro-American Cult." Anthropological Quarterly (38:2, Apr., 1965), pp. 72-78. DHU
Trinidad.

9016. ----- "Two Forms of Afro-Cuban Divination." Acculturation in the Americas, Tax, Sol (ed.). Proceedings and Selected Papers of the 29th International Congress of Americanists. (Chicago Press, 1952). V. 1, pp. 169-79. DAU; DCU/AN; DGU
Reprinted, New York: Cooper Square Publishers, 1967.

9017. Herrick, E. P. "Witchcraft in Cuba." Southern Workman (36:7, Jl., 1907), pp. 401-5. DLC; DHU/MO
How witchcraft was imported into Cuba from Western Africa.

9018. Herskovits, Melville J. Life in a Haitian Village. Introduction by Edward Brathwaite. Garden City, N. Y.: Doubleday, 1971. DHU/R; IC/H; NNCor; NjP
Part 3, Haitian Religion, Chapter 14, Catholicism and Vodun, and Appendix I, The Gods of the Vodun Pantheon.

9019. ----- "Trinidad Proverbs ("Old Time Saying so")." Journal of American Folk-Lore (58:299, Jl.-Sept., 1945), pp. 195-207.
                                                                NNC; DHU/R
        Microcard.

9020. ----- "The Trinidad Shouters: Protestant-African Synthesis." Frances S. Herskovits, (ed.). The New World Negro (Bloomington: Indiana University Press, 1966), pp. 329-53.   DHU/R

9021. ----- "What is 'Voodoo'?" Frances S. Herskovits, (ed.). The New World Negro (Bloomington: Indiana University Press, 1966), pp. 354-61.   DHU/R

9022. Hill, Clifford S. Black Churches: West Indian and African Sects in Britain. London: British Council of Churches, Community and Race Relations Unit, 1971.   DLC

9023. ----- "From Church to Sect: West Indian Religious Sect Development in Britain." Journal for the Scientific Study of Religion (10:2, Sum., 1971), pp. 114-23.   DHU/R
        "Written by a Fellow of the Martin Luther King Foundation," London, England.

9024. ----- West Indian Migrants and the Churches. London: Oxford University Press, 1963.   NNCor; DHU/AA
        Church and race problems, London.

9025. Hinton, John H. Memoir of William Knibb, Missionary in Jamaica. London: Houlston & Stoneman, 1849.
                                                NN; CtY; RPB; LU; DLC

9026. Hoetink, H. The Two Variants in Caribbean Race Relations. London: Published for the Institute of Race Relations, London by Oxford University Press, 1967.   DHU/R
        See index under Church and Religion, Missionaries, etc.

9027. Hogg, Donald William. "The Convince Cult in Jamaica." Sidney Mintz, (ed.). (Papers in Caribbean Anthropology, University Publications in Anthropology, no. 58, 1960). New Haven: Yale Dept. of Anthropology, 1960), pp. 3-24.
            MH-P; FMU; NNC; OU; FU; TCU; DCU; CtY

9028. ----- Jamaican Religions: A Study in Variations. Doctoral dissertation. Yale University, 1964.

9029. ----- "Statement of a Ras Tafari Leader." Caribbean Studies (6:1, Apr., 1966), pp. 37-38.
                                    Pam. File, DHU/R; DAU; DGU

9030. Holder, Geoffrey. Black Gods, Green Islands. Garden City, N.Y.: Doubleday, 1959.   DHU/MO
        Religion in Trinidad.

9031. Holly, James Theodore, (bp.), and J. Dennis Harris. Black Separatism and the Caribbean, 1860. Edited with an Introduction by Howard H. Bell. Ann Arbor: The University of Michigan Press, 1970.   DHU/R
        Includes "a vindication of the capacity of the Negro race for self-government and civilized progress" by Bishop Holly.

9032. ----- (bp.). Facts About the Church's Mission in Haiti; A Concise Statement. New York: Thomas Whittaker, 1897.
                                                                DHU/MO
        Written by first Negro bishop of Protestant Episcopal Church.

9033. Horowitz, Michael M., (ed.). Peoples and Cultures of the Caribbean, An Anthropological Reader. Garden City, N.Y.: Published for the American Museum of Natural History by the Natural History Press, 1971.   DHU/MO
        Includes information on religion and folklore.

9034. Horsford, John. A Voice from the West Indies: Being a Review of the Character and Results of Missionary Efforts in the British and other Colonies in the Caribbean Sea. With Some Remarks. London: Alexander Heylin, 1856.
                                            NN; IEG; NcD; ICarbS

9035. Hoster, William. "Our Mission Work in Porto Rico and the Virgin Islands." Spirit of Missions (91: , Ja., 1926), pp. 19-26.
                                                        NN; DHU/R

9036. Hughes, Henry Brackenbury Louis. Christian Missionary Societies in the British West Indies during the Emancipation Era. Doctoral dissertation. University of Toronto, 1944.

9037. ----- "The Impact on Jamaica of the Evangelical Revival." Jamaican Historical Review (1:1, Je., 1945), pp. 7-23.   NNM

9038. Hulse, Hiram H. "The History of the Church in Cuba." Historical Magazine of the Protestant Episcopal Church (6; 1937), p. 249-.   DLC

9039. Hurbon, Laënnec. Dieu dans le Vaudou Haitien. Préf. de Geneviève Calme-Griaule. Paris: Payot, 1972. NNCor; NjP
        Voodooism.

9040. Hurston, Zora Neale. Voodoo Gods. London: J. M. Dent, 1939.   NN/Sch; A&M
        An inquiry into native myths and magic in Jamaica and Haiti.

9041. Huxley, Francis. The Invisibles: Voodoo Gods in Haiti. New York: McGraw-Hill, 1969. DHU/R; NjP; MiBsA; TSewU-T; NNCor; PPT

9042. Inman, Samuel Guy. Trailing the Conquistadores. New York: Friendship Press, 1930.   MNtcA
        Missions in the West Indies.

9043. International Missionary Council, Caribbean Consultation, Inter-American University, San German, P. R., 1957. The Listening Isles; Records of the Caribbean Consultation, May 17-24, 1957, Held Under the Auspices of the International Missionary Council with the Cooperation of the World Council of Christian Education and Sunday School Association. (Edited by J. W. Decker) New York: International Missionary Council, 1957.   DHU/R

9044. ----- Dept. of Social and Economic Research. The Church in the New Jamaica; a Study of the Economic and Social Basis of the Evangelical Church in Jamaica; J. Merle Davis, Director. New York, London: Dept. of Social and Economic Research and Counsel, International Missionary Council, 1942.   DHU/R

9045. ----- The Cuban Church in a Sugar Economy; a Study of the Economic and Social Basis of the Evangelical Church in Cuba. J. Merle Davis, (dir.). New York, London: Dept. of Social and Economic Research & Counsel, International Missionary Council, 1942.   DHU/R

9046. Ivy, James W. "The Wisdom of the Haitian Peasant." Journal of Negro History (26:4, Oct., 1941), pp. 485-98.
                                                Pam. File, DHU/R

9047. Jan, Jean Marie. Les Congregations Religieuses à Saint-Dominique, 1681-1793. Port-au-Prince: n. p., n. d. NN/Sch

9048. Jay, E. H. "The Christian Church in Jamaica." International Review of Missions (51; 1962), pp. 471-78.   DHU/R

9049. Jekyll, Walter, (ed.). Jamaica Song and Story. Annancy Stories, Digging Sings, Ring Tunes, and Dancing Tunes. London: Folk-Lore Society, 1907. DHU/MO; DLC; CaBVaU; NIC; OrU; TxU; NN; TU

9050. Jesuits. Letters from Missions. Mission de Cayenne et de la Guyane Francaise. Avec une carte géographique. Paris: Julien, Lanier, Cosnard et oe., 1857.   NN/Sch

9051. "John Calvin's Gospel." Newday (Jamaica). (3:7, Jl., 1959), pp. 33-35.   DHU/MO
        Discusses Jamaican Presbyterianism.

9052. Johnson, G. E. Hickman. "Christian Work in Jamaica." International Review of Missions (24; 1935), pp. 344-48.
                                                                DHU/R

9053. Johnson, John H. "Folklore from Antigua, British West Indies." Journal of American Folklore (34:131, Ja.-Mr., 1921), pp. 40-88.   DHU/R

9054. Josselin de Jong, J. P. B. "Folklore van Suriname." West-Indische Gids (20; 1938), pp. 1-8.   NNC

9055. Julien, Claude. "Church and State in Cuba: Development of a Conflict." Cross Currents (11; Sept., 1961), pp. 186-92.   DHU/R
Catholicism in Cuba.

9056. Kiemen, Mathias C. "Catholic Schools in the Caribbean." A. Curtis Wilgus, (ed.). The Caribbean: Contemporary Education /Papers delivered at the Tenth Conference on the Caribbean held at the University of Florida, Dec. 3-5, 1959/ (Gainesville: University of Florida Press, 1960), pp. 51-64.   NNRIS

9057. Kiev, Ari. "Beliefs and Delusions of West Indian Immigrants to London." British Journal of Psychiatry (109:460, My., 1963), pp. 356-63.   NNRIS

9058. ----- "Psychotherapeutic Aspects of Pentecostal Sects Among West Indian Immigrants of England." British Journal of Sociology (15:2, Je., 1964), pp. 129-38.   NNRIS

9059. Kilpatrick, J. W. Protestant Missions in Jamaica: A Critical Survey of Mission Policy from 1754 to the Present Day. Doctoral dissertation. University of Edinburgh, 1944.

9060. King, James Ferguson. Negro Slavery in Viceroyalty of New Granada: Masters thesis. Univ. of California (Berkeley), 1939.

9061. King, R. O. C. "The Church in the British West Indies." International Review of Missions (37:145, Ja., 1948), pp. 80-85.   NN

9062. King, William Francis Henry. Addington Venables Bishop of Nassau. A Sketch of His Life and Lobours for the Church of God. London: W. W. Gardner, 1878.   NN/Sch

9063. Kitzinger, Sheila. "The Prophets: a Revivalistic Folk Religious Movement in Puerto Rico." Michael M. Horowitz, (ed.). Peoples and Cultures of the Caribbean, An Anthropological Reader (Garden City, New York: Pub. for the American Museum of Natural History, 1971), pp. 580-88.   DHU/MO

9064. ----- "Protest and Mysticism: the Rastafari Cult of Jamaica." Journal for the Scientific Study of Religion (8:2, Fall, 1969), pp. 240-62.   DHU/R

9065. Klingberg, Frank J. "The Lady Mico Charity Schools in the British West Indies, 1833-1842." The Journal of Negro History (24; 1939), pp. 291-344.   DHU/R

9066. Knapp, M. Diary Letters; a Missionary, (sic), Trip Through the West Indies and to South America. Cincinnati: God Revivalist Office, 1918.   NN/Sch

9067. Knox, John P. A Historical Account of St. Thomas, W. I., with its Rise and Progress in Commerce; Missions and Churches; Climate and its Adaptation to Invalids... New York: C. Scribner, 1852.   DHU/MO

9068. Lachatañeré, Rómulo. ...Manual de Santeria; el Sistema de Cultos' Lucumis. La Habana, Cuba: Editorial Caribe, 1942.   NN/Sch
Negroes in Cuba and their religion.
Negro author.

9069. ----- "El Sistema Religioso de los Lucumis y Otras Influencias en Cuba." Estudios Afrocubanos (5; 1945-46), pp. 191-215.   DHU/MO; NN; NNC

9070. Laguerre, Michel. "The Drum and Religious Dance in Christian Liturgy in Haiti." Freeing the Spirit (1:2, Spr., 1972), pp. 11-15.   DHU/R

9071. ----- "An Ecological Approach to Voodoo." Freeing the Spirit (3:1, Spr., 1974), pp. 4-12.   DHU/R

9072. ----- "Le Tambour et la Danse Religieuse dans la Liturgie Chrétienne en Haiti." Revue du Clergé Africain (27; 6, Nov., 1972), pp. 587-603.   DHU/R
Religious ritual in Haiti.

9073. ----- "Voodoo as Religious and Revolutionary Ideology." Freeing the Spirit (3:1, Spr., 1974), pp. 23-28. DHU/R
Voodoo in Haiti was a politico-religious movement and was one of the critical factors that helped make the Haitian revolution successful.

9074. Larsen, Jens Peter Mouritz. Virgin Islands Story; a History of the Lutheran State Church, Other Churches, Slavery, Education, and Culture of the Danish West Indies, Now the Virgin Islands. Philadelphia: Muhlenberg Press, 1950. NN/Sch

9075. Lawaetz, Herman. ...Brodremenighedens Mission i Dansk-Vestindien, 1769-1848; Bidrag Til en Charakteristik af Brodrekirkin og dens Gerning og af den Farvede Races Stilling til Christendommen. Kobenhaven: O. B. Wroblewski, 1902.   NN/Sch
Missions, Virgin Islands.

9076. Leach, Mae Edward. "Jamaican Duppy Lore." Journal American Folk-Lore (74:293, Jl.-Sept., 1961), pp. 207-15.   DHU/R
Microcard.
African survival of spirit beliefs.

9077. "Letter From Jamaica: What is Being Done for the Blacks; Day-schools, - Sunday-schools, - Denominational Work." Southern Workman (6:11, Nov., 1877), p. 87. DLC; DHU/MO
Letter written to the editor by Geo. Sargeant, Chairman of District and General Superintendent of Missions and schools for Wesleyan Churches of Jamaica.

9078. "Letters Showing the Rise and Progress of the Early Negro Churches of Georgia and the West Indies." Journal of Negro History (1:1, Ja., 1916), pp. 69-92.   DHU/MO

9079. Levo, John Ernest. Black and White in the West Indies. London: Society for the Propagation of the Gospel in Foreign Parts, 1930.   CtY-D

9080. ----- The Romantic Isles: A Sketch of the Church in the West Indies. London: The Society for the Propagation of the Gospel in Foreign Parts, 1937.   CtY/DML

9081. Levy, Babette M. "The West Indies and Bahamas: Puritanism in Conflict with Tropical Island Life." Proceedings of the American Antiquarian Society V. 70 (Worcester, Mass.: n.p., 1960), pp. 278-348.   NNC

9082. Livingston, Noel B. "Records of the Kingston Vestery." Jamaican Hisotrical Review (1:2, Dec., 1946), pp. 181-86.   NNC

9083. Loederer, Richard A. Voodoo Fire in Haiti. Garden City, N.Y.: Doubleday, Doran & Co., Inc., 1935. DHU/MO; IC/H; DHU/R; PPT

9084. Love, J. Robert. Is Bishop Holly Innocent? Charges Specific Arguments, Canon Laws Involved in an Ecclesiastical Trial Held in Holy Trinity Church, Port-au-Prince, Haiti, the 4th of Sept., 1882. n.p., n.d.   NN/Sch
First Negro Bishop in the Protestant Episcopal Church.

9085. MacDonald, John Stuart and Leatrice D. MacDonald. "Transformation of African and Indian Family Traditions in the Southern Caribbean." Comparative Studies in Society and History (15:2, 1973), pp. 171-98.   DHU/R

9086. Malden, K. S. The Broken Bonds: The S. P. G. and the West Indian Slaves. London: The Society for the Propagation of the Gospel in Foreign Parts, 1933.   CtY-D

9087. Marcelin, Milo. "Les Grands Dieux du Vodou Haitien."
Journal de la Societé des Americanistes (36; 1947), pp. 51-135.
                                                                      DCU/A

9088. ----- Mythologie Vodou, Rite Arada. Port-au-Prince: Ed.
Haitiennes, 1949.   NjP; NNCor; DHU/MO

9089. Marrat, Jabez. In the Tropics; or, Scenes and Incidents
of West Indian Life. London: Wesleyan Conference Office,
1876.   NN/Sch

9090. Mars, Jean Price. Ainsi Parla l'Oncle; Essais d'Ethnographie. New York: Parapsychology Foundation, 1954.
                                                     NjP; NNCor
        Folk-lore in Haiti.

9091. Mars, Louis. La Crise de Possession; Essais de Psychiatrie
Comparées. Port-au-Prince, Haiti: Impr. de l'Etat, 1955.
                                               DHU/MO; PPT
        Voodooism and demonic possession.

9092. Martin, Juan L. Ecué, Changó y Yemayá (Ensayos Sobre la
Sub-Religion de los Afro-Cubanos). Habana: Cultural, 1930.
                                               NNCor; DHU/MO
        Voodooism.

9093. Maximilien, L. Le Vodou Haitien: Rite Rada-Kanzo.
Port-au-Prince: n.p., 1945.   DHU/MO

9094. McDaniel, Cecilia. "The Trinidadian Yoruba: An Inquiry
into a Belief System." Renaissance 2: A Journal of Afro-
American Studies (3; 1973), p. 613.

9095. McGavran, Donald Anderson. Church Growth and Missions
in Jamaica. n.p.: Menier, 1958.   KyLxCB

9096. McKenzie, Azariah. "Baptists of the Caribbean and Their
Attitude Toward Other Christians." Foundations (17:1, Ja.-Mr.,
1974), pp. 51-57.   DHU/R

9097. McNeill, George. The Story of Our Missions: The West
Indies. Edinburgh: Foreign Mission Committees at the Offices
of the United Free Church of Scotland, 1911.   NNUT

9098. Mead, Frank Spencer. On Our Door Step. New York:
Friendship Press, 1948.   NN/Sch
        Missions in the Virgin Islands.

9099. Meikle, H. B. "Mermaids and Fairymaids or Water Gods
and Goddesses of Tobago." Caribbean Quarterly (5:2, Feb.,
1958), pp. 103-8.   NNRIS

9100. Mennesson-Rigaud, Odette. "Étude sur le Culte des Marassa
en Haiti." Zaire (6:6, Je., 1952), pp. 597-621. DCU/AN; DLC;
ICU; NN; DHU/MO

9101. ----- "The Feasting of Gods in Haitian Vodu." Primitive
Man (19; 1946), pp. 1-58. CtY; ICU; DGU; NN; NNC; OU; NjP;
OrU

9102. Métraux, Alfred. "The Concept of Soul in Haitian Vodu."
Southwestern Journal of Anthropology (Spr., 1946), pp. 84-92.
CLU; ICU; NN; NNC; NjP; OO; OrU

9103. ----- "Croyances et Pratiques Magiques dans la Vallee de
Marbial, Haiti." Societe des Americanistes de Paris Journal
(42-43; 1953), pp. 135-98.   DLC

9104. ----- Haiti. Black Peasants and Voodoo. New York:
Universe Books, 1960.   DHU/MO

9105. ----- "Rites Funeraires des Paysans Haitiens." Arts et
Traditions Populaires (2-3:4, Oct.-Dec., 1954), pp. 289-306.
                                            DLC

9106. ----- Voodoo in Haiti. New York: Schocken Books, 1972.
DHU/R; NjP; Ic/H; MiBsA; FU; DLC; CLU; MiU; ICLI; PPT
        Reprint of New ork: Oxford University Press, 1959 edition.

Review by George E. Simpson in Journal of American Folk-
Lore (73:289, Jl.-Sept., 1960), pp. 265-6. Microcard,
DHU/R

9107. Mischel, Frances O. "African 'Powers' in Trinidad: the
Shango Cult." Anthropological Quarterly (30:2, Apr., 1957),
pp. 45-59.   DHU; NNC

9108. ----- "Faith Healing and Medical Practice in the Southern
Caribbean." Southwestern Journal of Anthropology (15; Wint.,
1958), pp. 407+.   DCU/A

9109. ----- A Shango Religious Group and the Problem of Prestige
in Trinidadian Society. Doctoral dissertation. Ohio State
University, 1958.

9110. Mischel, Walter and Frances Mischel. "Psychological Aspects of Spirit Possession." American Anthropoligist (60:2,
pt. 1, Apr., 1958), pp. 249-60.   NNC; DCU/A; DHU
        Trinidad.

9111. Mitchell, David I. Principles and Policies for a Program of
Leadership Education for the Sunday Church Schools of the Methodist Church in English-Speaking Caribbean. Doctoral dissertation. Columbia University, 1964.

9112. Moister, William. Memorials of Missionary Labours in Africa and the West Indies: with Historical and Descriptive Observations. New York: Lane & Scott, 1851. NN/Sch; CtY

9113. Moore, Joseph Graessle and George E. Simpson. "A Comparative Study of Acculturation in Morant Bay and West Kingston,
Jamaica." Zaire (9-10; 1957), pp. 979-1019; (11; 1958), pp. 65-
87.

9114. Morgan, Carol McAfee. Rim of the Caribbean. New York:
Firendship Press, 1942.   NN/Sch
        Missions in the West Indies and Central America.

9115. Necheles, Ruth F. The Abbe Gregoire, 1787-1831: The
Odyssey of an Egalitarian. Westport, Conn.: Greenwood
Press, Inc., 1973.   DHU/MO
        Constitutional Bishop of Santo Domingo
        (French Colony).

9116. Neehall, Roy. Presbyterianism in Trinidad; a Study of the
Impact of Presbyterianism on the Island of Trinidad in the
19th Century. Masters thesis. Union Theological Seminary
(New York), 1958.

9117. Nelson, Robert G. Disciples of Christ in Jamaica 1858-
1958: A Centennial of Missions is the "Gem of the Caribbean."
St. Louis: Bethany Press, 1958. KyLxCB; CtY-D; NjPT;
MH-AH

9118. ----- A Historical Study of the American Christian Missionary
Society and its Work in Jamaica, British West Indies. Bachelor
of Divinity paper. Texas Christian University, 1953.

9119. Nettleford, Rex. "Pocomania in Dance-Theater." Freeing
the Spirit (3:1, Spr., 1974), pp. 16-19.   DHU/R
        How the ritual of dance in this Jamaican revival cult has
        influenced the dance theater in Jamaica.

9120. "New Day for Caribbean Churches." Presbyterian Outlook
(155:47, Dec. 24, 1973), pp. 3-4.   Pam. File, DHU/R
        Sixteen churches, Protestant, Roman Catholic and Orthodox
        form the Caribbean Conference of Churches.

9121. Newell, William W. "Myths of Voodoo Worship and Child
Sacrifice in Hayti." Journal of American Folk-Lore (1:1, Apr.
-Je., 1888), pp. 16-30.   DHU/R
        Microcard.

9122. Norris, Katrin. Jamaica: The Search for an Identity.
London: Institute of Race Relations, Oxford University Press,
Inc., 1962.   DHU

9123. Noussane, Henri de. La France Missionnaire Aux Antilles: Guadeloupe, Martinique, Trinidad. Paris: P. Lethielleux, 1935.   NN

9124. Oliver, Vere Langford. The Monumental Inscriptions in the Churches and Churchyards of the Island of Barbados, British West Indies. London: Mitchell, Hughes and Clarkes, 1915.   NN

9125. Oriol, Jacques. Les Survivances du Totemisme dans le Vodou Haitien. Port-au-Prince, Haiti: Impr. Théodore, 1967.
                                                   NNCor
     Voodooism.

9126. Orjala, Paul R. Haiti Diary: The Intimate Story of a Modern Missionary Couple's First Two Years in a Foreign County. Compiled from the letters of Paul Orjala and edited by Kathleen Spell. Kansas City, Mo.: Beacon Hill Press, 1953. NN/Sch

9127. ----- Some Implications of Haitian Culture for Leadership Education in the Evangelical Church in Haiti. Masters thesis. Hartford Seminary Foundation, 1956.

9128. Ortiz-Fernandez, Fernando. La Africania de la Musica Folklorica de Cuba. Habana: Ministerio de Educacion, Direccion de Cultura, 1950.   DHU/MO

9129. ----- Los Bailes y el Teatro de los Negros en el Folklore de Cuba. Habana: Ministerio de Educacion, Direccion de Cultura, 1951.   DHU/MO

9130. ----- "Los Cabildos Afro-Cubanos." Revista Bimestre Cubana (16' 1921), pp. 5-39.   CU

9131. ----- "La Fiesta Afro-Cubana del 'dia de Reyes'." Revista Bimestre Cubana (15; 1920), pp. 5-26.   CU

9132. ----- Hampa Afro-Cubana; Los Negros Brujos (Apuntes Para Un Estudio de Etnologia Criminal) Con Una Carta Prólogo de Lombroso. Madrid: Editorial-América, 1917.   NNCor
     Voodooism.

9133. ----- "La Musica Religiosa de las Yoruba entre los Negros Cubanos." Estudios Afrocubanos 5. Havana: Sociedad de Estudios Afrocubanos, 1945-46.   NN; NNC

9134. ----- Los Negros Brujos. Madrid: Libreria de Fernando Fe, 1906.   DHU
     An aspect of Afro-Cuban religion.

9135. Osborne, Edward W. "A Visit to the Church in Cuba." Spirit of Missions (76; Dec., 1911), pp. 996-1001; (77; Ja., 1912), pp. 16-23.   DLC; DHU/R

9136. The Other Revolution; the Dramatic Story of Another Revolution in the Dominican Republic. Compiled by Juan M. Isais. Waco, Tex.: Word Books, 1970.   DLC

9137. Ottley, Carlton, R. Legends: True Stories and Old Sayings from Trinidad and Tobago. Port of Spain: College Press, 1962.   NNRIS

9138. ----- Tobago Legends and West Indian Lore. Georgetown: Daily Chronicle, 1950.   NNRIS

9139. Panhuys, L. C. Van. "Folklore in Nederlandsch West-Indie." West-Indische Gids (14; 1932/33), pp. 124-30.   NNC

9140. ----- "Folklore in Suriname." West-Indische Gids (16; 1934-35), pp. 17-32.   NNC

9141. Parsons, Elsie C. "Barbados Folklore." Journal of American Folklore (38:148, Apr., 1925), pp. 267-92. NNC; DLC

9142. ----- "Spirit Cult in Haiti." Journal de la Societe des Americanistes de Paris (20; 1928), pp. 157-79. DCU/A; DAU; DCU/AN; DGU

9143. ----- "Spirituals and Other Folklore From the Bahamas." Journal of American Folklore (41:162, Oct.-Dec., 1928), pp. 453-524.   DHU/R
     Microcard.

9144. ----- "Spirituals From the 'American' Colony of Samana Bay, Santo Domingo." Journal of American Folklore (41:162, Oct.-Dec., 1928), pp. 525-8.   DHU/R
     Microcard.

9145. Paul, Emmanuel Casseus. Panorama du Folklore Haitien; Presence Africaine en Haiti. Port-au-Prince: Impr. de l'Etat, 1962.   PPT

9146. Payne, Ernest A. Freedom in Jamaica: Some Chapters in the Story of the Baptist Missionary Society. 2nd ed. London: Carey Press, 1946.   NNUT; DHU/MO

9147. Penard, F. P. and A. P. "Negro Riddles From Surinam." West-Indische Gids (7; 1926-27), pp. 411-32.   NNC

9148. Petitjean-Roget, Jacques. "Les Protestants à la Martinique sous l'Ancien Régime." Revue d'Historie des Colonies (40:3, 1956), pp. 220-65.   NNRIS

9149. Pierre-Louis, Ulysse. Sortilèges Afro-Haitiens (Contes et Legendes). Pref. du Jean Price Mars. Port-au-Prince: Imp. de l'État, 1961.   NjP
     Haitian folklore.

9150. Pilkington, Frederick. "The Church in Jamaica." Congregational Quarterly (35:1, 1957), pp. 65-72.   DHU/R

9151. ----- Daybreak in Jamaica. London: Epworth Press, 1950.
                                                   NN/Sch

9152. Pinnington, John E. "Parties and Priorities: The Background to Anglican Failure to Evangelize the Negro Population of Barbados and Antigua in the Years Immediately Following the Creation of the Diocese of Barbados." Historical Magazine of the Protestant Episcopal Church (42:2, Je., 1973), pp. 155-69. DHU/R

9153. "Pocomania: a Little Madness. A Startling Report on a Strange Jamaican Cult." New York: Time Life Films, n.d. 16mm., B&W., 22 min.
     Film.

9154. Pollak-Eltz, Angelina. "The Shango Cult in Grenada, British West Indies." Proceedings, 8th International Congress of Anthropological Sciences (3; 1968), pp. 59-60.

9155. Post, Ken. "The Bible as Ideology: Ethiopianism in Jamaica, 1930-38." Christopher Allen and R. W. Johnson (eds.). African Perspectives (New York: Cambridge University Press, 1972), pp. 185-207.   DHU/MO
     "Colonial misfortune and religious response."

9156. Pressoir, Catts. Le Protestantisme Baftien... Port-au-Prince: Impe. de la Société Biblique et des Livres Religieux d'Hafri, 1945. V. 1, pt. 2.   NN/Sch

9157. Price, Ernest. Bananaland; Pages from the Chronicle of an English Minister in Jamaica. London: Carey Press, 1930.
                                                   NN/Sch

9158. Price, Richard. "Magie et Pêche à la Martinique." L'Homme. Revue Francaise d'Anthropologie (4:2, My.-Ag., 1964), pp. 84-113.   NNRIS

9159. Prins, J. "De Islam in Suriname: een Oriëntatie." Nieuwe West-Indische Gids (41:1, 1961-62), pp. 14-37. NNC

9160. Reckord, M. Missionary Activity in Jamaica Before Emancipation. Doctoral dissertation. University of London, King's College, 1964.

9161. Reece, J. E. and C. G. Clark-Hunt, (eds.). Barbados Diocesan History. London: West India Committee, 1925.
                                                   MWA

9162. Reily, D. A. "William Hammett Missionary and Founder
of the Primitive Methodist Connection." Methodist History
(10:1, Oct., 1971), pp. 30-43.   DHU/R
     Methodist preacher and missionary in the West Indies.

9163. Religious Persecution in Jamaica. Report of the Speeches
of the Rev. Peter Duncan, Wesleyan Missionary and the Rev.
W. Knibb, Baptist Missionary at a Public Meeting of the Friend
of Christian Missions, Held at Exeter-Hall, August 15, 1832.
London: S. Bagster, 1832.   DHU/MO

9164. Reminiscences of the West India Islands. By a Methodist
Preacher... Edited by D. P. Kiddler. New York: Pub. by
Land & Scott for the Sunday School Union of the Methodist
Episcopal Church, 1849.   NN/Sch

9165. "Report on the 'Rastas.'" Newday (Jamaica) (4:8, Ag., 1960),
pp. 26-29.   DHU/MO

9166. Revert, Eugene. De Quelques Aspects Du Folk-Lore Martini-
quais: La Magic Antillaire. Paris: Editions Bellenand, 1951.
                                                   NNRIS

9167. Rigaud, Milo. Secrets of Voodoo. New York: Arco Publishing
Company, 1969.   DHU/R; NjP; NNCor

9168. ----- La Tradition Voudoo et le Voudoo Haïtien: Son Temple,
Ses Mystères, sa Magie. Paris: Niclaus, 1953. NjP; PPT;
DHU/MO

9169. Robb, Alexander. Gospel to the Africans: a Narrative of
the Life and Labours of the Rev. William Jameson in Jamaica
and Old Calabar. London: Hamilton and Adams, 1862. CtY

9170. Rodriquez, Manuel Tomas. El Haiti Brujo (Voudou, Misterios,
Desapariciones, Hechicerias, Cuentos, etc.). Habana: Rambla,
Couza, 1936.   NNCor
     Voodooism.

9171. Rogers, Cornish. "The Caribbean Churches: Celebrating
a Vital Unity." The Christian Century (90:43, Nov. 28, 1973),
pp. 1166-67.   DHU/R
     Negro author.

9172. ----- "West Indian Christianity: A Neglected Opportunity."
Christian Century (89:35, Oct. 4, 1972), p. 978.   DHU/R

9173. ----- "Youth Women Press for New Caribbean 'Man'." The
Christian Century (90:44, Dec. 5, 1973), pp. 1187-88. DHU/R
     Informatin on the first assembly of the Caribbean Conference
     of Churches held in Kingston, Jamaica, Nov. 13-16, 1973.

9174. Rossi, Vicente. Cosas de Negros [Los Orijenes del Tango
y Otros Aportes al Folklore Rioplatense. Rectificaciones
Históricas]. Buenos Aires: Hachette, 1958.   NjP

9175. Roumain, Jazques. Le Sacrifice du Tambour-Assorto(r).
Port-au-Prince, Haiti: Imprimerie de l'Etat, 1943. DHU/MO
     Voodooism in Haiti.
     Negro author.

9176. Russell, H. O. "Indigenous Mission: The Jamaica Baptist
Missionary Society." The Baptist Quarterly (125:2, Apr., 1973),
pp. 86-93.   DHU/R

9177. Ryall, D. A. The Organization of Missionary Societies and
the Recruitment of Missionaries in Britain, and the Role of
Missionaries in the Diffusion of British Culture in Jamaica
During the Period 1834-1865. Doctoral dissertation. University
of London, 1960.

9178. Rycroft, W. Stanley. "The Contribution of Protestantism in
the Caribbean." A Curtis Wilgus (ed.). The Caribbean: Its
Culture (papers delivered at the Fifth Conference on the Caribbean
Held at the University of Florida, Dec. 2-4, 1954). (Gainesville:
University of Florida Press, 1955), pp. 158-68.

9179. Samuel, Peter. Wesleyan-Methodist Missions in Jamaica
and Honduras Delineated; Containing a Description of the Prin-

cipal Stations, Together with a Consecutive Account of the Rise
and Progress of the Work of God at Each. London: Partridge,
1850.   TxFTC; NjNbt; MiU

9180. Schermerhorn, William David. The Christian Mission in
the Modern World. New York: The Abingdon Press, 1933.
                                                   DHU/R
     Includes sections on Africa and on the Caribbean.

9181. Schutz, John A. and Maud E. O'Neil, (eds.). "Arthur Holt,
Anglican Clergyman, Reports on Barbados." Journal of Negro
History (31:4, Oct., 1946), pp. 444-69.   NNC; DHU/MO

9182. Schwartz, Barton M. "Ritual Aspects of Caste in Trinidad."
Anthropological Quarterly (37:1, Ja., 1964), pp. 1-15. NNC;
DHU

9183. Seabrook, William Buehler. The Magic Island. New York:
Harcourt Brace and Co., 1929.   NjP; DHU/MO; NNCor;
PPT
     Voodooism and witchcraft in Haiti.

9184. Seaga, Edward. "The Rastafarian Movement, Its Influence
Belies its Numbers." Encore, the Monthly Magazine (2:9,
Sept., 1973), pp. 58-61. Pam. File, DHU/R; DHU/MO

9185. Sereno, Renzo. "Obeah: Magic and Social Structure in the
Lesser Antilles." Psychiatry (11:1, Feb., 1948), pp. 15-31.
NNC

9186. "Shango." Fritz Henle, 1953. Released by Brandon Films,
1956. 10 min., sd., color, 16 mm.   DLC
     Film.
     "A representative of a ritual West Indies voodoo dance.
     Filmed in Trinidad."

9187. Sherlock, Philip M. "Jamaica Superstitions." Living Age
(423:4169, Dec. 6, 1924), pp. 529-34.   NN

9188. Shilstone, E. M. "Parish Churches in Barbados." Journal
of the Barbados Museum and Historical Society (4:1, Nov., 1936),
pp. 5-8.   NNM

9189. Shorrocks, Francis. "History of the Catholic Church in Barbados During the 19th Century." Journal of the Barbados Museum
and Historical Society (25:3, My., 1958), pp. 102-22. NNM

9190. A Short Account of the Late Hurricane in the West Indies, as
Far as Relates to the Missions of the Brethren in the Islands
of St. Croix and St. Christopher. London: n.p., 1785. NN/Sch

9191. Simpson, George E. "The Acculturative Process in Jamaican
Revivalism." F. C. Anthony Wallace, (ed.). Men and Cultures:
Selected Papers of the Fifth International Congress of Anthropological and Ethnological Sciences, Philadelphia, Sept. 1-9,
1956 (Philadelphia: University of Pennsylvania Press, 1957),
pp. 332-41.   NNRIS

9192. ----- "The Acculturative Process in Trinidadian Shango."
Anthropological Quarterly (37:1, Ja., 1964), pp. 16-27.
                                                   NNRIS

9193. ----- "Baptismal 'Mourning,' and 'Building' Ceremonies
of the Shouters in Trinidad." Journal of American Folklore
(79; 1966), pp. 537-50.   CLU; ICU; NN; RPB

9194. ----- "The Belief System of Haitian Vodun." American
Anthropologist (47; 1945), pp. 37-56. CtY; DCU; DHU; DLC;
ICU; NN; OrU; TxD

9195. ----- "Cult Music in Trinidad." Folkways Records and
Service Corp., 1961.
     Phono-disc.

9196. ----- "Culture Change and Reintegration Found in the Cults
of West Kingston, Jamaica." Proceedings of the American
Philosophical Society (99:2, Apr., 1955), pp. 89-92. NNRIS

9197. ----- "Four Vodun Ceremonies." Journal of American Folk-Lore (59: 232, Apr.-Je., 1946), pp. 154-67. DHU/R; NN/ RPB; CLU; ICU
   Haiti.
   Microcard.

9198. ----- "Jamaican Cult Music." Folkways Records and Service Corp., 1945.
   Phono-disc.

9199. ----- "Jamaica Revivalist Cults." Social and Economic Studies (5:4, Dec., 1956), pp. i-iii. DAU; DCU/AN; DCU/SW; DHU; DHU/MO

9200. ----- "Loup Garou and Loa Tales From Northern Haiti." Journal of American Folk-Lore (55:218, Oct.-Dec., 1942), pp. 219-27.   DHU/R
   Microcard.
   Vodun in Haiti.

9201. ----- "Magical Practices in Northern Haiti." Journal of American Folk-Lore (67:266, Oct.-Dec., 1954), pp. 395-403.
                                    DHU/R
   Microcard.

9202. ----- "The Nine Night Ceremony in Jamaica." Journal of American Folk-Lore (70:278, Oct.-Dec., 1957), pp. 329-35. DHU/R; NNRIS
   Microcard.
   Spirit beliefs.

9203. ----- "Political Cultism in West Kingston, Jamaica." Social and Economic Studies (4:2, Sept., 1955), pp. 133-49.
                       DCU/AN; DCU/SW; DHU
   Rastifarian movement.

9204. ----- "The Rastafari Movement in its Millenial Aspect." Comparative Studies in Society and History (Supplement: 2, 1962), pp. 160-65.   DLC; NN/Sch

9205. ----- "The Rastafari Movement in Jamaica." Social Forces (34:2, 1953), pp. 167-71.   DAU; DCU/SW; DHU

9206. ----- Religious Cults of the Caribbean; Trinidad, Jamaica, and Haiti. Rio Piedras: Institute of Caribbean Studies, University of Puerto Rico, 1970.   DHU/R; DLC; CtY

9207. ----- The Shango Cult in Trinidad. Rio Piedras: Institute of Caribbean Studies, University of Puerto Rico, 1965. DLC; IU; Ni; DAU; FU; PPULC; OO
   Also in: African Notes (3:1, Oct., 1965), pp. 11-21. DHU/MO

9208. ----- "Two Vodun-Related Ceremonies." Journal of American Folklore (61:239, 1948), pp. 49-52. Pam. File, DHU/R

9209. ----- "The Vodun Cult in Haiti." African Notes (3:2, Ja., 1966), pp. 11-21.   DHU/MO

9210. ----- "The Vodun Service in Northern Haiti." American Anthropologist (42:2, Apr.-Je., 1940), pp. 236-54. CtY; DCU; DHU; DLC; ICU; NN; OrU; TxD; DCU/AN

9211. ----- and Peter B. Hammond. "The African Heritage in the Caribbean." Vera Rubin, (ed.). Caribbean Studies: A Symposium (Institute of Social and Economic Research, University of the West Indies, Jamaica, 1957), pp. 46-53. DHU/MO

9212. Sitahal, H. The Mission of the Church in Trinidad. Masters thesis. McGill University, 1964.

9213. Smith, Clayton Cheyney. The Jamaica Mission of the Christian Woman's Board of Missions. Indianapolis: CWBM, 1896.
                                    TN/DCHS
   Disciples of Christ (Christian Churches) and missions in the West Indies.

9214. Smith, Clayton Cheyney. What to Teach, and How to Uplift Jamaica. Kingston, Jamaica: Sollas & Cocking, 1906.
   TN/DCHS

   Disciples of Christ (Christian Churches) and missions in the West Indies.

9215. Smith, George W. Conquests of Christ in the West Indies: A Short History of Evangelical Missions. Brown's Town, St. Ann, Jamaica: n.p., 1937.   CtY; NNUT

9216. Smith, Michael G. Dark Puritan. Kingston: Dept. of Extra-mural Studies, University of the West Indies, 1963.
                                    NNRIS

9217. ----- Kinship and Community in Carriacou. New Haven: Yale Univ. Press, 1962.   DCU/AN
   Caribbena series, 5.

9218. ----- The Plural Society in the British West Indies. Berkeley: University of California Press, 1965.   DCU/AN

9219. ----- Stratification in Grenada. Berkeley: Univ. of Calif. Press, 1965.   DCU/AN

9220. ------ West Indian Family Structure. Seattle: Univ. of Wash. Press, 1962.   DCU/AN

9221. ----- and Rog Augier, et alii. The Ras Tafari Movement in Kingston, Jamaica. Mona, Jamaica: Institute of Social and Economic Research, 1960. IU; CU; CtY; FU; CLU; NN/Sch

9222. Smith, Pamela Coleman. "Two Negro Stories From Jamaica." Journal of American Folk-Lore (9:35, Oct.-Dec., 1896), p. 278.
                                    DHU/R
   Microcard.
   Kingston, Jamaica.

9223. Sosis, Howard. The Colonial Environment and Religion in Haiti: An Introduction to the Study of Negro Religious Syncretism in Colonial Saint Dominique. Doctoral dissertation. Columbia University, 1970.

9224. Souffrant, Claude. "La Religion du Paysan Haitien De l'Antheme au Dialogue." Social Compass (19:4, 1972), pp. 585-97.   DHU/R
   "Religion in Haiti."

9225. Staehelin, Felix, (ed.). Die Missions der Brudergemeine in Suriname und Berbice im Achtzehnten Jahrhundert; Eine Missionsgeschichte Hauptachlich in Briefen und Originalberichten. Herrnhut: Verein fur Brudergeschichte in Kommission der Unitatsbuchhandlung in Gnadau, 1912.   NN/Sch

9226. Stewart, J. A View of the Past and Present State of the Island of Jamaica: With Remarks on the Moral and Physical Conditions of the Slaves and on the Abolition of Slavery in the Colonies. Edinburgh: Oliver, 1823.   MBBC

9227. Stone, Ronald. "A Black - Liberation Theology From Jamaica." Christian Century (91:27, Jl. 31, 1974), pp. 750-51.
                                    DHU/R

9228. Stowell, Jay Samuel. Between the Americas. New York: Council of Women fro Home Missions and Missionary Education Movement, 1930.   DLC; NcD
   Methodist Episcopal Church and mission work in Jamaica.

9229. Stycos, J. Mayone and Durt Back. "Contraception and Catholicism in Jamaica." Eugenics Quarterly (5:4, Dec., 1958), pp. 216-20.   NNRIS

9230. Talbot, Frederick Hilborn. "Thanksgiving in Guyana for Bishop Fred Talbot's Election to Bishop of the A. M. E. Church." Voice of Missions (81:1 & 2, Sept.-Oct., 1972), pp. 110-12.   DHU/R

9231. Taylor, A. Wingrove. "Missionary's Role in West Indian Theological Education." Evangelical Missions Quarterly (9; Spr., 1973), pp. 169-76.   DAU/W

9232. Thoby-Marcelin, Philippe. The Pencil of God. Boston: Houghton Mifflin, 1951.   InU; DLC; DHU/MO
The church and voodooism in Haiti.

9233. Thompson, Augustus C. Moravian Missions. Twelve Lectures. New York: Charles Scribner's Sons, 1890. DHU/R
Includes mission to the West Indies and South Africa.

9234. Thompson, E. W. "Eyes on the West Indies." International Review of Missions (32; 1943), pp. 293-300.   DHU/R
Christian missions.

9235. ----- "The Return of the West Indies." International Review of Missions (29; 1940), pp. 452-62.   DHU/R
British Christian missions.

9236. Trowbridge, Ada Wilson. "Negro Customs and Folk-Stories of Jamaica." Journal of American Folk-Lore (9:35, Oct.-Dec., 1896), pp. 279-87.   DHU/R
Microcard.

9237. Tschuy, Theo. "The Cuban Miracle and the Church's Prison." Cross Currents (21:3, Sum., 1971), pp. 335-39.   DHU/R
The Roman Catholic Church and the Cuban Revolution.

9238. Tucker, Leonard, (comp.). "Glorious Liberty": The Story of a Hundred Years' Work of the Jamaica Baptist Mission. London: Baptist Missionary Society, 1914.   NNUT; CtY

9239. Underhill, Edward Bean. Life of James Mursell Phillippo, Missionary in Jamaica. London: Yates and Alexander, 1881.
NNMR

9240. ------ The West Indies: Their Social and Religious Condition. London: Jackson, Walford, and Hodder, 1862.
DHU/MO

9241. Underwood, Frances W. The Vodun Complex of the West Indies; a Study of Persistence. Doctoral dissertation. Yale University, 1947.

9242. Vandercook, John Womack. "White Magic and Black, the Jungle Science of Dutch Guiana." Harper's Magazine (151; Oct., 1925), pp. 548-54.   NNC

9243. Verschueren, Jacques. La Republique d'Haiti. Wettern: Scaldis, 1948.   NNCor; NjP
Voodooism in Haiti.

9244. Voorhoeve, Jan. "Missionary Linguistics in Surinam." Bible Translator (8:4, Oct., 1957), pp. 179-90.   NN

9245. Voullaire, W. R. Surinam: Le Pays, les Habitants et la Mission Morave. Lausanne: Impr. La Concorde, 1926. NNAG

9246. Waddell, Hope M. Twenty-Nine Years in the West Indies and Central Africa, a Review of Missionary Work and Adventure. London: T. Nelson & Sons, 1836.   DHU/MO; NN/Sch

9247. Walker, Frank Deaville. The Call of the West Indies; the Romance of Methodist Work and Opportunity in the West Indies and Adjacent Regions. London: Cargate Press, 193-. NN/Sch

9248. Walker, James B. "Notes on the Politics, Religion and Commerce of Old Calabar." Journal of Anthropoligical Institute (61; 1877), pp. 110-24.   DCU/AN

9249. Wallbridge, Edwin Angel. The Demerara Martyr. Memoirs of the Rev. John Smith, Missionary to Demerara. London: C. Gilpin, 1848.   CtY-D

9250. Watson, G. Llewellyn. "Patterns of Black Protest in Jamaica; The Case of the Ras - Tafarians." Journal of Black Studies (4:3, Mr., 1974), pp. 329-43.   Pam. File, DHU/R; DHU/MO

9251. Williams, Alfred W. "A Miracle Play in the West Indies." Journal of American Folk-Lore (9:33, Apr.-Je., 1896), pp. 117-20.   DHU/R
Microcard.

9252. Williams, Joseph J. Psychic Phenomena of Jamaica. New York: Dial Press, 1934.   NNM

9253. ----- Voodoos and Obeas; Phases of West Indian Witchcraft. New York: Dial Press, 1932. DHU/MO; NjP; IC/H; NNRIS

9254. ----- Whisperings of the Caribbean: Reflections of a Missionary. New York: Benziger, 1925.   DHU/MO; DLC

9255. Williams, Sheldon. Voodoo and the Art of Haiti. London: Morland Lee Ltd., 1969.   NjP; PPT

9256. Wipfler, William L. "Religious Syncretism in the Caribbean: A Study of the Persistence of African and Indian Belief." Occasional Bulletin, Missionary Research Library (19:1, Ja., 1968), pp. 1-13.   DHU/R

9257. Wirkus, Faustin and Taney Dudley. The White King of La Gonave. Garden City, N.Y.: Doubleday, Doran and Co., 1931. NjP; DHU/MO; NNCor; PPT
Voodooism in Haiti.

9258. "Witch Doctor." Ritter Young Lerner Associates, 1952. Released by Brandon Films, 1956. 10 min., d., b & w, 16 mm. Film.
"Jean Leon Destine performsa dance stylization of a voodoo rite performed by a Haitian witch doctor."

9259. "A Woman, A Slum, and the Gospel." New Covenant (4:2, Ag., 1974), pp. 17-18.   DHU/R
Community church project in Puerto Rico.

9260. World Council of Churches. Commission on World Mission and Evangelism. The Christian Ministry in Latin America and the Caribbean. Geneva, London and New York: Commission on World Mission and Evangelism. World Council of Churches, 1962.   DHU/R
"Report of a survey of theological education in the Evangelical Churches undertaken Feb.-May, 1961."

9261. Wright, Philip. Knibb 'the Notorious': Slaves' Missionary, 1803-1845. London: Sidgevick & Jackson, 1973.   DHU/R
About William Knibb, English Baptist missionary in Jamaica.

9262. Young, Robert. A View of Slavery in Connection With Christianity: Being the Substance of a Discourse Delivered in Wesleyan Chapel, Stoney-Hill, Jamaica, Sept. 19, 1824. With an Appendix Containing the Resolutions of the Missionaries in that Connection, at a General Meeting Held in Kingston, Sept. 6, 1824. Jamaica: A Aikman, June, 1824. London: Reprinted for Smith, Elder, 1825.   NNCor
Slavery and the Methodist Church.

3. Other areas

9263. Bascom, William R. "La Religion Africaine au Nouveau Monde." Les Religions Africaines Traditionelies (Paris: Editions du Seuil, 1965), pp. 119-37.

9264. ----- Shango in the New World. Austin: African and Afro-American Research Institute, University of Texas at Austin, 1972.   DHU/AA; DHU/R

9265. Bastide, Roger. African Civilisations in the New World. New York: Harper & Row, 1971. DHU/R; NjP; NNCor; PPT; NN/Sch
Describes African religions and how they survived in the Americas. The Fanti-Ashanti, Bantu and Yoruba in addition to Voodoo is included.

9266. ----- Les Amériques Noires, les Civilizations Africaines Dans Le Nouveau Monde. Paris: Pay t, 1967. DHU/MO

9267. ----- Las Américas Negras: las Civilzaciones Africanas en Nuevo Mundo. Madrid: n.p., 1969. NN/Sch

9268. ----- "La Theorie de la Reincarnation chez les Afro-Americains." Janheinz Jahn, (ed.). Reincarnation et Vie Mystique en Afrique Noire (Paris: n.p., 1965), pp. 9-29.

9269. Beltran, Gonzalo A. "La Etnohistoria y el Estudio del Negro en Mexico." Sol Tax, (ed.). Acculturation in the Americas New York: Cooper Square Publishers, Inc., 1967), pp. 161-68. DHU/R

9270. Bolton, H. Carrington. "Gombay, a Festal Rite of Bermudian Negroes." Journal of American Folklore (3:3, Jl.-Sept., 1890), pp. 222-26. Pam. File, DHU/R

9271. Bonino, Miguez Jose. "A Latin American Attempt to Locate the Question of Unity." Ecumenical Review (26:2, Apr., 1974), pp. 210-21. DHU/R
Author, a theologian discusses the Latin American situation concerning the problem of Christian unity.

9272. Borda, Orlando Fals. "The Social Sciences and the Struggle for Liberation." The Ecumenical Review (26:1, Ja., 1974), pp. 60-69. DHU/R
Author is a member of Group for Social Research and Action, Bogatá, Columbia.

9273. Bratcher, Lewis Malen. An Outline of Protestant Missions in South America. Doctoral dissertation. Southern Baptist Theological Seminary, 1918.

9274. Brett, William Henry and Leonard Lambert, (eds.). Guiana Legends. London: Society for the Propagation of the Gospel in Foreign Parts, 1931. NN

9275. Brown, Lawrence A. A Study of the Growth and Development of Protestantism in South America. Doctoral dissertation. Gol-Gate Baptist Theological Seminary, 1951.

9276. Calley, Malcolm J. C. God's People: West Indian Pentecostal Sects in England. New York: Oxford University Press, 1965. DHU/R

9277. Calmon, Pedro. Os Males, a Insurreicao das Senzales. Rio de Janeiro: Niteroi, 1933. NC; DLC; InU
Male is a believer in Islam of African origin.

9278. Canargo, Candido Procopio Ferreira de. Kardecismo e Umbanda. Biblioteca Pionera de Ciencias Sociais. Sao Paulo: Livraria Editora, 1961. CtY; IU; TxU; NIC; CLSU
Catechism of Umbanda of South America.

9279. Cappelle, H. van. "Surinaamsche Negervertellingen." Bijdragen tot de Taal-Land-en Volkenkunde van Nederlandsch-Indie (72; 1916), pp. 233-379. PPAmP
"Folktales of the Surinam Negroes."

9280. Carámbula, Rubén. Negro y Tambor; Poemas, Pregones, Danzas y Leyendas Sobre Motivos del Folklore Afro-rioplatense, Melodías y Anotaciones Rítmicas del Autor. Ensayo Literario Sobre el Candombe; Estudio Sobre el Lenguaje Afrocriollo de Los Negros Rioplatenses. Buenos Aires?: Editorial Folklorica Americana, 1952. NjP

9281. Carlson, Donald Arthur. Great Britain and the Abolition of the Slave Trade to Latin America. Doctoral dissertation. Univ. of Minneapolis, 1964.

9282. Carvalho-Neto, Paulo de. El Negro Uruguayo. Quito: Editorial Universitaria, 1965. DHU
Folklore, pp. 291-328.

9283. Chamlee, Roy Zebulon, Jr. A Comparison of Roman Catholic Influence in the United States and Latin America. Masters thesis. Southern Baptist Theological Seminary, 1961.

9284. "Controversy Arises Over Voodoo Legalization Issue." Jet (45:25, Mr. 14, 1974), p. 46. Pam. File, DHU/R
Prime Minister of Guyana is considering the legalization of Obeah, a form of voodoo.

9285. Costa, Arquedas. "El Folklore Negro en Bolivio." Tradicion (6:11, 1954), CLU; INU; NN

9286. Davis, John Merle. The Evangelical Church in the River Plate Republics. A Study of the Economic and Social Basis of Evangelical Church in Argentina and Uruguay. New York: International Missionary Council. Dept. of Social and Economic Research and Counsel, 1943. DHU/R

9287. Durkee, Arthur Albert. An Introductory Study of Roman Catholicism and Its Effects Upon Evangelical Missions in Latin America. Masters thesis. Golden Gate Baptist Theological Seminary, 1961.

9288. Fiorenza, Francis P. "Latin American Liberation Theology." Interpretation (28:4, Oct., 1974), pp. 441-57. DHU/R
"Liberation theology suggests new interpretations of the symbols of faith and calls for a radical transformation of man and society."

9289. Glover, R. F. "Religious Education and the Third World." Spectrum (48:2, Mr.-Apr., 1972), pp. 8-9. DHU/R

9290. Gray, Arthur Romeyn. That Freedom; A Study of Democracy in the Americas. New York: The National Council, 1925. NN/Sch

9291. Herskovits, Melville J. "Bush-Negro Art." Frances S. Herskovits, (ed.). The New World Negro (Bloomington: Indiana University Press, 1966), pp. 157-67. DHU/R
Also in Arts (17:51, 1930), pp. 25-37+.

9292. ----- "The Concept of the Soul." Frances S. Herskovits, (ed.). The New World Negro (Bloomington: Indiana University Press, 1966), pp. 268-275. DHU/R
Religion among Blacks in Suriname.

9293. ----- "Divination." Frances S. Herskovits, (ed.). The New World Negro (Bloomington: Indiana University Press, 1966), pp. 276-80. DHU/R
Religion among Blacks in Suriname.

9294. ----- "Gods and Familiar Spirits." Frances S. Herskovits, (ed.). The New World Negro (Bloomington: Indiana University Press, 1966), pp. 280-304. DHU/R
Religion among Blacks in Suriname.

9295. ----- "Magic, Good and Evil." Frances S. Herskovits, (ed.). The New World Negro (Bloomington: Indiana University Press, 1966), pp. 305-14. DHU/R
Religion among Blacks in Suriname.

9296. ----- "The Spirits of the Dead." Francis S. Herskovits, (ed.). The New World Negro (Bloomington: Indiana University Press, 1966), pp. 315-19. DHU/R
Religion among Blacks in Suriname.

9297. ----- Surinam Folk-Lore. New York: AMS Press, 1969. DCU/AN
Also published as Volume 27, Columbia University Contributions to Anthropology, 1943.

9298. Howard, George Parkinson. Religious Liberty in Latin America? Philadelphia: The Westminster Press, 1944. TSewU-T

9299. Johnson, John Albert. "African Methodism in Bermuda." The African Methodist Episcopal Church Review (81:221, Jl.-Sept., 1964), pp. 15-23. DHU/R
Negro author.

9300. Junker, L. "De Godsdienst der Boschnegers." West-Indische Gids (7; 1925/26), pp. 81-95+. NNC
The Religion of the Bush Negroes in Surinam, South America.

9301. Kalff, S. "Westindische Predikanten." West-Indische Gids
(10; 1928/29), pp. 412-26.   NNC
      West Indian preachers in Surinam and Curacao.

9302. Morpurgo, A. J. "Folklore in Surinam." West-Indische Gids
(19; 1935), pp. 116-26.   NNC

9303. Nida, Eugene A. "African Influence in the Religious Life of
Latin America." Practical Anthropology (13:3, My. -Je., 1966),
pp. 133-8.   DHU/R

9304. Panhuys, L. C. Van. "The Heathen Religion of the Bush Ne-
groes in Dutch Guiana." Actes do IVe Congrés International
D'Histoire Des Religions, Leide, Sept., 1912. (Leiden: E.J.
Brill, 1913), pp. 53-7.   NN

9305. Pinnington, John E. "Factors in the Development of the
Catholic Movement in the Anglican Church in British Guiana."
Historical Magazine of the Protestant Episcopal Church (37:4,
Dec., 1968), pp. 355-69.   DHU/R

9306. Pollak-Eltz, Angelina. "Religiones Africanas en las Americas." Boletin de la Asociacion Cultural Humboldt (4; 1969),
pp. 51-65.   DLC

9307. Riffey, John Leslie. Factors in the Development of Protestantism in Latin America. Doctoral dissertation. Southern
Baptist Theological Seminary, 1932.

9308. Rivera, Juan Marcos. "An Experiment in Sharing Personnel
From Historical Church to Pentecostal Movement." International Review of Mission (62:248, Oct., 1973), pp. 446-56.
                                                    DHU/R
      Written by a Puerto Rican pastor of the Christian Church
      (Disciples of Christ) and his work with the Venezuelan
      Pentecostal Union.

9309. Rosecrans, Wayne. Latin American Mission Fields Entered
by Southern Baptists Since 1940. Masters thesis. Central Baptist Theological Seminary, 1955.

9310. Sojo, Juan Pablo. "Algunas Supervivencias Negro - Culturales
en Venezuela." Revista Venezolana de Folklore (1:2, Jl. -Dec.,
1947), pp. 145-58.   DLC

9311. Speer, Robert E. Christian Work in South America: Official
Report of the Congress on Christian Work in South America at
Montevideo, Uruguay, April, 1925. New York: Revell, 1925.
                                                    DLC

9312. Steger, Hanns-Albert. El Trasfondo Revolucionario del
Sincretismo Criollo. Aspectos Sociales de la Transformacion
Clandestina de la Religion en Afroamerica Colonial y Post-
colonial. Cuernavaca, Mexique: Ed. du CIDOC, 1972. (Coll.
Sondeos, no. 86).

9313. "The Task of the Church in South America." International
Review of Missions (36; 1947), pp. 344-56.   DHU/R
      Brazil not included.

9314. Taylor, Clyde W. and Wade T. Coggins, (eds.). Protestant
Missions in Latin America. Washington, D. C.: Evangelical
Foreign Missions Association, 1961.   DHU/R

9315. Theisen, Gerald. "The Case of Torres Restrepo." Journal
of Church and State (16:2, Spr., 1974), pp. 300-15.   DHU/R
      Latin America.

9316. Unesco. Introduccion a la Cultura Africana en América Latina.
(Paris: Organizacion de las Naciones Unidas para la Educación,
1970).   DHU/R
      Includes lists of organizations and scholars engaged in re-
      search of the survival of African culture in Brazil, Carib-
      bean and South America. Information on cults, religion
      and folklore.

9317. Velasquez, R. M. "Leyendas y Cuentos de la Raza Negra."
Revista Colombiana de Folclor (2:4, 1960), pp. 67-120.
                                                    DCU/AN
      Legends and tales of Colombian Blacks.

9318. Whitten, Norman E., Jr. Class, Kinship, and Power in an
Ecuadorian Town: The Negroes of San Lorenzo. Stanford,
Calif.: Stanford University Press, 1965.   DHU/MO

C. CHURCH AND RELIGIOUS ORGANIZATIONS—RACE RELATIONS (including home missions)

1. Churches

a. Baptist

9319. Allen, W. C. "A Better View Concerning the Race Issue."
(Editorial) The Baptist Courier (70; Sept. 15, 1938), p. 2.
                                                    LNB; NcWfSB

9320. ----- "Unwise Negro Leadership." Editorial. The Baptist
Courier. (70; Je. 30, 1938), p. 21   LNB; NcWfSB

9321. American Baptist Home Mission Society. Forty Years' Work
for the Negroes. New York: American Baptist Home Mission
Society, 1901.   DHU/MO

9322. "Baptist Colleges for Negro Youth." Editorial. Southern
Workman (56:7, Jl., 1927), pp. 306-7.   DLC; DHU/MO

9323. Barnette, Henlee H. "Southern Baptist Churches and Segregation." Baptist Standard (76; Feb. 12, 1964), p. 7. LNB; TxFS

9324. Beall, Noble Y. "Educating the Negro Baptist Preacher."
Religious Herald (109; Je. 11, 1936), p. 17.   TND; ViU

9325. ----- "A New Awakening in Home Missions." Southern
Workman (65: 5, My., 1936), pp. 131-34. DLC; DHU/MO
      "The Southern Baptist Convention was organized in Augusta,
      Ga., in 1845. The Convention instructed the Home Mission
      Board to use all prudent means to bring about the evangel-
      ization and education of the Negroes."

9326. Bryan, Gainer E., Jr. "Southern Baptists Should Identify
with Negro Cause." Editorial. The Maryland Baptist (48;
My. 13, 1965), p. 8.   LNB; NcWfSB

9327. Bumsted, John M. and Charles E. Clark. "New England's
Tom Paine: John Allen and the Spirit of Liberty." William
and Mary Quarterly (3rd. Series, 21; Oct., 1964), pp. 561-70.
                                                    ViU
      About English Baptist minister who was critical of New
      England Baptist Church and their treatment of Negroes.

9328. Burton, Joe W. Epochs of Home Missions: Southern Baptist
Convention, 1845-1945. Atlanta, Ga.: Home Mission Board,
Southern Baptist Convention, 1945.   KKcB; NcWsW

9329. Burroughs, Nannie H. "Black Women and Reform." The
Crisis (10:4, Ag., 1915), p. 187.   DLC; DHU/MO
      Secretary of the Women's Auxiliary for the National Baptist
      Convention.

9330. Campbell, Stephen C. The Influence of Negro Baptists on
Secondary Education in South Carolina. Masters thesis. Wayne
University, 1947.

9331. Carver, William O. The Furtherance of the Gospel. Nashville, Tenn.: The Sunday School Board of the Southern Baptist
Convention, 1935.   NcD

9332. Chaplin, Jeremiah. Duncan Dunbar; the Record of an Earnest Ministry. A Sketch of the Life of the Late Pastor of the Mc-Dougal St. Baptist Church, New York... 4th ed. New York: U. D. Ward, 1878.   DHU/MO
Chapters 3, 5, & 15 contain accounts of the minister's association with and feelings about the Negro.

9333. Coward, Donald B. "The Vanishing Color Line in American Life." Missions: An International Baptist Magazine (148:2, Feb., 1950), pp. 83-5.   Pam. File, DHU/R

9334. Culpepper, Hugo H. "Missions in the Twentieth Century." Review and Expositor (70:1, Wint., 1973), pp. 87-98. DHU/R
Examines the theology of missions within the Southern Baptist Convention.

9335. Dahlberg, E. T. "Memorandum From the Desk of Dr. Dahlberg; Second Baptist Church." National Council Outlook (8; Je., 1958), p. 16.   DAU/W

9336. Daniel, W. Harrison. "Virginia Baptists and the Negro in the Early Republic." Virginia Magazine of History and Biography (64; Ja., 1972), p. 60.   ICMcC

9337. Dawson, Joseph Martin. "Baptist Liberals Given Setback." Christian Century (53: 22, My. 27, 1936), pp. 774-75. DHU/R

9338. "Education" The Crisis (8: 2, Je., 1912), p. 59. DLC; DHU/MO
Completion of building of the Birmingham Baptist College for Negroes.

9339. Eighmy, John Lee. Churches in Cultural Captivity; a History of the Social Attitudes of Southern Baptists. Knoxville: University of Tennessee Press, 1972.   NjP

9340. ----- The Social Conscience of Southern Baptist from 1900 to the Present as Reflected in Their Organized Life. Doctoral dissertation. University of Missouri, 1959.

9341. Falls, Helen E. "The Vocation of Home Missions 1845-1970." Baptist History and Heritage (7:1, Ja., 1972), pp. 25-32.   DHU/R
Author is professor of Mission at New Orleans Baptist Theological Seminary. History of the Southern Baptist Convention Board of Domestic Missions. Includes work among blacks.

9342. Foss, A. T. and E. Matthews. ...Facts for Baptist Churches. Collected, Arranged and Reviewed... Utica: Pub. by the American Baptist Free Mission Society, 1850. DHU/MO

9343. Foy, Valentine. A Historical Study of Southern Baptists and Race Relations, 1917-1947. Doctoral dissertation. Southwestern Baptist Theological Seminary, 1950.

9344. Gambrell, J. B. "Some New Phases of the Race Question in America." Baptist Standard (33; Feb. 24, 1921), p. 6.   LNB; TxFS

9345. Grant, J. Marse. "Southern Baptist Convention Must Share Responsibility for Climate in South." Editorial. Biblical Recorder (134; Apr. 13, 1968), p. 3.   LNB

9346. Grier, Woodrow A. "Southern Baptist Survey." Christian Century (80:49, Dec. 4, 1963), pp. 1526-27.   DHU/R
Survey conducted by the Southern Baptist on Negro membership.

9347. Gwaltney, L. L. "Race Relations." Editorial. The Alabama Baptist (98; Jl. 20, 1933), p. 3.   LNB; TND

9348. Hayne, Coe Smith. Race Grit; Adventures on the Borderland of Liberty. Ed. by the Dept. of Missionary Education, Board of Education of the Northern Baptist Convention... Philadelphia: The Judson Press, 1922.   CtY-D

9349. Hickman, Thomas Lloyd. A Study of the Status of Negroes as Members of White Baptist Churches in the State of North Carolina, 1776-1863. Master's thesis. School of Religion, Howard University, 1947.

9350. Hill, Davis C. Southern Baptist Thought and Action in Race Relations. Doctoral dissertation. Southern Baptist Theological Seminary, 1952.

9351. Hill, Samuel S. Jr. Baptists North and South. Valley Forge: Judson Press, 1964.   NcD

9352. Holt, A. J. "The Baptists of the South and the Negro." Editorial. Florida Baptist Witness (30; Ag. 2, 1917), p. 6.   FU; LNB; TND

9353. Hughes, John Edward. History of the Southern Baptist Convention's Ministry to the Negro: 1845-1904. Doctoral dissertation. Southern Baptist Theological Seminary, 1971.

9354. Hunter, R. M. "Treating the Negro Wrong." The Alabama Baptist 96th year (Jl. 28, 1932), p. 9.   LNB; TND

9355. Johnson, Charles Price. Southern Baptists and the Social Gospel Movement. Doctoral dissertation. Southwestern Baptist Theological Seminary, 1948.

9356. Jones, Terry Lawrence. Attitudes of Alabama Baptists Toward Negroes, 1890-1914. Masters thesis. Standford University, 1968.

9357. Kelsey, George D. Social Ethnics Among Southern Baptists, 1917-1969. Metheun, N. J.: Scarecrow Press, 1973. IObNB; DHU/R
Chapter 8, Race.
Negro author.

9358. Knight, Ryland. "The Historic Baptist Principle in Race Relations." Religious Herald (109; Jl. 23, 1936), p. 4. TND; ViU

9359. Kolb, Ernest C. Four Major Efforts to Change the Polity of the Southern Baptist Convention, 1900-1919. Masters thesis. Duke University, 1929.

9360. Leathers, W. W. "Ways to Aid the Negro." The Baptist Courier (63; Sept. 3, 1931), p. 6.   LNB; NcWfSB

9361. "Liberation on Sunday: The Black Christian Experience." Home Missions (43:4, Apr., 1972).   Pam. File, DHU/R

9362. Lipsey, P. I. "The Anti-Lynching Bill." Editorial. The Baptist Record (24; Ja. 19, 1922), p. 4.   LNB; TND

9363. ----- "Righteousness Among Races." Editorial. The Baptist Record (22; Sept. 9, 1920), p. 4.   LNB; TND

9364. Lunceford, Bill E. An Historical Study of the Development of Theological Education for Negro Baptist Ministers in the South from 1619 until 1954. Masters thesis. Southern Baptist Theological Seminary, 1955.

9365. Magruder, Edith C. A Histroical Study of the Educational Agencies of the Southern Baptist Convention, 1845-1945. New York: Bureau of Publications, Teachers College, Columbia University, 1951. No. 974.   NcD

9366. Martin, Theodore. The Administration of Instruction in Southern Baptist Colleges and Universities. Nashville: Bureau of Publications, George Peabody College for Teachers, 1949. NcD

9367. McBeth, Leon. "Southern Baptists and Race Since 1947." Baptist History and Heritage (7; Jl., 1972), pp. 155-69. DHU/R

9368. McGlothlin, W. J. "The 75 Million Campaign and Negro Education." The Baptist Courier (50; Oct. 9, 1919), p. 2.   LNB; NcWfSB

9369. "Mob Murders." Report of the Social Service Commission of the Southern Baptist Convention, Annual of the Southern Baptist Convention (Nashville, 1931), p. 122.   NNUT

9370. Moore, Elton. An Investigation of the Mississippi Baptist Seminary. Masters thesis. New Orleans Baptist Theological Seminary, 1950.

9371. Moore, J. D. "Interracial Problems." Editorial. Baptist and Reflector (88; Ja. 5, 1922), p. 2.   KyLoS; TND

9372. More, Joanne Patterson. In Christ's Stead: On Life and Work Among the Negroes of the Southern States, Autobiographical Sketches. Chicago: Woman's Baptist Home Mission Society, 1902.   NRAB; DHU/MO

9373. Morgan, David. "Alongside Us Caucasians." Biblical Recorder (106; Nov. 6, 1949), p. 9.   LNB; NcWfSB

9374. Morgan, Thomas J. Africans in America. New York: American Baptist Home Mission Society, 1898.   DLC

9375. ----- "After Thirty Years. A Review of the Educational, Social and Religious Status of our Colored People"   CtY; NN; ICU
Reprinted from the Baptist Home Mission Monthly, March, 1894.

9376. ----- Education of the Negro. An Address Before the American Baptist Home Missionary Society at Boston, Mass., May 17, 1890.   RPB
Mim.

9377. ----- "Negro Education: The Purpose, Spirit and Method of the American Baptist Home Mission Society." New York: n. p., n. d.   NRAB
Mim.

9378. Myers, Lewis A. "Equal Education for Negro." Editorial. The Arkansas Baptist (41; Mr. 5, 1942), p. 3.   TND

9379. Nannes, Caspar. "Black Cleric Demand Baptists Elect Negro." Evening Star (My. 30, 1968).   Pam. File, DHU/R

9380. Northern Baptist Convention. Board of Education. Department of Missionary Education. The Road to Brotherhood...
New York: n. p., 1924.   CtY-D

9381. "Pastors Adopt Statement on 'Human Equality'." The Maryland Baptist (41; Nov. 15, 1958), p. 14.   LNB; NcWfSB

9382. Posey, Walter Brownlow. The Baptist Church in the Lower Mississippi Valley, 1776-1845. Lexington: University of Kentucky Press, 1957.   NN/Sch

9383. "Race." Report of the Social Service Commission of the Southern Baptist Convention. Annual of the Southern Baptist Convention (Nashville, 1943), p. 107.   NNUT

9384. "The Racial Crisis," Report of the Christian Life Commission of the Southern Baptist Convention, Annual of the Southern Convention (1965), pp. 246-57.   NNUT

9385. Report of the Committee on Race Relations, Annual of the Southern Baptist Convention (Nashville, 1947), pp. 342-43.   NNUT

9386. "Resolutions, Concerning Lynching and Race Relations." Annual of the Southern Baptist Convention (Nashville, 1939), p. 141.   NNUT

9387. Riley, Benjamin Franklin. Memorial History of the Baptists of Alabama; Being an Account of the Struggles and Achievements of the Denomination from 1808 to 1923. Philadelphia: American Baptist Pub. Society, Judson Press, 1923.   DLC
Work among Negroes.

9388. Rouse, John E., Jr. "The Role of Segregation in Southern Baptist Polity." The Journal of Religious Thought (29:2, Aut. - Wint., 1972), pp. 19-38.   DHU/R

9389. Rutledge, Arthur B. Mission to America, A Quarter Century of Southern Baptist Home Missions. Nashville; Tenn.: Broad-

man Press, 1969.   DHU/R
Work with Negroes, pp. 133-42.

9390. Seawell, Joseph L. Law Tales for Laymen and Wayside Tales from Carolina. Raleigh, N. C.: A. Williams, 1925.
                                        NcC; NcD-L; NcU
Relates how Thomas Blacknall, a free Negro of Franklin, N. C., a Presbyterian, later served as a Baptist deacon where he led the largely white congregation in services.

9391. Shurden, Walter B. Not a Silent People; Controversies That Have Shaped Southern Baptists. Nashville: Broadman Press, 1972.   NjP

9392. ----- "The What About the Blacks Controversy." The Student: The Changing Church. (50:3, Dec., 1970), pp. 42-4.
                                        DHU/R
Southern Baptist Convention and the Black Revolution.

9393. Slattery, John R. "The Negroes and the Baptists." The Catholic World Magazine (63:37, My., 1896), pp. 265-70.
                                        DGU; DLC

9394. "Social Uplift." The Crisis (10:4, Ag., 1915), p. 165.
                                        DLC; DHU/MO
Mrs. Mary Church Terrell was one of the principal speakers at the session of the Baptist Council of Women for Home Missions, which was held at the Panama Exposition.

9395. Southern Baptist Convention. Annual Report of the Southern Baptist Convention 1932. 77th Session 87th Year. St. Petersburg, Fla. May 13-16, 1932. n. p., 1932.   DHU/MO

9396. ----- "Recommendations No. 3 -- Concerning the Supreme Court Decision on Public Education, "Report of the Christian Life Commission of the Southern Baptist Convention." Annual of the Southern Baptist Convention (Nashville, 1954), p. 407.
                                        NNUT

9397. "Southern Baptists Denounce Klan." Editorial. Christian Century (66:37, Sept. 14, 1949), pp. 1059-60.   DHU/R

9398. "Southern Baptists Open Seminaries to Negroes." Christian Century (68; Apr., 1951), pp. 452+.   DHU/R

9399. Spain, Rufus B. At Ease in Zion, Social History of Southern Baptist 1865-1900. Nashville: Vanderbilt Press, 1961.
                                        DHU/R; INU; NcD
Chapter 2, Segregation in the Churches.

9400. Spencer, Dwight. Home Missions and the Negroes. New York: American Baptist Home Missions Society, n. d.
                                        SCBHC

9401. Starr, Edward C. A Baptist Bibliography. Rochester, N. Y.: American Baptist Historical Society, 1947-.   DHU/R
Being compiled by the curator of the Samuel Colgate Baptist Historical Collection. Volumes are issued by alphabetical letters of surname of authors.

9402. Storey, John W. The Negro in Southern Baptist Thought, 1865-1900. Doctoral dissertation. University of Kentucky, 1968.

9403. Stripling, Paul Wayne. The Negro Excision from Baptist Churches in Texas: 1861-1870. Doctoral dissertation. Southwestern Baptist Theological Seminary, 1967.

9404. Tinnin, Finley W. "Effects of Dangerous Negro Leadership." Editorial. Baptist Message (55; Jl. 21, 1938), p. 2. LNB; TND

9405. ----- "Wild-eyed Social Equality, Vaporings." Editorial. Baptist Message (60; Apr. 29, 1943), p. 2.   LNB; TND

9406. ----- "World Alliance President and Civil Rights." Editorial. Baptist Message (65; Mr. 18, 1948), p. 2.   LNB; TNB

9407. Tonks, Alfred R. History of the Home Mission Board of the Southern Baptist Convention, 1845-1882. Masters thesis. Southern Baptist Theological Seminary, 1968.

9408. Tupper, H. A. The Foreign Mission of the Southern Baptist Convention. Philadelphia: American Baptist Publication Society, n. d.   DHU/MO
      African Missions, pp. 265-438.

9409. Valentine, Foy Dan. A Historical Study of Southern Baptist and Race Relations, 1917-1947. Doctoral dissertation. Southwestern Baptist Theological Seminary, 1949.

9410. Warnock, Henry Y. Modern Racial Thought and Attitudes of Southern Baptists and Methodists, 1900-1921. Doctoral dissertation. Northwestern University, 1963.

9411. ----- "Prophets of Change: Some Southern Baptist Leaders and the Problem of Race, 1900-1921." Baptist History and Heritage (7:3, Jl., 1972), pp. 172-83.   DHU/R
      "Reaction to Paper of Henry Y. Warnock." (7:3, Jl., 1972), pp. 184-85.

9412. Whipple, Phila M. Negro Neighbors, Bond and Free. Lessons in History and Humanity. Boston: Woman's American Baptist Home Mission Society, 1907.   NN/Sch; CtY-D

9413. White, Charles Lincoln. The Retaining of a Race; An Address Delivered at Des Moines, Iowa, May 24th, 1912, Commemorating the 50th Anniversary of the Work of the American Baptist Home Mission Society Among the Negroes. New York: American Baptist Home Mission Society, 1912.   DLC

9414. Woman's American Baptist Home Mission Society, Chicago. Thirty-Six Years' Work Among Negroes, 1877-1911. Chicago: Ill.: Woman's American Baptist Home Mission Society, 1913.   CtY-D

9415. ----- Twenty-Nine Years' Work Among Negroes. Chicago: Women's Baptist Home Mission Society, 1906.   NN/Sch

b. Congregational (United Church of Christ)

9416. Alley, Joe K. Churches of Christ in Mississippi, 1836-1954. Booneville, Miss.: By the author, 1953.

9417. Allison, Madeline G. "The Churches." The Crisis (22: 4, Ag., 1921), p. 178.   DHU/MO; DLC
      Progress report of Plymouth Congregational Church, Washington. Pastor, Rev. Dr. A. C. Garner, retired.

9418. Catchings, L. Maynard. "The Participation of Racial and Nationally Minority People in Congregational Churches." Journal of Negro Education (15; Fall, 1946), pp. 681-84.   DHU/MO
      Negro author.

9419. "A Christian Program of Race Relations." The Crisis (40: 5, My., 1933), p. 107.   DHU/MO; DLC
      Congregationalists Young People's Conference discuss race problems.

9420. "Churches." The Crisis (7:4, Feb., 1914), p. 167.   DHU/MO; DLC
      The Council of the Congregational Church will contribute $30,000 annually for church work among colored people.

9421. "City of Necessity." Produced by Robert Newman for the Board of Homeland Ministries of the United Church of Christ, National Council of Protestant Episcopal Church and Chicago City Missionary Society. 26 min. color. 16mm. Film.

9422. "Colored Congregationalists Will Meet in Chicago." The Christian Century (39:30, Jl. 27, 1922), p. 952.   DHU/R

9423. Congregational Christian Churches. General Council. "Resolutions on Race Relations." Voted Without Dissent, Je. 25, 1952, Claremont, Calif.   Pam. File, DHU/R

9424. ----- "Resolution of the General Council of the Congregational Christian Church." Cleveland, O., Je. 22-26, 1950.   Pam. File, DHU/R

9425. "The Congregational National Council." Voice of the Negro (2:1, Ja., 1905), p. 661.   DHU/MO

9426. Dutton, W. S. "The National Council of Congregational Churches." The New Englander (24, Jl., 1865), p. 531. DLC
      "The end of the war opens the South for evangelism. The Whites, on account of ignorance and barbarism, need evangelization as much as the newly freed men. Our Church structure rejects permanent national councils but this special situation allows one to be summoned."

9427. "Equality Education: The Contribution of Our United Church of Christ Black Colleges." United Church Herald (15:5, My., 1972), pp. 23-31.   DHU/R

9428-29. Gowin, Edward F. "One Hundred Years of Negro Congregationalism in New Haven, Connecticut." Crisis (19:4, Feb., 1920), pp. 177-81   DHU/MO

9430. Hargett, James H. The Black Ministries Resource Book. New York: United Church of Christ, 1970. Pam. File, DHU/R Mim.
      "The Black Situation in the United Church of Christ."

9431. Herring, Hubert C. "Seminar Discusses Negro in America." Christian Century (45:17, Apr. 26, 1928), p. 552. DHU/R; DLC
      Congregational Church.

9432. Hotchkiss, Wesley A. "Congregationalists and Negro Education." Journal of Negro Education (45; Sum., 1960). Reprint.   Pam. File, DHU/R

9433. Lawson, Jennifer. "Washington, D.C., Congregation Taps 17/76 Goal." A. D. United Church Herald Edition (2:9, Sept., 1973), pp. 19-22.   DHU/R
      Plymouth U. C. C. Church in Washington, D. C., a Negro church is in the vanguard of an Achievement Fund, a campaign authorized by the 8th General Synod to support a network of overseas educational institutions and six colleges related to the American Missionary Association.

9434. Long, Herman, H. Fellowship for Whom? A Study of Racial Inclusiveness in Congregational Christian Churches. New York: n. p., 1958.   NNUT
      "A report by the Race Relations Department, Division of Higher Education and the American Missionary Association Board of Home Missions of the Congregational Christian Churches in cooperation with the Council for Social Action and Research Office of the Board of Home Missions."

9435. Raney, G. Wesley. Black Congregationalism: Its Past and Future. Bachelor of Divinity Paper. Andover Newton Theological School, 1969.

9436. Rankin, Jeremiah Eames. God's Guarantee About Children. A Sermon in the First Congregational Church, Washington, D. C. April 30, 1832. Washington, D. C.: Pilgrim Press Assoc., 1882.   DHU/MO

9437. Sheares, Reuben. "New UCC Office for Church Life and Leadership to be Directed by Reuben Sheares." David A. Tillyer. "Pulpit and Pew Together." A. D. United Church, Herald Edition (2:11, Nov., 1973), pp. 24-27.   DHU/R

9438. Shinn, Roger L. The Educational Mission of Our Church. Boston: United Church Herald, 1962.   DHU/R

9439. Springfield, Massachusetts. St. John's Congregational Church. The History of St. John's Congregational Church, 1844-1962. Springfield, Mass.: St. John's Congregational Church, 1962.   A&M; DHU/MO

9440. Washington, D. C. Plymouth Congregational Church. Manual of the Church Adopted and Issued by the Church. Washington, D. C.: R. L. Pendleton, 1892.   DHU/MO
      Black United Church of Christ.

9441. Weaver, Galen R. "A Denominational Emphasis on Race Relations." Social Action (13:1, Ja., 1947), pp. 25-30.   DHU/R
Efforts of Congregational Christian denomination in race
relations.

9442. West Rutland, Vt. First Congregational Church. Manual of
the First Congregational Church, West Rutland, Vermont. Rutland, Vt.: Dodge, Printer, 1904.   NN/Sch
Manual of Lemuel Haynes' church, a Negro Congregationalist minister to Negroes and Whites in the eighteenth and
early nineteenth centuries.

9443. "White and Negro Churches in Georgia." The Congregationalist (78:38, Spet. 21, 1893), p. 374.   DHU/R
Race relations in Congregational Churches.

9444. Whittaker, John W. "Are Other Than Baptist and Methodist
Churches Adapted to the Present Negro?" Daniel W. Culp.
Twentieth Century Negro Literature. (Miami, Fla.: Mnemo-
syne Publishing Co., Inc., 1969), pp. 359-63.   DHU/MO
Reprint of 1902 edition.
Negro Congregationalist minister and former chaplin at
Tuskegee Institute.

9445. Williams, Charles H. "The Negro Church and Recreation."
Southern Workman (55:2, Feb., 1926), pp. 58-69.
DLC; DHU/MO
The Rev. William N. DeBerry, pastor of the St. John's
Congregational Church of Springfield, Mass., shows one of
the best examples of Church recreation work.

c. Disciples of Christ (Christian Churches)

9446. Azlein, Arthur A. A History of the Disciples of Christ in
the National Capital Area. Washington, D.C.: By the author,
1963.   TN/DCHS

9447. Barber, William Joseph. Disciple Assemblies of Eastern
North Carolina. St. Louis: The Bethany Press, 1966. DHU/R;
TN/DCHS; TxDaM; KyLxCB
History of a group of Negro Disciples of Christ (Disciple-
Assemblies of Eastern North Carolina). Negro author.

9448. Benjamin, T. Garrott Jr. "Disciples and the Black Comminity." World Call (54:4, Apr., 1972), pp. 29-31. DHU/R

9449. Bostick, Sarah Lue (Howard) Young. Beginning of the Mis-
sionary Work and Plans in Arkansas, 1896. 25 Years Service,
Historical Sketch Up to 1918. n.p.: n.p., 19? TN/DCHS
Disciples of Christ and Negroes.

9450. Cunningham, Effie L. Harris. Work of Disciples of Christ
with Negro Americans. St. Louis: UCMS, 1922? TN/DCHS

9451. "Disciples in Louisville: Democracy at Work.: Christian
Century (88:48, Dec. 1, 1971), pp. 1426-28.   DHU/R
Disciples of Christ.

9452-53. Eckstein, Stephen Daniel, Jr. History of the Churches
of Christ in Texas, 1824-1950. Austin, Tex.: Firm Foundation Publishing House, 1963.   TN/DCHS

9454. Eppse, Merl Raymond. The Disciples of Christ and the
Negro. n.p., 1940.   TN/DCHS

9455. ----- A Guide to the Study of the Negro in America. Nashville: National Educational Publishing Society, 1953. TN/DCHS
Disciples of Christ and the Negro.

9456. Fiers, A. Dale. "Race Relation in Global Perspective."
World Call (39:6, Je., 1957), pp. 21-22.   DHU/R

9457. Harmon, Marion Franklin. A History of the Christian
Churches in Mississippi. Aberdeen, Miss.: n.p., 1929.
TN/DCHS

9458. Jones, Richard B. "Steem: a Workable Model for Ministerial Enlistment." Ethnic Ministry (2:1, Sept- ct., 1974),
pp. 13-21.   DHU/R

Short-term Employment Experience in Ministry (STEEM),
program of the Disciples of Christ to enlist more black
and Hispanic young people for professional leadership in the
church.

9459. Lewis, Elmer C. A History of Secondary and Higher Edu-
cation in Negro Schools Related to the Disciples of Christ.
Doctoral dissertation. University of Pittsburgh, 1957.
TN/DCHS

9460. Liverett, Alice. Biographical Sketches of Leaders of
the Disciples of Christ. Indianapolis: Dept. Of Missionary
Education, UCMS, 19?   TNDC

9461. Long, John C. The Disciples of Christ and Negro Education.
Doctoral dissertation. University of Southern California, 1960.

9462. Lyda, Happy C. Development of the Black Churches in the
Christian Church. Doctoral dissertation. Vanderbilt University, 1971.

9463. Nance, Ellwood Cecil. Florida Christians: Disciples of
Christ. Winter Park, Fla.: College Press, 1941. TN/DCHS
Negro Disciples of Christ.

9464. Nunnelly, Donald Alfred. The Disciples of Christ in Alabama,
1860-1910. Masters thesis. The College of the Bible, 1954.
TN/DCHS

9465. Penabaz, Fernando. Crusading Preacher From the West.
Tulsa, Okla.: Christian Crusade, 1965.   TN/DCHS

9466. Smith, Clayton Cheyney. Negro Education and Evangelism.
Indianapolis: CWBM, 1909.   TN/DCHS
Disciples of Christ (Christian Churches) and race relations.

9467. Smith, Samuel Leonard. Builders of Goodwill. Nashville:
Tennessee Book Co., 1950.   TN/DCHS
Disciples of Christ Christian Churches and race relations.

9468. Smoot, Mareta. Chi Rho Fellowship Studies, Christian
World Outreach. Africa: Home Missions and Human Rights,
1952-1953. Indianapolis: UCMS, 1952.   TN/DCHS
Disciples of Christ (Christian Churches) and race relations.

9469. ----- The Christian and Race. Missionary Education Sug-
gestions for the CYF. Indianapolis: UCMS, n.d. TN/DCHS
Christian Youth Fellowship Studies.
Disciples of Christ (Christian Churches) and race relations.

9470. Smythe Lewis, (ed.). Southern Churches and Race Relations.
Report of the Fourth Interracial Consultation held at The College
of the Bible, July 16-20, 1962. Lexington, Ky., The College
of the Bible, 1963.   Pam. File, DHU/R

9471. Spencer, Justina K. Synoptic History (One Half Century)
Christian Church. Roanoke, Va.: Roanoke Tribune, 1959.
TN/DCHS

9472. Taylor, Marilyn. "Third Christian is Beautiful." World
Call (52:2, Feb., 1970), pp. 24+.   DHU/R
A Disciple of Christ Church of Philadelphia and its inter-
racial church and its social action program.

9473. Tuggle, Annie C. Our Ministers and Song Leaders of the
Church of Christ. Detroit: Author, 1945.   TN/DCHS
About Blacks in the Disciples of Christ.

9474. Walker, Claude. Negro Disciples in Kentucky, 1840-1925.
Bachelor's Paper. The College of the Bible, 1959. TN/DCHS

9475. Ware, Charles Crossfield. North Carolina Disciples of
Christ. St. Louis: CBP, 1927.   TN/DCHS

9476. West, Robert Frederick. Preaching on Race. St. Louis:
Bethany Press, 1962.   TN/DCHS
Disciples of Christ (Christian Churches) and race relations.

9477. Whitfield, Charles Randolph Davis. Brief History of the
Negro Disciples of Christ in Eastern North Carolina, Past
Achievements and Future Aims. Kinston, N.C.: Whitfield
Frintery, n.d.
          Negro author.

d. Eastern Orthodox

9478. Florovsky, Georges. "Social Problem in the Eastern
Orthodox Church." Journal of Religious Thought (8:1, Aut.
-Wint., 1950-51), pp. 41-51.   DHU/R

e. Friends—Quakers
9479 The African's Friend. For the Promotion of Religion and
Morality. No. 1-149; 1886-98. Philadelphia, 1886-98. NN/Sch
          "Religious tracts and wirtings, selected and published by
certain members of the Yearly meeting of the Friends of
Philadelphia, appointed trustees under the will of Charles L.
Willits, deceased, to select, print and distribute such writings
among the colored people of the southern states and Liberia."
Title varies: no. 1, 1886, The Willits Journal ... no. 2-149,
1886-98, The African's Friend. No more published.

9480. Bowden, James. Religion in America: The History of the
Society of Friends in America. New York: Arao Press, 1972.
                                                DHU/R

9481. Cadbury, Henry J. "Negro Membership in the Society of
Friends." Journal of Negro History (21:2, Apr., 1936), pp.
151-213.   DHU/R

9482. Chace, Elizabeth (Buffum). Two Quaker Sisters. From the
Original Diaries of Elizabeth B. Lovell, with an Introduction by
Malcolm R. Lovell, foreword by Rufus Jones. New York:
Liveright Publishing Corp., 1937.   DHU/MO; CtY-D

9483. Daniels, John. "How Deep Our Concern?" Friends Journal
(18:3, Feb. 1, 1972), p. 99.   DHU/R
          Black Developing funds of the Friends Yearly Meeting activ-
ities for racial justice.

9484. ----- "Why So Few Black Friends in New York?" Friends
Journal (18:21, Dec. 15, 1972), p. 686.   DHU/R
          Society of Friends and Negroes.

9485. DuBois, William E. B. "Puritans and Quakers." The Crisis
(37:12, Dec., 1930), p. 426.   DHU/MO; DLC
          How the Puritan and Quakers have shared and help the Amer-
ican Negro.

9486. Dunbar, Barrington. "Why Blacks are Getting Together."
Friends Journal (18: 18, Nov. 1, 1972), pp. 573-74. DHU/R
          A personal assessment of Quaker concerns over the lack
of understanding between Blacks and whites.

9487. Dunlap, William Cook. Quaker Education in Baltimore and
Virginia Yearly Meetings, with an Account of Certain Meetings
of Delaware and the Eastern Shore Affiliated with Philadelphia.
Based on the manuscript sources. Philadelphia: Science Press
Printing Co., 1936.   NN/Sch
          Issued also as thesis (Ph.D.) University of Pennsylvania.

9488. Endy, Melvin B. William Penn and Early Quakerism: A
Theological Study. Doctoral dissertation. Yale University,
1969.

9489. "Friends and Blacks." Friends Journal; Quaker Thought
and Life Today (19:18, Nov. 1, 1973), pp. 546-75. DHU/R
          Whole issue, "Focus: Friends and Blacks."

9490. Friends, Society of. American Friends Service Committee.
Race and Conscience in America; a Review... Norman:
University of Oklahoma Press, 1959. DHU/MO; CoDI; O

9491. ----- American Friends Service Committee. Some Quaker
Approaches to the Race Problem. Philadelphia: American
Firnds Service Committee, 1946.   DLC; NN/Sch; DHU/MO

9492. Pharr, Julia Marietta. The Activities of the Society of Friends
in Behalf of Negro Education. Masters thesis. Howard University, 1937.

9493. Perry, David B. "Black Men and the Quaker Bag." Friends
Journal (16:1, Ja. 1, 1970), pp. 6-7.   DHU/R

9494. Pumphrey, Stanley. Missionary Work in Connection With the
Society of Friends; an Address. Delivered in New York... 12th
Month, 1879. Philadelphia: n.p., 1880.   DHU/R

9495. Simpkins, Patrick L. "North Carlina Quakers and Blacks:
Education and Membership." Negro History Bulletin (35:11,
Nov., 1972), pp. 160-62.   DHU/MO

9496. Taylor, Richard K. Friends and the Racial Crisis.
Wallingford, Pa.: Pendle Hill, 1970.   PPT

f. Judaism
9497. Baldwin, James. "The Harlem Ghetto." Commentary (5:1,
Feb., 1948), pp. 65-70.   DHU/R
          Negro and Jewish relations.

9498. Clark, Kenneth B. "Candor on Negro-Jewish Relations."
Commentary (1:4, Feb., 1946), pp. 8-14.   DHU/R

9499. Elliot, John H. Building Bridges Between Groups That Differ
in Faith, Race, Culture. New York: American Brotherhood
Commission on Relgious Organizations, The National Conference of Christians and Jews, 1948.   O

9500. Freeman, John D. "Will Jewry Be Warned?" Editorial.
Western Recorder (119; Feb. 22, 1945), p. 8. LNB; TND

9501. Gwaltney, L. L. "The Jews and the Crucifixion." Editorial.
The Alabama Baptist (113; Apr. 1, 1948), p. 3. LNB; TND
          Editorial.

9502. Masters, Victor I. "The Jew and Public Opinion." Editorial.
Western Recorder (108; Nov. 22, 1934), p. 7. LNB; TND
          Editorial.

9503. ----- "The Jew and the Persecution Complex." Editorial.
Western Recorder (108; Apr. 26, 1934), p. 8. LNB; TND

9504. "Negro and Jew." Editorial. The Christian Century (39:38,
Sept. 21, 1922), pp. 1150-52.   DHU/R
          "What will become of the alliance of the two?"

9505. Pierce, David H. "Is the Jew a Friend of the Negro?"
Crisis (30; Jl., 1925), pp. 184-86.   DHU/MO

9506. Sheppard, Harold L. "The Negro Merchant: A Study of
Negro Anti-Semitism." American Journal of Sociology (53;
Sept., 1947), pp. 96-99.   DHU

g. Lutheran
9507. Achaller, Lyle E. "Nine Years of Advent." The Lutheran
(7:23, Dec. 3, 1969), pp. 5-8.   Pam. File, DHU/R
          All-Black Lutheran church -- Cleveland, Ohio.

9508. Bakke, N. J. Illustrated Historical Sketch of Our Colored
Missions. St. Louis: N.p., 1914.   DLC; NB;
MSL/CHI

9509-10. Bost, Raymond Morris. The Reverend John Bachman
and the Development of Southern Lutheranism. Masters thesis.
Yale, 1963.   TSewU-T

9511. Cooper, John C. "The Black Man's Burden." Metanoia
(4: 1, Mr., 1972), pp. 2-6.   DHU/R
          "Blacks and the Lutheran Church in South Carolina."

9512. ----- "Lutheran Church and the Unchurched Negro."
Lutheran Quarterly (11; Ag., 1959), pp. 274-51. DHU/R

9513. Cromer, Voigt R. Christian Action in Human Relations. New York: The United Lutherna Church in America. The Board of Social Missions, n. d.   Pam. File, DHU/R

9514. Drewes, C. F. Half a Century of Lutheranism Among Our Colored People. St. Louis: Concordia Publishing House, 1927. DHU/R; MSL/CHI; NN/Sch; NcD; DLC

9515. Fritz, John Henry Charles. The Lutheran Church and the Negro. n. p.: Missionary Board of the Lutheran Synodical Conference of North America, n. d.   MOSL/CHI

9516. Hill, Charles Leander, (trans.). Philip Melanchthon. The Loci Communes of Philip Melanchton, With a Critical Introduction by the Translator, Charles Leander Hill... Boston: Meador Publishing Co., 1944.   DHU/MO
        "Doctrines of the Lutheran Church."
        Negro minister translator.

9517. Huber, Ed. "The Diary of an Urban Priest." Metanoia (4:1, Mr., 1972), pp. 7-9.   DHU/R
        "Blacks and the Lutheran Church."

9518. Johnson, Art. "Lutherans Working Together. 'Goal' in Omaha is Start of a Metropolitan Ministry." The Lutheran (8: 12, Je., 17, 1970), pp. 40.   Pam. File, DHU/R
        Lutherans unite in Omaha.

9519. Kampschmidt, William H. "Why the Evangelical Lutheran Church Established and Maintains a College for Negroes." Journal of Negro Education (20; Sum., 1960), pp. 299-306.   DHU

9520. Krebs, Ervin E. The Lutheran Church and the American Negro. Columbus, O.: Board of American Missions, 1950.   DHU/MO

9521. Luecke, Jessie Rayne. Twenty-Eight Years in Negro Missions. Fort Dodge, Iowa: Joselyn Press, 1953.   MSL/CHI

9522. The Lutheran Church Missouri Synod. Our Colored Missions (Forward in Colored Missions). St. Louis: Evangelical Lutheran Synod of Missouri, Ohio, and Other States, n. d.   MSL/CHI

9523. Meyer, L. The Facts Behind the Figures. St. Louis: Evangelical Lutheran Synod of Missouri, Ohio, and other States, n. d.   MSL/CHI
        Race relations and the Lutheran Church.

9524. ----- Your Church at Work. St. Louis: Evangelical Lutheran Synod of Missouri, Ohio, and Other States, n. d. MSL/CHI
        Lutheran Church and race relations.

9525. Mueller, John T. A Brief History of the Origin, Development and Work of the Evangelical Lutheran Synodical Conference of North America. St. Louis: Concordia Publishing House, 1948.   MSL/CHI

9526. Nau, John F. "The Lutheran Church in Louisiana." Concordia Historical Institute Quarterly (25:1, Apr., 1952), pp. 30-35.   MSL/CHI

9527. Nothstein, Ira C. Adventuring for Christ. Philadelphia: The United Lutheran Publication House, 1932. MSL/CHI

9528. Piepkorn, Arthur C. "Here I Stand." Valparaiso, Ind.: Institute on Human Relations, n. d.   MSL/CHI
        Lutheran Church and race relations.

9529. Repp, Arthur G. "Beginnings of Lutheranism in Houston, Texas." Concordia Historical Institute Quarterly (26:2, Jl., 1953), pp. 69-72.   MSL/CHI

9530. Ritchie, M. A. F. "Churches and Community Relations." Lutheran Quarterly (9; My., 1957), pp. 110-24.   DHU/R

9531. Rooks, Charles Shelby. "The Black Church: Its Implications for Lutheran Theological Education." Concordia Theological Monthly (40:10, Nov. 1969).   DHU/R

9532. Scherer, James A. Mission and Unity in Lutheranism. Philadelphia: Fortress Press, 1969.   MSL/CHI
        Lutheran church and race relations.

9533. Schulze, Andrew. My Neighbor of Another Color. St. Louis: Andrew Schulze, 1941.   MSL/CHI
        Lutheran Church and race relations.

9534. ----- Race Against Time: A History of Race Relations in the Lutheran Church-Missouri Synod From the Perspective of the Author's Involvement 1920-1970. Valparaiso, Ind.: Lutheran Human Relations Association of America, 1972. MSL/CHI

9535. Sease, Rosalyn Summer. What About Race Relations? Six Forum Programs. Philadelphia: Women's Missionary Society, United Lutheran Church in America, Education Division, 1949.   NN/Sch

9536. Singmaster, Elsie. The Story of Lutheran Missions. Columbia, S.C.: Survey Publishing Company, 1917.   MSL/CHI
        Lutheran Church and race relations.

9537. Wolf, L. B., (ed.). Missionary Heroes of the Lutheran Church. Philadelphia: The Lutheran Publication Society, 1911.   MSL/CHI

h. Methodist Episcopal (United Methodist)

9538. Allen, L. Scott. "Toward Preserving the History of the Central Jurisdiction." Methodist History (7; Oct., 1968), pp. 24-30.   ISAR; DHU/R

9539. Allison, Madeline G. "The Churches." The Crisis (19: 6, Apr., 1920), p. 337.   DHU/MO; DLC
        M. E. Church and the Methodist Church South agreed to unite.

9540. ----- "The Horizon." The Crisis (23: 5, Mr., 1922), p. 222.   DHU/MO; DLC

9541. "Are the Methodist Being Tricked?" Christian Century (54; Oct. 27, 1937), p. 1318.   DHU/R

9542. Arnold, W. E. A History of Methodism in Kentucky. Louisville: Herald Press, 1936.   IEG
        pp. 268, 312 statements on Negro members.

9543. Atkins, D. "The Unification of the Methodist Episcopal Church and the Methodist Episcopal Church, South." Methodist Review Quarterly (73:2, Apr., 1924), pp. 276-99. DHU/R

9544. Bascom, Henry Bidleman, (bp.). The Methodist Church Property Case; Report of the Suit of and others, Heard Before Judges Nelson and Betts, in the Circuit Court, United States, for the Southern District of New York, May 18-29, 1851, by R. Sutton. Richmond: J. Early for the Methodist Episcopal Church, South, 1851.   NNCor

9545. Beach, Waldo. "Methodist General Conference: A Second Glance." Christianity and Crisis (16; Je. 11, 1956), pp. 73-74.   DHU/R

9546. Betts, Albert Dreems. History of South Carolina Methodism. Columbia, S.C.: Advocate Press, 1952.   IEG
        Chapters on "The Negro's Share in Methodism" and "Our Brother in Black."

9547. "Bishop Kern Reassures Southern Methodists." Christian Century (54:45, Nov. 10, 1937), p. 1380.   DHU/R

9548. "Bishops' Mission Brings Race Together in Tennessee." Together (8; Feb., 1964), p. 6.   DAU/W

9549. "Board of Methodist Church Studies Negro Problem." Christian Century (39:21, My. 25, 1922), pp. 664-66. DHU/R

9550. Bowen, John Wesley Edward, (ed.). An Appeal for Negro Bishops but No Separation. New York: Eaton and Marns, 1912. NN/Sch; DHU/MO; DLC

Negro author.
An appeal on the Methodist Episcopal Church for Negro bishops.

9551. Bradley, David H. "Francis Asbury and the Development of African Churches in America." Methodist History (10:1, Oct., 1971), pp. 3-29.   DHU/R

9552. Brashares, Charles W. "Racism and the Methodist Church." Social Question Bulletin (37; Feb., 1947), p. 20. CtY-D; DLC
Favors "permissive legislation" to make possible unsegregated Methodist work in the North.

9553. Brewer, Earl D. C. "Sect and Church in Methodism." Social Forces (30; 1952), pp. 400-08.   DHU
"Sect type religious organization can only be partly identified with folk culture."

9554. Briggs, Frederick W. Bishop Asbury: A Biographical Study for Christian Workers. London: n.p., 1879. IEG; NcD
Many references to the Bishop's attitude toward slavery in the Methodist Church.

9555. Brooks, William E. History and Highlights of Florida Methodism. Ft. Lauderdale, Fla.: Tropical Press, Inc., 1965.   ISAR
Chapter on "Work Among Slaves, Freedman's Aid and Development of the Central Jurisdiction."

9556. Bucke, Emory S. "Will Methodism Continue Segregation." Zions Herald (124; Mr. 13, 1946), p. 247.   DLC

9557. Butler, O. G. "Should Negroes Leave the Methodist Church?" Christian Century (53; Mr. 11, 1936), p. 403.   DHU/R

9558. Caldwell, John H., (bp.). "Negroes and Methodist Episcopal Church." Southern Methodist Quarterly Review (26; 1866), pp. 418+.   DLC; NcD

9559. ----- (bp.). "Relations of the Colored People to the Methodist Episcopal Church, South." Methodist Quarterly Review (48; 1866), pp. 418-43.   DLC; CtY-D

9560. Cameron, Richard M. Methodism and Society in Historical Perspective. New York: Abingdon Press, 1961. DHU/R
See chapter IV for Slavery; chapter V for Civil War and Reconstruction and chapter VII for Race Relations.

9561. Carrington, Charles L. "Methodist Union and the Negro." Crisis (43:5, My., 1936), pp. 135+.   DHU/MO

9562. ----- "The Problem of the Negro in the Methodist Church." Christian Advocate (137; Ag. 15, 1962), pp. 2+. Pam. File, DHU/R

9563. Carter, Paul A. "The Negro and Methodist Union." Church History (21:1, Mr., 1952), pp. 55-69.   DHU/R

9564. Centennial Methodist Conference, Balto., Md., 1884. Proceedings, Sermons, Essays, and Addresses of the... Held in Mt. Vernon Place Methodist Episcopal Church, Baltimore, Md., December 9-17, 1884. With a Historical Statement. Ed. by H. K. Carroll, W. Harrison, and J. H. Bayless. New York: Phillips & Hunt, 1885.   NN/Sch; ITC

9565. "Churches." The Crisis (3:3, Ja., 1912), p. 97. DHU/MO; DLC
"Agitation inside the Methodist Episcopal Church concerning its colored Membership still continues."

9566. ----- The Crisis (4:2, Je., 1912), p. 60. DLC; DHU/MO
"The general conference of the Methodist Episcopal Church held in Minneapolis discusses the question of electing colored bishops."

9567. Clair, Matthew W. (bp.). "Methodism and the Negro." Wm. K. Anderson, (ed.). Methodism (Nashville: The Metho-

dist Pub. House, 1947), pp. 245-50.   ISAR; DHU/R
Negro author.

9568. Cliffe, Albert. The Glory of Our Methodist Heritage. Nashville: Abingdon, 1958.   NcD
History of St. George's Methodist Church, Philadelphia by one of its former ministers. The church which Richard Allen and his followers left to organize the A.M.E. church.

9569. Corson, Fred Pierce. "St. George's Church; The Cradle of American Methodism." American Philosophical Society Transactions (43:1, 1953), pp. 230-36. DGU; DGW
The Methodist Church in Philadelphia from which Richard Allen and his followers left to organize the African Methodist Episcopal Church.

9570. Cox, James M. "What Progress Did the American White Man Make, in the Nineteenth Century, Along the Line of Conceding to the Negro His Religious, Political, and Civil Rights?" Daniel W. Culp. Twentieth Century Negro Literature (Miami, Fla.: Mnemosyne Pub. Co., Inc., 1969), pp. 295-98.   DHU/MO
Reprint of 1902 edition.
First student to receive the B.D. degree from Gammon Theological Seminary; Methodist Episcopal minister, teacher and President of Philander-Smith College, Little Rock, Arkansas.

9571. Cranston, Earl. Breaking Down the Walls. New York: Methodist Book Concern, 1915.   DHU/R
Chapter VIII, The Role of the Negro in the Unification of the Methodist Church.

9572. ----- (bp.). The Dynamic of a United Methodism. Evanston: n.p., 1915.   IEG

9573. Crum, Mason. The Negro in the Methodist Church... New York: Editorial Department, Division of Education and Civilization, Board of Missions and Church Extension, Methodist Church, 1951.   NcD; OWibfU; A&M

9574. Culver, Dwight W. Negro Segregation in the Methodist Church. New Haven: Yale University Press, 1953. DHU/R; INF; INU; NN/Sch; NjP
Also issued as a thesis at Yale University.

9575. ----- "Segregation in the Methodist Church." Christian Century (65; Apr. 14, 1948), pp. 325-6.

9576. Daniel, W. Harrison. "Methodist Episcopal Church and the Negro in the Early National Period." Methodist History (11:1, Ja., 1973), pp. 40-53.   DHU/R

9577. "Decisions Confronting the Methodists." Christian Century (53; Ja. 1, 1936), pp. 147+.   DHU/R

9578. Deems, Charles Force. Annals of Southern Methodism... New York: J. A. Gray's Printing Office, 1865. NN/Sch
V. 2, pp. 190-209, Negroes and missions.

9579. Diffendorfer, Ralph E., (ed.). The World Service of the Methodist Episcopal Church. Council of Boards of Benevolence. Committee on Conservation and Advance. Chicago: n.p., 1923. DHU/R
Part II, Board of Education for Negroes.

9580. Downey, David George, (ed.). Militant Methodism; the Story of the First National Convention of Methodist Men, Held at Indianapolis, Indiana, October Twenty-Eight to Thirty-One Nineteen Hundred and Thirteen... New York: The Methodist Book Concern, 1913.   NN/Sch

9581. Durham, E. C. "A Friendly Consideration of the Negro." Methodist Review (69:4, Oct., 1920), p. 682. DHU/R

9582. Ecumenical Methodist Conference. Wash., D.C. 1891. 2nd. Proceedings of the Second ... held in Metropolitan Methodist Church, October, 1891. New York: Hunt and Eaton, 1892.

(Ecumenical Methodist Conf. cont.)
OWibfU
Conference included Negro delegates for the A. M. E.,
C. M. E., A. M. E. Zion and Methodist Episcopal Church.

9583-84. Ecumenical Methodist Conference, Toronto, 1911. 4th.
Proceedings of the Fourth ... held in Metropolitan Methodist
Church, October 4-17, 1911. Cincinnati: Jennings and Graham,
1911.   OWibfU

9585. Edwards, John E. "Petersburg, Virginia, and Its Negro
Population." Methodist Quarterly Review (64; Apr., 1882), pp.
320-37.   DLC; CtY-D

9586. Edwards, S. J. Celestine. From Slavery to a Bishopric,
or the Life of Bishop Walter Hawkins. London: John Kensit,
1891.   IEG; DHU/MO
Bishop of the British Methodist Episcopal Church of Canada.
Negro author.

9587. Emerson, Harriet E. Annals of a Harvester, Reviewing
Forty Years of Home Missionary Work in Southern States.
East Andover, N. H.: A. W. Emerson, Sons & Co., 1915.
NcD

9588. Etheridge, J. W. The Life of Rev. Thomas Coke. London:
1860.   DLC; TxU; IU; ICU
Held strong views toward emancipation of slaves.

9589. Fair, Harold Lloyd. Southern Methodist on Education and
Race, 1900-1920. Doctoral dissertation. Vanderbilt University,
1971.   DHU/R

9590. Farish, Hunter D. The Circuit Rider Dismounts: A Social
History of Southern Methodism 1865-1900. Richmond: Dietz
Press, 1938.   DHU/MO
A Southern Methodist attitude toward Negro Methodists.

9591. Faulkner, Clyde Wheeler, Jr. A Study of the Relationships
Between Selected Attributes of Local Methodist Church Leaders
and Their Attitudes Toward Inclusiveness in the Methodist Church.
Doctoral dissertation. Emory University, 1971.

9592. "Favor the Admission Negro Students." Zions Herald (129;
Mr. 21, 1951), p. 227.   DLC; CtY-D

9593. Federal Council of the Churches of Christ in America. Dept.
of Research and Education. "The Race Issue in Methodist
Unification." Information Service (16; Apr. 3, 1937), pp. 1-4.
DHU/R

9594. Felton, Ralph Almon. The Ministry of the Central Jurisdiction of the Methodist Church... Madison, N.J.: n.p., 1954.
NcD

9595. Fish, John Olen. Southern Methodism in the Progressive Era:
A Social History. Doctoral dissertation. University of Georgia,
1969.   DHU/R

9596. Fox, Henry J. "Our Work in the South." Methodist Review
(Ja., 1874), pp. 31-2.   DHU/R

9597. "Garrett Launches Clinical Education Center for Blacks."
The Link (31:6, Je., 1973), p. 59.   Pam. File, DHU/R
An accredited Clinical Pastoral Education Center for Black
Seminarians and Pastors in Evanston, Illinois.

9598. George Peabody College for Teachers, Nashville. Division
of Surveys and Field Studies. Negro Colleges and Schools Re-
lated to the Methodist Church; A Survey Report... Nashville:
Div. of Surveys and Field Studies, George Peabody College for
Teachers, 1943.   NN/Sch
"Report on the Survey of Negro Colleges and Schools Related
to the Board of Education and the Woman's Division of
Christian Service to the Methodist Church."

9599. Gibson, Joseph Kermit. The Methodist Evangelistic Movement Among Negroes in America. Bachelor of Divinity thesis.
Livingstone College, 1948.   DLC

9600. Gordon, David M. The Lexington Conference and the Negro
Migration. Evanston: n.p., 1957.   IEG

9601. Graham, John H. A Study of Wesley Methodist Church, York,
South Carolina. Atlanta: Dept. of Sociology, Gammon Theological Seminary, 1959.   DAU; GAITH

9602. Gravely, William B. "The Afro-American Methodist Tradition: A Review of Sources in Reprint." Methodist History
(9:3, Apr., 1971), p. 214.   DHU/R; GAITH

9603. ----- "A Black Methodist On Reconstruction in Mississippi:
Three Letters by James Lynch in 1868-1869." Methodist History (11:4, Jl., 1973), pp. 3-18.   DHU/R

9604. ----- Gilbert Haven, Methodist Abolitionist; A Study in Race,
Religion and Reform, 1850-1880. Nashville: Abingdon Press,
1973. MiBsa; TSewU-T; NNCor; CDU; DHU/R

9605. Grissom, W. L. History of Methodism in North Carolina
From 1772 to the Present Time. Nashville: Publishing House
of the Methodist Episcopal Church, South, 1905.   IEG
Chapter XIV, Negroes.

9606. Gulfside, Waveland, Mississippi. A Summer Assembly and
Camp Ground for Religious, Educational and Recreational Pur-
poses. n.p., 1927.   NN/Sch
Conducted, for Negroes, by the Dept. of Rural Works, Board
of Home Missions and Church Extension, Methodist Episcopal
Church.

9607. Hagood, Lewis Marshall. The Colored Man in the Methodist
Episcopal Church. New York: Hunt & Eaton, 1890. DHU/R;
NN/Sch
Negro author.

9608. Hall, Prince. "Extract from a Charge Delivered to the African Lodge, June 24th, 1797, at Menotomy, (Now West Cambridge,) Mass. by the Right Worshipful Prince Hall." Leslie
H. Fishel, Jr. and Benjamin Quarles. The Black American
(rev. ed.) (N.Y.: William Morrow & Co., Inc., 1970), pp.
78-79.   DHU/R; DHU/MO
Written by Methodist minister of Massachusetts, considered
founder of first Black Masonic orders.

9609. Harmon, Ja. A. "The Negro: Our Duty and Relation to Him."
Methodist Review Quarterly (75:1, Ja., 1926), pp. 56-66.
DHU/R

9610. Harris, William Frederick. "Methodism and Her Secession"
Methodist Review (Quarterly) (77:1, Ja., 1928), pp. 72-81.
DHU/R
Includes brief section on Negro Secessions.

9611. Hartzell, Joseph C., (bp.). "Methodism and the Negro in
the United States." Journal of Negro History (8:3, Jl., 1923),
pp. 301-15.   DHU/MO

9612. Haygood, Atticus G. Address of the Rev. Atticus G. Haygood,
D. D., LL. D. of the Methodist Episcopal Church, South, at
the Fourth Annual Opening of the Gammon School of Theology,
Atlanta, Ga., Oct. 27, 1886.   NH; OFH

9613. ----- Our Brother in Black: His Freedom and His Future.
Nashville: Southern Methodist Publishing Co., 1881. DHU/MO

9614. Hazzard, Walter R. "Why Negroes Want Integration."
Central Christian Advocate (131: 12, Je. 15, 1956), pp. 4-6.
DHU/R

9615. Henzlik, William C. "Youth Black Coalition Triggers Missions Debate." Christian Advocate (13:17, Sept. 4, 1969),
p. 24.   Pam. File, DHU/R

9616. Hodges, Goerge Washington. Touchstones of Methodism.
New York: The Compact Reflector Press, 1947. NN/Sch
Negro author.

9617. Holmes, Edward H. The Influence of Methodism on the Negroes of the Delaware Conference Area From 1766-1866. Masters thesis. Temple University, 1958.

9618. Holsey, Lucius Henry, (bp.). "Methodist Means of Grace." Henry King Carroll, (ed.). Proceedings, Sermons, Essays, and Addresses of the Centennial Methodist Conference Held in Mt. Vernon Methodist Episcopal Church, Baltimore, Md., December 9-17, 1884. Cincinnati: n. p., 1885. GAU; NN/Sch

9619. Hoss, Elijah E. Methodist Fraternity and Federation. Nashville: Publishing House, Methodist Episcopal Church, South, 1913. DLC

9620. Jason, William C. "The Delaware Annual Conference of the Methodist Church 1864-1965." Methodist History (4:4, Jl., 1966), pp. 26-40. DHU/R; ISAR

9621. Jenkins, Warren M. Steps Along the Way; the Origin and Development of the South Carolina Conference of the Central Jurisdiction of the Methodist Church. Columbia, S. C.: Socamead Press, 1967. NcD
        Negro author.

9622. John Street Methodist Episcopal Church: Centenary Memorial... New York: n. p., 1868. NN/Sch
        Records include information on Negro Methodists and Peter Williams, Sr.

9623 Johnson, Henry M. The Methodist Episcopal Church and the Education of the Southern Negroes, 1862-1900. Doctoral dissertation. Yale University, 1939.

9624. Joint Commission on Unification of the Methodist Episcopal Church and the Methodist Episcopal Church, South. Proceedings. New York: Methodist Book Concern, 1918-24. DLC

9625. Jones, Donald Gene. The Moral, Social, and Political Ideas of the Methodist Episcopal Church from the Closing Years of the Civil War Through Reconstruction 1864-1876. Doctoral dissertation. Drew University, 1969.

9626. Jones, John G. A Complete History of Methodism as Connected with the Mississippi Conference. Baton Rouge: Claitors Book Store, 1966. IEG
        Brief statements about Negro work.

9627. Kaufer, Sonya F. You Hold the Key to Human Rights. Cincinnati: Woman's Division of Christian Service, Board of Missions and Church Extension, Methodist Church, 1953. NN/Sch

9628. Kennedy, Gerald Hamilton. The Methodist Way of Life. Englewood Cliffs, N. J.: Prentice-Hall, 1958. NN/Sch

9629. Kent, Juanita Ray. Our Negro Neighbors; a World Friendship Unit for Primary Children. Nashville, Tenn.: Cokesbury Press, 1936. NN/Sch

9630. King, Willis J., (bp.). "The Negro Membership of the (Former) Methodist Church in the (New) United Methodist Church." Methodist History (7; Apr. 3, 1969), pp. 32-43. ISAR
        Negro author.

9631. Kirkland, H. Burnham. The Methodist Church and the Negro. Bachelor of Divinity thesis. Union Theological Seminary, 1944.

9632. Lazenby, Marion Elias. History of Methodism in Alabama and West Florida. n. p.: n. p., 1960. ISAR
        See chapter 32.

9633. Luccock, Halford E. and Paul Hutchinson. The Story of Methodism. New York: Abingdon-Cokesbury Press, 1949. DHU/R
        Chapter 23, Methodism and the Negro.

9634. Lyon, Ernest. Autonomy. n. p.: Afro-American Co., n. d. DHU/MO
        Negro author.

9635. ----- The Negro's View of Organic Union. New York: Methodist Book Concern, 1915. DHU/R; NN/Sch
        "The question of organic union of the Methodist Episcopal Church, and the Methodist Church, South."

9636. Madron, Thomas W. "John Wesely on Race: A Christian View of Equality." Methodist History (2; Jl., 1964), pp. 24-34. DHU/R

9637. Martin, Isaac P. History of Methodism in the Holston Conference. Nashville: Holston Conference. Nashville: Holston Conference Historical Society, 1945. IEG
        Negroes and the Methodist Episcopal Church, South.

9638. Matlack, Lucius C. "The Methodist Episcopal Church in the Southern States." Methodist Review (Ja., 1872), pp. 103-26. DHU/MO

9639. May, William W. The Methodist Church and the Present Racial Crisis: An Analysis of Response and Action. Doctoral dissertation. Drew University, 1967.

9640. McFerrin, John B. History of Methodism in Tennessee. Nashville: Southern Methodist Publishing House, 1879. IEG
        See pp. 85-196.

9641. McMillan, William Asbury. The Evolution of Curriculum Patterns in Six Senior Negro Colleges of the Methodist Church. Doctoral dissertation. University of Michigan, 1957.

9642. McPheeters, A. A. "Interest of the Methodist Church in the Education of Negroes." Phylon (10:4, 4th Quarter, 1949), pp. 343-50. DHU/MO

9643. The Methodist Church. General Board of Social and Economic Relations. Interracial Conference Reports, 1955-1959. DHU/R Microfilm.

9644. Methodist Episcopal Church. Board of Foreign Missions. The Centenary Survey of the Board of Foreign Missions. The Methodist Episcopal Church. New York: Joint Centenary Committee, Methodist Episcopal Church, 1918. NN/Sch

9645. Methodist Church (United States). Board of Social and Economic Relations. The Road to Brotherhood; Views on Race Relations With Resources and Suggestions for Action. Chicago: The General Board of Social and Economic Relations, 1958. MiBsA

9646. Methodist Episcopal Church. Board of Missions. Journal of the Annual Meeting. NN/Sch; DLC; DHU/MO

9647. ----- Division of National Missions. Reports 194-. NN/Sch; GAU; NJMD

9648. ----- Freedmen's Aid Society. Annual Reports ... NcD-D; DHU/MO; NN/Sch; OO; GAU

9649. ----- The Freedmen's Aid and Southern Education Society. Progress. Report and Appeal for Funds. Cincinnati: Western Book Concern, 1904. CoDI

9650. ----- Minutes of the Lexington Conference of the Methodist Episcopal Church; Held in Park Street Methodist Episcopal Church, Cinn., Ohio, March 25-30, 1908. Adopted by the Conference as its Official Record. Cincinnati: John W. Robinson, Edited and Published, 1908. DHU/MO; GAU; NN/Sch

9651. ----- Official Journal of State Conferences... DHU/MO; NN/Sch; GAU

9652. ----- (United States). Dept. of Research and Survey. The Church in the Racially Changing Community. Robert L. Wilson and James H. Davis. New York: Abingdon Press, 1966. NjP

9653. "Methodist Episcopal Negro Bishops." Voice of the Negro (1:7, Jl., 1904), pp. 270+. DHU/MO

9654. "Methodist Negro City Workers Hold Conference." Editorial. The Christian Century (39:24, Je. 15, 1922), p. 761.   DHU/R

9655. "Methodist School for Negroes Has New President." Editorial. The Christian Century (39:40, Oct. 5, 1922), p. 1232.
DHU/R
J. W. Simmons elected president or Clark Univeristy, Atlanta, Ga.

9656. "Methodists and Race." Newsweek (54; Sept. 14, 1959), p. 70.   DHU

9657. "Methodists and Segregation." Time (75; My. 9, 1960), p. 53.   DHU

9658. "Methodists: Proposed Merger Called Segregation of Negroes." Newsweek (9; Feb. 13, 1937), p. 21.   DHU; DLC

9659. "Mishmash and Renewal: The Methodists in St. Louis." The Christian Century (87: 18, My. 6, 1970), pp. 556-58.
DHU/R

9660. Mitchell, Frank J. The Virginia Methodist Conference and Social Issues in the Twentieth Century. Doctoral dissertation. Duke University, 1962.

9661. Moore, John M. The Long Road to Methodist Union. New York: Abingdon-Cokesbury Press, 1943.   DHU/R
A history of unification by a Southern Methodist Bishop who played a prominent part in the movement.

9662. Mount Zion M. E. Church. History of Mount Zion M. E. Church, 1816-96 and Official Program of the 80th Anniversary, Oct. 11-18, 1896. Washington, D.C.: Press of R. L. Pendleton, n. d.   DHU/MO

9663. "Move Toward Church Unity; Methodists Appoint Negroes to Jersey, Iowa Bishoprics." Ebony (20:4, Feb., 1965), pp. 54-60.   DHU/MO

9664. Mudge, James. Historical Sketch of the Missions of the Methodist Episcopal Church. n. p.: American Methodist Mission Press, 1877.   OWibfU

9665. Nail, Olir. W. History of Texas Methodism. Austin: Capital Printing Co., 1961.   IEG
Methodism and the Negroes by I. B. Loud.

9666. Nanna, John C. The Centennial Services of Asbury Methodist Episcopal Church. Wilmington, Del.: Delaware Pub. Co., 1889.   NcD-D
Information about the African Union Methodist Protestant Church Organized in 1865. Disciplines of 1871 and 1895 contain information on it also.

9667. "Negro Methodists Consider Union." Christian Century (55: 28, Jl. 12, 1939), p. 867.   DHU/R
Reviews the decision of Negro Methodist to merge.

9668. Nelson, Clarence T. R. A Study of Current Relgious Education in the Lexington Conference of the Methodist Church. Masters thesis. Garrett Theological Seminary, 1951.

9669. Newell, Frederick B. "The Negro and the Methodist Church..." The Drew Gateway (18:2, Wint., 1947), pp. 17-21.
NNUT; NjD

9670. Oakes, Henry N. Black Accommodation in the Methodist Episcopal Church: the Career of Robert E. Jones, 1904-1944. Doctoral dissertation. University of Iowa, 1972.

9671. Olson, Arnold O. The Social Attitudes and Social Action of Some Ministers of the New York Conference of the Methodist Church. Doctoral dissertation. Yale University, 1953.

9672. Patterson, John William. The Right of Man or the Chastening Rod ... Two Lectures in One. Edited by Evelyn Patterson Burrell. Wash., D.C.: n. p., 1916.   DHU/MO

Written by a Negro Methodist Episcopal minister and edited by his daughter with a biographical sketch of his life.

9673. Perez, Joseph A. Some Effects of the Central Jurisdiction Upon the Movement to Make the Methodist Church an Inclusive Church. Doctoral dissertation. Boston University, Graduate School, 1964.

9674. Pleasants, D. M. "The Negro Methodist Since 1784." Central Christian Advocate (135:23, Dec. 1, 1960), pp. 4-6.
DHU/R

9675. Pool, Frank Kenneth. The Southern Negro in the Methodist Episcopal Church. Doctoral dissertation. Duke University, 1939.

9676. Posey, Walter Brownlow. The Development of Methodism in the Old Southwest, 1883-1924. Tuscaloosa, Ala.: Weatherford Printing Co., 1933.   IEG
Chapter, "Negro and the Methodist Church."

9677. Prestwood, Charles M. Social Ideas of Methodist Ministers in Alabama Since Unification. Doctoral dissertation. Boston University, Graduate School, 1960.

9678. Quayle, W. A. The Black Man and Christ. n.p.: Freedmen's Aid Society of the Methodist Episcopal Church, n. d.   IEG

9679. Reed, John Hamilton. Racial Adjustments in the Methodist Episcopal Church. New York: The Neale Publishing Co., 1914.
DHU/MO; TNF; NcD

9680. Ridout, D. L. "Study Methodist Racial Attitudes." Christian Century (74; Ja. 30, 1957), pp. 147-48.   DHU/R

9681. Riley, Negail Rudolph. Attitude Patterns of Negro Ministers Experiencing Desegregation in the North Central Jurisdiction of the Methodist Church. 1967.   NjP
Film.
Also author's doctoral dissertation, Boston University School, 1967.

9682. Riley, Walter H. Forty Years in the Lap of Methodism; History of Lexington Conference of Methodist Episcopal Church. Louisville, Ky.: Mayes Printing Co., 1915.   NN/Sch

9683. Rogers, Henry Wade. "The Status of the Negro." Methodist Review Quarterly (67:4, Oct., 1918), pp. 657-69. DHU/R

9684. Rumbough, Constance. Negro Americans; a World Friendship Unit for Junior Girls and Boys. Nashville, Tenn.: Cokesbury Press, 1936.   NN/Sch

9685. Rust, Richard Sutton. The Freedmen's Aid Society of the Methodist Episcopal Church. New York: Tract Department, 1880.   DLC

9686. "St. Mark's M. E. Church." Crisis (23:5, Mr., 1922), p. 222.   DHU/MO
William H. Brooks, pastor of St. Mark's M. E. Church in New York City plans celebration for fifty-sixth anniversary of the Church.

9687. Scott, Allen L. "Toward Preserving the History of the Central Jurisdiction." Methodist History (7; Oct., 1968), pp. 24-30.   DHU/R

9688. Shaw, Daniel Webster. Should the Negroes of the Methodist Episcopal Church be Set Apart in a Church by Themselves. New York: Eaton & Mains, 1912.   DHU/MO
Negro author.

9689. Shaw, James Beverly Ford. The Negro in the History of Methodism. Nashville: Parthenon Press, 1954. DHU/MO; DHU/R; NN/Sch; DLC; IEG

9690. Shipp, Albert M. A History of Methodism in the Holston Conference. Nashville: Holston Historical Conference, 1945.
IEG

9691. Shockley, Grant S. "Methodism, Society and Black Evangel-
ism in America: Retrospect and Prospect." A. M. E. Zion
Quarterly Review (86:2, Summer, 1974), pp. 145-82. DHU/R
Negro author.

9692. Simms, James. "The Union of White Methodism." The
Crisis (20:1, May., 1926), pp. 14-17. DHU/MO; DLC
Controversey over the Negro jurisdiction in the Methodist
Church.

9693. Sketon, D. E. History of Lexington Conference. n.p.,
1950.   ISAR
Former All-Negro conference of the United Methodist Church.

9694. Smith, Eugene L. "Personal Racism Remains Problem for
United Methodism." Christian Advocate (17; Ja. 4, 1973), pp.
9-10.   Pam. File, DHU/R

9695. Soper, Edmund D. Racism: A World Issue. New York:
Abingdon-Cokesbury Press, 1947.   DHU/R
United Methodist Church and race relations.

9696. Southall, Eugene P. "The Attitude of the Methodist Episcopal
Church, South, Toward the Negro from 1844 to 1870." The
Journal of Negro History (16; Oct. 1931), pp. 359-70. DHU/MO

9697. Stepp, Diane. "Methodist Tag $46,000 for Negro Church Aid."
Consititution (Oct. 31, 1968).   Pam. File, DHU/R

9698. Stevens, Francis B. "A Sign of Change in Mississippi
Methodism." Concern (7:15, Sept. 1, 1965), pp. 8-9+. DHU/R

9699. Stotts, Herbert E. and Paul Deats. Methodism and Society:
Guidelines for Strategy. New York: Abingdon Press, 1962.
                                            DHU/R
Statistics on Negroes in the Methodist Church, p. 316.

9700. Stowell, Jay S. J. W. Thinks Black... New York: The
Methodist Book Concern, 1922.   FSU; DHU/R
The work of the Methodist Episcopal Church among American
Negroes.

9701. ----- Methodist Adventures in Negro Education. New York:
The Methodist Book Concern, 1922.   DHU/R; A & M; FSU

9702. Sweet, William Warren. "Methodist Church Influence in
Southern Politics." Mississippi Valley Historical Review (1:4,
Mr., 1915), pp. 546-60.   DHU

9703. ----- Virginia Methodism. A History. Richmond: Whittel
& Shepperson, 1955.   IEG

9704. Taylor, Winston H. "An Inclusive Church: Up Ahead Some-
where." Engage / Social Action (2:8, Ag., 1974), pp. 10-17.
                                            DHU/R
"How thorough has desegregation in the United Methodist
Church been?"

9705. Thirkield, Mary Haven. Elizabeth Lounes Rust. Cincinnati:
Jennings & Pay, 1903.   GAITH

9706. Thirkield, Wilbur Patterson, (bp.). The Negro and the Organic Union of Methodism... An Address before the Working
Conference on the Organic Union of Methodist Held at Northwestern University, 1916, Under the Auspices of the John
Richard Lindgun Foundation. n.p., 1916.   DHU/MO

9707. -----(bp.). Rev. Eleza H. Gammon. Atlanta: n.p., 1892.
                                            IEG

9708. ----- (bp.). Separation of Continuity, Which? or A Colored
Man's Reply to Bishop Foster's Book, "The Union of the Episcopal Methodisms." Baltimore: H. H. Smith, 1893. NJMD

9709. Thomas, Isaac Lemuel. Methodism and the Negro. New York:
Eaton & Main, 1910.   DHU/R; DLC; MiBsa
Negro author.

9710-11. Thomas, James S. "Rationale Underlying Support of
Negro Private Colleges by the Methodist Church." Journal of
Negro Education (29; Sum., 1960), pp. 252-59.   DHU

9712. Thrift, Charles T. On the Trial of the Florida Circuit Rider.
Lakeland, Fla.: Florida College Press, 1944.   ISAR
See section on St. John's River Conference.

9713. Tindley, Charles A. "Church That Welcomes 10,000 Strangers."
World Outlook (5; Oct., 1919), pp. 5-6.   DLC; CtY-D; DHU/MO
Written by the pastor, East Calvary Methodist Episcopal
Church, Philadelphia, Pa.

9714. Tucker, Frank C. The Methodist Church in Missouri, 1798-
1839. Joint Committee on the Historical Societies of the Missouri East and Missouri West Annual Conference, 1966. IEG
Negro Methodists included.

9715. "Unification." Opportunity (2; 1924), p. 217.   DHU/MO
Concerns the Negro question and its implications on uni-
fication of the Methodist Church, South, with the Methodist
Church.

9716. United Methodist Church. Arizona District. Southern California-Arizona Conference. Human Relations Seminar. Central Methodist Church, Phoenix, Arizona, January 12-23, 1958.
                                    Pam. File, DHU/R

9717. ----- Board of Christian Social Relations. Interracial Lead-
ership Conference. Reports of... Conferences at Columbus,
Ohio, 1957-59; Austin, Texas, 1957; Detroit, Mich., 1957;
Florida, 1959; Indianapolis, 1957; Milwaukee, Wisconsin, 1958;
Pittsburgh, Pa., 1957; St. Louis, Mo., 1957; Atlanta, Ga.
1957.   Pam. File, DHU/R
Mim.

9718. Vernon, Walter H. Methodism Moves Across North Texas.
Nashville: Parthenon, 1967.   IEG
Negro members and preachers in the Conference.

9719. Wakely, Joseph B. Lost Chapters Recovered from the Early
History of American Methodism. New York: Pr. by the Author,
1858.   DHU/MO; NN/Sch
"Colored People in New York City in the Infancy of American Methodism." Biography of Peter Williams, Negro
minister.

9721. Waters, James O. A Planned Program for the Junior High
Class of Shiloh Community Methodist Church, Newburg, Maryland. B. D. paper. School of Religion, Howard University,
1966.
Negro author.

9722. West, Anson. A History of Methodism in Alabama. Nashville: Publishing House, Methodist Episcopal Church, South,
1893.   ISAR
Chapters 27 and 35.

9723. "What the Methodist Church is Doing for the Negro."
World Outlook (5; Oct., 1919), p. 31.   DLC; Cty-D

9724. Whitehead, C. L. Negro Bishop Agitation of the Methodist
Episcopal Church and Colored Members in Convention at
Nashville, Tennessee, October 22-23, 1914. n.p., 1914.
                                            TNMph

9725. "Will Negro Methodists Set Up a New Church?" Christian
Century (55:8, Feb. 23, 1938), pp. 229+.   DHU/R

9726. Williams, John B. L. "To What Extent is the Negro Pulpit
Uplifting the Race?" Daniel W. Culp. Twentieth Century Ne-
gro Literature. (Miami, Fla.: Manemosyne Publishing Co.,
Inc., 1969), pp. 120-22.   DHU/MO
Reprint of 1902 edition.
Negro Methodist Episcopal minister and teacher.

9727. Williams, Robert Moten. "Methodist Union and the Negro."
Crisis (43:5, My., 1936), pp. 134+.   DHU/MO; DLC

9728. Wilson, W. W. "The Methodist Episcopal Church in Her Relations to the Negro in the South." Methodist Review (75; Sept.-Oct., 1941), pp. 713-23.   DLC; Cty-D

9729. Wingeier, Douglas E. The Treatment of Negro-White Relations in the Curriculum Materials of the Methodist Church for Intermediate Youth, 1941-1960. Doctoral dissertaion. Boston University, Graduate School, 1962.

9730. Winton, G. B. Sketch of Bishop Atticus G. Haygood, 1915.   DHU/MO

9731. Wogaman, J. Philip. Methodism's Challenge in Race Relations; a Study of Strategy. Washington: Public Affairs Press, 1960.   NN/Sch; CtY-D; DHU/MO

i. Presbyterian

9732. Allison, Madeline G. "The Churches." The Crisis (20: 1, My., 1920), p. 68.   DHU/MO; DLC
Presbyterian Church adopts budget for Negroes.

9733. Anderson, Matthew. Presbyterianism: Its Relation to the Negro. Illustrated by the Berean Presbyterian Church, Philadelphia, with a Sketch of the Church and Autobiography of the Author. With Introduction by F. J. Grimke and John M. White. Philadelphia: John M. White, Publisher, 1897. DHU/MO; CtY-D

9734. Barber, Jesse Belmont. Climbing Jacob's Ladder; Story of the Work of the Presbyterian Church U.S.A. Among the Negroes. New York: Board of National Missions, Presbyterian Church in the U.S.A., 1952.   DHU/MO; DLC; NN/Sch
Negro author.

9735. ----- A History of the Work of the Presbyterian Church Among the Negroes in the United States of America. New York: Boards of National Missions, Presbyterian Church in the U.S.A. 1930.   PLuL

9736. Bell, John L. "The Presbyterian Church and the Negro in North Carolina." North Carolina Historical Review (40; Ja., 1963), pp. 15-36.   DHU

9737. "Biddle Institute." Editorial. The Southern Workman (1:6, Je., 1872).   DLC; DHU/MO
Microfilm.
Presbyterian school for Negroes.

9738. Boyer, Arthur Truman, (comp.). Brief Historical Sketch of the First African Presbyterian Church of Philadelphia. Philadelphia: n.p., 1944.   NN/Sch

9739. Cass, Michael M. "Charles C. Jones, Jr., and the 'Lost Cause.'" Georgia Historical Quarterly (55:2, Sum., 1971), pp. 222-233.   DGW
"Famous Presbyterian evangelist to blacks seen as anti-industrial, anti-New South in his critique of American conditions."

9740. Catto, William Thomas. A Semi-Centenary Discourse and History of the First African Presbyterian Church, Philadelphia, May, 1857, From Its Organization, Including a Notice of Its First Pastor, John Gloucester, Also Appendix Containing Sketches of All the Colored Churches in Philadelphia. Phila.: Joseph M. Wilson, 1857.   DHU/MO; DHU/R
Reprinted: Freeport, N.Y.: Books for Libraries Press, 1971.
Negro author.

9741. A Christian Manifesto of Some United Black Presbyterians of Birmingham and Their Pastor to the United Presbyterian Church in the United States of America. Birmingham, Ala.: n.p., 197?   Pam. File, DHU/R
Mim.

9742. "Churches." The Crisis (4:2, Je., 1912), p. 60. DLC; DHU/MO
Colored Cumberland Presbyterian Church admitted to the Council of Reformed Churches of America.

9743. ----- The Crisis (5:3, Ja., 1913), p. 118. DLC; DHU/MO
105th anniversary of the First African Presbyterian Church of Philadelphia.

9744. Davis, I. D. "To What Extent is the Negro Pulpit Uplifting the Race?" Daniel W. Culp. Twentieth Century Negro Literature (Miami, Fla.: Mnemosyne Pub. Co., Inc., 1969), p. 124.   DHU/MO
Reprint of 1902 edition.
Negro Presbyterian minister, teacher and Moderator of Catawba Synod, N.C.

9745. "Dedication of a Colored Church." The Church at Home and Abroad (2; Sept., 1887), p. 272.   DHU/R
Dedication of Negro Presbyterian Church in Tennessee.

9746. "Dedication of a Colored Church and Installation of a Colored Pastor." The Church at Home and Abroad (3; Ja., 1888), p. 62.   DHU/R
Announcement of dedication of a Negro Presbyterian Church in Baltimore.

9747. "Dedication of Mary Allen Seminary." The Church at Home and Abroad (4; Sept., 1888), pp. 261-63.   DHU/R
Announcement of the dedication of a boarding school for Negro girls by the Presbyterian Church.

9748. Edwards, Vetress Bon. Go South--With Christ; a Study in Race Relations. New York: Exposition Press, 1959.   DHU/MO; DLC
Negro author.

9749. "Evangelize the Negroes." (Freedmen). The Church at Home and Abroad (2; 1887), p. 60.   DHU/R
Presbyterian Church.

9750. Faulkner, L. E. "Reasons Why the Presbyterian Church (U.S.) Should Withdraw from the Federal Council of the Churches of Christ in America." Southern Presbyterian Journal (Ag. 15, 1947).   DLC

9751. Ferry, Henry. "Racism and Reunion: A Black Protest by Francis James Grimke." Journal of Presbyterian History (50: 2, Sum., 1972), pp. 77-88.   DHU/R

9752. Fisher, Samuel Jackson. The American Negro. Pittsburgh, Pa.: n.p., n.d.   NN/Sch

9753. ----- The Negro: An American Asset. Pittsburgh, Pa.: Board of Missions for Freedmen of the Presbyterian Church in the U.S.A., 1918.   NN/Sch; CtY-D; DHU/MO

9754. Flickinger, Robert Elliott. The Chocktaw Freedmen and the Story of Oak Hill Industrial Academy... Pittsburgh, Pa.: Under the Auspices of the Presbyterian Board of Missions for Freedmen, 1914.   DHU/MO; DHU/R
Chapters, IV and VI, the American Negro.

9755. Floyd, R. W. "Role of the Church in 'de facto' Segregation." Christian Advocate (8; Dec. 3, 1964), p. 7.   DHU/R; DAU/W

9756. Frazer, William H. "Why I Favor Preserving the Southern Church." Southern Presbyterian Journal (11; Jl. 23, 1952).   DLC; KyLXCB

9757. Garfield, James Walker. Presbyterianism and the Negro. n.p.: n.p., n.d.   DHU/MO

9758. "The General Assembly of 1862, The Presbyterian Church in the United States of America." The Danville Quarterly Review (2, Je., 1862), pp. 301- .   IEG
"This treason is contrary to the will of God and natural religion. Christians are obligated to whatever government under which their lots are cast."

9759. Gittings, James A. "A Respectable Kind of Reconciliation." A.D. United Presbyterian Edition (3:6, Je., 1974), pp. 54-58.   DHU/R

Author describes Clinton Marsh's year as moderator of the 185th general assembly of the United Presbyterian Church. Reverend Marsh is a Black Presbyterian minister.

9760. "Giving Out of Deep Poverty." (Freedmen). The Church at Home and Abroad (1; 1887), p. 448.   DHU/R
Negro Presbyterian. The Olivet Church, Charleston, S. C.

9761. "Gleanings at Home and Abroad." The Church at Home and Abroad (23; 1898), pp. 170-72.   DHU/R
Notes on Presbyterian missionary efforts.
Includes Africa.

9762. Glocester, S. H. A Discourse Delivered on the Occasion of the Death of Mr. John Frotren (Forten), Sr. in the Second Presbyterian Church of Colour of the City of Philadelphia... Philadelphia: n. p., 1843.   NN/Sch

9763. Gloucester, John. A Sermon Delivered in the First African Presbyterian Church in Philadelphia on the First of January, 1930, Before the Different Coloured Societies of Philadelphia. Philadelphia: n. p., 1839.   DHU/MO

9764. Grimke, Francis James. An Argument Against the Union of the Cumberland Presbyterian Church and the Presbyterian Church in the United States of America... Washington, D. C.: Hayworth Publishing House, 1904.   NN/Sch

9765. ----- Last Quadrennial Message to the Race. Washington, D. C.: The Author, 1929.   DHU/MO

9766. ----- Lincoln University Alone of Negro Institutions Shuts Out of Its Trustee Board and Out of Its Professorships. Pub. by the Author, 1916.   DHU/MO

9767. ----- The Shame of Lincoln University. Washington, D. C.: The Author, 1926.   DHU/MO

9768. ----- Wilson College Presbytery of Washington City... Colorphobia. Washington, D. C.: The Author, n. d.   DHU/MO

9769. Halloway, Harriette R. Suggestions to Leaders of Mission Study Classes Using "An African Trail." New York: Board of Foreign Missions and Woman's Boards of Foreign Missions of the Presbyterian Church in the U. S. A., 1917.   NN/Sch

9770. "A Historic Building." (Freedmen). The Church at Home and Abroad (23; 1898), p. 516.   DHU/R
Zion Presbyterian Church, Charleston, S. C.

9771. "An Independent Colored Presbytery." (Freedmen). The Church at Home and Abroad (4; 1888), p. 569.   DHU/R
"A circular was published announcing the formation of a Presbytery of Negro Presbyterians in the state of Texas."

9772. Johnson, Thomas C. History of the Southern Presbyterian Church. New York: The Christian Literature Co., 1894.   DHU/R
"American Church History Series, Volume XI."

9773. Jones, Robert E. Fifty Years in the Lombard Street Central Presbyterian Church. Philadelphia: Edward Stern, 1894.   DHU/MO
History of Second African Presbyterian Church with biographies of Negro Presbyterians.

9774. Little, John. "Lessons from Experience; Presbyterian Colored Missions, Louisville, Ky." Missionary Review (59; Je., 1936), pp. 312-15.   DHU/R

9775. ----- "The Work of the Southern Presbyterian Church for the Negro." Southern Workman (33:8, Ag., 1904), pp. 439-48.   DLC; DHU/MO
The training of colored ministers; by the colored missions of Louisville, Ky.

9776. Logan, S. C. Correspondence Between the Rev. S. C. Logan, Pittsburgh, Pa., and the Rev. Dr. J. Leighton Wilson, Colum-

bia, S. C. Colombia, S. C.: Printed at the Office of the Southern Presbyterian, 1868.   NNUT

9777. Love, H. Lawrence. "The Church and Human Rights." Southern Presbyterian Journal (11; Oct. 8, 1952), p. 9.   DLC; KyLxCB

9778. Macrae, David. Among the Darkies, and Other Papers. Glasgow: John S. Marr & Sons., 1881. Pam. File, DHU/R; DHU/MO
pp. 39-48, a night in the United Presbyterian Synod also description of religious service conducted by an early Negro preacher.

9779. McCloud, J. Oscar. "Perspective on Reunion." Church and Society (60:5, My.-Je., 1970), pp. 29-38.   DHU/R
Concerns the role that Black members will play in a "New United" Presbyterian Church.

9780. Mounger, Dwyn. "Racial Attitudes in the Presbyterian Church in the United States, 1944-54." Journal of Presbyterian History (48:1, Spr., 1970), pp. 38-68.   DHU/R

9781. Murray, Andrew E. Presbyterians and the Negro -- A History. Philadelphia: Presbyterian Historical Society, 1966.   DHU/MO; InU; CtY-D; NjP

9782. "Negro." (Freedmen). The Church at Home and Abroad (3; 1888), pp. 373-4.   DHU/R
Discussion of the term [Presbyterian Church periodical.]

9783. "Negro Presbyterian." Southern Workman (8:11, Nov., 1879), p. 106.   DLC; DHU/MO
Letter to the editor written by Orra Langhorne on the "dedication of the First Colored Presbyterian Church in Virginia which was recently established by the assistance of the white Church of which it was a mission chapel."

9784. "The Negroes of Our Country." The Church at Home and Abroad (4; 1888), p. 485.   DHU/R
Exhortation to evangelization, Presbyterian Church.

9785. Payne, H. N. "Our Colored Synods." The Church at Home and Abroad (4; 1888), pp. 165-6.   DHU/R
Presbyterian church.

9786. Pennington, James W. C. Christian Zeal. A Sermon Preached Before the Third Presbytery of New York in Thirteenth Street Presbyterian Church, July 3, 1853. (New York: Printed by Zuille and Leonard, 1854).   DHU/MO

9787. Phillips, A. L. The Presbyterian Church in the United States. "The Southern Presbyterian Church." and the Colored People... Acts viii:27. Birmingham, Ala.: Roberts and Son, 1890.   NNUT

9788. Phraner, Wilson. "School Work in the South." The Church at Home and Abroad (5; 1889), pp. 541-43.   DHU/R
The (Presbyterian) Board of Home Missions.

9789. Presbyterian Church Confederate States of America. Minutes of the General Assembly. Augusta, Ga.: Steam Power Press Chronicle & Sentinel, 1861. Vol. 1.   DHU/R
Reports of the Executive Committee on Domestic Missions including work with Negroes.

9790. Presbyterian Church in the U. S. A. Annual Reports of the Presbyterian Committee of Missions for 1871-82. Committee Incorporated under the Name of the Presbyterian Board of Missions for Freedom. Pittsburgh: n. p., 1883.

9791. ----- (N. S.) Committee of Home Missions. Freedmen's Department. ...Annual Report of the Freedmen's Department of the Presbyterian Committee of Home Missions. New York: Presbyterian Publication Committee, n. d.   NNUT

9792. ----- Executive Committee of Colored Evangelization. Annual Report. Birmingham, Ala.: n. p., n. d.   NNUT

9793. Randall, Virginia Ray. Shadows and Lights; the American Negro, also Program Material... New York: Board of National Missions of the Presbyterian Church in the United States of America, 1941.   NN/Sch

9794. Rice, Joseph S. The Challenge of the Negro to the Southern Presbyterian Church. Masters thesis. Princeton Seminary, 1946.

9795. Richards, James McDowell. Brothers in Black. A Sermon Preached as Retiring Moderator Before the Presbytery of Atlanta. Atlanta: Southern Regional Council, 1946. NN/Sch

9796. Savage, Theodore F. The Presbyterian Church in New York City. New York: Presbytery of New York, 1949.   DLC
        Includes brief history of early Negro Presbyterian churches.

9797. Schmelz, Annie M. "A Presbyterian Conference for Colored Women." Southern Workman (54:9, Sept., 1925), pp. 416-18.
                                                    DLC; DHU/MO
        "The following subjects were discussed: Sunday-School Methods, Vacation Bible Schools, Organization of Parent-Teacher Associations, Community Clubs, Recreation."

9798. Seville, Janet Elizabeth. Like a Spreading Tree; the Presbyterian Chruch and the Negro. New York: Board of National Missions, Presbyterian Church in the U.S.A., 1936. NN/Sch

9799. Shankman, Arnold. "Converse, The Christian and Civil War Cencorship." Journal of Presbyterian History (52:3, Fall, 1974), pp. 227-44.   DHU/R

        About Amasa Converse, editor of the Christian Observer and an ordained minister affiliated with the New School of the Presbyterian Chruch. He was pro-slavery and uses his editorial columns to criticize the North and abolitionists.

9800. "Southern Presbyterians Take Racial Lead." Christian Century (67; Jl. 12, 1950), p. 836.   DHU/R

9801. Steele, Algernon Odell. Shifts in the Religious Beliefs and Attitudes of Students in two Presbyterian Colleges. Doctoral dissertation. University of Chicago, 1942.   DLC
        Negro author.

9802. Swift, David E. "Black Presbyterian Attacks on Racism: Samuel Cornish, Theodore Wright and Their Contemporaries." Journal of Presbyterian History (51:4, Wint., 1973), pp. 433-70.   DHU/R

9803. Thompkins, Robert Edwin. A History of Religious Education Among Negroes in the Presbyterian Church in the United States of America. Doctoral dissertation. University of Pittsburgh, 1950.

9804. Thompson, Ernest Trice. "Black Presbyterians, Education and Evangelism After the Civil War." Journal of Presbyterian History (51:2, Sum., 1973), pp. 174-98.   DHU/R

9805. ----- "Christian Relations Among Races." Presbyterian Outlook (134; Je. 30, 1952).   DLC; NN/Sch; NcD

9806. ----- "Jesus Among People of Other Races." Presbyterian Outlook (131; Mr. 21, 1949), pp. 13-14. NN/Sch; DLC; NcD

9807. United Presbyterian Church of North America. Historical Sketch of the Freedmen's Missions of the United Presbyterian Church, 1862-1904. Knoxville, Tenn.: Printing Dept., Knoxville College, 1904.   NN/Sch

9808. Walker, James Garfield. Presbyterians and the Negro... Greensboro, N.C., n.p., n.d.   DHU/MO

9809. West, C.S. "A Colored Church Self-Sustaining." The Church at Home and Abroad (4; 1888), p. 43. DHU/R
        Presbyterian Church. Sumter County, South Carolina.

9810. Wilson, Frank T., (ed.). "Living Witnesses: Black Presbyterians in Ministry." Journal of Presbyterian History (51:4, Wint., 1973), pp. 347-91.   DHU/R

9811. Worcester, John. "Southern Blacks and Reunion." The Presbyterian Outlook (154:43, Nov. 27, 1972), p. 6.
                                        Pam. File, DHU/R; NjP

9812. Wright, Theodore S. "A Pastoral Letter, Addressed to the Colored Presbyterian Church, in the City of New York, June 20th, 1832." Dorothy B. Porter, (ed.). Early Negro Writings, 1760-1837 (Boston: Beacon, 1971), pp. 472-77.   DHU/MO
        Negro minister.

9813. Yohan, Walter. Presbyterians and Social Class in the Atlanta Metropolitan Area. Doctoral dissertation. Emory University, 1969.

j. Protestant Episcopal

9814. Allison, Madeline G. "The Episcopal Church Appropriation." The Crisis (24:2, Jr., 1922), p. 78.   DHU/MO; DLC
        Appropriations to Okolona Industria School in Mississippi.

9815. Baltimore, Maryland. Saint James' First African Protestant Episcopal Church. Origination, Constitution, and By-Laws of St. James' First African Episcopal Church in the City of Baltimore. Adopted Apr. 22, 1829. Baltimore: Pr. by William Woody, 1829.   NcD

9816. Bennett, Robert A. "Black Episcopalians: A History From the Colonial Period to the Present." Historical Magazine of the Protestant Episcopal Church (43:3, Sept., 1974), pp. 231-45.
                                                        DHU/R

9817. Bishop, Samuel H. "The Church and the Negroes." Spirit of Missions (74:3, Mr., 1909); (74:11, Nov., 1909), pp. 207-09; 931-33.   DHU/R
        Report on the schools for Negroes under the Protestant Episcopal Church.

9818. Bishop, Sheldon Hale. "A History of St. Philip's Church, New York City." Historical Magazine of the Protestant Episcopal Church (15; 1946), p. 298.
        Written by Negro Protestant Episcopal priest.

9819. "Bishop Tuttle Memorial House." Editorial. Southern Workman (54:6, Je., 1925), pp. 245-46.   DLC; DHU/MO
        "A new venture in church educational work is being undertaken on the campus of St. Augustine's School, Raleigh, N.C., by the National Council of the Episcopal Church in the contruction of a national school the training of colored women church workers."

9820. Bolivar, William C. A Brief History of St. Thomas' P.E. Church. Philadelphia: The Author, 1908.   NN/Sch

9821. Bragg, George Freemen. The Attitude of the Conference of Church Workers Among Colored People Toward the Adaption of the Episcopate to the Needs of the Race. n.p., 1904.
                                                    DHU/MO
        Contains a list of ordinations of colored men to the ministry of the church.
        Negro author.

9822. ----- "The Church's Early Work for the Colored Race." Living Church (65; Jl. 16, 1921), pp. 351-54.   DLC; CtY

9823. ----- The Colored Harvest in the Old Virginia Diocese. n.p., 1901.   DHU/MO

9824. ----- "The Episcopal Church and the Negro Race." Historical Magazine of the Protestant Episcopal Church (4; 1935), p. 45+.   DLC
        Negro author.

9825. ----- History of the Afro-American Group of the Episcopal Church. New York: Church Advocate Press, 1922.
                                            DHU/R; INU; DLC
        Reprint 1968, Johnson Reprint Co.

9826. ----- The Story of Old Stephen's, Petersburg, Va. & the Origin of the Bishop Payne Divinity School. Baltimore: n.p., 1917.   DHU/MO

9827. ----- "The Whittingham Canon" The Birth and History of the Missionary District Plan. Baltimore: n. p., n. d. NN/Sch

9828. ----- Yearbook and Church Directory of St. James First African Episcopal Church. Baltimore: Pub. by the Rector, 1934.   DHU/MO

9829. Bratton, Theodore DuBose, (bp.). Wanted-Leaders! A Study of Negro Development. New York: Protestant Episcopal Church in the U. S. A., Department of Missions and Church Extension, 1922.   TSewU-T

9830. Brooklyn. St. Philip's Church (Protestant Episcopal). Golden Jubliee Album of St. Philip's P. E. Church (McDonough Street) Brooklyn, New York. Published in Connection with the 50th Anniversary of the Founding of the Church. New York: Dodd Bros., Printers, 1949.   NN/Sch

9831. Brown, William M., (b. p.). Crucial Race Question; or Where and How Shall the Color Line Be Drawn. Little Rock, Ark.: Churchman's Pub. Co., 1907.   DHU/ MO
       White Episcopal bishop of Arkansas.

9832. Brydon, George McClaren. The Church's Ministry to the Negroes. n. p.: n. p., 1959.   TSewU-T

9833. ----- The Episcopal Church Among the Negroes of Virginia. Richmond, Va.: Richmond Press, Inc., Printers, 1937.
                                          NN/Sch; NcD; DHU/MO

9834. Caution, Tollie L. "Protestant Episcopal Church: Policies and Rationale upon which Support of its Negro Colleges is Predicated." Journal of Negro Education (29; Sum., 1960), pp. 274-83.   DHU
       Negro author.

9835. Chitty, Arthur Ben. "St. Augustine's College, Raleigh, North Carolina." Historical Magazine of the Protestant Episcopal Church (35:3, Sept. 1966), pp. 207-19.   DHU/R

9836. The Church Standard. The Church and the Negro; Five Editorials from the Church Standard. Reprinted by Request. Philadelphia: n. p., 1906.   NN/Sch; DLC
       Contents. -I. Race Separation; II. Religions division of races; III. the Opportunity of the Episcopal Church; IV. Evangelization; V. Bishop Nelson on church work among Negroes.

9837. "Churches." The Crisis (5:8, Ag., 1913), p. 166.
                                          DLC; DHU/MO
       Archdeacon Bragg, of Baltimore, recommends the consecration of a colored bishop for Episcopalians in Boley and other Negro communities in Oklahoma.

9838. ----- The Crisis (7:1, Dec., 1913), p. 62.   DLC; DHU/MO
       Home for young colored cripples, The House of St. Michael and all Angels in Philadelphia, Episcopal Church.

9839. ----- The Crisis (17: 4, Feb., 1919), p. 196.   DHU/MO;
                                                          DLC
       "The Rev. Frank Norman Fitzpatrick, first Negro to be ordained a priest (Episcopal Church) in this country by a colored bishop."

9840. ----- The Crisis (3: 5, Mr., 1912), p. 186. DLC; DHU/MO
       Episcopal Council of South Carolina recommends a Negro suffragan bishop.

9841. Crummell, Alexander. A Defense of the Negro Race in America from the Assaults and Charges of Rev. L. J. Tucker, D. D., of Jackson, Miss. in Paper before the "Church Congress" of 1882 on the Relation of the Church to the Colored Race. Prepared and published at the request of the colored clergy of the Protestant Episcopal Church... Washington: Judd & Detweiler, 1883.   DHU/MO
       Negro author.

9842. ----- The Shades and the Lights of a Fifty Years Ministry. Jubliate...St. Luke's Church, Washington, D. C. Washington, D. C.: R. L. Pendleton, printer, 1894.   OO; NN/Sch; DLC

9843. De Costa, Benjamin Franklin. Three Score and Ten. The Story of St. Philip's Church, New York City. A Discourse Delivered in the New Church, West Twenty-Fifth St., at its Opening, Sunday Morning, February 17, 1889. New York: Pr. for the Parish, 1889.   NN/Sch

9844. Demby, Edward Thomas, (b. p.). The Mission of the Episcopal Church Among the Negroes of the Diocese of Arkansas. Little Rock, Ark.: n. p., 190-?   NN/Sch
       Negro author.

9845. "Episcopal Church in the South Officially Inclusive (as to Race). Its Witness has been Stifled by Culturally-Conditioned Laymen." Christianity and Crisis (18; Mr. 3, 1958), pp. 18-20.   DHU/R

9846. "Episcopal Convention and the Negroes." Independent (63; Sept. 19, 1907), pp. 703-04.   DHU

9847. Fairly, John S. The Negro in His Relations to the Church... Charleston, S. C.: Walker Evans & Cogswell Co., Printers, 1889.   NN/Sch

9848. Foley, Judy Mathe. "Modeste in Motion." The Episcopalian (134:11, Nov., 1969), pp. 24+.   DHU/R
       Leon E. Modeste, Director, General Convention Special Program of Protestant Episcopal Church (minority self-help).

9849. Franklin, John Hope. Negro Episcopalians in Ante-Bellum North Carolina. New Brunswick, N. J.: n. p., 1944.
                                          DHU/MO; NN/Sch; DHU/R
       Reprinted from the Historical Magazine of the Episcopal Church (13; Sept., 1944).
       Negro author.

9850. Gailor, Thomas F. "Problem of the Racial Episcopate." The East and The West (12; Ja., 1914), pp. 67-72.   DHU/R
       U. S. A. - Post-Civil War.

9851. Gay, Milton Ferdinand. The Application of Laboratory Techniques in a Black Episcopal Parish. Masters thesis. Howard University, 1971.
       Written by Negro episcopal priest.

9852. "The Ghetto." The Crisis (8:1, My., 1914), p. 12. DLC;
                                                          DHU/MO
       Trinity Vestry, in New York City, made arrangements to provide for a separate place of worship for the colored members. At present all worship at the same place...

9853. Hayden, J. Carleton. Reading, Religion and Racism: The Mission of the Episcopal Church to Blacks in Virginia, 1865-1877. Doctoral dissertation. Howard University, 1972.
       Negro author.

9854. Holzhammer, Robert E. "The Formation of the Domestic and Foreign Missionary Society." Historical Magazine (40:3, Sept., 1971), pp. 259-72.   DHU/R
       Missions in Protestant Episcopal Church.

9855. ----- A History of the Missionary Expansion of the Episcopal Church in America, 1835-1970. Masters thesis. University of the South, Graduate School of Theology, Sewanee, Tenn., 1971.

9856. Hood, Robert E. The Placement and Deployment of Negro Clergy in the Episcopal Church; a Report Compiled for the Episcopal Society for Cultural and Racial Unity. 1967. TSewU-T
       Mim.

9857. Kater, John Luther. The Episcopal Society for Cultural and Racial Unity and its Role in the Episcopal Church in the United States, 1959-70. Doctoral dissertation. McGill University, 1972.

9858. Kershaw, J. "Negro Clergy, Rights of in Protestant Episcopal Convention of South Carolina." Church Review (46; 1885), p. 466.   DLC

9859. McCarriar, Herbert G., Jr. "A History of the Missionary Jurisdiction of the South of the Reformed Episcopal Church." Historical Magazine (41:2, Je., 1972), pp. 197-220.   DHU/R
"The work of the Reverend Peter F. Stevens, founder of the Missionary Jurisdiction."

9860. Miller, George Frazier. A Reply to "The Political Plea" of Bishop Cleland K. Nelson and Bishop Thomas F. Gailor, at the Cathedral of St. John the Divine in the City of New York, Sunday Evening, October 19, 1913. A Sermon by Rev. George Frazier Miller, Rector of St. Augustine's Church, Brooklyn, Sunday Morning October 26, 1913. Brooklyn: Interboro Press, 1913.   NN/Sch
Negro author.

9861. ----- The Sacredness of Humanity. Annual Sermon of the Conference of Church Workers (Episcopal) Among Colored People at St. Philips Church, New York. Brooklyn: Frank R. Chisholm, Printer, 1914.   DHU/MO

9862. Mitchell, Leonel L. "The Episcopal Church and the Christian Social Movement in the Nineteenth Century." Historical Magazine of the Protestant Church (30, 1961), pp. 173-82.
DHU/R

9863. Modeste, Leon. "The Church is ..." Black World (23:3, Ja., 1974), pp. 86-87.   DHU/MO
The General Convention of the Protestant Episcopal Church and Negroes since 1973.

9864. "Negro Episcopalians." The Episcopalian (127:3, Mr., 1962), pp. 19-42.   DHU/R

9865. Newton, John B. The Commission on Work Among the Colored People, its Work and Prospects. Alexandria, Va.: Hill Print, 1888.   NN/Sch
Protestant Episcopal Church in the U.S.A. Detached from the Virginia Seminary Magazine, v. 1, no. 2. January, 1888.

9866. "Open Church to Negroes: Episcopal Council Says All Equal in Worship and Work of Church." Christian Century (60:9, Mr. 3, 1943), p. 276.   DHU/R

9867. Patton, Robert Williams. An Inspiring Record in Negro Education; Historical Summary of the Work of the American Church Institute for Negroes Delivered to the National Council of the Protestant Episcopal Church, at the Request of the Presiding Bishop, the R. Rev. Henry St. George Tucker, D.D., February 14, 1940. New York: The National Council, Protestant Episcopal Church, 1940.   NN/Sch

9868. Philadelphia, Pa. St. Thomas African Church. "Constitution and Rules to be Observed and Kept by the Friendly Society of St. Thomas's African Church, of Philadelphia, 1797." Dorothy B. Porter, (ed.). Early Negro Writing, 1760-1837 (Boston: Beacon Press, 1971), pp. 28-32. DHU/MO; DHU/R

9869. Protestant Episcopal Church in the U.S.A. "Black Institutions." George F. Bragg. History of the Afro-American Group of the Episcopal Church. Balto., Md.: Chruch Advocate Press, 1922.   DHU/R

9870. ----- "Clergy, Biographical Sketches." George F. Bragg. History of the Afro-American Group of the Episcopal Church. Balto., Md.: Church Advocate Press, 1922.   DHU/R

9871. ----- Conference on the Relation of the Church to the Colored People of the South. n.p., 1883.   DHU/MO

9872. ----- Proceedings of the First Convocation of Colored Clergy, 1883.   OWibfU; NN/Sch
In Arnett Papers, v. 76.

9873. ----- Church Congress, Chicago, 1933. Chicago Papers...
Spencer, Mass.: The Heffernan Press, 1933.   DLC

"How far should national and racial distinctions be fostered in the church."

9874. ----- Church Congress, San Francisco, 1927. Christ in the World of To-day... New York: C. Scribner's Sons, 1927. DLC
Chapter entitled, "How can the Church Satisfy the Religious Needs of All Races?"

9875. ----- Commission of Home Missions to Colored People...
Annual Report of the Commission of Home Missions to Colored People, Protestant Episcopal Church. n.p.: n.p., n.d.
NNUT

9876. ----- Convention, 62nd, New York City. Journal of the Proceedings of the Sixty-Second Convention of the Protestant Episcopal Church in the Diocese of New York, Held in St. John's Chapel in the City of New York, Wednesday, Sept. 12 to Saturday, October 3, inclusive, A.D. 1846. New York: Henry M. Onderdonk & Co., 1846.
(In: The Negro and the Church, v. 3.)

9877. ----- Dept. of Missions and Church Extension. ...Liberia..
New York: The National Council of the Protestant Episcopal Church, Dept. of Missions, 1924.   NN/Sch
Handbook of the Missions of the Episcopal Church.

9878. ----- Liturgy and Ritual. Book of Common Prayer. Even-Prayer. ...Centennial Service of the New York African Society for Mutual Relief, St. Philip's Church, Whit-Sunday Evening, June Seventh, Nineteen Hundred and Eight. New York: n.p., 1903.   NN/Sch

9879. ----- National Council. The Christian Fellowship in Action... New York: The National Council, Protestant Episcopal Church, 1945.   NN/Sch

9880. ----- National Council. Woman's Auxiliary. Toward Understanding Negro American. Leader's Manual... New York: The National Council, Protestant Episcopal Church, 1936.
CtY-D
"Prepared by Leila W. Anderson, Esther Brown, field secretaries, Woman's Auxiliary."

9881. Reimers, David Morgan. "Negro Bishops and Diocesan Segregation in the Protestant Episcopal Church, 1870-1954." Historical Magazine (31:3, Sept., 1962), pp. 231-42. DHU/R

9882. Roberts, Elizabeth Hill. Hand-Book. Colored Work in Dioceses of the South. For Practical Purposes. Philadelphia: For sale, Jacobs' Book Store, 1915.   NN/Sch
Protestant Episcopal Church in the U.S.A. National Council. Woman's Auxiliary. Pennsylvania Branch, Colored Committee.

9883. "The St. Paul School." Editorial. Southern Workman (55:7, Jl., 1926), pp. 295-96.   DLC; DHU/MO
St. Paul Normal and Industrial School at Lawrenceville, Va., founder and principal, Archdeacon James S. Russell.

9884. Teba, Wea. The Book of Hymns; Selected Verses from the Protestant Episcopal Church, with New Hymn Tunes by Wea Teba (Taylor). New York: LeMers Music Publishers, 1959.
NN/Sch
Negro composer.
"Permission to use several of the enclosed hymn words was graciously granted by the church hymnal corporation."

9885. Thomas, Albert S. A Historical Account of the Protestant Episcopal Church in South Carolina, 1820-1957, Being A Continuation of Dalcho's Account, 1670-1820. Colombia: n.p., 1957.   DLC

9886. Thompson, John W. B. The Uses of the Past. Atlanta: The Episcopal Society for Cultural and Racial Unity, 1963.
TSewU-T

9887. Tucker, Joseph Louis. The Relations of the Church to the Colored Race. Speech of the Rev. J. L. Tucker Before the Church Congress, Held in Richmond, Va., on the 24-27 Oct.,

1882. Jackson, Miss.: C. Winkley, Steam Book and Job
Print., 1882.   DHU/MO; NN/Sch

9888. Turner, Franklin D. "St. George's Episcopal Church, Washington, D.C." Faith and Form (3; Apr., 1970), pp. 16-19.
                                 DHU/R

9889. Weston, M. Moran. Social Policy of the Episcopal Church
in the Twentieth Century. New York: Seabury Press, 1964.
                                 DHU/R
     Also Ph.D. thesis, Columbia Univ., 1954.

9890. Whipple, Henry Benjamin, (bp.). Sermon Preached Before
the Society for the Promotion of Church Work Among the Colored
People. Bishop of Minnesota, at their Annual Meeting Held at
St. John's Church, Washington, D.C., Sept. 27, 1877. Pub. by
the Society. Baltimore: F. A. Hanzsche, 1877.   NN/Sch

9891. Williams, Edwin M. "The Parishes of the Protestant Episcopal Church in the District of Columbia." John Clagett Proctor. Washington Past and Present V. 2 (New York: Lewis
Historical Publishing Co., 1930), pp. 806-25.   DLC

9892. Williams, Peter, Jr. Protestant Episcopal Church in the
U.S.A. New York (Diocese). Journal of ... Convention of the
Protestant Episcopal Church in the Diocese of New York. (New
York: n.p., n.d.), pp. 77+.   NN/Sch
     Protestant Episcopal Negro minister.

9893. Wilson, Arthur. Thy Will be Done; the Autobiography of an
Episcopal Minister. New York: Dial Press, 1960.   NN/Sch
     Missions in Cincinnati.

9894. Woodward, Joseph Herbert. The Negro Bishop Movement in
the Episcopal Diocese of South Carolina. McPhersonville, S.C.:
H. Woodward, 1916.

k. Roman Catholic
9895. Achille, Louis T. "The Catholic Approach to Interracialism
in France." American Catholic Sociological Review (3; My.,
1942), pp. 22-27.   DCU/TH; DGU
     Negro author.

9896. ----- "Race Prejudice." Catholic Mind (40; My., 22, 1942),
pp. 6-14.   DGU
     Negro author.

9897. Adams, Elizabeth Laura. Dark Symphony. New York: Sheed
& Ward, 1942.   DHU/MO; NN/Sch
     A Negro's woman's account of her conversion to Roman
     Catholicism.

9898. Aldrich, Gustave B. "Another View of Separate Churches."
Chronicle (3; Mr., 1930), pp. 55-57. ICU; NNC; NNUT; NjPT
     Catholic church.
     Negro author.

9899. ----- "Colored Cathechists." Interracial Review (7; Dec.,
1934), pp. 140-41.   DCU/SW
     "Let the colored Catholic, as a form of Catholic Action, in-
     terest himself in the conversion of the race."
     Negro author.

9900. ----- "Negro Statues for Catholic Negro Churches." Chronicle (3; Ja., 1930), pp. 9-10.   ICU; NNC; NNUT; NjPT
     "There is abundance of material for statues to Negro saints."
     Negro author.

9901 "An Angel." Editorial. The Crisis (16:2, Je., 1918) p. 61.
                                 DHU/MO
     Father Vernimont expresses himself on the Negro problem
     to the editor of the Little Rock Daily News.

9902. Bede, (Brother). A Study of the Development of Negro Education under Catholic Auspices in Maryland and the District of
Columbia. Baltimore: Johns Hopkins University Press, 1935.
                                 DLC; DCU

9903. Bennett, M. (Sister). "A Negro University and a Nun."
Community (25; Mr., 1966), pp. 10-12.   DHU/MO

9904. Bernard, Raymond. "Some Anthropological Implications of
the Racial Admission Policy of the U.S. Sisterhoods." American Catholic Sociological Review (19; Je., 1958), pp. 124-33.
                                 DCU/SW

9905. "Birth of a Bishop: West Indian Priest Becomes First Named
Prelate in U.S." Ebony (8; Ag., 1953), pp. 25-28.   DHU/MO

9906. "Black Catholic Pastor: A 'Cool' Priest." The Lamp (68:2,
Feb. 1970), pp. 16-19.   DHU/R
     Discusses Fr. Salmon, deputy vicar of Harlem and first
     black pastor in Archdiocese of New York.

9907. "The Black Catholics." Newsweek (Ja. 27, 1969), p. 55.
                                 Pam. File; DHU/R

9908. Boniface, M. "Sisters of the Holy Family." Sepia (8; My.,
1960), pp. 31-35.   DHU/MO; NN/Sch

9909. Broderick, William D. The Catholic Church and Black Amer-
icans in 1970, A Case Study. Washington, D.C.: U.S. State
Department, Senior Seminar in Foreign Policy, Twelfth Session,
Washington, D.C., 1969-1970.   Pam. File; DHU/R
     Also in Interracial Review (40:1, Fall, 1970), pp. 6-30.

9910. Bowman, John Walter. "Mouton Switch." St. Augustine's
Messenger (19; Nov., 1941), pp. 219-21.   DHU/R
     Negro author.
     New Negro Catholic mission founded beside a railroad siding
     four miles from Lafayette, La.

9911. ----- "Where the West Begins." St. Augustine's Messenger
(19; Sept., 1941), pp. 170-4.   DHU/R
     Christian Creoles of Duson and Scott, La.
     Negro author.

9912. ----- "A Year and a Day." St. Augustine's Messenger (20;
Sept., 1942), pp. 171-4.   DCU; DHU/R
     An account of a year's progress in a new Negro Catholic
     mission.
     Negro author.

9913. Brooks, Jerome. "The Negro Priest In White Parishes."
Religious Education (59:1, Ja.-Feb., 1964), pp. 73-76. DHU/R
     Catholic church and the race problem.
     Negro author.

9914. Brown William M. (bp.). The Catholic Church and the Color
Line... New York: Thomas Whittaker, 1910. TNF; OCTWHi;
                                 DHU/MO; NN/Sch; MB
     Written by the Episcopalian bishop of the diocese of Arkansas,
     Protestant Episcopal Church.

9915. Brunini, J. G. "Negro Mission Jubilee; Church of St. Benedict the Moor." Commonweal (19; Dec. 8, 1933), pp. 158-9.
                                 DHU/R

9916. Bryan, C. Braxton. "The Negro in Virginia." A Paper read
before the Discesan Council in Petersburg, Va., June, 1904.
Southern Workman (34: 1-3, Ja.-Mr., 1904-1905), pp. 51-54;
100-08; 170-79.   DLC; DHU/MO

9917. Buetow, Harold A. "The Underprivileged and Roman Catholic Education." Journal of Negro Education (40:4, Fall, 1971),
pp. 373-89.   DHU/R

9918. Butsch, Joseph. "Catholics and the Negro." Journal of Negro
History (2; Oct., 1917), pp. 393-410.   DHU/MO

9919. ----- "Negro Catholics in the United States." The Catholic
Historical Review (3:1, Apr., 1917), pp. 33-51.   DHU/R

9920. Calvez, Jean Yves and Jacques Perrin. The Church and Social
Justice: The Social Teachings of the Popes from Leo XIII to
Pius XII, 1878-1958. Chicago: H. Regnery Co., 1961. IU; DLC

9921. Campbell, Robert, (ed.). Spectrum of Catholic Attitudes. Milwaukee: Bruce Publishing Co., 1969.   DHU/R
Views on racial integration and anti-semitism, pp. 121-33.

9922. Cantwell, Daniel M. "Race Relations--As Seen by a Catholic." The American Catholic Sociological Review (7; Dec., 1946), pp. 242+.   DHU

9923. Carletti, Giuseppe. Life of St. Benedict Surnamed "the Moor", the Son of a Slave, Canonized by Pope Pius VII, May 24th, 1807. Phila.: P. F. Cunningham & Son, 1875.   NN/Sch

9924. Casey, John. "Mission Work Among the Negroes." St. Meinrad Historical Essays (1; 1932), pp. 216-23.   DCU/ST

9925. "The Catholic Church and Negroes. A Correspondence." (letters to the editor). The Crisis (30:3, Jl., 1925), pp. 120-21.
                                                          DLC; DHU/MO

9926. ----- Crisis (30; Jl., 1925), pp. 120-24.   DHU/MO

9927. "The Catholic Church and the Negro." Ebony (13; Dec., 1957), pp. 19-22.   Pam. File, DHU/R

9928. "Catholic Church and the Negro Priest." Crisis (19; Ja., 1920), pp. 122-23.   DHU/MO

9929. ----- (letter to the editor). The Crisis (19: 3, Jan., 1920), pp. 122-23.   DHU/MO; DLC
Letter to the editor written by George Joseph Mac William.

9930. Catholic Church in the United States. Commisssion for Catholic Missions Among the Colored People and the Indians. Appeal in Behalf of the Negro and Indian Missions in the United States. Clayton, Delaware: Printed at St. Joseph's Industrial School for Colored Boys, 1902.   DLC

9931. ----- Our Negro and Indian Missions. Annual Report of the Secretary. NN/Sch; DHU/MO; DCU; DLC (1892, 1893, 1917, 1918, DHU/R, 1927-62.)
Title varies: Mission work among the Negroes and the Indians.

9932. The Catholic Digest. Catholic Digest Reader; Selected by the Editors. Garden City, N. Y.: Doubleday, 1952.   NN/Sch

9933. Catholic Interracial Council. Sermons on Interracial Justice; Compiled by the Catholic Interracial Council of New York City, Under the Direction of the Reverend John La Farge. n. p., 1957.
                                                          NN/Sch

9934. "The Catholic Negro." The Crisis (11: 6, Apr., 1916), pp. 316-17.   DLC; DHU/MO

9935. "Catholicism Among Negroes." Harry A. Ploski, (ed.). Reference Library of Black America (New York: Bellwether Pub. Co., Inc., 1971), Book 2, pp. 203-04.   DHU

9936. "Catholicism and the Negro." Jubilee. (Sept., 1955).
                                                NN/Sch; DGU; DCU/HU
Special issue.

9937. "Churches." The Crisis (3:6, Apr., 1912), p. 230.
                                                          DLC; DHU/MO
Cardinals Gibbons and Farley and Archbishop Prendergast issued an appeal for support for Negro and Indian missions.

9938. ----- The Crisis (10:4, Ag., 1915), p. 167.   DLC; DHU/MO
Catholic Board for Colored Missions.

9939. ----- The Crisis (5:1, Nov., 1912), p. 62.   DLC; DHU/MO
The Catholic Church considers the conferring of sainthood upon black Christians.

9940. Code, Joseph B. "Negro Sisterhood in the United States." America (58; 1938), pp. 318-19.   DHU

9941. Collins, Daniel F. "Black Conversion to Catholicism: Its Implications for the Negro Church." Journal for the Scientific Study of Religion (10:3, Fall, 1971), pp. 208-19.
                                        DHU/R; DAU/W; DCU/SW; DGU; DGW

9942. Congar, Marie Joseph. The Catholic Church and the Race Question. Paris: UNESCO, 1953. CtY-D; DHU/R; NN/Sch; DLC

9943. Connell, Francis J. "Rights of the Catholic Negro." American Ecclesiastical Review (114; 1946), pp. 459-62.   DHU/R

9944. Cooley, Leo P. Bishop England's Solution of the Negro Problem. Masters thesis. St. John's University, 1940.

9945. Cooper, Harold L. "Priests, Prejudice, and Race." Catholic Mind (57; 1959), pp. 499-505.   DLC

9946. Dedeaux, Mary Liberata (Sister). The Influence of Saint Frances Academy on Negro Catholic Education in the Nineteenth Century. Masters thesis. Villanove University, 1944.

9947. DeHueck, Catherine. Friendship House. New York: Sheed and Ward, 1946.   NN/Sch

9948. "Detroit's Black Catholics." America (124; Je. 12, 1971), p. 603.   DHU/R

9949. Didas, James F. "Negro Challenge to the Church." Catholic Mind (50; 1952), pp. 257-62.

9950. Diggs, M. A. Catholic Negro Education in the United States. Washington: Pub. by the Author, 1936.   DHU/MO
Negro author.

9951. Doherty, Joseph F. Moral Problems of Interracial Marriage. Washington, D. C.: The Catholic University of America Press, 1949.   DCU; NN/Sch

9952. DuBois, William E. B. "The Catholic Church." Crisis (37: 4, Apr., 1930), p. 138.   DHU/MO

9953. Dunne, William. "Roman Catholic Church: The Rationale and Policies Underlying the Maintenance of Higher Institutions for Negroes." Journal of Negro Education (29; Sum., 1960), pp. 307-14.   DHU

9954. Emerick, A. J. "The Colored Mission of Our Lady of the Blessed Sacrament." Woodstock Letters (42; 1913), pp. 69-82, 175-88, 352-62; (43; 1914), pp. 10-23, 181-94.   DGU

9955. The Epistle. The Conversion of the Negro. New York: Saint Paul Guild, 1945.   NN/Sch
Issue of the Epistle (11:2, Spr., 1945).

9956. Fahey, Frank Joseph. The Sociological Analysis of a Negro Catholic Parish. Doctoral dissertation. University of Notre Dame, 1959.

9957. Falls, Arthur Grand Pré. "Better Race Relations from the Catholic Viewpoint." Interracial Review (6; Oct., 1933), pp. 183-4.   DCU/SW
Negro author.

9958. ----- "Industrial and Social Problems." Chronicle (4; Dec., 1931), pp. 678-81.   DCU/SW
Negro author.
A resume of Catholic methodology for the amelioration of distress among Negroes.

9959. Farnum, Mable. The Street of the Half-Moon. The Story of Saint Peter Claver, Apostle of the Negroes... Milwaukee: Bruce Publishing Co., 1940.   DHU/MO

9960. Fegin, Joe R. Black Catholics in the United States: An Exploratory Analysis. Hart M. Nelson & Raytha L. Yokley, (eds.). The Black Church in America (New York: Basic Books, 1971), pp. 246-54.   DHU/R
Also in his Slavery in the Cities in the South, 1820-1860.
                                                          DHU/R

9961. Fey, Harold E. "Catholicism and the Negro." Christian Century (61:51, Dec. 20, 1944), pp. 1476-79.   DHU/R

9962. ----- "Does the Catholic Church Fear Too Many Negro Converts?" (Affirmative answer; with Rev. John La Farge giving negative.) Christian Century (Dec. 20, 1944), condensed in Negro Digest (Apr., 1945), pp. 29-34.   DHU/R

9963. Fichter, Joseph H. "The Catholic South and Race." Religious Education (59:1, Ja.-Feb., 1964), pp. 30-33.   DHU/R

9964. ----- The Catholic Viewpoint on Race Relations. Chicago: University of Chicago Press, 1954.   DCU

9965. Foley, Albert S. "Bishop Healy and the Colored Catholic Congress." Interracial Review (28; 1954), pp. 79-80. DGU

9966. ----- The Catholic Church and the Washington Negro. Doctoral dissertation. University of North Carolina, 1950.

9967. ----- God's Men of Color: The Colored Catholic Priests of the U. S. 1854-1954. New York: Farrar, Straus, 1955.
          DHU/R; InU

9968. ----- Negro Americans: A Mission Investigation. Cincinnati: n. p., 1948.   ATI

9969. ----- "Negro and Catholic Higher Education." Crisis (64; Ag.-Sept., 1957), pp. 413-19.   DHU/MO

9970. ----- "St Elizabeth's Full Circle." Interracial Review (24; 1951), pp. 120-22.   DGU

9971. ----- "Status and Role of the Negro Priest in the American Catholic Church." American Catholic Sociological Review (16; Je., 1955), pp. 83-92.   DGU

9972. ----- "U. S. Colored Priests: Hundred Years Survey." America (49; Je. 13, 1953), pp. 295-97.   DGU

9973. Garvey, A. J. "A Condition--No Crisis." The Chronicle (3:5, My., 1930), pp. 105.   DHU/MO
          The Catholic Church and the reason there are so few Negro priests.

9974. Gaynor, W. C. "The Catholic Negro in Louisiana." Anthropos (9; 1914), pp. 539-45.   DCU/AN

9975. Gillard, John Thomas. The Catholic Church and the American Negro; Being an Investigation of the Past and Present Activities of the Catholic Church in Behalf of the 12,000,000 Negroes in the U. S., With and Examination of the Difficulties which Affect the Work of the Colored Missions. Baltimore: St. Joseph's Society Press, 1929.   DHU/MO

9976. ----- "Catholicism and the Negro." Interracial Review (12; Je., 1939), pp. 89-91.   DHU/MO

9977. ----- Colored Catholics in the United States, an Investigation of Catholic Activity in Behalf of the Negroes in the United States and a Survey of the Present Condition of the Colored Missions. Baltimore: The Josephite Press, 1941.   DHU/R; CtY-D

9978. ----- "First Negro Parish in the United States." America (50; 1934), pp. 370-72.   DGU

9979. ----- The Negro American; a Mission Investigation. Rev. by Josephite Fathers. Cincinnati: Catholic Students' Mission Crusade, 1935.   NN/Sch; CtY-D; DHU/MO

9980. ----- "Negro Looks to Rome." Commonweal (21; Dec. 14, 1934), pp. 193-95.   DHU/R

9981. "A Glance at the Negro Apostlate." Editorial. St. Augustine's Messenger (30:9, Nov. 1953), pp. 260+.   DHU/R

9982. Granger, Lester B. "Catholic Negro Relations." Opportunity (25:3, Sum., 1947), pp. 136-49.   DHU/MO

9983. Harte, Thomas J. Catholic Organizations Promoting Negro-White Race Relations in the United States. Doctoral dissertation. Catholic University of America, 1944.
          DCU; DHU/MO; NN/Sch
          Catholic University of America: Studies in Sociology, V. 20.
          Also published by Catholic University Press, 1947.
          DHU/MO

9984. Heithaus, C. H. "Jim Crow Catholicism." Time (55; Feb. 20, 1950), pp. 58-59.   DHU/R

9985. Hepburn, D. "Negro Catholic of New Orleans." Our World (5; Apr., 1950), pp. 14-31.   DLC; DHU/MO

9986. Herr, Dan. Realities, Significant Writing from the Catholic Press. Edited and with Introduction by Dan Herr and Clem Lane. Milwaukee: Bruce Publishing Co., 1958.
          DHU/MO
          Christianity and the Negro by John LaFarge, pp. 251-64.

9987. Herz, S. "Racism: Catholic Should Fight False Dogmas of Race Superiority." Commonweal (28; Jl. 8, 1938), pp. 296-97.   DHU

9988. Hogan, John A. "Church Work Among the Negroes: Letter dated Galveston, Texas, Aug. 3, 1901." Woodstock Letters (30; 1901), pp. 223-30.   DGU

9989. Howard, Clarence J. "Anniversary in Louisana." St. Augustine's Messenger (21; Dec., 1943), pp. 220-23.
          DCU/ST; DHU/R
          A progress report of Negro Missions in the Diocese of Lafayette, La. on its twenty-fifty anniversary.
          Negro author.

9990. Huggins, Willia Nathaniel. "The Catholic Church and the Negro." Opportunity (10:9, Sept., 1932), pp. 272-75.
          DHU/MO

9991. ----- The Contribution of the Catholic Church to the Progress of the Negro in the United States. Doctoral dissertation. Fordham University, 1932.   NN/Sch

9992. Hunton, George K. All of Which I Saw, Part of Which I Was; the Autobiography of Geoge K. Hunton as Told to Gary MacEoin. Garden City, N. Y.: Doubleday, 1967. InU; NcD

9993. Hyland, Philip. "The Field of Social Justice." The Thomist (1; 1939), pp. 295-330.   DCU/TH

9994. Janssens, Francis. "The Negro Problem and the Catholic Church." Catholic World (44; Mr., 1887), pp. 721-26.
          DCU/HU; DHU/R

9995. Kelly, Gerald, S. J. ... Guidance for Religion. Westminster, Md.: Newman Press, 1956.   NN/Sch
          "How to think and act about the race problem," pp. 303-16.

9996. Kelly, Laurence J. "Negro Missions in Maryland." Woodstock Letters (38; 1909), pp. 239-44.   DGU

9997. LaFarge, John. "The Cardinal Giggons Institute." Commonweal (15; Feb. 17, 1932), pp. 433-34.   DLC

9998. ----- "Caste in the Church: The Roman Catholic Experience." Survey Graphic (36; Ja., 1947), pp. 61+.
          DUH; CU; MA; DGW; OO

9999. ----- A Catholic Interracial Program. New York: The American Press, 1939.   DHU/MO

10000. ----- The Catholic Viewpoint on Race Relations. Garden City, N. Y.: Hanover House, 1960. DHU/MO; InU; CtY-D; DLC

10001. ----- "Development of Cooperative Acceptance of Racial
Integration." Journal of Negro Education (21; Sum., 1952),
pp. 430-33.   DHU

10002. ----- Interracial Justice: A Study of the Catholic Doctrine
of Race Relations. New York: America Press, 1937.
                                                    DHU/R

10003. ----- A John LaFarge Reader; Selected and Edited by
Thurston N. Davis and Joseph Small. New York: America
Press, 1956.   NN/Sch

10004. ----- The Maner is Ordinary. New York: Harcourt,
Brace, 1954.   NN/Sch

10005. ----- "Negro Apostolate." Commonweal (22; Jl. 5, 1955),
pp. 257-59.   DHU

10006. ----- No Postponement; U. S. Moral Leadership and the
Problem of Racial Minorities. New York: Longmans, Green
& Co., 1950.   NN/Sch; INU

10007. ----- The Race Question and the Negro. New York:
Longmans, Green & Co., 1945.   DHU/R;
                                                    CtY-D
    Catholic Doctrine on interracial justice...

10008. ----- ...The Religious Education of the American Negro..
Brussels: International Centre for Studies in Religious Education, 1947.   NN/Sch

10009. ----- Sermons on Interracial Justice. New York:
Catholic Interracial Council, 1957.   NN/Sch

10010. La Salle, Edward. "Continuing Problem." Interracial
Review (6; Feb., 1933), pp. 26-27.   DCU/SW
    Formation of Catholic interracial bodies for better race
    relations in America.
    Negro author.

10011. Markoe, William M. "Catholic Aid for the Negro." America (26; Feb. 18, 1922), pp. 417-18.   DLC

10012. ----- 'Catholics, the Negro, a Native Clergy." America
(25; Sept. 24, 1921), pp. 535-37.   DLC

10013. ----- "Negro and Catholicism." America (30; Feb. 23,
1924), pp. 449-50.   DLC

10014. Marx, Gary Trade. The Social Basis of the Support of a
Depression Era Extremist: Father Coughlin. Berkeley:
Survey Research Center, Univ. of California, 1962.   O

10015. Matthews, Dom Basil. "Vodun and Catholicism." Catholic
World (158; Oct., 1943), pp. 65-72. DCU/HU; DGU; DHU/R
    "Many of its (Vodun's) views are not unorthodox and can be
    an invaluable asset to the Catholic Church."
    Negro author.

10016. McAvoy, Thomas Timothy, (ed.). Roman Catholicism and
the American Way of Life. Notre Dame, Ind.: University of
Notre Dame, 1960.   InU
    pp. 156-63, Catholic Church and race relations.

10017. McCorry, V. P. "Word; Catholic Position on Racial Discrimination." America (100; Nov. 8, 1958), pp. 175-76.
                                                    DHU

10018. McGroarty, Joseph G. "Census Findings in a Negro Parish."
Catholic World (156:933, Dec., 1942), pp. 325-29.   DHU/R

10019. McKay, Claude. Right Turn to Catholicism. n.p.: n.p.,
1946.   NN/Sch
    Negro author.

10020. Meehan, Thomas Francis. "Mission Work Among Colored
Catholics." Catholic Mind (20; Apr. 22, 1922), pp. 141-52.
                                                    DLC

Also in Catholic Historical Society, Historical Records
and Studies, v. 8 (New York: n.p., 1915), pp. 116-28.
                                                    NN/Sch

10021. Merwick, Donna. "The Broken Fragments of Afro-American History: A Study of Catholic Boston, 1850-1890." Mc-
Cormick Quarterly (22:4, My., 1969), pp. 239-52. DHU/R

10022. Misch, Edwardo J. The American Bishops and the Negro
From the Civil War to the Third Plenary Council of Baltimore
(1865-1884). Roma: Pontificia Universitas Gregoriana Facul-
tas Historiae Ecclestiasticae, 1968.   NjP

10023. "Missionary in Alabama; Catholic Priest Builds Schools and
Churches for Negroes, Cajans Deep in Southern Backwoods."
Ebony (7; Ja., 1952), pp. 65-70.   DHU/MO

10024. Moody, Joseph N. "Salvation by Cooperation in the Maryland Counties." America (70; Ja. 22, 1944).   DHU

10025. Moroney, T. B. "The Condition of the Catholic Colored
Mission in the United States." American Ecclesiastical
Review (61; 1919), pp. 640-48.   DGU

10026. Murphy, Edward F. Yankee Priest, an Autobiographical
Journey, with Certain Detours, from Salem to New Orleans.
Garden City, N. Y.: Doubleday, 1952.   NN/Sch

10027. Murphy, John Clarence. An Analysis of the Attitudes of
American Catholics Toward the Immigrant and the Negro,
1825-1925. Doctoral dissertation. Catholic University, 1940.
                                                    DHU/MO

10028. Murphy, Miriam T. "Catholic Missionary Work Among the
Colored People of the United States, 1766-1866." American
Catholic Historical Society of Philadelphia Records (35; 1924),
pp. 101-36.   DGU

10029. "The Negro and the Roman Catholic Church." The Crisis
(20:1, My., 1920), pp. 17-22.   DHU/MO; DLC
    Letter to the editor written by Rt. Rev. John E. Burke,
    Director Gen., Catholic Board for Mission work among
    the Colored people in reply George J. MacWilliam "attack
    on the Catholic Church."

10030. "Negro Apostolate." Commonweal (50; Ag. 26, 1949), p.
488.   DCU/SW; DGU; DGW; DHU

10031. "Negro Catholics Looking and Listening." Crisis (65:4,
Apr., 1958), pp. 216-23.   DHU/MO

10032. "Negroes and Catholics United by Outrage." Christian
Century (43:44, Nov. 4, 1926), p. 1374.   DHU/R
    Ku Klux Klan threaten Catholic priest.

10033. "Negroes and the Roman Catholic Church." Catholic
World (27; 1883), pp. 374+.   DCU/HU

10034. Nolan, J. T. "Black and White Parish." Commonweal
(57; Feb. 20, 1953), pp. 496-97. DCU/SW; DGU; DGW; DHU

10035. O' Connel, Jeremiah Joseph. Catholicity in the Carolinas
and Georgia. New York: Sadler & Co., 1879. DLC; ICN

10035. O'Hanlon, Mary Ellen (Sister). The Heresy of Race. River
Forest: Rosary College, 1950.   NN/Sch

10037. O'Neill, Joseph Eugene. A Catholic Case Against Segregation. New York: Macmillan, 1961. DHU/R; CtY-D; DLC

10038. "Open Confession. A Negro Minister Charged With Teaching Catholicism Among Negroes." The Crisis (24:1, My.,
1922), pp. 36-37.   DHU/MO; DLC

10039. O'Reilly, Charles T. Race Prejudice Among Catholic
College Students in the United States and Italy; a Comparative
Study of the Role of Religion and Personality in Inter-Group
Relations. Doctoral dissertation. Notre Dame University,
1954.

10040. ----- "Religious Beliefs of Catholic College Students and their Attitude Toward Minorities." Journal of Abnormal and Social Psychology (49; 1954), pp. 378-80.   DAU; DHU

10041. Osborne, William A. The Race Problem in the Catholic Church in the United States. Doctoral dissertation. Teachers College, Columbia University, 1954.

10042. Ostheimer, Anthony Leo. Christian Principles and National Problems. New York: Sadler, 1945.   NN/Sch

10043. Penetar, Michael Palmo. The Social Thought of the Catholic Worker on the Negro. Doctoral dissertation. Catholic University, 1952.

10044. Perry, Galbraith B. Twelve Years Among the Colored People; A Record of the Work of Mt. Calvary Chapel of St. Mary the Virgin, Baltimore. New York: James Pott, 1884.   OWibfU; NN/Sch

10045. Reemer, Theodore, (Fr.). The Catholic Church in the United States. St. Louis: Herder, 1950.   NN/Sch

10046. Reynolds, Edward D. Jesuits for the Negro. New York: America Press, 1949.   DHU/R; NcD; CtY-D; NN/Sch

10047. Riley, Helen (Caldwell). Color, Ebony. New York: Sheed & Ward, 1951.   NN/Sch
    Discusses Catholic converts.
    Negro author.

10048. Roche, Richard J. Catholic Colleges and the Negro Student. Washington, D. C.: Catholic University of America, 1948.   INU; O; NCD; DHU/MO

10049. Romero, Emanuel A. "The Negro in the New York Arch-diocese." Catholic World (172:1, 030, Ja., 1951), pp. 6-12.   DHU/R

10050. Rouse, Michael Francis. A Study of the Development of Negro Education under Catholic Auspices in Maryland and the District of Columbia. The John Hopkins University Studies in Education, no. 22. Baltimore: The John Hopkins Press, 1935.   DHU/MO; DHU/R

10051. Roy, Ralph Lord. "Roman Catholicism, Protestantism, and the Negro." Religion in Life (33; Aut., 1964), pp. 577+.   DHU/R; DAU/W; DGW

10052. Scally, Mary Anthony. Negro Catholic Writers, 1900-1943. Detroit: Walter Romig & Company, 1945.   DHU/R; Ic/H

10053. Sesser, Robert. Primer on Interracial Justice. Baltimore: Helicon Press, 1932.   NN/Sch

10054. Shea, George W. "Black Students at Catholic Colleges." America (131:6, Sept. 14, 1974), pp. 108-13.   DHU/R
    "Blacks and Catholic colleges must work together for change."

10055. Sherwood, Grace H. The Oblates' Hundred and One Years. New York: The Macmillan Co., 1931.   DHU/MO
    The Founding of the Colored Order of the Oblate Sisters of Providence in Baltimore, Md., 1829.

10056. Slattery, John Richard. The Catholic Church and the Colored Race. Baltimore, Md.: Press of St. Joseph's Seminary for the Colored Mission, 189-.   NN/Sch

10057. ----- "The Catholic Church and the Negro Race." J. H. Barrows, (ed.). The World's Parliament of Religions. V. 2 (Chicago: Parliament Publishing Co., 1893), pp. 1104-06.   DHU/R

10058 ----- "Josephites and Their Work for the Negroes." Catholic World (5; Apr., 1890), pp. 101-11.   DCU/HU

10059. ----- "Native Clergy." Catholic World (52; Mr. 1891), pp. 882-93.   DCU/HU

10060. ----- "Roman Catholic College for Negro Catechists." Catholic World (70; 1900), pp. 1+.   DHU; DCU/HU

10061. ----- "The Seminary for the Colored Missions." Catholic World (46; 1888), pp. 541-50.   DHU/R

10062. "Southern States and Catholic Negroes." The Crisis (1:6, Apr., 1911), p. 10.   DHU/MO; DLC

10063. Spalding, David. "The Negro Catholic Congresses, 1889-1894." Catholic Historical Review (55:3, Oct., 1969), pp. 337+.   DHU/R
    Also: Freeing the Spirit (1:3, Sum., 1972), pp. 7-16.   DHU/R

10064. Staab, Giles J. The Dignity of Man in Modern Papal Doctrine; Leo XIII to Pius XII, 1878-1955. Washington, D. C.: The Catholic University of America Press, 1957.   DCU

10065. Tarry, Ellen. "The City of Jude." Catholic Digest (5; Oct., 1941), pp. 73-76.   DCU/ST; DGU
    Father Harold Purcell's town for Negroes of Montgomery, Ala., including church, school, clinic and social center. Negro authroess.

10066. ----- "Why is Not the Negro Catholic?" Catholic World (150:899, Feb., 1940), pp. 542-46.   DHU/R

10067. Theobald, Stephen L. "Catholic Missionary Work Among the Colored People of the United States (1776-1876)," American Catholic Historical Society of Philadelphia Records (35; 1924), pp. 324-44.   DGU

10068. ----- "Our Hopes and Aspirations." Chronicle (4; Nov. 1931), pp. 656-9.   DCU/SW
    Negro author.
    "Race prejudice is contrary to the principles of the Catholic Church, the only institution able to solve the race problem."

10069. Thering, M. Rose Albert (Sister). "Religious Education in Race Relations: A Catholic Viewpoint." Religious Education (59: 1, Ja.-Feb., 1964), pp. 50-55.   DHU/R

10070. Thomas, John Lawrence. The American Catholic Family. Englewood Cliffs, N. J.: Prentice-Hall, 1956.   DLC; CtY-D

10071. Toinette Eugene, (Sister). "Reflections of a Black Sistuh!" Freeing the Spirit (3:2, Sum., 1974), pp. 11-15.   DHU/R
    Author is a pastoral associate at St. Benedict's Church in Oakland, California.

10072. Turner, Thomas Wyatt. "Actual Conditions of Catholic Education among the Colored Laymen." Catholic Educational Association Bulletin (16; Nov., 1919), pp. 431-40. DCU; NN
    Negro author.

10073. ----- "The Social Order and the Catholic Negro." Chronicle (4; Nov., 1931), pp. 650-4.   DCU/SW
    "The Negro in relation to birth-control, native clergy, Catholic education, as stated in the Encyclicals."
    Negro author.

10074. ----- "Spirit of the Federated Colored Catholics." Chronicle (5; My., 1932), p. 92.   DCU/SW
    "Chief aim: to contribute out part in the promotion of Catholic Action as a concrete fact in our daily lives."
    Negro author.

10075. ----- "A Visit to Catholic New Orleans." Chronicle (5; Mr., 1932), pp. 52-3.   DGU/SW
    "Brief account of the outstanding Catholic enterprises in the city."

10076. United States. Congress. Senate. Discussion by the Senate on the Position of the Roman Catholic Church on

(United States cont.)
> Race Relations. 71st Cong., 2nd Ses., Feb. 7, 1930.
> Congressional Record, 3237.   DHU/L

10077. Vader, Anthony J. Racial Segregation Within Catholic Institutions in Chicago: A Study in Behavior and Attitudes. Masters thesis. University of Chicago, 1962.   DHU/R

10078. Washington, Curtis. "Miami Mission." St. Augustine's Messenger (Ja., 1946), pp. 1-2.   DHU/MO

10079. "Will Negroes Become Roman Catholic?" Editorial. The Christian Century (39:19, My. 11, 1922), pp. 580-1.   DHU/R

10080. Williams, Alberta. "White Priest Among Negroes." Survey Graphic (My., 1944).   DHU

10081. Wojiak, Edward J. Atomic Apostle, Thomas M. Morgan, S. V. D. Techny, Ill.: Divine Word Publications, 1957.
                                                          NN/Sch
> Missions - Negroes, pp. 212-52.

l. Seventh Day Adventist

10082. Cleveland, E. Edward. The Middle Wall. Washington, D.C.: Review and Herald, 1969.   MiBsa
> Seventh-day Adventist and segregation.

10083. Graybill, Ronald Duane. E. G. White and Church Race Relations. Washington, D.C.: Review and Herald, 1970.
                                                          MiBsA
> Seventh-day adventist and race relations.

10084. ----- Mission to Black America; the True Story of Edson White and the Riverboat Morning Star. Mountain View, Calif.: Pacific Press Pub. Association, 1971.   NjP

10085. Lee, W. S. Quiet Meditations in Human Relations. n.p.: n.p., 1961?   MiBsA
> Church and Race Problems - Seventh-day Adventists.

10086. MacKaye, William R. "Tolerated Segregation Charged to Adventists." Washington Post (Feb. 24, 1968). Pam. File,
                                                          DHU/R

10087. Nichol, Francis D. Reasons For Our Faith. A Discussion of Questions Vita. ... of Certain Seventh-Day Adventist Teachings. Takoma Park, Washington: Review and Herald Pub. Assn., 1947.
                                                          DHU/R
> Adventist and World Betterment, pp. 124-28.

10088. Peterson, Frank L. "Why the Seventh-Day Adventist Church Established and Maintains a Negro College (and Schools far below College grade)." Journal of Negro Education (29; Sum., 1960), pp. 284-88.   DHU

m. General

10089. Albert, Aristides E. "The Church in the South." Methodist Review (74; Mr., 1892), pp. 229-40.   DHU/R
> "Colored Denominations," pp. 237-40.

10090. Allison, Madeline G. "Social Progress." The Crisis (21: 3, Ja., 1921), p. 129.   DHU/MO; DLC
> Gov. Morrow of Kentucky designated an "Inter-racial Sunday."

10091. Andrews, C. F. "Race Within the Church." The East and the West (12; Oct., 1914), pp. 411-20.   DHU/R

10092. The Asheville Conference. A Conference of Christian Workers. Asheville, N.C.: n.p., 1898.   DHU/MO

10093. Backus, Edwin B. The Church and the Social Question. Bachelor thesis. Meadville Theological School, 1912.

10094. Bailey, Kenneth K. Southern White Protestantism in the Twentieth Century. New York: Harper, 1964. DHU/R; INU

10095. Bratton, Theodore DuBose, (bp.). "The Racial Episcopate." The East and the West (12; Apr., 1914), pp. 159-68. DHU/R

10096. Bristow, Edmund J. "Sanctified Prejudice." Crisis (27:1, Nov., 1923), pp. 19-20.   DHU/MO

10097. "Christian Science Church Adopts Jim Crowism." The Crisis (45:12, Dec., 1938), pp. 386-87.   DLC; DHU/MO
> "The Crisis purposely has omitted the name of the colored Christian Scientist to whom these letters were addressed. The correspondence grew out of one of the frequent protests made to The Mother Church against a brass plate on a Christian Science Church in Harlem bearing the word "colored."

10098. Cohn, Werner. "Jehovah's Witnesses and Racial Prejudice." The Crisis (63:1, Ja., 1956), pp. 5-9.   DLC; DHU/MO
> "The author explains why it is wrong to speak of Jehovah's Witnesses as a 'religion of integration.'"

10099. Cole, Marley. "Jehovah's Witnesses - Religion of Racial Integration." The Crisis (60:4, Apr., 1953), pp. 205-11; 253-55. DLC; DHU/MO
> "Makes racial integration an essential part of its central doctrine."

10100. Convention for Bible Missions, Syracuse, N.Y., 1846. Proceedings of the Convention for Bible Missions. n. p. :n. p., 1846?   NNCor

10101. Cotes, Sarah Jeannette. Progressive Missions in the South, and Addresses. Atlanta: Franklin Print. & Pub. Co., 1906.
                                                          NcD

10102. Cort, Cyrus. "Losing Caste Preaching for Darkies." The Christian Intelligencer (83:25, Je. 19, 1912), p. 392. DHU/R
> Reformed Church mission among Negroes in southern U.S.A.

10103. Dabbs, James McBride. Haunted by God. Virginia: John Knox Press, 1970.   DHU/R
> Part II, Spiritual Values of the American Southerner.

10104. "Farmers' and Ministers' Conference." Editorial. Southern Workman (49:8, Ag., 1920), pp. 346-48.   DHU/MO; DLC
> Work toward the progress of sound racial solidarity and community progress through organization.

10105. Goodykoontz, Colin B. Home Missions on the American Frontier. Caldwell, Idaho: Caxton Printers, 1939. DLC; PPT; PU; NcD

10106. Haselden, Kyle Emerson. "11 a.m. Sunday is Our Most Segregated Hour." NY Times Magazine (Ag. 2, 1964), p. 9+.
                                                          DHU

10107. "Home Mission Conference." Editorial. Southern Workman (57:3, Mr., 1928), pp. 109-10.   DLC; DHU/MO

10108. Industrial Mission School Society, Charleston, S.C. Prospectus and Appeal of the Industrial Mission School Society, Chartered, Charleston, S.C., September 22, 1887, for the Purpose of Endeavoring to Improve the Mental, Moral, Social and Religious Condition of the Negroes in the Diocese of South Carolina. Charleston, S.C.: Walker, Evans & Cogswell Co., Print, 1888.
                                                          NN/Sch

10109. Interchurch World Movement of North America. Survey Department. World Survey Conference: Atlantic City, January 7 to 10, Prepared by Survey Department-Home Missions Division. New York: 1920.   NN/Sch; DHU/MO

10110. Johnson, Richard Hanson. A Critical Study of Religious Work Among Negroes of St. Mary's County, Maryland Since 1865, with Special Reference to the Catholic, Episcopal and Methodist Churches. Masters thesis. Howard University, 1948.

10111. Kelsey, George D. Protestantism and Democratic Intergroup Living." Phylon (8:1, 1st Quarter, 1947), pp. 77-82. DHU/MO
> Negro author.

10112. Kitagawa, Daisuke. Race Relations and Christian Mission. New York: Friendship Press, 1964. DLC; DHU/R; DHU/MO; NN/Sch

10113. Kincheloe, Samuel C. The American City and Its Church. New York: Friendship Press, 1940. Pam. File, DHU/R
See Chapters IV, "What Cities do to Churches;" V, "What Churches do for Cities."

10114. Kramer, Alfred S. "Pattern of Racial Inclusion Among the Churches of Three Protestant Denominations." Phylon (16:3, 1955), pp. 285-94. DHU/MO

10115. Lehman, Joel Baer. The Paradoxical in Christianity as Illustrated in Negro Missions. (n.p., n.d.) TN/DCHS

10116. Little, John. "City Mission For Colored People." Arcadius S. Trawick, (ed.). The New Voice in Race Adjustments (New York: Student Volunteer Movement, 1914), pp. 132-39. DHU/R

10117. Loescher, Frank S. "Racial Policies and Practices of Major National Protestant Denominations." Phylon (8:3, 3rd Quarter, 1947), pp. 233-50. DHU/MO

10118. Low, A. Ritchie. "What Your Church Can Do About the Race Question: An Interview with Dr. George E. Haynes, An Outstanding Negro Leader." The Community Churchman (12:1, Apr., 1932), pp. 6-7. DHU/R

10119. Luiden, Anthony. "Helping Negroes, Radio Programs, and the Institutes." Intelligencer Leader (5:205, Oct. 14, 1938), p. 24. DHU/R
Reformed Church in America.

10120. Massiah, J. Bowden. The General Convention and the Negro Problem; a Review of the Controversy over Missionary Districts for Negroes of the Church with Comments. Chicago: The Convention, 1913. TNF

10121. McDowell, Edward Allison. Southern Churches and the Negroes... n.p.: n.p., 1946. NNUT; CtY-D

10122. Melish, William Howard. Strength for Struggle; Social Witness in the Crucible of our Times. New York: Bromwell Press, 1953. NN/Sch

10123. Miller, Robert Moats. An Inquiry into the Social Attitudes of American Protestantism 1919-1939. Doctoral dissertation. Northwestern University, 1955.

10124. Moyer, Elgin Sylvester. Missions in the Church of the Brethren; Their Development and Effect Upon the Denomination. Doctoral dissertation. Yale University, 1929.

10125. Muckle, Coy. That Negro Problem. Charlotte, N.C.: n.p., 1946. DLC; NRAB
Written by a minister.

10126. "Negro Issue Stirs Detroit Churches." Editorial. The Christian Century (47:3, Ja. 15, 1930), p. 89. DHU/R
Negro membership in white church.

10127. "Negroes in the Bronx." Christian Intelligencer (102; Sept., 1931), p. 567. DHU/R
Work of the Reformed Church among Negroes in New York City.

10128. Olkham, Joseph H. "Christian Missions and the Education of the Negro." International Review of Missions (7; 1918), pp. 242-47. DHU/R
Books reviews of two books discussing the contributions of Christian Missions to the education of Negroes.

10129. Oniki, S. Garry. "Interracial Churches in American Protestantism." Social Action (16; Ja., 1950), pp. 4-22. DHU/R

10130. Owens, I.V. "And Forbid Them Not." Crisis (57:2, Feb., 1950), pp. 78-82. DHU/MO

The merger of the Presbyterian and Protestant Episcopal Church in Cincinnati in organizing an interracial church.

10131. Reed, Richard Clark. "A Sketch of the Religious History of the Negroes in the South." Papers of the American Society of Church History, 2nd Series (New York: G. P. Putnam's Sons, 1914), v. 4, pp. 177-204. CtY-D; DHU/R; DLC
Account of White Missionary activities to Negroes in the South from the Colonial Period to circa 1900.

10132. Reimers, David Morgan. Protestant Churches and the Negro: a Study of Several Major Protestant Denominations and the Negro From World War One to 1954. Doctoral dissertation. University of Wisconsin, 1961.

10133. Smith, Lillian. "The White Christian and His Conscience." Presbyterian Outlook (127; Jl. 23, 1945), pp. 5-6. NN/Sch; DLC; NcD DH
Reprinted in South Today.

10134. Spann, M.C. "Work Among the Colored People." The Christian Intelligencer (82:17, Apr. 26, 1911), p. 264. DHU/R
Reformed Church mission among Negroes in the U.S.A.

10135. Speer, Robert Elliott. Race and Race Relations: a Christian View of Human Contacts. New York: Revell, 1924. CtY-D
"An abbreviated edition of this book was issued in the spring as a mission study text book by the Missionary Education Movement and the Council of Women for Home Missions." CtY-D

10136. Stalker, James. "Mission Work Among the Colored People." The Christian Intelligencer (76:35, Ag. 30, 1905), p. 556. DHU/R
Christian missions among the Negroes in the U.S.A.

10137. Tapp, Robert B. Religion Among the Unitarian Universalists. Converts in the Stepfathers' House. New York: Seminar Press, 1973. DHU/R
Attitudes toward racism, pp. 95-96.

10138. Taylor, Alva W. "The Trend of the Races." The Christian Century (39:37, Sept. 14, 1922), pp. 1130-31. DHU/R
"A new text on the trend of the races for study classes under the missionary education movement has been written by Dr. George E. Haynes, a Negro ..."

10139. Taylor, Edward B. Calls to Christians of the New South, in Duty of Extending Help to the Weaker Race by Promoting the Education in Morals and Manners of its Members. n.p.: n.p., n.d. DHU/MO

10140. Tinney, James S. "Nazarenes: Black Quest." Christianity Today (18:5, Dec. 7, 1973), pp. 53-54. DHU/R

10141. "Training for Colored Church Workers." Editorial. Southern Workman (52:5, My., 1923), pp. 207-08. DHU/MO; DLC
"Churches of all denominations realize the importance of having trained workers who will assist the regularly ordained clergy."

10142. Vail, T. H. "Missionary Bishops for Negroes." Church Review (41; 1883), p. 301. DLC

10143. Weatherford, Willis Duke. Present Forces in Negro Progress. New York: Association Press, 1912. NN/Sch; CtY-D; DHU/MO
Missions to Negroes, pp. 145-65.

10144. Weaver, Galen R. "Church Experiments in Community Action." Social Action (16:1, Ja. 15, 1950), p. 3. DHU/R

10145. "What Can the Church Do?" Social Action (9:1, Ja. 15, 1943), pp. 44-45. DHU/R

10146. Washington, Joseph R., Jr. "The Negro in America." (Notes and Reviews). Cross Currents (16:2, Spr., 1966), pp. 237-40. DHU/R
Christian churches and the Negro.

10147. White, Ronald C. Social Christianity and the Negro in the Progressive Era, 1890-1920. Doctoral dissertation. Princeton University, 1972.

10148. Williams, Hugh Ross. Pronouncements on Race Relations in Selected Ecumenical Documents: 1928-1954. Master's thesis. Southeastern Baptist Theological Seminary, 1959.

n. Mormons

10149. Bowles, Carey C. Experiences of a Negro Convert. Newark, N.J.: n.p. 1970.   NjP
Mormon church.

10150. ----- A Mormon Negro Views the Church. Newark: n.p., 1968.   NjP

10151. Brewer, David L. "The Mormons." Donald R. Cutler (ed.). The Religious Situation: 1968 (Boston: Beacon Press, 1968), pp. 518-554.   DHU/R; DLC
Mormons and Negroes, pp. 518-519, 523-524, 532-534, 536-538, 547, 549-551.
Mormons and Slavery, pp. 521-522.
Mormons and Civil Rights Programs, p. 540.

10152. ----- Utah Elites and Utah Racial Norms. Doctoral dissertation. Univ. of Utah, 1966.

10153. Brodie, Fawn McKay. Can We Manipulate the Past? Salt Lake City, Utah: n.p., 1970.   NjP; IAU
Includes information on Mormons and race relations.

10154. "The Changing Image of Mormonism." Dialogue (3; Wint., 1968), pp. 45-58.   DHU/R

10155. Christiansen, James W. The Construction of a Mormon Idological Commitment Scale. Masters thesis. University of Utah, 1966.

10156. Davidson, G. W. "Mormon Missionaries and the Race Question; Condemned by NAACP." Christian Century (82; Sept. 29, 1965), pp. 1183-86.   DHU/R

10157. Douglas, Norman. "The Sons of Lehi and the Seed of Cain: Racial Myths in Mormon Scripture and Their Relevance to the Pacific Islands." Journal of Religious History (8:1, Je., 1974), pp. 90-104.   DHU/R

10158. Hatch, William W. There is No Law. A History of Mormon Civil Relations in the Southern States, 1865-1905. New York: Vantage Press, 1968.   DHU/R
Deals with the persecution inflicted upon the Mormons because of their views on polygamy.

10159. Jonas, F. H. "Matter of Opinion: Mormonism's Negro Policy." The American West (8; Nov., 1971), p. 48. DGU

10160. Linn, William Alexander. The Story of the Mormons, From the Date of their Origin to the Year 1901. London: The Macmillan Co., 1902.   DHU/R

1061. Lund, John Lewis. The Church and the Negro; A Discussion of Mormon Negroes and the Priesthood. Salt Lake City: Paramount, 1967.   NjP; INU; DLC

10162. Mauss, Armand L. "Mormonism and Secular Attitudes Toward Negroes." Pacific Sociological Review (9; Fall, 1966), pp. 91-99.   DCU/SW; DGW; DAU; NcD

10163. ----- "Mormonism and the Negro Faith Folklore and Civil Rights." Dialogue (2; Wint., 1967), pp. 9-39.   DLC

10164. McMurrin, Sterling Moss. The Negroes Among the Mormons, Address Given Before the Annual Banquet of the Salt Lake City Chapter of the National Association for the Advancement of Colored People, June 21, 1968. Salt Lake City: Chapter of NAACP, 1968.   NjP

10165. "Mormon Policy Toward Negroes." Harry A. Ploski (ed.). Reference Library of Black America (New York: Bellwether Pub. Co., 1961), Book 2, pp. 206-07.   DHU

10166. "Mormons -- Racial Policy." New York Times (Apr. 6, 1972), p. 4.   DHU; DLC

10167. "NAACP Convention Urged by Salt Lake City Delegation to Ask South American, Asian and African Nations to Bar Mormon Missionaries because of Churches' Alleged Doctrine of Non-White Inferiority, and to Refuse Visas to Mormon Missionaries." New York Times (Jl. 2, 1965), p. 2.   DHU

10168. Nelson, Lowry. "Mormons and Blacks." Editorial. Christian Century (91:35, Oct. 16, 1974), pp. 949-50. DHU/R

10169. ----- "Mormons and the Negro." The Nation (174:21, My. 24, 1952), p. 490.   DHU; DGW; DGU

10170. Nye, Joseph S. "Memo From a Mormon; in Which a Troubled Young Man Raised the Question of His Church's Attitude Toward Negroes." Look (27; Oct. 22, 1963), pp. 45+. DGW
"Discussion." Look (27; Oct. 22, 1963), p. 79; (27; Dec. 3, 1963), p. 17.   DGW

10171. Quaintance, Charles W. "Race Evolution and Mormonism." Christian Century (88:19, My. 12, 1971), pp. 586-89. DHU/R

10172. Stewart, John J. Mormonism and the Negro; an Explanation and Defense of the Doctrine of the Church of Jesus Christ of Latter-Day Saints in Regard to Negroes and Others of Negroid Blood. With a Historical Supplement, The Church and the Negroid People, by Wm. E. Berrett. Orem, Utah: Bookmark Division, Community Press, Pub. Co., 1963. DHU/MO; CtY-D; NN/Sch

10173. Taggart, Stephen G. Mormonism's Negro Policy: Social and Historical Origins. Salt Lake City, Utah: University of Utah Press, 1970. DHU/R; NjP; InU; DLC; IC/H; TSewU-t

10174. Tanner, Jerald and Sandra. Mormons and Negroes. Salt Lake City: Modern Microfilm Co., 1970.   NjP

10175. ----- The Negro in Mormon Theology. Salt Lake City: Modern Microfilm Co., 1967.   NjP

10176. Turner, Wallace. The Mormon Establishment. Boston: Houghton Mifflin, 1966.   NN/Sch
"The anti-Negro doctrine:" p. (218)-245.
"Will the Negro doctrine change?" pp. 246-66.

10177. Whalen, William Joseph. The Latter-Day Saints in Modern World; an Account of Contemporary Mormonism. New York: John Day Co., 1964.   NN/Sch
"Mormonism and the Negro," pp. 245-57.

10178. White, O. Kendall, Jr. "Mormonism's Anti-Black Policy and Prospects for Change." The Journal of Religious Thought (29:2, Aut.-Wint., 1972), pp. 39-60.   DHU/R

10179. ----- The Social Psychological Bases of Mormon Neo-Orthodoxy. Doctoral dissertation. University of Utah, 1967.

10180. Widtsoe, John A. Discourses of Brigham Young... Salt Lake City, Utah: Deseret Book Co., /1925/.   DHU/R
Scattered statements as to his views on Negroes.

2. Organizations

a. American Missionary Association

10181. American Missionary Association. Annual Report.
DHU/MO (1922, 27, 28, 32, 33) DLC; NcD; CtY-D

10182. ----- The Eighty-Sixth Annual Report...and the Proceedings of the Annual Meeting Held at the First Congregational Church, Oak Park, Ill., Nov. 1, 2, 3, 1932. New York: American Missionary Assoc., 1932. DHU/MO

10183. ----- Forty Years of Missionary Work. The Past and Present, by Secretary Strieby. New York: n. p., 1886.
CtY-D
(Its Pamphlet no. 10)

10184. ----- History of the American Missionary Association: Its Churches and Educational Institutions Among the Freedmen, Indians and Chinese, with Illustrative Facts and Anecdotes. New York: S. W. Green, 1874. DHU/MO; DLC

10185. ----- The Nation Still in Danger; or, Ten Years After the War. A Plea by the American Missionary Association, with Confirmatory Articles by Rev. T. D. Woolsey...Hon. Frederick Douglass, Rev. Washington Gladden, Gov. D. H. Chamberlain, and Hon. J. P. Hawley. New York: Amer. Missionary Assoc., 1875. DLC

10186. ----- Ninety Years After. New York: The American Missionary Assoc., n. d. DHU/MO

10187. "The American Missionary Association and the Congregationalists have Established Educational Foundations in Southern States." The Southern Workman (5:7, Jl., 1876), p. 50.
DHU/MO; DLC

10188. Bailey, Falvius Josephus. Policies of the American Missionary Association in Negro Education. Masters thesis. Howard University, 1933. DHU/MO

10189. Beard, August Field. A Crusade of Brotherhood. A History of the American Missionary Association. New York: Pilgrim Press, 1909. DHU/MO

10190. Blanchard, F. Q. "A Quarter Century in the American Missionary Association." Journal of Negro Education (6:2, Apr., 1937), pp. 152-56. DHU/R; DHU/MO

10191. Brownlee, Frederick L. Heritage of Freedom, A Centenary Story of Ten Schools Offering Education in Freedom. Philadelphia: United Church Press, 1963. DHU/R
American Missionary Association and Negro education.

10192. ----- New Day Ascending. Boston: The Pilgrim Press, 1946. CtY-D
American Missionary Association.

10193. Cable, George Washington. What the Negro Must Learn. Address of Geo. W. Cable at the Annual Meeting of the American Missionary Association, held in Northhampton, Oct. 21-23, 1890. New York: American Missionary Association, 1890. NN/Sch

10194. Dewey, H. P. Race Problems and Their Christian Solution. Sermon Delivered at the Annual Meeting of the American Missionary Association, Held in Des Moines, Iowa, Oct. 16, 1904. New York: American Missionary Association, 1904. DHU/MO

10195. Drake, Richard Bryant. The American Missionary Association and the Southern Negro, 1881-1888. Masters thesis. Emory University, 1957.

10196. Fairchild, Edward Henry. God's Designs for and Through the Negro Race. New York: American Missionary Association, 1882. CtY-D
(American Missionary Association Pamphlet no. 7)

10197-98. "Hampton in Africa." Southern Workman (6:7, Jl., 1877), p. 50. DLC; DHU/MO

The Rev. G. D. Pike of the American Missionary Association believes "that the two-fold work of the Christian civilization of Africa can be best accomplished by native workers."

10199. Hubbard, Henry W. American Missionary Association. Work Among the Colored People of the South. New York: Congregational Rooms, n. d. DHU/MO

10200. Johnson, Charles S. "American Missionary Association Institute of Race Relations." Journal of Negro Education (13; Fall, 1944), pp. 568-74. DHU
Negro author.

10201. ----- Into the Main Stream, A Survey of Best Practices in Race Relations in the South. Chapel Hill: The University of North Carolina Press, 1947. DHU/R; NN/Sch; CtY-D
Survey conducted by the Race Relations Div., American Missionary Association.

10202. ----- "Race Relations Program of the American Missionary Association." Journal of Negro Education (13:2, Spr., 1944), pp. 248-52. DHU

10203. Johnson, Clifton Herman. American Missionary Association Archives as a Source for the Study of American History. New York: n. p., 1966. CtY-D

10204. ----- The American Missionary Association, 1846-1861: A Study of Christian Abolitionism. Doctoral dissertation. University of North Carolina, 1959. DHU/R; MNtcA

10205. LeMoyne College, Memphis, Tenn. Our American Missionary Association Heritage. Memphis: n. p., 1966.
T Sew U-T
American Missionary Association.

10206. Moxom, Phillip Stafford. Our Problem With the Negro in America. Sermon at the 57th Annual Meeting of the American Missionary Association, Oct. 20, 1903. New York: Holt, 1903. MB; NN/Sch

10207. Patterson, Joseph N. A Study of the History of the Contribution of the American Missionary Association to the Higher Education of the Negro-with Special Reference to Five Selected Colleges Founded by the Association. Doctoral dissertation. Cornell University, 1956.

10208. Richardson, Joe M. "Christian Abolitionism: The American Missionary Association and the Florida Negro." Journal of Negro Education (40:1, Wint., 1971), pp. 35-44. DHU/R

10209. Salisbury, Albert. "Some Conclusions Concerning the Education of the American Negro." Andover Review (6; 33, Sept., 1886), pp. 256-64. DHU/R
Written by a worker of the American Missionary Association.

10210. Storrs, Richard Salter. Our Nation's Work for the Colored People. A Discourse Delivered in the Church of the Pilgrims, Brooklyn, N. Y., in Behalf of the American Missionary Association... New York: Holt Bros., 1890.
DHU/MO; NN/Sch

b. Federal Council of Churches

10211. "Anti-Lynching Bill Making Progress." Editorial. The Christian Century (39:10, Mr. 9, 1922), pp. 293-94. DHU/R
The Federal Council of Churches sponsors an anti-lynching bill.

10212. Clemens, Eugene P. The Social Gospel Background of the Federal Council of Churches. Doctoral dissertation. University of Pennsylvania, 1970.

10213. "Dr. Cadman Speaks for Racial Goodwill." Christian
Century (43:1, Ja. 7, 1926), p. 28.   DHU/R
President of the Federal Council of Churches.

10214. Federal Council of the Churches of Christ in America.
Annual Report, 1919. "Committee on Negro Churches:
Report," pp. 155-58.   DHU/R

10215. ----- Annual Report, 1921. "The Church and Race Relations," pp. 79-82.   DHU/R

10216. ----- Annual Report, 1922. "United Work for Better
Race Relations," pp. 49-52.   DHU/R

10217. ----- Annual Report, 1923. "The Church and Race Relations," pp. 59-66.   DHU/R

10218. ----- Annual Report, 1925. "The Church and Race Relations," pp. 32-39.   DHU/R

10219. ----- Biennial Report, 1934. "Department of Race Relations: Report," pp. 58-62.   DHU/R
Also, pp. 75-79.

10220. ----- Biennial Report, 1936. "Department of Race Relations: Report," pp. 45-50.   DHU/R

10221. ----- Biennial Report, 1940. "Department of Race Relations," pp. 41-46.   DHU/R
Also pp. 95-100.

10222. ----- Biennial Report, 1942. "Department of Race Relations: Report," pp. 102-06.   DHU/R

10223. ----- Biennial Report, 1944. "Department of Race Relations: Report," pp. 86-90.   DHU/R

10224. ----- The Church and Race Relations: An Official Statement Approved at a Special Meeting, Columbus, Ohio, March
5-7, 1946. New York: Federal Council of the Churches of
Christ in America, Dept. of Race Relations, 1946.
                                              NN/Sch; DLC

10225. ----- Official Handbook for the Quadrennial Meeting, 1932.
"Recommended by the Commission on Race Relations," pp.
68-71.   DHU/R

10226. ----- Official Handbook for the Quadrennial Meeting,
1933. "Recommended by the Commission on Race Relations,"
pp. 68-71.   DHU/R

10227. ----- Official Handbook for Biennial Meeting, 1934. "Department of Race Relations," pp. 35-40.   DHU/R

10228. ----- Report to the Biennial Meeting, 1942. "Department
of Race Relations," pp. 58-62.   DHU/R

10229. ----- Reports Submitted to the Annual Meeting of the
Executive Committee, 1930. "Race Relations," pp. 30-33.
                                              DHU/R

10230. ----- Reports Submitted to the Annual Meeting of the Executive Committee, 1931. "Race Relations," pp. 24-28.
                                              DHU/R

10231. ----- Twenty Years of Church Federation: Report of
the Federal Council of the Churches of Christ in America,
1924-1928.   DHU/R
"The Church and Race Relations," pp. 107-19.

10232. ----- Commission on the Church and Minority Peoples.
Negro Churchmen Speak to White Churchmen. New York:
n. p., 1944.   DHU/R

10233. ----- Commission on the Church and Race Relations.
What Was Said and Done at the First National Interracial
Conference. Cincinnati: Pub. by the Commission, 1926.
                                              DHU/R

10234. ----- Committee on Race Relations. Report of the Conference on the Betterment of Race Relations in Washington,
D. C. ... n. p., 1935.   DHU/MO

10235. ----- Dept. of Race Relations. Along the Interracial
Front, by George Edmund Haynes, Executive Secretary,
Dept. of Race Relations. New York: n. p., 1945.
                                              DHU/R; NN/Sch

10236. ----- Dept. of Race Relations. Annual Report. (1919,
1921, 1923, 1925).   DHU/R; NN/Sch; DLC

10237. ----- Dept. of Race Relations... Biennial Report.
(1934, 1936, 1940, 1942, 1944).   DHU/R; NN/Sch

10238. ----- Dept. of Race Relations... Glimpses of Negro
Americans. New York: n. p., 1936.   DHU/R; NN/Sch

10239. "Federal Council Opposes Klu Klux Klan." Editorial. The
Christian Century (39: 43, Oct. 26, 1922), p. 1336.   DHU/R

10240. Flow, J. E. "The Federal Council and Race Segregation."
Southern Presbyterian Journal (5; My. 15, 1946; 10, Oct. 17,
1951), pp. 10, 17.   DLC; KyLxCB

10241. Greater New York Federation of Churches. The Negro
Churches of Manhattan. New York: n. p., 1930. NN/Sch
Typescript.

10242. Haynes, George Edmund. Address... Nation Interracial
Conference. Toward Interracial Cooperation (New York:
Little & Ives Co., 1926), pp. 168-73.   DHU/MO
Negro secretary of the Federal Council of Churches in
America. Dept. of Race Relations.

10243. ----- ... Along the Interracial Front. N. Y.: Dept. of
Race Relations, Federal Council of Churches, 1945. NN/Sch

10244. ----- "Changing Racial Attitudes and Customs." Phylon
(2:1, First Quarter, 1941), pp. 28-43.   DHU/MO; DLC

10245. ----- The Christian Association and Natives of South
Africa. N. Y.: n. p., 1930.   NN/Sch

10246. ----- "The Churches and Racial Peace." The Crisis
(25:3, Ja., 1923), pp. 113-16.   DHU/MO; DLC

10247. ----- The Clinical Approach to Race Relations; How to
Promote International Health in Your Community. New York:
Dept. of Race Relations, the Federal Council of the Churches
of Christ in America, 1946.   NH; DLC; NcGU; OWibfU

10248. ----- Continent of the Future. N. Y.: H. W. Wilson,
1954.   NN/Sch

10249. ----- "Conditions Among Negroes in the Cities." Annals
of the American Academy of Political and Social Science (49;
Sept., 1913), pp. 104-19.   DHU/R; NN/Sch

10250. ----- Enlistment for Brotherhood in Your Community.
New York: Dept. of Race Relations, the Federal Council of
Churches of Christ in America, 1947.   DHU/MO

10251. ----- "Lily-white Social Security." Crisis (42; Mr., 1935),
pp. 85-86.   DHU/MO

10252. ----- Migration of Negroes Into Northern Cities. Pittsburgh: National Conference of Social Work, 1917. NH; TNF

10253. ----- ... The Negro and the National Recovery Act...
New York: Federal Council of Churches, 1933-34. NN/Sch

10254. ----- "The Negro at Work: A Development of the War and
a Problem of Reconstruction." Review of Reviews (59; Ag.,
1919), pp. 389-93.   DLC

10255. ----- The Negro at Work During the World War and During Reconstruction... Washington: U. S. Dept. of Labor,
1921.   OWibfU; NN/Sch

10256. ----- "Negro Labor and the New Order." National Conference of Social Work. Proceedings (New York: 1919),
pp. 531-38.   DHU/MO

10257. ----- "Negro Migration." Opportunity (2; Sept., 1924),
pp. 303-06; 118-24.   DHU/MO

10258. ----- Negro Migration and Its Implications North and
South, an Address by George E. Haynes... Before the 77th
Annual Meeting of the American Missionary Association,
Springfield, Massachusetts, October 23, 1923. New York:
American Missionary Association, 1923.   NH; DLC

10259. ----- Negro Migration in 1916-17. Wash., D. C.: Govt.
Printing Office, 1919.   DHU/MO

10260. ----- Negro New-comers in Detroit, Michigan; a Challenge to Christian Statesmanship. New York: Home Mission
Council, 1918. NH; NN; DHU/MO; MiD-B, MiD; NNC

10261. ----- "Negroes and the Ethiopian Crisis." Christian
Century (52; Nov. 20, 1935), pp. 1485-86.   DHU/R
Discusses Black Church's reaction to Italian invasion of
Ethiopia.

10262. ----- "Negroes Move North: Their Departure from the
South." Survey (40; My. 4, 1918), pp. 115-22. (41; Ja. 4,
1919), pp. 455-61.   DHU/MO

10263. ----- "The Opportunity of Negro Labor." Crisis (18;
Sept., 1919), pp. 236-38.   DHU/MO

10264. ----- "Public Approbation as a Means of Changing Interracial Attitudes and Customs." Social Forces (24; Oct.,
1945), pp. 105-10.   DHU/MO

10265. ----- "South African Students Face Their Race Problem."
Crisis (37; Nov., 1930), pp. 370-72.   DHU/MO

10266. ----- Toward Interracial Peace: a Description of the
Movement in the Federal Council of the Churches of Christ
in America, to Discover Methods and Techniques for Ap-
plying Justice and Goodwill in Race Relations Through the
Evangelical Churches of the United States. New York: n. p.,
1940.   NN/Sch

10267. ----- "William E. Harmon Awards for Distinguished
Achievement." Opportunity (4; Apr., 1926), p. 129.
                                                      DHU/MO
Also: Crisis (31; Feb., 1926), pp. 174-75; (33; Ja.,
1927), pp. 156-57.   DHU/MO
Negro secretary of the Federal Council of Churches in
America. Dept. of Race Relations.

10268. ----- What Price American Progress? n. p.: n. p.,
1938.   NH; NN

10269. ----- .... The Work of the Commission on Race Relations, Federal Council of Churches of Christ in America.
N. Y.: n. p., 1932.   NN/Sch

10270. ----- and Benson Y. Landis, et alii. Cotton Growing
Communities... Studies no. 1. Case Studies of 9 Rural Communities and 30 Plantations in Alabama. New York: Federal Council of Churches of Christ in America, 1934.
                                             DHU/MO; NN/Sch

10271. ----- Cotton Growing Communities Study no. 2. Case
Studies of 10 Rural Communities and 10 Plantations in Arkan-
sas. New York: Federal Council of Churches of Christ in
America, 1935.   DHU/MO; NN/Sch

10272. Hunt, Lura Esther (Aspinwall). Race Relations Sunday.
New York: Dept. of Race Relations, Federal Council of the
Churches of Christ in America, n. d.   TN/DCHS

10273. Johnson, Frederick E. The Social Work of the Churches:
A Handbook of Information. New York: Department of Re-
search and Education, Federal Council of the Churches of
Christ in America, 1930.   DHU/R

10274. "Negro Churches to From Own Federal Council." Christian Century (51:5, Ja. 31, 1934), p. 139.   DHU/R; DLC

10275. Piper, Jr., John F. "The Formation of the Social Policy of the Federal Council of Churches." Journal of Church
and State (11:1, Wint., 1969), pp. 63-82.
                                       DHU/R; DAU/W; DGU; DGW

10276. "Preachers Speak for Ku Klux Klan." Editorial. The
Christian Century (39:43, Oct. 26, 1922), p. 1337. DHU/R
"...the Federal Council opposing the Ku Klux Klan...
astonishing to find some preachers...advocate."

10277. Reddis, Jacob L. The Negro Seeks Economic Security
Through Cooperation. An Address Delivered before the
National Seminar Consumer's Cooperation of the Federal
Council of Churches of Christ in America, Indianapolis,
Ind., Jan. 1, 1936. Chicago, Ill.: Pub. by Central States
Cooperative League, 1936.   DHU/MO

10278. Sidelights on Negro Soldiers. By Charles H. Williams.
B. J. Brimmer Co., Boston, Mass. The Crisis (27:4,
Feb., 1924), pp. 175-76.   DLC; DHU/MO
Author served as an investigator under the joint auspices
of the Federal Council of Churches in America and the
Phelps-Stokes Fund for racial strife in the Army.

c. National Council of Churches of Christ in the U.S.A.

10279. Fey, Harold E. "N. C. C. Acts on Racial Crisis." Christian Century (80:25, Je. 19, 1963), pp. 797-98.

10280. Jacquet, Constant H. Man Amidst Change; A Consultation
Held at Airlie House, Warrenton, Virginia, May 3-6, 1962.
New York: National Council of the Churches of Christ in the
U. S. A., 1963.   DHU/R

10281. Lewis, Philip C. White to White; a Docudrama. New York:
Council Press for the Department of Educational Development,
National Council of Churches of Christ in the U. S. A., 1969.
                                                      TSewU-T

10282. National Council of Churches of Christ in the United States
of America. American Christian Responsibility Toward Africa
(n. p., N. C. C. U. S. A., Je. 6, 1956). Pam. File, DHU/R
Mim.

10283. ----- The Churches and Segregation (n. p., N. C. C. U. S. A.,
Dec. 5, 1957). Pam. File, DHU/R
Mim.

10284. ----- Churches and Social Welfare. New York: n. p., 1955.
                                                      DHU/R

10285. ----- The Churches' Concern for People Without the Necessities of Life (n. p., N. C. C. U. S. A., Dec. 8, 1960), Pam. File,
                                                      DHU/R
Mim.

10286. ----- Growing Together; A Manual for Councils of Churches.
New York: n. p., 1955.   DHU/R

10287. ----- Human Rights (n. p., N. C. C. U. S. A., Dec. 6, 1963.)
                                       Pam. File, DHU/R
Mim.

10288. ----- A Pronouncement, a Policy Statement: Religious
and Civil Liberties in the U. S. A. Adopted by the General
Board, Oct. 5, 1955.   Pam. File, DHU/R

10289. ----- Commission on Religion and Race. Reports... V. 1-
1965-   NcD; CtY-D

10290. ----- Department of Education for Missions. "Crescend,
a Filmstrip on the Negro Protest Movement in America."
Filmstrip and phonodisc.

10291. ----- Dept. of Racial and Cultural Relations. About Racially
Inclusive Churches. Partial Statistical Survey of a Cross Sec-

(----Dept. of Racial and Cultural Relations cont.)
tion of Racially Inclusive Churches in the United States (1950).
                                        Pam. File, DHU/R
      Mim.

10292. ----- Dept. of Racial and Cultural Relations. Denominational Statements on Fair Employment Practices: 1955.
                                        Pam. File, DHU/R
      Typescript.

10293. ----- Dept. of Racial and Cultural Relations. Denominational Statements with Reference to a Racially Inclusive Fellowship. (Feb., 1955).   Pam. File, DHU/R

10294. ----- Dept. of Racial and Cultural Relations. Statements
Adopted by Religious Groups (re) Segregation in the Public
Schools. (Interracial Publication. no. 84, Oct., 1954). Pam.
File, DHU/R
      "Gives resolutions on race adeopted by various denominations."

10295. ----- Dept. of Youth Ministry. Racism in American Society.
White Plight? Youth Week Resource Youth Organization, Youth
Ministry, Natl. Counc. of Churches.   Pam. File, DHU/R
      Ecumenical ways in which youth and adults can work together
      in the struggle against racism. "A pamphlet: Youth Against
      Racism."

10296. ----- Division of Foreign Missions. The Christian Mission
for Today. New York: n.p., 1958?   DHU/R

10297. ----- Division of Foreign Missions. Study of the Common
Christian Responsibility Toward the Areas of Rapid Social
Change. 1959.   DHU/R

10298. ----- Division of Home Missions. Every Tribe and
Tongue... New York: Friendship Press, 1960.   DHU/R

10299. ----- Division of Overseas Ministries. Agricultural
Missions. Commonwealth Africa. Regional Youth Seminar.
"Youth and Development in Africa. A Report of the ... Nairobi,
November, 1969." Occasional Bulletin, Missionary Research
Library (21:11, Nov., 1970), pp. 1-8.   DHU/R

10300. ----- Governing Board. "Proposal for NCC Convocation
of Conscience for the Poor." Church and Society (63:5, My.
-Je., 1973), pp. 61-62.   DHU/R

10301. ----- Interfaith Center on Corporate Responsibility. An
Open Letter to the European-American Banking Corporation.
New York: National Council of Churches, 1974. Pam. File,
                                        DHU/R
      W. Sterling Cary, President of NCC and nine other church
      leaders call on the board to cancel its massive loan to the
      South African government.

10302. "NCC Takes Race Action." Christian Advocate (8; Apr. 23,
1964), pp. 23+.   DAU/W; DHU/R

10303. "National Council Changing With Times, an A.D. Interview
With the Council's President, W. Sterling Cary." A.D. United
Presbyterian Edition (3:6, Je., 1974), pp. 36-38.   DHU/R
      Black president of council explains his program after one
      year in office.

10304. "The National Council of Churches and Civil Rights." The
African Methodist Episcopal Church Review (8:222, Oct.-Dec.,
1964), pp. 5-7.   DHU/R

10305. "National Council of Churches Plans for Work in Poverty,
Narcotics, Race." Methodist Story (9; Mr., 1965), p. 46.
                                        DAU/W

10306. "National Council of Churches Steps Up Race Protest Moves."
Christian Advocate (7; Jl. 18, 1963), p. 24. DAU/W; DHU/R

10307. "National Council of Churches Unit Asks Us Jurisdiction in
Civil Rights Slayings." Concern (7; Oct. 15, 1965), pp. 16+.
                                        DAU/W

10308. "Negro Churches Enter Council." Editorial. The Christian
Century (47:9, Feb. 26, 1930), pp. 280-1.   DHU/R
      The council of churches receive Negro churches into the
      council.

10309. "Racism Workshops Set for Five Areas." Tempo Newsletter
(3:10, Ja., 1974), pp. 1-.   DHU/R

10310. Richardson, Lincoln. "Fine Vines in Doing Fine." Presbyterian Life (25:8, My., 1972), pp. 16-18.   DHU/R
      National Council of Churches and Mississippi Action for
      Community Education (MACE) brought together 14 Delta
      organizations and projects and set-up a black-run jeans
      factory in the Mississippi Delta.

10311. Rogers, Cornish. "The Politics of Holiness." Christian
Century (89:44, Dec. 6, 1972), pp. 1234-35.   DHU/R
      Council of Churches, N.Y. agreed to set up a 30-member
      task force to combat racism after a week of demonstrations
      by blacks.

d. World Council of Churches

10312. Adler, Elisabeth. A Small Beginning: An Assessment of the
First Five Years of the Programme to Combat Racism. Geneva,
Switzerland: WCC Publications Office, 1974.   DHU/R

10313. Biersteker, H. "WCC Tugs at the Vines of Investments in
Southern Africa." Christian Century (89; Oct. 4, 1972), pp.
987-88.   DHU; DAU/W; DCU; DGU; DGW
      World Council of Churches and action in South America.

10314. "A 'Dialogue' Breaks Down." Presence (5:2, 1971), pp.
36-37.   DHU/R
      "Excerpts from the exchange of letters concerning a proposed
      meeting between the World Council of Churches and its South
      African Members."

10315. Duff, Edward. The Social Thought of the World Council of
Churches. New York: Association Press, 1956. DHU/R

10316. Dunne, George H. "The Sin of Segregation. Exposing the
Sophistry Underneath Well-Worn Arguments." Commonweal
(99: 7, 1973), pp. 169-70.   DHU/R
      Written by a Catholic priest, former founding general sec-
      retary of Sodepax, a Geneva based agency sponsored by the
      Pontifical Commission on Justice and Peace of the World
      Council of Churches.

10317. "Executive Committee Acts on Race, Mideast, Good Crisis,
Development." Ecumenical Press Service (6; Mr., 1974),
pp. 12-13.   DHU/R
      World Council of Churches in their annual Meeting approved
      funds to provide poor countries with low-interest develop-
      ment loans.

10318. Gentz, William H. The World of Philip Potter. New York:
Friendship Press, 1974.   DHU/R

10319. Kraemer, Hendrik. World Cultures and World Religions;
The Coming Dialogue. London: Lutterworth Press, 1960.
                                        DHU/R

10320. Martin, J. A. "The Ecumenical Conference and Race
Relations." The Crisis (40:12, Dec., 1931), pp. 423+.
                                   DHU/MO; DLC

10321. Mays, Benjamin Elijah. "Amsterdam on the Church and
Race Relation." Religion in Life (9:1, Wint., 1940), pp. 95-
104.   DHU/R
      Negro author.
      World Council of Churches held in Amsterdam, Holland.

10322. ----- "Second Assembly of the World Council of Churches."
Journal of Religious Thought (10:2, Spr.-Sum., 1953), pp.
144-48.   DHU/R

10323. Nelson, J. Robert. "An Open Letter to Philip Potter."
The Christian Century (89:31, Sept. 6, 1972), pp. 873-74.
                                        DHU/R

World Council of Churches comments on the election of
Philip Potter, a West Indian as general secretary.

10324. ----- "The World Council and Race: Give the Black Man
his Own Turf." Catholic World (209:1254, Sept. 1, 1969),
pp. 256-61.   DHU/R

10325. Nolde, Otto. Free and Equal; Human Rights in Ecumenical
Perspective. With Reflections on the Origin of the Universal
Declaration of Human Rights by Charles Habib Malik. Geneva,
Switzerland: World Council of Churches, 1968.   DHU/R

10326. Paton, Alan. "Church Amid Racial Tensions. Issue Confronting the 1954 World Council Assembly." Christian Century
(71; Mr., 31, 1954), pp. 393-94.   DHU/R

10327. Payne, Ernest A. "Violence, Non-Violence and Human
Rights." Ecumenical Review (23:3, Jl., 1971), pp. 222-36.
                                                          DHU/R
World Council of Churches and grants to certain oppressed
racial groups.

10328. Potter, Philip. "Christ's Mission and Ours in Today's
World." International Review of Missions (62:246, Apr.,
1973), pp. 144-57.   DHU/R
Written by Jamaican General Secretary of the World Council
of Churches.

10329. ----- "The Third World in the Ecumenical Movement."
Ecumenical Review (24; Ja., 1972), pp. 55-71.
DCU/TH; DGU; DGW; DHU/R

10330. "Second Largest Dutch Church Supports Anti-Racism Fund."
Ecumenical Press Service (10/41, Apr. 4, 1974), p. 5.
                                                          DHU/R
The Synod of the Reformed Churches in the Netherlands
approved 49 to 22 a three-pronged resolution including
support for the World Council of Churches' Special Fund
to Combat Racism."

10331. Shepherd, George W., Jr. "Controversy Over the WCC
Program to Combat Racism." IDOC International North
American Edition (Apr. 24, 1971), pp. 71-78.   DHU/R

10332. Smith, Francis S. "World Council Struggles with Racism."
United Church Herald (12:11, Nov., 1969), pp. 46-47.
                                                          DHU/R

10333. "South African Churches Sending Representatives to WCC
Committee." Ecumenical Press Service (40:17, Je., 1973),
pp. 4-5.   DHU/R
World Council of Churches and South African Churches.

10334. "Special Fund to Combat Racism: World Council of
Churches." IDOC, International (Dec. 12, 1970), pp. 7-28.
                                                          DHU/R

10335. Stauderman, Albert P. "The World Council Takes a New
Tack." The Lutheran (10:19, Sept. 20, 1972), pp. 19-21.
                                         Pam. File; DHU/R
"Cooperation and Unity, rather than merger of Churches,
seen as goals for ecumenical movement."

10336. Thompson, Betty. "Philip Potter: Phase III for the WCC."
The Christian Century (89:30, Ag. 30, 1972), p. 839. DHU/R
Commentary on the selection of the first black general sec-
retary of the WCC, a West Indian Methodist.

10337. "Violence, Nonviolence and the Struggle for Social Justice."
The Ecumenical Review (25:4, Oct., 1973), pp. 430-46. DHU/R
Result of a two-year study undertaken by W. C. C. Central
Committee (Addis Ababa, 1971) Church and Society Com.
on the problems and potentialities of violence and nonviolence
in the struggle for social justice.

10338. World Council of Churches. Central Committee. Committee
to Combat Racism. "Background Paper on the Special Fund
and Letter, 'Committed to Fellowship, a Letter to the
Churches'." Ecumenical Press Service (26; Sept. 21, 1972), pp.
1-9.   DHU/R

10339. ----- Commission on World Mission and Evangelism.
The Christian Ministry in Latin America and the Caribbean;
Report of a Survey of Theological Education in the Evangelical
Churches, Undertaken Feb.-May, 1961, on Behalf of the
International Missionary Council (now the Commission on World
Mission and Evangelism of the World Council of Churches).
New York: n.p., 1962.   DHU/R

10340. ----- Dept. on Studies in Evangelism. Planning for Mission;
Working Papers on the New Quest for Missionary Communities.
New York: U.S. Conference for the World Council of Churches,
1966.   DHU/R

10341. ----- Ecumenical Statements on Race Relations; Develop-
ment of Ecumenical Thought on Race Relations, 1937-1964.
Geneva: n.p., 1965. MiBsA; MNtcA; DHU/R; DLC; NcD;
CtY-D

10342. ----- Secretariat for Migration. Division of Inter-Church
Aid, Refugee and World Service. "An Ecumenical Programme
to Combat Racism." Migration Today (13; Aut., 1969), pp.
54-59.   Pam. File, DHU/R

10343. ----- Secretariat on Racial and Ethnic Relations. "Race
Relations in Ecumenical Perspective." No. 3, Geneva, Switzerland, Sept.-Nov., 1963.   Pam. File, DHU/R

e. United Nations and Agencies

10344. Bennett, John Coleman. Christian Social Ethics in a
Changing World; An Ecumenical Theological Inquiry. New York:
Association Press, 1966.   DHU/R

10345. Cruise O'Brien, Conor. To Katanga and Back: A UN Case
History. New York: Grosset & Dunlap, 1966.   DHU/R
A Study by U. N. at Katanga, Congo (Province).

10346. Hummon, John Peter. Protestants and Point Four: the
Churches' Response to U.S. Programs of Aid to the Underde-
veloped Countries. Doctoral dissertation. University of
Michigan, 1958.

10347. Nixon, Justin Wroe. The United Nations and Our Religious
Heritage. New York: Church Peace Union, 1953. DHU/R

10348. Stuntz, Hugh Clark. The United Nations Challenge to the
Church. Nashville: Abingdon-Cokesbury Press, 1948.
DHU/R; NN/Sch

10349. United Nations Educational, Scientific and Cultural Organization. Human Rights, Comments and Interpretations; A Symposium. London: A. Wingate, 1949.   DHU/R

10350. ----- Dept. of Mass Communication. What is Race? Evidence from Scientists. Based on Race and Biology. Paris,
1952.   DHU/R

f. General
10351. Aery, William Anthony. "Industrial "Y" For Negro Ship-
builders." Southern Workman (20:1, Ja., 1921), pp. 17-26.
                                           DLC; DHU/MO
Y. M. C. A.

10352. African Mission School Association, New York. A Mission
School Among the Colored People of New York. New York:
n. p., 1868.   NN/Sch

10353. "The Alice Johnson Colored Young Men's Christian Association in Knoxville, Tenn. Advertises." The Crisis (2:3, Jl.,
1911), p. 98.   DHU/MO; DLC

10354. American Church Institute for Negroes. Annual Report
for 1927 of the American Church Insitutue for Negroes. New
York: Church Missions House, 1928.   DHU/MO

10355. ----- Down Where the Need is Greatest. A Record in the
Field of Negro Education Through Divinity School, College,
Junior Colleges, Industrial High and Normal Schools, Training
School for Nurses, Summer Schools and Farmers' Confer-
ences. New York: n.p., 1937?   NN/Sch; CtY-D

10356. ----- Our Church Industrial High School for Negroes.
The Bishop Payne Divinity School, the Junior College, Under
the Supervision of the American Church Institute for Negroes,
the Accredited Auxiliary to the National Council of the Protestant Episcopal Church. New York: Abbott Press, 1925.
                                                          NN/Sch

10357. ----- Spirit of Missions (74:6, Je., 1909), p. 485. DHU/R

10358. American Moral Reform Society, Philadelphia. The Minutes and Proceedings of the 1st Annual Meeting of the American
Moral Reform Society. Held at Philadelphia in the Presbyterian Church in 7th St., below Shippen, from the 14th to 19th
of August, 1897. Philadelphia: Merriher & Gunn, 1937.
                                                          DHU/MO

10359. "American Negro Ministers at the Ecumenical Council of
Methodism, in London." (portrait). The Crisis (23:1, Nov.,
1921), p. 33.   DHU/MO; DLC
          Portraits of Bishops Coppin, Smith and Jones; secretaries
          Hawkins and Wright; Dr. W. S. Scarborough; Mrs. J. F.
          Hurst; and others.

10360. Archibald, Helen Allen, (ed.). Negro History and Culture;
Selections for Use with Children. Chicago: Dept. of Cirricu-
lum Development, Chicago City Missionary Society, 1964.
                                                          CtY-D

10361. Arthur, George R. Life on the Negro Frontier; A Study
of the Objectives and the Success of the Activities Promoted
in the Young Men's Christian Association Operating in "Rosenwald" Buildings. New York: Association Press, 1934.
          NN/Sch; DHU/MO; DHU/R

10362. ----- "The Young Men's Christian Association Movement
Among Negroes." Opportunity (1:3, Mr., 1923), pp. 16-18.
Negro Executive Secretary, Wabash Avenue (Chicago)
Branch, Y. M. C. A.

10363. Association for the Benefit of Colored Orphans, New York.
Annual Report. New York: n. p., n. d.   NNUT

10364. Baker, Paul Earnest. Negro-White Adjustment; An Investigation and Analysis of Methods in the Interracial Movement
in the United States; the History, Philosophy, Program, and
Techniques of Ten National Interracial Agencies. Methods
Discovered Through a Study of Cases, Situations, and Projects
in Race Relations... New York: Association Press, 1934.
                                                          DHU/R; CtY-D; DHU/MO

10365. Batterham, E. Rose. "Negro Girls and the Y. W. C. A."
Southern Workman (48:9, Sept., 1919), pp. 437-41.
                                                          DLC; DHU/MO
          The Y. W. C. A. War Work Council and how colored wo-
          men were employed.

10366. "The Christian Endeavor Union on the Evil of Lynching."
The Crisis (2: 2, Je., 1911), p. 53.   DHU/MO; DLC

10367. "Church Leaders Adopt Recommendations." The Crisis
(51:5, My., 1944), p. 174.   DLC; DHU/MO
          National Conference of Church Leaders request legislations
          on Church and civil matters be passed. A permanent Fair
          Employment Practice Committee be formed is one of the
          recommendations.

10368. "Colored Student. Y. W. C. A. Conference." Editorial.
Southern Workman (45:8, Ag., 1916), pp. 442-43. DLC; DHU/
                                                          MO
          "The first colored student conference of the Y. W. C. A.
          was held at Spelman Seminary, Atlanta, Ga., from May
          26 to June 5, 1916."

10369. Commission on Inter-Racial Cooperation, Inc. Cooperation
in Southern Communities; Suggested Activities for Country and
City Inter-Racial Committees, Ed. by T. J. Woofter, Jr. and
Isaac Fisher. Atlanta, Ga.: Commission on Inter-Racial
Cooperation, 1921.   NN/Sch; DHU/MO

10370. ----- "Repairers of the Breach;" A Story of Interracial
Cooperation between Southern Women, 1935-1940... Prepared
by Jessie Daniel Ames, and Bertha Payne Newell (Mrs. W.
A. Newell), Atlanta: n. p., 1940.   NN/Sch

10371. Committee on Negro Churches. Report of Commission on
Christian Education, Commission on Evangelism, Commission
on the Church and Social Service, Commission on the Church
and Country Life. Committee on Negro Churches, Commission on Temperance. New York: n. p., n. d.   DHU/MO

10372. Council of Christian Associations. Christian Principles
and Race Relations: a Discussion Course for College Groups
Council of Christian Associations, Student Council, Y. W.
C. A. ... Student Department, Y. M. C. A. ... New York:
Association Press, 1926.   NN/Sch

10373. ----- "Race Issue Rocks Detroit Conference." Christian
Century (48:2, Ja. 14, 1931), pp. 62-63.   DHU/R
          Also pp. 49-50, The Race Issue at Detroit.

10374. "County Y. M. C. A. Work." Southern Workman (42:2,
Mr., 1913), p. 128.   DLC; DHU/MO
          The colored people of Brunswick County, Lawrenceville,
          Va. gather to organize the County committee of Colored
          Y. M. C. A.

10375. Craver, William C. "The Y. M. C. A. in Negro Schools."
Southern Workman (56:2, Feb., 1927), pp. 80-82.
                                                          DLC; DHU/MO

10376. Cuming, G. J., (ed.). The Mission of the Church and the
Propagation of the Faith. Cambridge: University Press,
1970.   DHU/R; DLC
          "Papers read at the Seventh Summer Meeting of the Eighth
          Winter Meeting of the Ecclesiastical History Society."

10377. Davis, Allison. The Negro Church and Association in the
Lower South; a Research Memorandum... The Negro Church
and Associations in Chicago; a Research Memorandum Prepared by J. G. St. Clair Drake... New York: n. p., 1940.
(Carnegie Myrdal Study), the Negro in America. NN/Sch
          Negro authors.

10378. Dean, Henry Talmadge. Christian Implications in the Program of the National Association for the Advancement of Colored People. Masters thesis. Howard University, 1939.

10379. Derrick, W. B. "The Work of Evangelization Among the
Negroes." Elias B. Sanford, (ed.), Church Federation:
Inter-Church Conference of Federation, New York, November
15-21, 1905. (New York: Fleming H. Revell Co., 1906), pp.
520-24.   DHU/R
          Negro author.

10380. Drake, St. Clair. Churches and Voluntary Associations
in the Chicago Negro Community. Report of Official Project
465-54-3-386 Conducted under the Auspices of the Work Projects Administration. Horace R. Clayton, Superintendent...
Chicago: n. p., 1940.   DHU/MO

10381. Dubois, William E. B. "The Problem of a Sacrifice."
The Crisis (25:2, Dec., 1922), pp. 56-57.   DHU/MO; DLC
          Rufus Meroney, Y. M. C. A. secretary for the colored,
          Brooklyn, N. Y. branch.
          Negro author.

10382. Gaines, Miriam. "The John Little Mission Louisville,
Ky." Southern Workman (62:4, Apr., 1933), pp. 161-70.
                                                          DLC; DHU/MO
          "The unusual character of this institution lies in the fact
          that its basic religious activities are marvelously inter-
          woven with a program of vocational, recreational, and
          educational training."

10383. "The Ghetto." The Crisis (7:4, Feb., 1914), p. 170.
                                                          DLC; DHU/MO
          Women's Home Missionary Society secures 162 signatures
          to a resolution against the Florida school law.

10384. Goodall, Norman. "The Inter-Racial Conference of Church Leaders: Witwatersrand, December, 1954." The International Review of Missions (35; 1955), pp. 193-97.   DHU/R

10385. Hammond, Lily Hardy. In the Vanguard of a Race. Council of Women for Home Missions and Missionary Education Movement. New York, 1922.   DHU/R; DLC; DHU/MO;O

10386. Hanson, J. W. (ed.). The World's Congress of Religions. Chicago: International Publishing Co., 1894.   DHU/MO
Addresses and papers delivered before the Parliament Ag. 25-Oct. 15, 1893 at the World's Columbia Exposition, Chicago. Many speeches were delivered by Negro ministers on race relations.

10387. Harlow, Harold C. Racial Integration of the YMCA: A Study of the Closing of Certain Negro YMCA's With Special Reference to the Role of Religious Factors. Doctoral dissertation. Hartford Seminary Foundation, 1961.

10388. Haskin, Sara Estelle. The Upward Climb. A Course in Negro Achievement. Missionary Education Movement of the U. S. and Canada. New York: n. p., 1927.   DHU/R

10389. Hayne, Coe Smith. For a New America. New York: Council of Women for Home Missions and Missionary Educations Movement of the United States and Canada, 1923.   CtY-D

10390. Home Missions Council. Annual Meeting of the Home Mission Council. 1920, 1922.   DHU/MO

10391. Hope, John. "Colored YMCA." Crisis (31; Nov., 1925), pp. 14-17.   DHU/MO

10392. ----- Relations Between the Black and White Races in America. New York: International Missionary Council, 1928.   CtY-D
At the Jerusalem meeting of the International Missionary Council, March 24-April 8, 1928. IV. The Christian Mission in the light of race conflict.

10393. Hopkins, C. Howard. History of the Y. M. C. A. in North America. New York: Association Press, 1951.   DHU/R
Includes information of Negro work and branches.

10394. Hunton, W. A. "Women's Clubs: Caring for Young Women" The Crisis (2:3, Jl., 1911), pp. 121-22.   DHU/MO; DLC
The Y. W. C. A.

10395. Imes, William Lloyd. "The Amateur Spirit in Religion." Southern Workman (62:2, Feb., 1933), pp. 61-64.   DLC; DHU/MO
"An address delivered on the opening of the new building of the 135th Street Branch Y. M. C. A. in the City of New York at the Evening in Honor of the Churches, Jan., 5, 1933 by a Presbyterian minister."

10396. "Julius Rosenwald and the Negro." The Crisis (24:5, Spet., 1922), pp. 203-10.   DHU/MO; DLC
The Y. W. C. A. Movement.

10397. Leevy, J. S., Jr. "Missionary Work of the Hampton Y. M. C. A." Southern Workman (34:7; Jl., 1905), pp. 412-3.   DLC; DHU/MO

10398. Macmillan, Elizabeth W. "An Institute for Racial Justice-- Results and Effects." The Y. M. C. A. Magazine (67:1, Ja., 1973), p. 25.   DHU/R

10399. Markoe, William M. "Claver Clubs for Colored People." America (29; Ag. 4, 1923), pp. 268-69.   DLC

10400. Mays, Benjamin Elijah. "The Church Surveys World Problems." The Crisis (44:10, Oct., 1937); (44:11, Nov., 1937), pp. 299+; 340+.   DLC; DHU/MO
"Delegates from fifty-six nations gathered at Oxford University, England, in July to consider religion and world problems. Mr. Mays reports here on the conference."

10401. McCulloh, James E., (ed.). Battling for Social Betterment, Southern Sociological Congress... Nashville: Southern Sociological Congress, 1914.   DHU/MO

10402. McCulloch, Margaret C. "Educational Programs for the Improvement of Race Relations: Seven Religious Agencies." Journal of Negro Education (13:4, Sum., 1944), pp. 305-15.   DHU/MO

10403. McGrew, J. H. "Y. M. C. A. Work for Virginia Negroes." Southern Workman (46:4, Apr., 1917), pp. 235-40.   DLC; DHU/MO

10404. Miller, Kelly. "The Negro Young Men's Christian Association." Southern Workman (33:2, Feb., 1904), pp. 93-9.   DLC; DHU/MO

10405. Mills, M. Gertrude. Christian Creative Science. Rendered at the State Federation of Colored Women Clubs. June 16-18, 1915. Palatka, Fla.: Fla. Printing Co., 1915.   NN/Sch

10406. Moorland, Jesse Edward. "Educational Work of the Colored Young Men's Christian Association." Southern Workman (35:4, Apr., 1906), pp. 244-46.   DLC; DHU/MO

10407. ----- "The YMCA With Colored Troops." Southern Workman (48:4, Apr., 1919), pp. 171-5.   DLC; DHU/MO

10408. ----- "The Young Men's Christian Association Among Negroes." Journal of Negro History (9:2, Apr., 1924), pp. 127-38.   DHU
Negro author.

10409. Morehouse, Henry Lyman. "A Survey of Twenty-five Years Work for the Colored People of the South." Address... at the special meeting of the American Baptist Historical Mission Society. Sept. 25, 1888. n. p.: 1888.   NRAB
Typescript.

10410. National Conference of Colored Men of the United States, Nashville, Tenn., 1879. Proceedings of the National Conference of Colored Men of the United States, Held in the State Capitol at Nashville, Tenn. May 6, 7, 8 and 9, 1879. Washington, D. C.: R. H. Darby, Printer, 1879.   NN/Sch

10411. National Conference on Religions in Independent Education. 7th Colorado Springs, 1962. Education for Decision. By Jas. Robinson. Editors: Frank R. Gaebelein... and others. New York: Seabury Press, 1963.   NN/Sch

10412. National Conference on the Christian Way of Life, New York. And Who is My Neighbor? An Outline for the Study of Race Relations in America... New York: Association Press, 1924.   DHU/MO

10413. Negro Young Peoples' Christian and Educational Congress. 1st. Atlanta, 1902. The United Negro: His Problems and His Progress... Held August 6-11, 1902. Atlanta, Ga.: D. E. Luther Pub. Co., 1902.   NN/Sch
Religion, pp. 382-88.

10414. ----- Souvenir Official Program and Music of the Young Peoples' Christian and Educational Congress. Held July 31 to August 5, 1906. Convention Hall, Washington, D. C. Edited by Corresponding Secretary, I. Garland Penn., n. d.   DHU/MO

10415. New York Colored Mission. Annual Report. 1st, 1869. New York: n. p., 1869.   NN/Sch

10416. ----- Report of the New York Colored Mission. New York: n. p., n. d.   NNUT

10417. North Carolina (Colony). The Colonial Records of North Carolina. Published under the Supervision of the Trustees of the Public Libraries by the Order of the General Assembly. Collected and edited by William L. Saunders, Secretary of State... Raleigh: P. M. Hale, 1886-90. NN; MB; NcD; MH-L
V. 6, information about John MacDowell, a missionary

(North Carolina (Colony) cont.)

    for the Society for the Propagation of the Gospel and his ministry with free Negroes in North Carolina.

10418. Protestant Council of the City of New York. Dpet. of Church Planning and Research. Profiles of Nassau County Communities; a Summary of Social, Economic and Housing Characteristics of 94 Nassau Counties, 1960... (Prepared for the Committee of Church Planning and Research, Nassau County Council of Churches). New York: n. p., 1964. NN/Sch

10419. ----- Dept. of Church Planning and Research. Upper Manhattan: a Community Study of Washington Heights. Robert Lee, Study Director; Clara Orr, Asst. to the Director. New York: n. p., 1954.   NN/Sch

10420. "The Race Issue at Detroit" Christian Century (48:2, Jan. 14, 1931), pp. 49-50.   DHU/R
    Editorial on racial problems of the Detroit Conference of the Council of Christian Associations. (Dec. 27-31, 1931).

10421. Racial Relations and the Christian Ideal; a Discussion Course for College Students. New York: Young Women's Christian Association, Young Men's Christian Association, 1923.
        DHU/MO; CtY-D; NN/Sch

10422. Ray, Charles B. ...Annual Report of City Missionary to the Destitute Colored Population. New York: n. p., n. d.
        NNUT

10423. "Religious Conventions Speak Out On Lynchings." Editorial. The Christian Century (39:22, Jl. 1, 1922), p. 698. DHU/R

10424. Religious Education Association. Education and National Character by Henry Churchill, Francis Greenwood Peabody, Lyman Abbott, Washington Gladden, and others. Chicago: Religious Education Association, 1908.   DHU/MO

10425. Russel, B. T. What are the Policies, Practices and Attitudes of the Foreign Mission Boards in North America with Reference to the Sending of American Negroes as Foreign Missionaries. Masters thesis. Presbyterian College of Christian Education, 1945.

10426. "Social Uplift." The Crisis (3:2, Dec., 1911), p. 51.
        DHU/MO; DLC
    In Indianapolis and Columbus, O., colored people raise money to build Y. M. C. A.'s.

10427. ----- The Crisis (3:5, Mr., 1912), p. 184. DLC; DHU/MO
    The Negro Christian Alliance.

10428. ----- The Crisis (5:5, Mr., 1913), p. 216. DHU/MO; DLC
    Julius Rosenwald offers $25,000 toward the building of Young Men's Christian Associations.

10429. Southern Society for the Promotion of the Study of Race Conditions and Problems in the South. Race Problems of the South; Report of the Proceedings of the First Annual Conference Held under the Auspices of the Southern Society for the Promoting of the Study of Race Conditions and Problems in the South, at Montgomery, Alabama, May 8, 9, 10, A. D. 1900. Richmond, Va.: B. F. Johnson Pub. Co., 1900.
        NN/Sch; DHU/MO

10430. Southern Sociological Congress. 2d Atlanta, 1913. The Challenge of Social Service. Edited by James E. McCulloch. Nashville: Southern Sociological Congress, 1913. NN/Sch
    The social problems of the church by Walter Rauschenbush.

10431. ----- The South Mobilizing for Social Service. Addresses Delivered at the Southern Sociological Congress, Atlanta, Georgia, April 25-29, 1913. Edited by James E. McCulloch. Nashville: Southern Sociological Congress, 1913. NN/Sch

19432. ----- 3d, Memphis, 1914. Battling for Social Betterment. Southern Sociological Congress, Memphis, Tennessee, May

6-10, 1914. Edited by James E. McCulloch. Nashville: Southern Sociological Congress, 1914.
        NN/Sch
    "The Southern Sociological Congress as a factor for social welfare by Booker T. Washington," pp. 154-59.

10433. ----- 5th, 7th, 1916-1918. Democracy in Earnest. Southern Sociological Congress, 1916-1918. Edited by James E. McCulloch. Washington, D. C.: Southern Sociological Congress, n. d.   NN/Sch
    Church and race problems.

10434. ----- 8th, Knoxville, Tenn., 1919. "Distinguished Service" Citizenship. Southern Sociological Congress, Knoxville, Tennessee. Edited by J. E. McCulloch. Washington, D. C.: Southern Sociological Congress, 1919.   NN/Sch
    Chapter 8, The Church conserving life.

10435. Speer, Robert Elliott. Of One Blood, a Short Study of the Race Problem. New York: Council of Women for Home Missions and Missionary Education Movement of the United States and Canada, 1924.   CtY-D; DHU/MO
    p. 147, race and religion.

10436. Sutherland, Robert L. Color, Class and Personality. Prepared for the American Youth Commission. Washington, D. C.: American Council on Education, 1942.   DHU/MO; CtY-D

10437. Thomasson, Maurice E. "The Negro Migration." Southern Workman (46:7, Jl., 1917), pp. 377-82.   DLC; DHU/MO
    "The Y. M. C. A. aids the Negro population in their migration from the South to the North."

10438. Tobias, Channing H. "A Decade of Student Y. M. C. A. Work." The Crisis (24:6, Oct., 1922), pp. 265-67.
        DHU/MO; DLC

10439. ----- "The Work of the Young Men's and Young Women's Christian Associations With Negro Youth." The Annals of the American Academy of Political and Social Science (140; Nov. 28, 1928), pp. 283-86.   DHU/R

10440. Washington Federation of Chruches. "An Approach Toward a Racially Inclusive Church; a Six Point Program."
        Pam. File, DHU/R
    Unanimous action by Board of Directors, Sept. 24, 1954, to accept this report and commend it to the member churches.

10441. Watson, James Jefferson. "Churches and Religious Organizations." The Annals of the American Academy of Political and Social Science (49; Sept., 1913), pp. 120-28.   DHU

10442. Wilkerson, Yolanda Barnett. Interracial Programs of Student YWCA's; an Inquiry Under Auspices of the National Student Young Women's Christian Association. New York: Woman's Press, 1948.   CtY-D

10443. Williams, Charles H. "Negro Y. M. C. A. Secretaries Overseas." Southern Workman (49:1, Ja., 1920), pp. 24-35.
        DLC; DHU/MO

10444. "Women of South May End Lynching." Editorial. Christian Century (39:18, My. 4, 1922), p. 548.   DHU/R
    A committee organized for race relations, by the Council on Religion.

10445. Wright, Richard Robert, Jr., (bp.). National Freedom Day Association. Philadelphia: n. p., 1942.   DHU/MO
    Bishop of the A. M. E. Church.

10446. "The Y. M. C. A., an Agent for Social Change." The Young Women's Christian Association (67:3, Mr.-Apr., 1973.)
    "Entire issue."

10447. "The Y. M. C. A. and the Negro." The Crisis (25:3, Ja., 1923), p. 120.   DHU/MO; DLC

10448. Yergan, Max. "A Y. M. C. A. Secretary in Africa." Southern Workman (47:8, Ag., 1918), pp. 401-3.
    Report from Mombassa, East Africa.

D. PREJUDICE, RACE RELATIONS AND SEGREGATION IN RELIGION,
HIGHER EDUCATION AND SOCIETY

10449. Ahmann, Mathew, (ed.). Race: Challenge to Religion. Chicago: Regnery, 1963. DHU/R
Speeches from a meeting of the National Conference on Religion and Race.

10450. Alexander, Will W. Racial Segregation in the American Protestant Church. New York: Friendship Press, 1946. DHU/MO

10451. Allport, Gordon W. "Prejudice: Is it Societal or Personal." Journal of Social Issues (18), pp. 130-32. DHU
Also in, Religious Education (59:1, Ja.-Feb., 1964), pp. 20-29. DHU/R

10452. ----- "Religion and Prejudice." Crane Review (2; 1959), pp. 1-10. DAU/W

10453. ----- and J. M. Ross. "Personal Religious Orientation and Prejudice." Journal of Personality and Social Psychology (5; 1967), pp. 432-43. DHU; DGU

10454. ----- "The Religious Context of Prejudice." Journal for the Scientific Study of Religion (5:3, Fall, 1966), pp. 447-57. DHU/R

10455. And Who is My Neighbor? An Outline for the Study of Race Relations in America. New York: Negro Universities Press, 1969. DHU/R

10456. Anthropology for the People; a Refutation of the Theory of the Adamic Origin of All Races. By Caucasian (pseud.). Richmond, Va.: Everett Woddey Co., 1891. TNF

10457. Argyle, M. Religious Behaviour. Glencoe, Ill.: Free Press, 1955. DHU/R
Racial prejudice, pp. 55-83.

10458. Ariel, Buckner H. Payne. The Negro: What is His Ethnological Status? Is He the Progeny of Ham? Is He a Descendant of Adam and Eve--What is His Relation to the White Race? Cincinnati: n.p., 1867. DHU/MO

10459. Armistead, W. S. The Negro is A Man, A Reply to Professor Charles Carroll's Book "The Negro is a Beast or in the Image of God." Atlanta, Ga.: Mutual Publishing Co., 1904. DHU/R; GEU; NcD

10460. Ashley Montagu, Montague Francis. Man's Most Dangerous Myth: The Fallacy of Race. New York: Columbia University Press, 1942. DHU/R

10461. Attaway, A. Henry. The Race Question, Another Angle. Jackson, Miss.: Herderman Brothers, n.d. OWibfU

10462. Atwood, Jesse H. The Attitudes of Negro Ministers of the Major Denominations in Chicago Toward Racial Division in American Protestantism. Doctoral dissertation. University of Chicago, 1930.

10463. Augusta, Marie (Sister). "Methods of Education in Race Relations." Religious Education (59:1, Ja.-Feb., 1964), pp. 43-46. DHU/R

10464. Baez-Carmargo, Gonzalo. "Christianity and the Race Problem." Henry C. Wallace, (ed.). Christian Bases of World Order. (New York: Abingdon-Cokesbury Press, 1943), pp. 101-24. DHU/R; CtY-D
Merrick lectures for 1943.

10465. Bailey, Hugh C. Edgar Gardner Murphy: Gentle Progressive. Coral Gables, Fla.: University of Miami Press, 1968. DHU/R
Biography of an early 20th century leader and pioneer in race relations, on the national level.

10466. Baldwin, James. "The Harlem Ghetto: Winter 1948." Commentary (5:2, Feb., 1948), pp. 165-170. DHU/R

10467. Bales, James David and Herbert Philbrick. Communism and Race in America. Searcy, Ark.: Bales Bookstore, 1965. TN/DCHS

10468. Barlow, William Harvey. Present Unrest of the Negro in the South. Doctoral Dissertation. Southern Baptist Theological Seminary, 1921.

10469. Barton, John W. "Negro Migration." Methodist Quarterly Review (74:1, Ja., 1925), pp. 84-101. DHU/R

10470. Beach, Waldo. "Ecclesiology and Race: In the Churches of Southern Protestantism." Union Seminary Quarterly Review (14; Ja., 1959), pp. 19-25. DHU/R

10471. ----- "Racial Crisis and the Prophet." New Christian Advocate (1:11, Ag., 1957), pp. 28-32.

10472. ----- "A Theological Analysis of Race Relation." Paul Ramsey, (ed.). The Theology of H. Richard Niebuhr. New York: Harper & Bros., 1957, pp. 205-24.

10473. Beard, August Field. What the North is Doing for the Christian Development of the Southern Negro. The Great Christian Denominational Agencies at Work in the South. New York: n.p., 190-. DLC
Also, Missionary Review (27; Sept., 1904), pp. 660-66. DHU/R; CtY-D

10474. Bell, L. Nelson. "Racial Tensions." Southern Presbyterian Journal (5; Feb. 15, 1947), pp. 2-3. DLC; KyLxCB

10475. Benedict, Ruth. Race: Science and Politics. New York: Modern Age Books, 1940. DHU/MO
pp. 158+ racism and Christianity.

10476. Bennett, Richard K. "Segregation and World Peace." Friends Intelligencer (109:22, My. 31, 1952), pp. 306-7. DHU/R

10477. "Bishop H. M. Turner on Negro Rights." The Crisis (1: 5, Mr., 1911), pp. 5-6. DHU/MO; DLC

10478. Blackburn, George Andrew. The Life Work of John L. Girardean, D.D. ... Columbia, S.C.: State Co., 1916. DLC
Professor, Presbyterian Theological Seminary, Columbia, S.C. and his view on race, pp. 82-4.

10479. Blum, B. S. and J. H. Mann. "The Effect of Religious Membership on Religious Prejudice." Journal of Social Psychology (52; 1960), pp. 97-101. DHU; DGU

10480. Booker, Merrel Daniel, Sr. and Carr Auburn. "White and Black Exchanged Parsonages and Pulpits." Missions: An International Baptist Magazine (148:2, Feb., 1950), pp. 82-84. Pam. File, DHU/R

10481. Booth, Newell Snow. Youth Guides on Races and Reconciliation. New York: Friendship Press, 19-? NN/Sch
Detailed plans for using these materials with youth groups in the local church, community, and in summer conferences.

10482. Bowen, John Wesley Edward. An Appeal to the King; the Address Delivered on Negro Day in the Atlanta Exposition, October 21, 1895. Atlanta; Ga.: n.p. 1895. DHU/MO

10483. ----- "An Apology for the Higher Education of the Negro." The Methodist Review (79; Sept., 1897), pp. 723-42. DHU/R; DLC; CtY-D

10484. ----- and Penn I. Garland. The United Negro: His Problems and Progress. Atlanta: D. E. Luther Pub. Co., 1902. DHU/MO

10485. Boyd, Malcolm. The Hunger, the Questions of Students and Young Adults. New York: Morehouse-Barlow, 1946. NN/Sch

10486. Braceland, Francis J. and Michael Stock. "The Deep Roots of Prejudice." Catholic World (198:1, 184, Nov., 1963), pp. 109-14.   DHU/R

10487. Brannon, Rena Avrette. A Study of Religious Beliefs, Attitudes and Practices Among College Students. Masters thesis. Howard University, 1940.
Negro author.

10488. Bratton, Theodore DuBose, (bp.). "The Christian South and Negro Education." Southern Workman (37:6, Je., 1908), pp. 331-36.   DLC; DHU/MO
An address delivered by Bishop Bratton of Mississippi before the Conference for the Education in the South, held at Memphis, Tenn., April 22-24.

10489. Breland, R. L. "The Children of Ham." The Baptist Record (32; Je. 5, 1930), p. 9.   KyLoS; LNB; TND

10490. Brown, James Russell. An Examination of the Thesis that Christianity in its Genesis was Technique of Survival for an Underprivileged Minority... B.D. paper. School of Religion, Howard University, 1935.

10491. Brown, Sarah D. Launching Beyond the Color Line ... Chicago: National Purity Association, 1905.   NN/Sch

10492. Brownell, Sally. "Racism in Children's Books." Friends Journal (19:8, Apr. 15, 1973), pp. 232-33.   DHU/R

10493. Bryson, Lyman. Approaches to Group Understanding. Sumposium of the Conference on Science, Philosophy and Religion. New York: Harper Bros., 1947.   DHU/R

10494. Burns, Aubrey. "Segregation and the Church." Reprinted from the Spring 1949 issue of Southwest Review, Pub. by University, Dallas, Texas.   DHU/R

10495. Buster, William. "Jap and Negro: A Similiarity of Social Problem." Methodist Review (Bimonthly) (87; Jl., 1905), pp. 576-81.   DHU/R

10496. Byrd, E. L. "Christianity and Segregation." The African Methodist Episcopal Church Review (70:181, J-.-Sept., 1954), pp. 72-79.

10497. Campbell, Ernest Q. "Moral Discomfort and Racial Segregation--An Examination of the Myrdal Hypothesis." Social Forces (Mr., 1961), p. 229.   DHU

10498. Campbell, Robert Fishburne. Some Aspects of The Race Problem in the South. N.C.: The Citizen Company, 1899.   NN/Sch

10499. Carhart, C. L. "Churches and Race Lines." Christian Century (50:26, Je. 28, 1933), pp. 849-50.   DHU/R
Dr. Kelly Miller quoted on the church and race prejudice.

10500. Carroll, Charles. The Negro A Beast; or, In the Image of God. St. Louis: American Book and Bible House, 1900; Miami, Fla.: Mnemosyne Pub. Co., 1969.   INu; DLC

10501. ----- The Tempter of Eve; or the Criminality of Man's Social, Political and Religious Equality with the Negro, and the Amalgamation to Which These Crimes Inevitably Lead. Discussed in the Light of the Scriptures. St. Louis: The Adamic Pub. Co., 1902.   DHU/MO

10502. Cartwright, Colbert S. "Church, Race and the Arts of Government." Christianity and Crisis (19; Feb. 16, 1959), pp. 12-14.   DHU/R

10503. ----- "The Southern Minister and the Race Question." New South (13; Mr. 1952), pp. 54-6.   DAU/W

10504. Catchings, L. Maynard. The Church Can Eliminate Discrimination and Segregation. n.p., n.d.   DHU/MO
Negro author.
Reprint. American Unity (v. 4 & 5, Jan. 1947).

10505. ----- "Interracial Activities in Southern Churches." Phylon (13; Mr., 1952), pp. 54-6.   DHU/MO

10506. Caudill, Rebecca. "The Plight of the Negro Intellectual." The Christian Century (47:33, Ag. 20, 1930), pp. 1912-14.   DLC; DHU/R
A Nashville, Tenn., interracial forum composed of scholastic and Church institutions discuss race problem.

10507. "Christian Morality and Race Issues." Life (56; Mr. 27, 1964), p. 4.   DHU

1508. "Christian Preaching and Race Relations." Interracial Review (37; Je., 1964), pp. 115-17.   DHU

10509. "Christian Strategy in Race Relations." Christian Century (48:4, Ja. 28, 1931), pp. 26-7.   DHU/R

10510. "Christians, White and Black." Opportunity (7:10, Oct., 1929), p. 303.   DHU/MO

10511. "The Church Speaks Out." Editorial. The Crisis (44:11, Nov., 1937), p. 337.   DLC; DHU/MO
"... good cause to castigate the church for its apathy on social issues."

10512. Clark, H. B. "Basic Sources of Race Relations Literature." Union Seminary Quarterly Review (20:3, Mr., 1965), p. 348.   DHU/R

10513. Clarke, William Francis. The Folly of Bigotry; an Analysis of Intolerance. Chicago: Non-Sectarian League for Americanism, 1940.   NN/Sch

10514. Clinchy, Everett Ross. All in the Name of God. Introd. by Newton D. Baker. New York: Day, 1934.   NN/Sch

10515. Clinton, George Wylie, (bp.). "To What Extent is the Negro Uplifting the Race." D. W. Culp. Twentieth Century Negro Literature. (Atlanta: Nicholson, 1902), pp. 115+. NcSalL; DHU/R

10516. Cohen, Henry. "Prejudice Reduction in Religious Education." Religious Education (59:2, Mr.-Apr., 1964), pp. 386-91.   DHU/R

10517. Cokes, George Louis. The Eagle and the Cross; the Racial Problem in Perspective. New York: Exposition Press, 1966. DHU/MO; NN/Sch; NjP

10518. Cole, Stewart Grant and Mildred W. Minorities and the American Promise: the Conflict of Principle and Practice. New York: Harper, 1954.   DHU/R
Church and race relations, pp. 192-200.

10519. Coleman, Charles Cecil, (bp.). Patterns of Race Relations in the South. New York: Exposition Press, 1949. NcSalL; DHU/MO
Negro author.

10520. "Condemn Segregation." Zions Herald (129; Feb. 14, 1951), p. 157.   DLC

10521. Conference of College Religious Workers. Report of Conference of College Religious Workers, Held at Fisk University, Nashville, Tenn. March 7-10, 1929. n.p., n.d.   DHU/MO

10522. Coogan, John E. "Christian Untouchables?" Review for Religious Research (5; 1946), pp. 107-13.   DCU/TH

10523. Cooper, Harold L. "Questions and Answers on Segregation." Social Order (6; 1956), pp. 432-33.   DCU/SW

10524. Cooper, John M. "Religion and the Race Problem." The Crisis (42:6, Je., 1935), pp. 170.   DLC; DHU/MO
"Author discusses the wolfishness of race to race, especially of the white race to the Negro race in our country."

10525. Coston, William Hilary. The Betrayal of the American Negroes as Citizens, as Soldiers and Sailors, by the Republican Party in Deference to the People of the Philippine Islands. n. p.: n. p., n. d.   DHU/MO

10526. Cromwell, John W. "The Early Convention Movement." n. p.: The American Academy, 1904.   NN/Sch "Occasional Papers, no. 9."

10527. Crummell, Alexander. "The Destiny of the Negro." The African Respository (53; Oct., 1887), pp. 97-107.   DHU/MO

10528. ----- Incidents of Hope for the Negro Race in America. A Thanksgiving Sermon. November 26th, 1895... Washington, D. C.: n. p., 1895.   DHU/MO; NN/Sch

10529. Curry, Jabez Lamar Monroe. ...Education of the Negroes Since 1860. Baltimore: n. p., 1894.   NN/Sch

10530. Dabbs, J. M. "Is a Christian Community Possible?" Christian Century (57; Jl. 10, 1940), pp. 874-6.   DHU/R

10531. Dabney, Robert Lewis. Ecclesiastical Relation of Negroes. Speech... in the Synods of Virginia, Nov. 9, 1867, Against the Ecclesiastical Equality of Negro Preachers in our Church and their Right to Rule over White Christians. Richmond: Pr. at the Office of the Boys and Girls' Montly, 1868.   NcD

10532. Davis, Allison. Children of Bondage; the Personality Development of Negro Youth in the Urban South. Prepared for the American Youth Commission. Washington, D. C.: American Council on Education, 1940.   CtY-D

10533. Davis, J. Arthur. Reformation and Unity... Can the Leopard Change His Spots... Washington, D. C.: Hamilton Printing Co., 1913.   NN/Sch "An open letter to the Afro-American ministry."

10534. Davison, Charles Clement. Race Friction in the South Since 1865. Doctoral dissertation. Southern Baptist Theological Seminary, 1922.

10535. Dean, John P. and Alex Rosen. A Manual on Intergroup Relations. Chicago: University of Chicago Press, 1955.   DHU/R

10536. Delaney, Lucy A. From the Darkness Commeth Light or Struggles for Freedom. St. Louis: J. T. Smith, n. d.   O WibfU

Written by an A. M. E. layman.

10537. Delany, Martin Robison. The Condition, Elevation, Emigration, and Destiny of the Colored People of the United States. New York: Arno Press, 1968c1852.   DHU/R; NNCor Includes short biographical material on early Black leaders in all professions.

10538. Dionisopoulies, P. Allan. Rebellion, Racism, and Representation; The Adam Clayton Powell Case and its Antecedents. Dekalb, Ill.: Northern Illinois Univ. Press, 1970.   INU; DLC; DHU/R

10539. Dorey, Frank David. The Church and Segregation in Washington, D. C., and Chicago, Illinois: A Prolegomenon to the Sociological Analysis of the Segregated Church. Doctoral dissertation. University of Chicago, 1950.   DHU/R

10540. Douglass, Frederick. "The Church and Prejudice." Philip S. Foner, (ed.). The Life and Writing of Frederick Douglass V. 1 (New York: International Publishers, 1950), pp. 103-05.   DHU/R A speech given at the Plymouth Church Anti-Slavery Society, December, 1841 and printed in the National Anti-Slavery Standard, December 23, 1841. Negro author.

10541. ----- Narrative of the Life of Frederick Douglass an American Slave. Benjamin Quarles, (ed.). Cambridge: Harvard University Press, 1967.   DHU/R; DHU/MO

In the appendix Douglass explains his position on Christianity and the hypocritical nature of its dealings with blacks.

10542. ----- Why is the Negro Lynched? Reprinted by Permission from "The A. M. E. Church Review" for Memorial Distribution, by a few of his English Friends. Bridgewater: Pr. by John Whitby, 1895.   DHU/MO Negro author.

10543. Dowd, Jerome. The Negro in American Life. New York: The Century Co., 1926.   NcD; DHU/MO Church and race.

10544. Doyle, Bertram Wilbur. The Etiquette of Race Relations in the South. Chicago: University of Chicago Press, 1937.   DHU/R

Chapter IV, Etiquette in the Church.

10545. DuBois, William E. B. "The Color Line and the Church." Crisis (36:11, Nov., 1929), pp. 387-88.   DHU/MO

10546. ----- The Revelation of Saint Orgne, the Damned. Nashville: Hamphill Co., 1939.   DHU/MO Negro author. Commencement Address Delivered at Fisk University, 1938. Indictment Against America for segregated churches.

10547. Duncan, Hannibal Gerald. The Changing Race Relationship in the Border and Northern States. Doctoral dissertation. Southern Baptist Theological Seminary, 1918.

10548. Dunn, James J. "Priests and Prejudice." Pastoral Life. (6; Mr. - Apr., 1958), pp. 29-31.   DCU/ST

10549. Eakin, Mildred Olivia (Moody). Sunday School Fights Prejudice, by Mildred Moody Eakin and Frank Eakin. New York: Macmillan, 1953.   DHU/R; NN/Sch

10550. Eddy, Sherwood. "The Ku Klux Klan." The Christian Century (39:22; 39:33, Aug., 10,17, 1922), pp. 993-5; 1021-3.   DHU/R

10551. Edwards, Lyford P. "Religious Sectarianism and Race Prejudice." American Journal of Sociology (41:2, Sept., 1935), pp. 167-79.   DHU

10552. Emil, Mary (Sister). "Race Relations and Higher Education." Religious Education (59:1, Ja. -Feb., 1964), pp. 107-11.   DHU/R

10553. Engle, Gerald. "Some College Students' Responses Concerning Negroes of Differing Religious Background." Journal of Social Psychology (74; Feb., 1968), pp. 275-83.   DHU/DGW; DAU

10554. Eutsler, Frederick B. "A Theological Analysis of the Concept of Equality in American Race Relations." Journal of Religious Thought (17; Wint. -Spr., 1960), pp. 3-14. DHU/R Also, Doctoral dissertation. Yale University, 1957.

10555. Falls, Arthur Grand Pré. "Interracial Cooperation in Chicago." Interracial Review (8; Ag., 1935), pp. 123-35.   DCU/SW Negro authro. Part 4-Discussion of religious groups in the movement.

10556. Farmer, James. The Relation Between Religion and Racism with a Special Reference to Christianity and the American Scene. Masters thesis. Howard University, 1941. Negro authro.

10557. Feagin, Joe R. "Prejudice and Religious Types: A Focused Study of Southern Fundamentalists." Journal for the Scientific Study of Religion (4:1, Fall, 1964), pp. 3-13.   DHU/R

10558. Fife, Robert Oldham. Teeth on Edge. Grand Rapids, Mich.: Baker Book House, 1971.   NjP Church and race problems in the United States.

10559. Fisher, Miles Mark. "Separated not Segregated." Chronicle (14:2, Apr., 1951), pp. 87-93.   SCBHC

10560. Flow, J. E. "Is Segregation Un-Christian?" Southern Presbyterian Journal (10; Ag. 29, 1951). DLC; DyLxCB

10561. Forsyth, David D. Christian Democracy for America. Cincinnati: The Methodist Book Concern, 1918. NN/Sch

10562. Frazier, E. Franklin. "Social Work in Race Relations." The Crisis (27:5, Mar., 1924), pp. 252-4.   DLC; DHU/MO
"...the present relations of the White and colored people in a so-called Christian nation presents to the world, have turned to the church..."

10563. Fuller, Thomas Oscar. Bridging the Racial Chasms; A Brief Survey of Inter-Racial Attitudes and Relations. Memphis: By the Author, 1937.   NcD; DHU/MO; ViU; TNF
Negro author.

10564. ----- Negro Education in Southern Cities. Memphis: n. p., n. d.   NcD

10565. Gaines, Wesley John, (bp.). The Negro and the White Man. Phila.: AME Pub. House, 1897. NN/Sch; DLC; InU; DHU/R
Written by A. M. E. bishop.

10566. Gallagher, Buell G. "Christianity and Color." Conference on Science, Philosophy and Religion, A Symposium, Vol. 6. New York: Harper, 1944.   DHU/R

10567. ----- Color and Conscience: The Irrepressible Conflict. New York: Harper, 1946.   DHU/R; NN/Sch
Christian integrationist position.

10568. ----- "Conscience and Caste: Racism in the Light of the Christian Ethic." Journal of Religious Thought (2:1, Aut.-Wint., 1945), pp. 20-29.   DHU/R

10569. ----- Portrait of a Pilgrim: A Search for the Christian Way in Race Relations. New York: Friendship Press, 1946.
DHU/MO; CtY-D

10570. ----- and Dwight Bradley. "The Question of Race: Interpreted by Science and Religion." Bulletin. Boston, General Theological Library (36:1, Oct., 1943), pp. 5-9. MBU

10571. Galloway, Charles B. The South and the Negro. New York: Southern Education Board, 1904.   DHU/MO

10572. Garnet, Henry Highland. "If You Must Bleed, Let it Come All at Once." Thomas Wagstaff, (ed.). Black Power. The Radical Response to White America. Beverly Hills: Glencol Press, 1909, pp. 32-40.   DHU/R
Negro author.

10573. Gillard, John Thomas. "Negro Challenges Christianity." Commonweal (16; Je. 1, 1932), pp. 129-31.   DHU

10574. Gillespie, G. T. A Christian View on Segregation. Greenwood, Miss.: Citizen's Council, 1957.   DHU/MO

10575. Gilligan, Francis James. The Morality of the Color Line. An Examination of the Right and the Wrong of the Discrimination Against the Negro in the United States. Washington, D. C.: Catholic University of America, 1928.   NN/Sch; DHU/R

10576. Gleason, Robert W. "The Immorality of Segregation." Thought (35; Aut., 1960), pp. 349-64.   DCU/HU

10577. Gordes, Robert. Race and the Religious Tradition. New York: Anti Defamation League, 1962.   DHU/R
Reprint from the Root and the Branch by Robert Gordes, University of Chicago Press, 1962.

10578. Gordon, Milton. Assimilation in American Life: The Role of Race and Religion and National Life. New York: Oxford University Press, 1964.   DHU/R

10579. Gorsuch, Richard L. and Daniel Aleshire. "Christian Faith and Ethnic Prejudice: A Review and Interpretation of Research." Journal for the Scientific Study of Religion (13:3, Sept., 1974), pp. 281-307.   DHU/R

10580. Gossett, Thomas F. Race: The History of an Idea in America. New York: Schocken Books, 1965.   DHU/R
Chapter 8, "The Social Gospel and Race" Clergyman and their refusal to attack racism in the church in the latter part of the nineteenth century and early twentieth century.

10581. Grant, George A. "Race Conflict." Methodist Review (Bimonthly) (92; My., 1910), pp. 423-30.   DHU/R

10582. Gray, D. B. and William Revelle. "A Multidimensional Religious Attitude Inventory Related to Multiple Measures of Race." Journal of Social Psychology (92; 1974), pp. 153-54.
DHU; DGU

10583. Griggs, Sutton E. Unfettered. Nashville: Orion Pub. Co., 1902. DHU/MO; NN/Sch; NcD; TNF; ViHoI; NcRR; OWibfU
Includes: Dorian's plan and a dissertation on the race problem.
Written by a Negro Baptist minister.

10584. Grimke, Francis James. The Afro-American Pulpit in Relation to Race Elevation. Washington, D. C.: n. p., n. d.
DHU/MO; DHU/R; NN/Sch
Also in Woodson, Carter G. Francis James Grimke, Washington, D. C.: Association Press, 1942.
Negro author.

10585. ----- The American Bible Society and Colorphobia. Washington, D. C.: n. p., 1916.   DHU/MO
Negro author.

10586. ----- The Atlanta Riot. A Discourse Delivered...Oct. 7, 1906.   DHU/MO

10587. ----- The Birth of a Nation. Washington, D. C.: n. p., 1915.   DHU/MO

10588. ----- The Brotherhood of Man, the Christian Church and the Race Problem in the United States of America. A Discourse delivered in the Fifteenth Street Presbyterian Church, Washington, D. C., March 20, 1921.   DHU/MO

10589. ----- Character, the True Standard by Which to Estimate Individuals and Races and by Which They Should Estimate Themselves and Others... Washington, D. C.: Pr. by R. L. Pendelton, n. d.   DHU/MO

10590. ----- Christianity and Race Prejudice. Two Discourses Delivered in the Fifteenth Street Church, Washington, D. C. Washington, D. C.: n. p., 1910.   NN/Sch
Also in Woodson, Carter G., Francis James Grimke. Washington, D. C., Association Press, 1942.

10591. ----- "Colored Men as Professors in Colored Institutions." Southern Workman (63; Dec., 1934), pp. 370-72.   DHU/MO

10592. ----- Equality of Rights for All Citizens: Black and White Alike. A Discourse Delivered in the Fifteenth Street Presbyterian Church, Washington, D. C., Sunday, Mr. 7, 1909. Washington, D. C.: n. p., 1909.   DHU/R; DHU/MO
Also in Woodson, Carter G. Francis James Grimke, Washington, D. C.: Association Press, 1942.

10593. ----- Excerpts from a Thanksgiving Sermon. Delivered Nov. 26, 1914 and Two Letters Addressed to Hon. Woodrow Wilson, President of the United States. Washington, D. C.: R. L. Pendelton, 1914.   DHU/R
Also in Woodson, Carter G. Francis James Grimke, Washington, D. C., Associated Press, 1942.

10594. ----- Fifty Years of Freedom. Washington, D. C.: The Author, 1913.   DHU/MO

10595. ----- Gideon Bands for Work Within the Race and for Work Without the United States. A Discourse in the Fifteenth Street

Presbyterian Church, Washington, D. C., Sunday, Mr. 2, 1913. Washington, D. C.: R. L. Pendelton, 1913. DHU/MO

10596. ----- God and the Race Problem. Delivered in the Fifteenth Street Presbyterian Church, Washington, D. C. May 3, 1903, on the Day Set Apart as a Day of Fasting, Prayer, and Humiliation for the Colored People. Throughout the United States. n. p., 1903.
Also in Woodson, Carter G. Francis James Grimke. Washington, D. C.: Association Press, 1942.

10597. ----- Jim Crow Christianity and the Negro. Washington, D. C.: n. p., n. d. DHU/MO

10598. ----- "The Lynching of Negroes in the South: Its Causes and Remedies." Carter G. Woodson, (ed.). The Works of Frances J. Grimke (Wash., D. C.: The Associated Pub., Inc., 1942), pp. 291-317. DHU/R
Negro author.

10599. ----- A Message to the Race... Delivered in the Fifteenth Street Presbyterian Church, Washington, D. C., Mr. 1, 1925. Washington, D. C.: n. p., 1925. DHU/MO

10600. ----- My Farewell Quadrennial Message to the Race. Delivered in the Fifteenth Street Presbyterian Church, Washington, D. C., Mr. 5, 1933. Subject: The Three Most Important Agencies in the Uplife of the Race. Washington, D. C.: n. p., 1933. DHU/MO

10601. ----- The Negro: His Rights and Wrongs, the Forces for Him and Against Him. Washington, D. C.: n. p., 1898. DHU/MO
"Sermons... delivered in the Fifteenth Street Presbyterian Church, Washington, D. C., Nov. 20 and 27, and Dec. 4 and 11, 1898."

10602. ----- "The Negro and His Citizenship," The Negro and the Elective Franchise. Washington, D. C.: The American Negro Academy, Occasional Papers, No. 11, 1905. DHU/MO

10603 ----- The Next Step in Racial Cooperation. A Discourse Delivered in the Fifteenth Street Presbyterian Church. Washington, D. C., Nov. 20, 1921. Washington, D. C.: n. p., 1921. DHU/MO; NN/Sch

10604. ----- Our Young People: How to Deal With Them. Washington, D. C.: n. p., n. d. DHU/MO

10605. ----- A Phase of the Race Problem, Looked at from Within the Race Itself... Delivered in the Fifteenth Street Presbyterian Church, Washington, D. C., Mr. 6, 1921. Washington, D. C.: n. p., 1921. DHU/MO; NN/Sch

10606. ----- The Progress and Development of the Colored People of our Nation. An Address Delivered Before the American Missionary Association, Wednesday... Oct. 21, 1908, at Galesburg, Illinois. n. p., 1908. DHU/MO

10607. ----- Quadrennial Message to the Race... Introductory Remarks by Dr. G. Lake Imes. Washington, D. C.: n. p., n. d. DHU/MO

10608. ----- The Race Problem as It Respects the Colored People and the Christian Church, in the Light of the Developments of the Last Year. A Discourse Delivered at a Union Thanksgiving Service Held at the Plymouth Congregational Church, Nov. 17, 1919. Washington, D. C.: n. p., 1919. NN/Sch; DHU/MO
Also in Woodson, Carter G. and Francis James Grimke, Washington, D. C.: Associated Press, 1942.

10609. ----- The Race Problem... Two Suggestions as to its Solution. Washington, D. C.: n. p., 1919. DHU/MO; DLC; DHU/R
Also in Woodson, Carter G. and Francis James Grimke, Washington, D. C.: Associated Press, 1942.

10610. ----- "Racism and Reunion: A Black Protest by Francis James Grimke." Henry Justin Ferry. Journal of Presbyterian History (50:2, Sum., 1972), pp. 77-88. DHU/R

10611. ----- "Segregation." Crisis (41; Je., 1932), pp. 173-4. DHU/MO

10612. ----- The Supreme Court's Decision in Regard to the Scottsboro Case. Washington, D. C.: n. p., n. d. DHU/MO

10613. ----- Theodore Roosevelt. An Address Delivered in the Fifteenth Street Presbyterian Church, Washington, D. C., Feb. 9, 1919. DHU/MO; DHU/R
Also in the Woodson, Carter G., Francis James Grimke, Washington, D. C., Associated Press, 1942.

10614. ----- The Young People of Today and the Responsibility of the Home in Regard to Them. Washington, D. C.: The Presbyterian Council, 1909. DHU/MO

10615. Hagood, Lewis Marahall. "The Southern Problem." The Methodist Review (Bimonthly) (7; My., 1891), pp. 428-34. DHU/R

10616. Hamilton, A. H. In the 20th Century. Alburquerque: n. p., n. d. Pam. File, DHU/R
A Black minister's account of slavery in the 20th Century.

10617. Hamm, Jack. Race... Twenty-Seven Drawings on the Subject of Race Relations. Waco, Texas: Religious Drawings, Inc., 1955. NN/Sch

10618. Hammond, J. D. "The Relation of the Southern White Man to the Education of the Negro in Church Colleges." Arcadius S. Trawick, (ed.). The New Voice in Race Adjustments (New York: Student Volunteer Movement, 1914), pp. 57-61. DHU/R

10619. Hammond, Lilly Hardy. "Human Races and the Race of Man." Methodist Review (Quarterly) (73:4, Oct., 1924), pp. 623-33. DHU/R

10620. Hardy, Arthur W. "Political Forces and the Christian Way." William S. Nelson, (ed.). The Christian Way in Race Relations (New York: Harper and Bros., 1948), pp. 77-96. DHU/R

10621. Harlow, S. Ralph. "The Color Bar in the Churches." Christian Century (47:22, My. 28, 1930), pp. 683-5. DLC; DHU/R

10622. Harris, Eugene. Two Sermons on the Race Problems, Addressed to Young Colored Men, by One of Them. Nashville, Tenn.: n. p., 1895. DHU/MO
Negro author.

10623. Haselden, Kyle Emerson. Mandate for White Christians. Richmond: John Knox Press, 1966. DHU/R; CtY-D; InU; DLC

10624. ----- The Racial Problem in Christian Perspective. New York: Harper, 1959. DHU/R; InU; NN/Sch

10625. Haynes, George Edmund. The Trend of the Races. New York: Council of Women for Home Missions and Missionary Education Movement of the United States and Canada, 1922. DHU/R; CtY-D
Negro author.

10626. ----- "The Unfinished Interracial Task of the Churches." Journal of Religious Thought (2:1, Aut.-Wint., 1945), pp. 53-59. DHU/R

10627. Heckman, Oliver S. Northern Church Penetration into the South, 1860-1880. Doctoral dissertation. Duke University, 1939.

10628. Hefley, J. Theodore. "Freedom Upheld: The Civil Liberties Stance of the Christian Century Between the Wars."

(Hefley, J. Theodore cont.)

Church History (37:2, Je., 1968), pp. 174-94.   DHU/R
An examination of the attitude of the liberal publication
which has been described as "Protestantism's most vigorous voice," towards civil rights issues that confronted
the nation between the two World Wars.

10629. Helm, Mary. The Upward Path: The Evolution of a Race.
New York: Young People's Missionary Movement of the United
States and Canada, 1909. DHU/MO; DLC; NN/Sch; CtY-D;
                                                            DHU/R
Revised edition of "From Darkness to Light."

10630. Henderson, George W. "The Southern Attitude Toward
the Education of the Negro." The Congregationalist (80:43,
Oct. 24, 1895), pp. 602-03.   DHU/R

10631. Herring, Hubert C. "An Adventure in Black and White."
The Christian Century (47:50, Dec. 10, 1930), pp. 1526-29.
                                                    DHU/R; DLC
An American interracial seminar of churchmen met in
nine southern cities and discussed the Negro in America.

10632. Hershberger, Guy Franklin. The Way of the Cross in
Human Relations. Scottdale, Pa.: Herald Pr., 1958. InU
Church and Race Problems, pp. 333-41.

10633. Hill, Samuel S., Jr. and Edgar T. Thompson, et alii.
Religion and the Solid South. Nashville: Abingdon Press,
1972.   DHU/R

10634. Hill, Timothy Arnold. "The Church and Industry." Opportunity (9:1, Ja., 1931), pp. 18-19.   DHU/MO
Negro author.

10635. Hodges, Louis W. Christian Analysis of Selected Contemporary Theories of Racial Prejudice. Doctoral dissertation.
Duke University, 1960.

10636. Holloway, Vernon H. "Christian Faith and Race Relations."
Religion in Life (14:2, Spr., 1945), pp. 340-50.   DHU/R

10637. Holly, James Theodore, (bp.). "The Auspicious Dawn of
Negro Rule." Carter G. Woodson, (ed.). Negro Orators
and Their Orations (Wash., D. C.: Associated Publishers,
1925), pp. 242-47.   DHU/MO; DHU

10638. Holmes, Dwight O. W. The Evolution of the Negro College.
New York: Teachers College, Columbia University, 1934.
                                                    DHU/MO
Negro author.

10639. Holsey, Lucius Henry, (bp.). "Race Segregation."
Washington Conference on the Race Problem in the United
States. National Sociological Society. How to Solve the Race
Problem (Washington, D. C.: Bersford, Printer, 1904),
pp. 40-66.   DHU/R
Bishop of the A. M. E. Church. Contains reaction by
race leaders to the paper. Negro author.

10640. Hood, James Walker, (bp.). "Greatest Need of the Negro
Race." William N. Hartshorn. An Era of Progress and Pro-
mise (Boston: The Priscilla Press, 1910), p. 395. DHU/MO
Includes biography of the author.
Written by A. M. E. Zion bishop.

10641. Houser, George M. "Racism Sits in the Pews." Fellowship (13; Feb., 1947), pp. 26+.   DGW

10642. Howard University, Washington, D. C. School of Religion.
... The Thirty-Fourth Annual Convocation, November 14-18,
1950. Theme: The Church, the State and Human Welfare...
Washington, D. C.: n. p., 1951.   NN/Sch; DHU/R

10643. Howe, Mark DeWolfe. The Garden and the Wilderness.
Religion and Government in American Constitutional History.
Chicago: The University of Chicago Press, 1965. DHU/R
Chapter V, Race, Religion, and Education.

10644. Huntley, Thomas Elliott. As I Saw it, not Communism
but Commonism; a Prophetic Appraisal of the Status Quo, a
Message for All Times, for America and for all Nations. New
York: Comet Press Books, 1955. DHU/MO; DLC; NN/Sch
Negro author.

10645. Imes, William Lloyd. The Black Pastures; An American
Pilgrimage in two Centuries; Essays and Sermons. Nashville:
Tenn.: Hemphill Press, 1957.   NN/Sch
Negro author.

10646. Institute for Religious Studies, Jewish Theological Seminary
of America. ... Civilization and Group Relationships, a Series
of Addresses and Discussions, Edited by R. M. MacIver. New
York: Institute for Religious Studies, Distributed by Harper
& Bros., 1945.   DHU/R; CtY-D
Religion and group tensions by John LaFarge.

10647. Interracial Consultation. 2d. College of the Bible, Lexington, Ky., 1960. Southern Churches and Race Relations;
Report of the Second Interracial Consultation Held at the College of the Bible, July 18-22, 1960. Edited by Lewis S. C.
Smythe. Lexington, Ky.: College of the Bible, 1960.
                                                    CtY-D

10648. "Is the Negro in a Trap?" Christian Century (50:16, Apr.
19, 1933), pp. 520-22.   DHU/R
Editorial on the Scottsboro Case.

10649. Ivy, A. C. and Irwin Ross. Religion and Race: Barriers
to College. New York: Anti-Defamation League of B'nai'B'
rith, 1949. (Public Affairs Pamphlet no. 153).
                            Pam. File, DHU/R

10650. Jack, Homer A. "The Emergence of the Interracial
Church." Social Action (13; Ja. 1947), pp. 31-37. DHU/R

10651. Jacks, M. L. God in Education. London: Rich & Cowan,
1939.   DLC

10652. Jackson, Olive Scott. God in the Flesh. Questions and
Answers About Women Jews, Negroes, and the Church. New
York: William-Frederick Press, 1958.   NN/Sch

10653. Jenkins, John J. The Structure and Function of the American Negro Church in Race Integration. Doctoral dissertation.
Boston, 1952.

10654. "Jim Crows Last Stand." Crisis (57; Je., 1950), pp. 349-
51.   DHU/MO

10655. Johnson, Charles S. Background to Patterns of Negro Segre-
gation. New York: Thomas Y. Crowell Co., 1970. DHU/R
Negro author.
Church Segregation, pp. 198, 276.

10656. ----- "Race Against Humanity." Social Action (9:1, Ja.
15, 1943), pp. 7-19.   DHU/R

10657. Johnson, Guion, Griffis. The Church and the Race Problem in the United States; a Research Memorandum Prepared
by Guion Griffis Johnson and Guy B. Johnson with the Assistance
of Edward Nelson Palmer... New York: n. p., 1940. NN/Sch

10658. Johnson, Henry Theodore. "How Can the Negroes be Induced to Rally More to Negro Enterprises and to Their Professional Men?" Daniel W. Culp. Twentieth Century Negro
Literature (Miami, Fla.: Mnemosyne Publishing Co., Inc.,
1969), pp. 186-89.   DHU/MO
Reprint of 1902 edition.
Written by A. M. E. minister, educator, author and
journalist.

10659. Johnson, Livingston. "Churches on Lynching." Biblical
Recorder (96; Nov. 5, 1930), p. 7.   LNB; NcWfSB

10660. ----- "The Crumbling Color Line." Editorial. Biblical
Recorder (95; Ag. 14, 1929), p. 7.   LNB; TND

10661. Johnson, William Decker, Sr., (bp.). Past and Present of the Negro Race in America. Everett, Mass.: n. p., 1897.
MH; TNF
Written by an A. M. E. bishop.

10662. Jones, David D. "Democracy, Race and the Church Related College." Zions Herald (118; Feb. 7, 1940), p. 125.
DLC; CtY-D

10663. Jordan, Winthrop D. The White Man's Burden: Historical Origins of Racism in the United States. New York: Oxford Univ. Press, 1974.   DHU/R
Chapter 5, "The Souls of Men: The Negro's Spiritual Nature."

10664. Kaplan, Harry. "Race Relations in College." Religious Education (59:1, Ja.-Feb., 1964), pp. 111-13.   DHU/R

10665. Kastler, Norman M. "The Church and the Color Line." Opportunity (10:1, Ja., 1932), pp. 8-11.   DHU/MO

10666. Kelsey, George D. "The Christian Way in Race Relations." Wm. S. Nelson, (ed.). The Christian Way in Race Relations (New York: Harper & Bros., 1948), pp. 29-48.   DHU/R
Negro author.

10667. Kennedy, Louise V. The Negro Peasant Turns Cityward: Effects of Recent Migrations to Northern Centers. New York: Columbia University Press, 1930.   DHU/R
The Church and the Migrant, pp. 202-06.

10668. King, Willis, J., (bp.). The Negro in American Life: An Elective Course. New York: The Methodist Book Concern, 1926.   PCC; JiU; NN; PP; PPE
For young people on Christian race relationships. Negro author.

10669. Kitagawa, Daisuke. "Christianity and Race." World Christian Handbook (London: Dominion Press, 1962), pp. 5-9.   DHU/R

10670. ----- "The Chruch and Race Relations in Biblical Perspective." Religious Education (59:1, Ja.-Feb., 1964), pp. 7-10.
DHU/R

10671. Knox, Ellis O. The Trend of Progress in the Light of New Educational Concepts in a Group of American Colleges Dominated by Religious Influences. Doctoral dissertation, University of Southern California, 1931.

10672. Kramer, Alfred S. Patterns of a Racial Inclusion Among Selected Congregations of Three Protestant Denominations: An Analysis of the Processes Through Which Congregations of Portestant Denominations Have Included Persons of Racial and Cultural Minority Groups. Doctoral dissertation. New York University, 1955.   DLC
Abstract, Phylon (16; Sum., 1955), pp. 283-97. DHU/MO

10673. "Ku Klux Klan Visits Chicago Church." Editorial. The Christian Century (39:39, Sept. 28, 1922), p. 1200. DHU/R

10674. Kyles, Josephine H. "Is There a Place for Church Supported School in the Life of the Negro?" The Negro Journal of Religion (4:6, Jl., 1938); (4:7, Ag., 1938), pp. 9; 5.   DHU/R
Negro author.

10675. La Farge, John. "How the Churches Suffer." R. M. MacIver, (ed.). Discrimination and National Welfare: A Series of Addresses and Discussions. Port Washington, N. Y.: Kennikat Press, 1969. pp. 77-81.   DHU/R

10676. Lambert, Rollin E. "Race Relations on the Campus." Religious Education (59:1, Ja.-Feb., 1964), pp. 114-16.
DHU/R

10677. Leavell, Ullin Whitney. Philanthropy in Negro Education. Nashville, Tenn.: George Peabody College for Teachers, 1930.
NN/Sch
Church and education.

10678. Lee, Davis. "A Negro Looks at Racial Issues." Southern Presbyterian Journal (8; Oct. 15, 1948), p. 5. DLC; KyLxCB

10679. Lee, Frank F. Negro and White in a Connecticut Town. New York: Bookman Associates, 1961.   CtY-D
"Based upon the writer's unpublished Doctoral dissertation... Yale University, 1953."

10680. Lee, J. Oscar. "Racial Inclusion in Church Related Colleges in the South." Journal of Negro Education (22; Win., 1953), pp. 16-25.   DHU
Negro author.

10681. Leek, Charles F. "Segregation or Subjugation." The Alabama Baptist (111; Nov. 28, 1946), p. 4.   LNB; TND

10682. Leftwich, W. M. "The Race Problem in the South." Quarterly Review (Methodist Episcopal Church, South), (6; Apr. 1889), p. 94.   DLC; CtY-D

10683. Lieffer, Murray H. "Segregation in Churches." Central Christian Advocate (131:8, Apr. 15, 1956), pp. 6-8. DHU/R

10684. Leiper, Henry. Blind Spots, Experiments in the Self-Cure of Race Prejudice. New York: Friendship Press, 1929. DHU/R
See Chapter VI, "Getting the Golden Rule Angle" written by an officer of The American Missionary Association.

10685. Leonard, Joseph T. Theology and Race Relations. Doctoral dissertation. Catholic University of America, 1963.

10686. Little, Sara. Youth Guide on Race Relations. New York: Friendship Press, 1957.   NN/Sch; DLC

10687. Loescher, Frank S. The Protestant Church and the Negro: A Pattern of Segregation. New York: Association Press, 1948.
DHU/R; INU; CtY-D

10688. ----- "The Protestant Church and the Negro: Recent Pronouncement." Social Force (26; Dec., 1947), pp. 197-201.
DAU; DCU/SW

10689. Logan, Rayford W. What the Negro Wants. Chapel Hill: The University of North Carolina Press, 1944.   DHU/R
Chapters on the church and race relations.

10690. Lord, Samuel Ebenezer Churchstone. God in a Troubled World. Amherst, Nova Scotia: News Sentinel Press, 1948.
NN/Sch
Negro author.

10691. MacArthur, Kathleen W. The Bible and Human Rights. New York: Woman's Press, 1959.   DHU/R
Chapter, The Biblical bases of human rights.

10692. Macklin, John M. Democracy and Race Friction. A Study in Social Ethics. New York: Macmillan Co., 1914. DHU/MO
pp. 41-43 Religious prejudice.

10693. Maffett, Robert Lee. The Kingdom Within, A Study of the American Race Problem and its Solution. New York: Exposition Press, 1955.   NN/Sch; DHU/R
Negro author.

10694. Manschreck, Clyde L. "Religion in the South: Problem and Promise." Francis B. Simkins, (ed.). The South in Perspective, Institute of Southern Culture Lectures at Longwood College, 1958. Farmville, Va.: Longwood College, 1959.   DLC

10695. Maritain, Jacques. "The Menace of Racialism." Interracial Review (10; 1937), pp. 70-71.   DCU/SW

10696. Markoe, John P. "A Moral Appraisal of the Color Line." Homiletic and Pastoral Review (48; 1948), pp. 828-36. DGU

10697. Martin, J. G. and F. W. Westie. "The Tolerant Personality." American Sociological Review (24; 1959), pp. 521-28.   DHU
Attempts to prove there is no relationship between religiosity and prejudice.

10698. Masters, Victor I. "Friendship and Social Apartness of Races in the South." Editorial. Western Recorder (112; Jl. 14, 1938), p. 6.   IObNB; KyLoS; LNB; TND

10699. ----- "Southern Christians and the Negro Problem." Editorial. Western Recorder (109; Nov. 28, 1935), p. 7. LNB; TND

10700. Maston, Thomas Bufford. Segregation and Desegregation: a Christian Approach. New York: Macmillan, 1959. CtY-D

10701. Mayer, M. "The Jim Crow Christ." Negro Digest (13; Feb. 1964), pp. 28-31.   DHU/MO

10702. Mayo, Amory D. The Work of Certain Northern Churches in the Education of the Freedmen, 1862-1900. Washington: Goot Printing Office, 1903.   DHU/MO; NN/Sch

10703. Mays, Benjamin Elijah. "A Centennial Commencement Address: Higher Education and the American Negro." Journal of Religious Thought (24:2, Aut.-Wint., 1967-68), pp. 4-12.   DHU/R

10704. ----- The Christian in Race Relations. West Haven, Conn.: Promoting Enduring Peace, Inc., 1952.   CtY-D
       Negro author.
       Lecture given at the Yale Divinity School.

10705. ----- "Christian Youth and Race." The Crisis (46:12, Dec., 1939), pp. 364-65; 370.   DLC; DHU/MO

10706. ----- "Christianizing and Democratizing America in This Generation." Journal of Negro Education (14:4, Fall, 1945), pp. 527-34.   DHU/MO
       Commencement address, Howard University, June 8, 1945.

10707. ----- "The Church and Racial Tensions." Christian Century (71:36, Sept., 1954), pp. 1068-69.   DHU/R

10708. ----- "In Pursuit of Freedom." The African Methodist Episcopal Church Review (80:219, Ja.-Mr., 1964), pp. 25-38.   DHU/R

10709. ----- "A Look at the Black Colleges." Foundations (17:3, Jl.-Sept., 1974), pp. 237-46.   DHU/R

10710. ----- "Obligation of Negro Christians in Relation to an Inter-racial Program." Journal of Religious Thought (2:1, Aut.-Wint., 1945), pp. 42-52.   DHU/R

10711. ----- "Present Status of and Future Outlook for Racial Integration in the Church Related White Colleges in the South." Journal of Negro Education (21; Sum., 1952), pp. 350-52.   DHU

10712. ----- "Realities in Race Relations." Christian Century (48:12, Mr. 25, 1931), pp. 404-06.   DHU/R

10713. ----- Seeking to Be Christian in Race Relations. New York: Friendship Press, 1946.   DLC; DHU/R; DHU/MO

10714. ----- "The South's Racial Policy." Presbyterian Outlook (132; Nov. 6, 1950), p. 5.   NN/Sch; DLC; NcD

10715. ----- "The Training of Negro Ministers." National Outlook Among Negroes (3:2, Nov.-Dec., 1939), pp. 16+. DHU/MO

10716. ----- "World Aspects of Race and Culture." Missions (147:2, Feb. 1949), pp. 83-7.   Pam. File; DHU/R

10717. McAfee, Joseph Ernest. "Church and Race Relations." Opportunity (7:2, Feb., 1929), pp. 39-41.   DHU/MO

10718. McColl, C. W. The Holy Ghost in the Church and in the Hearts of Believers. Germantown, Philadelphia: Press of the Germantown Telegraph Co., 1903.   DHU/MO

10719. McCreary, Edward Daniel, Jr. The Church and Race Prejudice. Bachelor of Divinity paper. Andover Newton Theological School, 1943.

10720. McCulloh, James E. "Cooperation of White and Negro Ministers for Social Service." Arcadius S. Trawick, (ed.). The New Voice in Race Adjustments (New York: Student Volunteer Movement, 1914), pp. 188-94.   DHU/R

10721. McDonough, John. "Manuscript Resources for the Study of Negro Life and History." Quarterly Journal of the Library of Congress (26:3, Jl., 1969), pp. 126-48.

10722. McDowell, Edward A. "The Color Line." Biblical Recorder (107; Apr. 2, 1941), p. 6.   LNB

10723. ----- "The Social Gospel of the New Testament." The Baptist Courier (66; Dec. 13, 1934), p. 8.   LNB; NcWfSB

10724. ----- Southern Churches and the Negroes. n.p., 194-?
                                                   CtY-D

10725. McGinnis, Frederick A. The Education of Negroes in Ohio. Wilberforce, O.: n.p., 1962.   DHU/MO
       pp. 15-29, sec. The Attitudes of religious denominations, p. 26-29.

10726. McGrath, Oswin. "The Theology of Racial Segregation." Catholic Mind (55; 1957), pp. 483-86.   DCU/TH

10727. McKeon, Richard M. "Social Attitudes and the Negro." St. Augustine's Messenger (31:7, Sept. 1954), pp. 222-25, 236+.   DHU/R

10728. McKinley, Carlyle. An Appeal to Pharaoh: The Negro Problem, and its Radical Solution. 3rd ed. Westport, Conn.: Negro Universities Press, 1970.   DHU/R
       Originally published in 1907 by the State Co., Columbia, S.C.

10729. McKinney, Richard I. Religion in Higher Education Among Negroes. New Haven: Yale University Press, 1945. DHU/R; DLC
       Negro author.

10730. McNeill, Robert B. God Wills Us Free: the Ordeal of a Southern Minister. Intro. by Ralph McGill. New York: Hill and Wang, 1965.   DLC; INU; DHU/MO
       Story of a white minister dismissed from his pulpit because of his stand on segregation.

10731. Meier, August. Negro Racial Thought in the Age of Booker T. Washington, circa 1880-1915... Doctoral dissertation. Columbia University, 1957.   NN/Sch
       Church and race relations, pt. 5.

10732. Mett, John Raleigh. Strategic Points in the World's Conquest; the Universities and Colleges as Related to the Progress of Christianity. Chicago: Fleming H. Revell Company, 1897.   NN/Sch

10733. Miller, George Frazier. A Discussion: Is Religion Reasonable? Mr. Clarence Darrow Says Not to the Blackman... Bishop Jones Says Yes... Brooklyn: The Henne Press, n.d. DHU/MO
       Negro author.

10734. Miller, Kelly. Radicals and Conservatives. New York: Sch Schocken Books, 1968.   DHU/R
       Negro author.
       Reprint of earlier edition.
       A chapter on religion as a solvent of the race problem.

10735. ----- Religion and Race.   DHU/MO
       Reprint: Student World. Geneva: Societe D'Imprimerie D'Ambilly-Annemasse (Haute-Savore), 1926.
       Negro author.

10736. ----- "Why Leave the Negro Out?" Christian Century (48:3, Ja. 21, 1931), pp. 89-90.   DHU/R
       Deals with Negro participation in Prohibition.

10737. Miller, Robert M. American Protestantism and Social Issues, 1919-1934. Chapel Hill: University of North Carolina Press, 1958.   DHU/R; INU; NN/Sch

10738. ----- The Attitudes of American Protestantism Toward the Negro." Journal of Negro History (41:3, Jl., 1956), pp. 215-40. DHU/MO

10739 ----- "The Protestant Churches and Lynching." Journal of Negro History (42:2, Apr., 1957), pp. 18-31. DHU/MO

10740. Mitchell, Edward Cushing. "Higher Education and the Negro." An Address Delivered before the American Baptist Home Mission Society, May 26, 1896. DHU; NH

10741-42. Montgomery, Ray. "Jim Crow Among the Christians." The Progressive (17; Ja., 1953), pp. 37-8.
Unable to locate.

10743. Moore, George W. The Redemptive Work for the Negro. n.p.: n.p., n.d. NN/Sch
In Lend a Hand (7:5, 1896), pp. 355-61.
Negro author.

10744. Mosely, Charles C., (Mrs.). The Negro in Mississippi History. Jackson, Miss.: Hederman Brothers, 1950. TN/DCHS

10745. Moton, Robert R. What the Negro Thinks. Garden City, N.Y.: Doubleday, Doran and Co., 1930. CtY-D
Negro author.

10746. Moxom, Philip Stafford. Our Problem with the Negro in America; Sermon by Rev. Philip S. Moxom, Delivered at the Fifty-Seventh Annual Meeting of the American Missionary Association, held in Cleveland, Ohio, October 20, 1903. New York: C. Holt, Printer, 1903. NN/Sch

10747. Murphy, Edgar Gardiner. The Basis of Ascendency. New York: Longmans Green & Co., 1909. DHU/MO
A Christian approach to the race problem.

10748. Muste, Abraham John. What the Bible Teaches About Freedom; A Message to the Negro Churches. New York

10749. Myer, Gustavus. History of Bigotry in the United States. New York: Random House, 1943. CtY-D

10750. National Educational Assembly, Ocean Grove, N.J. Christian Educators in Council. Sixty Addresses by American Educators; with Historical Notes Upon the National Education Assembly held at Ocean Grove, N.J., August 9-12, 1883. Also Illeteracy and Education Tables from Census of 1880. Compiled and Edited by Rev. J. C. Hartzell, D.D. New York: Phillips & Hunt; Cincinnati: Cranston & Stowe, 1883. NN/Sch

10751. "Negro Christians Face a Grave Decision." Christian Century (52; Sept. 11, 1935), pp. 1134-5. DHU/R

10752. "Negro Education Improving, But not for Ministry." Christian Century (45:48, Nov. 29, 1928), p. 1448. DLC; DHU/R

10753. Nelson, John O. "New Testament Power for Social Change." Journal of Religious Thought (15:1, Aut.-Wint., 1957-58), pp. 5-14. DHU/R

10754. Nelson, William Stuart. Bases of World Understanding, An Inquiry Into the Means of Resolving Racial, Religious, Class, and National Misapprehensions and Conflicts. /Baliygunge, Calcutta/ Calcutta University, 1949. DHU/R
Negro author.

10755. ----- "The Image of the College and World Trends." The African Methodist Episcopal Church Review (78:217, Jl.-Sept., 1963), pp. 39-46. DHU/R
Negro author.

10756. ----- "Our Racial Situation in the Light of the Judeo-Christian Tradition." Repr. of Religious Education (Mr.-Apr., 1944), pp. 74-77. Pam. File, DHU/R
Negro author.

10757. ----- "Religion and Racial Tension in America Today." Conference on Science, Philosophy and Religion. (New York:

Harper, 1945). DHU/R
Negro author.
Also in, Journal of Religious Thought (2:2, Spr.-Sum., 1945), pp. 164-78. DHU/R

10758. Newby, Idus. Jim Crow's Defense. Baton Rouge, La.: University of Louisiana Press, 1965. DHU/R
Bible justification for segregation.

10759. Oldham, Joseph Houldsworth. Christianity and the Race Problem. New York: Doran, 1925. DHU/R; NN/Sch

10760. Olson, Bernard E. Faith and Prejudice. Intergroup Problems in Protestant Chruches. New Haven: Yale University Press, 1963. DHU/R
Review, Commentary (35; My., 1963), pp. 455-60. DHU
Reply: Olson, B. E. Commentary (36; Sept., 1963), pp. 197-9. DHU

10761. Orr, Elbert L. "The Church and Race Relations." Southern Workman (55:11, Nov., 1926), pp. 489-94. DLC; DHU/MO

10762. Orrell, Julian Stokes. An Inquiry into the Moral Aspects of the Race Problem. Masters thesis. Southern Baptist Theological Seminary, 1956.

10763. Orser, W. Edward. "Racial Attitudes in Wartime: the Protestant Churches During the Second World War." Church History (41:3, Sept., 1972), pp. 337-53. DHU/R

10764. Orton, Hazel V. The American Negro: A Series of Worship Services to be Used in the Junior Department of the Church. New York: Methodist Book Concern, 1929. NN/Sch

10765. "Outlaw Color Segregation." Christian Century (63; Ag. 21, 1946), pp. 1010-11. DHU/R

10766. Owen, Robert Russell. Christianity and Race Relations, a Study of the Negro-White Problem. Bachelor of Divinity Paper. Andover Newton Theological School, 1943.

10767. Parker, J. Kenton. "Christian Relations Among Races." Southern Presbyterian Journal (10; Ag. 22, 1951), p. 7. DLC; KyLXCB

10768. Parry, H. J. "Protestants, Catholics and Prejudice." International Journal for Opinion and Attitude Research (3; 1949), pp. 205-13. DLC

10769. Parsons, Talcott. "Racial and Religious Differences as Factors in Group Tensions." Conference on Science, Philosophy and Religion, A Symposium (New York: Harper, 1945, vol. 5). DHU/R

10770. Paschal, George W. "Another Phase of the Race Problem." Editorial. Biblical Recorder (104; Jl. 20, 1938), p. 7. LNB; TND

10771. Paton, Alan. "The Person in Community." Edmund Fuller, (ed.). The Christian Idea (New Haven: Yale University Press, 1957), pp. 101-24. DHU/R; CtY-D

10772. Payne, Buckner H. The Negro: What is His Ethnological Status? Is He the Progeny of Ham? Is He a Descendant of Adam and Eve? ...What is His Relation to the White Race? Enl., With A Review of His Reviewers, Exhibiting the Learning of "The Learned." By Ariel, Pseud... Cincinnati: Pub. for the Proprietor, 1872. DHU/MO

10773. Pearne, Thomas H. "The Race Problem--The Situation." Methodist Quarterly Review (71; Sept.-Oct., 1890), pp. 690-705. DLC; CtY-D

10774. Pennington, James W. C. A Textbook of the Origin and History...of the Colored People (Hartford: Skinner, Printer, 1841). DHU/MO
Xerox copy.

10775. Perry, Rufus Lewis. The Cushite; or, The Descendants of Ham as Found in the Sacred Scriptures, and in the Writings of Ancient Historians and Poets from Noah to the Christian Era. Springfield, Mass.: Wiley & Co., 1893. DHU/MO;
OWibfU; DLC
Negro author.

10776. Peterson, Frank L. The Hope of the Race. Nashville, Tenn.: Southern Publishing Association, 1934.   DHU/MO

10777. Pettigrew, Thomas F. "Regional Differences in Anti-Negro Prejudice." Journal of Abnormal and Social Psychology (59; 1959), pp. 28-36.   DHU; DAU

10778. ----- "Wherein the Church has Failed in Race." Religious Education (59:1, Ja.-Feb., 1964), pp. 64-75. DAU/W; DCU/TH;
DHU/R

10779. Phillips, Randolph. The Use of the Bible in Contemporary Interpretations of Race Relations by Selected Writers in the United States. Masters thesis. Southeastern Baptist Theological Seminary, 1960.

10780. Pickens, William. "Christianity as a Basis of Common Citizenship." Arcadius Trawick, (ed.) The New Voice in Race Adjustments. (New York: Student Volunteer Movement, 1914), pp. 34-40.   DHU/R
Negro author.

10781. Pike, Esther, (ed.). Who is My Neighbor? Greenwich, Conn.: Seabury Press, 1960.   NN/Sch
"The Subjugated, by Michael Schoot, pp. 215-30.

10782. Pinch, Pearse. "The Color Line in Worship: Testimony of the Educated Negro." Andover Review (7:41, My., 1887), pp. 491-504.   DHU/R

10783. Plecker, W. A. "Interracial Brotherhood Movement, Is It Scriptual?" Southern Presbyterian Journal (5; Ja. 1, 1947), pp. 9-10.   DLC; KyLxCB

10784. Pope, Liston. "Caste in the Church: The Protestant Experience." Survey Graphics (36; Ja., 1947), pp. 59+.
DHU

10785. ----- "A Check of Procedures for Racial Integration." Social Action (13:1, Ja. 1947), pp. 38-43.   DHU/R
Discusses what churches can do to aid integration.

10786. Powdermaker, Hortense. "The Channeling of Negro Aggression by the Cultural Progress." Clyde Kluckhohn and Henry A. Murray, (eds.). Personality in Nature, Society, and Culture (New York: Alfred A. Knopf, 1949), pp. 473-84.   DHU/R

10787. Powell, Adam Clayton, Jr. Marching Blacks. New York: Dial Press, 1945.   DHU/MO
Negro author.

10788. Powell, Raphael Philemon. The Prayer for Freedom: a Memorial of the Prayer Pilgrimage, May 14, 1957. New York: n.p., 1957.   DHU/MO
Negro author.

10789. Price, Joseph C., (bp.). "The Race Problem Stated." Carter G. Woodson. Negro Orators and Their Orations (New York: Russell & Russell, 1969), pp. 448-501. DHU/R

10790. Price, Thomas. Christianity and Race Relations. London: SCM Press, 1954.   NN/Sch; CtY-D

10791. "The Protestant Ku Klux Klan." Editorial. The Christian Century (39:10, Mr. 9, 1922), pp. 293-94.   DHU/R

10792. Prothro, E. Terry and John A. Jensen, et alii. "A Comparison of Ethnic Attitudes of College Students and Middle Class Adults from the Same State." Journal of Social Psychology (36; 1952), pp. 53-58.   DHU
Finds no relationship between religiosity and prejudice.

10793. ----- "Comparison of Some Ethnic and Religious Attitudes of Negro and White College Students in the Deep South." Social Forces (30:4, My., 1952), pp. 426-28.   DHU

10794. Queen, Stuart A. and D. B. Carpenter. The American City. New York: McGraw-Hill Book Co., Inc., 1953.   DLC
Social stratification and religion.

10795. "Race and the Christian." United Church of Christ. 70 frames, color.
Filmstrip.

10796. "Race Relations and Religious Education." Religious Education (59:1, Ja.-Feb., 1964), p. 2.   DHU/R

10797. "Racial Christianity." Time (48; Dec. 9, 1946), p. 73.
DHU

10798. "Racial Prejudice on the Increase." The Christian Century (39:22, Ag. 10, 1922), p. 989.   DHU/R

10799. "Racial Questions in Process of Solution in South." Editorial. The Christian Century (39:35, Ag. 31, 1922), p. 1078.   DHU/R
Commission on Interracial Cooperation is the first sign of a solution.

10800. "Racism Seen as Emerging from Planned Effect; Denounced by Protestant Leaders." Interchurch News (1; Feb., 1960), p. 3.   DLC

10801. Randolph, A. Philip. "The Negro in American Democracy." Social Action (9:1, Ja. 15, 1943), pp. 22-29.   DHU/R
Discusses among other topics the "Un-Christian Practices" of the White Church.
Negro author.

10802. Ransom, Reverdy Cassius, (bp.). John Greenleaf: A Plea for Political Equality. Centennial Oration...in Faneuil Hall, 1907. Boston: n.p., n.d.   NcD

10803. ----- "The Negro and Socialism." A. M. E. Church Review (13; Oct., 1896), pp. 192-200.   DLC
Written by forty-eighth Bishop of the A. M. E. Church.

10804. ----- The Negro: The Hope and Despair of Christianity. Boston, Mass.: Ruth Hill Publisher, 1935.   NN/Sch

10805. Read, Margaret. "Inter-Group Relations--The Church Amid Racial and Ethnic Tensions." Ecumenical Review (6:1, Oct., 1953), pp. 40-7.   DHU/R

10806. Reid, Ira De A. "The Chruch and Education for Negroes." Trevor Bowen. Divine White Right. A Study of Race Segregation and Interracial Cooperation in Religious Organizations and Institutions. (New York: Harper & Bros., 1934). DHU/MO
Negro author.

10807. "Report on the Special Seminar on: The Spiritual Implications of Race and Culture." Social Action (9:1, Ja. 15, 1943), pp. 37-43.   DHU/R

10808. A Resemblance and a Contrast Between the American Negro and the Children of Israel in Egypt; or, the Duty of the Negro to Contend Earnestly for His Rights Guaranteed Under Constitution. n.p.: n.p., 1902.   DHU/MO

10809. Richards, James McDowell. "The Golden Rule and Racial Relationship." Presbyterian Outlook (129; Apr. 21, 1947), pp. 5-6.   NN/Sch; NcD; DLC

10810. Ridout, Lionel U. "The Church, the Chinese and the Negroes in California, 1849-1892." Historical Magazine (28:2, Je., 1959), pp. 115-38.   DHU

10811. Riley, Benjamin Franklin. The White Man's Burden; a Discussion of the Interracial Question with Special Reference to the Responsibility of the White Race to the Negro Problem. New York: Negro Universities Press, 1969.   DHU/R

Originally published in 1910.
Discusses the duty of organized religion to help solve the race problem.

10812. Roberts, James Deotis. "The Christian Conscience and Legal Discrimination." The Journal of Religious Thought (19:2, 1962-63), pp. 157-61.   DHU/R
"A careful examination of the nature of the 'Christian conscience' both in life and thought."
Negro author.

10813. Robertson, William J. The Changing South. New York: Boni and Liveright, 1927.   DLC

10814. Robinson, James Herman. "Social Practices and the Christian Way." William S. Nelson, (ed.). The Christian Way in Race Relations. (New York: Harper & Bros., Publishers, 1948), pp. 97-108.   DHU/R; DHU/MO
Negro author.

10815. Robinson, William C. "Christ Our Peace in Race Relations." Southern Presbyterian Journal (4; Jl., 1945). DLC; DyLxCB

10816. Rokeach, Milton. "Political and Religious Dogmatism: An Alternate to the Authritarian Personality." Psychological Monographs (70:18, 1956), pp. 1-43.   DHU

10817. Roman, Charles Victor. "Racial Self-Respect and Racial Antagonism." Methodist Review (Quarterly) (62:4, Oct., 1913), pp. 768-77.   DHU/R
Negro author.

10818. ----- Science and Christian Ethic. Part I. Statement of Principles. Part II. Religion a Necessity to Man; Defense of a Creed. Part III. Racial Antagonism; Principles Applied to the Solution of a Socioethico-economic Condition. n. p., 1943.
DHU/MO; NN/Sch

10819. Roosevelt, Eleanor. "Race, Religion and Prejudice." New Republic (106; My., 1942), pp. 630+.   DHU

10820. "The Roots of Immorality in Race Relations." Religious Education (58; Mr.-Apr., 1963), pp. 91-6.   DHU/R

10821. Rose, Arnold M. The Negro's Morale. St. Paul: University of Minnesota Press, 1949.   DHU/R

10822. Rose, Stephen C. "Religion and Race." Christianity and Crisis (23; Feb. 4, 1963), pp. 39-43.   DHU/R

10823. Rosenblum, A. L. "Ethnic Prejudice as Related to Social Class and Religiosity." Sociology and Social Research (43; 1948), pp. 272-75.   DHU

10824. Rowland, Stanley J. "Jim Crow in Church." Nation (182; My. 19, 1956), pp. 426-8.   DHU

10825. Sanford, Elias B., (ed.). Church Federation. Inter-Church Conference on Federation. New York: Fleming H. Revell Co., 1906.   DAU/R
Bishop W. B. Derrick, Negro made a plea for White sympathy for the Negro, pp. 520-24.

10826. Scarlett, William, (bp.). Toward a Better World. Philadelphia: Winston, 1946.   NN/Sch
The Negro problem, pp. 43-52.

10827. Schuyler, G. S. "Black America Begins to Doubt." American Mercury (25; Apr., 1932), pp. 423-30.   DHU

10828. Sease, Rosalyn Summer. Adult Guide on Christ, the Church, and Race. New York: Friendship Press, 1957.   NN/Sch

10829. "Segregation and the Churches." Time (65; Je. 30, 1955), pp. 54+.   DHU

10830. Sellers, James E. The South and Christian Ethics. New York: Association Press, 1962.   DHU/R; INU; CtY-D

10831. Shaffer, Helen B. "Segregation in Churches." Brief of Report Issued Sept. 3, 1954. Editorial Research Reports (2: 11, Sept. 3, 1954).   Pam. File, DHU/R

10832. Shaner, Donald Wayne. The Marxian Doctrine and Practice of Race Relations in the Light of the Theology of Reinhold Niebuhr. Doctoral dissertation. Drew University, 1970.

10833. Shannon, Alexander Harvey. The Racial Integrity of the American Negro. Washington, D. C.: Public Affairs Press, 1953.   NN/Sch

10834. Shaw, Alexander P. Christianizing Race Relation as a Negro Sees It. Los Angeles: Wetzer Pub. Co., 1928.
DHU/MO
Negro author.

10835. Sheerin, John B. "Is Segregation at the End of Its Rope?" Catholic World (183; Apr., 1956), pp. 1-5.   DHU/R

10836. Sherman, Anthony C. "A Virginian's Shame." Religious Education (59:1, Ja.-Feb., 1964), pp. 97-100.   DHU/R
A critique on the Church's silence in the face of segregation in Virginia.

10837. Sheild, R. N. "A Southern View of the Race Question." Quarterly Review Methodist Episcopal Church, South (8; Jl., 1890), p. 335.   DLC; CtY-D

10838. Silver, Abba Hillel. "America's Minority Groups in War and Peace." Social Action (9:1, Ja. 15, 1943), pp. 30-6.
Pam. File, DHU/R

10839. Simms, James. "The Union of White Methodism." Crisis (20; My., 1920), pp. 14-17.   DHU/MO

10840. Simons, Norman G. "Origin of the Negro." Message Magazine (35:4, Jl., 1969), pp. 12+.   DHU/R

10841. Simpson, Geoge Eaton and J. Milton Yinger. Racial and Cultural Minorities, An Analysis of Prejudice and Discrimination. New York: The Macmillan Co., 1944.   DHU/R
Chapter 18, Minorities and religion.

10842. Simpson, J. David. "Non-Segregation Means Eventual Inter-Marriage." Southern Presbyterian Journal (6; Mr. 15, 1948).   DLC

10843. Smith, Charles Spencer, (bp.). Lecture. "A Hot Time in the Old Town Tonight; or The Conflict Between John and Tony." A Review of the "Race Question" from 1620 to the Present. Nashville: n. p., 1899.   TNF

10844. ----- Race Question Reviewed. Nashville: n. p., 1899.
TNF
Written by twenty-eighth bishop of the A. M. E. Church.

10845. Smith Hilrie Shelton. In His Image, But...: Racism in Southern Religion, 1780-1910. Durham, N. C.: Duke University Press, 1972.   DHU/R

10846. Smith, Lillian. "Humans in Bondage." Social Action (10:2, Feb. 15, 1944), pp. 6-29.   DHU/R
A discussion of effects of prejudice. Includes a section, "The Church must dream a new dream."

10847. ----- There Are Things to Do. Clayton, Ga.: n. p., 1943. Reprinted from South Today (Wint., 1943).   DHU/MO
Religion and race.

10848. Smith, Robert Edwin. Christianity and the Race Problem. New York: Fleming H. Revell Co., 1922. DHU/MO; CtY-D

10849. Sperry, Willard Learoyd, (ed.). Religion and our Racial Tensions; One of a Series of Volumes on Religion in the Post-War World. By Clyde Kluckhohn, Everett R. Clincy, Edwin R. Embree and Others... Cambridge: Harvard University Press, 1945.   DHU/R; CtY-D

10850. Spilka, Bernard and J. Reynolds. "Religion and Prejudice: A Factor Analytic Study." Review of Religious Research (6; 1965), pp. 163-68.   DHU/R

10851. "The Spiritual Implication of Race and Culture in Our Democracy." Social Action (9:1, Ja. 15, 1943), pp. 20-21.   DHU/R
     Findings of a meeting in Cleveland, Ohio, Dec. 8-9, 1942, sponsored by "Eight Cooperating Interdenominational Bodies."

10852. Spoerl, D. T. "Some Aspects of Prejudice as Affected by Religion and Education." Social Psychology (33; 1951), pp. 69-76.   DAU

10853. Stirewalt, M. L. "Observations on the Church and Segregation." Lutheran Quarterly (9; Ag., 1957), pp. 254-59.   DHU/R

10854. Stoutmeyer, John Howard. Religion and Race Education. Doctoral dissertation. Clark University, 1910.

10855. Street, Elwood. "Southern Social Problems." Southern Workman (46:9, Sept., 1917), pp. 473-8.   DLC; DHU/MO
     "Wartime social problems vied with the questions of race relations and the participation of the church in social service, as the chief concerns in the minds of the delegates and speakers from 26 states who attended the Sixth Annual Southern Sociological Congress, held in Blue Ridge and Ashville, North Carolina, July 30 to August 3."

10856. Stringfellow, William. "Idolatry in Our Churches." Together (8; Sept. 1964), pp. 14+.   DAU/W
     Written by an Episcopalian layman.

10857. Tanenbaum, Marc H. "The American Negro: Myths and Realities." Religious Education (59:1, Ja.-Feb., 1964), pp. 33-36.   DHU/R

10858. Tarplee, Cornelius C. "Education and the Challenge of Prejudice." Religious Education (59:1, Ja.-Feb., 1964), pp. 47-9.   DHU/R

10859. Taylor, Alva W. "Inter-Racial Conciliation in the South." The Christian Century (39:17, Apr. 27, 1922), pp. 531-32.   DHU/R
     Attempts to translate the ethics of Christianity into the the race situation.

10860. ----- "The Ku Klux Klan." The Christian Century (39:27, Jl. 6, 1922), pp. 850-51.   DHU/R

10861. ----- "What Color Is the Church?" Christian Century (43:6, Feb. 11, 1926), pp. 175-76.   DHU/R

10862. "Teens Talk About Race, Religion and Prejudice." Negro Digest (11; Jan., 1962), pp. 71-81.   DHU/MO

10863. Thomas, George Finger. Christian Ethics and Moral Philosophy New York: Scribner, 1955.   NN/Sch; DHU/R
     Chapter. Race Problems and Christianity.

10864. Thompson, Edgar T. and A. M. Race and Religion: A Descriptive Bibliography compiled with Special Reference to the Relations between Whites and Blacks in the United States. Chapel Hill: University of North Carolina Press, 1949.

10865. Thompson, James J., Jr. "Erskine Caldwell and Southern Religion." Southern Humanities Review (5:1, Wint., 1971), pp. 33-43.   DLC

10866. Thompson, John Harry. The Negro Problem in Light of New Testament Teachings. B. D. Thesis. Graduate Seminary, Phillips University, 1932.

10867. Thurman, Howard. "God and the Race Problem." Rufus M. Jones. Together (Nashville: Abingdon-Cokesbury Press, 1946), pp. 118-20.   DHU/R; DHU/MO
     Negro author.

10868. ----- Jesus and the Disinherited. New York: Abingdon-Cokesbury Press, 1949.   DHU/R

10869. ----- "Judgement and Hope in the Christian Message." William S. Nelson, (ed.). The Christian Way in Race Relations. (New York: Harper & Bros., 1948), pp. 229-35.   DHU/R

10870. ----- The Luminous Darkness; a Personal Interpretation of the Anatomy of Segregation and the Ground of Hope. New York: Harper & Row, 1965.   DHU/R; DLC; INU; CtY-D
     Negro author.

10871. ----- "Racial Roots and Religion: An Interview with Howard Thurman." Mary E. Goodwin. Christian Century (90:19, My. 9, 1973), pp. 533-35.   DHU/R

10872. Tilson, Everett. Segregation and the Bible. New York: Abingdon Press, 1958.   INU; DHU/R; DHU/MO; CtY-D

10873. Tinnin, Finley W. "Racial Prejudice Bugaboo Again." Editorial. Baptist Message (49; Jl. 30, 1942), p. 2.   LNB; TND

10874. Tottress, Richard E. Heaven's Entrance Requirements for Races. New York: Comet Press Books, 1957.   DHU/R
     Negro author.

10875. Trawick, Arcadius McSwain. "The Good and Bad of Race Prejudice." Methodist Quarterly Review (74:2, Apr., 1925), pp. 243+.   DHU/R

10876. Triandis, Harry C. and Leigh M. "Race, Social Class, Religion, and Nationality as Determinants of Social Distance." Journal of Abnormal and Social Psychology (Jl.; 1960), pp. 110-18.   DHU; DAU

10877. Tuhl, Curtis G. The American Church and the Negro Problem. Master's thesis. Graduate Seminary, Phillips University, 1946.

10878. Turner, Henry McNeal, (bp.). The Black Man's Doom. The Two Barbarous and Cruel Decisions of the United States Supreme Court, Declaring the Civil Rights Act Unconstitutional and Disrobing the Colored Race of all Civil Protection. The Most Cruel and Inhuman Verdict Against a Loyal People in the History of the World, Consigned to Railroad Cars, in Most Instances Not Fit for Dogs to Ride In. Also the Powerful Speeches of Hon. Frederick Douglass and Col. Robert G. Ingersoll... Phila.: J. B. Rodgers Printing Co., 1896.   DHU/R; DHU/MO
     Negro author.
     First edition published under title: The Barbarous Decision of the United States Supreme Court.

10879. ----- Fifteenth Amendment. A Speech on the Benefits Accruing From the Ratification on the Fifteenth Amendment and Its Incorporation Into the United States Constitution, Delivered at the Celebration Held in Macon, Ga., April 19, 1890. n.p.: n.p., 1870.   DLC

10880. ----- The Negro in All Ages. A Lecture Delivered in the Second Baptist Church of Savannah, Ga... April 8th, 1873... Savannah: D. G. Patton, 1873.   MH

10881. ----- The Negro in Slavery, War and Peace... Phila.: A. M. E. Book Concern, 1913.   NN/Sch

10882. ----- "The Outrage of the Supreme Court: A Letter From Henry M. Turner." Thomas R. Frazier, (ed.). Afro-American History: Primary Sources (New York: Harcourt, Brace & World, Inc., 1970), pp. 184-91.   DHU/R; DHU/MO

10883. ----- A Speech on the Present Duties and Future Destiny of the Negro Race. Delivered Sept. 2, 1872. n.p.: n.p., 1872.   MH

10884. Van Deusen, John George. The Black Man in White America. Washington, D. C. Associated Publishers, 1938.
NN/Sch

10885. Vanecko, J. J. "Religious Behavior and Prejudice: Some Dimensions and Specifications of the Relationship." Review of Religious Research (8; 1966), pp. 27-37. DHU/R

10886. Vernon, William Tecumseh. (bp.). Democracy and the Negro and a Plea for Suspension of Judgment. n. p., n. d.
OWibfU
Bishop of the A. M. E. Church.

10887. Voight, Robert J. Thomas Merton: A Different Drummer. Liquor, Mo.: Liquori Publications, 1972. DHU/R
Chapter 3, Racism.

10888. Waldraven, Robert U. "Racial Friction in America." Methodist Review (Quarterly) (70:1, Ja., 1921), pp. 31-43. DHU/R

10889. Wamble, G. Hugh. "Negroes and Missouri Protestant Churches," Missouri Historical Review (Apr., 1967).
DC U/SW
A study of the relation of Negroes to Protestant churches in Missouri based on the congregational records of thirty-five churches including Grace Episcopal Church, Jefferson City.

10890. Warner, W. Lloyd and B. H. Junker. Color and Human Nature: Negro Personality Development in a Northern City. Washington, D. C.: American Council on Education, 1941.
DHU/MO

10891. Warren, Robert Penn. Segregation. New York: Random House, 1956. DHU/MO

10892. Washington Conference on the Race Problem in the United States. National Sociological Society. How to Solve the Race Problem. The Proceedings of the... Held at the Lincoln Temple Congregational Church; Nineteenth Street Baptist Church and Metropolitan A. M. E. Church. Washington, D. C.: Nov. 9-12, 1903. Washington, D. C.: Beresford, Printer, 1904. DHU/R

10893. Watson, Frank D. A Quest in Interracial Understanding by Frank D. Watson. Foreword by Henry J. Cadbury. October, 1935. Prepared under Direction of Sub-commission for Race Relations and Attitudes of the Five Years Meeting and the Committee on Race Relations of Philadelphia Yearly Meetings. INRE

10894. Weatherford, Willis Duke. Race Relations; Adjustment of Whites and Negroes in the United States. Boston; New York: D. C. Heath & Co., 1934. CtY-D
Moral condition of Negroes.

10895. ----- "A Social Work Worth While." Southern Workman (43; Dec., 1914), pp. 665+. DHU/MO

10896. Weaver, Robert C. "Community Action Against Segregation." Social Action (13:1, Ja., 1947), pp. 4-24. DHU/R
Includes discussion of Church action in Chicago.
Negro author.

10897. Weaver, Rufus W. "The Salvation of the White Races." The Christian Index (101; Je. 16, 1921), p. 8.
LNB; NcWfSB

10898. Weeks, Louis B., III. "Racism, World War I and the Christian Life: Francis J. Grimke in the Nation's Capital." Journal of Presbyterian History (51:4, Wint., 1973), pp. 471-88. DHU/R

10899. Weimer, G. Cecil. "Christianity and the Negro Problem." Journal of Negro History (16:1, Ja., 1931), pp. 67-78. DHU/MO

10900. Wentzel, Fred De Hart. Epistle to White Christians. Philadelphia: Christian Education Press, 1948.
CtY-D; NN/Sch; DHU/R

10901. West, James. Plainville, U. S. A. New York: Columbia University Press, 1945. NNC
Social stratification and religion.

10902. Whitam, Frederick L. "Subdimensions of Religiosity and Race Prejudice." Review of Religious Research (3; 1962), pp. 166-74. DHU/R

10903. White, Frank L. The Integration of Negro Chaplains in the Armed Forces. M. Div. Paper. School of Religion, Howard University, 1968.
Negro author.

10904. White, P. J. "Jim Crow's Last Stand." Crisis (57; Je., 1950), pp. 349-51. DHU/MO

10905. Whitsett, Dan C. "A Deep South Pastor Looks at Segregation." New Christian Advocate (2:2, Feb., 1958), pp. 8-11. DHU/R
Steps a church can take to break segregation.

10906. Wicklein, John. "The Church in the South and Segregation." New York Times (Jl. 5-8, 1959). DHU/R

10907. "Will the Church Remove the Color Line?" Christian Century (49; Dec. 9, 1931), pp. 1554-56. DHU/R

10908. Williams, Alice Elizabeth. An Analysis of the Ethical Theory and Social Thought of Buell Gallagher as Foundation Principles for Religious Education in Race Relations. Master's thesis. Howard University, 1964.

10909. Williams, Robin Murphy. The Reduction of Inter-group Tensions: A Survey of Research on Problems of Ethnic, Racial, and Religious Group Relations. Prepared Under the Direction of the Committee on Techniques for Reducing Group Hostility. New York: n. p., 1947. CtY-D

10910. Wilson, Cody. "Extrinsic Religious Values and Prejudice." Journal of Abnormal and Social Psychology (Mr., 1960), pp. 286-91. DHU

10911. Wilson, Frank T. "The Present Status of Race Relations in the United States." Journal of Religious Thought (2:1, Aut.-Wint., 1945), pp. 30-41. DHU/R
Negro author.

10912. Wilson, W. C. "Extrinsic Religious Values and Prejudice." Journal of Abnormal and Social Psychology (60; 1960), pp. 286-87. DAU; DHU

10913. "Wolf or Shepherd? Church Segregation in Alabama." Newsweek (65; Apr. 12, 1965), pp. 66-7. DHU

10914. Wood, Violet. In the Direction of Dreams. Stories, N. Y.: Friendship Press, 1949. NN/Sch
Church and race relations, pp. 65-93.

10915. Woodson, Carter Goodwin. The Education of the Negro Prior to 1861. Washington, D. C.: The Associated Publishers, 1919. DHU/R
"Chapters II and VIII role of churches in Educating Negroes." Negro author.

10916.   Woodward, C. Vann. "The Southern Ethic in a Puritan
World." William and Mary Quarterly (Jl. , 1968).   DAU
Professor Woodward undertakes a fresh examination of
the venerable dispute regarding Southern myths and their
relation to the Southern ethic.

10917.   Wright, Richard Robert, Jr., (bp.).   Brief Historical
Sketch of Negro Education in Georgia. Savannah, Ga.:
Robinson Print. House, 1894.   DHU/MO
Negro author.

10918.   ----- "Overcoming Racial and Religious Prejudice."
World Fellowship of Faiths. International Congress. Addresses. (New York: Livenght Pub. Corp. , 1935), pp. 319-
22.   DHU/MO

10919.   Yale Divinity School Seminar. Whither the Negro Chruch?
Seminar held at Yale Divinity School, New Haven, Conn.,
April 13-15, 1931. New Haven: City Printing Co., Inc.,
1932.   DHU/MO; CtY-D; NN/Sch

10920.   Yard, James M. "Color Tests the Church." Christian
Century (60; Sept. 29, 1943), pp. 1100+.   DHU/R

10921.   Yinger, J. Milton and G. E. Simpson.   Racial and Cultural Minorities: An Analysis of Prejudice and Discrimination. New York: Harper and Brothers, 1953.   DHU/R
pp. 574-89, the Negro Church.

10922.   Young, Andrew J., Jr. "The Church and Citizenship:
Education of the Negro in the South." Lewis S. C. Smythe,
(ed.).   Southern Churches and Race Relations. (Lexington,
Ky., The College of the Bible, 1963), pp. 64-81.
                                     Pam. File, DHU/R
Negro author.

10923.   Zaugg, E. J. "The Present Race Problem." Reformed
Church Review (3:3, Jl. , 1924), pp. 281-307.   DHU/R

IV. THE CIVIL RIGHTS MOVEMENT, 1954-1967

A. THE CHURCH, SYNAGOGUE AND INTEGRATION

1. Baptist

10924. Barnette, Henlee H. "What Can Southern Baptists Do About the Racial Issue?" Christianity Today (1; Je. 24, 1957), pp. 14-16. DHU/R

10925. Bryant, Baxton. "Where We Are in Civil Rights." Baptist Student (47:5, Feb., 1968), pp. 21-23. DHU/R

10926. Cole, James F. "Freedom Riders." Editorial. The Baptist Message (78; Je. 29, 1961), p. 2. LNB; TND

10927. Davis, William P. "Race Issue: Where Are We?" Baptist Student (47:9, Je., 1968), pp. 11-15. DHU/R

10928. Gaddy, Jerrel Dee. "Desegregation Versus Integration." Baptist Standard (75; Oct. 16, 1963), pp. 6-7. LNB; TxFS

10929. Gillies, J. "Justice, Southern Style; Ashton Jones vs. Atlantas First Baptist Church." (Discussion) Christian Century (81; Feb. 26, 1964. 82; Je. 9, 1965), pp. 270-2, 732. DHU/R

10930. Gritz, Jack L. "What About Integration?" Editorial. The Baptist Messenger (45; Mr. 8, 1956), p. 2. LNB

10931. Hollis, Alexander N., Jr. Southern Baptist Churches Desegregation in Our Public Schools. Master's thesis. Southern Baptist Theological Seminary, 1955.

10932. Hudson, R. Lofton. "Is Segregation Christian?" Baptist and Reflector (120; Ag. 5, 1954), p. 4. KyLoS; TND

10933. "In a Spirit of Repentance: Admission of Sin Regarding Racial Issues by Southern Baptist Convention." Time (85; Je. 11, 1965), p. 68. DHU

10934. Jackson, Joseph Harrison. Unholy Shadows and Freedom's Holy Light. Nashville: Towsend Press, 1967. DHU/R
President of the National Baptist Convention, U. S. A., Inc., gives his views on the civil rights struggle. Negro author.

10935. McClendon, James William, Jr. "The Civil Rights Bill: A New Opportunity for Baptists?" Baptist and Reflector (130; Ag. 6, 1964), p. 8. KyLoS; TND

10936. McCord, Louis A. "What do Southern Baptist Fear?" Christian Century (73:47, Nov. 21, 1956), pp. 1353-54. DHU/R

10937. "Negro Baptist May Go Political." Atlanta Constitution (Ag. 14, 1968). Pam. File, DHU/R

10938. Nichols, S. "Richmond Church Suit Dismissed; Admission of Negroes to Membership in First Bpatist Church." Christian Century (83; Mr. 30, 1966), pp. 411-12. DHU/R

10939. "Southern Baptists Break Silence." Christian Century (81; Jl. 22, 1964), p. 925. DHU/R

10940. Steele, Henry M. "The Time is Now." Baptist Leader (32:1, Apr., 1970), p. 2. DHU/R
Baptists Conv. to serve as catalyst to help churches.

10941. "Texas Baptist for Racial Justice." Christian Century (73; Sept. 26, 1956), pp. 1091+. DHU/R

10942. Tinnin, Finley W. "A Sane View of Segregation." Editorial. Baptist Message (73; Sept., 1956), p. 2. LNB; TND

2. Church of the Brethren

10943. Crouse, M. "Integration in the Church of the Brethen." Brethen Life and Thought (4; Spr., 1959), pp. 41-51. DAU/W

10944. Gardner, R. B. "Evangelical Christianity and Racial Tensions." Brethen Life and Thought (4; Aut., 1959), pp. 47-51. DAU/W

3. Congregational (United Church of Christ)

10945. Artopoeus, Otto F. "Nonviolence-Struggle Without Hate." United Church Herald (6:8, Apr. 18, 1963), pp. 16-17. DHU/R

10946. Barber, Carroll G. "Human Rights and Public Interest." United Church Herald (5:21, Nov. 15, 1962), pp. 14+. DHU/R

10947. Congregational Christian Churches; Council for Social Action. "Christian Social Action in the Congregational Christian Chruches, 1955-56." Pam. File; DHU/R

10948. Gibbons, R. and H. F. Flemme. "For such a Time as This Prospectus for Social Action in the United Church of Christ." Social Action (23; Je. 1957), pp. 12-22. DHU/R

10949. Hackett, Allen. "Let Us Worship Him Together." Social Action (25:5, Ja., 1959), pp. 12-15. DHU/R
"A Relection on Herman Long's report: Racial Inclusiveness in Congregation Christian Churches."

10950. Heacock, Roland T. Understanding the Negro Protest. New York: Praeger Publishers, 1965. DHU/MO
Written by Negro Congregational minister.

10951. Maddocks, Lewis I. "Civil Rights--1966." United Chruch Herald (9:2, Ja. 15, 1966), pp. 33+. DHU/R
Written by Washington secretary for the U. C. C. Council for Social Action.

10952. "March on With Might." United Church Herald (8:9, My. 1, 1965), pp. 2-3. DHU/R

10953. Parker, E. C. "United Church of Christ General Synod." Christian Century (84; Ag. 9, 1967), pp. 1026-8. DHU/R

10954. "Recommendations by U. C. C. Ministers for Racial and Social Justice." Social Action (34:1, Sept., 1967), pp. 36-39. DHU/R

315

10955. Schulz, Larold K. "The United Church of Christ Responds." Social Action (31:3, Nov., 1964), pp. 23-29. DHU/R
Discusses denomination's response to Mississippi Summer, 1964.

10956. United Church of Christ. Council for Christian Social Action. "Call to Christian Action in Society." Social Action (26; Sept., 1959), pp. 5-10. DHU/R
Section II Social Action (27; Oct., 1960), pp. 22-3.

10957. Weaver Galen R. "Racial Practices in Congregational Christian Chruches." Social Action (25:5, Ja., 1959), pp. 3-11. DHU/R

4. Disciples of Christ (Christian Churches)
10958. Bingham, Walter. "Black Men Discover Themselves." World Call (51:6, Je., 1969), pp. 22-23. DHU/R
Negro author.

10959. Cartwright, Colbert S. "Christian Churches (Disciples of Christ) as Racial Ferment (in the South) Accelerates Pastors and Congregations Take Divided Stand on Issue." Christianity and Crisis (18; Mr. 3, 1958), pp. 18-20. DHU/R

10960. "The 'Christian Churches' Become a 'Church'." Christianity Today (13:1, Oct. 11, 1968), pp. 40-41. DHU/R
Disciples of Christ.
Church's urban crisis program.

10961. Fey, Harold E. "Disciples on Civil Rights; International Convention of Christian Churches." Christian Century (80:44, Oct. 30, 1963), pp. 1326-27. DHU/R

10962. Wallace, David M. "Beyond Boycotts." World Call (50:1, Je., 1968), pp. 16-18. DHU/R
Author, program director of Operation Breadbasket in Chicago, is a Disciple of Christ minister.

5. Friends—Quakers
10963. Burton, John W. Nonalignment. New York: J. H. Heineman, 1966. DHU/MO
Papers from a series of discussions held by the Friends of Peace and International Relations Committee in London, 1963.

10964. Forbursh, Bliss. "Integration in Baltimore Friends School." Friends Intelligencer (112:1, Ja. 1, 1955), pp. 7-8. DHU/R

10965. Friends, Society of. American Friends Service Committee. Fair Housing Handbook; A Practical Manual for Those Who Are Working to Create and Maintain Inclusive Communities. Philadelphia: n. p., 1964. DHU/MO

10966. ----- Community Relations Program. The Public School System of Washington, D. C. Prepared by Irene Osborne Community Relations Program, American Friends Service Committee. September, 1953. Washington, D. C.: n. p., 1954. NN/Sch

10967. ----- Toward the Elimination of Segregation in the Nation's Capital; The Report of an AFSC Community Relations Project with Public Schools and Recreation Areas, 1951-1955. Philadelphia: American Friends Service Committee, Community Relations Program, 1955. NN/Sch

10968. ----- Peace Committee. Philadelphia. "A Perspective on Nonviolence." Friends Journal (3:14, Apr. 6, 1957), pp. 220-29. DHU/R
"A practical study and an inquiry into nonviolence, now in America." Suggested for First -day School classes and study groups.

10969. Hortenstine, Virgie B. "Message from a Tennessee Prison." Friends Journal (8:10, My. 15, 1962), pp. 209-10. DHU/R

10970. ----- "Work, Violence, and Faith in Fayette County." Friends Journal (9:22, Nov. 15, 1963), pp. 484-86. DHU/R

10971. Pemberton, John De J. "The Civil Rights Revolution." Friends Journal (10:11, Je. 1, 1964), pp. 246-48. DHU/R

10972. Rose, Ralph. American Friends and Race Relations. London: Friends Home Service Committee, 1954. INRE

10973. Taylor, Richard K. "Religion and Race." Friends Journal (9:4, Feb. 15, 1963), pp. 81-2. DHU/R

10974. Tolles, Frederick B. "Friends and Racial Discrimination." Friends Journal (3:33, Ag. 17, 1957), pp. 533-34. DHU/R

10975. Wixom, Robert L. "Letter from Little Rock." Friends Journal (4:19, My. 10, 1958), pp. 298-300. DHU/R
Also, (4:20, My. 17, 1958), pp. 313-15 and (4:18, My. 3, 1958), pp. 282-3. DHU/R

10976. Yungblut, John. "Triple Revolution in Atlanta." Friends Journal (10:13, Jl. 1, 1964), pp. 293-4. DHU/R

6. Judaism
10977. Bernards, Solomon S. "Race Relations in the Jewish School Curriculum." Religious Education (59:1, Ja. - Feb., 1964), pp. 60-63. DHU/R

10978. Brickner, Balfour. "Projects Under Synagogue Auspices." Religious Education (59:1, Ja. -Feb., 1964), pp. 76-80. DHU/R
Discusses Jewish projects for racial justice.

10979. "Charles Mantinband, Hebrew Prophet of Longview." William H. Crook and Ross Coggins. Seven Who Fought (Waco, Texas: Word Books, 1971), pp. 103-20. DHU/R
Rabbi of temples in the south was constantly threatened by the White Citizens councils because of his activities in the civil rights movement.

10980. Cohen, Henry. Justice, Justice: A Jewish View of the Black Revolution. New York: Union of American Hebrew Congregations, 1969. DHU/R

10981. Friedman, Murray. "Virginia Jewry in the School Crisis: Anti-Semitism and Desegregation." Commentary (27, Ja., 1959), pp. 17-22. DHU/R

10982. Glazer, Nathan. "Negroes and Jews: The New Challenge to Pluralism." Commentary (38; Dec., 1964), pp. 19-34. DHU/R

10983. Greenleaf, R. "National Conference on Religion and Race." Chicago Jewish Forum (21; Spr., 1963), pp. 194-6. DLC
Jews and Negroes.

10984. Halpern, Ben. "Emancipated and the Liberated." Symposium. Jewish Frontier (31; Mr., 1964), pp. 7-11. DLC
Jews and Negroes.

10985. Himmelfort, Milton. "Negroes, Jews and Muzhiks." Commentary (42; Oct., 1966), pp. 83-86. DHU/R

10986. Johnson, Willard. Minorities in our Nation. New York: National Conference of Christians and Jews, 1952. TN/DCHS

10987. Kahn, B. M. "Jewish Community and Civil Rights." Jewish Heritage (7; Sum., 1964), pp. 21-26. DLC

10988. Knoll, Erwin. "Washington: Showcase of Integration." Commentary (27:3, Mr., 1959), pp. 194-202. DHU/R

10989. Kogan, Lawrence A. "The Jewish Conception of Negroes in the North: A Historical Approach." Phylon (28; Wint., 1967), pp. 376-85. DHU/MO

10990. Korey, William and Charlotte Lubin. "Arlington--Another Little Rock? School Integration Fight on Washington's Doorstep." Commentary (26:3, Sept., 1958), pp. 201-09.
DHU/R

10991. Kyle, Keith. "Desegregation and the Negro Right to Vote." Commentary (24:1, Jl., 1957), pp. 15-19.   DHU/R

10992. "Liberalism and the Negro. A Round-Table Discussion." Commentary (37:3, Mr., 1964), pp. 25-42.   DHU/R
Participants: James Baldwin, Nathan Glazer, Sidney Hook and Gunnar Myrdal.

10993. Lubell, Samuel. "The Negro and the Democratic Coalition." Commentary (38:2, Ag., 1964), pp. 19-27.   DHU/R

10994. Malev, William S. "The Jew of the South in the Conflict on Segregation." Conservative Judaism (13; Fall, 1958), pp. 35-46.
DLC

10995. Mantinband, Charles. "From the Diary of a Mississippi Rabbi." American Judaism (13; Fall, 1958), pp. 35-46.
DLC

10996. Maslow, W. "Negro and Jew in America." World Jewry (7; Ja.-Feb., 1964), pp. 9-10.   DLC

10997. Muravchik, E. "Growing Estrangement Between Jews and Negroes." Jewish Digest (8; Jl., 1963), pp. 69-76.
DLC

10998. "Negro Youths Attack Jews at Yeshiva in Harlem." Jewish Observer (13; My. 8, 1964), p. 8.   DAU

10999. "Negroes and Jews in a Common Struggle." Reconstructionist. (30; Je. 26, 1964), pp. 5-6.   DLC

11000. "Negroes in Williamsburg, New York Attack Jews; Jews Urge Action on Civil Rights Bill." Editorial. Reconstructionist (30; My. 15, 1964), p. 6.   DLC

11001. Pettigrew, Thomas F. "Parallel and Distinctive Changes in Anti-Semitic and Anti-Negro Attitudes." Charles H. Stember, (ed.). Jews in the Mind of America (New York: Basic Books, 1966), pp. 377-403.   DLC

11002. Pilch, Judah. "Civil Rights and Jewish Institutions." Religious Education (59:1, Ja.-Feb., 1964), pp. 86-89.   DHU/R

11003. Podhoretz, Norman. "My Negro Problem--and Ours." Commentary (35:2, Feb., 1963), pp. 93-101.   DHU/R
Editorial opinion.

11004. Prinz, J. "Negro March for Freedom Has Lessons for Jews." World Jewry (6; Sept.-Oct., 1963), p. 7.   DLC

11005. "Rabbi Says Civil Rights Movement Belongs to All." Washington Afro-American (Apr. 13, 1968).   Pam. File, DHU/R

11006. Rabinowicz, R. A. "Sons of Solomon." Jewish Digest (9; Nov., 1963), pp. 71-2.   DLC
Jewish and Negro relations.

11007. Rinder, Irwin D. Jewish Identification and the Race Relations Cycle. Doctoral dissertation. University of Chicago, 1953.

11008. Ringer, Benjamin B. "Jews and the Desegregation Crisis." Charles H. Stember, (ed.). Jews in the Mind of America (New York: Basic Books, 1966), pp. 197-207.   DLC

11009. Robinson, James Herman and Kenneth B. Clark. "What Negroes Think About Jews." Anti-Defamation League Bulletin (14; Dec., 1957), pp. 4-8.   DLC

11010. Rubenstein, R. L. "Rabbia dn Social Conflict." Religious Education (59; Ja.-Feb., 1964), pp. 100-06.   DHU/R

11011. Shapiro, M. S. "Probing the Prejudices of American Jews; the Negro Revolution and Jews." Jewish Digest (10; Nov., 1964), pp. 1-6.   DLC

11012. Simpson, Richard. "Negro-Jewish Prejudice: Authoritarianism and Some Social Variables as Correlates." Social Problems (7; Aut., 1959), pp. 138-46.   DHU

11013. Teller, J. L. "Negroes and Jews: A Hard Look." Conservative Judaism (21; Aut., 1966), pp. 13-20.   DAU/W

11014. Ungar, Andre. "To Birmingham and Back." Conservative Judaism (18; Fall, 1963), pp. 1-17.   DLC
Story of 19 Rabbis' trip to Birmingham.

11015. Vorspan, Albert. "Segregation and Social Justice." American Judaism (7; Ja., 1958), pp. 10-11.   DLC

11016. Walden, Theodore. "Intervention by a Jewish Community Relations Council in a Negro Ghetto: A Case Illustration." Journal of Jewish Communal Service (44; Aut., 1967), pp. 49-63.   DHU

11017. Wilkins, Roy. "Jewish-Negro Relations: An Evaluation." American Judaism (12:3, Spr., 1963), pp. 4-5.   DLC

11018. Zinkin, T. "Black and White Jews of Cochin." Jewish Digest (9; Nov., 1963), pp. 12-4.   DLC
Black Jews.

7. Lutheran

11019. Ferrer, J. M. "N. E. T.'s A Time for Burning: Involvement of the Augustana Lutheran Church, Omaha, with Civil Rights." Life (62; Feb. 10, 1967), p. 12.   DHU

11020. Letts, Harold C. The United Lutheran Church Looks at Desegregation. New York: n. p., 1956.   NNUT

11021. "Lutheran View of Race Crisis." America (118; Feb. 3, 1968), p. 139.   DHU

11022. "Lutheran Seek Negroes for the Ministry." Atlanta World (Mr. 27, 1968).   Pam. File; DHU/R

11023. "New Lutheran Spirit; Pledge to Support Agencies Promoting Integrated Housing." Newsweek (70; Jl. 24, 1976), pp. 70-1.
DHU

11024. "A Time For Burning." Lutheran Film Associates. Made by Quest Productions. Released by Contemporary Films, 1966. 58 min. sd. b&w. 16mm.   DLC
Film.
"A study of racial conflicts and understanding as portrayed in Omaha, Neb., when the pastor of an all-white Augustana Lutheran Church took an initial step toward desegregation."

11025. "Two-Edged Sword; a Time for Burning, Film on Racial Patterns in a Lutheran Parish." America (115; Nov. 19, 1966), pp. 643-4.   DHU

8. Methodist Episcopal (United Methodist)

11026. "Action Now: Integration Proposal to be Debate at General Conference." Together (7; Nov. 1963), pp. 3-6.
DAU/W; DHU/R

11027. "Adopt Race Statement." Methodist Laymen (24; My., 1964), p. 24.   DAU/W

11028. "Adopt Strong Race Stand to Study Church State." Christian Advocate (8; My. 21, 1964), p. 4+.   DAU/W; DHU/R

11029. "Aid to Race Workers." Christian Advocate (8; Sept. 24, 1964), p. 24.   DAU/W; DHU/R

11030. "Alabama Bishop Calls for Responsibility and Patience." Concern (7; Apr. 1, 1965), p. 14.   DAU/W

11031. "All Persons May Attend Methodist Service." Concern
(7; My. 15, 1965), p. 15.   DAU/W

11032. "Attempt to Integrate Churches Result in Arrest." Together (7; Dec., 1963), p. 8.   DAU/W; DHU/R

11033. Bagby, Grover C. "Methodism's Fears of Racial Merger."
Central Christian Advocate (142:1, Ja. 1, 1967), pp. 9+.
                                    Pam. File, DHU/R

11034. Bennett, Anne McGrew. Beyond the Barriers of Nation,
Race and Sex. Evanston: The Yellow Ribbon, United Methodist Women's Caucus, 1973.   MNtcA

11035. "Beyond Lip Service: Methodist Church's General Conference." Time (83; My. 15, 1964), p. 53.   DHU

11036. Bibbons, J. C. "Analysis of Current Nonviolence Movements." Central Christian Advocate (138; Sept. 15, 1963),
pp. 4+.   DAU/W; DHU/R

11037. "Bi-racial Church Council Reorganized." Concern (4;
Jl. 1, 1962), p. 17.   DAU/W

11038. "Bishop Asks Methodist to Help Ease Tension." Christian
Advocate (8; Jl. 16, 1964), p. 22.   DHU/R; DAU/W

11039. "Bishop Calls for Phalanx of Freedom Riders." Central
Christian Advocate (136; Sept. 15, 1961), p. 7. DAU/W; DHU/R

11040. "Bishops Seek to Bolster Council Stand on Race." Christian Advocate (8; Apr. 23, 1964), p. 21.   DHU/R; DAU/W

11041. Campbell, Will D. "Starting Place is Christian Race Relations." Motive (22; My. 1962), p. 31+.   DHU/R

11042. "Christian Social Concerns Uphold 'Right of Protest' In
Discipline." Central Christian Advocate (139; Apr. 15,
1964), p. 14.   DHU/R; DAU/W

11043. "Church Segregation Denounced by Bishops." Central
Christian Advocate (139; Ja. 1, 1964), p. 3. DHU/R; DAU/W

11044. "Churches Pledge to Welcome All." Concern (4; My. 1,
1962), p. 17.   DAU/W

11045. "Clergyman Counsels Students on Integration." Central
Christian Advocate (136; Feb. 1, 1961), p. 15. DAU/W

11046. Collins, D. E. "Christian Race Relations." Central
Christian Advocate (139; My. 15, 1964), p. 6. DAU/W

11047. "Conference Adopts Statements on Race." Central Christian Advocate (139; Ja. 1, 1964), pp. 22+. DAU/W; DHU/R

11048. Crum, Jack. "Why I Favor Integration." New Christian
Advocate (1:5, Feb., 1957), pp. 34-6.   DHU/R

11049. "Dallas A. Blanchard, Don't Ask Me to Feel Guilty."
William H. Crook and Ross Coggins. Seven Who Fought
(Waco, Texas: Word Books, 1971), pp. 45-67.   DHU/R
White Methodist minister in the South "who fought for
integration and brotherhood within the framework of his
church."

11050. "Demonstration Defused by Methodist Bishops." Christian Century (80; Dec. 4, 1963), pp. 1498-1501. DHU/R

11051. Dennis, Joseph J. "Need for Brotherhood." Central
Christian Advocate (133:23, Dec. 1, 1958), pp. 4-6. DHU/R

11052. Dennison, Doris. "Prophets in Action." Wesley Quarterly (20; Jl. -Sept., 1961), pp. 8+.   DHU/R

11053. Dunbar, L. W. "That They May Be Free." Concern
(5; Sept. 1, 1963), pp. 9+.   DAU/W

11054. Garnett, Bernard E. Black Protest: Will it Split the
United Methodists? Nashville, Tenn.: Race Relations Information Center, November, 1969. Pam. File, DHU/R;
                                                  IEG

11055. Gordh, G. "Conversion and the Southern Conscience."
Concern (7; Ag. 1-15, 1965), pp. 4+.   DAU/W

11056. Gordon, Mamye. "Christianity and the Race Problem."
Central Christian Advocate (133:20, Oct. 15, 1958), pp. 5-6.
                                                  DHU/R

11057. Haywood, J. W. "Watching Desegregation at Work." Central Christian Advocate (132:19, Oct. 1, 1957), pp. 6-7. DHU/R

11058. "Hold Thanksgiving Service After Passage of Civil Rights
Bill." Central Christian Advocate (13; Ag. 15, 1964), pp. 12+.
                                          DAU/W; DHU/R

11059. Howard, Tilman J. "The Racial Issue Before Methodism."
Christian Advocate (139; Feb. 15, 1964), pp. 5+. Pam. File,
                                                  DHU/R

11060. "Integrating Methodism; Elimination of Central Jurisdiction."
Christian Century (83; Jan. 5, 1966), pp. 3-4.   DHU/R

11061. "Jackson Chruch Bishop Breaks Color Bar." Christian Advocate (9; Nov. 18, 1965), pp. 21+.   DAU/W; DGW

11062. Jackson, J. H. "Christ, the Church and Race." Central
Christian Advocate (136:8, Apr. 15, 1961), pp. 4+.
                                          DHU/R; DAU/W

11063. Jordan, David M. Gradual Racial Integration in the Methodist Church. n. p., 1956.   IEG

11064. King, J. T. "Challenge to Christian Leadership." Central
Christian Advocate (136; Feb. 1, 1961), pp. 7+. DHU/R;
                                                  DAU/W

11065. ----- "Christianity and Social Justice." Central Christian
Advocate (136; Nov. 1, 1961), p. 5.   DHU/R; DAU/W

11066. Kitly, H. "Where Were Methodists at the March?" Concern (5; Oct. 15, 1963), p. 12.   DAU/W

11067. "Kneel Ins." Concern (5; Nov. 1, 1963), p. 12. DAU/W

11068. Mathews, J. K. "Bishops Speak on Race." Church Advocate (8; Ja. 2, 1964), pp. 7+.   DHU/R; DAU/W

11069. ----- "Easter in Jackson; Methodist Bishops Barred from
Galloway Memorial Methodist Chruch." Christian Century
(81; Apr. 15, 1964), pp. 478-80.   DHU/R

11070. "McComb Methodists Aid Negro Rights." Christian Advocate (8; Dec. 3, 1964), p. 24.   DHU/R; DAU/W

11071. "Methodist Affirm Civil Disobedience as Citizen's Right."
New York Times (My. 4, 1968).   Pam. File, DHU/R

11072. Methodist Chruch, Department of Research and Survey.
The Church and the Racially Changing Community, by Robert
L. Wilson and James H. Davis, Jr. New York: Abingdon Pr.,
1966.   INU; NcD; DLC; NN/Sch

11073. "Methodist, Others Rally to Aid in Birmingham." Christian Advocate (7; Oct. 10, 1963), p. 24.   DAU/W; DHU/R

11074. "Methodist Racial Unit Defines Goals." Christian Century
(79; My. 9, 1962), pp. 592-3.   DHU/R

11075. "Methodist React to California Riots." Central Christian
Advocate (140; Oct. 15, 1965), p. 11.   DHU/R; DAU/W

11076. "Methodist Students Helped Ease Tensions at University
of Georgia." Christian Advocate (5; Feb. 2, 1961), p. 24.
                                          DAU/W; DHU/R

11077. "Methodist Study Race Relations." *Afro American* (Nov. 15, 1960).
Pam File, DHU/R

11078. "Methodists Relax Law View." *The Washington Post* (My. 4, 1968).
Pam. File, DHU/R

11079. "Methodists Vote Four-Year Integration." *Christian Century* (81; My. 13, 1964), p. 630.
DHU/R

11080. "Ministers Endorse Maryland Sit-Ins." *Concern* (3; Dec. 15, 1961), p. 4.
DAU/W

11081. "Ministers Endorse Sit-in Demonstrations." *Central Christian Advocate* (137; Ja. 15, 1962), p. 15. DHU/R; DAU/W

11082. "Mississippi Church Admits Negroes." *Concern* (7; Nov. 15, 1965), p. 16.
DAU/W

11083. "Mississippians Repudiate Religious Fredom, Capital Street Methodist Church in Jackson, Miss." *Christian Century* (80; Nov. 20, 1963), pp. 1425-6.
DHU/R

11084. Mitchell, E. O. "Interpretation: Action for Brotherhood." *Concern* (6:11, Dec. 1, 1964).
DAU/W

11085. Mooth, V. "True Brotherhood is Found in Christ." *Chruch Advocate* (Ag., 1968), p. 11.
DHU/R

11086. "Plan Strategy on Race." *Christian Advocate* (7; Dec. 19, 1963), pp. 21+.
DHU/R; DAU/W

11087. "Press Fair-Housing Drive After Admendment of Law." *Christian Advocate* (8; Dec. 17, 1964), pp. 23+. DHU/R; DAU/W

11088. "Race Lines Must Fade in Churches." *Journal and Guide* (My. 12, 1956).
Pam. File, DHU/R
"Methodists abolish All Negro Central Conference."

11089. "Racists Challenge Methodists; Methodst Bishop Barred from Galloway Chruch, Jackson, Miss." *Christian Century* (81; Apr. 8, 1964), p. 454.
DHU/R

11090. Ragan, Roger. "Methodist and Residential Segregation of the Negro." *Concern* (5; J. 15, 1963), pp. 4+. DAU/W

11091. "Religion and Race, Advocate Special Report." *Christian Advocate* (7; Feb. 28, 1963), p. 7. DAU/W; DHU/R

11092. Roy, Ralph Lord. "Methodists: Crisis of Conscience." *Nation* (198; Mr. 16, 1964), pp. 262-5.
DHU

11093. Schooler, R. "Missionary's Witness and Civil Rights." *Central Christian Advocate* (139; Nov. 15, 1964), pp. 12+.
DAU/W; DHU/R

11094. "Segregated Worship Hit." *Concern* (7; Sept. 15, 1965), p. 15.
DAU/W

11095. "Segregation To Be Out After Merger With EUB." *Central Christian Advocate* (140; Oct. 1, 1965), p. 14. DAU/W; DHU/R

11096. Seller, J. E. "Christian and Human Relations." *Roundtable* (12; Feb., 1964), p. 31. DAU; DCU/ST; DGW; DGW; DGU

11097. "6 Methodist Chruches Sign Welcoming Statement." *Central Advocate* (37; My. 1, 1962), pp. 15+. DHU/R; DAU/W

11098. "Southern Methodists Would Retain Race Divisions." *Christian Century* (72; Feb. 23, 1955), pp. 229+. DHU/R

11099. Thompson, T. "Another Pilgrimage to Jackson; Seven Ministers Barred from Capitol Street Methodist Chruch." *Christian Century* (81; Apr. 22, 1964), pp. 511-12. DHU/R

11100. "To Picket Segregated Chruches in Oklahoma City." *Central Christian Advocate* (136; Sept. 15, 1961), pp. 16+.
DHU/R; DAU/W

11101. "Trinity Church in Orangeburg Movement." *Central Christian Advocate* (139; Feb. 15, 1964), pp. 18+. DHU/R; DAU/W

11102. "12 Jailed in Mississippi for Appearance at Church and Sunday School." *Concern* (5; Nov. 1, 1963), p. 15. DAU/W

11103. United Methodist Chruch. General Board of Social Economic Relations. Methodist Youth Interracial Conference. *Living and Working Together*. Detroit, Mich., Apr. 18-20, 1958.
Mim. Pam. File, DHU/R

11104. "Urges Some Rightists Investigated, Lauds Poise of Religious Demonstrators." *Central Christian Advocate* (139; Nov. 1, 1964), pp. 9+.
DHU/R; DAU/W

11105. Waid, W. L. Interpretation: Conversion and the Southern Conscience (reply to Conversion and the Southern Conscience, by G. Gordh). *Concern* (7; Oct. 15, 1965), pp. 10+. DAU/W

11106. Walker, E. J. "Methodist Urban Convocation." *Christian Century* (75; Mr. 12, 1958), pp. 319-20.
DHU/R

11107. Warnock, Henry Y. "Southern Methodists, the Negro, and Unification: The First Phase." *Journal of Negro History* (52:4, Oct., 1967), pp. 287-304.
DHU

11108. Washington University. Social Science Institute. *Background for St. Louis Race Relations Conference of the Methodist Church, May 9-10, 1957*.
Mim. DHU/R
Negro population, work and housing.

11109. "White Parish's Negro Rector Cites High Morale, Support." *Central Christian Advocate* (140; Jl. 15, 1965), pp. 10+.
DHU/R; DAU/W

11110. Wilkins, R. "Church Renewal and Race by Interracial Council of Methodist." *Concern* (5; Sept. 1, 1963), pp. 9+.
DAU/W

11111. Wogaman, J. Philip. "Focus on Central Jurisdiction." *Christian Century* (80; Oct. 23, 1963), pp. 1296-98. DHU/R
Former Negro division of the Methodist Church.

11112. ----- *A Strategy for Racial Desegregation in the Methodist Church*. Doctoal dissertation. Boston University, Graduate School, 1960.

9. Presbyterian

11113. Calhoun, M. P. "Presbyterian Chruch, U. S., after Division and Silence, Its Ministers are again Speaking Against Racism." *Christianity and Crisis* (18; Mr. 3, 1958), pp. 24-6.
DHU/R

11114. "The Church and Race: A Promising First Step." *Presbyterian Life* (12:10, My. 15, 1959), pp. 26-28. DHU/R

11115. "Churches Challenged; National Council of Churches and Southern Presbyterians." *America* (112; Ja. 2, 1965), p. 4.
DHU

11116. "Civil Rights: The Backlash That Wasn't There." *Presbyterian Life* (17:12, Je. 15, 1964), pp. 19-22. DHU/R
Report of the 176th General Assembly of the Presbyterian Church.

11117. "Concern V. Concerned; Presbyterian Group Fear Church's Increasing Involvement in Social Issues." *Time* (90; Oct. 13, 1967), p. 50.
DHU

11118. "Death in the Sunday School." *Presbyterian Life* (Editorial) (16:19, Oct. 15, 1963), pp. 4+.
DHU/R
Opinion on the shooting of six black children at the Sixteenth Street Baptist Church in Birmingham, Alabama.

11119. Gittings, James A. "Clergymen Demonstrate in Hattiesburg, Mississippi." *Presbyterian Life* (17:4, Feb. 15, 1964), pp. 30-3.
DHU/R

11120. Ikeler, Bernard. "Troubleshooters of the Racial Crisis." Presbyterian Life (15:11, Je. 1, 1962), pp. 21-23. DHU/R

11121. Michie, Doyne E. "Hattiesburg: Trial and Debate." Presbyterian Life (17:7, Apr. 1, 1964), pp. 28-29. DHU/R

11122. Nelsen, Hart M. and Raytha L. Yokely. "Presbyterians Civil Rights and Church Pronouncements." Review of Religious Research (12:1, Fall, 1970), pp. 43-50. DHU/R
Results of a questionnaire to 3221 elders distributed in 1967.

11123. "No Private Domain; Racism at Home Viewed from the Churches' Mission Posts Abroad; Statements of the Presbyterian Board of World Missions." Christian Century (81; Feb. 5, 1964), p. 184. DHU/R

11124. "Presbyterian Vote $100,000 for Fund to Aid Poor People." New York Times (My. 21, 1968). Pam. File, DHU/R

11125. "Presbyterians Hold Line on School Prayers; Racial Justice." Christian Century (80; Dec. 11, 1963), p. 1538. DHU/R

11126. "Race Relations: Churchmen Take the Lead." Presbyterian Life (10:3, Feb. 2, 1957), p. 18. DHU/R

11127. Reimers, David Morgan. "The Race and Presbyterian Union." Chruch History (31:2, Je., 1962), pp. 203-15. DHU/R

11128. Sissel, H. B. "Civil Rights Legislation." Presbyterian Life (16:21, Nov. 1, 1963), pp. 27-28. DHU/R

11129. ------ "Days of Preparation." Presbyterian Life (17:9, My. 1, 1964), pp. 7-8. DHU/R
Predicts a new era in civil rights lies just ahead.

11130. ----- "Segregation in Sumter, South Carolina." Presbyterian Life (10:1, Ja. 5, 1957), pp. 6+. DHU/R

11131. Smylie, James H. "Conflict of Concerns; Tensions Affecting Southern Presbyterians." Christian Century (82:52, Dec. 29, 1965), pp. 1602-06. DHU/R

11132. "Southern Presbyterians Strengthen Race Stand." Presbyterian Life (17:11, Je. 1, 1964), pp. 31-2. DHU/R

11133. Wright, Paul S. "Desegregating Human Hearts." Presbyterian Life (17:9, My. 1, 1964), pp. 19+. DHU/R

10. Protestant Episcopal

11134. "Bells in the Delta; Episcopal Civil Rights Activists." Time (85; Feb. 26, 1965), p. 71. DHU

11135. "Church and Race." Christian Social Relations Bulletin (2:7, Je., 1965). Pam. File, DHU/R
Whole issue deals with race and the protestant Episcopal Church.

11136. "Duncan Gray, Too Smart to Scare, Too Mean to Kill." William H. Crook and Ross Coggins. Seven Who Fought (Waco, Texas: Word Books, 1971), pp. 1-25. DHU/R
White Recctr of St. Peter's Episcopal Church in Oxford, Mississippi and his fight against white racism at the University of Mississippi when James Meredith entered the university.

11137. National Council of the Episcopal Church. Just, Right & Necessary. New York: The National Council, 1955. DHU/R
A study of reactions to the Supreme Court decision on segregation.

11138. Osgood, Charles and Willie Charles. "When Blacks Join Whites." The Episcopalian (135:5, My., 1970), pp. 24+. DHU/R
Case study of Grace Protestant Episcopal Church, Syracuse, New York.

11139. Protestant Episcopal Church in the U. S. A. National Council. "Bridge Building in Race Relations: What the Episcopal Church Has Said and Done." Pam. File, DHU/R

11140. ----- The Church Speaks on Race: Official Statements of the Episcopal Church and the Anglican Communion, 1940-58. New York: n. p., 1959. NNUT

11141. "To Right a Wrong; Call for Episcopalians to Respond Creatively to Racial Riots." Newsweek (70; Sept. 25, 1967), p. 116. DHU

11. Roman Catholic

11142. Abbott, Walter M. "The Bible Abused." Interracial Review (36; Feb. 1963), pp. 26+. DCU/SW
White Catholics who resisted school desegregation.

11143. Ahmann, Mathew. "Catholics and Race." Commonweal (73; Dec. 2, 1960), pp. 247-50. DHU
Reply, W. V. D'Antonio (73; Ja. 6, 1961), pp. 390-1.

11144. ----- "Catholics and Racism in the North." Catholic World (195; Ag. 1962), pp. 266-74. DHU/R

11145. "Apostolic Delegate on Race." America (105; Je. 3, 1961), p. 387. DHU

11146. Ball, William B. "New Frontiers of Catholic Community Action." Interracial Review (35; Feb., 1962), pp. 49-51. DCU/SW

11147. Barrett, P. "Nuns in the Inner City; Force for Freedom and Creativity." Christian Century (83; Ag. 31, 1966), pp. 1050-3. DHU/R

11148. Bernard, Raymond. "The Negro Prospects." Social Order (7; Mr., 1957), pp. 135-6. Review of The Negro Potential by Eli Genzberg, and statement of the responsibility of Southern Catholics.

11149. "Bishop Jeanmard and the Erath La. Case." St. Augustine's Messenger (33:1, Jan., 1956), 24-7. DHU/R
"Decree issued to the parishioners on violence to Negroes in parish by Bishop of Lafayette."

11150. "Bishops Condemn Racial Injustice." America (100; Nov. 29, 1958), p. 264. DHU

11151. "Bishops on Race." Commonweal (69; Nov. 28, 1958), p. 219. DHU

11152. "Bishops on Racism." America (109; Ag. 10, 1963), p. 127. DHU

11153. Canavan, Francis P. "Civil Rights: Are They Moral Rights, Too?" Catholic World (187:1, 119, Je., 1958), pp. 166-72. DHU/R

11154. "Cardinal in Harlem." America (109; Jl. 17, 1963), p. 86. DHU

11155. "Cardinal McIntyre: A Ramparts Special Report." Ramparts (3; Nov., 1964), pp. 35-44. DHU
Effect of Cardinal McIntyre's refusal to support racial equality in Southern California.

11156. "The Catholic Church in the Modern World. Statement Against Racism." Interracial Review (37; Dec., 1964), pp. 226. DHU/MO

11157. "Catholic Know-Nothings; Integrationists and the Churches Racial Crisis in Chicago." Newsweek (68; Ag. 29, 1966), pp. 641+.

11158. "Catholic Sisters Have A Unique Opportunity as Teachers to Help Solve the Racial Problem." Interracial Review (29; Je. 1960), p. 161. DHU/MO

11159. "Catholic View on Segregation; Tablet of London Editorial."
U. S. News (43; Oct. 4, 1957), p. 124.   DHU
Reply. R. J. L'Hoste and A. J. Pilie (43; Nov. 8, 1957),
p. 135.

11160. "Catholics and Negroes." America (106; Dec. 9, 1961), p.
354.   DHU

11161. "Catholics and Race." America (109; Jl. 13, 1963;
110; Feb. 29, 1964), p. 33; pp. 276-7.   DHU

11162. "Catholics and Racial Bias." America (108; Mr. 16, 1963),
p. 351.   DHU

11163. "Caution on Civil Rights; Opposition to Clerical Involvement."
Times (88; Ag. 26, 1966), p. 58.   DHU

11164. "Church and Changing Urban Parish: Five Vignettes; Symposium." Catholic World (208; Dec. 1968), pp. 117-28.
                                                 DHU/R

11165. "Civil Rights Mass." America (104; Nov. 19, 1960), p. 253.
                                                 DHU

11166. Clark, D. "City Catholics and Segregation." America
(107; My. 19, 1962), pp. 269-71. Reply: Baroni, G. C. (107;
Je. 30, 1962), p. 431.   DHU

11167. ----- "Philadelphia, Still Closed; Catholic Attitudes Toward Racial Changes." Commonweal (80; My. 1, 1964).
                                                 DHU

11168. "Clergy and Nuns March; No Outsiders." America (112;
Mr. 27, 1965), p. 411.   DHU

11169. "Cody All Alone." Christian Century (84; 10, Mr., 1967),
p. 302.   DHU/R
Withdrawal of support from the Catholic interracial Council of Chicago by Archbishop Cody.

11170. Connelly, Joel R. and Howard Dooley. "The Priest and
the President." The Progressive (37: 2, Feb., 1973), pp.
27-31.   DHU/R
An interview with Reverend Theodore M. Hesburgh, Chairman of the Civil Rights Commission, about his resigna-
tion.

11171. Cronin, J. F. "Interracial Justice: The Catholic Record."
Social Order (11; Oct., 1961), pp. 345-55.   DHU

11172. "Discrimination and the Christian Conscience." Journal
of Negro Education (28:1, Wint., 1959), pp. 66-9. DHU/R
Position of Catholic bishops in the United States.
Also in: Crisis (66:1, Ja., 1959), pp. 15-19. DHU/MO

11173. "Doing is the Difference; Student Interracial Ministry."
America (112; Jan. 9, 1965), p. 33.   DHU

11174. "Episcopal Leadership, Cardinal Cushing on Religious and
Moral Responsibility of Catholics." America (111; Sept. 12,
1964), p. 249.   DHU

11175. "Evasive Answers About Racial Change Given by Local
Catholic Leaders." Interracial Review (Feb., 1960), pp. 34-
7.   DHU/MO

11176. "For West Bishops on Race." America (111; Sept. 12,
1964), p. 244.   DHU

11177. Froncek, Tom. "American Catholics and the American
Negro." Catholic Mind (64; Ja., 1966), pp. 4-11. DGU

11178. "The Full Catholic Teaching in Racial Justice." Interracial
Review (35; Oct., 1962), pp. 224-5.   DCU/SW
Syllabus prepared by the Diocesan Department of Educa-
tion, Charleston, S. C.

11179. Gasnick, Roy M. "Franciscan Pledge to Interracial Justice." Social Order (12; Apr., 1962), pp. 173-77. DHU

11180. ----- "The Pope Speaks on Racism." The Homiletic and
Pastoral Review (59; Je., 1959), pp. 827-31.   DGU

11181. Germillion, Joseph B. The Journal of A Southern Pastor.
Chicago: Fides Publishers Association, 1957.   NN/Sch

11182. Gibbons, R. W. "Blacklash and the Catholic Vote; Miller's
Catholicism." Christian Century (81; Oct. 21, 1964), pp. 1303-
5.   DHU/R

11183. Gillard John Thomas and John Lafarge, et al. Catholic
Students' Missions Crusade, U. S. A. Apostolate to Negro
America. Cincinnati: n. p., 1959.   NNUT

11184. Greeley, Andrew M. "White Parish--Refuge on Resource."
Interracial Review (35; Jl., 1962), pp. 168-9. DHU/R

11185. Groppi, James E. "The Church and Black America."
Conversations (Special Issue; Aut., 1973), pp. 17-19.
                                   Pam. File, DHU/R

11186. Harbutt, Charles. "The Church and Integration." Jubilee
(6; Feb., 1959), pp. 6-15.   DGU

11187. Hartnett, Robert C. "The Divine Doctrine of Brotherhood."
Interracial Review (35; Apr., 1962), pp. 96-7. DHU/R

11188. "Heart of the Matter; Pastoral Letter Officially Banning
Racial Discrimination." Nation (196; Mr. 16, 1963), p. 218.
                                                 DHU

11189. Hellwig, M. "Crash Attack on Prejudice, Suggestions for
a Parish Effort During Lent." America (120; Feb. 15, 1969),
pp. 193-94.   DHU

11190. Hesburgh, Theodore M. "Father Hesburgh's Program for
Racial Justice." The Y. W. C. A. Magazine (67:2, Feb.,
1973), pp. 13-15.   DHU/R
Written by President of Notre Dame University and Chairman of the U. S. Commission on Civil Rights.

11191. Holden, Anna. "A Call to Catholics." Interracial Review
(35; Je., 1962), pp. 140-43.   DHU
To participate in nonviolent direct action movement.

11192. "How Catholic Groups Should Work to Integrate the Negro."
Interracial Review (38; Apr., 1965), pp. 74+. DHU/MO

11193. "How do Churches Get Involved?" Christian Century
(80; Apr. 3, 1963), p. 420.   DHU/R

11194. Hurley, Denis E. "Second Vatican and Racism." Interracial Review (36; Dec., 1963), p. 11.   DHU/R

11195. "Indicative Concession." Christian Century (84; My. 22,
1967), p. 709.   DHU/R
Unfavorable treatment given Catholic Interracial Council
by Chicago Roman Catholic Archdiocese.

11196. "Integration and the Christian Conscience." Catholic Mind
(57; Oct., 1959), p. 469.   DLC

11197. "Interracial Council; Request for Amendment Specify that
It is Un-Christian to Discriminate on Grounds of Race."
America (109; Nov. 9, 1963), p. 544.   DHU

11198. "Interracial Franciscans; Third Order of St. Francis."
America (105; Apr. 29, 1961), p. 206.   DHU

11199. "Interracial Justice." Catholic International Outlook
(17; 1956), pp. 21-22.   DCU/ST

11200. "Is Segregation at the End of Its Rope?" Catholic World
(183; Apr., 1956), pp. 2-3.   DHU/R

11201. Kearney, John. "Interracial Justice and the Indwelling of
Christ Among All Men of Earth." Interracial Review (35;
Dec., 1962), p. 263.   DCU/SW

11202. La Farge, John. "American Catholics and the Negro."
Social Order (12; Apr., 1962), pp. 153-61.   DHU

11203. ----- "Direct Action." Interracial Review (36; Sept.,
1963), pp. 159f.   DCU/SW

11204. ----- "Pope John on Racism." Interracial Review (36;
Je., 1963), pp. 110+.   DCU/SW

11205. ----- "Translating into Action." Interracial Review
(35; Apr., 1962), pp. 92-95.   DCU/SW

11206. ----- "Why Say 'Interracial'?" Interracial Review (35;
Feb., 1962), pp. 44-45.   DCU/SW

11207. Leonard, Joseph T. Theology and Race Relations. Milwaukee: Bruce Pub. Co., 1963. DHU/R; NN/Sch; CtY-D

11208. Mallette, D. "White Priest in the Black Revolution."
Community (24; Oct., 1964), pp. 6-7.   DCU/SW

11209. Mattingly, T. "Gwynn Oak; Nine Catholic Priests Startled
Baltimore by Joining with the Pickets to Protest Segregation
at an Amusement Park." America (109; Ag. 10, 1963), pp.
136-7. Reply Gallagher, F. K. (109; Sept. 14, 1963), p. 249.
                                                    DHU

11210. McDermott, J. A. "Chicago Catholic Asks: Where Does
My Church Stand on Racial Justice?" Look (30; Nov. 1,
1966), pp. 82+.   DHU

11211. McIlvane, D. W. "Racial Balance in Catholic Schools."
Community (25; My., 1966), p. 7.   DHU/MO

11212. McLees, A. V. "Catholic and the NAACP." Crisis (63;
Je.-Jl., 1956), pp. 325-27+.   DHU/MO

11213. McManus, Eugene P. Studies in Race Relations. Baltimore: Josephite, 1961.   DHU/MO
An appeal for Christian principles in race relations.
                                                    DLC

11214. Mehan, Joseph. "Catholic Perspectives on Interracialism."
Interracial Review (35; Oct., 1962), pp. 222-23.   DCU/SW

11215. "Mockery of Tokenism; Meeting of Catholic Negroes and
Whites in Memphis." America (112; Apr. 3, 1965), p. 444.
                                                    DHU

11216. "Moral Miracle; Cardinal Cushing's Plea for Change of
Attitude Toward Negroes." America (110; Je. 6, 1964), p.
785.   DHU

11217. "National Catholic Conference for Interracial Justice Commitment." (Jl.-Ag., 1969).   Pam. File, DHU/R

11218. "The National Catholic Conference for Interracial Justice
Launches a New Project to Use Church Buying Power to
Fight Bias in Employment Against Negroes, Jews and
Other Minorities." Interracial Review (37; Oct., 1964),
pp. 178.   DHU/MO

11219. National Catholic Conference for Interracial Justice, Project Equality Council. Affirmative Action for Equal Employment Opportunity Through Churches, Synagogues and Related
Institutions. Chicago: NCCIJ, 1967.   Pam. File, DHU/R

11220. "Negro Dilemma: The Catholic Parish." Interracial Review (36; Sept., 1963), pp. 167-69+.   DHU/MO

11221. "New Catholic Bishop." Editorial. Crisis (72; Oct.,
1965), p. 485.   DHU/MO

11222. "No Postponement; Concerning Jesuit Letter on the Race
Question." America (109; Dec. 14, 1963), pp. 762-3. DHU

11223. "Nuns at Selma Sister Thomas Marguerite." America
(112; Apr. 3, 1965), pp. 454-6.   DHU

11224. O'Connor, John J. "Catholic Interracial Movement."
Social Order (10; Sept., 1960), pp. 290-95.   DCU/SW

11225. Osborne, William A. The Segregated Convenant; Race
Relations and American Catholics. New York: Herder and
Herder, 1964. BLGTL; DLC; NjP; DHU/MO; NcD

11226. Palms, Charles L. "A Harlem Priest Reports on Selma."
Catholic World (201:1, 203, Je., 1965), pp. 171-76. DHU/R
An interview with Fr. Edward T. Dugan.

11227. Patterson, Bernardin J. "Reflection of a Negro Priest."
Catholic World (200:1, 199, Feb., 1965), pp. 269-76. DHU/R

11228. Pohlhaus, J. Francis. "Catholic Involvement in Civil
Rights Legislation." Interracial Review (36; Oct., 1963),
pp. 192-95.   DCU/SW

11229. "Priestly Witness; Protest Against Failure of the Arch-
diocese to Take Leadership on Civil Rights Issues." America
(112; Ja. 16, 1965), pp. 66+.   DHU

11230. "Priests in Protest." America (109; Jl. 27, 1963), p. 91.
                                                    DHU

11231. "Priests' Pledge on Race." America (109; Oct., 1963), p.
376.   DHU

11232. "Priests' Protest." Time (85; Jan. 8, 1965), p. 38.
                                                    DHU

11233. "Racial Agenda for Catholics." Christianity Today (12;
My. 24, 1968), p. 39.   DHU/R

11234. "Racial Polls; Attitude of Catholics." America (111; Nov.
7, 1964), p. 541.   DHU

11235. "Religion and Race." America (110; My. 16, 1964), p. 662.
                                                    DHU

11236. "Religion and Race; Moves of Protestant Communions to
Foster Racial Unity." America (110; Je. 6, 1964), p. 785.
                                                    DHU

11237. Schuyler, Joseph B. "Apostolic Opportunity." Interracial
Review (35; Ja., 1962), pp. 20-21.   DCU/SW

11238. Senser, Robert. Primer on Interracial Justice. Baltimore:
Helicon, 1962.   DHU/MO
Catholic viewpoint.

11239. Sheerin, John B. "Catholic Involvement in Civil Rights."
Catholic World (201:1, 201, Apr., 1965), pp. 93-96. DHU/R

11240. Split-Level Lives; American Nuns Speak on Race, edited
by Sister Mary Peter Traxler. Techny, Ill.: Divine Word
Publications, 1967.   DHU/MO
Essays developed from lectures, experiences and seminars
by members of traveling workshop teams sponsored by the
National Catholic Conference for Interracial Justice.

11241. Sullivan, Kathryn (Mother). "Sacred Scripture and Race."
Religious Education (59:1, Ja.-Feb., 1964), pp. 10-13.
                                                    DHU/R

11242. Thomas, Howard E. Organizing for Human Rights; a Handbook for Teachers and Students, by Howard E. Thomas and
Sister Mary Peter. Dayton, O.: G. A. Pflaum, 1966. DLC

11243. Thornman, Donald J. "Catholic Approach to the Race Problem." America (95; My. 5, 1956), pp. 133-34.   DHU

11244. "Toward Open Hiring; Anti-Discrimination Pledges in
Church Contracts." Commonweal (81; Ja. 15, 1965), p. 500.
                                                    DHU

11245. "William Gerard Warthling, A Capacity for Outrage."
William H. Crook and Ross Coggins. Seven Who Fought (Waco,
Texas: Word Books, 1971), pp. 68-87.   DHU/R

White Catholic priest, asst. pastor at St. Nicholas Roman
Catholic Church, Buffalo, New York and his struggles
with his Bishop to bring racial justice to his ministry.

11246. Woods, Frances Jerome (Sister). "The Pope on Minority
Rights." Social Order (8; 1958), pp. 465-72. DGU; DCU/SW

12. Seventh Day Adventist

11247. Blake, Donald F. The Inner City; a Brief Synopsis of its
Complex Composition. n.p.: n.p., 1968.   MiBsA
Church and race problems, Seventh Day Adventists.

11248. Ford, Leighton. "Evangelism in a Day of Revolution."
The Message Magazine (36:4, Jl., 1970), pp. 4-7.
Pam. File; DHU/R
"What the position of a Church should be in an age of
revolution."

11249. Keidel, Levi O. "Where America's Racial Troubles Began." Message Magazine (35:4, Jl., 1969), pp. 22+. DHU/R

11250. Motley, Constance B. "Progress in Race Relations." The
Message Magazine (31:4, Jl., 1965), pp. 7+.   DHU/R
Negro author.

11251. Smith, Norma J. "Will Slavery Come Back in Disguise?"
The Message Magazine (29:5, Ag., 1963), pp. 13+.   DHU/R

13. Unitarian Universalist Association

11252. Atkins, James. "New Voice in Birmingham." Unitarian
Register and the Universalist Leader (141:3, Mr., 1962), pp.
5-7.   DHU/R

11253. Blanshard, Mary H. "The Outlook for Equal Rights."
Unitarian Register and the Universalist Leader (141:3, Mr.,
1962), pp. 13-15.   DHU/R

11254. Harrington, Donald. "Black and White Action." Now:
The Magazine of the Unitarian Universalist Association (50:
5, Aut., 1969), p. 4.   DHU/R

11255. Hemstreet, Robert. "We Shall Overcome." Unitarian
Universalist Register Leader (145:9, Nov., 1963), pp. 4-6.
DHU/R
Unitarian and Universalists join Washington March for
jobs and freedom.

11256. Hoffman, Clifton G. "On Trial in Mississippi." Unitarian
Register and the Universalist Leader (140:7, Mid-Sum., 1961),
pp. 3-5.   DHU/R
Report of trial shows basis for sentencing of twenty-seven
Freedom Riders.

11257. "How 'Open' is the Unitarian Door?" Christian Register
(Apr., 1954), Repr.   DHU/R

11258. Howlett, Duncan. "A Lover of His Fellow Man: Two
Tributes to James J. Reeb." Register-Leader (147:5, My.,
1965), p. 5.   DHU/R
Tribute to Associate Minister of All Souls Church, Washington, D.C. who was shot in Selma, Alabama participating in a freedom march.

11259. ----- No Greater Love: The James Reeb Story. New
York: Harper & Row, 1966.   DHU/R
Story of a Unitarian minister and the "Civil Rights
Movement, 1954-67."

11260. MacLean, Angus H. The Wind in Both Ears. Boston:
Beacon Press, 1965.   DHU/R
Unitarian Universalist minister discusses religious
liberals.

11261. Merrill, Charles. "Negro Pressure and White Liberals."
Register-Leader (149:6, Je. 1967), pp. 3-6.   DHU/R

11262. Ulman, Joseph N. "Two Days in Alabama--1965." Register-Leader (147:5, My., 1965), pp. 6-9.   DHU/R

14. General

11263. Abrams, Charles. "Civil Rights in 1956." Commentary
(22:2, Ag., 1956), pp. 101-09.   DHU/R

11264. "Action for Interracial Understanding." Franciscan Herald and Forum (42; Oct., 1963), p. 289.   DCU

11265. Adkins, Rufus. The Role of the Minister in the Civil Rights
Movement of Little Rock Arkansas. B.D. Paper, School of
Religion, Howard University, 1966.

11266. Assenheimer, R.C. "Doing is the Difference; Student
Interracial Ministry Reply." America (112; Apr. 14, 1965),
pp. 560-1.   DHU

11267. "Atlanta Manifesto." Theology Today (15:2, Jl., 1958),
pp. 165-6.   DHU/R
Statement by clergymen in Georgia on racial integration.

11268. "Atlanta Ministers Ask Racial Calm." Christian Century
(74; Nov. 13, 1957), p. 1340.   DHU

11269. Baggett, Hudson. "Recent Riots, The Harvest of False
Hopes." Editorial. The Alabama Baptist (131; Ag. 11, 1966),
p. 2.   LNB; TND

11270. Baitzell, E. Digby. The Protestant Establishment: Aris-
tocracy and Caste in America. New York: Random House,
1964.   DHU/R

11271. Banner, William Augustus. "An Ethical Basis for Racial
Understanding." Religious Education (59:1, Ja.-Feb., 1964),
pp. 17-19.   DHU/R

11272. Barbee, J.M. "Pastor Faces Racial Change." Christian
Advocate (5:2, 1961), pp. 7+.   DAU/W; DHU/R

11273. Bennett, John C. "The Demand for Freedom and Justice
in the Contemporary World Revolution." Walter Leibrecht
(ed.). Religion and Culture (New York: Harper and Brothers,
Publishers, 1959), pp. 321-34.   DHU/R
Essays in honor of Paul Tillich.

11274. Berger, Morroe. "Desegregation, Law, and Social Science."
Commentary (23:5, My., 1957), pp. 471-77.   DHU/R

11275. Bernard, Raymond. "Protestant Work in Race Relations."
Interracial Review (27; Ja., 1954), pp. 7-8.   DHU/MO

11276. Berrett, William Edwin. The Church and the Negroid
People. Orem, Utah: Bookmark Division, Community Press
Pub. Co., 1963.   DLC

11277. Bettelheim, Bruno. "Sputnik and Segregation." Commentary (26:4, Oct., 1958), pp. 332-39.   DHU/R
An experienced psychologist and educator examines this
two-fold problem and suggests that there may be a tendency
to replace the color-line by a new kind of social discrimination.

11278. Bickel, Alexander M. "The Civil Rights Act of 1964." Commentary (48:2, Ag., 1964), pp. 33-39.   DHU/R

11279. "Biracial Membership Exchange Scores Hit!" Pittsburgh
Courier (Jl. 24; 1965).   Pam. File; DHU/R

11280. "Bishop Deplores Worshippers Shut-Out." World Outlook
(24; Ja., 1964), p. 49.   DHU/R; DAU/W

11281. "The Black American. Pt. 5: Struggle for Civil and Hu-
man Rights." Alpha Corp. of America, 1968. 52 fr. color.
35 mm. & phonodisc: 2s.   DLC
Filmstrip.
"Describes various events in the struggle being waged by
Negroes for civil and human rights. Includes scenes of
sit-ins and riots, of James Meredith, of Martin L. King,
Jr., and of Thurgood Marshall."

11282. "----- Pt. 6: Cultural and Social Aspects of Struggle for Civil Rights." Alpha Corp. of America, 1968. 46 fr. color 35 mm. & phonodisc: 2 s.   DLC
Filmstrip.
"Describes the cultural and social aspects of the struggle for civil rights, and discusses the role of the church in this struggle."

11283. Blake, E. C. "Should Churches Speak Out on Race Problems Here and Abroad?" Excerpts from Address, April 18, 1960. U. S. News & World Report (48; My. 2, 1960), pp. 100-03.   DHU

11284. Blanchard, E. D. "National Council in Mississippi, Special Report." Christian Advocate (8; Ag., 13, 1964), p. 3.   DAU/W; DHU/R

11285. Bland, T. A. "Role of the Local Church In Human Relations." Review and Expositor (56; Jl., 1959), pp. 271-79.   DLC; CtY-D

11286. Boggs, Marion. "The Crucial Test of Christian Citizenship." New South (12; Jl.-Ag., 1957), pp. 7-8.   DHU/W
Little Rock minister denounces legal hindrance toward solving the problem in America.

11287. Boyle, Sarah Patton and John Howard Griffin. "The Racial Crisis: An Exchange of Letters." Christian Century (My. 22, 1968), pp. 679-83.   DHU/R

11288. Bradley, Sam. "Martin Luther King and Freedom." Friends Journal (7:18, Sept. 15, 1961), pp. 370+.   DHU/R

11289. Brennecke, Gerhard. "Inter-Group Relations--The Church Amid Racial and Ethnic Tensions." Ecumenical Review (7:1, Oct., 1954), pp. 49-55.   DHU/R

11290. Brink, William and Louis Harris. The Negro Revolution in America. New York: Simon & Schuster, 1963. DHU/R; INU
                                                               CtY-D
Chapter 6, "The Role of the Negro Church," pp. 96-110.

11291. Brown, Robert Raymond (bp.). "Little Rock and the Churches." Union Seminary Quarterly Review (13:2, Ja., 1958), pp. 19-27.   DHU/R
Discusses the Church's role in the crisis over integration.

11292. Bryant, F. "On Integration in the Churches." Review and Expositor (53; Apr., 1956), pp. 200-06.   DLC; CtY-D

11293. Buchanan, H. A. "Church and Desegration (Sermon)." Review and Expositor (52; Oct., 1955), pp. 475-82.
                                                               DLC; CtY-D

11294. ----- and B. W. Brown. "Integration: Great Dilema of the Church." Ebony (21; Je., 1966), pp. 163-4.   DHU

11295. Burns, Haywood. "The Rule of Law in the South." Commentary (40:3, Sept., 1965), pp. 80+.   DHU/R

11296. Burt, C. B. "From Grenda, Mississippi, a Minister Warns Christians: Stand up or Get Out!" Look (30; Dec. 27, 1966), pp. 34+.   DHU

11297. Caldwell, Gilbert H. "Black Folk in White Churches." Christian Century (86:7, Feb. 12, 1967), pp. 209-11. DHU/R

11298. Calhoun, D. "Human Freedom: Religion is the Enemy." Liberation (2; Jl.-Ag., 1957), 24-5.   DHU/R

11299. Campbell, Ernest Q. and Thomas F. Pettigrew. Christians in Racial Crisis; a Study of Little Rock's Ministry. Including Statements on Desegregation and Race Relation by the Leading Religious Denominations of the United States. Washington: Public Affairs Press, 1959. DHU/R; CtY-D; TSewll-T

11300. ----- "Racial and Moral Crisis; The Role of Little Rock Minsters." American Journal of Sociology (64; Mr., 1959), pp. 509-16.   DHU

11301. Cartwright, Colbert S. "Band Together for Genuine Unity." New South (16; Ja., 1961), pp. 6-10.   DAU/W
Little Rock minister's speech at Conference on Community Action.

11302. "Chicago Chruches Try Integration." Christian Century (73; Sept. 19, 1956), pp. 1080-81.   DHU

11303. "'Christian Guide' to Race Attitudes." New South (13:5, My., 1958), pp. 3-7.   DHU/MO
Text of Guide adopted by Gainesville-Hall County Ministerial Association, Georgia.

11304. "Christian Views of Civil Rights." America (115; Ag. 20, 1966), p. 167.   DHU

11305. "Church and Civil Rights." America (111; Ag. 8, 1964), p. 122.   DHU

11306. "Church and Segregation." Life (41; Oct. 1, 1956), pp. 46+.   DHU

11307. "Church Elements in the Segregation Struggle." Christian Century (72; Je. 1, 1955), pp. 644+.   DHU

11308. "A Church Looks at Civil Rights in North Carolina." New South (18:4, Apr., 1963), pp. 13-15.   DHU; DHU/R

11309. "Churches in the Civil-Rights Fight." The Crisis (67:2, Fe., 1960), pp. 87-88.   DLC; DHU/MO
"The Zion Baptist Chruch of Philadelphia, Pa., of which the Rev. Leon H. Sullivan is minister, is one of the nation's outstanding church supporters of the NAACP and its civil-rights program."

11310. "Churches Teaching on Race." America (115; Dec. 3, 1966), p. 730.   DHU

11311. Churchill, A. A. "Church Wavers in the South." Christian Century (73; Apr. 18, 1956), pp. 493+.   DHU/R

11312. "Churchmen and the Albany Movement." Christianity Today (6; Sept. 28, 1962), pp. 41-2.   DHU/R; DLC

11313. "Civil Rights and Religion." America (111; Jl. 25, 1964), p. 79.   DHU

11314. "Civil Rights Movement- Mississippi Summer Project." Richard Beymer. Released by Encyclopedia Britannica Eudcational Corp., 1966. 17 min. sd. b. & w. 16 mm.
Film.
"Depicts the civil rights movement in a single Mississippi community and highlights vital issues, such as the freedom schools set up by volunteers, labor exploitation, police brutality, voter registration and the challenge of achieving racial peace."

11315. "Civil Rights Movement- the North." National Broadcasting Co. Released by Encyclopedia Britannica Educational Corp., 1966. 23 min. sd. b & w. 16 mm.
Film.
"Presents news footage taken in Chicago when Negroes moved into a white area."

11316. "Civil Rights Movement, the Personal View." National Broadcasting Co. Released by Encyclopedia Britannica Educational Corp., 1966. 25 mm. s d. b & w. 16mm.
Film.
"Reveals attitudes of fear, hate, and suspicion between Negroes and whites."

11317. "Civil Rights Movement- The South." National Broadcasting Co. Released by Encyclopedia Britannica Educational Corp., 1966. 28 min. sd. b & w. 16 mm.
Film
"Examines the representative movements in the history of the protest, such as the Montgomery, Ala., bus boycott and the lunch sounter sit-ins."

11318. Clark, Thomas D., (ed.). The South Since Reconstruction. Indianapolis: The Bobbs-Merrill Co., Inc., 1973.   DHU/R
"A Christian view of Segregation, 1954," pp. 449-53;
"The Moral Aspects of Segregation," pp. 466-73.

11319. "Clubs, Pistols and Rifles Block Prayer Meet at Alabama Capitol." Journal and Guide (Mr. 12, 1961), Pam. File, DHU/R

11320. Cobb, Charles Earl. "Now More than Ever: the Church is Challenged." Social Action (33:4, Dec., 1966), pp. 12-22.
                                                        DHU/R
Negro author.

11321. Cogley, John. "The Clergy Heeds a New Call." New York Times Magazine (My. 2, 1965).   DHU
Selma, Ala., march and church leaders involvement in the civil rights movement.

11322. Cox, Harvey. "Letter from Williamston." Christian Century (80:49, Dec. 4, 1963), pp. 1516-18.   DHU/R
North Carolina and protest.

11323. Creger, Ralph and Erwin McDonald. A Look Down the Lonesome Road. Garden City, N.Y.: Doubleday, 1964.
                                                        DHU/R
Fundamentalist Baptist minister offers a solution to the "moral problem of integration."

11324. Crook, William H. and Ross Coggins. Seven Who Fought. Waco, Tex.: Word Books, 1971.   NjP; DHU/R
Biographies of white ministers who fought against white racism in their churches and communities.

11325. Danzig, David. "The Meaning of Negro Strategy." Commentary (37:2, Feb. 1964), pp. 41-46.   DHU/R

11326. Davies, Everett F. S. "The Negro Protest Movement: The Religious Way." Journal of Religious Thought (24:2, Aut.-Wint., 1967-68), pp. 13-25.   DHU/R

11327. Davis, J. A. "American Negro and Africa." Jewish Frontier (31; Mr., 1964), pp. 11-15.   DLC
Jewish and Negro relationships.

11328. Davis, Lloyd. "The Religious Dimension of Interracial Justice." Interracial Review (35; Feb., 1962), pp. 46-8.
                                                        DHU/R

11329. "Dealing with Racial and Ethnic Tensions." Christian Action (19; Feb., 1964), pp. 6+.   ICU

11330. DeMille, D. "All Race Chruch." Sepia (7; Ag., 1959), pp. 68-70.   NN/Sch

11331. Denham, John. "A Christian Educator's Involvement in the Race Crisis." Religious Education (59:1, Ja.-Feb., 1964), pp. 95-7.   DHU/R

11332. Dinwoodie, W. "Missions' Council Considers Issue: Desegregation of Churches." Christian Century (72; Feb. 9, 1955), pp. 190+.   DHU/R

11333. Dollen, Charles, (ed.). Civil Rights; a Source Book. Boston: St. Paul Editions, 1964.   NN/Sch
A compilation of excerpts from writing of modern Popes, statements from American Bishops, and quotations from the New Testament dealing with the subject of civil rights.

11334. "Don't Come Unto Me: Negro Admissions Cause Clergy Sacking in Macon, Ga." New Republic (155; Nov. 12, 1966), pp. 9-10.   DLC

11335. "Drive on Discrimination Shows Ecumenical Approach." Central Christian Advocate (139; Feb. 15, 1964). DHU/R; DAU/W

11336. Eckhardt, Kenneth W. "Religiosity and Civil Rights Militancy." Review of Religious Research (2:3, Spr., 1970), pp. 197-203.   DHU/R

11337. Eddy, Elizabeth M. "Student Perspectives on the Southern Church." Phylon (25:4, Wint., 1964), pp. 369-81.
                                                        DHU/MO

11338. Ellison, John Malcus. They Sang Through the Crisis. Chicago: Judson Press, 1961.   DHU/MO; DLC
Negro author.

11339. Fey, Harold E. "Churches Meet Racial Crisis; with Test of Statement to Churches." Christian Century (80: 51, Dec. 18, 1963), pp. 1572-73.   DHU/R

11340. ----- "For Brotherhood and Union." Christian Century (71:24, Je. 16, 1954), pp. 726-28.   DHU/R

11341. Fichter, Joseph H. "American Religion and the Negro." Daedalus: Journal of the American Academy of Arts and Sciences. (94:4, Fall, 1965), pp. 1085-1106. DHU/R; INU
"Role of organized religion in the current Negro freedom movement."

11342. ----- and George L. Maddox. "Religion in the South, Old and New." John McKenney and Edgar Thompson, (eds.). The South in Continuity and Change. Durham, N.C.: Duke University Press, 1965.   NcD

11343. Fontaine, William Thomas. Refelctions on Segregation, Desegregation, Power and Morals. Springfield, Ill.: Thomas, 1967.   O

11344. Foot, S. H. "On Reconciling Races and Nations." World Outlook (22; Mr., 1962), pp. 30+.   DAU/W

11345. Foshey, Gerald. "Divided Flocks in Jackson." Christian Century (80:27, Nov. 27, 1963), pp. 1469-71.   DHU/R
Blacks attempt to enter white churches in the South.

11346. Frady, M. "God and Man in the South; Church's Indifference to Civil Rights Movement." Atlantic Monthly (219; Ja., 1967), pp. 37-42.   DHU

11347. Frakes, Margaret. "Two Church Unafraid." Christian Century (73:15, Apr. 11, 1956), pp. 450-52.   DHU/R
Two all-white churches in Chicago become inter-racial.

11348. Franklin, John Hope and Isidore Starr. The Negro in the 20th Century; A Reader on the Struggle for Civil Rights. New York: Vintage Books, 1967.   DHU/R
Pp. 203-07, religious leaders and civil rights.
Also Martin Luther King and S. C. L. C.
Negro author.

11349. Fraser, Thomas P. "Desegregation and the Church." Union Seminary Quarterly Review (11:3, Mr. 1956), pp. 37-9.
                                                        DHU/R

11350. Fry, H. W. "On Race Relations." Christian Century (81; Sept. 9, 1964), pp. 1121-2.   DHU/R

11351. Gardner, E. C. "Justice and Love." Theology Today (14:2, Jl., 1957), pp. 212-22.   DHU/R

11352. Garfinkel, Herbert. When Negroes March; the March on Washington Movement in the Organizational Politics for FEPC. Glencoe, Ill.: Free Press, 1959.   O

11353. Gerner, Henry L. A Study of the Freedom Riders with Particular Emphasis Upon Three Dimensions: Dogmatism, Value Orientation and Religiosity. Doctoral dissertation. Pacific School of Religion, 1963.

11354. Gilbert, A. "Biblical Teaching About Race Relations - an Old Testament Perspective." Religious Education (59; Ja.-Feb., 1964), pp. 14-17.   DHU/R

11355. Glazer, Nathan. "Is 'Integration' Possible in the New York Schools?" Commentary (30:3, Sept., 1960), pp. 185-93.   DHU/R

11356. Glock, Charles Y. "Religion and the Integration of Society." Review of Religious Research (2:2, Fall, 1960), pp. 49-61.   DHU/R

11357. "Glorius Opportunity; Establishment of Emergency Commission on Religion and Race." Newsweek (62; Jl. 8, 1963), p. 55.   DHU

11358. Goodman, D. "Churches and Civil Rights." Central Christian Advocate (140; Oct. 15, 1965), pp. 5+. DAU/W; DHU/R

11359. Goodman, Paul. "The Children of Birmingham." Commentary (36:3, Sept., 1963), pp. 242-44.   DHU/R

11360. Gordon, Albert I. Intermarriage; Interfaith, Interracial, Interethnic. Boston: Beacon, 1964.   DHU/MO

11361. Graham, Billy. "Why Don't Our Churches Practice the Brotherhood They Preach?" Reader's Digest (77; Ag. 1960), pp. 52-6.   DHU

11362. Gremley, W. "Negroes in Your Parish." America (107; Sept. 1962), pp. 817-19. Reply. Ahmann, M. (107; Apr. 14, 1962), p. 35.   DHU

11363. Grier, Woodrow A. "Calm Desegregation." Christian Century (79:43, Oct. 24, 1962), p. 1302.   DHU/R

11364. Groppi, James E. "The Church and Civil Rights." Malcolm Boyd, ed. The Underground Church (New York: Sheed & Ward, 1968), pp. 70-83.   DHU/R

11365. Hadden, Jeffrey K. "Clergy Involvement in Civil Rights." Annals of the American Academy of Political & Social Science (387; Ja., 1970), pp. 118-27.   DHU

11366. Halvorsen, Lawrence W. The Church in a Diverse Society. Minneapolis: Augsburg Pub. House, 1964.   CtY-D

11367. Handlin, Oscar. "Civil Rights After Little Rock." Commentary (24:5, Nov., 1957), pp. 392-96.   DHU/R

11368. Hanish, Joseph J. "Catholics, Protestants and the American Negro." Nuntius Aulae (43; 1961), pp. 98-115. Pam. File.   DHU

11369. Harding, Vincent. Must Walls Divide? New York: Friendship Press, 1965.   DHU/R
       Questions for Christians about race relations. Negro author.

11370. ----- "Toward the Other Shore; Freedom Movement as Seen by a Church Leader." Reporter (29: Oct. 10, 1963), pp. 27-31.
                                        DGW; DCU/SW; DGW

11371. Haselden, Kyle E. "Religion and Race." Christian Century (80:5, Ja. 30, 1963), pp. 133-35.   DHU/R

11372. Hays, Brooks. A Southern Moderate Speaks. Chapel Hill: University of North Carolina Press, 1959.   NN/Sch
       Church and Race Relations, pp. 195-215.

11373. Henderlite, R. "Christian Way in Race Relations." Theology Today (14; Jl., 1957), pp. 195-211   DHU/R

11374. Herberg, Will. "A Religious 'right' to Violate the Law?" National Review (16; Jl. 14, 1964), p. 579. DAU; DCU/SW;
                                                  DGU; DHU

11375. Hill, Samuel S., Jr. Southern Churches in Crisis. New York: Holt, Rinehart and Winston, 1969.   DLC; DHU/R
       Negro church, pp. 92+.

11376. ----- "Southern Protestantism and Racial Integration." Religion in Life (33:3, Sum., 1964), pp. 421-29. DHU/R

11377. ----- "The Uses of Religion in the South." Cross Currents (16:3, Sum., 1966), pp. 339-48.   DHU/R
       A chapter from the author's book, Southern Churches in Crisis.

11378. Hinwood, Bonaventura. Race: the Reflections of a Theologian. Rome: Herder, 1964.   NNCor

11379. "Historic Pulpit Swap; Negro and White Pastors Exchange Homes, Too." Ebony (12:12, Oct. 1957), pp. 69-70+.   DHU/MO

11380. "Hollow Gesture or Omens of Unity? Election of Negroes to Highest Honorary Posts in White-Dominated Protestant Churches." Christian Century (82:27, Jl. 14, 1965), pp. 884-85.   DHU/R

11381. Horchler, Richard. "The Layman's Role in the Changing Community." Interracial Review (35; Ja., 1962), pp. 12-13.   DHU/R

11382. Hughley, Judge Neal. "The Church, the Ministry, and the Negro Revolt." Journal of Religious Thought (22:2, 1965-66), pp. 121-40.   DHU/R
       Negro author.

11383. ----- "Integration in the Church." Theology Today (14:2, Jl., 1957), pp. 223-28.   DHU/R

11384. Hurley, Phillip S. "Role of the Churches in Integration." Journal of Intergroup Relations (1; Sum., 1960), pp. 41-6.   DLC

11385. Ianniello, Lynne. Milestones Along the March; Twelve Historic Civil Rights Documents From World War II to Selma... New York: F. A. Praeger, 1966.   O

11386. "Integration Hits the Churches." Ebony (13; My., 1958), pp. 43-4.   DHU/MO

11387. "Integration Lacks in Northern Churches." Christian Century (72; Oct. 12, 1955), pp. 1165+.   DHU/R

11388. James, E. S. "Desegregation, Yes - By Legislation, No." Editorial. Baptist Standard (75; Jl. 24, 1963), p. 3.
                                                  LNB; TxFS

11389. Johnson, Philip A. Call Me Neighbor, Call Me Friend: the Case History of the Integration of a Neighborhood on Chicago's South Side. Garden City, N. Y.: Doubleday, 1965.   INU; DHU/R; DLC; CtY-D

11390. Jordan, Clarence. "Christian Community in the South." Journal of Religious Thought (14:1, Aut. -Wint., 1956-57), pp. 27-36.   DHU/R

11391. Joseph, James A. "The Rebellion Against Absolutes." The Journal of the Interdenominational Theological Center (1:1, Fall, 1973), pp. 50-54.   DHU/R
       Black rebellion and theology in the sixties. Commencement address at the Interdenominational Theological Center, Atlanta, Ga., May 6, 1973.

11392. Keedy, T. C. "Anomic and Religious Orthodoxy." Sociology and Social Research (43; 1958), pp. 34-7.
                                                       DHU

11393. Kelley, James Robert. The Church and Segregation. Bachelor of Divinity Paper. Andover Newton Theological School, 1959.

11394. Kelsey, George D. "Churches and Freedom." Journal of Religious Thought (14:1, Aut. -Wint., 1956-57), pp. 17-26.   DHU/R
       Negro author.

11395. ----- "The Ethico-Cultural Revolution in American Race Relations." Religion in Life (26:3, Sum., 1957), pp. 335-44.   DHU/R

11396. King, C. H. "Negro Ministers Have Not Failed. Have Sociologists?" Negro Digest (13; Nov., 1963), pp. 43-4.
                                                     DHU/MO

11397. Kitagawa, Daisuke. "The Pastor and the Race Issue."
Motive (26; Oct. , 1965), pp. 54+.   DHU/R; DAU/W
Book Review.

11398. ----- "Theological and Non-Theological Factors in Race
Relations." Ecumenical Review (13:3, Apr. , 1961), pp. 335-41.
DHU/R

11399. Kramer, Alfred S. "The Churches and Race Relations."
News Service (34; Ja. -Feb. , 1963), pp. 4-5.
NN/Sch; CtY-D

11400. ----- "For Those Who Inherit." Religious Education (59:1,
Ja. -Feb. , 1964), pp. 56-59.   DHU/R
The religious educator's responsibility in dealing with
racial prejudice.

11401. Kraus, C. Norman. Integration: Who's Prejudiced?
Scottdale, Pa.: Mennonite Publishing House, 1958.
DHU/R
The author, a Mennonite, "examines racial prejudice
in light of reason and Christian faith."

11402. Kruuse, Elsa. "The Churches Act on Integration."
National Council Outlook (7; Mr. , 1957), pp. 6-8.
DHU/R

11403. Lawrence, N. "Racially Inclusive Churches."
National Council Outlook (4; Dec. , 1954), pp. 10-12.
DHU/R

11404. Lee, Carlton Lafayette. "Religious Roots of the Negro
Protest." Arnold Rose (ed.). Assuring Freedom to the
Free: A Century of Emancipation. (Detroit: Wayne State
University Press, 1964), p. 47.   DHU/R
Negro author.

11405. Lee, J. Oscar. "Churches and Race Relations."
Christianity and Crisis (17; Feb. 4, 1957), pp. 4-7.
Negro author.   DAU/W

11406. ----- "The Freedom Movement and the Ecumenical Movement." The Ecumenical Review (17:1, Ja. , 1965), pp. 18-28.
DHU/R

11407. ----- "Racism: Effects, Origins, Remedies: The Time for
All-Out, Massive Effort to Eliminate Racial Discrimination is
Now." The African Methodist Episcopal Church Review (78:218,
Oct. -Dec. , 1963), pp. 30-34.   DHU/R

11408. ----- "The Status of the Racial Integration in Religious
Institutions." Reprint: Journal of Negro Education (23:3, Sum. ,
1954), pp. 231-41.   Pam. File, DHU/R; DHU/MO

11409. "A Legacy of Creative Protest." The Massachusetts
Review (4; Aut. , 1962), p. 43   DHU

11410. "Let Justice Roll Down." Nation (200; Mr. 15, 1965),
p. 269.   DHU; DGW; DGU; DCU/SW; DAU

11411. Lincoln, Charles Eric. "The American Protest
Movement for Negro Rights." John P. Davis, (ed.).
The American Negro Reference Book (Englewood-Cliffs,
N. J.: Prentice-Hall, Inc. , 1966), pp. 458-83 DHU/R
Negro author.

11412. ----- "Five Fears for Integration." Central Christian Advocate (132:17, Sept. 1, 1957), pp. 4-7.   DHU/R

11413. Lippincott, H. H. "Still Jimcrow Churches?"
Christian Century (72; Feb. 9, 1955), pp. 172+ DHU/R

11414. Liu, William T. "The Community Reference System,
Religiosity, and Race Attitudes." Social Forces (39;
My. , 1961), pp. 324-28.   DHU

11415. Loescher, Frank S. "Racism in the Northern City
Churches." Christian Century (73:6, Feb. 8, 1956),
pp. 174-76   DHU/R

11416. ----- "A Religious Approach to Discrimination." Friends
Journal (1:23, Dec. 3, 1955), p. 364.   DHU/R

11417. Long, Herman H. "Beyond Tokenism." Social Action
(30:1, Sept. , 1963), pp. 5-13.   DHU/R
Negro author.

11418. "Looking at the Other Side of Church Inclusiveness."
Central Christian Advocate (140; Jl. 1, 1965), p. 3.
DAU/W; DHU/R

11419. "Love Shall Overcome." Presbyterian Survey (58:6,
Je. , 1968), entire issue. Pam. File   DHU/R

11420. "Many Methodists March." Central Christian Advocate
(138; Oct. 15, 1963), p. 14.   DHU/R; DAU/W

11421. Marcis, C. L. "Next Steps for Churches in Race
Relations." Social Action (26; Sept. , 1959), pp. 24-27.
DHU/R

11422. Marx, Gary T. "Religion: Opiate or Inspiration of
Civil Rights Militancy." Hart M. Nelsen & Raytha L.
Yokley, et alii. The Black Church in America (New
York: Basic Books, 1971), pp. 150-60.   DHU/R

11423. ----- "Religion: Opiate or Inspiration of Civil Rights
Militancy Among Negroes." Benjamin Quarles. The Negro in
the Making of America (New York: Macmillan, 1964), pp. 362-
75.   DHU/MO

11424. ----- "Religion: Opiate or Inspiration of Civil Rights
Militancy Among Negroes?" Marcel L. Goldschmidt, (ed.).
Black Americans and White Racism; Theory and Research
(New York: Holt, Rinehart and Winston, 1970), pp. 366-75.
DHU/MO
Marx's chapter also in: Edward Greer. Black Libera-
tion Politics: A Reader.

11425. Mather, P. B. "Religion and Race; Local Efforts."
Christian Century (80; Mar. 27, 1963), pp. 412-14.
DHU/R

11426. Mays, Benjamin Elijah. "The Church Amidst Ethnic
and Racial Tensions." The African Methodist Episcopal
Church Review (10:182, Oct. -Dec. , 1954), pp. 86-88.
DHU/R
Negro author.

11427. ----- "Church Will be Challenged at Evanston." Christianity and Crisis (14:14, 1954), pp. 106-08.   DHU/R

11428. ----- "Churches Will Follow." Christian Century (81; Apr.
22, 1964), pp. 513-14.   DHU/R

11429. McCoy, C. "Way Toward Integration." Christian
Century (75; Feb. 12, 1958), pp. 195-7.   DHU

11430. McCutcheon, James N. "Jesus Christ and Civil
Rights." Crisis (80:9, Nov. , 1973), pp. 303-06.
DHU/R; DHU/MO

11431. McGill, Ralph. "The Agony of the Southern Minister."
New York Times Magazine (Sept. 27, 1959).   DHU

11432. McMillan, G. "Silent White Ministers of the South."
N. Y. Times Magazine (Apr. 5, 1964), pp. 22+. DHU

11433. McNeill, Robert B. God Wills Us Free: the
Ordeal of a Southern Minister. New York: Hill and Wang,
1965.   PPT; DLC; INU; DHU/MO

11434. Memmi, Albert. Dominated Man. New York: Orion
Press, 1968.   DHU/R; DHU/MO
    Chapter 1, The Paths of the Revolt, is a commentary
    on the historic TV show (later published as The Negro
    Protest) which presented the views of James Baldwin,
    Malcolm X and Martin Luther King. (This essay
    appeared as the French intro. to THE NEGRO PROTEST);
    Chapter 2, A Total

11435. Merton, Thomas. "The Hot Summer of Sixty-Seven."
Katallagete (Wint., 1967-68), pp. 28-34.   DHU/R
    A Catholic's criticism of black militancy and a call
    for the return to Dr. King's philosphy of non-violence.

11436. "Methodist Bishops Evade Big Issues." Christian
Century (73; My. 9, 1956), pp. 573+.   DHU/R

11437. Meyer, A. C. "Integration in Church Schools."
Integrated Education (2; Je.-Jl., 1964), pp. 45-46.
                                               DHU/MO

11438. Meyers, R. N. "Christian Service Corp." Christianity
Today (8; Jl. 17, 1964), pp. 11-13.   DHU/R

11439. "Michigan Council Releases Policy Statement on Civil
Rights, 1960." Interchurch News (1; Ag., 1960), p. 4.
                                               DLC

11440. "Militant Clergy; Critics Fire Back." U. S. News
(63; Nov. 27, 1967), pp. 66-8.   DHU

11441. Miller, F. P. "Southern Protestants and Desegregation." New Republic (141; Nov. 2, 1959), pp. 17-18.
                                               DGU

11442. Miller, William Robert. Nonviolence; A Christian
Interpretation. New York: Association Press, 1964.
                                               DHU/R

11443. Minear, L. "Hattiesburg: Toward Reconciliation;
Hattiesburg Minister's Project." Christian Century
(81; Mar. 11, 1964), pp. 340-41.   DHU/R

11444. "Ministers' Statement of Conviction on Race."
New South (12; Apr., 1957), pp. 3-6.   DAU/W
    Ministers Association of Richmond, Va.

11445. "Miracle in Kentucky; In Blue Grass State Black and
White Work, Pray, Eat and Sleep Together." Our World
(8; Ag. 1953), pp. 20-26+.   DLC; DHU/MO

11446. Mitchell, Henry H. "Toward a New Integration."
Christian Century (85; Je. 12, 1968), pp. 780-82.
    Negro author.

11447. Moellering, Ralph Luther. Christian Conscience and
Negro Emancipation. Philadelphia: Fortress Press,
1965.   NcD; CtY-D; NN/Sch; DLC; A&M

11448. Morgenthau, M. J. "Coming Test of American
Democracy." Commentary (37; Ja., 1964), pp. 61-3
                                               DHU/R

11449. "National Council Churches Launches Interfaith Movement in Race Crisis." Christian Advocate (7; Jl. 4, 1963),
p. 22.   DHU/R; DAU/W

11450. "Negro Kneel-ins in White Churches in Savannah, Ga."
New South (20; Jl.-Aug., 1965), pp. 2+.   DHU/R

11451. "Negro-White Church Union Brings Melee." Washington
Post (Je. 1, 1953). Pam. File.   DHU/R

11452. Nelson, J. Robert. "Race and Denomination--One
Issue." Christian Century (78; Dec. 27, 1961),
pp. 1554-55.   DHU/R

11453. "New Commitments of Religions in Civil Rights; John
LaFarge Institute Report." America (114; Feb. 26, 1966),
pp. 292-93.   DHU

11454. Nichols, L. and L. Cassels. "Churches Repent."
Harper's (211; Oct., 1955), pp. 53-7.   DLC

11455. Northwood, Lawrence K. "Ecological and Attitudinal
Factors in Church Desegregation." Social Problems
(6; Fall, 1958), pp. 150-63.   DAU

11456. "183 Churches: No Color Bar." Christian Advocate
(6; Mr. 15, 1962), pp. 23+.   DHU/R; DAU/W

11457. Osborne, William A. "The Church and Negro: A
Crisis in Leadership." Cross Currents (15; Wint., 1965),
pp. 129-50.   DHU/R

11458. "The Other Mississippi." New South (18; Mr., 1963),
pp. 1+.   DHU/R

11459. Parker, J. "The Interaction of Negroes and
Whites in an Integrated Church Setting." Social Forces
(46; 1968), pp. 359-66.   DHU; DGU

11460. Poinsett, Alex. "What the Bible Really Says About
Segregation." Ebony (17; Jl., 1962), pp. 73-6. DHU/MO

11461. Porteous, A. C. "Seminary and the Racial Crisis; Consultation on the Church and the Racial Crisis." Christian Century
(81; Jan. 29, 1964), pp. 147-8   DHU/R

11462. Poteat, Edwin McNiell. "Current Perspectives on the Race
Problem." Biblical Recorder (122; Feb. 4, 1956), pp. 2-3.
                                          LNB; NcWfSB

11463. "Prayers on Steps of Harlem Hospital." Amsterdam News
(Ag. 4, 1956).   DHU/MO

11464. "Preaching on Civil Rights." America (111; Oct. 31, 1964),
p. 506.   DHU

11465. "President Calls Churchmen on Race." Christian Advocate
(7; Jl. 4, 1963), p. 24.   DAU/W

11466. Prestwood, Charles M. "Dilemas of the Deep South Clergy."
Christianity Today (5; Ja., 1961), pp. 8-9.   DLC

11467. "Protestant-Jewish-Roman Catholic Conversation on the
Sit-Ins." Presbyterian Outlook (142; Mr. 20, 1960), pp. 3-7.
                                               NNUT

11468. "Protestantism Speaks on Justice and Integration." Christian
Century (75; Feb. 5, 1958), pp. 164-6.   DHU/R

11469. "Race and Religion." Commonweal (64; Je. 22, 1956),
pp. 290+.   DHU/R

11470. "Race and Religion." Nation (197; Dec. 7, 1963), p. 378.
                                               DHU

11471. "Race Held Major Challenge to U. S. Protestantism."
Concern (7; Mr. 15, 1965), p. 15.   DAU/W

11472. "Race Relations." Concordia Films, 1962. 15 min., sd.,
b & w., 16mm.
Film.
    "Raises questions regarding the Christian attitudes toward
    racial prejudice and bigotry."

11473. Race Relations in the USA, 1954-68. New York: Charles
Scribner's Sons, 1970.   DHU/R
    See pp. 63-8, "Churches Denunciation of Racial Segregation,"
    pp. 84-8, "Desegregation of Public and Roman Catholic
    Schools, 1961-63." Chapter 10, The Death of Martin Luther
    King.

11474. "Racial Integration in the Churches." Social Action (22;
Dec., 1955), p. 27.   DHU/R

11475. "Racism and the Council." America (109; Nov. 2, 1963),
p. 507.   DHU

11476. "Racism; the Nations's False Religion." Christian Century
(80; Feb. 6, 1963), p. 166.   DHU/R

11477. "Reformed Churches Take Strong Stand on Race." Christian
Century (81; Sept. 2, 1964), p. 1077.   DHU/R

11478. "Religious Leaders Demand Civil Rights Bill." Christian
Century (81; My. 13, 1964), p. 631.   DHU/R

11479. "Religious Leaders Give Thanks for Civil Rights Bill Passage." Concern (6:14, Jl., 1964).   DAU/W

11480. Reston, James. "The Churches, the Synagogues, and the
March on Washington." Religious Education (59:1, Ja.-Feb.,
1964). pp. 5+.   DHU/R; DAU/W; DCU/TH

11481. Reuter, George Sylvester. One Blood; the Christian Approach
to the Civil Rights. New York: Exposition Press, 1964.
DHU/MO; CtY-D; DLC; INU

11482. "Rich Long Island's Church." Color (11; Apr., 1957),
pp. 42-3.   TNF

11483. Rorty, James. "Desegregation Along the Mason-Dixon Line."
Commentary (18:6, Dec. 1954), pp. 493-503.   DHU/R

11484. ----- "Desegregation: Prince Edward County, Va." Commentary (21:11, My. 1956), pp. 431-38.

11485. Rose, Peter Isaac. They and We, Racial and Ethnic Rela-
tions in the United States. New York: Random House, 1964
DHU/R
Religious groups in the United States, pp. 64-6.

11486. Rose Stephen C. "Epitaph for an Era." Christianity and
Crisis (23:10, Je. 10, 1963), pp. 103-10.   DHU/

11487. ----- "N. C. C. Visits Clarksdale." Christian Century
(80; Sept. 11, 19633), pp. 1104-6.   DHU/R

11488. Rountree, Malachi D. The Ecumenical Movement and the
Racial Problem in the Greater Washington Area. B. D. Paper.
School of Religion, Howard University, 1964.
Negro author.

11489. Roy, Ralph Lord. "Church Race Policies Compared." The
Christian Century (73:22, My. 30, 1956), pp. 664-5. DHU/R

11490. Ruark, G. "Carolinians See Racial Progress." Christian
Century (71; Dec. 1, 1954), pp. 1472+.   DHU/R

11491. Rustin, Bayard and Tom Kahn. "Civil Rights." Commentary
(39:6, Je., 1965), pp. 43-46.   DHU/R

11492. Salten, David G. "Education in Race Relations." Religious
Education (59:1, Ja.-Feb., 1964), pp. 37-43.   DHU/R

11493. Schneider, Louis, (ed.). Religion, Culture and Society.
New York: Wiley, 1964.   DHU/R
Negro ministers and the civil struggle.

11494. Schomer, H. "Race and Religion in Albany." Christian
Century (79; Sept. 26, 1962), pp. 1155-6.   DHU

11495. Schulz, Larold K. "The Delta Ministry." Social Action
(31: 3, Nov., 1964), pp. 30-34.   DHU/R

11496. Schuyler, Joseph B. Northern Parish. A Sociological and
Pastoral Study. Chicago: Loyola University Press, 1961 DCU
Survey of a Bronx parish, showed majority favoring racial
equality.

11497. "Selma, Civil Rights and the Church Militant." Newsweek
(65; Mr. 29, 1965), pp. 75-76.   DHU

11498. "Seven Protestant Denominations Join Forces in Seattle
Through CURE." Concern (6; Feb. 15, 1964), p. 15. DAU/W

11499. Seymour, R. "Interracial Ministry in North Carolina; What
it was Like for a Southern White Church to have a Negro Assistant on its Staff." Christian Century (80; Sept. 15, 1962),
p. 109.   DHU

11500. Shepherd, Wilhelmina. "A Simple, Easy Way to Improve
Racial Understanding." Religious Education (59:1, Ja.-Feb.,
1964), pp. 84-5.   DHU/R

11501. Shriver, Donald W. The Unsilent South: Prophetic Preaching
in Racial Crisis. Richmond: John Knox Press, 1965.
INU; DHU/R; CtY-D; NN/Sch; DLC; MMtcA

11502. Smith, Earnest A. "The Church and the 1967 Civil Rights
Bill." Concern (9:11, Je. 15, 1967), pp. 4-6.   DHU/R

11503. Smith, Elwyn A. "Stalemate in Selma." Christian Century
(82: 34, Ag. 25, 1965), pp. 1031-33. Pam. File. DHU/R
A perceptive analysis of the frustration which followed the
marches in Selma, Alabama.

11504. Southard, S. "Are Southern Churches Silent." Christian
Century (80; Nov. 20, 1963), pp. 1429-32.   DHU/R

11505. "Southern Desegregation; Protestant Churches." Time
(84; Dec. 4, 1964), pp. 94+.   DHU

11506. Spike, Robert W. The Freedom Revolution and the Churches.
New York: Association Press, 1965.   DHU/R; INU; NcD; DLC

11507. ----- "Mississippi: an Ecumenical Ministry." Social
Action (31:3, Nov., 1964), pp. 16-18.   DHU/R

11508. ----- "Our Churches Sin Aginst the Negro." Look (My.,
1965)   DHU

11509. Stahl, David (ed.). Community and Racial Crisis. New
York: Practicing Law Institute, 1966.   DHU/SW

11510. "Stand and be Counted; Roman Catholics, Jews and Protestants Support Civil Rights Bill." Newsweek (63; My. 11, 1964),
p. 90.   DHU

11511. Stark, Rodney, and Charles Y. Glock. "Prejudice and the
Churches." Charles Y. Glock and Ellen Siegelman, (eds.).
Prejudice U.S.A. (New York: Praeger Publishers, 1969),
pp. 70-95.   DHU/R

11512. Stringfellow, William. "Race Religion and Revenge; Negroes
in New York's Harlem." Christian Century (79; Feb. 14,
1962), pp. 192-4.   DHU/R

11513. Student Interracial Ministry Committee. Statement of
Purpose. New York: Union Theological Seminary.
Pam. File.   DHU/R
mim.
Union Theological students organize to play a constructive
role in the present racial crisis.

11514. "Student Perspectives on the Southern Church." Phylon
(25; Wint., 1964), pp. 369-81.   DHU/MO

11515. Sullivan, H. T. "The Christian Concept of Race Relations."
The Baptist Message (74; Oct. 10, 1957), pp. 1, 4. LNB; TND

11516. "Summit Conference on Race, Religion." Ebony (18; Apr.,
1963), pp. 43-44.   DHU/MO

11517. Survey by Protestant Council of the City of New York of
Interracial Aspects of the City's Protestant Churches. New
York Times (Feb. 10, 1957).   DLC; DHU

11518. Taft, A. A. "Miami Spurns Integration." Christian Century
(72; Oct. 19, 1955), pp. 1220+.   DHU/R

11519. Teel, Charles. A Profile of Civil Disobedient Clergy,
1956-68. Doctoral Dissertation. Boston University, 1972.

11520. ----- A Study of Selected United States Clergymen on the
Problem of Norms and Limits for Civil Disobedience. Doctoral
dissertation. Boston University Graduate School, 1971

11521. Thielicke, Helmut. Between Heaven and Earth Conversations
with American Christians. New York: Harper & Row, 1965.
                                                                    DHU/R
        Chapter VII, "Racial Integration and the Christian."

11522. Thomas, Mary S. "The Ordeal of Koinonia Farm."
Progressive (21; Ja., 1957), pp. 23-25.   DLC
        An account of the attacks on a Georgia religious and inter-
        racial camp and community.

11523. Thurman, Howard. "The Role of the Christian Religion in
the Negro's Struggle for Freedom" Ebony (18:11, Sept., 1963),
pp. 58+.   DHU/MO

11524. Tilson, Everett. "A Christian Brief for Integration."
Journal of Religious Thought (18: 2, 1961-62), pp. 149-66.
                                                                    DHU/R

11525. "Toward Integration; Christian Life Commission." Time
(86; Nov. 26, 1965), p. 68.   DHU

11526. Travers-Ball, I. "India and the Negro Question; Here's
How Birmingham and Montgomery Look to People Around the
World." America (109; Jl. 13, 1963), pp. 44-5. DHU

11527. Vander Zanden, James W. Race Relations in Transition;
the Segregation Crisis in the South. New York: Random House,
1965.   DHU/MO

11528. Visser't Hooft, Willem Adolph. The Ecumenical Movement
and the Racial Problem. Paris: UNESCO, 1954.
                                        DHU/R; NN/Sch; CtY-D

11529. Vries, Egbert de. Man in Community; Christian Concern
for the Human in Changing Society. New York: Association
Press, 1966.   DHU/R

11530. Waltz, Alan K. and Robert L. Wilson. "Ministers Attitudes
Toward Integration." Phylon (19; Sum., 1958), pp. 195-98.
                                                                    DHU/MO

11531. Warder, V. G. "Bounce Away From Church Integration."
Music Ministry (5; Apr., 1964), pp. 12+. DAU/W; DHU/R

11532. Watters, Pat. Down to Now; Reflections on the Southern
Civil Rights Movement. New York: Random House, 1971
                                                                    DHU/R

11533. Weaver, Galen R. "Racial Integration in the Churches."
Social Action (22:4, Dec., 1955), pp. 6-19.   DHU/R

11534. ----- "There is Something You Can do For Human Relations
in Your Church, in Your Community." New York Dept. of Race
Relations, n. d.   Pam. File, DHU/R

11535. Webb, Maurice. "Race Tensions: Is a New Approach
Possible?" Ecumenical Review (8:4, Jl., 1956), pp. 458-61
                                                                    DHU/R

11536. Westin, Alan R. Freedom Now! The Civil Rights Struggle in
America. New York: Basic Books, 1964.   INU
        pp. 297-306, the church and civil rights.

11537. "When U. S. Churches Face Up to Integration." U. S. News
& World Report, (48; My. 16, 1960), pp. 61-3. DHU

11538. White, Henry Eugene. Racialism in the New Testament
Church. Master's thesis. Southern Baptist Theological
Seminary, 1957.

11539. White, W. L. "Los Angeles Aftermath Churches Respond to
Racial Riots." Christian Advocate (9; Sept. 9, 1965), pp. 24+.
                                                        DHU/R; DAU/W

11540. Whitman, A. "How the Civil Right Struggle Challenges Our
Churches." Redbook (125; Ag. 1965), pp. 55-7+. DLC

11541. Wilmore, Gayraud S., Jr. "The New Negro and the Church."
The African Methodist Episcopal Church Review (78:216, Apr.-
Je., 1963), pp 60-65.   DHU/R
        Negro author.

11542. Windham, Festus F. A Bible Treatise on Segregation; an
Analysis of Biblical References to Determine the True Relationship of the Races. New York: William-Frederick Press,
1957.   TSewU-T

11543. Winter, Gibson. "Theology of Demonstration; Interrelation Between Freedom Movement and Christianity."
Christian Century (82; Oct. 13, 1965), pp. 1249-52. DHU/R

11544. Wofford, H. "Non-Violence and the Law; the Law Needs
Help." Journal of Religious Thought (15:1, Aut.-Wint., 1957-
58), pp. 25-36.   DHU/R
        Churches role in non-violence.

11545. Woodward, C. Vann. "The Great Civil Rights Debate."
Commentary (24:4, Oct., 1957), pp 283-91.   DHU/R

B. SOUTHERN CHRISTIAN LEADERSHIP CONFERENCE AND MARTIN LUTHER KING, JR.

11546. Abernathy, Ralph David. "My Last Letter to Martin."
Ebony (23:9, Jl., 1968), pp. 58-61.   DHU/MO
        Negro author.

11547. "Acceptance Speech of Martin Luther King, Jr. of the Nobel
Peace Prize on December 10, 1964." Negro History Bulletin
(31; My., 1968), pp. 20-21.   DHU/MO

11548. "Accused Killer, a Clumsy Man with Closed Eyes." Life
(64; Apr. 26, 1968), p. 42B.   DHU

11549. Adams, S. J. "Measuring Up the Catholic Press and Rev.
Dr. Martin Luther King, Jr." America (118; My. 4, 1968),
p. 624.   DHU
        Discussion. (118; Je. 22, 1968), p. 781.

11550. "Aim: Registration; Promoting Desegregation in Selma, Ala."
Time (85; Jan. 29, 1965), pp. 20-1.   DHU

11551. Alexander, Mithrapuram K. Martin Luther King; Martyr for
Freedom. New Delhi: New Light Publishers, 1968.
                                        DCU; NNCor; NcD

11552. "American Dream: Address, June 6, 1961." Negro History
Bulletin (31:5, My., 1968), pp. 10-15.   DHU/MO
        A transcription of the Commencement Address delivered by
        Martin Luther King, Jr. at Lincoln University on June 6, 1961.

11553. "American Negro Pathfinders." Santa Monica, Calif.: BFA
Educational Media, 1971. Color.
        Filmstrip, Dr. Martin Luther King, Jr.: Non-Violent Cru-
        sader.

11554. "As 150,000 Said Farewell to Dr. King." U. S. News (64;
Apr. 22, 1968), pp. 38-9.   DHU

11555. Ashmore, Harry S. "Martin Luther King, Spokesman for the
Southern Negro." New York Herald Tribune Book Review (Sept.
21, 1958), p. 5.   DHU; DGW

11556. "Assassination According to Capote." Time (91; My. 10, 1968), p. 65.   DHU

11557. "Assassins: Who Did It, and Why? Ray: Ninety-Nine Years and a Victory." Newsweek (73; Mr. 24, 1969), pp. 28-32.   DHU

11558. Baldwin, James. "Dangerous Road Before Martin Luther King." Harper (222; Feb., 1961), pp. 33-42.   DHU
Negro author.

11559. Bales, James David. The Martin Luther King Story. Oklahoma Christian, 1967.   DHU/MO; TN/DCHS

11560. Balk, A. "What Memorial to Martin Luther King? Ways of Rectifying Injustices." Saturday Review of Literature (51; My. 4, 1968), p. 18.   DHU

11561. Bartlett, Robert Merrill. They Stand Invincible; Men Who Are Re-shaping Our World. New York: Crowell, 1959.
                                        OO; IU; NN; NIC; OCl
A chapter on Martin Luther King.

11562. "Beauty for Ashes; Committee of Concern Organized to Re-build Negro Churches Bombed and Burned in Mississippi." Time (85; Feb. 5, 1965), p. 61.   DHU

11563. Bedau, Hugo Adam. Civil Disobedience Theory and Practice. New York: Pegasus, 1969   DHU/R

11564. Bennett, John C. "Martin Luther King, Jr. 1929-1968." Christianity and Crisis (28:6, Apr. 15, 1968), pp. 69-70.
                                        DHU/R

11565. Bennett, Lerone, Jr. "The King Plan for Freedom" Ebony (11; Jl., 1956), p. 65.   DHU/MO
Martin Luther King.
Negro author.

11566. ----- "Martyrdom of Martin Luther King, Jr." Ebony (23; My., 1968), pp. 174-81.   DHU/MO

11567. ----- What Manner of Man: A Biography of Martin Luther King, Jr. Chicago: Johnson Publishing Co., 1964.
                                        INU; DHU/R

11568. Berio, Luciano. Sinfonia for Eight Voices and Orchestra. London: Universal Edition, 1969.   NNCor
Reproduction of the composer's Masters score. Second movement is a tribute to Martin Luther King, Jr.

11569. "Big Man is Martin Luther King, Jr." Newsweek (62; Jl. 29, 1963), pp. 30-2.   DHU

11570. Bims, Hamilton. "A Sculptor Looks at Martin Luther King." Ebony (28:6, Apr., 1973), pp. 95-96+.
                        DHU/MO; Pam. File; DHU/R
"Chicago artist Geraldine Mc Cullogh creates a controversial monument which will be placed in Chicago in the Lawndale area."

11571. Bishop, Jim. The Days of Martin Luther King, Jr. New York Putnam, 1971.   DHU/MO; NjP
Review, Christian Century (89:9, Mr. 1, 1972), p. 256.

11572. Blair, Clay. The Strange Case of James Earl Ray, the Man who Murdered Martin Luther King. n.p.; Bantam Books, 1969.
                                        IC/H; PPT

11573. Bleiweiss, Robert M. and Jaqueline L. Harris, et alii, (eds.). Marching to Freedom; the Life of Martin Luther King, Jr. Middletown, Conn.: American Education Publications, 1968.
                                        NjP; PPT

11574. Booker, Simeon. "50,000 March on Montgomery." Ebony (20; My. 1965), pp. 46-8+.   DHU/MO

11575. Bosco, Teresio. Martin Luther King. Torino: Societa editrice internazionale, 1969.   NjP; DLC

11576. Boutelle, Paul and George Novak, et alii. Murder in Memphis; Martin Luther King and the Future of the Black Liberation Struggle. New York: Merit Publishers, 1969.   IC/H

11577. "Boycotts Will Be Used: Interview with Martin Luther King." U. S. News and World Report (56; Feb. 24, 1964), pp. 59-61.
                                        DLC

11578. Bradford, D. "Martin Luther King says: 'I'd Do it All Again!.'" Sepia (10; Dec., 1961), p. 15.   DHU/MO; NN/Sch

11579. Brantley, Susan K. Civil Disobedience: Thoreau, Gandhi, and King. Masters thesis. Texas Christian University, 1967.

11580. Brenneck, H. E. "Memorial to Dr. King." Negro History Bulletin (31; My., 1968), p. 8.   DHU/MO

11581. Buckley, William F. "Memorial for Dr. King." National Review (21; Oct. 21, 1969), p. 1078.   DGU

11582. ----- "On Bugging Martin Luther King." National Review (21; Jl. 15, 1969), p. 714.   DGU

11583. Burns, W. Haywood. The Voices of Negro Protest in America. New York: Oxford University Press, 1963.
                                        DHU/R; IC/H
Chapter 3, "We Shall Overcome," Martin Luther King and non-violent protest movement.

11584. Buskes, Johannes Jacobus. Martin Luther King. Den Haag: Kruseman, 1965.   NjP; MH

11585. Cameron, J. M. "British View on Martin Luther King." Commonweal (88; Apr. 26, 1968), p. 164.   DHU/R

11586. Campbell, Will D. "The Sit-Ins: Passive Resistance or Civil Disobedience." Social Action (27:5, Ja., 1961) pp. 14-18.
                                        DHU/R

11587. Chandler, Russell. "King in the Capital." Christianity Today (15; Ja. 5, 1968), pp. 44-6.   DHU/R

11588. "Children's Tribute to Dr. Martin Luther King, Jr." Negro History Bulletin (31; My., 1968), p. 2.   DHU/MO

11589. Childress, James F. "Nonviolent Resistance: Trust and Risk-Taking." The Journal of Religious Ethics (1; Fall, 1973), pp. 87-112.   DHU/R
Author discusses nonviolence and resistance, from the standpoint of trust and risk-taking. Uses Martin Luther King and Gandhi theories to analyze his theory.

11590. "Churchmen Defend Sit-in Student." Christian Century (80; Je. 26, 1963), p. 821. Discussion (80; Sept. 11, Oct. 9, 1963), pp. 1239+.   DHU/R

11591. Clarke, Autstin. The Confessed Bewilderment of Martin Luther King. Canada: Al Kitah Sudan, 1968.   INU; CtY; DLC

11592. Clarke, J. W. and J. W. Soule. "How Southern Children Felt About King's Death." Trans-Action (5; Oct., 1968), pp. 34-5.   DCU/SW

11593. Clayton, Edward Taylor. Martin Luther King: The Peaceful Warrior. Englewood Cliffs, N. J.: Prentice-Hall, Inc., 1968
                                        INU; DHU/R

11594. Cleaver, Eldridge. "The Death of Martin Luther King: Requiem for Nonviolence." Robert H. Binstock and Katherine Ely (eds.). The Politics of the Powerless (Cambridge, Mass.: Winthrop Publishers, 1971), pp. 285-88.   DHU/MO
Negro author.

11595. Cleghorn, Reese. "Martin Luther King, Jr., Apostle of Crisis." Saturday Evening Post (Je. 15, 1963). DLC; DHU

11596. Collins, L. J. "Biography of Martin Luther King." Contemporary Review (208; Je., 1966), p. 326.
                                        DAU; DGU; DGE; DHU

11597. "Conner and King." Newsweek (61; Apr. 22, 1963), p. 28+.
DHU

11598. Cook, Bruce. "King in Chicago." Commonweal (84:6, Apr. 29, 1966), pp. 175-77.
DHU/R

11599. Cook, Samuel Du Bois. "Is Martin Luther King, Jr. Irrelevant?" New South (26:2, Spr., 1971), pp. 2-14. DHU/R

11600. ----- "King, Martin Luther." Journal of Negro History (53:4, Oct., 1968), pp. 348-54.
DHU

11601. Crawford, Fred Roberts and Roy Norman, et alii. A Report of Certain Reactions by the Atlanta Public to the Death of the Reverend Doctor Martin Luther King, Jr. Atlanta: Emory University, Center for Research in Social Change, 1969. NjP

11602. Cunningham, George, Jr. The Poor Black People. Hamtramck: Sherwood Forest Publishers, 1968. DHU/MO; NjP
Essays and picture of the effect of Dr. King on the lives of poor Black people.

11603. Davis, Jerome. World Leaders I Have Known. New York: Citadel Press, 1963.
DLC
Includes biography of Martin Luther King.

11604. "Dear Dr. King..." A Tribute in Words and Pictures by Children of the Richard J. Bailey School. Including "The Journey to Oslo," Documenting the Presentation of the Nobel Peace Prize to Dr. Martin Luther King, Jr. Jamaica, N. Y.: Buckingham Enterprises, 1968.
IC/H

11605. DeKay, James T. Meet Martin Luther King, Jr. New York: Random House, 1969.
DHU/R

11606. "Dispute Between Hoover and King: The FBI's Answer to Criticisms; FBI Analysis of Telegram." U. S. News (57; Dec. 6, 1967), pp. 46+.
DHU

11607. "Doctor King: A Year Later; California Senate Refuses to Honor Dr. King's Memory." Nation (208; Apr. 14, 1969), p. 453.
DHU

11608. "Doctor King and the Paris Press." Editorial. America (2; Nov. 13, 1965), p. 560.
DLC

11609. "Doctor King Carries Fight to Northern Slums." Ebony (21; Apr., 1966

11610. "Doctor King: in Tribute; Excerpts From his Writings." Christian Century (85; Apr. 17, 1968), p. 503. DHU/R

11611. "Doctor King's Case for Nonviolence." America (115; Nov. 12, 1966), p. 578.
DHU

11612. "Doctor King's Closed Session Set the Strategy." Life (58; Mr. 19, 1965), p. 35+.
DHU

11613. "Doctor King's Disservice to His Cause." Life (62:16, Apr. 21, 1967), p. 4.
DHU/R

11614. "Doctor King's Murder: Nagging Questions Remain." U. S. News (66; Mr. 24, 1969), p. 13
DHU

11615. "Doctor King's Nobel Prize." America (111; Oct. 31, 1964), p. 503.
DHU

11616. Douglas, Carlyle C. "Ralph Abernathy." Ebony (25:3, Ja., 1970), pp. 40-50.   Pam. File, DHU/R
A Negro Baptist Minister fights to keep Martin Luther King's dream alive.

11617. "Dream Still Unfulfilled." Newsweek (73; Apr. 14, 1969), pp. 34-5.
DHU

11618. Duckett, Alfred. "Daddy King's Boy Comes Home." Equal Opportunity (7:2, Wint., 1973-74), pp. 48-55; 58-63.
Pam. File, DHU/R
About Martin Luther King, Jr.

11619. Dugan, George, "Abernathy Asks Presbyterians to Give $10 Million for the Poor." New York Times (My. 18, 1968).
Pam. File, DHU/R

11620. Dunbar, E. "Visit With Martin Luther King." Look (27; Feb. 12, 1963), pp. 92-6.
DHU

11621. Duvalier, Francois. A Tribute to the Martyred Leader of Non-Violence: Reverend Martin Luther King, Jr. Port-au-Prince, Haiti: Press Nationals, 1968.
DHU/R

11622. "Endorse Dr. King for Nobel Prize." Christian Century (81; Ag. 12, 1964), p. 1308.
DHU

11623. "Equality is Not Negotiable." Christian Century (80; Sept. 4, 1963), p. 1069.
DHU/R

11624. Evtushenko, E. A. "In Memory of Dr. Martin Luther King." Negro History Bulletin (31; My., 1968), p. 14. DHU/MO

11625. "Execution of Dr. King." Ramparts Magazine (6; My., 1968), pp. 46-7.
DHU/R

11626. "An Experiment in Love." Jubilee (6:5, Sept., 1958), pp. 11-17.
DCU
"Reaffirmation of the logic and wisdom behind the facts and success of nonviolent resistance."

11627. Fager, C. E. "Delemma for Dr. King." Christian Century (83; Mr. 16, 1966), pp. 331-2
DHU

11628. Fairfax, Jean. "Martin Luther King, Jr.: One Year Later." Christian Advocate (13:7, Apr. 3, 1969), p. 13.
Pam. File, DHU/R

11629. Feuerlicht, Robert S. Martin Luther King, Jr.; a Concise Biography. New York: American R. D. M. Corp., 1966 IC/H

11630. "The First Word 'Do We Dare?'" Friends Journal (20:7, Apr. 1, 1974), pp. 195-200.   DHU/R
Photographic essay with passages from Where Do We Go From Here in memory of Martin Luther King, Jr. Society of Friends memorial to Martin Luther King, Jr.

11631. "Four Poets on Martin Luther King." Nation (206; Je. 24, 1968), p. 831.
DHU

11632. Frank, Gerold. An American Death; the True Story of the Assassination of Dr. Martin Luther King, Jr. and the Greatest Manhunt of Our Time. Garden City, New York: Doubleday, 1970.
NjP; PPT; IC/H; T SewU-T; NNCor; MNTCA

11633. Franklin, Ben A. "Mourning for Dr. King Ended; Abernathy Now Man in Charge." New York Times, Sunday, Ag. 17, 1969.
Pam. File, DHU/R

11634. "Free at Last, Free at Last." Brotherhood LP 2001.
Audiotape.
Martin Luther King, Jr.

11635. "From the Birmingham Jail; Excerpt from Letter." Negro History Bulletin (31; My., 1968), p. 19. DHU/MO

11636. Galphin, Bruce M. "Does Martin Luther King Have a Future in Politics." Negro Digest (20; Ja., 1962), pp. 41-7.
SCBHC; DHU/MO

11637. ----- "Political Future of Dr. King." The Nation (Sept. 23, 1961).
DLC

11638. Garber, Paul R. "Too Much Taming of Martin Luther King?" Christian Century (91:22, Je. 5, 1974), p. 616. DHU/R
"Book review."

11639. Garland, Phyl. "I've Been to the Mountaintop." Ebony (23:7, My., 1968), pp. 124+.
DHU/R

11640. Gaudnault, Gerard. L'Engagement de L'Eglise Dans la Revolution d'Apres Martin Luther King, Jr. Montreal: Fides, 1971.
PPT

11641. "Georgia Imprisons Martin Luther King, Jr.: Christian
Century (77; Nov. 9, 1960), p. 1300.   DHU

11642. "Georgia Justice." Nation (191; Nov. 5, 1960), pp. 338-9.
DHU

11643. "Georgia Whodunit." Newsweek (60; Jl. 23, 1962), pp. 18-19.
DHU

11644. Gerasimov, G. Fire Bell in the Night. By G. Gerasimov,
G. Kuznetsov and V. Morev. Moscow: Novosti Press Agency
Pub. House, 1968.   NcD

11645. Gerbeau, Hubert. Martin Luther King. Paris: Editions
Universitraires, 1968.   CNoS; CoFS; CSt; NN; NNCor

11646. Gessell, J. M. "Memphis in Holy Week." Christian Century
(85; My. 8, 1968), pp. 19-20.   DHU/R

11647. "Gift of Love" McCall's Magazine (94; Dec., 1966), pp. 146-7.
DLC

11648-49. Good, Paul. "Chicago Summer: Bossism, Racism and
Dr. King." Nation (203; Sept. 19, 1966), pp. 237-42.   DHU

11650-51. ----- "No Man Can Fill Dr. King's Shoes--But Abernathy
Tries." August Meier and Elliott Rudwick (eds.). Black Protest in the Sixties (Chicago: Quadrangle Books, 1950), pp. 284-
301.   DHU/R

11652. Goodman, G. "Doctor King, One Year After: He Lives, Man!'
Look (33; Apr. 15, 1969), pp. 29-31.   DGW

11653. Goodwin, Bennie E. "In Memory of Dr. Martin Luther King,
Jr.: A Tribute and a Selected Bibliography." Perspective (13:2,
Spr., 1972), pp. 102-10.   DHU/R

11654. "Graham and King as Ghettomates." Christian Century (83;
Ag. 10, 1966), p. 976.   DHU

11655. Griffin, John Howard. "Martin Luther King's Moment,
Excerpts from Thirteen for Christ." Sign (42; Apr., 1963),
p. 28.   DCU/HU; DGU

11656. Grosse, Henrich Wilhelm. Die Macht der Armen. Martin
Luther King und der Kampf für Sociale Gerechtigkeit. Hamburg:
Furche Verlag, 1971.   MNtcA; PPT

11657. Härtel, Klaus-Dieter. Martin Luther King; Vorkämpfer für
Frieden und Menschenwurde. Giessen: Brunnen-Verlag, 1968.
NjP

11658. Halberstam, David. "Notes from the Bottom of the Mountain.'
Harper's (236; Je., 1968), pp. 40-2.   DHU

11659. ----- "The Second Coming of Martin Luther King." Harper's
(235:1407, Ag., 1967), pp. 39-51.

11660. ----- "Are You Guilty of Murdering Martin Luther King?"
New York Times Magazine (Je. 9, 1968), pp. 27-9+.
DHU

11661. "Hammer of Civil Rights." Nation (198; Mr. 9, 1964), pp.
230-4.   DHU

11662. "Hanh, Nhat. "A Letter to Martin Luther King from a Bud-
dhist Monk." Liberation (10:9, Dec., 1965), pp. 18-19 DHU/R

11663. Hanigan, James P. Martin Luther King, Jr., and the Ethics
of Militant Non-Violence. Doctoral dissertation Duke University, 1971.

11664. Hare, Alexander P. Nonviolent Direct Action, American
Cases: Social-Psychological Analyses. Washington, D. C.:
Corpus Books, 1968.   DHU/R
Includes protests led by Martin Luther King.

11665. Harnett, Rodney T. and Carol U. Libby. "Agreement With
Views of Martin Luther King, Jr. Before and After His Assassination." Phylon (33:1, 1st Quarter, 1972), pp. 79-87. DHU/MO

11666. Harrison, Deloris. We Shall Live in Peace: the Teachings
of Martin Luther King, Jr. New York: Hawthorn Books, 1968.
DLC

11667. "Hate is Always Tragic: Martin Luther King's Challenge."
Time (80:5, Af. 3, 1962), p. 13.
Address before the National Press Club, Washington, D. C.

11668. Heinz, H. John, (ed.). Crises in Modern America; A Series
of Lectures on Two Areas of Conflict in Our Society: Civil
Rights and Economic Life. New Haven: Yale University Alumni-
Sponsoring Committee, 1959.   CtY-L; DLC

11669. Hendrick, George. "Dr. King's Pilgrimage to Nonviolence."
Gandhi Magazine (3; Ja., 1959), pp. 63-5.   DHU

11670. ----- "Gandhi and Dr. Martin Luther King." Gandhi Magazine (3; Ja., 1959), pp. 18-22   DHU

11671. Hentoff, Nat. "Peaceful Army." Commonweal (72; Je. 10,
1960), pp. 275-8   DHU

11672. Hepburn, Dave. "Rat Pack Gives $50,000 to Reverend Martin
Luther King." Sepia (9; Apr., 1961), pp. 42-47.   DHU/MO

11673. Hodgetts, Colin. We Will Suffer and Die if We Have to; a
Folk Play for Martin Luther King. Valley Forge, Pa.: Judson
Press, 1969.   T Sew U-T; PPT

11674. "Hoover-King Meeting." Newsweek (64; Dec. 14, 1964),
p. 22+.   DHU

11675. Houck, J. B. "Nonviolence and Christian Tradition."
Comminity (27; Dec., 1967), p. 4.   DHU/MO

11676. "How Martin Luther King won the Nobel Peace Prize." U. S.
News (58; Feb. 8, 1965), pp. 76-7.   DHU

11677. "How Some Clergymen Who Campaigned in '65 See Poor
People's March." National Observer (My. 27, 1968).
Pam. File, DHU/R

11678. Howard, R. "Requiem to Dr. Martin Luther King, Jr."
Negro History Bulletin (32; Apr. 1969), p. 17.   DHU/MO

11679. Huie, William B. "Story of James Earl Ray and the Plot
to Assassinate Martin Luther King." Look (32; Nov. 12;
Nov. 26, 1968), pp. 90-7+, pp. 86-7+.   DHU

11680. ----- and A. C. Hanes; P. Foreman. "Why James Earl
Ray Murdered Doctor King." Look (33; Apr. 15, 1969), pp. 102-
4+.   DHU

11681. ----- He Slew the Dreamer; My Search for the Truth About
James Earl Ray and the Murder of Martin Luther King. New
York: Delacorte Press, 1970.   NjP; PpT; NNCor; M. Bea

11682. Hunt, James D. "Gandhi and the Black Revolution."
Christian Century (86:40, Oct. 1, 1969), pp. 1242-44 DHU/R
A comparison between Martin Luther King and Gandhi.

11683. "I Have A Dream; Original Address from the March on
Washington, August, 1963." Twentieth Century Fox 3201.
Audiotape.
Speech by Martin Luther King.

11684. "'I Have a Dream...': The Life of Martin Luther King."
Santa Monica, Calif.: BFA Educational Media, 1971. 35min.
B&W Film.

11685. "International Evening: Martin Luther King." Publishers
        Weekly (191; Je. 19, 1967), p. 52.   DAU; DCW; DCU/LS

11686. Italiaander, Rolf. Die Friedensmacher. Drei Neger Er-
        hielten den Friedens-Nobelpreis. (Ralph Bunche, Martin Luther
        King, Albert John Luthuli) Mit Originalbeiträgen von A. J.
        Toynbee. Kassel: Oncken, 1965.   NNCor; PPT

11687. ----- Martin Luther King. Berlin: Colloquium-Verlag,
        1968.   MU; WaU; WU; CU; CU-S; NNCor; NjP

11688. Jackson, Jesse L. "Completing the Agenda of Dr. King."
        Ebony (28:8, Je., 1974), pp. 116-20. Pam. File, DHU/R

11689. Jackson, Mahalia. "The Best Loved Songs of Dr. Martin
        Luther King, Jr."
        Phonodisc.

11690. "Johnson, King and Ho Chi Minh." Christianity Today (12;
        Ja. 5, 1968), pp. 24-5.   DHU/R

11691. Jones, J. "Priests, Sisters, and Martin Luther King."
        Community (25; Sept., 1965), pp. 4-6.   DHU/MO

11692. Jones, Lawrence N. "Interpreters of Our Faith: Martin
        Luther King, Jr." A. D. United Church Herald Edition (2:4,
        Apr., 1973), pp. 18-22.   DHU/R
            Contains "A Letter to American Christians" by Martin Luther
            King, Jr. as an epistle from the Apostle Paul from the book,
            Strength to Love, 1963.

11693. Jordan, Eddie. "A Black Re-Evaluation of King's Intellectual
        Evolution." Black Collegian (3:1, Sept.-Oct., 1972), pp. 20-22+.
                                          Pam. File, DHU/R
            Martin Luther King, an evaluation of his work.

11694. Josca, Guiseppe. Martin Luther King. Milano: Della Volpe,
        1968.   NjP

11695. Karr, Albert R. "Northern Rights Drive by King Might Stall
        in Some Large Cities." Wall Street Journal (165; Je. 7, 1965),
        p. 1.   DAU; DGU

11696. "Kennedy to Mrs. King: Did a Phone Call Elect Kennedy
        President?" Negro Digest (11; Nov., 1961), pp. 45-9. DHU/MO

11697. Kiely, H. C. "Judgement and Grace in Selma." Concern
        (7; Apr. 1, 1965), pp. 6+.   DAU/W

11698. "King Acts for Peace." Christian Century (82; Sept. 29,
        1965), pp. 1180+.   DHU/R

11699. "King Announces Plan to Move to Atlanta." Southern School
        News (6; Ja., 1960), p. 9.   DAU/W; DGU/LW

11700. "King Comes to Chicago." Christian Century (82; Ag. 11,
        1965), pp. 974+.   DHU/R

11701. King, Coretta. "How Many Men Must Die?" Life (64:16, Apr.
        19, 1968), pp. 34-5.   Pam. File, DHU/R
            Negro author.

11702. ----- "The Legacy of Martin Luther King, Jr." Theology
        Today (27:2, Jl., 1970), pp. 129-39.   DHU/R

11703. ----- My Life with Martin Luther King, Jr. New York:
        Holt, Rinehart and Winston, 1969.   DHU, R; NjP; MntcA

11704. "King is the Man, Oh Lord." Newsweek (71; Apr. 15, 1968).
                                                    DHU
            "A detailed look at the life of Martin Luther King, Jr."

11705. King, Martin Luther, Jr. "Black Power." Ross & Barker.
        The Afro-American Readings. New York: Van Nostrand, Rein-
        hold Co., 1950, pp. 389-403.   DHU/MO
            Negro author.

11706. ----- "Bold Design for a New South." Nation (196; Mr. 30,
        1963), pp. 259-62.   DAU

11707. ----- "The Burning Truth in the South." Progressive (24;
        My., 1960), pp. 8-10.   DGU

11708. ----- "Case Against Tokenism." New York Times Magazine
        (Ag. 5, 1962), p. 11+.   DHU

11709. ----- A Comparison of the Conceptions of God in the Think-
        ing of Paul Tillich and Henry Nelson Wieman. Doctoral disser-
        tation. Boston University, 1955.

11710. ----- "The Current Crisis in Race Relations." New South
        (13; Mr., 1958), pp. 8-12.   DAU/W; DHU/MO

11711. ----- "Dreams of Brighter Tomorrows." Ebony (20; Mr.,
        1965), pp. 35-6+.   DHU/MO

11712. ----- "Facing the Challenge of a New Age." Phylon (18;
        Spr., 1957), pp. 25-34.   DHU/MO

11713. ----- "Freedom's Crisis; Last Steep Ascent." Nation (202;
        Mr. 14, 1966), pp. 288-92.   DHU

11714. ----- "Fumbling on the New Frontier." Nation (194; Mr. 3,
        1962), pp. 190-3.   DHU

11715. ----- "The Future of Integration." James A. Moss, (ed.).
        The Black Man in America (New York: Dell Publishing Co.,
        1971), pp. 31-42.   DHU/MO

11716. ----- "The Great March to Freedom." Gordy 906, 1963.
        2 s. 12 in. 33 1/3 rpm.
        Phonodisc.
        "The author's speech at Detroit, June 23, 1963."

11717. ----- "Hate is Always Tragic; Excerpts from Address."
        Time (80; Ag. 3, 1962), p. 13.   DHU

11718. ----- "I Have a Dream." John Hope Franklin and Isidore
        Starr. The Negro in the 20th Century (New York: Vintage
        Books, 1967), pp. 143-47.   DHU/R

11719. ----- "In Search of Freedom." Mercury SR 61170.
        Audiotape.

11720. ----- "I've Been to the Mountaintop." Freeing the Spirit
        (1:4, 2:1, Fall-Wint., 1972, Spr., 1973), pp. 14-21. DHU/R

11721. ----- "A Legacy of Creative Protest." Jules Chametzky and
        Sidney Kaplan, (eds.). Black and White In American Culture;
        An Anthology from The Massachusetts Review (Amherst, Mass.:
        University of Massachusetts Press, 1969), p. 105. DHU/MO
            The influence of Henry David Thoreau and his beliefs about
            civil disobedience.

11722. ----- "Let Justice Roll Down." Nation (200; Mr. 15, 1965),
        pp. 269-73.   DHU

11723. ----- "Letter from Birmingham Jail." Robert H. Binstock
        and Katherine Ely, (eds.). The Politics of the Powerless
        (Cambridge, Mass.: Winthrop Publishers, 1971), pp. 265-77.
                                                    DHU/MO

        Excerpt from King's Why We Can't Wait.

11724. ----- "Letter from Birmingham City Jail." Ruth Miller,
        (ed.). Black American Literature (California: Glencoe Press,
        1971), pp. 456-75.   DHU/R; DHU/MO

11725. ----- "Letter from Birmingham Jail." Thomas R. Frazier,
        (ed.). Afro-American History: Primary Resources (New York:
        Harcourt, Brace & World, Inc., 1970), pp. 392-405.
                                             DHU/R; DHU/MO

11726. ----- "Love, Law and Civil Disobedience." New South
        (16; Dec., 1961), pp. 3-11.   DAU/W

11727. ----- "Love Your Enemies. A Sermon Delivered by Dr. Martin Luther King, Jr. ... in the Andrew Rankin Memorial Chapel, Howard University, Washington, D. C. on Sunday, Morning, Nov. 10, 1957. Journal of Religious Thought (27:2, Sum. Suppl., 1970), pp. 31-41.   DHU/R

11728. ----- "The Luminous Promise." Progressive (26; Dec., 1962), pp. 34-7.   DGU

11729. ----- "Man in a Revolutionary World." William Robert Miller (ed.). Contemporary American Protestant Thought, 1900-1970. (New York: The Bobbs-Merrill Co., Inc., 1973), pp. 491-504.   DHU/R
    An address delivered July 6, 1965, at the General Synod of the United Church of Christ.

11730. ----- "The Man of Love." Produced by Nathanial Montague. Buddah record.
    Phonodisc.

11731. ----- "Martin Luther King at Zion Hill." (Compton, Calif.: Public Information Communications Ass'n., 1962), 2 s. 12 in. 33.   DLC
    Phonodisc.
    The author's address in Zion Hill Baptist Church, Los Angeles, June 17, 1962 on Civil rights.

11732. ----- "Martin Luther King Defines Black Power." New York Times Magazine (Je. 11, 1967).   DLC

11733. ----- A Martin Luther King Treasury. Yonkers: Educational Heritage, 1964.   DHU/MO; NN/Sch

11734. ----- The Measure of a Man. Philadelphia: Pilgrim Press, 1968.   DHU/R

11735. ----- "Memorial Issue to Martin Luther King." Negro History Bulletin (31:5, My., 1968).   DHU/MO

11736. ----- "The Montgomery Bus Boycott." Bradford Chalmers. Chronicles of Black Protest (New York: The New American Library, 1968), pp. 177-87.   DHU/MO
    Includes also "I Have a Dream."

11737. ----- "The Negro is Your Brother." Arthur C. Littleton and Mary W. Burger, (eds.). Black Viewpoints (New York: New American Library, 1964), pp. 230-45.   DHU/R

11738. "Martin Luther King, Jr.: The New International Year Book, A Compendium of the World's Affairs for the Year 1963. (New York: Funk and Wagnalls, 1964).   DLC

11739. King, Martin Luther, Jr. "A New Sense of Direction." Worldview (15:4, Apr., 1972), pp. 5-12.   DHU/R
    This article has never been printed before, made available by Mrs. Coretta Scott King for this printing.

11740. ----- Our Struggle; the Story of Montgomery. New York: Congress of Racial Equality (Core), 1957.   NNCor

11741. "Martin Luther King, Jr., President, Southern Christian Leadership Conference (SCLC)." Harry A. Ploski, (ed.). Reference Library of Black America (New York: Bellwether Pub. Co., Inc., 1971), Book 2, pp. 15-18.   DHU

11742. King, Martin Luther, Jr. "Racism and the White Backlash." Nick Aaron Ford, (ed.). Black Insights: Significant Literature by Black Americans - 1760 to the Present. (Waltham, Mass.: Ginn and Co., 1971), pp. 227-39.   DHU/R
    Excerpt from Where Do We Go From Here? by Martin Luther King.

11743. "Martin Luther King, Jr. Rare Tribute." Time (85:6, Feb 5, 1965), p. 24.   DHU

11744. King, Martin Luther, Jr. "The Role of the Behavioral Scientist in the Civil Rights Movement." Marcel L. Goldschmid, (ed.). Black Americans and White Racism; Theory and Research

(New York: Holt, Rinehart and Winston, 1970), pp. 8-14.   DHU/MO

11745. ----- "Showdown for Non-Violence." Arthur C. Littleton and Mary W. Burger, (eds.). Black Viewpoints (New York: New American Library, 1964), pp. 332-42.   DHU/R

11746. ----- "Religious Commitment for Racial Equality." United Church Herald (6; Mr. 7, 1963), pp. 8-10.   DHU/R

11747. ----- "Splendid Victory for the 'Concerned'." Life (58:6, Feb. 12, 1965), p. 4.   DHU

11748. ----- Strength to Love. New York: Harper & Row, 1963.   DHU/R; DLC; INU

11749. ----- Stride Toward Freedom; the Montgomery Story. New York: Harper, 1958.   CtY-D; DHU/R

11750. ----- "Three Dimensions of a Complete Life. William M. Philpot, (ed.). Best Black Sermons (Valley Forge: Judson Press, 1972), pp. 7-17.   DHU/R
    A sermon.

11751. ----- "Time for Freedom Has Come." New York Times Magazine (Sept. 10, 1961), pp. 25+.   DHU

11752. ----- The Trumpet of Conscience. New York: Harper & Row, 1968.   CtY-D; DHU/R

11753. ----- "The Un-Christian Christian." Ebony Editors. The White Problem in America (Chicago: Johnson Publishing Co., 1966), pp. 57-64.   DHU/MO; DHU/R

11754. ----- "The Voice of Greatness. Excerpts from his Most Famous Speeches with the Clara Ward Singers." Phonodisc.

11755. ----- "We Are Still Walking." Liberation (1; Dec., 1956), pp. 6-9.   DHU/R

11756. ----- Where Do We Go From Here: Chaos or Community? New York: Harper & Row, 1967.   DHU/R
11757. ----- "Who is Their God?" Nation (195; Oct. 13, 1962), pp. 209-10.   DHU

11758. ----- Why We Can't Wait. New York: Harper & Row, 1964.   CtY-D; DHU/R

11759. "King Moves North." Time (85; Apr. 30, 1965), pp. 32-3.   DHU

11760. "King." New Yorker (41; My. 1, 1965), pp. 35-7.   DLC

11761. "King Proposed for Peace Prize." Christian Century (81; Feb. 12, 1964), p. 198.   DHU/R

11762. "King Receives Nobel Prize." Christian Century (81; Oct. 28, 1964), p. 1324.   DHU/R

11763. "King Speaks for Peace." Christian Century (84; Apr. 19, 1967), pp. 492-93.   DHU/R

11764. "King Wants White Demonstrators." Christian Century (81; Je. 3, 1964), pp. 724-5.   DHU/R

11765. "King's Last March." Time (91; Apr. 19, 1968), pp. 18-19.   DHU

11766. "King's Last Tape: Excerpts." Newsweek (72; Dec. 18, 1968), pp. 34+.   DHU

11767. "King's Targets." Newsweek (63: Je. 22, 1964), pp. 26+.   DHU

11768. Kirk, R. "Plight of the Colored Clergy; Incidents at Selma, Alabama." National Review (17; Je. 29, 1965), p. 551.   DGU; DAU

11769. Knight, Janet M., (ed.). 3 Assassinations: the Deaths of John & Robert Kennedy and Martin Luther King. New York: Facts on File, 1971.   NjP

11770. Koch, Thilo. Fighters for a New World: John F. Kennedy. Martin Luther King. Robert F. Kennedy. New York: Butnam, 1969.   DHU/MO; MiBsa; NjP

11771. Krasnow, Erwin G. "Copywrights, Performers' Rights and the March on Civil Rights: Reflections on Martin Luther King, Jr., versus Mister Maestro." Georgetown Law Journal (53; Wint., 1965), pp. 403-29.   DHU/L

11772. "The Legacy of Martin Luther King." Life (64:19, Apr., 1968), pp. 28-33.   DHU

11773. "Letter from Birmingham Jail." Christian Century (80; Je. 12, 1963), pp. 763-73; Ebony (18; Ag., 1963), pp. 23-26; Time (83; Ja., 3, 1964), p. 15; Negro History Bulletin (27; Mr., 1964), p. 156.   DHU
       Also: Why We Can't Wait. Thomas Frazier. Afro-American History ... 1970. Robert Binstock. The Politics of the Powerless.

11774. Lewis, David L. King: a Critical Biography New York: Praeger, 1970. DHU/R; NjP; T Sew U-T; MiBsA; NNCor; MNtcA

11775. Lincoln, Charles Eric. Martin Luther King, Jr., A Profile. New York: Hill & Wang, 1970.   DHU/R
       Negro author.

11776. ----- "Weep for the Living Dead." Christian Century (85:18, My. 1, 1968), p. 578.   DHU/R

11777. Lokos, Lionel. House Divided; the Life and Legacy of Martin Luther King. New Rochelle, N. Y.: Arlington House, 1968.   DHU/MO; NcD

11778. Lomax, Louis E. To Kill a Black Man. Los Angeles: Holloway House, 1968.   DHU/MO; NjP; NNCor
       "Martin Luther King, Jr."

11779. Lorew, Joseph. "I've Been to the Mountaintop." Life (64:12, Apr., 1968), pp. 74-84.   DHU

11780. Lorit, Sergio C. Martin Luther King: Il Sogno Finito della Non Violenza? Roma: Citta Nuova, 1970.   NjP

11781. Maguire, John David. "Martin Luther King and Vietnam." Christianity and Crisis (27:7, My. 1, 1967), pp. 89-90 DHU/R

11782. ----- "Martin Luther King, Jr., 1929-1968." Chrisitanity and Crisis (28:6, Apr. 15, 1968), pp. 69-70. DHU/R

11783. "Man of Conflict Wins a Peace Prize." U. S. News (57; Oct. 26, 1964), p. 24.   DHU

11784. "Man of Peace Leads - a Second March That Ends In A Prayer." Life (58:11, Mr. 19, 1965), pp. 32-34.   DHU
       Martin Luther King, Jr.

11785. "March on Washington: What to Expect." U. S. News (64; Mr. 18, 1968), pp. 44+.   DHU/R

11786. "Martin Luther King; a Candid Conversation with the Nobel Prize-Winning Leader of the Civil Rights Movement." Playboy (12:1, Ja., 1965), pp. 65-68.   DHU/EG

11787. "Martin Luther King." BBC-TV. New York: Time-Life, Inc., 16 mm. B & W. 30 min.
       Film.

11788. "Martin Luther King Defines Black Power." New York Times Magazine (Je. 11, 1967), p. 26. DAU; DCU/RE; DGU; DGW; DHU

11789. "Martin Luther King, Jr." Britannica Book of the Year. 1958. 1963. 1964. 1965. 1966. Chicago: Encyclopedia Britannica, Inc.   DAU; DGU; DGW

11790. "Martin Luther King, Jr." C. Eric Lincoln, The McGraw-Hill Encyclopedia of World Biography. (New York: McGraw-Hill Book Co., 1973), pp. 204-07.   DLC

11791. "Martin Luther King, Jr." Charles Emerson Boddie. God's Bad Boys. (Valley Forge: Judson Press, 1972), pp. 77-92
                                                        DHU/R
       Baptist minister.

11792. "Martin Luther King, Jr." Charles Moutz, (ed.). Current Biography (26:5, My., 1965), p. 220.   DHU

11793. "Martin Luther King, Jr." Current Biography, 1965. (New York: H. Wilson, 1966), pp. 220-23.   DHU

11794. "Martin Luther King, Jr." Davis, John P. (ed.). The American Negro Reference Book. (Englewood Cliffs, N. J.: Prentice-Hall, 1966), pp. 469-70+.   DHU/R

11795. "Martin Luther King, Jr." Edgar A. Toppin. Biographical History of Blacks in America Since 1528. (New York: David McKay Co., 1971), pp. 346-9.   DHU/R

11796. "Martin Luther King, Jr.: From Montgomery to Memphis." Santa Monica, California. BFA Educational Media, 1971. 26 1/2 min. B & W.
       Film.

11797. "Martin Luther King, Jr." The International Who's Who, 1966-67. (London: Europa Publications Ltd., 1968), p. 645.
                                                  DHU; DLC

11798. "Martin Luther King, Jr. Man of 1963." Negro History Bulletin (27:6, Mr., 1964), pp. 136-37.   DHU/MO

11799. "Martin Luther King, Jr." Marcus H. Boulware. The Oratory of Negro Leaders, 1900-1968. (Westport, Conn.: Negro Universities Press, 1969), pp. 423-75. DHU/R; DHU/MO

11800. Martin Luther King: Memorial. New York: Country Wide Publications, 1968.   IC/H

11801. "Martin Luther King, Jr., Peace Medal; Awarded St. Francis Peace Medal." Catholic Messenger (81; Oct. 17, 1963), p. 12.   DCU/RE

11802. "Martin Luther King, Jr." Robert M. Bartlett. They Stand Invincible. (New York: Crowell, 1959), pp. 235-56.   DLC

11803. "Martin Luther King, Jr. Who he is... What he Believes." U. S. News (58; Apr. 5, 1965), pp. 18+.   DHU

11804. "Martin Luther King, Jr. and Mahatma Gandhi." Negro History Bulletin (31; My., 1968), pp. 4-5.   DHU/MO

11805. "Martin Luther King and the Right to Know." America (120; Mr. 22, 1969), p. 323.   DHU

11806. "Martin Luther King Memorial in Central Park." Pacifica Archives ALW 725.
       Audiotape.

11807. "Martin Luther King." New York: Time Life Films, n.d. 16 mm. 30 min.
       Film.

11808. "Martin Luther King's Reaction - A Statement and a Disagreement." U. S. News and World Report (57; Nov. 18, 1964), p. 58.   DHU; DLC
       Reply to J. Edgar Hoover's Nov. 18, 1964, conference, to defend accusations and to complain of FBI disinterest in civil rights crimes.

11809. "Martin Luther King, the Man of Love." Produced by Nathaniel Montague. Buddah Record.
       Phonodisc.

11810. "Martin Luther King's Acceptance Speech at Oslo (1964)." Harry A. Ploski, (ed.). Reference Library of Black America.

(New York: Bellwether Pub. Co., Inc., 1971), Book 2, pp. 131-35.   DHU

11811. A Martin Luther King Treasury. Yonkers, N. Y.: Educational Heritage, 1964.   DHU/R; NNCor

11812-13. "Martyrdom Comes to America's Moral Leader." Christian Century (85; Apr. 17, 1968), p. 475.   DHU/R

11814. Matthews, Jim (ed.). Five Dark Days in History: Biography of a Non-violent Warrior. Dr. Ralph Abernathy Carries on. Los Angeles: Creative Advertising Media, 1968. IC/H

11815. McClendon, James William, Jr. "M. L. King: Politician or American Church Father?" Journal of Ecumenical Studies (8:1, Wint., 1971), pp. 115-21.   DHU/R

11816. McKee, Don. Martin Luther King, Jr. New York: G. P. Putnam's Sons, 1969.   DHU/R

11817. Meier, August. "On the Role of Martin Luther King." New Politics (4:1, Wint., 1965), pp. 52-9.   DLC

11818. Meltzer, Milton, (ed.). In Their Own Words: A History of the American Negro 1916-1966. New York: Thomas Y. Crowell Co., 1967.   DHU/R
        Martin Luther King speaks on Bus Boycott, 1954 and Demands of "March on Washington."

11819. "Memo to Martin Luther King." National Review (19:49, Dec. 12, 1967), pp. 1368-69.   DGU; DGW

11820. "Memphis March Leads to Riot." Senior Scholar (92; Apr. 11, 1968), pp. 22-3.   DHU/R

11821. "Men Behind Martin Luther King." Ebony (20; Je., 1965), pp. 104-06.   DHU/MO

11822. Millender, Dharathula H. Martin Luther King, Jr., A Boy With A Dream. Indianapolis: Bobbs Merril, 1969.   DLC

11823. Miller, Perry. "The Mind and Faith of Martin Luther King." The Reporter (Oct. 30, 1958).   DLC

11824. Miller, William Robert. Martin Luther King, Jr.: His Life, Martyrdom and Meaning for the World. New York: Weybright and Talley, 1968.   DHU/MO

11825. "Mourns Death of Martin Luther King." Editorial. Life (64:5, Apr. 12, 1968), p. 4   DHU

11826. Muller, Gerald Francis. Martin Luther King, Jr., Civil Rights Leader. Minneapolis: Denison, 1971 MNtcA; NjP

11827. Munshaw, Joe A. "Martin Luther King, Jr.: The Development of a Philospher and Spokesman." The Missouri Honors Review (6; My., 1969), pp. 21-38.   Pam. File, DHU/MO

11828. Nelson, William Stuart. "Mohandas K. Gandhi: The Non-Violent Answers." Friends Journal (15: 18, Oct. 1, 1969), pp. 548+.   DHU/R
        Negro author.

11829. "New Tack for Dr. King; Broader Issues, Wider Goals." U. S. News and World Report (58:18, My. 3, 1965), p. 18. DLC

11830. "No False Moves for King." Christian Century (80; Je. 17, 1963), p, 919.   DHU

11831. "No Peace For Winner of Peace Prize." U. S. News (58; Feb. 1, 1965), pp. 19+.   DHU

11832. Noack, Hans Georg. Der Gewaltlose Aufstand. Martin Luther King und der Kampf der Amerikanischen Neger. Baden-Baden: Signal-Verlag, 1965.   NNCor; PPT
        Martin Luther King, Jr.

11833. ----- L'Insurrection Pacifique de Martin Luther King, le combat de Martin Luther King Pour la Liberté et les

Droits des Noirs Américains. Traduit de l'allemand par Fernand Lambert. Paris: Editions Alsatia, 1967. NjP

11834. "Nobelman King." Newsweek (64; Oct. 26, 1964), p. 77.
                                                         DHU

11835. Nonviolence After Gandhi; A Study of Martin Luther King, Jr. Edited by G. Ramachandran and T. K. Mahadevan. New Delhi: Gandhi Peace Foundation, 1968.   NcD; NNCor

11836. "Nonviolence: The Only Road to Freedom." Ebony (21; Oct., 1966), pp. 27-30.   DHU/MO

11837. "Now Dr. King's Marchers Turn North." U. S. News (58; My. 3, 1965), pp. 8+.   DHU

11838. Nuby, C. "He Had a Dream." Negro History Bulletin (31; My., 1968), p. 21.   DHU/MO

11839. O'Dell, J. H. "Charleston's Legacy to the Poor Peoples Campaign." Freedomways (9:3, Sum., 1969), pp. 197-211.
                                                         DHU/R
        Southern Christian Leadership Conference Role in Charleston, S. C.

11840. "Off Hoover's Chest: With Excerpts from Press Conference." Newsweek (64; Nov. 30, 1964), p. 30   DHU

11841. "On to Montgomery." Newsweek (65; Mr. 29, 1965), pp. 21-2.   DHU

11842. Osborne, J. "Doctor King's Memorial." New Republic (161; Oct. 11, 1969), pp. 9-10   DHU

11843. Patterson, Lillie. Martin Luther King, Jr., Man of Peace. Champaign, Ill.: Garrard Pub. Co., 1969. DHU/R; NcD

11844. "Peace Prize Causes Controversy: Reactions in Atlanta." Christian Century (82; Ja. 13, 1965), p. 39. DHU/R

11845. "Peace With Justice." Commonweal (78; My. 31, 1963), p. 268.   DGU

11846. "Peaceful Kingdom." National Review (16; Dec. 29, 1964), p. 1135   DAU

11847. "Pertinent Momorials." Christian Century (86; Apr. 2, 1969), p. 459.   DHU/R

11848. Peters, W. "Man Who Fights Hate With Love." Redbook (117; Sept., 1961), pp. 36-7.   DLC

11849. "Pilgrimage to Non-Violence." Christian Century (77; Apr. 13, 1960), pp. 439-41.   DHU

11850. Pilpel, H. F. "Copyright Case Material; Unauthorized Recording of Speech by M. L. King." Publisher's Weekly (185; Apr. 6, 1964), p. 28.   DHU

11851. Pitcher, Alvin. "Martin Luther King Memorial." Criterion (7:2, Wint., 1968).   DLC

11852. ----- and David Wallace, et al.   "The Breadbasket Story." Church in Metropolis (No. 16, Spr., 1968), pp. 3-5; 10.
                                                         DHU/R
        Reverend Jesse Jackson and SCL's Operation Breadbasket program.

11853. "Posthumous Pillory." Time (96:7, Ag. 17, 1970), pp. 12-13.
                                                         DHU/R
        Commentary on the book, The King God Didn't Save, by John Williams (New York: Coward-McCann, 1970).

11854. Preece, Harold "Hatred for Whites and Preachers Led to Stabbing of Martin Luther King." Sepia (7:52, Ja., 1959), pp. 24-29.   DHU/MO

11855. Preston, Edward. Martin Luther King: Fighter for Freedom. New York: Doubleday, 1968. DHU/MO; DHU/AA; MNtcA; O; PPT

11856. "Prince of Peace Is Dead." Ebony (23; My., 1968), p. 172.
DHU/MO

11857. "Prophetic Ministry?" Newsweek (60; Ag. 20, 1962),
pp. 78-9.   DHU

11858. Quarles, Benjamin. "Martin Luther King in History." Negro
History Bulletin (31; My., 1968), p. 9.   DHU/MO

11859. Rahming, Philip A. The Church and the Civil Rights Movement
in the Thought of Martin Luther King, Jr. Master's thesis.
Southern Baptist Theological Seminary, 1971.

11860. Ramsy, Paul. Christian Ethics and the Sit-In. New York:
Association Pr., 1961.   CtY-D; DHU/R; INU

11861. Ray, J. E. "Deepening Mystery of Dr. King's Assassination."
U. S. News (64; My. 27, 1968), p. 10.   DHU

11862. "Reactions to the Slaying of Martin Luther King: Symposium."
America (118; Apr. 20, 1968), pp. 534-6.   DHU

11863. Reagin, Ewell. "The Southern Christian Leadership Conference: Strategy and Purpose." National Council of the Churches
of Christ in the U.S.A. (ed.). Manpower for Mission, New
Forms of the Church in Chicago (New York: Council Press,
1967), pp. 183-213.   DHU/R

11864. Reddick, Lawrence D. Crusader Without Violence: A Biography of Martin Luther King, Jr. New York: Harper and Row,
1959.   DHU/R
Negro author.

11865. "Revolt Without Violence: the Negroes New Strategy; Interview." U. S. News (48; Mr. 21, 1960), pp. 76-8.   DHU

11866. Richardson, W. H. "Martin Luther King, Unsung Theologian."
Commonweal (88; My. 3, 1968), pp. 201-03.   DHU

11867. Rogers, Cornish. "Dr. King's Legacy: A Gospel of Freedom."
Christian Century (88:5, Feb. 3, 1971), p. 148.   DHU/R

11868. ----- "Martin Luther King and Jesse Jackson: Leaders to
Match Mountains." Christian Century (89:2, Ja., 1972), p. 29.
DHU/R

11869. ----- "SCLC: Rhetoric or Strategy?" Christian Century
(87:35, Sept. 2, 1970), p. 1032.   DHU/R

11870. ----- "SCLC's 15th Convention: The Last Hurrah?" The
Christian Century (89:30, Ag. 30, 1972), pp. 839-40.   DHU/R

11871. Rohler, J. "Life and Death of Martin Luther King." Christianity Today (12; Apr. 26, 1968), pp. 37-40.   DHU/R

11872. Romero, P. W. "Martin Luther King and his Challenge to
White America." Negro History Bulletin (31; My., 1968),
pp. 6-8.   DHU/MO

11873. "Roundup: Foreign Tribute to Dr. King." Christian Century
(85; My. 8, 1968), pp. 629-30.   DHU/R

11874. Rowan, Carl T. "Heart of a Passionate Dilemma." Saturday Review (42; Ag. 1, 1959), pp. 20-1.   DHU
Negro author.

11875. ----- "Martin Luther King's Tragic Decision." Reader's
Digest (91:545, Sept., 1967), pp. 37-42.   DHU

11876. Rowe, Jeanne A. An Album of Martin Luther King, Jr.
New York: F. Watts, 1970.   NjP

11877. Schrag, P. "Uses of Martyrdom." Saturday Review of
Literature (51; Apr. 20, 1968), pp. 28-9.

11878. Schulz, W. "Martin Luther King's March on Washington."
Reader's Digest (92; Apr., 1968), pp. 65-9.   DHU

11879. Scott, Robert L. The Rhetoric of Black Power. New York:
Harper & Row, 1969.   DHU/R
Negro author.
Chapter 3, Martin Luther King, Jr. writes about the
birth of the Black power slogan.

11880. Sharma, Mohan Lal. "Martin Luther King: Modern
America's Greatest Theologian of Social Action." Journal of
Negro History (53:3, Jl., 1968), pp. 259-63.   DHU/MO

11881. Shaw, Rodney. "On the Freedom Road." Concern (7:7,
Apr. 15, 1965), pp. 6-8.   DHU/R

11882. "Showdown for Non-Violence." Look (32; Apr. 16, 1968),
pp. 23-5.   DHU

11883. Siegmeister, Elie. I Have a Dream; Canta for Mixed
Chorus... New York: MCA Music, 1968.   NNCor
Text by Edward Mabley based on a speech by Martin Luther
King, Jr.

11884. Sitton, C. "Doctor King, Symbol of the Segregation Struggle."
New York Times Magazine (Ja., 1962), pp. 10+.   DHU

11885. Slack, Kenneth. Martin Luther King. London: S.C.M.
Press, 1970.   MH-AH; DHalR

11886. Smith, Donald Hugh. "An Exegesis of Martin Luther King,
Jr.'s Social Philosophy." Phylon (31; Spr., 1970), pp. 89-97.
DHU/MO

11887. ----- Martin Luther King, Jr.: Rhetorician of Revolt.
1964.   NjP
Film.
Also, Doctoral dissertation, University of Wisconsin, 1964.

11888. Smith, Kenneth L. and Ira G. Zapp, Jr. Search for the
Beloved Community: The Thinking of Martin Luther King, Jr.
Valley Forge, Pa.: Judson Press, 1974.   DLC

11889. Smylie, James H. "On Jesus, Pharoahs, and the Chosen
People. Martin Luther King as Biblical Interpreter and
Humanist." Interpretation (24:1, Ja. 1970), pp. 74+.   DHU/R

11890. Southern Christian Leadership Conference. "The Fight for
the Vote." Carlene Young (ed.). Black Experience (San
Rafael, Cal.: Leswing Press, 1972), pp. 252-53.   DHU/R

11891. Southern Christian Leadership Conference. Indianapolis
Affiliate. Wealth, Power and Authority in Indianapolis.
Indianapolis: S.C.L.C., 1973.   DHU/R

11892. Spillers, Hortense J. "Martin Luther King and the Style
of the Black Sermon." The Black Scholar (3:1, Sept., 1971),
pp. 14-27.   DHU/R
"Second Prize, the Black Scholar Essay Contest."

11893. Stackhouse, Max L. "Reflections of a White Christian on
the Death of Dr. Martin Luther King, Jr." Andover Newton
Quarterly (9:2, Nov., 1968), pp. 10-14.   MNtcA; NN

11894. Steinkraus, Warren E. "Martin Luther King's Personal-
ism and Non-Violence." Journal of the History of Ideas (34:1,
Ja.-Mr., 1973), pp. 97-111.   DHU/R

11895. Tallmer, Jerry. "Martin Luther King, Jr., His Life and
Times." New York Post (Apr. 8, 1968).   NN

11896. Thomas, Charles Walker. "Nobel Peace Prize Goes to
Martin Luther King." Negro History Bulletin (28; Nov.,
1964), p. 35.   DHU/MO

11897. "Tribute to the Rev. Martin Luther King, Jr.: Ebony
(16; Apr., 1961), pp. 91-2+.   DHU/MO

11898. Tull, James E. Shapers of Baptist Thought. Valley
Forge: Judson Press, 1972.   DHU/R
A presentation of the thought of "representative Baptist
thinkers." Includes Martin Luther King, Jr.

11899. Turner, Otis. Reconciliation and Community in M. L. King, Jr., and Black Power. Doctoral Dissertation. Emory University, 1972.

11900. Turner, W. W. "Some Disturbing Parallels; Assassinations of M. L. King and J. F. Kennedy." Ramparts Magazine (6; Ja. 29, 1968), pp. 33-6   DHU/R

11901. "Two Perspectives, One Goal; Accepts Peace Prize." Time (84; Dec. 18, 1964), p. 21.   DHU

11902. "Un-Christian Christian." Ebony (20; Ag. 1965), pp. 76-80.
                                                                DHU/MO

11903. Vidal Alcover, Jaume. El Dedo Asesino. Barcelona: Editorial Linosa, 1969.   NNCor
        About the death of Martin Luther King.

11904. Vivian, Octavia. Coretta: The Story of Mrs. Martin Luther King, Jr. Philadelphia: Fortress Press, 1970.   DHU/R

11905. Wainwright, L. "Martyr of the Sit-Ins." Life (49; Nov. 7, 1960), pp. 123-24+.   DHU
        Also in Negro History Bulletin (24; Apr., 1961), pp. 147-51+.

11906. "Waiting for Miracles." Time (80; Ag. 3, 1962), pp. 12-13.
                                                                DHU

11907. Walton, Hanes, Jr. The Political Philosophy of Martin Luther King, Jr. Westport, Conn.: Greenwood, 1971.
        DHU/MO; MNtcA; NjP; Ic/H; MiBsA; NNCor

11908. Warren, Mervyn Alonzo. A Rhetorical Study of the Preaching of Doctor Martin Luther King, Jr., Pastor and Pulpit Orator. n. p.: n. p., 1966.   MiBsA

11909. Warren, Robert Penn. Who Speaks for the Negro. New York: Random House, 1965.   DHU/R
        Scattered referenced to Black Church and Martin Luther King, Jr.

11910. Washington, D. C. Wesley Theological Seminary. The Third Annual Martin Luther King Memorial Lecture, by the Rt. Rev. Colin O'Brian Winter, Bishop of Damaraland-in-Exile, Nov. 15, 1972.   Pam. File, DHU/R

11911. Weaver, Galen R. "Rebuke to Dr. King? Negro Official Speaks Out; Excerpts from Address, Aug. 19, 1965." U. S. News and World Report (59; Ag. 30, 1965), pp. 16+.   DHU

11912. Weisberg, Harold. Frame-Up, the Martin Luther King/ James Earl Ray Case. New York: Outerbridge & Dienstfrey, 1969.   DHU/R; NNCor

11914. White, John. Reflections on Certain Aspects of Dr. Martin Luther King's Thoughts. Masters thesis. Howard University, School of Religion, 1973.

11915. Whitehead, Brady B. Preaching Response to the Death of Martin Luther King, Jr. Doctoral dissertation. Boston University, 1972.

11916. "Why They Follow King." Christian Advocate (9; Apr. 8, 1965), pp. 2+.   DHU/R; DAU/W

11917. "Will This Prophet Be Heard?" America (118; Apr. 20, 1968), p. 532.   DHU

11918. Williams, Jim. "King: A Filmed Record - Montgomery to Memphis." Freedomways (10:3, Third Quarter, 1970), pp. 226-36.   DHU/R

11919. Williams, John A. The King God Didn't Save. Coward McCann, 1970.   DHU/R
        "Reflections on the life and death of Martin Luther King."

11920. Wills, G. "Martin Luther King is Still on the Case." Esquire (70; Ag., 1968), pp. 98-104+.   DLC

11921. "Year of Homage to Martin Luther King." Ebony (24; Apr., 1969), pp. 31-4+.   DHU/MO

11922. "Year Later: Honors for Dr. King; Violence Too." U. S. News and World Report (66; Apr. 14, 1969), p. 8.   DHU

11923. Yglesias, Jose. "Dr. King's March on Washington Part II." August Meier and Elliott Rudwick (eds.). Black Protest in the Sixties (Chicago: Quadrangle Books, 1970), pp. 267-83.
                                                                DHU/R

11924. Young, Andrew J., Jr. "Demonstrations: A Twentieth Century Christian Witness." Social Action (30; My., 1964), pp. 5-12.   DHU/R
        Negro author.

11925. ----- "Hope in the Quest for Economic Justice." Tempo (1:25, Oct. 15, 1969, pp. 5+.   DHU/R

11926. ----- "Results of Frustration." Tempo (1:3, Dec. 1, 1968).
                                                                DHU/R

11927. Young, Margaret B. The Picture Life of Martin Luther King, Jr. New York: Franklin Watts, 1967.   DHU/MO

11928. Young, Peter. "Who Killed Rev. King? An Interview with Rev. Bevel." Liberator (9:3, Mr., 1969), pp. 4-5.   DH/R

11929. Zepp, Ira Gilbert, Jr. The Intellectual Sources of the Ethical Thought of Martin Luther King, Jr., as Traced in His Writings With Special Reference to the Beloved Community. Doctoral Dissertation. Ecumenical Institute of Theology of St. Mary's Seminary and University, 1971.   DHU/R

C. SOCIAL ACTION

11930. Abrecht, Paul. The Churches and Rapid Social Change. Garden City, N. Y.: Doubleday, 1961.   DHU/R
        Bibliography: p. (208)-216.
        "The Church and the Conflict of Nationalism and Colonialism." p. (95)-112.

11931. Adams, J. L. "Theological Bases of Social Action." Journal of Religious Thought (8:1, Aut.-Wint., 1950-51), pp. 6-21.
                                                                DHU/R

11932. Alexander, Raymond P. "The Church: A Symbol of Commitment." Negro History Bulletin (28; Ja., 1965), pp. 77-8+.
                                                                DHU/MO

11933. Alford, Neal B. The Invisible Road to Peace. Boston: Meador Pub. Co., 1957.   DHU/MO
        Negro author.

11934. Allan, Alfred K. "The Community Church of New York City." The Crisis (64:8, Oct., 1957), pp. 473-77. DLC; DHU/MO

11935. "Argument Returns to Dynamite; Koinonia Farm." Christian Century (74; Je. 26, 1957), p. 780.   DHU

11936. Asch, Sidney H. Civil Rights & Responsibilities under the Constitution. Rev. ed. New York: Arco, 1970.   DHU/R
        Chapter 3 entitled "Freedom of Religius Conviction."

11937. Bates, Daisy. The Long Shadow of Little Rock: A Memoir. New York: David McKay Co., 1962   DHU/R
        Negro author.
        "Minister action in the tragedy that placed Little Rock on the world stage." pp. 156-60.

11938. Bennett, John C. "Faith and Responsibility." Christian
Century (75:49, Dec. 3, 1958), pp. 1394-97.   DHU/R

11939. "Black Is Beautiful." Warren Schloat Productions, 1970.
117 fr. color. 35 mm. & phonodisc: 1s., 12 in., 33 1/3 rpm.,
15 min.   DLC
      Filmstrip
      "Presents dominant events and personalities in the civil
      rights movements, including the Black Muslim movement,
      black power, Ossie Davis at the funeral of Malcolm X,
      Stokely Carmichael and SNCC, Dr. Ralph Abernathy and
      the 1968 poor people's campaign, Mayor Carl Stokes of
      Cleveland, and Mayor Richard Hatcher of Gary, Indiana."

11940. "Blacklash Hits the Churches." Christian Century
(81; Ag. 12, 1964), pp. 1004-05.   DHU/R

11941. Blanton, Paul. Toward a Christian Strategy for Social
Change Based on the Program of Community Organization as
Practiced by Saul D. Alinsky. Doctoral dissertation. Clare-
mont Graduate School, 1972.

11942. Bloom, J. The Negro Church and the Movement for Equality. Masters thesis. University of California (Berkeley), 1966.

11943. Brazier, Arthur M. Black Self-Determination: The Story
of the Woodlawn Organization. Grand Rapids, Mich.: William
B. Eerdmans Pub. Co., 1969.   DHU/R; DLC
      Negro author.

11944. Brown, Charles S. Negro Protest and White Power Structure: A Study of the Boston School Controversy 1963-1966.
Doctoral dissertation. Boston University, 1968.

11945. Burney, H. L. "Drop-Out Problem and the Churches."
Central Christian Advocate (140; Dec. 15, 1964), p. 4.
                                          DHU/R; DAU/W

11946. Bush, J. B. "Is America Christian?" Negro History
Bulletin (27; Apr., 1964), p. 173+.   DHU/MO

11947. Campbell, H. W. "Communication: The Pastor in Social
Unrest." Christian Advocate (9; Nov. 4, 1965), pp. 15+.
                                          DAU/W; DHU/R

11948. Campbell, Will D. "The Role of Religion in Segregation
Crises." New South (15:1, Ja., 1960), pp. 3-11. DHU/MO

11949. Church and Race Problems-- U. S. Addresses, Essays,
Lectures. The Church and the Urban Racial Crisis. Edited
by Mathew Ahmann and Margaret Roach. Techny, Ill.: Divine
Word Publications, 1967.   NNCor

11950. "The Church and the Race Crisis." Christian Century (75:
41, Oct. 8, 1958), pp. 1140-41.   DHU/R

11951. Clark, Henry B. "Churchmen and Residential Desegregation." Review of Religious Research (5:3, Spr., 1964), pp. 157-
64.   DHU/R

11952. Clark, Kenneth B. The Negro Protest: James Baldwin,
Malcolm X, Martin Luther King Talk With Kenneth B. Clark.
Boston: Beacon Press, 1963.   DHU/R

11953. Clark, Mary T. Discrimination Today; Guidelines for
Civic Action. Foreword by John J. Wright. New York: Hobbs,
Dorman, 1966   DHU/MO; INU; DLC; Nj

11954. Clarke, Jacquelyne J. These Rights They Seek. n. p.:
n. p., 1962.   DLC
      "About the Alabama Christian Movement for Human Rights,
      the Montgomery Improvement Association and the Tuskeegee
      Civic Association."

11955. "Company Capitulates to Demands of Clergy." Central
Christian Advocate (137; My. 1, 1962), p. 19.   DAU/W; DHU/1

11956. "Council Rescinds Restrictions; Clergymen's Participation
in Racial Justice Projects." Christian Century (82; Mr. 10,
1965), p. 293.   DHU/R

11957. "Court Cases Brought by Christian Movement for Human
Rights Against Commissioner of Public Safety in Birmingham."
Race Relations Law Reporter (5; Wint., 1960), pp. 1150-52.
                                                 DHU/L

11958. Crawford, Evans E. "Some Sociological Perspectives of
Social Change in the Negro Religious Community and its
Leadership." Journal of Religious Thought (18;1, 1961), pp. 67-
77.   DHU/R
      Negro author.

11959. Crowell, George Harvey. "American Cultural Values
Obstructing Christian Social Action." Doctoral dissertation.
Union Theological Seminary, 1967.

11960. Cuninggim, Merrimon. "The Southern Temper." New South
(13; Jl.-Ag., 1958), pp. 7-8   DHU/R

11961. "Delta Ministry." World Outlook (24; Ag., 1964), pp. 14+.
                                                 DAU/W

11962. "Division to 'Do-Sponsor' U. N. Seminar on World View of
Race Relations." Concern (4; Dec. 15, 1962), p. 12.   DAU/W

11963. Dodds, Elizabeth D. Voices of Protest and Hope. New York:
Friendship Press, 1965.   DHU/R
      Chapter 7, The Church, voice of hope.

11964. Dodson, Dan. "The Church, Power and Saul Alinsky."
Nashville, Religion in Life (36:1, Spr., 1967), pp. 108-18.
                                                 DHU/R
      A discussion of Alinsky's power/conflict approaches to
      community organization and their relationship to the church
      and its use of the so-called "integrative processes."

11965. "A Dream Deferred." Student Nonviolent Coordinating Com-
mittee and Harvey Richards, Released by Student Nonviolent
Coordinating Committee, 1964. 37 min., sd. b & w. 16 mm.
Film.
      "Describes the work of field secretaries for SNCC who are
      engaged in voter registration, and other projects in the
      South."

11966. Duff, E. "Boston's St. Joseph Retreat League." Social
Order (8; Je., 1958), pp. 265-68.   DCU/SW; DGU

11967. ----- "Social Action in the American Environment."
Social Order (9; Sept., 1959), pp. 297-308. DCU/SW; DGU

11968. "Education: A Perennial Priority." Editorial. Message
Magazine (29:7, Oct., 1963), pp. 5-6.   DHU/R
      "Equal opportunity for each individual to obtain a sound
      and suitable education."

11969. Egerton, John. "Lucius Pitts and U. W. Clemon." New
South (25:3, Sum., 1970), pp. 9-20.   DHU/R
      The role Miles College president and students played in
      the civil rights struggle in Birmingham, Alabama.

11970. Ellison, Virginia H. "It Happened in Shippensburg!"
Religious Education (59:1, Ja.-Feb., 1964), pp. 80-83. DHU/R
      An incident of segregation in Pennsylvania and the
      subsequent action of churchmen is discussed.

11971. "Facing the Challenge of a New Age." The Phylon Quarterly
(17:1, Apr., 1957), pp. 25-34.   DHU/MO
      Substance of an address on combining peacefulness and
      action to speed the coming of the new age of Negro rights,
      First Annual Institute on Non-Violence and Social Change,
      Montgomery, Ala., December, 1956.

11972. "Faith and Prejudice in Georgia; Lovett Schools Whites-Only
Admission Policy." Time (82; Nov. 15, 1963), p. 94.   DHU

11973. Fichter, Joseph H. Social Relations in the Urban Parish. Chicago: University Press, 1954.   DHU/R

11974. Fiske, Edward B. "Social Action for the Parish." New York Times (Oct. 13, 1968).   Pam. File, DHU/R

11975. "Fresh Look at Black America; Conference of the National Council of Churches." Christian Century (84; Oct. 25, 1967), pp. 1340-1.   DHU

11976. Friedrichs, David W. The Role of the Negro Minister in Politics in New Orleans. Doctoral dissertation. Tulane University, 1967.

11977. Friedrichs, R. W. "Christians and Residential Exclusion." Journal of Social Issues (15; 1959), pp. 14-23.   DHU/R

11978. Gandy, Samuel L. "Youth Establishments and Protest." Theology Today (23:2, Jl., 1966), pp. 316-23.
     Pam. File; DHU/R
     The younger generation and its relation to religious organizations.
     Negro author.

11979. Garman, Harold W. A Theory of Responsible Action for Boston Clergymen in Relation to the 1963 March on Washington. Doctoral dissertation. Boston University Graduate School, 1965.

11980. Gehres, M. "Cleveland's Project Friendship." Presbyterian Life (21; Ag. 1, 1968), p. 5.   DAU/W

11981. Gilliam, W. A. "Prepare Christians for Revolution." United Evangelical Action (24; Dec., 1965), pp. 9-11.   KyLoS

11982. Glock, Charles Y. and B. B. Ringer. "Church Policy and the Attitudes of Ministers and Parishioners, on Social Issues." American Sociological Review (21; Apr., 1956), pp. 148-56.   DHU

11983. ----- "The Political Role of the Church as Defined by its Parishioners." Public Opinion Quarterly (18; Wint., 1954-55), 337-47.   DHU

11984. Graham, Billy. "Billy Graham Makes Plea for an End to Intolerance." Life (41; Oct. 1, 1956), pp. 138+.   DHU

11985. Green, C. A. "Negro Church: A Power Institution." Negro History Bulletin (26:1, Oct., 1962), pp. 20-22+.   DHO/MO

11986. Gusweller, J. A. "Church and Community Action, Church of St. Timothy and St. Matthew, New York." Christian Century (76; Jl. 15, 1959), pp. 824-5.   DHU

11987. Hamblin, Dora Jane. "Crunch in the Church." Life (Oct. 4, 1968), pp. 79-87.   Pam. File, DHU/R
     Protestant ministers and social action.

11988. Hare, Nathan. "Have Negro Ministers Failed Their Roles?" Negro Digest (12:9, Jl., 1963), pp. 11-19.
     Pam. File, DHU/R; NN/Sch

11989. Harmon, John J. "Towards a Style for the White Church." Church in Metropolis (17; Sum., 1968), pp. 1-3.   DHU/R

11990. Harper, L. Alexander. "School Integration--Search for a Christian Context." Social Action (32:1, Sept., 1965), pp. 31-37.   DHU/R

11991. Harriman House, New York. Discrimination, What Can Churches Do? A Handbook and Report on the Religious Leadership Conference of Equaltiy of Opportunity. Harriman House, N. Y. Arden House. Apr. 28-29, 1958.   DHU/MO

11992. Hart, W. C. "Negro in the Christian Ministry." Christian Century (76:11, Mr. 18, 1959), p. 319.   DHU/R

11993. Hecht, James L. "Open Housing: A Challenge to the Church." The Christian Century (89:36, Oct. 11, 1972), pp. 1010-14.   DHU/R

11994. Hedgeman, Anna A. The Trumpet Sounds. A Memoir of Negro Leadership. New York: Rinehart and Winston, 1964. Negro author.

11995. Height, Dorothy Irene. The Christian Citizen and Civil Rights; a Guide to Study and Action. By Dorothy L. Height and J. Oscar Lee... New York: Woman's Press, 1949. (Public Affairs News Service, v. 12, no. 4.).   NN/Sch
     Negro author.

11996. Hill, Samuel S., Jr. "The South's Culture Protestantism." Christian Century (79:37, Sept. 12, 1962), pp. 1094-96.   DHU/R

11997. Holmes, Willie Lawsie. Negro Minister and His Community Contacts. Masters thesis. Southern Baptist Theological Seminary, 1957.

11998. Humphrey, Hubert Horatio. Integration vs. Segregation. New York: Crowell, 1964.   DHU/MO

11999. "Interchurch Social Mission; Forming Interreligious Committee Against Poverty." America (114; Feb. 19, 1966), p. 246.   DHU

12000. Jeffries, Vincent and Clarence E. Tygart. "The Influence of Theology, Denomination, and Values upon the Positions of Clergy on Social Issues." Journal for the Scientific Study of Religion (13:3, Sept., 1974), pp. 309-24.   DHU/R
     Includes opinions of clergymen on civil rights movement.

12001. Keenan, C. "Church Leaders on School Segregation." America (11; Jl. 10, 1954), pp. 378-9   DHU

12002. Kenealy, William J. "Racism Desecrates Liberty, Perverts Justice and Love." Social Order (13; My., 1963), pp. 5-20.   DHU
     By a professor of law, Loyola University, Chicago.

12003. Killian, Lewis M. and Charles Grigg. Racial Crisis in America: Leadership in Conflict. Englewood Cliffs, N. J.: Prentice Hall, 1964.   DHU/R

12004. ----- and Charles U. Smith. "Negro Protest Leaders in Southern Community." Social Forces (38; Mr., 1960), pp. 253-57.   DHU

12005. King, C. H. "Growing Rebellion in the Negro Church." Negro Digest (12; Mr., 1963), pp. 38-45.   DHU/MO; DLC

12006. Kirk, W. Astor. "Responsible Use of Social Power by the Church in Race Relations." Central Christian Advocate (138; Ag. 15, 1963), pp. 4+.   DAU/W; DHU/R
     Negro author.

12007. Kobben, A. J. F. "Prophetic Movements as an Expression of Social Protest." International Archives of Ethnography (49; 1960), pp. 117-64.   DCU/AN

12008. Kretzschmer, R. "Church in Disadvantaged Communities." World Outlook (25; Dec., 1964), pp. 11+.   DAU/W

12009. Lee, Robert, (ed.). Religion and Social Conflict. New York: Oxford Univ. Press, 1964.   INU
     Pp. 37-54, race and church.

12010. Lenox, C. Merrill. "Civil Rights Marches in Detroit." Christian Century (80:37, Sept. 11, 1963), p. 1112.   DHU/R

12011. Lester, Julius. Revolutionary Notes. New York: Richard W. Baron, 1969.   DHU/R
     "Martin Luther King, Jr." pp. 82-90. "The Poor People's Campaign and Radicals," pp. 124-27.
     "Jewish Racism and Black Anti-Semitism," pp. 181-84.
     Negro author.

12012. Lindsey, A. J. "Church and Social Action." United Evangelical Action (17; Jl. 15, 1958), pp. 227-30.   KyLoS

12013. Martin, William C. "Shepherds vs. Flocks; Church Involvement in Fight Assault on Kodak." Atlantic Monthly
(220; Dec., 1967), pp. 53-9.   DHU

12014. McDowell, Edward A. "What About Race Relations in the
South Today?" Religious Herald (127; Ja. 14, 1954), pp. 4-5.
TND; ViU

12015. McPeak, William. "Social Problems are Human Problems."
Interracial Review (35; Nov., 1962), pp. 253-4.
DCU/SW; DCU

12016. Meier, August. "Negro Protest Movements and Organizations." Journal of Negro Education (32:4, Fall, 1963), pp. 437-
ro.   DHU/MO

12017. ----- and Elliot Rudwick. The Making of Black America.
New York: Atheneum Press, 1969.   DHU/R

12018. "A Missionary Presence in Mississippi 1964." Social
Action (31; Nov., 1964), pp. 1-48.   DHU/R
The National Council of Churches and the Mississippi
Summer Project.

12019. National Conference on Race and Religion, Chicago, 1963.
Race: Challenge to Religion, an Original Essay and an
Appeal to the Conscience. Chicago: H. Regnrey Co., 1963
INU

12020. "Negro Churches Lead Mass 'Get Out the Vote' Drive."
Atlanta World (Oct. 24, 1968). Pam. File; DHU/R

12021. Nelson, William Stuart. "Gandhian Values and the
American Civil Rights." Paul F. Power, (ed.). The
Meaning of Gandhi (Hawaii: The University Press of Hawaii,
1971), pp. 153-64.   DHU/R
Negro author.

12022. ----- "Thoreau and American Nonviolent Resistance."
Jules Chamezky, and S. Kaplan, (eds.). Black and White in
American Culture. An Anthology from the Massachusetts Review. (n. p., The University of Massachusetts Press, 1969),
pp. 106-10   DHU/R

12023. Nerberg, Well. "Religion in a Secularized Society." Review of Religious Research (3:4, Spr., 1962), pp. 145-58.
DHU/R

12024. Niebuhr, Reinhold. "The Negro Minority and its Fate in a
Self-Righteous Nation." McCormick Quarterly (22:4, My.,
1969), pp. 201-10   DHU/R
Article makes a plea for the church to engage in full struggle
for justice.
Also in, Social Action (35:2, Oct., 1968), pp. 53-64.
DHU/R

12025. Niebuhr, Richard R. "Theologians Comments on the Negro
in America." Reporter (15; Nov. 29, 1956), pp. 24-5.
Discussion (15; Dec. 27, 1956), p. 3.   DHU/R

12026. "No Panacea." Editorial. Christian Century (82:34, Ag.
25, 1965), pp. 1027-28.
Comments on the civil disturbances in Watts and the possible inadequacies of the Civil Rights Act of 1964 and the
Voting Rights Act of 1965.

12027. Norman, Clarence. A Study of How the East Harlem
Protestant Is Trying to Solve Some of the Social and Religious
Problems of an Inner City Parish. Bachelor of Divinity Paper.
School of Religion, Howard University, 1964.

12028. Nygren, Malcolm. "The Church and Political Action.
Christianity Today (13:12, Mr. 14, 1969), pp. 9-12.
DHU/R

12029. Parsonage, R. R. "Blacklash and Christian Faith."
Christian Century (81; Oct. 21, 1964), pp. 1300-02.   DHU/R

12030. Payton, Benjamin F. "Civil Rights and the Future of
American Cities." Social Action (33:4, Dec., 1966), pp. 6-11.
DHU/R
Negro author.

12031. Powell, Ingeborg B. Ideology and Strategy of Direct Action:
A Study of the Congress of Racial Equality. Doctoral dissertation. University of California, 1965.

12032. Proctor, Samuel D. The Young Negro in America, 1960-
1980. New York: Association Press, 1966.   DHU/R
Negro author.

12033. "Progress in Little Rock." Christian Century (80; My. 8,
1963), p. 606.   DHU/R

12034. Purnell, J. M. In his Pavilions. Reflections Upon Religion
and Modern Society. New York: Exposition Press, 1959.
DHU/MO

Negro author.

12035. Putney, Snell and Russell Middleton. "Rebellion, Conformity, and Parental Religious Ideologies." Sociometry (24; Je.,
1961), pp. 125-36.   DHU

12036. Rainwater, Lee and William L. Yancey. The Moynihan
Report and the Politics of Controversy. Cambridge: M. I. T.
Press, 1967.   DHU/MO

12037. "Reconciliation Through Anger: Delta Ministry." Time
(86; Jl. 2, 1965), pp. 70-1.   DHU

12038. "Religion and Politics." WCBS-TV and Columbia University. Released by Holt, Rinehart and Winston, 1969. 30 min.
sd. b & w. 16 mm.   DLC
Film.
"Dr. C. Eric Lincoln discusses the role of ministers in the
social protest of black Americans in urban ghettos during
the period, 1945-1954, and the effect of two wars, the N. A.
A. C. P., and other factors in shaping political ideologies."

12039. "Religious Revolution and the Void." Bloomington, Ind.:
Indiana Univ., National Education Television, 1971.
16mm. 60 min. b & w.
Film.
Civil Rights, jazz, new social forms.

12040. "Report of a Housing Project Undertaken by the Monthly
Meeting of the Religious Society of Friends in Syracuse, New
York, 1954-55.   Pam. File, DHU/R
"One Quaker Group's Efforts to Integrate and Make Avail-
able Better Housing for Negroes."

12041. "The Role of the National Council of Churches in the Mississippi Summer Project." Social Action (31:3, Nov., 1964),
pp. 10-15.   DHU/R

12042. Rooks, Charles Shelby. "The Bible and Citizenship."
Social Action (25:2, Oct., 1958), pp. 13-21.
Pam. File, DHU/R

12043. Root, Robert. Struggle of Decency: Religion and Race
in Modern America. New York: Friendship Press, 1965.
CtY-D; DHU/MO; NN/Sch; DHU/R; NcD

12044. Rose, Arnold M. The Negro Protest. Philadelphia: The
American Academy of Political and Social Science, 1965. DHU/R
Annals of the American Academy of Political and Social
Science. (Ja., 1965).

12045. Ross, Harry. Souls Don't Have Color. Detroit, Mich.:
Pub. and distributed by UAW-CIO Fair Practices and Anti-
Discrimination Department, 1953.   NcD

12046. Ruoss, Meryl. Citizen Power and Social Change. The
Challenges to Churches. New York: The Seabury Press,
1968.   DHU/R

12047. "Sanctuary and Spear: the Church in the Revolution."
Ann Arbor: University of Michigan, Television Center,
197?. 29 min. b & w.   DHU/AA; MiU
Story of the Black Church.
Film.

12048. Schaller, Lyle E. Planning for Protestantism in Urban
America. New York: Abingdon Press, 1965.   DHU/R

12049. "School Integration is Proceeding: Churches Face Many
Problems on Desegregation." Christian Century (71; Oct. 6,
1954), pp. 1195+.   DHU/R

12050. See, Ruth D. What Can We Do? New York: Friendship
Press, 1965.   DHU/R
"Directed to Christian youth within the church who are
looking for solutions to the perplexing questions of race
prejudice and suspicion that are consistent with their
faith."

12051. Sellers, James E. "Love, Justice and the Non-violent
Movement." Theology Today (18:4, Ja., 1962), pp. 422-34.
                                            DHU/R

12052. Shuttlesworth, Fred L. "Birmingham Revisited." Ebony
(24:10, Ag., 1971), pp. 114-18.   Pam. File, DHU/R
Rev. Shuttlesworth who took a leading role in demonstrating
against segregation in Birmingham, Alabama "returns to
the city to view a decade of change".

12053. Silberman, Charles E. "Up from Apathy-- The Woodlawn
Experiment: Self-Help in a Slum Neighborhood." Commentary
(37:5, My., 1964), pp. 51-58.   DHU/R
Adapted from author's: Crisis in Black and White.
New York: Random House, 1964.   DHU/R

12054. "Southern Ministers Stand Up to Mobs." Christian Century
(73; Oct. 10, 1956), pp. 1155+.   DHU/R

12055. Spike, Robert W. "Civil Rights Involvement, Model for
Mission: A Message to Churchmen." Detroit Industrial Society
(No. 9, Nov., 1965).   Pam. File, DHU/R
A series of occasional papers on Christian Faith and
Industrial Society.

12056. ----- "Fissures in the Civil Rights Movement." Christianity and Crisis (26:2, Feb. 21, 1966), p. 21. DHU/R

12057. Spivey, R. A. "Integration and the South: the South as a
Cultural Unit." Union Seminary Quarterly Review (11; Mr.,
1956), pp. 33-36.   DHU/R

12058. Stagg, Paul Leonard. "A Minister's Involvement in the
Racial Crisis." The Journal of Religious Thought (16:2,
Sum.-Aut., 1959), pp. 77-94.   DHU/R

12059. Stepp, Diane. "Ministers to Picket Food Chain." Atlanta
Journal (Nov. 2, 1968),   Pam. File, DHU/R

12060. Stevick, Daniel B. Civil Disobedience and the Christian.
New York: Seabury Press, 1969.   DHU/R

12061. Sullenger, Earl T. "The Church in an Urban Society."
Sociology and Social Research (41:5, My.-Je., 1957), pp. 361-
66.   CLU; TxD; PPi; VaU

12062. "Support for Mississippi Volunteers Reaffirmed by National
Council of Churches." Concern (6; Jl. 15, 1964), pp. 14+.
                                            DAU/W

12063. Sweeney, Odile. "Sit Ins" American Students Seek Freedom
from Indignity." Social Action (27:5, Ja., 1961), pp. 5-13.
                                            DHU/R

12064. "'3rd Society' Held Forgotten in Racial Tension." New York
Times (Nov. 18, 1968).   Pam. File, DHU/R

12065. Thomas, Howard E. and Mary Peter. Organizing for Human
Rights; a Handbook for Teachers and Students. Dayton, Ohio:
G. A. Pflaum, 1966.   PPT

12066. Tillman, James A. Not by Prayer Alone; a Report on the
Greater Minneapolis Interfaith Fair Housing Program. Philadelphia: United Church Press, 1964.   DHU/R; DLC; CtY-D

12067. Towne, Anthony. "Revolution and the Marks of Baptism."
Katallegete (Sum., 1967), pp. 2-13.   DHU/R

12068. Ullman, V. "In Darkest America: Delta Ministry Programs
in Mississippi." Nation (205; Sept. 4, 1967), pp. 177-80.
                                            DHU

12069. United Lutheran Church in America. Board of Social
Missions. A Statement on Human Relations Adopted by the
Board of Social Missions and the Executive Board of the
United Lutheran Church in America. New York: Board of
Social Missions, 1956?   NNUT

12070. Valentine, Foy Dan. "The Court, The Church, and the
Community." Review and Expositor (53; Oct., 1956), pp. 536-
50.   DLC; CtY-D

12071. Vernon, Robert. The Black Ghetto. Preface by Rev. Albert
B. Cleage, Jr., Introduction by James Shabazz. New York:
Merit Publishers, 1965.   DHU/R
"Articles originally appeared in the socialist newspaper,
The Militant.

12072. "Walk in My Shoes, Pts. 1 & 2." ABC News. Released by
McGraw-Hill Book Co., 1963. 54 min. sd. b & w. 16 mm.
Film.
Views for and against the Black Muslins, Martin Luther King,
The Freedom Riders and rapid integration and the NAACP.

12073. Wallace, Helen K. Keys in Our Hands. Valley Forge: The
Judson Press, 1967.   DHU/R
Dedicated to Dr. Leon H. Sullivan, Negro minister, and
the work of the Opportunities Industrialization Center,
founded by him.

12074. Weaver, Galen R. "Racial Change and Relevant Religious
Faith and Action." Religious Education (59:1, Ja.-Feb., 1964),
pp. 91-4.   DHU/R

12075. Wharton, W. E. "Change Through Non-Violent Resistance."
The African Methodist Episcopal Church Review (78:214,
Oct.-Dec., 1962), pp. 50-52.   DHU/R
Negro author.

12076. Wilmore, Gayraud S., Jr. The Secular Relevance of the
Church. Philadelphia: Westminster Press, 1962.   DHU/R
Negro author

12077. Wine, S. T. "Humanistic Religious Institutions and Political
Power." Religious Humanism (2:3, Sum., 1968), p. 124.
                                            DHU/R

12078. Wright, Nathan, Jr. Ready to Riot. New York: Holt, Rinehart & Winston, 1968.   DHU/R
Account of the factors that led to the riots in Newark, N. J.,
by a former Prtoestant Epicopal priest.

12079. Younger, G. D. "Church and Urban Renewal." Commonweal
(82; Jl. 23, 1965), p. 540.   DHU

12080. Zeuner, R. W. "Pastor and Social Acion." Christian Advocate (9; Ag. 26, 1965), pp. 9+.   DAU/W; DHU/R

12081. Zietlow, Carl P. "Race, Students, and Non-Violence."
Religious Education (59:1, Ja.-Feb., 1964), pp. 116-20. DHU/R

12082. Zinn, Howard. SNCC, The New Abolitionists. Boston:
Beacon Press, 1964.   DHU/R
A study of the members of the Student Nonviolent Coordinating Committee in action and a suggestion as to their contribution to American civilization.

V. THE CONTEMPORARY RELIGIOUS SCENE

A. CHURCH, URBAN CRISIS AND SOCIAL ACTION

12083. Abernathy, Ralph D. "Leisure Time for the Poor."
Spectrum (48:1), pp. 11-14. DHU/R
Negro author.

12084. ----- "Some International Dimensions of the Peace Movement." Freedomways (2:3, 1971), pp. 237-42.
DGW; DHU/R

12085. ----- (Speech.) Imamu Amiri Baraka (LeRoi Jones), (ed.).
African Congress. A documentary of the First Modern Pan-
African Congress (New York: Wm. Morrow & Co., 1972),
pp. 9-11. DHU/R

12086. Adams, Donald Conrad. A Comparative Study of the Social
Functions of the Highway Church of Jesus of the Apostlic Faith
of T. B., Maryland and the Grace Methodist Church of Chapel
Hill, Maryland. B. D. Paper. School of Religion, Howard
University, 1966.

12087. Adams, John Hurst. "Saturday Ethnic School, A Model."
Spectrum (47:4, Jl., 1971), pp. 8+. DHU/R
The article concerns the opeerations of the Educational
Growth Organization, a system of Saturday ethnic schools
operated by a cluster of 8 Black Churches in Los Angeles.

12088. Adams, John P. "The Church Must Read the Riot Act."
Concern (9:6, Oct. 1, 1967), pp. 7-13, 19-21. DHU/R

12089. ----- "A Letter from the Milwaukee Ghetto: Put it Down
in Black and White." Concern (9:17, Oct. 15, 1967), pp. 4-11.
DHU/R

12090. ----- "A Report from Milwaukee." Concern (9:19, Nov.
15, 1967), pp. 4-5+. DHU/R

12091. ----- "Thoughts on a Bombing." Concern (10:1, Ja. 1-15,
1968), pp. 6-9. DHU/R

12092. "After South Bend, A Sampling of Comments on the Main
Issue." The Episcopalian (34:11, Nov. 1969), pp. 33+. DHU/R

12093. Ahmann, Mathew. "Church and the Urban Negro." America
(118; Feb. 10, 1968), pp. 181-5. Discussion (118; Apr. 13, 1968),
p. 456. DHU

12094. ----- and Margaret Roach (ed.). The Church and the
Urban Racial Crisis. Techny, Ill.: Divine Word Publications,
1967. NjP

12095. "Angela and the Presbyterians." Christian Century, Edit-
orial. (88:27, Je. 7, 1971), p. 823. DHU/R
Synod of United Presbyterian Church contributes to Angela
Davis defense fund.

12096. Ashbrook, James B. A New Day Has Taken Place. An Interpretive Description of the Crisis in Black and White. Rochester, N. Y.: Colgate Rochester Divinity School, 1969. NNtcA
Church and race problems.

12097. Austin, Ann. "The Crisis Parish of East Harlem." Social
Action (16:1, Ja. 15, 1950), pp. 23-33. DHU/R

12098. Baldwin, James. "Our Divided Society: A Challenge to
Religious Education." Religious Education (64:5, Sept.-Oct.,
1969), pp. 342-46. DHU/R

12099. ----- "White Racism or World Community?" Religious
Education (64:5, Sept.-Oct., 1969), pp. 342+. DHU/R

12100. Barnhart, Phil. Don't Call Me Preacher; for Laymen and
Other Ministers. Grand Rapids: Eerdmans, 1972. NNtcA
Church and race problems in Atlanta, Georgia.

12101. Bartlett, Bob. The Soul Patrol. Plainfield: Lagos International, 1970. DHU
"Youth group of Philadelphia that goes into city areas to
help people discover the real power of the Christian religion."

12102. Beach, Waldo. Christian Community and American Society.
Philadelphia: Westminster Press, 1969. CtY-D

12103. "Bearers of Christ. Address on the Role of the Catholic
Church and Other Churches in the Struggle for Racial Improve-
ment in Our Society." New South (20; Sept., 1965), pp. 13-15.
DHU/R

12104. Berger, Peter L. and Brigitte Berger. "The Assault on
Class." World View (15:7, Jl., 1972), pp. 20-25. DHU/R
Current confusions of "class" and "race" and how they may
reverse the drive for social justice in America.

12105. Bervine, J. W. "Christian Concern and Black Business."
United Evangelical Action (28; Fall, 1969), pp. 31-33. McMjHi

12106. Beukema, George G. "Inner City Shared Ministry." The
Reformed Review (23:1, Fall, 1969), pp. 51-55. DHU/R

12107. Billingsley, Andrew W. Black Families and the Struggle
for Survival: Teaching Our Children to Walk Tall. New York:
Friendship Press, 1974. DHU/R
Published for the National Council of Churches. Committee
on Ministries with Blacks.
Negro author.

12108. "Black Americans at Work: Shelvin Hall, Minister." Cor-
onet Instructional Films, 1970. 51 fr. color. 35 mm. & Phonodisc: 1 s., 12 in., 33 1/3 rpm., 12 min. DLC
Filmstrip.
"Presents Negro life in the city as seen through the eyes of
a black minister who relates his early struggles to build a
Church in Chicago and describes the dilemma facing black
people today."

12109. Booker, Merrel Daniel, Sr., et alii. Cry at Birth. Collected
and edited by the Bookers. New York: McGraw-Hill, 1971.
DHU/R
An anthology of prose and poetry by Negro youths. See especially, "Ghetto Service," and "A Prayer," poems which reflect

(Booker, Merrel Daniel cont.)
   religious sentiment.
   Negro authors.

12110. Boomershine, Tom. "The Rich and the Poor in Theological
   Education." Motive (30: 5, Feb., 1970), pp. 20-30. DHU/R
   Union Theological Seminary, New York, ask Board of Directors to appropriate funds to help aleviate the economic
   condition of blacks in Harlem."

12111. Boyd, Bob. "Breaking Down the Wall of Fear." Tempo
   (2:8, Feb. 1, 1970), pp. 3+.   DHU/R
   Young Lutheran group and Black Youth Unlimited visit
   the Delta Ministry in Mississippi.

12112. Breeden, Jim. "Church, Racism and Boston." Tempo
   (1:5, Dec. 15, 1968), p. 8.   DHU/R
   An interview.

12113. Breen, Jay. "Parish in Hades." Negro Digist (9:6, Apr.,
   1951), pp. 75-8.   DHU/MO
   Work of three Protestant ministers in East Harlem, New
   York City.

12114. Brisbane, Robert H. Black Activism. Valley Forge, Pa.:
   Judson Press, 1974.   DHU/R
   Includes information on Malcolm X's movement and Martin
   Luther King, Jr.

12115. Brockway, Allan R. "Riotous Judgment of God." Concern
   (7:15, Sept. 1, 1965), pp. 12-13.   DHU/R; DAU/W

12116. ----- "The Urban Riots, the Church and the Future."
   Concern (9:16, Oct. 1, 1967), p. 4.   DHU/R

12117. Brown, Geneva N. "The James Varick 1.6 Million Dollar
   Multi-Purpose Community Center is Dedicated." The A.M.E.
   Zion Quarterly Review (86:1, Spr., 1974), pp. 7-11. DHU/R
   This center located in Harlem, New York, sponsored by
   the mother Zion Church offers educational, social, cultural
   and recreational programs for all age levels.

12118. Brown, H. C., Jr., (comp.). The Cutting Edge; Critical
   Questions for Contemporary Christians. Waco, Texas: Word
   Books, 1969.   MiBsA

12119. Brown, John W. "The Church Casts Its Shareholders Votes
   for Equal Employment." Contact (5:3, Sum., 1974), pp. 29-30.
                                        Pam. File, DHU/R

12120. Brown, R. "The Christian and the Riot Report." Pulpit
   (Feb., 1969), p. 11.   DAU/W

12121. Bucher, Glenn R. "Leberation, Male and White: Initial
   Reflections." The Christian Century (91:11, Mar. 20, 1974),
   pp. 312-16.   DHU/R
   Written by assistant professor of religion at the College of
   Wooster, Ohio.

12122. Burke, Carl. God is For Real, Man. New York: Association Press, 1966.   DHU/R
   Prayers of ghetto children in their own language.

12123. Byrd, Cameron Wells. Black Power, Black Youth, the
   City's Rebellion. Implication for Youth Ministry. An Address
   by the Pastor of Christ United Church of Christ. Detroit:
   n.p., n.d.   Pam. File, DHU/R
   Negro author.

12124. Campbell, James. "Black Community Developers' Search
   for Roles." Christian Advocate (13:23, Nov. 27, 1969), p. 28.
                                                   DAU/W

12125. Carling, Francis. "Move Over," Students, Politics, Religion. New York: Sheed & Ward, 1969.   DHU/R
   Chapter IV, Religion and Rebellion.

12126. Castle, Robert W. Prayers for the Burned-Out City. New
   York: Sheed & Ward, 1968.   DLC; DHU/R

12127. Cater, D. G. "Church and the Reliefers; Urban Negro Slum
   Dwellers." Christian Century (82; Feb. 24, 1965), pp. 232-5
                                                   DHU/R

12128. "Catholics and Urban Problems." America (115; Ag. 20,
   1966), p. 168.   DHU

12129. Cave, Clarence L. "The Theological Significance of Racial
   and Cultural Pluralism." Church and Society (62:5, My.-Je.,
   1972), pp. 53-56.   DHU/R

12130. Chandler, E. Russell. "Putting Treasure Where the Heart
   Is." Liberty (66:6, Nov.-Dec., 1971), pp. 12-12.
                                        Pam. File, DHU/R
   "Story of how concerned Christians are making the church
   come alive in urban ghettos."

12131. Charland, William A. "Contracts and Covenants: A Model
   for Interracial Social Action." Pastoral Psychology (21: 204,
   My., 1970), pp. 39+.   DHU/R

12132. Chatman, Jacob L. "A Black Pastor Speaks to the Issues
   of His Community." Baptist Leader (31:12, Mr., 1970), pp. 6+.
                                                   DHU/R

12133. Chauncey, George C. "Violence and the Judgement of God."
   Ceaser D. Coleman, (ed.). Beyond Blackness to Destiny:
   Study Guide (Memphis: Printed by Wimmer Bros., n. d.),
   pp. 55-60.   Pam. File, DHU/R

12134. Childress, James F. The Basis and Limits of Political Obligation: A Theological and Philosophical Analysis of Civil
   Disobedience. Doctoral dissertation. Yale University, 1969.

12135. Chisholm, Shirley. "The Relationship Between Religion and
   Today's Social Issues." Religious Education (69:2, Mr.-Apr.,
   1974), pp. 117-23.   DHU/R
   Written by Negro member of Congress, 12th District of
   New York; U. S. House of Representatives.

12136. "The Church and Social Change." Joint Strategy and Action
   Committee Grapevine. (5:3, Sept., 1973), pp. 1-6.

12137. The Church and the Urban Racial Crisis. Edited by Matthew
   Ahmann and Margaret Roach. Techney, Ill.: Divine Word Publications, 1967.   DLC; DHU/R
   "The major addresses and background papers prepared for
   the August, 1967, convention of the National Catholic Conference for Interracial Justice held at Rockhurst College in
   Kansas City, Missouri."

12138. "Church Heads Urged to Promote Education of Black Young-
   sters." Chicago Daily Defender (Ja. 14, 1969).
                                        Pam. File, DHU/R

12139. "Church Money for the Slums." America (119; Nov. 9, 1968),
   p. 425.   DHU

12140. "Churches Confront Urban Crisis." Christianity Today
   (12; Je. 21, 1968), pp. 26-28.   DHU/R

12141. Clark, Henry B. The Church and Residential Desegregation:
   a Case Study of an Open Housing Covenant Campaign. New Haven,
   Conn.: College & University Press, 1965. DHU/R; InU; NN/Sch

12142. Clark, Kenneth B. Dark Ghetto; Dilemmas of Social Power.
   New York: Harper & Row, 1965.   DHU/R
   Negro author.
   Negro church, pp. 174-83.

12143. Coburn, John E. Time For Turning. New York: Seabury,
   1969.   T Sew U-T
   Church and Society.

12144. Coggins, Ross. "On the Street Where You Live." Baptist
   Student (49:8, My., 1970), pp. 26+.   DHU/R
   Article deals with Christians on fair housing.

12145. Coleman, Ceasar D. "The Crisis in the Nation: Study Guide
and Outline for Church and Community Use. "
Pam. File; DHU/R
Written by secretary of Christian Methodist Episcopal
Church, Bd. of Christian Education.

12146. Coles, Robert. "The Lord of the Ghettos. The God Who
Asked People to Cross Rivers and Deserts. " Commonweal
(93:7, Nov. 13, 1970), pp. 167-74.   DHU/R

12147. Comer, James P. Beyond Black and White. New York: A
New York Times Company, 1972.   DHU/R
Religion and the Church, pp. 15-20; 179-89.

12148. Conant, Ralph E. "Black Control: A White Dilemma. "
Perspective (10:1, Spr., 1969), pp. 9-21.   DHU/R

12149. Crawford, Evans Edgar. "The Response of Black Churchmen. " J. Philip Wogaman, (ed.). The Population Crisis
and Moral Responsibility (Washington, D. C.: Public Affairs
Press, 1973), pp. 327-29.   DHU/R
Negro author.

12150. Cully, Kendig B. and F. Nile Harper. Will the Church Lose
the City? New York: The World Publishing Co., 1969. DHU/R
Chapter 10, the Black Church in search of a new theology.

12151. Cutting, Tom. "A Presbytery Considers Project Equality. "
The Chicago Theological Seminary Register (62:4, Sept., 1972),
pp. 31-39.   Pam. File, DHU/R
Subtitled, "A Case Study in Educating and Organizing Around
Social Issues. " The article examines the John Knox Presbytery's attempt at instituting "Project Equality, as a program of the religious community.

12152. Daughtry, J. "The Pulpit and the Picket Line. " His (31:1,
Oct. 1970), p. 10+.   DOBNB

12153. Delk, Yvonne Virginia. The Inner-City: a Challenge to the
Church. Masters thesis. Andover Newton Theological School,
1963.

12154. ----- "Liberating Resources for Church Education, A
Bibliography. " Colloquy (4:10, Nov., 1971), pp. 30-32.
DCU/TH; DHU/R
"Resources for liberation and for those persons who are
committed to the creation of a world where racial justice
is a reality. "

12155. Di Gangi, Mariano. "The Church and the Inner City. " David
McKenna, (ed.). The Urban Crisis (Grand Rapids, Mich.:
Zondervan, 1969), pp. 108-20.   DHU/R

12156. "District of Columbia. " Christian Century (80:22, My. 29,
1963), pp. 725-26.   DHU/R
Rally at Mt. Shiloh Baptist Church urged a call for leadership of the Black community.

12157. Drummond, Eleanor. "Lady Dynamo in Los Angeles. "
Presbyterian Life (23:8, Apr. 15, 1970), pp. 14+.   DHU/R
Work of Mrs. Francis L. Hollis, Synod of Southern Calif-
ornia Committee on Urban & Specialized Ministries.

12158. Dugan, George. "Billions for Poor Urged by Leaders of
Four Religions. " New York Times (Apr. 29, 1968).
Pam. File; DHU/R

12159. ----- "Interfaith Group to Aid Urban Negroes. " New York
Times (My. 15, 1968).
Pam. File, DHU/R

12160. ----- "Presbyterians Define Role in Welfare Program. "
New York Times (My. 20, 1968). Pam. File, DHU/R

12161. Dulin, Robert O., Jr. "Social Contexts for Black Christian
Education. " Spectrum (47: 4, Jl.-Aug., 1971), pp. 19-21
DHU/R

12162. Duncan, W. J. "Non-Profit Organization; Church in the
Inner City. " Commonweal (89; Dec. 20, 1968), pp. 400-02.
DHU/R

12163. The Edge of the Ghetto; a Study of Church Involvement in
Community Organization. By John Fish and others. New York:
Seabury Press, 1968.   DLC

12164. Edwards, David L. "Religion and Change. " Theology Today
(26:3, Oct., 1969), pp. 353+.   DHU/R

12165. Ehrenhalt, Alan. "Chicago Priest Fights for White Neighborhood. " Chicago Daily Defender (Dec. 29, 1968).
Pam. File, DHU/R

12166. Elder, Frederick. Crisis in Eden: A Religious Study of
Man and Environment. Nashville: Abingdon, 1970 DHU/R

12167. Ellison, John M. "The Negro Preacher as A Social Prophet. "
The Baptist Herald (30: 5, 6, My.-Je., 1973), pp. 3-7.
Pam. File, DHU/R

12168. Ellul, Jacques. Violence; Reflections from a Christian
Perspective. New York: The Seabury Press, 1969. DHU/R

12169. Evans, Walter. A Critical Analysis of Black Social Movement Leadership in the U. S. A. Masters thesis. Washington,
D. C., Howard University, 1972.

12170. Fabian, Johannes: "Religion and Change. " John N. Paden
and Edward W. Soja (eds.). The African Experience. (Evanston: Northwestern Univ. Press, 1970), Vol. 1, pp. 381-99.
DHU

12171. Felton, Carroll M., Jr. "The Black Church and Economic
Development. " The Church School Herald-Journal (56:3, Je.-
Jl.; Ag., 1972), pp. 5-7.   DHU/R
A. M. E. Zion periodical.

12172. Fiske, Edward B. "Rites, Echo, War and Racial Strife. "
New York Times (Apr. 13, 1968). Pam. File, DHU/R

12173. Friedrichs, Robert. "Decline in Prejudice among Church-
Goers Following Clergy-Led Open-Housing Campaign. "
Journal for the Scientific Study of Religion (10:2 Sum., 1971),
pp. 152-56.   DHU/R

12174. Fry, John R. Fire and Blackstone. Philadelphia: J. B. Lip-
pincott Co., 1969.
The Woodlawn Organization of the First Church, Presbyterian,
Southside Chicago and the "Blackstone Rangers. "

12175. ----- Locked-Out Americans. New York: Harper & Row
Publishers, Inc., 1973.   DHU/R
Includes a chapter on the criminal church. The program
of the Blackstone Rangers and the first Presbyterian Church
of Chicago.

12176. Gannon, Thomas M. "What the Black Community Wants. "
America (121; Dec. 6, 1969), pp. 558-62.   DHU

12177. Gittings, James A. "True Stories About Blacks for Children. " A. D. Presbyterian Life Edition (1:4, Dec., 1972), pp.
40-42.   DHU/R
The New Day Press, Black owned developed in Cleveland,
Ohio with the help of the Presbyterian Church to publish
books that teach Black history.

12178. Goldman, Peter. Report From Black America. New York:
Simon & Schuster, 1970.   DHU/MO
Chapter 3, Directions: Jesse Jackson.

12179. Gooden, Winston. "The Black Church in Liberation. "
Reflections (69: 2, Ja., 1972), Pam. File, DHU/R
Author is second year student in the M. Div. program at
Yale University Diviinity School.

12180. Greeley, Andrew M. "Changing City." Catholic World
(188; Mr., 1959), pp. 481-7.   DHU

12181. "City Life and the Churches." America (103: Ag. 27, 1960),
pp. 573-74.   DHU

12182. Grimes, Alan P. Equality in America; Religion, Race and
the Urban Majority. New York: Oxford University Press, 1964.
                                                     INU

12183. Hall, Clarence W. "Must Churches Finance Revolution?"
Moody Monthly (72:4, Dec., 1971), pp. 18-21.
                                    Pam. File, DHU/R

12184. Harding, Vincent. "I Hear Them ... Calling (And I Know
What It Means)." Katallagete Be Reconciled Journal of the
Committee of Southern Churchmen (4:2-3, Fall-Wint., 1972),
pp. 21-25.   DHU/R
   About his religious convictions and the black community.

12185. Hargraves, J. Archie. Stop Pussyfooting Through a Revolution: Some Churches That Did. New York: United Church
Board for Homeland Ministries, n.d. Pam.File, DHU/R

12186. Harley, Philip A. "Being Practical in Preparing Black
Youth for Ministry." Christian Advocate (14:17, Sept. 13, 1973),
pp. 11-12.   Pam. File, DHU/R

12187. Harper, F. Nile. "Social Power and the Limitation of
Church Education." Religious Education (64:5, Sept.-Oct.,
1969), pp. 390-98.   DHU/R

12188. Harris, Janette Hoston. Black Religious Leaders in
Politics in Washington, D. C. from 1950 to 1972. Masters
thesis. Howard University, 1972

12189. Harrison, James Haygood. "The Campus Ministry as
Change Agent: an Imperative in the Liberation Struggle."
Toward Wholeness (1:1, Sum., 1972), pp. 30-32. DHU/R
   Written by Vice-President and Director of Institutional
   Planning and Resource Development, Morgan State College.

12190. Harrod, Howard L. "The Culture of Poverty." Concern
(7:8, My. 1, 1965), pp. 13-15.   DHU/R

12191. ----- The Ghetto, the Churches and Social Change: An
Evaluation of the Community Service Project, Washington,
D. C., August, 1965. Mim.   DHU/R
   Report on the Howard University Community Service Pro-
   ject, begun in 1961 in cooperation with some local ministers
   of the Washington, D. C. area.

12192. Hensman, C. R. "Joining the Struggle for Social Justice."
International Review of Missions (61:243, Jl, 1972), pp. 257-62.
                                                     DHU/R
   Pointing out the social injustices of the oppressed and the
   need of all to join their cause.

12193. Herberg, Will. Protestant, Catholic, Jew. Garden City,
N. Y.: Doubleday, 1955.   DHU/R
   Chapter on the Negro problem in Protestant city churches.

12194. Hessel, Dieter T. Reconciliation and Conflict: Church
Controversy Over Social Involvement. Philadelphia: The Westminister Press, 1969.   DHU/R
   Church's mandate to concern itself with race as well as other
   social problems in the world.

12195. Hilton, Bruce. The Delta Ministry. New York: Macmillan,
1969.   CtY-D; DHU/R; DLC

12196. Hitchcock, James. "The Christian and Change." Christian
Century (87:1, Ja. 7, 1970), pp. 7-11.   DHU/R

12197. Hofmann, Paul. "Clergymen Meeting Strong: Resistance
to Involvement in Secular Causes." New York Times (Apr. 12,
1968).   Pam. File, DHU/R

12198. Hoge, Dean R. and D. A. Luideus. "Religion and Alienation
as Factors in Student Activism (bibliog)." Sociological Analysis (33; Wint., 1972), pp. 217-29.
                           DAU; DCU/SW; DGU; DHU

12199. Hook, H. Phillip. "Biblical Mandate for an Inner City Ministry." Bibliotheca Sacra (127: 506, Apr.-Je., 1970), pp. 140+.
                                                     DHU/R

12200. Hoover, Theressa. "Keepers of the Faith and Changing
Society." The Church Woman (35:9, Nov., 1969), pp. 25-28.
                                    Pam. File; DHU/R

12201. "How to Carry Out a Conviction; Episcopal Church Poverty
Programs for Urban Ghettos." Time (90; Sept. 29, 1967),
pp. 53-4.   DHU

12203. "In Harlem Slum Area, Canaan Church Has Big Uplift Program." Journal and Guide (Ja. 12, 1974), p. 4.
                                    Pam. File; DHU/R
   Pastor, Dr. T. Wyatt Walker expanded church program to
   include all areas of social action needed in this slum
   district.

12204. Jackson, Jesse L. "Rev. Jesse Jackson Raps on Youth and
Keeping the Faith." Sepia (19; Oct., 1970), pp. 18-20.
                           DHU/MO; DLC; NN/Sch

12205. James, G. M. "Seminar in the Slums." Christian Life
(29; Je., 1967), pp. 34+.   DHU/R

12206. Janey, Pat. "Haven House, 'An Avenue of Compassion.'"
American Baptist Magazine (172:4, Apr., 1974), pp. 20-21.
                                                     DHU/R
   About the work of 59th St. Baptist Church's (West Philadelphia) community house program to furnish supportive
   services to the Blacks in the neighborhood.

12207. Jeffers, Robert A. "The 'Poor of God' and the Black
Christian in America." Catholic World (213: 1275, Je., 1971),
pp. 126-29.   DHU/R

12208. Johnson, Benton. "Ascetic Protestantism and Political
Preference in the Deep South." American Journal of Sociology
(69; Ja., 1964), pp. 359-66.
   Tie between Republicans and fundamentalist.

12209. Jones, Madison. "On the Neighborhood Level." Interracial
Review (35; Ja., 1962), pp. 1262-3.   DHU/R
   Relationships between Negroes and Catholics.

12210. Karsch, Carl G. "The Meaningful Minority." Presbyterian
Life (23:4, Feb. 15, 1970), pp. 8+.   DHU/R
   In suburban Washington, D. C. several denominations or-
   ganized programs for social action.

12211. Katoke, Israel K. "Encounter of the Gospel and Cultures."
The Black Church (1:2, 1972), pp. 49-71.   DHU/R

12212. Kenrick, Bruce. Come Out the Wilderness; the Story of
East Harlem Protestant Parish. Drawing by Joseph Papin.
New York: Harper, 1962. INU; DHU/R; NN/Sch; CtY-D

12213. King, Douglas W. Ethos and Chaos: Toward an Ethic of
Social Change. Doctoral dissertation. Vanderbilt University,
1972.

12214. Kirk, W. Astor. "Povety, Powerlessness, the Church."
Concern (7:8, My. 1, 1965), pp. 10-12.   DHU/R
   Negro author.

12215. Kochman, Thomas, (ed.). Rappin' and Stylin' Out Communication in Urban Black America. Urbana: Univ. of
Illinois Press, 1972.   DHU/R

12216. Kostyu, Frank A. "Accent Local Church: The Bugle Blows
for Action." United Church Herald (15:2, Feb., 1972), pp. 16-
22.   DHU/R

12217. Kotz, Nick. "At the Doorstep of 'the Great Society': The Poor people's Campaign in Washington." Robert H. Binstock and Katherine Ely, (eds.). The Politics of the Powerless (Cambridge, Mass.: Winthrop Publishers, 1971), pp. 75-92.
DHU/MO

12218. Kovarsky, Irving. Black Employment, the Impact of Religion, Economics Theory, Politics, and Law. Ames, Iowa: State University Press, 1970.   INU

12219. Kuehn, B. H. "Inner City: An Evangelical Eye-Opener." Christianity Today (13; Ja. 3, 1969), pp. 31-2.   DHU/R

12220. Lambert, Herbert H. "Two Days in the Inner City." World Call (52:2, Feb., 1970), pp. 23+.   DHU/R

12221. Lambert, I. C. "Businessmen Churches and the Ghetto." Christian Century (85; Feb. 7, 1968), pp. 181-2.   DHU/R

12222. Lee, Robert, (ed.). Cities and Churches: Readings on the Urban Church. Philadelphia: Westminister, 1962. DHU/R

12223. Lefever, Harry G. Ghetto Religion. Doctoral dissertation. Emory University, 1971.

12224. Leslie, B. "God Loves the Inner City." Christian Life (35; Jl., 1973), pp. 27+.   ICMB; IEG; IES

12225. Lincoln, Charles Eric. "How Now America?" Christianity and Crisis (28:4, Apr. 1, 1968), pp. 56-59.   DHU/R
"Racism" the mother of crime."
Negro author.

12226. ----- Is Anybody Listening to Black America? New York: Seabury Press, 1968.   DHU/MO

12227. Locke, Hubert G. The Care and Feeding of White Liberals. Paramus, N. J.: Paulist/Newman Press, 1972.   DHU/R
Written by a Negro minister.

12228. Lowe, J. R. "Power of Your Purse; Project Equality: Encourager of Fair Employment Practices." McCall's Magazine (95; Apr., 1968), p. 7.

12229. Lutze, Karl E. To Mend the Broken; the Christian Response to the Challenge of Human Relations Problems. St. Louis: Concordia Pub. House, 1966.   NcD; DLC

12230. Maddocks, Lewis J. "Panthers vs. Police. Challenge to the Christian. The Nature of the Conflict." Social Action (37:3, Nov., 1970), pp. 17-29.   DHU/R

12231. Marshall, Kenneth E. "White Boom-Black Depression." Social Action (36:6, Feb., 1970), pp. 7-17.   DHU/R

12232. Mathe, Judy. "A City Only Needs One Riot." The Episcopalian (133:8, Ag., 1968), pp. 12-14.   Pam. File, DHU/R
A discussion of Northcott Neighborhood House in Milwaukee and its problems and achievements.

12233. Mayhew, Bruce H., Jr. Religion and Fertility in a Negro Ghetto; A Study in Micro-Demography. Doctoral Dissertation. Kentucky State University, 1964.

12234. Mays, Benjamin Elijah. "The Black Man's Environment and his Minority Status, A Challenge to the Black Church." The Black Church (1:1, 1972), pp. 7-16.   DHU/R

12235. McCord, William and John Howard. Life Styles in the Black Ghetto. New York: W. W. Norton & Co., Inc. 1969. DHU/R
pp. 107-17, religion.

12236. McDaniel, Charles-Gene. "The Ghetto Nightmare." Christian Century (89:1, Ja. 5, 1972), pp. 15-16.   DHU/R

12237. McKenna, David L. The Urban Crisis: A Symposium on the Racial Problem in the Inner City. Grand Rapids, Mich.: Zondervan Pub. House, 1970.   DHU/R

Chapter 1, The church and communication within the urban society.

12238. McKenney, Theodore R. The Role of the Black Church in the Contemporary Urban Community. Masters thesis. 1971
TNSB

12239. McKinney, Richard I. "The Ethics of Dissent." The Journal of Religious Thought (29:2, Aut.-Wint., 1972), pp. 68-79.
DHU/R

12240. McLaurin, Dunbar S. "The Ghediplan: An Approach to Ghetto Economic Development." Social Action (36:6, Feb., 1970), pp. 27-31.   DHU/R
Practical guidelines of how the churches can help in attaining overall economic development.

12241. McManus, Michael J. "Barn Raising in the Ghetto." Christian Herald (93:4, Apr., 1970), pp. 21-8.   DHU/R

12242. McPeak, Francis W. "The Churches and Public Housing in Washington." Social Action (10:9, Nov. 15, 1944), pp. 4-26.   DHU/R

12243. Mearns, John G. "Changes in the Black Ghetto--II: Cleveland." Saturday Review (53:31, Ag. 1, 1970), pp. 13-15.
DHU/R

12244. Meister, Richard J. The Black Ghetto. Lexington, Mass.: Heath, 1972.   MCE

12245. "Men for Others." Bloomington, Ind.: Indiana Univ., National Education Television, 1971. 16mm. 60 min. B & W. Film.
Woodlawn Organization in Chicago & Peace Corps workers in Africa helping their fellowman.

12246. Middeke, Raphael. "Black and Poor in Cairo." Commonweal (90:17, Jl. 25, 1969), pp. 453-54. Pam. File, DHU/R

12247. Millea, Thomas V. Ghetto Fever. Milwaukee: Bruce Pub. Co., 1968.   DLC; NcD

12248. Miller, Douglas. The Justifiability of Civil Violence: The Moral Dialectic and Depiction of Violent Resistance in a Democracy. Doctoral dissertation. Claremont Graduate School, 1972.

12249. "Minister Defends Aid to Slum Gangs." New York Times (Je. 25, 1968),   Pam. File, DHU/R

12250. "Mission: Chicago." WMAQ-TV. Released by NBC, 1966. 30 min. sd. color. 16 mm.
Film.
"New joint church effort to attack the problems of poverty, hunger, and ignorance within the inner-city through the work of foreign missionaries in Chicago."

12251. Mitchell, Donald E. "Urban Renewal- Opportunity or Disaster." World Call (54:6, Je., 1972), pp. 19-20. DHU/R
The Christian Church (Disciples of Christ) Board of Church Extension program to aid its churches located in urban communities.

12252. Mitchell, Henry H. and Eddie S. O'Neal. "A Tale of Two Cities." Christian Century (88:5, Feb., 1971), pp. 156-58.
DHU/R
Two Black Clergymen relate their experiences in urban churches where Blacks were replacing Whites in the congregation.

12253. Moberg, David O. "The Church and the Urban Crisis." David McKenna, (ed.). The Urban Crisis (Grand Rapids, Mich.: Zondervan, 1969), pp. 32-47.   DHU/R

12254. ----- The Church as a Social Institution; The Sociology of American Religion. Englewood Cliffs, N. Y.: Prentice Hall, 1962.   NN/Sch
"The Church and social problems," pp. 445-80.

12255. Moore, LeRoy, Jr. "From Profane to Sacred America: Religion and the Cultural Revolution in the United States." Journal of the American Academy of Religion (39:3, Sept., 1971), pp. 321-38.   DHU/R

12256. Moss, Otis, Jr. "Between Symbol and Substance." Home Missions (43:4, Apr., 1972), pp. 28-9. Pam. File, DHU/R
    "The Black Church teaches that liberation is salvation."

12257. Murray, Michael H. "Holy Week in Kansas City." Church in Metropolis (No. 17, Sum., 1968), pp. 4-7+. DHU/R

12258. ----- "MICA, Kansas City." Church in Metropolis (No. 17, Sum., 1968), pp. 8-10.   DHU/R

12259. National Council of Churches of Christ in the United States of America. Dept. of Social Justice. "The Church and the Urban Crisis."   Pam. File, DHU/R
    mim.
    Includes Declaration of Black Churchmen, Declaration of White Churchmen in response. Resolution on the Crisis in the Nation by General Board.

12260. "Negro Churches Seek Power." Washington Post (Nov. 25, 1968).   DHU

12261. Newby, Donald O. "Tulsa Metropolitan Ministry: Vision of the New Jerusalem." International Review of Missions (43:250, Apr., 1974), pp. 264-7.   DHU/R

12262. O'Brien, David. "Parish For Others." New Catholic World (216:1288, Ja.-Feb., 1973), pp. 9-11+.   DHU/R
    Social action and the Catholic Church.

12263. Odell, Brian N. "Ghetto Ethnic." Catholic World (210:1, 259, Feb. 1970), pp. 213-15.   DHU/R

12264. Oglesby, Jacob. An Analysis of the Concept of Ministry in an Inner City Church (A Case Study of the Greater Christ Baptist Church, Detroit, Michigan). Doctor of Ministry dissertation. Howard University, School of Religion, 1973.

12265. Ostling, Richard N. "Racial Chic Goes to Church." Christian Herald (94:7, Jl., 1971), pp. 14-20.   DHU/R
    Protestant Episcopal Church and its role in current social issues.

12266. "Our Spiritual and Cultural Future." WCBS-TV and Columbia University. Released by Holt, Rhinehart and Winston, 1969. 30 min. sd. b & w. 16 mm.   DLC
    Film.
    "Dr. Vincent Harding serves as moderator as Rev. Albert Cleage and John Henrik discuss the meaning of cultural and religious life as it will affect the future of black Americans. They describe the various efforts of black artists and religious leaders to give cultural substance to the black liberation movement.

12267. Outen, George H. "Trusting Our Evangelists in the Black Community." Christian Advocate (17; Ja. 4, 1973), pp. 7-8.
                                       Pam. File, DHU/R

12268. Paul, Joan. "The Bishop Who Speaks for the Poor." The Lamp, A Christian Unity Magazine (69:4, Apr., 1971), pp. 16-25.   DHU/R
    About Bishop Michael R. Dempsey, Auxiliary Bishop of Chicago.

12269. Payne, Ethel L. "Father Groppi, A Latter Day John Brown." Chicago Daily Defender (Sept. 30-Oct. 6, 1967).
                                       Pam. File, DHU/R

12270. "The People and the Church Take on the Law and the Vigilantes." Interreligious Foundation for Community Organization News (3:4, Jl.-Ag., 1972), p. 7.
    The struggle of Rev. Ben Chavis, pastor of the First African Temple of the Black Messiah in Wilmington, N. C.

12271. People United to Save Humanity (PUSH). "Monitoring Industry." National Black Monitor (Pilot issue, no. 1, 1972), pp. 16-17.   DHU/MO
    "Rev. Jesse Jackson of Operation PUSH (People United to Save Humanity) made big economic news for black Americans three times recently." Announces agreements made for jobs with Joseph Schlitz Brewing Co. and General Foods.

12272. Perez, Joseph A. "Social Action Means Confronting Institutions." Christian Advocate (14:6, Mr. 19, 1970). DHU/R

12273. Powell, Don. "We Stayed in the Inner City." HIS (30:2, Nov., 1969), pp. 18-19.   Pam. File, DHU/R

12274. "Presbyterians Aid Negro Business." New York Times (Apr. 27, 1968).   Pam. File, DHU/R

12275. "Project Equality in New York." America (119; Jl. 20, 1968), pp. 27-28.   DHU

12276. Protestant Episcopal Church in the U.S.A. Executive Council. Showdown at Seattle. New York: Seabury Press, 1968.   DHU/R
    Prepared under the auspices of Executive Council of the Episcopal Church, an account of the women of the Church to Presiding Bishop John Hines plea to the people gathering at the Triennial Convention to deal with the urban problems in America.

12277. Ranck, Lee. "The SCLC and UMC Social Action Resolutions: Speaking to the Church--and the World." Engage/Social Action (1:6, Jl., 1973), pp. 35-47.   DHU/R
    Resolutions on assassination on martyred leaders, pp. 45-47.

12278. Rashford, N. J. "Parishes in the Central City." America (117; Oct. 7, 1967), pp. 381-3.   DHU

12279. "Religions Join in War on Job Discrimination." Pittsburgh Courier (Sept. 21, 1968).   Pam. File, DHU/R

12280. Rhodes, Rhoda. "Accent Local Church: Taking a Giant Step into the Business World." United Church Herald (14:5, My., 1971), pp. 14-17.   DHU/R

12281. Richardson, Lincoln. "Fighting an American Famine." A. D. United Church Herald Edition (1:2, Oct., 1972), pp. 20-23.   DHU/R

12282. ----- "Rochester's White Activists." Presbyterian Life (Ag. 1, 1968), p. 12.   DAU/W

12283. "The Riot Report and the Churches." Christian Century (85:13, Mr. 27, 1968), pp. 379-80.   DHU/R

12284. "Riot Report and the 'Hit' Churches." Christianity Today (12; Feb. 2, 1968), p. 44.   DHU/R

12285. Roberts, Harriet C. "Root Out Racial Malpractice." Christian Century (80:2, Feb., 1971), pp. 72-3. DHU/R

12286. Rodgers, Johnathan. "The North. Hustler, Preacher, Panther." Newsweek (73:26, Je. 30, 1969), pp. 32-33.
                                               DLC; DHU
    "Black Militant's views on the churches in a Chicago ghetto."

12287. Rogers, Cornish R. "Black Students' Identity Crisis." The Christian Century (89:25, Je. 28, 1972), pp. 705-06. DHU/R
    Discusses the "need at this time for an effective ministry to black students on college campuses."

12288. ----- "Copping Out on Social Action." Christian Century (90:19, My. 9, 1973), pp. 524-25.   DHU/R
    "Religious agencies retreat from progressive social programming."

12289. ----- "The Minister and Social Action" Christian Ministry (3:6, Nov., 1972), pp. 10-11   DHU/R
    Negro author.

12290. Rooks, Charles Shelby. "New Ministers for the New City."
Christian Ministry (1:2, Ja., 1970), pp. 12-17.
                                    Pam. File; DHU/R
        Negro author.

12291. ----- "The Rebirth of Hope." National Elementary Principal (48:1, Sept., 1968), pp. 44-50. Pam. File; DHU/R
        Negro minister in keynote speech at Princeton, N. J., for
        parents, teachers and community on race relations.

12292. ----- "Response to a Speech of George Cabot Lodge."
Anglican Theological Review (50:1, Ja., 1968), pp. 47-51.
                                                        DHU/R
        Speech describes the steps the United States should take to
        solve its social problems.

12293. Ross, Jack C. & Raymond H. Wheeler. Black Belonging.
A Study of the Social Correlates of Work Relations Among
Negroes. Westport, Conn.: Greenwood Pub. Corp., 1971.
                                            DHU/R; DLC
        Chapter 6, Church and union.

12294. "Roundup. Religious Agencies and the Urban Crisis."
Christian Century (86; Feb. 12, 1969), pp. 223-24+. DHU/R

12295. Ruether, Rosemary R. "Radical Social Movement and the
Radical Church Tradition." Colloquium, Bethany Theological
Seminary Monograph Series (1; Nov., 1970).
                                    Pam. File, DHU/R

12296. ----- "Sad Songs of Zion Beside the Waters of Babylon."
Journal of Religious Thought (28:2, Aut.-Wint., 1971), pp. 112-
18.

12297. Ryan, Joseph A. "Why Don't They Respond Like Whites?"
Christianity Today (17:14, Apr. 13, 1973), pp. 7-13. DHU/R
        "Community problems between black and white believers."

12298. Sanders, Russell C. "Bridging Church and Ghetto." World
Call (54:9, Oct., 1972), pp. 21-22.   DHU/R
        "Mr. Sanders is a minister on the staff of First Christian
        Church in Minneapolis, Minnesota."

12299. Saunders, F. Brooks. "The Church and Communication
with the Urban Society." David McKenna, (ed.). The Urban
Crisis (Grand Rapids, Mich.: Zondervan, 1969), pp. 61-76.
                                                        DHU/R

12300. Schoonover, Melvin E. Making All Things Human; a
Church in East Harlem. New York: Holt, Rinehart and Winston, 1969.   DHU/R; BMGTL

12301. "Second Chance for Suburbia." Christian Century (85;
Oct. 16, 1968), p. 1296.   DHU/R

12302. Senn, Milton. "Race, Religion and Suburbia." Journal of
Intergroup Relations (3; Spr., 1962), pp. 159-70. DLC

12303. Shipley, David O. Neither Black Nor White, The Whole
Church for a Broken World. Waco, Tex.: Word Books, 1971.
                                                        DHU/R

12304. Simms, David M. "Ethnic Tensions in the Inner-City
Church." Journal of Negro Education. (31; Fall, 1962), pp.
448-54.   DHU/MO

12305. Simon, A. "Gospel and the Urban Crisis." Concordia
Theological Monthly (40; Je., 1969), pp. 493-500. DHU/R

12306. Slater, Jack. "The School That Beat the Odds: Militant
Holy Angels in Chicago Demonstrates Black Parent Power."
Ebony (28:7, My., 1973), pp. 64-72.
                                    Pam. File, DHU/R; DHU/MO

12307. Southern Christian Leadership Conference. Indianapolis
Affiliate. Wealth, Power, and Poverty in Indianapolis.
Indianapolis: SCLC, 1973.   Pam. File, DHU/R

12308. Spurlock, Frank. "New Jobs, New Understanding."
Presbyterian Life (23:19, Oct. 1, 1970), pp. 22-24. DHU/R
        White Presbyterian Church opens a training center for
        blacks in Kansas City, Mo.

12309. Steele, James E. and Neigel Scarborough, et alii. I Have
a Ghetto in my Heart. Cleveland, Tenn.: Pathway Press,
1973.   DHU/R
        Story of inner city pastor of the Chicago Tabernacle Church
        and his program.

12310. Stepp, Diane. "Baptist Deny Failing to Act on Social Ills."
Atlanta Constitution (Sept. 5, 1968). Pam. File, DHU/R

12311. Stokes, Olivia P. "Blacks, Engagement, and Action."
Religious Education (67:1, Ja.-Feb., 1972), pp. 22-25.
                                                        DHU/R
        Negro author.

12312. Stone, Michael. "Project Equality Today: A Case Study of
the Church in the Social Order." Christian Century (87:3, Ja.
21, 1970). pp. 79-82.   DHU/R
        "A case study of the Church in the social order."

12313. Stromberg, Jerome. "The Church and the Urban Family."
David McKenna, (ed.). The Urban Crisis (Grand Rapids,
Mich.: Zondervan, 1969), pp. 96-107.   DHU/R

12314. Stuber, Stanley Irving. Human Rights and Fundamental
Freedoms in Your Community. New York: Association Press,
1968.   DHU/R

12315. Sullivan, Leon H. Alternatives to Despair. Valley Forge,
Pa.: Judson Press, 1972.   DHU/R; CLU; MNtcA
        The theological basis for the clergyman's devoting his work
        to the social and economic development of his people.
        Negro author.

12316. ----- Build Brother Build. Chicago: Ebony Bookshop,
1970.   DHU/R
        Opportunities Industrialization Center, founder explains
        program.
        Negro minister of Philadelphia.

12317. ----- "Conquering Poverty Through Self-Help." Christian
Economics (21:18, Sept. 30, 1969).   DHU/R
        Clergyman-educator shares his tested formula for an effec-
        tive answer to poverty.

12318. Tharp, Clifford, Jr. "The Parish Minister of Education:
An Examination of Roles." Religious Education (67:4, Jl.-Ag.,
1972), pp. 289-97.   DHU/R
        Author is Research Associate, Research Services Depart-
        ment, Southern Baptist Convention.

12319. Thornton, Jeannye. "Black America Today - Who's in
Charge." The Christian Science Monitor (Sat. Mr. 17, 1973),
p. 9.   DHU
        Jesse Jackson and Elijah Muhammed are included.

Trexler, Edgar R. "The Crisis is Over in Omaha." The Lutheran
(8:11, Je. 3, 1970), pp. 14-17.   Pam. File, DHU/R
        Lutherans projects in inner city of Omaha.

12320. Trexler, Edgar R. "The Crisis is Over in Omaha." The
Lutheran (8:11, Je. 3, 1970), pp. 14-17. Pam. File, DHU/R
        Lutherans projects in inner city of Omaha.

12321. ----- "Life Off the Main Road." The Lutheran (9:2, Ja. 20,
1971), pp. 6-10.   Pam. File, DHU/R
        "South Carolina Lutherans fight the cycle of rural poverty."

12322. "Un-Ghettoing Suburbia." Tempo (Nov. 15, 1968).
                                    Pam. File, DHU/R

12323. United Presbyterian Church in the United States. Education
in the City Church. Philadelphia: The United Presbyterian
Church, U.S.A. Bd. of Christian Education, 1967. DHU/R

(United Presbyterian Church--- cont.)
     Project in the inner-city churches of Chicago, its purpose
     for a possibility of a truly evangelical impact on the people
     of the city.

12324. Van Ness, Paul. "An Experimental Church Related Coun-
     seling Program for the Inner City." Pastoral Psychology
     (20:198, Nov. 1, 1969), pp. 15+.   DHU/R

12325. Verlich, Edward. "Mix in Pittsburgh: Unions, Black Work-
     men, and the Church." Presbyterian Life (Je. 1, 1970), p. 16+.
                                         DAU/W; DHU/R

12326. Wagner, C. Peter. "Black Beauty and Church Integration."
     Other Side (10:1, Ja. -Feb., 1974), pp. 14-17+.   TxDaTS
     Also: Eternity (23:9, Sept., 1972), pp. 17-19. IoBNB

12327. Walker, Lucius. "Church Renewal in Rural and Urban
     America." International Review of Mission (58:230, Apr.,
     1969), pp. 158-64.   DHU/R

12328. ----- "Mass Based Organization: A Style for Christian
     Mission." Church in Metropolis (No. 17, Sum., 1968), pp.
     21-6.   DHU/R

12329. ----- "Opportunities for Minority Development." Church
     and Society (41:3, Ja. -Feb., 1971), pp. 22-26.   DHU/R
     Presbyterian's role in church and race.

12330. Walker, Margaret. "Religion, Poetry, and History Found-
     ations for a New Educational System." Floyd B. Barbour,
     (ed.). The Black Seventies (Boston: Porter Sargent Publisher,
     1970), pp. 284-95.   DHU/MO

12331. Washington, Betty. "Milwaukee Struggle Nears Crisis."
     Chicago Daily Defender (Sept. 23-29, 1967),
                                   Pam. File, DHU/R
     About a white priest, Fr. James E. Groppi, leader of open
     housing demonstrations in Milwaukek.

12332. Washington, Joseph R., Jr. "The Role of the Theologian
     in a Time of Religious Crisis." Washington Star-News Tuesday
     Magazine (My., 1974), pp. 10+.   Pam. File, DHU/R
     "Part four of a series."
     Negro author.

12333. Waterman, Kenneth S. "The Church in the Ghetto." Church
     in Metropolis (No. 15, Wint., 1967), pp. 23-7. DHU/R

12334. "What We Have Learned About Housing." Social Action
     (39:3, Nov., 1972), pp. 3-32.   DHU/R
     Issue devoted to discussion of adequate housing by the Social
     Action Committee of the United Church of Christ.

12335. Whelan, Charles M. "The Fleischmann Report: Race and
     Religion." America (126:8, Feb. 26, 1972), pp. 195-98.
                                               DHU/R
     "The Fleischmann Commission wants the government to
     use the schools to end racial and ethnic religious discrim-
     ination."

12336. Williams, Preston N. "Ethnic Pluralism or Black Sep-
     aratism." Social Progress (60:1, Sept. -Oct., 1969), pp. 32-39.
                                   Pam. File, DHU/R
     Negro author.

12337. ----- "Criteria for Decision-Making for Social Ethics in
     the Black Community." Journal of the Interdenominational
     Theological Center (1:1, Fall, 1973), pp. 65-79.   DHU/R
     Negro author.

12338. ----- "The Price of Social Justice." Christian Century
     (90:19, My. 9, 1973), pp. 529-33.   DHU/R
     Negro author.

12339. Willie, Charles V. Church Action in the World: Studies in
     Sociology and Religion. New York: Morehouse-Barlow Co.,
     1969.   DHU
     "Crisis in American cities--a call for church action,"
     pp. 119-38.

12340. Wilmore, Gayraud S., Jr. "From Protest to Self-Develop-
     ment?" Church and Society (41:3, Ja. -Feb., 1971), pp. 6-13.
                                               DHU/R
     Chairman of United Presbyterian Division of Church and
     Race analyzes some of the factors that are basic to racial
     justice.

12341. Wilson, Robert L. and James H. Davis. The Church and the
     Racially Changing Community. Nashville: Abingdon Press, 1966.
                                               DHU/MO

12342. Winter, Gibson. The Suburban Captivity of the Churches.
     Garden City, N. Y.: Doubleday & Co., 1961. DHU/R; TNU
     Negro churches, pp. 112-18.

12343. Winthrop, W. "Scientific, Intentional Communities Can
     Save Democracy and Religion." Social Order (13; My., 1963),
     pp. 21-31.   DGU

12344. Witmer, Lawrence. "Studies in Cooperative Ministry for
     Urban Mission." National Council of the Churches of Christ
     in the U. S. A., (ed.) Manpower for Mission, New Forms of
     the Church in Chicago (New York: Council Press, 1967), pp.
     132-51.   DHU/R

12345. Wynn, Daniel W. The Black Protest Movement. N. Y.:
     Philosophical Library Inc., 1974.   DHU/R
     Negro author.

12346. Yoder, John H. "Exodus and Exile: The Two Faces of
     Liberation." Cross Currents (23:3, Fall, 1973), pp. 297-309.
                                               DHU/R
     "We seek more creatively to describe what can best be done
     by creative minorities in a society they don't control."

12347. "You Have Been Set Free." American Baptist Films, 1971.
     94 fr. color. 35 mm. & phonodisc: 1 s., 10 in., 33 rpm.,
     14 min.   DLC
     Filmstrip.
     "Discusses the development of the relationship between
     blacks and whites in America, the difference between civil
     rights and black economic development, and ways in which
     the Church can relate to black economic development."

12348. Younger, George D. "The Mission of Christ and the Work
     of the Church in Chicago." International Review of Missions
     (43:250, Apr., 1974), pp. 256-63.   DHU/R

B. BLACK IDENTITY

1. Black Theology, Black Power, and Black Religion

12349. Adams, Charles G. "The Burden of the Black Religion."
     Tempo (2:5; 6, Dec. 15-Ja. 1, 1970), p. 15. DHU/R

12350. ----- "Some Aspects of Black Workshop." Andover
     Newton Quarterly (11:3, Ja., 1971), pp. 124-38.
                                   Pam. File, DHU/R
     Negro author.

12351. Adams, John Hurst. "Black Power Situation--Judgement-
     Summons." The African Methodist Episcopal Church Review
     (93:235, Apr.-Je., 1968), pp. 64-71.   DHU/R
     Negro author. "Minister of the First A. M. E. Church,
     Seattle, Wash."

12352. Alexander, Fred A. and John F. Alexander. "A Manifesto For White Christians---or What Do We Do Now That Integration Has Failed." Other Side (10:1, Ja.-Feb., 1974), pp. 4-6+.
TxDaTS

12353. Allen, Blanche T. An Analysis and Interpretation of Thirty-One Poems of James Weldon Johnson -- Implications for Black Religious Experience. Masters thesis. School of Religion, Howard University, 1971.
Negro author.

12354. Alston, Jon P. "Religiosity and Black Militancy." Journal for the Scientific Study of Religion (11:3, Sept., 1972), pp. 252-61.   DAU/W; DCU/SW; DGU; DGW; DHU/R

12355. Alston, Percel O. "Black and Third World Perspectives in Church Education." Andover Newton Quarterly (14:2, Nov., 1973), pp. 143-152.   DHU/R

12356. "Artists Portray a Black Christ." Ebony (26:6, Apr., 1971), pp. 177-80.   DHU/R

12357. Bailey, Leroy. A Comparative Analysis of the Negro Church in America, by E. Franklin Frazier and Black Religion, by Joseph R. Washington, Jr. Masters thesis. Howard University, 1971.
Negro author.

12358. "Baldwin Excoriates Church for Hypocritical Race Stance." Afro-American (Jl. 16, 1968).   Pam. File, DHU/R

12359. Balazar, Eulalio R. The Dark Center; A Process Theology of Blackness. Paramus, N. J.: Paulist Press, 1973.
DHU/R

12360. Banks, Walter R. "Two Impossible Revolutions? Black Power and Church Power." Journal for the Scientific Study of Religion (8:2, Fall, 1969), pp. 263+.   DHU/R

12361. Banks, William L. "Reparations, Black Power, and 'Black Theology.'" Moody Monthly (72:8, Apr., 1972), pp. 30-31.
DHU/R

12362. ----- "The Social Gospel and the Black Preacher." Other Side (8:2, Mar.-Apr. 1972), pp. 14-17+.   IOBNB

12363. Barbour, Floyd B., (ed.). The Black Power Revolt: A Collection of Writings on "Black Power." Boston: Extending Horizons Books, 1968.   DHU/R
Contains articles by Black theologians.

12364. Barndt, Joseph R. Why Black Power. New York: Friendship Press, 1968.   DHU/R
Chapter 6: "Freedom, Power and the Church."

12365. Barnett, Hanlee H. Crucial Problems in Christian Perspective. Philadelphia: Westminster Press, 1970. DHU/R
Chapter 7, Black Power and the church.

12366. Becker, William H. "Black Power in Christological Perspective." Religion in Life (38:3, Aut., 1969), pp. 404-14.
DHU/R

12367. Bedingfield, R. W. "A Religious Response to Racism." Navy Chaplains Bulletin (No. 1; 1975), pp. 3-4+. DHU/R

12368. Behm, R. and C. Salley. "Bible and Black Theology." His (30:4, Mr., 1970), pp. 1-4.   IOBNB

12369. Bennett, Robert A. "Black Experience and the Bible." Theology Today (27:4, Ja., 1971), pp. 422-33.   DHU/R

12370. Berry, Benjamin D. "Soul Brothers, Unite: Comments on the Black Church." Katallagate (2:2, Fall, 1969), pp. 30-33.
DHU/R

12371. Bethea, Joseph B. "The Black Church: 1973." The Duke Divinity School Review (39:1, Wint., 1974), pp. 21-26. DHU/R

12372. ----- "Black Church Studies." Duke Divinity School Review (38; Spr., 1973), pp. 96-100.   NcD

12373. Birch, Bruce C. "Black Theology Means Liberation for All." Christian Advocate (18:13, Je., 21, 1973), pp. 13-14
Pam. File, DHU/R

12374. "The Black Christian Nationalist Church." Black World (23:3, Ja., 1974), pp. 88-89.   DHU/R
Jaramogi Abebe Agyeman, formerly known as the Reverend Albert B. Cleage, Jr., press conference. Included is the creed for the new church.

12375. "Black Baptist Demands Met." Journal and Guide (Je. 8, 1968).   Pam. File, DHU/R
"Demands of the delegates to the American Baptist Convention for more representation."

12376. Black Church/Black Theology. Summation of Lectures Given in Washington, D. C., Spring 1969 at Georgetown University. J. Deotis Roberts, Walter Yates, Joseph R. Washington and Preston Williams.   Pam. File, DHU/R
Mim.
Negro author.

12377. "The Black Church." Journal of Negro Education of the A. M. E. Church. (30:3, Mr.-My., 1970), pp. 2+.   DHR/R
Editorial on Contributions of traditional "Negro Church."

12378. "Black Church: Three Views - C. Marshall, J. H. Jackson, and S. W. Williams." Time (95; Apr. 6, 1970), pp. 71-73.
DAU; DCU/SW; DGU; DGW; DHU

12379. Black Militancy and the University; Report of a Conference for Campus Clergy, November 29-December 1, 1968 at Shaw University, Raleigh, N. C. Washington: National Newman Apostolate, 1969.   NjP; MiBsA; Pam. File, DHU/R; DLC
"Racism and its theological implications."

12380. "Black Power in the Pulpit." Time (90; Nov. 17, 1967), p. 87.   DHU

12381. "Black Power Moves on Churches." U. S. News and World Report (65; Ag. 26, 1968), pp. 46-48.
DCU; DHU, Pam. File, DHU/R

12382. "Black Power Restated by United States Presbyterians." Chicago Daily Defender. (Ag. 19-19, 1966). Pam. File, DHU/R

12383. "Black Prayer; Gospel of Black Nationalism." Newsweek (71; Ja. 15, 1968), p. 71.   DAU; DLC; DHU; DGW

12384. "The Black Religious Experience and Theological Education for the Seventies: A Report of the Special AATS Committee." Theological Education (6:3, Spr., 1970), Suppl.   DHU/R

12385. Bone, Richard. "A Black Man's Quarrel With the Christian God." New York Times Book Review (Sept. 11, 1966). DHU

12386. Bosch, David J. "The Case for Black Theology." Pro Veritate (11:4, 1972), pp. 3-8.   DLC

12387. Bourguignon, Erika. "Afro-American Religions: Tradition and Transformation." John F. Szwed, (ed.). Black America (New York: Basic Books, 1970), pp. 190-202.   DHU/SW

12388. Bracey, John H. and August Meier, et alii., (eds.). Conflict and Competition: Studies in the Recent Black Protest Movement. Belmont, California: Wadsworth, 1971.
InU; DLC

12389. Bradford, C. E. "Christianity and the Black Man." The Message Magazine (39:8, Nov.-Dec., 1973), pp. 14-17.
Pam. File, DHU/R

12390. Bradley, I. T. "God's Redeeming Love." Perspective (13:2, Spr., 1972), pp. 118-26.   DHU/R
Sermon delivered at a Black Preaching Seminar.

12391. Breitman, George and George Novack. Black Nationalsim and Socialism. New York: Merit Publishers, 1968. DHU/MO

12392. Brow, Robert. "The Curse of Ham -- Capsule of Ancient History." Christianity Today (18:2, Oct. 26, 1973), pp. 8-10. DHU/R
Thesis is that Genesis 10 cannot be applied to black people.

12393. Brown, Clifton F. "Black Religion, 1968." Hart M. Nelsen and Raytha L. Yokley, et alii. The Black Church in America (New York: Basic Books, 1971). DHU/R
Negro author.

12394. ----- "Black Religion--1968." Patricia Romero, (ed.). In Black America (Washington, D. C.: United Publishing Co., 1969), pp. 345-53. DHU/R

12395. Brown, Grayson. "On Black Liturgy." Freeing the Spirit (1:1, Ag., 1971), pp. 6-13. DHU/R

12396. Brown, Harold O. J. "Evolution, Revolution or Victory." Christianity Today (14:14, Apr. 10, 1970), pp. 10-15. DHU/R
"Written by a Negro Evangelist taken from his address on Evangelism to the U. S. Congress of Evangelism."

12397. Browne, Robert S. "The Case for Black Separatism." Cross Currents (18:4, Fall, 1968), pp. 471-82. DHU/R

12398. Bruce, Calvin E. "Refocusing Black Religious Education." Religious Education (69:4, Jl.-Ag., 1974), pp. 431-32. DHU/R

12399. Bucher, Glenn R. "Liberation in the Church: Black and White." Union Seminary Quarterly Review (29:2, Wint., 1974), pp. 91-105. DHU/R

12400. Burg, P. "Military and the Black Survival Agenda." Christian Century (90:20, My. 16, 1973), p. 580. DHU/R
Response to editorial by Cornish Rogers.

12401. Caldwell, Erskine. Deep South Memory and Observation. New York: Weybught & Talley, 1968. CLU
Part I was first published in England under the title "In the Shadow of the Steeple".
Religion and the South.

12402. Caldwell, Gilbert H. "The Black Church in White Structures." The Black Church (1:2, 1972), pp. 11-15. DHU/R

12403. ----- "Black Churchmen Find African, American Links." Christian Advocate (15:17, Sept. 16, 1971), p. 19. DAU/W; DHU/R

12404. California Black Leadership Conference. "Role of the Church in the Black Revolution." Pacifica Archives AP 1181. Audiotape.

12405. Campbell, James. "Black Budget Woes Linked to the Pulpit." Christian Advocate (15:2, Ja. 21, 1971), p. 24. Pam. File, DHU/R
Financial assistance given to Black Churches by General Board of the United Methodist Church.

12406. ----- "Blacks Told Self-Neglect is Sin." Christian Advocate (14:23, Dec. 10, 1970), p. 22. Pam. File, DHU/R

12407. ----- "Pastoral Supply Dwindles for Black Inner-City Churches." Christian Advocate (16:13, Jl. 6, 1972), p. 24. Pam. File, DHU/R

12408. Campen, Henry C., Jr. "Black Theology: The Concept and Its Development." The Lutheran Quarterly (23:4, Nov., 1971), pp. 388-99. DHU/R

12409. Carey, John J. "Black Theology, An Appraisal of the Internal and External Issues." Theological Studies (33:4, Dec., 1972), pp. 684-97. DHU/R

12410. ----- "What Can We Learn From Black Theology?" Theological Studies (35:3, Sept., 1974), pp. 518-28. DHU/R
Written by professor of religion at Florida State University.

12411. Carruthers, Ben F. "At the Shrine of the Black Madonna, A Portfolio of Impressions." Tuesday at Home (1:12, Mr., 1972), pp. 7-8+. Pam. File, DHU/R
Report of a trip to the Basilica of Montserrat, home of the Black Madonna, forty miles from Barcelona, Spain.

12412. Cassels, Louis. "Black Power Becoming Force in Religious Life." Chicago Daily Defender (Nov. 1, 1968). Pam. File, DHU/R

12413. Chandler, Russell. "Church Militants Fashion a New Black Theology." The Evening Star (Nov. 2, 1968). Pam. File, DHU/R

12414. Chapman, G. Clarke, Jr. "American Theology in Black: James H. Cone." Cross Currents (22:2, Spr., 1972), pp. 139-57. DHU/R

12415. ----- "Black Theology and Theology of Hope: What Have They to Say to Each Other?" Union Seminary Quarterly Review (29:2, Wint., 1974), pp. 107-29. DHU/R

12416. ----- "Peaceniks, Abolitionists and the Institutional Beast." The Christian Century (89:15, Apr. 12, 1972), pp. 424-26. DHU/R
Explores the moral sensibilities of youth in the peace movement, abolitionists and Black power advocates.

12417. Chauncey, George. "Black Power." Ceasar D. Coleman, (ed.). Beyond Blackness To Destiny: Study Guide (Memphis: Printed by Wimmer Bros., n.d.), pp. 17-20. Pam. File, DHU/R

12418. "The Church and Black Economics Development. A New Era of Secular Concern sees Increased Use of Cold Cash." Black Enterprise (3:5, Dec., 1972), pp. 17-20. Pam. File, DHU/R

12419. Cleage, Albert B., Jr. Black Christian Nationalism: New Directions for the Black Church. New York: William Morrow & Co., Inc., 1972. DHU/R; DHU/MO; TSewU-T; MNtcA
Negro author.

12420. ----- Black Messiah. New York: Sheed & Ward, 1968. DHU/R; DLC
Review: Robert Batchelder. Encounter (31:1, Wint., 1970), p. 79. DHU/R

12421. ----- "The Black Messiah and the Black Revolution." James J. Gardiner and J. Deotis Roberts, Sr. (eds.). Quest for a Black Theology (Philadelphia: United Press, 1971), pp. 1-21. DHU/MO; DHU/R

12422. ----- "Black U. C. C. Clergyman Organizes New Denomination." United Church Herald (1:3, Nov., 1972), p. 52. DHU/R
New denomination called the Black Christian Nationalist Church, Inc. Mr. Cleage has taken the Swahili name Jaramogi Adebe Agyeman.

12423. ----- "Interview: Al Cleage on Black Power." United Church Herald (Feb., 1968). Pam. File, DHU/R

12424. "Clergy Meet Shows Black Power Growth." Afro-American (Oct. 29, 1968). Pam. File, DHU/R

12425. Cochrane, Eric. "The Church and Black Power." New City (6; My., 1968), pp. 17-22. DT

12426. Coleman, Ceasar D. "Agenda for the Black Church." Beyond Blackness to Destiny: Study Guide (n. p.: Printed by Wimmer Bros., Memphis, n.d.). Pam. File, DHU/R

12427. ----- "Understanding Black Power." Beyond Blackness to Destiny: Study Guide (Memphis: Printed by Wimmer Bros., n.d.).   Pam. File, DHU/R

12428. Coleman, William E. "Religion, Protest, and Rhetoric." Foundations (16:1, Ja.-Mr., 1973), pp. 40-56.   DHU/R

12429. "Color God Black." New York Times (Nov. 10, 1968).
                                              Pam. File, DHU/R

12430. Cone, Cecil Wayne. The Identity Crisis in Black Theology: an Investigation of the Tensions Created by the Efforts to Provide a Theological Interpretation of the Black Religious Experience in the Works of Joseph Washington, Albert Cleage, J. Deotis Roberts and James Cone. Doctoral dissertation. Emory University, 1972.

12431. Cone, James H. "The Black Church and Black Power." Raytha Yokley and Anne Nelsen, (eds.). The Black Church In America. (New York: Basic Books, 1971), pp. 335-54.
                                                             DHU/R
       Negro author.

12432. ----- "Black Consciousness and the Black Church." Christianity and Crisis (30:18, Nov. 2 & 16, 1970), pp. 244-50.
                                                             DHU/R

12433. ----- "Black Consciousness and the Black Church: A Historical-Theological Interpretation." The Annals of the American Academy of Political and Social Science (37; Ja., 1970), pp. 49-55.   DHU/R

12434. ----- "Black Power, Black Theology, and the Study of Theology and Ethics." Theological Education (6:3, Spr., 1970), pp. 202-15.   DHU/R

12435. ----- "Black Theology and Black Liberation." The Christian Century (87:37, Sept. 16, 1970), pp. 1084-88. DHU/R
       "Black power is not only consistent with the gospel of Jesus Christ: it is the gospel of Jesus Christ."

12436. ----- "Black Theology and Black Power." Christian Century (86:51, Dec. 17, 1969), pp. 1619+.   DHU/R
       A Review.

12437. ----- "Black Theology and Black Power". New York: Seabury Press, 1969.   DHU/R; DLC

12438. ----- "Black Theology and Violence." The Tower, Alumni Magazine, Union Theological Seminary (Spr., 1969).   NNUT

12439. ----- A Black Theology of Liberation. Philadelphia: Y. B. Lippincott & Co., 1970.   DHU/R

12440. ----- "Black Theology on Revolution, Violence and Reconciliation." Dialog: A Journal of Theology (12:2, Spr., 1973), pp. 127-33.   DHU/R

12441. ----- "Black Theology: We Were Not Created for Humiliation." Ladies Home Journal (86:12, Dec., 1969), pp. 132+.
                                                    DLC; DMLK

12442. ----- Christ in Black Theology. Pittsburgh: Thesis Theological Cassettes, 1970.   TSewU-T
       Thesis theological cassettes, V. 2, no. 2.

12443. ----- "Christian Theology and the Afro-American Revolution." Christianity and Crisis (30:10, Je. 8, 1970), pp. 123-35+.   DHU/R

12444. ----- "Christianity and Black Power." C. Eric Lincoln (ed.). Is Anybody Listening to Black America? (New York: Seabury Press, 1968), pp. 3-9.   DHU/R

12445. ----- "The Dialectic of Theology and Life or Speaking the Truth." Union Quarterly Review (29:2, Wint., 1974), pp. 75-89.   DHU/R

12446. ----- "Failure of the Black Church." Liberator (9:5, My., 1969), pp. 14-17; 22+.   DHU/R

12447. ----- "Freedom, History and Hope." The Journal of the Interdenominational Theological Center (1:1, Fall, 1973), pp. 55-64.   DHU/R

12448. ----- "Theological Reflections on Reconciliation." Christianity and Crisis (32:24, Ja. 22, 1973), pp. 303-05. DHU/R

12449. ----- "Toward a Black Theology." Ebony (25:10, Ag., 1970), pp. 113-16.   DHU/R

12450. ----- "Toward a Constructive Definition of Black Power." Student World (42: 3-4, 1969), pp. 314-33.   DHU/R

12451. ----- and William Hordern. "Dialogue on Black Theology." Christian Century (88: 37, Sept. 15, 1971), pp. 1079+.
                        DAU/W; DCU/TH; DGU; DGW; DHU/R

12452. Copher, Charles B. "The Black Man in the Biblical World." Journal of the Interdenominational Theological Center (1:2, Spr., 1974), pp. 7-16.   DHU/R
       Negro author.

12453. ----- "Perspective and Questions: The Black Religious Experience and Biblical Studies." Theological Education (6:3, Spr., 1970), pp. 181-88.   DHU/R

12454. Culverhouse, Patricia. "Black Religion: Folk or Christian. Foundations: A Baptist Journal of History and Theology. (13:4, Oct.-Dec., 1970), pp. 295-315.   DHU/R

12455. Curry, Norris S. "When the Subject is the Negro Church." Guest Editorial. The Christian Index (103:9, Apr. 30, 1970), pp. 3-4.   DHU/R

12456. Davis, Emory G. "Religion and Black Power." Chicago Daily Defender (Sept. 9-15, 1967).   Pam. File, DHU/R

12457. Dickinson, Richard. "Black Theology and Black Power Encounter (3:4, Aut., 1970), pp. 387-92.   DHU/R
       "Review of James Cone's Black Theology and Black Power (New York: Seabury Press, 1969)."

12458. Dixon, Norman R. "Will White Theological Schools Meet the Black Challenge?" Perspective (13:2, Spr., 1972), pp. 164-81.   DHU/R

12459. "Dr. Benjamin Mays Gives Black Power's Definition." Journal and Guide (My. 11, 1968).   Pam. File, DHU/R

12460. Dole, Kenneth. "Pastor Sees 'Black Theology' in Militants." Washington Post (Dec. 14, 1968).   Pam. File, DHU/R

12461. Draper, Theodore. The Rediscovery of Black Nationalism. New York: The Viking Press, 1970.   DHU/R
       Discusses the role religion has played in Black nationalists movements.

12462. Duke, Robert W. "Black Theology and the Experience of Blackness." Journal of Religious Thought (29:1, Spr.-Sum., 1972), pp. 28-42.   DHU/R

12463. Eichelberger, William L. "The Black Messiah." The Black Church (2:3, Fall, 1974), pp. 14-16.   DHU/R

12464. ----- Reality in Black and White... Philadelphia: The Westminster Press, 1969.
       Black Presbyterian minister advocates Black Power liberation movement and believes that it will eventually transform itself into a human rights movement.

12465. ----- "Reflections on the Person and Personality of the Black Messiah." The Black Church (2:1, 1972), pp. 51-63.
                                                             DHU/R

12466. Eugene, Toinette. "Training Religious Leaders for a New Black Generation." Freeing the Spirit (1:4, 11:1, Fall-Wint., 1972, Spr., 1973), pp. 52-55.   DHU/R

12467. Evans, Randall H., Jr. A Practical Theology for the Black Based on the Philosophical Anthropology of Paul Ricouer. Doctoral dissertaion. University of Chicago Divinity School, 1970.

12468. Fish, John H. Black Power/White Control: The Struggle of the Woodlawn Organization in Chicago. Princeton: Princeton University Press, 1973.   NjP; DHU/R

12469. ----- The Edge of the Ghetto; a Study of Church Involvement in Community Organization. New York: Seabury Press, 1968.   MiBsA; MNtcA; DHU/MO

12470. Fiske, Edward B. "The Black-White Power Struggle in the Church." Tempo (22:1, Sept. 1, 1969), pp. 3+.   DHU/R

12471. ----- "The Messiah is Black." Tempo (1:4, Dec. 1, 1968), p. 5.   DHU/R

12472. ----- "Now a Challenge to the Church From the Blacks." Pam. File, DHU/R
    mim.

12473. Fleming, John W. "Faith and the Black Experience." Home Missions (43:4, Apr., 1972), pp. 27-28.
                    Pam. File, DHU/R

12474. Flournoy, Ray. Black Christian Studies V. 1 Denver, Colo.: The Church of the Black Cross, 1971.
                    Pam. File, DHU/R

12475. Foster, Isaac & Leon Howell. "On Growing Up Black in Mississippi." Tempo (1:22, Sept. 1, 1969), pp. 6-7. DHU/R
    Memories of Isaac Foster, founder and administrator of "Freedom City."

12476. Fraser, Thomas P. "Black Studies for the Local Church." Social Progress (60:1, Sept.-Oct., 1969), pp. 26-31.
                    Pam. File, DHU/R
    Has outline of a suggested course.

12477. Fry, John R. "Soul." McCormick Quarterly (23:2, Ja., 1970), pp. 123-29.   DHU/R
    Theological implications of the usage of the word "Soul" by Blacks.

12478. Gardiner, James J. and James Deotis Roberts. Quest for a Black Theology. Philadelphia: Pilgrim Press, 1971.
                    DHU/R

12479. Geltman, Max. The Confrontation: Black Power, Anti-Semitism, and the Myth of Integration. Englewood Cliffs, N. J.: Prentice-Hall, 1970.   DHU/R; NjP

12480. Gelzer, David Georg. "Random Notes on Black Theology and African Theology." The Christian Century (87:37, Sept. 16, 1970), pp. 1091-93.   DHU/R

12481. Georgetown University, Washington, D. C. Black Church/ Black Theology. Summation of Lectures given by James D. Roberts, Walter L. Yates, Joseph R. Washington, Jr., and Preston Willaims at a Institute sponsored by the Graymoor Ecumenical Institute and the Georgetown Univeristy, Department of Theology. Feb., 1970. Mim. Pam. File; DHU/R

12482. Goodwin, Bennie E. "Black Power and Education." Perspective (13:2, Spr., 1972), pp. 156-63.   DHU/R

12483. Gqubule, T. Simon N. "What is Black Theology?" Journal of Theology for Southern Africa (8; Sept., 1974), pp. 16-23.
                    DHU/R

12484. Grant, Daniel R. "Black Power's Many Faces." The Alabama Baptist (133; Oct. 10, 1968), p. 7. LNB; TND

12485. Gray, Ocam J. An Analysis of Revivalism in America With Special Reference to Charles G. Finney and the Black Religious Perspective. Masters thesis. School of Religion, Howard University, 1971.
    Negro author.

12486. Gregory, Dick. "Knowing the Truth." The Episcopalian (133:4, Apr., 1968), pp. 14-15.   Pam. File; DHU/R

12487. Groves, Richard. "Black Power in the Church." The Student: The Changing Church (50:3, Dec. 1970), pp. 45-7.
                    DHU/R

12488. Hamilton, Charles V. The Black Preacher in America, 1972. N. Y.: Morrow, 1972.   DHU/R

12489. Hanson, Geddes. "Black Theology and Protestant Thought." Social Progress (Sept.-Oct., 1969), pp. 5-12.   DLC

12490. Harding, Vincent. "Black Power and the American Christ." Christian Century (84:1, Ja. 4, 1967), pp. 10-13.   DHU/R
    Negro author.

12491. ----- "Black Power and the American Christ." Floyd Barbour, (ed.). The Black Power Revolt (Boston: Extending Horizon Books, 1968), pp. 85-93.   DHU/R

12492. ----- "The Gift of Blackness." Repr. New York: Dept. of Publication Services, 1967.   Pam. File; DHU/R
    Also in Katallagete (Sum., 1967), pp. 17-22.   DHU/R

12493. ----- "Reflections and Meditations on the Training of Religious Leaders for the New Black Generation." Theological Education (6:3, Spr., 1970), pp. 189-201. DHU/R

12494. ----- "The Religion of Black Power." Donald R. Cutler, (ed.). The Religious Situation. 1968. (Boston: Beacon Press, 1969), pp. 3-37.   DHU/R

12495. Hare, Nathan. "Emptiness of Negro Middle Class Church Life." Negro Digest (14; Ag., 1965), pp. 34-9. DHU/MO
    Negro author.

12496. Hargraves, J. Archie. "Blackening Theological Education." Christianity and Crisis (29; Apr. 14, 1969), pp. 93-8.
                    DHU/R

12497. Harrington, M. "Religion and Revolution." Commonweal (91; Nov. 14, 1969), pp. 203-04.   DHU/R

12498. Harrison, Bob and Jim Montgomery. When God Was Black. Grand Rapids, Mich.: Zondervan Publishing House, 1971.
                    DHU/R; NjP
    Written by a Negro evangelist, singer and speaker. His organization is called "Bob Harrison Ministries."

12499. Hatcher, Richard. "Black Power is an Attitude." Lutheran Standard (129; Feb. 2, 1971), p. 3.   IMC

12500. Haughley, J. "Black Theology." America (120:20, My. 17, 1969), p. 583.   DHU

12501. Hawke, Gwendolyn. "Silently the Giants Have Grown." The Black Church (2:3, Fall, 1974), pp. 22-25.   DHU/R
    Historical surveys of four Negro churches in Boston, Mass.

12502. Hayashi, Janet W. "Thinking Black About the Old Testament Heritage." United Methodists Today (1:5, My., 1974), pp. 31-34.   Pam. File, DHU/R

12503. Henry, Hayward. "Toward a Religion of Revolution." The Black Scholar (2:4, Dec., 1970), pp. 27-31.   DHU
    Negro author.

12504. Herzog, Frederick. "The Liberation of White Theology." The Christian Century (91:11, Mar. 20, 1974), pp. 316-17.
                    DHU/R
    Written by professor of systematic theology at Duke Univer-

sity. Author of Liberation Theology; Liberation in the Light of the Fourth Gospel.

12505. ----- Liberation Theology in the Light of the Fourth Gospel. New York: Seabury Press, 1973.   DHU/R

12506. ----- "Liberation Theology or Culture Religion?" Union Seminary Quarterly Review (29:3&4, Spr. & Sum., 1974), pp. 233-44.   DHU/R

12507. ----- "The Political Gospel," Christian Century (87:46, Nov. 18, 1970), pp. 1380-83.
Professor of Systematic Theology at Duke University asks what has gone wrong with white theology.

12508. ----- "Theology of Liberation." Continuum (7:4, Wint., 1970), pp. 515-24.   DHU/R

12509. Hickman, Garrison M. A Critique of Black Theology. Masters thesis. School of Religion, Howard University, 1971. Negro author.

12510. Hill, Bob. "The Dilemma of the Black Christian." Moody Monthly (69:11, Sept., 1969), pp. 34-37.   DHU/R
Responses to Article (70:4, Dec., 1969), pp. 30-31.

12511. Hill, Edward V. "White Liberals Behind Black Militancy." Christian Economics (23:3, Feb. 11, 1970), pp. 2+.   DHU/R
Article by Negro minister of Watts, California.

12512. Hobbs, Helen. "Who Speaks for America's Blacks?" Christian Herald (92:8, Ag., 1969), pp. 16-21.   DHU/R

12513. Hodges, William H. "Not by White Might Nor by Black Power." Christianity Today (15:1, Oct. 9, 1970), pp. 5-10.
DHU/R

12514. Hodgson, Peter C. and William S. Ellis. Black Liberation and Christian Faith. Phila., Pa.: Fortress Press, 1973.
DHU/R

12515. Horton, Frank L. "Reclaiming the Richness of the Black Church Heritage." Christian Advocate (15:19, Oct. 14, 1971), pp. 11-12.   DLC; Pam. File, DHU/R

12516. ----- "Teaching Black History in the Local Church." Christian Advocate (14:3, Feb. 5, 1970), pp. 11-12.
Pam. File, DHU/R

12517. Hough, Joseph C. Black Power and White Protestants; a Christian Response to the New Negro Pluralism. New York: Oxford University Press, 1968.   DHU/R; INU

12518. Howard, Walden. "How One Church Rose to the Challenge of a Young Black Minister." Faith/at Work (85:5, Oct., 1972), pp. 6-8.   IOBB; IOBNB

12519. "In Search of a Black Christianity." Time (94:1, Jl. 4, 1969), pp. 57-8.   Pam. File; DHU/R

12520. Ingham, Lee Lindsay John. Black Liberation: The Ethical Implications of Employing "Any Means Necessary" as a Just Means of Attaining Black Liberation in America. Masters thesis. Howard University, School of Religion, 1973.

12521. "An Interview with C. Eric Lincoln: A Top Scholar Comments on Black Church and Theology." Black Enterprise (3:5, Dec., 1972), pp. 31-34+.   DHU/R

12522. Jackson, Jesse L. "Black Power and White Churches." Arther C. Littleton and Mary W. Burger, (eds.). Black Viewpoints (New York: New American Library, 1964), pp. 354-59.
DHU/R

12523. ----- "Black Power and White Churches." Church in Metropolis (16; Spr., 1968), pp. 6-9.   DHU/R
Negro author.

12524. Johnson, Joseph A., (bp.). "Jesus, the Liberator." James J. Gardiner and J. Deotis Roberts, Sr., (eds.). Quest for a Black Theology (Philadelphia: United Church Press, 1971), pp. 97-111.   DHU/MO; DHU/R

12525. ----- (bp.). "Jesus: The Liberator." Andover Newton Quarterly (10:3, Ja., 1970), pp. 58-96.   DHU/R
"Quest for the Black Jesus and the limitations of White Theology."

12526. ----- (bp.). "The Legitimacy of Black Theology." Christian Index (103:7, Apr. 9, 1970), pp. 3-4.   DHU/R
Negro author.

12527. Johnson, Otis S. "The Evolving Black Church." The Savannah State College Bulletin (27:2, Dec., 1973), pp. 101-09.
Pam. File, DHU/R
"Faculty Research Edition."
Negro author.

12528. Johnson, Thomas A. "Black Religion Seeks Own Theology." The New York Times (Ja. 20, 1971), p. 29.   DHU/ DLC

12529. Johnson, William R. "A Black Prayer and Litany." Theology Today (26:3, Oct., 1969), pp. 262-65.   DHU/R

12530. Johnstone, Ronald L. Militant and Conservative Community Leadership Among Negro Clergymen. Doctoral dissertation. University of Michigan, 1963.

12531. Jones, Lawrence N. "Black Churches in Historical Perspective." Christianity and Crisis (30:18, Nov. 2 & 16, 1970), pp. 226-28.   DHU/R
Author is President and Professor of Afro-American Church History at Union Theological Seminary, New York.
Negro author.

12532. Jones, Major J. "Black Awareness: A Theology of Hope. Nashville: Abington Press, 1971.   DHU/R

12533. ----- "Black Awareness: Theological Implications of the Concept." Religion in Life (38:3, Aut., 1969), pp. 389-403.
DHU/R
Negro author.

12534. ----- Christian Ethics for Black Theology. Nashville: Abingdon Press, 1974.   DHU/R

12535. Jones, Miles J. "Why a Black Seminary." Christian Century (89:5, Feb. 2, 1972), pp. 124+.   DHU/R

12536. Jones, William A. "The Negro Church." Foundations (10:2, Apr.-Je., 1967), pp. 108-10.   DHU/R

12537. Jones, William R. Is God a White Racist? A Preamble to Black Theology. Garden City, N. J.: Doubleday, 1973.
DHU/R
Negro author.

12538. ----- "Reconciliation and Liberation in Black Theology: Some Implications for Religious Education." Religious Education (67:5, Sept.-Oct., 1972), pp. 383-89.   DHU/R

12539. ----- "Theodicy and Methodology in Black Theology: A Critique of Washington and Cleage." Harvard Theological Review (64:4, Oct., 1971), pp. 541-57.   DHU/R

12540. ----- "Theodicy: The Controlling Category for Black Theology." Journal of Religious Thought (30:1, Spr.-Sum., 1973), pp. 28-38.   DHU/R

12541. ----- "Toward an Interim Assessment of Black Theology." The Christian Century (89:18, My. 3, 1972) pp. 513-17.
DHU/R

12542. Joseph, James A. "Has Black Religion Lost Its Soul?" Floyd B. Barbour, (ed.). The Black Seventies (Boston: Porter Sargent Publisher, 1970), pp. 69-83.   DHU/MO

12543. Kennedy, Robert F. "Suppose God is Black." Look (Ag. 23, 1966), pp. 45-7.   Pam. File; DHU/R

12544. Kilgore, Thomas. "The Black Church." Ebony (25:10, Ag., 1970), pp. 106-10.   DHU/MO

12545. Killinger, J. "The Black Man and the White God." Religion in Life (39:4, Wint., 1970), pp. 498-521.   DHU/R

12546. Knight, E. "On Being and Being Black." Motive (30:6, Mr., 1970), pp. 52.   DHU/R

12547. Kucharsky, David. "Black Evangelicals: Possessing the Land." Christianity Today (17:16, Myl, 1973), pp. 44-45.
                                                                   DHU/R

12548. Kuhn, Harold B. "Does Theology Come in Colors?" Christianity Today (15:15, Apr. 23, 1971), pp. 43-44.
                                                                   DHU/R

12549. ----- "Examining Black Theology." Christianity Today (14; Mr., 1970), p. 34.   DAU/W; DCU/TH; DHU/R

12550. Kuhn, Thomas W. "Black Chaplain Responses." Navy Chaplains Bulletin (No. 1; 1975), pp. 5-7+.   DHU/R

12551. Ledit, Joseph H. "Dark Madonnas." The Chronicle: Official Organ of the Federated Colored Catholics (5:1, Ja., 1932), pp. 2-4.   DHU/MO; DHU/R

12552. Lee, Carlton Lafayette. "Toward a Sociology of the Black Religious Experience." The Journal of Religious Thought (29: 2, Aut.-Wint., 1972), pp. 5-18.   DHU/R
        Negro author.

12553. Le Mone, Archie. "Quest for a Black Theology: a Review Article." World Christian Education (4: 1st Qt., 1972), pp. 50+.   DHU/R

12554. Lincoln, Charles Eric. "Black Consciousness and the Black Church in America." Missiology: An International Review (1:2, Apr., 1973), pp. 7-20.   DHU/R
        Negro author.

12555. ----- (ed.). The Black Experience in Religion: A Book of Readings. New York: Harper & Row, 1974.   DHU/R

12556. ----- "Black Nationalism and Christian Conscience." Concern (5; Sept. 15, 1963), pp. 5+.   DAU/W

12557. ----- "The Power in the Black Church." Cross Currents (24:1, Spr., 1974), pp. 3 21.   DHU/R

12558. Long, Charles H. "The Black Reality: Toward a Theology of Freedom." Criterion (8:2, Spr.-Sum., 1969), pp. 2-7.
                                            Pam. File, DHU/R
        Nathan A. Scott, Jr. "Response to Charles Long's Paper." Criterion (8:2, Spr.-Sum., 1969), pp. 8-11.

12559. ----- "The Death of God: Creativity of Decadence, a Modest Reflection." Criterion (7:3, Spr., 1968), pp. 15-18.
                                            Pam. File; DHU/R

12560. ----- "Perspectives for a Study of Afro-American Religion in the United States." History of Religions (11:1, Ag., 1971), pp. 54-66.   DHU/R

12561. ----- Signs of Wholeness in the Black Religious Tradition. Summary of Two Addresses on Agenda for the Black Church, Nashville, Tennessee, April 2, 1971. Nashville: n.p., 1971.
                                                                   TSewU-T
        Typescript.

12562. Longcope, Kay. "Toward a New Black Church." Tempo (1:4, Dec. 1, 1968), p. 3.   DHU/R

12563. Lyke, James. "Black Liturgy/Black Liberation." Freeing the Spirit (1:1, Ag., 1971), pp. 14-17.   DHU/R
        Negro minister.

12564. "The Magic of..."Black Nativity." Sepia (14; Je., 1965), pp. 36-41.   DHU/MO

12565. Marshall, Calvin B. "The Black Church--Its Mission is Liberation." The Black Scholar (2:4, Dec., 1970), pp. 13-19.
                                                                   DHU/R
        Negro author.

12566. Mazrui, Ali A. World Culture and the Black Experience. Seattle: University of Washington Press, 1974. DHU/R

12567. McCall, Emmanuel L. The Black Christian Experience. New York: Broadman Press, 1972. DHU/R; TSewU-T; DLC

12568. ----- "The Black Struggle, How can You Help?" The Baptist Student (49:2, Nov., 1969), pp. 19+. DHU/R

12569. ----- "New Dimensions in Freedom." Home Missions (43:4, Apr., 1972), pp. 35-36.   Pam. File, DHU/R
        Article deals with the several options before the Black Church Tradition in the Contemporary world.

12570. McClain, William B. "The Genius of the Black Church." Christianity and Crisis (30:8, Nov. 2 & 16, 1970), pp. 250-2.
                                                                   DHU/R

12571. McDonnell, Jane. "Contemporary Black Themes: Social, Historical, Hopeful." Cross Currents (21:4, Fall, 1971), pp. 469-75.   DHU/R
        Critique of five books on Black Theology.

12572. McKinney, Richard I. "The Black Church, Its Development and Present Impact." The Harvard Theological Review (64:4, Oct., 1971), pp. 452-81.   DHU/R

12573. McPherson, James M. Blacks in America: Bibliographical Essays. Garden City, New York: Doubleday & Co., 1971.
        Includes information on the Black Church.

12574. McQuilkin, Frank. Think Black, An Introduction to Black Political Power. New York: Bruce Publishing Co., 1970.
                                                                   DHU/R
        Chapter 9, Back to Africa; Chapter 10, Black Pilgrimage; Chapter 11, Malcolm X; Chapter 12, The Black Muslims.

12575. Marcel, J. W. God, the Bible and Black Liberation Struggle. Washington, D. C.: Institute of Black History and Religion, 1971.   DHU/AA

12576. Mason, William. "Hermeneutics and the Black Experience." Reformed Review (23:4, Sum., 1970), pp. 217+. DHU/R

12577. Massey, James E. "Christian Theology and the Social Experience of Being Black." Christian Scholar's Review (1; Spr., 1971), pp. 207-16.
        Negro author.

12578. ----- "The Relational Imperative: Black Theology and Redemptive Relations." Spectrum (47:4, Jl.-Ag., 1971), p. 15-17.   DHU/R
        Negro author.

12579. Mays, Benjamin Elijah. "The Church: New Challenges for Survival." Washington Star-News. Tuesday Magazine (Feb., 1974), pp. 12-15.   Pam. File, DHU/R

12580. Mbiti, John. "An African Views American Black Theology." Worldview (17:8, Ag., 1974), pp. 41-44.   DHU/R

12581. Merton, Thomas. Seeds of Destruction. New York: Macmillan, 1967.   NcD; DHU/MO; INU; DLC; NN/Sch
        The Black Revolution.

12582. Miranda, Osmundo Afonso. Apocalyptico-Eschatological Hope, the Theology of the Oppressed; an Enquiry into Some Aspects of Popular Black Religion. Tuscaloosa, Ala.: n.p., 1971.   Pam. File, DHU/R

Mim.
"Paper read at the annual meeting of the Southeast Area of the American Academy of Religion in the University of Tennessee. March 19, 1971."

12583. "Miracle in Atlanta--A Black Christ." Ebony (24:2, Dec., 1968), pp. 33-40.   Pam. File, DHU/R

12584. Mitchell, Henry H. Black Belief. New York: Harper & Row, 1974.   DHU/R
Negro author.

12585. ----- "Black Christianity in the Post-Christian Era., U. S. A." The Black Scholar 2:4, Dec., 1970), pp. 43-9.   DHU

12586. ----- "Black Power and the Christian Church." pp. 1-8.
                                              Pam. File, DHU/R
mim.
"Written by the pastor of Calvary Baptist Church, Santa Monica, Calif. for seminary students at American Baptist related theological schools."

12587. ----- "Issues and Perspectives: The Practical Field and its Relationship to the Black Man's Practice of the Christian Faith." Theological Education (6:3, Spr., 1970), pp. 216-23.
                                                            DHU/R

12588. Moore, Basil. "Jesus and Black Oppression." World Student Christian Federation (A WSCF Book) (2:2, 1972), pp. 46-65.   DHU/R

12589. Moss, James A. "The Negro Church and Black Power." An Address. Journal of Human Relations (2: Spr., 1964), pp. 152-61.   DAU/DCU/SW

12590. Moss, Leonard W. and Stephen C. Cappannari. "The Black Madonna: An Example of Culture Borrowing." Scientific Monthly (76:6, Je., 1953), pp. 319-24.
                                              Pam. File; DHU/R
Based on a paper presented to the Anthropology Section of the American Association for the Advancement of Science. December 28, 1952, St. Louis, Missouri.

12591. Mshana, Eliewaha E. "The Challenge of Black Theology and African Theology." Africa Theological Journal (5; Dec., 1972), pp. 19-30.   DHU/R

12592. Murray, Michael H. "White Churches and Black Power." Church in Metropolis (no. 16, Spr., 1968), pp. 1-3. DHU/R

12593. National Committee of Black Churchmen. "Black Power." Ceasar D. Coleman, (ed.). Beyond Blackness to Destiny: Study Guide (Memphis: Printed by Wimmer Bros., n.d.).
                                              Pam. File, DHU/R
Negro author.

12594. Nelsen, Hart M. and Raytha Yokley, (eds.)., et alii. The Black Church in America. New York: Basic Books, Inc., 1971.
                                                            DHU/R
Collection of writings previously published by social scientists and journalists selected to reveal the complex nature of the black church.

12595. Nelson, C. Ellis. "Can Protestantism Make it with the Now Generation?" Ceasar D. Coleman, (ed.). Beyond Blackness to Destiny: Study Guide (Memphis: Printed by Wimmer Bros., n.d.).   Pam. File, DHU/R

12596. Neuhaus, Richard J. "Liberation Theology and the Captivities of Jesus." Worldview (16:6, Je., 1973), pp. 41-48. DHU/R
Review of Gustavo Gutieviez A Theology of Liberation. Author discusses place of his conclusions for Latin America with James Cone's Black Theology.

12597. Newman, Richard A. "Black Power and White Liberals." Register-Leader (148:9, Nov. 1966), pp. 7-8.   DHU/R

12598. ----- "Black Power, Black Nationalism, Black Rebellion." Concern (9:16, Oct. 1, 1967), pp. 5-6.   DHU/R

12599. ----- "Black Power." Concern (8:15, Sept. 1, 1966), p. 4.
                                              Pam. File, DHU/R

12600. Nix, Roscoe N. "Wanted: A Radical Black Church." The Black Church (1:2, 1972), pp. 39-47.   DHU/R

12601. Norman, Clarence. A Constructive Study of the Concept of Liberation in Contemporary "Black Religion" With Special Preference to the Thought of James Cone, Vincent Harding and James Deotis Roberts. Doctor of Religion Paper. School of Religion, Howard University, 1971.
Negro author.

12602. Norton, W. "Black Power Gospel." Christian Life (Oct., 1968), pp. 39+.   DHU/R

12603. ----- "A Day in the Life of a Black Fundamentalist." Eternity Magazine (22:9, Sept., 1971), pp. 22+.   IOBNB

12604. Offer, Henry J. "Black Power, A Great Saving Grace." American Ecclesiastical Review (159: Sept., 1968), pp. 193-201.
                                                        CtY; DCU

12605. Oglesby, Enoch H. "Ethical and Educational Implications of Black Theology in America." Religious Education (69:4, Jl.-Ag., 1974), pp. 403-12.   DHU/R

12606. Oliver, C. Herbert. "Black Power; What Does it Mean?" Journal of the American Scientific Affiliation (22:2, Je., 1970), pp. 44-45.   DHU/R
Deals with the political, social and religious ramification of Black Power.

12607. Oliver, Kenneth D. The History and Philosophy of Radical Black Theology. Masters thesis. Western Evangelical Seminary, 1973.

12608. Olson, Howard S. "The Development of Black Theology in America." Africa Theological Journal (5; Dec., 1972), pp. 8-18.   DHU/R

12609. Olsson, Karl A. "Black Christ." Lutheran Standard (128: Apr. 14, 1970), p. 37.   IMC

12610. Opocensky, Milan. "The Afro-American Revolution and Black Theology." Communio Viatorum (15:1, Spr., 1972), pp. 67-70.   DHU/R

12611. ----- "Lessons from Black Theology." This Month (Ecumenical Press Service) (15; Je., 1973), pp. 3-5.   DHU/R

12612. Owens, Milton E. "Black Awareness: Re-Established Dignity-- An Educational Experience in Blackness and the Bible." Spectrum (49; Spr., 1973), pp. 16-20.   DHU/R

12613. Parker, J. A. "Two Views of Black Religion." Christianity Today (17; My. 25, 1973), p. 37.   DHU/R

12614. Payne, Ethel L. "Survey Shows Role of Blacks in the Church." Chicago Daily Defender (Ja. 16, 1969). Pam. File; DHU/R

12615. Peeks, Edward. The Long Struggle for Black Power. New York: Charles Scribner's Sons, 1971.   DHU/R
The prominent role of the black churches in the movement is discussed.

12616. Poinsett, Alex. "The Black Revolt in White Churches." Ebony (23:11, Sept., 1968), pp. 63-8.   Pam. File, DHU/R

12617. ----- "The Quest for a Black Christ." Ebony (24:3, Mr., 1969), pp. 170-8.   DHU/MO

12618. Potter, Ron. "Black Christian Separatism." Other Side (10; 7, Ja.-Feb., 1974), pp. 30-33+.   TxDaTS

12619. Powell, Adam Clayton, Jr. "Black Power in the Church." The Black Scholar (2:4, Dec., 1970), pp. 32-4. DHU/R
Negro author.

12620. ----- "Can There Be Any Good Thing Come Out of Nazareth?"
A. L. Smith, (ed.). Rhetoric of Black Revolution (Boston:
Allyn and Bacon, 1969), pp. 154-60.   DHU/MO
    Also: Arther C. Littleton and Mary W. Burger, (eds.).
    Black Viewpoints (New York: New American Library, 1964),
    pp. 218-25.   DHU/R

12621. Price, Jo-Ann. "Churches Have 'Betrayed' Negroes, James
Baldwin Tells World Assembly." Washington Post (Jl. 8, 1968).
                                    Pam. File, DHU/R

12622. Rashke, Richard. "Black Theology: A Gospel of Confrontation." The Lamp/A Christian Unity Magazine (68:5, My., 1971),
pp. 2-4.   DHU/R
    The White Adminstrator of the International Research and
    Self-Study Team of the Divine Word Missionaries.

12623. Reece, Robert D. "Black Theology and Social Ethics."
Norbert Brockman and Nicholas Piediscalzi. Contemporary
Religion and Social Responsibility (New York: Alba House,
1973), pp. 265-74.   DHU/R

12624. "Regarding the Race Cirisis (Tom Skinner Cites Need for
Negro Christian Responsibility). Wesleyan Advocate (Feb. 10,
1969), p. 6.   DAU/W

12625. "Religion; The Black Church; Three Views." Time (95:14,
Apr. 6, 1970), pp. 71+.   Pam. File, DHU/R

12626. Relyea, Harold C. "The Theology of Black Power." Religion in Life (38:3, Aut., 1969), pp. 415-20.   DHU/R

12627. Roberts, James Deotis, Sr. "Afro-Arab Islam and the Black
Revolution." Journal of Religious Thought (28:2, Aut.-Wint.,
1971), pp. 95-111.   DHU/R

12628. ----- "Black Consciousness in Theological Perspective."
James J. Gardiner and J. Deotis Roberts, Sr. (eds.). Quest
for a Black Theology (Philadelphia: United Church Press, 1971),
pp. 62-81.   DHU/MO; DHU/R

12629. ----- A Black Political Theology. Phila.: Westminster
Press, 1974.   DHU/R

12630. ----- "Black Theological Education Programming for Liberation." Christian Century (91:5, Feb. 6, 1974), pp. 117-18.
                                             DHU/R

12631. ----- "Folklore and Religion: The Black Experience."
Journal of Religious Thought (27:2, Sum. Suppl., 1970), pp. 5-
15.   DHU/R
    Negro author.

12632. ----- "The Implications of Black Theology for Campus
Ministry.' Toward Wholeness (1:1, Sum., 1972), pp. 23-29.

12633. ----- Liberation and Reconciliation: A Black Theology.
Philadelphia: Westminster Press, 1971.
                           DHU/R; TSewU-T; MNtcA

12634. ----- Liberation Theology. New York: Seabury, 1972.
                                             DHU/R
    Review of Religious Education (68:4, Jl.-Ag., 1973), pp.
    518-21.   DHU/R

12635. ----- "Religio-Ethical Reflections Upon the Experiential
Components of a Philosophy of Black Liberation." Journal of
the Interdenominational Theological Center (1:1, Fall, 1973),
pp. 80-94.   DHU/R
    Negro author.

12636. ----- "Theology of Religions: The Black Religious Heritage." Journal of the Interdenominational Theological Center
(1:2, Spr., 1974), pp. 54-68.   DHU/R

12637. Roberts, Joseph L., Jr. "The Black Church in the South:
A Few Challenges of the '70's." The Black Church (1:2, 1972),
pp. 17-36.   DHU/R

12638. Robinson, Louie. "Glide to Glory: San Francisco Minister
Turns on Masses With Rock and Relevancy." Ebony (26:9, Jl.,
1971), pp. 41-52.   Pam. File, DHU/R

12639. Robison, B. James. "A Tillichian Analysis of James Cone's
Black Theology." Religious Studies (1:1, Spr., 1974), pp. 15-28.
                                             DHU/R

12640. Rogers, Cornish. "Black Religion Group Probes African
Roots; Society for the Study of Black Religion." Christian Century (90; Nov. 7, 1973), p. 1092.   DHU/R

12641. ----- "Pan-Africanism and the Black Church: a Search for
Solidarity." Christian Century (88:46, Nov. 17, 1971), pp. 1345-
47.   DHU/R

12642. ----- "Tom Bradley and the Black Churches." Christian
Century (90:24, Je. 13-20, 1973), p. 668.   DHU/R

12643. ----- "Where are the Black Chaplains?" Christian Century
(90:14, Apr. 4, 1973), p. 381.   DHU/R

12644. Rogers, Jefferson P. "The Crisis in the American Church."
The Black Church (1:1, 1972), pp. 1-5.   DHU/R

12645. ----- "The Church in Crisis." Church and Society (55:5,
My.-Je., 1970), pp. 24-28.   DHU/R
    "In the True church there can be no basic divisions between
    the black church and the white church."

12646. Rollins, Metz. "Revolution, Ecumenicity and the Black
Church." The Black Church (1:2, 1972), pp. 3-9.   DHU/R

12647. Rooks, Charles Shelby. "The Black Church and Theological Education." Nexus (12:3, Spr., 1969), pp. 13-16+.
                                    Pam. File, DHU/R
Negro author.

12648. ----- "The Black Church Looks Ahead."
                                    Pam. File, DHU/R
mim.
    Sermon preached at Lincoln Memorial Temple United Church
    of Christ, Nov. 30, 1969, Washington, D. C.

12649. ----- "Crisis in Church Negro Leadership." Theology
Today (22: 3, Oct., 1965), pp. 323-35. Pam. File, DHU/R

12650. ----- "The First Dozen Years are the Hardest." Journal
of the Interdenominational Theological Center (1:1, Fall, 1973),
pp. 95-102.   DHU/R

12651. ----- "From Genesis to Revelation: Black Identity in the
Church." Shawensis (Sum., 1969), pp. 30-34.
                                    Pam. File, DHU/R

12652. ----- "God's Grace and New Beginnings." Dimension;
Theology in Church and World (6:1, Fall, 1968), pp. 34-40.
                                    Pam. File, DHU/R

12653. ----- "Implications of the Black Church for Theological
Education." Voice (61:1, Ja., 1969), pp. 3-5+.
                                    Pam. File, DHU/R

12654. ----- "Theological Education and the Black Church."
Christian Century (8:7, Feb. 12, 1969), pp. 212-16.   DHU/R

12655. ----- "Toward the Promised Land." Scott Lecture, Texas
Christian University, 1972. Held at Texas Christian University,
February 15-17, 1972.   Pam. File, DHU/R
    Mim.
    "Lectures revolve around Joseph Washington's Black Religion,
    James Cones's Black Theology, Albert Cleage's Black Mess-
    iah and J. Deotis Roberts' Liberation and Reconciliation."
    Also The Black Church (2:1, 1972), pp. 1-48.   DHU/R

12656. ----- "Why a Conference on the Black Religious Experience."
Theological Education (6:3, Spr., 1970), pp. 173-80.   DHU/R

12657. Ross, James Robert. The War Within. New York: Sheed
& Ward, 1971.   DHU/R
"Black Theology."
Negro author.

12658. Ruether, Rosemary R. "Black Theology and Black Church."
Religious Education (64:5, Sept.-Oct., 1969), pp. 347-51.
DHU/R

12659. ----- "Black Theology and Black Church." The Journal of
Religious Thought (26:2, Sum. Suppl, 1969), pp. 26-33.
DHU/R

12660. ----- "The Black Theology of James Cone." Catholic
World (214:1, 279, Oct., 1971), pp. 18-20. DHU/R

12661. ----- "Crisis in Sex and Race: Black Theology vs. Feminist Theology." Christianity and Crisis (34:6, Apr. 15, 1974),
pp. 67-73.   DHU/R

12662. ----- Liberation Theology. Human Hope Confronts Christian History and American Power. New York: Paulist Press,
1972.   DHU/R
Chapter 9, "Is There a Black Theology? The Validity and
Limits of a Racial Perspective."

12663. Rutenber, C. G. "American Baptists Respond to Black
Power Challege." Christian Century (85:27, Jl. 3, 1968),
pp. 878-80.   DHU/R

12664. Satterwhite, John H. Will the Black Experience Make Meth-
odists One People?   Pam. File, DHU/R/
Speech made at Annual Meeting of Commission on Ecumen-
ical Affairs, Western N. C. Conference, United Methodist
Church, Duke University, Gradaute Center, Wednesday,
October 28, 1970.
Negro author.

12665. Schackern, Harold. "Toward a New Black Theology."
Tempo (Dec. 1, 1968).   Pam. File, DHU/R

12666. Scott, Julius. "Campus Ministries to Blacks: Some Ob-
servations." Toward Wholeness (1:1, Sum., 1972), pp. 33-34.
DHU/R
Written by former director, Martin Luther King Memorial
Center, Associate Professor of History, Spelman College.

12667. Seagraves, Amelia. "A Lay Woman's Reflection on Black
Liturgy." Freeing the Spirit (1:1, Ag., 1971), p. 30. DHU/R

12668. "A Separate Black Church Ahead?" Christianity Today
(13:4, Nov. 22, 1968), pp. 40-42.   Pam. File, DHU/R

12669. Serrin, William. "Cleage's Alternative." Reporter (38;
My. 1968), pp. 20-30.   DHU
Black clergyman left United Church of Christ to organize
the Church of the Black Madonna and the Black Christian
movement in Detroit.

12670. Setiloane, Gabriel M. "About Black Theology." World
Student Christian Federation (2:2, 1972), pp. 66-71. DHU/R

12671. Sheares, Reuben A. "Beyond White Theology." Chrisitanity and Crisis (30:18, Nov. 2 & 16, 1970), pp. 229-35. DHU/R
"The Black Church has always existed and functioned out-
side of or beyond white theology."

12672. Shockley, Grant S. "Black Awareness: A Theology of Hope."
Major J. Jones. Christian Advocate (41; Ja. 20, 1972), p. 17.
DHU/R
Book review.
Negro author.

12673. ----- "Religious Education and the Black Experience."
The Black Church (2:1, 1972), pp. 91-111.   DHU/R

12674. Sleeper, Charles Freeman. Black Power and Christian
Responsibility; Some Biblical Foundations for Social Ethics.
Nashville: Abingdon Press, 1969.   DHU/R; CtY-D

12675. Smith, Allen H. "Black Liberation and Black Churches."
Reflection (69:2, Ja., 1972),   Pam. File, DHU/R
Author is administrative assistant and lecturer in Pastoral
Theology at Yale Divinity School.

12676. Smith, Elwyn A. What the Religious Revolutionaries Are
Saying. Philadelphia: Fortress Press, 1971.   DHU/R
Black Power in the Church, pp. 34-39.

12677. "SNCC Position Paper on Black Power. "Who is the Real
Villain--Uncle Tom or Simon Legree?: Thomas Wagstaff,
(ed.). Black Power: The Radical Response to White America
(Beverly Hills: Glencoe Press, 1969), pp. 11-118. DHU/R

12678. Snider, David J. Can Christian Realists Support Black
Power Strategies. Doctoral dissertation. Emory University,
1969.

12679. Solomon, Walker. "Theological Education From the Black
Perspective." Reflection (69:2, Ja., 1972).
Pam. File, DHU/R
Third-year student in M. Div. program at Yale Divinity
School.

12680. Soulen, Richard N. "Black Worship and Hermeneutic."
Christian Century (87:6, Feb. 11, 1970), pp. 168+. DHU/R

12681. "Sound and Song and Soul." Home Missions (43:4, Apr.,
1972), pp. 9-13.   Pam. File, DHU/R
Black Church worship service.

12682. Speaks, Ruben L. "The Church and Black Liberation."
A. M. E. Zion Quarterly Review (83:3, Fall, 1971), pp. 138-
48.   DHU/R

12683. Spivey, Charles S., Jr. "Cocu and the 'Black Problem'."
The Black Church (1:1, 1972), pp. 79-82.   DHU/R

12684. Starr, Paul. "Black Panthers and White Radicals." Commonweal (92:12, Je. 12, 1970), pp. 294-97.   DHU/R

12685. Stiles, B. J. "Where Have All the Negroes Gone?" Motive
(28:4, Ja., 1968), pp. 4-5.   DHU/R

12686. Stokes, Olivia Pearl. "Education in the Black Church: Design for Change." Religious Education (69:4, Jl.-Ag., 1974),
pp. 433-45.   DHU/R

12687. Swomley, John M., Jr. Liberation Ethics. New York:
MacMillan, 1973.   DHU/R

12688. "Symposium on Black Power." Lutheran Quarterly (20:2,
My., 1968), pp. 152-60.   DHU/R

12689. "Theological Education and the Black Church." Information
Service (48: Mr. 8, 1969), p. 6.   CtY; DLC

12690. Thibodeaux, Mary Roger, (Sister). A Black Nun Looks at
Black Power. New York: Sheed and Ward, 1972. DHU/R

12691. Thomas, George. "Black Theology: Vanguard of Pan-
African Christianity in America." Journal of the Interdenom-
inational Theological Center (1:2, Spr., 1974), pp. 69-77.
DHU/R

12692. ----- "Three R's in Theology." Spectrum (47:4, Jl., 1971),
p. 13.   DHU/R
A brief article containing resources, references, and reflections on Black religion.

12693. Thomas, Harold A. "The Ideology of Black Power." Dimension: Theology in Church and World (5:1, Fall, 1968), pp. 47-
60.   Pam. File, DHU/R

12694. Thomas, Neil. "White Church and Black Business." Commonweal (90:19, Ag. 22, 1969), pp. 503-04.   DHU/R

12695. Thompson, J. Earl. "Black Studies and White Americanism."
Andover Newton Quarterly Review (62:2, Nov., 1969), pp. 56-65.
Pam. File, DHU/R

12696. Tinney, James S. "Black Christianity Being Redefined Now."
The Washington Afro-American (Ag. 18, 1973), p. 17.
Pam. File, DHU/R

12697. Tischler, Nancy M. Black Masks: Negro Characters in
Modern Southern Fiction. University Park, Pa.: Pennsylvania
State University Press, 1969.   DHU/MO
Chapter 6, The Black Christ.

12698. Traynham, Warner R. "Black Studies in Theological Education: The Camel Comes of Age." Harvard Theological Review
(66:2, Apr., 1973), pp. 257-71.   DHU/R

12699. ----- Christian Faith in Black and White; A Primer in Theo-
logy from the Black Perspective. Wakefield, Mass.: Parameter
Press, Inc., 1973.   DHU/R
Written by a Negro Catholic priest.

12700. ----- "Power and Violence." The Black Church (2:2, Spr.,
1974), pp. 14-20.   DHU/R

12701. Trueblood, Roy W. "Union Negotiations Between Black
Methodists in America." Methodist History (8:4, Jl., 1970),
pp. 18-29.   DHU/R

12702. Turner, Harold W. "Resource Materials on African Spiritual
Heritage." Council on the Study of Religion, Bulletin (3:4, Oct.,
1972), pp. 14-17.   DHU/R

12703. Tutu, Desmond. "God--Black or White." Ministry (11:4,
1971), pp. 111-15.   CLWM; CLoIC

12704. Vaughn, Napoleon N. "To Be Black on November 20, 1967."
African Methodist Episcopal Church Review (93:235, Apr.-Je.,
1968), pp. 42-49.   DHU/R

12705. Vincent, John. "A Renaissance for Theology Through Racism.
Christian Advocate (14:9, Apr. 30, 1970), pp. 7-8.   DHU/R

12706. Vincent, Theodore G. Black Power and the Garvey Movement. California: Ramparts Press, n.d.   DHU/R

12707. Vivian, C. T. Black Power and the American Myth. Phila-
delphia: Fortress Press, 1970.   DHU/R
Chapter 4, "Christian love and Christian hate."
Negro author.

12708. Wagner, C. Peter. "Church Integration and Black Beauty."
Eternity (23:9, Sept., 1972), pp. 16-18.   IOBNB
See also "Four Spokesmen Answer Wagner," Eternity (23:9
Sept., 1972), pp. 18-19+.

12709. Wallace, W. J. L. "The Black Church: Past and Present."
The A. M. E. Zion Quarterly Review (82:2, Sum., 1970), pp.
63-72.   DHU/R

12710. ----- "The Mission of the Black Church." The A. M. E.
Zion Quarterly Review (82:2, Sum., 1970), pp. 73-76.   DHU/R

12711. Ward, Hiley H. Prophet of the Black Nation. Philadelphia:
Pilgrim Press, 1969.   DHU/R
Chapters on black God, black gospel and strife at the shrine.
DHU/R

12712. Washington, Joseph R., Jr. Black and White Power Subrep-
tion. Boston: Beacon Press, 1969.   DHU/R
Negro author.

12713. ----- Black Religion: the Negro and Christianity in the
United States. Boston: Beacon Press, 1964.
DHU/R; DHU/Sp; InU; OWibfU; DLC

12714. ----- "The Black Religious Crisis." The Christian Century
(91:17, My. 1, 1974), pp. 472-75.   DHU/R

12715. ----- "How Black is Black Religion." James J. Gardiner
and J. Deotis Roberts, Sr., (eds.). Quest for a Black Theology
(Philadelphia: United Church Press, 1971), pp. 22-43.
DHU/MO; DHU/R

12716. ----- The Politics of God. Boston: Beacon Press, 1967.
DHU/R; DLC; NcD
Part II, Chapter VI, "Irrational Color Prejudice: America's
Preconscious White Folk Religion."

12717. ----- "The Roots and Fruits of Black Theology." Theology
Today (30:2, Jl., 1973), pp. 121-129.   DMU/R

12718. ----- "Shafts of Light in Black Religious Awakening." Religion in Life (43:2, Sum., 1974), pp. 150-60.   DHU/R

12719. ----- "Revolution Not Resuscitation." Religious Education
(59:2, Mr.-Apr., 1964), pp. 171-73.   DHU/R
Future role of Black Church.

12720. ----- "Youth and the Black Religious Crisis." Washington
Star-News, Tuesday Magazine (Apr., 1974), pp. 17-18.
Pam. File, DHU/R
"Part three of a series."

12721. Washington, Paul M. "Liberation: Theology Comes fo Life."
Colloquy (4:10, Nov., 1971), pp. 10-11.   DHU/R
Written by the rector of the Episcopal Church of the Advocate
in North Philadelphia.

12722. Watkin, E. "Black Power in the Church in Harlem." U. S.
Catholic (Mr., 1969), pp. 30+.   DCU

12723. Watts, Leon W. "The Black Church Yes! COCU No!"
Renewal (10:3, Mr., 1970), pp. 10-11.   DHU/R

12724. Wheeler, Lillian. "Rev. Eaton Gives Views on Religion's
Role in Black University." The Hilltop (Nov. 22, 1968).
Pam. File, DHU/R
Negro author.

12725. White, Andrew. "Random Notes on the Black Theology of
Liberation and Hope." Journal of Religious Education of the A.
M. E. Church (31:3, Fall, 1971), pp. 16-17.   DHU/R

12726. ----- "The Role of the Black Church in the Liberation
Struggle." Spectrum (47:4, Jl.-Ag., 1971), pp. 10-12.   DHU/R

12727. Williams, A. Cecil. "Blacks Are Not for Sale." Black
Scholar (2:4, Dec., 1970), pp. 35-42.   DHU/R
Minister employs jazz rhythm and blues and African dance in
his church services in San Francisco.
Negro author.

12728. Williams, A. Roger. "A Black Pastor Looks at Black Theology." Harvard Theological Review (64:4, Oct., 1971), pp. 559-
67.   DHU/R

12729. Williams, Preston N. "Black Church, Origin, History and
Present Dilemma." McCormick Quarterly (22:4, My., 1969),
pp. 223-37.   DHU/R

12730. ----- "The Black Experience and Black Religion." Theology
Today (26:3, Oct., 1969), pp. 246-61.   DHU/R

12731. ----- "Black Theology." Communion Viatorum (14:2-3,
Sum., 1971), pp. 192-204.   DHU/R

12732. ----- "The Ethical Aspects of the Black Theology Phenomenon," Journal of Religious Thought (26:2, Sum. Suppl., 1969),
pp. 34-45.   DHU/R

12733. ----- "Ethics and Ethos in the Black Experience." Christianity and Crisis (31:9, May 1971), pp. 104-09.   DHU/R
"Victimization and the search for Black identity."

12734. ----- "The Ethics of Black Power." James J. Gardiner and
J. Deotis Roberts, Sr. (eds.). Quest for a Black Theology

(Philadelphia: United Church Press, 1971), pp. 82-96.
DHU/MO; DHU/R

12735. ----- "James Cone and the Problem of a Black Ethic."
Harvard Theological Review (65:4, Oct., 1972), pp. 483-94.
DHU/R

12736. ----- "The New Black Politics Needs Revision." The Christian Century (89:33, Sept. 20, 1972), pp. 913-14. DHU/R
Negro author.

12737. ----- "Toward a Sociological Understanding of the Black Re-
ligious Community." Soundings (54:3, Fall, 1971), pp. 260-70.
DHU/R
Author is Houghton Professor of Theology and Contemporary
Change, Harverd Divinity School.

12738. Williams, Robert C. "Moral Suasion and Militant Aggression
in the Theological Perspectives of Black Religion." Journal of
Religious Thought (30: Fall-Wint., 1973-74), pp. 27-50. DHU/R

12739. Williamson, Joseph C. "Theology and Revolution." Andover
Newton Quarterly (10:2, Nov. 2, 1969). Pam. File, DHU/R

12740. Wilmore, Gayraud S., Jr. Black Religion and Black Radicalism. New York: Doubleday, 1972. DHU/R; TSewU-T
Book review in: Christian Century (90:13, Mr., 1973), pp.
369-72.   DHU/R
Negro author.

12741. ----- "Black Theology." William M. Philpot, (ed.). Best
Black Sermons (Valley Forge: Judson Press, 1972), pp. 87-94.
DHU/R
A sermon.
Presbyterian minister.

12742. ----- "Black Theology: Its Significance for Christian Mission Today." International Review of Missions (43:250, Apr.,
1974), pp. 211-31.   DHU/R

12743. ----- "The Case for a New Black Church Style." Hart M.
Nelsen & Reytha L. Yokley, et alii. The Black Church in Amer-
ica (New York: Basic Books, 1971), pp. 324-34.   DHU/R
Also in Church in Metropolis (18; Fall, 1968), pp. 18-22.
Negro author.

12744. ----- "The Search of a New Theology." Kendig B. Cully
and F. Nile Harper. Will the Church Lose the City? (New York:
World Publishing Co., 1969), pp. 137-39.   DHU/R
Negro author.

12745. ----- "Stalking the Wild Black Theologues." Social Progress (60:1, Sept.-Oct., 1969), pp. 3-4+. Pam. File, DHU/R
Negro author.

12746. ----- "White Church and the Search for Black Power."
Social Progress (Mr.-Apr., 1967).   ICMcC

12747. Wilson, Frank T. "The Black Revolution: Is There a Black
Theology?" The Journal of Religious Thought (26:2, Sum.

Suppl., 1969), pp. 5-14.   DHU/R
Negro author.

12748. Winston, J. P. The Relevance of Black Power to the Church
n.p.: n.p., 1969.   MiBsA
Church and race problems, Seventh-Day Adventists.

12749. Witheridge, D. "Why Neglect the Negro Churches?" Christian Century (85:42, Oct. 16, 1968), p. 1303.   DHU/R

12750. Woodruff, James E. P. "Black Power Vis-a-Vis "The Kingdom of God." Malcolm Boyd, (ed.). The Underground Church
(New York: Sheed & Ward, 1968), pp. 84-101. DHU/R

12751. World Council of Churches. "Black Theology Conference Set
for May." Ecumenical Press Service (8; Mr. 22, 1973), p. 6.
DHU/R
Four day symposium on "Black Theology and Latin American
Theology."

12752. Wren, Christopher S. "Black Power Shakes the White
Church." Look (Ja. 7, 1969).   Pam. File, DHU/R

12753. Wright, Leon E. "Black Theology or Black Experience?"
Journal of Religious Thought (26:2, Sum. Suppl., 1969), pp. 46-
56.   DHU/R
Negro author.

12754. Wright, Nathan, Jr. "Black Power: A Creative Necessity."
Arthur C. Littleton and Mary W. Burger, (eds.). Black View-
points (New York: New American Library, 1964), pp. 381-89.
DHU/R

12755. ----- "Black Power: A Creative Necessity." Catholic
World (204:1, 219, Oct., 1966), pp. 46-51.   DHU/R

12756. ----- "Black Power...a Creative Necessity." Phyllis M.
Banks and Virginia M. Bruke, (eds.). Black Americans:
Images in Conflict (New York: Bobbs-Merrill Co., 1970), pp.
48-52.   DHU/R

12757. ----- Black Power and Urban Unrest: Creative Possibilities. New York: Hawthorn Books, 1967.   DHU/R; CtY-D
"Negro ministers: Statement on Black power."

12758. ----- "Black Power: Crisis or Challenge for the Churches?"
Paul T. Jersild and Dale A. Johnson, (eds.) Moral Issues and
Christian Response (New York: Holt, Rinehart and Winston,
1971), pp. 288-96.   DHU/R

12759. ----- "Black Power What? Why? How?" Social Action
(34:5, Ja., 1968), pp. 23-31.   DHU/R

12760. ----- "Power and Reconciliation." Concern (9:16, Oct. 1,
1967), pp. 14-16.   DHU/R

12761. ----- "Why Black Power?" The Christian Science Monitor
(Sept. 18, 1967).   Pam. File, DHU/R

12762. Zulu, Alphaeus. "Whither Black Theology?" Pro Veritate
(Johannesburg) (11:11, 1973), pp. 11-13.   NNMR

2. Black Caucuses

12763. "Black Catholic Caucus; Joint Convention of the National
Black Catholic Clergy Caucus and the National Black Catholic
Lay Caucus." America (125; Sept. 4, 1971), p. 107.
DAU; DGU

12764. "Black Caucus Speakers at All Souls." Afro-American (Ja.
18, 1969).   Pam. File, DHU/R

12765. "Black Manifesto Demand from U. S. Catholics." Catholic
Mind (67, Je., 1969), pp. 4-6.   DGU

12766. Campbell, James. "Caucuses Mergers Remain Thorny
Issues." Christian Advocate (15:24, Dec. 23, 1971), p. 19-20.
Pam. File, DHU/R

12767. Davis, Joseph Morgan. "Disparate Unanimity/ The Common
Goal." Freeing the Spirit (1:3, Sum., 1972), pp. 52-54. DHU/R
DHU/R
"Continuation of the reflections on the Black Caucus Move-
ment."

12768. ----- "Reflections on a Central Office for Black Catholicism." Freeing the Spirit (1:3, Sum., 1972), pp. 31-38.
DHU/R

12769. ----- "The Resolutions of the National Convention of Black
Lay Catholics." Freeing the Spirit (1:3, Sum., 1972), pp. 41-
42.   DHU/R

12770. ----- "Statement of the Black Catholic Clergy Caucus."
Freeing the Spirit (1:3, Sum., 1972), pp. 27-28.   DHU/R

12771. Felder, Cain Hope. "Sweetback, the Campus and the
Caucus." Toward Wholeness (1:1, Sum., 1972), pp. 13-15.
                                    DHU/R
    Written by Executive Director, Black Methodists for
    Church Renewal, Atlanta, Ga.
    Negro author.

12772. "Forging Directions. A National Black Catholic Convention."
Signs of Soul; Newsletter of the National Black Sisters Conference (5:2, Fall, 1973), pp. 10-11.   DHU/R

12773. Garnett, Bernard E. "Black Catholics Work for Change."
Race Relations Reporter (2:1, Ja., 1971), pp. 9-11. DHU/MO
    See next issue for "Report on the Church's Response to the
    Black Movement."

12774. Gopaul, F. "A Black Priest Looks at His Racist Church."
U. S. Catholic (Jl., 1969), p. 13.   DCU

12775. Griffin, John Howard. "The Position of the Catholic Church
in the Black Community." The Church and the Black Man
(Dayton, O.: Pflaum Press, 1969), pp. 118-32.   DHU/R
    Position paper of Catholic Black Caucus, January 1969.

12776. Grey, M. (Sister Martin De Perres). "A Black View: The
Politics of Black Catholic Radicalism." New Catholic World
(215:1283, Mr.-Apr., 1972), pp. 55-56.   DHU/R
    Author is president of National Black Sisters Conference.

12777. Haughey, John C. "Black Catholicism." America (120:
Mr. 22, 1969), pp. 325-27.   DHU

12778. Henry, Hayward. "Black Affairs Council." Now: The
Magazine of the Unitarian Universalist Association (50:15, Aut.,
1969), pp. 12-15.   DHU/R
    Negro author.

12779. Kiely, P. "A Cry for the Black Nun Power." Commonweal
(88:22, Sept. 27, 1968), p. 650.   DHU/R

12780. Lucas, Lawrence E. "Developing Black Independence."
The Advocate: Christian Community of the Arch-diocese of
Newark (22:42, Oct. 12, 1972),   Pam. File, DHU/R

12781. The Lutheran Church. Missouri Synod. A Consultation
of Black Lutheran Clergymen. Chicago, Ill., May, 1968.
Report.   MSL/CHI

12782. "Office for Black Catholics: Formation of National Office
for Black Catholics." America (121; Nov. 29, 1969), p. 516.
                                  DCU; DHU

12783. "On Dow and Calico." Editorial. Christian Century (86:50,
Dec. 10, 1969), pp. 1571.   Pam. File, DHU/R
    United Methodist Church and the Black Churchmen.

12784. Park, J. P. "Black Nuns Relate to Black Power: National
Black Sisters Conference." Christian Century (85:42, Oct. 16,
1968), pp. 1320-22.   DHU/R

12785. Rashke, Richard. "Trust for Black Catholics." Commonweal (92:2, Mr. 20, 1970), pp. 35-37.   DHU/R

12786. Roberts, James Deotis, Sr. "The Black Caucus and the
Failure of Christian Theology." The Journal of Religious
Thought (26:2, Sum. Suppl., 1969), pp. 15-25.   DHU/R
    Negro author.

12787. Tinney, James S. "Many Whites Attend Black Congress."
Christianity Today (15:1, Oct. 9, 1970), pp. 43-4. DHU/MO
    Black Congress on Evangelism called by black pastors.

12788. "The White Liberal and the Black Rebellion: A Study in
Anguish." Respond (1:3, Fall, 1967).   Pam. File, DHU/R
    "This issue discusses Unitarianism and the 'Black Caucus'."

3. Reparations

12789. Abernathy, Ralph David. "A Black Preacher Looks at the
Black Manifesto." Christian Century (86:33, Ag. 13, 1969),
pp. 1064-65.   DHU/R

12790. Atkins, Anselna. "Christians: James Forman Wants Your
Shirt." The Lamp (67:9, Sept. 1969), pp. 21-23; 30. DHU/R

12791. Belford, Lee A. "Questions About the Black Manifesto."
The Churchman (183:9, Nov., 1969), pp. 6-7.   DHU/R

12792. Bittker, Boris L. The Case for Black Reparations. New
York: Random House, 1973.   DHU/R
    Author, professor of law at Yale, makes a plea for payment
    to blacks for state segregation in public education and other
    facilities.

12793. "The Black Manifesto." Tempo (1:16, Je. 1, 1969), pp. 4+.
                                    DHU/R
    The complete text as adopted by National Black Economic
    Development Conference.

12794. "The Black Manifesto." Floyd B. Barbour (ed.). The
Black Seventies (Boston: Porter Sargent Publishing, 1970), pp.
296-308.   DHU/MO
    "This document was presented by James Foreman to the
    National Black Economic Development Conference in De-
    troit, Michigan, and adopted on April 26, 1969."

12795. "The Black Manifesto and Its Aftermath." Tempo (1:16, Je.
1, 1969), pp. 3+.   Pam. File, DHU/R

12796. "'Black Manifesto' Declares War on Churches." Christianity Today (13:17, My. 23, 1969), p. 29.
                                DHU/R; DAU/W; DCU/TH

12797. "The Black Manifesto (1969)." Harry A. Ploski (ed.). Reference Library of Black America (New York: Bellwether Pub.
Co., Inc., 1971), Bood 2, pp. 152-55.   DHU

12798. "The Black Manifesto." Thomas R. Frazier (ed.). Afro-
American History: Primary Resources (New York: Harcourt
Brace & World, Inc., 1970), pp. 501-11.   DHU/R DHU/MO
    "From James Forman, "Black Manifesto," a speech delivered
    at the National Black Economic Development Conference in
    Detroit, Michigan, April 26, 1969."

12799. "Black Manifesto's Birthday: Frosting on the Cake?"
Christianity Today (14:17, My. 22, 1970), p. 37.
                                DAU/W; DCU/TH; DHU/R

12800. "Black Over White." Commonweal (90:11, My. 30, 1969),
pp. 308-09.   DHU/R
    A critique of the "Black Manifesto."

12801. Campbell, Ernest T. "The Case for Reparations." Theology
Today (26:3, Oct., 1969), pp. 266-83.   DHU/R

12802. "Church and State in the Black Manifesto." Church and State
(21:10, Nov., 1969), pp. 11+.   DHU/R

12803. "Did We Endorse the Black Manifesto?" Editorial. Christian Century (86:27, Jl. 2, 1969), p. 894.   DHU/R

12804. Dowey, Edward A., Jr. "The Black Manifesto: Revolution,
Reparation and Separation." Theology Today (26:3, Oct., 1969),
pp. 288-93.   DHU/R

12805. Edwards, John. "Jesuits Pay Bonds for Exploited Blacks."
Modern Society (13:1, Ja.-Feb., 1970), pp. 7+.
                                Pam. File, DHU/R

12806. "Episcopalians Hold Special Convention: Historic Session."
Christian Century (86:40, Oct. 1, 1969), pp. 1262-63. DHU/R
Reparation payment made by this denomination.

12807. Foley, Judy Mathe. "Church and Race: More on the Manifesto." Episcopalian (134:8, Ag., 1969), p. 19. DHU/R

12808. ----- "Dealing with a Manifesto." Episcopalian (134:7, Jl.,
1969), pp. 11-12.   DHU/R

12809. Forman, James. "The Black Manifesto." Arthur C. Littleton and Mary W. Burger (eds.). Black Viewpoints (New York:
New American Library, 1964), pp. 393-400.   DHU/R

12810. ----- The Making of Black Revolutionaries. New York:
The Macmillan Co., 1972.   DHU/R
Roots and text of the "Black Manifesto."

12811. ----- The Political Thought of James Forman. Detroit:
Black Star Publishing, 1970.   DHU/MO
Negro minister, author of Black Manifesto.

12812. Goetz, Ronald. "Black Manifesto: The Great White Hope."
Christian Century (86:25, Je. 18, 1969), pp. 832-33. DHU/R

12813. Green, Mark. "Reparations for Blacks." Commonweal
(90:13, Je., 1969), pp. 359-62.   DHU/R

12814. Grizzard, R. Stuart. "Reparations, Restitution and Repentance." Religious Herald (142; Nov. 6, 1969), pp. 12-13.
                                                  TND; ViU

12815. "A Hammer for a House." Dick McCutcheon. Released by
Mass Media Associates, 1969. 20 min. sd. color. 16 mm. DLC
Film.
"A survey of the feelings that were triggered by James Fore-
man's presentation of his Black manifesto to the Inter-Faith
Center in New York in 1969."

12816. Holland, Darrell W. "Massachusetts Conference Commits
$1 Million to Black Churchmen." United Church Herald (13:1,
Ja. 1, 1970), pp. 36-7.   DHU/R

12817. "How to Rob a Church." Presbyterian Journal (Je. 18, 1969),
pp. 12+.   DLC
"Reparations."

12818. Howell, Leonard and Robert S. Lecky. "Reparation Now?"
Christianity and Cisis (29:9, My. 26, 1969), p. 141. DHU/R

12819. Joseph, James A. "Black Manifesto and the Ethics of Reparation." Christian Ministry (1:4, Myl, 1970), pp. 36-40. DHU/R

12820. Kempton, Murray. "The Black Manifesto." New York Review of Books (13; Jl. 10, 1969), pp. 31-32. DGW; DAU

12821. Lecky, Robert S. Black Manifesto, Religion Racism and
Reparations. New York: Sheed & Ward, 1969. DHU/R; CtY-D

12822. Lovelace, John A. "The Black Manifesto." Christian Advocate (13:14, Jl. 10, 1969), pp. 3, 21-22. DHU/R

12823. Lester, James A. "The Black Manifesto." Editorial.
Baptist and Reflector (135; Je. 12, 1969), p. 6. KyLoS; TND

12824. "Manifesto (of National Black Economic Development Conference) Information Service (48; My. 17, 1969), p. 1.
                                                  DLC; CtY

12825. "Methodists Vow New Priorities. Funding Still Uncertain."
Christianity Today (15:17, My. 22, 1970), pp. 763+. DHU/R

12826. Montgomery, Ray. "Slavery and the Claimed Reparations."
American Opinion (Nov., 1970), p. 37.   DGW

12827. Morsell, John A. "The NAACP and Reparations." The
Crisis (77:3, Mr., 1970), pp. 96-101.

12828. Mulder, John M. "The Church as a Financial Institution or
Forgive Us Our Debts." Theology Today (26:3, Oct., 1969),
pp. 294-98.   DHU/R

12829. "N. A. A. C. P. Executive Urges Churches to Reject Demands
for Reparations." Christian Century (86:45, Nov. 5, 1969),
p. 1413.   DHU/R

12830. "The NCC and the Black Manifesto." Tempo (1:19, Jl. 15,
1969), pp. 3-5.   Pam. File, DHU/R

12831. "National Council of Churches' General Board Responds to
the Black Manifesto." Tempo (1:24, Oct. 1, 1969), pp. 4+.
                                                  DHU/R

12832. "Negro Church Rejects Plan." Denver Post (Ag. 8, 1969),
                                       Pam. File, DHU/R
A. M. E. Church rejects the plan of James Forman for
"reparations".

12833. Nelson, J. Robert. "Preparation for Separation and Reparation; the Churches Response to Racism?" Demands on the
World Council of Churches. Christian Century (86; Feb. 14,
1969), pp. 862-65.   DHU/R

12834. Oursler, Will. Protestant Power and the Coming Revolu-
tion. New York: Doubleday & Co., 1971. DHU/R; DLC
Black Manifesto, Delta Ministry and Welfare and the
Churches.

12835. Rensenbrink, Dorothy. "Two Crowded Days in Indianapolis."
Tempo (1:24, Oct. 1, 1969), pp. 3+.   DHU/R

12836. "Reparations, Tactics and the Churches; Some Comments."
Tempo (1:16, Je., 1, 1969), p. 6-7.   DHU/R

12837. "The Requests Were Severe But the Tone was Gentle."
Christian Advocate (14:9, Apr. 30, 1970, p. 6.   DHU/R

12838. "Riverside Replys." Information Service (48; My. 17,
1969), p. 7.   CtY
(Relates to Black Manifesto demands.)

12839. Roddy, Sherman S. "Black Manifesto -- A Reappraisal."
Church and Society (60:5, My.-Je., 1970), pp. 39-50. DHU/R
Discusses the Black Manifesto's relationship to changing
attitudes in the church.

12840. Rose, Stephen C. "The Manifesto and Renewal." Christianity and Crisis (29:9, My. 26, 1969), pp. 142-43. DHU/R

12841. ----- "Suggested Soulful Responses to the Black Manifesto:
Reparation Now!"   Pam. File, DHU/R
mim.

12842. ----- "Wake-ing up the Church." Christian Century (87;
Ja. 14, 1970), p. 50.
General Assembly Meeting, 1969 Black Manifesto.

12843. "Roundup: The Year of the Black Manifesto." Christian
Century (87:6, Feb. 11, 1970), pp. 185-88. DHU/R

12844. "Roy Wilkins on Reparations." Living Church (Ja. 11,
1970), p. 8.   ViAlTh

12845. Sayre, Charles A. "A Crossroads--Nonviolence or Black
Manifesto." Christian Advocate (14:5, Mr. 5, 1970), pp. 18+.
                                                  DHU/R; DAU/W

12846. Schomer, H. "The Manifesto and the Magnificat."
Christian Century (86:26, Je. 25, 1969), pp. 866-67.   DHU/R

12847. Schuchter, Arnold. Reparations: The Black Manifesto
and its Challenge to White America. Philadelphia: J. B. Lippincott Co., 1970.

12848. "Some Comments on the Black Manifesto." Church Herald
(Jl. 11, 1969), p. 6.   DHU/R

12849. Stackhouse, Max L. "Reparations: A Call to Repentance." Colloquy (3:2, Feb., 1970), pp. 18-26.   DHU/R

12850. "Synagogue Council Responds to Manifesto." Information Service (48; My. 17, 1969), p. 8.   CtY; DLC

12851. Text of Demands Made to Riverside Church (relates to Black Manifesto demands)." Information Service (48; My. 17, 1969), p. 6.   CtY; DLC

12852. "Unitarians Approve Negro-Lead Council; Allocate $1 Million." New York Times (My. 28, 1968).
          Pam File, DHU/R

12853. United Church of Christ. Office of the President. "A Report from the Seventh General Synod, 1969."
          Pam. File, DHU/R
     "Resolutions taken on social change. A letter addressed to James Forman in reply to the request for 'reparation'. "

12854. United Methodist Church. Board of Health and Welfare Ministries. "One Million Dollars for Black Health Welfare." Christian Advocate (13:22, Nov. 13, 1969), pp. 23+.   DHU/R

12855. Vorspan, Albert. "How James Forman Lost His Cool But Saved Religion in 1969: A Modern Bible Story." Christian Century (86:32, Ag. 6, 1969), p. 1042.   DHU/R

12856. Wells, Charles A. "Black Reparations How and To Whom." Friends Journal (16:3, Feb. 1, 1970), pp. 69+.   DHU/R

12857. White, Andrew. "The Role and Future of the Negro Church." Editorial. Journal of Religious Education of the African Meth-

odist Episcopal Church (29:4, Je.-Ag., 1969), pp. 2-5.
     Editor discussed Black Manifesto.
     Negro author.

12858. ----- "Way the Church Should Evangelize Youth." Religious Education (64:6, Nov.-Dec., 1969), pp. 446-50.   DHU/R

12859. Whiten, Bennie E. "Reparations and the Contribution of the Church." Social Action (36:6, Feb., 1970), pp. 18-26.
          DHU/R

     Negro author.

12860. "Will the Black Manifesto Help Blacks?" Christian Century (86:21, My. 21, 1969), p. 701.   DHU/R

12861. Wilmore, Gayraud S., Jr. "Black Manifesto Revisited." Christian Century (88:14, Apr. 7, 1971), pp. 452-53.   DHU/R
     Negro author.

12862. ----- "The Church's Response to the Black Manifesto." Ceasar D. Coleman, (ed.). Beyond Blackness to Destiny: Study Guide (Memphis: Printed by Wimmer Bros., n.d.), pp. 95-109.   Pam. File, DHU/R
     Negro author.

12863. ----- "Reparations: Don't Hang up on the Word." Theology Today (26:3, Oct., 1969), pp. 284-87.   DHU/R

12864. Wogoman, Philip. "Testing the Rhetoric of the Black Manifesto." Christian Advocate (13:17, Sept. 4, 1969), pp. 9-10.
          Pam. File, DHU/R

4. National Committee of Black Churchmen—Local Groups

12865. "Bishop Shaw Urges New Direction for Churchmen." Afro-American (Nov. 12, 1968).   Pam. File, DHU/R
     "Speech when elected president of the National Committee of Black Churchmen. "

12866. "The Black Church Acts." National Black Monitor (Pilot issue, no. 1, 1972), p. 23.   DHU/MO
     Report of Conference held by National Committee of Black Churchmen (NCBC) in New York, 9-13, October 1972.

12867. "Black Churchmen Achieve Recognition." The United Church Herald (12:8, Ag., 1969), pp. 12-13.   DHU/R

12868. Black Methodiss For Church Renewal. "BMCR's Central Aim: Strengthen Black Church." Christian Advocate (18:7, Mr. 29, 1973), p. 20.   Pam. File, DHU/R

12869. "Black Methodists for Church Renewal: Black Churchmen Build Unity." Together (14:1, Ja., 1969), pp. 10+.   DHU/R

12870. "Black Power: Statement by National Committee of Negro Churchmen." Concern (8:15, Sept. 1, 1966), pp. 5-7. DHU/R

12871. Boynton, Ernest. "Christianity's Black Power." Church in Metropolis (no. 19; Wint., 1968), pp. 20-24. DHU/R
     A discussion of the Black Caucus Movement as reflected at the second annual convocation of Black Churchmen in St. Louis, 1968.

12872. Campbell, James. "NCBC: On Verge of Demise?" Christian Advocate (15:23, Dec., 1971), p. 19.   DAU/W
     "National Committee of Black Churchmen. "

12873. Campbell, Will D. "A Conversation With Will Cambell: Prophet Poet, Preacher-at-Large." The Student (50:3, Dec. 1970), pp. 291.   DHU/R
     A conversation with the director of the Committee of Southern Churchmen on the future of the black church.

12874. Chapman, Robert C. "The Black Church Now." The Black Church Quarterly Journal of the Black Ecumenical Commission of Massachusetts (1:1, 1972), pp. 45-57.   DHU/R

12875. "Chicago's Black Churchmen: How Their New Executive Sees Their Role." Christian Century (87:18, My. 6, 1970), pp. 578-80.   DHU/R

12876. Committee on Theological Prospectus, National Committee of Black Churchmen. "Black Theology: A Statement of the National Committee of Black Churchmen." Christian Century (86:42, Oct. 15, 1969), p. 1310.   DHU/R

12877. Goodman, Grace Ann. Ecumenism in Wahington, D. C. in the 1960's. United Presbyterian Church, U. S. A. Board of National Missions, Institute of Strategic Studies, 1970.
          Pam. File, DHU/R
     Typescript.
     pp. 12-15, The Council of Churches and Black Churchmen.

12878. Grey, M. (Sister Martin de Porres). "The Church Revolution and Black Catholics." The Black Scholar (2:4, Dec., 1970), pp. 20-4.   DHU/R
     Negro author.

12879. "Happening at St. Louis." Editorial. Tempo (1:4, Dec. 1, 1968), p. 2.   DHU/R
     "The Second Annual Convocation of the National Committee of Black Churchmen. "

12880. Lester, Julius. "Come, Come, Ye Saints All Is Well." Katallagete: Be Reconciled Journal of the Committee of Southern Churchmen (5:1, Spr., 1974), pp. 4-15.   DHU/R

12881. "Local Colored Church Withdraws After Merger of Colored and White." The Ecclesiastical Court Digest (8:11, Nov., 1970), p. 1.   DHU/R

12882. "A Message to the Churches from Oakland." Tempo (2:4, Dec. 1, 1969), pp. 10-14.   DHU/R

12883. "Methodism Under Siege." Christianity Today (14:16, My.
8. 1970), pp. 36-7.   DHU/R
Rev. James M. Lawson, president of Black Methodists for
Church Renewal, announces that his organization requests
$21,500.00 from the church to equalize social and economic
justice for blacks.

12884. "Methodist Vow New Priorities." Christianity Today (14:
17, My. 22, 1970), pp. 31-2.   DHU/R
Rev. James M. Lawson, president of the Black Methodists
for Church Renewal, request for "reparations" is debated
in General Conference.

12885. Metropolitan Boston Committee of Black Churchmen. Report to the Membership. By Cameron Wells Byrd, Chairman.
February 6, 1972.   Pam. File, DHU/R
6 pp. Mim.

12886. National Committee of Negro Churchmen. "Black Power."
Paul T. Jersild and Dale A Johnson, (eds.). Moral Issues
and Christian Response (New York: Holt, Rinehart and Winston, 1971), pp. 280-86.   DHU/R

12887. National Committee of Black Churchmen. "Black Theology."
Paul T. Jersild and Dale A. Johnson, (eds.). Moral Issues and
Christian Response (New York: Holt, Rinehart and Winston,
1971), pp. 286-88.   DHU/R

12888. "National Committee of the Black Churchmen." Constitution
                                     Pam. File, DHU/R
mim.

12889. "The National Committee of Negro Churchmen." Harry A.
Ploski, (ed.). Reference Library of Black America (New
York: Bellwether Pub. Co., 1971), Book 2, pp. 216-21.   DHU

12890. National Committee of the Black Churchmen. "Reflections
on Some Documents..." Renewal (10:7, Oct.-Nov., 1970).
                                                      DHU/R
Complete issue devoted to NCBC.

12891. National Committee of the Black Churchmen. Third Annual
Convocation. Nov. 11-14, 1969. Oakland, Calif.
                                     Pam. File, DHU/R

12892. "Racist Church? Black Clergy Conference." Commonweal
(88:8, My. 10, 1968), p. 222.   DHU

12893. Ranck, Lee. "I Want to Use Your Blackness." Engage/
Social Action (2:3, Mr., 1974), pp. 14-27.   DHU/R
A report on the United Methodist National Convocation on
the Black Church held in Atlanta, Georgia, in December,
1973.

12894. Rollins, J. Metz. "Black Churchmen Meet in Atlanta."
Presbyterian Life (24:2, Ja., 1971), pp. 30-31.   DHU/R

12895. "School Ouster Charges by Black Priests." Chicago Daily
Defender (Je. 1-7, 1968).   Pam. File, DHU/R

12896. "Seven Negro Priests Criticise Church." New York Times
(Feb. 18, 1968).   Pam. File, DHU/R

12897. Shockley, Grant S. "Ultimatum and Hope: The Black
Churchmen's Convocation; An Interpretation." Christian
Century (8:71, Feb. 12, 1969), pp. 217-19.
                                     Pam. File, DHU/R

12898. Stone, Michael. "Chicago's Black Churchmen: How Their
New Executive Sees Their Role." The Christian Century (87:
18, My. 6, 1970), pp. 578-80   DHU/R

12899. Tilly, Andrew W. The Black Churchmen. California:
Crescent Publications, 1973.   DHU/R
Negro author.

12900. "Toward An Authentic Black Catholic Preaching Tradition."
Freeing the Spirit (1:4, 11:1, Fall-Wint., 1972, Spr., 1973),
pp. 3-4.   DHU/R

12901. United Methodist Church. Board of Missions. "Youth Black
Coalition Trigger Missions Debate." Christian Advocate (13:22,
Nov. 13, 1969), pp. 24+.   DHU/R

12902. "A Vicariate for Black Catholics." Divine Word Messenger
(50:4, Aut., 1973), p. 69.   Pam. File, DHU/R

12903. Watts, Leon W. "The National Committee of Black Churchmen." Christianity and Crisis (30:18, Nov. 2 & 16, 1970),
pp. 237-43.   DHU/R

12904. Williams, Preston N. "The Atlanta Document: An Interpre-
tation." Christian Century (86:42, Oct. 15, 1969), pp. 1311-12.
                                                      DHU/R
A reaction to the statement on Black Theology by National
Committee of Black Churchmen.
Negro author.

12905. ----- "Black Theology: A Statement of the National Committee of Black Churchmen." Christian Century (86:42, Oct.
15, 1969), p. 1310.   DHU/R

12906. Wilmore, Gayraud S., Jr. "Africa and Afro-Americans:
Report of Conversations Between NCBC Officials and Members
of the All Africa Conference of Churches." Christian Century
(87:22, Je. 3, 1970), p. 686.
Negro author.

C. THE JEW AND THE NEGRO

12907-08. "Advice to Jews." Chicago Daily Defender (Nov. 15,
1968).   Pam. File, DHU/R
Rabbi Bernard Weinberger makes a plea for better relations
between Jews and Blacks.

12909. "American Jewish Congress Names Urban-Affair Aide."
New York Times (Dec. 8, 1968).   Pam. File, DHU/R
"Will guide programs aimed at reducing community ten-
sions."

12910. "Anti-Semitism Mounting in Harlem Area of New York."
World Over (25; Mr. 27, 1964), p. 5.   DGU; DLC
Negroes and Jews.

12911. Baldwin, James. Black Anti-Semitism and Jewish Racism.
New York: R. W. Baron, 1969.   NjP; DHU/MO; DHU/R; DLC
Negro author.

12912. Becker, William H. "Black and Jew: Ambivalence and
Affinities." Soundings (53:4, Wint., 1970), pp. 413-39. DHU/R

12913. Bender, Eugene I. "Reflections on Negro-Jewish Relationships: the Historical Dimension." Phylon (30:1, Spr., 1969),
pp. 56-65.   DHU/MO

12914. Berson, Lenora A. The Negroes and the Jews. New York:
Random House, 1971.   DHU/R
Review, City Magazine of Urban Life and Environment.
(Jl.-Ag., 1971), by Clifton F. Brown.

12915. "Black Jew-Hatred in Historical Perspective." Jewish
Spectator (Ja., 1969), pp. 2+.   NN

12916. "Blacks, Jews, and Violence." Jewish Spectator (Je.,
1969), pp. 2+.   NN

12917. Bontemps, Alex. "Black Jewish Conflicts: The Fisk Consultation." Editorial. Christian Century (91:27, Jl. 31, 1974),
pp. 740-42.   DHU/R

12918. "Boycott by Negro Churches." Together (6:5, My., 1962),
p. 73.   DHU/R; DAU/W

("Boycott by Negro Churches." cont.)
      Boycott of some 200 Negro Churches in Baltimore, Md. of
      businesses practicing discrimination in employment.

12919. Brandow, Jonathan. "Jewish Radicals and Self-Hatred."
Jewish Spectator (Je., 1970), pp. 12-14.   NN; OCH

12920. Clark, Kenneth B. The Negro Protest: James Baldwin,
Malcolm X, Martin Luther King Talk With Kenneth B. Clark.
Boston: Beacon Press, 1963.   DHU/R

12921. Cohen, J. "Jews and Blacks--A Response to Ben Halpern."
Jewish Frontier (Sept., 1971), pp. 17+.
      ICU; KyLoU; MdBE; MiU; NN; NNJ; OCU; PPT; WU

12922. Conference on Negro Jewish Relations in the United States,
New York, 1964. Negro Jewish Relations in the United States:
Papers and Proceedings. New York: Citadel Press, 1966.
      NjP; O; InLL

12923. Cuddihy, John M. "Jews, Blacks and the Cold War at the
Top." Worldview (15:2, Feb., 1972), pp. 30-40.   DHU/R

12924. Davies, Alan T. "The Contemporary Encounter of Christians and Jews." The Ecumenist (10:4, My.-Je., 1972), pp.
56-59.   DHU/R

12925. Dugan, George. "Negroes and Jews Seek an Accord."
New York Times (Dec. 7, 1968). Pam. File, DHU/R

12926. Estes, Joseph R. "Jewish-Christian Dialogue as Mission."
Review and Expositor, A Baptist Theological Journal (68:1,
Wint., 1971), pp. 5-16.   DHU/R

12927. Featherstone, Joseph. "Inflating the Threat of Black Anti-
Semitism." New Republic (160; Mr. 8, 1969), pp. 14-15.
      DHU; DGW; DCU/SW

12928. Fineberg, S. Anhil and Benjamin F. McLaurin. "We Want
Integration Now." United Church Herald (14:8, Ag., 1971),
p. 44.   DHU/R
      Fineberg (a rabbi and consultant to the National Conference
      of Christians and Jews) and McLaurin, a Negro (director of
      New York City's Labor Services) discuss Christian and
      Church responsibility.

12929. "Forward Together; Protestant-Catholic-Jewish Cooperation." Commonweal (76; Jl. 13, 1962), p. 389. DHU

12930. Glazer, Nathan. "Blacks, Jews and the Intellectuals."
Commentary (47; Apr., 1969), pp. 33-39.   DHU/R

12931. Glock, Charles Y. and Rodney Stark. Christian Beliefs
and Anti-Semitism. New York: Harper & Row, 1969.
      DLC; ICU

12932. Halpern, Ben. "The Ethnic Revolt." Midstream, A Quarterly Jewish Review. (17; Ja., 1971), p. 3.   DAU; DHU

12933. ----- Jews and Blacks: The Classic American Minorities.
New York: Herder & Herder, 1971.   DHU/R

12934. Harris, Louis and Bert E. Swanson. Black Jewish Relations in New York City. New York: Praeger Publishers, 1970.
      NN/Sch
      "Praeger's special studies in U. S. economic and social
      development."

12935. Hentoff, Nat. Black Anti-Semitism and Jewish Racism.
New York: Richard W. Baron, 1970.   DHU/R

12936. Hollander, Judith. "Black Consciousness and Jewish
Conscience." Reconstructionist (32; Feb. 3, 1967), pp. 7-14.
      NN; NNC; NNJ; OKS

12937. "Jewish and Negro Clergy Meet on School Tensions." New
York Times (Nov. 13, 1968).   Pam. File, DHU/R

12938. "Jewish Congress to Press Support of Aid to Negroes."
New York Times (Dec. 16, 1968).   Pam. File, DHU/R

12939. "Jews and Blacks: Together Again?" Editorial. Christian
Century (88:43, Oct. 27, 1971), p. 1251.   DHU/R

12940. "Jews are Advised to Ease Tensions." New York Times
(Oct. 27, 1968).   Pam. File, DHU/R
      "Rabbi Weinberger advises Jewish people to give up ex-
      plosive businesses in ghetto areas."

12941. Kopkind, Andrew. "Blacks vs. Jews." New Statesman
(77; Feb. 7, 1969), pp. 175-76.   DHU

12942. Kovach, Bill. "Facist and Anti-Semite Strain Old Negro-
Jewish Ties." New York Times (Sept. 23, 1968).
      Pam. File, DHU/R

12943. Krasner, Barbara. "Jew and Black in Christian America:
A Study in Separation." Renewal (9; Mr., 1969), pp. 6-9.
      DAU/W

12944. Leo, J. "Black Anti-Semitism." Commonweal (89:19,
Feb. 14, 1969), pp. 618-20.   DHU/R

12945. Majdalany, Gebran. "Reflections on Racism, Anti-Semitism, and Zionism." Liberation (14:8, Nov., 1968), pp. 36-40.
      DHU/R

12946. Marx, Gary T. Protest and Prejudice. A Study of Belief
in the Black Community. New York: Harper & Row, 1969.
      DHU/R
      "Negroes and Jews, pp. 126-67."

12947. McKay, Claude. "Anti-Semitism and the Negro." Wayne
F. Cooper, (ed.). The Passion of Claude McKay... (New
York: Schocken Books, 1973), pp. 257-61.   DHU/R
      "An essay."
      Negro author.

12948. Negro and Jew; an Encounter in America; a Symposium
Compiled by Midstream Magazine. New York: Macmillan,
1967.   DHU/MO; OU; InU; FSU

12949. "Negro Leaders Here Urged to Reject Anti-Jew Leaflet."
New York Times (Dec. 13, 1968). Pam. File, DHU/R

12950. Poussaint, Alvin F. "Blacks and Jews: An Appeal for
Unity." Ebony (29:9, Jl., 1974), pp. 120-24+.
      Pam. File, DHU/R
      Negro author.

12951. Raab, Earl. "The Black Revolution and the Jewish Question." Commentary (47:1, Ja., 1969), pp. 23-33.
      Pam. File, DHU/R

12952. "Rights Expert Tells Jewish Congress Liberals Fail
Negro." New York Times (My. 17, 1968).
      Pam. File, DHU/R

12953. Rubenstein, Richard L. "Jews, Negroes and the New
Politics." Reconstructionist (33; Nov. 17, 1967), pp. 7-16.
      NN; NNC; NNJ; OKS

12954. Rustin, Bayard. "American Negroes and Israel."
Crisis (81; 4, Apr., 1974), pp. 115-18.   DHU/R
      Written by executive director of the A. Philip Randolph
      Institute.
      Negro author.

12955. Selznick, Gertrude J. and Stephen Steinberg. The Tenacity
of Prejudice; Anti-Semitism in Contemporary America. V. 4
New York: Harper and Row, Publishers, 1969. DHU/R
      Chapter 9, Anti-Semitism and Anti-Negro Prejudice.

12956. Sengstacke, John H. "Negroes and Jews." Editorial.
Chicago Daily Defender (Dec. 19, 1968). Pam. File, DHU/R

12957. Spiegel, Irving. "B'nai B'rith Head Scores Militants." New York Times (Sept. 8, 1968).   Pam. File, DHU/R

12958. ----- "Jewish Unit Sets a Negro Aid Drive." New York Times (Apr. 3, 1968).   Pam. File, DHU/R

12959. ----- "Jews in Suburbia Scored as Racist." New York Times (My. 25, 1968).   Pam. File, DHU/R

12960. ----- "Jews Told Aid is 'Imperative' in Negroes Fight for Equality." New York Times (Oct. 28, 1968).
                                    Pam. File, DHU/R

12961. ----- "Rabbis Here Urge Rights for Negro." New York Times (Apr. 9, 1968).   Pam. File, DHU/R

12962. ----- "Rabbis Score School Decentralization." New York Times (Feb. 1, 1968).   Pam. File, DHU/R

12963. ----- "Zionists Deplores Black Extremists." New York Times (Sept. 13, 1968).   Pam. File, DHU/R

12964. Stark, Rodney and Bruce D. Foster et. al. Wayward Shepherds: Prejudice and the Protestant Clergy. New York: Harper and Row, 1971.   DHU/R; INU
        5 year study of Anti-Semitism in the U. S.

12965. Still, Lawrence A. "Black Anti-Semitism? Realignment or Alienation." Renewal ((; Mr., 1969), pp. 4-5.   DAU/W

12966. Stringfellow, William. "Negro Anti-Semitism." World Call (49:1, Ja., 1967), p. 29.   DHU/R

12967. "Tension Between Blacks, Jews Deplored." Chicago Daily Defender (Dec. 14, 1968).   Pam. File, DHU/R

12968. "Unity Group Deplores Negro Bias, Reaction." Washington Post (Nov. 15, 1968).   Pam. File, DHU/R
        "President of National Conference of Christians and Jews warns against rising passions of Negro anti-semitism."

12969. Vorspan, Albert. "The Negro Victory and the Jewish Failure." American Judaism (13:1, Fall, 1963).
                            DLC; Pam. File, DHU/R

12970. Weisbord, Robert G. and Arthur Stein. Bittersweet Encounter, the Afro-American and the American Jew. Wesport, Conn: Negro Universities Press, 1970.   DHU/R; NjP
        "Contribution in Afro-American and African studies, no. 5."

12971. Weiss-Rosemarin, Trude. "Jewish Backlash." Jewish Spectator (My., 1970), pp. 2-6+.   NN; OCH

12972. ----- "Negro Anti-Semitism." Jewish Spectator (29; Mr., 1964), pp. 3-4.   DLC

D. RACISM AND CONTEMPORARY CHURCH

12973. Anderson, John F. "A Time to Heal: A Southern Church Deal With Racism." International Review of Mission (59:235, Jl., 1970), pp. 304-10.   DHU/R
        Presbyterian Church in the United States and its racial policy.

12974. Bailey, Donald R. "Race Relations: Major Factor in Pastor Defections." Engage / Social Action (2; 4, Apr., 1974), pp. 42-9.   DHU/R
        Results of a study begun at Emory University 1964-65 and completed in 1972. Author's conclusion "seminary experience had a general liberalizing effect on the respondents as a whole."

12975. Barbour, Russell B. Black and White Together; Plain Talk for White Christians. Philadelphia: United Church Press, 1967.   DHU/R CtY-D; NcD; DLC

12976. Barr, William R. "The Shape of a White Liberation Theology." Lexington Theological Quarterly (9:4, Oct., 1974), pp. 113-27.   Pam. File, DHU/R

12977. Bastide, Roger. "Color, Racism and Christianity." John Hope Franklin, (ed.). Color and Race (Boston: Beacon Press, 1968), pp. 34+.   DHU/R

12978. Beckwith, John Q. The Race Problem and the South; Five Lectures, January-February 1958. Washington, D. C.: Organizing Committee, Chrisitanity and Modern Man Lectures, 1958.
                                    CtY-D
        (A Chrisitanity and modern man publication, 26.)

12979. Beeson, Trevor. "Dutch Prescription for Racial Harmony." The Christian Century (89:31, Sept. 6, 1972), pp. 866-67.
                                    DHU/R

12980. Berrigan, Philip. No More Strangers. New York: Macmillan, 1965.   DHU/R; INU; NcD
        Racial patterns and the Christian.

12981. ----- A Punishment for Peace. New York: Macmillan, 1969.   CtY-D
        Chapter IV, Racial patterns and the Christians.

12982. Blau, Joseph L. "Religion and the Two Faces of America." Roger L. Shinn. Search for Identity Essays on the American Character. (New York: Harper & Row, 1964), pp. 29-38.
                                    DHU/R

12983. Boyd, Malcolm, (ed.). On the Battle Lines. New York: Morehouse-Barlow, 1964.   NN/Sch

12984. ----- The Underground Church. New York: Sheed & Ward, 1968.   DHU/R
        Contains chapters on Race and Church.

12985. Brink, William. Black and White: A Study of United States Racial Attitudes Today. New York: Simon Press, 1967.   DHU/R

12986. Brown, Harold O. J. Christianity and the Class Struggle. Introductory Note by Billy Graham. Grand Rapids, Mich.: Zondervan Pub. House, 1971.   DHU/R
        Chapter 4, Racial Classes.

12987. Brown, John Pairman. The Liberated Zone. A Guide to Christian Resistance. Richmond, Va.: John Knox Press, 1969.
                                    DHU/R

12988. Brown, Robert Raymond, (bp.). Bigger Than Little Rock. Greenwich, Conn.: Seabury Press, 1958.
                            DLC; DHU/R; NYP/Sch; CtY-D
        Section 6 "Religion and Segregation."

12989. Bucher, Glenn R. "Social Gospel Christianity and Racism." Union Seminary Quarterly Review (28:2, Wint., 1973), pp. 146-57.   DHU/R

12990. Burnham, Kenneth E. "Racial Prejudice in Relation to Education, Sex, and Religion." Journal for the Scientific Study of Religion (8:2, Fall, 1969), p. 318.

12991. Campbell, Will D., (comp.) The Failure and the Hope; Essays of Southern Churchmen. Edited with an introduction by Will D. Campbell and James Y. Holloway. Grand Rapids: Eerdmans, 1972.   MNtcA; PPT.

12992. ----- Race and the Renewal of the Church. Philadelphia: Westminister Press, 1962.   DHU/R; CtY-D

12993. Carcich, Theodore. "This Would End Racism." The Mess-age Magazine (40:6, Sept., 1974), pp. 37-40.   DHU/R
"The time has come for the gospel of Jesus Christ to be shared with the whole world."

12994. Christmas, Faith C. "Appoint Black Pastor, Priests Urge Cody." Chicago Daily Defender (Dec. 12, 1968).
Pam. File, DHU/R

12995. "Church and Race; Letter to the Editor." Christian Century (80; Ag., 21, 1963), p. 1032.   DHU/R

12996. "Churches Must Play Key Role in Quest for Racial Justice." Afro-American (Apr. 6, 1968).   Pam. File; DHU/R

12997. Churchill, Rhona. White Man's God. New York: Morrow, 1962.   DLC

12998. "Confronting the Racial Crisis." Editorial. Christianity Today (12:10, Feb. 16, 1968), pp. 26-28.   DHU/R

12999. Dalzell, Bonnie. "The Church's Record in Black and White." Christian Herald (96:7, Jl., 1973), pp. 4+.   DHU/R

13000. Daniels, Joseph. "The Psychodynamics of Racism." Chris-tianity Today (15:1, Oct. 9, 1970), pp. 12-14.   DHU/R

13001. Davies, Alfred T. (ed.). The Pulpit Speaks on Race. New York: Abingdon Press, 1965.   DHU/R; DHU/MO; DLC; CtY-D

13002. Davies, Lawrence E. "Wide Bias Found in Church People." The New York Times (Mr. 26, 1968).   Pam. File, DHU/R

13003. Davis, Joseph M. "Can Blacks Expect Anything From the Churches?" New Catholic World (217:1300, Jl.-Ag., 1974), pp. 152-55.   DHU/R

13004. "Demonstration by 'Action' - 'Black Sundays'--Inside Cath-olic Church." The Ecclesiastical Court Digest (8:1, Ja., 1970), p. 1.   DHU/R

13005. Denhardt, Robert B. and Jerome J. Salomone. "Race, In-authenticity, and Religious Cynicism." Phylon (33:1, 2nd Quarter, 1972), pp. 120-31.   DHU/MO

13006. Dennis, Lane and Ebeth Dennis. "Integration In the North Woods." Other Side (10:1, Ja.-Feb., 1974), pp. 34-39.
TxDaTS

13007. Deschner, John. "Ecclesiological Aspects of the Race Problem." International Review of Missions (59:235, Jl., 1970), pp. 285-95.   DHU/R

13008. De Wolf, L. Harold. Galatians: A Letter for Today. Grand Rapids, Mich.: William B. Eerdmans Publishing Co., 1971.   DHU/R
Describes the steps by which twentieth century man recog-nizes God's message to us. Throws light on many issues and among them the agony of friction between races.

13009. "A Dialogue on Race." Creative Resources CRC. 07,000 1971.   DLC
Phonotape.
Includes "The Liberation has Come" by Tom Skinner.

13010. Dittes, James E. Bias and Pious; the Relationship Between Prejudice and Religion. Minneapolis: Augsburg Pub. House, 1973.   MiBsA; MNtcA

13011. "Dr. Taylor Addresses World Meet, Liberia, Hits Racism." Pittsburgh Courier (Ag. 24, 1968).   Pam. File, DHU/R
President of the Progressive National Baptist Convention delivered an Address on "Racial Justice."

13012. Dole, Kenneth. "Baptist Image on Equality Disturbs Cleric." The Washington Post (Apr. 27, 1968).   Pam. File, DHU/R

13013. Doty, Robert C. "Pope Asks Vietnam Peace; Calls for an End of Racism." New York Times (Apr. 15, 1968).
Pam. File, DHU/R

13014. Dugan, George. "18 Negro Priests in Antibias Move." New York Times (Jl. 28, 1968).   Pam. File, DHU/R

13015. Dumond, Dwight Lowell. "Democracy and Christian Ethics." Journal of Negro History (46:1, Ja., 1961), pp. 1-11.   DHU

13016. Dunn, Larry. "Racism in the United States." Ceasar D. Coleman, (ed.). Beyond Blackness to Destiny: Study Guide (n.p.: Printed by Wimmer Bros., Memphis. n.d.).
Pam. File, DHU/R

13017. Duval, Armand. "Anthropologie a l'assaut du Racisme." Revue du Clerge Africain (36:2, Mr., 1971), pp. 113-41.   DHU/R

13018. Edwards, Herbert O. "Racism and Christian Ethics in America." Katallagete (Wint., 1971), pp. 15-24.   DHU/R
Negro author.

13019. Epps, B. Crandell. "Church can Heal Racial Injustice." Christian Science Journal (88:5, My., 1970), pp. 252-54.
DHU/R

13020. Ezell, Humphrey K. The Christian Problem of Segrega-tion. New York: Greenwich Book Publishers, 1959.
NN/Sch; CtY-D

13021. Faramelli, Norman J. "Needed in the Seventies: A Miss-ionary Strategy for the White Majority." Anglican Theological Review (Supplementary Series 2; Sept., 1973), pp. 1-15.
ViAlTH

13022. Fullinwider, S. P. The Mind and Mood of Black America. Homewood, Ill.: The Dorsey Press, 1969.   DHU/MO; DHU/R
Chapter 21, Racial Christianity.

13023. Gilmore, J. Herbert. They Chose to Live, The Racial Agony of an American Church. Michigan: William B. Eerd-mans Publishing Co., 1972.   DHU/R; NNCor; MNtcA; PPT
The tragedy and heroism of a Baptist Congregation's use of the gospel to deal with the problem of color.

13024. ----- When Love Prevails; a Pastor Speaks to a Church in Crisis. Grand Rapids: Eerdmans, 1971.
MiBsa; MNtcA; PPT
"Sermons were preached in the First Baptist Church in Birmingham, Alabama."

13025. Goodson, James Lenard. The Ideology of American Racial Integration. Masters thesis. Southwestern Baptist Theological Seminary, 1970.

13026. Graham, Jewel. "One Imperative - To Eliminate Racism." Y.M.C.A. Magazine (67:4, My.-Je., 1973), pp. 7-8. DHU/R
Report of the vice-president of Racial Justice Task Force of the Y.M.C.A.

13027. Greeley, A. "Civil Religion and Ethnic Americans." World View (Feb., 1973), p. 21.   DHU/R

13028. Grier, William and Price Cobbs. The Jesus Bag. New York: McGraw-Hill Book Co., 1971.   DHU/R
Chapter on Religion and the American Black Man.
Negro author.

13029. Griffin, John Howard. The Black Church and the Black Man. Dayton, O.: Pflaum, 1969.   DHU/R
Includes a recorded commentary of Rev. James Groppi and Rev. Albert Cleage.

13030. Hackett, Allen. For the Open Door. Philadelphia: United Church Press, 1964.   DLC

13031. Hadden, Jeffrey K. The Gathering Storm in the Churches. Garden City, N.Y.: Doubleday, 1969.   DHU/R

13032. Harrell, David E., Jr. White Sects and Black Men in the Recent South. Nashville: Vanderbilt University Press, 1971.
DHU/R

13033. Hill, Clifford, S. Race: A Christian Symposium; Edited by Clifford S. Hill & David Mathews. London: Gollanca, 1968.
DLC

13034. Hoge, Dean R. and Jackson W. Carroll. "Religiosity and Prejudice in Northern and Southern Churches." Journal for the Scientific Study of Religion (12:2, Je., 1973), pp. 181-97.
DHU/R

13035. Holtrop, Donald. Notes on Christian Racism. Grand Rapids, Mich.: Wm. B. Eerdmans Pub. Co., 1969.   DHU/R

13036. Hoover, Arlie J. "Science Joins Religion in Ranks of Prejudice." Christianity Today (17:6, Dec., 1972), pp. 12-15.
DHU/R

13037. Hyde, G. "Grace for Race." These Times (79; Nov., 1971), pp. 29+.
INE
Church and Christian responsibility

13038. Jackson, Jesse. "Christianity, the Church, and Racism." Religious Education (65:2, Mr.-Apr., 1970), pp. 90-98.
DJI/R

Negro author.

13039. Johnson, Wayne G. "Religion, Racism, and Self-Image: the Significance of Beliefs." Religious Education (68:5, Apr., 1970), pp. 620-30.
DHU/R

13040. Jones, G. Curtis. "Is Racism a Sin?" Link: A Magazine For Armed Forces Personnel (29:11, Nov., 1971), pp. 32-38.
Pam. File, DHU/R

13041. Jones, Howard O. Shall We Overcome? A Challenge to Negro and White Christians. Westwood, N. J.: F. F. Revell Co., 1966.   DLC; NN/Sch; DHU/R; DHU/MO

13042. Jurji, E. "Religious Convergence and the Course of Prejudice." Journal of the American Academy of Religion (37:2, (Je., 1969), pp. 119+.
DHU

13043. Kelsey, George D. Racism and the Christian Understanding of Man. New York: Scribner, 1965.
NcD; DHU/R; NN/Sch; CtY-D

13044. Kitagawa, Daisuke. The Pastor and the Race Issue. New York: Seabury Press, 1965.
DHU/R; InU; DLC; NN/Sch; CtY-D

13045. ----- "Racial Man in the Modern World." Paul T. Jersild and Dale A. Johnson, (eds.). Moral Issues and Christian Response (New York: Holt, Rinehart and Winston, 1971), pp. 241-49.
DHU/R

13046. Knowles, Louis L. and Kenneth Prewitt. Institutional Racism in America. Englewood Cliffs, N. J.: Prentice-Hall, Inc., 1969.
DHU/R

13047. Krebs, A. V. "Prejudice in the Pews; Sociologists Report." America (118; Je. 15, 1968), pp. 715-6.   DHU

13048. Kucharsky, David. "Evangelicals on Justice Socially Speaking..." Christianity Today (28:6, Dec., 21, 1973), pp. 38-40.
DHU/R
Adopted an order to strike out racism in the Church.

13049. Labbé, Dolores E. Jim Crow Comes to Church; the Establishment of Segregated Catholic Parishes in South Louisiana. Lafayette, La.: University of Southwestern Louisiana, 1971.
PPT

13050. Lecky, Robert S. and H. Elliott Wright. Can These Bones Live? New York: Sheed & Ward, 1969.   DHU/R
Pp. 142-159, "Black Man - White Church."

13051. LeDoux, Jerome. "The Roman Catholic Church and Black Self-Determination." Toward Wholeness: A Journal of Ministries to Blacks in Higher Education (2:1&2, Spr.-Sum., 1973), pp. 22-24.
DHU/R

13052. Legg, Sam. "Black Mistrust and White Justice." Friends Journal (15:23, Dec. 15, 1969), pp. 714-15.   DHU/R

13053. Lincoln, Charles Eric. "Aspects of American Pluralism." Journal of the Interdenominational Theological Center (1:2, Spr., 1974), pp. 17-26.   DHU/R
Black religion and the religious mainstream in America.

13054. Littell, Franklin H. Wild Tongues, A Handbook of Social Pathology. London: The Macmillan Co., 1969. DHU/R
Suggestions as to how the church can fight racism.

13055. Lucas, Lawrence. E. Black Priest, White Church; Catholics and Racism. New York: Random House, 1970.   DHU/R

13056. Maranell, Gary M. "An Examination of Some Religious and Political Attitude Corelates of Bigotry." Social Forces (45; Mr., 1967), pp. 356-62.   DHU

13057. Marrow, Alfred J. Changing Patterns of Prejudice. A New Look at To-Day's Racial Religious and Cultural Tensions. Philadelphia: Chilton, 1962.   DHU/R

13058. Martin, Douglas L. "The White Protestant Church and Black Freedom." Foundations (13:2, Apr.-Je., 1970), pp. 159-74.
DHU/R

13059. Martin, William C. Christians in Conflict. Chicago: Center for the Scientific Study of Religion, 1972.   MiBsA; DHU/R
Church and race problems in Rochester, New York.

13060. Mason, Philip. Chrisianity and Race. New York: St. Martin's Press, 1957.   DHU/R; DLC

13061. Mays, Benjamin Elijah. Disturbed About Man. Richmond, Va.: John Knox Press, 1969.   DHU/R
Last chapter, "The Church Amidst Ethnic and Racial Tensions."
Negro author.

13062. McDermott, Patrick P. "A New Encyclical on Social Justice." Christian Century (88:24, Je., 16, 1971), pp. 748-51. DHU/R
Includes statement on "Institutional Racism."

13063. McDowell, Edward A. "Myths About Race We Must Give Up." Baptist and Reflector (134; Jl. 18, 1968), p. 9.
KyLoS; TND

13064. ----- "The Race Problem and the Gospel." Baptist and Reflector (134; Je. 27, 1968), p. 5.   KyLoS; TND

13065. McFerran, D. "The Limits of Confrontation." Commonweal (97:2, Mr. 2, 1973), pp. 498-500.   DHU/R
A report on a classroom experiment in race and religion.

13066. "Missionaries Urged to Include Race Problems, Objectors in Program." Chicago Daily Defender (Dec. 21, 1968).
Pam. File, DHU/R

13067. Mitchell, Henry H. "The Cold, White Church." Register-Leader (148:7, Midsummer, 1966), pp. 14-15. DHU/R
Written by Negro Baptist minister, author of Black Preaching.

13068. Monsma, G. "The Christian, Discrimination, and Economic Injustice." Banner (Mr. 24, 1972), p. 16.   CtY-D; NN

13069. Morrison, George. "St. Louis Militants Tell Aims." Washington Post (Je. 2, 1969).   Pam. File, DHU/R
Demonstrate to show "Racism in Churches."

13070. Mott, Paul E., (ed.). American Society; Religion, Reward, and Race. Columbus, Ohio: Merrill, 1973.   ICT

13071. Mueller, Samuel A. and Joyce A. Swean. "Omnis America in Partes Tres Dursa Est." Christian Century (86:43, Oct. 22, 1969), pp. 342+.   DHU/R
"The nation is not divided into white and black camps; there is an important, if rather small middle camp, the white non-Christian."

13072. Mulder, John M. "Is White Racism Declining?" Theology Today (29:3, Oct., 1972), pp. 318-22.   DHU/R

13073. Nashville, Tenn. Vanderbilt University Divinity School. Racism, Racists and Theological Education. Nashville: Vanderbilt University Divinity School, 1971.   Pam. File, DHU/R Mim.
Papers and comments from Colloquium compiled in Nashville, Tenn. by Kelly Miller Smith, Asst. Dean. Held Feb. 11-12, 1971.

13074. National Conference on the Christian Way of Life. And Who is My Neighbor? An Outline for the Study of Race Relations in America. New York: Negro Universities Press, 1969.
                                                                DHU/R
Originally published in 1924. Includes Information on race and religious prejudice.

13075. "Negro Priest Assails Catholic Church as Racist." New York Times (Apr. 19, 1968).   Pam. File, DHU/R

13076. Norris, Hoke, (ed.). We Dissent. New York: St. Martin's Pr., 1963.   INU

13077. Oliver, C. Herbert. No Flesh Shall Glory. Nutley, N. J.: Presbyterian and Reformed Pub. Co., 1959.   CtY-D

13078. Pannell, William E. My Friend, the Enemy. Waco, Tex.: Word Books, 1968.   DLC

13079. Parham, T. David. "Removing Racial and Social Barriers Through Charismatic Renewal." New Covenant (3:12, Je., 1974), pp. 14-15.   DHU/R
Negro author.

13080. Paton, Alan. The Christian Approach to Racial Problems in the Modern World. London: Christian Action, 1959?
                                                                NN/Sch
"One of the Christian Action Stafford Cripps Memorial Lectures entitled 'The Christian and This World' which were delivered in St. Paul's Cathedral, in the autumn of 1959, before the St. Paul's Lecture Society."

13081. Pawlikowski, John T. Catechetics and Prejudice: How Catholic Teaching Materials View Jews, Protestants and Racial Minorities. Parmus, N. J.: Paulist/Newman Press, 1973.
                                                                DHU/R

13082. Pitcher, Alvin. "White Racism and Black Development." Religious Education (65:2, Mr.-Apr., 1970), pp. 84-89.
                                                                DHU/R

13083. Pope, Liston. The Kingdom Beyond Caste. New York: Friendship Press, 1957.   DHU/R; CtY-D
P. 81 - Church, race and democracy.

13084. "Precious in His Sight." Newsweek (76:6, Ag. 10, 1970), pp. 69-70.   DHU/R
Segregation in a Birmingham Baptist Church.

13085. Presbyterian Church in the United States. General Assembly. "Race, Racism and Repression." Church and Society (61: 1, Sept.-Oct. 1970), pp. 12-20.   Pam. File, DHU/R

13086. Race: Nation: Person, Social Aspects of the Race Problem. Freeport, N. Y.: Books For Libraries Press, 1971. DHU/R
Chapter 1, Racism, Law and Religion.

13087. "The Racial Crisis." Social Action (36:1, Sept. 1, 1969), pp. 23-29.   DHU/R

13088. Racism and White Christians; a Resource Study, by Students at Chicago Theological Seminary. Chicago: Chicago Theological Seminary, 1968.   PPT; I; DLC

13089. Reimers, David Morgan. White Protestantism and the Negro. New York: Oxford University Press, 1965.
                                        DHU/R; DLC; CtY-D; NN/Sch

13090. Religious Leadership Conference on Equality of Opportunity. Harriman, New York. Discrimination. What Can Churches Do? A Handbook and Report on the Religious Leadership Conference ...Arden House. Aug. 28-29, 1958. New York: Commission Against Discrimination, 1958.   DHU/MO

13091. Rice, Gene. "God in the Storm." The Journal of Religious Thought (26:2, Sum. Suppl., 1969), pp. 70-74.
A comparison of psalm 29 and present race relations in America.

13092. Robinson, James Herman. ... Love of This Land. Illustrated by Elton C. Fax. Philadelphia: Christian Education Press, 1956.   DHU/R
Church and race relations.
Negro author.

13093. Rogers, Cornish. "White Ethnics and Black Empowerment." Christian Century (87:46, Nov. 18, 1970), pp. 1380-81.   DHU/R

13094. Root, Meganne. "Racism in the Curriculum - An Attempt at Change." The Y.W.C.A. Magazine (66:3, Mr., 1972), pp. 8+.
                                                                DHU/R

13095. Root, Robert. Progress Against Prejudice; the Church Confronts the Race Problem. New York: Friendship Press, 1957.
                                        DHU/R; DLC; NN/Sch

13096. Rose, Benjamin Lacy. Racial Segregation in the Church. Richmond, Va.: Outlook Pub., 1957.   CtY-D

13097. Rowland, Stanley J. Land in Search of God. New York: Random House, 1958.   NN/Sch

13098. Roy, Ralph Lord. Apostles of Discord; a Study of Organized Bigotry and Disruption on the Fringes of Protestantism. Boston: Beacon Press, 1953.   DLC
Beacon studies in church and state. "Originally...the author's thesis."

13099. Russell, Jean. God's Lost Cause: A Study of the Church and the Racial Problem. London: S. C. M. Press, 1968.
                                        DHU/R; DLC; CtY-D; NcD

13100. Saffen, Wayne. "Campus Ministry and the University in the Mutual Task of Liberation." Concordia Theological Monthly (43:7, Jl.-Ag., 1972, pp. 419-29.   DHU/R
Author is Lutheran campus pastor, University of Chicago. Challenges both the Church and the University to become agents of God's program of setting people free.

13101. St. Julien, Aline. "Holy Mother the Church ... An Unfit Mother?" Freeing the Spirit (3:2, Sum., 1974), pp. 5-9.
                                                                DHU/R
Written by a black Catholic. Questions if Black Catholics can keep their identity in a white racist church.

13102. Salley, Columbus & Ronald Behm. Your God is Too White. Downers Grove, Ill.: Inter-Varsity Press, 1970. DHU/R
Racial Crisis in America written by two evangelicals, one black and the other white.

13103. Satterwhite, John H. "For Authentic Freedom: COCU and Black Churches." Christian Century (87:8, Feb. 25, 1970), p. 236.   DHU/R

13104. Schulze, Andrew. Fire From the Throne: Race Relations in the Church. St. Louis: Concordia Pub. House, 1968.
                                        NcD; DLC; MiBsA; NNCor; PPT

13105. Scott, Charles E. "The Experience of Racism." Religion in Life (41:2, Sum., 1972), pp. 179-85.   DHU/R
Author is professor of philosophy at Vanderbilt University.

13106. Scott, James A. "Racism, the Church, and Educational Strategies." Foundations (17:3, Jl.-Sept., 1974), pp. 268-80.
DHU/R

13107. Seiler, J. E. "The Church-Racist or Christian." Church Management (46:5, Feg., 1970), pp. 22+.   DHU/R

13108. Sessions, R. P. "Are Southern Ministers Failing in the South?" Saturday Evening Post (234; My. 13, 1961), p. 37.
DHU

13109. Setiloane, Gabriel M. "A Personal Encounter With Racism." International Review of Mission (59:235, Jl. 1970), pp. 324-32.
DHU/R
African minister discusses racism and church in England.

13110. Shockley, Donald G. "First Baptist, Birmingham; A Case Study of Wineskins Bursting." Christian Century (87:48, Dec. 2, 1970), pp. 1462-3.   DHU/R
White minister resigns because church membership refuses to adopt open membership.

13111. Shriver, Donald W. "Southern Churches in Transition." New South (25:1, Wint., 1970), pp. 40-47.   DHU/R

13112. Skinner, Tom. Black and Free. Grand Rapids, Mich.: Eerdman's, 1968.   DHU/R
Negro author.

13113. ----- "Called to be a Miltant." Lutheran Standard (129; Nov., 1971), pp. 3+.   IMC

13114. ----- "Christ is the Answer." The American Baptist (171:9, Oct., 1973), pp. 7-8+.   DHU/R
Written by a Negro evangelist.

13115. ----- "Evangelism, Racial Crisis and World Evangelism." The Message Magazine (40:6, Sept., 1974), pp. 40-48.   DHU/R

13116. ----- How Black is the Gospel? Philadelphia: J. B. Lippincott Co., 1970.   DHU/R

13117. ----- "I Preach the White Man's Religion." Christian Life (28; Jl., 1966), pp. 21-25.   Pam. File, DHU/R

13118. ----- Now I'm Free. Seattle, Wash.: Life Messengers, 1968.   Pam. File, DHU/R

13119 ----- "Why We Must Win the American Negro." Moody Monthly (68; Apr., 1968), pp. 34-7.   DHU/R

13120. ----- Words of Revolution. Grand Rapids, Mich.: Zondervan Pub. House, 1970.   DHU/R

13121. Spear, Allan H. Black Chicago: The Making of a Negro Ghetto, 1890-1920. Chicago: The University Press, 1967.
DHU/R
For a treatment of the Black Church in Chicago as an aspect of the Institutional Ghetto, see pp. 91-97; and the effect of Negro migration from the South on ghetto churches in Chicago, pp. 174-79.

13122. Spivey, Charles S., Jr. "Ecumenism and Racism." Christian Century (91:16, Apr. 24, 1974), pp. 459-60.   DHU/R
Letter to the editor written by black executive director of the Chicago Church Federation.

13123. Stauffer, Robert E. "Civil Religion Technocracy, and the Private Sphere: Further Comments on Cultural Integration in Advanced Societies." Journal for the Scientific Study of Religion (12; 4, Dec., 1973), pp. 415-25.   DHU/R

13124. Stegall, W. "Baptism, Race and the East Bay." Pulpit (Feb., 1969), p. 4.   DAU/W

13125. Stith, Moses. "Ministering to Blacks in a White Setting." Toward Wholeness: A Journal of Ministries to Blacks in Higher Education (2:1&2, Spr.-Sum., 1973), pp. 25-28.   DHU/R

13126. Strickland, Bonnie R. and Sallie Cone Weddell. "Religious Orientation and Prejudice Among Baptists and Unitarians." Journal for the Scientific Study of Religion (11:4, Dec., 1972), pp. 395-99.   DHU/R

13127. Stringfellow, William. "Harlem Rebellion and Resurrection." Christian Century (87:45, Nov. 11, 1970), pp. 1345-48.   DHU/R
Fourteenth article in a series, How My Mind Has Changed.

13128. ----- My People is the Enemy: An Autobiographical Polemic. New York: Holt, 1964.   DHU/R; CtY-D
An indictment of the Christian response to racial crisis.

13129. Swan, C. "Integration Begins With the Individual." Christian Science Journal (89:5, My., 1971), pp. 225-28.   DHU/R

13130. Tate, Eugene. "More Prejudice in Church? Yes and No." Christian Advocate (18:7, Mr. 29, 1973), pp. 11-13.
Pam. File, DHU/R; DAU/W

13131. "Their Brother's Brother." Home Missions (43:4, Apr., 1972), pp. 37-39.   Pam. File, DHU/R

13132. United Methodist Church. Commission on Religion and Race. An Experiment in Relevance. Black Community Developers.
Pam. File, DHU/R
Mim.
"A report to the 1972 General Conference of the United Methodist Church."

13133. Vanderbilt University. Divinity School. Racism, Racists and Theological Education.   Pam. File, DHU/R
mim.
"Kelly Miller Smith, Asst. Dean, editor. Speeches given at Colloquium, February 11 and 12, 1971."

13134. Verkuyl, Johannes. Break Down the Walls; a Christian Cry for Racial Justice. Grand Rapids: W. B. Eerdmans Pub. Co., 1973.   MiBsA; DHU/R; MNtcA

13135. Vivian, C. T. America's Joseph. Philadelphia: Fortress Press, 1971.   DHU/R
Parallels the social and religious situation today with the O. T. account of Joseph and his brothers.
Negro author.

13136. Walker, Jerald C. "White Racism: An Overstress?" Christian Advocate (13:1, Ja. 9, 1969), pp. 9-10.   Pam. File, DHU/R

13137. Watson, Bill. "Digging at the Roots of White Racism." Friends Journal (16:6, Sept. 15, 1970), p. 500.
Formation of Society of Friends new race relations committee, Friends for Human Justice.

13138. West, Elmer S., Jr. "Will Your Church Have a Race Relations Emphasis?" Church Administration (14:5, Feb., 1972), pp. 32-33.   DHU/R

13139. "What the Churches Are Doing on the Crisis Front." Journal of Religious Education (29:4, Je.-Ag., 1969), p. 13.   DHU/R

13140. "White Churches." Harry A. Ploski (ed.). Reference Library of Black America (New York: Bellwether Pub. Co., Inc., 1971), Book 2, p. 204.   DHU

13141. White, Ellen G. "The Gospel Jesus Disapproves of Hatred and Bigotry." The Message Magazine (40:6, Sept., 1974), pp. 36-37.   DHU/R

13142. White, Willie. "Separate Unto God." Christian Century (91:6, Feb. 13, 1974), pp. 179-81.   DHU/R
"Its God's purpose that stands opposed to any thorough going ecumenical approach between the black and white churches of America."

13143. Whitman, Frederick L. "Subdimensions of Religiosity and Race Prejudice." Review of Religious Research (3; Spr., 1962), pp. 166-74.   DHU/R

13144. Witt, Raymond H. It Ain't Been Easy, Charlie. New York: Pageant Press, 1965.   DHU/MO; DLC
       Church and race problems, Chicago.

13145. Wood, J. R. "Personal Commitment and Organizational Constraint; Church Officials and Racial Integration." Sociolog-

ical Analysis (33; Fall, 1972), pp. 142-51.
                                    DHU; DGU; DCU; DAU

13146. Wright, Nathan. Let's Face Racism. Camden, N. J.: Thomas Nelson, 1970.   DHU/R
       Negro author.

13147. Young, Andrew J., Jr. Racism in the Church. Pittsburgh: Thesis Theological Cassettes, 1970.   T Sew U-T
       Thesis theological cassettes, v. 2. no. 2.

E. GENERAL

13148. Ames, Wilmer C. "Directions in Religion." Essence (4:8, Dec., 1973), pp. 40-41+.   Pam. File, DHU/R
       Christianity and Christmas.

13149. "Baptists are Urged to Study Carefully Before Casting Vote." Atlanta Constitution (Sept. 7, 1968).   Pam. File, DHU/R

13150. Basen, Carol. Showdown at Seattle. New York: Seabury Press, 1968.   DLC; NcD
       Prepared under the auspices of the Executive Council of the Episcopal Church.
       Reports, including excerpts from the proceedings, of the meeting of the women of the church during the National Convention of the Protestant Episcopal Church in the U. S. A., Seattle, September 1967.

13151. Beasley, Yvonne. "Black Youth Ministries." Colloquy (6:3, Mr., 1973), pp. 32-33.   DHU/R

13152. Becker, William H. "The Black Church: Manhood and Mission." Journal of the American Academy of Religion (40:3, Sept., 1972), pp. 316-33.   DHU/R

13153. Bennink, Richard John. "The Minister and His Role." The Reformed Review (23:1, Fall, 1969), pp. 56+.   DHU/R

13154. Block, Arthur. "Sister, Are You Black or White." America (128:3, Ja., 1973), pp. 60-63.   DHU/R
       A white Catholic sister experiences as a teacher in race relations.

13155. Boyd, Malcolm. Human Like Me, Jesus; Prayers with Notes on the Humanistic Revolution. New York: Simon and Schuster, 1971.   DHU/R
       "Prayers in a black student center," pp. 69-81.

13156. Camara, Helder. The Church and Colonialism; the Betrayal of the Third World. Denville, N. J.: Dimension Books, 1969.
                                                            DLC

13157. Carr, Oscar C. "The Church, Mission, Race and Me." The Lamp (68:3, Mr., 1970), pp. 20+.   DHU/R
       A concerned churchman and southerner makes a plea for love and understanding of all men - even racists.

13158. Carroll, Edward G. "Spiritual Training in the Seminary." Nexus, Alumni Magazine of Boston University, Sch. of Theology (16:1, Wint., 1972-73), pp. 6-7+.   Pam. File, DHU/R
       Written by Negro bishop of the Boston area of U. Methodist Church.

13159. Chamberlain, Gary L. "Has 'Benign Neglect' Invaded the Churches?" Christian Century (91:16, Apr. 24, 1974), pp. 448-51.   DHU/R
       "Despite the appointment or election of some blacks to key positions... Church programs by and large have failed to deal at the parish level with the issue of racism."

13160. ----- Institutional Change and Christian Social Ethics: Model for Racial Justice. Doctoral Dissertation. Graduate Theological Union, 1972.

13161. Cobb, Charles E. "Racial Justice." Christian Century (91:1, Ja. 2-9, 1974), p. 8.   DHU/R
       Written in a series of articles, "What's in Store for 74?"

by the executive director of the UCC's Commission for Racial Justice.

13162. Cone, James H. "Political Christian Theology." James R. Ross, (ed.). The War Within (New York: Sheed & Word, 1971), pp. 90-111.   DLC
       Negro author.

13163. Conrad, Robert L. "Race and the Institutional Church." Concordia Theological Monthly (39:2, Dec., 1968), pp. 762-71.
                                                            DHU/R

13164. Davis, Joseph Morgan. "Getting Ourselves Together." Freeing the Spirit (1:3, Sum., 1972), pp. 43-49.   DHU/R

13165. ----- "The Position of the Catholic Church in the Black Community." Freeing the Spirit (1:3, Sum., 1972), pp. 19-24.
                                                            DHU/R

13166. De Laney, Moses N. Social Interaction of Three Denominations in the Inner City. Doctoral dissertation. Shaw University, 1959.

13167. Del Negro, Helena. "A Genuinely Integrated Church. Christian Science Journal (89:10, Oct., 1971), pp. 524-26.
                                                            DHU/MO

13168. Dole, Kenneth. "Reason Urged on Racial Unit." Washington Post (Feb. 24, 1968).   Pam. File, DHU/R

13169. Ekaete, Genevieve. "Growing Up With Two Religions and Ending Up With None." Essence (4:8, Dec., 1973), pp. 58-59+.
                                            Pam. File, DHU/R
       Negroes and religion in America.

13170. Freire, Paulo. "Cultural Action for Freedom." Harvard Educational Review (40:2, My., 1970), pp. 205-26.   DHU

13171. Gayle, Addison. The Black Situation. New York: Horizon Press, 1970.   DLC

13172. Hanson, Geddes. "Black Seminarians and the Crisis Theological Education." Dimension, Theology in Church and World (6:1, Fall, 1968), pp. 41-6.   Pam. File, DHU/R

13173. Hargrove, Barbara W. Reformation of the Holy; A Sociology of Religion. Philadelphia: F. A. Davis Co., 1971.   DHU/R
       Chapter 16, The Black Church.

13174. Harrison, Ira E. Church Types Among Negroes in Syracuse, New York. Syracuse, N. Y.: Youth Development Center, Syracuse University, Apr., 1962.   NSyU
       Mim.

13175. Harwell, Jack U. "Prayer, Patience Needed in School Integration." (Editorial) The Christian Index (148; Jl. 24, 1969), p. 6.   DHU/R

13176. Hecht, James L. "A Catholic Challenge: Open Housing." America (128:5, Feb. 10, 1973), pp. 112-14.   DHU/R

13177. Henderson, Lawrence W. "The Identity Crisis of African and American Churches." Missionary Research Library Occasional Bulletin (22:11, Nov. 9, 1971), pp. 1-6.   DHU/R

13178. Herzog, Frederick. "The Burden of Southern Theology: A Response." Duke Divinity School Review (38:3, Fall, 1973), pp. 151-70.   Pam. File, DHU/R

13179. Hicks, Richard Ross. "New Mood of College Students; a Black View Point." Christian Century (90:19, My. 9, 1973), pp. 538-9.
DHU/R
Negro author.

13180. ----- "Problems Related to Funding Local Ministries on Predominantly Black Campuses." Toward Wholeness: A Journal of Ministries to Blacks in Higher Education (2:1&2, Spr. -Sum., 1973), pp. 15-17.   DHU/R

13181. Horton, Frank L. "The Black Church and Community Colleges. Toward Wholeness: A Journal of Ministries to Blacks in Higher Education (2:1&2, Spr.-Sum., 1973), pp. 18-21.   DHU/R

13182. Jackson, Agnes M. "To See the "Me" in "Thee"; Challenge to All White Americans, or, White Ethnicity From a Black Perspective and a Sometimes Response to Michael Novak." Soundings (56:1, Spr., 1973), pp. 21-44.   DHU/R

13183. Jackson, Harold A., Jr. "Religious Symbols and the Black Experience." Religion in Life (61:1, Spr., 1972), pp. 29-36.
DHU/R

13184. Jackson, Jesse. (Speech.) Imamu Amiri Baraka (LeRoi Jones), (ed.). African Congress. A Documentary of the First Modern Pan-African Congress (New York: Wm. Morrow & Co., 1972), pp. 22-34.   DHU/R

13185. Jefferson, Frederick D. "Faith and Reconciliation in Black and White." McCormick Quarterly (22:4, My., 1969), pp. 253-62.   DHU/R

13186. Jenks, Philip E. "Evangelical Social Concerns." The American Baptist Magazine (172:4, Apr., 1974), pp. 42+.   DHU/R
"A Declaration of Evangelical Social Concern which exhorts evangelicals to demonstrate the social and political injustice of our nation. Signed by many conservative evangelists."

13187. Jones, Lawrence N. "To Seize the Times." Theological Education (9:4 suppl., Sum., 1973), pp. 333-39.   DHU/R
Black scholars, students and theological education.
Negro author.

13188. Kaufmann, Leonard. "Theological Education in the 1970's." African Ecclesiastical Review (15:3, 1973), pp. 250-58. DHU/R
Article questions changes necessary to make Catholicity significant in the Third World.

13189. Keeley, Benjamin J. "Reactions of a Group of White Parishioners Toward the Acceptance of a Negro as Pastor." Sociology and Social Research (55:2, 1971), pp. 216-28.
DAU/ DCU/SW; DGU; DGW; DHU

13190. Kenyatta, Mary. "On Liberation and Black Women." Church and Society (62:3, Ja.-Feb., 1972), pp. 21-24.   DHU/R
Author is co-director of Project WIL (Women in Leadership), Board of Christian Education United Presbyterian Church, U. S. A.

13191. Knight, Walker L. "The Unfiltered Experience." Home Missions (43:4, Apr., 1972), p. 40.   Pam. File, DHU/R
The changing relationships between Southern Baptists and Blacks.

13192. Korby, Kenneth F. "Different Ministries, Different Means, One God: A Theological Opinion on the Racial Issue." Concordia Theological Monthly (41:2, Feb., 1970), pp. 86+.   DHU/R

13193. Kuhn, Harold B. "Subcultures and Counterculture, a Christian Response." Asbury Seminarian (25; Oct., 1971), pp. 6-19.
IEG; IW

13194. Langhorne, George. "The Black Campus Minister, A Pastoral Counselor." Toward Wholeness: A Journal of Ministries to

Blacks in Higher Education (2:1&2, Spr. -Sum., 1973), pp. 31-33.
DHU/R

13195. Leas, Speed B. "The Missionary and the Black Man." Malcolm Boyd, (ed.). The Underground Church (New York: Sheed & Ward, 1968), pp. 159-76.   DHU/R
"The ghetto church's ministry must be a mission not only to the colonized but also to the colonizers."

13196. Leffall, Dolores C. Focus on The Black Church. An Annotated Bibliography. Wash., D. C.: Minority Research Center, Inc., 1973.   DHU/R; DHU/MO
"Minority Group Series."
Negro author.

13197. Lester, W. Sybel. The Black Church Gang. Phila.: House of Geminia, 1972.   ULC
Includes material on black clergy.

13198. "Let the Church Say Amen!" Produced and directed by David W. Briddell and St. Clair Bourne. A Chamba Productions Film for the United Methodist Church, 1973.
Color. 78 minutes film.
Black people and how they see the role of contemporary Black church.

13199. Lincoln, C. Eric. The Black Church Since Frazier. New York: Schocken Books, 1974.   DHU/R

13200. Lyles, James V. "Black Survival at Stake." The Christian Century (89:29, Ag. 16, 1972), pp. 815-16.   DHU/R
"Metropolitan Negro minister of the United Methodist Church's Milwaukee district." Comments on the "recent disclosure of U. S. Public Health Service study in which 400 black men were denied treatment for syphillis".

13201. Marr, Warren, II. "Which Way to Equality?" United Church Herald (13:3, Mr. 1, 1970), p. 13.   DHU/R
Present racial program of American Missionary Association.

13202. Mayo, Robert. "Symbols and the Ministry to Blacks in Higher Education." Toward Wholeness (1:1, Sum., 1972), pp. 16-19.
DHU/R

13203. Mbiti, John. "Theological Impotence and the Universality of the Church." Lutheran World (21:3, 1974), pp. 251-60.
Pam. File, DHU/R

13204. Merton, Thomas. Faith and Violence, Christian Teaching and Christian Practice. Notre Dame, Ind.: University of Notre Dame, 1968.   DHU/R
Part I includes, "Non-violence and the Christian Conscience,"; Part III, "From Non-Violence to Black Power" and "Religion and Race in the United States."

13205. Metropolitan New York Conference on Religion and Race: 1964. Proceedings. New York: Conference Secretariat, New York City Youth Board, 1964.   DLC; NNUT

13206. Mid-Peninsula Christian Ministry. "Institutional Racism in American Society." Paul T. Jersild and Dale A. Johnson (eds.). Moral Issues and Christian Response (New York: Holt, Rinehart, and Winston, 1971), pp. 254-68.   DHU/R

13207. Mitchell, Henry H. "Key Term in Theological Education for the Negro: Compensatory." Christian Century (84:17, Apr. 26, 1967), pp. 530-33.   DHU/R

13208. Mueller, Samuel A. "Busing, School Prayer, and Wallace: Some Notes on Right-Wing Populism." Christian Century (89: 16, Apr. 19, 1972), pp. 451-54.   DHU/R

13209. National Conference of Catholic Bishops. "What the Bishops Did and Didn't." America (127:18, Dec. 2, 1972), pp. 462-65.
DHU/R
Includes discussions on civil rights, sanctions against Rhodesia and the question of Uganda.

13210. Nelsen, Hart M. and Lynda Dickson. "Attitudes of Black Catholics and Protestants; Evidence for Religious Identity." Sociological Analysis (33; Fall, 1972), pp. 152-65.
DAU; DCU/SW; DGU; DHU
A bibliography.

13211. "New Black History Museum Is a Part of Unitarian-Universalist History." Unitarian-Universalist Association (Oct. 28, 1969), p. 6.   Pam. File, DHU/R

13212. Ntwasa, Sabelo. "Some Thoughts on the Training of Black Ministers Today." Presence (5:3, 1972), pp. 30-32.   DHU/R

13213. ----- "Training of Black Ministers Today." International Review of Mission (61:242, Apr., 1972), pp. 177-82.   DHU/R

13214. Perkins, Benjamin Paul. Black Christians' Tragedies. New York: Exposition Press, 1972.
MNtcA; MH-AH; MBU-T; DHU/R; NjP; CLU
"An analysis of black youth and their churches."

13215. Perkins, John. "Integration or Development." Other Side (10:7, Ja.-Feb., 1974), pp. 10-13.   TxDaTS

13216. "Progressive National Baptists Elect Dr. E. R. Searcy, President." Atlanta World (Sept. 10, 1968).
Pam. File; DHU/R

13217. Quebedeaux, Richard. "Evangelicals: Ecumenical Allies." Christianity and Crisis (31:22, Dec., 1971), pp. 286-88.
Pam. File, DHU/R
Article about the acceptance of Blacks and other minorities into ecumenical leadership.

13218. "Race Rift Grows, Lindsay Asserts." New York Times (Apr. 23, 1968).   Pam. File, DHU/R
Governor's Speech to Inter-Faith Group.

13219. Roberts, James Deotis, Sr. Opening Closed Doors. Missouri: Christian Board of Publication, 1973.   DHU/R
Chapter V, Black/White Encounter.

13220. Rogers, Cornish. "Is the Church Failing the Black Students." Christian Century (90:17, Apr. 25, 1973), pp. 469-70. DHU/R

13221. ----- "Toward Tribalism?" The Christian Century (89:27, Jl. 19, 1972), pp. 769-70.   DHU/R
Relates how the various religious, social, and racial groups tend to work only for their own interests.

13222. Rogers, Robert L. "Chicago Ecumenism: Changes in Style and Agenda." Christian Century (88:20, My. 19, 1971), pp. 626-28.
Author analyzes the changes in Chicago's "ecumenism" around the issue of race.

13223. Rooks, Charles Shelby. "Crisis in Theological Education." City of God (3:1, Ag., 1970), pp. 7-17.   Pam. File; DHU/R
Negro author.

13224. Ruether, Rosemary R. "Liberation Theology and the Third World. Rich Nations/Poor Nations and the Exploitation of the Earth." Dialog: A Journal of Theology (13:3, Sum., 1974), pp. 201-07.   DHU/R

13225. ----- "The Messianic Core." Commonweal (91:15, Ja. 16, 1970), pp. 423+.   DHU/R
The left tradition in church and society.

13226. ----- "The Search for Soul Power in the White Community." Christianity and Crisis (30:7, Apr. 27, 1970), pp. 83-5. DHU/R

13227. Simms, James. "Black Preaching on the College Campus." Toward Wholeness: A Journal of Ministries to Blacks in Higher Education (2:1&2, Spr.-Sum., 1973), pp. 29-30.   DHU/R

13228. Smith, Cecil R., Jr. "Black Separatism and the Future of Integration." Friends Journal (19:11, Je. 1-15, 1973), pp. 324-25.   DHU/R

13229. Snowden, R. Grady, Jr. "An Appraisal of the Inter-racial Bible Conference." Florida Baptist Witness (86; Nov. 20, 1969), p. 10.   FU; LNB; TND

13230. Stepp, Diane. "Decatur Baptist Became Relevant." Atlanta Constitution (Ag. 31, 1968).   Pam. File; DHU/R

13231. Stokes, Olivia P. "Education of Blacks in the Household of Faith." Spectrum (47:4, Jl., 1971), pp. 5-7+.   DHU/R

13232. "Survey of Church Union Negotiations, 1969-1971." The Ecumenical Review (24:3, Jl., 1972), pp. 353-58. DHU/R

13233. "Transfer of Church and Property by Church Society to Black Group." The Ecclesiastical Court Digest (8:9, Sept., 1970), p. 2.   DHU/R.
About the Unitarian Church.

13234. Travis, Paul D. "Baptist Higher Education and Minorities: Finding a Future in the Past." The Southern Baptist Educator (36; Nov., 1972), pp. 3+.

13235. Trudgian, Raymond. "Religious Education for a Multi-Racial Society. Learning for Living (9:1, Sept., 1969), pp. 19+.
DHU/R

13236. "Unrest Hits America's Negro Churches." U. S. News and World Report (73; Sept. 25, 1972), pp. 45-48.   DHU

13237. Warren, Mervyn Alonzo. "Civil Wars and the Church." Frontier (16; Feb., 1973), pp. 7-10.   DCU/TH

13238. Wattenberg, Ben J. & Richard M. Scammon. "Black Progress and Liberal Rhetoric." Commentary (55:4, Apr., 1973), pp. 35-44.   DHU/R

13239. White, Woodie W. "Black and White Merger at Any Cost." Christian Advocate (13:20, Oct. 16, 1969), p. 9.   DHU/R

13240. Whittington, Frank J. "Rebellion, Religiosity, and Racial Prejudice." Afro-American Studies (1:2, Oct., 1970), pp. 139-46.   DHU/MO

13241. Williams, Hosea L. "The Relevancy of the Black Church to the New Generation." William M. Philpot (ed.). Best Black Sermons (Valley Forge: Judson Press, 1972), pp. 78-86.
DHU/R
A sermon. Baptist minister.

13242. Williams, Willard A. (ed.) Educational Ministry in the Black Community. Resource Booklet. Nashville, Tenn.: Board of Education of the United Methodist Church, 1972.
DHU/R
Program for use in local churches to upgrade Christian Education in the Black Community.

I-B.   Davis, Raymond J. Fire on the Mountains. Grand Rapids, Mich.: Zondervan Pub. Co., 1966. DHU/R; MN+CA
       The story of a miracle in the church of Ethiopia. Written by the general director of the Sudan Interior Mission, who has been a missionary in Africa since 1934.

I-E1a. Christol, Frank. ...Quatre ans au Cameroun. Paris: Société des Missions Evangéliques de Paris, 1922. NN/Sch

I-E1p. "Crisis in the Soudan." The Christian Intelligencer (78:52, Dec. 23, 1908), p. 849.   DHU/R
       Call for Christian evangelism in the Soudan.

I-E1p. Dieterlen, Germaine. Essai sur la Religion Bambara. Paris: Presses Universitaires de France, 1951.   DHU/MO
       An account of the religious myths and beliefs of the Bambara tribe in the Sudan.

I-E1p. Moor, Vincent de. La Croisière Bleue et les Missions d'Afrique. Paris: Desclee, De Bourwer & cie, 1932.
                                                               NN/Sch

I-E1s. Clayborn, John H. Two in One, Bright and Dark Side of West Africa, by John H. Clayborn Presiding Bishop, 14th Episcopal District. Little Rock, Ark.: D. M. Wells & Sons, 1945.   OWibfU
       "Report to the bishops of the A. M. E. Church of the first visit to the 14th Episcopal District to Africa."

I-E1s. Presbyterian Church in the U.S.A. Synod of New York and New Jersey. An Address to the Public, on the Subject of the African School, Lately Established Under the Care of the Synod of New York and New Jersey. By the directors of the Institution. New York: Printed by J. Seymour, 1816.
                                                               NNUT
       "Signed by James Richards, President. Edward D. Griffin, Sec. Newark, N.J. Oct. 21, 1816."

I-E2.   Fraser, Elizabeth. "The Ahmadiyya Movement in Nigeria." K. Kirbwood, (ed.). African Affairs (St. Antony's Papers, No. 10) London: Chatto and Windus, 1961, pp. 60-88.
                                                               DHU/MO

I-E3b. O'Grady, Desmond. "Conscience Crunch in Mozambique." U. S. Catholic (38:6, Je., 1973), pp. 30-33. Pam. File.
                                                               DHU/R

I-E3b. Perret, Edmond. "The Faithful Witness of the Presbyterian Church of Mozambique." Church and Society. (64:6, Jl.-Ag., 1974), pp. 8-17.   DHU/R

I-E3b. "Shedding the Protector." America (124; Je. 19, 1971), p. 622.   DHU/R
       "Missions in Mozambique."

I-E3b. Triggs, W. "Rome and Colonialism; the Protesting Missionaries in Mozambique." Christian Century (88; Jl. 7, 1971), pp. 824-25.
                                                               DHU/R

I-E3b. Wright, Marcia. "Nyakusa Cults and Politics in the Later Nineteenth Century." Terence O. Ranger and I. Kimambo, (eds.). Historical Study of African Religion (Berkeley: Univ. of Calif. Press, 1972), pp. 153-70.   DHU/R

I-E3c. Harlin, Tord. Spirit and Truth. Religious Attitudes and Life Involvements of 2,200 African Students. Uppsala: Scaninavian Institute of African Studies, 1973.   DLC

I-E3c. Lehmann, Dorothea. "Alice Lenshina Mulenga and the Lumpa Church." John V. Taylor and Dorothea Lehmann. Christians of the Copperbelt (London: n.p., 1961), pp. 248-68.   DHU/R

I-E3d. Cruise O'Brien, Donal B. The Mourides of Senegal. Oxford: Clarendon Press, 1971.   DHU/R; DLC
       A sociological account of the structure of religious authority and of the relations surrounding economic production of the Brotherhood.

I-E3e. "Black Churchmen Demand Reparation." African Opinion (10; Oct./Nov., 1973), p. 6.

II-D15. Bourne, George. Man Stealing and Slavery Denounced by the Presbyterian and Methodist Churches, Together with an Address to All the Churches. Boston: Garrison & Knapp, 1834.   DHU/MO; DLC; NN/Sch; NcD

III-A1a.i Caldwell, Josiah S., (bp.). "Financial Department of the A. M. E. Zion Church." I. G. Penn. The United Negro (Atlanta: Luther, 1902), pp. 524+.
       Negro author.

III-C1e. DuBois, William E. B. "How Negroes Have Taken Advantage of Educational Opportunities Offered by Friends." Journal of Negro Education (6:1, Ja. 1938), pp. 124-131.
                                                               DHU/MO

       Negro author.

III-D. Ashley Montagu, M. F. "Racism, Religion and Anthropology." Phylon (8:3, 3rd Quarter, 1947), pp. 230-38.
                                                               DHU/MO

IV-B.   "A Good Journey to Martin Luther King, Jr." Liberation (3:12, Feb., 1959), p. 19.   DHU/R

IV-B.   "When Dr. King Went to Jail Again." U. S. News and World Report (53; Jl. 23, 1962), p. 10.   DHU

Africa Inter-Mennonite Mission, Inc. (Formerly Congo Inland Mission). Reports of work in Zaire from 1911-. InELkB

African Methodist Episcopal Church. Controversy between A. M. E. Church and Methodist Episcopal Church in Philadelphia. PHi

---- Publications of this Body Printed in America Before 1801 are Available in this Library in the Readex Microprint Edition of Early American Imprints Published by the American Antiquarian Society.
This Collection is Arranged According to the Numbers in Charles Evans' American Bibliography. DLC

---- Unpublished materials and manuscripts. OWibfU

African Methodist Episcopal Zion Church. Unpublished materials and manuscripts. NcSalL; NN

Richard Allen. Sermons, letters and church records of Mother Bethel A. M. E. Church, Philadelphia, Pa. PHi

---- and Absalom Jones. To the People of Colour. Mms. NN/Sch

American Baptist Missionary Union. Annual Reports, 1826-1906. 20 Vols. Proceedings of the Baptist Board of Foreign Missions. Also, proceedings of its successor after 1845, the American Baptist Mission Society. Includes information relating to mission work in Africa and Negro Baptists in America. PV

American Board of Commissioners for Foreign Missions. Records, 1810-. MH-H

American Church Records. Personnel statistics and development in microfilm. Collected and edited by A. T. Degroot. Many church periodicals otherwise unavailable. DLC
Microfilms available in most theological libraries.

American Colonization Papers. Includes information on Negro ministers and churches. DLC

American Home Missionary Society. See Congregational Home Missionary Society.

American Missionary Association Archives. Letters, reports, minutes and other archival materials on the A. M. A. Also information on evangelistic abolitionism (particularly as it affected the Northern Protestant Churches). LOAA

American Negro Historical Society. Records, 1790-1901. Ca. 3000 items. Includes material on the First and Second African Presbyterian Churches of Philadelphia. PHi

American Sunday School Union. Records, 1877-1932. Includes letters and reports from missionaries regarding their work with Indians and Negroes in frontier areas, and foreign lands. PPPrHi

Anti-Slavery Materials. Mms. Letters, diaries. Tract Repository (24-issues, 1893-1895). Issued at Philadelphia to furnish Freedmen with reading material. INRE

Atlanta, Georgia. Negro Young People's Christian and Educational Congress. Scrapbook and newspaper clippings of meeting held August 6-12, 1902. DHU/MO

Gustav Auzenne Papers, 1929-45. (Professor of Business, Howard University). Letters written to the Pope requesting that a church and school for Negroes be erected at Frilot Cove, St. Landry Parish, Louisiana. DHU/MO

Baltimore, Md. St. James First African Protestant Episcopal Church. Records, September 15, 1826 to May 29, 1829. Record of founding, constitution and deed. DHU/MO

John Bennett Papers, 1900-1957. (Author, illustrator of Charleston, S. C.). Manuscripts and notes on local folklore of Gullah Negroes. Musical compositions included. ScHi

Edward W. Blyden. Mms. DLC; NjP; NN/Sch
Also: Rhodes House Library, Oxford University College; London School of Economics; Salisbury Court London EC1; Public Records Office, England; University of Ibadan, Nigeria.

---- see also George L. Ruffin Papers.

John Wesley Edward Bowen Papers. (1855-1933). (Methodist Episcopal minister and President of Gammon Theological Seminary.) GAU/ITC

George Freeman Bragg Papers. (1863-1940.) DHU/MO; MH

Brethren in Christ Church. Reports and correspondence of mission work in Rhodesia and Zambia. PGraM

Calvin Scott Brown Papers. (1884-1934.). Includes reports of Lott Carey Baptist Foreign Mission Convention. DHU/MO

Neill Brown Papers. (North Carolina Presbyterian minister.). Includes "A Letter Apparently Written by a Slave to Hugh Brown, Reproaching Him for Turning his Back on the Slaves and Preaching Only to Whites." NcD

John E. Bruce Papers. (African Methodist Episcopal Zion layman and lawyer). NN/Sch

John C. Burruss. (Methodist minister of Virginia and Mississippi.) Family Papers. Includes unpublished materials relating to the Methodist Episcopal Church. Views on Slavery in America. (Justification). L

Archibald James Carey Papers, 1909-1966. (Lawyer, judge, A. M. E. minister, Chicago, Ilinois). Ministerial correspondence, particularly during his presidency of the A. M. E. Connectional Council. Also includes his political activities. ICHi

Eli Washington Caruthers Papers. (North Carolina Presbyterian minister). Includes an unpublished, Anti-Slavery manuscript, "American Slavery and the Immediate Duty of Southern Slaveholders. Written at the request of his Friends.
NcD

John Chavis. (Negro Ante-bellum Presbyterian minister and teacher of North Carolina). Correspondence with his benefactor, Willie P. Mangum, U. S. Senator, North Carolina.
NcHiC; DLC

---- Manuscripts and unpublished writings.
NcMHi; NcD; NcU; PPPrHi

Christian and Missionary Alliance. Foreign Department. Includes reports from missionaries in Brazil, Gabon, Zaire, Mali, Upper Volta and Ivory Coast.   NN-CMA

Christian Methodist Episcopal Church. Manuscripts and unpublished materials.   GAuP; TJaL

Church and Race Relations. Manuscripts, letters and unpublished materials. Includes "Slaves Bible."   TNF

The Church of Jesus Christ of Latter Day Saints. Religious activities of mission work in Africa.   USID

Churches. (Histories of individual churches). Check State Historical Associations for histories compiled by the U. S. Works Project Aministration, Historical Records Survey.

Churches and Race Relations in the Old South. Manuscripts and unpublished materials.   GAuP

Thomas Clarkson Papers, 1760-1846. (English philanthropist and abolitionist). Mms.   DHU/MO; CSmH

Daniel Coker. (Negro minister, migrated to Sierra Leone). Journal kept on the West Coast of Africa, April 21 to Sept. 21, 1821.   DLC

Colonization Society of Virginia. Records, 1823-59.   ViHi

Congregational Home Missionary Society (Until 1893, called American Home Missionary Society). Archives, 1826 to 1907. (750,000 items).   LNAA

Conservative Baptist Foreign Mission Society. Letters from mission staff in Senegal, Ivory Coast, Zaire, Uganda and Madagascar.   IW-CBFMS

John Francis Cook Papers. (Minister, teacher, pastor of Union Bethel A. M. E. Church and Fifteenth Street Presbyterian Church, Wash., D. D.). Diary.   DHU/MO

Anna Julia Cooper Papers, 1881-85. Clippings and notes used in her book on the Grimke family.   DHU/MO

Levi Jenkins Coppin Papers. (African Methodist Episcopal Bishop).
OWibfU

Alexander Crummell Papers.   NN/Sch

John C. Dancy Papers, 1916-49. (Director, Detroit Urban League). Includes information on Negro Churches in Detroit during World War II and the post-war period.   MiU-H

Delaware Church Records, 1707-. Transcripts made by the Historical Records Survey. Includes registers, minutes and histories, principally of churches in New Castle and Sussex Counties. Some Negro Churches included.   DE-Ar

John Miller Dickey Papers. (Presbyterian minister, founder of Lincoln University, Chester County, Pa.). PLuL; PCarlD

Disciples of Christ (Christian Churches). Manuscripts, correspondences, annual reports and issues of the Christian Evangelist, from 1866-1958. Includes information on the home and foreign missions in Africa.   TN/DCHS

District of Columbia. Historical Records Survey. Inventory of the Church records of the Protestant Episcopal Church.
WNa; WHi

Paul Lawrence Dunbar Papers. Letter to Alexander Crummell, September 9, 1894.   NN/Sch

James Stanley Durkee Papers, 1837-38. (Protestant Episcopal minister and president of Howard University).   DHU/MO

John Emory Papers. Letters include information on Negro Methodists in Philadelphia.   PHi

Evangelical Lutheran Synodical Conference of North America. Missionary Board. Records, 1906-1953. Missionary work among Negroes in the South and among Ibesikpo Tribe in Nigeria.   MoSCH; NNUT

Evangelical United Brethren Church. (Merged with United Methodist Church in 1968). see United Methodist Church.

John G. Fee Papers. (Presbyterian clergyman, founder of Berea College, Berea, Kentucky).   KyBB

Free Will Baptists Records. Includes information on church's views on slavery in America.   OHi

Friends, Society of. Association of Friends for the Free Instruction of Adult Colored Persons. Minutes, 1789-1822; 1878-91.
PSCH-Hi

---- Baltimore Society for the Protection of Free People of Color. Minutes, with Constitution and By-Laws. 1827-29.   MdBFr

---- Beehive School for Colored Children. Managers Minutes, 1865-1888.   PSC-Hi

---- Friends Freedmen's Association. 1863-1935. Papers on educational work among Negroes.   PSC-Hi

---- Indiana Yearly Meeting. Records, 1821-1920. Includes minutes of the Committee on the Concerns of the People of Colour.
InRE

---- Institute for Colored Youth. First Minute Book, 1837-59. Original draft of Minutes, 1850-58. Minutes of Board Instruction, 1868-97.   PSC-Hi

---- New England Yearly Meeting. Abolition Society Book. Includes petitions and other papers relating to slavery; an account of the African School and Meeting House in Providence (printed). Covers years 1798-1830.   RPB

---- Quaker protest literature on the importation of slaves. (1698).
PFL

---- Society of Women Friends for the Free Instruction of African Females. Minutes, 1795-1845.   PSC-Hi

---- David Ethan Frierson Papers, 1839-96. 272 items. Sermons, notes and lectures and an account of the first General Assembly of the Presbyterian Church, Confederate States of America. Includes a catechism for Negroes.   ScU

Henry Highland Garnet Papers. (Early Negro Presbyterian minister). Letters and speeches.   NN/Sch

Henry Highland Garnet. Unpublished materials and letters. See also William Lloyd Garrison Papers.

William Lloyd Garrison Papers.   MB

William Goodell Papers, 1737-1882. (Abolitionist). Sermons, essays and notebooks.   OO

Francis Grimke Papers and Sermons, 1834-1937. 26 Boxes. Included in the Grimke Family Papers.   DHU/MO

Cornelius Mack Hall Correspondence and Records of Milwaukee's Inner City Development Project, 1965-66. 25 ft. Microfilm, 530 items, 16 mm.   WMCHi

William and Benjamin Hammett Papers. (Methodist ministers of Charleston, South Carolina). Includes confession of Benjamin Hammett's slave concerning the "threatened slave uprising" in Charleston, 1822.   NcD

Lemuel Haynes Papers. (Early Negro minister to whites in New England).   NN/Sch

Roland T. Heacock Papers. (Negro Congregationalist minister and author, Massachusetts, Philadelphia and Connecticut).   LNAA

James A. Healy. (Black Catholic Bishop appointed assistant to the Papal Throne in 1900). 2 diary manuscripts, 1849, 1891. Also sermons and lectures.   DHC

James M. Henderson. (A. M. E. minister). Sermon, delivered at Indiana Annual Conference, August, 1886.   OWibfU

Charles Leander Hill Papers, 1948-1956. (A. M. E. minister, theologian, author and president of Wilberforce University).   OWibfU

Mildred J. Hill. See Avery Robinson Papers.

Nicholas Hood. (Pastor, Negro Church, New Orleans, Louisiana). See Central Christian Church.

Isabella Hume Child Development Community Center. See Central Christian Church, New Orleans, Louisiana.

Anna Marie Hansen Jamison Papers, 1917-1937. (Teacher with the American Missionary Association). Reports to the association, yearbooks and newspaper clippings.   LNAA

Jesuit Museum. Manuscripts on this order of the Catholic Church. Includes some materials on race relations. 700 Howder Mill Rd., St. Louis, Mo.

Charles Colcock Jones Papers, 1831-93. (Minister of South Carolina and author Religious Instruction to Slaves).   NcD

Thomas Jesse Jones. (Educational director of Phelps-Stokes Fund). See Phelps-Stokes Fund.

Josephite Motherhouse Archives. Manuscripts on Negroes in this order. 1130 Calvert St., Balto., Md.

Albert Lee Papers, 1922-1926. (A. M. E. minister). 1 Box. Correspondence, notes and programs. Also papers on Masonic Order.   IU

Lilly Family Papers, 1924-60. Correspondence, sermons and other archival materials relating to the Presbyterian Church and the Negro.   NcMHi

Charles Eric Lincoln Papers.   GAU

Lott Carey Baptist Mission Society in the Interest of Home and Foreign Missions. Complete set of Lott Carey Herald, minutes and other archival materials. Office: 1501- 11th St., N. W., Washington, D. C.

Benjamin Lundy Papers. (Member of the Society of Friends and abolitionist). Papers, 1814-39 on the Free Produce and Free Cotton Society.   NNCor

Lutheran Church in America. Missouri Synod. Unpublished materials.   MoSCH; NNUT

Willie Person Mangum Papers. See John Chavis.

John and William Markoe Papers. (Catholic brothers active in integrating Negroes into the Catholic Church).   MoSU

Mennonite Brethren, Missions Services. Archives of Home Missions.   KH-MBMS

Mennonite Brethren Churches. See also Africa-Inter-Mennonite Missions, Inc.

Methodism. Extensive Collection manuscripsts, books and pamphlets.   IEG

Methodist Episcopal Church. Border States. Conference Reports.   DLC

---- California Conferences. California records, 1849-1939.   CBPac

---- Freedmen's Aid Society. Papers, 1865-1877. GAU; LNAA

---- Missions and Mission Conferences. South Central Africa. Angola District records, 1885-1897.   CBPac

---- See also United Methodist Church.

Methodist-Presbyterian United Mission Library. Archival materials, reports of foreign and home missions.   NN-MPUML

Michigan. Historical Records Survey. Inventory of the church archives.   NNCor

Henry Miles Papers, 1839-1865. (A Quaker abolitionist). Letters and documents dealing with the Anti-Slavery movement, Fugitive Slave Law and the Freedmen's Aid Association.   NcD

Milwaukee's Inner City Development Project. Records. See Cornelius Mack Hall Correspondence.

Missionary Research Library. Reports, documents and journals of missionaries in Africa, Brazil and Cuba.   NNMRL

Winfield Henry Mixon. (African Methodist Episcopal minister and editor of the Dallas Post). 12 vols. including a diary.   NcD

Thomas Montgomery Papers, 1841-1907. (Union soldier). Letters written to family in Cleveland, Minnesota, while serving in the Civil War. Describes religious activities of Negro soldiers in the service.   MnHi

Jesse Edward Moorland Papers. (Graduate of Howard University Medical School, minister and Donor of Moorland Negro Collection to Howard University Library). Correspondence and documents dealing with Y. M. C. A., J. E. K. Aggrey, Negro ministers and churches.   DHU/MO

Lucretia Mott (Coffin) Papers, 1834-1896. (Quaker abolitionist).   PSC-Hi

Robert Hamill Nassau Papers. (Presbyterian missionary to Africa).   PLuL

Negroes in New Orleans, 1850-1865. Card index from newspapers. Includes information on churches and ministers.   LND

New Orleans Catholic Council on Human Relations. Records, 1961-1964.   LNAA

New Orleans, Louisiana. Central Christian Church. Papers and reports of the church and its minister, Rev. Nicholas Hood, 1949-58. Information on the Isabella Hume Child Development Community Center.   LNAA

Richard Nisbet. Manuscript copy of, "Slavery not Forbidden by Scripture, 1773."   MH

North Carolina Legislative Papers. 1870-1860. Includes information, petitions, correspondence and bills concerning free Negro ministers in the State.   NcHiC

Maurice Ouellet Papers. (Catholic priest, active in Civil Rights Movement in Alabama). Correspondence, sermons and newspaper clippings concerning his removal from his church by the bishop.   LNOA

Theodore Parker Papers. (Massachusetts Unitarian minister). Letters and other manuscripts.   DHU/MO; DLC; MB

Daniel A. Payne. Letters to George Whipple.   LNAA

Daniel A. Payne Papers.   OWibfU; NN/Sch; DHU/MO

Amos Agustus Phelps Papers. Letters relating to missions organized by former Oberlin College students near Kingston, Jamaica in 1839, after the British Act of Emancipation. Phelps was sent by the American Missionary Association.
                                                                  LNAA

Philadelphia, Pa. Mt. Olive A. M. E. Church. Minutes and other church records, 1911-18.   DHU/MO

Presbyterian and Reformed Churches, Inc. See United Presbyterian Church in the U. S. Synods.

Presbyterian Church in the U. S. A. Board of Missions for Freedmen. Annual Reports, 1866-1923. (Heritage Patron Micropublications). 35 mm. film.   PHi

---- West Africa Mission. Selected minutes, reports and correspondence, 1902-1966. (Heritage Patron Micropublications). 35 mm. film.   PHi

---- See also United Presbyterian Church in the U. S. A.

Henry Hugh Proctor Papers, 1868-1905. (Negro pastor of First Congregational Church, Atlanta, Ga. and Nazarene Congregational Church, Brooklyn, N. Y., vice-president of the American Missionary Association).   LNAA

Protestant Episcopal Church in the U. S. A. The Church Historical Society. Church records, and other archival materials including Negro ministers and churches.   TXCH/SPEC

---- Freedman's Commission. Annual reports.   DLC; DHU/MO

---- Proceedings of first convocation of Colored Clergy. 1883.
                                                                  OWibfP

---- Provinces. Northwest. Records, 1914-42. Correspondence and journals relating to missions, maintained by the church. Includes a survey of the Negro population, religious education programs and list of the clergy.   MnHi

---- Unpublished autobiography of Rev. Paul Trapier describing his work as an Episcopal minister among South Carolina Negroes and his role in guiding the church in the Confederate and post-bellum period.   ScHi

Reverdy Cassius Ransom Papers. (Bishop of African Methodist Episcopal Church).   OWibfFU

John Stark Ravenscroft. Personal letters of Ravenscroft, first Protestant Episcopal Bishop of North Carolina. Included is a letter addressed to Gavin Hoag, a young minister of Raleigh, advising him to sell the Bishop's slaves.   NcD

E. Y. Reese Papers, 1858-61. (Methodist minister of Baltimore, Md.). Letters to Rev. R. B. Thompson of Lynchburg, Va. Information on Methodist Episcopal Church and the attitude of the church on the question of slavery.   NcD

Charles Lenox Remond. See George L. Ruffin Papers.

Avery Robinson Papers, 1895-1964. Includes two notebooks of Negro humns collected and annotated by Mildred J. Hill. OrU

James H. Robinson, 1907-1972. (Negro Presbyterian minister and executive director of Crossroads Africa). Letters, sermons and manuscripts of published writings.   LNAA

John S. Rock. See George L. Ruffin Papers.

Roman Catholic Church. Missionary work among Negroes. MsBsS

George L. Ruffin Papers. Includes papers of E. W. Blyden, C. L. Remond, John S. Rock and George W. Williams. 291 mms.
                                                                  DHU/MO

William Sanders Scarborough Papers. 936 mms.   OWibfP

S. S. Schmucker. Manuscript copy of, "Memorial of Professor S. S. Schmucker Relative to Binding Out Minor Colored Children. "   MOSCH

Seabury Family Papers, 1823-1916. Correspondence of Samuel Seabury as editor of The Churchman and his correspondence (1864) with Bishop Alonzo Potter relating to the "Slavery Question. "   NHi

Seventh Day Baptist. Historical Society. Correspondence, reports and other archival materials of mission work in Nyasaland and Malawi.   NjPlaSDB

Shelter for Aged and Infirm Colored Persons. First and second annual reports, 1883-1884.   OWibfP

Moses Sheppard Papers, 1794-1927. (Quaker humanitarian). Correspondence on the subjects of anti-slavery, the Colonization Society and Liberia.   PSC-Hi

Edwin Chalmers Silsby Papers, 1851-1937. (Educator of Alabama). Correspondence relating to Talladega College and the work of the American Missionary Association with Negroes in Alabama.
                                                                  ATC

Simms Family Papers, 1802-65. Records include information on development of Methodism in Washington, D. C. and the formation of the First African Methodist Episcopal Church.
                                                                  DHU/MO

Matthew Simpson Papers. Includes correspondence of white abolitionists and missionaries to freedmen in post-war South.
                                                                  DLC

Slavery and Abolitionists' Papers, 1792-1865.   DHU/MO; OO

Slavery and Secession. Unpublished materials on the position the Methodist Church and other denominations took on seccession from the Union.   MdHi

Slavery Not Immoral: A Letter to James Haughton. By Philanthropos, [pseud.] Mms.   MH

Simon Peter Smith. See Edward F. Williams Papers.

Society for the Propagation of the Gospel. Letters, reports and correspondence relating to Africa.   MWA

Southern Baptist Convention. Church records and other archival materials.   TN/SBCHC

Thomas McCants Stewart Papers. (Lawyer and African Methodist Episcopal minister).   DHU/MO

Anson Phelps Stokes Papers. (Chairman of the Anson Phelps-Stokes Fund). Includes correspondence with missionaries and Negro administrators.   LNAA; CtY

Edward F. Stratton Papers, 1750-1961. 207 mms. Includes Quaker documents letters and reports of Edward Williams and wife, teachers in schools for freedmen in Mississippi and Texas.   PSC

Henry Howard Summers Papers. (A. M. E. minister and teacher). Box. Correspondence, biography, photographs and clippings. Includes information on Wilberforce University and Paine Theological Seminary.   DHU/MO

Robert Tallant Papers, 1936-59. (Author of New Orleans). Papers relating to voodoo, spiritualism and Negro folklore.   LN

Benjamin T. Tanner. See Carter G. Woodson Collection.

Lewis Tappan Papers. Contains minister's correspondence on abolition.   DLC

Mary Church Terrell Papers, 1888-1954. Includes correspondence and papers about her activities with the Washington Federation of Churches.   DHU/MO

Henry McNeal Turner Papers.   DHU/MO; NN/Sch

---- See also Benjamin W. Arnett Papers and Carter G. Woodson Papers.

Thomas Wyatt Turner Papers. (Negro Catholic layman, Ph. D. in Botany, active in Colored Federated Catholic Organization). ViHa

Underground Railroad. Mms. Miscellaneous file on Levi Coffin and Underground Railroad.   INRE

United Church of North America. Board of American Missions. Board of Missions to the Freedmen, financial records, 1920-38 and 1941-58.   PPPrHi

United Methodist Church. For manuscripts and other unpublished materials dealing with this denomination's foreign mission work in Africa.   DOUM/EUB

---- Board of Global Ministries. Extensive manuscripts relating to home and foreign missions. Includes materials relating to former United Brethren Church.   NNMB

United Presbyterian Church in the U. S. A. Papers dealing with slavery, schools for Negroes and mission.   PLuL

---- Synod of New York and New Jersey. Extract from minutes of the directors of the African School established by this group.   NjPT

---- Synods. Minutes, 1788-1956. Includes minutes of the Afro-American Synod, 1916.   NcMHi

Washington, D. C. Galbraith African Methodist Episcopal Zion Church. Scrapbook of James Guy Tyson, 1899-1970. DHU/MO

---- Fifthteen Presbyterian Church. 3 Vols. Xerox copies of church records, 1841-1868 and 1874-1890.   DHU/MO

---- First Congregational Church. Sermons and attitudes of Church relative to the admission of Colored people.   DHU/MO

---- Metropolitan African Methodist Episcopal Church. Records including minutes of meetings.   DHU/MO

---- Union Bethel A. M. E. Church. Records, 1825-1972. See Washington, D. C. Metropolitan A. M. E. Church.   DHU/MO

Charles Harris Wesley. Typescript carbon of "The Negro Church in the United States." n. p.: Institute of Social and Religious Research, 1928. This study was compiled by using Baltimore, Md. as an urban type and Suffolk, Va. as a rural type.
                                                        DHU/MO

Western Anti-Slavery Society Papers, 1834, 1835, 1837-46. DLC

Edward Williams Correspondence. See Edward F. Stratton Papers.

George W. Williams. See George L. Ruffin Papers.

Carter G. Woodson Collection of Negro Papers and Related Documents. Includes manuscript materials on Negro ministers and churches.
                                                            DLC

Writers Program. West Virginia. Includes papers, correspondences and clippings of Negroes. Also folklore of the Negro.
                                                            WvU

Brantley York. (Free Negro of North Carolina). Unpublished autobiography. Describes practice of whites of providing church services to slaves and free Negroes.   NcD

ABDEL RAHMAN EL-MAHDI

J. A. Rogers. World's Great Men of Color (N. Y.: J. A. Rogers, 1946), p. 545.   DHU/MO; DHU/R
Religious leader of the (UMMA) Independence Party of the Anglo-Egyptian Sudan.

New York Times (Nov. 14, 20, 1946).   DLC; DHU

ABERNATHY, RALPH D.

The editors of Ebony. The Ebony Success Library: 1,000 Successful Blacks (Nashville: The Southwestern Co., 1973), V. 1, p. 2.   DHU
Baptist minister and president of SCLC.

Harry A. Ploski, (ed.). Reference Library of Black America (New York: Bellwether Pub. Co., 1971), Book 2, pp. 18-19.   DHU

ABUNE THEOPHILOS

A Biographical Sketch of His Holiness Abune Theophilos Patriarch of Ethiopia. n. p.: n. p., n. d.   DHU/R

ADAMS, GEORGE S.

James W. Hood. One Hundred Years of the A. M. E. Zion Church (New York City: A. M. E. Zion Book Concern, 1895), pp. 444-47.   DHU/MO
A. M. E. Zion minister.

ADAMS, HENRY

William J. Simmons. Men of Mark (Cleveland, C.: George M. Rewell & Co., 1887), p. 798.   DHU/R
Baptist minister.

ADAMS, WILLIAM HENRY

Albert S. Foley. God's Men of Color (New York: Farrar, Straus & Co., 1955), pp. 270-73.   DHU/R
Catholic priest.

ADKINSON, L. G.

G. F. Richings. Evidences of Progress Among Colored People (Phila.: G. S. Ferguson, 1904), p. 107.   DHU/MO
Methodist Episcopal minister; President of New Orleans University Medical School.

AGBEBI, W. MOJOLO

William H. Ferris. The African Abroad V. 2 (New Haven, Conn.: Tuttle, Morehouse, & Taylor Press, 1913), p. 848.   DHU/MO
Minister of Lagos, West Africa, director of the Niger Delta Mission and president of the Baptist Union of West Africa.

AGGREY, JAMES E. K.

Edwin W. Smith. Aggrey of Africa; a Study in Black and White (New York: Doubleday, Doran & Co., Inc., 1929).   DHU/MO
A. M. E. Zion minister.

Kenneth King. "James E. K. Aggrey: Collaborator, Nationalist, Pan African." Canadian Journal of African Studies (3:3, Fall, 1970), pp. 511-30.   DHU/MO

William John Waterman Roome. Aggrey, the African Teacher (London: Marshall, Morgan & Scott, 1934).   PU

AKINYELE, A. B.

Bayo Adebiyui. The Beloved Bishop ... (Ibadan: Day-star Press, 1969).   DLC

ALBERT, ARISTIDES ALPHONSO E. P.

(Indianapolis) Freeman (1:24, Feb. 2, 1889; 1:29, Mr. 9, 1889), p. 4; 5.   DHU/MO
Editor of The South Western Advocate, Methodist Episcopal minister and President of the Board of Trustees of New Orleans University.

Irvine G. Penn. The Afro-American Press and Its Editors. (Springfield, Mass.: Willey & Co., 1891), pp. 223-27.   DHU/R; DHU/MO

Portrait on p. 225.

ALEXANDER, DANIEL R.

William R. Scott. Going to the Promised Land. Afro-American Immigrants in Ethiopia 1930-1935.
Paper delivered at the 14th Annual Meeting of the African Studies Association, Denver, Colorado, November, 1971.
About Missouri born Negro who settled in Ethiopia.

ALEXANDER, S. C.

H. F. Kletzing. Progress of a Race (Atlanta: J. L. Nichols & Co., 1901), p. 406.   DHU/MO
Presbyterian minister and teacher.

ALEXANDER, W. G.

    Henry F. Kletzing. Progress of a Race (Atlanta: J. L.
Nichols & Co., 1901), pp. 505-07.   DHU/MO
A. M. E. minister.

ALLEN, ALEXANDER JOSEPH

    Richard R. Wright, The Bishops of the A. M. E. Church
(Nashville: AME Sunday School Union, 1963), pp. 41-44.
                              DHU/R
Sixty-second Bishop of A. M. E. Church; Pres. of Wilber-
force U. Board of Trustees.

ALLEN, G. W.

    W. N. Hartshorn. An Era of Progress and Promise. (Boston:
Priscilla Publ. Co., 1910), p. 470.   DHU/MO
A. M. E. minister.

ALLEN, J. O.

    Samuel W. Bacote. Who's Who Among the Colored Baptists
(Kansas City, Mo.: F. Hudson Co., 1912), pp. 197-98.
                              DHU/MO
Baptist minister, vice-pres., South Carolina Baptist Conven-
tion.

ALLEN, JOHN CLAUDE, (bp.).

    What Manner of Man (n. p.: n. p., n. d.), pp. 1-64.
                    Pam. File, DHU/R
Bishop of the Third Episcopal District of the C. M. E. Church.

ALLEN, LUKE, JR.

    William Hicks. The History of Louisiana Negro Baptists from
1804-1914 (Nashville, Tenn.: National Baptist Publishing
Board, n. d.), p. 190.   DHU/R
Baptist minister.

ALLEN, LUKE, SR.

    William Hicks. The History of Louisiana Negro Baptists from
1804-1914. Nashville, Tenn.: National Baptist Publishing
Board, n. d.), pp. 156-59.   DHU/R
Baptist minister and State missionary.

ALLEN, RICHARD, (bp.).

    Richard Robert Wright, Jr., (bp.). Bishops of the A. M. E.
Church (Nashville: A. M. E. Sunday School Union, 1963), pp.
46-76.   DHU/R
First Bishop of the African Methodist Episcopal Church.

    The African Methodist Episcopal Church Review (72:186, Oct. -
Dec., 1955), pp. 7-16.   DHU/R

    Benjamin G. Brawley. Early Negro American Writers (Chapel
Hill, N. C.: Univ. of N. C. Press, 1937), pp. 87-95.
                              DHU/MO

    Benjamin W. Arnett. The Budget...Biographical Sketches...
(Dayton, Ohio: Christian Pub. House, 1882), p. 141. DHU/MO

    Charles Harris Wesley. Richard Allen, Apostle of Freedom
(Washington, D. C.: The Associated Publishers, Inc., 1935).
           DHU/R; GAU; TNF; NN/Sch; NjP
Negro author.

    Edgar A. Toppin. A Biographical History of Blacks in America
Since 1528 (New York: David McKay Co., 1971), pp. 247-48.
                              DHU/R

    Edward A. Johnson. School History of the Negro Race in
America (Raleigh: Edward & Broughton, 1890), p. 147.
                              DHU/MO

    Frederick Douglass. "The Place of Richard Allen in History."
The African Methodist Episcopal Church Review (80:219, Ja. -
Mr., 1964), p. 75.   DHU/R

    Harry A. Ploski, (ed.). Reference Library of Black America
(New York: Bellwether Pub. Co., Inc., 1971), Book 2, p. 212.
                              DHU

    Howard V. Harper (ed.). Profiles of Protestant Saints (New
York: Fleet Press, 1968), pp. 56-76.   DHU/R

    Isaiah H. Welch. The Heroism of the Rev. Richard Allen ...
and Rev. Daniel Coker ... (Nashville: A. M. E. Sunday
School Union, 1910).   NN/Sch

    Leslie H. Fishel, Jr. The Black American (New York: Wil-
liam Morrow, 1970), pp. 141-42+.   DHU/MO
Formerly entitled The Negro American.

    The Life Experience and Gospel of the Rt. Rev. Richard Allen.
To Which is Annexed the Rise and Progress of the African
Methodist Episcopal Church in the United States of America.
Containing a Narrative of the Yellow Fever in the People of
Color in the United States. Written by Himself and Published
by His Request. With an Introduction by Geo. A. Singleton.
(New York: Abingdon Press, 1960).
          DHU/R; A&M; DHU/MO; OWibfU

    Mary E. Moxcey. Philip Henry Lotz, (ed.). Rising Above
Color (New York: n. p., 1943).   NcD

    Miles Mark Fisher. Crisis (44:7, Jl., 1937), pp. 198-99+.
                        DHU/MO; DLC

    Montrose W. Thornton. The African Methodist Episcopal
Church Review (78:213, Jl.-Sept., 1962), pp. 25-27. DHU/R

    Richard Bardolph. "Social Origins of Distinguished Negroes,
1770-1865." Journal of Negro History (40:3, Jl., 1955), p. 221.
                            DHU/MO

    Richard Robert Wright, Jr., (bp.). Allen Day Address;
Greatest Negro Born in America, Richard Allen, 1760-1831
(Philadelphia: The Author, n. d.)   DHU/MO

    W. H. Prince. The Stars of the Century of African Methodism
(Rutland, Oregon: n. p., 1916).   NN/Sch

    Who Was Who, Historical Volume 1607-1896 (Chicago: The
A. N. Marquis Co., 1907), p. 88.   DLC

    Wilhelmena S. Robinson. Historical Negro Biographies (New
York: Publishers Co., 1967), pp. 5-6.   DHU/MO

    William H. Ferris. African Abroad (New Haven, Conn.:
Tuttle, Morehouse & Taylor Press, 1913), p. 766. DHU/MO

    William J. Simmons, (ed.). Men of Mark (Cleveland, O.:
Geo. M. Rewell & Co., 1887), p. 491.   DHU/R

    William W. Brown. The Rising Son (Miami, Fla.: Mnemo-
syne Pub. Co., Inc., 1969), pp. 337-38. DHU/R; DHU/MO

    Marcia M. Mathews. Richard Allen (Baltimore: Helicon,
1963).   NN/Sch; NcD; DLC

ALLEN, WILLIE B.

The editors of Ebony. The Ebony Success Library: 1,000 Successful Blacks V. 1 (Nashville: The Southwestern Co., 1973), p. 10.   DHU
Baptist minister.

ALLENSWORTH, A. M.

William J. Simmons, (ed.). Men of Mark (Cleveland, O.: George M. Rewell & Co., 1887), p. 843.   DHU/R
Baptist minister and chaplain.

ALSTORK, JOHN WESLEY, (bp.).

G. F. Richings. Evidences of Progress Among Colored People (Phila.: Geo. S. Ferguson Co., 1904), p. 391.
                                        DHU/MO; DHU/R
A. M. E. Zion bishop.

James W. Hood. One Hundred Years of the A. M. E. Zion Church (New York City: A. M. E. Zion Book Concern, 1895), pp. 374-77.   DHU/MO

ALVORD, J. W.

G. F. Richings. Evidences of Progress Among Colored People (Philadelphia: Geo. S. Ferguson Co., 1904), p. 83.
                                                DHU/MO
Congregationalist minister and one of the organizers of the Educational Commission.

AMIGER, WILLIAM THOMAS

Samuel W. Bacote. Who's Who Among the Colored Baptists (Kansas City, Mo.: F. Hudson Co., 1912), pp. 30-32.
                                                DHU/MO
Baptist minister of State University, Louisville, Kentucky.

AMOS, THOMAS H.

G. F. Richings. Evidences of Progress Among Colored People (Philadelphia: Geo. S. Ferguson Co., 1904), pp. 181-83.
                                                DHU/MO
Pastor of the First African Presbyterian Church, Philadelphia and later principal of Ferguson Academy, South Carolina.

ANDERSON, D. W.

James J. Pipkin. The Negro in Revelation, in History and in Citizenship (N. Y.: Thompson Publishing Co., 1902), pp. 86-87.   DHU/MO
Baptist minister.

Leila A. Pendleton. A Narrative of the Negro (Wash., D. C.: Press of R. L. Pendleton, 1912), p. 177.   DHU/MO

ANDERSON, FLOYD J.

W. N. Hartshorn. An Era of Progress and Promise (Boston: Priscilla Publ. Co., 1910), p. 493.   DHU/MO
Presbyterian minister, teacher and editor of Afro-American Presbyterians.

ANDERSON, J. F.

G. F. Richings. Evidences of Progress Among Colored People (Philadelphia: Geo. S. Ferguson Co., 1904), p. 68.
                                                DHU/MO
Principal of Hearne Academy, Hearne, Texas and Baptist minister.

ANDERSON, J. H.

David H. Bradley, Sr. A History of the A. M. E. Zion Church V. II 1872-1968 (Nashville: Parthenon Press, 1970),
                                                DHU/R
A. M. E. Zion minister.

D. W. Culp. Twentieth Century Negro Literature (Atlanta: J. L. Nichols & Co., 1902), p. 323.   DHU/MO

H. F. Kletzing. Progress of a Race (Atlanta: J. L. Nichols & Co., 1901), p. 578.   DHU/MO

James W. Hood. One Hundred Years of the A. M. E. Zion Church (N. Y.: A. M. E. Zion Book Concern, 1895), pp. 238-40.   DHU/MO

Samuel W. Bacote. Who's Who Among the Colored Baptists (Kansas City, Mo.: Franklin Hudson Pub. Co., 1912), pp. 188-89.   DHU/MO

ANDERSON, MATTHEW

(Indianapolis) Freeman (2:15, Je. 1, 1889), p. 4.   DHU/MO
Presbyterian minister, includes portrait.

ANDERSON, ROBERT

The Life of Rev. Robert Anderson, Born the 22n Day of February in the Year of Our Lord 1819, and joined the Methodist Episcopal Church in 1839. This Book Shall be Called The Young Men's Guide; or The Brother in White ... Atlanta, Ga.: Foote & Davies Co., 1900.   NN/Sch; DHU/MO; GAU
Minister of the M. E. Church.

ANDERSON, THOMAS

James M. Simms. The First Colored Baptist Church in North America (Phila.: J. B. Lippincott Co., 1888), pp. 253-54.
                                                DHU/R
Baptist minister.

ANDERSON, W. H.

Irvine G. Penn. The Afro-American Press and Its Editors. (Springfield, Mass.: Willey & Co., 1891), pp. 246-48.
                                        DHU/MO; DHU/R
Baptist minister and editor of Baptist Watchtower.

ARMISTEAD, JOHN MAURICE

Lewis G. Jordan. Negro Baptist History, U. S. A. (Nashville: Sunday School Publ., 1930), p. 56.   DHU/MO
President of Virginia Baptist Convention and minister.

The Crisis (26:1, Nov., 1922), p. 30   DHU/MO; DLC

ARMISTEAD, THOMAS

Carter G. Woodson. The History of the Negro Church (Wash., D. C.: Associated Publishers, 1921), p. 46.
                                        DHU/R; DHU/MO
Baptist minister.

ARMSTRONG, ESTHER

Benjamin T. Tanner. An Apology for African Methodism (Baltimore: n.p., 1867), pp. 461-63.   DHU/MO
Religious worker.

ARMSTRONG, JOSIAH HAYNES, (bp.).

 Richard R. Wright. The Bishops of the A. M. E. Church
 (Nashville: A. M. E. Sunday School Union, 1963), p. 77.
 DHU/R
 Twenty-fourth bishop of the A. M. E. Church.

ARMSTRONG, SAMUEL CHAPMAN

 Robert R. Moton. "An Apostle of Good Will." Southern
 Workman (46:3, Mr., 1917), pp. 162-68. DLC; DHU/MO
 Founder of Hampton Institute, General Armstrong.
 Negro author.

ARNETT, BENJAMIN WILLIAM, (bp.).

 Benjamin T. Tanner. An Apology for African Methodism
 (Baltimore: n.p., 1867), pp. 285-89.   DHU/MO
 Seventeenth bishop of A. M. E. Church.

 Charles Alexander. One Hundred Distinguished Leaders
 (Atlanta: The Franklin Printing & Publishing Co., 1899), p.
 56.   DHU/MO

 G. F. Richings. Evidences of Progress Among Colored People
 (Philadelphia: Geo. S. Ferguson Co., 1904), p. 385. DHU/MO

 H. F. Kletzing. Progress of a Race (Atlanta: J. L. Nichols
 & Co., 1898), pp. 500+.   DHU/MO

 Henry D. Northrop. College of Life (Chicago: Chicago Publ.
 & Lithograph, 1895), p. 131.   DHU/MO

 James T. Haley. Afro-American Encyclopedia (Nashville:
 Haley & Florida, 1895), pp. 570-71.   DHU/MO

 Lucretia H. Newman Coleman. Poor Ben, A Story of Real
 Life (Nashville: Publishing House of the A. M. E. Sunday
 Union, 1890).   DHU/MO

 Richard R. Wright. The Bishops of the A. M. E. Church
 (Nashville: A. M. E. Sunday School Union, 1963), pp. 78-82.
 DHU/R

 William J. Simmons, (ed.). Men of Mark (Cleveland, O.:
 George M. Rewell & Co., 1887), p. 883.   DHU/R

 Winfield S. Montgomery. Historical Sketch of Education for
 the Colored Race in D. C. 1807-1905 (Wash.: Smith Brothers,
 Printers, 1907), pp. 17-18.   DHU/MO

ASHER, JEREMIAH

 An Autobiography with Details of a Visit to England and Some
 Account of the History of the Meeting Street Baptist Church,
 Providence, Rhode Island, and of the Shiloh Baptist Church,
 Philadelphia (Philadelphia: By the Author, 1862).
 DHU/MO; DLC; MB; NiC

 Christian Recorder (Aug. 6, 1865), p. 135.
 Obituary.

 Incidents in the Life of Rev. J. Asher: Pastor of Shiloh
 (Colored) Baptist Church, Philadelphia. With an Introduction
 by Wilson Armistead (London: C. Gilpin, 1850). DLC; NcD
 Baptist minister.

BABER, GEORGE WILBUR, (bp.).

 Richard R. Wright. The Bishops of the A. M. E. Church.
 (Nashville: A. M. E. Sunday School Union, 1963), pp. 83-86.
 DHU/R
 Sixty-third bishop of the A. M. E. Church.

BACKUS, J. TRUMBULL

 Presbyterian Reunion: 1837-1871 (New York: De W. C. Lent
 & Co., 1870), p. 506.   DHU/MO
 Presbyterian minister of Schenectady, N. Y.

BACOTE, ALBERT R.

 Samuel W. Bacote. Who's Who Among the Colored Baptists
 (Kansas City, Mo.: F. Hudson Co., 1912), pp. 142-43.
 DHU/MO
 Baptist minister and teacher.

BAILEY, J. W.

 Samuel W. Bacote. Who's Who Among the Colored Baptists
 (Kansas City, Mo.: F. Hudson Co., 1912), pp. 169-70.
 DHU/MO
 Baptist minister and evangelist, superintendent of missions for
 State of Texas.

BAILEY, RICHARD H.

 Wendell P. Dabney. Cincinnati's Colored Citizens (Cincinnati,
 Ohio: The Dabney Pub. Co., 1926), p. 263.   DHU/MO
 Baptist minister.

BAKER, GEORGE (Father Divine).

 A Biographical History of Blacks in America Since 1528 (N. Y.:
 Davic McKay Co., 1971), pp. 279-80.   DHU/R
 Cult leader of "Father Divine's Peace Mission."

 Marcus Boulware. The Oratory of Negro Leaders 1900-1968
 (Westport, Conn.: Negro Universities Press, 1969), p. 206.
 DHU/MO

 Wilhelmena S. Robinson. Historical Negro Biographies (New
 York: Publishers Co., 1967), p. 190.   DHU/MO

 The Washington Evening Star (Sept. 10, 1965), p. B-3-4.
 Pam. File, DHU/MO

 The New York News (Mr. 21, 1935).   DLC

 Harry A. Ploski, (ed.). Reference Library of Black America
 (New York: Bellwether Pub. Co., Inc., 1971), Book 2, p. 212.
 DHU

 Edgar A. Toppin. A Biographical History of Blacks in America Since 1528 (New York: David McKay Co., 1971), pp. 279-
 80.   DHU/MO

BAKER, HARRIET

 John H. Acornley. The Colored Lady Evangelist; Being the
 Life, Labors and Experiences of Mrs. Harriet Baker (Brook-
 lyn: n.p., 1892).   OWibfU
 Evangelist.

BAKER, RICHARD

 Emanuel K. Love. History of the First African Baptist Church
 (Savannah, Ga.: Morning News Print, 1888), p. 173. DHU/MO
 Deacon of the First African Baptist Church.

BALAY, W. D.

 H. F. Kletzing. Progress of a Race (Atlanta, Ga.: Nichols
 & Co., 1898), p. 507.   DHU/MO
 Baptist minister and organizer of the Afro-American Indus-
 trial Union of America.

BALL, CHARLES CHESTER EVERETT

Albert S. Foley. God's Men of Color (New York: Farrar, Straus & Co., 1955), pp. 229-30.   DHU/R
Catholic priest.

BALL, WILLIAM FRANKLIN, (bp.).

Richard R. Wright. The Bishops of the A. M. E. Church (Nashville: A. M. E. Sunday School Union, 1963), pp. 87-91.
                                                                 DHU/R
Seventy-seventh Bishop of the A. M. E. Church.

BANKS, J. H.

James W. C. Pennington. A Narrative of Events of the Life of J. H. Banks, An Escaped Slave from the Cotton State, Alabama in America (Liverpool: M. Rourke, Printer, 1861).
                                                                 DHU/MO

BARBOUR, AARON

Lewis G. Jordan. Negro Baptist History U. S. A. (Nashville, Tenn.: The Sunday School Publishing Board, N. B. C., 1930), p. 144.   DHU/MO; DHU/R
Baptist minister, Galveston, Texas. President of Texas Sunday School Convention.

BARBOUR, RUSSELL CONWELL

Charles Emerson Boddie. God's "Bad Boys" (Valley Forge: Judson Press, 1972), pp. 17-30.   DHU/R
Baptist minister.

BARKSDALE, JAMES D.

James T. Haley. Afro-American Encyclopedia (Nashville: Haley & Florida, 1895), pp. 594-95.   DHU/MO
A. M. E. preacher and teacher.

BASFIELD, TITUS

Martin R. Delany. The Condition, Elevation, Emigration, and Destiny of the Colored People of the United States (New York: Arno Press, 1968), p. 131.   DHU/R; DHU/MO
Negro minister who migrated to Canada and became pastor to a Scotch Congregation.

BASSETT, SHADRACK

Alexander W. Waymon. My Recollections of African Methodist Episcopal Ministers (Phila.: African Methodist Episcopal Book Rooms, 1881), pp. 1-4.   DHU/MO
A. M. E. minister.

BAYLOR, RICHARD W.

James T. Haley. Afro-American Encyclopedia (Nashville: Haley & Florida, 1895), pp. 609-11.   DHU/MO
Baptist minister of S. C.

BAYNES, LAURA

Adoh B. Thomas. Pathfinders (Phila.: G. S. Ferguson, 1929), p. 96.   DHU/MO
"First Colored Missionary Nurse to enter Bangassou, Africa."

BEARDEN, HAROLD IRVING

The African Methodist Episcopal Church Review (Jl. -Sept., 1963), pp. 34-36.   DHU/R
Bishop of the A. M. E. Church.

The editors of Ebony. The Ebony Success Library: 1,000 Successful Blacks (Nashville: The Southwestern Co., 1973), Vol. 1, p. 22.   DHU

BEATTY, CHARLES C.

Presbyterian Reunion 1837-1871 (N. Y.: De W. C. Lent & Co., 1870), pp. 505-06.   DHU/MO
Presbyterian minister and evangelist.

BECK, GUY

William Hicks. The History of the Louisiana Negro Baptist from 1804-1914 (Nashville, Tenn.: National Baptist Publishing Board, n. d.), p. 194.   DHU/R
Baptist minister.

BECKER, C. E.

G. F. Richings. Evidences of Progress Among Colored People (Phila.: G. S. Ferguson, 1904), p. 32.   DHU/MO
Baptist minister and principal of Benedict College, Columbia, South Carolina, 1881-82.

BECKETT, WILLIAM WESLEY, (bp.).

Richard R. Wright. The Bishops of the A. M. E. Church (Nashville: AME Sunday School Union, 1963), pp. 92-93.
                                                                 DHU/R
Fortieth Bishop of the A. M. E. Church.

BECKHAM, WILLIAM

Lewis G. Jordan. Negro Baptist History, U. S. A. (Nashville: Sunday School Publishing Board, N. B. C., 1930), p. 392.   DHU/R; DHU/MO
Baptist minister of Texas and field secretary of the National Baptist Convention.

Samuel W. Bacote. Who's Who Among the Colored Baptists (Kansas City, Mo.: F. Hudson Co., 1912), pp. 56-57.
                                                                 DHU/MO

BECRAFT, MARIA

U. S. Dept. of Education. Special Report (Washington: Government Print. Off., 1871), pp. 204-05.   DHU/MO
"Founder of the First Seminary for Girls, D. C., Sister of Providence-Catholic Church and teacher."

BEEBE, JOSEPH A., (bp.).

Charles H. Phillips. History of the Colored Methodist Church in America (Jackson, Tenn.: Pub. House, C. M. E. Church, 1898), pp. 208-12.   DHU/R; DHU/MO
Bishop of the C. M. E. Church.

BELL, G. H. S.

James W. Hood. One Hundred Years of the A. M. E. Zion Church (N. Y.: A. M. E. Zion Book Concern, 1895), pp. 315-21.   DHU/MO
A. M. E. Zion minister.

BELL, MARK M.

James W. Hood. One Hundred Years of the A. M. E. Zion Church (New York: A. M. E. Book Concern, 1895), pp. 544-47.   DHU/MO
A. M. E. Zion minister.

BEMAN, AMOS GERRY

Benjamin Quarles. Black Abolitionists (New York: Oxford Univ. Press, 1969), pp. 68+.   DHU/MO; DHU/R
Minister of a Congregational Church, Connecticut, abolitionist and son of Jehiel C. Beman.

Robert A. Warner. New Haven Negroes: A Social History (New Haven: Yale Univ. Press, 1940), pp. 88-97+.   DHU/R

Robert A. Warner. "Amos Gerry Beman 1812-1874: A Memoir of a Forgotten Leader." Journal of Negro History (22; 1937), pp. 200-21.   DHU/MO

William H. Ferris. African Abroad V. 2 (New Haven, Conn.: Tuttle, Morehouse & Taylor Press, 1913), p. 699.   DHU/MO

BEMAN, JEHIEL C.

Benjamin Quarles. Black Abolitionists (New York: Oxford University Press, 1969), pp. 26+.   DHU/MO
Abolitionist and father of Amos Gerry Beman.

BENDAU, S. M.

William Hicks. The History of Louisiana Negro Baptists from 1804-1914. (Nashville, Tenn.: National Baptist Publishing Board, n. d.), p. 188.   DHU/R
Baptist minister.

BENDICT THE MOOR, Saint

Harold Robert Perry. "St. Benedict the Moor." St. Augustine's Messenger (21; Ja., 1943), pp. 8-9.   DGU/ST; DHU/R
St. Benedict, Protector of the Negroes of the United States, was a Negro monk in the Franciscan Monastery of Palermo, Italy, canonized in 1807.
Negro author.

Gustave B. Aldrich. Chronicle (4; Jl., 1931), pp. 385-86.
                                                                                 DCU/SW

Joel A. Rogers. World's Great Men of Color V. 2 (New York: J. A. Rogers, 1947), pp. 17-23.   DHU/R
Black Saint of the Catholic Church, 1524-1589.

M. L'Abbe J. Hardy. La Morale en Action des Noir. Paris: Jacques Le Coffre et Cie, Libraires, 1846.

Sabine Baring-Gould. Lives of the Saints V. 10 (New York: Longmans, Green, and Co., 1898), pp. 329-37.   DHU/R

BENNET, JACOB R.

Lewis G. Jordan. Negro Baptist History U. S. A. (Nashville, Tenn.: The Sunday School Pub. Board, N. B. C., 1930), p. 392.   DHU/R; DHU/MO
Baptist minister.

BENNETT, MARION D.

The editors of Ebony. The Ebony Success Library. 1,000 Successful Blacks (Nashville: The Southwestern Co., 1973), Vol. 1, p. 25.   DHU
United Methodist minister.

BENOIT THE BLACK, Saint

Henri Gregoire. An Inquiry Concerning the Intellectual and Moral Faculties and Literature of Negroes ... (Brooklyn: Printed by Thomas Kirk, 1810), pp. 82-84.   DHU/MO
A saint and divine healer of Palermo.

John E. Bruce. A Short Biographical Sketches of Eminent Negro Men and Women (Yonkers, N. Y.: Gazette Press, 1910), pp. 14-15.   DHU/MO

Wilson A. Armistead. A Tribute for the Negro (Miami, Fla.: Mnemosyne Pub. Co., Inc., 1969), p. 397.
                                                                        DHU/R; DHU/MO
Reprint of 1848 edition.

BENSON, LLOYD

Benjamin T. Tanner. An Apology for African Methodism (Balto: n. p., 1867), pp. 234-46.   DHU/MO
A. M. E. minister.

BENTLEY, DANIEL S.

Irvine G. Penn. The Afro-American Press and Its Editors (Springfield, Mass.: Willey & Co., 1891), pp. 150-51.
                                                                        DHU/MO; DHU/R
A. M. E. minister and president of Spokesman Stock Company and frequent contributor to the Christian Recorder.

BESA, DAVID

Georgina A. Gollock. Sons of Africa (New York: Friendship Press, 1928), pp. 178-81.   DHU/R; DHU/MO
Lutheran pastor of Togoland.

BETTIS, ALEXANDER

Alfred William Nicholson. Brief Sketch of the Life and Labors of Rev. Alexander Bettis; Also an Account of the Founding and Development of the Bettis Academy (Trenton, S. C.: The Author, 1913).   DHU/MO
Baptist slave minister and founder of Bettis Acadamy, South Carolina.

BIAS, JAMES J. G.

James A. Handy. Scraps of African Methodist History (Philadelphia, Pa.: A. M. E. Book Concern, n. d.), pp. 346-47.
                                                                                 DHU/MO
A. M. E. minister.

BIBB, HENRY

"Autobiographical Narrative of the Life and Adventures of Henry Bibb." Ruth Miller, (ed.). Black American Literature (California: Glencoe Press, 1971), pp. 62-66.   DHU/R
A fugitive slave writes of his suffering as a slave.

Narrative of the Life and Adventures of Henry Bibb, an American Slave, Written by Himself (New York: n. p., 1850).
                                                                            NcD; DHU/MO

William Wells Brown. The Black Man (Miami, Fla.: Mnemosyne Pub., Inc., 1969), pp. 86-88.   DHU/R

BIDDLE, WILLIAM T.

James W. Hood. One Hundred Years of the A. M. E. Zion Church (New York: A. M. E. Book Concern, 1895), pp. 605-08.   DHU/MO
A. M. E. Zion minister.

BILAL

Joel A. Rogers. World's Great Men of Color (New York:
J. A. Rogers, 1946), pp. 74-77.   DHU/MO; DHU/R
"First Muezzin and treasurer of Islam, 600 A. D. "

BIRCHMORE, SAMUEL

James W. Hood. One Hundred Years of the A. M. E. Zion
Church (New York: A. M. E. Book Concern, 1895), pp. 254-
55.   DHU/MO; DHU/R
A. M. E. Zion minister.

David Bradley, Sr. A History of the A. M. E. Zion Church
1872-1968 V. 2 (Nashville: Parthenon Press, 1970), pp. 32+.
                              DHU/R; DHU/MO

BIRD, FRANKLIN K.

David H. Bradley, Sr. A History of the A. M. E. Zion Church
1872-1968 V. 2 (Nashville: Parthenon Press, 1970), p. 158.
                              DHU/R
Minister of the A. M. E. Zion Church and manager of the
Publishing House.

James W. Hood. One Hundred Years of the A. M. E. Zion
Church (New York: A. M. E. Book Concern, 1895), pp. 307-
11.   DHU/MO

BISHOP, CECIL

The editors of Ebony. The Ebony Success Library: 1,000 Successful Blacks (Nashville: The Southwestern Co., 1973), Vol. 1,
p. 28.   DHU
A. M. E. Zion minister.

BISHOP, HUTCHENS C.

George F. Bragg. History of the Afro-American Group of the
Episcopal Church (Balto., Md.: Church Advocate Press,
1922), pp. 88-89.   DHU/R
Protestant Episcopal priest.

The Crisis (2:3, Jl., 1911), p. 102.   DHU/MO; DLC

BISHOP, JOSIAH

Carter G. Woodson. The History of the Negro Church (Wash.,
D. C.: Associated Publishers, 1921), p. 46+. DHU/R; DHU/MO
Baptist minister.

BISHOP, WILLIAM H. (bp.).

James W. Hood. One Hundred Years of the A. M. E. Zion
Church (New York: A. M. E. Zion Book Concern, 1895), p.
84.   NcD
Bishop of the A. M. E. Zion Church.

J. B. F. Shaw. The Negro in the History of Methodism (Nashville: Parthenon Press, 1954), p. 76.   NcD

Minutes of the 27th Annual New England Conference (A. M. E.
Zion Church) (My. 6, 1874), p. 33.   NcSalL

BLACK, JAMES L.

Wendell L. Dabney. Cincinnati's Colored Citizens (Cincinnati,
Ohio: The Dabney Pub. Co., 1926), p. 269.   DHU/MO
A. M. E. Zion minister.

BLACKBURN, GIDEON

Presbyterian Reunion 1837-1871 (N. Y.: De W. C. Lent & Co.,
1870), pp. 209-11.   DHU/MO

BLACKMAN, T. F. H.

James W. Hood. One Hundred Years of the A. M. E. Zion
Church (New York: A. M. E. Book Concern, 1895), pp. 313-
15.   DHU/MO
A. M. E. Zion minister.

BLACKNALL, THOMAS

John Hope Franklin. The Free Negro in North Carolina (N.
Y.: W. W. Norton & Co., 1943), p. 176.   DHU/R
Presbyterian and later Baptist minister in Franklin, N. Caro-
lina during the ante-bellum period.

BLACKWELL, GEORGE LINCOLN, (bp.).

David H. Bradley, Sr. A History of the A. M. E. Zion Church
1872-1968 V. 2 (Nashville: Parthenon Press, 1970), p. 89.
                              DHU/R
Bishop of the A. M. E. Zion Church.

James W. Hood. One Hundred Years of the A. M. E. Zion
Church (N. Y.: A. M. E. Book Concern, 1895), pp. 245-49.
                              DHU/MO

Wilhelmena S. Robinson. Historical Negro Biographies (New
York: Publishers Co., 1967), p. 52.   DHU/MO

William N. Hartshorn. An Era of Progress and Promise
(Boston: The Priscilla Pub. Co., 1910), p. 409.   DHU/MO

BLAKE, JOSEPH

L. A. Pendleton. A Narrative of the Negro (Wash., D. C.:
Press of R. L. Pendleton, 1912), p. 47.   DHU/MO
A missionary in Liberia.

BLAKELY, ULYSSES BUCKLEY, SR.

The editors of Ebony. The Ebony Success Library: 1,000 Successful Blacks (Nashville: The Southwestern Co., 1973), Vol. 1,
p. 30.   DHU
Presbyterian minister.

BLUE, JOSIAH

William T. Catto. Catto's Semi-Centenary Discourse (Phila.:
Joseph M. Wilson, 1857), p. 107.   DHU/R
Minister and founder of Wesley Methodist Episcopal Church.

BLYDEN, EDWARD WILMOT

Joel A. Rogers. World's Great Men of Color V. 2 (New York:
J. A. Rogers, 1947), pp. 294-97.   DHU/MO
Native of Virgin Islands and Presbyterian minister. Emigrated
to Africa "Minister of Truth", Ambassador, author, and
educator.

Edith Holden. Blyden of Liberia. An Account of the Life and
Labors of ... (New York: Vantage Press, 1966).   DHU/R

Henry F. Kletzing. Progress of a Race (Atlanta, Ga.: J. L.
Nichols & Co., 1898), pp. 498; 578.   DHU/MO

(Blyden, Edward Wilmont cont.)

    Hollis R. Lynch. Edward Wilmot Blyden. Pan-Negro Patriot
1832-1912 (London: Oxford University Press, 1970).   DHU/R

    John W. Cromwell. The Negro in American History. (Wash-
ington, D. C.: The American Negro Academy, 1914), pp. 235-
39.   DHU/R; NN/Sch

    James T. Haley. Afro-American Encyclopedia (Nashville,
Tenn.: Haley & Florida, 1895), pp. 38-40.   DHU/MO

    Wilhelmena S. Robinson. Historical Negro Biographies (New
York: Publishers Co., 1967), p. 53.   DHU/MO

    Hollis Lynch, (ed.). Black Spokesman (New York: Human-
ities Press, 1971), no. 13.   DHU/MO

BODDIE, CHARLES E.

    Giant in the Earth: A Biography (Berne, Ind.: Berne Wit-
ness Co., 1944).   DHU/MO
Baptist minister.

BODDIE, JAMES TOMOTHY

    Charles Emerson Boddie. God's "Bad Boys" (Vally Forge:
Judson Press, 1972), pp. 31-46.   DHU/R
Baptist minister.

BOLDEN, JESSE F.

    Lewis G. Jordan. Negro Baptist History U. S. A. (Nashville,
Tenn.: The Sunday School Pub. Bd., N. B. C., 1930), p. 392.
                                                DHU/MO
Organizer of the Baptists of Mississippi.

BONNER, ISAIAH HAMILTON, (bp.).

    Richard R. Wright. The Bishops of A. M. E. Church (Nash-
ville: A. M. E. Sunday School Union, 1963), pp. 94-96.
                                                DHU/R
Sixty-eighth bishop of the A. M. E. Church.

    The editors of Ebony. The Ebony Success Library: 1,000 Suc-
cessful Blacks (Nashville: The Southwestern Co., 1973), Vol. 1,
p. 33.   DHU

BOOKER, EMMER H.

    The African Methodist Episcopal Church Review (81:221, Jl. -
Sept., 1964), p. 61.   DHU/R
A. M. E. minister.

BOOKER, JOSEPH A.

    Irvine G. Penn. The Afro-American Press and Its Editors
(Springfield. Mass.: Willey & Co., 1891), pp. 258-.
                                                DHU/R; DHU/MO
President of Arkansas Baptist College and editor of Baptist
Vanguard and Baptist minister.

    G. F. Richings. Evidences of Progress Among Colored People
(Phila.: G. S. Ferguson, 1904), pp. 63-65.   DHU/R; DHU/MO

    Henry F. Kletzing. Progress of a Race (Atlanta, Ga.: J. L.
Nichols & Co., 1898), p. 508.   DHU/MO

BOOTH, C. O.

    Irvine G. Penn. The Afro-American Press and Its Editors
(Springfield, Mass.: Willey & Co., 1891), p. 262.   DHU/R
Associate editor of The Conservator and minister.

BOOTH, VENCHAEL L.

    The editors of Ebony. The Ebony Success Library: 1,000 Suc-
cessful Blacks (Nashville: The Southwestern Co., 1973), Vol. 1,
p. 35.   DHU
Baptist minister.

BORDERS, J. S.

    Lewis G. Jordan. Negro Baptist History U. S. A. (Nashville:
The Sunday School Publishing Board, N. B. Co., 1930), p. 368.
                                                DHU/R; DHU/MO
Baptist minister.

BORDERS, JAMES B.

    E. R. Carter. The Black Side. (Atlanta: n. p., 1894), pp.
208 -10.   DHU/MO
Negro Baptist minister and teacher.

BORDERS, WILLIAM HOLMES

    James W. English. Handyman of the Lord: The Life and Min-
istry of the Rev. William Holmes Borders (N. Y.: Meredith
Press, 1967).   InU; DLC
Negro Baptist minister

    The editors of Ebony. The Ebony Success Library: 1,000 Suc-
cessful Blacks (Nashville: The Southwestern Co., 1973), Vol. 1,
p. 35.   DHU

BOSTON, NOAH

    William Joseph Barber. Disciple Assemblies of Eastern North
Carolina (St. Louis: The Bethany Press, 1966), pp. 249-51.
                                                DHU/R
Black Disciples of Christ minister.

BOUEY, HARRISON N.

    Lewis G. Jordan. Negro Baptist History U. S. A. (Nashville:
The Sunday School Publishing Board, N. B. C., 1930), p. 392.
                                                DHU/MO; DHU/R
Baptist minister of South Carolina, and one of the pioneers of
West Africa Foreign Mission among Negro Baptists.

    James J. Pipkin. The Negro in Revelation in History and in
Citizenship (N. Y.: Thompson Pub. Co., 1902), p. 114.
                                                DHU/MO

    William J. Simmons, (ed.). Men of Mark (Cleveland, O.:
Geo. M. Rewell & Co., 1887), p. 951.   DHU/R

BOULDEN, JESSE FREEMAN

    William J. Simmons, (ed.). Men of Mark (Cleveland, O.:
George M. Rewell & Co., 1887), p. 707.   DHU/R

BOURGES, ANTHONY

    Charles B. Rousseve. The Negro in Louisiana (New Orleans:
The Xavier University Press, 1937), p. 141.   DHU/MO
Catholic priest.

Albert S. Foley. God's Men of Color (New York: Farrar,
Straus & Co., 1955), pp. 149-56.   DHU/R

BOURNE, IDA SHARP

The Crisis (4:5, Sept., 1912), p. 220.   DHU/MO; DLC
A negro missionary in Africa.

BOWEN, H. W.

Lewis G. Jordan. Negro Baptist History U. S. A. (Nashville,
Tenn.: The Sunday School Pub. Bd., N. B. C., 1930), p. 144.
                                             DHU/MO; DHU/R
Baptist minister and Mississippi President of State Convention.

BOWEN, JOHN WESLEY EDWARD

Benjamin G. Brawley. Negro Builders and Heroes (Chapel
Hill: Univ. of N. C. Press, 1937), p. 204. DHU/MO; DHU/R
Methodist Episcopal minister.

G. F. Richings. Evidences of Progress Among Colored People
(Phila.: G. S. Ferguson, 1904), p. 116.   DHU/MO

Henry F. Kletzing. Progress of a Race (Atlanta, Ga.: J. L.
Nichols & Co., 1898), pp. 550-52+.   DHU/MO

James L. Nichols. The New Progress of a Race (N. Y.:
Arno Press, 1929), p. 335.   DHU/MO

Thomas Culp. Twentieth Century Negro Literature (Atlanta:
Nicholson & Co., 1902), p. 29.   DHU/MO

Who's Who of the Colored Race (Chicago: n.p., 1915), p. 32.
                                             DHU/MO

William H. Ferris. African Abroad V. 2 (New Haven, Conn.:
The Tuttle, Morehouse, & Taylor Press, 1913), p. 790.
                                             DHU/MO

Wilhelmena S. Robinson. Historical Negro Biographies (New
York: Publishers Co., 1967), p. 54.   DHU/MO

BOWENS, WILLIAM B.

David H. Bradley, Sr. A History of the A. M. E. Zion Church
1872-1968 V. 2. (Nashville: Parthenon Press, 1970), p. 222.
                                             DHU/R
Minister of the A. M. E. Zion Church.

James W. Hood. One Hundred Years of the A. M. E. Zion
Church (New York: A. M. E. Book Concern, 1895), pp. 261-
64.   DHU/MO

BOWERS, JOSEPH O., (bp.).

Albert S. Foley. God's Men of Color (New York: Farrar,
Straus & Co., 1955), pp. 216-19.   DHU/R
Negro bishop of the Catholic Church.

BOWLES, CHARLES

John W. Lewis. The Life, Labors, and Travels of Elder
Charles Bowles, of the Free Will Baptist Denomination ...
(Watertown, N. Y.: Ingall & Stowell's Steam Press, 1952).
                                             NcD
Black Free Will Baptist minister.

Booker T. Washington. A. New Negro for a New Century
(Chicago, Ill.: American Publishing House, 1900), p. 133.
                                             DHU/MO

BOWMAN, JOHN WALTER

Albert S. Foley. God's Men of Color (New York: Farrar,
Straus & Co., 1955), pp. 187-92.   DHU/R
Catholic priest, chaplain in World War II.

BOYD, HENRY A.

G. F. Richings. Evidences of Progress Among Colored People
(Phila.: G. S. Ferguson, 1904), pp. 564-67. DKU/R; DHU/MO
Baptist minister and General Secretary of the National Baptist
Publishing Board.

James L. Nichols. The New Progress of a Race (New York:
Arno Press, 1929), pp. 336-37.   DHU/MO

Thomas O. Fuller. Pictorial History of the American Negro
(Memphis, Tenn.: Pictorial History, Inc., 1933), p. 249.
                                             DHU/MO

BOYD, RICHARD H.

Samuel W. Bacote. Who's Who Among the Colored Baptists
(Kansas City, Mo.: Franklin Hudson Publishing Co., 1913),
pp. 73-76.   DHU/MO
Negro Baptist minister and founder of the National Baptist
Convention Publishing House.

Lewis G. Jordan. Negro Baptist History U. S. A. (Nashville,
Tenn.: The Sunday School Pub. Bd., N. B. C., 1930), p. 392.
                                             DHU/MO

John L. Hill. When Black Meets White (Chicago: Argyle
Publishers, 1922), p. 78.   DHU/MO

Thomas O. Fuller. Pictorial History of the American Negro
(Memphis, Tenn.: Pictorial History, Inc., 1933), p. 241.
                                             DHU/MO

William N. Hartshorn. An Era of Progress and Promise
(Boston: The Priscilla Pub. Co., 1910), p. 517. DHU/MO

BOYD, WILLIAM M.

Leila A. Pendleton. A Narrative of the Negro (Wash., D. C.:
Press of R. L. Pendleton, 1912), p. 177.   DHU/MO
Presbyterian minister.

BRACKETT, N. C.

G. F. Richings. Evidences of Progress Among Colored People
(Phila.: G. S. Ferguson, 1904), pp. 38-40. DHU/R; DHU/MO
Free-will Baptist minister and first President of Storer Col-
lege, Harpers Ferry, West Va.

BRADDAN, WILLIAM S.

Harold F. Gosnell. Negro Politicians (Chicago, Ill.: Univ.
of Chicago Press, 1935), pp. 99-100.   DHU/MO
Baptist minister, Illinois. Political activist.

BRADLEY, MARK A.

David H. Bradley, Sr. A History of the A. M. E. Zion Church
1872-1968 V. 2 (Nashville: Parthenon Press, 1970., p. 206.
                                             DHU/R
Minister of the A. M. E. Zion Church

James W. Hood. One Hundred Years of the A. M. E. Zion
Church (N. Y.: A. M. E. Zion Book Concern, 1895), pp. 219-
22.   DHU/MO

BRAGG, GEORGE F.

Benjamin G. Brawley. Negro Builders and Heroes (Chapel Hill, N. C.: Univ. of N. C. Press, 1937), p. 208.   DHU/MO Rector of St. James Episcopal Church; author of History of the Afro-American Group of the Episcopal Church (1922) and Men of Maryland (1914).

Mildred Louise McGlotten. Rev. George Freeman Bragg, a Negro Pioneer in Social Welfare. Masters thesis. Howard University, 1948.

Thomas Culp. Twentieth Century Negro Literature (Atlanta, Ga.: Nicholson & Co., 1902), p. 357.   DHU/MO

BRANCH, DOROTHY SUTTON

The editors of Ebony. The Ebony Success Library: 1,000 Successful Blacks (Nashville: The Southwestern Co., 1973), Vol. 1, p. 39.   DHU

BRAWLEY, EDWARD M.

William J. Simmons. Men of Mark ... (Cleveland, Ohio: George M. Rewell, 1887), pp. 908-12.   DHU/R; DHU/MO Baptist minister, President of Selma University and editor of Baptist Tribune.

Benjamin G. Brawley. Negro Builders and Heroes (Chapel Hill: The Univ. of N. C. Press, 1937), p. 201.   DHU/MO

Daniel W. Culp. 20th Century Negro Literature (Atlanta: Nicholson & Co., 1902), p. 243.   DHU/MO

Edward A. Johnson. A School History of the Negro Race in America From 1619 to 1890 (Raleigh: Edward & Broughton, Printers, 1890), p. 148.   DHU/MO

Henry F. Kletzing. Progress of a Race (Atlanta, Ga.: J. L. Nichols & Co., 1898), p. 518.   DHU/MO

Lewis G. Jordan. Negro Baptist History U. S. A. (Nashville: Sunday School Publishing Board, N. B. C., 1930), p. 392.   DHU/R; DHU/MO

Thomas O. Fuller. Pictorial History of the American Negro (Memphis: Pictorial History Inc., 1933), p. 83.   DHU/MO

William H. Ferris. African Abroad (New Haven, Conn.: Tuttle, Morehouse, Taylor Press, 1913), p. 787.   DHU/MO

BRAXTON, P. H. A.

William J. Simmons, (ed.). Men of Mark (Cleveland, O.: George M. Rewell & Co., 1887), p. 1046.   DHU/R Baptist minister and author, Baltimore, Maryland.

BRIGHT, JOHN DOUGLAS, (bp.).

Richard R. Wright. Bishops of A. M. E. Church (Nashville: A. M. E. Sunday School Union, 1963), pp. 97-104.   DHU/R Seventy-ninth bishop of the A. M. E. Church.

Voice of Missions (81:1 & 2, Sept.-Oct., 1972), pp. 6-7.   DHU/R

BRIGHTWELL, ROBERT B.

E. R. Carter. The Black Side. (Atlanta: n. p., 1894), pp. 230-32.   DHU/MO Negro Baptist minister and businessman.

BROCKETT, JOSHUA A.

William H. Ferris. African Abroad V. 2 (New Haven, Conn.: Tuttle, Morehouse, & Taylor Press, 1913), p. 801.   DHU/MO Minister and orator, Boston.

BROOKINS, H. HARTFORD

The African Methodist Episcopal Church Review (78:218, Oct.-Dec., 1963), p. 1.   DHU/R A. M. E. Minister. Also: (78:208, Apr.-Je., 1961), pp. 66-77.   DHU/R

BROOKS, CHARLES WILLIAM

William Hicks. The History of Louisiana Negro Baptists from 1804-1914 (Nashville, Tenn.: National Baptist Publishing Board, n. d.), pp. 166-69.   DHU/R Baptist minister and state missionary of Louisiana.

BROOKS, J. D., (bp.).

David Bradley, Sr. A History of the A. M. E. Zion Church 1872-1968 V. 2 (Nashville: Parthenon Press, 1970), pp. 54+.   DHU/R Bishop of the A. M. E. Zion Church.

James W. Hood. One Hundred Years of the A. M. E. Zion Church (New York: A. M. E. Book Concern, 1895), pp. 182-84.   DHU/MO

BROOKS, L. W.

U. S. Dept. of Education. Special Report (Wash., D. C.: Government Printing Office, 1871), p. 286.   DHU/MO Baptist minister and teacher.

BROOKS, W. F.

The Church at Home and Abroad (23; 1898), pp. 109-10.   DHU/R Negro minister of Presbyterian Church and professor at Biddle University.

BROOKS, WALTER H.

Thomas O. Fuller. Pictorial History of the American Negro (Memphis: Pictorial History Inc., 1933), p. 75.   DHU/MO Baptist minister of Washington, D. C.

Benjamin G. Brawley. Negro Builders and Heroes (Chapel Hill: The Univ. of N. C. Press, 1937), p. 203.   DHU/MO

The Crisis (24:2, Je., 1922), p. 78.   DHU/MO; DLC

James L. Nochols. The New Progress of a Race (New York: Arno Press, 1929), p. 339.   DHU/MO

Who's Who in Colored America (N. Y.: Who's Who in Colored American Corp., 1938-1940), pp. 81-82.   DHU/R

Who's Who in the Colored Race V. 1. (Chicago: Half Century Anniversary of Negro Freedom in U. S., 1915), p. 39.   DHU/MO

William N. Hartshorn. An Era of Progress and Promise (Boston: The Priscilla Pub. Co., 1910), pp. 498-99.   DHU/MO

BROOKS, WILLIAM HENRY

    James L. Nichols. The New Progress of a Race (New York:
Arno Press, 1929), pp. 341-42.   DHU/MO
C. M. E. minister.

BROOKS, WILLIAM SAMPSON, (bp.).

    Richard Robert Wright, Jr., (bp.). Bishops of the A. M. E.
Church (Nashville: A. M. E. Sunday School Union, 1963),
pp. 105-10.   DHU/R
Forty-fourth Bishop of the African Methodist Episcopal Church.

BROWN, AARON

    The A. M. E. Zion Quarterly Review (84:4, Wint., 1972),
pp. 236-39.   DHU/R
Active layman of the A. M. E. Z. Church.

BROWN, B. J.

    Samuel W. Bacote. Who's Who Among the Colored Baptists
(Kansas City, Mo.: F. Hudson Co., 1912), pp. 195-96.
                                                            DHU/MO
Baptist minister and editor of the Northwestern Baptist
Informer.

BROWN, CALVIN S.

    Irvine G. Penn. The Afro-American Press and Its Editors
(Springfield, Mass.: Willey & Co., 1891), pp. 305-08.
                                                   DHU/R; DHU/MO
Baptist minister and editor of The Samaritan Journal, The
Chowan Pilot, and The Baptist Pilot.

    Charles Alexander. One Hundred Distinguished Leaders
(Atlanta, Ga.: The Franklin Printing & Publishing Co., 1899),
p. 57.   DHU/MO

    William N. Hartshorn. An Era of Progress and Promise
(Boston: The Priscilla Pub. Co., 1910), pp. 488-89.
                                                            DHU/MO

    Thomas O. Fuller. Pictorial History of the American Negro
(Memphis, Tenn.: Pictorial History Inc., 1933), p. 78.
                                                            DHU/MO

BROWN, CYRUS

    E. R. Carter. The Black Side (Atlanta, Ga.: n. p., 1894),
pp. 96-98.   DHU/MO
Ex-slave and Baptist minister.

BROWN, D. M.

    William Hicks. History of Louisiana Negro Baptists from
1804-1914 (Nashville, Tenn.: National Baptist Publishing
Board, n. d.), pp. 122-25.   DHU/R
Baptist minister.

BROWN, FREDERICK T.

    Presbyterian Reunion 1837-1871 (N. Y.: De W. C. Lent & Co.,
1870), pp. 511-12.   DHU/MO
Presbyterian minister, evangelist, and missionary.

BROWN, H. B. N.

    William Hicks. The History of Louisiana Negro Baptists from
1804-1914 (Nashville, Tenn.: National Baptist Publishing
Board, n. d.), pp. 174-75.   DHU/R
Baptist minister, editor of Louisiana Baptist.

BROWN, JOHN H.

    Emanuel K. Love. History of the First African Baptist Church
(Savannah, Ga.: Morning News Print, 1888), pp. 181-82.
                                                            DHU/MO
Deacon of the First African Baptist Church and Superintendent
of the Sunday School.

    Edgar G. Thomas. The First Baptist Church of North America
(Savannah, Ga.: By the Author, 1925), pp. 136-37. DHU/MO

    G. F. Richings. Evidences of Progress Among Colored People
(Phila.: G. S. Ferguson, 1904), p. 70.   DHU/MO; DHU/R

BROWN, JOHN MIFFLIN, (bp.).

    Richard R. Wright. Bishops of the A. M. E. Church (Nash-
ville: A. M. E. Sunday School Union, 1963), pp. 111-14.
                                                            DHU/R
Eleventh Bishop of the A. M. E. Church and editor of the
Christian Recorder.

    Benjamin Arnett. The Budget ... Biographical Sketches Pro-
ceeding ... (Dayton, Ohio: Christian Pub. House, 1882), pp.
19-23.   DHU/MO

    Irvine G. Penn. The Afro-American Press and Its Editors
(Springfield, Mass.: Willey & Co., 1891), p. 79.   DHU/R

    James A. Handy. Scraps of African Methodist History (Phila.,
Pa.: A. M. E. Book Concern, n. d.), p. 339.   DHU/MO

    William J. Simmons, (ed.). Men of Mark (Cleveland, O.:
George M. Rewell & Co., 1887), p. 1113.   DHU/R

    William W. Brown. The Rising Son (Boston: A. G. Brown
& Co., 1874), pp. 449-50.   DHU/MO; DHU/R

BROWN, MORRIS, (bp.).

    Richard Robert Wright, Jr. (bp.). Bishops of the A. M. E.
Church (Nashville: A. M. E. Sunday School Union, 1963),
pp. 115-18.   DHU/R
Second Bishop of the A. M. E. Church.

    Benjamin G. Brawley. Negro Builders and Heroes (Chapel
Hill: Univ. of N. C. Press, 1937), p. 98. DHU/R; DHU/MO

    Benjamin W. Arnett. The Budget ... Biographical Sketches
Preceeding ... (Dayton, Ohio: Christian Pub. House, 1882),
p. 7+.   DHU/MO

    Carter G. Woodson. The History of the Negro Church (Wash.,
D. C.: Associated Publishers, 1921), pp. 77-8.
                                                   DHU/R; DHU/MO

    Marina Wikramanayake. A World in Shadow; the Free Black
in Ante-Bellum South Carolina (Columbia, S. C.: University
of S. C. Press, 1973), pp. 74+.   DHU/MO

    Richard Bardolph. "Social Origins of Distinguished Negroes,
1770-1865." Journal of Negro History (40:3, Jl., 1955), p.
223.   DHU/MO

    Who Was Who in America, Historical Volume, 1607-1907
(Chicago: The A. N. Marquis Co., 1907), p. 79.   DLC

    Ulrich B. Phillips. American Negro Slavery (Baton Rough,
La.: University Press, 1966), pp. 420-22.   DHU/MO

    William W. Brown. The Rising Son (Boston: A. G. Brown
& Co., 1874), pp. 337-38.   DHU/R; DHU/MO

BROWN, ROBERT TURNER

    O. O. Sarver. Leaders of the Colored Race in Alabama (Mobile, Ala.: News Publishing Co., 1928), p. 14.   DHU/MO
C. M. E. minister.

    Charles H. Phillips. History of the Colored Methodist Episcopal Church (Jackson, Tenn.: Pub. House, C. M. E. Church, 1898), pp. 570-73.   DHU/MO

BROWN, SAMUEL ALBERT

    Wendell P. Dabney. Cincinnati's Colored Citizens (Cincinnati, Ohio: The Dabney Pub. Co., 1926), p. 252.   DHU/MO
Negro Presbyterian minister and U. S. Army Chaplain.

    William N. Hartshorn. An Era of Progress and Promise (Boston: Priscilla Pub. Co., 1910), p. 441.   DHU/MO

BROWN, STERLING NELSON

    Daniel W. Culp. 20th Century Literature (New York: Arno Press, 1969), pp. 68-69.   DHU/MO
Professor of Bible, Howard University and Congregational minister of Washington, D. C.

BROWN, THOMAS ANTHONY

    James T. Haley. Afro-American Encyclopaedia (Nashville: Haley & Florida, 1895), pp. 602-03.   DHU/MO
A. M. E. minister.

BROWNE, GEORGE D., (bp.).

    The Episcopal Church Annual (New York: Morehouse-Barlow, 1971), p. 241.   PPPD; ViA1TH
Protestant Episcopal bishop of Liberia.

BROWNE, WILLIAM WASHINGTON

    G. F. Richings. Evidences of Progress Among Colored People (Phila.: G. S. Ferguson, 1904), pp. 335-39.   DHU/R; DHU/MO
Minister and founder of the Grand Fountain, United Order of True Reformers in Virginia.

    Charles Alexander. One Hundred Distinguished Leaders (Atlanta, Ga.: The Franklin Printing & Publishing Co., 1899), pp. 20+.   DHU/MO

    Daniel W. Davis. The Life and Public Services of Rev. William Washington Browne: Founder of the Grand Fountain U. O. of True Reformers and Organizer of the First Distinctive Negro Bank in America (Philadelphia: A. M. E. Book Concern, 1910).   OWibfU

BROWNLEE, FREDERICK L.

    Henry Curtis McDowell. Frederick L. Brownlee: Heritage of Freedom (Philadelphia: United Church Press, 1963).   DHU/R
Negro missionary to Angola.

BROYLES, R. A.

    Samuel W. Bacote. Who's Who Among the Colored Baptists (Kansas City, Mo.: F. Hudson Co., 1912), pp. 136-37.   DHU/MO

Baptist minister and welfare worker.

BRYAN, ANDREW

    Benjamin G. Brawley. Negro Builders and Heroes (Chapel Hill: Univ. of N. C. Press, 1937), p. 200 DHU/R; DHU/MO
Ex-slave and Baptist minister.

    Carter G. Woodson. The History of the Negro Church (Wash., D. C.: The Associated Publishers, 1921), pp. 47-53.   DHU/R; DHU/MO

    Edgar G. Thomas. The First African Baptist Church of North America (Savannah, Ga.: By the Author, 1925), pp. 33-43.   DHU/MO

    Emanuel K. Love. History of the First African Baptist Church (Savannah, Ga.: Morning News Print, 1888), pp. 1-2.   DHU/MO

    James M. Simms. The First Colored Baptist Church in North America (Phila.: J. P. Lippincott Co., 1888), pp. 234-37.   DHU/R

    John W. Davis. "George Liele and Andrew Bryan, Pioneer Baptist Preachers." Journal of Negro History (3:2, Apr., 1918), pp. 119-27.   DHU/MO

    Richard Bardolph. "Social Origins of Distinguished Negroes, 1770-1865." Journal of Negro History (40:3, Jl., 1955), p. 222.   DHU/MO

BRYAN, PRISCILLA

    Thomas O. Fuller. Pictorial History of the American Negro (Memphis, Tenn.: Pictorial History, Inc., 1933), p. 21.   DHU/MO

Missionarist (Picture).

BRYANT, GLOSTER R.

    Wendell P. Dabney. Cincinnati's Colored Citizens (Cincinnati, Ohio: The Dabney Pub. Co., 1926), p. 277.   DHU/MO
Methodist Episcopal minister.

BRYANT, HARRISON JAMES, (bp.).

    The editors of Ebony. The Ebony Success Library: 1,000 Successful Blacks (Nashville: The Southwestern Co., 1973), Vol. 1, p. 48.   DHU
Bishop of the A. M. E. Church.

BULKLEY, WILLIAM LEWIS

    H. F. Kletzing. Progress of a Race (Atlanta, Ga.: J. L. Nichols & Co., 1898), pp. 491-94.   DHU/MO
Methodist Episcopal minister and educator.

BULLARD, ARTEMAS

    Presbyterian Reunion 1837-1871 (N. Y.: De W. C. Lent & Co., 1870), pp. 237-40.   DHU/MO
Presbyterian minister and missionary.

BUMSTEAD, HORACE

    G. F. Richings. Evidences of Progress Among Colored People (Phila.: G. S. Ferguson, 1904), p. 248.   DHU/R; DHU/MO
Minister and President of Atlanta University, Atlanta, Ga.

BUNTON, HENRY CLAY, (bp.).

The editors of Ebony. The Ebony Success Library: 1,000 Successful Blacks (Nashville: The Southwestern Co., 1973),
Vol. 1, p. 50.   DHU
Bishop, C. M. E. Church.

Robert Lewis Douglass. The Life and Thought of Bishop Henry Clay Bunton (Bachelor of Divinity paper. School of Religion, Howard University, 1968).

BURGAN, ISAAC M.

William J. Simmons, (ed.). Men of Mark (Cleveland, O.:
George M. Rewell & Co., 1887), p. 1086.   DHU/R
A. M. E. minister and college president.

BURGESS, JOHN MELVILLE, (bp.).

Edgar A. Toppin. A Biographical History of Blacks in America Since 1528 (N. Y.: David McKay Co., 1971), pp. 261-62.
                                                                DHU/R
Negro Bishop of the Protestant Episcopal Church, Boston,
Mass.

The editors of Ebony. The Ebony Success Library: 1,000 Successful Blacks (Nashville: The Southwestern Co., 1973), Vol. 1,
p. 50.   DHU

Time (80; Dec. 21, 1962), pp. 37-38.
                      DAU; DCU/SW; DGU; DGW; DHU

The Episcopal Church Annual (New York: Morehouse-Barlow,
1964), p. 422.   PPPD; ViAlTH

BURGESS, JOSEPH C.

Albert S. Foley. God's Men of Color (New York: Farrar,
Straus & Co., 1955), pp. 72-80.   DHU/R
Catholic priest and missionary to Haiti.

BURKE, JOHN E.

Torch (21; Jl.-Ag., 1937), pp. 2+.   CtY; NN
Father Burke, priest to Blacks for 42 years, worked for a
native clergy and the promotion of the canonization of Blessed
Martin de Porres.

BURNS, ANTHONY

Benjamin Brawley. A Short History of the American Negro
(New York: The Macmillan Company, 1939), pp. 81-82.
                                                                DHU/MO
A slave and Baptist minister.

Leslie H. Fishel, Jr. The Negro American ... (New York:
Wm. Morrow, 1970), pp. 199-202.   DHU/MO; DHU/R

BURNS, FRANCIS, (bp.).

Leila A. Pendleton. A Narrative of the Negro (Wash., D. C.:
Press of R. L. Pendleton, 1912), p. 149.   DHU/MO
M. E. bishop and missionary to West Africa.

James J. Pipkin. The Negro in Revelation, in History, and
in Citizenship (New York: Thompson Pub. Co., 1902), pp.
95-96.   DHU/MO

BURRELL, J. L.

William Hicks. The History of Louisiana Negro Baptists from
1804-1914 (Nashville, Tenn.: National Baptist Publishing
Board, n. d.), pp. 165-66.   DHU/R
Baptist minister and president of the Louisiana Baptist State
Convention.

BURROUGHS, NANNIE HELEN

The Worker, A Missionary and Educational Quarterly (24:110,
Oct.-Dec., 1961).   Pam. File, DHU/R
Memorial edition on life and work of Nannie Helen Burroughs.

BURSON, RICHARD H.

E. R. Carter. The Black Side. (Atlanta: n. p., 1894), pp.
85-87.   DHU/MO
Georgia State missionary and Negro Baptist minister.

BUTLER, DANIEL H.

G. F. Richings. Evidences of Progress Among Colored
People (Phila.: G. S. Ferguson, 1904), pp. 140-41.
                                                  DHU/R; DHU/MO
African Methodist Episcopal minister and President of Campbell College, Jackson, Mississippe.

BUTLER, PAUL

Albert S. Foley. God's Men of Color (New York: Farrar,
Straus & Co., 1955), p. 300.   DHU/R
Catholic priest.

BUTLER, POMPEY H.

Emanuel K. Love. History of the First African Baptist Church
(Savannah, Ga.: Morning News Print, 1888), pp. 175-75.
                                                                DHU/MO
Minister of the First African Baptist Church.

BUTLER, WILLIAM F.

William Wells Brown. The Rising Son ... (Miami, Fla.:
Mnemosyne Pub., Inc., 1969), pp. 525-26.   DHU/R
A. M. E. Zion minister.

BYRD, GEORGE

William Hicks. History of Louisiana Negro Baptists from
1804-1914 (Nashville, Tenn.: National Baptist Publishing
Board, n. d.), p. 195.   DHU/R
Baptist minister.

CAIN, RICHARD HARVEY, (bp.).

Benjamin W. Arnett. The Budget ... Biographical Sketches
Preceding ... (Dayton, Ohio: Christian Pub. House, 1882),
pp. 24+.   DHU/R
Fourteenth Bishop of the A. M. E. Church, editor and State
Congressmen.

Benjamin G. Brawley. Negro Builders and Heroes (Chapel
Hill, N. C.: Univ. of N. C. Press, 1937), p. 123.
                                                  DHU/R; DHU/MO

Concise Dictionary of American Biography (New York:
Charles Scribner, 1964), p. 135.   DHU

(Cain, Richard Harvey, (bp.) cont.)

Irvine G. Penn. The Afro-American Press and Its Editors
(Springfield, Mass.: Willey & Co., 1891), pp. 108-09.
DHU/MO; DHU/R

James C. Embry and W. B. Derrick. "The Late Bishop Cain."
A. M. E. Church Review (3:4, Apr., 1887), pp. 337-50.
DHU/MO

James J. Pipkin. The Negro in Revelation, in History and in
Citizenship (New York: Thompson Pub. Co., 1902), p. 62.
DHU/MO

Leila A. Pendleton. A Narrative of the Negro (Wash., D. C.:
Press of R. L. Pendleton, 1912), pp. 170+.   DHU/MO

Richard R. Wright. Bishops of the A. M. E. Church (Nashville: A. M. E. Sunday School Union, 1963), pp. 119-22.
DHU/R

Wilhelmana S. Robinson. Historical Negro Biographis (N. Y.:
Publishers Co., 1967), p. 59.   DHU/MO

William H. Ferris. The African Abroad (New Haven, Conn.:
Tuttle, Morehouse & Taylor Press, 1913), p. 761.   DHU/MO

William J. Simmons. Men of Mark (Cleveland, O.: George
M. Rewell & Co., 1887), p. 866.   DHU/R

William W. Brown. The Rising Son (Boston: A. G. Brown
and Co., 1874), pp. 544-45.   DHU/R; DHU/MO

CALDWELL, J. S., (bp.).

David H. Bradley, Sr., (bp.). A History of the A. M. E.
Zion Church 1812-1968 V. II (Nashville: Parthenon Press,
1970), pp. 89+.   DHU/R
Bishop of the A. M. E. Zion Church.

James W. Hood. One Hundred Years of the A. M. E. Zion
Church (N. Y.: A. M. E. Book Concern, 1895), pp. 222-23.
DHU/MO

William N. Hartshorn. An Era of Progress and Promise
(Boston: The Priscilla Pub. Co., 1910), p. 399.   DHU/MO

CALLAHM, PETER A.

Samuel W. Bacote. Who's Who the Colored Baptists (Kansas
City, Mo.: F. Hudson Co., 1912), pp. 84-86.   DHU/MO
Baptist minister.

CAMPBELL, ALEXANDER

Anti-Slavery Bugle. (3:15, Nov. 19, 1847), p. 27.   DLC
Founder of an indigenious American religious body, The
Disciples of Christ (Christian Church). Views on slavery and
his debate with Robertson, an American abolitionist.

CAMPBELL, ISRAEL

An Autobiography. Bond and Free: or Yearnings for Freedom, From my Green Brier House ... (Philadelphia: by
the Author, 1861).   SCBHC

CAMPBELL, J. S.

William H. Heard. The Bright Side of African Life (N. Y.:
Negro Universities Press, 1969), p. 91.   DHU/R
Presbyterian minister.

CAMPBELL, JABEZ PITT, (bp.).

Benjamin W. Arnett. The Budget ... Biographical Sketches
Preceding ... (Dayton, Ohio: Christian Pub. House, 1882),
pp. 16+.   DHU/MO

James A. Handy. Scraps of African Methodist History (Phila.,
Pa.: A. M. E. Book Concern, n. d.), pp. 340-41.   DHU/MO

Irvine G. Penn. The Afro-American Press and Its Editors
(Springfield, Mass.: Willey & Co., 1891), pp. 78-79.
DHU/MO; DHU/R

Richard R. Wright. Bishops of the A. M. E. Church (Nashville: A. M. E. Sunday School Union, 1963), pp. 123-26.
DHU/R

William J. Simmons, (ed.). Men of Mark (Cleveland, O.:
George M. Rewell & Co., 1887), p. 1031.   DHU/R

William W. Brown. The Rising Son (Boston: A. G. Brown
and Co., 1874), pp. 446-47.   DHU/MO

CAMPBELL, JOHN N.

Presbyterian Reunion 1837-1871 (N. Y.: De W. C. Lent & Co.,
1870), pp. 164-68.   DHU/MO
Presbyterian minister.

CAMPBELL, LEE L.

Samuel W. Bacote. Who's Who Among the Colored Baptists
(Kansas City, Mo.: F. Hudson., 1912), pp. 90-92. DHU/MO
Baptist minister and politician.

Benjamin T. Tanner. An Apoligy for African Methodism
(Balto., Md.: n. p., 1867), pp. 159-73.   DHU/MO

CAMPBELL, MATTHEW

William J. Simmons, (ed.). Men of Mark (Cleveland, O.:
Geo. M. Rewell & Co., 1887), p. 719.   DHU/R
Baptist minister.

CAMPBELL, WILLIAM J.

Edgar G. Thomas. The First Baptist Church of North America
(Savannah, Ga.: n. p., 1925), pp. 76-81.   DHU/MO
Pastor of the First African Baptist Church.

Emanuel K. Love. History of the First African Baptist Church
(Savannah, Ga.: Morning News Print, 1888), pp. 57-82; 165.
DHU/MO

CAMPHOR, ALEXANDER PRIESTLY, (bp.).

James L. Nichols. The New Progress of a Race (New York:
Arno Press, 1929), p. 346.   DHU/MO
Methodist Episcopal Bishop who served as president of the
College of West Africa and Central Alabama Institute.

The Crisis (19:5, Mr., 1920), p. 273.   DHU/MO; DLC

CANFIELD, L. W.

William Hicks. The History of Louisiana Negro Baptists from
1804-1914 (Nashville, Tenn.: National Baptist Publishing
Board, n. d.), p. 190.   DHU/R
Baptist minister.

CANNON, DAN W.

Lewis G. Jordan. Negro Baptist History, U. S. A. (Nashville, Tenn.: The Sunday School Pub. Bd., N. B. C., 1930), p. 392.   DHU/MO; DHU/R
Baptist minister of Georgia and Pres. of the S. S. & B. Y. P. U. Congress of the National Baptist Convention.

CANNON, GEORGE E.

Dennis Clark. "Black Churchman, Physician, and Republican Politician." Journal of Presbyterian History (57:4, Wint., 1973), pp. 411-32.   DHU/R

CANNON, NOAH C. W.

Alexander W. Wayman. My Recollections of African Methodist Episcopal Ministers (Phila., Pa.: African Methodist Episcopal Book Rooms, 1881), pp. 7-11.   DHU/MO
A. M. E. minister.

CAPERS, L. C.

William Hicks. The History of Louisiana's Negro Baptists from 1804-1914 (Nashville, Tenn.: National Baptist Publishing Board, n.d.), p. 193.   DHU/R
Baptist minister.

CAPTEIN, JACOBUS E. J.

Henry Gregoire. Inquiry Concerning the Intellectual and Moral Faculties and Literature of Negroes (Brooklyn: Thomas Kirk, 1810), pp. 196-207.   DHU/MO
African slave from Gold Coast ordained a Christian minister in Amsterdam.

Albert Eekhof. De Negerpredikant Jacobus Elisa Joannes Capitein, 1717-1749 (Gravenhage: M. Nijhoff, 1917).
                                                  CtY-D; DHU/MO

F. L. Bartels. Transactions of the Historical Society of Ghana (4:3-13, 1959), part 1.   DHU/MO

John Edward Bruce. Short Biographical Sketches of Eminent Negro Men and Women (Yonkers, N. Y.: Gazette Press, 1910), pp. 18-20.   DHU/MO

Wilhelmena S. Robinson. Historical Negro Biographies (N. Y.: Publishers Co., 1967), p. 10.   DHU/MO

William A. Armistead. A Tribute for the Negro (Manchester, Eng.: William Irwin, 1848), pp. 126-27+.   DHU/MO

CAREY, ARCHIBALD JAMES, (bp.).

Marcus H. Boulware. The Oratory of Negro Leaders 1900-1968 (Westport, Conn.: Negro Universities Press, 1969), p. 165.   DHU/MO
Forty-third Bishop of the A. M. E. Church.

Harold F. Gosnell. Negro Politicians (Chicago, Ill.: Univ. of Chicago Press, 1935), pp. 49-51+.   DHU/MO

Richard R. Wright. Bishops of the A. M. E. Church (Nashville: A. M. E. Sunday School Union, 1963), pp. 127-29.
                                                  DHU/R

CAREY, ARCHIBALD JAMES, JR.

The editors of Ebony. The Ebony Success Library: 1, 000 Successful Blacks (Nashville: The Southwestern Co., 1973), Vol. 1, p. 58.   DHU

CAREY, LOTT

Benjamin Griffith Brawley. Short History of the American Negro (New York: Macmillan, 1931), pp. 201-02.   DHU/MO
First American missionary to Africa. Name sometimes spelled Cary.

Abigail Field Mott. Narratives of Colored Americans (N. Y.: Boune & Co., 1882), pp. 191-99.   DHU/MO

Abigail Mott. Biographical Sketches and Interesting Anecdotes of Persons of Color (New York: M. Day, 1839), pp. 179-89.
                                                  DHU/MO

American Colonization Society. Memorial of the Semi-Centennial Anniversary of the American Colonization Society, Celebrated at Washington, January 15, 1867. With Documents Concerning Liberia (Washington: The Society, 1867), p. 178.
                                                  DHU/MO

Benjamin G. Brawley. Negro Builders and Heroes (Chapel Hill, N. C.: The Univ. of N. C. Press, 1937), p. 200.
                                                  DHU/MO

C. C. Boone. Liberia As I Know It (Richmond, Va.: The Author, 1929), pp. 25-37.   DHU/MO

Chambers' Miscellany of Useful and Entertaining Tracts (Edinburgh: William and Robert Chambers, 1845), pp. 13-15.
                                                  DHU/MO

Charles Huberich. The Political and Legislative History of Liberia (New York: Central Book Co., 1947), pp. 368-72.
                                                  DHU/MO

Death of Lott Carey (Philadelphia, Pa.: J. MacFarlan, n.d.).
                                                  DHU/MO

George Winfred Hervey. Story of Baptist Missions in Foreign Lands, From the Time of Carey to the Present Date, With an Introduction by A. H. Burlingham (St. Louis: C. A. Barnes, 1886), pp. 199-207.   DHU/MO

Hollis R. Lynch. "Pan-Negro Nationalism in the New World, Before 1862." August Meier and Elliott Rudwick, (eds.). The Making of Black America V. 1 (New York: Athenaeum, 1969), pp. 47-48.   DHU/R

James Brainerd Taylor. Lives of Virginia Baptist Ministers (Richmond: Yale and Wyatt, 1837), pp. 396-444.   DHU/MO

Miles Mark Fisher. Journal of Negro History (7:4, Oct., 1922), pp. 380-418.   DHU

Miles Mark Fisher. Lott Cary (Philadelphia: Foreign Mission Board, National Baptist Convention Publishers, 1921).   PCC

Nathaniel R. Richardson. Liberia's Past and Present (London: Diplomatic Press, 1959), pp. 25-26.   DHU/MO

Ralph Randolph Gurley. Life of Jehudi Ashmun, Late Colonial Agent in Liberia. With an Appendix, Containing Extracts From His Journal and Other Writings; With a Brief Sketch of the Life of the Rev. Lott Carey (Washington: Printed by J. C. Dunn, 1835), pp. 156-60.   DHU/MO

Who Was Who in America, Historical Volume, 1607-1907 (Chicago: The A. N. Marquis Co., 1907), p. 98.   DLC

William A. Poe. Church History (39:1, Mr., 1970), pp. 49-61.   DHU/R

William H. Ferris. African Abroad V. 2 (New Haven, Conn.: Tuttle, Morehouse, Taylor Press, 1913), p. 713.   DHU/MO

William J. Simmons, (ed.). Men of Mark (Cleveland, O.: Geo. M. Rewell & Co., 1887), p. 506.   DHU/R; DHU/MO

Carey, Archibald James, Jr. cont.)

Wilson Armistead, (ed.). A Tribute for the Negro: Being a Vindication of the Moral, Intellectual, and Religious Capabilities of the Colored Portion of Mankind ... (Conn.: Negro Univ. Press, 1848), pp. 427-31.   DHU/R
Baptist minister who emigrated back to Africa to become a missionary to Africans.

CARLETON, FREDERICK L.

E. R. Carter. The Black Side (Atlanta, Ga.: n.p., 1894), pp. 180-84.   DHU/MO
Baptist minister and evangelist.

CARNES, JAMES ROBINSON

H. F. Kletzing. Progress of a Race (Atlanta, Ga.: J. L. Nichols & Co., 1897), p. 510.   DHU/MO
A. M. E. minister.

CARR, ALTHEUS

Harriet Parks Miller. Pioneer Colored Christians (New York: Books for Libraries, 1971), pp. 39-46.   DHU/R
Reprint of 1911 edition.
Second minister of Mount Zion Baptist Church, Port Royal, Tennessee.

CARR, HORACE

Harriet Parks Miller. Pioneer Colored Christians (New York: Books for Libraries Press, 1971), pp. 15-22.   DHU/R
Reprint of 1917 edition. Negro Baptist preacher of Port Royal, Tennessee, who organized Mount Zion Baptist Church in 1867.

CARR, JAMES WESLEY

Edgar G. Thomas. The First African Baptist Church of North America (Savannah, Ga.: By the author, 1925), pp. 110-13.
                                              DHU/MO
Baptist minister.

CARR, JAMES WILLIAM

Harriet Parks Miller, Pioneer Colored Christians. (New York: Books for Libraries Press, 1971), Reprint of 1911 edition.   DLC; DHU/R
Sixth pastor of First African Baptist Church of Savannah.

CARROLL, RICHARD

Leila A. Pendleton. A Narrative of the Negro (Wash., D. C.: Press of R. L. Pendleton, 1912), p. 184.   DHU/MO
Chaplain of U. S. Army.

CARROTHERS, S. L.

James W. Hood. Centennial of African Methodism (N. Y.: A. M. E. Zion Book Concern, 1895), pp. 434-35.   DHU/MO
A. M. E. Zion minister.

CARSON, W. R.

Benjamin W. Arnett. The Budget ... Biographical Sketches Proceeding ... (Dayton, O.: Christian Publishing House, 1882), p. 34.   DHU/MO
A. M. E. minister.

CARTER, ALBERT R.

Charles H. Phillips. History of the Colored Methodist Episcopal Church (Jackson, Tenn.: Pub. House, C. M. E. Church, 1898), pp. 566-68.   DHU/MO
C. M. E. minister.

CARTER, EDWARD R.

William H. Ferris. African Abroad V. 2 (New Haven: The Tuttle, Morehouse & Taylor Press, 1913), p. 790.   DHU/MO
Baptist minister.

Benjamin G. Brawley. Negro Builders and Heroes (Chapel Hill, N. C.: Univ. of N. C. Press, 1937), pp. 203-04.
                                        DHU/MO; DHU/R

Henry F. Kletzing. Progress of a Race ... (Atlanta, Ga.: J. L. Nichols & Co., 1898), pp. 508-09+.   DHU/MO

CARTER, GEORGE C.

James W. Hood. One Hundred Years of the A. M. E. Zion Church (New York: A. M. E. Book Concern, 1895), pp. 587-89.   DHU/MO
A. M. E. Zion minister.

CARTER, I. A.

William Hicks. The History of Louisiana Negro Baptists from 1804-1914 (Nashville, Tenn.: National Baptist Publishing Board, n.d.), pp. 184-86.   DHU/R
Baptist minister.

CARTER, J. W.

Samuel W. Bacote. Who's Who Among the Colored Baptists (Kansas City, Mo.: F. Hudson Co., 1912), pp. 173-74.
                                              DHU/MO
Baptist minister, Texas.

CARTER, JAMES MONROE

William Hicks. The History of Louisiana Negro Baptists from 1804-1914 (Nashville, Tenn.: National Baptist Publishing Board, n.d.), pp. 180-81.   DHU/R
Baptist minister and editor.

CARTER, PETER J.

Albert S. Foley. God's Men of Color (New York: Farrar, Straus & Co., 1955), pp. 288-93.   DHU/R
Catholic priest.

CARTWRIGHT, A.

William H. Heard. The Bright Side of African Life (New York: Negro Universities Press, 1969), p. 16+.
                                        DHU/R; DHU/MO
A. M. E. Zion minister in Brewersville, Liberia.

CARTWRIGHT, CARRIE E. SAWYER

Lawson A. Scruggs. Women of Distinction (Raleigh: L. A. Scruggs, 1893), pp. 259-61.   DHU/MO
A. M. E. Zion church layman and missionary to Africa.

CARTWRIGHT, PETER

    Autobiography of Peter Cartwright, the Backwoods Preacher
(Cincinnati: Cranston & Curts, 1856).
                DHU/R; DHU/MO; NN/Sch
Methodist circuit rider and evangelist who was uncompromis-
ing in his hatred of slavery, but despised abolitionism. He
preferred moral persuasion for abolishing slavery.

CARY, WILLIAM STERLING

    The editors of Ebony. The Ebony Success Library: 1,000 Suc-
cessful Blacks (Nashville: The Southwestern Co., 1973),
Vol. 1, p. 61.   DHU
Executive director of National Council of Churches

    Missionary Seer (72:1, Ja., 1973), pp. 3.   DHU/R

    Voice of Missions (79:4, Dec., 1972), p. 9.   DHU/R

CASTLE, T. A.

    Samuel W. Bacote. Who's Who Among Colored Baptists
(Kansas City, Mo.: F. Hudson Co., 1912), pp. 249-50.
                DHU/MO
Founder of Rescue Home, Bryan, Texas, an institution for
girls.

CATTO, WILLIAM T.

    William T. Catto. Catto's Semi-Centenary Discourse
(Phila.: Joseph M. Wilson, 1857), p. 101.   DHU/R
Presbyterian minister of the First African Presbyterian
Church in Philadelphia.

    Martin R. Delany. The Condition, Elevation, Emigration
and Destiny of the Colored People of the United States (New
York: Arno Press, 1968), pp. 125-26.   DHU/R; DHU/MO

CATTRELL, ELIAS, (bp.).

    Charles H. Phillips. History of Colored Methodist Episcopal
Church (Jackson, Tenn.: Pub. House, C. M. E. Church,
1898), pp. 227-33.   DHU/MO; DHU/R

CAVINESS, THEOPHILUS E.

    The editors of Ebony. The Ebony Success Library: 1,000 Suc-
cessful Blacks (Nashville: The Southwestern Co., 1973),
Vol. 1, p. 62.   DHU
Baptist minister.

CHACHERE, CARMEN GEORGE

    Albert S. Foley. God's Men of Color (New York: Farrar,
Straus & Co., 1955), pp. 203-10.   DHU/R
Catholic priest.

CHACHERE, EARL

    Albert S. Foley. God's Men of Color (New York: Farrar,
Straus & Co., 1955), pp. 210-15.   DHU/R
Catholic priest.

CHAMBERLAIN, HOLBROOK

    William Hicks. History of Louisiana Negro Baptists from 1804-
1914 (Nashville: National Baptist Publishing Board, n.d.), pp.
200-01.   DHU/R
Baptist minister and founder of Leland University.

CHAMBERS, W. H.

    James W. Hood. One Hundred Years of the A. M. E. Church
(New York: A. M. E. Book Concern, 1895), pp. 593-96.
                DHU/MO
A. M. E. Zion minister.

CHAPPELLE, WILLIAM DAVID, (bp.).

    Daniel Wallace Culp. 20th Century Negro Literature (New
York: Arno Press, 1969), pp. 62-63.   DHU/MO
Thirty-seventh Bishop of the A. M. E. Church

    G. F. Richings. Evidences of Progress Among Colored People
(Phila.: G. S. Ferguson, 1904), p. 389.   DHU/MO

    John R. Wilson. A Brief Sketch of the Life and Career of the
Rt. Rev. William David Chappelle (Columbia, S. C.: n. p.,
n. d.).   OWibfU

    Richard R. Wright. Bishops of the A. M. E. Church (Nash-
ville: A. M. E. Sunday School Union, 1963), pp. 130-33.
                DHU/R

CHAVERS, JOHN D.

    G. F. Richings. Evidences of Progress Among Colored People
(Phila. G. S. Ferguson, 1904), p. 113. DHU/MO; DHU/R
M. E. minister and president of Bennett College.

    E. A. Johnson. A School History of the Negro Race in
America from 1619 to 1890 ... (Phila.: Sherman & Co., 1892),
pp. 189-91.   DHU/MO; DHU/R

    William H. Ferris. African Abroad (New Haven, Conn.:
Tuttle, Morehouse, Taylor Press, 1913), p. 689. DHU/MO

CHAVIS, BENJAMIN

    Colman McCarthy. "At the Expense of Justice." Engage /
Social Action (2:8, Ag., 1974), pp. 7-9.   DHU/R
U. C. C. Black minister, Washington director of the United
Church of Christ's Commission for Racial Justice, and cen-
tral member of the Wilmington, N. C. 10 defendants on trial
for nonviolent resistance.

    Freedomways (14:2, 1974), pp. 104-05.   DHU/R

CHAVIS, JOHN

    John Hope Franklin. The Free Negro in North Carolina 1790-
1860 (New York: Norton, 1943), pp. 170-77.
             DHU/R; DLC; DHU/MO
Antebellum Negro Presbyterian preacher and teacher.

    Carter G. Woodson. The History of the Negro Church (Wash.,
D. C.: The Associated Pub., 1921), pp. 67-70. DHU/MO

    Charles Lee Smith. History of Education in North Carolina.
Circular of Information, No. 2, 1888 (Wash., D. C.: Bureau
of Education, 1888), pp. 138-41.   DLC

    Christine Towne Tools. The Life and Times of John Chavis
(Masters thesis. University of North Carolina, 1956).

    Daniel L. Boyd. Free Born Negro, the Life of John Chavis
(Bachelor's thesis. Princeton University, 1947).

    Edgar A. Toppin. A Biographical History of Blacks in Ameri-
ca Since 1528. (New York: David McKay Co., Inc., 1971).
pp. 102, 268-69.   DHU/R

    Edgar W. Knight. The Academy Movement in the South
(Durham: n. p., 1920), pp. 21-22.   DLC

(Chavis, John cont.)

Edgar W. Knight. "John Chavis: A Negro Teacher of Southern Whites." The Baltimore Sun (Dec. 8, 1929).

Edgar W. Knight. North Carolina Historical Review (7:3, Jl., 1930), pp. 326-43.   Pam. File, DHU/R

Edgar W. Knight. "Notes on John Chavis." North Carolina Historical Review (7; 1930), pp. 326-45.
                                   DHU; Pam. File, DHU/R

George C. Shaw. John Chavis, 1763-1838, a Remarkable Negro Who Conducted a School in North Carolina for White Boys and Girls. (Binghamton, N. Y.: Printed by the Vail - Ballori Press, 1931)

Gossie Harold Hudson. A Black Man for Slavery: John Chavis (Association for the Study of Afro-American Life and History, 58th Annual Convention, New York City, October 18-21, 1973).
Speech delivered by the chairman, History Department, Lincoln University, Jefferson City, Missouri.

---- Blacks in Southern Politics Before 1861: John Chavis and Others (Pittsburgh, Pa.: Dusquesne University, Duquesne History Forum, Nov. 4, 1972).   PPiB
Speech delivered by chairman, History Department, Lincoln University, Jefferson City, Missouri.

----John Chavis: Black Federalist and Proslaverist During the Ante-Bellum Period, 1820-1838. (Moorehead, Minn: Moorehead State College, Northern Great Plains History Conference, Nov. 4, 1971).
Speech delivered by chairman, History Department, Lincoln University, Jefferson City, Missouri.

Henry T. Shanks, (ed.). The Mangum Papers (Chapel Hill, N. C.: University of North Carolina, Dept. of History, 1950), V. 1.   DLC; NcD; NcU

John Spencer Bassett. Slavery in the State of North Carolina (Baltimore: The Johns Hopkins Press, 1899).
                              DHU/MO; CoU; GU; MB

Joseph L. Seawall, "Black Teacher of Southern Whites." The New York Times Magazine (My. 18, 1924), p. 8. DHU

M. Grant Batey. John Chavis Masters thesis. (Durham, N. C.: North Carolina College, 1954).

Middleton A. Harris. The Black Book (New York: Random House, 1974), p. 86.   DHU/R

National Cyclopedia of American Biography V. 7 (New York: J. T. Wyatt & Co., 1897), p. 123.   DLC

Penelope McDuffie. "Chapters in the Life of Wiley Person Mangum." The Trinity College Historical Society Papers (15; 1925), pp. 13-14.   NcD; MB; PU

Richard Bardolph. "Social Origins of Distinguished Negroes, 1770-1865." Journal of Negro History (40:3, Jl., 1955), p. 224.   DHU/MO

Samuel A'Cour Ashe. History of North Carolina (Raleigh: Edwards and Broughton Printing Company, 1925), p. 21.
                                   ViU; DLC

Stephen B. Weeks. "John Chavis: Antebellum Negro Preacher and Teacher." Southern Workman (43:2, Feb., 1914), pp. 101-06.   DLC; DHU/MO

W. H. Quick. Negro Stars in All Ages of the World (Richmond: n. p., 1898), pp. 103-10.   DLC

Washington and Lee University Bulletin (Mr., 1929), p. 22.
                                   DLC

William K. Boyd. History of North Carolina (Chicago: The Lewis Pub. Co., 1919), p. 221.   DLC

CLAIBORNE, SMITH

David H. Bradley, Sr. A History of the A. M. E. Zion Church 1872-1968 V. 2 (Nashville: Parthenon Press, 1970), p. 116.
                                   DHU/R
Minister of the A. M. E. Zion Church.

James W. Hood. Centennial of African Methodism (N. Y.: A. M. E. Book Concern, 1895), pp. 265-68.   DHU/MO

CLAIR, MATTHEW W., (bp.).

Irvine G. Penn. The Afro-American Press and Its Editors (Springfield, Mass.: Willey & Co., 1891), pp. 330-33.
                              DHU/R; DHU/MO
Bishop of the Methodist Episcopal Church and editor of the Methodist Banner.

Thomas O. Fuller. Pictorial History of the American Negro (Memphis, Tenn.: Pictorial History, Inc., 1933), p. 81.
                                   DHU/MO

CLANTON, SOLOMON TRUMBULL

William Hicks. The History of Louisiana Negro Baptists from 1804-1914 (Nashville, Tenn.: National Baptist Publishing Board, n. d.), pp. 144-46.   DHU/R
Baptist minister; District Secretary of American Baptist Publication Society.

William J. Simmons, (ed.). Men of Mark (Cleveland, O.: Geo. M. Rewell & Co., 1887), p. 419.   DHU/R

CLARK, CAESAR A. W.

The editors of Ebony. The Ebony Success Library: 1, 000 Successful Blacks (Nashville: The Southwestern Co., 1973), Vol. 1, p. 67.   DHU
Baptist minister.

CLARK, CHARLES H.

Samuel W. Bacote. Who's Who Among the Colored Baptists (Kansas City, Mo.: F. Hudson Co., 1912), pp. 24-27.
                                   DHU/MO
Baptist minister, teacher, and co-founder of the National Baptist Publishing House.

CLARK, GEORGE V.

James T. Haley. Afro-American Encyclopaedia (Nashville: Haley & Florida, 1895), pp. 615-17.   DHU/MO
Congregational preacher and teacher.

H. F. Kletzing. Progress of a Race (Atlanta, Ga.: J. L. Nichols & Co., 1898), p. 513.   DHU/MO

CLARK, W. G.

Emanuel K. Love. History of the First African Baptist Church (Savannah, Ga.: Morning News Print, 1888), pp. 190-91.
                                   DHU/MO
Minister of the First African Baptist Church.

CLAYBORN, JOHN HENRY, (bp.).

Richard R. Wright. Bishops of the A. M. E. Church (Nashville: A. M. E. Sunday School Union, 1963), pp. 134-38.
DHU/R
Sixty-fourth Bishop of the A. M. E. Church.

CLAYTON, M. C.

Lewis G. Jordan. Negro Baptist History U. S. A. (Nashville, Tenn.: The Sunday School Publishing Board, N. B. C., 1930), p. 392.   DHU/MO
"Founder of the First African Church of Baltimore, Maryland."

CLEAGE, ALBERT B.

Hiley H. Ward. Prophet of the Black Nation: A Biography of the Reverend Albert B. Cleage, Jr. (Phila.: United Church Press, 1969).   DHU/R
Former Congregational minister and founder of "Shrine of the Black Madonna."

The editors of Ebony. The Ebony Success Library: 1,000 Successful Blacks (Nashville: The Southwestern Co., 1973), Vol. 1, p. 70.   DHU

CLEAVES, NELSON C.

Charles H. Phillips. History of the Colored Methodist Episcopal Church (Jackson, Tenn.: Pub. House, C. M. E. Church, 1898), pp. 568-70.   DHU/MO
C. M. E. minister.

CLEMENT, GEORGE C., (bp.).

Thomas O. Fuller. Pictorial History of the American Negro (Memphis, Tenn.: Pictorial History Inc., 1933), p. 77.
DHU/MO
Bishop of the A. M. E. Zion Church.

CLEMENTS, GEORGE H.

The editors of Ebony. The Ebony Success Library: 1,000 Successful Blacks (Nashville: The Southwestern Co., 1973), Vol. 1 p. 71.   DHU
Catholic priest.

CLIFTON, E. G.

David H. Bradley, Sr. A History of the A. M. E. Zion Church 1872-1968 V. 2 (Nashville: Parthenon Press, 1970), p. 350.
DHU/R; DHU/MO
A. M. E. Zion minister.

James W. Hood. One Hundred Years of the A. M. E. Zion Church (New York: A. M. E. Book Concern, 1895), pp. 218-19.   DHU/MO

CLINTON, FRANKLIN A.

James W. Hood. One Hundred Years of the A. M. E. Zion Church (New York: A. M. E. Zion Book Concern, 1895), pp. 425-29.   DHU/MO
A. M. E. Zion minister.

CLINTON, GEORGE W.

G. F. Richings. Evidences of Progress Among Colored People (Phila.: G. S. Ferguson, 1904), p. 391. DHU/R; DHU/MO
A. M. E. Zion minister and editor of Afro-American Spokesman.

Irvine G. Penn. The Afro-American Press and Its Editors (Springfield, Mass.: Willey & Co., 1891), pp. 309-12.
DHU/MO; DHU/R

James J. Pipkin. The Negro in Revelation, in History and Citizenship (New York: Thompson Pub. Co., 1902), p. 361.
DHU/MO

James T. Haley. Afro-American Encyclopedia (Nashvill: Haley & Florica, 1895), pp. 118-24.   DHU/MO

James W. Hood. One Hundred Years of African Methodism (New York: A. M. E. Zion Book Concern, 1895), pp. 268-74.
DHU/MO

William N. Hartshorn. An Era of Progress and Promise (Boston: Priscilla Pub. Co., 1910), p. 397.   DHU/MO

CLINTON, ISOM C., (bp.).

B. T. Washington. The Story of the Negro V. 2 (New York: Association Press Co., 1909), pp. 39-40.   DHU/MO
A. M. E. Zion bishop.

G. F. Richings. Evidences of Progress Among Colored People (Phila.: G. S. Ferguson, 1904), p. 390. DHU/MO: DHU/R

James W. Hood. One Hundred Years of the A. M. E. Church (New York: A. M. E. Book Concern, 1895), pp. 207-09.
DHU/MO

W. H. Quick. Negro Stars in All Ages of the World (Richmond: Adkins, 1898), p. 214.   NN/Sch

CLINTON, JOSEPH J., (bp.).

James J. Pipkin. The Negro in Revelations in History, and Citizenship ... (New York: Thompson Pub. Co., 1902), p. 89.   DHU/MO
A. M. E. Zion bishop.

James W. Hood. One Hundred Years of the A. M. E. Zion Church (New York: A. M. E. Book Concern, 1895), pp. 172-73.   DHU/MO

John J. Moore, (bp.). History of the A. M. E. Zion Church in America ... (York, Pa.: Teachers Journal Office, 1894), pp. 362-67.   DHU/MO

L. A. Pendleton. A Narrative of the Negro ... (Wash., D. C.: Press of R. L. Pendleton, 1912), p. 177.   DHU/MO

William W. Brown. The Rising Son (Boston: A. G. Brown & Co., 1874), pp. 528-29.   DHU/MO

COAN, JOSEPHUS R.

R. R. Wright, Jr. The Encyclopedia of the African Methodist Episcopal Church (Phila.: Book Concern of the A. M. E. Church, 1947), p. 68.
A. M. E. minister, writer and theologian.

COBBS, CLARENCE

The editors of Ebony. The Ebony Success Library: 1,000 Successful Blacks (Nashville: The Southwestern Co., 1973), Vol. 1, p. 73.   DHU
Minister of the Spiritualist Church of Christ.

COFFEE, T. W.

Irvine G. Penn. The Afro-American Press and Its Editors (Springfield, Mass.: Willey & Co., 1891), pp. 265-67.
DHU/R; DHU/MO
A. M. E. minister and editor of The Christian Era or Birmingham Era and The Methodist Vindicator.

COKER, DANIEL

Richard Bardolph. "Social Origins of Distinguished Negroes, 1770-1865." Journal of Negro History (40:3, Jl., 1955), pp. 221-22.   DHU/MO
A. M. E. minister. Left America in 1820 and migrated to Sierra Leone and built a church.

Isaiah H. Welch. The Heroism of the Richard Allen, Founder and First Bishop of the A. M. E. Church in the United States of America and Rev. Daniel Coker, Co-founder and First Missionary to Africa ... (Nashville: A. M. E. Sunday School Union, 1910).   NN/Sch

Journal of Daniel Coker ... Baltimore: Edward J. Cole, Publisher, 1820.   DHU/MO

L. A. Pendleton. A Narrative of the Negro (Wash., D. C.: Press of R. L. Pendleton, 1912), p. 46.   DHU/MO

COLBERT, JESSE B.

James W. Hood. One Hundred Years of the A. M. E. Zion Church (New York: A. M. E. Book Concern, 1895), pp. 256-58.   DHU/MO
A. M. E. Zion minister and secretary of the Foreign Mission Board, 1898-1904.

COLBY, LEWIS

G. F. Richings. Evidences of Progress Among Colored People (Phila.: G. S. Ferguson, 1904), p. 32.   DHU/MO; DHU/R
Baptist minister and Principal of Benedict College, Columbia, S. C.

COLE, CAIN PETER

The African Methodist Episcopal Church Review (78:210, Oct.-Dec., 1961), pp. 8-9.   DHU/R
A. M. E. minister.

COLEMAN, ALEXANDER J.

James W. Hood. One Hundred Years of the A. M. E. Zion Church (New York: A. M. E. Zion Book Concern, 1895), pp. 592-93.   DHU/MO
A. M. E. Zion minister.

COLEMAN, GORDON C.

Walter F. Watkins. The Cry of the West: the Story of the Mighty Struggle for Religious Freedom in California (Saratoga: R. & E Research Associates, 1969), pp. 23-24. DHU/R
Baptist minister.
Reprint.
Negro author.

COLEMAN, O. L.

William Hicks. The History of Louisiana Negro Baptists from 1804-1914 (Nashville, Tenn.: National Baptist Publishing Board, n. d.), pp. 161-63.   DHU/R
Baptist minister and founder of Coleman College.

COLEMAN, WARREN C.

James W. Hood. One Hundred Years of the A. M. E. Zion Church (New York: A. M. E. Zion Book Concern, 1895), pp. 403-07.   DHU/MO
A. M. E. Zion minister.

COLES, R. H.

Irvine G. Penn. The Afro-American Press and Its Editors (Springfield, Mass.: Willey & Co., 1891), p. 378.
DHU/MO; DHU/R
Editor of the Baptist Journal, Baptist minister.

COLES, SAMUEL B.

Preacher With a Plow (Boston: Houghton Mifflin, 1957).
DHU/R
Alabama born son of slave parents who became missionary for the Congregational Church in Angola, Africa.

COLES, W. R.

G. F. Richings. Evidences of Progress Among Colored People (Phila.: G. S. Ferguson, 1904), pp. 171-73.   DHU/MO; DHU/R
Presbyterian minister, superintendent of the Immanuel Training School and founder of Immanuel Presbyterian Church in Aiken, S. C.

COLES, WALTER C.

Silas Zavier Floyd. Life of Charles T. Walker (New York: Negro Universities Press, 1969), pp. 109-10.   DHU/R
Reprint of 1902 edition.
Presbyterian minister and first secretary of New York City, Y. M. C. A.; Colored Men's Branch.

COLLETT, J. H.

G. F. Richings. Evidences of Progress Among Colored People (Phila.: G. S. Ferguson, 1904), p. 389.   DHU/MO; DHU/R
A. M. E. minister and business manager of the A. M. E. Publishing House.

COLLEY, WILLIAM W.

Lewis G. Jordan. Negro Baptist History U. S. A. (Nashville, Tenn.: The Sunday School Pub. Bd., N. B. C., 1930), p. 56.
DHU/MO
First Corresponding secretary and first missionary to Africa of the National Baptist Convention.

COLLINS, C. S.

William Hicks. The History of Louisiana Negro Baptists from 1804-1914 (Nashville, Tenn.: National Baptist Publishing Board, n. d.), pp. 148-49.   DHU/R
Baptist minister and president of Houma Academy Educational Board.

COLLINS, GEORGE NAPOLEON, (bp.).

Richard R. Wright. Bishops of the A. M. E. Church (Nashville: A. M. E. Sunday School Union, 1963), pp. 139-42.
DHU/R
Eightieth Bishop of the A. M. E. Church.

COLSTON, JAMES ALLEN

Frank T. Wilson. "Living Witnesses: Black Presbyterians in Ministry." Journal of Presbyterian History (51:4, Wint., 1973), pp. 370-73.   DHU/R
Presbyterian layman, president of Knoxville College.

COMFORT, SAMUEL J.

William N. Hartshorn. An Era of Progress and Promise (Boston: The Priscilla Publishing Co., 1910), pp. 499-500.
                                              DHU/MO

Baptist minister and teacher.

CONE, JAMES H.

The editors of Ebony. The Ebony Success Library: 1,000 Successful Blacks (Nashville: The Southwestern Co., 1973), Vol. 1, p. 77.   DHU
Black theologian and professor of Union Theological Seminary, N. Y.

CONNOR, JAMES MAYER, (bp.).

Richard R. Wright. Bishops of the A. M. E. Church (Nashville: A. M. E. Sunday School Union, 1963), pp. 143-45.
                                              DHU/R
Thirty-ninth Bishop of the A. M. E. Church.

CONYERS, JOSEPH

E. R. Carter. The Black Side (Atlanta, Ga.: n.p., 1894), pp. 316-19.   DHU/MO
Baptist minister.

COOK, JOHN FRANCIS, SR.

John W. Cromwell. The Negro in American History (Washington: The American Negro Academy, 1914), pp. 229-30.
                                              DHU/MO
Presbyterian minister of Washington, D. C.

Martin R. Delany. The Condition, Elevation, Emigration, and Destiny of the Colored People of the United States (New York: Arno Press, 1968), pp. 114-15.   DHU/R
Reprint of 1858 edition.

Wilhelmena S. Robinson. Historical Negro Biographies (New York: Publishers Co., 1967), p. 66.   DHU/MO

William H. Ferris. African Abroad V. 2 (New Haven: Tuttle, Morehouse & Taylor Press, 1913), p. 698.   DHU/MO

Winfield S. Montgomery. Historical Sketch of Education for the Colored Race in D. C. 1807-1905 (Washington: Smith Brothers, 1907), pp. 9-10.   DHU/MO

COOKSEY, A. P.

Samuel W. Bacote. Who's Who Among the Colored Baptists (Kansas City, Mo.: F. Hudson Co., 1912), p. 157. DHU/MO
Baptist minister.

COPPIN, LEVI JENKINS, (bp.).

G. F. Richings. Evidences of Progress Among Colored People (Phila.: G. S. Ferguson Co., 1904), pp. 359-60+.
                                        DHU/MO; DHU/R
Thirtieth Bishop of the A. M. E. Church and editor of the A. M. E. Church Review.

(Indianapolis) Freeman (1:24, Feb. 2, 1889); (2:14, My. 25, 1889), p. 5; p. 8.   DHU/MO

Irvine G. Penn. The Afro-American Press and Its Editors (Springfield, Mass.: Willey & Co., 1891), pp. 216-17.
                                        DHU/R; DHU/MO

Richard R. Wright. Bishops of the A. M. E. Church (Nashville: A. M. E. Sunday School Union, 1963), pp. 146-50.
                                              DHU/R

William N. Hartshorn. An Era of Progress and Promise (Boston, Mass.: The Priscilla Pub. Co., 1910), p. 391.
                                              DHU/MO

CORDEN, GEORGE FRANKLIN

William Joseph Barber. Disciple Assemblies of Eastern North Carolina (St. Louis: The Bethany Press, 1966), pp. 248+.
                                              DHU/R
Black Disciples of Christ minister.

CORNELIUS

Abigail Mott. Biographical Sketches and Interesting Anecdotes of Persons of Color (N. Y.: M. Day, 1839), pp. 156-56.
                                              DHU/MO
An African assistant Christian Missionary in St. Thomas, Virgin Islands.

Wilson A. Armistead. Tribute for the Negro (Miami: Mnemosyne Pub., Inc., 1969), pp. 433-36+.   DHU/MO; DHU/R

CORNISH, SAMUEL

David E. Swift. "Black Presbyterian Attacks on Racism: Samuel Cornish, Theodore Wright and Their Contemporaries." Journal of Presbyterian History (51:4, Wint., 1973), pp. 433-70.   DHU/R
Black Presbyterian minister, editor of Freedom's Journal and Rights of All.

Benjamin Quarles. Black Abolitionists (New York: University Press, 1969), pp. 6-7+.   DHU/R

Benjamin G. Brawley. The Negro Genius (New York: Dodd, Mead & Co., 1937), p. 34.   DHU/R; DHU/MO

----- Negro Literature and Art (Atlanta, Ga.: n.p., 1910), p. 40.   DHU/MO

Frederick Cooper. "Elevating the Race: The Social Thought of Black Leaders, 1827-50." American Quarterly (24; 1972), pp. 604-25.   DHU; DGW

Gerald Sorin. The New York Abolitionists: A Case Study of Political Radicalism (Westport, Conn.: Greenwood Pub. Corp., 1971), pp. 92-3.   DHU/MO

Irvine G. Penn. The Afro-American Press and Its Editors (Springfield, Mass.: Willey & Co., 1891), pp. 28-30+.
                                        DHU/R; DHU/MO

Leslie H. Fishel, Jr. The Negro American (New York: William Morrow & Co., 1940), p. 157.   DHU/R; DHU/MO

Wilhelmena S. Robinson. Historical Negro Biographies (New York: Publishers Co., 1967), p. 68.   DHU/MO

CORR, JOSEPH M.

    A. M. E. Church Review (68: 176, Apr. - Je. , 1953), cover
page.   DHU/R
In 1835 wrote and published 1, 000 copies of the discipline,
hymnals, and minutes of the A. M. E. Church. Died at an
early age, Dec. , 1835.

CORROTHERS, JAMES DAVID

    Who's Who of the Colored Race (Chicago: n. p. , 1915), p. 77.
                                DHU/MO
    Baptist minister.

CASEY, A. A.

    Samuel W. Bacote. Who's Who Among the Colored Baptists
(Kansas City, Mo. : F. Hudson Co. , 1912), pp. 171-72.
                                DHU/MO
    Baptist minister.

COTTON, H. C.

    William Hicks. History of Louisiana Negro Baptists from
1804-1914 (Nashville, Tenn. : National Baptist Publishing
Board, n. d.), pp. 113-16.   DHU/R
Baptist minister, President of Louisiana Baptist State Convention and founder of Houma Academy and Israel Academy.

COTTRELL, ELIAS, (bp.).

    William N. Hartshorn. An Era of Progress and Promise
(Boston, Mass. : Priscilla Publishing Co. , 1910), p. 406.
                                DHU/MO
    C. M. E. bishop and teacher.

COUNCIL, WILLIAM HOPPER

    William J. Simmons. Men of Mark ... (Cleveland, O. :
George M. Revell, 1887), pp. 390-94. DHU/R; DHU/MO
Negro educator, editor, lawyer and clergyman.

COWLES, JESSE S.

    David H. Bradley, Sr. A History of the A. M. E. Zion Church
1872-1968 V. 2 (Nashville: Parthenon Press, 1970), p. 342.
                                DHU/R
    A. M. E. Zion minister.

    James W. Hood. One Hundred Years of the A. M. E. Zion
Church (N. Y. : A. M. E. Book Concern, 1895), pp. 613-15.
                                DHU/MO

CRAVATH, ERASTUS MILO

    Charles Alexander. One Hundred Distinguished Leaders (At-
lanta, Ga. : The Franklin Printing & Pub. Co. , 1899), p. 58.
                                DHU/MO
    Clergyman, educator, and president of Fisk University.

CRIDER, WALTER A.

    African Methodist Episcopal Church Review (78:215, Ja. -Mr. ,
1963), pp. 65-67.   DHU/R
    A. M. E. minister.

CROCKETT, NERO A.

    James W. Hood. One Hundred Years of the A. M. E. Zion
Church (N. Y. : A. M. E. Zion Book Concern, 1895), pp.
362-64.   DHU/MO
A. M. E. Zion minister.

CROWTHER, SAMUEL ADJAI, (bp.).

    The African Slave Boy. A Memoir of the Rev. Samuel Crow-
ther, Church Missionary at Abbeokuta, Western Africa (London: n. p. , 1852).

    Georgina A. Gollocks. Sons of Africa (New York: Friendship
Press, 1928), pp. 43-57.   DHU/R; DHU/MO
First African to be ordained minister in the Church of England,
later appointed Bishop.

    "A Second Narrative of Samuel Ajayi Crowther's Early Life. "
The Bulletin of the Society for African Church History (2:1,
Dec. , 1965), pp. 5-14.   DHU/R

    The African Slave Boy. A Memoir of the Rev. Samuel Crow-
ther, Church Missionary at Abbeokuta, Western Africa (London: n. p. , 1852).

    Adjai; or the True Story of a Little African Slave-Boy (Lon-
don: S. P. C. K. , 1882).

    Frederick Tomkins. Jewels in Ebony (London: S. W. Pat-
ridge, n. d.), pp. 60-2.   DHU/MO

    Herman K. Kumm. African Missionary Heroes and Heroines
(New York: Macmillan Co. , 1917), pp. 43-57.   DHU/R

    Jesse Page. The Black Bishop, Samuel Adjai Crowther (Lon-
don: Simpkin, Marshall, Hamilton, Kent and Co. , 1910).
                         DHU/MO; NN/Sch

    Joel A. Rogers. World's Great Men of Color (New York: J.
A. Rogers, 1946), pp. 206-11.   DHU/MO

    John McKay. The Life of Bishop Crowther, First African
Bishop of the Niger (London: Sheldon Press, 1932).
                             NN/Sch

    John R. Milsome. Samuel Adjai Crowther, Bishop of Courage
(Ibadan: Oxford University Press, 1968).   DLC

    Leila A. Pendleton. A Narrative of the Negro (Wash. , D.
C. : Press of R. L. Pendleton, 1912), pp. 29; 42. DHU/MO

    P. E. H. Hair. "Archdeacon Crowther and the Delta Pastor-
ate, 1892-1899. " Sierra Leone Bulletin of Religion (5:1, Je. ,
1963), pp. 18-27.   DHU/MO

    Southern Workman (6;7, Jl. , 1877), p. 52. DLC; DHU/MO

    William H. Ferris. African Abroad (New Haven, Conn. :
Tuttle, Morehouse, Taylor Press, 1913), p. 588. DHU/MO

    William W. Brown. The Rising Son (Boston: A. G. Brown
& Co. , 1874), pp. 106-36.   DHU/MO

CRUMMELL, ALEXANDER

    William Wells Brown. The Rising Son or the Antecedents and
Advancement of the Colored Race (Miami, Fla. : Mnemosyne
Pub. , Inc. , 1969), pp. 455-57.   DHU/R
Protestant Episcopal priest.

    Benjamin G. Brawley. Early Negro American Writers
(Chapel Hill, N. C. : Univ. of N. C. Press, 1935), pp. 299-
305.   DHU/R; DHU/MO

Benjamin G. Brawley. Negro Builders and Heroes (Chapel Hill: Univ. of N. C. Press, 1937), pp. 207-08.
DHU/R; DHU/MO

Benjamin G. Brawley. The Negro Genius (New York: Dodd, Mead & Co., 1937), pp. 101-05.   DHU/R; DHU/MO

Benjamin G. Brawley. Negro in Literature and Art (Atlanta, Ga.: n. p., 1910), p. 106.   DHU/R; DHU/MO

Elizabeth Haynes. Unsung Heroes (New York: DuBois & Dill Publishers, 1921), pp. 263-66.   DHU/MO

Henry D. Northrop. College of Life (Phila.: Nat. Pub. Co., 1895), p. 44.   DHU/MO

Henry L. Phillips. In Memoriam of the Late Rev. Alex Crummell, D. D. of Washington, D. C. An Address Delivered Before the American Negro Historical Society, of Phila., Nov., 1898, With an Introduction Address by Rev. Matthew Anderson (Philadelphia: Coleman Printery, 1899).
DHU/MO

James T. Haley. Afro-American Encyclopeadia (Nashville: Haley & Florida, 1895), pp. 561-62.   DHU/MO

John W. Cromwell. Negro in American History (Wash., D. C.: American Negro Academy, 1914), pp. 130-38.
DHU/MO

Kathleen O'Mara Whale. "Alexander Crummell: Black Evangelist and Pan-Negro Nationalist." Phylon (29; 1968), pp. 388-95.   DHU/MO

Leslie H. Fishel, Jr. The Negro American (New York: William Morrow, 1970), p. 352.   DHU/R; DHU/MO

Otey M. Scruggs. We the Children of Africa in This Land; Alexander Crummell. (Wash., D. C.: Howard University, Dept. of History, 1972.)   DHU/R

William E. B. DuBois. The Souls of Black Folk (Greenwich, Conn.: Fawcett Publications, Inc., 1961), pp. 157-65.
DHU/R; DHU/MO

William H. Ferris. African Abroad (New Haven, Conn.: Tuttle, Morehouse, Taylor Press, 1913), pp. 206; 590-92+.
DHU/MO

William H. Ferris. Alexander Crummell: an Apostle of Negro Culture. (Wash., D. C.: Published by the Academy, 1920.)   DHU/MO

William J. Simmons. Men of Mark... (Cleveland, Ohio: George M. Rewell, 1887), pp. 530-35.   DHU/R; DHU/MO

William W. Brown. The Black Man (New York: T. Hamilton, 1863), pp. 165-69.   DHU/MO

William W. Brown. The Rising Son (Boston: A. G. Brown & Co., 1874), pp. 455-57.   DHU/R; DHU/MO
Protestant Episcopal priest of Africa and Wahington, D. D.

Wilson A. Armistead. A Tribute for the Negro (Miami, Fla.: Mnemosyne Pub. Co., Inc., 1969), pp. 139; 479-90.

CUFFE, PAUL

John W. Cromwell. The Negro in American History (Wash., D. C.: The American Negro Academy, 1914), pp. 98-104.
DHU/MO

Abigail F. Mott. Biographical Sketches and Interesting Anecdotes of Persons of Color (New York: M. Day, 1826), pp. 39-46.   DHU/MO

Henry N. Sherwood. Journal of Negro History (8; Apr., 1923), pp. 152-232.   DHU/MO

Sheldon H. Harris. Paul Cuffe: Black America and the African Return (New York: Simon Schuster, 1972).   DHU/R
Includes letter to Richard Allen and his activities with the African Methodist Episcopal Church.

Narrative of the Life and Adventures of Paul Cuffe, A Pequot Indian: During Thirty Years Spent at Sea, and in Traveling in Foreign Lands (Vernon: H. N. Bill, 1839).   DHU/MO
Abolitionist.

Wilson Armistead. Tribute for the Negro (Westport, Conn.: Negro Universities Press, 1970), pp. 460-75.   DHU/R

CUNNINGHAM, LEONARD

Albert S. Foley. God's Men of Color (New York: Farrar, Straus & Co., 1955), p. 302.   DHU/R
Catholic priest.

CURRY, E. H.

James W. Hood. One Hundred Years of the A. M. E. Zion Church (N. Y.: A. M. E. Zion Book Concern, 1895), pp. 556-59.   DHU/MO
A. M. E. Zion minister and president of Livingstone College.

CURRY, G. C. F.

Samuel W. Bacote. Who's Who Among the Colored (Kansas City, Mo.: F. Hudson Co., 1912), pp. 64-65.   DHU/MO
Baptist minister.

CURRY, GEORGE EDWARD, (bp.).

Richard R. Wright. Bishops of the A. M. E. Church (Nashville: A. M. E. Sunday School Union, 1963), pp. 151-52.
DHU/R
Sixtieth Bishop of the A. M. E. Church.

CURRY, GEORGE W.

G. F. Richings. Evidences of Progress Among Colored People (Phila.: G. S. Ferguson, 1904), p. 262.   DHU/MO; DHU/R
Baptist minister.

CURTIS, L. C.

William H. Heard. The Bright Side of African Life (N. Y.: Negro Universities Press, 1969), p. 91.   DHU/R
A. M. E. minister, graduate of Howard University who migrated to Liberia.

CUTHBERT, J. J.

William H. Heard. The Bright Side of African Life (N. Y.: Negro Universities Press, 1969), p. 32.   DHU/R
Baptist minister, Careyburg, Liberia.

DANEY, JOHN C.

(Indianapolis) Freeman (1:24, Feb. 2, 1889); (1:29, Mr. 9, 1889), p. 5; p. 11.   DHU/MO
Editor of the Star of Zion and A. M. E. Zion minister.

Irvine G. Penn. The Afro-American Press & Its Editors (Springfield, Mass.: Willey & Co., 1891), pp. 197-200. Portrait, p. 199.   DHU/R; DHU/MO

DARDEN, ROBERT L.

    E. R. Carter. The Black Side (Atlanta, Ga.: n.p., 1894),
    pp. 67-69; 72.   DHU/MO
    Baptist minister.

DART, J. L.

    William N. Hartshorn. An Era of Progress and Promise
    (Boston, Mass.: The Priscilla Publishing Co., 1910), p. 462.
                                DHU/MO
    Baptist minister and educator.

DAUPHINE, JOHN W.

    Albert S. Foley. God's Men of Color (New York: Farrar,
    Straus & Co., 1955), pp. 219-22.   DHU/R
    Catholic priest.

DAVIDSON, FRANCIS JAMES

    William Hicks. The History of Louisiana Negro Baptists from
    1804-1914 (Nashville, Tenn.: National Baptist Publishing
    Board, n.d.), pp. 141-44.   DHU/R

DAVIS, DANDRIDGE F.

    A. R. Green. The Life of the Rev. Dandridge F. Davis of the
    African Methodist Episcopal Church, and His Ministerial Labor
    (Pittsburgh, Pa.: Pr. at Herald Office, 1850).
                           DHU/MO; NN/Sch

DAVIS, DANIEL W.

    Lewis G. Jordan. Negro Baptist History (Nashville: The
    Sunday School Pub. Board, N. B. C., 1930), p. 392. DHU/MO
    Baptist minister, educator, poet, lecturer and philosopher.

    Benjamin G. Brawley. The Negro Genius (New York: Dodd,
    Mead & Co., 1937), p. 167.   DHU/MO

    H. F. Kletzing. Progress of a Race (Atlanta, Ga.: J. L.
    Nichols & Co., 1898), p. 579.   DHU/MO

    William N. Hartshorn. An Era of Progress and Promise
    (Boston: The Priscilla Pub. Co., 1910), p. 454. DHU/MO

DAVIS, H. L.

    William Hicks. History of Louisiana Negro Baptists from
    1804-1914 (Nashville, Tenn: National Baptist Publishing
    Board, n.d.), p. 196.   DHU/R
    Baptist minister.

DAVIS, JAMES A.

    James T. Haley. Afro-American Encyclopaedia (Nashville:
    Haley & Florida, 1895), pp. 584-87.   DHU/MO
    A. M. E. minister

    H. F. Kletzing. Progress of a (Atlanta: J. L. Nichols &
    Co., 1898), p. 507.   DHU/MO

DAVIS, JEREMIAH B.

    E. R. Carter. The Black Side (Atlanta, Ga.: n.p., 1894),
    pp. 91-94.   DHU/MO
    Ex-slave and Baptist minister.

DAVIS, MONROE HORTENSIUS, (bp.).

    Richard R. Wright. Bishops of the A. M. E. Church (Nash-
    ville: A. M. E. Sunday School Union, 1963), pp. 153-54.
                           DHU/R
    Fifty-third bishop of the A. M. E. Church.

DAVIS, NOAH

    A Narrative of the Life of Rev. Noah Davis, a Colored Man.
    Written by Himself, at the Age of Fifty-Four. Printed Solely
    for the Author's Benefit (Baltimore: John F. Weishample,
    Jr., 1859).   SCBHC

DAVIS, RICHARD H.

    Wendell P. Dabney. Cincinnati's Colored Citizens (Cincinnati,
    Ohio: The Dabney Pub. Co., 1926), p. 257. DHU/MO
    Negro Disciples of Christ minister.

DAVIS, WALTER C.

    African Methodist Episcopal Church Review (80:220, Apr.-
    Je., 1964), p. 55.   DHU/R
    A. M. E. minister.

DAWSON, J. M.

    U. S. Dept. of Education. Special Report (Wash., D. C.:
    Government Printing Office, 1871), p. 286. DHU/MO
    Baptist minister and teacher.

DAY, WILLIAM H.

    Irvine G. Penn. The Afro-American Press and Its Editors
    (Springfield, Mass.: Willey & Co., 1891), pp. 108+.
                         DHU/R; DHU/MO
    A. M. E. Zion Layman and editor of The Zion Standard,
    Weekly Review and Our National Progress.

    G. F. Richings. Evidences of Progress Among Colored People
    (Phila.: G. S. Ferguson, 1904), p. 391. DHU/R; DHU/MO

    Henry F. Kletzing. Progress of a Race (Atlanta, Ga.: J. L.
    Nichols & Co., 1898), pp. 513-14.   DHU/MO

    James W. Hood. One Hundred Years of the A. M. E. Zion
    Church (N. Y.: A. M. E. Book Concern, 1895), pp. 321-27.
                         DHU/MO

    U. S. Dept. of Education Special Report (Wash., D. C.:
    Gov't. Printing Office, 1871), p. 336. DHU/MO

    William C. Nell. Colored Patriots of the American Revolu-
    tion (Boston: R. F. Wallcut, 1855), pp. 278-85. DHU/MO

    William H. Ferris. African Abroad V. 2 (New Haven, Conn.:
    Tuttle, Morehouse, Taylor Press, 1913), p. 697. DHU/MO

    William J. Simmons. Men of Mark (Cleveland, Ohio: Rewell
    & Co., 1887), pp. 978-84.   DHU/R; DHU/MO

    William W. Brown. The Rising Son (Boston: A. G. Brown &
    Co., 1874), pp. 499-500.   DHU/R; DHU/MO

    Wilson A. Armistead. A Tribute for the Negro (Miami, Fla.:
    Mnemosyne Pub., Inc., 1969), p. 138. DHU/MO; DHU/R

    Leila A. Pendleton. A Narrative of the Negro (Wash., D. C.
    Press of R. L. Pendleton, 1912), p. 216. DHU/MO
    Minister.

DE BAPTISTE, RICHARD

Irvine G. Penn. The Afro-American Press and Its Editors
(Springfield, Mass.: Willey & Co., 1891), pp. 262-65.
                                    DHU/MO; DHU/R
Editor of The Conservator, The Western Herald and on
editorial staff of The Brooklyn Monitor. Statistical secretary
of the National Baptist Association and Baptist minister.

Henry D. Northrop. The College of Life (Phila.: Nat. Pub.
Co., 1895), pp. 43-44.   DHU/MO
Editor of The Conservator, The Western Herald and on
editorial staff of The Brooklyn Monitor. Statistical secretary
of the National Baptist Association and Baptist minister.

Lewis G. Jordan. Negro Baptist History U. S. A. (Nashville,
Tenn.: The Sunday School Pub. Board, N. B. C., 1930), p.
392.   DHU/MO; DHU/R
Editor of The Conservator, The Western Herald and on editor-
ial staff of The Brooklyn Monitor. Statistical secretary of the
National Baptist Association and Baptist minister.

William J. Simmons. Men of Mark (Cleveland, O.: Rewell,
1887), p. 352.   DHU/R; DHU/MO

DECKER, GEORGE DOVE

William H. Heard. The Bright Side of African Life (N. Y.:
Negro Universities Press, 1969), p. 179.   DHU/R
A. M. E. minister in Freetown, Sierra Leone.

DE GRASSE, ISAIAH G.

George F. Bragg. History of the Afro-American Group of
the Episcopal Church (Balt., Md.: Church Advocate Press,
1922.   DHU/R
Protestant Episcopal priest.

Henry H. Garnet. Memorial Discourse ... (Phila.: Joseph
M. Wilson, 1865), pp. 69-91.   DHU/MO

DELAMOTTA, C. L.

Edgar G. Thomas. The First Baptist Church of North America
(Savannah, Ga.: By the author, 1925), pp. 135-36. DHU/MO
Deacon of the First African Baptist Church.

Emanuel K. Love. History of the First African Baptist Church
(Savannah, Ga.: Morning News Print, 1888), p. 169. DHU/MO

DELANY, HENRY B., (bp.).

George F. Bragg. History of the Afro-American Group of the
Episcopal Church (Baltimore, md.: Church Advocate Press,
1922), p. 213.   DHU/MO
Bishop Suffragan of North Carolina and Archdeacon for the
Colored Work of North Carolina, Protestant Episcopal Church.

DELILE, HENRIETTE

Rudolphe L. Desdunes. Nos Hommes et Notre Histoire ...
(Montreal: Arbour & Dupont, 1911), p. 136. DHU/MO
"Founder of the Holy Family Order of First Mother Superior."

DEMBY, EDWARD THOMAS, (bp.).

The Crisis (17:2, Dec., 1918), p. 75.   DHU/MO; DLC
Protestant Episcopal Bishop.

George F. Bragg. History of the Afro-American Group of
the Episcopal Church (Baltimore, Md.: Church Advocate
Press, 1922), p. 212.   DHU/MO; DHU/R

Thomas O. Fuller. Pictorial History of the American Negro
(Memphis: Pictorial History Inc., 1933), p. 82.   DHU/MO

DEMPSEY, (Father)

Hazel McDaniel Teabeau. "Father Dempsey - Priest of Charity." Interracial Review ((; My., 1936), pp. 76-78.
                                    DCU/SW; DGU
"He reared a great temple of charity and gave his life to admin-
istering it himself." --Archbishop Glennon.
Negro author.

DEPUTIE, R. M. J.

William H. Heard. The Bright Side of African Life (N. Y.:
Negro Universities Press, 1969), p. 32.   DHU/R
Presbyterian minister in Careyburg, Liberia.

DERRICK, WILLIAM BENJAMIN, SR., (bp.).

G. F. Richings. Evidences of Progress Among Colored People
(Phila.: G. S. Ferguson, 1904), pp. 387-88. DHU/R; DHU/MO
Twenty-third Bishop of the A. M. E. Church.

Benjamin T. Tanner. An Apology for African Methodism
(Baltimore: n.p., 1867), pp. 229-31.   DHU/MO

The Crisis (6:2, Je., 1913), p. 72.   DHU/MO; DLC

Richard R. Wright. Bishops of the A. M. E. Church (Nashville: A. M. E. Sunday School Union, 1963), pp. 155-57.
                                    DHU/R

William J. Simmons, (ed.). Men of Mark (Cleveland, O.:
George M. Rewell & Co., 1887), p. 88.   DHU/R
Negro author.

William N. Hartshorn. An Era of Progress and Promise
(Boston: The Priscilla Pub. Co., 1910), p. 408.   DHU/MO

DERRICKS, AUGUSTINE

Albert S. Foley. God's Men of Color (New York: Farrar,
Straus & Co., 1955), pp. 111-14.   DHU/R
West Indian priest, assistant priest in the Italian parish of St.
Ann's in Bristol, Pa.

DERRY, SOLOMON

James W. Hood. One Hundred Years of the A. M. E. Zion
Church (N. Y.: A. M. E. Zion Book Concern, 1895), pp.
370-74.   DHU/MO
A. M. E. Zion minister.

DESHONG, J. M. W.

James T. Haley. Afro-American Encyclopaedia (Nashville:
Haley & Florida, 1895), pp. 593-94.   DHU/MO
Presbyterian, editor and publisher of The Colored Cumber-
land Presbyterian.

DEVOUX, JOHN BENJAMIN

James M. Simms. The First Colored Baptist Church in North
America (Phila.: J. B. Lippincott Co., 1888), pp. 256-58.
                                    DHU/R

Baptist minister

DICKERSON, WILLIAM FISHER, (bp.).

    Richard R. Wright. Bishops of the A. M. E. Church (Nashville: A. M. E. Sunday School Union, 1963), pp. 158-59.
                                  DHU/R
    Thirteenth Bishop of the A. M. E. Church.

    Benjamin T. Tanner. An Apology for African Methodism (Baltimore, Md.: n. p., 1867), pp. 437-38.   DHU/MO

    Benjamin W. Arnett. The Budget ... Biographical Sketches Proceeding ... (Dayton, Ohio: Christian Pub. House, 1882), pp. 23-24+.   DHU/MO

    Leila A. Pendleton. A Narrative of the Negro (Wash., D. C.: Press of R. L. Pendleton, 1912), p. 177.   DHU/MO

    William H. Ferris. African Abroad (New Haven, Conn.: Tuttle, Morehouse, & Taylor Press, 1913), p. 764. DHU/MO

DICKSON, MOSES

    Leila A. Pendleton. A Narrative of the Negro (Wash., D. C.: Press of R. L. Pendleton, 1912), pp. 127-28.   DHU/MO
    A. M. E. minister

DICKSON, SIMEON F.

    James W. Hood. One Hundred Years of the A. M. E. Church (N. Y.: A. M. E. Book Concern, 1895), pp. 600-02. DHU/MO
    A. M. E. Zion minister.

DINKINS, CHARLES S.

    J. J. Pipkin. The Negro in Revelation, in History, and in Citizenship (New York: Thompson Pub. Co., 1902), p. 400.
                                    DHU/MO
    "Teacher, Pastor, Pres. Alabama Baptist Colored Univ. at Selma. "

DISNEY, RICHARD RANDOLPH, (bp.).

    Richard R. Wright. Bishops of the A. M. E. Church (Nashville: A. M. E. Sunday School Union, 1963), pp. 160-61.
                                    DHU/R
    Fifteenth bishop of the A. M. E. Church.

DIXON, SAMUEL M.

    World Call (53:11, Dec., 1971), p. 15.   DHU/R
    Layman installed as first Black President of the Chicago Disciples of Christ.

DIXON, WILLIAM T.

    E. A. Hohnson. School History of the Negro Race in America (Raleigh: Edward Broughton, 1890), p. 172. DHU/R; DHU/MO
    Baptist minister of New York and early organizer of first units of the National Baptist Convention.

    Lewis G. Jordan. Negro Baptist History U. S. A. (Nashville: Sunday School Publishing Board, N. B. C., 1930), p. 392.
                             DHU/R; DHU/MO

    William J. Simmons. Men of Mark (Cleveland: O. Rewell, 1887), pp. 713-18+.   DHU/MO

D'NLAZI, ERNEST

    Thomas O. Fuller. Pictorial History of the American Negro (Memphis, Tenn.: Pictorial History Inc., 1933), p. 21.
                                    DHU/MO
    Minister of South Africa.

DODGE, TIMOTHY S.

    G. F. Richings. Evidences of Progress Among Colored People (Phila.: G. S. Ferguson, 1904), p. 32.   DHU/MO
    Baptist minister and principal of Benedict College, Columbia, S. C.

D'ORLANDO, ALBERT

    William H. Crook and Ross Coggins. Seven Who Fought (Waco, Texas: Word Books, 1971), pp. 88-102.   DHU/R
    White Unitarian minister who survived the bombing of his church and home in New Orleans because of his efforts to make the relationship between the races better.

DORSEY, JOHN HENRY

    The Crisis (17:3, Ja., 1919), p. 140.   DHU/MO; DLC
    Catholic priest.

    Albert S. Foley. God's Men of Color (New York: Farrar, Straus & Co., 1955), pp. 52-62.   DHU/R

    J. L. Nichols. The New Progress of a Race (Naperville, Ill.: J. L. Nichols & Co., 1929), pp. 365-66. DHU/MO

    James J. Pipkin. The Negro in Revelation, in History, and in Citizenship (New York: Thompson Pub. Co., 1902), pp. 64-65.   DHU/MO

DORSEY, THOMAS M.

    E. R. Carter. The Black Side (Atlanta: n. p., 1894), pp. 87-89.   DHU/MO
    Negro Baptist minister and teacher.

DOUGLASS, JACOB M.

    William Douglass. Annals of the First African Church in the U. S. A. (Phila.: King and Bair Printers, 1862), p. 128.
    Minister of the first African Episcopal Church of St. Thomas, Phila.

DOUGLASS, WILLIAM

    William W. Brown. The Black Man (N. Y.: T. Hamilton, 1863), pp. 271-72.   DHU/MO
    Episcopalian minister and pastor of St. Thomas African Church, Philadelphia.

    George F. Bragg. History of the Afro-American Group of the Episcopal Church (Balto., Md.: Church Advocate Press, 1922), p. 71.   DHU/R

    William Douglass. Annals of the First African Church in the U. S. A. (Phila.: King & Bair Printers, 1862.) DHU/MO

    William C. Nell. Colored Patriots of the American Revolution (Boston: R. F. Wallcut, 1855), pp. 193-94. DHU/MO

    William W. Brown. The Rising Son (Boston: A. G. Brown & Co., 1874), pp. 338-9.   DHU/MO; DHU/R

DOZIER, JOHN

    Wilhelmena S. Robinson. <u>Historical Negro Biographies</u> (N. Y.: Publishers Co., 1967), p. 75.   DHU/MO
Ex-slave, Baptist minister and Reconstructionist politician.

DUFFIELD, GEORGE

    <u>Presbyterian Reunion 1837-1871</u> (N. Y.: Dew C. Lent & Co., 1870), pp. 232-37.   DHU/MO
Presbyterian minister.

DUKETTE, NORMAN

    Albert S. Foley. <u>God's Men of Color</u> (New York: Farrar, Straus & Co., 1955), pp. 115-23.   DHU/R
Catholic priest.

DUNBAR, ALBERT P.

    Samuel W. Bacote. <u>Who's Who Among the Colored Baptists</u> (Kansas City, Mo.: F. Hudson Co., 1912), pp. 286-89.
        DHU/MO
Baptist minister and teacher.

DUNBAR, BARRINGTON

    Elizabeth Cattell. "A Quaker Portrait: Barrington Dunbar." <u>Friends Journal</u> (16:9, My. 1, 1970), pp. 257-58.   DHU/R
Ghanaian, member of the Society of Friends in America.

DUNTON, L. M.

    G. F. Richings. <u>Evidences of Progress Among Colored People</u> (Phila.: G. S. Ferguson, 1904), p. 105.   DHU/MO; DHU/R
M. E. minister and president of Claflin University, Orangeburg, S. C.

DUPEE, GEORGE W.

    Lewis G. Jordan. <u>Negro Baptist History U. S. A.</u> (Nashville: Sunday School Publishing Board, N. B. C., 1930), p. 392.   DHU/MO
Baptist minister of Kentucky, editor, and moderator of General Association of Kentucky.

    James T. Haley. <u>Afro-American Encyclopedia</u> (Nashville: Haley & Florida, 1895), p. 611.   DHU/MO

    William J. Simmons, (ed.). <u>Men of Mark</u> (Cleveland, O.: Geo. M. Rewell & Co., 1887), p. 847.   DHU/R

DURHAM, JACOB J.

    Samuel W. Bacote. <u>Who's Who Among the Colored Baptists</u> (Kansas City, Mo.: F. Hudson, 1912), pp. 114-17. DHU/MO
Baptist minister and physician, president of South Carolina Baptist State Convention, and pastor of Calvary Baptist Church, Columbia, S. C.

    Lewis G. Jordan. <u>Negro Baptist History U. S. A.</u> (Nashville, Tenn.: The Sunday School Pub. Board, N. B. C., 1930), p. 152.   DHU/MO; DHU/R

    William J. Simmons. <u>Men of Mark</u> (Cleveland, O.: Rewell, 1887), pp. 878-82.   DHU/MO

DYSON, ROBERT H. G.

    David H. Bradley, Sr. <u>A History of the A. M. E. Zion Church 1872-1968</u> V. 2 (Nashville: Parthenon Press, 1970), p. 138.   DHU/R; DHU/MO
A. M. E. Zion minister.

    James W. Hood. <u>One Hundred Years of the A. M. E. Zion Church</u> (N. Y.: A. M. E. Zion Book Concern, 1895), pp. 227-33.   DHU/MO

EARLY, JORDAN

    Sarah J. W. Early. <u>The Life and Labors of Rev. Jordan Early.</u> Edited by George A. Singleton (Nashville Publishing House, A. M. E. Church Sunday School Union, 1894).
        DHU/R; INF; OWibfU; NN/Sch

EAST, J. E.

    Thomas O. Fuller. <u>Pictorial History of the American Negro</u> (Memphis, Tenn.: Pictorial History Inc., 1933), p. 89.
        DHU/MO
Baptist minister and secretary of the Foreign Mission Board, National Baptist Convention.

ECHOLS, E. J.

    Thomas O. Fuller. <u>Pictorial History of the American Negro</u> (Memphis, Tenn.: Pictorial History Inc., 1933), p. 80.
        DHU/MO
Minister of Buffalo, N. Y.

EDWARDS, J. E.

    Charles Alexander. <u>One Hundred Distinguished Leaders</u> (Atlanta, Ga.: The Franklin Print. & Pub. Co., 1899), p. 22+.
        DHU/MO
Negro minister.

EIDSON, PLEASANT W.

    Wendell P. Dabney. <u>Cincinnati's Colored Citizens</u> (Cincinnati, Ohio: The Dabney Pub. Co., 1926), p. 325. DHU/MO
Negro Baptist minister who pastored in the United States and Canada.

EIKERENKOETTER, FREDERICK J.

    James Morris. <u>The Preachers</u> (New York: St. Martin's Press, 1973), pp. 173-85.   DHU/R
Rev. Dr. Frederick J. Eikkrenkoetter II, Black evangelist, pastor of the United Church in Washington Heights, New York, Leader of Science of Living Institute and radio preacher.

    C. Clare Campbell. "Who is Rev. Ike???" <u>The Black Church</u> (2:3, Fall, 1974), pp. 10-12.   DHU/R

ELIZABETH

    <u>Colored Minister of the Gospel, Born in Slavery</u> (Philadelphia: Tract Association of Friends, 1889).   NN/Sch
Tract no. 170.

ELLIOTT, DAVID

> Presbyterian Reunion: 1837-1871 (N. Y.: De W. C. Lent &
> Co., 1870), pp. 528-30.   DHU/MO
> Presbyterian minister and president of Washington College,
> Pa.

ELLIOTT, G. M.

> G. F. Richings. Evidences of Progress Among Colored People
> (Phila.: G. S. Ferguson, 1904), pp. 183-84.   DHU/MO
> Presbyterian minister and president of Harbison Institute,
> Beaufort, S. C.

ELLIS, HARRISON W.

> Martin R. Delany. The Condition, Elevation, Emigration and
> Destiny of the Colored People of the United States (New York:
> Arno Press, 1968), p. 165.   DHU/MO; DHU/R
> Ex-slave, Presbyterian minister, missionary and educator.

EMBRY, JAMES CRAWFORD, (bp.).

> G. F. Richings. Evidences of Progress Among Colored People
> (Phila.: G. S. Ferguson, 1904), p. 387.   DHU/MO
> Twenty-fifth bishop of the A. M. E. Church.

> A. M. E. Church Review (14; Oct., 1897), pp. 269+.   NN/Sch

> Richard R. Wright. Bishops of the A. M. E. Church (Nash-
> ville: A. M. E. Sunday School Union, 1963), pp. 162-63.
>   DHU/R

ENGLES, WILLIAM M.

> Presbyterian Reunion 1837-1871 (N. Y.: Dew C. Lent & Co.,
> 1870), pp. 161-64.   DHU/MO
> Presbyterian minister, missionary, and editor of the Presby-
> terian and the Presbyterian Board of Publication.

ERSKINE, GEORGE M.

> Leila A. Pendleton. A Narrative of the Negro (Wash., D. C.:
> Press of R. L. Pendleton, 1912), p. 47.   DHU/MO
> Presbyterian minister.

ESNARD, ADRIAN

> Albert S. Foley. God's Men of Color (New York: Farrar,
> Straus & Co., 1955), pp. 63-71.   DHU/R
> Catholic priest.

ESTELL, ERNEST COBLE

> Charles Emerson Boddie. God's "Bad Boys" (Valley Forge:
> judson Press, 1972), pp. 46-60.   DHU/R
> Baptist minister.

EVANS, HENRY

> John Hope Franklin. The Free Negro in North Carolina,
> 1790-1860 (New York: Norton, 1971), pp. 178-79.
>   DHU/R; DHU/MO; DLC
> Pioneer Negro preacher of North Carolina.

> Carter G. Woodson. History of the Negro Church (Washing-
> ton, D. C.: Associated Publishers, 1921), p. 56.
>   DHU/MO; DLC

EVANS, MARY

> Our World (6; Feb., 1951), pp. 42-45.   DHU/MO; DLC
> About Reverend Mary Evans, minister of Chicago's Cosmo-
> politan Community Church.

EVANS, P. S.

> Lewis G. Jordan. Negro Baptist History U. S. A. (Nash-
> ville, Tenn.: The Sunday School Pub. Board, N. B. C.,
> 1930), p. 392.   DHU/MO; DHU/R
> Baptist minister of Mississippi and secretary of Baptist
> Convention.

FADUNA, ORESHATUKEH

> Charles Alexander. One Hundred Distinguished Leaders
> (Atlanta, Ga.: The Franklin Print. & Pub. Co., 1899), p. 59.
>   DHU/MO
> Born in West Africa, attended Yale Divinity School. Minister
> and teacher in Africa and America.

> William H. Ferris. African Abroad (New Haven, Conn.:
> The Tuttle, Morehouse, Taylor Press, 1913), p. 570. DHU/MO

FARMER, G. B.

> James W. Hood. One Hundred Years of the A. M. E. Zion
> Church (N. Y.: A. M. E. Zion Book Concern, 1895), pp.
> 550-51.   DHU/MO
> A. M. E. Zion minister.

FARRIS, BENJAMIN W.

> William N. Hartshorn. An Era of Progress and Promise
> (Boston: The Priscilla Publishing Co., 1910), p. 489.
>   DHU/MO
> Baptist minister and chaplain of the Kentucky State Legisla-
> ture.

FAULKNER, WILLIAM J.

> Louis B. Reynolds. Look to the Hills (Nashville, Tenn.:
> Southern Pub. Assn., 1960), pp. 38-42.   DHU/R
> Black Congregationalist minister.

FAUSTINA, JOHN MARCELLUS

> Albert S. Foley. God's Men of Color (New York: Farrar,
> Straus & Co., 1955), pp. 243-47.   DHR/R
> Catholic priest.

FENDERSON, WILLIAM B.

> James W. Hood. One Hundred Yeard of the A. M. E. Zion
> Church (N. Y.: A. M. E. Zion Book Concern, 1895), pp. 259-
> 61.   DHU/MO
> A. M. E. Zion minister.

FERGUSON, KATY

> John W. Olcott. "Recollections of Katy Ferguson." Southern
> Workman (52; Sept., 1923), p. 463.   DHU/MO; CtY-D; DLC
> About the Negro woman who founded the first Sunday School in
> New York City.

FERGUSON, SAMUEL DAVID, (bp.).

Leila A. Pendleton. A Narrative of the Negro (Wash., D. C.:
Press of R. L. Pendleton, 1912), pp. 49-50+.   DHU/MO
Protestant Episcopal Bishop of Liberia.

George F. Bragg. History of the Afro-American Group of
the Episcopal Church (Blato., Md.: Church Advocate Press,
1922), pp. 201-04.   DHU/MO

William H. Heard. The Bright Side of African Life (N. Y.:
Negro Universities Press, 1969), pp. 79-85.   DHU/R

FERGUSON, W. H.

James W. Hood. One Hundred Years of the African Metho-
dist Episcopal Zion Church (N. Y.: A. M. E. Zion Book
Concern, 1895), pp. 561-64.   DHU/MO
A. M. E. Zion minister.

FERRILL, LONDON

William J. Simmons, (ed.) Men of Mark (Cleveland, O.:
George M. Rewell & Co., 1887), p. 321.   DHU/R
Baptist minister.

FERRIS, WILLIAM HENRY

Who's Who of the Colored Race (Chicago: n.p., 1915), p. 102.
Methodist Episcopal minister and author.

FIELDS, J. B.

William J. Simmons, (ed.). Men of Mark (Cleveland, O.:
George M. Rewell & Co., 1887), p. 1016.   DHU/R
Baptist minister.

FIGARO, EGBERT

Albert S. Foley. God's Men of Color (New York: Farrar,
Straus & Co., 1955), p. 303.   DHU/R
Catholic priest.

FIGARO, MARK

Albert S. Foley. God's Men of Color (New York: Farrar,
Straus & Co., 1955), p. 302.   DHU/R
Catholic priest.

FINCH, WILLIAM M.

E. R. Carter. The Black Side (Atlanta, Ga.: n. p., 1894),
pp. 74-77.   DHU/MO
African Methodist Episcopal minister, businessman and first
Negro member of the Atlanta City Council.

Leslie H. Fishel. The Negro American. (New York: Wm.
Morrow, 1967), p. 260.   DHU/MO

FISHBACK, CHARLES GENTRY

Samuel W. Bacote. Who's Who Among the Colored Baptist
(Kansas City, Mo.: F. Hudson Co., 1912), pp. 295-96.
                                      DHU/MO
Baptist minister, field secretary of Foreign Mission Board,
National Baptist Convention.

FISHER, CHARLES L.

William N. Hartshorn. An Era of Progress and Promise
(Boston: Priscilla Publishing Co., 1910), p. 494.   DHU/MO
Baptist minister, professor, and editor of Sparks.

Samuel W. Bacote. Who's Who Among Colored Baptists
(Kansas City, Mo.: F. Hudson Co., 1912), pp. 241-43.
                                      DHU/MO

FISHER, ELIJAH JOHN

Miles Mark Fisher. The Master's Slave, Elijah John Fisher
(Philadelphia: The Judson Press, 1922).   DHU/MO
Pastor of Olivet Baptist Church, Georgia, written by his son,
pastor of White Rock Baptist Church, Durham, N. C.

FISHER, MILES MARK

Friends; Pictorial Report of Ten Years Pastorate (1933-1943)
(Durham, N. C.: White Rock Baptist Church, 1943).   DLC
Negro Baptist minister.

FISHER, SAMUEL

Presbyterian Reunion 1837-1871 (N. Y.: Dew C. Lent & Co.,
1870), pp. 198-205.
Presbyterian minister.

FLEGLER, S. F.

William H. Heard. The Bright Side of African Life (N. Y.:
Negro Universities Press, 1969), p. 17.   DHU/R
A. M. E. minister, Brewersville, Liberia.

FLEMINGS, J. H.

William Hicks. History of Louisiana Negro Baptists From
1804-1914 (Nashville, Tenn.: National Baptist Publishing
Board, n. d.), pp. 111-13.   DHU/R
Baptist minister and moderator of the First District Association, Louisiana.

FLIPPER, JOSEPH SIMEON, (bp.).

Richard R. Wright. Bishops of the A. M. E. Church (Nashville: A. M. E. Sunday School Union, 1963), pp. 164-67.
                                      DHU/R
Thirty-third Bishop of the A. M. E.

Daniel W. Culp. Twentieth Century Negro Literature (Atlanta,
Ga.: Nicholson & Co., 1902), pp. 256-57.

William N. Hartshorn. An Era of Progress and Promise
(Boston: Priscilla Pub. Co., 1910), p. 393.   DHU/MO

FLOOD, AUDER BACK

William Hicks. History of Louisiana Negro Baptists From
1804-1914 (Nashville: National Baptist Publishing Board, n. d.),
pp. 131-33.   DHU/R
Baptist minister and president of Louisiana Baptist State Convention.

FLYNN, H. R.

William Hicks. History of Louisiana Negro Baptists From
1804-1914 (Nashville, Tenn.: National Baptist Publishing
Board, n. d.), pp. 196-98.   DHU/R
Baptist minister.

FOOTE, JULIA A. J.

A Brand Plucked from the Fire. An Autobiographical Sketch
(New York: G. Hughes & Co., 1879).   DHU/MO; DLC
Evangelist.

FORD, ARNOLD JOSIAH

R. Landes. "Negro Jews in Harlem." Jewish Journal of
Sociology (8; Dec., 1964).   DCU
Black leader of a group of converted Jews in Harlem.

FORD, JERRY W.

The editors of Ebony. The Ebony Success Library: 1,000 Successful Blacks (Nashville: The Southwestern Co., 1973), V. 1,
p. 114.   DHU
A. M. E. minister and pastor of Bethel A. M. E. Church, Los
Angeles, Calif.

FORD, JOHN ELIJAH

Samuel W. Bacote. Who's Who Among the Colored Baptists
(Kansas City, Mo.: F. Hudson Co., 1912), pp. 283-85.
                                              DHU/MO

Baptist minister and educator.

FOSSETT, PETER F.

Wendell P. Dabney. Cincinnati's Colored Citizens (Cincinnati, Ohio: The Dabney Pub. Co., 1926), pp. 349-50. DHU/MO
Baptist minister and businessman.

Lewis G. Jordan. Negro Baptist History U. S. A. (Nashville, Tenn.: The Sunday School Pub. Board, N. B. C.,
1930), p. 392.   DHU/MO

FOSTER, WILLIAM W.

G. F. Richings. Evidences of Progress Among Colored People
(Phila.: G. S. Ferguson, 1904), p. 109. DHU/R; DHU/MO
Methodist Episcopal minister and President of Rust University,
Holly Springs, Mississippi.

FOUNTAIN, WILLIAM ALFRED, (bp.).

Richard R. Wright. Bishops of the A. M. E. Church (Nashville: A. M. E. Sunday School Union, 1963), pp. 168-70.
                                              DHU/R
Forty-sixth Bishop of the A. M. E. Church.

FOWLER, PHILEMON H.

Presbyterian Reunion: 1837-1871 (N. Y.: De W. C. Lent &
Co., 1870), p. 516.   DHU/MO
Presbyterian minister and trustee of Hamilton College, N. Y.
and Theological Seminary, Auburn, N. Y.

FRANCIS, HENRY

Carter G. Woodson. The History of the Negro Church (Wash.,
D. C.: Associated Publishers, 1921), p. 44. DHU/R; DHU/MO
Slave and pastor of the Second African Baptist Church of
Savannah.

FRANCIS, JOSEPH ABEL

Albert S. Foley. God's Men of Color (New York: Farrar,
Straus & Co., 1955), pp. 274-77.   DHU/R
Catholic priest.

FRANCIS, ROBERT B.

Samuel W. Bacote. Who's Who Among the Colored Baptists
(Kansas City, Mo.: F. Hudson Co., 1912), pp. 110-11.
                                              DHU/MO
Baptist minister and vice president of the Baptist State Con-
vention of Texas.

FRANCIS, SAMUEL L. M.

Samuel W. Bacote. Who's Who Among the Colored Baptists
(Kansas City, Mo.: F. Hudson Co., 1912), pp. 124-25.
                                              DHU/MO
Baptist minister and race advocate.

FRANCISCO JOVIER DE LUNA VICTORIA, (bp.).

The Crisis (11:1, Nov., 1915), p. 11.   DLC; DHU/MO
Catholic bishop of Panama and Peru.

Carter G. Woodson. The History of the Negro Church (Wash.,
D. C.: Associated Publishers, 1921), p. 3. DHU/R; DHU/MO

FRANKLEN, B. A.

(Indianapolis) Freeman (2:8, Je. 22, 1889), p. 4.   DHU/MO
Editor of the Golden Eagle, Baptist minister and associate
editor of The Tribune, Springfield, Mo.

FRANKLIN, MARTIN R., (bp.).

David H. Bradley, Sr. A History of the A. M. E. Zion Church
1872-1968 V. 2 (Nashville: Parthenon Press, 1970), pp. 391-
92.   DHU/R
Bishop of the A. M. E. Zion Church.

James W. Hood. One Hundred Years of the A. M. E. Zion
Church (N. Y.: A. M. E. Zion Book Concern, 1895), pp.
597-98.   DHU/MO

FRAZER, EDWARD

Wilson A. Armistead. A Tribute for the Negro. (Miami,
Fla.: Mnemosyne Pub. Inc., 1969), p. 140.   DHU/MO
Ex-slave and Wesleyan minister of Parham, Antigua.

FRAZER, GARRISON

James M. Simms. The First Colored Baptist Church in North
America (Phila.: J. B. Lippincott Co., 1888), pp. 261-62.
                                              DHU/R
Baptist minister.

FRAZIER, CHARLES P.

Wendell P. Dabney. Cincinnati's Colored Citizens (Cincinnati, Ohio: The Dabney Pub. Co., 1926), p. 292. DHU/MO
African Methodist Episcopal Zion minister and businessman.

FRAZIER, D. W.

William H. Heard. The Bright Side of African Life (N. Y.:
Negro Universities Press, 1969), p. 88.   DHU/R
Presbyterian minister, organizer of a mission at Greenville,
Sinoe County, Liberia.

FRAZIER, MARTIN F.

Wendell P. Dabney. Cincinnati's Colored Citizens (Cincinnati, Ohio: The Dabney Pub. Co., 1926), p. 336.   DHU/MO
Negro Disciples of Christ minister.

FREEMAN, RALPH

George W. Purefoy. A History of the Sandy Creek Baptist Association, from its Organization in AD 1758 to AD 1858 ... (New York: Sheldon & Co., 1859), p. 328.   DLC
Ex-slave, Baptist minister and missionary who traveled through counties in N. C. in the antebellum period.

John Hope Franklin. The Free Negro in North Carolina 1790-1860 (N. Y.: W. W. Norton & Co., 1943), p. 180. DHU/R

FRENCH, M.

G. F. Richings. Evidences of Progress Among Colored People (Phila.: G. S. Ferguson, 1904), p. 83.
                                                     DHU/R; DHU/MO
Congregationalist minister and organizer of the Educational Commission.

FRIERSON, TAYLOR

William Hicks. History of Louisiana Negro Baptists from 1804 - 1914 (Nashville, Tenn.: National Baptist Publishing Board, n.d.), p. 191.   DHU/R
Baptist minister.

FULLER, CAROLINER

William Hicks. The History of Louisiana Negro Baptists from 1804 - 1914 (Nashville, Tenn.: National Baptist Publishing Board, n.d.), pp. 150-51.   DHU/R
Baptist minister.

FULLER, JACKSON J.

William Hicks. History of Louisiana Negro Baptists from 1804-1914 (Nashville, Tenn.: National Baptist Publishing Board, n.d.), pp. 129-31.   DHU/R
Baptist minister; moderator of Northwest Association No. 2.

FULLER, THOMAS O.

Samuel W. Bacote. Who's Who Among the Colored Baptists (Kansas City, Mo.: F. Hudson Co., 1912), pp. 121-23.
                                                     DHU/MO
Baptist minister, college president, author and senator.

Thomas O. Fuller. Pictorial History of the American Negro (Memphis, Tenn.: Pictorial History, Inc., 1933), pp. 279+.
                                                     DHU/MO

Twenty Years in Public Life, 1890-1910, North Carolina-Tennessee (Nashville, Tenn.: National Baptist Publishing Board, 1910).   DHU/MO; DLC

William N. Hartshorn. An Era of Progress and Promise (Boston, Mass.: The Priscilla Publishing Co., 1910), p. 482.

GADDIE, DANIEL A.

Lewis G. Jordan. Negro Baptist History U. S. A. (Nashville, Tenn.: The Sunday School Publishing Board, N. B. C., 1930), p. 392.   DHU/MO; DHU/R
Baptist minister and Kentucky moderator of the General Association.

William J. Simmons. Men of Mark (Cleveland: O. Revell, 1887), pp. 647-50.   DHU/MO; DHU/R

GAINES, ABRAHAM LINCOLN, (bp.).

Richard R. Wright. Bishops of the A. M. E. Church (Nashville: A. M. E. Sunday School Union, 1963), pp. 171-72.
                                                     DHU/R
Forty-seventh Bishop of the A. M. E. Church.

GAINES, JOHN WESLEY, (bp.).

Benjamin W. Arnett. The Budget ... (Dayton, Ohio: Christian Pub. House, 1882), pp. 24-27.   DHU/MO
Sixteenth bishop of A. M. E. Church.

African Methodist Episcopal Church Review (78:212, Apr.-Je., 1962), p. 77.   DHU/R

E. A. Johnson. School History of the Negro Race in America (Raleigh: Edward & Broughton, Printers, 1890), pp. 145-47.
                                                     DHU/MO; DHU/R

G. F. Richings. Evidences of Progress Among Colored People (Phila.: G. S. Ferguson, 1904), p. 385.   DHU/MO; DHU/R

James J. Pipkin. The Negro in Revelation, in History, and in Citizenship (New York: Thompson Pub. Co., 1902), pp. 106-07.
                                                     DHU/MO

William N. Hartshorn. An Era of Progress and Promise (Boston, Mass.: The Priscilla Pub. Co., 1910), pp. 386-88.
                                                     DHU/MO

Richard R. Wright. Bishops of the A. M. E. Church (Nashville: A. M. E. Sunday School Union, 1963), pp. 173-78.
                                                     DHU/R

GAINES, MATT.

John Mason Brewer. Negro Legislators of Texas and Their Descendants; a History of the Negro in Texas Politics From Reconstruction to Disfranchisement. (Dallas, Texas: Mathis Publishing Co., 1935), pp. 50-52.
Activist politician, Texas State Senator, former slave and minister.

GALBRAITH, GEORGE, (bp.).

A. M. E. Zion Quarterly Review (62; 1952), p. 224.   NcSalL

Carter G. Woodson. The History of the Negro Church (Washington, D. C.: Associated Publishers, 1921), p. 92.
                                                     DHU/R; NcSalL
A. M. E. Zion Bishop.

James B. F. Shaw. The Negro in the History of Methodism (Nashville: Parthenon Press, 1954), p. 76.   DHU/R

John J. Moore. History of the A. M. E. Zion Church in America (York, Pa.: Teachers Journal Office, 1884), pp. 355-62.
                                                     DHU/MO

GARDINER, T. MOMOLU, (bp.).

George F. Bragg. History of the Afro-American Episcopal Church (Baltimore, Md.: Church Advocate Press, 1922), p. 214.
                                                     NN/Sch
Bishop Suffragan of Liberia, Protestant Episcopal Church.

The Crisis (22:5, Sept., 1921), p. 216.   DHU/MO; DLC

GARDNER, CHARLES

William T. Catto. Catto's Semi'Centenary Discourse (Phila.: Joseph M. Wilson, 1857), pp. 84-86.   DHU/R
Presbyterian minister, the First African Presbyterian Church, Philadelphia.

The Christian Recorder (Apr. 11, 1863), p. 58.

GARNET, HENRY HIGHLAND

William Wells Brown. The Black Man (Miami, Fla.: Mnemo-syne Pub. Co., Inc., 1969), pp. 149-51.   DHU/R
Black Presbyterian minister and ardent abolitionist editor.

Alfred Nevin, (ed.). Encyclopedia of the Presbyterian Church (Phila.: Presbyterian Pub. Co., 1884), p. 257.   NjP; NNUT

Benjamin G. Brawley. Negro Builders and Heroes (Chapel Hill, N. C.: Univ. of N. C. Press, 1937), pp. 208-09.   DHU/MO

Benjamin W. Arnett. The Budget ... (Dayton, Ohio: Christ-ian Pub. House, 1882), p. 126.   DHU/MO

Benjamin G. Brawley. Early Negro American Writers (Chapel Hill, N. C.: Univ. of N. C. Press, 1935), p. 124.   DHU/MO

Benjamin G. Brawley. The Negro Genius (New York: Dodd, Mead & Co., 1937), pp. 47-50.   DHU/MO

Carter G. Woodson. Dictionary of American Biography V. 4 (New York: Scribner's & Co., 1932), pp. 154-55.   DHU

Carter G. Woodson. The History of the Negro Church (Wash., D. C.: The Associated Publishers, 1921), pp. 175-76.
DHU/MO

Earl Ofari. Let Your Thoughts be Resistance: The Life and Thought of Henry Highland Garnet (Boston: Beacon Press, 1972.)   DHU/R

Hallie Q. Brown. Homespun Heroines and Other Women of Distinction (Xenia, O.: The Aldine Pub. Co., 1926), pp. 110-14.   DHU/MO

Henry D. Northrop. The College of Life (Phila.: Nat. Pub. Co., 1895), p. 43.   DHU/MO

Irvine G. Penn. The Afro-American Press and Its Editors (Springfield, Mass.: Willey & Co., 1891), pp. 52-54.
DHU/R; DHU/MO

James A. Handy. Scraps of African Methodist History (Phila., Pa.: A. M. E. Book Concern, n. d.), pp. 404-05.   DHU/MO

James McCune Smith. Sketch of the Life and Labors of Rev. Henry Highland Garnet (Phila.: Joseph M. Wilson, 1865), pp. 17-68.   DHU/MO

John W. Cromwell. The Negro in American History (Wash., D. C.: The American Negro Academy, 1914), pp. 126-29.
DHU/MO

Journal of Negro History (13; Ja., 1928), pp. 36-52.
DHU; DLC

Leila A. Pendleton. A Narrative of the Negro (Wash., D. C.: Press of R. L. Pendleton, 1912), pp. 50+.   DHU/MO

Martin R. Delany. The Condition, Elevation, Emigration and Destiny of the Colored People of the U. S. (New York: Arno Press, 1968), p. 127.   DHU/R; DHU/MO

Richard K. MacMaster. "Henry Highland Garnet and the Af-rican Civilization Society." Journal of Presbyterian History (48; Sum., 1970), pp. 95-112.   DHU/R

Who Was Who in America, Historical Volume, 1607-1907 (Chicago: The A. N. Marquis Co., 1907), p. 198.   DLC

Wilhelmena S. Robinson. Historical Negro Biographies (New York: Publishers Co., 1967), p. 82.   DHU/MO

William J. Simmons. Men of Mark (Cleveland, O.: George M. Rewell & Co., 1887), p. 656.   DHU/R

William W. Brown. The Rising Son (Boston: A. G. Brown & Co., 1874), pp. 457-59.   DHU/MO

Wilson A. Armistead. A Tribute for the Negro (Miami, Fla.: Mnemosyne Pub. Co., Inc., 1969), pp. 139+.   DHU/MO

GARNIER, LUC, (bp.).

The Episcopal Church Annual (New York: Morehouse-Barlow, 1972), p. 235.   PPPD; ViAlTH
Protestant Episcopal bishop of Haiti.

GARVEY, MARCUS

Joel A. Rogers. World's Great Men of Color V. 2 (New York: J. A. Rogers, 1947), pp. 415-31. DHU/MO; DHU/R
'Back to Africa' leader and a 'Messiah' to his large following.

Arther P. Davis and Sauders Redding, (eds.). Cavalcade: Negro American Writing from 1760 to the Present (Boston: Houghton Mifflin, 1971), pp. 264-68.   DHU/MO
Negro author.

Edgar A. Toppin. A Biographical History of Blacks in Amer-ica Since 1528 (New York: David McKay Co., 1971), pp. 302-04.   DHU/MO; DHU/R

Edmund D. Cronon. Black Moses, the Story of Marcus Garvey ... (Madison, Wisc.: The University of Wisconsin Press, 1969).   DHU/R; DHU/MO
Garvey's ideas on religion, pp. 177-83; 215.

Ruth Miller, (ed.). Black American Literature 1760-Present (Beverly Hills, Cal.: Glencoe Press, 1971), pp. 191-98.
DHU/MO

The Universal Negro Improvement Association (UNIA). Harry A. Ploski, (ed.). Reference Library of Black America (New York: Bellwether Pub. Co., Inc., 1971), Bood 2, pp. 26-28.
DHU

GEDDA, J. R.

William H. Heard. The Bright Side of African Life (N. Y.: Negro Universities Press, 1969), p. 17.   DHU/R
A. M. E. minister in Brewersville, Liberia.

GEORGE, ARTHUR HENRY

Frank T. Wilson. "Living Witnesses: Black Presbyterians in Ministry." Journal of Presbyterian History (51:4, Wint., 1973), pp. 361-64.   DHU/R
Presbyterian minister, teacher and dean of Johnson C. Smith Seminary.

GEORGE, DAVID

Carter G. Woodson. The History of the Negro Church (Wash., D. C.: The Associated Publishers, 1921), pp. 42-43. DHU/MO
A Negro Baptist slave preacher. Associated with First Baptist Church in North America and founder of the First Baptist Church in Sierra Leone.

GEORGE, ELIZA DAVIS

The African Methodist Episcopal Church (80:220, Apr.-Je.,
1964), pp. 43-46.   DHU/R
Story of a Texas Black woman who devoted half a century to
missionary work in Africa.

GIBBONS, GEORGE

Emanuel K. Love. History of the First African Baptist Church
(Savannah, Ga.: Morning News Print, 1888), p. 168. DHU/MO
Deacon and assistant pastor of the First African Baptist Church.

Edgar G. Thomas. The First Baptist Church of North America (Savannah, Ga.: By the author. 1925), pp. 82-85.
                                                       DHU/MO

GIBBS, CAREY ABRAHAM, (bp.).

Richard R. Wright. Bishops of the A. M. E. Church (Nashville: A. M. E. Sunday School Union, 1963), pp. 179-84.
                                                       DHU/R
Seventieth Bishop of the A. M. E. Church.

GIBBS, EMILY V.

Frank T. Wilson. "Living Witnesses: Black Presbyterians in
Ministry." Journal of Presbyterian History (51:4, Wint., 1973),
pp. 381-83.   DHU/R
Presbyterian church executive and program consultant.

GIBBS. JONATHAN C.

The Christian Recorder (Mr. 17, 1866), p. 42.
Presbyterian pastor in Philadelphia and Troy, N. Y.

GILBERT, MATTHEW W.

William N. Hartshorn. An Era of Progress and Promise.
(Boston: The Priscilla Publishing Co., 1910), p. 490.
                                                       DHU/MO
Baptist minister and one-time Vice-President of the Southern
Baptist Annual Association.

G. F. Richings. Evidences of Progress Among Colored People
(Philadelphia: G. S. Ferguson, 1904), p. 53.
                                                       DHU/MO; DHU/R

GLASCO, BENJAMIN FRANKLIN

Frank T. Wilson. "Living Witnesses: Black Presbyterians in
Ministry." Journal of Presbyterian History (51:4, Wint.,
1973), pp. 357-58.   DHU/R
Presbyterian evangelist, Berean Presbyterian Church in Philadelphia, Pa.

GLOUCESTER, JEREMIAH

William Douglass. Annals of the First African Church in the
U. S. A. (Philadelphia: King and Baird Printers, 1862), p.
126.   DHU/MO
Presbyterian minister and son of John Gloucester, minister of
the First African Presbyterian Church

GLOUCESTER, JOHN

Carter G. Woodson. The History of the Negro Church (Wash.,
D. C.: Associated Publishers, 1921), p. 56+.
                                                       DHU/R; DHU/MO
Founder of First African Presbyterian Church in Philadelphia
in 1802.

Benjamin Quarles. Black Abolitionists (New York: University Press, 1969), pp. 3-5+.   DHU/R

E. H. Gillett. History of the Presbyterian Church in the
United States of America, V. 1 (Phila.: Presbyterian Board
of Publication, 1864), pp. 486-87.   DHU/R

GLOUCESTER, STEPHEN

Wilson Armistead. A Tribute for the Negro (Miami, Fla.:
Mnemosyne Pub. Inc., 1969), p. 139.   DHU/MO
Presbyterian minister and son of John Gloucester, minister
of the First African Presbyterian Church.

Benjamin Quarles. Black Abolitionists (New York: University Press, 1969), pp. 45-46+.   DHU/R

GOLER, WILLIAM H.

David H. Bradley, Sr. A History of the A. M. E. Zion
Church 1872-1968 V. 2 (Nashville: Parthenon Press, 1970),
pp. 32+.   DHU/R
President of Livingstone College, Salisbury, N. C., A. M. E.
Zion college.

James W. Hood. One Hundred Years of the A. M. E. Zion
Church (N. Y.: A. M. E. Zion Book Concern, 1895), pp.
447-55.   DHU/MO

GOMEZ. JOSEPH, (bp.).

Richard R. Wright. Bishops of the A. M. E. Church (Nashville: A. M. E. Sunday School Union, 1963), pp. 185-97.
                                                       DHU/R
Sixty-seventh Bishop of the A. M. E. Church.

GOODALL, THOMAS JEFFERSON

Edgar G. Thomas. The First African Baptist Church of North
America (Savannah, Ga.: By the author, 1925), pp. 118-21.
                                                       DHU/MO
Baptist minister.

GOODE, GEORGE WASHINGTON

Samuel W. Bacote. Who's Who Among the Colored Baptists.
(Kansas City, Mo.: F. Hudson Co., 1912), pp. 204-06.
                                                       DHU/MO
Baptist minister and president of General Association of Vir-
ginia.

GOODWIN, GEORGE A.

Samuel W. Bacote. Who's Who Among Colored Baptists (Kansas City, Mo.: F. Hudson Co., 1912), pp. 164-66. DHU/MO
Baptist minister and professor.

GOODWIN, J. J.

Samuel W. Bacote. Who's Who Among Colored Baptists (Kan-
sas City, Mo.: F. Hudson Co., 1912), pp. 161-62. DHU/MO
Baptist minister, clerk, moderator and president of East Texas
Bethel Association.

GOODWIN, KELLY OLIVER PERRY

The editors of Ebony. The Ebony Success Library: 1,000 Successful Blacks (Nashville: The Southwestern Co., 1973), V. 1,
p. 127.   DHU
Baptist minister and pastor of Mount Zion Baptist Church,
Winston-Salem, N. C.

GOPAUL, PAUL

Albert S. Foley. God's Men of Color (New York: Farrar,
Straus & Co., 1955), p. 303.   DHU/R
Catholic priest.

GORDON, CHARLES B. W.

William Henry Sherwood. Life of Charles B. W. Gordon, Pas-
tor of the First Baptist Church, Petersburg, Virginia, and
History of the Church (Petersburg: J. B. Edge Steam, Printer,
1885).   NN/Sch
Includes sermon by Charles B. W. Gordon. Author, Negro
Evangelist

Charles Alexander. One Hundred Distinguished Leaders.
(Atlanta, Ga.: The Franklin Printing and Publishing Co., 1899),
p. 60.   DHU/MO

Irvine G. Penn. The Afro-American Press and Its Editors.
(Springfield, Mass.: Willey & Co., 1891), pp. 194-96.
                                    DHU/MO; DHU/R

Samuel W. Bacote. Who's Who Among the Colored Baptists.
(Kansas City, Mo.: F. Hudson Co., 1912), pp. 211-13. DHU/MO

GOW, FRANCIS HERMAN, (bp.).

Richard R. Wright. Bishops of the A. M. E. Church (Nashville: A. M. E. Sunday School Union, 1963), pp. 188-90.
                                                   DHU/R
Seventy-fourth Bishop of the A. M. E. Church

GRACE, CHARLES MANUEL (Daddy Grace).

Marcus H. Boulware. The Oratory of Negro Leaders 1900-
1968 (Westport, Conn.: Negro Universities Press, 1969), p.
208.   DHU/MO
Cult leader of the "House of Prayer For All People."

Life (19; Oct. 1, 1945), pp. 51-56+.   DHU/MO

GRAHAM, D. A.

James D. Northrop. College of Life (Phila.: National Pub.
Co., 1895), pp. 51-52.   DHU/MO
A. M. E. minister.

GRAHAM, WESLEY F.

William N. Hartshorn. An Era of Progress and Promise
(Boston, Mass.: The Priscilla Publishing Co., 1910), p. 442.
                                                 DHU/MO
Baptist minister and ex-slave.

GRANDY, MOSES

William L. Katz, (ed.). Five Slave Narratives (New York:
Arno Press, 1969), pp. 35-36.   DHU/MO

GRANNUM, STANLEY E.

Wendell P. Dabney. Cincinnati's Colored Citizens (Cincinnati, Ohio: The Dabney Pub. Co., 1926), p. 279. DHU/MO
Methodist Episcopal minister.

GRANT, ABRAM, (bp.).

Richard R. Wright. Bishops of the A. M. E. Church (Nashville: A. M. E. Sunday School Union, 1963), pp. 191-92.
                                                   DHU/R
Nineteenth Bishop of the A. M. E. Church.

The Crisis (1:5, Mr., 1911), p. 9.   DHU/MO; DLC

James J. Pipkin. The Negro in Revelation, in History and in
Citizenship (N. Y.: Thompson Publishing Co., 1902), pp.
107-08.   DHU/MO

William N. Hartshorn. An Era of Progress and Promise
(Boston, Mass.: The Priscilla Publishing Co., 1925), p. 394.
                                                 DHU/MO

GRANT, DANIEL T.

When the Melon is Ripe. Autobiography of a Georgia Negro
High School Principal and Minister. New York: Exposition
Press, 1955.   DHU/MO; NcD
Negro author.

GRANT, ROBERT ALEXANDER, (bp.).

Richard R. Wright. Bishops of the A. M. E. Church (Nashville: A. M. E. Sunday School Union, 1963), pp. 193-94.
                                                   DHU/R
Fiftieth Bishop of the A. M. E. Church

GRAU, WILLIAM C.

Albert S. Foley. God's Men of Color (New York: Farrar,
Straus & Co., 1955), pp. 181-87.   DHU/R
Catholic priest and chaplain in World War II.

GRAY, ARTHUR D.

The editors of Ebony. The Ebony Success Library: 1,000 Successful Blacks (Nashville: The Southwestern Co., 1973), Vol. 1,
p. 130.   DHU
Congregationalist minister and president of Talladega College,
1952-62.

GRAY, LEE W.

Wendell P. Dabney. Cincinnati's Colored Citizens (Cincinnati, Ohio: The Dabney Pub. Co., 1926), p. 283. DHU/MO
Negro Baptist minister and teacher.

GREEN, A. R.

Irvine G. Penn. The Afro-American Press and Its Editors
(Springfield, Mass.: Willey & Co., 1891), p. 456.
                                    DHU/MO; DHU/R
A. M. E. minister and editor of the Christian Herald.

GREEN, ELISHA W.

Life of the Rev. Elisha W. Green. One of the Founders of the
Kentucky Normal and Theological Institute and Other Thirty
Years Pastor of the Colored Baptist Churches (Maysville,
Ky.: The Republican Printing Office, 1888).
                                         NG; DLC; NCWSW
Baptist minister.

GREEN, FRANCES P.

Wendell P. Dabney. Cincinnati's Colored Citizens (Cincinnati, Ohio: The Dabney Pub. Co., 1926), p. 280. DHU/MO
Baptist minister

GREEN, N. J.

James W. Hood., One Hundred Years of the A. M. E. Zion Church (N. Y.: A. M. E. Zion Book Concern, 1895), pp. 245-50.   DHU/MO
A. M. E. Zion minister.

GREEN, THOMAS E.

Benjamin T. Tanner. An Apology for African Methodism (Baltimore: n. p., 1867), pp. 236-39.   DHU/MO
A. M. E. minister

GREENE, SHERMAN LAWRENCE, (bp.).

Richard R. Wright. Bishops of the A. M. E. Church (Nashville: A. M. E. Sunday School Union, 1963), pp. 195-98.
                                                      DHU/R
Fifty-first Bishop of the A. M. E. Church.

GREGG, JOHN ANDREW, (bp.).

Richard R. Wright. Bishops of the A. M. E. Church (Nashville: A. M. E. Sunday School Union, 1963), pp. 199-202.
                                                      DHU/R
Forty-ninth Bishop of the A. M. E. Church.

African Methodist Episcopal Church Review (68:176, Apr.-Je., 1953), pp. 3-8.   DHU/R

GRÉGOIRE, HENRI BAPTISTE, (bp.).

Apolijie de Berthélemy de Las-Casas, Evêque de Chiappa ... Paris: Baudouin, 1802.   NN/Sch
Bishop of Blois, who campaigned for the liberation of slaves.

M. Carnot. Memoires de Grégoire, Ancien Evêque de Blois ... (Paris: E. Legrand & Descauriet, 1837).
                      DLC; NcU; WaU; NjP; NIC; NN

Memoires de Grégoire, Ancien Evêque de Blois ... Précédes d'une Notice Historique sur l'auteur (Paris: E. Legrand & Descauriet, 1837).   DLC; NcU; WaU; NjP; NIC; NN

Paul F. J. Grumebaum. Henri Grégoire, l'Ami des Hommes de Toutes les Couleurs ... (Paris: n. p., 1948).
                          MH; CtY; CU; IEN

GREGORY, B. F.

William Joseph Barber. Disciple Assemblies of Eastern North Carolina (St. Louis: The Bethany Press, 1966), pp. 254-55.
                                                      DHU/R
Disciples of Christ minister.

GRIGGS, AARON R.

Lewis G. Jordan. Negro Baptist History, U. S. A. (Nashville, Tenn.: The Sunday School Publishing Board, N. B. C., 1930), p. 392.   DHU/R

James J. Pipkin. The Negro in Revelation, in History, and in Citizenship (N. Y.: Thompson Pub. Co., 1902), p. 113.
                                                      DHU/MO

GRIGGS, E. M.

Samuel W. Bacote. Who's Who Among the Colored Baptists (Kansas City, Mo.: F. Hudson Co., 1912), pp. 54-55.
                                                      DHU/MO
Baptist minister, district secretary of Nat. Bapt. Conv. and State organizer, State Negro Business League of Texas.

GRIGGS, SUTTON ELBERT

The Mission Herald (36; Feb., 1933), p. 9.   DHU/MO
Author and baptist minister.

GRIMES, LEONARD A.

Carter G. Woodson. The History of the Negro Church (Wash., D. C.: Associated Publishers, 1921), pp. 159-60.
                                          DHU/MO; DHU/R
Baptist minister.

Lewis G. Jordan. Negro Baptist History U. S. A. (Nashville, Tenn.: The Sunday School Publishing Board, N. B. C., 1930), p. 392.   DHU/MO; DHU/R

William H. Ferris. African Abroad V. 2 (New Haven, Conn.: The Tuttle, Morehouse, Taylor Press, 1913), p. 695.
                                                      DHU/MO

William Wells Brown. The Black Man (Miami, Fla.: Mnemosyne Pub., Inc., 1969), pp. 217-20.   DHU/R

William Wells Brown. The Rising Son (Miami, Fla.: Mnemosyne Pub., Inc., 1969), pp. 534-35.   DHU/R

GRIMKE, FRANCES J.

Leslie H. Fishel. The Negro American (N. Y.: William Morrow, 1970), pp. 390-91.   DHU/MO
Presbyterian minister and author of Washington, D. C.

Benjamin G. Brawley. Negro Builders and Heroes (Chapel Hill, N. C.: Univ. of N. C. Press, 1937), p. 209. DHU/MO

Clifton E. Olmstead. Hugh T. Kerr, (ed.). Sons of the Prophets (Princeton, N. J.: Princeton University Press, 1963).
                                                      DHU/R

Daniel W. Culp. Twentieth Century Negro Literature (Atlanta: Nicholson & Co., 1902), p. 426.   DHU/MO

Henry J. Ferry. Francis James Grimke: Portrait of a Black Puritan (Doctoral dissertation. Yale University, Graduate School, 1970).

Louis B. Weeks. "Racism, World War I and the Christian Life: Francis J. Grimke in the Nation's Capital." Journal of Presbyterian History (51:4, Wint., 1973), pp. 471-88. DHU/R

Wilhelmena S. Robinson. Historical Negro Biographies (N. Y.: Publishers Co., 1967), pp. 86-87.   DHU/MO

William H. Ferris. African Abroad (New Haven, Conn.: The Tuttle, Morehouse, Taylor Press, 1913), p. 219. DHU/MO

William J. Simmons. Men of Mark (Cleveland: O. Rewell, 1887), pp. 608-12.   DHU/MO

GUDGER, B. M.

James W. Hood. One Hundred Years of the A. M. E. Zion Church (N. Y.: A. M. E. Zion Book Concern, 1895), pp. 559-61.   DHU/MO
A. M. E. Zion minister.

GUNNER, BYRON

    The Crisis (24:1, My., 1922), p. 28.   DHU/MO; DLC
Pastor of the Colored Presbyterian Church, Reading, Pa.

GURLEY, PHINEAS DENSMORE

    Presbyterian Reunion: 1837-1871 (N. Y.: De W. C. Lent &
Co., 1870), pp. 188-95.   DHU/MO
Presbyterian minister.

HAGAN, WILLIAM T.

    William H. Heard. The Bright Side of African Life (N. Y.:
Negro Universities Press, 1969), pp. 33-34.   DHU/R
Minister and presiding elder of M. E. Church in Careysburg,
Liberia.

HALL, PRINCE

    Edgar A. Toppin. A Biographical History of Blacks in Amer-
ica Since 1528 (N. Y.: David McKay Co., 1971), pp. 309-10.
                              DHU/R
Methodist minister of Massachusetts, considered founder of
first Black Masonic orders.

    The Negro American (N. Y.: William Morrow, 1970), pp.
78-79.   DHU/MO

HAMILTON, FAYETT M., (bp.).

    The Freeman (Indianapolis) (2:9, Apr. 20, 1889), p. 1.
                              DHU/MO
Bishop of the C. M. E. Church and editor of The Christian
Index.

    Irvine G. Penn. The Afro-American Press and Its Editors
(Springfield, Mass.: Willey & Co., 1891), pp. 278-80.
                              DHU/MO; DHU/R

HAMLETT, JAMES ARTHUR

    Charles H. Phillips. History of the Colored Methodist Episco-
pal Church (Jackson, Tenn.: Pub. House, C. M. E. Church,
1898), pp. 574-76.   DHU/MO
C. M. E. minister.

HAMMOND, EDWARD W. S.

    Henry D. Northrop. College of Life (Phila.: Nat. Pub. Co.,
1895), p. 55.   DHU/MO
A. M. E. minister and editor of Southwestern Christian Advocate.

    Benjamin T. Tanner. An Apology for African Methodism
(Baltimore: n. p., 1867), pp. 438-42.   DHU/MO

HAMPTON, CHARLES N.

    Samuel W. Bacote. Who's Who Among the Colored Baptists
(Kansas City, Mo.: F. Hudson Co., 1912), pp. 132-33.
                              DHU/MO
Baptist minister.

HANDY, JAMES ANDERSON, (bp.).

    Benjamin W. Arnett. The Budget ... (Dayton, Ohio: Chris-
tian Pub. House, 1882), p. 141.   DHU/MO
Twenty-second Bishop of the A. M. E. Church.

Benjamin T. Tanner. An Apology for African Methodism
(Baltimore: n. p., 1867), pp. 222-26.   DHU/MO

    The Crisis (34:1, Nov., 1911), p. 19.   DHU/MO; DLC

    G. F. Richings. Evidences of Progress Among Colored Peo-
ple (Phila.: G. S. Ferguson, 1904), pp. 386-87.
                              DHU/R; DHU/MO

    Henry D. Northrop. The College Of Life (Phila.: Nat. Pub.
Co., 1895), pp. 34-35.   DHU/MO

    James A. Handy. Scraps of African Methodist History (Phila.:
A. M. E. Book Concern, n. d.), pp. 5-10.   DHU/MO

    Richard R. Wright. Bishops of the A. M. E. Church (Nash-
ville: A. M. E. Sunday School Union, 1963), pp. 203-08.
                              DHU/R

    William N. Hartshorn. An Era of Progress and Promise
(Boston, Mass.: The Priscilla Pub. Co., 1910), p. 394.
                              DHU/MO

HARRIS, ANDREW

    Benjamin Quarles. Black Abolitionists (New York: Oxford
University Press, 1969), pp. 34+.   DHU/MO; DHU/R
Minister, Second African Church, Philadelphia.

    Religious Services in the Second African Church, Philadelphia
V. 8, pt. 5 (Phila.: Isaac Ashmead, 1841).   DHU/MO
Ordination services of the pastor.

HARRIS, C. R., (bp.).

    Henry F. Kletzing. Progress of a Race (Atlanta, Ga.: J. L.
Nichols & Co., 1898), pp. 504-05.   DHU/MO
Bishop of the A. M. E. Zion Church.

    G. F. Richings. Evidences of Progress Among Colored
People (Phila.: G. S. Ferguson, 1904), pp. 146-49+.
                              DHU/MO

    James W. Hood. One Hundred Years of the A. M. E. Zion
Church (N. Y.: A. M. E. Zion Book Concern, 1895), pp.
212-07.   DHU/MO

    William N. Hartshorn. An Era of Progress and Promise
(Boston, Mass.: The Priscilla Publishing Co., 1910), pp. 400-
01.   DHU/MO

HARRISON, SAMUEL

    Rev. Samuel Harrison. His Life Story, Told by Himself
(Pittsfield, Mass.: Press of the Eagle Pub. Co., 1899.)
                              DHU/MO
Negro minister, 1818-1900.

    Life Story as Told by Himself (Pittsfield, Mass.: n. p., 1899).
                NH; MH; MHi; MWA; NN/Sch

HARRISON, ZACHARIAH

    James T. Haley. Afro-American Encyclopaedia (Nashville,
Tenn.: Haley & Florida, 1895), pp. 597-99.   DHU/MO
Baptist minister.

HARRY (Black Harry).

    Carter G. Woodson. The History of the Negro Church (Wash.,
D. C.: The Associated Pub., 1921), pp. 48-49.
                              DHU/MO; DHU/R
Methodist minister accompanying Bishop Asbury.

"African Methodism's Adventures in Missions: A Black Pioneer in Christian Missions." The African Methodist Episcopal Church Review (94:236, Jl.-Sept., 1968), pp. 57-58.
DHU/R

HARVEY, WILLIAM J.

The editors of Ebony. The Ebony Success Library: 1,000 Successful Blacks (Nashville: The Southwestern Co., 1973), Vol. 1, p. 144.
DHU

HATCHER, EUGENE CLIFFORD, (bp.).

Richard R. Wright. Bishops of the A. M. E. Church (Nashville: A. M. E. Sunday School Union, 1963), pp. 209-13.
DHU/R
Seventy-third bishop of the A. M. E. Church.

The African Methodist Episcopal Church Review (18:202, Apr.-Je., 1961), p. 65.
DHU/R

HAWKINS, EDLER GARNETT

Frank T. Wilson. "Living Witnesses: Black Presbyterians in Ministry." Journal of Presbyterian History (51:4, Wint., 1973), pp. 373-75.
DHU/R
Minister, moderator, United Presbyterian Church and professor, Princeton Seminary.

HAYES, J. O.

William H. Heard. The Bright Side of African Life (N. Y.: Negro Universities Press, 1969), p. 91.
DHU/R
Baptist minister in Liberia.

HAYGOOD, ATTICUS GREENE

Atticus Green Haygood: Methodist Bishop, Editor and Educator (Athens: University of Georgia Press, 1965). DHU/MO
Chapter XI, an account of the Bishop's views on Negroes in the Methodist Church and higher education.

HAYNES, GEORGE EDMUND

Crisis (4; Jl., 1912), p. 119.
DHU/MO
Negro secretary of the Federal Council of Churches in America. Dept. of Race Relations.

HAYNES, LEMUEL B.

E. F. Chittenden. "Black Missionary to White Vermont."
Negro History Bulletin (35:?, Nov., 1972), pp. 163-65.
DHU/MO
Negro Congregationalist minister to Negroes and Whites in the eighteenth and early nineteenth centuries.

Appleton's Cyclopedia of American Biography V. 3 (New York: D. Appleton & Co., 1888), pp. 145-46. DLC; DHU

Benjamin G. Brawley. Negro Builders and Heroes (Chapel Hill, N. C.: Univ. of N. C. Press, 1937), pp. 209-10.
DHU/MO

Benjamin G. Brawley. The Negro Genius (New York: Dodd, Mead & Co., 1937), p. 33.
DHU/R; DHU/MO

Carter G. Woodson. The History of the Negro Church (Wash., D. C.: The Associated Publishers, 1921), pp. 61-5.
DHU/R; DHU/MO

George Smith. A Short Treatise Upon the Most Essential and Leading Points of Wesleyan or Primitive Methodism (Poultney, Vt.: L. J. Reynolds, Printer, 1830), p. 35. NN/Sch

James L. Nichols. The New Progress of a Race (Naperville, Ill.: J. L. Nichols and Co., 1929), pp. 385-86.
DHU/MO

John L. Hill. When Black Meets White... (Chicago: The Argyle Publishers, 1922).
DHU/MO

Journal of Negro History (4:1, Ja., 1919), pp. 22-32. DHU/MO

Leila A. Pendleton. A Narrative of the Negro (Wash., D. C.: Press of R. L. Pendleton, 1912), pp. 96-97.
DHU/MO

Lucius E. Chittenden. Personal Reminiscences 1840-1890, Including Some Not Hiterto Published of Lincoln and the War (New York: Richmond, Croscup & Co., 1893), p. 335.
DHU/MO

Richard Bardolph. "Social Origins of Distinguished Negroes, 1770-1865." Journal of Negro History (40:3, Jl., 1955), p. 225.
DHU/MO

Sherman Roberts Moulton. The Boorn Mystery, an Episode From the Judicial Annals of Vermont (Montpelier: Vermont Historical Society, 1937).
NN/Sch

Timothy M. Cooley. Sketches of the Life and Character of the Rev. Lemuel Haynes (New York: Harper & Brothers, 1837).
DHU/MO; NN/Sch; DHU/R

Wilbur H. Siebert. Vermont's Anti-Slavery and Underground Railroad Record, With a Map and Illustrations (Columbus, O.: The Spahr & Glenn Co., 1937).
NN/Sch

Wilhelmena S. Robinson. Historical Negro Biographies (New York: Publishers Co., 1967), pp. 22-3.
DHU/MO

William C. Nell. Colored Patriots of the American Revolution (Boston: R. F. Wallcot, 1855), pp. 123-23. DHU/MO

William H. Ferris. African Abroad (New Haven, Conn.: The Tuttle, Morehouse, Taylor Press, 1913), p. 687. DHU/MO

HEAD, WILLIAM

William Hicks. The History of Louisiana Negro Baptists from 1804-1914 (Nashville, Tenn.: National Baptist Publishing Board, n. d.), p. 189.
DHU/R
Baptist minister.

HEALY, ALEXANDER SHERWOOD

Albert S. Foley. God's Men of Color (New York: Farrar, Straus & Co., 1955), pp. 13-22.
DHU/R
Catholic priest.

HEALY, JAMES A., (bp.).

Charles B. Rousseve. The Negro in Louisiana (New Orleans: The Xavier Univ. Press, 1937), p. 140.
DHU/MO
Black Catholic bishop, appointed assistant to the Papal Throne in 1900.

Albert S. Foley. Bishop Healy: Beloved Outcast (New York: Farrar, Strauss & Young, 1954).
DHU/R

Albert S. Foley. God's Men of Color (New York: Farrar, Straus & Co., 1955), pp. 1-12.
DHU/R

Edgar A. Toppin. A Biographical History of Blacks in America Since 1528 (New York: David McKay, 1971), pp. 317-19.
DHU/MO; DHU/R

(Healy, James A., (bp.) cont.)

Josephine Kelly. Dark Shepherd (Paterson, N. J.: St. Anthony Guild Press, 1967).   NN/Sch; DCU

Wilhelmena S. Robinson. Historical Negro Biographies (N. Y.: Publishers Co., 1967), p. 89.   DHU/MO

HEALY, PATRICK FRANCIS

Edgar A. Toppin. A Biographical History of Blacks in America Since 1528 (New York: David McKay, 1971), p. 317.
                                                        DHU/R
Taught at St. Joseph's College in Philadelphia and was president of Georgetown University from 1871 to 1883. Black Catholic priest.

Albert S. Foley. God's Men of Color (New York: Farrar, Straus & Co., 1955), pp. 23-31.   DHU/R

HEARD, WILLIAM HENRY, (bp.).

The Crisis (9:4, Feg., 1915), p. 167.   DLC; DHU/MO
Thirty-fifth Bishop of the A. M. E. Church.

Daniel W. Culp. Twentieth Century Negro Literature (Atlanta: Nicholson & Co., 1902), p. 442.   DHU/MO

National Cyclopedia of American Biography. (12; 1935), p. 212.
                                                        DLC

Richard R. Wright. Bishops of the A. M. E. Church (Nashville: A. M. E. Sunday School Union, 1963), pp. 214-20.
                                                        DHU/R

Thomas O. Fuller. Pictorial History of the American Negro (Memphis, Tenn.: Pictorial History, Inc., 1933), p. 74.
                                                        DHU/MO

William H. Heard. The Bright Side of African Life (N. Y.: Negro Universities Press, 1969), p. 48.   DHU/R

William N. Hartshorn. An Era of Progress and Promise (Boston: The Priscilla Publishing Co., 1910), p. 393.
                                                        DHU/MO

HEATH, ANDREW

William J. Simmons. Men of Mark (Cleveland: O. Rewell, 1887), pp. 185-93.   DHU/MO; DHU/R
Baptist minister.

HEMINGWAY, LAWRENCE HENRY, (bp.).

Richard R. Wright. Bishops of the A. M. E. Church (Nashville: A. M. E. Sunday School Union, 1963), pp. 221-23.
                                                        DHU/R
Sixty-fifth Bishop of the A. M. E. Church.

HENDERSON, ELO LEON

Frank T. Wilson. "Living Witnesses: Black Presbyterians in Ministry." Journal of Presbyterian History (51:4, Wint., 1973), pp. 376-78.   DHU/R
Presbyterian minister and church administrator.

HENDERSON, JAMES M.

G. F. Richings. Evidences of Progress Among Colored People (Philadelphia: G. S. Ferguson, 1904), p. 136.
                                                        DHU/MO; DHU/R
A. M. E. minister and president of Morris Brown College.

HENDERSON, JOHN HARRIS

Samuel W. Bacote. Who's Who Among the Colored Baptists (Kansas City, Mo.: F. Hudson Co., 1912), pp. 293-94.
                                                        DHU/MO
Baptist minister and dean of Theological Dept. of Coleman College, Gibsland, La.

William Hicks. The History of Louisiana Negro Baptists from 1804-1914 (Nashville, Tenn.: National Baptist Publishign Board, n.d.), pp. 181-84.   DHU/R

HENDERSON, THOMAS W.

William N. Hartshorn. An Era of Progress and Promise (Boston: Priscilla Publishing Co., 1910), p. 440.   DHU/MO
A. M. E. minister and publisher of the Colored Radical.

HENDON, I. M.

Samuel W. Bacote. Who's Who Among Colored Baptists (Kansas City, Mo.: F. Hudson Co., 1912), pp. 254-55. DHU/MO
Baptist minister, secretary, General Baptist State Convention of Texas and Chairman of Church Extension Board.

HENRY, ALBERT

William H. Crook and Ross Coggins. Seven Who Fought (Waco, Texas: Word Books, 1971), pp. 121-43.   DHU/R
White baptist minister and his attempt to bring the races together.

The History of Louisiana Negro Baptists from 1804-1914 (Nashville, Tenn.: National Baptist Publishing Board, n.d.), pp. 151-53.   DHU/R
Baptist minister.

HENSON, JOSIAH

Benjamin Brawley. Early Negro American Writers (Chapel Hill, N. C.: Univ. of N. C. Press, 1935), pp. 160-67.
                                                        DHU/MO; DHU/R
Exslave and minister of the Methodist Episcopal Church.

An Autobiography of the Reverend Josiah Henson (Reading, Mass.: Addison-Wesley Publishing Co., 1969).   DHU/R

Benjamin G. Brawley. The Negro Genius (N. Y.: Dodd, Mead, & Co., 1937), pp. 65-66.   DHU/MO

Benjamin Brawley. Negro in Literature and Art (Atlanta, Ga.: n. p., 1910), p. 39.   DHU/MO

Black Pioneers in American History in the Nineteenth and Twentieth Century. Read by Diana Sands and Moses Gunn. Phonodisc.

Elizabeth Haynes. Unsung Heroes (New York: DuBois & Dill Pub., 1921), pp. 191-206.   DHU/MO

Wilhelmena S. Robinson. Historical Negro Biographies (New York: Publishers Co., 1967), p. 89.   DHU/MO

HICKMAN, ERNEST LAWRENCE, (bp.).

Richard R. Wright. Bishops of the A. M. E. Church (Nashville: A. M. E. Sunday School Union, 1963), pp. 224-28.
                                                        DHU/R
Seventy-fifth Bishop of the A. M. E. Church.

HIGGINBOTHAN, MAURICE JAMES

The editors of Ebony. The Ebony Success Library: 1,000 Successful Blacks (Nashville: The Southwestern Co., 1973), Vol. 1, p. 152.   DHU
A. M. E. minister.

HIGGINS, G. W.

G. F. Richings. Evidences of Progress Among Colored People (Philadelphia: G. S. Ferguson, 1904), pp. 531-32.
                                                    DHU/MO; DHU/R
A. M. E. Zion minister.

HIGGINS, SAMUEL RICHARD, (bp.).

Richard R. Wright. Bishops of the A. M. E. Church (Nashville: A. M. E. Sunday School Union, 1963), pp. 229-30.
                                                                DHU/R
Seventy-sixth Bishop of the A. M. E. Church.

HILL, DANIEL GRAFTON

Toward Wholeness (1:1, Sum., 1972), p. 8.   DHU/R
Dean Emeritus, Howard University School of Religion.

HILL, JAMES MONROE

David H. Bradley, Sr. A History of the A. M. E. Zion Church 1872-1968 V. 2 (Nashville: Parthenon Press, 1970), pp. 158+.   DHU/R
Minister of the A. M. E. Zion Church and manager of the Publishing House.

James W. Hood. One Hundred Years of the A. M. E. Zion Church (N. Y.: A. M. E. Zion Book Concern, 1895), pp. 407-12.   DHU/MO

HILL, JOHNSON W.

William N. Hartshorn. An Era of Progress and Promise (Boston, Mass.: The Priscilla Pub. Co., 1910), p. 433.
                                                            DHU/MO
Baptist minister and physician.

HILL, PLEASANT S.

Wendell P. Dabney. Cincinnati's Colored Citizens (Cincinnati, Ohio: The Dabney Pub. Co., 1926), pp. 276-77.
                                                            DHU/MO
African Methodist Episcopal minister and teacher.

HILL, WARNER WASHINGTON

William Hicks. The History of Louisiana Negro Baptists from 1804-1914 (Nashville: National Baptist Publishing Board, n.d.), pp. 146-48.   DHU/R
Baptist minister and moderator of the Tenth District Association of Louisiana.

HITCHCOCK, HENRY L.

Presbyterian Reunion: 1837-1871 (New York: De W. C. Lent & Co., 1870), p. 517.   DHU/MO
Presbyterian minister and president of Western Reserve College, Hudson, Ohio.

HOARD, J. H.

Samuel W. Bacote. Who's Who Among the Colored Baptists (Kansas City, Mo.: F. Hudson Co., 1912), pp. 140-41.
                                                            DHU/MO
Baptist minister, Oklahoma.

HODGE, W. J.

"Never Enough Time." Home Missions (43:4, Apr., 1972), pp. 23-25.   Pam. File, DHU/R
Pastor of Louisville's Fifth Street Baptist Church, one of the nation's oldest Black Churches.

HODGES, JACOB

A. D. Eddy. "Black Jacob." A Monument of Grace. The Life of Jacob Hodges, an African Negro, Who Died in Canadaigua, New York, February, 1842 (Philadelphia: American Sunday School Union, 1842).   NcD

HOKE, J. H.

James J. Pipkin. The Negro in Revelation, in History, and in Citizenship (New York: Thompson Pub. Co., 1902), p. 110.
                                                            DHU/MO
Slave, Baptist minister, teacher, founder of Arkansas Baptist College, Little Rock.

HOLLIDAY, JOHN, (bp.).

David H. Bradley, Sr. A History of the A. M. E. Zion Church 1872-1968 V. 2 (Nashville: Parthenon Press, 1970), pp. 61+.
                                                                DHU/R
Bishop of the A. M. E. Zion Church.

James W. Hood. One Hundred Years of the A. M. E. Zion Church (New York: A. M. E. Zion Book Concern, 1895), pp. 542-44.   DHU/MO

HOLLOMAN, JOHN LAWRENCE SULLIVAN

John M. Ellison. Journal of Religious Thought (27:2, Sum. Suppl., 1970), pp. 19-22.   DHU/R
Negro minister of Washington, D. C.

HOLLY, JAMES, T., (bp.).

Benjamin G. Brawley. Negro Builders and Heroes (Chapel Hill, N. C.: Univ. of N. C. Press, 1937), p. 207. DHU/MO
Protestant Episcopal bishop.

Alonzo Holly. God and the Negro (Nashville: National Baptist Publishing Board, 1937),   DHU/R

Appleton's Cyclopedia of American Biography V. 3 (New York: D. Appleton & Co., 1888), p. 238.   DHU

George F. Bragg. History of the Afro-American Group of the Episcopal Church (Balto., Md.: Church Advocate Press, 1922), pp. 192-97.   DHU/R

Lelia A. Pendleton. A Narrative of the Negro (Wash., D. C.: Press of R. L. Pendleton, 1912), pp. 62-63+.   DHU/MO

Newman White and Walter Johnson, et alii. The History of the Negro Church (Wash., D. C.: The Associated Publishers, 1921), pp. 179-80.   DHU/
Protestant Episcopal minister.

(Holly, James T. cont.)

    Richard P. Duane. The Rt. Rev. James Theodore Holly, D. D., First Bishop of the National Haitian Church (New York: n.p., 1874).   PBL

    The Southern Workman (5:4, Apr., 1876), p. 31.
                DHU/MO; DLC

    W. W. Brown. The Black Man (New York: T. Hamilton, 1863), pp. 274-76.   DHU/MO

HOLMES, HENRY

    Walter F. Watkins. The Cry of the West: the Story of the Mighty Struggle for Religious Freedom in California (Saratoga: R. & E Research Associates, 1969), pp. 25-26. DHU/R
    Baptist minister. Reprint. Negro author.

HOLMES, J. ALEXANDER

    Irvine G. Penn. The Afro-American Press and Its Editors. (Springfield, Mass.: Willey & Co., 1891), pp. 140-41.
                DHU/R; DHU/MO
    M. E. minister and editor of The Central Methodist.

HOLMES, JAMES H.

    William J. Simmons. Men of Mark (Cleveland, O.: George M. Rewell & Co., 1887), p. 666.   DHU/R
    Ex-slave and Baptist minister.

HOLMES, ZAN WESLEY, JR.

    The editors of Ebony. The Ebony Success Library: 1,000 Successful Blacks (Nashville: The Southwestern Co., 1973), Vol. 1, p. 156.   DHU
    United Methodist Church minister.

HOLSEY, LUCIUS H., (bp.).

    Benjamin G. Brawley. Negro Builders and Heroes (Chapel Hill: Univ. of N. C. Press, 1937), pp. 206-07.
                DHU/R; DHU/MO
    Fourth Bishop of the C. M. E. Church.

    Autobiography, Sermons, Addresses, and Essays of Bishop L. H. Holsey (Atlanta, Ga.: Franklin Printing and Publishing Co., 1898).   DHU/MO; NN/Sch

    Charles Alexander. One Hundred Distinguished Leaders (Atlanta, Ga.: Franklin Print. & Pub. Co., 1899), pp. 49+.
                DHU/MO

    Charles H. Phillips. History of Colored Methodist Episcopal Church (Jackson, Tenn. Pub. House, C. M. E. Church, 1898), pp. 213+.   DHU/MO

    Crisis (35; Feb., 1928), p. 53.   DHU/MO

    Daniel W. Culp. Twentieth Century Negro Literature (Atlanta, Ga.: Nicholson & Co., 1902), pp. 46-47. DHU/MO

    Henry F. Kletzing. Progress of a Race (Atlanta: J. L. Nichols & Co., 1898), pp. 494-96.   DHU/MO

    James T. Haley. Afro-American Encyclopaedia (Nashville: Haley & Florida, 1895), pp. 599-601.   DHU/MO

    John B. Cade. Holsey, The Incomparable (New York: Pageant Press, 1964).   DLC; DHU/MO; A&M

    William H. Ferris. African Abroad V. 2 (New Haven, Conn.: Tuttle, Morehouse, & Taylor Press, 1913), p. 806. DHU/MO

    William N. Hartshorn. An Era of Progress and Promise (Boston: Priscilla Pub. Co., 1910), p. 402.   DHU/MO

HOOD, JAMES W. (bp.).

    David H. Bradley, Sr. A History of the A. M. E. Zion Church 1872-1968 V. 2 (Nashville: Parthenon Press, 1970), pp. 31+.
                DHU/R
    Bishop of the A. M. E. Zion Church and author of One Hundred Years of the A. M. E. Zion Church.

    Benjamin G. Brawley. Negro Builders and Heroes (Chapel Hill, N. C.: Univ. of N. C. Press, 1937), pp. 204-05.
                DHU/MO; DHU/R

    Daniel W. Culp. Twentieth Century Negro Literature (Atlanta: Nicholson & Co., 1902), p. 51.   DHU/MO

    G. F. Richings. Evidences of Progress Among Colored People (Phila.: G. S. Ferguson, 1904), pp. 144-45+. DHU/MO

    William N. Hartshorn. An Era of Progress and Promise (Boston: Priscilla Pub. Co., 1910), p. 395.   DHU/MO

HOOPER, JOHN

    James W. Hood. One Hundred Years of the A. M. E. Zion Church (New York: A. M. E. Zion Book Concern, 1895), pp. 548-50.   DHU/MO
    A. M. E. Zion minister.

HORACE, J. L.

    Thomas O. Fuller. Pictorial History of the American Negro (Memphis, Tenn.: Pictorial History, Inc., 1933), p. 82.
                DHU/MO
    Baptist minister of Hot Springs, Arkansas.

HORNE, GEORGE

    G. F. Richings. Evidences of Progress Among Colored People (Philadelphia: G. S. Ferguson, 1904), p. 36.
                DHU/MO; DHU/R
    Baptist minister and principal of Dawes Academy.

HOUSTON, ULYSSES L.

    Lewis G. Jordan. Negro Baptist History U. S. A. (Nashville: Sunday School Pub. Bd., N. B. C., 1930), p. 392. Baptist minister in Georgia, organizer of the Georgia State Convention, and vice-president of the Georgia Legislature.

    James M. Simms. The First Colored Baptist Church in North America (Phila.: J. B. Lippincott Co., 1888), pp. 262-64.
                DHU/R

HOWARD, CLARA A.

    Lawson A. Scruggs. Women of Distinction (Raleigh, N. C.: L. A. Scruggs, 1893), pp. 256-59.   DHU/MO
    Missionary to the Congo and teacher.

    Henry F. Kletzing. Progress of a Race (Atlanta, Ga.: J. L. Nichols & Co., 1898), pp. 381-83.   DHU/MO

HOWARD, CLARENCE J.

    Albert S. Foley. God's Men of Color (New York: Farrar, Straus & Co., 1955), pp. 193-202.   DHU/R
    Catholic priest.

HOWARD, EDWARD J., (bp.).

> Richard R. Wright. Bishops of the A. M. E. Church (Nashville: A. M. E. Sunday School Union, 1963), p. 231. DHU/R
> Fifty-eighth Bishop of the A. M. E. Church.

HOWARD, W. J.

> James J. Pipkin. The Negro in Revelation, in History, and in Citizenship (New York: Thompson Pub. Co., 1902), pp. 96-97. DHU/MO
> Baptist minister.

HOWARD, WILLIAM D.

> Presbyterian Reunion: 1837-1871 (New York: De W. C. Lent & Co., 1870), pp. 507-08. DHU/MO
> Presbyterian minister, trustee of Washington College and Western University and director of Western Theological Seminary, Pa.

HOWZE, JOSEPH LAWSON, (bp.).

> The editors of Ebony. The Ebony Success Library: 1,000 Successful Blacks (Nashville: The Southwestern Co., 1973), Vol. l, p. 160. DHU
> Bishop of Roman Catholic Church.

HUBERT, G. J.

> Thomas O. Fuller. Pictorial History of the American Negro (Memphis, Tenn.: Pictorial History Inc., 1933), p. 321. DHU/MO
> Minister and civic leader.

HUDSON, JAMES

> Toward Wholeness (1:1, Sum., 1972), p. 9. DHU/R
> Brief biographical data given as Hudson is honored by the Ministries to Blacks in Higher Education on its Roll of Honor.

HUGHES, P. H.

> Samuel W. Bacote. Who's Who Among Colored Baptists (Kansas City, Mo.: F. Hudson Co., 1912), pp. 261-62. DHU/MO
> Evangelist and minister.

HUGHES, S. R.

> William N. Hartshorn. An Era of Progress and Promise (Boston: The Priscilla Publishing Co., 1910), p. 443. DHU/MO
> M. E. minister and teacher.

HUGHES, W. A. C.

> William N. Hartshorn. An Era of Progress and Promise (Boston, Mass.: The Priscilla Publishing Co., 1910), p. 456. DHU/MO
> M. E. minister.

HUNTER, WILLIAM H.

> Benjamin T. Tanner. An Apology for African Methodism (Baltimore: n.p., 1867), pp. 219-21. DHU/MO
> Army chaplain and Elder of the A. M. E. Church.

HURST, JOHN H., (bp.).

> Alonzo P. B. Holly. God and the Negro ... (Nashville, Tenn.: National Baptist Pub. Board, 1937), p. 3. DHU/R
> Thirty-sixth Bishop of the A. M. E. Church.

> Richard R. Wright. Bishops of the A. M. E. Church (Nashville: A. M. E. Sunday School Union, 1963), pp. 232-33. DHU/R

IMES, WILLIAM LLOYD

> Frank T. Wilson. "Living Witnesses: Black Presbyterians in Ministry." Journal of Presbyterian History (51:4, Wint., 1973), pp. 359-61. DHU/R
> Presbyterian minister.

> Crisis (31; Nov., 1925), p. 22. (4; Mr., 1934), p. 72. DHU/MO

> "William Lloyd Imes, a City Pastor." Mary Jenness. Twelve Negro Americans (New York: Friendship Press, 1936), pp. 35-52. DLC; DHU/MO

IRONS, CLEMENT

> William H. Heard. The Bright Side of African Life (N. Y.: Negro Universities Press, 1969), p. 26. DHU/R
> A. M. E. minister, Millsburg, Liberia.

ISAAC, E. W. D.

> William N. Hartshorn. An Era of Progress and Promise (Boston: The Priscilla Publishing Co., 1910), p. 487. DHU/MO
> Baptist minister and editor of the National Baptist Union.

JACK (Uncle Jack)

> Carter G. Woodson. The History of the Negro Church (Wash., D. C.: Associated Publishers, 1921), p. 47. DHU/MO; DHU/R
> Negro Baptist preacher from Virginia. Appreciatiative of his preaching, Whites bought his freedom and a small plantation for him in Virginia.

> M. S. Wood and Abigail Mott. Narratives of Colored Americans (N. Y.: Bownes & Co., 1872), p. 46. DHU/MO

> William S. White. The African Preacher: An Authentic Narrative (Philadelphia: Presbyterian Board of Publications, 1849), Rare Book Room. TxW; NcD; DHU/MO

JACKSON, ALEXANDER S.

> William Hicks. The History of Louisiana Negro Baptists From 1804-1914 (Nashville, Tenn.: National Baptist Publishing Board, n.d.), pp. 175-76. DHU/R
> Baptist minister and president of the Louisiana Baptist State Convention.

> Samuel W. Bacote. Who's Who Among the Colored Baptists (Kansas City, Mo.: F. Hudson Co., 1912), pp. 61-63. DHU/MO

JACKSON, CAMERON W.

> The editors of Ebony. The Ebony Success Library: 1,000 Successful Blacks (Nashville: The Southwestern Co., 1973), Vol. l, p. 166. DHU
> A. M. E. Zion minister.

JACKSON, DOCK B.

Samuel W. Bacote. Who's Who Among the Colored Baptists
(Kansas City, Mo.: F. Hudson Co., 1912), p. 162. DHU/MO
Baptist minister and teacher.

JACKSON, E. FRANKLIN

The Full Grown Minister. A Synopsis of a Minister's Life
for Twenty-one Years (n.p.: n.p., n.d.).
                                        Pam. Fiel, DHU/R
Written when the author was pastor of St. Luke's A. M. E.
Zion Church, Buffalo, New York.

JACKSON, G. N.

Samuel W. Bacote. Who's Who Among Colored Baptists
(Kansas City, Mo.: F. Hudson Co., 1912), pp. 190-91.
                                        DHU/MO
Baptist minister, Kansas.

JACKSON, J. C.

Samuel W. Bacote. Who's Who Among Colored Baptists
(Kansas City, Mo.: F. Hudson Co., 1912), pp. 154-56.
                                        DHU/MO
Evangelist, statistician of New England Baptist Convention.

JACKSON, JAMES H.

James W. Hood. One Hundred Years of the A. M. E. Zion
Church (N. Y.: A. M. E. Zion Book Concern, 1895), pp.
580-81.   DHU/MO
A. M. E. Zion minister.

JACKSON, JESSE L.

The editors of Ebony. The Ebony Success Library: 1,000 Suc-
cessful Blacks (Nashville: The Southwestern Co., 1973), 1,
Vol. 1, p. 158.   DHU
Baptist minister, former member of SCLC, (Southern Christ-
ian Leadership Conference) national director of Operation
Breadbasket, President of Operation PUSH (People United to
Save Humanity).

Claude Lewis. "Reverend Jesse Jackson: Passage to Progress." Tuesday (Jl., 1968), pp. 6-8+. Pam. File, DHU/R

Ernest Dunbar. Look (35:20, Oct. 5, 1971), pp. 17-20.
                                        DHU/R

Harry A. Ploski, (ed.). Reference Library of Black America
(New York: Bellwether Pub. Co., Inc., 1971), Book 2, pp. 19-
21.   DHU

Joel Dreyfull. "Where Is Jesse Jackson Going?" Black Enterprise (5:3, Oct., 1974), pp. 23-27. Pam. File, DHU/R

Warren Halliburton. The Picture Life of Jesse Jackson (New
York: Franklin Walts, Inc., 1972).   DHU/R

JACKSON, JOSEPH H.

The editors of Ebony. The Ebony Success Library: 1,000 Suc-
cessful Blacks (Nashville: The Southwestern Co., 1973),
Vol. 1, p. 168.   DHU
Baptist minister, pastor of Olivet Baptist Church, Chicago,
Ill., president of National Baptist Convention, U. S. A.

Harry A. Ploski. Reference Library of Black America (New
York: Bellwether Pub. Co., Inc., 1971), Book 2, p. 213.
                                        DHU

Willa Mae Rice. "Black Separatists Preaching 'KKK Gospel'
J. H. J. Warns." Pittsburgh Courier (Sept. 21, 1968).
                                        Pam. File, DHU/R

JACKSON, LAWRENCE R.

The editors of Ebony. The Ebony Success Library: 1,000 Successful Blacks (Nashville: The Southwestern Co., 1973),
Vol. 1, p. 169   DHU
Baptist minister and pastor of Lilydale Progressive Missionary Church in Chicago, Ill.

JACKSON, RAYMOND S.

James E. Massey. Raymond S. Jackson; A Portrait (n. p.:
Privately printed by the Author, 1967).   DHU/R
Church of God minister.

JACOB, H. P.

Lewis G. Jordan. Negro Baptist History U. S. A. (Nashville,
Tenn.: The Sunday School Pub. Board, N. B. C., 1930), p.
392.   DHU/MO; DHU/R
Baptist minister of Mississippi.

JACOBS, FRANCIS

William W. Brown. The Rising Son (New York: T. Hamilton,
1874), pp. 337-38.   DHU/MO; DHU/R
Minister and one of the founders of A. M. E. Zion Church.

JACOBS, FREDERICK M.

James W. Hood. One Hundred Years of the A. M. E. Zion
Church (New York: A. M. E. Zion Book Concern, 1895),
pp. 346-53.   DHU/MO
A. M. E. Zion minister.

JACOBUS, MELNACTHON W.

Presbyterian Reunion: 1837-1871 (New York: De W. C. Lent
& Co., 1870), pp. 530-32.   DHU/MO
Presbyterian minister and author.

JAMES, JOSEPH ISRAEL, SR.

William Joseph Barber. Disciple Assemblies of Eastern North
Carolina (St. Louis: The Bethany Press, 1966), pp. 255-56.
                                        DHU/R
Disciples of Christ minister.

JAMES, WILLIAM ANTHONY

William Joseph Barber. Disciple Assemblies of Eastern
North Carolina (St. Louis: The Bethany Press, 1966), pp.
256-57.   DHU/R
Disciples of Christ minister. Negro author.

JAMES, WILLIAM M.

The editors of Ebony. The Ebony Success Library: 1,000 Suc-
cessful Blacks (Nashville: The Southwestern Co., 1973),
Vol. 1, p. 172.   DHU
Minister of United Methodist Church, former president of New
York City branch of N. A. A. C. P.

JAMES, WILLIAM ROBERT

William Joseph Barber. Disciple Assemblies of Eastern North Carolina (St. Louis: The Bethany Press, 1966), pp. 257-59.
DHU/R
Disciples of Christ minister.

JAMISON, MONROE F. (bp.).

Charles H. Phillips. History of the Colored Methodist Episcopal Church (Jackson, Tenn.: Pub. House, C. M. E. Church, 1898), pp. 563-64.
DHU/MO
C. M. E. bishop.

Autobiography and Work of Bishop Monroe F. Jamison ...
(Nashville: Pr. for the Author, 1912).   DHU/MO; CoDI

JASPER, JOHN J.

Encyclopedia of Southern Baptists V. 1 (Nashville, Tenn.: Broadman Press, (1958-71)), p. 699.   DLC
Baptist minister of Richmond, Va.

Benjamin G. Brawley. Negro in Literature and Art (Atlanta, Ga.: n.p., 1910), pp. 51-52.   DHU/MO

Benjamin G. Brawley. Negro Builders and Heroes (Chapel Hill: Univ. of N. C. Press, 1937), pp. 80+.   DHU/MO

Edwin Archer Randolph. The Life of Rev. John Jasper, Pastor of Sixth Mt. Zion Baptist Church, Richmond, Va. From His Birth to the Present Time, with his Theory on the Rotation of the Sun. (Richmond, Va.: R. T. Hill & Co., 1884).   DHU/MO

H. H. Smith. Methodist Quarterly Review (72:2, Jl., 1923), pp. 466+.   DHU/R

Henry D. Northrop. College of Life (Phia.: Nat. Pub. Co., 1895), pp. 54-55.   DHU/MO

Howard Harper Harlan. John Jasper-- a Case History in Leadership (Charlottesville: University of Va., 1936).
NcD; DLC; DHU/MO

James J. Pipkin. The Negro in Revelation, in History, and in Citizenship (N. Y.: Thompson Pub. Co., 1902), pp. 89-95.   DHU/MO

Richard Ellsworth Day. Rhapsody in Black (Philadelphia: Judson Press, 1953).   DHU/MO; DHU/R

William E. Hatcher. John Jasper, the Unmatched Negro Philosopher and Preacher (Westport, Conn.: Negro Univ. Press, 1969).   InU; DLC
Reprint of 1908 edition.

William J. Simmons. Men of Mark (Cleveland, O.: George M. Rewell & Co., 1887), p. 1064.   DHU/R

JASON, WILLIAM C.

G. F. Richings. Evidences of Progress Among Colored People (Phila.: G. S. Ferguson, 1904), p. 247.
DHU/R; DHU/MO
Minister and President of Delaware State College.

JENIFER, JOHN THOMAS

The Crisis (4:2, Je., 1912), p. 69.   DLC; DHU/MO
A. M. E. minister.

G. F. Richings. Evidences of Progress Among Colored People (Phila.: Geo. S. Ferguson, 1904), p. 390.   DHU/MO

Henry D. Northrop. College of Life (Phila.: Nat. Pub. Co., 1895), pp. 35-36.   DHU/MO

James T. Haley. Afro-American Encyclopaedia (Nashville: Haley & Florida, 1895), pp. 562-63.   DHU/MO

JERNAGIN, W. H.

Samuel W. Bacote. Who's Who Among the Colored Baptists (Kansas City, Mo.: F. Hudson Co., 1912), p. 86.   DHU/MO
Baptist evangelist, president of Oklahoma Constitutional League and treasurer, National B. Y. P. U. Board.

JETER, HENRY NORVAL

William J. Simmons. Men of Mark (Cleveland: O. Rewell, 1887), pp. 588-89.   DHU/R
Baptist minister of Newport, Rhode Island.

JOHN, JOSEPH ALEXANDER

Albert S. Foley. God's Men of Color (New York: Farrar, Straus & Co., 1955), pp. 105-11.   DHU/R
West Indian Catholic priest, worked in America and Trinidad.

JOHNS, VERNON

Charles Emerson Boddie. God's "Bad Boys" (Valley Forge: Judson Press, 1972), pp. 61-76.   DHU/R
Baptist minister of Virginia.

JOHNSON, A. M.

Samuel W. Bacote. Who's Who Among the Colored Baptists (Kansas City, Mo.: F. Hudson Co., 1912), pp. 263-64.
DHU/MO
Baptist minister and president of General Baptist Convention.

JOHNSON, ARTHUR LEE

The editors of Ebony. The Ebony Success Library: 1,000 Successful Blacks (Nashville: The Southwestern Co., 1973), Vol. Vol. 1, p. 175.   DHU
Baptist minister.

JOHNSON, CHARLES JOHNSON

Newman I. White and Walter C. Johnson. An Anthology of Verse by Negro Americans (Durham, N. C.: Trinity College Press, 1924), pp. 189 & 224.   DHU/MO
Baptist minister

Robert T. Kerlin. Negro Poets and Their Poems (Wash., D. C.: Associated Pub. Inc., 1923), pp. 95-99.   DHU/MO

JOHNSON, CHARLES H.

Lewis G. Jordan. Negro Baptist History (Nashville: Sunday School Publishing Board, N. B. C., 1930), p. 144.
DHU/MO; DHU/R
Baptist minister, Indianapolis, Indiana.

JOHNSON, HARVEY

Lewis G. Jordan. Negro Baptist History U. S. A. (Nashville: Sunday School Publishing Board, N. B. C., 1930), p. 392.
DHU/MO; DHU/R
Baptist minister of Maryland and founder of Clayton Williams Academy.

G. F. Richings. Evidences of Progress Among Colored People (Phila.: G. S. Ferguson, 1904), p. 26.
DHU/MO; DHU/R

Wilhelmena S. Robinson. Historical Negro Biographies (N. Y.: Publishers Co., 1967), p. 91.   DHU/MO

William J. Simmons. Men of Mark (Cleveland: O. Rewell, 1887), p. 729.   DHU/R; DHU/MO

JOHNSON, HENRY THEODORE

G. F. Richings. Evidences of Progress Among Colored People (Phila.: G. S. Ferguson, 1904), pp. 355-7+.
DHU/R; DHU/MO
Minister and founder of Slater College.

JOHNSON, J. A.

William H. Heard. The Bright Side of African Life. (N. Y.: Negro Universities Press, 1969), p. 91.   DHU/R
Baptist minister and pastor of Providence Baptist Church, Monrovia.

JOHNSON, JAMES B.

James W. Hood. One Hundred Years of the A. M. E. Zion Church (N. Y.: A. M. E. Zion Book Concern, 1895), pp. 332-36.   DHU/MO
A. M. E. Zion minister.

JOHNSON, JOHN ALBERT, (bp.).

William N. Hartshorn. An Era of Progress and Promise (Boston, Mass.: The Priscilla Publishing Co., 1910), p. 409.
DHU/MO
Thirty-fourth Bishop of the A. M. E. Church.

JOHNSON, JOSEPH A., JR (bp.).

The editors of Ebony. The Ebony Success Library: 1,000 Successful Blacks (Nashville: The Southwestern Co., 1973), Vol. 1, p. 178.   DHU
Bishop of Fourth Episcopal District (Mississippi and Louisiana) of Christian Methodist Episcopal Church.

JOHNSON, JOY JOSEPH

The editors of Ebony. The Ebony Success Library: 1,000 Successful Blacks (Nashville: The Southwestern Co., 1973), Vol. 1, p. 179.   DHU
Baptist minister and North Carolina State legislator.

JOHNSON, MORDECAI WYATT

Edwin R. Embree. 13 Against the Odds (New York: The Viking Press, 1944), pp. 175-95.   DHU/R
Biography of Baptist minister and former president of Howard University.

Daniel G. Hill. "Tribute to the President Emeritus." Journal of Religious Thought (18; Wint.-Spr., 1961), p. 3. DHU/R

JOHNSON, PETER

Lewis G. Jordan. Negro Baptist History U. S. A. (Nashville: The Sunday School Publishing Board, N. B. C., 1930), p. 392.
DHU/MO; DHU/R
Baptist minister of Georgia; member of the Springfield Church, which is possibly the oldest Negro church on the continent.

JOHNSON, W. D.

E. R. Carter. The Black Side (Atlanta, Ga.: n.p., 1894), pp. 104-08.   DHU/MO
Negro Baptist minister.

JOHNSON, W. H.

Samuel W. Bacote. Who's Who Among Colored Baptists (Kansas City, Mo.: F. Hudson Co., 1912), pp. 256-57.
DHU/MO
Baptist minister and evangelist, president of Friendship District Sunday-School Convention.

JOHNSON, WILLIAM BISHOP

Irvine G. Penn. The Afro-American Press and Its Editors. (Springfield, Mass.: Willey & Co., 1891), pp. 235-37.
DHU/MO; DHU/R
Baptist minister and editor of the Wayland Alumni Journal and the Baptist Companion.

William H. Ferris. African Abroad V. 2 (New Haven, Conn.: Tuttle, Morehouse, & Taylor Press, 1913), pp. 871-72.
DHU/MO

JOHNSON, WILLIAM DECKER, SR., (bp.).

Biographical Sketches of Prominent Negro Men and Women of Kentucky ... With Introductory Material of the Author, and Prefatory Remarks Showing the Difference Between American and British Slaveholders; Also Opinion of Leading Thinkers of the Race. Lexington: The Standard Print, 1897.   TNF
There were two William Decker Johnsons of this era. Both were of the A. M. E. Church, but only one a bishop. The two were often confused.

Richard Robert Wright, Jr., (bp.). Bishops of the A. M. E. Church. (Nashville: A. M. E. Sunday School Union, 1963), pp. 236-38.   DHU/R

JOHNSON, WILLIAM T.

Samuel W. Bacote. Who's Who Among the Colored Baptists (Kansas City, Mo.: F. Hudson Co., 1912), pp. 251-53.
DHU/MO
Baptist minister, president of Friends' Orphan Asylum, and chairman of the Lott Carey Foreign Mission Board.

JOHNSTON, CAESAR

Lewis G. Jordan. Negro Baptist History U. S. A. (Nashville, Tenn.: The Sunday School Pub. Board, N. B. C., 1930), p. 392.   DHU/MO; DHU/R
Baptist minister of North Carolina, and first president of the North Carolina State Convention.

JOHNSTON, ELIJAH

Leila A. Pendleton. A Narrative of the Negro (Wash., D. C.: Press of R. L. Pendleton, 1912), p. 47.   DHU/MO
Missionary to Liberia.

JOHNSTON, LEWIS

    G. F. Richings. Evidences of Progress Among Colored
People (Phila.: G. S. Ferguson, 1904), p. 188.
                      DHU/MO; DHU/R
Presbyterian minister and principal of Richard Allen Institute,
Pine Bluff, Arkansas.

    Charles Alexander. One Hundred Distinguished Leaders (At-
lanta, Ga.: Franklin Printing & Publishing Co., 1899), p. 61.
                      DHU/MO

JONES, ABSALOM

    George F. Bragg. History of the Afro-American Group of
Episcopal Church (Baltimore: Church Advocate Press, 1922),
p. 72.   DHU/MO; DHU/R
Ex-slave and first rector of the St. Thomas African Episcopal
Church, Philadelphia.

    Benjamin Brawley. Early Negro American Writers (Chapel
Hill: Univ. of N. C. Press, 1935), pp. 87-95. DHU/MO

    George Freeman Bragg. Heroes of the Eastern Shore: Absa-
lom Jones, the First of the Blacks ... (Baltimore, Md.: The
Author, 1939).   CtY-D

    George F. Bragg. The Story of the First of the Blacks, the
Pathfinder, Absalom, 1746-1818 (Baltimore, Md.: n.p.,
1929).   DHU/MO

    Leila A. Pendleton. A Narrative of the Negro (Wash., D. C.:
Press of R. L. Pendleton, 1912), p. 97.   DHU/MO

    Leslie H. Fishel. The Negro American (N. Y.: William
Morrow, 1967), pp. 164-66.   DHU/MO

    Richard Bardolph. "Social Origins of Distinguished Negroes,
1770-1865." Journal of Negro History (40:3, Jl., 1955), p.
221.   DHU/MO

    Wilhelmena S. Robinson. Historical Negro Biographies (N.
Y.: Publishers Co., 1967), p. 74.   DHU/MO

JONES, DANIEL

    William J. Simmons, (ed.). Men of Mark (Cleveland, O.:
Geo. M. Rewell & Co., 1887), p. 583.   DHU/R
Methodist Episcopal minister.

JONES, EDWARD

    George F. Bragg. History of the Afro-American Group of the
Episcopal Church (Balto., Md.: Church Advocate Press,
1922), p. 186.   DHU/R
Negro Protestant Episcopal priest who migrated to Africa.

JONES, EDWARD P.

    William N. Hartshorn. An Era of Progress and Promise
(Boston, Mass.: The Priscilla Publishing Co., 1910), p. 440.
                      DHU/MO
Baptist minister and grand master of the Grand United Order
of Odd Fellows of Mississippi.

JONES, F. L.

    G. F. Richings. Evidences of Progress Among Colored
People (Phila.: G. S. Ferguson, 1904), p. 51. DHU/MO
Baptist minister and Principal of Arkadelphia Academy, Ark-
adelphia, Arkansas.

JONES, J. A.

    Charles Alexander. One Hundred Distinguished Leaders
(Atlanta, Ga.: The Franklin Printing & Publishing Co., 1899),
p. 61.   DHU/MO
"Clergyman, educator."

JONES, J. E.

    Irvine G. Penn. The Afro-American Press and Its Editors.
(Springfield, Mass.: Willey & Co., 1891), pp. 164-69.
                      DHU/MO; DHU/R
Baptist minister and professor at Richmond Theological Seminary. Member of Editorial staff of the Baptist Companion and
editor of African Missions.

JONES, JOHN

    William Hicks. The History of Louisiana Negro Baptists
from 1804-1914 (Nashville, Tenn.: National Baptist Publishing Board, n. d.), pp. 178-80.   DHU/R
Baptist minister.

JONES, JOSEPH H.

    Presbyterian Reunion 1837-1871 (N. Y.: Dew C. Lent & Co.,
1870), pp. 156-61.   DHU/MO
Presbyterian minister.

JONES, JOSHUA H., (bp.).

    Richard R. Wright. Bishops of the A. M. E. Church (Nash-
ville: A. M. E. Sunday School Union, 1963), pp. 239-43.
                      DHU/R
Thirty-eighth Bishop of the A. M. E. Church.

JONES, N. J.

    E. R. Carter. The Black Side (Atlanta: n.p., 1894), pp. 38-
42.   DHU/MO
Negro Baptist minister, business man and social worker.
Founder of the Colored Men's Protective Association (C. M.
P. A.) Lodge.

JONES, RAYMOND LUTHER, (bp.).

    A. M. E. Zion Quarterly Review (84:2, Sum., 1972), pp. 94-
96.   DHU/R
Bishop of the A. M. E. Zion Church.

JONES, RICHARD A.

    Irvine G. Penn. The Afro-American Press and Its Editors
(Springfield, Mass.: Willey & Co., 1891), pp. 292-95.
                      DHU/R; DHU/MO
Editor of the Cleveland Globe and one of the founders of St.
Andrews Episcopal Church of Cleveland, Ohio and U. S.
Deputy Marshall for the Northern district of Ohio.

JONES, S. S.

    Samuel W. Bacote. Who's Who Among Colored Baptists
(Kansas City, Mo.: F. Hudson Co., 1912), pp. 152-53.
                      DHU/MO
Baptist minister of largest church in Oklahoma, pres. of
Baptist State Convention and Muskogee Fruit and Bottling Co.,
editor of the Baptist Informer.

JONES, SINGLETON T., (bp.).

Irvine G. Penn. The Afro-American Press and Its Editors.
(Springfield, Mass.: Willey & Co., 1891), p. 108.
                                        DHU/R; DHU/MO
Bishop of the A. M. E. Zion Church and editor of The Zion
Standard and Weekly Review.

G. F. Richings. Evidences of Progress Among Colored
People. (Phila.: G. S. Ferguson, 1904), p. 148.
                                        DHU/R; DHU/MO

Henry F. Kletzing. Progress of a Race. (Atlanta: J. L.
Nichols, 1898), p. 580.   DHU/MO

James W. Hood. One Hundred Years of the A. M. E. Zion
Church (N. Y.: A. M. E. Book Concern, 1895), pp. 178-80.
                                        DHU/MO

John J. Moore. History of the A. M. E. Zion Church in
America (York, Pa.: Teachers Journal Office, 1884), pp.
373-74.   DHU/MO

William W. Brown. The Rising Son. (Boston: A. G. Brown
& Co., 1874), p. 531.   DHU/R; DHU/MO

JONES, T. L.

Samuel W. Bacote. Who's Who Among Colored Baptists
(Kansas City, Mo.: F. Hudson Co., 1912), pp. 181-82.
                                        DHU/MO
Baptist minister, organizer of first Teacher's Assoc. of Tenn-
essee and president of Nashville Sunday-School Union.

JONES, THELDON FRANCIS

Albert S. Foley. God's Men of Color (New York: Farrar,
Straus & Co., 1955), pp. 170-72.   DHU/R
Catholic priest.

JONES, THOMAS C.

Albert S. Foley. God's Men of Color (New York: Farrar,
Straus & Co., 1955), pp. 297-300.   DHU/R
Catholic priest.

JONES, WILLIS L.

E. R. Carter. The Black Side. (Atlanta: n.p., 1894), pp. 98-
101.   DHU/MO
Negro Baptist minister.

Edgar G. Thomas. The First African Baptist Church of
North America (Savannah, Ga.: By the author, 1925), pp.
114-17.   DHU/MO

JORDAN, FREDERICK DOUGLASS, (bp.).

Richard Robert Wright, Jr., (bp.). Bishops of the A. M. E.
Church (Nashville: A. M. E. Sunday School Union, 1963),
pp. 244-50.   DHU/R
Seventy-second Bishop of the A. M. E. Church.

JORDAN, LEWIS GARNETT

William N. Hartshorn. An Era of Progress and Promise
(Boston, Mass.: Priscilla Publishing Co., 1910), p. 483.
                                        DHU/MO
Baptist minister and corresponding secretary of the Foreign
Mission Board of the National Baptist Convention.

On Two Hemispheres Being the Life Story of Lewis G. Jordan
as Told by Himself. n. p., n. d.

Thomas O. Fuller. Pictorial History of the American Negro
(Memphis, Tenn.: Pictorial History Inc., 1933), p. 81.
                                        DHU/MO

JUDKINS, R. C.

William N. Hartshorn. An Era of Progress and Promise
(Boston, Mass.: The Priscilla Publishing Co., 1910), p. 486.
                                        DHU/MO
Baptist minister and editor of the Colored Alabamian.

JUNKIN, GEORGE

Presbyterian Reunion 1837-1871 (N. Y.: Dew C. Lent & Co.,
1870), pp. 142-48.   DHU/MO
Presbyterian minister.

KAPO (Mallica Reynolds).

Alex Gradussov. "Cult Leader, Sculptor, Painter Kapo."
Freeing the Spirit (3:1, Spr., 1974), pp. 29-31. DHU/R
Jamaican prophet, preacher "in the manner of the Zion Re-
vival."

KEALER, A. G.

James W. Hood. One Hundred Years of the A. M. E. Zion
Church (N. Y.: A. M. E. Zion Book Concern, 1895), pp. 339-
46.   DHU/R
A. M. E. minister.

KEEBLE, MARSHALL

Biography and Sermons of Marshall Keeble, Evangelist (Nashville: Gospel Advocate Co., 1931).   TN/DCHS
Disciples of Christ Negro minister.

KEELING, ULYSSES SIMPSON

Samuel W. Bacote. Who's Who Among the Colored Baptists
(Kansas City, Mo.: F. Hudson Co., 1912), pp. 207-08.
                                        DHU/MO
Baptist minister, president of Old Landmark District B. Y.
P. U. Convention.

KELLY, EDMUND

William J. Simmons, (ed.). Men of Mark (Cleveland, O.:
Geo. M. Rewell & Co., 1887), p. 291.   DHU/R
Baptist minister.

KELLY, I. H.

Samuel W. Bacote. Who's Who Among the Colored Baptists
(Kansas City, Mo.: F. Hudson Co., 1912), pp. 67-68.
                                        DHU/MO
Baptist minister, president of B. Y. P. U. State Convention
and trustee of Guadalupe College.

KENNEDY, PAUL H.

James T. Haley. Afro-American Encyclopaedia (Nashville:
Haley & Florida, 1895), p. 613.   DHU/MO
Baptist minister, State Missionary for Kentucky, author and
publisher of the Baptist Directory and Year Book of Kentucky.

Henry F. Kletzing. Progress of a Race (Atlanta, Ga.: J. L.
Nichols & Co., 1898), p. 512.   DHU/MO

KERSH, J. F.

    Samuel W. Bacote. <u>Who's Who Among Colored Baptists</u> (Kansas City, Mo.: F. Hudson Co., 1912), pp. 216-17.
                                          DHU/MO
    Baptist minister and secretary of State Baptist Convention of Oklahoma.

KEYS, FRANK

    William Joseph Barber. <u>Disciple Assemblies of Eastern North Carolina</u> (St. Louis: The Bethany Press, 1966), pp. 259-60.
                                          DHU/R
    Disciples of Christ minister.

KEYS, I. V.

    William Joseph Barber. <u>Disciple Assemblies of Eastern North Carolina</u> (St. Louis: The Bethany Press, 1966), pp. 259-60.
                                          DHU/R
    Black Disciples of Christ minister.

KEYS, W. D., (bp.).

    Robert L. Friedly. <u>The Disciple</u> (1:16, Ag. 4, 1974), pp. 9-10.
                                          DHU/R
    Negro Bishop of the Disciples of Christ Church in North Carolina.

KILGORE, THOMAS, JR.

    The editors of Ebony. <u>The Ebony Success Library: 1,000 Successful Blacks</u> (Nashville: The Southwestern Co., 1973), Vol. 1, p. 191.
                                          DHU
    Baptist minister and senior pastor of Second Baptist Church, Los Angeles, Calif.

KING, C. A.

    James W. Hood. <u>One Hundred Years of the A. M. E. Zion Church</u> (N. Y.: A. M. E. Zion Book Concern, 1895), pp. 570-80.
                                          DHU/MO
    A. M. E. Zion minister.

KING, G. M. P.

    G. F. Richings. <u>Evidences of Progress Among Colored People</u> (Phila.: G. S. Ferguson, 1904), p. 25.   DHU/MO
    Baptist minister and president of Wayland Seminary, Washington, D. C.

KING, MARTIN LUTHER, SR.

    The editors of Ebony. <u>The Ebony Success Library: 1,000 Successful Blacks</u> (Nashville: The Southwestern Co., 1973), p. 194.
                                          DHU

KING, WILLIS J., (bp.).

    <u>The Foundation Magazine</u> (34:3, Jl., 1944), pp. 1-2.
                            Pam. File, DHU/R
    Picture and biographical information on Negro bishop of the United Methodist Church.

KING, WILLIS J., (bp.).

    <u>The Foundation Magazine</u> (34:3, Jl., 1944), pp. 1-2.
                            Pam. File, DHU/R
    Picture and biographical information on Negro bishop of the United Methodist Church.

KIRBY, J. W.

    James J. Pipkin. <u>The Negro In Revelation, In History, and In Citizenship</u> (N. Y.: Thompson Pub. Co., 1902), p. 98.
                                          DHU/MO
    Baptist minister.

KIRUBULAYA, APOLO

    Georgina A. Gollock. <u>Sons of Africa</u> (N. Y.: Friendship Press, 1928), pp. 173-78.   DHU/MO; DHU/R
    Evangelist to Toro and vice-pres. of the Church Missionary Society.

KLUGH, DAVID S.

    E. R. Carter. <u>The Black Side</u> (Atlanta: n.p., 1894), pp. 94-6.
                                          DHU/MO
    Negro Baptist minister and teacher.

KNOX, JOHN EDWARD

    Samuel W. Bacote. <u>Who's Who Among the Colored Baptists</u> (Kansas City, Mo.: F. Hudson Co., 1912), pp. 174-76.
                                          DHU/MO
    Baptist minister and president of Brinkley Academy.

LABEAU, J. T. B.

    William Hicks. <u>The History of Louisiana Negro Baptists from 1804-1914</u> (Nashville, Tenn.: National Baptist Publishing Board, n.d.), pp. 190-91.   DHU/R
    Baptist minister.

LACEY, J. W.

    David H. Bradley, Sr. <u>A History of the A. M. E. Zion Church 1872-1968</u> V. 2 (Nashville: Parthenon Press, 1970), p. 32.
                                          DHU/R
    Minister and missionary of the A. M. E. Zion Church.

    James W. Hood. <u>One Hundred Years of the A. M. E. Zion Church</u> (N. Y.: A. M. E. Zion Book Concern, 1895), pp. 277-79.
                                          DHU/MO

LAMBERT, ROLLINS

    Albert S. Foley. <u>God's Men of Color</u> (New York: Farrar, Straus & Co., 1955), pp. 278-87.   DHU/R
    Catholic priest.

LAMPTON, EDWARD WILKINSON, (bp.).

    Richard R. Wright. <u>Bishops of the A. M. E. Church</u> (Nashville: A. M. E. Sunday School Union, 1963), pp. 251-52.
                                          DHU/R
    Thirty-first bishop of the A. M. E. Church.

    G. F. Richings. <u>Evidences of Progress Among the Colored People</u> (Phila.: G. S. Ferguson, 1904), p. 389. DHU/MO

    James J. Pipkin. <u>The Negro in Revelation in History and in Citizenship</u> (N. Y.: Thompson Pub. Co., 1902), p. 191.
                                          DHU/MO

    William N. Hartshorn. <u>An Era of Progress and Promise</u> (Boston: Priscilla Pub. Co., 1910), p. 392.   DHU/MO

LANDRY, PIERRE

    Henry D. Northrop. <u>College of Life</u> (Philadelphia: National
Pub. Co., 1895), pp. 45-47.   DHU/MO
M. E. minister and politician.

LANE, ISAAC, (bp.).

    Charles N. Phillips. <u>History of the Colored Methodist Church</u>
(Jackson, Tenn.: Pub. House, A. M. E. Church, 1898), pp.
218-22.   DHU/MO; DHU/R
Fifth Bishop of the Christian Methodist Episcopal Church.

    <u>Autobiography of Bishop Isaac Lane, LL. D.; with a Short
History of the C. M. E. Church in America and of Methodism</u>
(Nashville, Tenn.: Printed for the Author, Publishing House
of the C. M. E. Church South, 1916). NjP; DHU/MO; ATI

    Horace C. Savage. <u>Life and Times of Bishop Isaac Lane</u>
(Nashville: National Publishing Co., 1958).   DHU/MO

    James T. Haley. <u>Afro-American Encyclopaedia</u> (Nashville:
Haley & Florida, 1895), p. 352.   DHU/MO

    Thomas O. Fuller. <u>Pictorial History of the American Negro</u>
(Memphis, Tenn.: Pictorial History Inc., 1933), p. 72.
         DHU/MO

    William N. Hartshorn. <u>An Era of Progress and Promise</u>
(Boston: Priscilla Pub. Co., 1910), pp. 405-06.   DHU/MO

LANE, LUNSFORD

    John Spencer Bassett. <u>"Anti-Slavery Leaders of North Caro-
lina</u> (Balto.: The Johns Hopkins Press, 1898), pp. 60-74.
         DHU/MO; DHU/R
Slave who became an active lecturer and abolitionist.

    <u>The Narrative of Lunsford Lane, Formerly of Raleigh, N. C.,
Embracing an Account of His Early Life, the Redemption by
Purchase of Himself and Family from Slavery, and his Banish-
ment from the Place of His Birth for the Crime of Wearing a
Colored Skin. Pub. by Himself</u> (Boston: Torrey Printer,
1842).   DHU/MO

    William George Hawkins. <u>Lunsford Lane: Another Helper
From North Carolina</u> (Boston: Crosby & Nichols, 1863).
         DHU/MO
Reprinted Miami, Fla.: Mnemosyne Press, 1969.

LANE, WILLIAM L.

    Albert S. Foley. <u>God's Men of Color</u> (New York: Farrar,
Struas & Co., 1955), pp. 172-75.   DHU/R
Catholic priest.

LANEY, LUCY CRAFT

    Frank T. Wilson. "Living Witnesses: Black Presbyterians
in Ministry." <u>Journal of Presbyterian History</u> (51:4, Wint.,
1973), pp. 348-50.   DHU/R

LAWRENCE, GEORGE

    The editors of Ebony. <u>The Ebony Success Library: 1,000 Suc-
cessful Blacks</u> (Nashville: The Southwestern Co., 1973),
Vol. 1, p. 197.   DHU

LAWRENCE, WILLIAM P.

    Samuel W. Bacote. <u>Who's Who Among the Colored Baptists</u>
(Kansas City, Mo.: F. Hudson Co., 1912), pp. 88-89.
         DHU/MO
Baptist minister, president of Progressive Building & Loan
Association, Orange, N. J. and Oakwood Home Asso., 1st
vice-pres. of New England Baptist Missionary Convention.

LAWS, WILLIAM J.

    William H. Ferris. <u>African Abroad</u> V. 2 (New Haven, Conn.:
Tuttle, Morehouse, & Taylor Press, 1913), p. 764. DHU/MO
A. M. E. minister and ex-president of Paul Quinn College,
Waco, Texas.

LAWTON, BRISTER

    James M. Simms. <u>The First Colored Baptist Church in North
America</u> (Phila.: J. B. Lippincott Co., 1888), p. 261.
         DHU/R
Baptist minister.

LAWTON, WILLIAM R.

    William H. Ferris. <u>African Abroad</u> V. 2 (New Haven, Conn.:
Tuttle, Morehouse, & Taylor Press, 1913), p. 775. DHU/MO
Presbyterian minister and writer for the <u>Brooklyn Press</u>.

LEDOUX, LOUIS

    Albert S. Foley. <u>God's Men of Color</u> (New York: Farrar,
Straus & Co., 1955), Farrar, Straus & Co., 1955), pp. 301-
02.   DHU/R
Catholic priest.

LEE BENJAMIN FRANKLIN, (bp.).

    Richard R. Wright. <u>Bishops of the A. M. E. Church</u> (Nash-
ville: A. M. E. Sunday School Union, 1963), pp. 253-55.
         DHU/R
Twentieth Bishop of the A. M. E. Church.

    Benjamin W. Arnett. <u>The Budget... Biographical Sketches
Proceeding...</u> (Dayton, Ohio: Christian Pub. House, 1882),
pp. 15-17.   DHU/MO; DHU/R

    G. F. Richings. <u>Evidences of Progress Among Colored
People</u> (Philadelphia: G. S. Ferguson, 1904), pp. 122-25+.
         DHU/MO; DHU/R

    Henry D. Northrop. <u>College of Life...</u> (Philadelphia:
National Pub. Co., 1895), pp. 33-34.   DHU/MO

    William J. Simmons, (ed.). <u>Men of Mark</u> (Cleveland, O.:
Geo. M. Rewell & Co., 1887), p. 922.   DHU/R

    William N. Hartshorn. <u>An Era of Progress and Promise</u>
(Boston, Mass.: The Priscilla Pub. Co., 1910), p. 191.
         DHU/MO

    William Steward and Theophilus Gould. <u>Gouldtown a Very
Remarkable Settlement of Ancient Date</u> (Philadelphia:
Lippincott, 1913), p. 18.   DHU/MO

LEE, GEORGE W.

    Lewis G. Jordan. <u>Negro Baptist History U. S. A.</u> (Nash-
ville, Tenn.: Sunday School Pub. Bd., N. B. C., 1930),
p. 392.   DHU/MO; DHU/R
Baptist minister, Washington, D. C.

LEE, JERENA

Dorothy B. Porter. Early Negro Writing, 1760-1837 (Boston: Beacon, 1971), pp. 494-514.   DHU/MO
An 1836 autobiographical account of the woman evangelist.

The African Methodist Episcopal Church Review (81:222, Oct. -Dec., 1964), pp. 2-4.   DHU/R

LEE, JOSEPH E.

Benjamin W. Arnett. The Budget... Biographical Sketches Proceeding... (Dayton, O.: Christian Publishing House, 1882), pp. 30-32.   DHU/MO
A. M. E. minister.

LEE, MARSHALL W.

American Baptist Magazine (172:6, Je., 1974), p. 43.   DHU/R
Founding pastor of St. Paul's Baptist Church in Conshohocken, Pa., and active civil rights worker and advisor to Martin Luther King, Jr.

LEE, THOMAS F.

The editors of Ebony. The Ebony Success Library: 1,000 Successful Blacks (Nashville: The Southwestern Co., 1973), Vol. 1, p. 199.   DHU
Baptist minister and pastor of Emmanuel Baptist Church, Chicago, Ill.

LEEDIE, ALEXANDER J.

Albert S. Foley. God's Men of Color (New York: Farrar, Straus & Co., 1955), pp. 241-43.   DHU/R
Catholic priest.

LEMON, WILLIAM

Carter G. Woodson. The History of the Negro Church (Wash., D. C.: Associated Publishers, 1921), p. 45.
                                                DHU/MO; DHU/R
Baptist minister.

LEONARD, CHAUNCEY

U. S. Dept. of Education. Special Report (Wash., D. C.: Government Printing Office, 1871), p. 241.   DHU/MO
Baptist minister and teacher.

LEWIS, H. C.

Samuel W. Bacote. Who's Who Among the Colored Baptists (Kansas City, Mo.: F. Hudson Co., 1912), pp. 112-13.
                                                          DHU/MO
Baptist minister, treasurer and trustee of Guadalupe College, Texas.

LEWIS, M. M.

Orrin C. Evans. The Crisis (52:6, Je., 1945), pp. 170-71.
                                                 DLC; DHU/MO
A. M. E. minister.

LEWIS, P. B.

William Hicks. History of Louisiana Negro Baptists from 1804-1914 (Nashville, Tenn.: National Baptist Publishing Board, n. d.), pp. 127-29.   DHU/R
Baptist minister.

LEWIS, WALTER A.

James T. Haley. Afro-American Encylopaedia (Nashville, Tenn.: Haley & Florida, 1895), pp. 572-74.   DHU/MO
A. M. E. minister and teacher.

H. F. Kletzing. Progress of a Race (Atlanta, Ga.: J. L. Nichols & Co., 1898), p. 575.   DHU/MO

LIELE, GEORGE

Carter G. Woodson. The History of the Negro Church (Wash., D. C.: Associated Publishers, 1921), pp. 37-40.
                                                 DHU/R; DHU/MO
Ex-American slave, Baptist minister who was active in Jamaica.

Benjamin Brawley. Negro Builders and Heroes (Chapel Hill: University of North Carolina Press, 1937), p. 200.
                                                 DHU/R; DHU/MO

Edgar G. Thomas. The First African Baptist Church of North America (Savannah, Ga.: By the Author, 1925), pp. 10-23+.   DHU/MO

Edward A. Holmes. "George Liele" Negro Slavery's Prophet of Deliverance." Foundations (9:4, Oct. -Dec., 1966), pp. 333-45.   DAU/W

Emanuel K. Love. History of the First African Baptist Church (Savannah, Ga.: Morning News Print, 1888), p. 1.
                                                          DHU/MO

James M. Simms. The First Colored Baptist Church in North America (Phila.: J. B. Lippincott Co., 1888), p. 14.
                                                          DHU/R

John P. Gates. "George Liele: a Pioneer Negro Preacher." The Chronicle (6; Jl., 1944), pp. 118-21.

John W. Davis. "George Liele and Andrew Bryan, Pioneer Negro Baptist Preachers." Journal of Negro History (3:2, Apr., 1918), pp. 119-27.   DHU/MO

Richard Bardolph. "Social Origins of Distinguished Negroes, 1770-1865." Journal of Negro History (40:3, Jl., 1955), p. 222.   DHU/MO

LIGHTS, F. L.

Samuel W. Bacote. Who's Who Among the Colored Baptists (Kansas City, Mo.: F. Hudson Co., 1912), pp. 71-72.   DHU/MO
Baptist minister and president of Orgen Banking Co. and Foreign Mission Convention.

LIPSCOMBE, E. H.

William J. Simmons, (ed.). Men of Mark (Cleveland, O.: George M. Rewell & Co., 1887), p. 959.   DHU/R
Baptist minister and editor.

LITTLE, MALCOLM (Malcolm X)

Marcus H. Boulware. The Oratory of Negro Leaders 1900-1968 (Westport, Conn.: Negro Universities Press, 1969), p. 234.   DHU/MO
Race activist and once Black Muslim minister.

Edward A. Toppin. A Biographical History of Blacks in America Since 1928 (New York: David McKay Co., 1971), pp. 358-63.   DHU/MO

Elton C. Fax. Contemporary Black Leaders (New York: Dodd, Mead, & Co., 1970), pp. 1-17.   DHU/R

LIVINGSTON, WILLIAM

　　George F. Bragg. History of the Afro-American Group of the
　　Episcopal Church (Balto., Md.: Church Advocate Press,
　　1922), pp. 90+.　　　　　　　　　　　DHU/R
　　First rector of St. James Protestant Episcopal Church, Balti-
　　more, Md.

LOGUEN, JERMAIN W., (bp.).

　　James W. Hood. One Hundred Years of the A. M. E. Zion
　　Church (N. Y.: A. M. E. Zion Book Concern, 1895), pp.
　　180-82.　　　　　　　　　　　　　　　DHU/MO
　　Bishop of the A. M. E. Zion Church and active in the Under-
　　ground Railroad.

　　The Rev. J. W. Loguen, As a Slave and As a Freeman (New
　　York: Negro Universities Press, 1968).　　DHU/R; FSU
　　Autobiography originally published in 1859.
　　Negro author.

　　Samuel J. May. Some Recollections of the Anti-Slavery Con-
　　flict (Miami, Fla.: Mnemosyne Publishing Co., 1969).
　　　　　　　　　　　　　　　　　　　　DHU/MO

　　William H. Ferris. African Abroad V. 2 (New Haven, Conn.:
　　Tuttle, Morehouse, Taylor Press, 1913), p. 692.　DHU/MO

　　William Wells Brown. The Rising Son or the Antecedents and
　　the Advancements of the Colored Race (Miami, Fla.: Mnem-
　　osyne Pub. Inc., 1969), pp. 531-32.　　DHU/MO; DHU/R

LOMAX, THOMAS H., (bp.).

　　E. A. Johnson, School History of the Negro Race in America
　　(Raleigh: Edward & Broughton, 1890), pp. 186-88.
　　　　　　　　　　　　　　　　DHU/MO; DHU/R
　　Bishop of the A. M. E. Zion Church.

　　James W. Hood. One Hundred Years of the A. M. E. Zion
　　Church (N. Y.: A. M. E. Zion Book Concern, 1895), pp.
　　191-95.　　　　　　　　　　　　　　DHU/MO

　　John J. Moore. History of the A. M. E. Zion Church in
　　America (York, Pa.: Teachers Journal Office, 1884), pp.
　　376-77.　　　　　　　　　　　　　　DHU/MO

LONG, GEORGE WALDO

　　Frank T. Wilson. "Living Witnesses: Black Presbyterians
　　in Ministry." Journal of Presbyterian History (51:4, Wint.,
　　1973), pp. 351-54.　　　　　　　　　DHU/R
　　Black Presbyterian Church, Mayesville, South Carolina.

LOUGHRIDGE, ALBERT

　　G. F. Richings. Evidences of Progress Among Colored People
　　(Phila.: G. S. Ferguson, 1904), p. 31.　　DHU/MO; DHU/R
　　Baptist minister and president of Bishop College, Marshall,
　　Texas.

LOVE, EMANUEL K.

　　Edgar G. Thomas. The First Baptist Church of North Amer-
　　ica (Savannah, Ga.: By the author, 1925), p. 86-108.
　　　　　　　　　　　　　　　　　　　　DHU/MO
　　Baptist minister and editor.

　　Lewis G. Jordan. Negro Baptist History U. S. A. (Nash-
　　ville, Tenn.: The Sunday School Pub. Board, 1930), p. 392.
　　　　　　　　　　　　　　　　DHU/MO; DHU/R

William J. Simmons. Men of Mark (Cleveland, Ohio:
Rewell, 1887), pp. 481-83.　　　　　　　DHU/R

LOVE, J. S.

　　William Hicks. The History of Louisiana Negro Baptists from
　　1804-1914 (Nashville, Tenn.: National Baptist Publishing
　　Board, n. d.), p. 186.　　　　　　　　DHU/R
　　Baptist minister.

LOVEJOY, ELIJAH P.

　　William T. Alexander. History of the Colored Race in Amer-
　　ica (N. Y.: Negro Universities Press, 1968), pp. 413-33.
　　　　　　　　　　　　　　　　　　　　DHU/MO
　　White Presbyterian minister and editor of the National Repub-
　　lican.

LOVELACE, WILLIAM FRANKLIN

　　Samuel W. Bacote. Who's Who Among the Colored Baptists
　　(Kansas City, Mo.: F. Hudson Co., 1912), pp. 227-29.
　　　　　　　　　　　　　　　　　　　　DHU/MO
　　Baptist minister.

LOWRY, W. S.

　　Irvine G. Penn. The Afro-American Press and Its Editors
　　(Springfield, Mass.: Willey & Co., 1891), pp. 148-50.
　　　　　　　　　　　　　　　　　　　　DHU/R
　　Business manager of the Afro-American Spokesman and min-
　　ister of the A. M. E. Church.

LUCAS, W. W.

　　Henry F. Kletzing. Progress of a Race (Atlanta, Ga.: J. L.
　　Nichols & Co., 1898.)　　　　　　　　DHU/MO
　　Secretary of the Stewart Missionary Foundation for Africa.

LUIS DE MOLINA

　　Bernard J. F. Lonergan. Encyclopedia Britannica V. 15
　　(Chicago: William Benton, 1970), pp. 665-66.　　DHU/R
　　Black religious reformer, professor of Moral Theology at
　　the University of Evora, Portugal in the seventeenth century.

　　F. L. Sheerin. New Catholic Encyclopedia V. 9 (Wash.,
　　D. C.: Catholic Univ., 1967), p. 1010.　　DHU/R

　　Joel A. Rogers. World's Great Men of Color (New York:
　　Joel A. Rogers, 1947), pp. 548-49.　　DHU/R

LUKE, LUCAS M.

　　Lewis G. Jordan. Negro Baptist History U. S. A. (Nashville,
　　Tenn.: The Sunday School Pub. Bd., N. B. C., 1930), p. 392.
　　　　　　　　　　　　　　　　DHU/MO; DHU/R
　　Baptist minister of Texas and first corresponding secretary
　　for the Foreign Mission Board of the National Baptist Conven-
　　tion.

LYNCH, JAMES

　　The African Methodist Episcopal Church Review (78:212,
　　Apr.-Je., 1962), p. 77.　　　　　　　　DHU/R
　　Negro Methodist minister. Editor of the Recorder, a popular
　　Methodist publication.

Irvine G. Penn. The Afro-American Press and Its Editors (Springfield, Mass.: Willey & Co., 1891), pp. 102+.
DHU/R; DHU/MO

William W. Brown. The Rising Son (Boston: A. G. Brown & Co., 1874), pp. 519-20.   DHU/MO; DHU/R

LYONS, C. H.

Lewis G. Jordan. Negro Baptist History U. S. A. (Nashville, Tenn.: The Sunday School Pub. Bd., N. B. C. 1930), p. 392.
DHU/MO; DHU/R
Baptist minister of Georgia and Secretary of the Georgia Baptist State Convention.

LYONS, ERNEST A.

William H. Ferris. African Abroad V. 2 (New Haven, Conn.: Tuttle, Morehouse, & Taylor Press, 1913), p. 796.   DHU/MO
United States Minister to Liberia and M. E. minister.

James L. Nichols. The New Progress of a Race (New York: Arno Press, 1929), pp. 403-04.   DHU/MO

Journal of Negro History (22:1, Ja., 1937), pp. 80-83; (23:4, Oct., 1938), p. 514.   DHU/MO

Leila A. Pendleton. A Narrative of the Negro (Wash., D. C.: Press of R. L. Pendleton, 1912), p. 50.   DHU/MO

MABANE, C. S.

G. F. Richings. Evidences of Progress Among Colored People (Philadelphia: G. S. Ferguson, 1904), pp. 168-70.
DHU/MO; DHU/R
Presbyterian minister, ex-slave, and founder and principal of Monticello Seminary, Monticello, Arkansas.

MACVICAR, M.

G. F. Richings. Evidences of Progress Among Colored People (Phila.: G. S. Ferguson, 1904), p. 28.
DHU/R; DHU/MO
Baptist minister and President of Virginia Union University, Richmond, Va.

MADDEN, B. F.

U. S. Dept. of Education. Special Report (Wash., D. C.: Government Printing Office, 1871), p. 291.   DHU/MO
Baptist minister.

MADDEN, S. W.

U. S. Dept. of Education. Special Report (Wash., D. C.: Government Printing Office, 1871), p. 239.   DHU/MO
Baptist minister.

Leila A. Pendleton. A Narrative of the Negro (Wash., D. C.: Press of R. L. Pendleton, 1912), p. 177.   DHU/MO

MADISON, WILLIAM

Samuel W. Bacote. Who's Who Among the Colored Baptists (Kansas City, Mo.: F. Hudson Co., 1912), pp. 273-74.
DHU/MO

Baptist minister.

MAGEE, J. H.

The Night of Affliction and Morning of Recovery. An Auto-biography. By Rev. J. H. Magee, Paster of the Union Baptist Church (Cincinnati, O.: Pub. by the Author, 1873).   SCBHC
Baptist minister.

MANLEY, JAMES H.

James W. Hood. One Hundred Years of the A. M. E. Zion Church (N. Y.: A. M. E. Zion Book Concern, 1895), pp. 356-58.   DHU/MO
Secretary of Foreign Mission Board of A. M. E. Zion Church, 1892-1896.

MANNING, CORNELIUS MAXWELL

William H. Heard. The Bright Side of African Life (N. Y.: Negro Universities Press, 1969), pp. 51+.   DHU/R
A. M. E. minister and secretary of the Legation of the U. S. at Monrovia, Liberia.

MAPOPE, CALVIN MATSIVI

Georgina A. Gollock. Sons of Africa (N. Y.: Friendship Press, 1928), pp. 185-88.   DHU/R
South African pastor and evangelist.

MARIN, PHILIP

Albert S. Foley. God's Men of Color (New York: Farrar, Straus & Co., 1955), pp. 176-80.   DHU/R
Catholic priest.

MARKS, JOHN

William Hicks. The History of Louisiana Negro Baptists From 1804-1914 (Nashville, Tenn.: National Baptist Publishing Board, n. d.), pp. 176-78.   DHU/R
Baptist minister and chairman of Southern Trustee Board of Leland University.

MARRANT, JOHN

"A Narrative of the Lord's Wonderful Dealings with John Marrant, a Black..." Dorothy B. Porter. Early Negro Writing, 1760-1837 (Boston: Beacon, 1971), pp. 427-47.
DHU/MO

"Perhaps the first Negro minister of the Gospel in North America."

MARRS, ELIJAH P.

G. F. Richings. Evidences of Progress Among Colored People (Phila.: G. S. Ferguson, 1904), p. 56.
DHU/R; DHU/MO
Baptist minister, Kentucky and business manager of State Univ. of Louisville, Kentucky.

Life and History of the Rev. Elijah P. Marrs (Miami, Fla.: Books for Libraries, 1969).   DHU/R
Reprint of 1885 edition.

William J. Simmons. Men of Mark (Cleveland: Geo. Rewell, 1887), pp. 579-81.   DHU/R; DHU/MO

MARS, JOHN

Methodist Episcopal Church. New England Conference.
Minutes (1885), pp. 81-82.   NjD
Mars was an antebellum preacher in New England, a missionary to the freedmen and later a pastor of a black Methodist
congregation in Boston.

MARSHALL, ANDREW

Emanuel K. Love. History of the First African Baptist Church
(Savannah, Ga.: Morning News Print, 1888), pp. 13-14, 41-56.
                                                            DHU/MO
Baptist minister.

Edgar G. Thomas. The First Baptist Church of North America
(Savannah, Ga.: By the author, 1925), pp. 43-52.   DHU/MO

James M. Simms. The First Colored Baptist Church in North
America (Phila.: J. B. Lippincott Co., 1888), pp. 237-242.
                                                            DHU/R

Lewis G. Jordan. Negro Baptist History U. S. A. (Nashville,
Tenn.: Sunday School Publishing Board, N. B. C., 1930),
p. 392.   DHU/MO

MARSHALL, JULIAN FRANKLIN

Henry D. Northrop. College of Life (Phila.: Nat. Pub. Co.,
1895), p. 53.   DHU/MO
A. M. E. minister.

MARTIN DE PORRES, Saint

Ellen Tarry. Martin de Porres: Saint of the New World (New
York: Farrar Straus & Co., 1963).   DHU/MO; NN/Sch
Declared a saint by the Catholic Church, May, 1962. A Negro
lay brother of the Dominican Order, Lima, Peru.

Gustave B. Aldrich. Chronicle (3; Sept., 1930), pp. 208-09.
                                        ICU; NNC; NNUT; NjPT

H. C. Kearns. The Life of Blessed Martin de Porres (New
York: Kennedy & Sons, 1937).   DHU/R

Leo Marie Preher, (Sister). The Social Implications in the
Work of Blessed Martin De Porres... (Doctoral dissertation.
Catholic University, 1941).   DCU

Norbert Georges. Meet Brother Martin. The Life of Blessed
Martin de Porres, Saintly American Negro (New York: The
Torch, 1936).   DHU/MO

Stanislas Fumet. Life of St. Martin De Porres, Patron Saint
of Interracial Justice (Garden City, N. Y.: Doubleday & Co.,
Inc., 1964).   DHU/R

MARTIN, J. A.

Samuel W. Bacote. Who's Who Among the Colored Baptists
(Kansas City, Mo.: F. Hudson Co., 1912), p. 302. DHU/MO
Baptist minister and representative of Alabama State Conven-
tion.

MARTIN, JOHN SELLA

William Wells Brown. The Black Man (N. Y.: T. Hamilton,
1863), pp. 241-45.   DHU/R

William Wells Brown. The Rising Son or the Antecedents and
the Advancement of the Colored Race (Miami, Fla.: Mnemosyne Pub. Inc., 1969), pp. 535-36.   DHU/R
Baptist minister and editor of National Era.

MARTIN, JOSEPH C.

Charles H. Phillips. History of the Colored Methodist Epis-
copal Church (Jackson, Tenn.: Pub. House, C. M. E.
Church, 1898), p. 573.   DHU/MO
C. M. E. minister.

MARTIN, LEANDER JOSEPH

Albert S. Foley. God's Men of Color (New York: Farrar,
Straus & Co., 1955), pp. 235-38.   DHU/R
Catholic priest.

MARTIN, RICHARD B., (bp.).

The Episcopal Church Annual (New York: Morehouse-Barlow,
1968), p. 241.   PPPD; ViA1TH
Protestant Episcopal Suffragan bishop of Long Island.

MASON, LENA DOOLIN

Daniel W. Culp. Twentieth Century Negro Literature (Miami,
Fla.: Mnemosyne Pub. Co., Inc., 1969), p. 445. DHU/MO
Reprint of 1902 edition.
Negro woman evangelist and lecturer who pastored Negro and
White congregations.

MASON, MADISON CHARLES BUTLER

G. F. Richings. Evidences of Progress Among Colored People
(Phila.: G. S. Ferguson, 1904), p. 117. DHU/R; DHU/MO
African Methodist Episcopal minister and first Negro to be
elected General Corresponding Secretary of the Freedman's
Aid and Southern Educational Society.

Benjamin G. Brawley. Negro in Literature and Art (Atlanta,
Ga.: n. p., 1910), p. 52.   DHU/MO

Charles Alexander. One Hundred Distinguished Leaders
(Atlanta, Ga.: Franklin Printing & Publishing Co., 1899),
p. 62.   DHU/MO

Henry D. Northrop. College of Life (Phila.: Nat. Pub. Co.,
1895), pp. 51-3.   DHU/MO

Henry F. Kletzing. Progress of a Race (Atlanta: J. L.
Nichols & Co., 1898), pp. 511-12.   DHU/MO

William H. Ferris. Africans Abroad (New Haven, Conn.:
Tuttle, Morehouse & Taylor Press, 1913), p. 791. DHU/MO

William N. Hartshorn. An Era of Progress and Promise
(Boston: Priscilla Publishing Co., 1910), p. 422. DHU/MO

MASSEY, WILLIAM

Samuel W. Bacote. Who's Who Among the Colored Baptists
(Kansas City, Mo.: F. Hudson Co., 1912), pp. 299-301.
                                             DHU/MO
Baptist minister.

MATTOCKS, J. H.

James W. Hood. One Hundred Years of the A. M. E. Zion
Church (N. Y.: A. M. E. Zion Book Concern, 1895), pp. 551-
53.   DHU/MO
A. M. E. Zion minister.

MAURICE OF AGANAUM, Saint

Gustave B. Aldrich. "St Maurice of Africa." Chronicle (3;
Ag., 1930), p. 183.   ICU; NNC; NNUT; NjPT

Joel A. Rogers. World's Great Men of Color V. 2. (New York: Macmillan & Co., 1972), pp. 11-15.   DHU/R

Wolfgang S. Seiferth. "St. Mauritius, African." Phylon (2:4, Fourth Quarter, 1941), pp. 370-76.   DHU/MO

MAXWELL, O. C.

Thomas O. Fuller. Pictorial History of the American Negro (Memphis, Tenn.: Pictorial History Inc., 1933), p. 86.
                                                        DHU/MO
Minister of St. Louis, Mo.

MAY, SAMUEL

William W. Brown. The Rising Son (Boston: A. G. Brown & Co., 1874), pp. 398-400.   DHU/R; DHU/MO
Unitarian minister and activist in the Anti-Slavery movement.

Danvers Historical Society. Old Anti-Slavery Days (Danvers, Mass.: Danvers Mirror Print, 1893), pp. 101-03.   DHU/MO

MAYES, ELIAS

John M. Brewer. Negro Legislators of Texas (Dallas, Tex.: Mathis Pub. Co., 1935), pp. 97-98.   DHU/MO
Negro minister; served two terms in the Texas State Legislature.

MAYFIELD, R. A.

William Hicks. History of Louisiana Negro Baptist from 1804-1914 (Nashville, Tenn.: National Baptist Publishing Board, n.d.), pp. 125-27.   DHU/R
Baptist minister and founder of Homer Normal, Industrial and Bible Training School.

MAYO, J. HASKEL

African Methodist Episcopal Church Review (81:221, Jl.-Sept., 1964), p. 60.   DHU/R
Minister of the A. M. E. Church.

MAYS, BENJAMIN ELIJAH

Marcus H. Boulware. The Oratory of Negro Leaders 1900-1968 (Westport, Conn.: Negro Universities Press, 1969), p. 187.   DHU/MO
Baptist minister, college president, and author.

MCALPINE, WILLIAM H.

Henry F. Kletzing. Progress of a Race (Atlanta: J. L. Nichols & Co., 1898), p. 404.   DHU/MO
Baptist minister, first president of the National Baptist Convention and founder and president of Selma University, editor of the Baptist Pioneer.

Lewis G. Jordan. Negro Baptist History U. S. A. (Nashville: The Sunday School Pub. Board, N. B. C., 1930), p. 56.
                                                DHU/R; DHU/MO

William J. Simmons. Men of Mark (Cleveland: O. Rewell, 1887), pp. 524-29.   DHU/R; DHU/MO

MCCLELLAN, GEORGE M.

Otelia Cromwell and Lorenzo D. Turner, et alii. Readings from Negro Authors for Schools and Colleges (New York: Harcourt, Brace & Co., 1931), p. 378.   DHU/MO
Graduate of Hartford Theological Seminary and principal of Paul Lawrence Dunbar High School, Louisville, Ky.

MCCOO, F. A.

James L. Nichols. The New Progress of a Race (Naperville, Ill.: J. L. Nichols & Co., 1929), p. 404.   DHU/MO
Baptist minister, Illinois.

MCCRACKEN, C. L.

G. F. Richings. Evidences of Progress Among Colored People (Phila.: G. S. Ferguson, 1904), p. 440.
                                        DHU/MO; DHU/R
United Presbyterian minister and principal of Henderson Normal Institute, Henderson, N. C.

MCCROREY, H. L.

William N. Hartshorn. An Era of Progress and Promise (Boston, Mass.: Priscilla Publishing Co., 1910), p. 443.
                                                        DHU/MO
Presbyterian minister and teacher.

Thomas O. Fuller. Pictorial History of the American Negro (Memphis, Tenn.: Pictorial History Inc., 1933), p. 103.
                                                        DHU/MO

MCDOWELL, JOHN

Presbyterian Reunion: 1837-1871 (New York: De W. C. Lent & Co., 1870), pp. 133-41.   DHU/MO
Presbyterian minister, director and trustee of Theological Seminary at Princeton.

MCDOWELL, WILLIAM ANDERSON

Presbyterian Reunion: 1837-1871 (N. Y.: De W. C. Lent & Co., 1870), pp. 141-42.   DHU/MO
Presbyterian minister and secretary of the Board of Domestic Missions.

MCEWEN, A. N.

Irvine G. Penn. The Afro-American Press and Its Editors (Springfield, Mass.: Willey & Co., 1891), pp. 300-05.
                                        DHU/MO; DHU/R
Editor of The Baptist Leader, the official organ of the Colored Baptists of Alabama. Baptist missionary minister.

MCEWEN, ALICE E.

Irvine G. Penn. The Afro-American Press and Its Editors, (Springfield, Mass.: Willey & Co., 1891), pp. 396-400.
                                                        DHU/MO
Associate editor of the Baptist Leader.

Lawson A. Scruggs. Women of Distinction. (Raleigh, N. C.: L. A. Scruggs, 1893), pp. 249-51.   DHU/MO

MCGUIRE, GEORGE ALEXANDER

Gavin White. "Patriarch McGuire and the Episcopal Church." Historical Magazine of the Protestant Church (38;2, Je., 1969), pp. 109-41.   DHU/R
West Indian born Archdeacon of the Convocation of Arkansas and later Chaplain-General of Marcus Garvey's Universal Negro Improvement Association. Founder of the African Orthodox Church.

MCINTOSH, P. J.

James W. Hood. One Hundred Years of the A. M. E. Zion Church (New York: A. M. E. Zion Book Concern, 1895), pp. 429-33.   DHU/MO
A. M. E. Zion minister and founder of McIntosh Institute, Anniston, Ala.

MCKENZIE, JOHN EMANUEL

>   Frank T. Wilson. "Living Witnesses: Black Presbyterians
>   in Ministry." Journal of Presbyterian History (51:4, Wint.,
>   1973), pp. 378-80.   DHU/R
>   Presbyterian rural minister of the Southeast.

MCKINNEY, GEORGE P.

>   G. F. Richings. Evidences of Progress Among Colored
>   People (Phila.: G. S. Ferguson, 1904), pp. 53-55. DHU/MO
>   Baptist minister and President of Florida Institute.

MCKINNEY, JOHN WESLEY

>   Henry F. Kletzing. Progress of a Race (Atlanta: J. L.
>   Nichols & Co., 1898), pp. 575-76.   DHU/MO
>   C. M. E. minister

>   Charles H. Phillips. History of the Colored Methodist Epis-
>   copal Church (Jackson, Tenn.: Pub. House, A. M. E.
>   Church, 1898), pp. 576-78.   DHU/MO

MCKINNEY, SAMUEL B.

>   The editors of Ebony. The Ebony Success Library: 1,000 Suc-
>   cessful Blacks (Nashville: The Southwestern Co., 1973),
>   Vol. 1, p. 211.   DHU
>   Baptist minister and pastor of Mt. Zion Baptist Church,
>   Seattle, Wash.

MCKNIGHT, ALBERT J.

>   The editors of Ebony. The Ebony Success Library: 1,000 Suc-
>   cessful Blacks (Nashville: The Southwestern Co., 1973),
>   Vol. 1, p. 212.   DHU
>   Catholic priest, president of Southern Cooperative Development
>   Fund, Lafayette, Louisiana.

>   Albert S. Foley. God's Men of Color (New York: Farrar,
>   Straus & Co., 1955), p. 303.   DHU/R

MCKNIGHT, ROBERT

>   Presbyterian Reunion: 1837-1871 (N. Y.: De W. C. Lent &
>   Co., 1870), pp. 520-21.   DHU/MO
>   Presbyterian minister and lawyer elected to House of Repre-
>   sentatives and 36th and 37th Congress.

MCNEIL, JESSE JAI

>   Charles Emerson Boddie. God's "Bad Boys" (Valley Forge:
>   Judson Press, 1972), pp. 93-105.   DHU/R
>   Baptist minister.

MCNEILL, ROBERT B.

>   William H. Crook and Ross Coggins. Seven Who Fought (Waco,
>   Texas: Word Books, 1971), pp. 26-44.   DHU/R
>   White minister of the First Presbyterian Church, Columbia,
>   Georgia and his attempt to bring the races together in his
>   church and community.

MCNORTON, L. J.

>   Samuel W. Bacote. Who's Who Among Colored Baptists
>   (Kansas City, Mo.: F. Hudson Co., 1912), pp. 209-10.
>   DHU/MO
>   Treasurer of women's dept., Northwestern Baptist Assoc.,
>   president of one of the largest Missionary societies in Texas.

MCQUEEN, STEPHEN

>   James M. Simms. The First Colored Baptist Church in North
>   America (Phila.: J. B. Lippincott Co., 1888), pp. 255-56.
>   DHU/R
>   Baptist minister.

MEDFORD, HAMPTON THOMAS, (bp.).

>   Biographical Encyclopedia of the World (New York: Institute
>   of Research, 1946), p. 818.   NcSalL
>   Bishop of A. M. E. Zion Church.

>   J. G. Schwarz. Religious Leaders of America (New York:
>   The Author, 1941-42), p. 779.   NcSalL; DHU/R

>   Who's Who in Colored America (New York: Who's Who in
>   Colored America, 1930-32).   NcSalL; DHU/R

MELDON, CHARLES MANLY

>   G. F. Richings. Evidences of Progress Among Colored
>   People (Phila.: G. S. Ferguson, 1904), p. 102. DHU/R
>   President of Clark Univ., Atlanta, Ga. and M. E. minister.

MERRILL, J. G.

>   G. F. Richings. Evidences of Progress Among Colored
>   People (Philadelphia: G. S. Ferguson, 1904), pp. 73-75.
>   DHU/R
>   White Congregationalist minister and president of Fisk Univ-
>   ersity, Nashville, Tennessee.

MERRY, NELSON

>   Lewis G. Jordan. Negro Baptist History U. S. A. (Nashville,
>   Tenn.: Sunday School Publishing Board, N. B. C., 1930), p.
>   392.   DHU/R
>   Baptist minister and pastor of Spruce Street Baptist Church,
>   Nashville, Tenn.

MEYER, PROSPER (Edward)

>   Albert S. Foley. God's Men of Color (New York: Farrar,
>   Straus & Co., 1955), pp. 253-57.   DHU/R
>   Catholic priest.

MICHAUX, SOLOMON LIGHTFOOT

>   Marcus H. Boulware. The Oratory of Negro Leaders 1900-
>   1968 (Westport, Conn.: Negro Universities Press, 1969), p.
>   204.   DHU/MO
>   Black radio evangelist of Washington, D. C.

>   Our World (5:1, Ja., 1950), pp. 44-47.   DHU/MO

>   The Washington Evening Star (Jl., 1938), p. 2.
>   Pam. File, DHU/MO

MILES, WILLIAM H., (bp.).

>   Charles N. Phillips. History of the Colored Methodist Epis-
>   copal Church in America (Jackson, Tenn.: Pub. House, A.
>   M. E. Church, 1898), pp. 196-204.   DHU/R
>   First Bishop of the Colored Methodist Episcopal Church.

MILLER, A. H.

G. F. Richings. Evidences of Progress Among Colored People
(Phila.: G. S. Ferguson, 1904), p. 515.   DHU/R
Ex-slave and Baptist minister in 1874 served in Arkansas Gen-
eral Assembly.

MILLER, D. D.

Carol Colliver. "The Black Pulpit--From Whence Cometh
the Dream." Midway, the Magazine of the Topeka Capital
Journal (Apr. 11, 1971), pp. 4-14. Pam. File, DHU/R
Pictorial article on Topeka's black churches and biography of
Rev. D. D. Miller, Baptist minister.

MILLER, GEORGE FRAZIER

James L. Nichols. The Progress of a Race (N. Y.: Arno
Press, 1909), pp. 405-06.   DHU/MO
"Reprint of earlier edition."
Protestant Episcopal minister of New York.

MILLER, SAMUEL

Presbyterian Reunion: 1837-1871 (N. Y.: Dew C. Lent & Co.,
1870), pp. 119-24.   DHU/MO
Presbyterian minister.

MILLER, THEODORE DOUGHTY

William J. Simmons. Men of Mark (Cleveland: Geo. Rewell,
1887), pp. 260-66.   DHU/R
Baptist minister and pastor of Cherry Street Baptist Church,
Philadelphia.

MILLER, WILLIAM, (bp.).

A. M. E. Zion Quarterly Review (62; 1952), p. 233. DHU/R
Bishop of the A. M. E. Zion Church.

David H. Bradley. A History of the A. M. E. Zion Church
(Nashville: Parthenon Press, 1956), p. 129.   DHU/R

Carter G. Woodson. The History of the Negro Church (Washington: Associated Publishers, 1945), pp. 68-69+.
                                        DHU/MO; DHU/R

Henry F. Kletzing. Progress of a Race (Atlanta: J. L.
Nichols & Co., 1898), p. 406.   DHU/MO

James B. F. Shaw. The Negro in the History of Methodism
(Nashville: Parthenon Press, 1954), p. 76.   DHU/R

James W. Hood. One Hundred Years of the A. M. E. Zion
Church (N. Y.: A. M. E. Z. Book Concern, 1895), pp. 70-
71.   DHU/MO

John J. Moore. History of the A. M. E. Zion Church in
America (York, Pa.: Teachers Journal Office, 1884), pp.
353-55.   DHU/MO

Leila A. Pendleton. A Narrative of the Negro (Wash., D.
C.: Press of R. L. Pendleton, 1912), p. 97. DHU/MO

William W. Brown. The Rising Son (Boston: A. G. Brown
& Co., 1874), pp. 337-38.   DHU/R

MILLS, CEDRIC, (bp.).

The Episcopal Church Annual (New York: Morehouse-Barlow, 1964), p. 425.   PPPD; ViAlTH
Protestant Episcopal bishop of Virgin Islands.

MILLS, HENRY

Presbyterian Reunion: 1837-1871 (N. Y.: Dew C. Lent &
Co., 1870), pp. 215-16.   DHU/MO
Presbyterian minister and teacher.

MITCHELL, EDWARD CUSHING

Henry F. Kletzing. Progress of a Race (Atlanta, Ga.: J. L.
Nichols & Co., 1898), p. 400.   DHU/MO
President of Leland University and minister.

MIXON, WINFIELD HENRY

Irvine G. Penn. The Afro-American Press and Its Editors
(Springfield, Mass.: Willey & Co., 1891), pp. 201-03.
                                        DHU/MO; DHU/R
Minister of the A. M. E. Church and editor of the Dallas Post.

M'KIRAHAN, WILLIAM

G. F. Richings. Evidences of Progress Among Colored
People (Phila.: G. S. Ferguson, 1904), pp. 438-39. DHU/R
Presbyterian minister and Principal of Norfolk Mission Coll-
ege.

MOFFAT, ROBERT

William T. Alexander. History of the Colored Race in America (New York: Negro Universities Press, 1968), pp. 66-90.
                                        DHU/MO
Christian missionary and minister.

MONFORT, JOSEPH G.

Presbyterian Reunion: 1837-1871 (N. Y.: De W. C. Lent &
Co., 1870), pp. 506-07.   DHU/MO
Presbyterian minister and director of Theological Seminary of
the Northwest.

MONTGOMERY, SIMON P.

Christian Century (72:42, Oct. 19, 1955), p. 1196. DHU/R
A Black pastor to an all white Methodist Church in Old Mystic,
Connecticut.

MOORE, B.

William Hicks. The History of Louisiana Negro Baptists From
1804-1914 (Nashville, Tenn.: National Baptist Publishing
Board, n.d.), pp. 188-89.   DHU/R
Baptist minister.

MOORE, E. W.

Madeline G. Allison. The Crisis (19:2, Dec., 1919), p. 84.
                                        DHU/MO; DLC
First Negro elected Gen. Supt. of the American Baptist Home
Mission Society.

MOORE, J. M.

G. F. Richings. Evidences of Progress Among Colored
People (Phila.: G. S. Ferguson, 1904), p. 439. DHU/R
Presbyterian minister and principal of Thyne Institute, Chase
City, Va.

MOORE, JOHN H.

Walter F. Watkins. The Cry of the West: the Story of the
Mighty Struggle for Religious Freedom in California (Sara-
toga: R. & E Research Associates, 1969), pp. 24-25. DHU/R
Baptist minister.

MOORE, JOHN J., (bp.).

David H. Bradley, Sr. A History of the A. M. E. Zion Church
V. II 1872-1968 (Nashville: Parthenon Press, 1970), p. 11+.
Bishop of the A. M. E. Zion Church.

Henry G. Kletzing. Progress of a Race (Atlanta: J. L. N
Nichols & Co., 1898), p. 580.   DHU/MO

James W. Hood. One Hundred Years of the A. M. E. Zion
Church (N. Y.: A. M. E. Zion Book Concern, 1895), pp. 172-
74.   DHU/MO

John J. Moore. History of the A. M. E. Zion Church in
America (York, Pa.: Teachers Journal Office, 1884), pp.
367-73.   DHU/MO

MOORE, JUNE

William H. Heard. The Bright Side of African Life (N. Y.:
Negro Universities Press, 1969), pp. 88-91.   DHU/R
Baptist minister, Vice-Pres. of Baptist Convention, Liberia.

MOORE, MORRIS MARCELLUS, (bp.).

Richard R. Wright. Bishops of the A. M. E. Church (Nashville: A. M. E. Sunday School Union, 1963), p. 256. DHU/R
Twenty-seventh Bishop of the A. M. E. Church

G. F. Richings. Evidences of Progress Among Colored
People (Philadelphia: G. S. Ferguson, 1904), p. 388.
                                     DHU/MO; DHU/R

MOORE, THOMAS PAGE R.

James W. Hood. One Hundred Years of the A. M. E. Zion
Church (N. Y.: A. M. E. Zion Book Concern, 1895), pp.
575-77.   DHU/MO
A. M. E. Zion minister.

MOORE, WILLIAM J.

James W. Hood. One Hundred Years of the A. M. E. Zion
Church (N. Y.: A. M. E. Zion Book Concern, 1895), pp.
285-87.   DHU/MO
A. M. E. Zion minister.

MOORLAND, JESSE E.

William N. Hartshorn. An Era of Progress and Promise
(Boston, Mass.: Priscilla Publishing Co., 1910), p. 428.
                                                 DHU/MO
Baptist minister, teacher and physician.

James L. Nichols. The New Progress of a Race (Naperville, Ill.: J. L. Nichols & Co., 1929), pp. 411-12. DHU/MO

MORRIS, ELIAS C.

G. F. Richings. Evidences of Progress Among Colored
People (Phila.: G. S. Ferguson, 1904), p. 568. DHU/R
Baptist minister and President of the National Baptist Con-
vention.

Benjamin G. Brawley. Negro Builders and Heroes (Chapel
Hill: Univ. of N. C. Press, 1927), pp. 201-02.
                                     DHU/R; DHU/MO

Henry F. Kletzing. Progress of a Race (Atlanta, Ga.:
Nichols & Co., 1898), pp. 437-39.   DHU/MO

James L. Nichols. The New Progress of a Race (Naperville,
Ill.: J. L. Nichols & Co., 1929), pp. 412-13.   DHU/MO

Lewis G. Jordan. Negro Baptist History (Nashville, Tenn.:
The Sunday School Publishing Board, N. B. C., 1930), p. 392.
                                                 DHU/MO

Samuel W. Bacote. Who's Who Among the Colored Baptists
(Kansas City, Mo.: F. Hudson Co., 1912), pp. 14-17.
                                                 DHU/MO

Thomas O. Fuller. Pictorial History of the American Negro
(Memphis, Tenn.: Pictorial History Inc., 1833), p. 75.
                                                 DHU/MO

Wilhelmena S. Robinson. Historical Negro Biographies (New
York: Publishers Co., 1967), p. 102.   DHU/MO

William N. Hartshorn. An Era of Progress and Promise
(Boston, Mass.: The Priscilla Pub. Co., 1910), p. 481.
                                                 DHU/MO

MORRIS, F. L.

Samuel W. Bacote. Who's Who Among the Colored Baptists
(Kansas City, Mo.: F. Hudson Co., 1912), pp. 151-52.
                                                 DHU/MO
Baptist minister of Texas.

MORRIS, GEORGE EDMUND

Samuel W. Bacote. Who's Who Among the Colored Baptists
(Kansas City, Mo.: F. Hudson Co., 1912), pp. 183-85.
                                                 DHU/MO
Baptist minister, president of the Afro-American State Con-
vention, and vice president of the National Baptist Convention.

MORRIS, ROBERT R.

David H. Bradley, Sr. A History of the A. M. E. Zion Church
1872-1968 V. 2 (Nashville: Parthenon Press, 1970), pp. 32-
33+.   DHU/R
Minister and missionary of the A. M. E. Zion Church.

James W. Hood. One Hundred Years of the A. M. E. Zion
Church (N. Y.: A. M. E. Zion Book Concern, 1895), pp. 414-
19.   DHU/MO

Leila A. Pendleton. A Narrative of the Negro (Wash., D. C.:
Press of R. L. Pendleton, 1912), p. 132.   DHU/MO

William W. Brown. The Black Man (N. Y.: T. Hamilton,
1863), pp. 227-30.   DHU/MO; DHU/R

MORTON, CHARLES E.

The editors of Ebony. The Ebony Success Library: 1,000 Suc-
cessful Blacks (Nashville: The Southwestern Co., 1973),
Vol. 1, p. 230.   DHU
Baptist minister and pastor of Metroplitan Baptist Church,
Detroit, Mich.

MOSELY, SAMUEL A.

Samuel W. Bacote. Who's Who Among the Colored Baptists
(Kansas City, Mo.: F. Hudson Co., 1912), pp. 220-21.
                                                        DHU/MO
Baptist minister

MOSES, (Saint)

Harold Robert Perry, (bp.). "St. Moses, Negro Hermit."
St. Augustine's Messenger (21; Oct., 1943), pp. 176-78.
                                                        DCU/ST

MOSES, WILLIAM HENRY

Samuel W. Bacote. Who's Who Among the Colored Baptists
(Kansas City, Mo.: F. Hudson Co., 1912), pp. 224-26.
                                                        DHU/MO
Baptist minister and editor of Baptist Statesman.

MOSLEY, JAMES

Albert S. Foley. God's Men of Color (New York: Farrar,
Straus & Co., 1955), p. 301.   DHU/R
Catholic priest.

MOSS. AARON W.

Who's Who Among the Colored Baptists (Kansas City, Mo.:
F. Hudson Co., 1912), pp. 289-90.   DHU/MO
Baptist minister.

MOSS, OTIS

The editors of Ebony. The Ebony Success Library: 1,000 Suc-
cessful Blacks (Nashville: The Southwestern Co., 1973),
Vol. 1, p. 230.   DHU
Baptist minister and pastor of Mount Zion Baptist Church,
Lockland, Ohio.

MURCHISON, ELISHA, (bp.).

The editors of Ebony. The Ebony Success Library: 1,000 Suc-
cessful Blacks (Nashville: The Southwestern Co., 1973),
Vol. 1, p. 232.   DHU
A Bishop of the Christian Methodist Episcopal Church.

MURDEN, AARON B. U. G.

E. R. Carter. The Black Side (Atlanta, Ga.: n.p., 1894),
pp. 109-14.   DHU/MO
Negro Baptist minister and teacher.

MURPHY, MAX E.

Albert S. Foley. God's Men of Color (New York: Farrar,
Straus & Co., 1955), pp. 163-70.   DHU/R
Catholic priest.

MURRAY, NICHOLAS

Presbyterian Reunion: 1837-1871 (N.Y.: Dew C. Lent & Co.,
1870), pp. 172-78.   DHU/MO
Presbyterian minister.

MUZOREWA, ABEL T., (bp.).

United Church Herald (13:11, Dec., 1970), p. 46.   DHU/R
"Methodist bishop of Rhodesia, first native-born Methodist
bishop and vigorous foe of white supremacy."

MYERS, CYRUS

Henry F. Kletzing. Progress of a Race (Atlanta, Ga.:
J. L. Nichols & Co., 1898), p. 576.   DHU/MO
Minister.

NANCE, S. D.

William Hicks. History of Louisiana Negro Baptists from
1804-1914 (Nashville, Tenn.: National Baptist Publishing
Board, n.d.), pp. 199-200.   DHU/R
Baptist minister.

NAZREY, WILLIS, (bp.).

Richard R. Wright. Bishops of the A. M. E. Church (Nashville: A. M. E. Sunday School Union, 1963), pp. 257-60.
                                                        DHU/R
Fifth Bishop of the A. M. E. Church.

NEAL, P. CARTER

Samuel W. Bacote. Who's Who Among the Colored Baptists
(Kansas City, Mo.: F. Hudson Co., 1912), pp. 128-29.
                                                        DHU/MO
Baptist minister, professor, and Y. M. C. A. worker.

NEILL, WILLIAM

Presbyterian Reunion: 1837-1871 (N. Y.: Dew C. Lent & Co.,
1870), pp. 128-33.   DHU/MO
Presbyterian minister.

NELSON, HENRY A.

Presbyterian Reunion: 1837-1871 (N. Y.: De W. C. Lent &
Co., 1870), pp. 518-19.   DHU/MO
Presbyterian minister and teacher.

NELSON, WARREN JULIUS

Frank T. Wilson. "Living Witnesses: Black Presbyterians in
Ministry." Journal of Presbyterian History (51:4, Wint.,
1973), pp. 354-56.   DHU/R
Black Presbyterian minister.

NEWBY, W. H.

James W. Hood. One Hundred Years of the A. M. E. Zion
Church (New York: A. M. E. Book Concern, 1895), pp. 358-
59.   DHU/MO
A. M. E. Zion minister.

NEWMAN, A. M.

William Hicks. The History of Louisiana Negro Baptists from
1804-1914 (Nashville, Tenn.: National Baptist Publishing
Board, n.d.), pp. 17.-74.   DHU/R
Baptist minister and founder of Providence Academy.

NEWMAN, WILLIAM P.

    Journal of Negro History (44; 1959), p. 125.   DHU/MO
    Editor of Provinical Freeman and Baptist minister.

NICHOLS, DECATUR WARD, (bp.).

    Richard R. Wright. Bishops of the A. M. E. Church (Nash-
    ville: A. M. E. Sunday School Union, 1963), pp. 261-63.
                                       DHU/R
    Fifty-ninth Bishop of the A. M. E. Church.

NIXON, B. A. J.

    Henry D. Northrop. College of Life (Phila: National Pub.
    Co., 1895), p. 53.   DHU/MO
    A. M. E. minister and educator.

NORMAN, MOSES W. D.

    Samuel W. Bacote. Who's Who Among the Colored Baptists
    (Kansas City, Mo.: F. Hudson Co., 1912), pp. 146-48.
                                         DHU/MO
    Dean of Theological School, Shaw Univ., pres., Roanoke
    Institue and Baptist minister.

    Henry F. Diezzing. Progress of a Race (Atlanta, Ga.: J. L.
    Nichols & Co., 1898), pp. 439-40.   DHU/MO

NOTT, ELIPHALET

    Presbyterian Reunion: 1837-1871 (N. Y.: De W. C. Lent &
    Co., 1870), ppl 124-28.   DHU/MO
    Presbyterian minister and teacher, president of Union College,
    Schenectady, N. Y.

OCCOMY, RUTH

    Adah B. Thoms. Pathfinders (Phila.: G. S. Ferguson,
    1929), p. 128.   DHU/MO
    Missionary nurse in Baptist Hospital, Liberia.

O'CONNELL, P.

    G. F. Richings. Evidences of Progress Among Colored
    People (Phila.: G. S. Ferguson, 1904), p. 110.
                               DHU/R; DHU/MO
    Minister and Principal of Princess Anne Academy, Baltimore,
    Md.

ODEN, A. G.

    James W. Hood. One Hundred Years of the A. M. E. Zion
    Church (N. Y.: A. M. E. Zion Book Concern, 1895), pp.
    620-22.   DHU/MO
    Ex-slave and A. M. E. Zion minister.

OFFLEY, G. W.

    James W. Hood. One Hundred Years of the A. M. E. Zion
    Church (N. Y.: A. M. E. Zion Book Concern, 1895), pp.
    236-38.   DHU/MO
    A. M. E. Zion minister and politician.

    Narrative of the Life and Laaors of the Rev. G. W. Offley,
    a Colored Man, and Local Preacher. Written by Himself
    (Hartford, Conn.: n.p., 1860).   TNF

OSBORN, A. C.

    G. F. Richings. Evidences of Progress Among Colored
    People (Phila.: G. S. Ferguson, 1904), p. 32.
                                 DHU/R; DHU/MO
    Baptist minister and President of Benedict College, Colum-
    bia, S. C.

OVER, D. E.

    Samuel W. Bacote. Who's Who Among Colored Baptists
    (Kansas City, Mo., 1912), pp. 265-66.   DHU/MO
    Baptist minister, Colorado.

OWEN, S. A.

    Thomas O. Fuller. Pictorial History of the American Negro
    (Memphis, Tenn.: Pictorial History Inc., 1933), p. 318.
                                    DHU/MO
    Minister.

OWENS, A. F.

    William Hicks. The History of Louisiana Negro Baptists from
    1804-1914 (Nashville, Tenn.: National Baptist Publishing
    Board, n.d.), pp. 160-61.   DHU/R
    Baptist minister, editor of Baptist Pioneer and Alabama Bap-
    tist Leader. Trustee of Selma University.

OXLEY, EDMUND H.

    Wendell P. Dabney. Cincinnati's Colored Citizens (Cincin-
    nati, Ohio: The Dabney Pub. Co., 1926), pp. 231-33. DHU/MO
    Negro Episcopal priest.

PACE, DINAH WATTS

    Elizabeth L. Davis. Lifting As They Climb (Chicago, Ill.:
    n. p., 1933), p. 421.   DHU/MO
    Negro ex-slave and missionary.

    G. F. Richings. Evidences of Progress Among Colored People
    (Phila.: G. S. Ferguson, 1904), pp. 239-41.   DHU/MO

    Lawson A. Scruggs. Women of Distinction (Raleigh: L. A.
    Scruggs. 1893), pp. 352-53.   DHU/MO

PAGE, WILBUR A.

    Wendell P. Dabney. Cincinnati's Colored Citizens (Cincin-
    nati, Ohio: The Dabney Pub. Co., 1926), p. 323. DHU/MO
    Baptist minister and Chaplain in Ohio National Guards.

PARHAM, THOMAS DAVID, JR.

    "Presbyterian Chaplain Helps Humanize the Navy." A. D.
    United Presbyterian Edition (3:10, Oct., 1974), p. 61.
                                   DHU/R

PARKER, G. W.

    U. S. Dept. of Education. Special Report (Wash., D. C.:
    Government Printing Office, 1871), p. 286.   DHU/MO
    Baptist minister and teacher.

PARKER, JOHN P.

    Autobiography by a Slave, John Parker (Brown County, Ohio:
    n. p., 1880).   NcD
    Black inventor and abolitionist in Ohio during nineteenth and
    early twentieth centuries.

Ohio History (80:2, Spr., 1971), pp. 155-62.
                              Pam. File, DHU/R; DGU; DCU

PARKS, HENRY BLANTON, (bp.)

Richard R. Wright. Bishops of the A. M. E. Church (Nashville: A. M. E. Sunday School Union, 1963), pp. 264-65.
                                                              DHU/R
Thirty-second Bishop of the A. M. E. Church.

G. F. Richings. Evidences of Progress Among Colored People
(Philadelphia: G. S. Ferguson, 1904), p. 389.   DHU/MO

T. W. Haigler. The Life and Times of Rt. Rev. H. B. Parks
Presiding Bishop of the Twelfth Episcopal District of the A. M.
E. Church (Nashville, Tenn.: A. M. E. Sunday School Union,
1909).   NN/Sch

PARKS, WESLEY G.

Lewis G. Jordan. Negro Baptist History, U. S. A. (Nashville,
Tenn.: The Sunday School Pub. Board, N. B. C., 1930), p.
392.
Baptist minister and vice-president of the National Baptist
Convention.

Samuel W. Bacote. Who's Who Among Colored Baptists
(Kansas City, Mo.: F. Hudson Co., 1912), pp. 22-24.
                                                              DHU/MO

PARRISH, CHARLES H.

William N. Hartshorn. An Era of Progress and Promise
(Boston, Mass.: The Priscilla Publishing Co., 1910), p. 483.
                                                              DHU/MO
Baptist minister and chairman of the Foreign Mission Board
of the National Baptist Convention.

Charles Alexander. One Hundred Distinguished Leaders
(Atlanta, Ga.: The Franklin Printing Co., 1899), p. 63.
                                                              DHU/MO

G. F. Richings. Evidences of Progress Among Colored
People (Phila.: G. S. Ferguson, 1904), pp. 218-24.
                                            DHU/MO; DHU/R

Samuel W. Bacote. Who's Who Among Colored Baptists
(Kansas City, Mo.: F. Hudson Co., 1912), pp. 36-37.
                                                              DHU/MO

William J. Simmons. Men of Mark (Cleveland, Ohio: O.
Rewell, 1887), pp. 1059-63.   DHU/MO

PARROTT, RUSSELL

William Douglass. Annals of the First African Church in the
U. S. A. (Phila.: King and Bair Printers, 1862), p. 124.
                                                              DHU/MO
Lay reader of the first African Church, African Episcopal
Church of St. Thomas, Phila.

Benjamin Quarles. Black Abolitionists (N. Y.: University
Press, 1969), pp. 3-5.   DHU/R

PATTERSON, BERNADINE

Albert S. Foley. God's Men of Color (New York: Farrar,
Straus & Co., 1955), p. 303.   DHU/R
Catholic priest.

PATTERSON, ROBERT W.

Presbyterian Reunion: 1837-1871 (New York: De W. C. Lent
& Co., 1870), p. 518.   DHU/MO
Presbyterian minister of Chicago, trustee of lake Forest
Univ. and Blackburn, Univ.

PATTERSON, S. J.

Alonzo Holly. God and the Negro (Nashville, Tenn.: Natl.
Baptist Pub. Board, 1937).   DHU/R
Presiding Elder of the A. M. E. Church.

PAUL, BENJAMIN

Howard Coles. The Cradle of Freedom: A History of the
Negro in Rochester (Rochester, N. Y.: Oxford Press, 1941),
pp. 68-71.   DHU/MO
Abolitionist and Baptist minister.

Austin Steward. Twenty-Two Years a Slave and Forty Years
a Free Man (Rochester, N. Y.: Allings & Cory, 1861), pp.
257-61.   DHU/MO

PAUL, NATHANIEL

Carter G. Woodson. The Mind of the Negro as Reflected in
Letters Written During the Crisis, 1800-1860 (New York:
Russell & Russell, 1969), pp. 163-70+.   DHU/MO

Austin Steward. Twenty-Two Years a Slave and Forty Years
a Free Man (Rochester, N. Y.: Allings & Cory, 1861), pp.
257-61.   DHU/MO

Charles Stuart. Remarks on the Colony of Liberia and the
American Colonization Society (London: Printed by J.
Messeder, 1832), pp. 15-16.   DHU/MO

Howard Coles. The Cradel of Freedom: A History of the
Negro in Rochester (Rochester, N. Y.: Oxford Press, 1941),
pp. 44-46.   DHU/MO

Robin Winks. The Blacks in Canada; A History (Montreal:
McGill-Queen's Univ. Press, 1971), pp. 158-61.   DHU/MO

William Pease and June. Black Utopia: Negro Communal
Experiments in America (Madison: State Historical Society,
1963), pp. 58-61.   DHU/MO

PAUL, THOMAS

Harry A. Ploski, (ed.). Reference Library of Black America
(New York: Bellwether Pub. Co., Inc., 1971), Book 2, pp.
213+.   DHU
First Negro Baptist minister to pastor an independent Negro
Church in the North.

Caleb H. Snow. History of Boston (Boston: A. Bowen,
1825), p. 342.   DLC

Carter G. Woodson. History of the Negro Church (Wash.,
D. C.: Associated Publishers, 1921), pp. 88-91.
                                            DHU/R; DHU/MO

David P. Adams, (ed.). Great Negroes Past and Present
(Chicago: Afro-Am. Publishing Co., 1963), p. 80.   DHU/R

John Dowling. "Sketches of New York Baptists: Rev. Thomas
Paul and the Colored Baptist Churches." Baptist Memorial
and Monthly Chronicles (8:9, Sept., 1849), pp. 295-301.
                                            SCBHC

(Paul, Thomas cont.)

Lee M. Freedman. "A Beacon Hill Synagogue." Old Time New England (33; Jl., 1942), pp. 2-4.   DLC; NN; CtY

Nathan Franklin Carter. The Native Ministry of New Hampshire. (Concord, N. H.: Rumford Printing Co., 1906), p. 239.   DLC; NC; ViU; CtY-D; NN

Ruby F. Johnson. The Development of Negro Religion. (New York: Philosophical Library, 1954), p. 34.   DHU/MO

Walter H. Brooks. "The Evolution of the Negro Baptist Church." Journal of Negro History (7; Ja., 1954), p. 17.
DHU/MO

William G. McLoughlin. New England Dissent 1630-1833. The Baptists and the Separation of Church and State (Cambridge, Mass.: Harvard University Press, 1971), pp. 765-66.
DGW; DGU

History of Weare, New Hampshire (n.p.: Lowell, 1888), pp. 283+.   DLC

PAYNE, CHRISTOPHER H.

William J. Simmons. Men of Mark (Cleveland: O. Rewell, 1887), pp. 363-74.   DHU/MO; DHU/R
Baptist minister and educator.

PAYNE, DANIEL ALEXANDER, (bp.).

Benjamin G. Brawley. Early Negro American Writers (Chapel Hill, N. C.: Univ. of North Carolina Press, 1935), pp. 147-59.   DHU/R
Sixth bishop of A. M. E. Church.

African Methodist Episcopal Church Review (68:172, Apr.-Je., 1952), pp. 5-15.   DHU/R
Also: (68:174, Oct.-Dec., 1952), pp. 18-22. (78:215, Ja.-Mr., 1963), pp. 62-64.

Benjamin Brawley. Negro Builders and Heroes (Chapel Hill: University of North Carolina Press, 1937), pp. 95+.
DHU/R; DHU/MO; DLC; NcD

Benjamin W. Arnett. The Budget. Biographical Sketches ... (Dayton, Ohio: Christian Pub. House, 1882), p. 141. DHU/MO

Benjamin Quarles. Black Abolitionists (New York: University Press, 1969), pp. 40+.   DHU/R

Booker T. Washington. A New Negro for a New Century (Chicago: Amer. Pub. House, 1900), p. 79.   DHU/MO

Ceremonies Attending the Unveiling of the Monument Erected in the Memory of Bishop Daniel Alexander Payne, Monday, May 21, 1894. At Laurel Cemetery, Baltimore, Maryland, Appendix-Sermon by Bishop A. W. Wayman, at the Funeral of Bishop Payne, Preached in Bethel A. M. E. Church, Baltimore, Dec. 5, 1893. Published by the Committee.
DHU/MO

Charles Spencer Smith, (bp.). The Life of Daniel Alexander Payne; With an Introduction by Bishop Abram Grant and a Poem, "In Memoriam," by Bishop James A. Handy (Nashville: School Union, 1894).   OWibfU

Douglas C. Strange. "Bishop Daniel Alexander: Protestation of American Slavery." Journal of Negro History (52:1, Ja., 1967), pp. 59-64.   DHU

Douglas C. Strange. "Bishop Daniel A. Payne and the Lutheran Church." Lutheran Quarterly (16:4, Nov., 1964), pp. 354-59.   DHU/R

E. A. Johnson. School History of the Negro Race in America (Raleigh: Edward & Broughton Printers, 1890), p. 172.
DHU/R

Edgar A. Toppin. A Biographical History of Blacks in America Since 1928 (New York: David McKay Co., 1871), pp. 384-85.   DHU/MO; DHU/R

Eugene G. Prater. "Bishop Payne of African Methodism." Journal of Religious Thought (15; Aut.-Wint., 1957-58), pp. 59-70.   DHU/R

G. F. Richings. Evidences of Progress Among Colored People (Phila.: Geo. S Ferguson Co., 1904), pp. 110-29.
DHU/R

H. H. Summers and I. H. Welch. "In Memoriam." A. M. E. Church Review (11; Jl., 1894), pp. 160-71. DHU/MO; DLC

Henry F. Kletzing. Progress of a Race (Atlanta, Ga.: J. L. Nichols & Co., 1898), pp. 510+.   DHU/MO

John Andrew Gregg, (bp.). The African Methodist Episcopal Church Review (68:172, Apr.-Je., 1952), pp. 20-21.
DHU/R
Negro author.

Josephus R. Goan. Daniel Alexander Payne: Christian Education (Philadelphia: A. M. E. Book Concern, 1935).
DHU/MO; NcD

Leila A. Pendleton. A Narrative of the Negro (Wash., D. C.: Press of R. L. Pendleton, 1912), p. 147.   DHU/MO

Lutheran Observer (46:20, My. 17, 1878), p. 6.   IMC

Martin R. Delany. The Condition, Elevation, Emigration and Destiny of the Colored People of the United States (New York: Arno Press, 1968), pp. 124-25.   DHU/MO; DHU/R

Reverdy Cassius Ransom, (bp.). African Methodist Episcopal Church Review (29; Apr., 1913), pp. 380-82.   DHU/MO

Reverdy Cassius Ransom, (bp.). Daniel Alexander Payne, The Prophet of an Era.   OWibfU

Richard R. Wright. Bishops of the A. M. E. Church (Nashville: A. M. E. Sunday School Union, 1963), pp. 266-79.
DHU/R

Wilhelmena S. Robinson. Historical Negro Biographies (New York: Publishers Co., 1967), pp. 106-07.   DHU/MO

William J. Simmons, (ed.). Men of Mark (Cleveland, O.: Geo. M. Rewell & Co., 1887), p. 1078.   DHU/R

William Wells Brown. The Black Man (Miami, Fla.: Mnemosyne Pub. Co., 1969), pp. 207-11.   DHU/R

William W. Brown. The Rising Son (Boston, Mass.: A. G. Brown & Co., 1874), pp. 454-55.   DHU/R

PAYNE, JOHN, (bp.).

George F. Bragg. History of the Afro-American Group of the Episcopal Church (Balto., Md.: Church Advocate Press, 1922), pp. 208-11.   DHU/MO
Bishop of the Protestant Episcopal Church.

John Payne. U. S. Dept. of Education. Special Report (Wash., D. C.: Govt. Print. Office, 1871), p. 272. DHU/MO

PEAKE, MARY S.

Lewis Lockwood. Mary S. Peake, the Colored Teacher at Fortress Monroe (Boston: American Tract Society, 189-?).
NN/Sch

PECK, E. W. S.

    Irvine Garland Penn. The Afro-American Press (Springfield,
Mass.: Willey & Co., 1891), pp. 255-56.   DHU/MO
Minister of M. E. Church, editor of The Welcome Friend and
The Washington Conference Journal.

PENN, IRVINE GARLAND

    Who's Who in Colored America, 1928-29 New York: Who's
Who in Colored America, Corp., 1930. p. 288.   DHU/MO
Author and minister of the M. E. Church.

    (Indianapolis) Freeman (2:4, Mar. 16, 1889), p. 1.   DHU/MO

    Irvine G. Penn. The Afro-American Press and Its Editors
(Springfield, Mass.: Willey & Co., 1891), DHU/MO; DHU/R

PENNINGTON, JAMES W. C.

    William W. Brown. The Rising Son (Boston: A. G. Brown
& Co., 1874), pp. 461-3.   DHU/R; DHU/MO
Ex-slave and Presbyterian minister.

    Benjamin G. Brawley. The Negro Genius (New York: Dodd,
Mead & Co., 1937), p. 67.   DHU/MO

    Dictionary of American Biography V. 7 (New York: Scribner's
& Co., 1932), pp. 441-42.   DHU

    Edward F. Gowin. "One Hundred Years of Negro Congrega-
tionalism in New Haven, Connecticut." Crisis (19; Feb.,
1920), pp. 177-81.   DHU/MO

    Free Presbyterian (Oct. 22, 1851).   OWoC

    The Fugitive Blacksmith: or, Events in the History of James
Pennington, Pastor of a Presbyterian Church, Formerly a
Slave in the State of Maryland, United States (London: Charles
Gilpin, 1850).   DLC; DHU/R

    James A. Handy. Scraps of African Methodist History (Phil-
adelphia: A. M. E. Book Concern, n. d.), p. 404.   DHU/MO

    Martin R. Delany. The Condition, Elevation, Emigration, and
Destiny of the Colored People of the United States (New York:
Arno Press, 1968), pp. 113-14.   DHU/R

    Who Was Who in America, Historical Volume, 1607-1907
(Chicago: The A. N. Marquis Co., 1907), p. 404.   DLC

    Wilhelmena S. Robinson. Historical Negro Biographies (New
York: Publishers Co., 1967), p. 108.   DHU/MO

    William H. Ferris. The African Abroad (New Haven, Conn.:
Tuttle, Morehouse & Taylor Press, 1913), p. 692.   DHU/MO

    William L. Katz, (ed.). Five Slave Narratives (New York:
Arno Press, 1969).   DHU/MO

    William Wells Brown. The Black Man (Miami, Fla.: Mnem-
osyne Pub. Co., 1969), pp. 276-78.   DHU/R

    Wilson A. Armstead. A Tribute for the Negro (Miami, Fla.:
Mnemosyne Publishing Co., Inc., 1969), p. 136+.   DHU/MO

PERRY, E. W.

    Thomas O. Fuller. Pictorial History of the American Negro
(Memphis, Tenn.: Pictorial History Inc., 1933), p. 88.
       DHU/MO

    Minister of Oklahoma City, Okla.

PERRY, HAROLD ROBERT, (bp.).

    Harry A. Ploski, (ed.). Reference Library of Black America
(New York: Bellwether Pub. Co. Inc., 1971), Book 2, p. 216.
       DHU
Negro Roman Catholic Bishop of New Orleans Archdiocese.

    Christian Century (82:42, Oct. 20, 1965), pp. 1277-78.
       DHU/R

    Ebony (21:4, Feb., 1966), pp. 62-66+.   DHU/MO

    Albert S. Foley. God's Men of Color (New York: Farrar,
Straus & Co., 1955), pp. 247-49.   DHU/R

PERRY, MAJOR

    David W. Roston. "The Sleeping Preacher" Major Perry,
1831-1925. "Saluda County's Sleeping Preacher Carries
Mystery to the Grave." (n. p., n. d.). Pam. File, DHU/R
C. M. E. minister.

PERRY, RUFUS L.

    Irvine G. Penn. The Afro-American Press and Its Editors.
(Sringfield, Mass.: Willey & Co., 1891), p. 108.
       DHU/R; DHU/MO
Baptist minister and editor of The National Monitor.

    William J. Simmons. Men of Mark (Cleveland, O.: George
M. Rewell & Co., 1887), p. 620.   DHU/R

    William Wells Brown. The Rising Son or the Antecedents
and the Advancement of the Colored Race. (Miami, Fla.:
Mnemosyne Publishing Co., Inc., 1969), p. 533.   DHU/R

PETER CLAVER, Saint

    Peter Claver: a Sketch of his Life and Labors in Behalf of
the African Slave. Boston: n. p., 1868.
Black Catholic saint.

    Angel Valtierra. Peter Claver. Saint of the Slaves (London:
n. p., 1960).

    Ann Roos. Peter Claver: Saint Among Slaves (New York:
Farrar, Straus & Giroux, 1965).   DHU/MO

    Katharine Chorley. "St. Peter Claver." Month (13; 1955),
pp. 325-41.

    Mariano Picon-Salas. Pedro Claver, el Santo de los Esclavos
(Mexico: n. p., 1949).

PETER, JESSE

    Leslie H. Fishel. The Negro American or the Black American
(New York: William Morrow, 1970), p. 42.   DHU/MO; DHU/R
One of the first Negro preachers to be licensed by Baptist
Church and minister, Silver Bluff, S. C., First Negro Bap-
tist Church in U. S.

    Carter G. Woodson. The History of the Negro Church (Wash.,
D. C.: Associated Publishers, 1921), p. 36+.
       DHU/R; DHU/MO

PETERSON, DANIEL H.

    The Looking-Glass: Being a True Report and Narrative of the
Life Travels of a Colored Clergyman (New York: Wright,
Printer, 1854).   DHU/MO

PETERSON, JOHN

Booker T. Washington. A New Negro for a New Century
(Chicago: American Publishing House, 1900), p. 79. DHU/R
Black minister of New York City, active as an educator.

PETTEY, CHARLES C., (bp.).

G. F. Richings. Evidences of Progress Among Colored People
(Phila.: G. S. Ferguson, 1904), p. 390. DHU/R; DHU/MO
Bishop of the African Methodist Episcopal Zion Church.

PETTIFORD, WILLIAM REUBEN

William J. Simmons, (ed.). Men of Mark (Cleveland, O.:
Geo. M. Rewell & Co., 1887), p. 460.   DHU/R

PETTIGREW, H. B.

James W. Hood. One Hundred Years of the A. M. E. Zion
Church (New York: A. M. E. Zion Book Concern, 1895),
pp. 566-68.   DHU/MO
Ex-slave and A. M. E. Zion minister.

PHILLIP, LEE C.

Toward Wholeness (1:1, Sum., 1972), p. 10.   DHU/R
Brief biographical data given as Phillip is honored by the
Ministries to Blacks in Higher Education on Negro minister.

PHILLIPS, CHARLES HENRY, (bp.).

The Crisis (21:4, Feb., 1921), p. 172.   DHU/MO; DLC
Pioneer bishop of the C. M. E. Church.

From the Farm to the Bishopric: An Autobiography (Nashville: Parthenon Press, 1937).   DHU/R; DHU/MO

G. F. Richings. Evidences of Progress Among Colored
People (Philadelphia: G. S. Ferguson, 1904), pp. 364-65.
                                   DHU/MO; DHU/R

James J. Pipkin. The Negro in Revelation, in History and
in Citizenship (New York: Thompson Publishing Co., 1902),
p. 221.   DHU/MO

PHILLIPS, D. W.

Henry F. Kletzing. Progress of a Race (Atlanta, Ga.: J. L.
Nichols & Co., 1898), p. 405.   DHU/MO
Baptist minister.

James J. Pipkin. The Negro in Revelation, in History, and
in Citizenship (New York: Thompson Pub. Co., 1902), p. 395.
                                              DHU/MO

G. F. Richings. Evidences of Progress Among Colored
People (Phila.: G. S. Ferguson, 1904), p. 21.
                                   DHU/R; DHU/MO

PHILLIPS, HENRY L.

The Crisis (5:1, Nov., 1912), pp. 16-17.   DLC; DHU/MO
The oldest colored American priest in point of services in the
Episcopal Church.

PHILLIPS, WILLIAM WIRT

Presbyterian Reunion: 1837-1871 (N. Y.: De W. C. Lent &
Co., 1870), pp. 153-56.   DHU/MO
Presbyterian minister, trustee and director of Theological
Seminary of Princeton, president of Board of Foreign Missions.

PINCKNEY, AURELIUS D.

The Romance of a Nobody (n. p.: Privately Printed by Author,
n. d.)   DHU/R
"Autobiography. "
Negro United Church of Christ minister, teacher, and administrator.

PIUS, NATHANIEL H.

G. F. Richings. Evidences of Progress Among Colored People
(Phila.: G. S. Ferguson, 1904), p. 46.   DHU/R; DHU/MO
Baptist minister and author of Outlines of Baptist History.
(only history of Negro Baptists before 1930)

William N. Hartshorn. An Era of Progress and Promise
(Boston: The Priscilla Pub. Co., 1910, p. 487. DHU/MO

PLANTEVIGNE, JOHN

Albert S. Foley. God's Men of Color (New York: Farrar,
Straus & Co., 1955), pp. 81-94.   DHU/R
Catholic priest.

PLUMMER, H. Z., (bp.).

Crisis (44:5, My., 1937), pp. 148-49.   DHU/MO
Bishop objects to "cult" classification given his church in
letter to the editor.

POINDEXTER, JAMES PRESTON

Lewis G. Jordan. Negro Baptist History U. S. A. (Nashville:
Sunday School Publishing Board, N. B. C., 1930), p. 392.
                                   DHU/R; DHU/MO
Baptist minister and director of Bureau of Forestry in Ohio

Leila A. Pendleton. A Narrative of the Negro (Wash., D. C.:
Press of R. L. Pendleton, 1912), p. 177.   DHU/MO

Richard Clyde Minor. James Preston Poindexter, Elder Statesman of Columbus, Ohio (Reprinted from the Ohio State Archaeological Historical Quarterly, Jl., 1947).   SCBHC

William J. Simmons. Men of Mark (Cleveland: O. Rewell,
1887), pp. 394-404.   DHU/MO; DHU/R

POLLARD, RANDALL T.

G. F. Richings. Evidences of Progress Among Colored People
(Phila.: G. S. Ferguson, 1904), p. 68.   DHU/MO; DHU/R
Baptist minister and president of Selma University.

Lewis G. Jordan. Negro Baptist History U. S. A. (Nashville,
Tenn.: The Sunday School Publishing Board, N. B. C., 1930),
p. 392.   DHU/R

POOLE, ELIJAH (Elijah Muhammad)

Edgar A. Toppin. A Biographical History of Blacks in America Since 1528 (New York: David McKay Co., 1971), pp. 372-
75.   DHU/MO; DHU/R

Harry A. Ploski, (ed.). Reference Library of Black America (New York: Bellwether Pub. Co., Inc., 1971), Book 2, p. 29.
DHU/R

Steve D. Abel. The Dynamics of Social Cohesion as Found in the Teaching of a Black Religious Thinker: Elijah Muhammad (Masters thesis. Howard University, Schol of Religion, 1973).
DHU/R

PORTER, HERMAN A. (Martin)

Albert S. Foley. God's Men of Color (New York: Farrar, Straus & Co., 1955), pp. 263-70.   DHU/R
Catholic priest.

POTTER, PHILIP A.

George G. Beazley, Jr. "A Big Man for a Big Job." World Call (54:10, Nov., 1972), pp. 21-2.   DHU/R
An interview with the new General Secretary of the World Council of Churches by the President of the Council of Christian Churches (Disciples of Christ).
Methodist minister.

Donald G. Roper. "World Council Names West Indian as Executive." A. D. United Church Herald Edition (1:2, Oct., 1972), pp. 25-26.   DHU/R

WCC Central Committee Elects West Indian General Secretary. Ecumenical Press Service (24; Sept., 1972), p. 14. DHU/R

World Parish (12:1, Oct., 1972), pp. 5-6.   DHU/R

POTTS, GEORGE

Presbyterian Reunion: 1837-1871 (New York: De W. C. Lent & Co., 1870), pp. 168-72.   DHU/MO
Presbyterian minister, director of Theological Seminary, Princeton and member of the Council of New York Univ.

POWELL, ADAM CLAYTON, JR.

Edgar A. Toppin. A Biographical History of Blacks in America Since 1528 (N. Y.: David McKay Co., 1971), pp. 388-91.
DHU/R
Baptist minister of Abyssinian Baptist Church in New York and Congressman.

Adam by Adam (New York: Dial Press, 1971).
DHU/AA; DHU/MO

"At Berkeley." Pacifica Archives. A 2376.
Audiotap.

Claude Lewis. Adam Clayton Powell (Greenwich, Conn.: Fawcett Press, 1963).   DHU/MO

Contact (3:8, Jl., 1972), pp. 37-38.   DHU/R

Ebony (4; Jl., 1949), pp. 39-41.   DHU/MO

Editorial. Freedomways (12:2, Second Quarter, 1972, pp. 101-02.   DHU/R

Freedomways (7; Sum., 1967), pp. 199-213.   DHU/R

Jack Slater. "Harlem Bids Farewell to Keeper of the Faith." Ebony (27:8, Je., 1972), pp. 31-42. Pam. File, DHU/R

Kent M. Weeks. Adam Clayton Powell and the Supreme Court (New York: Dunellen Pub. Co., 1971).   DHU/R

Marcus H. Boulware. The Oratory of Negro Leaders 1900-1968 (Westport, Conn.: Negro Universities Press, 1969), p. 169.   DHU/MO

Neil Hickey. Adam Clayton Powell and the Politics of Race (New York: Fleet, 1965).   DHU/R

The New York Age (Ag. 5, 1944).   DHU/MO; NN/Sch

Social Progress (57; Mr.-Apr., 1967), pp. 39-46.   DAU

Wayne F. Cooper, (ed.). The Passion of Claude McKay... (New York: Schocken Books, 1973), pp. 250-52.   DHU/R

POWELL, ADAM CLAYTON, SR.

Benjamin G. Brawley. Negro Builders and Heroes. (Chapel Hill: Univ. of N. C. Press, 1937), pp. 203-04.
DHU/MO; DHU/R
Baptist minister of Abyssinian Baptist Church, New York.

Against the Tide; an Autobiography (New York: R. R. Smith, 1938).   TNF; DHU/MO

Ben Richardson. Great American Negroes. (New York: Thomas Crowell Co., 1945), pp. 200-10. Pam. File, DHU/R

Harry A. Ploski (ed.). Reference Library of Black America. (New York: Bellwether Pub. Co., Inc., 1971), Book 2, p. 216.
DHU

James L. Nicholas. The New Progress of the Race. (Naperville, Ill.: J. L. Nichols & Co., 1929), pp. 420-21. DHU/MO

Thomas O. Fuller. Pictorial History of the American Negro. (Memphis: Pictorial History Inc., 1933), p. 312.   DHU/MO

Wilhelmena S. Robinson. Historical Negro Biographies. (New York: Publishers Co., 1967), pp. 237-38.   DHU/MO

PRESLEY, H. E. HARRIS

Lawson A. Scruggs. Women of Distinction (Raleigh: L. A. Scruggs, 1893), pp. 158-61.   DHU/MO
Missionary.

PRESTON, FRANCES E.

Elizabeth L. Davis. Lifting As They Climb (Chicago, Ill.: n. p., 1933), p. 236.   DHU/MO
Baptist layman and active organizer of women and children in the church.

Henry D. Northrop. College of Life (Phila.: Nat. Pub. Co., 1895), p. 106.   DHU/MO

PRICE, JOSEPH C.

Benjamin Brawley. Negro Builders and Heroes (Chapel Hill: Univ. of N. C. Press, 1937), pp. 205-06. DHU/MO; DHU/R
A. M. E. Zion minister. President of Livingstone College, Salisbury, N. C.

Benjamin G. Brawley. The Negro Genius (N. Y.: Dodd, Mead & Co., 1937), pp. 121-22.   DHU/R; DHU/MO

Benjamin G. Brawley. Negro Literature and Art (Atlanta: n. p., 1910), p. 53.   DHU/R; DHU/MO

Booker T. Washington. A New Negro for a New Century (Chicago: American Publishing House, 1900), p. 90.
DHU/MO; DHU/R

(Price, Joseph C. cont.)

E. A. Johnson. School History of the Negro Race in America
(Raleigh: Edward & Broughton Printers, 1890), pp. 177-78.
DHU/MO; DHU/R

G. F. Richings. Evidences of Progress Among Colored People
(Phila.: G. S. Ferguson, 1904), pp. 143-53+.   DHU/MO

Henry F. Kletzing. Progress of a Race (Atlanta: J. L.
Nichols & Co., 1898), p. 402+.   DHU/MO

Irvine G. Penn. The Afro-American Press & Its Editors
(Springfield, Mass.: Willey & Co., 1891), pp. 124-26+. Portrait, p. 125.   DHU/R; DHU/MO

John W. Cromwell. Negro in American History (Wash.:
American Negro Academy, 1944), pp. 171-78.   DHU/MO

Walter L. Yates, (ed.). He Spoke Now and They Speak: A
Collection of Speeches and Writings of and on the Life and
Works of J. C. Price (Salisbury, N. C.: Rowan Printing Co.,
1952).   DHU/R

William B. Gravely. Encyclopedia of World Methodism V. 2
(Nashville: n.p., 1974), p. 1950.   CoDU; NjD

William J. Simmons, (ed.). Men of Mark (Cleveland, O.:
Geo. M. Rewell & Co., 1887), p. 754.   DHU/R

PRIMM, HOWARD THOMAS, (bp.).
Richard R. Wright. Bishops of the A. M. E. Church (Nash-
ville: A. M. E. Sunday School Union, 1963), pp. 280-82.
DHU/R
Seventy-first Bishop of the A. M. E. Church

PRIMO, QUINTIN E., JR., (bp.).

The editors of Ebony. The Ebony Success Library: 1,000 Suc-
cessful Blacks (Nashville: The Southwestern Co., 1973), Vol.
Vol. 1, p. 254.   DHU
Bishop of Episcopal Diocese of Chicago, Ill.

The Episcopal Church Annual (New York: Morehouse-Barlow,
1973), p. 242.   PPPD; ViAlTH

PRITCHARD, NATHAN

The Crisis (10:2, Je., 1915), p. 62.   DLC; DHU/MO
A white church at Mesick, Wexford County, Mich., called the
Rev. Nathan Pritchard, a colored man, to be its pastor. It
has a membership of nearly 100 and belongs to the Free Methodist denomination.

PROCTOR, HENRY H.

Henry F. Kletzing. Progress of a Race (Atlanta, Ga.: J. L.
Nichols & Co., 1898), pp. 501-103.   DHU/MO
Congregationalist minister and first Black to speak at a Yale
University graduation exercise.

William N. Hartshorn. Era of Progress and Promise. (Boston: The Priscilla Publishing Co., 1910), p. 459.   DHU/MO

PROCTOR, SAMUEL DE WITT

The editors of Ebony. The Ebony Success Library: 1,000 Suc-
cessful Blacks (Nashville: The Southwestern Co., 1973), Vol.
Vol. 1, p. 255.   DHU
Baptist minister and pastor of Abyssinian Baptist Church,
New York City.

PROUT, S. T.

William H. Heard. The Bright Side of African Life (N. Y.:
Negro Universities Press, 1969), p. 35.   DHU/R
M. E. minister in Marshall, Liberia.

PULLETT, FROST

U. S. Dept. of Education. Special Report (Wash., D. C.:
Government Printing Office, 1871), p. 291.   DHU/MO
A. M. E. minister.

PURCE, CHARLES L.

G. F. Richings. Evidences of Progress Among Colored
People (G. S. Ferguson, 1904), pp. 57-9.   DHU/R; DHU/MO
Baptist minister and President of State University of Louis-
ville, Kentucky and Selma University, Selma, Ala.

Charles Alexander. One Hundred Distinguished Leaders.
(Atlanta: The Franklin Printing and Publishing Co., 1899),
p. 63.   DHU/MO

James J. Pipkin. The Negro in Revelation in History and in
Citizenship. (New York: Thompson Pub. Co., 1902), p. 430.
DHU/MO

Lewis G. Jordan. Negro Baptist History U. S. A. (Nashville:
The Sunday School Publishing Board, N. B. C., 1930), p. 392.
DHU/MO; DHU/R

William J. Simmons. Men of Mark... (Cleveland, O.:
George M. Rewell & Co., 1887), pp. 454-56.   DHU/MO

PURVIS, W. B.

William Hicks. The History of Louisiana Negro Baptists from
1804-1914 (Nashville, Tenn.: National Baptist Publishing
Board, n. d.), pp. 133-35.   DHU/R
Baptist minister; principal of Pleasant Hill Colored School and
President of N. W. No. 2 S. S. Association.

QUARLES, FRANK

Lewis G. Jordan. Negro Baptist History U. S. A. (Nashville,
Tenn.: The Sunday School Publishing Board N. B. C., 1930),
p. 392.   DHU/MO
Minister of Friendship Baptist Church, Atlanta and moderator
of Ebenezer Baptist Association.

QUINN, WILLIAM PAUL, JR., (bp.).

Richard R. Wright. Bishops of the A. M. E. Church. (Nash-
ville: A. M. E. Sunday School Union, 1963), pp. 283-86.
DHU/R
Fourth Bishop of the A. M. E. Church.

Benjamin T. Tanner. An Apology for African Methodism.
(Baltimore: n.p., 1867), pp. 144-47.   DHU/MO

Benjamin W. Arnett. The Budget... Biographical Sketches
Proceedings... (Dayton, Ohio: Christian Pub. House, 1882),
p. 8+.   DHU/MO

Effie Lee Newsome. The Negro Journal of Religion (5:7,
Sept., 1939), p. 9.   DHU/R

William Wells Brown. The Rising Son; or the Antecedents and
Advancement of the Colored Race. (Miami, Fla.: Mnemosyne
Pub. Inc., 1969), pp. 432-33.   DHU/R

RANDOLPH, FLORENCE

    James L. Nichols. The New Progress of a Race (Naperville, Ill.: J. L. Nichols & Co., 1929), p. 423. DHU/MO
A. M. E. Zion minister, chaplain of Northeastern Federation of Colored Women's Clubs and president of Women's Home and Foreign Missionary Society.

RANDOLPH, PETER

    From Slave Cabin to Pulpit: the Autobiography of Rev. Peter Randolph: The Southern Question Illustrated and Sketches of Slave Life (Boston: James H. Earle, 1893).
        NcD; OClWHi; MB; ViU

    Denvers Historical Society. Old Anti-Slavery Days (Danvers, Mass.: Mirror Print, 1893), pp. 126-31. DHU/MO
Baptist minister and ex-slave.

RANSOM, REVERDY CASSIUS, (bp.).

    Richard R. Wright. Bishops of the A. M. E. Church (Nashville: A. M. E. Sunday School Union, 1963), pp. 287-92.
        DHU/R
Forty-eighth Bishop of the A. M. E. Church.

    Benjamin G. Brawley. The Negro Genius (New York: Dodd, Mead & Co., 1937), p. 194. DHU/MO; DHU/R

    Ebony (5; Mr., 1950), pp. 72-80. DHU/MO

    Irvine G. Penn. The Afro-American Press and Its Editors (Springfield, Mass.: Willey & Co., 1891), p. 148.
        DHU/MO; DHU/R

    James L. Nichols. The Progress of a Race (New York: Arno Press, 1969), p. 424. DHU/MO

    Joseph Gomez, (bp.). The African Methodist Episcopal Church Review (75:200, Apr.-Je., 1959), pp. 70-74. DHU/R

    S. P. Fullenwider. The Mind and Mood of Black America (Homewood, Ill.: Dorsey Press, 1969), Chapter 2. DLC

    Thomas O. Fuller. Pictorial History of the American Negro (Memphis, Tenn.: Pictorial History Inc., 1933), p. 276.
        DHU/MO

    William E. B. DuBois. The African Methodist Episcopal Church Review (75:200, Apr.-Je., 1959), pp. 8-9. DHU/R

RAPHAEL, ROBERT JOSIAS MORGAN

    J. L. Nichols. The New Progress of a Race (Naperville, Ill.: J. L. Nichols & Co., 1929), pp. 424-25. DHU/MO
Protestant Episcopal minister who became the only Negro of the Greek Orthodox Catholic Church. Founder and Superior of the Order of the Cross of Golgotha, a religious Fraternity.

    Who's Who of the Colored Race (Chicago: n.p., 1915), p. 226.
        DHU/MO

RAY, CHARLES B.

    Carter G. Woodson. The History of the Negro Church (Wash., D. C.: The Associated Publishers, 1921), pp. 152-53.
        DHU/MO; DHU/R
Congregational minister edited The Colored American. Active in the anti-slavery movement & underground railroad.

    Benjamin Quarles. Black Abolitionists (N. Y.: Oxford Univ. Press, 1969), p. 310. DHU/MO

    Carleton Mabee. Black Freedom: the Non-violent Abolitionist From 1830 Through the Civil War (N. Y.: Macmillan Co., 1970), p. 435. DHU/MO

    The Colored American (1; Mr. 4, Apr. 15, Nov. 18, 1837; 2; Je. 2, 1838; 3; Jl. 13, 1839.) DHU/MO

    Dictionary of American Biography V. 8, 1963. DHU/MO

    Florence T. Ray and Henrietta Ray. Sketch of the Life of Rev. Charles B. Ray (N. Y.: Press of J. J. Little & Co., 1887), p. 79. DHU/MO

    Gerald Sorin. The New York Abolitionists (Westport, Conn.: Greenwood Pub. Corp., 1971), p. 172+. DHU/MO

    Gerrit Smith. An Address to the Three Thousand Colored Citizens of New York... (N. Y.: n. p., 1846), nos. 4-6.
        DHU/MO

    Horatio T. Strother. The Underground Railroad in Connecticut (Middletown, Conn.: Wesleyan Univ. Press, 1962), p. 262+. DHU/MO

    Irvine G. Penn. The Afro-American Press and Its Editors (N. Y.: Arno Press, 1969), p. 565. DHU/R; DHU/MO

    Leila A. Pendleton. A Narrative of the Negro (Wash., D. C.: Press of R. L. Pendleton, 1912), p. 217+. DHU/MO

    Who Was Who in America, Historical Volume, 1607-1907 (Chicago: The A. N. Marquis Co., 1907), p. 433. DLC

    William Ferris. The African Abroad (New Haven, Conn.: The Tuttle, Morehouse & Taylor Press, 1913), p. 697.
        DHU/MO

    Wilbur H. Siebert. The Underground Railroad From Slavery to Freedom (N. Y.: Macmillan Co., 1898), p. 478. DHU/MO

    William W. Brown. The Rising Son (Boston: A. G. Brown & Co., 1874), pp. 472-73. DHU/R; DHU/MO

RAY, JOSEPH EUGENE SOLOMON

    Frank L. Keegan. Blacktown, U. S. A. (Boston: Little, Brown, 1971), pp. 194-205. DHU/MO

    "Planning a program for the restoration of the ideals of Marcus Garvey in the 1970's."

RAY, SANDY FREDERICK

    The editors of Ebony. The Ebony Success Library: 1, 000 Successful Blacks (Nashville: The Southwestern Co., 1973), Vol. 1, p. 259. DHU
Baptist minister and vice-pres. of National Baptist Convention.

RAYMOND, JOHN F.

    William T. Catto. Catto's Semi-Centenary Discourse (Phila.: Joseph M. Wilson, 1857), p. 108. DHU/R
Minister of Shiloh Baptist Church, Philadelphia

RAYMOND, JOHN T.

    U. S. Dept. of Education. Special Report (Washington, D. C.: Government Printing Office, 1871), p. 394. DHU/MO
Baptist minister and teacher.

    Leila A. Pendleton. A Narrative of the Negro (Wash., D. C.: Press of R. L. Pendleton, 1912), p. 132.

READ, GEORGE E.

    Samuel W. Bacote. <u>Who's Who Among the Colored Baptists</u> (Kansas City, Mo.: F. Hudson Co., 1912), pp. 192-94.
                              DHU/MO

    Baptist minister and educator.

REASON, CHARLES L.

    William Wells Brown. <u>The Black Man</u> (Miami, Fla.: Mnemosyne Pub., Inc., 1969), pp. 246-50.   DHU/R
    Black abolitionist and writer.

REED, VILLEROY D.

    <u>Presbyterian Reunion: 1837-1871</u> (N. Y.: De W. C. Lent & Co., 1870), pp. 509-11.   DHU/MO
    Presbyterian minister, teacher and president of Alexander College, Dubuque, Iowa.

REEVE, JOHN BUNYAN

    William J. Simmons. <u>Men of Mark</u> (Cleveland, O.: Geo. M. Rewell & Co., 1887), pp. 199-202.   DHU/R
    Presbyterian minister appointed by American Missionary Society to organize the Theology Department at Howard University in 1871.

    Alfred Nevin, (ed.). <u>Encyclopedia of the Presbyterian Church</u> (Phila.: Presbyterian Pub. Co., 1884), p. 747.
                              NjP; NNUT

REID, FRANK MADISON, SR. (bp.).

    Richard R. Wright. <u>Bishops of the A. M. E. Church.</u> Nashville: A. M. E. Sunday School Union, 1963), pp. 293-95.
                              DHU/R
    Sixty-first bishop of the A. M. E. Church.

    <u>The African Methodist Episcopal Church Review</u> (75:200, Apr.-Je., 1959), pp. 3-4.   DHU/R

REID, WILLIAM

    Isaac S. Harrell. "Gates County to 1860." <u>Historical Papers of the Trinity College Historical Society.</u> (Durham, N. C.: n.p., 1916), p. 67.   DLC; NH; NcD; CoU; OCI
    Negro Baptist minister and pastor of New Hope Baptist Church, Gates County, N. C. early twentieth century.

    John Hope Franklin. <u>The Free Negro in North Carolina 1790-1860</u> (N. Y.: W. W. Norlin & Co., 1843), p. 176.   DHU/R

REMOND, CHARLES L.

    William W. Brown. <u>The Rising Son</u> (Miami, Fla.: Mnemosyne Pub. Co., 1969), pp. 403-04.   DHU/R
    Negro abolitionist.
    Originally published in 1874.

RESPES, ABEL

    "Black Rabbi Drops Conversion Idea." <u>Baltimore Afro-American</u> (Jl., 1973).   Pam. File, DHU/R

REVELS, HIRAM R.

    Benjamin G. Brawley. <u>Negro Builders and Heroes.</u> (Chapel Hill: Univ. of N. C. Press, 1937), pp. 123, 125-26. DHU/R
    A. M. E. minister and first Negro to sit in the United States Senate.

    Elizabeth Lawson. <u>The Gentleman From Mississippi; Our First Negro Congressman, Hiram R. Revels</u> (New York: The Author, 1960).   DHU/MO

    Joseph A. Borome. "The Autobiography of Hiram Rhoades Revels Together With Some Letters By and About Him." <u>Midwest Journal</u> (5:1, Wint., 1952-53), pp. 79-92. DHU/MO

    <u>New Era</u> (1:14, 1912; 1:22, 1912), p. 2; p. 1.   DHU/MO

    <u>New National Era</u> (4:2, Ja. 16, 1873), p. 2.   DHU/MO

    Harry A. Ploski (ed.). <u>Negro Almanac</u> (New York: The Bellwether Co., 1971), pp. 307-08.   DHU/R
    Methodist Episcopal minister, first Negro to serve in U. S. Senate, from Mississippi and president of Alcorn University.

    William H. Ferris. <u>African Abroad.</u> (New Haven, Conn.: The Tuttle, Morehouse & Taylor Press, 1913), p. 741.

    William Wells Brown. <u>The Rising Son.</u> (Boston: A. G. Brown & Co., 1874), pp. 500-03.   DHU/MO

    James J. Pipkin. <u>The Negro in Revelation in History and in Citizenship</u> (N. Y.: Thompson Pub. Co., 1902), p. 62.
                              DHU/MO

    Arthur Huff Fauset. <u>For Freedom; a Biographical Story of the American Negro</u> (Philadelphia: Franklin Pub. and Supply Co., 1927), p. 79.   DHU/MO

    Thomas O. Fuller. <u>Pictorial History of the American Negro</u> (Memphis, Tenn.: Pictorial History, Inc., 1933), p. 63.
                              DHU/MO

RICHARD, JAMES

    Emanuel K. Love. <u>History of the First African Baptist Church</u> (Savannah, Ga.: Morning News Print, 1888), p. 168. DHU/MO
    Deacon of the First African Baptist Church.

RICHARDSON, ROBERT B.

    William H. Heard. <u>The Bright Side of African Life</u> (N. Y.: Negro Universities Press, 1969), p. 88.   DHU/R
    Baptist minister, Secretary of Baptist Convention, President of Ricks Institute, Associate Justice of Supreme Court, Liberia.

RICHARDSON, TIMOTHY

    <u>Ebony</u> (28:9, Jl., 1972), pp. 80+.   Pam File, DHU/R
    About a young black Catholic friar from Pittsburgh, Pa., who "serves his faith," "guarding sacred treasures and traditions" "in Ancient Bethlehem."

RIDDICK, JOHN HUDSON

    William J. Simmons. <u>Men of Mark</u> (Cleveland: O. Rewell, 1887), pp. 752-53.   DHU/R; DHU/MO
    Ex-slave and M. E. minister and educator.

RIDGEL, A. L.

    William H. Heard. <u>The Bright Side of African Life</u> (N. Y.: Negro Universities Press, 1969), p. 17.   DHU/R
    A. M. E. minister in Brewersville, Liberia.

RIEVES, ROBERT STEPHEN

    James W. Hood. <u>One Hundred Years of the A. M. E. Zion Church</u> (N. Y.: A. M. E. Zion Book Concern, 1895), pp. 412-14.   DHU/MO
    A. M. E. Zion minister.

RIVERS, DAVID FOOTE

Journal of Negro History (26:4, Oct., 1941), pp. 548-49.
                          Pam. File, DHU/R
Politician and baptist minister who served Berean Baptist
Church, Washington, D. C.

ROBERTS, CHARLES L.

William Hicks. The History of Louisiana Negro Baptists from
1804-1914 (Nashville, Penn.: National Baptist Publishing
Board, n.d.), pp. 169-70.   DHU/R
Baptist minister and president of Cheyneville Academy.

Samuel W. Bacote. Who's Who Among the Colored Baptists
(Kansas City, Mo.: F. Hudson Co., 1912), pp. 78-79.
                                             DHU/MO

ROBERTS, ISAAC

James M. Simms. The First Colored Baptist Church in
North America (Phila.: J. B. Lippincott Co., 1888), pp. 258-
60.   DHU/R
Baptist minister.

ROBERTS, JOHN WRIGHT, (bp.).

Leila A. Pendleton. A Narrative of the Negro (Wash., D. C.:
Press of R. L. Pendleton, 1912), p. 49.   DHU/MO
Methodist Episcopal Bishop.

James J. Pipkin. The Negro in Revelation, in History, and
in Citizenship (New York: Thompson Pub. Co., 1902), p. 96.
                                             DHU/MO

ROBERTS, Z. B.

William H. Heard. The Bright Side of African Life (N. Y.:
Negro Universities Press, 1969), pp. 68-71.   DHU/R
Baptist minister appointed Chief Justice in 1895 of Liberia.

ROBINSON, A. R.

Lewis G. Jordan. Negro Baptist History U. S. A. (Nashville:
Sunday School Publishing Board, N. B. C., 1930), p. 88.
                                 DHU/MO; DHU/R
Baptist minister and chairman of the Foreign Mission Board.

The Crisis (27:3, Ja., 1924), pp. 132-33.   DLC; DHU/MO

W. Bacote. Who's Who Among the Colored Baptists (Kansas
City: F. Hudson Co., 1912), pp. 33-35.   DHU/MO

ROBINSON, C.

U. S. Dept. of Education. Special Report (Wash., D. C.:
Government Printing Office, 1871), p. 286.   DHU/MO
Baptist minister.

ROBINSON, J. P.

Thomas O. Fuller. Pictorial History of the American Negro
(Memphis, Tenn.: Pictorial History Inc., 1933), p. 83.
                                             DHU/MO
Minister of Little Rock, Arkansas.

ROBINSON, JAMES HERMAN

Frank T. Wilson. "Living Witnesses: Black Presbyterians in
Ministry." Journal of Presbyterian History (51:4, Wint.,
1973), pp. 367-70.   DHU/R
Presbyterian minister, author and director of "Operation
Crossroads Africa."

Road Without Turning. The Story of Reverend James H. Robinson; an Autobiography (New York: Farrar Straus, 1950).
                                 DHU/R; DLC

ROBINSON, L. M.

Lewis G. Jordan. Negro Baptist History U. S. A. (Nashville,
Tenn.: The Sunday School Publishing Board N. B. C., 1930),
p. 392.   DHU/R; DHU/MO
Baptist minister, Georgia.

ROBINSON, WARREN

"Elder Warren Robinson, Founder of Jewish Cult has Promised
to Rise in 60 Days." Amsterdam News (Jl. 1, 1931). NN/Sch

ROCK, CALVIN BOVELL

The editors of Ebony. The Ebony Success Library: 1,000 Successful Blacks (Nashville: The Southwestern Co., 1973), Vol. 1,
p. 267.   DHU
Seventh Day Adventist minister and president of Oakwood
College, Huntsville, Ala.

ROCKWELL, J. EDSON

Presbyterian Reunion: 1837-1871 (N. Y.: De W. C. Lent &
Co., 1870), pp. 512-13.   DHU/MO
Presbyterian minister, author and editor of The Sabbath School
Visitor.

RODGERS, WILLIAM

Albert S. Foley. God's Men of Color (New York: Farrar,
Straus & Co., 1955), p. 301.   DHU/R
Catholic priest.

ROGERS, E. PAYSON

Carter G. Woodson. The History of the Negro Church (Wash.,
D. C.: Associated Publishers, 1921), p. 158.
                                 DHU/R; DHU/MO
Presbyterian minister in New Jersey.

William W. Brown. The Black Man (N. Y.: T. Hamilton,
1863), p. 272.   DHU/R; DHU/MO

ROSE, JAMES EVERETT

Charles Emerson Boddie. God's "Bad Boys" (Valley Forge:
Judson Press, 1972), pp. 105-16.   DHU/R
Baptist minister

ROSS, ISAAC NELSON, (bp.).

Richard R. Wright. Bishops of the A. M. E. Church (Nashville: A. M. E. Sunday School Union, 1963), pp. 296-98.
                                             DHU/R
Forty-first Bishop of the A. M. E. Church.

ROSS, MAJOR H. D.

 James W. Hood. One Hundred Years of the A. M. E. Zion
 Church (N. Y.: A. M. E. Zion Book Concern, 1895), pp. 616-
 18.   DHU/MO
 Ex-slave and A. M. E. Zion minister and author.

ROUSSEVE, MAURICE L.

 Charles B. Rousseve. The Negro in Louisiana (New Orleans:
 The Xavier Univ Press, 1937), p. 141.   DHU/MO
 Catholic priest.

 Albert S. Foley. God's Men of Color (New York: Farrar,
 Straus & Co., 1955), pp. 124-38.   DHU/R

ROWE, GEORGE C.

 Benjamin C. Brawley. The Negro Genius (N. Y.: Dodd,
 Mead & Co., 1937), pp. 122-23.   DHU/R
 Pastor of Plymouth Congregational Church of Charleston, S. C.
 and author of Thoughts in Verse and Patriotic Poems.

 Charles Alexander. One Hundred Distinguished Leaders
 (Atlanta, Ga.: The Franklin Printing & Publishing Co., 1899),
 p. 65.   DHU/MO

 Henry F. Kletzing. Progress of a Race (Atlanta, Ga.: J.
 L. Nichols & Co., 1898), p. 580.   DHU/MO

 James T. Haley. Afro-American Encyclopaedia (Nashville: Haley & Florida, 1895), pp. 589-90.   DHU/MO

RUSH, CHRISTOPHER, (bp.).

 Henry F. Kletzing. Progress of a Race (Atlanta, Ga.: J. L.
 Nichols & Co., 1898), p. 581.   DHU/MO
 Bishop of A. M. E. Zion Church

 A. M. E. Zion Quarterly Review (62; 1952), p. 229. DHU/R

 A. M. E. Zion Church. New England Conference. Minutes
 (My. 6, 1874), p. 33.   NcSalL

 Carter G. Woodson. The History of the Negro Church (Wash.,
 D. C.: The Associated Publishers, 1921), pp. 89-90.
                                     DHU/MO; DHU/R

 James B. F. Shaw. The Negro in the History of Methodism
 (Nashville: Parthenon Press, 1954), p. 75.   DHU/R

 James W. Hood. One Hundred Years of the A. M. E. Zion
 Church (N. Y.: A. M. E. Zion Book Concern, 1895), pp.
 168-71.   DHU/MO

 John J. Moore. History of the A. M. E. Zion Church in
 America (York, Pa.: Teachers Journal Office, 1884), pp.
 349-53.   DHU/MO

RUSSELL, JAMES SOLOMON

 Charles Alexander. One Hundred Distinguished Leaders
 (Atlanta, Ga.: The Franklin Printing & Publishing Co.,
 1899), p. 65.   DHU/MO
 Founder of St. Paul's Normal & Industrial School. A graduate of Hampton and an Archdeacon in the Episcopal Church.

 G. F. Richings. Evidences of Progress Among Colored
 People (Phila.: G. S. Ferguson, 1904), pp. 88-91.
                                     DHU/R; DHU/MO

 Southern Workman (52:10, Oct., 1923), pp. 474-76.
                                     DLC; DHU/MO

 Southern Workman (54:2, Feb., 1925), pp. 49-58.
                                     DLC; DHU/MO

RUSSELL, S. D.

 (Indianapolis) Freeman (1:27, Feb. 23, 1889), p. 5. DHU/MO
 Minister of the A. M. E. Church and editor of The Southern
 Guide, The Torchlight Appeal, The Texas Reformer and The
 Herald of Truth.

 Irvine G. Penn. The Afro-American Press and Its Editors
 (Springfield, Mass.: Willey & Co., 1891), pp. 267-69.
                                     DHU/R; DHU/MO

RUST, RICHARD SUTTON

 G. F. Richings. Evidences of Progress Among Colored People
 (Phila.: G. S. Ferguson, 1904), pp. 118-19. DHU/R; DHU/MO
 Methodist Episcopal minister, member of the first Board of
 Trustees and first active President of Wilberforce University,
 Wilberforce, Ohio.

 Dictionary of American Biography V. 2 (New York: Charles
 Scribner's & Sons, 1935), pp. 253-54.   DHU

SALES, GEORGE

 G. F. Richings. Evidences of Progress Among Colored People
 (Phila.: G. S. Ferguson, 1904), p. 29.   DHU/R
 Baptist minister and President of Atlanta Baptist Seminary.

 Leila A. Pendleton. A. Narrative of the Negro (Wash., D. C.:
 Press of R. L. Pendleton, 1912), p. 51.   DHU/MO

SALTER, MOSES BUCKINGHAM, (bp.).

 Richard R. Wright. Bishops of the A. M. E. Church. (Nashville: A. M. E. Sunday School Union, 1963), pp. 299-300.
                                              DHU/R
 Twenty-first Bishop of the A. M. E. Church.

 G. F. Richings. Evidences of Progress Among Colored People
 (Phila.: G. S. Ferguson, 1904), p. 386.   DHU/MO; DHU/R

 William N. Hartshorn. An Era of Progress and Promise.
 (Boston, Mass.: The Priscilla Pub. Co., 1910), p. 107.
                                              DHU/MO

SAMPSON, JOHN P.

 Irvine G. Penn. The Afro-American Press and Its Editors
 (Springfield, Mass.: Willey & Co., 1891), pp. 89-91. DHU/MO
 Minister, abolitionist, and editor of the Colored Citizen.

 William W. Brown. The Rising Son (Miami, Fla.: Mnemosyne
 Pub. Co., 1969), pp. 514-17.   DHU/R
 Originally published in 1874.

SAMUELS, A. H.

 William Hicks. The History of Louisiana Negro Baptists from
 1804-1914 (Nashville, Tenn.: National Baptist Publishing Board,
 n. d.), pp. 140-41.   DHU/R
 Baptist minister and moderator of the thirteenth District Association.

SANDERS, D. J.

 The Church at Home and Abroad (23; 1898), p. 109. DHU/R
 Rev. D. J. Sanders, President of Biddle University.

SAN PEDRO

José Antonio Fernandez. Vida de San Pedro de la Compañia de Jesus, Apóstol de los Negros ... Refundida y Acrescentado por el P. Juan Maria Sola ... (Barcelona: n. p. , 1888).

SATTERFIELD, DAVID JANKER

Charles Alexander. One Hundred Distinguished Leaders (Atlanta, Ga. : The Franklin Printing & Publishing Co. , 1899), pp. 63-64.   DHU/MO
A white Presbyterian minister.

SAUNDERS, D. J.

Irvine G. Penn. The Afro-American Press and Its Editors (Springfield, Mass. : Willey & Co. , 1891), pp. 299-300.
                                                          DHU/MO
Presbyterian minister, founder and editor of The Afro-Amer-ican Presbyterian, associate editor of The Southern Evange-list and President of Biddle University, Charlotte, N. C.

Henry F. Kletzing. Progress of a Race (Atlanta: J. L. Nich-ols & Co. , 1898), pp. 341-42.   DHU/MO

G. F. Richings. Evidences of Progress Among Colored People (Phila.: G. S. Ferguson, 1904), pp. 180-81. DHU/R; DHU/MO

SAUNDERS, JOHN CARROLL

James W. Hood. One Hundred Years of the A. M. E. Zion Church (N. Y.: A. M. E. Zion Book Concern, 1895), pp. 583-85.   DHU/MO
Ex-slave and A. M. E. Zion minister and editor of the Star of Zion.

SAUNDERS, PRINCE

William Douglass. Annals of the First African Church in the U. S. A. (Phila.: King & Bair Printers, 1862), p. 123.
                                                          DHU/MO
Lay reader of the African Episcopal Church of St. Thomas, Phila.

Wilhelmena S. Robinson. Historical Negro Biographies (N. Y.: Publishers Co. , 1867), p. 32.   DHU/MO

SAVAGE, JOHN A.

Evidences of Progress Among Colored People (Phila.: G. S. Ferguson, 1904), p. 178.   DHU/MO; DHU/R
Presbyterian minister and President of Albion Academy.

SAYLES, BARTHOLOMEW (John B. Letory)

God's Men of Color (New York: Farrar, Straus & Co. , 1955), pp. 250-53.   DHU/R
Catholic priest.

SCHELL, ROBERT

E. R. Carter. The Black Side (Atlanta, Ga. : n. p. , 1894), pp. 114-16.   DHU/MO
Black Baptist minister.

SCHENCK, WILLIAM EDWARD

Presbyterian Reunion: 1837-1871 (N. Y.: De W. C. Lent & Co. , 1870), pp. 508-09.   DHU/MO
Presbyterian minister, superintendent of Church Extension, Philadelphia and corresponding secretary of Board of Pub-lication.

SCOTT, DANIEL

William T. Catto. Catto's Semi-Centenary Discourse (Phila.: Joseph M. Wilson, 1857), pp. 108- 09. DHU/R
Founder and minister, Union Baptist Church, Philadelphia.

SCOTT, DANIEL A.

Samuel W. Bacote. Who's Who Among the Colored Baptists (Kansas City, Mo. : F. Hudson Co. , 1912), pp. 51-53.
                                                          DHU/MO
Baptist minister, president of Houston College, editor of Texas Headlight and Truth, Sunday-School missionary of American Baptist Publication Society.

SCOTT, ISAIAH B. , (bp.).

Booker T. Washington. A New Negro for a New Century (Chicago, Ill. : American Publishing House, 1900), p. 257.
                                                          DHU/MO
Methodist Episcopal bishop, third Negro to be elected a missionary bishop.

G. F. Richings. Evidences of Progress Among Colored People (Phila.: G. S. Ferguson, 1904), p. 368.
                                                DHU/R; DHU/MO

James J. Pipkin. The Negro in Revelation, in History and in Citizenship (New York: Thompson Pub. Co. , 1902), p. 62.
                                                          DHU/MO

William N. Hartshorn. An Era of Progress and Promise (Boston, Mass.: Priscilla Publishing Co. , 1910), p. 401.
                                                          DHU/MO

SCOTT, RUEBEN

Home Missions (43:4, Apr. , 1972), pp. 31-33.
                                        Pam. File, DHU/R
Baptist pastor in Fresno, Calif.

SCOTT, WARREN

Toward Wholeness (1:1, Sum. , 1972), p. 11.   DHU/R
Brief biographical data given as Scott is honored by the Min-istries to Blacks in Higher Education on its Roll of Honor. Episcopal campus minister, Atlanta University Center

SCRUGGS, ENOS L.

G. F. Richings. Evidences of Progress Among Colored People (Phila.: Geo. S. Ferguson, 1904), pp. 43-45.
                                                          DHU/MO
Baptist minister and president of Western College.

James J. Pipkin. The Negro in Revelation, in History, and in Citizenship (N. Y.: Thompson Pub. Co. , 1902), pp. 419-20.   DHU/MO

SEARCY, THOMAS JEFFERSON

James T. Haley. Afro-American Encyclopaedia (Nashville: Haley & Florida, 1895), pp. 574-75.   DHU/MO
Baptist minister; organizer and president of the Tennessee State Convention.

SEVORRES, JAMES J.

Emanuel K. Love. History of the First African Baptist Church (Savannah, Ga.: Morning News Print, 1888), p. 189. DHU/MO
Baptist minister.

SEWARD, JOHN H.

    Thomas O. Fuller. Pictorial History of the American Negro
(Memphis, Tenn.: Pictorial History Inc., 1933), p. 319.
                                       DHU/MO
Minister and dentist.

SEYMOUR, WILLIAM J.

    Walter J. Hollenweger. The Pentecostals; the Charismatic
Movements in the Churches (Minneapolis: Augsburg Publishing House, 1972), pp. 22, 24, 47, 43, 338, 350, 495.
                                       DHU/R
Seymour, a black Pentecostal minister credited with establishing in Los Angeles the original place of worship of the Pentecostal Movement.

    Nils Bloch-Hoell. The Pentecostal Movement, Its Origin,
Development, and Distinctive Character (New York: Humanities Press, 1964).   DHU/R

SHAFFER, CORNELIUS THADDEUS, (bp.).

    Richard R. Wright. Bishops of the A. M. E. Church (Nash-
ville: A. M. E. Sunday School Union, 1963), pp. 301-03.
                                       DHU/R
Twenty-ninth Bishop of the A. M. E. Church.

    G. F. Richings. Evidences of Progress Among Colored
People (Philadelphia: G. S. Ferguson, 1904), pp. 380-84.
                                       DHU/R

    William N. Hartshorn. An Era of Progress and Promise
(Boston: Priscilla Publishing Co., 1910), p. 389. DHU/MO

SHAFTER, GEORGE H.

    Benjamin W. Arnett. The Budget... Biographical Sketches
Proceeding... (Dayton, O.: Christian Publishing House,
1882), pp. 21-24.   DHU/MO
A. M. E. minister.

SHAW, ALEXANDER PRESTON, (bp.).

    James Beverly Ford Shaw. Life and Work of Bishop Alexander
Preston Shaw (Nashville: Parthenon Press, 1954).
                      NcLjHi; DHU/MO; DHU/R
Bishop of the Methodist Episcopal Church.

SHAW, ALVIA A.

    The editors of Ebony. The Ebony Success Library: 1,000 Suc-
cessful Blacks (Nashville: The Southwestern Co., 1973),
Vol. 1, p. 279.   DHU
A. M. E. minister and pastor of St. James A. M. E. Church,
Cleveland, Ohio.

SHAW, HERBERT BELL, (bp.).

    The editors of Ebony. The Ebony Success Library: 1,000 Suc-
cessful Blacks (Nashville: The Southwestern Co., 1973),
Vol. 1, p. 279.   DHU
Bishop of A. M. E. Zion Church.

    Biographical Encyclopedia of the World (New York: Institute
of Research, 1946), p. 817.   NcSalL

    O. O. Sarver. Leaders of the Colored Race in Alabama
(Mobile, Ala.: The News Pub. Co., 1928), pp. 12-13. DHU/R

    Who's Who in Colored America (New York: Who's Who in
Colored America Corp., 1938-40; 1950), pp. 464+.
                         NcSalL; DHU/R

SHAW, JAMES B.

    Presbyterian Reunion: 1837-1871 (N. Y.: De W. C. Lent &
Co., 1870), pp. 516-17.   DHU/MO
Presbyterian minister of Utica, N. Y. and member of the
General Assembly.

SHEFTALL, ADAM

    Emanuel K. Love. History of the First African Baptist Church
(Savannah, Ga.: Morning News Print, 1888), p. 164. DHU/MO
Deacon of the First African Baptist Church.

SHELTON, C. S.

    William Hicks. The History of Louisiana Negro Baptists from
1804-1914 (Nashville, Tenn.: National Baptist Publishing
Board, n. d.), p. 188.   DHU/R
Baptist minister.

SHELTON, WALLACE

    Lewis G. Jordan. Negro Baptist History U. S. A. (Nashville:
Sunday School Pub. Board N. B. C., 1930), p. 392.
                       DHU/MO; DHU/R
Baptist minister, Ohio

    Leila A. Pendleton. A Narrative of the Negro (Wash., D. C.:
Press of R. L. Pendleton, 1912), p. 177.   DHU/MO

SHEPARD, MARSHALL L., SR.

    Charles Emerson Boddie. God's "Bad Boys" (Valley Forge:
Judson Press, 1972), pp. 117-25.   DHU/R
Baptist minister and Recorder of Deeds in Washington, D. C.

    Al Smedley. "The Preacher in City Hall." The Crisis (60:2,
Feb., 1953), pp. 98-99+.   DHU/MO; DLC

SHEPHERD, HARVEY (Walter)

    Albert S. Foley. God's Men of Color (New York: Farrar,
Straus & Co., 1955), pp. 257-61.   DHU/R
Catholic priest.

SHEPPARD, WILLIAM H.

    Crisis (10:1, My., 1915), p. 15.   DLC; DHU/MO
Presbyterian minister and missionary to Belgian Congo.

    Leila A. Pendleton. A Narrative of the Negro (Wash., D. C.:
Press of R. L. Pendleton, 1912), pp. 33-34. DHU/MO

SHERMAN, ODIE LEE, (bp.).

    Richard R. Wright. Bishops of the A. M. E. Church (Nash-
ville: A. M. E. Sunday School Union, 1963), pp. 304-06.
                                     DHU/R
Seventy-fifth Bishop of the A. M. E. Church.

    The editors of Ebony. The Ebony Success Library: 1,000 Suc-
cessful Blacks (Nashville: The Southwestern Co., 1973),
Vol. 1, p. 280   DHU

SHIRLEY, LEMUEL B., (bp.).

    The Episcopal Church Annual (New York: Morehouse-Barlow,
1972), p. 236.   PPPD; ViAlTH
Protestant Episcopal bishop of Panama.

SHORTER, JAMES ALEXANDER, (bp.).

Richard R. Wright. Bishops of the A. M. E. Church. (Nashville: A. M. E. Sunday School Union, 1963), pp. 307-10.
DHU/R
Ninth bishop of the A. M. E. Church

Alexander Walker Wayman, (bp.). The Life of Rev. James Alexander Shorter, One of the Bishops of the African Methodist Episcopal Church (Baltimore: J. Lanahan, 1890).
DHU/MO

Benjamin T. Tanner. An Apology for African Methodism. (Baltimore: n.p., 1867), pp. 282-85.   DHU/MO

Benjamin W. Arnett. The Budget ... Biographical Sketches Proceeding... (Dayton: Christian Pub. House, 1882), pp. 16-19.   DHU/MO

G. F. Richings. Evidences of Progress Among the Colored People. (Phila.: G. S. Ferguson, 1904), p. 120.
DHU/MO; DHU/R

James A. Handy. Scraps of African Methodist History. (Phila.: A. M. E. Book Concern, n.d.), pp. 341-43.
DHU/MO

Leila A. Pendleton. A Narrative of the Negro. (Wash., D. C.: Press of R. L. Pendleton, 1912), p. 177.   DHU/MO

U. S. Dept. of Education Special Report. (Wash., D. C.: Govt. Printing Office, 1871), p. 217.   DHU/MO

SHUTTLESWORTH, FRED. L.

The editors of Ebony. The Ebony Success Library: 1,000 Successful Blacks (Nashville: The Southwestern Pub. Co., 1973), V. 1, p. 281.   DHU
Baptist minister and pastor of Greater New Light Baptist Church, Cincinnati, Ohio.

SIMMONS, JAMES

David H. Bradley, Sr. A. History of the A. M. E. Zion Church 1872-1968 V. 2 (Nashville: Parthenon Press, 1970), pp. 11+.   DHU/R; DHU/MO
Minister of the A. M. E. Zion Church.

John J. Moore. History of the A. M. E. Zion Church in America (York, Pa.: Teachers Journal Office, 1884), p. 367.   DHU/MO

SIMMONS, ROBERT HARRISON

James W. Hood. One Hundred Years of the A. M. E. Zion Church (N. Y.: A. M. E. Zion Book Concern, 1895), pp. 301-07.   DHU/MO
A. M. E. Zion minister.

SIMMONS, WILLIAM J.

Benjamin G. Brawley. Negro Builders and Heroes (Chapel Hill: Univ. of N. C. Press, 1937), pp. 200-01.
DHU/R; DHU/MO
Baptist minister, author and President of State University, Louisville, Ky., and editor of Our Women and Children.

Benjamin G. Brawley. The Negro Genius (New York: Dodd, Mead & Co., 1937), p. 111.   DHU/R; DHU/MO

E. A. Johnson. A School History of the Negro Race in America (Raleigh, N. C.: Edward & Broughton, Printers, 1890), p. 179.   DHU/R; DHU/MO

G. F. Richings. Evidences of Progress Among Colored People (Phila.: G. S. Ferguson, 1904), pp. 218-24.
DHU/MO

Henry D. Northrop. College of Life (Phila.: Nat. Pub. Co., 1895), pp. 129-30.   DHU/MO

Irvine G. Penn. The Afro-American Press and Its Editors (Springfield, Mass.: Willey & Co., 1891), pp. 120-23.
DHU/R; DHU/MO

(Indianapolis) Freeman (1:24, Feb. 2, 1889), p. 5. DHU/MO

Lewis G. Jordan. Negro Baptist History U. S. A. (Nashville, Tenn.: Sunday School Publishing Board, N. B. C., 1930), p. 392.   DHU/MO

SIMMS, JAMES M.

Edgar G. Thomas. The First Baptist Church of North America (Savannah, Ga.: By the author, 1925), pp. 134-35. DHU/MO
Minister of the First African Baptist Church.

Emanuel K. Love. History of the First African Baptist Church (Savannah, Ga.: Morning News Print, 1888), p. 165. DHU/MO

SIMON, LAURENCE CYRUS

William Hicks. History of Louisiana Negro Baptists from 1804 to 1914 (Nashville, Tenn.: National Baptist Publishing Board, n.d.), pp. 121-22.   DHU/R
Baptist minister, moderator of the 7th District Baptist Association and founder of the 7th District Baptist Association and founder of Opelousas Academy.

SIMPSON, ALLEN MATTHEW

Albert S. Foley. God's Men of Color (New York: Farrar, Straus & Co., 1955), pp. 294-97.   DHU/R
Catholic priest.

SIMPSON, JACK

Emanuel K. Love. History of the First African Baptist Church (Savannah, Ga.: Morning News Print, 1888), p. 164.
DHU/MO
Deacon of the First African Baptist Church.

SIMS, DAVID HENRY, (bp.).

Richard R. Wright. Bishops of the A. M. E. Church (Nashville: A. M. E. Sunday School Union, 1963), pp. 311-16.
DHU/R
Fifty-fifth Bishop of the A. M. E. Church

SINCLAIR, WILLIAM A.

William N. Hartshorn. An Era of Progress and Promise (Boston, Mass.: Priscilla Publishing Co., 1910), p. 439.
DHU/MO
Ex-slave, minister of the Congregational Church, physician, financial secretary of Howard Univ., and author of The Aftermath of Slavery.

William H. Ferris. African Abroad V. 2 (New Haven, Conn.: The Tuttle, Morehouse & Taylor Press, 1913), p. 791.
DHU/MO

SINGLETON, BENJAMIN, (Pat)

Roy Garvin. "Benjamin or 'Pap' Singleton and his Followers."
Journal of Negro History (33:1, 1948), pp. 7-23.   DHU/MO
Negro organizer of the United Transatlantic Society. Led a
group of Negroes from the South to Kansas to settle for better
opportunities. Early 19th century.

Walter L. Fleming. "Pat Singleton, the Moses of the Colored
Exodus." American Journal of Sociology (15; Jl., 1909), pp.
61-82.   DHU/MO

SINGLETON, GEORGE A.

Marcus H. Boulware. The Oratory of Negro Leaders 1900-
1968 (Westport, Conn.: Negro Universities Press, 1969), p.
128.   DHU/MO
A. M. E. minister and editor of the Christian Recorder.

The Autobiography of George A. Singleton (Boston: Forum
Pub. Co., 1964).   DHU/R

SINGLETON, HERBERT

Albert S. Foley. God's Men of Color (New York: Farrar,
Straus & Co., 1955), p. 303.   DHU/R
Catholic priest.

SLEDGE, ANDREW

John Mason Brewer. Negro Legislators of Texas and Their
Descendants; a History of the Negro in Texas Politics From
Reconstruction to Disfranchisement. (Dallas, Texas: Mathis
Publishing Co., 1935), pp. 50-52.
Negro Baptist minister. A member of the Sixteenth Legisla-
ture of Texas and president of State Baptist Convention of
Texas for several years.

SMALL, J. B.

G. F. Richings. Evidences of Progress Among Colored
People (Phila.: G. S. Ferguson, 1904), p. 391.
                                       DHU/R; DHU/MO
A. M. E. minister.

SMALL, JOHN BRYAN, JR.

James W. Hood. One Hundred Years of the A. M. E. Zion
Church (N. Y.: A. M. E. Zion Book Concern, 1895), pp. 233-
36.   DHU/MO
A. M. E. Zion minister.

SMITH, AMANDA

African Methodist Episcopal Church Review (80:219, Ja.-Mr.,
1964), pp. 3-7.   DHU/R
A. M. E. evangelist.

An Autobiography (Chicago: Meyers & Bros., 1893). DHU/MO

Elizabeth L. Davis. Lifting as They Climb (Chicago, Ill.:
n. p., 1933), pp. 293-94.   DHU/MO

Hallie Q. Brown. Homespun Heroines and Other Women of
Distinction (Xenia, O.: Aldine Publishing Co., 1926), pp.
128-32.   DHU/MO

James A. Handy. Scraps of African Methodist History (Phila.:
A. M. E. Book Concern, n. d.), p. 347.   DHU/MO

Lawson A. Scruggs. Women of Distinction (Raleigh: L. A.
Scruggs, 1893), pp. 57-61.   DHU/MO

N. H. Cadbury. The Life of Amanda Smith (Birmingham,
Ala.: Cornish, 1916).   NcNjHi

SMITH, CHARLES H

James W. Hood. One Hundred Years of the A. M. E. Zion
Church (N. Y.: A. M. E. Zion Book Concern, 1895), pp.
608-10.   DHU/MO
A. M. E. Zion minister.

James L. Nichols. The New Progress of a Race (Naperville,
Ill.: J. L. Nichols & Co., 1929), p. 431.   DHU/MO

SMITH, CHARLES SPENCER, (bp.).

G. F. Richings. Evidences of Progress Among Colored
People (Phila.: Geo. S. Ferguson, 1904), p. 388.
                                       DHU/MO; DHU/R
Bishop of the A. M. E. Church, founder and manager of the
Sunday School Union and author of The History of the A. M. E.
Church.

Benjamin W. Arnett. The Budget... Biographical Sketches
Proceeding... (Dayton, Ohio: Christian Pub. House, 1884),
p. 177.   DHU/MO

The Crisis (20:2, Je., 1920), pp. 90-92.   DHU/MO

Henry F. Kletzing. Progress of a Race (Atlanta: J. L.
Nichols & Co., 1898), p. 581.   DHU/MO

Richard R. Wright. Bishops of the A. M. E. Church (Nashville: A. M. E. Sunday School Union, 1963), pp. 317-22.
                                                       DHU/R

William N. Hartshorn. An Era of Progress and Promise
(Boston: Priscilla Pub. Co., 1910), p. 408.   DHU/MO

SMITH, DAVID

Benjamin W. Arnett. The Budget... Biographical Sketches
Proceeding... (Dayton, O.: Christian Publishing House,
1882), p. 127.   DHU/MO
A. M. E. minister.

Biography of Rev. David Smith, of the A. M. E. Church;
Being a Complete History, Embracing Over Sixty Years
Labor in the Advancement of the Redeemer's Kingdom on
Earth. Including "The History of the Origin and Development
of Wilberforce University" (Xenia, O.: Pr. at the Xenia
Gazette Office, 1881).   NN/Sch

SMITH, E. N.

G. F. Richings. Evidences of Progress Among Colored
People (Phila.: G. S. Ferguson, 1904), p. 70.
                                       DHU/R; DHU/MO
Baptist minister and Principal of Howe Institute, New Iberia,
La.

SMITH, EZEKIEL EZRA

James L. Nichols. The New Progress of a Race (Naperville,
Ill.: J. L. Nichols & Co., 1929), p. 431-32.   DHU/MO
Baptist minister. Resident and Consul-General of Liberia,
president of Farmer's and Mechanic's Building & Loan Assoc.
and Cape Fear Investment Co.

SMITH, G. W.

Samuel W. Bacote. Who's Who Among the Colored Baptists (Kansas City, Mo.: F. Hudson Co., 1912), pp. 96-97.
DHU/MO
"Pioneer minister", Texas.

SMITH, HARDIN

Samuel W. Bacote. Who's Who Among the Colored Baptists (Kansas City, Mo.: F. Hudson Co., 1912), pp. 82-83.
DHU/MO
"Pioneer preacher", organizer of ten Baptist churches.

SMITH, J. BRINTON

G. F. Richings. Evidences of Progress Among Colored People (Phila.: G. S. Ferguson, 1904), p. 95.
DHU/MO; DHU/R
Episcopal minister of the diocese of Pennsylvania and founder of St. Augustine's School, Raleigh, N. C.

SMITH, JOHN W., (bp

David H. Bradley, Sr. A History of the A. M. E. Zion Church 1872-1968 V. 2 (Nashville: Parthenon Press, 1970), pp. 390-91.
DHU/R
Bishop of the A. M. E. Zion Church and editor of the Star of Zion

G. F. Richings. Evidences of Progress Among Colored People (Phila.: G. S. Ferguson, 1904), p. 357.
DHU/R; DHU/MO

James W. Hood. One Hundred Years of the A. M. E. Zion Church (N. Y.: A. M. E. Zion Book Concern, 1895), pp. 240-43.
DHU/MO; DHU/R

William N. Hartshorn. An Era of Progress and Promise (Boston: Priscilla Pub. Co., 1910), p. 398.
DHU/MO

SMITH, JOSEPH

Presbyterian Reunion: 1837-1871 (N. Y.: De W. C. Lent & Co., 1870), pp. 148-53.
DHU/MO
Presbyterian minister and president of Franklin College, Harrison County, Ohio.

SMITH, KELLY MILLER, SR.

The editors of Ebony. The Ebony Success Library: 1,000 Successful Blacks (Nashville: The Southwestern Co., 1973), Vol. 1, p. 285.
DHU
Baptist minister and pastor of First Baptist Church, Nashville, Tenn.

SMITH, KENNETH B.

The editors of Ebony. The Ebony Success Library: 1,000 Successful Blacks (Nashville: The Southwestern Co., 1973), Vol. 1, p. 285.
DHU
United Church of Christ minister and pastor of Church of the Good Shepherd in Chicago, Ill.

SMITH, LORENZO

William Hicks. The History of Louisiana Negro Baptists from 1804-1914 (Nashville, Tenn.: National Baptist Publishing Board, n.d.), pp. 153-54.
DHU/R
Baptist minister.

SMITH, OWEN W. L.

James J. Pipkin. The Negro in Revelation, in History, and in Citizenship (N. Y.: Thompson Pub. Co., 1902), p. 335.
DHU/MO
A. M. E. Zion minister.

James W. Hood. One Hundred Years of the A. M. E. Zion Church (N. Y.: A. M. E. Zion Book Concern, 1895), pp. 287-89.
DHU/MO

Leila A. Pendleton. A Narrative of the Negro (Wash., D. C.: Press of R. L. Pendleton, 1912), p. 50.
DHU/MO

SMITH, S. P.

Irvine G. Penn. The Afro-American Press and Its Editors (Springfield, Mass.: Willey & Co., 1891), p. 152.
DHU/R; DHU/MO
Editor of The People's Advocate and minister.

SMITH, SILAS

E. R. Carter. The Black Side. (Atlanta: n.p., 1894), pp. 103-04.
DHU/MO
Negro Baptist minister.

SMITH, SIMON

A Sketch of the Life, Death and Funeral of the Rev. Simon Smith, a Man of Colour and a Member of the Methodist Episcopal Church (n.p.: n.p., [1818]).
NN/Sch
Minister of the Methodist Episcopal Church.

SMITH, STEPHEN

G. F. Richings. Evidences of Progress Among Colored People. (Phila.: G. S. Ferguson, 1904), pp. 407-08.
DHU/MO; DHU/R
Businessman and Methodist Episcopal minister of Philadelphia.

Benjamin T. Tanner. An Apology for African Methodism. (Balto.: n.p., 1867), pp. 196-99.
DHU/MO

Henry F. Kletzing. Progress of a Race (Atlanta: J. L. Nichols & Co., 1898), p. 581.
DHU/MO

Leila A. Pendleton. Narrative of the Negro. (Wash., D. C.: Press of R. L. Pendleton, 1912), p. 129.
DHU/MO

William W. Brown. The Rising Son. (Boston: A. G. Brown & Co., 1874), pp. 545-47.
DHU/MO; DHU/R

SMITH, VINCENT (Father Mary Simon)

Albert S. Foley. God's Men of Color (New York: Farrar, Straus & Co., 1955), pp. 139-48.
DHU/R
Negro trappist priest, 1894-1952.

SNELSON, F. G.

William H. Heard. The Bright Side of African Life (N. Y.: Negro Universities Press, 1969), p. 179.
DHU/R
A. M. E. minister in Sierra Leone, Liberia.

SPILLER, RICHARD

G. F. Richings. Evidences of Progress Among Colored People (Phila.: G. S. Ferguson, 1904), p. 70.
DHU/R; DHU/MO
Baptist minister, Virginia. Organizer of Virginia Baptist State Convention.

(Spiller, Richard cont.)

Lewis G. Jordan. Negro Baptist History U. S. A. (Nashville, Tenn.: Sunday School Publishing Board, N. B. C., 1930), p. 392.   DHU/R; DHU/MO

STARR, FREDERICK, JR.

Presbyterian Reunion: 1837-1871 (N. Y.: De W. C. Lent & Co., 1870), pp. 240-43.   DHU/MO
Presbyterian minister and missionary of Missouri.

STEELE, ROBERT W.

Presbyterian Reunion: 1837-1871 (N. Y.: De W. C. Lent & Co., 1870), p. 526.   DHU/MO
Presbyterian minister of Dayton, Ohio; trustee of Miami Univ. and director in Lane Theological Seminary.

STEPHENSON, JOHN W.

William J. Simmons. Men of Mark (Cleveland, O.: George M. Rewell & Co., 1887), p. 820.   DHU/R
A. M. E. minister and physician.

STEVENSON, ALLEN

William Hicks. The History of Louisiana Negro Baptists from 1804-1914 (Nashville, Tenn.: National Baptist Publishing Board, n. d.), p. 156.   DHU/R
Baptist minister and president of the Board of Trustees of Leland Academy, Donaldsonville, La.

STEWARD, AUSTIN

Twenty-two Years a Slave and Forty Years a Freeman (Rochester, N. Y.: Alling, 1857.)   DHU/MO
(Name sometimes spelled Stewart.) Ex-slave and A. M. E. minister.

Leila A. Pendleton, A Narrative of the Negro (Wash., D. C.: Press of R. L. Pendleton, 1912), p. 147.   DHU/MO
Name sometimes spelled Stewart.

STEWARD, THEOPHILUS GOULD

The African Methodist Episcopal Church Review (78:212, Apr.-Je., 1962), p. 77.   DHU/R
A. M. E. minister

STEWARD, WILLIAM H.

Samuel W. Bacote. Who's Who Among the Colored Baptists (Kansas City, Mo.: F. Hudson Co., 1912), pp. 281-82.
                                                          DHU/MO
Secretary of Natl. Baptist Convention, Sunday-School missionary and editor of American Baptist.

STEWART, CHARLES

Samuel W. Bacote. Who's Who Among the Colored Baptists (Kansas City, Mo.: F. Hudson Co., 1912), pp. 277-78.
                                                          DHU/MO
"Journalist and press agent for the National Baptist Convention and the Negro race."

STEWART, DARNEAU V.

The editors of Ebony. The Ebony Success Library: 1,000 Successful Blacks (Nashville: The Southwestern Co., 1973), Vol. 1, p. 292.   DHU
A. M. E. minister and pastor of People's Community Church, Detroit, Mich.

STEWART, GEORGE W.

Charles H. Phillips. History of the Colored Methodist Episcopal Church (Jackson, Tenn.: Pub. House C. M. E. Church, 1898), pp. 564-66.   DHU/MO
C. M. E. minister.

STEWART, J. W.

Samuel W. Bacote. Who's Who Among Colored Baptists (Kansas City, Mo.: F. Hudson Co., 1912), pp. 214-15.
                                                          DHU/MO
Baptist minister and missionary of Oklahoma.

STEWART, JOHN

Carter G. Woodson. The History of the Negro Church (Wash., D. C.: Associated Publishers, 1921), pp. 49-52.
                                                          DHU/R; DHU/MO
Methodist Episcopal minister.
Evangelist to Wyandot Indians.

John H. Satterwhite. "John Stewart and the Mission to the Wyandott Indians." Forever Beginning (Lake Junaluska, N. C.: Association of Methodist Historical Societies, 1967).
                                                          DHU/R

Joseph Mitchell. A Missionary Pioneer or a Brief Memoir of the Life and Labors and Death of John Stewart (Man of Color) Founder Under God of the Missions Among the Wyandotts, at Upper Sandusky, Ohio (New York: J. C. Totten, 1827).   TAMph; DLC; DHU/R; DHU/MO

STEWART, THOMAS MCCANTS

African Methodist Episcopal Church Review (71:185, Jl.-Spt., 1955), pp. 70-71.   DHU/R
A. M. E. minister, lawyer and author.

STILLS, E. S.

William Hicks. The History of Louisiana Negro Baptists From 1804-1914 (Nashville, Tenn.: National Baptist Publishing Board, n. d.), p. 186.   DHU/R
Baptist minister.

STILLWELL, W. M.

James J. Pipkin. The Negro in Revelation, in History and in Citizenship (N. Y.: Thompson Pub. Co., 1902), p. 89.
                                                          DHU/MO
A. M. E. Zion minister.

STITT, R. HAYWOOD

James W. Hood. Centennial of African Methodism (N. Y.: A. M. E. Zion Book Concern, 1895), pp. 420-23. DHU/MO
A. M. E. Zion minister and founder and organizer of youth organizations ... Progressive Literary, Sons and Daughters of Zion and Christian Endeavor.

STOKES, ANDREW J.

Lewis G. Jordan. Negro Baptist History U. S. A. (Nashville, Tenn.: Sunday School Publishing Board N. B. C., 1930), p. 392.   DHU/MO
Baptist minister, editor of South Carolina Baptist and Helping Hand, president of Montgomery Academy, treasurer of National Baptist Convention.

Samuel B. Bacote. Who's Who Among the Colored Baptists (Kansas City, Mo.: F. Hudson Co., 1912), pp. 38-39.
                                                          DHU/MO

STRONG, J. W.

Samuel W. Bacote. Who's Who Among Colored Baptists (Kansas City, Mo.: F. Hudson Co., 1912), pp. 179-80.
DHU/MO
Baptist minister and president of Central Texas College.

STROYER, JACOB

William L. Katz, (ed.). Five Slave Narratives (New York: Arno Press, 1969).   DHU/MO
A. M. E. minister

STULMM, C. C.

Irvine G. Penn. The Afro-American Press (Springfield, Mass.: Wiley & Co., 1891), pp. 248-54.   DHU/R; DHU/MO
President of Bowling Green Academy and Baptist minister. Editor of The Baptist Moniter and The Christian Banner, children's column of the American Baptist.

SULLIVAN, LEON H.

Phyl Garland. "The Unorthodox Ministry of Leon Sullivan." Ebony (26:7, My., 1971), pp. 112-20. Pam. File, DHU/R
Negro Baptist minister founder of O. I. C.

The editors of Ebony. The Ebony Success Library: 1, 000 Successful Blacks (Nashville: The Southwestern Co., 1973), Vol. 1, p. 296.   DHU

SUMPTER, Q. T.

William Hicks. The History of Louisiana Negro Baptists from 1804-1914 (Nashville, Tenn.: National Baptist Publishing Board, n.d.), p. 191.   DHU/R
Baptist minister.

SWANN, DARIUS LEANDER

Frank T. Wilson. "Living Witnesses: Black Presbyterians in Ministry." Journal of Presbyterian History (151:4, Wint., 1973), pp. 386-89.   DHU/R
Presbyterian missionary to India, China and theology professor.

SWANN, J. B.

G. F. Richings. Evidences of Progress Among Colored People [Phila.: G. S. Ferguson, 1904), pp. 184-5.   DHU/R; DHU/MO
Presbyterian minister and educator.

SWANN, VERA POE

Frank T. Wilson. "Living Witnesses: Black Presbyterians in Ministry." Journal of Presbyterian History (51:4, Wint., 1973), pp. 386-89.   DHU/R
Missionary to India, China and civil rights activist.

TALBOT, SAMPSON DUNBAR, (bp.).

William W. Brown. The Rising Son (Boston: A. G. Brown & Co., 1874), pp. 549-50.   DHU/MO; DHU/R
Bishop of the A. M. E. Zion Church.

James W. Good. One Hundred Years of the African Methodist Episcopal Church (N. Y.: A. M. E. Zion Book Concern, 1895), pp. 184-85.   DHU/MO

TALIAFERRO, GRANVILLE L. P.

Lewis G. Jordan. Negro Baptist History U. S. A. (Nashville, Tenn.: Sunday School Publishing Board, N. B. C., 1930), p. 152.   DHU/R; DHU/MO
Baptist minister owned and edited the Christian Banner. Organized the Banner Publishing Co., Banner Real Estate Co., Northern Aid Society - an insurance company. Director in Republic Trust Co.

TANNER, BENJAMIN TUCKER, (bp.).

Richard R. Wright. Bishops of the A. M. E. Church (Nashville: A. M. E. Sunday School Union, 1963), pp. 323-26.
DHU/R
Eighteenth Bishop of the A. M. E. Church and author.

G. F. Richings. Evidences of Progress Among Colored People. (Phila.: G. S. Ferguson, 1904), p. 384.
DHU/MO; DHU/R

Henry F. Kletzing. Progress of a Race. (Atlanta: J. L. Nichols & Co., 1898), pp. 500-01.   DHU/MO

Irvine G. Penn. The Afro-American Press and Its Editors (Springfield, Mass.: Willey & Co., 1891), pp. 120-21.
DHU/MO; DHU/R

James J. Pipkin. The Negro in Revelation in History and in Citizenship (New York: Thompson Pub. Co., 1902), pp. 104-05.   DHU/MO

Leila A. Pendleton. A Narrative of the Negro (Wash., D. C.: Press of R. L. Pendleton, 1912), p. 173.   DHU/MO

William J. Simmons. Men of Mark (Cleveland, Ohio: Rewell & Co., 1887), p. 985.   DHU/R; DHU/MO

William N. Hartshorn. An Era of Progress and Promise (Boston: Priscilla Publishing Co., 1910), p. 407.   DHU/MO

William W. Brown. The Rising Son (Boston: A. G. Brown & Co., 1874), pp. 530-31.   DHU/R

TAPPAN, JOHN, (bp.).

John J. Moore. History of the A. M. E. Zion Church in America (York, Pa.: Teachers Journal Office, 1884), p. 367.
DHU/MO
A. M. E. Zion bishop.

TATE, HENRY W.

Wendell P. Dabney. Cincinnati's Colored Citizens (Cincinnati, Ohio: The Dabney Pub. Co., 1926), pp. 301-02.
DHU/MO
Methodist Episcopal minister and teacher.

TATE, JAMES

E. R. Carter. The Black Side (Atlanta: n.p., 1894),
DHU/MO
Negro Baptist minister. Present at the Formation of the first Colored Baptist Church in Atlanta in 1868.

TAYLOR, BARTLETT

William J. Simmons. Men of Mark (Cleveland, Ohio: Rewell & Co., 1887), pp. 626-30.   DHU/R; DHU/MO
A. M. E. minister.

TAYLOR, G. E.

Evidences of Progress Among Colored People (Phila.: G. S.
Ferguson, 1904), p. 389.   DHU/MO; DHU/R
A. M. E. minister and editor of the Southern Christian.

TAYLOR, GARDNER C.

Marcus H. Boulware. The Oratory of Negro Leaders 1900-
1968 (Westport, Conn.: Negro Universities Press, 1969), p.
197.   DHU/MO; DHU/R
Black Baptist minister and former president of Progressive
National Baptist Convention, Inc.

TAYLOR, JORDAN

William Hicks. The History of Louisiana Negro Baptists from
1804-1914 (Nashville, Tenn.: National Baptist Publishing
Board, n.d.), pp. 191-93.   DHU/R
Baptist minister.

TAYLOR, MARSHALL W.

Irvine G. Penn. The Afro-American Press and Its Editors
(Springfield, Mass.: Willey & Co., 1891), p. 132+.
                                              DHU/MO; DHU/R
Editor of the Southwestern Christian Advocate and the Ken-
tucky Methodist.
Minister of the A. M. E. Church.

(Indianapolis) Freeman (1:29, Mr. 9, 1889),   DHU/MO

Leila A. Pendleton. A Narrative of the Negro (Wash., D.
C.: Press of R. L. Pendleton, 1912), p. 177.   DHU/R

William J. Simmons. Men of Mark (Cleveland: O. Rewell,
1887), p. 933.   DHU/R; DHU/MO

TAYLOR, PRESTON

William J. Simmons. Men of Mark (Cleveland, Ohio: Rewell
& Co., 1887), pp. 296-301.   DHU/R; DHU/MO
Disciples of Christ minister.

G. F. Richings. Evidences of Progress Among Colored
People (Philadelphia: G. S. Ferguson, 1904), pp. 269-70.
                                              DHU/MO

Henry D. Northrop. College of Life (Phila.: Nat. Pub. Co.,
1895), p. 48.   DHU/MO

James T. Haley. Afro-American Encyclopaedia (Nashville:
Halley & Florida, 1895), pp. 215-20.   DHU/MO

William N. Hartshorn. An Era of Progress and Promise
(Boston, Mass.: Priscilla Publishing Co., 1910), p. 445.
                                              DHU/MO

TAYLOR, ROBERT

William Hicks. The History of Louisiana Negro Baptists from
1804-1914. (Nashville, Tenn.: National Baptist Publishing
Board, n.d.), p. 188.   DHU/R
Baptist minister.

TAYLOR, W. M.

William Hicks. History of Louisiana Negro Baptists from
1804-1914 (Nashville, Tenn.: National Baptist Publishing
Board, n.d.), pp. 135-38.   DHU/R
Baptist minister; Vice-President of La. State Baptist Convention.

TAYLOR, WILLIAM L.

William N. Hartshorn. An Era of Progress and Promise
(Boston: Priscilla Publishing Co., 1910), p. 455. DHU/MO
Ex-slave, Baptist minister, Grand Master of the United
Order of True Reformers, and member of the executive com-
mittee of National Negro Business League.

G. F. Richings. Evidences of Progress Among Colored
People (Phila., Pa.: G. S. Ferguson, 1904), pp. 336-37.
                                              DHU/MO; DHU/R

TEFFT, LYMAN B.

G. F. Richings. Evidences of Progress Among Colored
People (Phila.: G. S. Ferguson, 1904), p. 34.
                                              DHU/R; DHU/MO
Baptist minister and president of Hartshorn Memorial College,
Richmond, Va.

TELESFORO, ISAAC, (bp.).

The Episcopal Church Annual (New York: Morehouse-Barlow,
1973), p. 239.   PPPD; ViAlTH
Protestant Episcopal bishop of Panama.

TEMPLETON, BENJAMIN FRANKLIN

Martin R. Delany. The Condition, Elevation, Emigration and
Destiny of the Colored People of the United States (New York:
Arno Press, 1968), pp. 126-27.   DHU/R; DHU/MO
Presbyterian minister.

TERESA JULIANA OF SAINT DOMINIC, (Chicaba)

John Joseph O'Gorman. "Chicaba: the African Princess,
Who later Became Ven. Sister Teresa Juliana of Saint Dominic." Missionary Annals, Rathmines (6; 1924); (7; 1925),
pp. 208-10+; 10-12.

THEOBALD, STEPHEN L.

Albert S. Foley. God's Men of Color (New York: Farrar,
Straus & Co., 1955), pp. 95-103.   DHU/R
Catholic priest.

THIRKIELD, WILBUR P., (bp.).

William H. Ferris. African Abroad V. 2 (New Haven:
Tuttle, Morehouse, & Taylor Press, 1913), p. 789. DHU/MO
President of Howard University and bishop of the M. E.
Church.

G. F. Richings. Evidences of Progress Among Colored
People (Phila.: G. S. Ferguson, 1904), p. 188.
                                              DHU/MO; DHU/R

THISTLE, TAYLOR

James H. O'Sonnell. Journal of Southern History (33; Feb.,
1967), pp. 68-84.   DHU
A former slave's letters (1872-1873) of thanks to those who
helped him in his training as a minister.

THOMAS, EDGAR GARFIELD

Edgar G. Thomas. The First African Baptist Church of North
America (Savannah, Ga.: By the author, 1925), pp. 122-31.
                                              DHU/MO
Baptist minister.

THOMAS, J.

U. S. Dept. of Education. Special Report (Wash., D. C.:
Government Printing Office, 1871), p. 286.   DHU/MO
Baptist minister and teacher.

THOMAS, JACOB

James W. Hood. Centennial of African Methodism (N. Y.:
A. M. E. Zion Book Concern, 1895), pp. 223-26. DHU/MO
A. M. E. Zion minister.

THOMAS, JAMES S., (bp.).

The editors of Ebony. The Ebony Success Library: 1, 000 Suc-
cessful Blacks (Nashville: The Southwestern Co., 1973),
Vol. 1, p. 302.   DHU
Bishop of Iowa area of United Methodist Church.

THOMAS, JOHN WESLEY

James W. Hood. One Hundred Years of A. M. E. Zion Church
(N. Y.: A. M. E. Zion Book Concern, 1895), pp. 584-86.
                                         DHU/MO

A. M. E. Zion minister.

THOMAS, M. G.

James W. Hood. One Hundred Years of the A. M. E. Zion
Church (N. Y.: A. M. E. Zion Book Concern, 1895), pp.
619-20.   DHU/MO
A. M. E. Zion minister and editor of Alabama Guide, Alabama
Enterprise and Southern Review.

THOMPSON, ABRAHAM

Leila A. Pendleton. A Narrative of the Negro (Wash., D. C.:
Press of R. L. Pendleton, 1912), p. 97.   DHU/MO
Co-organizer of New York City branch of A. M. E. Zion
Church.

THOMPSON, JOSEPH P., (bp.).

James W. Hood. Centennial of African Methodism. (N. Y.:
A. M. E. Zion Book Concern, 1895), pp. 188-91. DHU/MO
Ex-slave and Bishop of the A. M. E. Zion Church.

John J. Moore. History of A. M. E. Zion Church in America
(York, Pa.: Teachers Journal Office, 1884), pp. 375-76.
                                         DHU/MO

THORNE, VANCE

Albert S. Foley. God's Men of Color (New York: Farrar,
Straus & Co., 1955), p. 303.   DHU/R
Catholic priest.

THURMAN, HOWARD

Marcus H. Boulware. The Oratory of Negro Leaders, 1900-
1968 (Westport, Conn.: Negro Univerisities Press, 1969), p.
184.   DHU/MO
Minister, author, professor and former dean of Marsh Chapel,
Boston University School of Theology.

The editors of Ebony. The Ebony Success Library: 1, 000 Successful Blacks (Nashville: The Southwestern Co., 1973),
Vol. 1, p. 304.   DHU

Elizabeth Yates. Portrait of a Practical Dreamer (New York:
John Day Co., 1964).   DHU/R

Toward Wholeness (1:1, Sum., 1972), p. 12.   DHU/R

Wilhelmena S. Robinson. Historical Negro Biographies (N.
Y.: Publishers Co., 1967), pp. 251-52.   DHU/MO

TINDLEY, CHARLES A.

The Crisis (24:2, Je., 1922), p. 79.   DHU/MO; DLC
Pastor of East Calvary M. E. church of Philadelphia, P.

TOLBERT, JAMES T.

Lewis G. Jordan. Negro Baptist History U. S. A. (Nashville,
Tenn.: Sunday School Publishing Board N. B. C., 1930), p.
392.   DHU/R; DHU/MO
Baptist minister, Georgia. Moderator of Storm Branch Association of S. C., treasurer of Georgia State Convention.

TOLTON, AUGUSTINE

Albert S. Foley. God's Men of Color (New York: Farrar,
Straus & Co., 1955), pp. 32-41.   DHU/R
Catholic priest and missionary.

Caroline Hemesath. From Slave to Priest: A Biography of
the Rev. Augustine Tolton (1854-1897), First Black Priest in
Illinois (Chicago: Franciscan Herald Press, 1973).   DHU/R

The Crisis (10:3, Je., 1915), p. 116.   DHU/MO; DLC

Henry D. Northrop. College of Life (Phila.: National Pub.
Co., 1895), pp. 47-48.   DHU/MO

Wilhelmena S. Robinson. Historical Negro Biographies (N.
Y.: Publishers Co., 1967), pp. 129-30.   DHU/MO

William J. Simmons. Men of Mark (Cleveland, Ohio: Revell
& Co., 1887), pp. 439-46.   DHU/R; DHU/MO

TONEY, G. W.

William Hicks. History of Louisiana Negro Baptists from 1804-
1914. (Nashville, Tenn.: National Baptist Publishing Board,
n.d.), p. 194.   DHU/R
Baptist minister.

TOOKES, HENRY YOUNG, (bp.).

Richard Robert Wright, Jr., (bp.). Bishops of the A. M. E.
Church. (Nashville: A. M. E. Sunday School Union, 1963),
pp. 327-28.   DHU/R
Fifty-sixth Bishop of the A. M. E. Church

TOPP, E. B.

Lewis G. Jordan. Negro Baptist History U. S. A. (Nashville, Tenn.: Sunday School Publishing Board, N. B. C.,
1930), p. 392.   DHU/MO; DHU/R
Baptist minister, Mississippi. African missionary, Pres.
of his state convention.

TOWNSEND, D. A.

Lewis G. Jordan. Negro Baptist History U. S. A. (Nashville,
Tenn.: Sunday School Publishing Board N. B. C., 1930), p.
392.   DHU/R; DHU/MO
Baptist minister, Tenn.

TOWNSEND, JAMES MATTHEW

William J. Simmons, (ed.). Men of Mark... (Cleveland, O.:
George M. Rewell & Co., 1887), pp. 1135-38.
                                                    DHU/R; DHU/MO
African Methodist Episcopal minister.

Benjamin W. Arnett. The Budget... Biographical Sketches
Proceeding... (Dayton: Christian Pub. House, 1884), pp.
141+.   DHU/R; DHU/MO

Henry D. Northrop. The College of Life. (Phila.: Nat. Pub.
Co., 1895), pp. 36-39.   DHU/MO

TRIMBLE, J. H.

James W. Hood. One Hundred Years of the A. M. E. Zion
Church (N. Y.: A. M. E. Zion Book Concern, 1895), pp.
596-97.   DHU/MO
A. M. E. Zion minister.

TROY, WILLIAM

Lewis G. Jordan. Negro Baptist History U. S. A. (Nashville,
Tenn.: Sunday School Publishing Board N. B. C., 1930), p.
392.   DHU/R; DHU/MO
Baptist minister, among first missionaries sent to the South
by the American Baptist Missionary Convention.

Henry F. Kletzing. Progress of a Race (Atlanta, Ga.: J. L.
Nichols & Co., 1898), p. 581.   DHU/MO

TUGGLE, WILLIAM H.

E. R. Carter. The Black Side (Atlanta: n.p., 1894), pp. 80-
82.   DHU/MO
Black Baptist minister.

TUNNELL, WILLIAM V.

William H. Ferris. African Abroad V. 2 (New Haven, Conn.:
Tuttle, Morehouse, & Taylor Press, 1913), p. 796.
Episcopal minister, president of King Hall, an Episcopal Theo-
logical Seminary in Washington, D. C.

TUPPER, H. M.

G. F. Richings. Evidences of Progress Among Colored
People (Phila.: G. S. Ferguson, 1904), p. 30.
                                         DHU/R; DHU/MO
Baptist minister and founder of Shaw University, Raleigh,
N. C.

Henry F. Kletzing. Progress of a Race (Atlanta: J. L.
Nichols & Co., 1898), p. 404.   DHU/MO

TURNER, HENRY MCNEAL, (bp.).

Richard Robert Wright, Jr., (bp.). Bishops of the A. M. E.
Church (Nashville: A. M. E. Church (Nashville: A. M. E.
Sunday School Union, 1963), pp. 329-41. DHU/R
Twelfth Bishop of the African Methodist Episcopal Church.

African Methodist Episcopal Church Review (78: 212, Ja.-
Mr., 1963), pp. 53-4.   DHU/R

Benjamin T. Tanner. An Apology for African Methodism
(Baltimore, n.p., 1867), p. 412.   DHU/MO

Benjamin W. Arnett. The Budget... Biographical Sketches
Preceeding... (Dayton: Christian Pub. House, 1882), p. 23.
                                         DHU/MO

Bishop Turner's Quarto Centennial (n.p.: n.p., 1905).
                                         DHU/MO
Tributes to Bishop by many ministers.

Carey H. Wynne. Bishop Henry McNeal Turner and Pan-
Africanism: Reinterpretations of the American Protestant
Experience, 1861-1898 (Doctoral dissertation. University of
Chicago, 1972).

Charles Alexander. One Hundred Distinguished Leaders
(Atlanta: Franklin Printing & Publishing Co., 1899), p. 66.
                                         DHU/MO

Church History (7:3, Sept., 1938), pp. 231-46. DHU/R

Daniel W. Culp. Twentieth Century Negro Literature (Atlanta,
Ga.: Nicholson & Co., 1902), p. 43.   DHU/MO

E. A. Johnson. School History of the Negro Race in America
(Raleigh: Edward & Broughton Printers, 1890), pp. 172-73.
                                         DHU/R; DHU/MO

Dictionary of American Biography (New York: 1928-36), pp.
65-66.   DHU

Edward A. Johnson. History of Negro Soldiers in the Spanish
American War (Raleigh: Capital Printing Co., 1899), p. 113.
                                         DHU/MO

Edwin S. Redkey. "The Flowering of Black Nationalism:
Henry McNeal Turner and Marcus Garvey." Nathan I. Huggins, (ed.). Key Issues in the Afro-American Experience
V. 1 (New York: Harcourt Brace Jovanovich, Inc. 1971), pp.
107-24.   DHU/MO

Edwin S. Redkey. Henry McNeal Turner; Bishop of the African Methodist Episcopal Church (Doctoral dissertation. Yale
University, 1967).

Encyclopedia Britannica Educational Corp., 1969. 54 fr.
color. 35 mm.   DLC
Filmstrip.

G. F. Richings. Evidences of Progress Among Colored People
(Phila.: G. S. Ferguson, 1904), pp. 136+. DHU/R; DHU/MO

Henry D. Northrop. The College of Life (Phila.: Nat. Pub.
Co., 1895), pp. 29-30.   DHU/MO

Henry F. Kletzing. Progress of a Race (Atlanta: J. L.
Nichols & Co., 1898), pp. 498-99+.   DHU/MO

Irvine G. Penn. The Afro-American Press and Its Editors
(Springfield, Mass.: Willey & Co., 1891), pp. 356-60.
                                         DHU/R; DHU/MO

James J. Pipkin. The Negro in Revelation in History and in
Citizenship (New York: Thompson Pub. Co., 1902), pp. 98-
100.   DHU/MO

Jane Herndon. "Henry McNeal Turner's African Dream: A Re-
evaluation." Mississippi Quarterly (33; Fall, 1969).
                                         DAU; DGW

Journal of Religious Education (30:1, Sept., 1969), p. 4.
                                         DHU/R

Josephus Roosevelt Coan. "Henry McNeal Turner: A Fearless Prophet of Black Liberation." Journal of the Interdenominational Theological Center (1:1, Fall, 1973), pp. 8-20.
                                         DHU/R

Leila A. Pendleton. A Narrative of the Negro (Wash., D. C.:
Press of R. L. Pendleton, 1912), p. 177. DHU/MO

Merton E. Coulter. Georgia Historical Quarterly (48; Dec.,
1964), pp. 371-410.   DGW

Wilhemena S. Robinson. Historical Negro Biographies (New York: Publishers Co., 1967), pp. 132-3.   DHU/MO

M. M. Ponton. Life and Times of Henry M. Turner. The Antecedent & Preliminary History of the Life & Times of Bishop H. M. Turner, His Boyhood Education & Public Career... (Atlanta: A. B. Caldwell Pub., 1917.)   DHU/MO; DHU/R

William H. Heard. The Bright Side of African Life (New York: Negro Universities Press, 1969), p. 92.   DHU/R

William N. Hartshorn. An Era of Progress and Promise (Boston: The Priscilla Publishing Co., 1910), pp. 388-89.   DHU/MO

William W. Brown. The Rising Son (Boston: A. G. Brown & Co., 1874), pp. 504-05.   DHU/R; DHU/MO

TURNER, JAMES H.

James T. Haley. Afro-American Encyclopaedia (Nashville: Haley & Florida, 1895), pp. 603-05.   DHU/MO
A. M. E. minister

TURNER, NAT

Joel A. Rogers. World's Great Men of Color V. 2 (New York: J. A. Rogers, 1947), pp. 325-31.   DHU/R; DHU/MO
Baptist minister and insurrection leader.

Edgar Toppin. A Biographical History of Blacks in America Since 1528 (N. Y.: David McKay Co., 1971), pp. 431-33.   DHU/R

TURNER, WILLIAM L.

James T. Haley. Afro-American Encyclopaedia (Nashville: Haley & Florida, 1895), pp. 579-80.   DHU/MO
Baptist minister and teacher.

TWIGGS, W. H.

Irvine G. Penn. The Afro-American Press and Its Editors (Springfield, Mass.: Willey & Co., 1891), p. 124.   DHU/MO; DHU/R
Minister and corresponding editor of the Afro-American Budget.

TYREE, EVANS, (bp.).

Richard Robert Wright, Jr., (bp.). Bishops of the A. M. E. Church. (Nashville: A. M. E. Sunday School Union, 1963), pp. 342-43.   DHU/R
Twenty-sixth Bishop of the A. M. E. Church

G. F. Richings. Evidences of Progress Among Colored People (Phila.: G. S. Ferguson, 1904), p. 388.   DHU/R; DHU/MO

William N. Hartshorn. An Era of Progress and Promise (Boston: Priscilla Pub. Co., n.d.), p. 390.   DHU/MO

UNCLES, CHARLES RANDOLPH

Albert S. Foley. God's Men of Color (New York: Farrar, Straus & Co., 1955), pp. 42-51.   DHU/R
First Negro Josephite Catholic priest.

UNDERHILL, IRVIN WINDFIELD, JR.

Frank T. Wilson. "Living Witnesses: Black Presbyterians in Ministry." Journal of Presbyterian History (51:4, Wint., 1973), pp. 364-67.   DHU/R
Presbyterian minister and missionary to West Africa

VALENTINE, GEORGE

William T. Catto. Semi-Centenary Discourse (Phila.: Joseph M. Wilson, 1857), p. 108.   DHU/R
Founder and minister John Wesley M. E. Church, Philadelphia.

VANDERHORST, RICHARD H.

Charles N. Phillips. History of Colored Methodist Episcopal Church (Jackson, Tenn.: Publishing House of the A. M. E. Church, 1898), pp. 204-08.   DHU/MO; DHU/R
C. M. E. minister.

VANDERVALL, RANDALL BARTHOLOMEW

William J. Simmons, (ed.). Men of Mark (Cleveland, O.: Geo. M. Rewell & Co., 1887), p. 572.   DHU/R

VANN, MICHAEL

James T. Haley. Afro-American Encyclopaedia (Nashville: Haley & Florida, 1895), pp. 605-09.   DHU/MO
Baptist minister and educator.

Lewis G. Jordan. Negro Baptist History U. S. A. (Nashville, Tenn.: Sunday School Pub. Board, 1930), p. 392.   DHU/MO; DHU/R

VARICK, JAMES, (bp.).

Carter G. Woodson. The History of the Negro Church (Wash., D. C.: Associated Publishers, 1921), p. 68+.   DHU/MO; DHU/R
One of the founders and first Bishop of the A. M. E. Zion Church.

B. F. Wheeler. The Varick Family (Pittsburgh: A. M. E. Zion Church, 1966).   DHU/R

Benjamin Brawley. Negro Builders and Heroes (Chapel Hill: Univ. of N. C. Press, 1937), pp. 198-99.   DHU/MO; DHU/R

Dictionary of American Biography (New York: Scribners), V. 19, pp. 225-26.   NcSalL; DHU

James B. F. Shaw. The Negro in the History of Methodism (Nashville: Parthenon Press, 1954), p. 76.   DHU/R

James W. Hood. Centennial of African Methodism (N. Y.: A. M. E. Zion Book Concern, 1895), pp. 162-68.   DHU/MO

John J. Moore. History of A. M. E. Zion Church in America (York, Pa.: Teachers Office, 1884), pp. 347-49.   DHU/MO

Leila A. Pendleton. A Narrative of the Negro (Wash., D. C.: Press of R. L. Pendleton, 1920), p. 97.

Negro History Bulletin (1; 1937); (5; 1941), p. 5; p. 28.   DHU/R

Richard Bardolph. "Social Origins of Distinguished Negroes, 1770-1865." Journal of Negro History (40:3, Jl., 1955), p. 223.   DHU/MO

(Varick, James, (bp.) cont.)

    W. H. Quick. Negro Stars in All Ages of the World (Richmond: Adkins, 1898), p. 115.   DHU/MO

    Wilhelmena S. Robinson. Historical Negro Biographies (N. Y.: Publishers Co., 1967), pp. 35-36.   DHU/MO

VAUGHN, C. C.

    William J. Simmons. Men of Mark... (Cleveland, O.: George M. Rewell, 1887), pp. 723-28.   DHU/R; DHU/MO
    Baptist minister and educator.

VERNON, WILLIAM TECUMSEH, (bp.).

    Richard Robert Wright, Jr., (bp.). Bishops of the A. M. E. Church. (Nashville: A. M. E. Sunday School Union, 1963), pp. 344-46.   DHU/R
    Forty-fifth Bishop of the A. M. E. Church

VIEIRA, ANTONIO

    World's Great Men of Color V. 2 (N. Y.: J. A. Rogers, 1947), pp. 40-53.   DHU/R
    Black Catholic priest and missionary of Portugal and Brazil.

VIVIAN, CORDY TINDELL

    The editors of Ebony. The Ebony Success Library: 1,000 Successful Blacks (Nashville: The Southwestern Co., 1973), Vol. 1, p. 314.   DHU
    Baptist minister and university minister at Shaw Univ., Raleigh, N. C.

WACTOR, JAMES W. WACTOR, (bp.).

    A. M. E. Zion Quarterly Review (84:3, Fall, 1972), pp. 162-63.   DHU/R
    Bishop of A. M. E. Zion Church.

WADDLES, CHARLESZETTA, (Mother)

    The editors of Ebony. The Ebony Success Library: 1,000 Successful Blacks (Nashville: The Southwestern Co., 1973), Vol. 1, p. 314.   DHU
    Evangelist of Detroit.

WADE, FRANCES GUY

    Albert S. Foley. God's Men of Color (New York: Farrar, Straus & Co., 1955), pp. 156-62.   DHU/R
    Catholic priest.

WAGNER, F. J.

    G. F. Richings. Evidences of Progress Among Colored People (Phila.: G. S. Ferguson, 1904), p. 112. DHU/R
    Methodist Episcopal minister and President of Morgan College, Baltimore, Md.

WALDEN, HARVEY E.

    African Methodist Episcopal Church Review (78:209, Jl. - Sept., 1961), pp. 66-67.   DHU/R
    A. M. E. minister.

WALDRON, J. MILTON

    William N. Hartshorn. An Era of Progress and Promise (Boston: Priscilla Publishing Co., 1910), p. 457.   DHU/MO
    Baptist minister and secretary of the Young Men's Christian Association.
    Baptist minister and secretary of the Young Men's Christian Association.

    William H. Ferris. African Abroad V. 2 (New Haven: Tuttle, Morehouse, & Taylor Press, 1913), p. 74. DHU/MO

WALKER, CHARLES T.

    Benjamin G. Brawley. Negro in Literature and Art (Atlanta, Ga.: n. p., 1910), p. 52.   DHU/MO
    Baptist minister, chaplain in the U. S. Army, and teacher.

    James L. Nichols. The New Progress of a Race (Naperville, Ill.: J. L. Nichols & Co., 1929), p. 442.   DHU/MO

    Leila A. Pendleton. A Narrative of the Negro (Wash., D. C.: Press of R. L. Pendleton, 1912), p. 184. DHU/MO

    Lewis G. Jordan. Negro Baptist History U. S. A. (Nashville, Tenn.: Sunday School Publishing Board, N. B. C., 1930), p. 392.   DHU/MO

    Samuel W. Bacote. Who's Who Among the Colored Baptists (Kansas City, Mo.: F. Hudson Co., 1912), pp. 43-46.   DHU/MO

    Silas Xavier. Life of Charles T. Walker, D. D. ("The Black Surgeon,") Pastor, Mt. Olivet Baptist Church (Nashville: National Baptist Publishing Board, 1902). DHU/MO; DHU/R
    Reprinted, Negro Univ. Press, 1969.

    William N. Hartshorn. An Era of Progress and Promise (Boston: Priscilla Publishing Co., 1910), p. 495. DHU/MO

WALKER, D. I.

    James W. Hood. One Hundred Years of the A. M. E. Zion Church (N. Y.: A. M. E. Zion Book Concern, 1895), pp. 572-75.   DHU/MO
    Ex-slave, A. M. E. Zion minister and state Senator in S. C.

WALKER, DOUGAL ORMONDE BEACONSFIELD, (bp.)

    Richard R. Wright. Bishops of the A. M. E. Church (Nashville: A. M. E. Sunday School Union, 1963), pp. 347-49.   DHU/R
    Sixty-sixth Bishop of the A. M. E. Church.

WALKER, GEORGE W.

    William Hicks. History of Louisiana Negro Baptists from 1804-1914 (Nashville, Tenn.: National Baptist Publishing Board, n. d.), pp. 116-19.   DHU/R
    Baptist minister; trustee of Leland University, life member of the Baptist Foreign Mission Convention.

WALKER, J. FRANKLIN

    Samuel W. Bacote. Who's Who Among the Colored Baptists (Kansas City, Mo.: F. Hudson Co., 1912), pp. 138-39.   DHU/MO

    Baptist minister and vice-president of National Baptist Convention.

WALKER, JOHN THOMAS, (bp.).

The editors of Ebony. The Ebony Success Library: 1,000 Successful Blacks (Nashville: The Southwestern Co., 1973), Vol. 1, p. 316.   DHU
Episcopal Bishop of the Episcopal Diocese of Washington, D. C.

The Episcopal Church Annual (New York: Morehouse-Barlow, 1972), p. 238.   PPPD; ViAlTH

WALKER, LUCIUS, JR.

The editors of Ebony. The Ebony Success Library: 1,000 Successful Blacks (Nashville: The Southwestern Co., 1973), Vol. 1, p. 316.   DHU
Baptist minister and executive director of Foundation for Community Organization in New York City.

WALKER, T. W.

Samuel W. Bacote. Who's Who Among the Colored Baptists (Kansas City, Mo.: F. Hudson Co., 1912), pp. 167-69.
                                          DHU/MO
Baptist minister; president of Union Mutual Association, Atlanta and New Era Baptist State Convention.

WALKER, WYATT TEE

The editors of Ebony. The Ebony Success Library: 1,000 Successful Blacks (Nashville: The Southwestern Co., 1973), Vol. 1, p. 317.   DHU
Baptist minister and pastor of Canaan Baptist Church, New York City.

WALLER, GARNETT RUSSELL

James J. Pipkin. The Negro in Revelation, in History, and in Citizenship (New York: Thompson Pub. Co., 1902), pp. 110-13.   DHU/MO
Baptist minister.

WALLER, OWEN MEREDITH

Daniel W. Culp. Twentieth Century Negro Literature (Atlanta: Nicholson & Co., 1902), p. 363.   DHU/MO
Protestant Episcopal minister.

WALLS, WILLIAM JACOB, (bp.).

The Missionary Seer (73:7, Sept., 1974), pp. 3+. DHU/R

Missionary Seer (72:9, Nov., 1973), pp. 3-4.   DHU/R
About A. M. E. Zion Bishop, founder and chief donor of "Heritage Hall", center for A. M. E. Zion History and Blacks in Africa and the United States, at Livingston College.

Biographical Encyclopedia of the World (New York: Institute of Research, 1946), p. 824.   NcSalL

WALTERS, ALEXANDER, (bp.).

Charles Alexander. One Hundred Distinguished Leaders (Atlanta, Ga.: Franklin Printing & Publishing Co., 1899), p. 66.   DHU/MO
Bishop Walters of the A. M. E. Zion Church

Carter G. Woodson. History of the Negro Church (Washington, D. C.: Associated Publishers, 1925), pp. 311-12.
                                      NcSalL; DHU/R

The Crisis (3:4, Feb., 1912), p. 146.   DLC/ DHU/MO
Also: (10:2, Je., 1915), p. 63.

Dictionary of American Biography (New York: Scribners), V. 19, no. 9.   NcSalL

G. F. Richings. Evidences of Progress Among Colored People (Phila.: G. S. Ferguson, 1904), p. 390.
                                      DHU/R; DHU/MO

Henry D. Northrop. The College of Life (Phila.: Nat. Pub. Co., 1895), pp. 30-31.   DHU/MO

James W. Hood. One Hundred Years of A. M. E. Zion Church (N. Y.: A. M. E. Zion Book Concern, 1895), pp. 209-12.   DHU/MO

My Life and Work (n. p.: n. p., 1917).   NcSalL

Who Was Who in America (New York: 1897-1942), p. 1295.
                                      NcSalL

Who's Who in America (Chicago: Marquis Co., 1908; 1912; 1914; 1916).

Who's Who in American Methodism (New York: E. B. Treat Co., 1916), p. 232.   NcSalL

William J. Simmons. Men of Mark (Cleveland: O. Rewell, 1887), pp. 340-44.   DHU/R; DHU/MO

William N. Hartshorn. An Era of Progress and Promise (Boston: Priscilla Pub. Co., 1910), p. 396.   DHU/MO

WALTERS, EDWARD

Benjamin W. Arnett. The Budget... Biographical Sketches Proceeding... (Dayton, O.: Christian Publishing House, 1882), p. 8.   DHU/MO
A. M. E. minister.

James A. Handy. Scraps of African Methodist History (Philadelphia: A. M. E. Book Concern, n. d.), p. 37.
                                      DHU/MO

WARD, CASSIUS A.

William N. Hartshorn. An Era of Progress and Promise (Boston: Priscilla Publishing Co., 1910), p. 492. DHU/MO
Baptist minister.

WARD, SAMUEL R.

Martin R. Delany. The Condition, Elevation, Emigration and Destiny of the Colored People of the United States (New York: Arno Press, 1968), p. 112.   DHU/R; DHU/MO
Congregational minister in New York and editor.

Wilson A. Armistead. A Tribute for the Negro (Miami, Fla.: Mnemosyne Pub. Co., 1848), p. 139.   DHU/MO; DHU/R

William W. Brown. The Black Man (N. Y.: T. Hamilton, 1863), pp. 284-85.   DHU/R

Who Was Who in America, Historical Volume, 1607-1907 (Chicago: The A. N. Marquis Co., 1907), p. 561.   DLC

Fred Landon. Dictionary of American Biography V. 7 (New York: Scribner's & Co., 1932), p. 440.   DHU

E. A. Johnson. School History of the Negro Race in America (Raleigh: Edward & Broughton, Printers, 1890), p. 80.
                                      DHU/MO

Benjamin Quarles. Black Abolitionists (New York: University Press, 1969), pp. 65+.   DHU/R

(Ward, Samuel, R. cont.)

    Autobiography of a Fugitive Negro (London: n.p., 1855).
                                   DHU/MO

    Reprint: New York: Arno Press, 1968.

    Wilhelmena S. Robinson. Historical Negro Biographies (N.
    Y.: Publishers Co., 1967), p. 140.   DHU/MO

WARD, THOMAS M. D., (bp.).

    Richard R. Wright. Bishop of the A. M. E. Church (Nash-
    ville: A. M. E. Sunday School Union, 1963), pp. 350-54.
                                     DHU/R
    Tenth Bishop of the A. M. E. Church

    Benjamin W. Arnett. The Budget ... Biographical Sketches
    ... (Dayton, Ohio: Christian Pub. House, 1882), p. 19.
                                     DHU/MO

    James A. Handy. Scraps of African Methodist History
    (Phila., Pa.: A. M. E. Book Concern, n.d.), p. 342.
                                     DHU/MO

WARNER, ANDREW J., (bp.).

    James W. Hood. Centennial of African Methodism (N. Y.:
    A. M. E. Zion Book Concern, 1895), pp. 553-56. DHU/MO
    Bishop of A. M. E. Zion Church.

    William N. Hartshorn. An Era of Progress and Promise
    (Boston: Priscilla Pub. Co., 1910), p. 409.   DHU/MO

WARRANT, JOHN

    Arthur A. Schomburg. "Two Negro Missionaries to the
    American Indians, John Warrant and John Stewart." Journal
    of Negro History (21:4, Oct., 1936), pp. 394-415. DHU/MO

WASHINGTON, CURTIS

    Albert S. Foley. God's Men of Color (New York: Farrar,
    Straus & Co., 1955), pp. 224-27.   DHU/R
    Catholic priest.

WASHINGTON, G. H.

    James W. Hood. Centennial of African Methodism (N. Y.:
    A. M. E. Zion Book Concern, 1895), p. 264.   DHU/MO
    A. M. E. Zion minister.

WASHINGTON, GEORGIA

    The Southern Workman (28:5, My., 1899), pp. 183-84.
                                  DHU/MO; DLC
    Missionary

WASHINGTON, JOHN H.

    Lewis G. Jordan. Negro Baptist History U. S. A. (Nash
    ville, Tenn.: Sunday School Publishing Board N. B. C.,
    1930), p. 392.   DHU/R; DHU/MO
    Baptist minister, North Carolina. First State missionary.

WASHINGTON, P. R.

    Samuel W. Bacote. Who's Who Among the Colored Baptists
    (Kansas City, Mo.: F. Hudson Co., 1912), pp. 149-50.
                                     DHU/MO
    Baptist minister; first vice-pres. of State Sunday School
    Convention.

WATKINS, WALTER F.

    The Cry of the West: the Story of the Mighty Struggle for
    Religious Freedom in California (Saratoga: R & E Research
    Associates, 1969), pp. 22-23.   DHU/R
    Baptist minister
    Reprint.
    Negro author.

WATKINS, WALTER THOMAS

    Samuel W. Bacote. Who's Who Among the Colored Baptists
    (Kansas City, Mo.: F. Hudson Co., 1912), pp. 93-95.
                                     DHU/MO
    Bjptist minister, New Jersey.

WATSON, A. W.

    William H. Heard. The Bright Side of African Life (New
    York: Negro Universities Press, 1969), p. 18. DHU/R
    A. M. E. minister in Virginia, Liberia, Africa.

WATSON, EDGAR BENTON, (bp.).

    Who's Who in Colored America (New York: Who's Who in
    Colored America Corp.), 1930-40.   NcSalL; DHU/R
    A. M. E. Zion bishop.

WATSON, S. E. J.

    Lewis G. Jordan. Negro Baptist History U. S. A. (Nash-
    ville, Tenn.: Sunday School Publishing Board, N. B. C.,
    1930), p. 120.   DHU/R; DHU/MO
    Baptist minister, Illinois. Chairman of Board of Evangelism
    of the National Baptist Convention. Writer for B. Y. P. U.

WAYLAND, H. L.

    Henry F. Kletzing. Progress of a Race (Atlanta: J. L.
    Nichols & Co., 1898), p. 405.   DHU/MO
    Baptist minister and teacher.

WAYMAN, ALEXANDER W., (bp.).

    James A. Handy. "Alexander Walker Wayman." The A. M.
    E. Church Review (12:4, Apr., 1896), pp. 491-95. DHU/MO
    Bishop of the A. M. E. Church and author.

    A. M. E. Church Review (2:1, Apr., 1896), pp. 495-99.
                                     NN/Sch; DLC

    Benjamin T. Tanner. An Apology for African Methodism
    (Baltimore: n.p., 1867), pp. 151-57.   DHU/MO

    Benjamin W. Arnett. The Budget (Dayton: Christian Pub.
    House, 1882), p. 141.   DHU/MO

    D. S. Bentley. "The Fruitful Life of a Christian Hero."
    The A. M. E. Church Review (12:4, Apr., 1896), pp. 495-99.
                                     DHU/MO

    Henry F. Kletzing. Progress of a Race (Atlanta: J. L.
    Nichols & Co., 1898), p. 581.   DHU/MO

    James A. Handy. The A. M. E. Church Review (12:1, Apr.,
    1896), pp. 491-95.   DLC

    James A. Handy. Scraps of African Methodist History (Phila.:
    A. M. E. Book Concern, n.d.), p. 340.   DHU/R

    Leila A. Pendleton. A Narrative of the Negro (Wash., D. C.:
    Press of R. L. Pendleton, 1912), p. 176.   DHU/MO

    Richard R. Wright. Bishops of the A. M. E. Church (Nash-
    ville: A. M. E. Sunday School Union, 1963), pp. 357-61.
                                     DHU/R

Who Was Who in America, Historical Volume, 1607-1907
(Chicago: The A. N. Marquis Co., 1907), p. 567.   DHU

William W. Brown. The Rising Son (Boston: A. G. Brown
& Co., 1874), pp. 440-41.   DHU/R; DHU/MO

WEATHINGTON, TITUS ATTICUS

James W. Hood. Centennial of African Methodism (N. Y.:
A. M. E. Zion Book Concern, 1895), pp. 377-79.   DHU/MO
A. M. E. Zion minister and President and founder of the
Mechanicville Literary Society.

WEAVER, WILLIAM H.

The Church at Home and Abroad (23; 1898), pp. 14-16.
                                                DHU/R
A special agent of the Board of Missions for Freedmen, Presbyterian church and minister.

WEBB, M. R. RODGERS

Lawson A. Scruggs. Women of Distinction (Raleigh: L. A.
Scruggs, 1893), pp. 287-89.   DHU/MO
Lecturer, missionary, minister and editor of the Texas Re-
former.

WELCH, I. H.

G. F. Richings. Evidences of Progress Among Colored
People (Phila.: G. S. Ferguson, 1904), p. 134.
                                        DHU/MO; DHU/R
A. M. E. minister and president of Wayman Institute,
Harrodsburg, Kentucky.

WELCH, T. L.

William Hicks. The History of Louisiana Negro Baptists from
1804-1914 (Nashville, Tenn.: National Baptist Publishing
Board, n. d.), pp. 120-21.   DHU/R
Baptist minister; Treasurer and Secretary of the Fifth District
Association.

WELLS, J. W.

William Hicks. The History of Louisiana Negro Baptists from
1804-1914 (Nashville, Tenn.: National Baptist Publishing
Board, n. d.), p. 189.   DHU/R
Baptist minister.

WEST, W. B.

Henry F. Kletzing. Progress of a Race (Atlanta: J. L.
Nichols & Co., 1898), p. 510.   DHU/MO
C. M. E. minister and editor of the Western Index.

WESTBERRY, RANSOM

John R. Wilson. Life and Speeches of Ransom Westberry...
(Atlanta, Ga.: A. B. Caldwell Pub. Co., 1921). DHU/MO
Deacon in the Baptist church and active in the Y. M. C. A.

WESTBROOK, B. J. F.

Samuel W. Bacote. Who's Who Among the Colored Baptists
(Kansas City, Mo.: F. Hudson Co., 1912), pp. 222-23.
                                        DHU/MO
Baptist minister, corresponding secretary of Foreign
Mission Convention of Oklahoma and Inter-State Press Asso.

WHALEY, J. W.

William Hicks. The History of Louisiana Negro Baptests from
1804-1914 (Nashville, Tenn.: National Baptist Publishing
Board, n. d.), p. 189.
Baptist minister and President of the Trustee Board of Coleman College.

WHEELER, B. F.

Henry F. Kletzing. Progress of a Race (Atlanta, G.: J. L.
Nichols & Co., 1898), p. 582.   DHU/MO
A. M. E. Zion minister.

James W. Hood. One Hundred Years of the A. M. E. Zion
Church (N. Y.: 396-99.   DHU/MO

WHITE, EDWARD D.

Lewis G. Jordan. Negro Baptist History U. S. A. (Nashville, Tenn.: Sunday School Publishing Board N. B. C., 1930),
p. 392.   DHU/R; DHU/MO
Baptist minister, South Carolina. One of Founders of Morris
College at Sumter and General State missionary.

WHITE, GEORGE L.

William N. Hartshorn. An Era of Progress and Promise
(Boston: Priscilla Publishing Co., 1910), p. 441.   DHU/MO
A. M. E. Zion minister and physician.

James M. Trotter. Music and some Highly Musical People
(N. Y.: C. T. Dillingham, 1878), p. 256.

WHITE, H. W.

William H. Heard. The Bright Side of African Life (New
York: Negro Universities Press, 1969), p. 35.   DHU/R
A. M. E. minister in Johnsonville, Liberia.

WHITE, HENRY

E. R. Carter. The Black Side (Atlanta, Ga.: n. p., 1894),
pp. 89-90.   DHU/MO
Black Baptist minister.

WHITE, JAMES T.

Lewis G. Jordan. Negro Baptist History U. S. A. (Nashville: Sunday School Publishing Board N. B. C., 1930), p.
392.   DHU/R; DHU/MO
Baptist minister - Arkansas, state senator, Editor; Organizer of the Missionary Baptist Convention.

William J. Simmons. Men of Mark (Cleveland: O. Rewell,
1887), pp. 590-93.   DHU/R; DHU/MO

WHITE, M. V.

E. R. Carter. The Black Side (Atlanta, Ga.: n. p., 1894),
pp. 79-80.   DHU/MO
Black Baptist minister.

WHITE, SAMPSON

Lewis G. Jordan. Negro Baptist History U. S. A. (Nashville, Tenn.: Sunday School Publishing Board N. B. C.,
1930), p. 392.   DHU/R; DHU/MO
Baptist minister of Pennsylvania.

Petersburg Progress Index (Ja. 3, 1939).

WHITE, W. J.

> Evidences of Progress Among Colored People (Phila.: G.
> S. Ferguson, 1904), p. 368.   DHU/MO; DHU/R
> Baptist minister and editor and business manager of The
> Georgia Baptist.

> (Indianapolis) Freeman (1:24, Feb. 2, 1889), p. 5.
>   DHU/MO

> Irvine G. Penn. The Afro-American Press and Its Editors
> (Springfield, Mass.: Willey & Co., 1891), p. 216+.
>   DHU/MO; DHU/R

> William J. Simmons, (ed.). Men of Mark (Cleveland, O.:
> Geo. M. Rewell & Co., 1887), p. 1095.   DHU/R

WHITFIELD, CHARLES RANDOLPH DAVIS

> William Joseph Barber. Disciple Assemblies of Eastern
> North Carolina (St. Louis: The Bethany Press, 1966), pp.
> 260-69.   DHU/R
> Disciples of Christ minister.

WHITFIELD, CLINTON LEAGO

> William Joseph Barber. Disciple Assemblies of Eastern
> North Carolina (St. Louis: The Bethany Press, 1966), pp.
> 266-69.   DHU/R
> Disciples of Christ minister.

WHITFIELD, EDGAR STONEWALL LAPADOTH

> William Joseph Barber. Disciple Assemblies of Eastern
> North Carolina (St. Louis: The Bethany Press, 1966), p.
> 263.   DHU/R
> Disciples of Christ minister.

WHITMAN, ALBERY A.

> Benjamin Brawley. Negro Builders and Heroes (Chapel Hill,
> N. C.: Univ. of N. C. Press, 1937), p. 234.
>   DHU/R; DHU/MO
> A. M. E. minister.

> Beatrice F. Wormley and Charles W. Carter. An Anthology
> of a Negro Poetry (W. P. A.) (Trenton: n.p., 1937), p. 18.
>   DHU/MO

> Benjamin Brawley. The Negro Genius (N. Y.: Dodd, Mead
> & Co., 1937), pp. 101-10.   DHU/R

> _____. Negro in Literature and Art (Atlanta: n.p., 1910), pp.
> 45-49.   DHU/MO; DHU/R

> Henry F. Kletzing. Progress of a Race (Atlanta: J. L.
> Nichols & Co., 1898), p. 582.   DHU/MO

> Newman I. White and Walter C. Jackson. An Anthology of
> Verse by Negro Americans (Durham, N. C.: Trinity College
> Press, 1924), p. 50.   DHU/MO

> Robert T. Kerlin. Negro Posts and Their Poems (Wash.,
> D. C.: Associated Publishers, Inc., 1923), p. 279. DHU/MO

> William J. Simmons. Men of Mark (Cleveland: O. Revell,
> 1887), pp. 1122-26.   DHU/MO; DHU/R

WHITTED, JOHN A.

> William N. Hartshorn. An Era of Progress and Promise
> (Boston: Priscilla Publishing Co., 1910), p. 497. DHU/MO
> Baptist minister, historian and president of the Education and
> Missionary Convention of North Carolina.

> James J. Pipkin. The Negro in Revelation, in History and
> Citizenship (N. Y.: Thompson Publishing Co., 1902), p. 97.
>   DHU/MO

WILEY, JAMES W.

> The African Methodist Episcopal Church Review (81:222,
> Oct.-Dec., 1964), pp. 68-69.   DHU/R
> A. M. E. minister and author.

WILEY, JAMES W.

> The African Methodist Episcopal Church Review (81:222,
> Oct.-Dec., 1964), pp. 68-69.   DHU/R
> A. M. E. minister and author.

WILKES, WILLIAM REID

> Richard Robert Wright, Jr., (bp.). Bishops of the A. M. E.
> Church (Nashville: A. M. E. Sunday School Union, 1963),
> pp. 362-67.   DHU/R
> Sixty-ninth Bishop of the A. M. E. Church.

> The editors of Ebony. The Ebony Success Library: 1,000 Suc-
> cessful Blacks (Nashville: The Southwestern Co., 1973),
> Vol. 1, p. 328.   DHU

WILLIAMS, CECIL A.

> The editors of Ebony. The Ebony Success Library: 1,000 Suc-
> cessful Blacks (Nashville: The Southwestern Co., 1973),
> Vol. 1, p. 329.   DHU
> Pastor of Glide Memorial United Methodist Church, San
> Francisco, Calif.

WILLIAMS, CHARLES W.

> Wendell P. Dabney. Cincinnati's Colored Citizens (Cincin-
> nati, Ohio: The Dabney Pub. Co., 1926), p. 338. DHU/MO
> Baptist minister.

WILLIAMS, CHARLEY

> William Hicks. The History of Louisiana Negro Baptists
> from 1804-1914 (Nashville, Tenn.: National Baptist Pub-
> lishing Board, n.d.), p. 195.   DHU/R
> Baptist minister.

WILLIAMS, D. A.

> (Indianapolis) Freeman (2:16, Je. 8, 1889), p. 4. DHU/MO
> Editor of The New Light; The People's Adviser.
> M. E. minister.

> Irvine G. Penn. The Afro-American Press and Its Editors
> (Springfield, Mass.: Willey & Co., 1891), p. 228-.
>   DHU/MO; DHU/R

WILLIAMS, EMPEROR

> Henry D. Northrop. College of Life (Phila.: National Pub.
> Co., 1895), pp. 48-50.   DHU/MO
> Ex-slave, Methodist Episcopal minister and one of the twelve
> organizers of the M. E. Church in New Orleans.

Henry F. Kletzing. Progress of a Race (Atlanta: J. L. Nichols & Co., 1898), pp. 514-15.   DHU/MO

WILLIAMS, FRANK M.

Emanuel K. Love. History of the First African Baptist Church (Savannah, Ga.: Morning News Print, 1888), p. 172.   DHU/MO Deacon of the First African Baptist Church.

WILLIAMS, GEORGE W.

Booker T. Washington. A New Century For a New Century (Chicago: American Publishing House, 1900), p. 187. Baptist minister, founder and President of Simmons University.

Benjamin G. Brawley. Negro Builders and Heroes (Chapel Hill: Univ. of N. C. Press, 1937), p. 237. DHU/R; DHU/MO

Benjamin G. Brawley. The Negro Genius (New York: Dodd, Mead & Co., 1937), pp. 100-10.   DHU/R; DHU/MO

Benjamin G. Brawley. Negro in Literature and Art (Atlanta, Ga.: n.p., 1910), p. 104.   DHU/MO

Benjamin W. Arnett. The Budget... Biographical Sketches Proceeding... (Dayton, Ohio: Christian Pub. House, 1882), p. 126.   DHU/MO

Lewis G. Jordan. Negro Baptist History U. S. A. (Nashville, Tenn.: Sunday School Publishing Board, N. B. C., 1930), p. 392.   DHU/R

William H. Ferris. African Abroad (New Haven: Tuttle, Morehouse, Taylor Press, 1913), p. 763.   DHU/R

WILLIAMS, HENRY

William Henry Johnson. A Sketch of the Life of Rev. Henry Williams, D. D., Late Pastor of the Gilfield Baptist Church, Petersburg, Virginia, with Ceremonies Incident to his Death, and to the Erection of a Monument to his Memory (Petersburg, Va.: Fenn & Owen, Printers, 1901). SCBHC

WILLIAMS, HENRY W.

Presbyterian Reunion: 1837-1871 (N. Y.: De W. C. Lent & Co., 1870), pp. 524-25.   DHU/MO Presbyterian minister and judge.

WILLIAMS, JOSEPH C.

Emanuel K. Love. History of the First African Baptist Church. (Savannah, Ga.: Morning News Print, 1888), pp. 180-81. DHU/MO Deacon of the First African Baptist Church.

WILLIAMS, LACEY KIRK

Benjamin Brawley. Negro Builders and Heroes (Chapel Hill: Univ. of N. C. Press, 1937), pp. 202-03. DHU/MO; DHU/R Ministers of the Olivet Baptist Church in Chicago. Became vice president of the Baptist World Alliance in 1928 and received a Harmon Award for "outstanding work in the religious field" in 1929.

James L. Nichols. The Progress of a Race (New York: Arno Press, 1969), p. 450.   DHU/MO Reprint of earlier edition.

Samuel W. Bacote. Who's Who Among the Colored Baptists (Kansas City, Mo.: F. Hudson Co., 1912), pp. 177-78.   DHU/MO

Thomas O. Fuller. Pictorial History of the American Negro (Memphis, Tenn.: Pictorial History, Inc., 1933), p. 311.   DHU/MO

WILLIAMS, MAXIM ANDREW

Albert S. Foley. God's Men of Color (New York: Farrar, Straus & Co., 1955), pp. 238-41.   DHU/R Catholic priest.

WILLIAMS, NOAH W., (bp.).

Richard Robert Wright, Jr., (bp.). Bishops of the A. M. E. Church (Nashville: A. M. E. Sunday School Union, 1963), pp. 368-70.   DHU/R Fifty-fourth Bishop of the A. M. E. Church.

WILLIAMS, PETER, JR.

Writers' Program. New York (City). Negroes of New York Biographical Sketches. New York: 1838-41. NN/Sch; DHU/MO Typescript. Protestant Episcopal priest.

Appleton's Cyclopedia of American Biography V. 6 (New York: D. Appleton & Co., 1888), p. 530.   DLC; DHU

Benjamin Brawley. Early Negro American Writers (Chapel Hill: Univ. of N. C. Press, 1935), p. 100.   DHU/R

Benjamin Brawley. The Negro Genius (N. Y.: Dodd, Mead & Co., 1937), p. 33.   DHU/MO

Benjamin Quarles. Black Abolitionists (New York: University Press, 1969), pp. 107+.   DHU/R

Emanuel K. Love. History of the First African Baptist Church (Savannah, Ga.: Morning News Print, 1888), p. 176. DHU/R; DHU/MO

George F. Bragg. History of the Afro-American Group of the Episcopal Church (Balto., Md.: Advocate Press, 1922), pp. 81-85.   DHU/R

William C. Nell. Colored Patriots of the American Revolution (Boston: R. F. Wallcut, 1855), pp. 320-23. DHU/MO

William W. Brown. The Rising Son (Boston: A. G. Brown & Co., 1874), pp. 338-99.   DHU/R

WILLIAMS, PETER, SR.

Carter G. Woodson. The History of the Negro Church (Wash., D. C.: Associated Publishers, 1921), pp. 67-68. DHU/R; DHU/MO M. E. minister whose name appears on charter of 1800 organizing the A. M. E. Zion Church in Philadelphia.

Joseph B. Wakely. Lost Chapters Recovered From the Early History of American Methodism (New York: By the author, 1858).   DHU/MO; NN/Sch

Writers Program. New York (City). Negroes of New York: Biographical Sketches (New York: 1838-41), NN/Sch; DHU/MO Typescript.

F. B. Upham. The Story of Old John Street M. E. Church, New York City, 1766-1932 (N. Y.: n.p., 1932).   NN/Sch

WILLIAMS, ROBERT S., (bp.).

Charles Phillips. History of Colored Methodist Church (Jackson, Tenn.: Pub. House, A. M. E. Church, 1898), pp. 222-27.   DHU/R; DHU/MO
Sixth Bishop of the C. M. E. Church

William N. Hartshorn. An Era of Progress and Promise (Boston: Priscilla Publishing Co., 1910), p. 403.   DHU/MO

WILLIAMS, W. HENRY

Wendell P. Dabney. Cincinnati's Colored Citizens (Cincinnati, Ohio: The Dabney Pub. Co., 1926), pp. 298-300.
                                                                       DHU/MO
Negro Baptist minister.

WILLS, JOSEPH

Leslie H. Fishel. The Negro American (New York: Wm. Morrow, 1970), p. 42.   DHU/R; DHU/MO
Negro Baptist minister reported to have "delivered the first Protestant sermon heard West of the Mississippi."

WILMORE, GAYRAUD STEPHEN, JR.

Frank T. Wilson. "Living Witnesses: Black Presbyterians in Ministry." Journal of Presbyterian History (51:4, Wint., 1973), pp. 383-86.   DHU/R
Minister, professor of Social Ethics, author and executive director of Council on Church and Race, Presbyterian Church.

WILSON, ELISHA ARLINGTON

Samuel W. Bacote. Who's Who Among the Colored Baptists (Kansas City, Mo.: F. Hudson Co., 1912), pp. 47-49.
                                                                       DHU/MO
Evangelist, president of Kansas Baptist Convention and asst. secretary of National Baptist Convention.

WILSON, GEORGE G.

Albert S. Foley. God's Men of Color (New York: Farrar, Straus & Co., 1955), pp. 222-24.   DHU/R
Catholic priest.

WILSON, MANNIE L.

The editors of Ebony. The Ebony Success Library: 1,000 Successful Blacks (Nashville: The Southwestern Co., 1973), Vol 1, p. 335.   DHU
Baptist minister and pastor of Convent Avenue Baptist Church, New York City.

WILSON, ROBERT E.

James W. Hood. Centennial of African Methodism (N. Y.: A. M. E. Zion Book Concern, 1895), pp. 274-76.   DHU/MO
Minister of A. M. E. Zion Church and educator.

WILTBANK, JAMES

William Douglass. Annals of the First African Church in the U. S. A. (Phila.: King and Bair Printers, 1862), p. 125.
                                                                       DHU/MO
Minister of the First African Church, African Episcopal Church of St. Thomas, Phila.

WINFIELD, C. W.

James W. Hood. Centennial of African Methodism (N. Y.: A. M. E. Zion Book Concern, 1895), pp. 564-66. DHU/MO
Minister of A. M. E. Zion Church.

WINTERS, ARTHUR C.

Albert S. Foley. God's Men of Color (New York: Farrar, Straus & Co., 1955), pp. 273-74.   DHU/R
Catholic priest.

WINTERS, RICHARD

Albert S. Foley. God's Men of Color (New York: Farrar, Straus & Co., 1955), pp. 227-28.   DHU/R
Catholic priest.

WISWELL, GEORGE F.

Presbyterian Reunion: 1837-1871 (N. Y.: De W. C. Lent & Co., 1870), p. 519.   DHU/MO
Presbyterian minister of Philadelphia, Pa.

WOLVERTON, N.

G. F. Richings. Evidences of Progress Among Colored People (Phila.: G. S. Ferguson, 1904), p. 31.
                                                             DHU/R; DHU/MO
Baptist minister and President of Bishop College, Marshall, Texas.

WOOD, CHARLES WINTER

James L. Nichols. The New Progress of a Race (Naperville, Ill.: J. L. Nichols and Co., 1929), pp. 453-54.
                                                                       DHU/MO
Minister, teacher and publicity manager of Tuskegee Institute.

WOOD, HENRY D.

G. F. Richings. Evidences of Progress Among Colored People (Phila.: G. S. Ferguson, 1904), pp. 174-76.
                                                             DHU/MO; DHU/R
Presbyterian minister and principal of Dayton Academy, Carthage, N. C.

WOOD, JOHN WESLEY, (bp.).

Who's Who in American Methodism (New York: Who's Who in America Corp., 1927-37). NcSalL; DHU/MO; DHU/R
Bishop of the A. M. E. Zion Church.

WOODS, J. S.

Irvine G. Penn. The Afro-American Press and Its Editors (Springfield, Mass.: Willey & Co., 1891), p. 124.
                                                             DHU/R; DHU/MO
Minister and editor of the Afro-American Budget.

WOODSON, LEWIS

Leila A. Pendleton. A Narrative of the Negro (Wash., D. C.: Press of R. L. Pendleton, 1912), p. 149.   DHU/MO
M. E. minister.

Floyd J. Miller. "Another Contender for the Father of Black Nationalism." William B. Hesseltine, (ed.). Civil War History V. 8, no. 2 (Kent, Ohio: Kent State Univ. Press, 1972).
                                                                       DLC

WOODSON, S. HOWARD, JR.

The editors of Ebony. The Ebony Success Library: 1,000 Successful Blacks (Nashville: The Southwestern Co., 1973), Vol. 1, p. 337.   DHU
Baptist minister and state legislator in New Jersey.

WOODSON, THOMAS

Martin R. Delany. The Condition Elevation Emigration and Destiny of the Colored People of the U. S. (N. Y.: Arno Press, 1968), p. 127.   DHU/MO; DHU/R
Editor of Colored Citizen and minister.

WOODWORTH, FRANK G.

G. F. Richings. Evidences of Progress Among Colored People (Phila.: G. S. Ferguson, 1904), p. 78.
                                                    DHU/R; DHU/MO
Congregationalist minister and president of Tougaloo University, Tougaloo, Miss.

WRIGHT, BRYANT

William Hicks. The History of Louisiana Negro Baptists from 1804-1914. (Nashville, Tenn.: National Baptist Publishing Board, n. d.), pp. 138-39.   DHU/R
Baptist minister; one of first Sunday School superintendents.

WRIGHT, CORNEIL W.

Wendell P. Dabney. Cincinnati's Colored Citizens (Cincinnati, Ohio: The Dabney Pub. Co., 1926), p. 253. DHU/MO
Negro Baptist minister and businessman.

WRIGHT, F. J.

Emanuel K. Love. History of the African Baptist Church (Savannah, G.: Morning News Print, 1888), pp. 188-89.
                                                    DHU/MO
Deacon of the First African Baptist Church.

WRIGHT, HAROLD L., (bp.).

The Episcopal Church Annual (New York: Morehouse-Barlow, 1974), p. 242.   PPPD; ViAlTH
Protestant Episcopal Suffragan bishop of New York.

WRIGHT, J. T.

William H. Ferris. African Abroad V. 2 (New Haven, Conn.: Tuttle, Morehouse, & Taylor Press, 1913), p. 793.
                                                    DHU/MO
Presbyterian minister and chaplain of State College, Orangeburg, S. C.

WRIGHT, RICHARD ROBERT, JR., (bp.).

Richard Robert Wright, Jr., (bp.). Bishops of the A. M. E. Church (Nashville: A. M. E. Sunday School Union, 1963), pp. 371-77.   DHU/R
Fifty-seventh Bishop of the A. M. E. Church

S. P. Fullenwider. The Mind and Mood of Black America (Homewood, Ill.: Dorsey Press, 1969), Chapter 2.

WRIGHT, THEODORE S.

Wilson A. Armistead. A Tribute for the Negro (Miami, Fla.: Mnemosyne Pub. Co., 1848), p. 139. DHU/R; DHU/MO
Presbyterian minister of New York and abolitionist.

Bella Gross. "Life and Times of Theodore S. Wright, 1797-1849." Negro History Bulletin (3:9, Je., 1940), pp. 133-38+.
                                                    DHU/MO

Benjamin Quarles. Black Abolitionists (New York: University Press, 1969), pp. 38+.   DHU/R

David E. Swift. "Black Presbyterian Attacks on Racism: Samuel Cornish Theodore Wright and their Contemporaries." Journal of Presbyterian History (51:4, Wint., 1973), pp. 433-70.   DHU/R

Gerald Sorin. The New York Abolitionists: A Case Study of Political Radicalism (Westport, Conn.: Greenwood Pub. Corp., 1971), pp. 81-85.

Wilhelmena S. Robinson. Historical Negro Biographies (N. Y.: Publishers Co., 1967), p. 148.   DHU/MO

YOUNG, ANDREW J., JR.

Ebony (28:4, Feb., 1973), pp. 82-84+. Pam. File, DHU/R
Black U. C. C. minister and U. S. Congressman.

Christian Century (89:42, Nov., 1972), p. 1176.   DHU/R

Audrey Miller. "Portraits of Angela Davis and Andrew Young." Colloquy (4:10, Nov., 1971), pp. 16-23.   DHU/R

YOUNG, GEORGE BENJAMIN, (bp.).

Richard R. Wright. Bishops of the A. M. E Church (Nashville: A. M. E. Sunday School Union, 1963), pp. 378-79.
                                                    DHU/R
Fifty-second Bishop of the A. M. E. Church.

YOUNG, ROBERT P.

Emanuel K. Love. History of the First African Baptist Church (Savannah, Ga.: Morning News Print, 1888), pp. 174-75.
                                                    DHU/MO
Deacon of the First African Baptist Church.

YOUNG, RUFUS KING, SR.

The editors of Ebony. The Ebony Success Library: 1,000 Successful Blacks (Nashville: The Southwestern Co., 1973), Vol. 1, p. 341.   DHU
A. M. E. minister and pastor of Bethel A. M. E. Church, Little Rock, Arkansas.

ZELLARS, JAMES E.

Wendell P. Dabney. Cincinnati's Colored Citizens (Cincinnati, Ohio: The Dabney Pub. Co., 1926), p. 332. DHU/MO
Baptist minister.

Alger, A. L.
5961
Alinsky, Saul D.
11941, 11964
All Africa Church Conference
3910, 3911, 3912
All African Conferences of
Churches
3545, 3915, 3916
Allan, Afred K.
11934
Alland, Alexander
7065
Allard, Paul
5219
Alldridge, Thomas J.
1991
Allen, Belle Jane
2571
Allen, Benjamin R.
4654
Allen, Blanche.
12353
Allen, Christopher
487, 9155
Allen, Cuthbert E.
5111
Allen, Easter W.
7531
Allen, George
4655, 4656, 5220, 5221,
5565
Allen, Helen B.
8057
Allen, Issac
4394
Allen, Jewett W.
8880, 8881
Allen, John
4616.
Allen, Joseph H.
5222
Allen, L. Scott
9538
Allen, Richard
5721, 5962, 6385, 6386,
6387, 6472, 6501, 8058,
8059, 8081, 8117, 8419
Allen, Robert L.
7243
Allen, Roland
488, 2572
Allen, W. C.
9319, 9320
Allen, William F.
5963
Allen, William G.
5223
Alley, Joe K.
9416
Alleyne, Cameron C.
1650, 8060, 8061, 8062
Allier, Raoul
2573, 3185
Allison, Madeline G.
1936, 2574, 6388, 6389,
6390, 6391, 6649, 6687,
6688, 6898, 9417, 9539,
9540, 9732, 9814, 10090
Allotte de la Fuÿe, Maurice
64
Allport, Gordon W.
10451, 10452, 10453, 10454
Almquist, Lars Adren
2364
Al-Rayyah Hashim, M. A.
489

Alston, Jon P.
12354
Alston, Leonard
2575
Alston, Percel O.
12355.
Alvares, Francisco.
70, 1581
Alves Correia, Manuel
1937
Alvord, John W.
5859
Ambali, Augustine
1800
American and Foreign Anti-
Slavery Society
5556, 5567, 5568
American Baptist Free Mission Society
4617, 4618, 4619
American Baptist Historical
Mission Society
10409
American Baptist Home Missions Society
9400, 9412, 9413, 9414,
9415, 7532
American Baptist Theological
Seminary
6979
American Board of Commis-
sions for Foreign Missions
2576
American Board of Commis-
sioners for Foreign Mis-
sions
2576, 5569, 5570
American Church Institute
6976
American Church Institute
for Negroes
10354-10057
American Colonization Society
5571, 5815, 5821
American Missionary Association
5224, 5860, 5861, 9434,
10181, 10182, 10183, 10184,
10185, 10186, 10187, 10946
American Moral Reform Society
10358
American National Baptist
Convention
6892
American Reform Tract and
Book Society
4395, 4396, 4397, 4398,
4399. 5573, 5574
American Society for Colonizing the Free People of Color
5794, 5797
American Sunday School Union
2292
American Tract Society
5226, 5575, 5576.
Amero, Constant
65
Ames, Wilmer C.
13148
Amiji, Hatim M.
3186
Amor, Frank.
2577
Amorium, Deolindo
490
Amu, E.
2578

Andersen, Esther
3187, 3455
Andersen, Knud Tage
67
Anderson, August Magnus
1565
Anderson, Benjamin J. K.
2579
Anderson, E. Hutts
8063
Anderson, Gerald H.
3918
Anderson, H. C.
6689
Anderson, Izett
8882
Anderson, J. N. D.
492
Anderson, James-Forrester
3188
Anderson, James H.
6604
Anderson, John F.
12973
Anderson, John Q.
5964
Anderson, Llewellyn K.
5965, 2580, 3189
Anderson, Matthew
9733
Anderson-Morshead, A. E. M.
2582
Anderson, Robert E.
1735
Anderson, Susan
1827
Anderson, Vernon Andry
493
Anderson, W. H.
2026
Anderson, William B.
3456, 3457
Anderson, William K.
9567
Anderson, William T.
2581
Andersson, Efraim
3256, 3412
Andre, Marie
2365
Andre, Pierre J.
494
Andrews, C. F.
10091
Andrews, Charles Freer
2027
Andrews, Rena M.
5112
Andriamanjato, R. R.
3919
Anet, Henri
2366, 2367
Ankrah, Kodwo E.
3547
Anozie, Ifeanyichukwu
3815
Anscombe, Francis C.
5862
Anstrey, Roger T.
3548
Anti-Slavery Convention of
American Women
4756, 5577
Antoine, Charles
8746
Antubam, Kofi
1651

Appia, Béatrice
705
Applegarth, Albert C.
4757
Apsey, Lawrence S.
8064
Aptheker, Herbert
4758, 5548, 5579
Arberry, A. J.
495
Arbousset, Jean Thomas
2028
Arce, Laurent d'
69
Archdeacon, Ward
496
Archibald, Helen A.
10360
Ardener, Edwin
497
Argyle, M.
10457
Argyle, William Johnson
1571
Ariel, Buckner H. P.
10458
Arinze, Francis A.
498
Armistead, W. S.
10459
Armistead, Wilson
5580, 5581, 5582
Armstrong, George D.
4400, 4975
Armstrong, Mary F.
5966
Armstrong, Roger D.
3920
Arnett, Benjamin W.
6394, 6395, 6396, 6397,
6398, 6399, 6478, 6900,
6901, 7535, 7536, 8065,
8066, 8067, 8068, 8069,
8070, 8071, 8072, 8073
Arnhard, Carl von
71
Arnold, Benjamin
7537
Arnold, Byron
5967
Arnold, S. G.
5863
Arnold, W. E.
9542
Arnot, Frederick Stanley
2368, 2369, 2584
Arnoux, P. Alex
499, 500, 501, 502, 503
Arras, Victor
72
Arthur, George R.
10361, 10362
Artopoeus, Otto F.
10945
Asamoa, E. A.
3921
Asbury, Francis
4872
Asch, Sidney H.
11936
Ashanin, C. B.
7538, 7539
Ashbrook, James B.
12096
Ashe, Robert P.
2370
Ashen, Jermiah
6690, 6837

Barr, Mary
2595

Barr, William R.
12976

Barreal, Isaac
8885

Barret, David B.
3263, 3264, 3265, 3266, 3267

Barrett, David B.
1701, 3928, 3929, 3930, 3931, 8886

Barrett, Harris
5988

Barrett, Leonard E.
7548, 8887

Barrett, P.
11147

Barron, Jack Terrill
2596

Barrow, A. H.
2597

Barrow, Alfred H.
3190

Barrow, David
4407

Barrows, John H.
6401

Barsotti, Giulio
1583

Bartels, Francis L.
1654

Bartlett, Bob
12101

Bartlett, Robert M.
1561

Bartlett, S. C.
2598

Bartlett, T. R.
4408

Bartnicki, Andrzej
1584

Barton, George A.
521

Barton, John W.
10469

Barton, William E.
5989, 5990

Bascom, Henry Bidleman
4875, 9544

Bascom, William R.
522, 523, 524, 525, 526, 527, 528, 529, 530, 531, 532, 533, 534, 535, 536, 3932, 5991, 8888, 8889, 8890, 8891, 8892, 9263, 9244

Bascon, John
5233

Basen, Carol
13150

Basker, Roosevelt A.
4979

Baskin, Wade
7067

Basom, William R.
6329

Bassett, George W.
4660

Bassett, John S.
4876, 5592, 5593

Bassett, William
4762, 4763

Bastide, Roger
540, 541, 542, 8749, 8750, 8751, 8752, 8753, 8754, 8755, 8756, 8757, 8758, 8759, 9265, 9266, 9267, 9268, 12977

Bastien, Remy
8956

Bates, Daisy
11937

Bates, Gerald E.
3933

Bates, William N.
5

Batterham, E. Rose
10365

Battey, D. S.
2032

Battle, Allen O.
7032

Battle, Vincent M.
2599

Baudert, S.
2600

Baudin, Noel
543, 544

Baugh, J. Gordon
6697

Baumann, Julius
2601

Baxter, Daniel M.
6402, 6403, 8081

Baxter, Richard
4409, 4410

Bayer, Wilheim.
6

Bayley, Solomon
8082

Bayliss, John F.
8083

Baynes, Hamilton
2033

Beach, Harlan P.
2602, 2603

Beach, Waldo
9545, 10470, 10471, 10472, 12102

Beacham, C.
2268

Beall, Noble Y.
9324, 9325

Beanland, Lillian L.
1542

Bearcroft, Phillip
4318

Beard, August Field
5865, 10189, 10473

Beardsley, Grace M. H.
7

Beasley, Delilah L.
8084

Beasley, Yvonne
13151

Beatti, John H. M.
545, 546, 547, 548, 549

Beatty-Brown, Florence R.
7549

Beaumont, Geoffrey
5992

Beaver, Robert P.
3934

Beavon, Harold W. E.
550

Becken, Hans-Jürgen
3191, 3268, 3269, 3554

Becker, C. H.
551

Becker, William H.
12366, 12912, 13152

Beckers, Gerhard
3555

Beckett, Lemuel Morgan
552, 8085

Beckham, Albert S.
5993

Beckingham, Charles F.
81, 82

Beckmann, David M.
7033

Beckmann, Klaus-Marten
3935

Beckwith, John Q.
12978

Beckwith, Martha W.
8893, 8894, 8895, 8896, 8897, 8898

Bedau, Hugo A.
11563

Bede, (Brother)
9902

Bedinger, Robert Dabney
2376

Bedingfield, R. W.
12367

Bedwell, H. Kenneth
2034

Beecham, John
553, 2604

Beecher, Charles
4411, 5234, 5594

Beecher, Henry W.
5595

Beecher, Leonard J.
1702, 3270

Beecher, Lyman
5235

Beeson, Lewis
4661, 4877

Beeson, Trevor
12979

Beethan, Thomas A.
3936

Behm, R.
12368

Behrman, Lucy C.
554

Beidelman, Thomas O.
556, 557, 558

Beiderbecke, Heinrich
3192

Beier, Ulli
559

Belfast Anti-Slavery Society
5596

Belford, Lee A.
12791

Belk, Leotis S.
8086

Bell, Barbara L.
8087

Bell, Henry Hesketh Joudou
560, 8899, 8900

Bell, Howard H.
5597

Bell, John
2378

Bell, John L.
9736

Bell, L. Nelson
10474

Bell, Lester C.
8760

Bell, Richard
561

Bell, T. M.
1994

Bell, W. B.
5866

Bell, William C.
2505, 2506

Beckham, Albert S.
5993

Bellamy, Donnie D.
7550

Bellamy, V. Nelle
1738

Bellinger, Lucius
5996

Belshaw, Harry
1655, 1656, 3818

Belstrom, Chester E.
7068

Beltram, Gonzalo A.
9269

Beman, Nathans
4980

Bender, C.
562

Bender, Eugene I.
12913

Bender, Lauretta
7069

Benedict, Burton
563

Benedict, Dan
7182

Benedict, David
6698

Benedict, Ruth
10475

Benezet, Anthony
4764, 4765, 4766, 4767, 4768, 4769, 4770, 4771

Bengston, Dale Raymond
564

Benham, Marian S.
2035

Benjamin, T. Garrott, Jr.
9448

Ben-Jochannan, Yosef
8, 566

Bennett, Ambrose A.
6699

Bennett, Anne M.
11034

Bennett, George
3937

Bennett, J. Harry
4257, 8901

Bennett, John
5997

Bennett, John C.
10344, 11273, 11564, 11938

Bennett, Lerone
11565, 11566, 11567

Bennett, M. (Sister)
9903

Bennett, Norman Robert
1703, 2607

Bennett, Richard K.
10476

Bennett, Robert A.
567, 5998, 9816, 12369

Bennink, Richard J.
13153

Benson, Stanley
3458

Bent, James T.
83

Bentley, D. S.
6404

Bentley, H. Margo
2379

Benton, Peggie
8761

Benz, Ernst
3271

Bunton, Henry C.
8134
Buntrock, Orville A.
2647
Burdette, Mary G.
6723
Buresh, B.
7287
Burger, Mary W.
7842
Burger, Nash K.
4323, 5085
Burgess, Andrew S.
3949, 3950
Burgess, Lois F.
8135
Burgess, Margaret E.
6911
Burgess, Thomas
5621
Burke, Carl
12122
Burke, Fred G.
3464
Burke, John E.
10029
Burke, M. E.
8914
Burkhardt, Gustav E.
2053, 2648, 3194
Burkle, Horst
3951
Burleigh, Charles C.
5257, 5622
Burlin, Natalie
6023
Burnet, Amos
3284
Burney, H. L.
11945
Burnham, Kenneth E.
7087, 12990
Burnham, L. E.
7288
Burns, Aubrey
10494
Burns, Haywood
11295
Burns, W. Haywood
7289, 11583
Burridge, William
2649, 2650
Burroughs, Margaret G.
7463
Burroughs, Nannie H.
8136, 8137, 9329
Burt, C. B.
11296
Burt, Jairus
5258
Burton, E. D.
2651
Burton, Joe W.
9328, 10963
Burton, Richard Francis
611
Burton, William F.
612, 2387, 2388, 2652
Bury, Herbert
4265
Bush, J. B.
11946
Bushnell, Horace
4667, 4668, 4669
Buskes, Johannes J.
11584

Buster, William
10495
Buswell, James O.
4428
Butcher, Charles S.
7587
Butcher, Vada E.
6164
Butel, Pierre
8915
Buthelegi, Manas
613
Butin, Romain Francois
614
Butler, Alfred J.
109
Butler, Annie R.
2653
Butler, O. G.
9557
Butler, Rosa Kate (Smith)
2654
Butler, William H. H.
6413
Butsch, Joseph
9918, 9919
Butt, G. E.
1957
Butt, Israel L.
6414
Butterfield, Kenyon Leech
2054
Butterfield, R.
7588
Butt-Thompson, Frederick
615
Buxton, David R.
110, 111, 112, 113, 114
Buxton, Jean
616
Buxton, T. F. V.
2389
Buxton, Thomas F.
8942
Byaruhanga-Akiiki, A. B. T.
617
Byers, Theodore F.
7589
Byrd, Cameron W.
12123
Byrd, E. L.
10496
Byrne, Donald E.
6024
Byrson, Lyman
7631
Cable, George W.
10193
Cabon, A.
8916
Cabrera, Lydia
618, 8917, 8918
Cadbury, Henry J.
8919, 8920, 8921, 8922,
8923, 8924, 8925, 8926,
9481
Cade, John B.
5259, 7630
Cade, Toni
8138
Cady, George L.
6912
Cagnolo, C.
619
Cain, Richard H.
5873, 5874, 6415

Cains, Earle Edwin
2055
Caines, H. S. de.
8927
Cairns, Earle E.
5260
Calcraft, G.
2390
Calder, Ralph F. G.
3573
Calderwood, Henry
2056
Caldwell, Ben
8139
Caldwell, Erskine
12401
Caldwell, Gilbert H.
11297, 12402, 12403
Caldwell, J. C.
6416
Caldwell, John H.
4888, 9558, 9559
Caldwell, Josiah S.
7590, 8140
Calhoun, D.
11298
Calhoun, M. P.
11113
Calabar
1839
Calkins, Thomas M.
3574
Callaway, Godfrey
620, 2057, 2058, 2059,
2060, 2061, 2062, 2063.
Callaway, T. F.
5261
Calley, Malcolm J. C.
9276
Calloway, Henry
621
Calmettes, Jean Loup
3285
Calmon, Pedro
9277
Calverley, Edwin E.
7292
Calvez, Jean Y.
9920
Camara, Helder
13156
Camargo, Candido Procopio F.
9778
Camboue, S. J., P. Paul
2299
Cameron, J. M.
11585
Cameron, James
2316
Cameron, Richard M.
9560
Cameron, W. M.
3286
Campbell, Alexander
4324, 4746, 5623
Campbell, Douglas
5195
Campbell, Dugald
623
Campbell, Ernest Q.
11299, 11300, 10497
Campbell, Ernest T.
12801
Campbell, H. W.
11947
Campbell, J. P.
8602

Campbell, James
12124, 12405, 12406,
12407, 12766, 12872
Campbell, James F.
7592
Campbell, John
2064, 2065, 2066
Campbell, Robert
1840, 2722, 9922
Campbell, Robert E.
1752
Campbell, Robert F.
10498
Campbell, Stephen C.
9330
Campbell, Will D.
11041, 11586, 11948, 12873,
12991, 12992
Campen, Henry C.
12408
Camphor, Alexander P.
624
Cancela, Luis Lourenco
1942
Candler, John
4266
Cannon, Noah Caldwell
4429, 6417-6418, 8141,
8142
Cantori, Louis Joseph
625
Cantril, Hadley
7088, 7089
Cantwell, Daniel M.
9922
Canzoneri, Robert
4593
Capen, Nahum
5262
Capitein, Jacobus Eliza J.
4430
Cappelle, H. van
9279
Capper, Joseph
2655
Caprasse, P.
3273
Carámbula, Rubén
9280
Carawan, Guy
6025
Carcich, Theodore
12993
Cardi, C. N. de (Comte)
626, 627
Cardinall, Allan Walsey
628
Cardoso, Vladimir
8790
Carey, Archibald J.
6913
Carey, John J.
12409, 12410
Carey, Walter
1707
Carhart, C. L.
10499
Carles, Fernand
629
Carleton, Stephen
5263
Carletti, Giuseppe
9923
Carlile, Gavin
8929
Carlile, Warrand
8929

Chitty, Arthur B.
9835
Chivers, W. R.
7611
Chojnacki, Stanislaw
132, 133, 134, 135, 136
Chome, Jules
3288
Chona, M. Mainza
3421
Chrisiza, Dunduza K.
3960
Christaller, J. G.
1658
Christensen, A. M. H.
6036
Christensen, James Boyd
651
Christensen, Thomas G.
652
Christian Anti-Slavery Convention
5631, 5632
Christian Council of Nigeria
1842, 3823
Christian, John
4624
Christian Methodist Episcopal
Church
6653, 6654, 6655, 6656,
6657, 6658, 6659, 6660,
6661, 6662, 6663
Christian Movement For Human
Rights Against Commissioner
of Public Safety in Birmingham.
11957
Christian, Paul
7097
Christian Science Church
10097
Christiansen, James W.
10155
Christiansen, Ruth
1958
Christie, John W.
4987
Christofersen, Arthur F.
2080
Christy, David
2671, 4436, 5270
Christzberg, A. M.
6914
Church Anti-Slavery Society
of the United States.
5633, 5634
Church Conference on African
Affairs, Otterbein.
1942
Church Conferences on African
Affairs.
1711
Church Missionary Society
1843
Church Missionary Society for
Africa and the East.
2674, 2675
Church of God in Christ
7037
Church of the Brethen.
10124
Church, Roberta
8155

Churches.
9420, 9565, 9566, 9662,
9686, 9732, 9742, 9745,
9746, 9760, 9770, 9773,
9783, 9809, 9817, 9837,
9838, 9839, 9840, 9891,
9937, 9938, 9939, 10044,
10291, 10889.
Churchill, Rhona
12997
Clair, Matthew W.
7616, 7617, 9567
Clanton, Solomon T.
6731, 6732
Clapham, Christopher
139
Claridge, W. Walton
1659
Clark, Calvin M.
4675
Clark, Charles E.
9327
Clark College
6978
Clark, D.
11166, 11167
Clark, Davis W.
8156
Clark, Edgar R.
6037, 6038
Clark, Elmer T.
4329, 4891, 7098
Clark, Henry B.
10512, 11951, 12141
Clark-Hunt, C. G.
9161
Clark, Joseph D.
6039
Clark, Joseph S.
5635
Clark, Kenneth B.
7294, 9498, 11009, 11952,
12142, 12920.
Clark, Leon E.
3462, 3964
Clark, M. M.
6422
Clark, Mary T.
11953
Clark, Michael
7295
Clark, Robert D.
8157
Clark, Rufus Wheelwright
5272, 5273
Clark, Samuel
2081
Clark, Thomas D.
11318
Clark, William A.
7618
Clarke, Austin
11591
Clarke, J. D.
653
Clarke, J. W.
11592
Clarke, Jacquelyne J.
11954
Clarke, James Freeman
5156, 5157, 5636
Clarke, John
8935, 8936
Clarke, John H.
7099, 7296

Clarke, Mary O.
6040
Clarke, Richard F.
5117
Clarke, Virginia Maltby
654, 2676
Clarke, Walter
5637
Clarke, William F.
10513
Clarkson, Thomas
4778, 4779, 5638, 5639
Classen, A. J.
3965
Clavel, M.
8937
Claver, Peter (St.)
9959
Clay, Cassius M.
5274
Clayson, Rodman R.
16
Clayton, Edward T.
11593
Cleage, Albert B.
7297, 12266, 12374, 12419,
12420, 12669.
Cleaveland, Elisha L.
4676
Cleaver, Eldridge
8158, 11594
Clebsch, William A.
4437
Cleene, Nide
655
Cleghorn, Reese
11595
Cleghorn, Robert
8938
Cleland, C. S.
1594
Clemens, Eugene P.
10212
Clement, George
8159
Clement, Rufus
7619
Clemes, W. W.
7620
Clendenen, Clarence C.
1528, 2677
Cleve, Hugh Craswall
140
Cleveland, Charles D.
4988, 5627
Cleveland, E. Edward
10082
Cleveland, James T.
6041
Cliffe, Albert
9568
Clifton, Danzil T.
5086
Clinch, B. J.
2303
Clinchy, Everett R.
10514
Cline, Catherine Ann
1545, 3423
Clinton, Desmond K.
2082
Clinton, George W.
7621, 7622, 7623, 7624,
10515
Clinton, Iris A.
2083

Cloete, Stuart
2678
Clough, Simon
5640
Clouzot, Henri G.
8939
Clyde, Nathana L.
7625
Coan, Josephus Roosevelt
2679, 3966, 6423, 6424
Coates, Austin
3593
Cobb, Charles E.
11320, 13161
Cobb, Howell
4438
Cobbs, Price
13028
Cobbs, Therion E.
8164
Cobern, Camden McCormick
656
Coburn, John E.
12143
Cochrane, Eric
12425
Cocke, Sarah J.
6042
Cockin, Frederic A.
7626
Code, Joseph B.
9940
Coger, Dalvan M.
2839
Coggeshall, Samuel W.
4892
Coggins, Ross
10979, 11324, 12144
Coggins, Wade T.
9314
Cogley, John
11321
Cohen, Chapman
5275
Cohen, Daniel
8940
Cohen, David W.
5641
Cohen, Henry
10516, 10980
Cohen, J.
12921
Cohen, Lily Y.
6043
Cohen, Sheldon S.
4331
Cohn, Werner
10098
Coillard, Francois
1959, 2680
Coke, Thomas
4269, 8165, 9588
Coker, Daniel
8166
Cokes, George L.
10517
Colclough, J. G.
6665
Coldham, Geraldine E.
2681
Cole, Arthur C.
5276
Cole, Charles C.
5642, 5643
Cole, Henry
2304

Cox, Emmett Dean
3824
Cox, Frances A.
4442
Cox, Harvey
11322
Cox, James M.
9570
Cox, John M.
6429
Cox, Melville Beveridge
1754
Coxill, H. Wakelin
2400, 2401
Crabb, J. A.
8957
Crabitès, P.
7303
Craige, John H.
8958
Crain, James A.
4747
Crane, Jonathan T.
4897
Crane, T. F.
6049
Crane, William H.
3291, 3971
Cranston, Earl
9571, 9572
Crapsey, Algernon S.
8183
Craver, William C.
10375
Crawford, Daniel
2697
Crawford, E. May
2698
Crawford, Evans Edgar
7636, 11958, 12149
Crawford, Fred R.
11601
Crawford, George W.
6050
Crawford, J. R.
671, 2402, 2403, 3424
Crawford, Marc
7304
Crawford, O. G. S.
1599
Crawshaw, C. J.
2089
Creger, Ralph
11323
Creighton, William F.
3595
Cripps, Arthur S.
2699
Crite, Allan R.
6051, 8184
Critendon, Harriet
7136
Crogman, William H.
8185, 8186, 8513
Cromer, Voight R.
9513
Cromwell, John W.
5549, 6924, 7637, 10526
Cronan, Edward P.
4443
Cronin, J. F.
11171
Cronk, Katharine
2700
Cronon, E. David
7103

Crook, Roger H.
7638
Crook, William H.
10979, 11324
Crooks, Kenneth B. M.
8960
Cross, Jasper W.
4989
Cross, Sholto
672, 3292
Crossley, John
673, 674
Crothers, Samuel
5279, 5280, 5281.
Crouse, M.
10943
Crouzet
2308
Crowder, Calvin Ray
675
Crowder, M.
676, 677
Crowell, George H.
11959
Crowley, Daniel J.
6053, 8961, 8962, 8963
Crowther, E.
3597
Crowther, Samuel Adjai
678, 1845, 1846, 1847,
1848, 1849, 1850, 2701,
2702, 2703
Croydon, Edward
2405
Cruise O'Brien, Conor
10345
Crum, Jack
11048
Crum, Mason
9573
Crummell, Alexander
1755, 1756, 1757, 2704,
2705, 2706, 2707, 2708,
7639, 8187, 8188, 8189,
8190, 8191, 8192, 8193,
8194, 8195, 10527, 10528.
Crummey, Donald E.
164, 679, 1601, 1602,
1603.
Cuddihy, John M.
12923
Cuffe, Paul
5811, 8196, 8714, 8715
Cuffel, Victoria
5282
Cullen, Countee
8569
Cullin, Steuart
6054
Cully, Kendig B.
12150
Culp, Daniel W.
7640, 7681
Culpepper, Hugo H.
9334
Cultrera, Samuele
2406
Culver, Dwight W.
9574, 9575
Culverhouse, Patricia
12454
Culwick, Arthur T.
2709
Cuming, G. J.
10376
Cummings, George D.
3196

Cundall, Frank
8882, 8964
Cuninggim, Merrimon
11960
Cunningham, Dorothy H.
6430
Cunningham, Effie L.
9450
Cunningham, George
11602
Cunningham, James Francis
2407
Cunningham, John C.
6431
Cunningham, Robert J.
3598
Cunnison, I.
681
Curran, Francis X.
7641
Currens, Gerald E.
3825
Current, William C.
7642
Curry, Daniel
5283
Curry, Jabez L. M.
10529
Curry, Norris S.
12455
Curtis, Anna L.
4780
Curtis, George T.
5284
Curtis, Richard
7305
Cushman, Mary Floyd
1946, 3599
Cushmeer, Bernard
7306
Cutting, Sewall S.
4627
Cuvelier, Jean
1527, 2408
Cuypers, L.
2409
Cuzuano, Ottobah
5653
Dabbs, J. M.
10530
Dabbs, James M.
10103
Dabney, Robert L.
10531
Dabney, Wendell P.
8197
Dachs, Anthony J.
2089
Dagadu, P. K.
2710
Dahlberg, E. T.
9335
Daigre, Father
3197
Dain, Ronald
3463
Dalbey, E. Gordon
3972
Dalcho, Frederick
4444
Dale, Godfrey
682, 683, 684
Dallimore, H.
3293
Daly, John
1851

Dalzell, Bonnie
12999
Dalziel, Jack
2090
Damboriena, Prudencio
3973
Dames, Jonathan A.
7643
Dammann, Ernst
685, 3294
Dana, James
5285
Dana, Marvin
6057
Dancy, John C.
7644
Daneel, Marthinus L.
686, 3295, 3296, 3297,
3298, 3299, 3300
Danforth, Mildred E.
4781
Dangerfield, Abner W.
7645
Daniel, Everard W.
8198
Daniel, Robert P.
6925, 6926
Daniel, Vattel Elbert
7108, 7646, 7647
Daniel, W. Harrison
4628, 9336, 9576
Daniel, William A.
6927, 7648
Daniell-Bainbridge, H. C.
2091
Daniels, George M.
3600, 3601, 3602, 3974,
3975
Daniels, Henry E.
8199
Daniels, John
9483, 9484
Daniels, Joseph
13000
Dann, Martin E.
8200
Danneskiold-Samsoe, A.
8965
Danquah, Joseph Boakye
687, 688
Danzig, David
11325
Daoud, Marcos
165, 166
Dapper, Olfert
689
Darby, Golden B.
7184
Dargitz, Robert E.
3976
Darrow, Clarence
7649
Daskalakis, Apostolos V.
167
Daughtry, J.
12152
Dauphine, John W.
1660
Davenport, Frederick Morgan
7650, 7651
Davenport, William H.
6610, 6611
Davidson, G. W.
10156
Davidson, Hannah Frances
2092

Diamond, John C.
8211
Diamond, Stanley
3464
Diara, Agadem L.
3829
Diaz, J. A.
7215
Dickey, James H.
4448
Dickinson, Charles H.
2726
Dickinson, James T.
4681
Dickinson, Noadiah S.
4682
Dickinson, Richard
12457
Dickson, Andrew Flinn
4333
Dickson, Kwesi A.
701, 702, 3987
Dickson, Lynda
13210
Dickson, Moses
8212, 8213, 8214
Didas, James F.
9949
Dieterlen, Germaine
703, 704, 705
Dieterlen, H.
2727
Dieu, Léon
2413
Diffendorfer, Ralph E.
9579
Di Gangi, Mariano
12155
Diggs, James R.
7656
Diggs, John R. L.
7657
Diggs, M. A.
9950
Dike, Kenneth O.
1854
Dillard, James A.
6065
Dillmann, August
174, 175, 176, 177
Dillon, Merton L.
4782, 5654
Dindinger, Johannes
3102
Dinwoodie, W.
11332
Dioisopoulies, P. Allan
10538
Diro, Mergia
135
Dittes, James E.
13010
Dix, Jabez
8980
Dixon, Norman R.
12458
Dixon, O. M.
20
Doane, Thomas W.
707
Dobbins, Frank Stockton
708
Dobie, James F.
6067, 6068
Dodds, Elizabeth D.
11963
Dodds, Fred W.
1855

Dodge, Ralph E.
2729, 3610, 3988
Dodson, Dan.
7658, 11964
Doering, Alma E.
2414
Doherty, Joseph F.
9951
Doi, A. R. I.
709, 710
Dole, Kenneth
7114, 12460, 13012, 13168
Dollar, George W.
5293
Dollard, John
7659
Dollen, Charles
11333
Dombrowski, Joanne
178
Dominion Sister
1960
Donald, Henderson H.
5879
Donaldson, Stuart A.
711
Donegan, Charles E.
3830
Donohugh, T. S.
1758
Dooley, Howard
11170
Doresse, Jean
21, 179, 180, 181
Dorey, Frank David
6930, 10539
Döring, Paul
2730
Dorman, C. E.
8659
Dornas, Joao
8783
Dorough, Charles D.
5294
Dorsainvil, Justin C.
8981
Dorsey, George A.
712
Dorson, Richard M.
6070, 6071, 6072, 6073
Dos Santos, Juana E.
8784
Doty, James E.
2731
Doty, Robert C.
13013
Dougall, James W. C.
1712, 2731, 2732, 2733,
2734, 2735, 2736, 2737,
3302, 3989, 3990.
Douglas, Arthur J.
1803
Douglas, Carlyle C.
11616
Douglas, Mary
713
Douglas, Norman
10157
Douglass, Frederick
5295, 5655, 8216, 10540,
10541, 10542
Douglass, Harlan P.
5880
Douglass, William
7660, 8217
Douglin, D.
8218

Doulophilus
4452
Doutte, Edmond
3200
Dovlo, C. K.
3991
Dowd, Jerome
7661, 10543
Dowey, Edward A.
12804
Dowling, John
6739
Dowling, Theodore Edward
183
Downes, Rupert M.
714
Downey, David G.
9580
Downs, Karl E.
7662
Doyle, Bertram W.
10544
Drach, George
2738, 2739
Drake, Richard B.
5881, 10195
Drake, St. Clair
7663, 7641, 10380
Drake, Thomas E.
4783, 4784
Draper, Charlotte
2741
Draper, Theodore
12461
Dreves, Francis M.
2415
Drew, Samuel
4274
Drewes, C. F.
9514
Driberg, Jack Herbert
715
Drimmer, Melvin
7314
Drisler, H.
4453
Drummond, Andrew L.
5296
Drummond, Eleanor
12157
Drury, Clifford M.
4992
Dubb, A. A.
3992
Dube, J. L.
2094
Duberman, Martin B.
5656
DuBois, Felix
1566
Dubois, Henri Marie
716, 2311, 2742, 2743
DuBois, William E. B.
717, 5657, 6740, 7665,
7666, 7667, 7668, 7669,
7670, 7671, 7672, 7673,
7674, 7675, 9485, 9952,
10381, 10545, 10546.
Dubose, Hampden C.
2744
Ducas, George
7315
Duckett, Alfred
11618
Dudley, Miss Mary
4454
Dudley, Taney
9257

Duensing, Hugo
184, 185
Duff, Douglass V.
186
Duff, E.
10315, 11966, 11967
Duffield, George
5297
Dugan, George
11619, 12158, 12159, 21260,
12925, 13014
Duignan, Peter
1528, 2677, 3967
Duke, Robert W.
12462
Dulin, Robert O.
12161
Dumond, Dwight L.
4987, 5298, 5590, 13015
Dunbar, Ann
4104
Dunbar, Barrington
9486
Dunbar, Duncan
9332
Dunbar, E.
11620
Dunbar, L. W.
11053
Dunbar, Paul L.
6075, 8521, 8550
Duncan, Hannibal G.
10547
Duncan, James
4455
Duncan, Peter
8982, 9163
Duncan, Sylvia
2416
Duncan, W. J.
12162
Dungee, John R.
6076
Dunger, George A.
718
Dunham, Chester F.
5659
Dunham, Dows
22
Dunham, Katherine
8983
Dunlap, William C.
9487
Dunlop, John
4683
Dunn, James J.
10548
Dunn, Larry
13016
Dunne, George H.
10316
Dunne, William
9953
Dunningan, A.
8984
DuPlessis, Johannes
2095, 2096, 2745
Du Preez, Andries Bernardus
3611, 3612
Durden, Lewis M.
6741
Durham, E. C.
9581
Durham, Harriet F.
8985
Durkee, Arthur A.
9287

Estes, Joseph R.
   12926
Esteves Pereira, Francisco
   Maria
   195, 196, 197
Etheridge, J. W.
   9588
Etherington, Norman Alan
   2101
Euba, Akin
   741
Eubank, Richard
   2754
Eubanks, John B.
   7692
Eucher, F.
   2421
Eugene, Toinette
   12466
Eutsler, Frederick B.
   10554
Evangelical Consociation
   5305
Evangelical Covenant Church
   of America
   2422
Evangelical Union Anti-slavery
   Society of the City of New
   York.
   5661
Evangelicus
   4464
Evans, David K.
   6082
Evans, John T.
   1961
Evans, Joshua
   5306
Evans, Luther
   25
Evans, Melvin O.
   742
Evans-Pritchard, Edward E.
   744, 745, 746, 747, 748
Evans, Randall H.
   12467
Evans, Ronald
   7327
   See also
   Esa, Raqi
Evans, Stanley George
   4005
Evans, St. John
   743
Evans, Walter
   12169
Evans, William
   4786
Even, A.
   749
Everett, E. E.
   6343
Evtushenko, E. A.
   11624
Ewald, Heinrich
   210
Ewart, David
   4465
Ewell, John L.
   8222
Ewing, Ethel E.
   750
Ezeanya, S. N.
   751, 752
Ezell, Humphrey K.
   13020

Fabian, Johannes
   3304, 12170
Fabunmi, M. A.
   753
Faduma, Orishetukeh
   754, 2756, 7694
Fage, J. D.
   1530
Fager, C. E.
   11627
Fahey, Frank J.
   9956
Fahim, Hussein
   956
Fahs, Charles Harvey
   2757
Fahs, Sophia Blanche
   2423
Fair, Harold L.
   9589
Fairbanks, Calvin
   8529
Fairchild, Edward H.
   10196
Fairfax, Jean
   11628
Fairly, John S.
   9847
Faitlovitch, Jacques
   211
Falkner, D.
   755
Falls, Arthur Grand Pré
   7695, 9957, 9958, 10555
Falls, Helen E.
   9341
Fanon, Frantz
   4007
Farag, Farag Rofail
   214
Faramelli, Norman J.
   13021
Farguhar, Charles W.
   1763
Farish, Hunter D.
   9590
Farmer, E.
   3305
Farmer, James
   10556
Farnum, Mable
   9959
Farrakhan, Louis
   7328
Farrar, P. A.
   8992
Farrow, S. S.
   756
Faublee, Jacques
   757
Faulk, John H.
   8223
Faulkner, Clyde W.
   9591
Faulkner, L. E.
   9750
Faulkner, Rose E.
   2758
Faulkner, William J.
   6083
Faupel, John Francis
   2424
Faure, Jean
   3203
Fauset, Arthur H.
   7121

Faust, Arthur J.
   758
Fave, Armand J.
   5123
Favre, Edouard
   2103, 2759
Fawcett, Benjamin
   5309
Fax, Elton C.
   7122, 13092
Feagin, Joe R.
   10557
Featherstone, Joseph
   12927
Federal Council of the Churches
   of Christ in America.
   9593, 9750, 10211, 10212,
   10214-10238, 10240
Federated Colored Catholics
   10074
Fedry, J.
   4008
Fee, John Gregg
   4466, 4467, 4468
Fegin, Joe R.
   9960
Fehderau, Harold W.
   3306, 3307, 3427
Felder, Cain H.
   12771
Feldmann, Susan
   761
Felton, Carroll M.
   12171
Felton, Ralph A.
   7696, 7697, 7698, 7699,
   9594
Fenton, Thomas
   3204
Ferguson, George P.
   2104
Ferguson, John
   759, 760, 3857
Ferm, Vergilius T.
   7700
Fernandes, Albino G.
   8786
Fernandes, Florestan
   8759
Fernandez, James W.
   762, 763, 764, 765, 766,
   767, 768, 3308, 3309,
   3310, 4009.
Ferrer, J. M.
   11019
Ferrere, F.
   769
Ferris, David
   4788
Ferris, William H.
   8224
Ferris, William R.
   6084, 6085
Ferry, Henry
   9751, 10610
Feurlicht, Robert S.
   11629
Fey, Harold E.
   9961, 9962, 10279, 10961,
   11339, 11340
Fiawoo, D. K.
   770
Fichter, Joseph H.
   9963, 9964, 11341, 11342,
   11973
Fickland, R. William
   7701

Fickling, Susan M. M.
   4335
Field, M. J.
   771
Fields, Arlene L.
   6086
Fiers, A. Dale
   9456
Fife, Robert O.
   4748, 10558
Figge, Horst H.
   8787
Figueired, Napolean
   8788
Findlay, G. G.
   2760
Findlay, L.
   217
Fineberg, S. Anhil
   12928
Finkelstein, Louis
   7631
Finley, James B.
   8225
Finley, Robert
   5617, 5618
Finnegan, Ruth
   772, 773
Finney, Charles G.
   4684, 5742
Finney, Rodney E.
   2761
Fintan, Father
   3205
Fiorenza, Francis P.
   9288
First African Baptist
   Church
   6697, 6720
First African Presbyterian
   Church, Phila., Pa.
   9738, 9740, 9743
Fischer, Oskar
   774
Fish, Carl R.
   5312
Fish, Henry C.
   5313
Fish, John H.
   12468, 12469
Fish, John O.
   9595
Fishel, Leslie H.
   8226
Fisher, A. B.
   2762
Fisher, Allan G. B.
   775
Fisher, George E.
   5314
Fisher, H. J.
   776
Fisher, Humphrey J.
   3311
Fisher, Lena Leonard
   2763
Fisher, Miles Mark
   2764, 6088, 6744, 6745,
   6746, 6934, 7123, 7703,
   7704, 7705, 7706, 8227,
   10559.
Fisher, Ruth B.
   3206
Fisher, Samuel Jackson
   9752, 9753
Fisher, William Singleton
   3207

Froncek, Tom
11177

Frost, Maria Goodell
4474

Frothingham, Frederick
5668

Frothingham, Octavius B.
5162, 5163, 5164, 5669

Froude, J. A.
8997

Frucht, Richard
7720

Fry, C. Luther
7721

Fry, H. W.
11350

Fry, John R.
12174, 12175, 12477

Fueter, Paul D.
4014

Fuhs, Hans Ferdinand
219

Fulani Bin Fulani
2783, 2784

Fuller, Bertha
8234

Fuller, Edward J.
5199

Fuller, Erasmus Q.
4903

Fuller, J. Latimer
2109, 2110

Fuller, James C.
4822

Fuller, Richard
4632

Fuller, Thomas O.
6750, 6751, 7722, 8235,
8236, 8237, 8238, 10563,
10564

Fuller, W. Harold
2274-75, 3469, 4015

Fullerton, William Young
2427

Fullinwider, S. P.
13022

Funk, F. X.
220

Furfey, Paul H.
5325

Furlong, C. W.
2785

Furman, Richard
4633

Furness, William Henry
5165, 5166, 5167, 5168,
5169, 5670, 5671

Fyfe, Christopher (Hamilton)
2786, 3840

Gaba, Christian R.
796, 797, 798, 799

Gaddy, Jerrel D.
10928

Gailor, Thomas F.
9850

Gaines, Miriam
10382

Gaines, Wesley J.
6444, 10565

Gainous, Albert
6445

Gairdner, G. D. A.
800

Gairdner, W. H.
801

Galbiati, Giovanni
1605

Gale, Hubert P.
2428

Gale, William K.
2319

Gallagher, Buel G.
10566, 10567, 10568,
10569, 10570, 10908

Gallagher, Joseph T.
802

Gallaudet, Thomas H
4475

Galloway, Charles B.
10571

Galphin, Bruce M.
11636, 11637

Galpin, William
5326, 5327

Galvao, Eduardo
8796

Gambrell, J. B.
9344

Gammon, Eleza H.
9707

Gammon Theological
Seminary
2789, 6939, 6940, 6978,
7004, 9612

Gamperle, Lukas
2320

Gamst, Frederick Charles
221

Gandhi, Mohandas K.
11682, 11828, 11835

Gandy, Samuel L.
7724, 8239, 8240, 11978

Gann, Lewis Henry
1962

Gannett, Ezra Stiles
5170, 5171, 5328, 5329

Gannett, William C.
5172

Gannon, Michael V.
5126

Gannon, Thomas M.
12176

Ganse, Hervey Doddridge
4476

Garber, Paul N.
4904

Garber, Paul P.
7124, 11638

Garcia, Samuel Ruiz
803

Gardiner, James J.
12478

Gardiner, John S.
8241

Gardiner, Marilyn
8998

Gardner, E. C.
11351

Gardner, R. B.
10944

Garfield, James W.
9757

Garfinkel, Herbert
11352

Garland, Phyl
8242, 11639

Garlick, Peter C.
4016

Garlick, Phyllis Louisa
2429, 5330

Garman, Harold W.
11979

Garner, R. O.
804

Garnet, Henry H.
5672, 5673, 5674, 5675,
5676, 8243, 8452, 10572.

Garnett, Bernard E.
7329, 11054, 12773

Garnier, Christine
805

Garrett, A. E. F.
3618

Garrettson, Freeborn
5677

Garrison, William L.
4477, 8525

Garritt, J. B.
2790

Gartlan, Jean
806

Garvey, A. J.
9973

Garvey, Marcus M.
5848, 7125, 7126, 7127,
12706

Gasnick, Roy M.
11179, 11180

Gatewood, R. D.
4017

Gaudnault, Gerard
11640

Gaustad, Edwin S.
5331

Gavan Duffy, Thomas
2791

Gay, Milton F.
9851

Gayle, Addison
13171

Gaynor, W. C.
9974

Gbadamosi, G. O.
807

Gebauer, Paul
808

Gehres, M.
11980

Gelfand, Michael
809, 810, 811, 812, 813,
814, 2111, 3210

Gelman, Martin
7128

Geltman, Max
12479

Gelzer, David Georg
1547, 12480

General Anti-Slavery Convention.
5772

Genischen, H. W.
4018

Gentz, William H.
10318

George, Arthur A.
6936

George, C. T. T.
2793

George, Carol V.
6446

George, Poikail John
2794

George, Thomas P.
8999

Georgia Writers' Project,
Work Projects Administration.
6095

Geppert, Dora H.
5895

Gerasimov, G.
11644

Gerbeau, Hubert
11645

Gerber, A.
6096

Gerbert, Martin
8797

Gerdener, Gustav A.
2112, 2113, 3619

Germillion, Joseph B.
11181

Germond, Robert C.
2114

Gerner, Henry L.
11353

Gerster, Georg
222, 223

Gessell, J. M.
11646

Getty, Marie Madeline of
Jesus (Sister)
28

Geyer, Franz Xaver
2276

Gholson, Edward
8244

Gianazza, Elvira
1606

Gibbons, James
5127

Gibbons, R.
10948

Gibbons, R. W.
11182

Gibbs, Jonathan C.
4994, 8245

Gibbs, Mifflin W.
5678

Gibson, A. B. B.
6447

Gibson, Alan G. S.
2115, 2116, 2117, 2118,
3315

Gibson, Bertha A.
5679

Gibson, DeLois
6937

Gibson, Edmund
4338

Gibson, John W.
7725

Gibson, Joseph K.
9599

(Keis) Gidada Solon
1607

Giddings, Joshua R.
4478

Giel, R.
224

Gielow, Martha S.
6098

Giffen, John Kelly
2277, 3211

Gifford, Edward S.
6099

Gilbert A.
11354

Gilbert, Arthur
5200

Gilbert, John W.
2796

Gilbert, Matthew W.
8247

Gilbert, Mercedes
6100

Gillard, John Thomas
225, 7726, 9975, 9976,
9977, 9978, 9979, 9980
10573, 11183

Green, Sue B.
5688
Greenberg, Joseph H
831, 832, 833
Greene, Lorenzo J.
4343
Greene, Sherman L.
6450
Greenleaf, Jonathan
6942
Greenleaf, R.
10983
Greenslade, Stanley L.
5343
Greenwood, Leonard
8801
Greenwood, Theresa
6106
Greer, Harold E.
9003
Gregg, Howard D.
6451
Gregor, A. James
7334
Gregorius (Bishop)
237
Gregory, Dick
12486
Gregory, John Walter
2807
Grenfell, W. D.
1948
Greschat, Hans-Jurgen
835, 3428, 3473
Greville, Robert K.
5344
Grey, M.
12776, 12878
Griaulle, Marcel
238
Grier, William
13028
Grier, Woodrow A.
9346, 11363
Griffin, Clifford S.
7736
Griffin, Edward D.
4999
Griffin, Eunice
6452
Griffin, John H.
11655, 11287, 12775, 13029
Griffin, Maude K.
7737
Griffith, Francis Llewellyn
836
Griffith, T. L.
8258
Grigg, Charles
12003
Griggs, John Paul
2808
Griggs, Leverett S.
5345
Griggs, Sutton E.
8259, 10583
Grill, C. Frederick
7738
Grimes, Alan P.
12182
Grimes, Leonard A.
5346
Grimes, William W.
6453
Grimke, Angelina E.
5347, 5689, 5690

Grimke, Francis J.
5898, 7739-48, 8260-98,
9751, 10584-10614, 10898
Grimley, John B.
3842
Grinstead, S. E.
6755
Grissom, Mary A.
7749
Grissom, W. L.
9605
Gritz, Jack L.
10930
Grizzard, R. Stuart
12814
Groffier, Valérien
3213
Groppi, James E.
11185, 11364, 12269, 12331
Grose, Howard B.
9004
Groselaude, Étienne
2321
Gross, Alexander
4906
Gross, Bella
5691
Grosvenor, Cyrus P.
5348
Groth, Siegfried
3623
Grout, L.
4344
Groves, Charles Pelham
2809, 2810, 2811
Groves, Richard
12487
Grubb, Norman Percy
2433
Gruber, Jacob
5550
Grundemann, R.
2812, 2813
Grunebaum, Gustave E.
837
Guebels, Léon
2434
Guersa, Israel B.
8993
Guggenheim, Hans
9005
Guice, John A.
4907
Guidi, Ignazio
239, 240, 241
Guidi, Michelangelo
242
Guilcher, Rene Francois
1575, 3214
Guinnes, Fanny Emma
2435, 2436
Gullins, William R.
6454
Gulliver, J. P.
4689
Gulliver, P. H.
838
Gulzow, Henneke
5349
Gunda, Zephania
3474
Gurley, Ralph R.
1768
Gusimana, Bartholome
3843
Gustafson, James M.
7750

Gusweller, J. A.
11986
Guthrie, John
5692
Gutieviez, Gustavo
12596
Gwaltney, Grace
7751
Gwaltney, L. L.
9347, 9501
Gwoehr, Wesley M.
7752
Gwynne, L. H.
2279
Haberland, E.
243
Hacker, C. Leroy
6756
Hackett, Allen
10949, 13030
Hadden, Jeffrey K.
11365, 13031
Hadfield, E. L.
3624
Hadfield, Percival
839
Hagood, Lewis M.
9607, 10615
Hague, William
4486
Hahn, Heinrich
1609
Haines, A. Grove
4023
Haines, C. R.
840
Hair, Paul E. H.
841, 1532, 1533, 2004,
2005, 3844
Haitz, Linn
842
Hake, A.
3475
Halberstam, David
11658, 11659, 11660
Halévy, J.
244
Haley, Alex
7246, 7336
Haley, James
6943
Haliburton, Gordon M.
1665, 1666, 3316, 3317
Hall, A. L.
8299
Hall, Barnes M.
4485
Hall, Clarence W.
12183
Hall, Edward B.
4690
Hall, Ernest N.
8300
Hall, Gwendolyn M.
9008
Hall, Julien A.
6108
Hall, Nathaniel
4691, 4692, 4693, 4694,
4695, 4696
Hall, P. W.
5350
Hall, W. H.
7753
Hallden, Erik
1548

Hallenbeck, Wilbur C.
7186
Hallencreutz, Carl F.
3941, 4024
Hallett, Robin
2814
Halliday, Fred
8802
Halloway, Harriette R.
9769
Hallpike, Christopher R.
843
Halpern, Ben
10984, 12932, 12933
Halsey, Abram W.
1549, 2815, 2816
Halvorson, Lawrence W.
11366
Hamblin, Dora J.
11987
Hambly, Wilfrid D.
844, 845
Hamer, John H.
245
Hamid, Idris
8928
Hamilton, A. H.
10616
Hamilton, Benjamin A.
2817
Hamilton, C. H.
7686, 7754
Hamilton, Charles V.
12488
Hamilton, Fayette M.
6667, 6668, 8301
Hamilton, R. A.
846
Hamilton, W. T.
4487
Hamilton, William
5693, 5694, 5695, 5696.
Hamm, Jack
10617
Hammelt, William
9162
Hammerschmidt, Ernst
246, 247, 248, 249, 250,
251, 252, 261
Hammon, Jupiter
5351, 5697, 6109, 7755,
8302, 8303, 8694
Hammond, E. W. S.
2818
Hammond, J. D.
10618
Hammond, Lilly H.
8304, 10385, 10619
Hammond, Peter B.
9211
Hampton Institute
6912, 6926, 6935, 6944
Hampton Negro Conference
6945
Hance, Gertrude Rachel
2121
Handler, Jerome S.
4278
Handlin, Oscar
11367
Handy, James A.
6455
Handy, Robert T.
6946, 7757
Hanish, Joseph J.
11368

Hays, Brooks
11372
Hayward, Victor E. W.
3318, 3319
Haywood, Charles
6115
Haywood, Dolores C.
1770, 1771
Haywood, J. W.
11057
Hazzard, Walter R.
9614
Heacock, Roland T.
8335, 8538, 10950
Heard, William H.
2830, 2831, 6459
Hearn, Winifred
8337
Heathcote, Charles W.
4864
Heaton, Jane
3628
Hecht, James L.
11993, 13176
Heckman, Oliver S.
10627
Hedding, Elijah
8156
Hedgeman, Anna A.
11994
Hedgley, David R.
7768
Hefele, Karl J.
5000
Hefly, J. Theodore
10628
Heggoy, W. N.
2832
Height, Dorothy I.
11995
Heimer, Haldor Eugene
3320
Heintzen, H.
866
Heinwick, J. O.
867
Heinz, H. John
11668
Heithaus, C. H.
9984
Helander, Gunnar
2122
Hellberg, Carl J.
2833
Hellberg, J. H.
4030
Hellwig, M.
11189
Helm, C.
7221
Helm, Mary
10629
Helm, T. G.
5701
Helper, Hinton R.
5355
Helser, Albert D.
1864, 1865, 2834, 2835,
2836
Helton, Charles L.
8338
Hemmens, Harry L.
2441
Hempel, Christa
261
Hemptinne, Jean Felix de
2442

Hemstreet, Robert
11255
Henderlite, R.
11373
Henderson, George E.
9011
Henderson, George W.
8339, 8340, 10630
Henderson, Lawrence W.
13177
Hendrick, George
11669, 11670
Hendrick, S. Purcell
9012
Hendrickson, Francis H.
2443
Hening, E. F.
2837
Henkle, Moses M.
4912
Henning, C. Garnett
7769
Henning, Thomas
5356
Henny, Jeanette
9013
Henriet, M.
4031
Henry, Caleb S.
8341
Henry, Frances M.
9014, 9015, 9016
Henry, Hayward
12503, 12778
Henry, Mellinger
6116
Henry, Romiche
8342
Hensey, Andrew F.
2444, 6117
Hensman, C. R.
12192
Henson, Herbert Hensley, (bp.)
4492
Henson, Josiah
8083, 8343
Hentoff, Nat
7338, 11671, 12935
Henzlik, William C.
9615
Hepburn, D.
9985
Hepburn, Dave
11672
Hepburn, James Davidson
3216
Herberg, Will
11374, 12193
Herbert, Mary Elisabeth
(A'Court), (Baroness)
262
Hernton, Calvin C.
7339
Herr, Dan
9986
Herrick, E. P.
9017
Herrick, Mary D.
4032
Herring, Hubert C.
9431, 10631
Hersey, John
5357
Hershberger, Guy F.
10632
Herskovits, Frances S.
869, 870, 8804, 8805,
8806-11, 9291-97.

Herskovits, Melville J.
523, 868, 6118, 7771,
8804-11, 9018-21, 9291-97.
Hertefelt, Marcel d'
2445
Hertlein, Siegfried
2838
Herz, S.
9987
Herzog, Frederick
12504, 12505, 12506, 12507,
12508, 13178
Herzog, H.
3321
Hesburgh, Theodore M.
11170, 11190
Hess, Mahlon M.
4033
Hess, Robert L.
263, 264, 2839
Hessel, Dieter T.
12194
Hester, William H.
6759
Heston, David
7772
Hetherwick, Alexander
871, 872, 3430
Hewitt, Doris W.
7773
Hewitt, Gordon
2840
Hewitt, James
2123
Hewson, Leslie A.
2124
Heyer, Friedrich
265
Heywood, R. S.
3479
Hibbert, Robert, Jr.
4279
Hickman, Garrison M.
12509
Hickman, Thomas L.
9349
Hickok, C. T.
7774
Hickok, Laurens P.
5358
Hicks, Elias
4823, 4824
Hicks, Richard R.
6119, 13179. 13180
Hicks, William
6760, 6761
Higginbotham, Maurice J.
6460
Higgins, Edward
3629, 3630
Higginson, Thomas W.
4493, 5359, 5360
High, Thomas O.
1866
Hilford, M. R.
2841
Hilger, Rothe
6121
Hilgers, Walter
2446
Hill, Andrew W.
6762
Hill, Bob
12510
Hill, Charles L.
6461, 8344, 8345, 8346,
8347, 8451, 9516

Hill, Clifford S.
9022, 9023, 9024, 13033
Hill, Daniel G.
7775, 7776, 8240, 8348,
8349
Hill, David
7232
Hill, Davis C.
9350
Hill, Edward V.
12511
Hill, Hilley
7191
Hill, John L.
8350
Hill, Leslie P.
8351
Hill, Richard
874
Hill, Richard H.
6763
Hill, Samuel S.
9351, 10633, 11375, 11376,
11377, 11996
Hill, Timothy A.
10634
Hillhouse, William
5361
Hillman, Eugene
4034
Hilton, Bruce
12195
Hilty, Hiram H.
4825
Himmelfort, Milton
19085
Himchcliff, Peter B.
2125, 3322, 4035
Hinchliff, P.
3631
Hinchliff, Peter B.
3323, 3631
Hinderer, Anna (Martin)
1867
Hine, J. E.
2842
Hine, Virginia H.
7045
Hinkle, J. Herbert
7777
Hinman, H. H.
5702
Hinnant, John
875
Hinsley, Arthur
266
Hinton, John H.
9025
Hinwood, Bonaventura
11378
Hippolytus
267
Hirsch, Leo H.
6949
Hiskett, Mervyn
876
Historia Missionum Ordinis
Fratrum Minorum
2843
Historical Records Survey
6462, 6741, 6950
Hitchcock, James
12196
Hitchens, William
873

Jones, David Benjamin, (Mrs.)
2880

Jones, David D.
10662

Jones, Donald Gene
9625

Jones, F. Melville
1875, 1876, 2381, 2882, 2883

Jones, G. Curtis
13040

Jones, Herbert G.
2450

Jones, Howard O.
13041

Jones, J. D. Rheinallt
2137

Jones, Jerome W.
4358

Jones, John G.
9626

Jones, John R.
4506

Jones, Lawrence N.
7809, 12531, 13187

Jones, Le Roi (Imamu Amiri Baraka)
4045, 6163, 7352

Jones, Madison
12209

Jones, Major J.
12532, 12533, 12534

Jones, Miles J.
12535

Jones, R. E.
7649

Jones, Raymond J.
7140

Jones, Rex R.
1615

Jones, Richard B.
9458

Jones, Robert E.
8404, 9773, 9670

Jones, Rufus M.
4829

Jones, Singleton T.
6624, 6625

Jones, Summerfield F.
7810

Jones, Terry
9356

Jones, Thomas C.
4507

Jones, Thomas Jesse
2884

Jones, William A.
12536

Jones, William R.
12537, 12538, 12539, 12540, 12541

Jones-Williams, Pearl
6164

Jordaan, Bee
2885

Jordan, Artishia
6477

Jordan, Casper L.
6478, 8405

Jordan, Clarence
11390

Jordan, David M.
11063

Jordan, Frederick D.
6479

Jordan, John P.
1877

Jordan, Lewis J.
1774, 6777, 6778, 6779, 6780

Jordan, Marjorie W.
4916

Jordan, Richard
4830

Jordan, Winthrop D.
7811, 7812, 10663

Jorns, Auguste
4831

Josca, Guissepe
11694

Joseph, Gaston
1695

Joseph, James A.
11391, 12542, 12819

Josselin de Jong, J. P. B.
9054

Jouen, Louis
2331

Jowers, Joseph B.
7813

Joy, Charles R.
2886

Juhnke, James C.
3647

Julien, Claude
9055

Jullan, George W.
5378

Jumbale, Anderson
939

Jump, Chester J.
2451

Jungmann, Josaf
281

Jungraithmayr, H.
3473

Junker, B. H.
10890

Junker, L.
9300

Junkin, George
4509

Junod, Henri A.
940, 941, 942, 943

Junod, Henri Philippe
944, 2138

Jurji, E.
13042

Kaan, Fred
1949

Kaberry, P. M.
785

Kabore, D. Y.
945

Kaemer, John
946

Kagame, Alexis
947, 948

Kaiser, Clyde V.
7814

Kahn, B. M.
10987

Kahn, Tom
11491

Kale, S. I.
949

Kalff, S.
9301

Kalilombe, Patrick A.
3648, 4046

Kallimachos, D.
282

Kamfer, Pieter
3485

Kamil, 'Abd-al-'Aziz 'Abd-al-Qādir
950

Kampschmidt, William H.
9519

Kanyua, Jesse Ndwiga
951

Kaplan, Harry
10664

Kaplan, Howard M.
7354

Kaplan, Sidney
8406

Kardiner, Abram
7141

Karefa-Smart, John
4047

Karefa-Smart, Rena
4048

Karmiris, Ioannis
283

Karon, Bertram P.
7815

Karpas, Melvin R.
7355

Karpozilos, Apostolos D.
284

Karr, Albert R.
11695

Karsch, Carl G.
12210

Kasozi, A. B. K.
952, 953

Kastler, Norman M.
10665

Kataza, Eugene
3519

Kater, John L.
9857

Katoke, Israel K.
12211

Kaufer, Sonya F.
9627

Kaufmann, Leonard
13188

Kaufnian, Ishi
7222

Kaula, Edna Mason
954

Kavulu, David
2453

Kay, John
5006

Kay, Stephen
955

Keable, Robert
3433

Kealing, Hightower T.
7816, 8407, 8408, 8409

Kearney, John
11201

Kearney, Vincent S.
4049

Keats, Ezra Jack
4050

Keck, Daniel
2332

Kedro, Milan J.
5905

Keedy, T. C.
11392

Keefer, Justus
4510

Keeley, Benjamin J.
13189

Keenan C.
12001

Keene, Calvin
4832

Keet, B.
3649

Kehler, L.
4051

Keidel, Levi O.
11249

Keil, Charles
7817

Keith, George
4833, 4834

Keith, Henry H.
8814

Keller, Jean
3434

Kellerman, A. P. R.
3650

Kellersberger, Julia L.
2454, 2455, 2456

Kelley, H.
7142

Kelley, James R.
11393

Kelly, Gerald S. J.
9995

Kelly, Herbert
2139

Kelly, Laurence J.
9996

Kelsey, George D.
9357, 10111, 10666, 11394, 11395, 13043

Kemble, Frances A.
5379

Kemp, Dennis
1669

Kemp-Blair, Henry J.
3651

Kempton, Murray
12820

Kendall, R. Elliott
3652

Kendrick, J. R.
5906

Kenealy, William J.
12002

Kennard, Richard
6781

Kennedy, Gerald H.
9628

Kennedy, John G.
956

Kennedy, John Herron
2887

Kennedy, Louise
6165

Kennedy, Louise V.
10666

Kennedy, P.
6782

Kennedy, Robert F.
12543

Kennedy, William B.
4052

Kennedy, William T.
6166

Kenrick, Bruce
12212

Kent, G. E.
6167

Kent, Juanita R.
9629

Kentucky Baptists
6893

Kenyatta, Jomo
957

Locke, Mary S.
4704
Lockley, Edith
7151
Lockwood, Ted
3663
Lods, Adolphe
303
Loeb, Edwin M.
1021, 1022
Loederer, Richard A.
9083
Loescher, Frank S.
10117, 10687, 10688,
11415, 11416
Loewen, Jacob A.
1023, 1024, 1025
Loewen, Melvin J.
2468
Löfgren, Oscar
304, 305, 306
Logan, Rayford W.
8425, 10689
Logan, S. C.
9776
Loguen, Jermain W.
5400
Lohrentz, Kenneth P.
3336
Løken, Andreas
3664
Lokos, Lionel
7394, 11777
Lomax, Alan
6179, 6180, 6205
Lomax, John A.
6180
Lomax, Louis E.
7395, 7396, 11778
Lombard, Pascal (Padre)
1623
London Emancipation Com-
mittee's Tract.
5735
London Missionary Society
5401
Long, Charles H.
974, 1026, 8426, 8427,
12558, 12559, 12560,
12561
Long, Charles S.
6485
Long, Edward L.
7152
Long, Herman H.
9434, 11417
Long, John C.
9461
Long, John D.
5402
Long, Norman
3665
Longcope, Kay
12562
Longstreet, Augustus B.
4516
Loram, Charles T.
2155, 3337
Lord, F. Townley
2926
Lord, John C.
5008
Lord, Nathan
5009
Lord, Samuel E. C.
7843, 10690
Lorew, Joseph
11779

Loring, Eduard N.
5403
Lorit, Sergio C.
11780
Lorraine, Guy
3666
Lory, Maris Joseph
2469
Loth, Heinrich
2927, 4070
Lott Carey Baptist Foreign
Mission Society
6786, 6787
Lotz, Adolf
5404
Louis-Jean, Antonio
6181
Lounsbury, Thomas
4517
Love, Edgar
7844
Love, Emanuel K.
6788
Love, H. Lawrence
9777
Love, Horace T.
5405
Love, J. Robert
9084
Love, James E.
7398
Love, William D.
5406
Lovejoy, Joseph C.
4518, 5736
Lovejoy, Owen
4519
Lovelace, C. C.
6182
Lovelace, John A.
12822
Lovell, John
6183
Lovett, Leonard
7050
Lovewell, Lyman
5407
Low, A. Ritchie
10118
Low, D. A.
2470, 3490
Lowe, J. R.
12228
Lowenstern, Edward S.
307
Lowrie, John C.
2928
Lubell, Samuel
10993
Lucas, George W.
6789
Lucas, Jonathan Olumide
1027, 1883
Lucas, Lawrence E.
12780, 13055
Lucatello, Enrico
1624
Luccock, Halford E.
9633
Luck, Anne
2929
Ludlow, Helen W.
5966
Ludwig, Charles
1718
Luecke, Jessie R.
9521

Lugira, A. M.
1028
Luiden, Anthony
10119
Luideus, D. A.
12198
Luijk, J. N. van
224
Luka, Ibrahim
308
Luke, James
2930
Lunceford, Bill E.
9364
Lund, John L.
10161
Lundgreen, F.
309
Lundy, John P.
4520
Lunn, Arnold H.
5408
Luntadila, Jean-Cl. L.
4071
Lupton, D. E.
5202
Luther, Ernest W.
310
The Lutheran Church,
Missouri Synod.
9522, 12781
Lutheran Church. South
Africa
3667, 3688
Lutheran Church. South
West Africa
3669
Luttig, Hendrik Gerhard
1029
Lutze, Karl E.
12229
Luykx, B.
4072
Luzbetak, Louis J.
1030
Lyda, Happy C.
9462
Lyke, James
12563
Lyles, James V.
13200
Lynch, Hollis R.
3856
Lynch, James
9603
Lynch, John R.
5911
Lyon, Ernest
5912, 9634, 9635
Lyon, James A.
5010, 5011
Lyons, Adelaide A.
4521
Lyons, Charles H.
2599
Lystad, Robert A.
1031
Mabie, Catharine Louise Roe
2471, 2472
Mabuda, Fanny
2158
MacArthur, Kathleen W.
10691
Macbeth, James
4522
Macdonald, Allan J.
2931

Macdonald, Duff
1807
Macdonald, Eugene M.
5409
MacDonald, James
1033, 1034
MacDonald, John S.
9085
MacDonald, Roderick J.
3338, 3670
MacDonnell, John de Courey
2473
MacDowell, John
10417
Macgregor, J. K.
2932
MacGregor-Hastie, Roy
2933
MacIver, R. M.
7631
Mackay, Alexander M.
2474
MacKaye, William R.
10086
MacKenzie, George S.
2475
MacKenzie, Agnes E.
1035, 1036, 1037
MacKenzie, D. R.
1038
MacKenzie, Jean Kenyon
1556, 1557, 2934, 2935
Mackenzie, John
2156
MacKenzie, William Douglas
2157
Mac Keown, Robert L.
1884
MacKerrow, P.
6790
MacKintosh, Catherine W.
1808, 1966, 2936
Macklin, John M.
10692
Mackrell, J. E. C.
1039
MacLean, Angus H.
11260
Maclean, Norman
1809
Mac Mahon, Edward Oliver
2338
MacMaster, Richard K.
4919, 5737
Macmillan, Elizabeth W.
10398
Macmillan, Margaret B.
4920, 4921
Macpherson, R.
1719
Macrae, David
9778
Maddocks, Lewis J.
10951, 12230
Maddox, George L.
11342
Maddry, Charles E.
1885
Madron, Thomas W.
9636
Madziyire, Salathiel
1040
Maesen, William A.
7399
Mafeja, Archie
1041

May, Samuel Joseph
4289, 5174, 5741

May, Sherry
8432

May, William W.
9639

Mayard, Aurora
8433

Mayer, Albert J.
7851

Mayer, M.
10701

Mayer, Philip
3677

Mayhew, Bruce F.
12233

Mayle, Bessie H.
6187

Mayo, Amory D.
10702

Mayo, Robert
13202

Mayr, F. R.
2166

Mays, Benjamin E.
5915, 6962-64, 7852-64,
8434-45, 10321, 10322,
10400, 10703-16, 11426-
28, 12234, 12459, 12579,
13061.

Maze, Jules
2944

Mazrui, Ali A.
1072, 3493, 12566

Mba, Cyriac S.
1073

Mbaeyi, P. M.
4086

Mbali, E. Z.
3678

Mbiti, John S.
1074-81, 4087-92, 12580,
13203

Mbunga, Stephen B. C.
1082

McAdams, Nettie F.
6188

McAfee, Joseph E.
10717

McAfee, Sara J.
6673

McAvoy, Thomas T.
10016

M'Caine, Alexander
4526

McAll, Samuel
5203

McAllister, Dorothy
3494

McBeth, Leon
9367

McCabe, Joseph
5415

McCabe, Lida R.
7865

McCall, Emmanuel L.
12567, 12568, 12569

McCarriar, Herbert G.
9859

McCarter, John M.
2167, 4929

McClain, William B.
12570

McClellan, G. E.
7866

McClelland, E. M.
1085

McClendon, James W.
10935, 11815

McCloud, J. Oscar
9779

McClure, William Donald
1629

McColl, C. W.
10718

McCord, Louis A.
10936

McCord, William
12235

McCorry, V. P.
10017

McCoy, C.
11429

McCreary, Edward D.
10719

McCulloch, Margaret C.
10402

McCulloh, James E.
10401, 10720

McCutcheon, James N.
11430

McDaniel, Cecilia
9094

McDaniel, Charles-Gene
8446, 2236

McDaniels, Geraldine
8447

McDermott, J. A.
11210

McDermott, Patrick P.
13062

McDonald, Erwin
11323

McDonnell, Jane
12571

McDonough, John
10721

McDowell, Edward A.
10121, 10722, 10723, 10724,
12014, 13063, 13064

McEwen, Able
4705

McFall, Ernest A.
4093

McFarlan, Donald Maitland
1888

McFerran, D.
13065

McFerrin, John B.
9640

McGarey, Margaret
3859

McGavran, Donald Anderson
2945, 9095

McGee, Daniel B.
6189

McGee, William
3208

McGhee, N. B.
6190

McGiffert, Arthur C.
5742

McGill, Alexander T.
5014

McGill, Ralph
11431

McGinnis, Frederick A.
10725

McGlothlin, W. J.
9368

McGrath, Oswin
4094, 10726

McGregor, A. W.
1720

McGrew, J. H.
10403

McGroarty, Joseph G.
10018

McGuire, U. M.
6681

McIlvane, D. W.
11211

McIntire, Robert L.
8827

McIntosh, Brian G.
1721, 3339

McIver, Isaiah
7509

McKay, Claude
6191, 6192, 7156, 7157,
10019, 12947

McKee, Don
11816

McKee, William
2946

McKeen, Silas
5416

McKelvey, Blake
5916

McKenna, David L.
12237

McKenney, Theodore R.
12238

McKenzie, Azariah
9096

McKenzie, P. R.
2947

McKeon, Richard M.
10727

McKiever, Charles
4837

McKinley, Carlyle
10728

McKinney, Richard I.
6565, 10729, 12239, 12572

McKinney, Samuel B.
6193

McKitrick, Eric L.
2948

McLanaham, Samuel
2948

McLaurin, Benjamin F.
12928

McLaurin, Dunbar S.
12240

McLean, David A.
1084

McLees, A. V.
11212

McLeod, Alexander
5015

McLeod, J. R.
6674

McLoughlin, William G.
4641, 4642, 4706, 5016,
5417

McManus, Eugene P.
11213

McManus, Michael J.
12241

McMillan, G.
11432

McMillan, William A.
9641

McMurrin, Sterling M.
10164

McNeil, Jesse Jai
8448, 8449

McNeile, R. F.
322

McNeill, George
9097

McNeill, Robert B.
10730, 11433

McNeilly, James H.
4930, 5418

McPeak, Francis W.
12242

McPeak, William
12015

McPheeters, A. A.
9642

McPherson, James M.
12573

McQuilkin, Frank
12574

McTyeire, H. N.
4364

McVeigh, Malcolm J.
1086, 4095

McWright, A.
4528

Mdlalose, W. J.
3679

Meacham, Standish
5419

Meachum, John B.
8450

Mead, Frank Spencer
6966, 7867, 9098

Mead, Margaret
1087

Meade, William
4365, 4366

Means, John E.
1088

Mearns, John G.
12243

Mears, W. J. Gordon
2168, 2169

Mears, Walter
3230

Mears, William
2170

Mechem, D.
3680

Medbery, Rebecca B.
2010

Medeiros, Jose
8828

Medford, Hampton T.
6628

Meeham, Thomas F.
10020

Meek, C. K.
1089, 1090

Mehan, Joseph
11214

Meier, August
5610, 7407, 7868, 7869,
10731, 11817, 12016, 12017,
12388

Meigs, Paul A.
7158

Meikle, H. B.
9099

Mein, David
8829

Meinardus, Otto F.
323, 324, 325, 1630

Meinerts, Oryn G.
3860

Meinhof, Carl
1091, 1092, 2949

Meister, Richard J.
12244

Moodie, T. D.
3685
Moody, Joseph N.
10024
Moon, Bertha L.
8456
Moon, Henry L.
7410
Moore, Basil
3686, 3687, 12588
Moore, Charlean DeBerry
36
Moore, Clark D.
4104
Moore, Dale H.
344
Moore, Edmund A.
5019
Moore, Eine
345
Moore, Elton
9370
Moore, Everett L.
7052
Moore, Frank L.
8457
Moore, G.
1129
Moore, George F.
2960
Moore, George W.
10743
Moore, H. E.
5422
Moore, J. D.
9371
Moore, James R.
4105
Moore, Joanne P.
9372
Moore, John J.
6631
Moore, John M.
9661
Moore, Joseph G.
8834, 9113
Moore, LeRoy, Jr.
6201, 12255
Moore, Loren Ellsworth
2478
Moore, R. J. B.
1130, 1972
Moore, Ruby A.
6202
Moore, Wilbert E.
5747
Moorehead, Alan
1131
Moorhead, James H.
5020
Moorhouse, Geoffrey
2961
Moorland, Jesse Edward
8458, 10406, 10407, 10408
Mooth, V.
11085
Morand, Paul
6203
Morant, John J.
8459
Morcelli, Stefano A.
2962
Modell, Albert
4838
Mordini, Antonio
320
Morel, Edmund D.
1133

Moret, Alexandre
37
Moretz, Rufus L.
346
Morgan, Carol M.
9114
Morgan, David
9373
Morgan, Joseph H.
6494, 8460
Morgan, Lily Mae Wingate
1894
Morgan, Thomas J.
9374, 9375, 9376, 9377
Morgan, Thomas M.
10081
Morgan, W. T. W.
3231
Morgenthau, M. J.
11448
Morill, Anson P.
5424
Morison, Samuel E.
5205
Morland, Kenneth J.
7879
Moroney, T. B.
10025
Morpurgo, A. J.
9302
Morrill, Madge (Haines)
2963
Morris Brown College
6990, 7024, 7025
Morris, Charles S.
6792, 6793
Morris, Colin M.
3439, 3688, 4106, 4107,
4108, 4109
Morris, Elias C.
8461
Morris, James W.
8835
Morris, Madison C. B.
8462
Morris, Robert
4707
Morris, Samuel S.
6495
Morrisey, Richard A.
4533, 4534
Morrison, Elizabeth J.
8463
Morrison, George
13069
Morrison, James H.
2964, 2965
Morrison, Lionel
3689
Morrison, S. A.
347
Morrow, Ralph E.
5918, 5919
Morse, Jedidiah
5425
Morse, Samuel F. B.
4535
Morse, Sidney Edwards
4536, 5426
Morsell, John A.
7411, 12827
Morshead, Anne E. M.
2175, 2966
Morton, Don
3690
Morton, Lena B.
8464

Morton-Williams, Peter
1134
Mosely, B. W.
5920
Mosely, Charles C.
10744
Moses, William H.
6794, 6795, 6796, 6797,
8465, 8466, 8467
Mosley, Leonard Oswald
348
Mosmans, Guy
1135
Mosothome, Ephraim K.
4110
Moss, James A.
12589
Moss, Leonard W.
12590
Moss, Otis, Jr.
8468, 8469, 12256
Mossell, Gertrude E. N.
8470
Motley, Constance B.
11250
Moton, Robert R.
10745
Motovu, Joachim
76
Mott, Abigail
8471
Mott, Lucretia
5748
Mott, John Raleigh
2967
Mott, Paul E.
13070
Mouezy, Henri
2968
Moulton, Phillips
5427
Mounger, Dwyn
9780
Mount Zion M. E. Church
9662
Moving Star Hall Singers
6204, 6205
Moxom, Phillip S.
10206, 10746
Moyd, Olin P.
6206, 6207, 6208
Moyer, Elgin S.
10124
Mpongo, Laurent
1136
Mgotsi, L.
3348
Mshana, Eliewaha E.
4111, 4112, 4113, 12591
Mtumishi
6209
Muckle, Coy
10125
Mudge, James
9664
Mudge, Zachariah A.
5749
Muelder, Walter
7880
Mueller, John Theodore
2969, 2970, 2971, 9525
Mueller, Samuel A.
13071, 13208
Mufassir, Sulayman S.
1137
Muga, Erasto
3498

Muhammed, Said Abdulla
1138
Mukendi, Placide
1139
Mukenge, Godefroid
1140
Mulago gwa Cikala Mushar-
hamina
1141
Mulago, Vincent
1142, 1143
Mulder, John M.
12828, 13072
Muller, Gerald F.
11826
Mullin, Gerald W.
5553
Mullin, Joseph
4115
Multi-Racial Conference on
Christian Responsibility
Toward Areas of Rapid
Social Change. Johannes-
burg, 1959.
3691
Mumba, Levi
1144
Munday, J. T.
1145
Munro, Eleanor C.
349
Munshaw, Joe A.
11827
Munthe, Ludvig
2340
Muravchik, E.
10997
Murdock, John N.
4643
Murphree, Marshall W.
1146
Murphy, Dubose
5101
Murphy, Edgar G.
10465
Murphy, Edward F.
10026
Murphy, John C.
10027
Murphy, Miriam T.
10028
Murray, Albert Victor
1895, 2972, 2973, 2974
Murray, Andrew E.
6967, 7881, 9781
Murray, Ellen
6210
Murray, Florence
7882
Murray, Jocelyn
3349
Murray, M. M.
4116
Murray, Michael H.
12257, 12258, 12592
Murray, V. W.
6968
Murray, William
4290
Musa, Thomas
4117
Mushanga, Musa T.
4118
Muste, Abraham J.
10748
Mutembei, Richard
3499

Mutwa, Credo Vusa'mazula
1147

Muzorewa, Abel
3692

Mveng, Englebert
1148

Mwanza, R.
1149

Mwasaru, Dominic
4119

Myer, Gustavus
10749

Myers, James G.
6211

Myers, John Brown
2479, 2480

Myers, Lewis A.
9378

Myrdal, Gunner
7883, 10992

N. A. A. C. P.
7884, 10164, 10167, 10378, 11212, 11309, 12038, 12827, 12829, 13094

Nabeeta, Tom
4120

Nadel, Siegfried F.
1150, 1151, 1152, 1896

Nail, Olin W.
9665

Nance, Ellwood C.
9463

Nanna, John C.
9666

Nannes, Caspar
9379

Nash, J. O.
2176, 3693

Nashville, Tenn. Vanderbilt University Divinity School
13073

Nass, Eef A. H.
3500

Nassau, Robert H.
1154, 1155, 1690, 2975, 2976, 3232

National Association for the Advancement of Colored People
see N. A. A. C. P.

National Baptist Convention of America
6894, 6895

National Baptist Convention, U. S. A. Inc.
6799, 6800, 6801, 6802, 6803, 6804, 6805, 6806, 6807, 6808, 6809.

National Baptist Publishing Board
6712, 6732, 6740, 6810

National Baptist Sunday School Convention of the U.S.
6811

National Catholic Conference for Interracial Justice
11217, 11218, 11219, 11240, 12137

National Committee of Black Churchmen
12593, 12887-12891

National Committee of Negro Churchmen
12886

National Conference of Catholic Bishops
13209

National Conference of Church Leaders
10367

National Conference of Colored Men of the United States
10410

National Conference on Race and Religion
12019

National Conference on the Christian Way of Life
10412, 13074

National Council of Churches of Christ in the United States of America
10279, 10282-10301, 10302, 11115, 11449, 11475, 11975, 12018, 12041, 12062, 12259, 12344, 12830, 12831

National Council of Congregational Churches
9426

National Council of the Episcopal Church
11137

National Negro Evangelical Association
6968

National Urban League
7886

Nau, Henry
1897

Nau, John F.
9526

Naylor, Wilson Samuel
2977

Nazarenes
10140

NCC
see also
National Council of Churches of Christ in the United States of America

Ncube, Pius A.
4121

N'Daye, Jean P.
7433

Neal, James H.
6213

Necheles, Ruth F.
9115

Neckebrouck, V.
2978

Needles, Edward
5750

Neehall, Roy
9116

Negaso Gidada
350

Negro Missionary Baptist in America
6761

Negro Young Peoples' Christian and Educational Congress
10413, 10414

Neher, Andrew
6221

Neill, Stephen C.
2979, 4122

Neilson, Peter
5430

Nelsen, Hart M.
11122, 12594, 13210

Nelson, Alice R.
6222, 7644

Nelson, C. Ellis
12595

Nelson, Clarence T. R.
9668

Nelson, Geoffrey K.
7161

Nelson, Isaac
5431

Nelson, J. Robert
351, 10323, 10324, 11452, 12833

Nelson, John O.
10753

Nelson, Lowry
10168, 10169

Nelson, Patricia D.
6223

Nelson, Robert G.
2482, 3694, 4123, 9117, 9118

Nelson, William S.
4537, 8476, 10754, 10755, 10756, 10757, 11828, 12021, 12022

Nemoy, Leon
352

Nenquin, Jacques
1156

Nerberg, Well
12023

Nesbitt, Lewis Mariano
1157

Nesbitt, Rozell W. P.
3695

Ness, John H.
3870

Nettleford, Rex
9119

Neuhaus, Richard J.
12596

Nevin, Edwin H.
5021

Nevin, John W.
5751

Nevin, Robert
4538

Nevinson, Henry W.
2980

New, Charles
3233

New England Colored Baptist Convention
6843

New England Missionary Baptist Convention
6818

New Jersey. Churches
7010, 7011

New York City
4709, 6821, 6822, 6823, 6824, 6825, 6826, 6827, 7897

New York Colored Mission
10415, 10416

New York, Missionary Research Library
2981

Newborn, Captolia D.
6675

Newby, Donald O.
12261

Newby, Idus
10758

Newcomb, Harvey
5432

Newell, Frederick B.
9669

Newell, William W.
6224, 6225, 6226, 6227, 6228

Newhall, Fales H.
5752

Newing, Edward G.
3501, 4126

Newman, Albert H.
6682

Newman, Edward W.
353

Newman, Henry Stanley
2341

Newman, Louis C.
4539

Newman, Richard A.
12597, 12598, 12599

Newport, R. I., Shiloh Baptist Church
6832

Newsome, Effie L.
8477-78

Newton, Alexander H.
6497

Newton, John B.
7898, 9865

Newton, Page
6184

Newton, Percy J.
8479

Ney, Joseph S.
3502

Ngindu, A.
3350, 4127

Ngoumou, P. C.
4128

Ngoyi, Louis
4129

Ngugi, James
4130

Nichol, Francis D.
10087

Nichol, John T.
7053

Nichols, Decatur W.
6498

Nichols, J. L.
8513

Nichols, L.
11454

Nichols, S.
10938

Nicholson, John
5921

Nicolas, Jacqueline
3861

Nida, Eugene A.
9303

Niebuhr, Helmut R.
6970

Niebuhr, Reinhold
12024

Niebuhr, Richard R.
12025

Niederberger, Oskar
3697

Niklaus, Robert L.
3440, 3441, 3442

Niles, John M.
4839

Nina Rodriques, Raymundo
8836, 8837

Nipperdey, H.
1158

Nisbet, Richard
4291

Nix, Roscoe N.
12600

Nixon, Justin W.
10347

Nketia, Joseph H.
1159, 1160, 1161, 1162,
1163, 4131
Noack, Hana G.
11832, 11833
Noble, Frederic Perry
2983, 2984
Noble, Lowell Lappen
1164
Noble, Walter James
3698
Noel, Baptist W.
4367
Nolan, J. T.
10034
Nolde, Otto
10325
Nomenyo, Seth
4132
Norbeck, Edward
1165
Nordby, Juel A.
4133
Norden, Hermann
354, 355
Norfolk, Va. First Baptist
Church
6709
Norman, Clarence
12027, 12601
Norris, H. T.
1166
Norris, Hoke
13076
Norris, J. Frank
8629
Norris, John W.
6499
Norris, Katrin
9122
North American Assembly
of African Affairs, Wit-
tenberg College, 1952.
4134
North American Baptist
General Conference
3862, 3863
North Carolina Churches
7030
North Carolina. General
Assembly
5433
North Carolina. Neuse River
Baptist Association
6902
North, Eric McCoy
2985
North West Rhodesia.
General Missionary Con-
ference.
1973
Northcott, William C.
2177, 2986, 2987, 4136
Northern Baptist Convention
9380
Northwood, Lawrence K.
11455
Norton, H. Wilbert
3443
Norton, W.
12602, 12603
Norvel, William
6230
Norwood, John N.
4937

Noshy, Ibrahim
356
Noss, Philip A.
1167
Nothstein, Ira C.
9527
Nott, Samuel
4710, 4711, 4712
Nottingham, John
1168
Noussanne, Henri de
9123
Novack, George
12391
Nsasak, I. V.
1898
Ntlabati, Gladstone
3699, 3700
Ntwasa, Sabelo
13212, 13213
Nuby, C.
11838
Nuermberger, Ruth A.
4841
Nukunya, K. G.
1169
Nunnelly, Donald A.
9464
Nunns, Theodora
2178
Nürnberger, Klaus
3701, 3702
Nwabara, Samuel N.
1170
Nyblade, Orville
2342, 2989
Nye, Joseph S.
10170
Nygren, Malcolm
12028
Nystrom, Gertrude E.
1722
Oak Hill Industrial Academy
9754
Oak, Liston M.
8370
Oakes, Henry N.
9670
Oates, J. F. A.
38
Obatala, J. K.
7231, 7442
Obiechina, Emmanuel
4137
Oblate Sisters
10055
O'Brien, David
12262
O'Brien, Donald C.
1172, 1173
Ochiagha, Gregory O.
1899
Ochsner, Knud
3503
O'Connel, Jeremiah J.
10035
O'Connell, James
1174, 1175, 1176
O'Connell, P.
7899
O'Connor, John J.
11224
Odell, Brian N.
12263
O'Dell, J. H.
11839

Odhiambo, Abel Ouma
4138
Odiong, Udo
1177
Odita, E. Okechukwu
1178
Odom, Edward J.
7900
Odonkor, S. S.
1674
O'Donohue, J.
1179
Odum, Howard W.
7901
Oduyoye, Mercy Amba
4139
Oduyoye, Modupe
1180, 1900
Oertel, Hanns
6231
Ofari, Earl
7443
Offer, Henry J.
12604
Officer, Morris
1778
Offley, Greenberg W.
5434, 8102
O'Gara, J.
7444
Oger, Louis
1181
Ogilvie, Charles F.
5922
Oglesby, Enoch H.
12605
Oglesby, Jacob
12264
Oglethorpe, James
2179
Ogot, B. A.
1182
Ogunba, Oyinade
1183
Ogutu, G. E. M.
1184
O'Hanlan, Douglas
357
O'Hanlon, Mary E.
10036
Ohio State Christian Anti-
Slavery
5753
Ohsberg, Harry O.
6828
Ojiako, J.
4140
Okafor-Omali, Dilim
4141
Okite, Odhiambo
3351, 4142
Oko, William
1185
Okon, Gabriel
1902
Okonji, D. Ogbulu
1186
Okullu, J. Henry
4143, 4144, 4145
Okuma, Thomas M.
1947
Olatunji, Kwame
1187
Olatunji, Olatunde
1903
Oldendorp, Christian G. A.
4292

Oldham, Joseph H.
2484, 2990, 2991, 2992,
2993, 2994, 10128, 10759
O'Leary, de Lacy Evans
358
Olinton, Desmond K.
2180
Olisa, Michael S. O.
1188
Oliver, Bernard J.
7055
Oliver, C. Herbert
12606, 13077
Oliver, Kenneth D.
12607
Oliver, Pearleen
6829
Oliver, R. A.
1530
Oliver, Revilo P.
7445
Oliver, Roland
3234
Oliver, Vere L.
9124
Olivet Baptist Church
6830
Olsen, Jack
7446
Olson, Arnold O.
9671
Olson, Bernard E.
10760
Olson, Gilbert W.
2013
Olson, Howard S.
12608
Olsson, Karl A.
12609
Olumide, Y.
4146
Oluwole, Isaac
1904
O'Mahoney, Kevin
1634
Omari, C. K.
1189, 1190
Omijeh, Matthew
1191, 1192
Omoyajowo, Joseph A.
1193, 1194
O'Neal, Eddie S.
12252
O'Neil, Maud E.
9181
O'Neil, Michael J.
8481
O'Neill, Joseph E.
10037
Ong, Walter J.
3864
Oniki, S. Garry
10129
Onokpasa, B. E.
3703
Onwuachi, P. Chike
4147, 7163
Oosthuizen, Gerhardus C.
2182, 3352, 3353, 4148,
4149, 4150, 4151
Opaleye, 'Biodun
4152, 4153
Opocensky, Milan
12610, 12611
Opoku, Kofi Asare
1195

Peabody, George Barh-Fofe
1781
Peabody, William B. O.
5762-63
Peacock, Amjogolo E.
2014
Peaden, W. R.
3355
Peak, Lynda S.
1910
Pearce, Gordon James M.
2487
Pearce, Ivy
364
Pearle, C. Baker
6517
Pearne, Thomas H.
5926, 10773
Pearson, Colbert H.
6977
Pearson, J. D.
1228
Pearson, Rcger
1229
Peck, George
4939
Peck, Nathaniel
5764
Peck, W. H.
7906
Peckard, Peter
5765
Pedersen, Odd Kvaal
3715
Pederson, Pernie C.
2185
Peeks, Edward
12615
Peel, John D. Y.
1230, 3356-58
Peeters, Paul
2488
Pegues, Albert W.
6833
Peirce, Alfred M.
6978
Peirot, Claude-Helene
1231
Pelt, Owen D.
6834
Peltola, Matti
3007
Pelton, Robert W.
6243
Pemberton, John De J.
10971
Penabaz, Fernando
9465
Penard, F. P.
9147
Pendleton, Louis
6244
Penetar, Michael P.
10043
Penick, C. C.
1232
Penn, Irvine G.
7590, 7907-08, 8491

Penn, Robert E.
6835
Pennell, William E.
13078
Pennington, Edgar L.
4371, 4372
Pennington, James W. C.
5766-74, 8083, 9786,
10774
Pentecost, E. C.
3359
People United to Save
Humanity (PUSH)
12271
Percy, Douglas Cecil
2287
Pereira, Manoel N.
8840
Pereira de Queiroz, M. I.
8841
Perez, Joseph A.
9673, 12272
Perham, Margery
365
Perkins, A. E.
6245, 7909
Perkins, Benjamin P.
13214
Perkins, Haven P.
4372
Perkins, John
13215
Perkins, Justin
5442
Perlo, Filippo
1724
Perraudin, Jean
3445
Perregaux, E.
1233
Perret, Edmond
3716
Perrin, Jacques
9920
Perrin-Jassy, Marie F.
4159
Perruchon, Jules
366
Perry, David B.
9493
Perry, Galbraith
10044
Perry, Grace N.
6518
Perry, H. J.
10768
Perry, Lewis
4550, 5775
Perry, Naomi
6519
Perry, Rufus L.
10775
Person, I. S.
6836
Person, Yves
1234
Peter, Mary
12065

Peters, Erna Alma
3010
Peters, G.
3011
Peters, W.
11848
Petersen, William J.
3012
Peterson, Frank L.
10088, 10776
Petitjean-Roget, J.
9148
Pétridès, Stephanos Pierre
367
Petrie, William M. F.
39-42
Pettay, Louanna
6012
Pettersson, Olof
1235-36
Pettey, Sarah D.
8492
Pettigrew, M. C.
6676
Pettigrew, Thomas F.
7910, 10777-78, 11001,
11299, 11300
Pharr, Julia M.
9492
Phelan, Macum
4940
Phelps, Amos A.
4551, 5776
Phenix, George P.
6246
Philadelphia, Pa.
4845, 5206, 6837-38,
6986, 9868
Philander Smith College
6937
Philbrick, Herbert
10467
Philip, John
2190, 5025
Philip, Robert
3013
(Abuna) Philippos
368
Philipps, Tracy
1238
Philips, H. E.
3251
Phillippo, James M.
9239
Phillips, A. L.
9787
Phillips, Charles H.
6677
Phillips, Earl H.
1911
Phillips, Gene D.
3014
Phillips, J. E. Tracy
1238
Phillips, Randolph
10779
Phillips, Ray E.
2191, 3360

Phillips, Romeo E.
6247, 6248
Phillips, Wendell
8523
Philpot, David
4160
Philpot, William M.
8493
Phipps, William E.
3446
Phraner, Wilson
9788
Pich, V. Merlo
1239
Pickens, Andrew L.
5026
Pickens, William
7911, 10780
Pickett, Clarence E.
4846
Piepkorn, Arthur C.
6839-40, 9528
Pierce, David H.
9505
Pierce, Elijah
6249
Pierce, Paul S.
5927
Pierpont, Ivan de
2489
Pierpont, John
5443
Pierre, C. E.
4373
Pierre-Louis, Ulysse
9149
Pierson, Arthur T.
2015, 3015-17
Pierson, Donald
8842-43
Pierson, Paul
8844
Pierson, Robert H.
8494
Pike, Esther
10781
Pike, G. D.
10198
Pilch, Judah
11002
Pilkington, Frederick
1912, 3866, 9150-51
Pilkington, George
5138
Pillsbury, Parker
5444, 5777, 5778
Pilpel, H. F.
11850
Pinch, Pearse
10782
Pineau, Henry
1810
Pinnington, John E.
9152, 9305
Pinnock, Samuel G.
1913
Pinto, Tancredo da Silva
8845-46

Shoemaker, Gertrude M.
3240
Shorrocks, Francis
9189
Shorter, Aylward
1335, 1336, 1337, 1338,
3519, 4203
Shorter, Susie I.
6538
Shrewsbury, William J.
4954
Shriver, Donald W.
11501, 13111
Shropshire, Denys W.
1339, 1340, 1341
Shurden, Walter B.
9391, 9392
Shuttlesworth, Charles E.
12052
Sibley, James L.
1792
Sibree, James
1342, 1343, 2348, 2349,
2350
Sicard, Harold von
2351, 2352, 4204
Sideboard, Henry Y.
6678
Sidney, Joseph
5812
Siebert, Wilbur H.
4850
Siegmeister, Elie
11883
Sievers, E. K.
4205
Sihler, Wilhelm
4573
Silberman, Charles E.
12053
Silva, Antonio da
1539
Silver, Abba H.
10838
Silver Bluff, S. C.
Silver Bluff Baptist Church
6721
Silver, James W.
5474
Simensson, Tord
4206
Simmons, George F.
5813
Simmons, William J.
8573
Simmons, William S.
1344
Simms, David M.
12304
Simms, James
9692, 10839, 13227
Simms, James M.
6861
Simms, Joseph D.
8574
Simon, A.
12305
Simon, Jean Marie
3071
Simon, Walter B.
7485
Simons, Norman G.
10840
Simonson, Jonathan D.
1730
Simoons, Frederick J.
400

Simor, George
7235
Simpkins, Patrick L.
9495
Simpson, Donald H.
3521
Simpson, George E.
1345-46, 3880, 9113, 9191-
9211, 10841, 10921
Simpson, J. David
10842
Simpson, Matthew
4955, 8157
Simpson, Richard
11012
Simpson, Robert B.
6282
Sims, Charles F.
4383
Sims, David
6995
Sinclair, George H.
7967
Sinclair, Margaret
1637
Sinclair, Upton
5475
Singh, Raman K.
7968
Singleton, Deborah
7171
Singleton, George A.
3073, 4384, 6539, 6540
Singleton, Michael
3377, 4207
Singmaster, Elsie
2700, 9536
Sipkins, Henry
5814
Sisk, Glenn N.
7969
Sissel, H. B.
11128, 11129, 11130
Sitahal, H.
9212
Sithole, Ndabaningi
3378, 3750
Sitton, C.
11884
Sketon, D. E.
9693
Skinner, Elizabeth
401
Skinner, Elliot P.
1347, 1348
Skinner, Tom
13009, 13112-13120
Skolaster, Hermann
1560
Slack, Kenneth
11885
Slade, Ruth N.
2506
Slater, Jack
12306
Slattery, John R.
9393, 10056, 10057, 10058,
10059, 10060, 10061
Sleeper, Charles F.
12674
Slicer, Henry
4956
Sloane, James R. W.
5053, 5054
Slosser, Gaius J.
5055
Sly, Virgil A.
2507, 2508

Small, John B.
8575-8578
Smart, Ninian
1349
Smectymnuus
4730, 5485
Smedes, Susan D.
4386
Smedley, Robert C.
5816
Smiley, Portia
6283
Smit, M. T. R.
2217
Smith, A. C. Stanley
2509
Smith, Alfred W.
1350
Smith, Allen H.
7970, 12675
Smith, Arthur L.
7469
Smith, Asa D.
5056
Smith, Brian H.
4208
Smith, Cecil R.
13228
Smith, Charles S.
1793, 2218, 3074, 6541-
6544, 8579-8580, 10843-
10844
Smith, Charles U.
12004
Smith, Cynthia
1351
Smith, Clayton C.
9213, 9214, 9466
Smith, Donald E.
4209
Smith, Donald H.
11886, 11887
Smith, E.
4578
Smith, Earnest A.
11502
Smith, Edward
5057
Smith, Edwin W.
1352-1355, 1985, 2219-
2223, 3075-3077, 3241
Smith, Eli
3078
Smith, Elwyn A.
11503, 12676
Smith, Emmitt M.
8581
Smith, Ernest
7027
Smith, Eugene L.
9694
Smith, Frances S.
10332
Smith, George
8582
Smith, George W.
9215
Smith, Gerrit
5058, 5059, 5486, 5817,
5818
Smith, Goldwin
4579
Smith, H. Sutton
2510, 2511
Smith, Henry B.
5487
Smith, Herbert Maynard
2353

Smith, Hilrie S.
5060, 5061, 10845
Smith, Hubert W.
8583
Smith, Inez W.
6545
Smith, J. Alfred
6862
Smith, J. Allister
2224
Smith, James H.
6546
Smith, Jeremiah
4580
Smith, John
1698, 9249
Smith, John W.
8594
Smith, Joseph F.
402
Smith, Kelly Miller
8585
Smith, Kenneth L.
11888
Smith, Lillian
10133, 10846, 10847
Smith, Lucius Edwin
1794
Smith, Marian W.
7172
Smith, Michael G.
9216-9221
Smith, Noel
1682
Smith, Norma J.
11251
Smith, Pamela C.
9222
Smith, Paul D.
8586
Smith, R. L.
6834
Smith, Robert
1356, 3079, 3080
Smith, Robert E.
10848
Smith, Robert W.
4301
Smith, S. R.
3081
Smith, Samuel L.
9467
Smith, Simon
8655
Smith, Timothy L.
5488, 5489, 7971
Smith, Vern E.
7057
Smith, William A.
5490
Smoot, Mareta
9468, 9469
Smothers, Felton C.
8587
Smucker, Orden C.
4851
Smulie, H.
5491
Smylie, James H.
5062, 11131, 11889
Smyth, Thomas
5063, 5064
Smythe, Lewis
9470
Smythe, Lewis S. C.
10647
SNCC
see also Student Nonviolent
Coordinating Committee

Stevens, Francis B.
9698
Stevens, George E.
7979
Stevens, R. S. O.
3883
Stevenson, J. D.
6997
Stevenson, J. W.
8595
Stevenson, R. C.
1368
Steward, Theophilus G.
6550, 8596, 8608
Steward, W. H.
6869
Stewart, Charles Cameron
1369
Stewart, Charles E.
6998
Stewart, J.
9226
Stewart, James
3093, 3244
Stewart, John
8552, 8609
Stewart, John J.
10172
Stewart, Maria W.
5940, 6870, 8610
Stewart, Thomas McCants
1796, 5823, 8611, 8612,
8613, 8614
Stewick, Daniel B.
12060
St. George Methodist Church
Philadelphia, Pa.
9568, 9569
St. George Protestant
Episcopal Church
9888
Stigand, Chauncey Hugh
409
Stiles, B. J.
12685
Stiles, Joseph C.
5068
Still, Lawrence A.
12965
Still, William
5824
Stinetorf, Louise A.
3094, 3095
Stirewalt, M. L.
10853
Stirling, Leader
2354
Stith, Moses
13125
Stitz, Voker
410
St. James First African
Protestant Episcopal Church
9815, 9828
St. John, Burton
2603, 3057
St. Julien, Aline
13101
St. Laurent, Phillip
48
Stock, Eugene
3096-3099
Stock, Michael
10486
Stock, Sarah G.
2516, 3100
Stokes, A. Jackson
8615
Stokes, James C.
4960

Stokes, Olivia P.
6871, 12311, 12686, 13231
Stone, Michael
12312, 12898
Stone, Michael E.
411
Stone, Ronald
9227
Stone, Thomas T.
5825
Stone, W. Vernon
3101, 3381
Stonehouse, Helena M.
6637
Stonelake, Alfred R.
2517, 2518
Stoney, S. G.
6300
Storey, John W.
9402
Storm, Herbert E.
5501
Storrs, Richard S.
4734, 10210
Stotts, Herbert E.
9699
Stoutemeyer, John H.
10854
Stow, N.
1370, 1371
Stowe, Charles E.
4387
Stowe, David M.
1732
Stowe, Harriet E.
5502, 5826
Stowe, Lyman B.
5827
Stowell, Jay S.
9228, 9700, 9701
St. Paul, Minn. Pilgrim
Baptist Church
6857
St. Paul Normal and Industrial
School
9883
St. Philip Protestant Episcopal
Church
9818, 9830, 9843
Straker, David A.
5535, 5941, 8616-8619
Strange, Douglas C.
4867
Strange, Robert
7980
Strassberger, Elfriede
2234
Strawbridge, Jean A.
2355
Street, Elwood
10855
Streeter, S. W.
4582
Streicher, Henri
2519
Streit, Robert
3102
Strelcyn, S.
412, 1372
Strickland, Bonnie R.
13126
Stringfellow, Thornton
4583, 4584
Stringfellow, William
10856, 11512, 12966, 13127,
13128
Stripling, Paul W.
9403
Stromberg, Jerome
12313

Strong, Josiah
5503
St. Thomas Protestant
Episcopal Church
9820, 9868
Stuart, Charles
4585, 5828
Stuart, M.
4586
Stuart, Richard G.
1373
Stuart-Watt, Eva
1374, 2356
Stuber, Stanley I.
12314
Stuckey, Sterling
6301
Student Christian Association
2235
Student Nonviolent Coordinating Committee
11965, 12082, 12677
Stuntz, Hugh C.
10348
Stuyvesant, Carolyn
4212
Stycos, J. Mayone
9229
Sudan United Mission
2288
Sulaymen, Shahid Mufassir
1375, 7489
Sullenger, Earl T.
12061
Sullivan, H. T.
11515
Sullivan, Kathryn (Mother)
11241
Sullivan, Leon H.
8242, 11309, 12073, 12315,
12316, 12317
Sulzer, Peter
2520
Summerlin, Claude
8863
Sumner, Charles
5829, 8658
Sumner, Claude
413, 414
Sunderland, LaRoy
4587, 5830
Sundermeier, Theo
3104, 4213
Sundkler, Bengt G. M.
3382-3384, 3761, 4214-15
Sutherland, Robert L.
7981, 10436
Suttles, William C.
5556
Swadley, Elizabeth
8864
Swan, C.
13129
Swaney, Charles B.
4961
Swanson, Bert E.
12934
Swanson, S. Hjalmar
2357
Swantz, Lloyd W.
3522
Swantz, Marja-Liisa
1376
Swean, Joyce A.
13071
Sweeney, Odile
12063
Sweet, Leonard I.
5106

Sweet, William W.
4648, 4917, 4962, 4963,
5504, 5942, 7000, 9702,
9703
Sweeting, Rachael
2521
Swift, David E.
9802
Swift, Job
8333, 8620
Swingle, Albert Edwin
1797
Swithenbank, Michael
1377
Swomley, John M.
12687
Synan, Vinson
7058
Szecsi, Ladislas
6202
Taddesse Tamrat
415-420
Taggart, Charles M.
5193
Taggart, Stephen G.
101703
Takla-Haymanot (Abba)
1643, 1644
Talbert, Horace
6551, 6559
Talbot, Edith A.
6303
Talbot, Frederick H.
9230
Talbot, Percy A.
1378-1380, 3104
Tallant, Robert
6304
Talley, Marshall A.
6686
Talley, Thomas W.
6305
Tallmadge, William H.
6306, 6307
Tallmer, Jerry
11895
Tamuno, Tekena
1381
Tanenbaum, Marc H.
10857
Tankerson, Richard E.
7001
Tannenbaum, Frank
5505
Tanner, Benjamin T.
8621-8628
Tanner, Carl M.
6556-6558
Tanner, Jerald
10174, 10175
Tanner, Ralph E. S.
1382, 1383, 3523, 4216
Tanner, Sandra
10174, 10175
Tapp, Robert B.
10137
Tappan, Lewis
5069, 5506, 5507, 5831
Tarplee, Cornelius
10858
Tarr, H.
7236
Tarry, Ellen
10065, 10066
Tarter, Charles L.
7982
Tasie, Godwin O.
1384, 1923, 3884
Tasoma Adara
422

Torbet, Robert G.
6876

Torrend, F. J.
1406

Torrend, Jules
1407

Torres, João Camilo
8866

Torrey, E. Fuller
1408, 1409

Tottress, Richard E.
10874

Tougaloo University
7008

Toupet, Charles
3887

Towne, Anthony
12067

Towne, Laura M.
5900

Townsend, Vince M.
6560

Tracy, Joseph
5837

Tracy, Nat
7062

Travers-Ball, I.
11526

Travis, Paul D.
13234

Trawick, Arcadius M.
7888, 7993, 7994, 10875

Trawick, Arch (Mrs.)
7995

Traxler, Mary Peter (Sister)
11240, 11242

Traynham, Warner R.
12698, 12699, 12700

Tremearne, Arthur J.
1410, 1411

Trent, William J.
7009

Trew, J. M.
4390

Trexler, Edgar R.
12320, 12321

Triandis, Harry C.
10876

Trimingham, John Spencer
1412-1420, 1645, 2289, 2290

Trobisch, Ingrid Hult
1562

Trobisch, Walter A.
4224

Trollope, Anthony
2241

Trollope, Frances
7996

Tross, Joseph S. N.
8654

Trowbridge, Ada W.
9236

Troxler, George
5838

Truby, David W.
3449

Trudgian, Raymond
13235

Trueblood, Roy W.
12701

Truly, Mary E.
3899

Truman, George
4303

Truss, Matthew B.
8655

Tschuy, Theo
9237

Tshibangu, Tharcisse
1421

Tucker, Alfred R.
2525, 2526, 3117

Tucker, Frank C.
9714

Tucker, Hugh C.
8867

Tucker, John T.
1954

Tucker, Joseph L.
9887

Tucker, Leonard
9238

Tucker, Sarah
1924

Tucker, Theodore
1955

Tuggle, Annie C.
9473

Tuhl, Curtis G.
10877

Tull, James E.
11898

Tupper, H. A.
6877, 9408

Turaev, Boris A.
428-434

Trunbull, Colin M.
1422

Turner, Edward R.
4855

Turner, Franklin D.
9888

Turner, Harold W.
1423, 1424, 3386-3396, 3890, 4226

Turner, Henry M.
1425, 3397, 5839, 5945-5947, 6561-6566, 8656-8666, 10477, 10878-10883, 12702

Turner, Maynard P.
8663

Turner, Otis
11899

Turner, Philip
1426

Turner, Ronny E.
7997

Turner, Thomas W.
10072-10075

Turner, Victor W.
1427, 1428, 1429, 1430

Turner, W. W.
11900

Turner, Wallace
10176

Tuskeegee Civic Association
11954

Tutu, Desmond
1431, 1432, 12703

Tutuola, Amos
3118

Tygart, Clarence E.
12000

Tyler, Alice
5515

Tyler, Edward B.
1434, 4596

Tyler, J.
1433

Tyler, Josiah
2243

Tyler, Lawrence L.
7497

Tyms, James D.
1435, 3891, 6878, 7177, 7998, 8664

Tyng, Stephen Higginson
2020

Tyson, Bryan
5516

Uba, Sam
4227, 4228

Uchendu, Victor C.
1925

Udo, Edet Akpan
1926

Uganda, J. J.
2527, 2528, 2529, 3119

Ullendorff, Edward
435-438

Ullman, V.
12068

Ulman, Joseph N.
11262

Umunna, V. N.
1436

Underhill, Edward B.
3120, 9239, 9240

Underwood, Frances W.
9241

Unesco
9316

Ungar, Andre
3767, 11014

Union Anti-Slavery
5077, 5517

Union Theological Seminary
7202

Unitarian-Universalists
10137, 13211, 13233

United Brethren Mission
2021

United Christian Missionary Society
2530

United Church of Christ
9427, 10946, 10956, 12334, 12853

United Church of Christ. Board of World Ministries
3769

United Church of Christ. Eighth General Synod
3770

United Lutheran Church in America
12069

United Methodist Church
9716, 9717, 12405, 12406, 12407, 12854, 12901, 13132

United Methodist Church see also Methodist Episcopal Church

United Missionary Conference on the Congo, 1902-1924
2531

United Nations Educational, Scientific and Cultural Organization
10349, 10350

United Presbyterian Church in the United States of America
1646, 9807, 12323

United States Census Bureau
7999-8001

United States Senate
8666, 10076

United States Works Progress Administration
7010, 7011

Universal Negro Improvement Association
8002

Universities' Mission to Central Africa
3121

Usher, Roland G.
1437

Uzoho, V. N.
1438

Vaagenes, Morris G. C., Jr.
2358

Vadasy, Tibor
439, 440

Vader, Anthony J.
10077

Vail, Stephen M.
4598, 4966

Vail, T. H.
10142

Valente, Waldemar
8868, 8869

Valentine, Foy D.
4597, 9409, 12070

Valentine, Rachel
6568

Van Binsbergen, Wim M. J.
1439

Van Catledge, John
6639

Vance, L. F.
6318

Vandegrift, Eileen Gordon
3122

Vanderbosch, Army
3947

Vandercook, John W.
9242

Van der Linde, Jan M.
5519

Van der Merwe, Willem J.
1440, 1441, 2246

Van der Post, Laurens
3398

Vander Velde, Lewis G.
5079

Vandervort, Eleanor
3123

Van der Westhuizen
1442

Vander Zanden, James W.
11527

Van Deusen, John G.
10884

Van Doren, Charles
7315

Van Dyke, D.
3124

Van Dyke, Henry J.
5078, 5841

Vanecko, J. J.
10885

Van Horne, Marion
4231

Vann, M.
6880

Van Ness, Paul
12324

Vanneste, A.
1443

Van Rensselaer, Cortland
3125

Van Ronsle, Camillus
2532

Van Velsen, Jaap
1815

Varney, Peter D.
3892

Vass, Samuel N.
6881, 7012, 7013

Vassal, Gabrielle M.
2533

Vassall, William F.
8667

Vaughan, Benjamin N. Y.
4231

Warren, Ebenezer W.
4603
Warren, Edwin R.
5525
Warren, Max
4239
Warren, Mervyn A.
8009, 11908, 13237
Warren, Robert B.
7510, 10891, 11909
Warthling, William G.
11245
Warvield, B. B.
5950, 5951
Wa Said, Dibinga
4233
Washington, Betty
12331
Washington, Booker T.
6571, 8010-8012, 8215,
8307, 8483, 8688-8690,
10731
Washington Conference on the
Race Problem in the
United States.
10892
Washington, Curtis
10078
Washington, D. C.
6883, 6884, 7943, 9433,
9440
Washington, D. C. Plymouth
Congregational Church
9440
Washington, D. C. Nineteenth
Street Baptist Church
6883
Washington, D. C. Shiloh
Baptist Church
6884
Washington Federation of
Churches
10440
Washington, Joseph R.
7178, 8013, 8691, 8692,
10146, 12332, 12376,
12712-12720
Washington, Kenneth S.
12333
Washington, L. Barnwell
5526
Washington, Paul M.
12721
Washington, R. Francis
6572
Waterbury, Maria
5952
Waterman, Richard A.
6328, 6329
Waters, James O.
9721
Watkin, E.
12722
Watkin, Edward
450
Watkins, Richard H.
4650
Watson, A.
1459
Watson, Andrew P.
6330
Watson, Bill
13137
Watson, Charles R.
1460, 1461, 2291
Watson, Frank D.
10893
Watson, G. Llewellyn
9250
Watson, Harmon C.
6331

Watson, James J.
8014, 8015, 10441
Watson, Richard
4305-4307
Watt, E. S.
1462
Watt, Rachel S.
3248
Wattenberg, Ben J.
13238
Watters, Pat
11532
Watts, C. C.
2251
Watts, Herman H.
8693
Watts, Hilstan
3655
Watts, Hilstan L.
3781
Watts, Leon W.
12723, 12903
Wayland, Francis
4604, 4651
Wayman, Alexander W.
6573-6576
Weatherford, Allen E.
8016
Weatherford, Willis D.
7017, 8017, 8018, 10143,
10894
Weatherhead, H. T. C.
2535
Weaver, Edwin I.
3402
Weaver, Galen R.
9441, 10144, 10957, 11533
11534, 11911, 12074
Weaver, Irene
3402
Weaver, Robert C.
7018, 10896
Weaver, Rufus W.
10897
Webb, Allan B.
3138
Webb, James M.
3139, 7512
Webb, Maurice
11535
Webber, W.
8019
Weber, Hans-Ruedi
3787
Webster, Allan Neill
2359
Webster, Hutton
1463
Webster, James B.
1932, 3403, 4240
Webster, Noah
5527
Webster, Sherman N.
7019
Wechsler, James A.
7513
Weeks, Annie F.
1933
Weeks, John H.
1464, 2536, 2537, 3140
Weeks, Louis B.
8020, 10898
Weeks, Stephen B.
4856
Wegelin, Oscar
8694
Weil, Ulrich
3787
Weimer, G. Cecil
10899

Weinberg, Arthur
7179
Weinberg, Lila
7179
Weisberg, Harold
11912
Weisbord, Robert G.
12970
Weischer, Bernd Manuel
451
Weisenburger, Francis P.
8021
Weiss, H.
4308
Weiss, John
4738, 4739, 5847
Weiss-Rosemarin, Trude
12971, 12972
Weitfrecht, H. U.
3141
Welbourn, Frederick B.
1465, 2538, 3142, 3404,
3405
Welch, F. G.
3406, 3533
Welch, Galbraith
1466
Welch, Isaiah H.
6577
Welch, James W.
1467, 1468, 1469, 3143
Welch, Sidney R.
1540, 1541
Weld, Alfred
1956
Weld, Theodore D.
4605
Welldon, J. E. C.
3144
Wellens, Stephen C.
1817
Weller, John C.
3145
Wellmer, G.
4241
Wells, Charles A.
12856
Wells, Goldie Ruth
2539
Welsh, David
2252
Welsh, Isabel M.
1470
Welton, Michael R.
1471, 3407
Wendt, Kurt
452, 453
Wengatz, John C.
8022
Wentzel, Fred D.
10900
Wenzel, Kristen
4242, 4243
Were, Gideon S.
1472
Werman, Henry
4244
Werner, Alice
1473
Werner, Douglas
1474, 1475
Werner, M. R.
5211
Wesley, Charles H.
8023, 8024
Wesley, John
4967, 9636
West African Conference
3146, 3147
West, Anson
9722

West Brookfield, Mass.
Anti Slavery Society
4740
West Brookfield, Mass.
First Church
4741
West, C. S.
9809
West Central African Regional
Conference
3148
West, E. Courtenay
3149
West, Elmer S.
13138
West, James
10901
West, Martin
3788, 4245
West, Ralph L.
1934
West, Richard
5848
West, Robert F.
9476
West Rutland, Vt. First
Congregational Church
9442
Westermann, Diedrich
1476-78, 3150, 3151
Westermarck, E. A.
1479
Westervelt, Josephine H.
3152
Westin, Alan R.
11536
Westink, D. E.
3534
Weston, Abraham
6578
Weston, M. Moran
9889
Westherell, Phyllis J.
3153
Whalen, William J.
7514, 10177
Whalum, W.
6333
Wharton, Vernon L.
8025
Wharton, W. E.
12075
Wheatley, Phillis
8695-8699
Wheaton, N. S.
4606
Wheeler, Benjamin F.
6647, 6648
Wheeler, Lillian
12724
Whelan, Charles M.
12335
Whipple, Charles K.
4742, 4968, 5528-5531,
5849
Whipple, Henry B.
9890
Whipple, Phila M.
9412
Whitam, Frederick L.
10902
Whitchurch, S.
6334
Whitcomb, William C.
4743
White, Ackrel E.
3155
White, Amos Jerome
2253